THE CAMBRIDGE THESAURUS OF AMERICAN ENGLISH

THE CAMBRIDGE THESAURUS OF AMERICAN ENGLISH

WILLIAM D. LUTZ
Rutgers University

CAMBRIDGE UNIVERSITY PRESS

Published by the Press Syndicate of the University of Cambridge
The Pitt Building, Trumpington Street, Cambridge CB2 1RP
40 West 20th Street, New York, NY 10011-4211, USA
10 Stamford Road, Oakleigh, Melbourne 3166, Australia

First published 1994

Printed in the United States of America

Library of Congress Cataloging-in-Publication Data
Lutz, William.
The Cambridge thesaurus of American English / William D. Lutz.
p. cm.
ISBN 0-521-41427-X (hard)
1. English language – United States – Synonyms and antonyms.
2. Americanisms – Dictionaries.   I. Title.
PE2832.L88   1994
423'.1 – dc20   93-31878
                                                        CIP

A catalog record for this book is available from the British Library.

ISBN 0-521-41427-X hardback

For
FRANK FINNEGAN
1951–1990

May you go safe, my friend, across that dizzy way
No wider than a hair, by which your people go
From earth to Paradise; may you go safe today
With stars and space above, and time and stars below.

("May You Go Safe," Edward John Moreton Drax Plunkett)

INTRODUCTION

The word *thesaurus* is from the Latin, meaning "treasury," or "storehouse." Peter Mark Roget's *Thesaurus of English Words and Phrases Classified and Arranged so as to Facilitate the Expression of Ideas and Assist in Literary Composition*, first published in 1852, was indeed a kind of treasury or storehouse. Using seventeenth-century philosophical and scientific principles, Roget classified all human concepts into 1,000 categories. He then listed all the synonyms he thought appropriate for each of these categories or subject indexes. Although a very popular book, Roget's work has over the years frustrated many writers as they tried to determine under which of Roget's categories to look for a synonym. Even after finding the proper subject index, readers were often referred to two or three places in the book for synonyms for any one sense of a word. Even then, a successful search would often lead to a large collection of synonyms, many of them obscure or unfamiliar, arranged in no particular order. Needless to say, this organization proved challenging for many users.

While Roget's book is a superb example of seventeenth-century philosophical thought, it does not function well as a handy, usable reference work. In response to Roget's organization, others collected and published alphabetically arranged lists of synonyms. Over the years, these lists have developed into the now familiar and popular dictionary-style thesaurus with entries arranged alphabetically. An alphabetical thesaurus allows readers to look words up quickly without having first to search through a complicated subject index. However, these alphabetical thesauruses are often brief, offering searchers too few synonyms to be really helpful.

The Cambridge Thesaurus of American English offers the easy-to-use alphabetical format combined with a full but discriminating list of synonyms for each entry word. The alphabetical arrangement allows readers to find quickly the word for which they need a synonym. In addition, the synonyms for an entry have been divided according to the important meanings of a word so that readers are not left to sort out a collection of synonyms for different meanings of the same word. Nor will readers have to turn to different sections of the book for each meaning of a word. Every attempt has been made to provide an ample number of apt synonyms for each entry, thus avoiding the overwhelming number found in Roget's book and the limited number of synonyms found in many alphabetical thesauruses.

By definition, synonyms are words having the same meaning. But, as has often been observed, there are no exact synonyms in English, because no two words are identical in meaning and therefore interchangeable in a variety of contexts. If two words were precisely identical in meaning, one of them could disappear without any loss to the language. Any thesaurus that attempted to list only exact synonyms would indeed be a very short book.

Therefore, a thesaurus does not provide users with a list of exact synonyms for a word. What, then, should a thesaurus do?

Users of a thesaurus are not searching for exact synonyms. They already have a perfectly usable word, but for any number of reasons they don't want to use that particular word. They may have used the word so many times in a piece of writing that they want to avoid using it again. Or they have thought of a word that is too general or abstract. In any case, they know what they want to say, but they are searching for suggested ways in which to express their thought.

A thesaurus works best not when it provides its users with a shopping list of words from which they choose but when it functions to prompt their thinking about which word best expresses what it is they want to say. The synonyms in *The Cambridge Thesaurus* have been arranged to provide users with a broad selection of synonyms that adhere closely to the meaning of the entry word. Care has been taken to provide a list of synonyms that will substitute in a variety of contexts, giving users a wide choice, but a choice that does not stray from the meaning of the entry word. The number of synonyms listed for each meaning of an entry word generally does not exceed ten. Rather than confuse users with long lists of synonyms, many of dubious aptness and value, we have attempted to confine the entries to those synonyms that are appropriate and above all familiar and useful.

We have paid special attention to including idioms and verb phrases both as entries and as synonyms. Users of this book will find most of the common idioms that are in current use, such as *when the chips are down, get carried away,* and *play it by ear.* There are also extensive entries covering verb phrases such as *choke up, ease off,* and *carry on.*

We have paid a great deal of attention to antonyms, because users of this thesaurus will find them useful in narrowing the range of meanings of the synonyms in an entry and in selecting the appropriate synonym for their needs. Just as there are no exact synonyms, there are no exact antonyms, and so we have selected the antonyms for each entry with care. In a number of instances there are no antonyms listed because no appropriate ones exist. Listing antonyms for a particular word can be tricky, as antonyms have a way of drifting away from the central meaning of an entry. While we have provided a number of antonyms, we have also taken care to see that no list of antonyms drifts from the meaning of the entry word.

Finally, we have chosen not to list types of things as synonyms. Users will not find, for example, lists of different cheeses under the entry for cheese, nor a list of flowers or a list of the muscles of the body under those entries. Such lists must of necessity be arbitrary, for which cheeses or flowers of the world should be included and which excluded? Such lists are not composed of synonyms and do little to aid the user who is seeking an appropriate synonym.

Guide to the Use of This Thesaurus

Entries appear in boldface type and are arranged in alphabetical order. The part-of-speech label immediately follows the entry and is abbreviated as follows: *n.*, noun; *v.*, verb; *adj.*,

Introduction

adjective; *adv.*, adverb; *prep.*, preposition; *interj.*, interjection. Phrases, such as *take care of*, are not labeled. If an entry can be more than one part of speech, it is listed separately for each in the following order: noun, verb, adjective, adverb. Thus, *taint* is listed first as a noun and then as a verb, and *early* is listed first as an adjective and then as an adverb. If an entry has more than one meaning, each meaning and the synonyms for each meaning are indicated by an arabic numeral. The first two or three synonyms listed for each meaning of an entry are those that should distinguish it from other meanings. Then the more common synonyms for the meaning are listed, followed by less familiar terms. In those instances where a synonym does not clarify the different meanings of a word, brief glosses are provided in parentheses. For example, the entry for the verb *scorn* provides users with the following glosses: *treat with scorn* and *refuse as a matter of principle*. The semicolon is used within a group of synonyms to indicate a closely related but submeaning within the same sense of an entry. For example, within the first meaning of the entry for the noun *labor*, *drudgery* and *effort* are set off by a semicolon from the other synonyms *work*, *chore*, *job*, and so on.

We have given special attention to slang terms, and to noun and verb phrases. Slang entries are identified by the label (*slang*) immediately following the entry. If one of the meanings of an entry is slang, the label (*slang*) immediately follows the number, indicating that when the word is used in that sense it is considered slang. Synonyms that are slang also carry the label (*slang*) immediately following the synonym. Occasionally, when there are a number of slang synonyms for a meaning, they are collected into a group after the slang label. Users should be aware that many entries and synonyms that may be considered informal or colloquial are not labeled. Users who have any question about the suitability of using a synonym in a particular context should consult a current dictionary.

Phrases are listed according to alphabetical order under the main word in the phrase. Verb phrases are listed after the appropriate verb entry; for example, the entries *take after, take apart, take in, take off, take on, take out, take over*, and so on follow the entry for the verb *take*. Where the main word in a phrase is a noun, the phrase is listed after the noun entry. For example, after the entry for the noun *ear* are the entries for the phrases *all ears, in one ear and out the other, lend an ear*, and *play it by ear*.

Antonyms are introduced by the abbreviation *ant.* and are listed following the synonyms for an entry. Where an entry has more than one meaning, the antonyms are listed after the synonyms for that meaning. Where no antonyms are appropriate, none are listed.

Acknowledgments

A work of the complexity of a thesaurus depends upon the skills and cooperation of a number of people, and I have been fortunate to have had the assistance of a number of talented and dedicated people in the preparation of this work. Brian Brown, Pamela Mertsock, Kathleen Volk-Miller, and Florence Werner labored long and hard, contributing their collective keen eye and sharp sense for words. This book would not have been possible without their many talents and their hard work. Ruth Koenigsberg's sharp and discriminating editorial acumen has left its imprint on just about every page of this book. My appreciation goes also to Sidney Landau, who demonstrated repeatedly what a good editor does to see such a large project through to the finish. Without his contributions, both tangible and intangible, this project would not have been possible. My thanks also to John Wright, who served as mediator, friend, and consultant. Finally, to my wife, Denise Gess, and my stepdaughter, Austen Leigh Gess, my thanks for their patience, understanding, and encouragement during the more trying times in writing a book they believed would never end.

A

aback *adv.* back, behind, to the rear, backward. **taken aback** surprised, startled, caught off guard.

abandon *v.* **1.** relinquish, discontinue, give up, quit, cease, let go, cast off *or* away *or* aside, discard, renounce, throw in the towel (*slang*), vacate, evacuate, withdraw from. **2.** leave, desert, forsake, back out on, leave behind, break up with (*slang*), disown, ostracize, leave in the lurch, leave in the cold, skip out on (*slang*), drop, dump.

abandoned *adj.* deserted, desolate, forsaken, neglected, cast out.

abase *v.* humble, humiliate, degrade, demean, belittle, debase, disgrace, mortify, shame; *ant.* honor.

abashed *adj.* embarrassed, chagrined, shamefaced, ashamed, taken back, disconcerted, bewildered, dismayed, nonplussed; *ant.* at ease, composed.

abate *v.* decrease, diminish, lessen, wane, taper off, weaken, dwindle, slacken, decline, ebb, fade, subside; *ant.* increase, strengthen.

abbey *n.* monastery, seminary, priory, convent, nunnery, friary, cloister.

abbreviate *v.* shorten, condense, contract, summarize, compress, cut, trim, précis.

abbreviation *n.* **1.** abridgment, synopsis, précis, condensation, sketch, abstract, summary, outline, reduction; *ant.* amplification, expansion. **2.** condensation, truncation, compression, reduction, contraction, shortening, paring down, pruning; *ant.* augmentation, expansion.

abdicate *v.* renounce, surrender, give up, resign, relinquish, vacate, forgo, abandon, yield.

abdomen *n.* stomach, midriff, belly, tummy (*slang*), gut, paunch.

abduct *v.* seize, kidnap, carry off, run off with, appropriate, snatch, spirit away.

aberrant *adj.* deviant, anomalous, different, perverse, atypical, irregular, odd, peculiar, divergent, incongruous, queer, quirky; *ant.* normal.

abet *v.* **1.** help, assist, aid, succor, encourage, support, countenance. **2.** incite, excite, instigate, urge, goad, spur.

abettor *n.* accomplice, helper, assistant, accessory, backer, supporter, second.

abeyance *n.* suspension, postponement, adjournment, remission, dormancy, inactivity, lull, deferral, recess; *ant.* activity, continuation.

abhor *v.* despise, detest, loathe, hate, recoil from, shudder at, shrink from, spurn; *ant.* adore, love.

abhorrence *n.* loathing, revulsion, aversion, disgust, distaste, hatred, repugnance, horror, odium; *ant.* adoration, love, attraction.

abhorrent *adj.* loathsome, repellent, offensive, abominable, heinous, horrid, repulsive, disgusting, revolting, odious; *ant.* attractive.

abide *v.* **1.** submit to, tolerate, suffer, bear, put up with. **2.** remain, continue, keep on, persevere, endure. **3.** lodge, stay at, room, dwell, sojourn, reside, inhabit, dwell, settle, tenant.

abide by agree to, comply with, obey, observe, stand by, submit to, adhere to, follow, go along with, acquiesce, conform to, live by.

abiding *adj.* unchanging, enduring, lasting, steadfast, constant, continuing, permanent, tenacious, indissoluble, fast; *ant.* transient, ephemeral.

ability *n.* skill, proficiency, capability, aptitude, faculty, expertise, forte, talent, facility, qualification, strength.

abject *adj.* base, low, ignoble, mean, miserable, degenerate, deplorable, despicable, contemptible, sordid, vile; *ant.* exalted.

abjuration *n.* disavowal, renunciation, retraction, recantation, eschewal, abnegation, denial.

abjure *v.* give up, forswear, forgo, forsake, disclaim, renounce, retract, disavow, deny, eschew, recant, abnegate, abandon.

ablaze *adj.* **1.** afire, aflame, on fire, burning, flaming, fiery, ignited, blazing, aglow, illuminated, glowing, incandescent. **2.** excited, exhilarated, impassioned, aroused, enthusiastic, stimulated, fervent.

able *adj.* capable, adept, skilled, qualified, proficient, competent, adroit, deft, talented, expert, masterful; *ant.* incapable, incompetent.

able-bodied *adj.* strong, robust, healthy, stalwart, hale, hardy, fit, sound, strapping, powerful; *ant.* delicate, infirm.

abnegate *v.* renounce, give up, forsake, abjure, concede, relinquish, surrender, eschew, forgo, reject, yield.

abnormal *adj.* irregular, different, atypical, odd, remarkable, strange, deviant, peculiar, aberrant, anomalous, queer, singular, unusual, uncommon, rare; *ant.* common, typical, normal.

abode *n.* domicile, habitat, home, house, quarters, residence, lodging.

abolish *v.* do away with, end, terminate, annul, nullify, void, eradicate, obliterate, destroy, overthrow, overturn, expunge, exterminate, eliminate; *ant.* continue, retain.

abominable *adj.* loathsome, vile, disgusting, abhorrent, horrid, repulsive, contemptible, foul, base, repugnant, revolting, atrocious; *ant.* desirable, delightful.

abominate *v.* despise, loathe, hate, detest, abhor, condemn; *ant.* adore, love, esteem.

abomination *n.* loathing, repugnance, disgust, hatred, abhorrence, aversion, odium, animosity, horror, revulsion; *ant.* adoration, delight.

aboriginal *adj.* indigenous, original, primal, native, earliest, primordial, ancient, primeval.

abort *v.* stop, terminate, halt, end, nullify, cancel, call off; thwart, arrest, check; *ant.* continue.

abortive *adj.* fruitless, unproductive, barren, ineffectual, sterile, useless, futile, vain, ill-starred, doomed; *ant.* successful.

abound *v.* be plentiful, luxuriate, multiply, brim over, teem, overflow, proliferate, thrive, flourish, swarm, run riot.

abounding *adj.* abundant, bountiful, luxuriant, ample, full, lavish, overflowing, prolific, replete, flourishing, teeming, profuse, rich, plenteous; *ant.* sparse, lacking.

about *adv.* approximately, roughly, nearly, more or less, in general.

about *prep.* concerning, regarding, in *or* with regard to, referring to, with reference to, related to, touching on.

above *adj.* **1.** upper, higher, superior, raised. **2.** previous, preceding, before, foregoing, earlier.

aboveboard *adj.* forthright, frank, honest, straightforward, candid, trustworthy, reputable, legitimate, honorable, open, fair, truthful; *ant.* shady, underhand.

abrade *v.* chafe, wear away, wear down, erode, scrape, rub off, grind, file, scour.

abrasive *n.* grinder, sander, file, grater, sharpener, cutter, millstone, grindstone, whetstone.

abrasive *adj.* **1.** sharpening, cutting, eroding, grinding, rough. **2.** (said of one's manner, personality, etc.) irritating, annoying, disturbing, caustic, harsh, grating, rude, brash, insensitive, tactless, hard to live with.

abreast *adj.* up-to-date, informed, knowledgeable, familiar, acquainted, in touch, au courant, on the ball (*slang*); *ant.* out of touch, unaware.

abridge *v.* shorten, compress, abbreviate, lessen, condense, summarize, synopsize, précis, cut down, circumscribe, reduce; *ant.* amplify, add to, pad.

abroad *adv.* out of the country, overseas, in foreign parts, at large.

abrogate *v.* abolish, end, cancel, nullify, terminate, void, retract, reverse, annul, override, dissolve, rescind.

abrupt *adj.* brusque, curt, blunt, brief, terse, precipitous, short, uncivil, rude, discourteous, impolite; *ant.* expansive, leisurely, gracious.

abscond *v.* run off, escape, flee, disappear, make off, *slang:* hightail it, skedaddle, clear out, scram.

absence *n.* **1.** truancy, vacancy, nonappearance, nonattendance, nonresidence, inexistence, loss, anesthesia; *ant.* presence, attendance, appearance. **2.** deficiency, inadequacy, need, lack, gap, hole, void, lacuna, missing part.

absent *adj.* gone, missing, nonexistent, not present, truant,

absent-minded *adj.* forgetful, distracted, preoccupied, engrossed, inattentive, unthinking, dreamy, oblivious, faraway, unaware, scatterbrained, wool-gathering; *ant.* attentive, focused.

absolute adj. **1.** complete, total, entire, unlim-ited, infinite, full, whole, comprehensive, thor-ough, unmitigated, unbounded. **2.** perfect, pure, faultless, unblemished, untarnished. **3.** authoritarian, supreme, domineering, auto-cratic, totalitarian, suppressive, controlling, im-perious, dictatorial, dogmatic, despotic; ant. lenient, democratic. **4.** (as of a truth) certain, positive, unquestionable, undeniable.

absolution n. forgiveness, pardon, vindication, acquittal, dispensation, emancipation, exon-eration, mercy, exemption, deliverance; ant. condemnation.

absolve v. forgive, acquit, pardon, clear, vindi-cate, exempt, exonerate, excuse, redeem, re-lease, set free, liberate, let off; ant. convict.

absorb v. **1.** take in, digest, suck or take or drink in or up, ingest, imbibe, swallow, con-sume; ant. expel, discharge. **2.** occupy, en-gross, engage, employ. **3.** learn, grasp, under-stand, assimilate, take in, fathom.

absorbent adj. retentive, porous, permeable, spongy, pervious, penetrable; ant. imperme-able.

absorbing adj. engrossing, arresting, riveting, gripping, enthralling, fascinating, captivating, spellbinding, intriguing, interesting; ant. bor-ing, off-putting.

abstain v. refrain, decline, deny, resist, forgo, give up, swear off, eschew, avoid; ant. indulge.

abstemious adj. temperate, moderate, re-strained, abstinent, disciplined, self-denying, sparing, sober; ant. gluttonous, intemperate.

abstinence n. temperance, abstemiousness, moderation, self-restraint, self-discipline, so-briety, forbearance, avoidance; ant. self-indulgence.

abstinent adj. temperate, moderate, abstemi-ous, self-controlled, self-disciplined, self-restrained, self-denying; ant. self-indulgent, vo-luptuous, wanton.

abstract n. summary, synopsis, précis, conden-sation, outline, recapitulation, essence.

abstract v. **1.** withdraw, separate, extract, re-move. **2.** summarize, condense, digest, de-crease, synopsize.

abstract adj. generalized, hypothetical, theoreti-cal, conceptual, indefinite, subtle, unrealistic; ant. concrete.

abstruse adj. recondite, incomprehensible, per-plexing, obscure, complex, enigmatic, puz-zling, deep, difficult, cryptic; ant. understand-able, obvious.

absurd adj. ludicrous, preposterous, ridiculous, nonsensical, silly, irrational, idiotic, illogical, implausible, incongruous, anomalous, fantas-tic, bizarre; ant. logical, sensible, rational.

abundance n. plenty, plethora, opulence, profu-sion, bounty, lavishness, affluence, ampleness, bonanza, copiousness, heap, glut, richness; ant. scarcity, dearth.

abundant adj. plentiful, ample, bountiful, copi-ous, well-supplied, profuse, generous, over-flowing, full, teeming, rich, exuberant; ant. scarce, sparse.

abuse n. **1.** (of actions) misuse, harm, debase-ment, degradation, desecration, violation, per-version, defilement, profanation, prostitution, ill-usage, maltreatment, malevolence; ant. re-spect, care. **2.** (of language) insult, offense, affront, outrage, attack.

abuse v. **1.** hurt, harm, damage, injure, insult, mistreat, wrong, persecute, victimize, violate, molest, ill-use. **2.** malign, libel, slander, vilify, insult, attack.

abusive adj. **1.** cruel, brutal, destructive, harm-ful, hurtful, injurious. **2.** scolding, reproach-ful, derisive, derogatory, disparaging, insulting, maligning, pejorative, vilifying, upbraiding; ant. complimentary.

abut v. conjoin, meet, touch, verge, adjoin, border, connect, meet, join.

abysmal adj. **1.** bottomless, endless, vast, boundless, yawning. **2.** unfathomable, immea-surable, infinite, incalculable.

abyss n. chasm, fissure, gulf, canyon, crater, pit, void.

academic adj. **1.** scholastic, scholarly, erudite, learned. **2.** conventional, formalistic, pedan-tic, speculative, theoretical, impractical.

accede v. go along with, assent, agree, consent, concede, concur, capitulate, succeed to, en-dorse, accept, acquiesce, comply, defer, yield; ant. demur, object.

accelerate v. speed up, quicken, expedite, has-ten, precipitate, facilitate, spur, step on the gas (slang); ant. delay, slow down.

accent n. **1.** pronunciation, inflection, intonation, modulation, enunciation, articulation. **2.** stress, emphasis, importance, significance, weight.

accent *v.* stress, emphasize, accentuate, underline, underscore.

accentuate *v.* highlight, intensify, emphasize, stress, underline, spotlight, strengthen, italicize.

accept *v.* **1.** receive, get, take, acquire. **2.** agree to, assent, consent to, acquiesce, approve. **3.** believe, hold, trust, affirm.

acceptable *adj.* satisfactory, passable, suitable, tolerable, agreeable, adequate, pleasing, admissible, welcome, all right; *ant.* unsatisfactory, unwelcome.

acceptance *n.* approval, consent, compliance, permission, tolerance, acknowledgment, recognition, belief, credence, seal *or* stamp of approval; *ant.* dissent, refusal.

accepted *adj.* agreed upon, recognized, received, sanctioned, approved, authorized, acceptable, customary, orthodox, standard, traditional, universal, conventional, kosher; *ant.* unorthodox.

access *n.* admission, entry, ingress, gateway, passageway, door, avenue, path, course, road, key; *ant.* egress, outlet.

accessible *adj.* attainable, procurable, obtainable, available, reachable, nearby, ready; friendly, approachable, sociable, agreeable, warm, genial; *ant.* inaccessible.

accession *n.* **1.** induction, installation, inauguration, advance, arrival. **2.** addition, increase, enlargement, augmentation.

accessory *n.* **1.** accomplice, partner, assistant, aide, associate, colleague, confederate, helper, adjunct, abettor. **2.** adornment, embellishment, frill, extra, trim, supplement.

accident *n.* **1.** calamity, mishap, misfortune, disaster, casualty, collision, crash, blow. **2.** fluke, chance, fortuity, happenstance, twist of fate.

accidental *adj.* inadvertent, uncalculated, unintended, unplanned, unexpected, unforeseen, unwitting, chance, fortuitous, serendipitous, random, fluky; *ant.* premeditated, intentional.

acclaim *n.* praise, commendation, honor, exaltation, applause, kudos, approbation, cheering, ovation, plaudits; *ant.* criticism, vituperation.

acclaim *v.* praise, commend, salute, honor, laud, hail, extol, exalt, crown, applaud, cheer; *ant.* denounce.

acclimate *v.* adapt, adjust, conform, accommodate.

acclimatize *v.* adapt, adjust, get used to, accustom, conform, attune, familiarize, naturalize, inure.

accolade *n.* praise, honor, laurels, kudos, award.

accommodate *v.* **1.** help, aid, comfort, serve, please, assist, cater to, provide, gratify, attend to, care for, oblige, do a favor for, pamper, see to; *ant.* neglect. **2.** harmonize, fit, attune, reconcile, adapt, modify, make suitable, adjust.

accommodating *adj.* agreeable, obliging, helpful, willing, complaisant; cooperative, considerate, hospitable, sympathetic, complying; *ant.* refractory, unhelpful.

accommodation *n.* **1.** compromise, reconciliation, agreement, settlement. **2.** convenience, ease, comfort, luxury.

accommodations *n.* lodging, rooms, quarters; seats, berth.

accompaniment *n.* accessory, complement, support, backup, background.

accompany *v.* escort, go with, consort, chaperon, usher, attend, complement, supplement.

accompanying *adj.* complementary, related, concurrent, joint, supplemental, appended, additional, attached, connected, attendant, associate.

accomplice *n.* conspirator, collaborator, abettor, ally, accessory, helper, partner, assistant, associate, colleague, confederate, henchman.

accomplish *v.* achieve, finish, produce, realize, complete, fulfill, obtain, bring about, do, attain, execute, effect.

accomplished *adj.* **1.** done, finished, completed, concluded, consummated. **2.** (of a person) proficient, skilled, expert, able. **3.** (of a manner or performance) cultured, cultivated, refined, exquisite, polished.

accomplishment *n.* **1.** achievement, triumph, feat, coup, realization, completion, deed, fulfillment, fruition; *ant.* failure. **2.** talent, forte, gift, skill.

accord *v.* bestow, grant, present, give, endow, render.

accordance n. agreement, harmony, accord, concert, conformity, rapport, unanimity, assent, congruence.

accordingly adv. appropriately, correspondingly, ergo, therefore, thus, as a result, consequently.

according to consistent with, in compliance with, in accord with, commensurate with, in keeping with, in light of, in relation to, in line with, in conformity with.

accost v. approach, greet, hail, address, confront, buttonhole, waylay, detain, halt, stop.

account n. narrative, story, tale, recital, chronicle, description, version, record, report.

account v. reckon, assess, consider, estimate, count, gauge, appraise, rate, value, weigh.

account for explain, clear up, answer for, justify, rationalize, vindicate, elucidate, clarify, excuse.

accountability n. liability, responsibility, amenability, chargeability, blameworthiness.

accountable adj. liable, responsible, amenable, answerable, blamable, obligated, charged with.

accoutrements n. adornments, ornamentation, trimmings, decorations, furnishings, outfit, paraphernalia, apparel, garb, gear.

accredit v. authorize, credit, endorse, recognize, certify, sanction, qualify, attribute, ascribe, assign, approve.

accretion n. addition, accumulation, accrual, growth, enlargement, amplification, augmentation, increase; ant. decrease, deduction.

accrue v. accumulate, increase, amass, grow, enlarge, be added, collect, gather, build up.

accumulate v. accrue, cumulate, amass, grow, gather, collect, stockpile, hoard, stash, assemble, multiply, increase; ant. disseminate, diffuse.

accuracy adj. correctness, exactness, precision, scrupulousness, minuteness, veracity, meticulousness, truthfulness, faithfulness, faultlessness, closeness.

accurate adj. correct, right, precise, unerring, sound, exact, proper, true, factual, faithful, letter-perfect; ant. wrong, inaccurate, vague.

accursed adj. 1. damned, cursed, doomed, jinxed, condemned, ill-fated, bedeviled, bewitched, hopeless, hapless, luckless; ant.

accusation n. allegation, complaint, charge, indictment, denunciation, attribution, citation, incrimination, impeachment.

accuse v. allege, charge, blame, impugn, indict, incriminate, cite, attribute, denounce, impeach, inform against, point a finger at.

accustom v. adapt, adjust, familiarize, habituate, inure, acclimatize, train, discipline, season, harden.

accustomed adj. 1. used to, adapted, habituated, inured, familiarized, given to. 2. routine, customary, established, conventional, acclimatized, acquainted.

ace n. expert, master, champion, specialist.

ace adj. excellent, outstanding, superb, fine, brilliant, great, expert, virtuoso, matchless, first-class, champion, nonpareil.

acerbic adj. 1. acidic, sour, tart, astringent, sharp, bitter. 2. harsh, mordant, caustic, rancorous, irritable, brusque, churlish.

ache n. 1. pain, hurt, anguish, throb, soreness, pang, twinge, pounding, smarting, grief, misery, sorrow, suffering. 2. yearning, longing, desire, need, pining, craving, hankering.

ache v. 1. pain, hurt, throb, pound, smart; agonize, grieve, mourn, sorrow, suffer. 2. yearn, hunger, long, desire, need, pine, crave, covet.

achieve v. accomplish, fulfill, succeed, win, complete, finish, reach, realize, do, execute, attain, bring about; ant. fail, miss.

achievement n. accomplishment, success, fulfillment, attainment, success, realization, fruition, feat, completion, execution.

achiever n. go-getter, doer, performer, self-starter, winner, success.

acid adj. 1. (said of a taste) sour, acerbic, acrid, sharp, tart, pungent, vinegary, astringent, bitter, corrosive. 2. (as of a comment) caustic, vitriolic, trenchant, acerbic, harsh, cutting, hurtful, biting, stinging, sharp, withering.

acidulous adj. 1. acid, sour, sharp, bitter, piquant. 2. caustic, sarcastic, ironical, mocking, satirical.

acknowledge v. 1. admit, confess, confirm,

concede, grant, profess, own up, declare; *ant.* deny. **2.** greet, hail, thank, notice, address, answer, recognize, respond to.

acknowledged *adj.* admitted, confessed, confirmed, recognized, accepted, sanctioned; received, accredited, approved, receipted.

acknowledgment *n.* acceptance, compliance, affirmation, recognition, assent, confirmation, acquiescence, assertion, confession, declaration, admission, concession, owning up.

acme *n.* apex, zenith, pinnacle, climax, peak, summit, apogee, culmination, high point, crown, vertex; *ant.* nadir.

acolyte *n.* altar boy, attendant, helper, follower, assistant.

acquaint *v.* accustom, familiarize, apprise, inform, introduce to, divulge, enlighten, brief, reveal, disclose, advise.

acquaintance *n.* **1.** colleague, friend, speaking acquaintance, neighbor. **2.** knowledge, conversance, awareness, familiarity.

acquainted on speaking terms, familiar with, introduced, conversant.

acquiesce *v.* agree, assent, concur, comply, consent, defer, accede, yield, give in, approve; *ant.* object, resist.

acquiescent *adj.* agreeable, amenable, accepting, consenting, complaisant, compliant, conforming, biddable, yielding, acceding; *ant.* resistant.

acquire *v.* obtain, take, get, earn, gain, amass, appropriate, buy, earn, receive, gather, collect; *ant.* lose, dispense.

acquired *adj.* **1.** (gotten by effort) collected, procured, obtained, reached, attained, won, learned, realized, earned, gotten by the sweat of one's brow (*slang*). **2.** given, inherited, accrued, granted, endowed, handed down, bequeathed, awarded, willed to, derived.

acquirements *n.* knowledge, skills, learning, qualifications, accomplishments, achievements, attributes, culture, erudition.

acquisition *n.* **1.** property, purchase, possession. **2.** appropriation, procurement, gain, attainment, takeover.

acquisitive *adj.* avaricious, greedy, covetous, grasping, materialistic, insatiable, voracious, grabby, grabbing, possessive; *ant.* generous.

acquit *v.* exonerate, clear, absolve, free, reprieve, dismiss, liberate, release, excuse, vindicate; *ant.* convict.

acquittal *n.* exoneration, reprieve, release, liberation, vindication, absolution, clearance, dispensation, deliverance; *ant.* conviction.

acreage *n.* land, grounds, property, real estate.

acrid *adj.* pungent, sharp, acerbic, acrimonious, sarcastic, sardonic, biting, caustic, trenchant, vitriolic, cutting, stinging, malicious, mordant.

acrimonious *adj.* bitter, biting, sarcastic, acerbic, sardonic, irascible, virulent, caustic, cutting, rancorous, peevish, mordant, churlish; *ant.* amicable, peaceable.

acrimony *n.* bitterness, resentment, rancor, acerbity, ill will, churlishness, virulence, petulance, sarcasm, asperity, harshness; *ant.* cordiality, goodwill.

across *adv.* crosswise, to the opposite side, transversely, on the other side, from side to side, from one side to another, athwart.

across *prep.* opposite (to), to the other side of, athwart, facing, in front of.

across-the-board *adj.* common, general, universal.

act *n.* **1.** action, deed, performance, exploit. **2.** law, judgment, order, announcement, edict, proposal, decree, ordinance. **3.** (part of a drama) scene, canto, segment, episode. **4.** pose, affectation, falsification, feigning, pretense, ruse, performance.

act *v.* **1.** do, execute, carry on, operate, accomplish, achieve, consummate, function, be in action, transact, do one's stuff (*slang*); *ant.* wait, rest. **2.** behave, seem, appear, carry *or* bear *or* comport oneself, give the appearance of, represent oneself as, play one's part, impress one as; put on airs, pretend.

act for do the work of, substitute, fill in.

act up cause trouble, misbehave, *slang:* horse around, mess around, make waves, rock the boat.

acting *adj.* substitute, surrogate, temporary, interim, provisional, standby, stopgap.

action *n.* **1.** activity, response, reaction, enterprise, vivacity, vigor, animation, energy, work, industry. **2.** (legal process) legal action, law-

actions *n.* behavior, conduct, deportment, ways, air, bearing, manners, mein.

suit, claim, litigation, trial, hearing, court case. 3. engagement, sortie, contest, conflict, battle, fight, skirmish.
bring action accuse, sue, take to court, file a lawsuit.
take action initiate, do, become active, act, instigate.

activate *v.* start, set in motion, spark, galvanize, initiate, propel, prompt, stimulate, initiate, arouse, begin, catalyze, invigorate, renew.

actor *n.* player, performer, character, impersonator, thespian, member of the cast, dramatis persona.

actress *n.* player, actor, performer, character, impersonator, thespian, member of the cast, ingenue.

actual *adj.* true, original, real, genuine; existent, tangible, factual, concrete, present, substantive; *ant.* imaginary, hypothetical.

acumen *n.* cleverness, astuteness, shrewdness, keenness, insight, discernment, acuteness, sagacity, intelligence, wisdom, perspicuity, wit, sensitivity, intuition.

acute *adj.* 1. crucial, decisive, critical, urgent, important, vital. 2. keen, shrewd, sharp, discerning, astute, clever, intuitive, penetrating, intelligent; *ant.* obtuse.

ad (*slang*) *n.* advertisement, announcement, display, notice.

adage *n.* maxim, saying, proverb, dictum, byword, axiom, aphorism, precept, motto.

adamant *adj.* resolute, inflexible, unrelenting, determined, obstinate, unyielding, insistent, steely, tough, hard, uncompromising, stony, firm, obdurate, fixed; *ant.* flexible, pliant, yielding.

adapt *v.* conform, modify, adjust, accommodate, reshape, alter, habituate, acclimatize, harmonize, refashion, change.

adaptable *adj.* malleable, pliant, amenable, compliant, conformable, changeable, flexible, modifiable, versatile, adjustable; *ant.* inflexible, refractory.

adaptation *n.* change, modification, conversion, transformation, variation, shift, rework-

ing, adjustment, alteration, naturalization, familiarization.

add *v.* 1. total, count, reckon, sum up, compute, calculate, tally. 2. join, attach, include, append, affix, interconnect, abut, combine, couple, juxtapose; *ant.* remove, separate.
add up 1. add, count, sum up, tally, compute, total, reckon, count up. 2. make sense, stand to reason, be plausible, ring true, hang together, be consistent, hold water.
add up to indicate, imply, mean, signify, amount to.

added *adj.* supplementary, additional, adjunct, extra, increased, new, fresh.

addendum *n.* attachment, postscript, appendage, addition, supplement, extension, epilogue, codicil, augmentation.

addict *n.* 1. (of drugs) user, *slang:* junkie, dope fiend, pothead, head, acidhead. 2. enthusiast, buff (*slang*), fan, follower, devotee, *slang:* nut, freak.

addicted *adj.* habituated, given *or* disposed to, hooked on (*slang*), accustomed, inclined, obsessed with, in the habit of, under the influence of, attached, prone; *ant.* averse to, disinclined.

addiction *n.* dependence, habit, craving, enslavement, obsession, a monkey on one's back (*slang*).

additional *adj.* added, extra, supplementary, appended, further, more, increased, new, fresh, spare, other.

addled *adj.* 1. bad, rotten, rancid, off, putrid. 2. unbalanced, mixed-up, befuddled, muddled, confused, perplexed, addlebrained, silly.

address *n.* 1. oration, speech, lecture, sermon. 2. residence, home, dwelling, headquarters, box number, street, house number, zip code.

address *v.* 1. label, mark, inscribe. 2. lecture, discourse, discuss, give *or* deliver a speech *or* address, pontificate, expatiate. 3. petition, appeal, write, plead, enter a plea.

adept *adj.* skilled, proficient, capable, expert, masterly, clever, able, adroit, deft, practiced; *ant.* inept.

adequate *adj.* sufficient, satisfactory, enough,

fit, acceptable, suitable, fair, requisite, efficacious.

adhere *v.* **1.** follow, be devoted to, obey, heed, abide by, comply with, observe, follow, maintain, respect, stand by, keep. **2.** cling, attach, hold fast, stick, cleave, hold fast, join.

adherent *n.* follower, supporter, disciple, aficionado, devotee, admirer, advocate, enthusiast, fan; *slang:* freak, nut.

adhesive *adj.* adherent, sticking, sticky, gluey, gummed, glutinous, viscid, tenacious.

ad infinitum endlessly, forever, ceaselessly, on and on, regularly.

adjacent *adj.* adjoining, abutting, nearby, juxtaposed, next, bordering.

adjacent to beside, alongside, next to, near, bordering on.

adjoin *v.* **1.** abut, join, lie beside, be adjacent to. **2.** unite, append, annex, join.

adjoining *adj.* adjacent, connecting, joined, interconnecting, bordering, neighboring, next, touching, near, abutting.

adjourn *v.* discontinue, recess, interrupt, suspend, delay, stay, put off, defer; *ant.* convene.

adjournment *n.* recess, suspension, break, postponement, deferment, delay, interruption, stay, pause.

adjudicate *v.* judge, arbitrate, decide, settle, determine, pronounce, referee, umpire.

adjudication *n.* judgment, decision, verdict, ruling, pronouncement, determination, finding, conclusion, arbitration, settlement.

adjunct *n.* supplement, complement, addition, accessory, extension, auxiliary.

adjure *v.* **1.** charge, command, direct, order. **2.** beseech, plead with, beg, entreat, implore, supplicate, pray, appeal to.

adjust *v.* adapt, modify, change, remodel, accommodate, conform, harmonize, suit, refashion, alter, fine-tune.

adjustable *adj.* malleable, alterable, adaptable, flexible, modifiable, tractable; *ant.* inflexible, fixed.

adjustment *n.* alteration, conversion, modification, adaptation, harmonization, naturalization, fitting, naturalization, refashioning, tuning.

adjutant *n.* assistant, helper, aide, auxiliary.

ad-lib *v.* improvise, extemporize, make up.

ad-lib *adj.* extemporaneous, spontaneous, off-the-cuff, unrehearsed, ad hoc.

administer *v.* **1.** direct, manage, conduct, control, command, govern, supervise, run. **2.** inflict, deal out, dispense, deliver.

administration *n.* **1.** supervision, direction, management, government, guidance, authority, policy, charge, control, policing, legislation. **2.** administrators, directors, officers, supervisors, superintendents, advisers, executives, officials, governing board. **3.** term of office, tenure, presidency, regime, reign, dynasty, incumbency, power.

administrative *adj.* managerial, executive, supervisory, regulatory, organizational, directorial, legislative, governmental, gubernatorial.

administrator *n.* manager, director, supervisor, overseer, governor, boss, controller, curator, custodian, trustee.

admirable *adj.* commendable, praiseworthy, laudable, estimable, worthy, fine, respected, deserving, superior, valuable; *ant.* despicable.

admiration *n.* esteem, reverence, respect, appreciation, praise, veneration, pleasure, wonder, adoration, affection, awe; *ant.* contempt.

admire *v.* esteem, revere, respect, applaud, appreciate, praise, venerate, laud, value, prize; *ant.* disdain.

admirer *n.* devotee, enthusiast, aficionado, fan, adherent, supporter, idolizer; wooer, boyfriend, beau, lover, sweetheart.

admissible *adj.* allowed, permissible, acceptable, justifiable, tolerable; *ant.* illegitimate.

admission *n.* **1.** entry, entrance, access, admittance, inclusion; *ant.* exclusion. **2.** disclosure, divulgence, acknowledgment, confession, exposé, revelation; *ant.* denial. **3.** fee, ticket, cover charge, dues, price.

admit *v.* **1.** let in, allow entrance to, welcome, receive. **2.** acknowledge, confess, disclose, reveal, divulge, lay bare, expose, make a clean breast of, own up, *slang:* spill the beans, open up, come clean; *ant.* deny.

admittance *n.* entrance, access, entree, passage, reception.

admonish *v.* **1.** reprimand, reproach, reprove, scold, upbraid, rebuke, chide, censure. **2.** caution, warn, counsel, advise, urge.

admonition *n.* **1.** reprimand, reproach, scold-

ado n. fuss, trouble, bother, commotion, flurry, stir, tumult, bustle, ceremony, excitement.

adolescence n. puberty, teens, juvenility, youth-fulness, immaturity; ant. senescence.

adolescent n. juvenile, teenager, minor, young-ster, youth.

adolescent adj. teenage, youthful, boyish, girlish, maturing, juvenile, immature, puerile; sophomoric.

adopt v. 1. take in, support, foster, father, mother, bring up, raise, rear. 2. embrace, appropriate, endorse, sanction, approve, ac-cept, back, espouse, hold, take as one's own.

adorable adj. lovable, captivating, enchanting, delightful, precious, appealing, bewitching, fetching, winsome, charming; ant. hateful.

adoration n. idolization, veneration, exalta-tion, glorification, reverence, worship, love, admiration, esteem, honor; ant. detestation, abhorrence.

adore v. idolize, revere, venerate, glorify, exalt, love, cherish, esteem, honor, worship, dote on; ant. hate, abhor.

adorn v. decorate, embellish, gild, beautify, bedeck, bejewel, emblazon, enhance, trim, doll up.

adornment n. accessory, decoration, ornamenta-tion, gilding, frippery, embellishment, trap-ping, trimming, frill, flounce.

adrift adj. directionless, aimless, at sea, an-chorless, rudderless, rootless, astray, off course, amiss, purposeless, spacey (slang); ant. an-chored, stable.

adroit adj. adept, deft, proficient, skillful, ex-pert, clever, cunning, masterful, quick, artful, dexterous; ant. inept, clumsy.

adulation n. fawning, sycophancy, flattery, boot-licking (slang), idolization, worship.

adulatory adj. fawning, sycophantic, servile, obsequious, flattering, bootlicking (slang), idolatrous, groveling, worshiping, slavish, blandishing.

adult n. (mature person) grown-up, woman, man.

adult adj. grown-up, mature, full-grown, of age, developed, ripened; ant. immature.

adulterate v. weaken, dilute, thin, water down, pollute, taint, contaminate, corrupt, bastard-ize, defile, devalue.

adulteration n. corruption, deterioration, con-tamination, pollution; ant. purity.

adultery n. infidelity, unfaithfulness, fornica-tion, cuckoldry.

adumbrate v. foreshadow, portend, hint at, outline, sketch, limn, suggest, foretell, indi-cate, presage, prophesy; veil, obscure.

advance n. 1. development, advancement, im-provement, breakthrough, progress, rise, bet-terment, increase, growth, gain, headway, pro-motion; ant. regression. 2. prepayment, down payment, deposit, credit, retainer, loan.

advance v. 1. progress, proceed, move on, forge ahead, march or push or press on, gain ground, continue; ant. recede, retreat, stag-nate. 2. propel, push, drive, launch. 3. lend, loan, provide with, furnish.

advanced adj. progressive, forward-looking, ahead, leading, higher, original, imaginative, avant-garde.

advancement n. growth, improvement, prog-ress, betterment, headway, development, gain, forward movement, promotion, maturation, onward movement; ant. demotion, retardation.

advances n. overtures, approach, proposition, proposal, attentions, addresses, moves.

advantage n. 1. luck, favor, approval, help, aid, assistance, leverage, precedence, upper hand, headstart, edge (slang); ant. hindrance, handicap. 2. dominance, superiority, suprem-acy, lead, preeminence, sway, power, upper hand. 3. benefit, good, gain, profit, welfare, boon, fruit.

take advantage of exploit, profit by, use, abuse, bully, intimidate.

advantageous adj. favorable, useful, worth-while, valuable, beneficial, opportune, profit-able, rewarding, helpful, gainful, convenient; ant. harmful, detrimental.

advent n. coming, arrival, accession, appear-ance, visitation, inception.

adventure n. venture, experience, undertaking, happening, story.

adventurer n. traveler, voyager, wanderer, fortune-hunter, opportunist, soldier of fortune, daredevil, knight-errant.

adventurous adj. adventuresome, venturesome, bold, audacious, daring, dauntless, plucky, risky, daredevil, game, reckless, enterprising; *ant.* cautious, prudent.

adversary *n.* enemy, antagonist, opponent, rival, competitor, foe, assailant, attacker; *ant.* ally, supporter.

adverse *adj.* 1. hostile, antagonistic, conflicting, unfriendly, contrary. 2. unfavorable, inopportune, disadvantageous, detrimental, unpropitious, unlucky, untoward, unfortunate, poor.

adversity *n.* misfortune, disaster, calamity, catastrophe, hard times, misery, suffering, sorrow, trouble, woe, tribulation, distress; *ant.* prosperity.

advertise *v.* 1. promote, herald, flaunt, praise, blazon, push, tout (*slang*), trumpet, plug (*slang*). 2. announce, broadcast, display, exhibit, publish, publicize, make known, declare.

advertised *adj.* announced, publicized, offered, displayed, presented, put on sale, exhibited, posted, noted, flaunted.

advertisement *n.* ad (*slang*), commercial, promotion, display, circular, handout, placard, handbill, propaganda, *slang:* plug, hype.

advice *n.* guidance, recommendation, counsel, help, do's and don'ts (*slang*), wisdom, word, instruction, direction, caution, admonition, warning, suggestion.

advisability *n.* suitability, fitness, propriety, appropriateness, wisdom.

advisable *adj.* appropriate, proper, desirable, prudent, wise, judicious, politic, seemly, sensible, desirable, beneficial, correct, apt, fit, called-for; *ant.* injudicious.

advise *v.* 1. counsel, recommend, caution, guide, instruct, forewarn, suggest, teach, tutor, urge, warn. 2. report, inform, notify, make known, apprise, tell.

advisedly *adv.* 1. consciously, thoughtfully, intentionally, deliberately. 2. carefully, discreetly, cautiously, prudently.

adviser *n.* counselor, consultant, guide, confidant, instructor, teacher, therapist, lawyer, mentor, coach, aide, tutor.

advisory *adj.* counseling, consultatory, advising, helping, recommending.

advocacy *n.* support, backing, assistance, encouragement, championing, advancement, pro-

motion, campaigning, espousal, recommendation.

advocate *v.* promote, support, champion, campaign for, endorse, espouse, plead for, subscribe to, recommend, defend, argue for; *ant.* disparage, impugn, deprecate.

aegis *n.* protection, shelter, sponsorship, umbrella, backing, advocacy, guardianship, support, patronage, favor.

aerial *adj.* airy, elevated, insubstantial, ethereal, lofty, unreal, incorporeal.

aesthetic *adj.* 1. beautiful, pleasing, lovely, tasteful. 2. artistic, refined, sensitive, appreciative.

affability *n.* amicability, friendliness, cordiality, geniality, graciousness, kindliness, pleasantness, warmth, accessibility, benevolence, congeniality, openness, sociability, gemütlichkeit; *ant.* reserve, reticence, coolness.

affable *adj.* amicable, friendly, open, genial, cordial, gracious, kind, pleasant, warm, approachable, benevolent, good-natured, sociable, clubbable, accessible; *ant.* unfriendly, reserved, reticent, cool.

affair *n.* 1. business, concern, responsibility, matter, interest, pursuit, occupation, profession, case, circumstance. 2. love affair, liaison, rendezvous, romance, relationship, intrigue, amour, dalliance, intimacy. 3. party, gathering, function, entertainment.

affect *v.* 1. influence, sway, move, impress, touch, stir. 2. feign, pretend, assume, put on, take on.

affectation *n.* pretense, pose, mannerism, posturing, simulation, deception, put-on (*slang*).

affected *adj.* 1. moved, touched, sympathetic, stimulated, stirred, struck, impressed, influenced, melted; *ant.* indifferent, unmoved, untouched. 2. insincere, pretentious, pedantic, melodramatic, self-conscious, overdone, ostentatious, stagy, rehearsed, superficial, put-on (*slang*); *ant.* natural, genuine.

affecting *adj.* touching, moving, poignant, stirring, impressive, pathetic, pitiful, troubling, saddening.

affection *n.* fondness, tenderness, warmth, feeling, regard, care, good will, partiality, desire, love, passion, devotion.

affectionate *adj.* caring, warm, loving, kind,

affectionate adj. friendly, solicitous, tender, amiable, warm-hearted, doting, passionate, responsive; ant. cold, indifferent.

affiliate v. associate, connect, join, incorporate, merge, unite, ally, band together, combine.

affiliation n. association, alliance, connection, relationship, coalition, union, confederation, incorporation, merger, union.

affinity n. 1. fondness, liking, attraction, closeness. 2. kinship, relationship, bond, tie, connection, alliance, association, attachment, union, fraternity, affiliation. 3. similarity, likeness, resemblance, correspondence, parallel.

affirm v. confirm, assert, attest, maintain, corroborate, certify, state, declare, pronounce, swear, testify, witness, depose.

affirmation n. corroboration, deposition, pronouncement, statement, certification, assertion, declaration, oath, testimony, confirmation, endorsement.

affirmative adj. assenting, agreeing, consenting, concurring, approving, corroborative, emphatic, positive; ant. dissenting, negative, contradictory.

affix v. join, connect, fasten, attach, bind, add, append, tack on, glue, paste; ant. detach.

afflict v. distress, plague, beset, burden, grieve, smite, torment, hurt, wound, trouble, strike, harrow, pain.

affliction n. pain, suffering, distress, hardship, illness, calamity, trouble, scourge, tribulation, sorrow, woe; ant. solace, comfort.

affluence n. wealth, prosperity, riches, fortune, plenty, opulence, abundance; ant. poverty.

affluent adj. wealthy, rich, prosperous, well-to-do, well-off, moneyed, comfortable, loaded (slang), flourishing, opulent, well-heeled (slang); ant. poor, impoverished.

afford v. 1. produce, provide, furnish, generate, supply, yield. 2. (have sufficient means for) spare, allow, manage, stand, bear, cope with, offer.

affray n. brawl, fracas, riot, melee, free-for-all, disturbance, fight, quarrel, skirmish, squabble, fray, feud.

affront n. insult, offense, slight, disrespect, indignity, provocation, slur, rudeness, snub, discourtesy, slap in the face; ant. compliment.

affront v. insult, offend, slight, pique, snub, incense, gall, irritate, nettle, vex, hurt, cold-shoulder (slang).

afoot adj., adv. in the air, in the wind, up, brewing, about, circulating, astir, forthcoming, going on, in progress.

aforesaid adj. preceding, previous, aforementioned.

afraid adj. 1. frightened, scared, fearful, alarmed, terrified, petrified, panic-stricken; ant. brave, bold. 2. reluctant, suspicious, uneasy, apprehensive, nervous, intimidated, anxious, hesitant; ant. confident. 3. sorry, regretful, unhappy.

afresh adv. again, once more, anew, newly, over again.

after adv. subsequently, afterwards, thereafter, later, next, post, below, behind.

after all finally, at last, when all is said and done, in the end.

afterlife n. life after death, eternity, heaven, afterworld, immortality.

aftermath n. fallout, upshot, outcome, wake, repercussion, consequences, results, aftereffects, end, backwash.

afterthought n. reconsideration, review, second thoughts.

afterward adv. later, after, subsequently, in a while, a while later, by and by, eventually, soon, ultimately, then, thereafter.

again adv. another time, once more, encore, ditto, anew, repeatedly, afresh.

again and again repeatedly, over and over, continuously, endlessly, ad infinitum.

against prep. 1. abutting, adjacent to, close to, facing, fronting, in contact with, touching, next to. 2. counter to, facing, opposite to. 3. contrary to, in opposition to, opposed to, adverse to, versus, hostile to, in defiance of.

age n. 1. era, date, time, years, period, epoch, generation. 2. elderliness, senescence, seniority, maturity, senility, dotage, decrepitude; ant. youth, salad days.

age v. mature, ripen, season, mellow, grow old, decline, deteriorate, obsolesce.

aged adj. old, senescent, antiquated, ancient, elderly, geriatric, venerable, age-old, time-worn, worn-out.

agency n. 1. office, firm, bureau, company,

organization, business. **2.** power, auspices, force, means, instrumentality, action.

agenda *n.* schedule, plan, timetable, program, calendar, list, menu, diary.

agent *n.* representative, executor, intermediary, surrogate, envoy, go-between, broker, promoter, assistant, attorney, appointee.

ages *n.* years, eons, centuries, decades, time.

aggrandize *v.* exaggerate, glorify, glamorize, exalt, magnify, amplify, elevate, inflate, enhance.

aggravate *v.* irritate, exasperate, vex, pester, provoke, harass, incense, annoy, tease, irk; *ant.* appease. **2.** intensify, heighten, magnify, worsen, exacerbate, increase; *ant.* alleviate.

aggravation *n.* **1.** (cause of discomfort) irritation, exasperation, annoyance, provocation; affliction, difficulty, trouble, worry, distress. **2.** worsening, exacerbation, intensification, heightening, sharpening, inflammation, deepening, strengthening; *ant.* amelioration.

aggregate *n.* whole, aggregation, collection, gathering.

aggression *n.* combativeness, belligerence, offense, pugnacity, hostility, antagonism, provocation, invasion, assault, attack, onslaught, encroachment, militancy.

aggressive *adj.* **1.** assertive, dynamic, bold, energetic, zealous, enterprising, vigorous, proactive. **2.** combative, bellicose, belligerent, pugnacious, argumentative, hostile, offensive, pushy, forceful, militant, jingoistic, intrusive, destructive; *ant.* peaceful, submissive.

aggressor *n.* attacker, assailant, assaulter, offender, invader, intruder, provoker; *ant.* victim.

aggrieved *adj.* wronged, offended, affronted, maltreated, ill-used, hurt, pained, insulted, harmed, disturbed, distressed, saddened, woeful.

aghast *adj.* shocked, alarmed, horrified, terrified, stupefied, stunned, dismayed, astonished, astounded, appalled, thunderstruck, frightened, afraid.

agile *adj.* nimble, quick, spry, lithe, lissome, limber, flexible, supple, sprightly, swift, clever, adroit, athletic, acrobatic; *ant.* stiff, clumsy.

agitate *v.* stir up, stimulate, arouse, excite, work up, incite, inflame, rouse, disconcert,

unnerve, unsettle, rattle, fluster; *ant.* calm, tranquilize, quiet.

agitated *adj.* anxious, flustered, disconcerted, uneasy, upset, perturbed, nervous, jumpy, ruffled, unnerved, distracted, flappable, restless, uptight (*slang*); *ant.* calm, composed, unflappable.

agitation *n.* confusion, tumult, clamor, commotion, turmoil, ferment, uproar, unrest, stir, alarm, anxiety, worry, excitement, outcry, tailspin; *ant.* tranquillity.

agitator *n.* instigator, rabble-rouser, troublemaker, revolutionary, agent provocateur, firebrand, demagogue, inciter, soap-box orator.

ago *adv.* before, gone, since, past.

agog *adj.* enthusiastic, eager, excited, expectant, in suspense, breathless.

agonize *v.* suffer, anguish, struggle, strain; trouble, torment, distress, pain, afflict, rack, harrow.

agony *n.* pain, misery, distress, anguish, suffering, tribulation, affliction, woe, paroxysm.

agrarian *adj.* agricultural, farming, georgic, praedial.

agree *v.* concur, acquiesce, assent, see eye to eye, harmonize, accord, coincide, correspond, match, jibe, suit, fit; *ant.* conflict.

agreeable *adj.* pleasing, satisfactory, acceptable, suitable, fitting, proper, amenable, amicable, willing, suitable, attractive, enjoyable; *ant.* incompatible, distasteful.

agreement *n.* **1.** harmony, concert, acceptance, unanimity, compliance, congruence, union, affinity, similarity, accord, consistency. **2.** contract, settlement, arrangement, covenant, understanding, deal, bargain, pact, treaty, trade-off, compromise.

agricultural *adj.* agrarian, farming, predial.

agriculture *n.* farming, agribusiness, agronomics, cultivation, husbandry, tillage.

aground *adj.* grounded, ashore, beached, high and dry, foundered, marooned, stranded; *ant.* afloat.

ague *n.* fever, malaria, fit.

ahead *adj.* advancing, progressing, leading, first, advanced, at the head, winning, superior, triumphant; *ant.* trailing, behind, last.

ahead of before, earlier than, preceding, in front of; *ant.* following.

aid n. **1.** help, assistance, succor, subsidy, patronage, contribution, donation, relief, benefit; support. **2.** assistant, aide, helper, adjunct, supporter, sidekick (slang).

aid v. help, assist, succor, abet, ease, boost, relieve, rally around, support, encourage, lend a hand to, pitch in, subsidize, facilitate; ant. impede, obstruct.

aide n. assistant, supporter, adjutant, advocate, aide de camp, follower, disciple, right-hand man or woman, adviser, sidekick (slang).

ailing adj. sick, ill, afflicted, infirm, debilitated, diseased, unsound, weak, languishing, valetudinarian; slang: out of sorts, under the weather; frail; ant. healthy, flourishing, robust.

ailment n. sickness, malady, illness, affliction, disease, infirmity, disability, weakness.

aim n. goal, objective, target, object, aspiration, intention, ambition, plan, scheme, purpose, desire, dream, wish.

aimless adj. desultory, goalless, pointless, undirected, adrift, unguided, unmotivated, rambling, random, wayward; ant. purposeful.

air n. **1.** atmosphere, oxygen, breeze, wind, blast, draft, waft, breath, heavens, sky. **2.** demeanor, manner, appearance, aura, bearing, character, impression, look, quality, style. **3.** ambiance, feeling, mood, tone. **4.** melody, aria, song, tune, strain.

up in the air undecided, unsettled, uncertain, unsure, unresolved, on tenterhooks, hanging fire.

air v. give vent to, disclose, make public, reveal, divulge, make known, expose, broadcast, proclaim, tell, declare, voice.

airily adv. lightheartedly, buoyantly, cheerfully, happily, jauntily, blithely, nonchalantly, unconcernedly, flippantly, ethereally, breezily, daintily, delicately; ant. concernedly, thoughtfully.

airless adj. unventilated, close, suffocating, stifling, oppressive, muggy, musty, stale, stuffy, breathless; ant. airy, fresh.

airs n. affectation, pretensions, staginess, posing, artificiality, pomposity, snobbishness, haughtiness, superciliousness, arrogance, hauteur.

get ahead succeed, advance, prosper, progress, move up (the ladder).

airtight adj. **1.** impenetrable, impermeable, closed, sealed, hermetic, tightfitting. **2.** certain, indisputable, irrefutable, incontestable, unassailable, unimpeachable, incontrovertible, absolute.

airy adj. **1.** ventilated, open, spacious, breezy, exposed, roomy, drafty, windy, gusty, aerial; **2.** sprightly, light, gay, whimsical, flippant, happy. **3.** delicate, fragile, frail, thin, dainty; ant. closed, stifling.

aisle n. lane, passage, path, corridor, division, walkway, gangway.

alacrity n. readiness, willingness, eagerness, enthusiasm, alertness, liveliness, quickness, speed, zeal, swiftness; ant. slowness, dilatoriness.

alarm n. **1.** warning, alert, notification, caution, siren, bell, signal, shout, yell, scream. **2.** fear, dread, fright, trepidation.

alarm v. frighten, scare, panic, startle, distress, dismay, daunt.

alas interj. alack, dear me, oh, my God, woe is me.

albeit conj. although, even though, notwithstanding that, though, even if.

album n. collection, registry, index, portfolio, notebook, scrapbook, photograph album, autograph book.

alchemy n. magic, witchcraft, sorcery, hermetics, wizardry.

alcohol n. liquor, spirits, slang: booze, hard stuff, moonshine, firewater, mountain dew, rotgut, hooch.

alcoholic n. inebriate, drunkard, tippler, hard drinker, drunk, boozer, slang: lush, wino, soak.

alcoholic adj. intoxicating, inebriating, distilled, fermented, hard, strong, spirituous, vinous.

alcoholism n. alcohol addiction, dipsomania, crapulence, vinosity.

alcove n. nook, niche, recess, bower, compartment, cubicle, corner, cubbyhole, booth, bay.

ale n. beer, stout, brew, malt, bitter.

alert n. signal, warning, alarm, admonition.

alert adj. vigilant, attentive, on the ball (slang), observant, ready, wary, watchful, on the qui vive.

put on airs brag, have pretensions, show off, strut, pose.

vive, circumspect, wide-awake; *ant.* listless, unwary.

alias *n.* pseudonym, assumed name, nom de plume, pen name, stage name, nickname, anonym.

alibi *n.* excuse, explanation, reason, defense, coverup, story.

alien *adj.* foreign, unfamiliar, strange, exotic, incongruous, outlandish, estranged.

alien *n.* foreigner, immigrant, outsider, stranger, newcomer; *ant.* native.

alienate *v.* estrange, disassociate, separate, withdraw, turn away, set against, antagonize, divorce; *ant.* unite, disarm.

alienation *n.* estrangement, disassociation, disjunction, indifference, remoteness, rupture, severance, withdrawal, turning away, separation, divorce; *ant.* reconciliation.

alight *v.* disembark, get down, dismount, land, touch down, perch, come to rest, come down, descend, settle, get off; *ant.* ascend, board, rise.

allay *v.* **1.** soothe, appease, mollify, pacify, ease, quell, quiet, subdue. **2.** lessen, soften, reduce, abate, moderate, decrease, mitigate, slake, assuage, diminish; *ant.* exacerbate, intensify.

allegation *n.* accusation, charge, claim, assertion, deposition, statement, testimony, declaration.

allege *v.* accuse, charge, claim, contend, maintain, put forward, state, assert, declare, depose, insist, profess.

alleged *adj.* supposed, reputed, described, suspect, reported, implied, purported, so-called, claimed, declared.

allegiance *n.* loyalty, fidelity, faithfulness, adherence, constancy, duty, homage, obedience, support, devotion, duty, obligation.

allegorical *adj.* symbolic, figurative, emblematic, representative, parabolic.

allegory *n.* symbol, parable, metaphor, analogy, emblem, story.

allot *v.* allocate, budget, designate, earmark, set aside, assign, dispense, distribute, render, grant, mete, share out.

allotment *n.* allocation, portion, share, ration, lot, percentage, allowance, quota, grant, appropriation.

all-out *adj.* intensive, full, total, optimum, exhaustive, no-holds-barred (*slang*), full-scale, complete, thorough, unrestrained, vigorous, determined, resolute; *ant.* half-hearted, perfunctory.

allow *v.* **1.** permit, let, grant *or* give permission to *or* for, sanction, have no objection, put up with, tolerate, endure, bear; *ant.* deny, forbid, prohibit. **2.** recognize, support, approve, admit, acquiesce. **3.** (give at lower rates) make allowance, concede, subtract, deduct.

allowable *adj.* acceptable, permissible, admissible, appropriate, legitimate, apt, legal, suitable, tolerable, sufferable; *ant.* unacceptable.

allowance *n.* **1.** portion, share, ration, quantity, quota. **2.** gratuity, salary, wage, commission, fee, recompense, remittance, stipend, pension, alimony, aid, honorarium.

make allowances for allow for, weigh, consider, rationalize, excuse, justify.

alloy *n.* compound, mixture, mix, hybrid, combination, amalgam, blend, coalescence, fusion, composite.

alloy *v.* **1.** combine, mix, blend, compound, fuse, amalgamate. **2.** devalue, debase, adulterate, impair.

all right **1.** adequate, satisfactory, enough, tolerable, acceptable, passable. **2.** agreed, yes, OK, of course, surely, definitely, positively. **3.** uninjured, well, unhurt, safe, whole. **4.** correct, exact, precise, accurate, right.

all-time *adj.* best, champion, unsurpassed, greatest, record-breaking.

all told in all, altogether, on the whole, in toto.

allude to imply, insinuate, hint, intimate, suggest, refer, touch upon, remark, cite, mention.

allure *v.* attract, entice, seduce, disarm, enchant, entrance, beguile, lure, tempt, fascinate, charm, persuade.

allusion *n.* intimation, reference, mention, hint, inference, implication, insinuation, connotation, denotation, innuendo, suggestion, citation.

ally *n.* confederate, partner, friend, associate, colleague, consort, abettor.

ally *v.* unite, join forces, band together, collaborate, affiliate, team up, fraternize.

almanac *n.* annual, yearbook, calendar, register.

almighty adj. all-powerful, omnipotent, absolute, supreme, invincible, great; ant. impotent, weak.

almost adv. close to, all but, very nearly, well-nigh, as good as, practically, virtually, approximately, about.

alone adj. 1. lone, solitary, abandoned, apart, by oneself, isolated, single, separate, detached, unattached; ant. accompanied, escorted. 2. unique, unparalleled, unequaled.

let alone 1. in addition, besides, not to mention or speak of, also. 2. ignore, isolate, leave, leave in peace, let be, slang: get off one's back, bug off.

let well enough alone forget, ignore, let alone.

alone adv. solely, singly, independently, single-handedly, solo.

along adv. ahead, on, onward, forth, forward.

all along from the beginning, all the time, constantly, regularly.

along with together with, with, accompanying, in addition to, simultaneously.

get along 1. prosper, get by, make ends meet, succeed. 2. progress, move on, advance, push ahead. 3. grow old, age, decline, decay. 4. be compatible, agree, stand together, accord.

alongside prep., adv. beside, by, near, close to, parallel to, at the side of, even with; ant. beyond, ahead (of), behind.

aloof adj. remote, indifferent, standoffish, distant, detached, unfriendly, unresponsive, unsociable, reticent, reserved, inaccessible, cold; ant. sociable, friendly, concerned.

aloud adv. out loud, audibly, sonorously, intelligibly, distinctly, clearly; ant. silently.

already adv. by this time, beforehand, by now, previously, at present, by then, by that time, heretofore, hitherto.

also adv. in addition, including, too, additionally, plus, as well, moreover, furthermore, besides, likewise, ditto, to boot.

alter v. change, adjust, revise, modify, shift, transform, convert, adapt, turn, amend, metamorphose.

alteration n. change, adjustment, modification, transformation, difference, revision, conversion, adaptation, amendment, reformation, shift, variation, metamorphosis.

altercation n. fight, dispute, disagreement, argument, quarrel, squabble, debate, controversy, clash, fracas, row, contention.

alternate n. replacement, substitute, equivalent, double.

alternate v. fluctuate, oscillate, take turns, vary, rotate, interchange, substitute, transpose.

alternate adj. alternative, reciprocal, substitute, second, rotating, every other, other, different.

alternation n. variation, transposition, interchange, shift.

alternative n. choice, option, recourse, substitute, backup.

although conj. though, even though, albeit, conceding that, admitting that, notwithstanding, while, even if, granted that.

altitude n. height, elevation, stature, tallness; ant. depth.

altogether adv. all in all, totally, completely, wholly, utterly, entirely, absolutely, in general, as a whole, collectively, all told.

altruistic adj. humanitarian, self-sacrificing, unselfish, benevolent, public-spirited, self-abnegating, charitable, philanthropic, generous, noble, noble-hearted, humane, kind.

altruism n. humanity, self-sacrifice, unselfishness, social conscience, public spirit, self-abnegation, philanthropy, generosity; ant. selfishness.

always adv. 1. forever, perpetually, endlessly, everlastingly, eternally, in perpetuum, evermore. 2. without exception, constantly, continually, regularly, invariably, unfailingly, consistently.

amalgam n. combination, mixture, blend, compound, composite, amalgamation, fusion, union, aggregate, coalescence, alloy.

amalgamate v. compound, blend, intermix, combine, coalesce, integrate, merge, synthesize, fuse, unify, homogenize, incorporate, alloy.

amalgamation n. alloy, compound, amalgam, mixture, blend, combination, fusion, synthesis, composite; coalescence, commingling, homogenization.

amass v. gather, compile, accumulate, assemble, collect, garner, hoard, pile up.

amateur n. novice, beginner, initiate, apprentice, nonprofessional, neophyte, aspirant, hopeful, dabbler, greenhorn, rookie (*slang*), tenderfoot.

amateurish *adj.* unskilled, crude, clumsy, incompetent, unprofessional, makeshift.

amatory *adj.* passionate, erotic, sensual, sexual, amorous, romantic, lascivious, libidinous, erogenous.

amaze *v.* astound, astonish, stun, wow (*slang*), flabbergast, floor, dumbfound, bewilder, confound, dismay, disconcert.

amazement *n.* astonishment, wonder, bewilderment, incomprehension, perplexity, stupefaction, shock, surprise, dismay, confusion.

amazing *adj.* astonishing, astounding, marvelous, incredible, unbelievable, stupendous, unusual; *ant.* ordinary.

ambassador *n.* representative, diplomat, agent, minister, emissary, envoy, deputy, consul, legate, plenipotentiary.

ambassadorial *adj.* representative, diplomatic, legatine, plenipotentiary.

ambiance *n.* atmosphere, mood, setting, tone, vibrations, impression, aura, environment, tenor, feeling, air, surroundings.

ambiguity *n.* vagueness, obscurity, equivocation, indefiniteness, dubiousness, ambivalence, confusion, doubt, inconclusiveness; *ant.* certainty, clarity.

ambiguous *adj.* vague, obscure, indefinite, indeterminate, unclear, unspecific, cryptic, equivocal, ambivalent, double-meaning, doubtful, confused.

ambit *n.* circuit, confines, scope, precincts, environs, compass.

ambition *n.* **1.** aspiration, goal, objective, dream, desire, intent, purpose, aim, design. **2.** ambitiousness, drive, enterprise, push, initiative.

ambitious *adj.* industrious, aspiring, enterprising, energetic, eager, enthusiastic, hardworking, diligent, fervid, intent, hard-driving, striving.

ambivalent *adj.* vacillating, inconsistent, of two minds, fluctuating, unresolved, warring, wavering, conflicted, confused, unsettled, unsure, mixed.

amble *n.* walk, stroll, meander, ramble, mosey, perambulate, wander, drift, dawdle.

ambush *n.* trap, snare, hiding place, concealment, shelter, cover.

ambush *v.* entrap, ensnare, surprise, trap, waylay, bushwhack.

ameliorate *v.* improve, enhance, better, elevate, raise, promote, benefit, advance.

amenable *adj.* **1.** complaisant, flexible, tractable, persuadable, obliging, acquiescent, agreeable, biddable, conformable, submissive, susceptible; *ant.* resistant, recalcitrant. **2.** responsible, answerable, accountable, liable, chargeable.

amend *v.* correct, rectify, emend, fix, better, remedy, revise, modify, qualify, repair, redress; *ant.* worsen, impair.

amendment *n.* addition, addendum, emendation, change, correction, appendix, postscript, rectification, clarification, redress, revision, betterment, improvement.

amends *n.* atonement, recompense, expiation, restitution, compensation, satisfaction, restoration, indemnity.

amenity *n.* comfort, convenience, service, attraction, facility, pleasantness, charm, refinement; *ant.* inconvenience.

amiable *adj.* sociable, approachable, friendly, kind, congenial, obliging, agreeable, good-tempered, affable; *ant.* hostile, abrasive.

amicable *adj.* friendly, peaceable, amiable, kind, sociable, cordial, easy, unreserved, fraternal, good-natured; *ant.* acrimonious.

amid *prep.* amidst, amongst, among, in the midst of, in the middle of, in the thick of, surrounded by.

amiss *adj.* wrong, awry, astray, improper, inaccurate, incorrect, faulty, untoward, false, erroneous, defective; *ant.* all right, well.

amity *n.* friendship, fellowship, goodwill, harmony, peace, fraternity, accord, comradeship, amicability, kindness, understanding, tranquillity; *ant.* discord, hostility.

amnesty *n.* pardon, reprieve, mercy, dispensation, immunity, lenience, forgiveness, absolution.

amok *adv.* amuck, crazy, wild, mad, in a frenzy, berserk, insane, like a madman, in a fury.

among *prep.* amid, amidst, amongst, in the midst of, in the middle of, between, with, surrounded by.

amoral adj. nonmoral, unrestrained, intemper-ate, uninhibited, free-living, lax, loose, aban-doned, profligate, wayward.

amorous adj. enamored, in love, amatory, af-fectionate, impassioned, loving, tender; lust-ful, erotic, ardent, randy; ant. indifferent, cold.

amorphous adj. 1. shapeless, formless, un-structured, characterless, featureless, un-formed. 2. unorganized, vague, chaotic, inde-terminate, nondescript, indistinct, indefinite, nebulous; ant. distinctive.

amount n. total, whole, entirety, lot, ex-panse, number, measure, sum, supply, mass, volume.

amount to add up to, come to, equal, total, be tantamount to, be equivalent to, become, purport.

amour n. love affair, relationship, romance, entanglement, intimacy, liaison, affaire de coeur.

ample adj. big, large, generous, expansive, full, plentiful, substantial, lavish, extensive, commo-dious, copious, voluminous.

amplification n. addition, augmentation, in-crease, elaboration.

amplifier n. microphone, loudspeaker, mega-phone, speaker, woofer, tweeter.

amplify v. increase, magnify, boost, expand, intensify, augment, add to, raise, strengthen, enlarge, enhance; ant. diminish, reduce.

amplitude n. 1. breadth, bulk, mass, volume, width, scope, capacity, range, reach, size, dimension, bulk. 2. abundance, plethora, am-pleness, profusion, copiousness, fullness, vast-ness, spaciousness, largeness, greatness, huge-ness, magnitude, plentifulness.

amply adv. liberally, fully, plentifully, substan-tially, abundantly, richly, thoroughly, suffi-ciently, unstintingly, generously, lavishly, hand-somely, greatly.

amputate v. sever, separate, cut or lop off, excise, truncate, remove.

amulet n. charm, talisman, fetish, juju, lucky charm.

amuse v. entertain, cheer, divert, delight, en-thrall, regale, gladden, tickle, charm, beguile, please; ant. bore.

amusement n. entertainment, diversion, distrac-tion, fun, recreation, lark, pastime, sport, game, enjoyment, hobby, merriment; ant. bore, boredom.

amusing adj. 1. entertaining, charming, de-lightful, diverting, enjoyable, interesting, pleas-ant, fun (slang); ant. boring, tedious. 2. funny, humorous, comical, laughable, ludicrous, droll, jolly, merry; ant. dour.

anachronism n. archaism, antique, fossil, dino-saur, fogey.

analogous adj. similar, alike, comparable, corre-sponding, reciprocal, equivalent, parallel, re-sembling, agreeing, like, homologous, related; ant. disparate.

analogy n. comparison, parallelism, resem-blance, similarity, correlation, equivalence, homology, relationship.

analysis n. evaluation, examination, study, test, review, scrutiny, explication, interpretation, in-quiry, breakdown, dissection, investigation.

in the final analysis lastly, finally, in conclu-sion, with everything considered.

analytical adj. logical, rational, perceptive, judi-cious, penetrating, philosophical, precise, sys-tematic, scientific, well-organized, reasonable, well-grounded, thorough, conclusive.

analyze v. examine, investigate, scrutinize, study, evaluate, dissect, consider, test, reduce.

anarchic adj. chaotic, lawless, ungoverned, nihilistic, revolutionary, rebellious, riotous, iconoclastic, disorganized, confused, disor-dered; ant. orderly, submissive.

anarchist n. revolutionary, rebel, nihilist, insur-gent, apostate, terrorist.

anarchy n. chaos, rebellion, revolution, lawless-ness, unrule, nihilism, riot, bedlam, confusion, pandemonium, apostasy, insurrection; ant. rule, control, order.

anathema n. 1. curse, denunciation, maledic-tion, condemnation, damnation, abhorrence, aversion. 2. (object of loathing) pariah, out-cast, persona non grata, abomination, enemy, bane.

anatomize v. dissect, analyze, examine, scruti-nize, vivisect, study, break down, pull apart, separate.

anatomy n. structure, composition, framework, construction, build, makeup, analysis.

ancestor n. forebear, predecessor, antecedent,

precursor, forefather, progenitor, forerunner; *ant.* descendant.

ancestral *adj.* genetic, lineal, hereditary, familial, genealogical, parental.

ancestry *n.* lineage, genealogy, heredity, origin, descent, blood, extraction, forebears, forefathers, race, roots, stock.

anchor *n.* **1.** grapnel, kedge, killick, mudhook. **2.** security, support, mainstay, pillar of strength.

anchor *v.* make fast, affix, moor, fasten, fix, attach.

anchorage *n.* harbor, mooring, port, shelter, refuge, sanctuary, protection.

ancient *adj.* antiquated, old, aged, archaic, primordial, immemorial, outmoded, superannuated, venerable, obsolete, fossilized, antediluvian; *ant.* modern.

ancillary *adj.* auxiliary, subsidiary, additional, supplementary, accessory, extra, secondary, subordinate.

and *conj.* plus, in addition to, together with, including, as well as; also, furthermore, moreover.

androgynous *adj.* hermaphroditic, epicene, gynandrous, bisexual.

anecdote *n.* story, tale, fable, yarn, reminiscence, sketch, episode, incident.

anemic *adj.* pale, pallid, wan; sickly, weak, frail, feeble, infirm.

anew *adv.* afresh, from the beginning, newly, again, once more, once again, in a different way *or* manner.

angel *n.* **1.** cherub, guardian spirit, divine messenger, archangel, saint, seraph; *ant.* devil, fiend. **2.** supporter, backer, benefactor. **3.** (good person) ideal, paragon, darling, treasure.

angelic *adj.* **1.** cherubic, celestial, ethereal, pious, pure, holy, innocent, saintly. **2.** heavenly, entrancing, divine, beautiful.

anger *n.* rage, wrath, fury, outrage, temper, pique, rancor, vexation, ire, dander, passion, gall, exasperation; *ant.* forbearance.

anger *v.* incense, infuriate, enrage, rile, antagonize, provoke, exasperate, madden, miff, needle, annoy, offend; *ant.* appease, calm, please.

angle *n.* **1.** corner, elbow, fork, notch, crotch, incline, divergence, right *or* acute *or* obtuse angle. **2.** view, perspective, outlook, standpoint, viewpoint.

angle for aim for, seek, be after, be out for, contrive, scheme, fish for, hunt, have one's eye on.

angler *n.* fisher, rodster, piscator.

angrily *adv.* infuriatingly, heatedly, irately, furiously, fiercely, sharply, grouchily, violently, hotly, bitterly, acidly, testily; *ant.* calmly, quietly, softly.

angry *adj.* furious, incensed, enraged, mad, irate, infuriated, outraged, rancorous, wrathful, miffed, irascible, splenetic, out of sorts, seeing red (*slang*).

angst *n.* anxiety, dread, apprehension, disquiet, foreboding, worry; agony, depression.

anguish *n.* distress, grief, pain, agony, misery, sorrow, tribulation, heartache, suffering, wretchedness, angst, anxiety; *ant.* solace, happiness.

anguished *adj.* distressed, miserable, wretched, suffering, stricken, afflicted, pained, agonizing, in a state.

angular *adj.* gaunt, bony, rawboned, lean, lanky, skinny.

animal *n.* **1.** beast, living creature, living thing, mammal, fish, crustacean, amphibian, vertebrate, invertebrate, wild animal, domestic animal. **2.** monster, beast, brute, savage.

animal *adj.* **1.** bestial, beastly, brutish, feral, savage, piggish, wild. **2.** corporeal, physical, bodily, carnal, fleshly, instinctive, sensual.

animate *v.* **1.** activate, vitalize, arouse, energize, galvanize, invigorate, reactivate, revive, spark, stimulate, enliven; *ant.* suppress. **2.** inspire, arouse, excite, urge, incite, stir, move, fire, goad, impel; *ant.* discourage.

animated *adj.* spirited, passionate, energetic, lively, vivacious, zestful, enthusiastic, excited, fervent, gay, alive, exuberant; *ant.* sluggish, inert.

animation *n.* life, vitality, exhilaration, passion, spirit, verve, zeal, energy, ebullience, fervor, sparkle, pep; *ant.* inertia, dullness.

animosity *n.* hostility, ill will, malice, spite, enmity, antagonism, malevolence, bitterness, hatred, acrimony, loathing, bad blood; *ant.* goodwill.

annals *n.* records, chronicles, registers, journals, reports, files, memoirs, archives, history.

annex *n.* addition, attachment, adjunct, supplement, addendum, appendix.

annex *v.* append, attach, affix, join, fasten, incorporate, add, acquire, appropriate, seize, take over, usurp.

annexation *n.* **1.** (act of adding on) addition, incorporation, merger, joining. **2.** attachment, increment, increase, addition, expansion, wing.

annihilate *v.* obliterate, abolish, destroy, nullify, demolish, exterminate, eliminate, eradicate, extinguish, wipe out, *slang:* rub out, zap.

annihilation *n.* obliteration, elimination, nullification, extinction, destruction, extermination, eradication, defeat.

annotate *v.* elucidate, gloss, note, comment, interpret, explain.

annotation *n.* marginalia, commentary, footnote, explication, elucidation, interpretation, note, gloss, apparatus criticus.

announce *v.* proclaim, state, declare, advertise, broadcast, publish, reveal, disclose, make known, intimate, divulge, report, leak; *ant.* suppress.

announcement *n.* notification, declaration, statement, advertisement, broadcast, publication, report, bulletin, revelation, disclosure.

announcer *n.* newscaster, reporter, broadcaster, commentator, anchor, messenger, harbinger, herald, crier.

annoy *v.* irritate, aggravate, pester, vex, badger, needle, harass, bother, plague, rile, provoke, exasperate, madden; *ant.* please.

annoyance *n.* irritation, nuisance, vexation, disturbance, bother, aggravation, harassment, pest, headache, pain, pain in the neck; *ant.* pleasure, joy, delight.

annoying *adj.* irritating, aggravating, troublesome, bothersome, disturbing, irksome, maddening, exasperating, pesky, vexatious.

annul *v.* negate, invalidate, rescind, retract, repeal, revoke, void, cancel, reverse; *ant.* restore, enact.

annulment *n.* nullification, invalidation, retraction, repeal, dissolution, cancellation, reversal, recall; *ant.* restoration, enactment.

anodyne *adj.* pain-relieving, numbing, deadening, desensitizing, pain-killing, analgesic, narcotic, sedative, dulling; *ant.* irritant.

anoint *v.* **1.** consecrate, sanctify, bless. **2.** oil, rub, smear, lubricate, daub, grease.

anointing *n.* consecration, blessing, sanctification, dedication, unction.

anomalous *adj.* abnormal, irregular, deviant, unusual, atypical, aberrant, odd, peculiar, incongruous, inconsistent, bizarre, rare; *ant.* normal.

anomaly *n.* abnormality, oddity, exception, aberration, deviation, irregularity, exception, rarity, peculiarity, anachronism, incongruity, freak, misfit.

anonymous *adj.* unidentified, unnamed, unsigned, unacknowledged, uncredited, unauthenticated, unknown, incognito, nondescript, faceless.

another *pron.* someone else, a different person, alternative, substitute, something else; *ant.* same.

another *adj.* **1.** additional, one more, extra, added, a further. **2.** different, distinct, separate, some other.

answer *n.* **1.** response, reply, acknowledgment, explanation, retort, rejoinder, comeback, refutation. **2.** solution, discovery, resolution, outcome, elucidation, explanation.

answer *v.* **1.** reply, respond, acknowledge, retort, rejoin, return, echo, say, come back (*slang*); *ant.* question, inquire. **2.** satisfy, fulfill, suffice, fill. **3.** solve, elucidate, clarify, explain.

answer for be held responsible for, take the blame, be accountable, accept responsibility, be liable, take the rap for (*slang*).

answer to be ruled by, be responsible to, respect the authority of, report to, respect, obey.

answerable *adj.* **1.** responsible, accountable, amenable, chargeable, liable, blameworthy, to blame. **2.** refutable, deniable, defensible, explicable, disprovable.

antagonism *n.* hostility, conflict, animosity, dissension, discord, friction, ill will, competition, rivalry.

antagonist *n.* adversary, opponent, enemy, rival, foe, competitor, contender; *ant.* ally, supporter.

antagonistic *adj.* hostile, adverse, conflicting, opposing, inimical, contentious, bellicose, belligerent.

ligerent, pugnacious, unfriendly, adversarial, unwelcome; *ant.* friendly, sympathetic.

antecedent *adj.* preceding, previous, prior, preliminary.

antecedents *n.* ancestors, descent, lineage, ancestry, forebears, forefathers, extraction, pedigree, stock, blood, background, progenitors.

antedate *v.* **1.** date back, predate. **2.** go before, forerun, precede.

antediluvian *adj.* ancient, primal, prehistoric, primitive, anachronistic, archaic, superannuated, primordial, obsolete, old-fashioned, out-of-date, passé, bygone, antiquated, primeval; *ant.* up-to-date, with it (*slang*).

anterior *adj.* preceding, antecedent, introductory, previous, former, prior, earlier, foregoing; *ant.* subsequent.

anthem *n.* chant, song, hymn, psalm, chorale.

anthology *n.* compilation, collection, selection, treasury, digest, miscellany.

antic *n.* caper, frolic, trick, joke, prank, lark, stunt.

anticipate *v.* **1.** foresee, expect, predict, look forward to, await, hope for, look for, forecast, bank on (*slang*), count on. **2.** preclude, forestall, intercept, prevent.

anticipation *n.* expectation, hope, awaiting, preconception, forethought; forewarning, apprehension, presentiment.

anticipatory *adj.* expectant, hopeful, preparatory, intuitive, proleptic.

anticlimax *n.* disappointment, letdown, disenchantment, bathos, comedown, fiasco.

antidote *n.* neutralizer, cure, detoxicant, countermeasure, remedy, counteragent, corrective, antitoxin, preventive.

antipathetic *adj.* abhorrent, loathsome, averse, hateful, horrible, disgusting, offensive, repellent, inimical, repulsive, revolting, distasteful; *ant.* sympathetic, agreeable, harmonious.

antipathy *n.* dislike, animosity, hatred, hostility, loathing, odium, enmity, aversion, bad blood, repugnance, ill will, incompatibility; *ant.* sympathy, rapport.

antiquarian *adj.* antiquary, collector, curator, archivist, archaist, classicist, savant, anthropologist, archaeologist, student of antiquity.

antiquary *n.* antiquarian, archaist, archaeologist, paleologist.

antiquated *adj.* old-fashioned, out-of-date, obsolete, outmoded, old-fogeyish, archaic, dated, anachronistic, ancient, superannuated, antediluvian; *ant.* modern, forward-looking.

antique *n.* antiquity, period piece, museum piece, heirloom, relic, rarity, curio.

antique *adj.* old, vintage, old-fashioned, quaint, aged, ancient, outdated, superannuated, obsolete.

antiquity *n.* ancient times, time immemorial, distant past, olden days.

antiseptic *n.* disinfectant, germicide, cleanser, purifier, bactericide, decontaminant.

antiseptic *adj.* **1.** disinfectant, bactericidal, germicidal, medicated. **2.** sterile, hygienic, sanitary, pure, germ-free; *ant.* contaminated.

antisocial *adj.* **1.** unfriendly, aloof, reserved, retiring, withdrawn, cold, distant; *ant.* approachable, communicative. **2.** antagonistic, hostile, belligerent, menacing. **3.** disruptive, anarchic, rebellious, disorderly, intractable, feral, wild.

antithesis *n.* **1.** (the state of being opposite) opposition, contradiction, inversion, polarity, contraposition. **2.** (something that is opposite) opposite, reverse, converse, contrary, opposite extreme, contrast, inverse.

antithetical *adj.* contradictory, conflicting, contrasting, counter, opposed, polarized, reverse, inverse, poles apart.

anxiety *n.* anxiousness, uneasiness, worry, misgiving, nervousness, fretfulness, distress, dread, tension, apprehension, angst, foreboding.

anxious *adj.* **1.** distressed, uneasy, worried, afraid, nervous, fearful, jumpy, on edge, apprehensive, fretful, concerned, tense, disturbed, troubled; *ant.* assured, serene. **2.** expectant, eager, enthusiastic, fervent, zealous, impatient, in suspense, intent, itching, yearning, desirous.

apace *adv.* swiftly, speedily, fast, quickly, rapidly, posthaste, expeditiously, at top speed, without delay.

apart *adj.* separated, disconnected, disassociated; distinct, separate, isolated, alone, aloof, individual, special.

apart *adv.* **1.** independently, individually, singly. **2.** aside, to one side, at one side; asunder, in two, into pieces.

apartment n. rooms, living quarters, flat, condominium, penthouse, tenement, suite, lodgings, pad (slang).

apathetic adj. 1. indifferent, unconcerned, dispassionate, uninterested, unfeeling, stoic, unresponsive, cold; ant. concerned, responsive, active. 2. listless, lethargic, unambitious, sluggish, torpid, unmotivated, passive; ant. driven, active.

apathy v. 1. indifference, unconcern, coldness, emotionlessness, uninterestedness, disdain, aloofness, unresponsiveness; ant. interest, concern. 2. listlessness, lethargy, passivity, inertia, sluggishness, torpor.

ape v. imitate, caricature, mock, parody, mirror, parrot, echo, copy, affect, take off on (slang).

aperture n. opening, hole, gap, breach, orifice, chink, rent, cleft, crack, space, vent, fissure, rift.

apex n. top, pinnacle, zenith, peak, summit, climax, vertex, crowning point, high point, crest, culmination, apogee, acme; ant. nadir, bottom.

aphorism n. maxim, adage, axiom, dictum, saying, proverb, saw, epigram, precept.

aplomb n. confidence, poise, savoir-faire, calmness, composure, equanimity, self-assurance, self-confidence, self-possession, sang-froid.

apocalyptic adj. ominous, threatening, prophetic, portentous, revelational, oracular, fatidic.

apocryphal adj. doubtful, spurious, fictitious, fabricated, unauthenticated, questionable, imaginary, phony, concocted, dubious, unproved, unlikely, false, unsubstantiated, unsupported; ant. certain, true, verified.

apogee n. zenith, peak, summit, pinnacle, apex, acme, high point, vertex, top, crest, culmination; ant. nadir, depths.

apologetic adj. repentant, contrite, remorseful, sorry, regretful, rueful, penitent, conscience-stricken; ant. defiant.

apologist n. defender, vindicator, supporter, justifier, advocate, champion, endorser, upholder.

apologize v. beg pardon, excuse oneself, make amends, atone, express regret, ask forgiveness, retract; ant. insult, offend.

apology n. 1. excuse, explanation, justification, defense, apologia, vindication, plea, extenuation. 2. confession, acknowledgment, regret, repentance.

apostle n. advocate, champion, promoter, missionary, preacher, proponent, proselytizer, propagator, evangelist, crusader.

apostasy n. perfidy, disloyalty, betrayal, renunciation, faithlessness, recreancy, heresy, defection, desertion, abandonment; ant. loyalty, orthodoxy.

apostate n. heretic, traitor, recreant, renegade, tergiversator, defector, turncoat, deserter.

apotheosis n. 1. deification, glorification, idolization, exaltation, idealization, immortalization, elevation. 2. ideal, paragon, model, exemplar.

apotheosize v. deify, glorify, idolize, exalt, idealize, immortalize, elevate.

apothecary n. pharmacist, druggist, chemist (Brit.).

appalling adj. disgusting, horrifying, amazing, dismaying, shocking, disconcerting, revolting, awful, horrible, dreadful, horrid, alarming, daunting, grim; ant. pleasant.

apparatus n. 1. appliance, machinery, tool, utensil, equipment, implement, gadget, contraption, device, gear, gizmo (slang). 2. bureaucracy, system, organization, framework, structure, setup, outfit, network.

apparel n. wardrobe, outfit, garments, clothing, attire, dress, vestments, accoutrements, trappings, garb, costume.

apparent adj. evident, obvious, visible, unmistakable, clear, plain, discernible, distinct, conspicuous, distinct, marked, noticeable, overt, outward, manifest; ant. obscure.

apparition n. specter, ghost, phantom, spirit, wraith, chimera, manifestation, phantasm, shade, visitation, presence.

appeal n. 1. attractiveness, interest, charm, engagingness, seductiveness, charisma, sexiness. 2. entreaty, plea, request, solicitation, petition, requisition, overture, proposal, bid, claim, suit.

appeal v. 1. ask, beg, request, urge, petition, beseech, entreat, plead. 2. fascinate, interest, engage, entice, captivate, intrigue, tantalize, tempt, enchant, beguile.

appear *v.* **1.** come into view, come to light, transpire, materialize, surface, emerge, come out, crop up, develop, loom, show, surface. **2.** seem, look, resemble, have the appearance. **3.** (be present or active) attend, perform, act, present oneself, be published, play, take part, turn up, be there, show one's face; *ant.* be absent, be missing, leave.

appearance *n.* **1.** look, countenance, bearing, mien, mannerism, demeanor, attitude, carriage, air, face, posture. **2.** mirage, vision, impression, image, reflection, façade, dream, illusion, apparition, phenomenon, ghost.

make an appearance be present, come, appear, show up.

appease *v.* **1.** satisfy, quell, quench, be enough, do, serve. **2.** calm, allay, soothe, assuage, ease, quiet, diminish, mollify, pacify, placate, quiet, soften; *ant.* provoke, anger.

appellation *n.* name, title, label, address, monicker, epithet, denomination, description, nickname, designation.

append *v.* add, attach, join, tack on, affix, fasten, annex.

appendage *n.* **1.** limb, member, extremity, prosthesis. **2.** addition, attachment, supplement, addendum, adjunct.

appendix *n.* addendum, supplement, codicil, excursus, attachment, index, bibliography, tables, notes.

appertaining *adj.* pertaining, related, germane, relevant, applicable, connected, characteristic, belonging.

appetite *n.* **1.** hunger, thirst, craving, taste, yearning, lust. **2.** desire, longing, craving, hankering, yearning, passion; predilection, proclivity, propensity, inclination.

appetizer *n.* hors d'oeuvre, aperitif, canapé, antipasto, cocktail, taste, sample, preview, tidbit, whet.

appetizing *adj.* tempting, appealing, mouthwatering, inviting, delicious, succulent, tasty, scrumptious, savory, yummy (*slang*); *ant.* disgusting.

applaud *v.* cheer, clap, commend, praise, laud, compliment, acclaim, extol, eulogize, congratulate; *ant.* disparage, jeer.

applause *n.* cheering, acclaim, praise, accolade, ovation, plaudits, eulogizing, commendation, kudos, approval, hand; *ant.* disparagement, jeering.

appliance *n.* device, gadget, machine, mechanism, implement, instrument, apparatus, contraption, tool, contrivance, gizmo (*slang*).

applicable *adj.* fitting, suitable, appropriate, apropos, apt, useful, valid, germane, legitimate, pertinent, proper, relevant, related.

applicant *n.* candidate, aspirant, interviewee, petitioner, inquirer, competitor.

application *n.* **1.** use, utilization, employment, purpose. **2.** request, appeal, entreaty, demand, petition.

applied *adj.* **1.** used, related, correlated, enforced, practiced, utilized, activated. **2.** practical, pragmatic, utilitarian, practicable; *ant.* theoretical.

apply *v.* **1.** request, demand, beg, appeal, petition. **2.** attach, place *or* put on *or* upon, affix, fasten, join, adjoin.

apply oneself attend to, dedicate oneself, address oneself, concentrate on, be occupied with, keep one's mind on, persevere *or* persist in, be industrious, buckle down.

appoint *v.* designate, select, nominate, ordain, assign, delegate, elect, name, commission, choose.

appointed *adj.* **1.** designated, selected, nominated, ordained, assigned, delegated, elected, commissioned, chosen. **2.** equipped, furnished, supplied, fitted out, fixed, set.

appointment *n.* **1.** selection, designation, election, nomination, assignment, installation, delegation, empowering, promotion, approval, choice. **2.** engagement, arrangement, meeting, rendezvous, invitation, conference, tête-à-tête, date.

appointments *n.* furnishings, fittings, gear, paraphernalia, accoutrements, trappings, fixtures, outfit.

apportion *v.* allot, allocate, distribute, ration, dispense, dole out, share, mete, divide, assign, award.

apposite *adj.* relevant, appropriate, apt, apropos, pertinent, germane, befitting, suited, proper, applicable.

appraisal *n.* estimation, assessment, review, sizing up, evaluation, inspection, examination, rating, once-over, opinion, assay, valuation.

appreciable *adj.* definite, discernible, evident, noticeable, obvious, substantial, undeniable, perceptible, measurable, considerable, apparent, clear-cut, pronounced; *ant.* negligible.

appreciate *v.* 1. acknowledge, thank, welcome, enjoy, be obliged, be indebted, give thanks; *ant.* find fault with, complain, object, minimize, complain. 2. admire, value, esteem, honor, extol, praise, applaud; *ant.* denigrate. 3. be sensitive to, have a taste for, have the faculty for, derive pleasure from, like, enjoy, respond to, dig (*slang*).

appreciation *n.* 1. gratitude, thankfulness, recognition, gratefulness. 2. sensitivity, taste, enjoyment, fascination, attraction, love, affection.

appreciative *adj.* 1. thankful, indebted, grateful, obliged, beholden. 2. responsive, perceptive, sensitive, sympathetic, aware, understanding.

apprehend *v.* arrest, capture, seize, catch, detain, hold, get, grab, nab, *slang:* bust, collar, run in.

apprehension *n.* fear, anxiety, concern, worry, unease, nervousness, trepidation, misgiving, doubt, suspicion.

apprehensive *adj.* fearful, afraid, anxious, uneasy, worried, nervous, suspicious, distrustful, alarmed, concerned, doubtful; *ant.* confident.

apprentice *n.* trainee, beginner, novice, neophyte, pupil, student, recruit; *ant.* expert.

apprise *v.* acquaint, brief, inform, tell, enlighten, notify, warn, tip off.

approach *v.* 1. appeal *or* apply to, address, speak *or* talk to, accost, request, propose, make advances *or* overtures to, buttonhole, corner, descend on *or* upon; *ant.* avoid, shun, turn away. 2. come near, drift *or* go *or* move toward, come up to, loom up, verge upon, close in, *ant.* leave, recede, depart. 3. be imminent *or* forthcoming, loom, await, impend, draw near.

approachable *adj.* 1. (of places or things) accessible, available, convenient, attainable, obtainable. 2. (of people) sociable, friendly, agreeable, warm, engaging, receptive, congenial; *ant.* aloof, standoffish, intimidating.

approbation *n.* 1. approval, admiration, high regard, esteem, favor. 2. sanction, consent, support, endorsement, permission.

appropriate *v.* 1. seize, take, secure, usurp. 2. allocate, allot, disburse, set aside *or* apart, apportion, budget, reserve.

appropriate *adj.* proper, fit, suitable, seemly, becoming, right, fitting, correct, meet.

appropriateness *n.* propriety, properness, correctness, felicitousness, pertinence, relevance, aptness, applicability, seemliness, suitability.

appropriation *n.* 1. seizure, commandeering, confiscation, misappropriation, usurpation, impoundment. 2. allocation, gift, award, grant, funding, bestowing, allotment, apportionment, donation, entitlement, sponsoring.

approval *n.* 1. regard, esteem, favor, admiration, praise, respect, acclaim, liking, appreciation. 2. sanction, endorsement, support, consent, permission, acquiescence, agreement, validation, OK, blessing, go-ahead, green light (*slang*).

approve *v.* 1. affirm, support, encourage, ratify, endorse, confirm, sanction, consent *or* agree *or* assent to, OK, give one's blessing, give the green light (*slang*); *ant.* oppose, reject, veto. 2. favor, recommend, praise, acclaim, applaud; *ant.* frown on.

approved *adj.* accepted, sanctioned, recommended, permitted, recognized, correct, authorized, official, prestige, preferred.

approximate *adj.* estimated, rough, loose, conjectural, guessed, ballpark (*slang*), inexact; *ant.* close, near, similar, comparable, relative; *ant.* exact, absolute.

approximately *adv.* relatively, about, more or less, around, roughly, nearly, almost, not far from, in the vicinity of, in the region of, close to, in round numbers, circa; *ant.* exactly.

approximation *n.* estimation, conjecture, rough calculation, rough idea, guesstimate (*slang*), extrapolation, *ant.* exactitude, precision.

appurtenance *n.* accessory, supplement, accompaniment, auxiliary, adjunct, addition, subsidiary, attachment.

appurtenances *n.* 1. accessories, accompaniments, appendages, additions. 2. equipment, paraphernalia, gear, trappings.

apropos *adj.* appropriate, fitting, germane, relevant, suitable, timely, apt, correct, right, seemly, to the point, applicable.

apt *adj.* 1. likely, inclined, prone, tending,

liable, disposed, given. 2. appropriate, suitable, fit, proper, applicable, apropos, germane, befitting, timely, pertinent, seemly, meet.

aptitude *n.* skill, talent, capability, ability, intelligence, proficiency, faculty, capacity, quickness.

aquatic *adj.* swimming, amphibious, marine, oceanic, of the sea, fishlike.

arbiter *n.* judge, arbitrator, mediator, intermediary, negotiator, referee, umpire.

arbitrary *adj.* 1. capricious, willful, fanciful, whimsical, superficial, irrational, erratic, random, inconsistent; *ant.* rational, reasonable, circumspect. 2. absolute, despotic, autocratic, dictatorial, tyrannical, dogmatic, domineering, imperious, overbearing.

arbitrate *v.* settle, decide, determine, adjudicate, judge, referee, umpire.

arbitration *n.* mediation, settlement, negotiation, adjudication, determination, judgment, decision.

arbitrator *n.* arbiter, adjudicator, negotiator, intermediary, mediator, moderator, judge, referee, umpire.

arcane *adj.* secret, hidden, mysterious, cryptic, obscure, private, esoteric, enigmatic, abstruse, recondite, profound, *ant.* open, obvious.

arch *n.* curve, arc, bend, bow, archway, cupola, dome, vault.

arch *v.* arc, bow, curve, bend, vault, extend.

arch *adj.* 1. principal, chief, first, foremost, main, primary, major, greatest, highest, leading. 2. mischievous, roguish, waggish, wily, provocative, sly, frolicsome, playful.

archaic *adj.* ancient, primitive, superannuated, obsolete, outdated, antiquated, antediluvian, outmoded, passé, démodé, old.

archetype *n.* prototype, model, pattern, original, precursor, standard, paradigm, exemplar, role model, type, form, ideal, classic, conception.

architect *n.* designer, planner, engineer, master builder, constructor, creator, originator, founder.

architecture *n.* structure, construction, design, composition, framework, building, style, architectonics.

archive *n.* repository, record office, library, museum.

archives *n.* records, ledgers, documents, annals, registers, muniments, memorabilia.

ardent *adj.* 1. passionate, fervent, impassioned, warm, hotblooded, avid, eager, zealous, vehement, fervent, fervid, enthusiastic, keen; *ant.* lukewarm, indifferent. 2. devoted, constant, loyal, true, faithful.

ardor *n.* enthusiasm, fervor, passion, warmth, intensity, spirit, lust, vehemence, zeal, fire, heat; *ant.* coolness, indifference.

arduous *adj.* difficult, hard, strenuous, exhausting, grueling, laborious, severe, taxing, enervating, draining, rigorous, trying, onerous, formidable; *ant.* easy.

area *n.* 1. expanse, stretch, distance, space. 2. section, lot, plot, zone, neighborhood, sector, block, precinct, ward, district, township, division.

arena *n.* stadium, coliseum, amphitheater, park, field, stage, ground, battleground, battlefield.

argot *n.* dialect, idiom, jargon, cant, slang, vernacular, lingo, terminology, vocabulary, usage.

argue *v.* 1. quarrel, bicker, fight, squabble, feud, fall out, haggle. 2. (give the pros and cons of) debate, clarify, discuss, talk about, question, dispute, thrash out, reason. 3. (make a case for) plead, appeal, justify, explain, elucidate, maintain, reason, show, convince, contend, claim, persuade, prove.

argument *n.* 1. (acrimonious verbal exchange) disagreement, spat, fight, dispute, quarrel, words, row. 2. evidence, reasons, exhibits, reasons, proof. 3. debate, discussion, exchange, contention, dialogue.

argumentative *adj.* disputatious, pugnacious, contentious, factious, quarrelsome, opinionated.

arid *adj.* 1. dry, sere, parched, baked, torrid, desert. 2. barren, infertile, sterile, lifeless, unproductive, waste.

aright *adv.* rightly, correctly, properly, accurately, duly, justly, exactly, truly.

arise *v.* 1. get up, wake up, awaken, rise, stand up. 2. ascend, go up, climb, soar, tower, mount. 3. result, emanate, begin, originate, derive, commence, ensue, come to light, crop up, follow, occur.

aristocracy *n.* nobility, gentry, upper class, ruling class, patricians, elite, gentility, upper crust, top drawer.

aristocratic *adj.* **1.** noble, genteel, blueblooded, titled, highborn, patrician, thoroughbred, elite. **2.** dignified, refined, well-bred, courtly, polished; haughty, lordly, imperious.

arm *n.* **1.** limb, appendage, wing, member, branch, rod, bough, offshoot, handle; bend, crook, projection. **2.** branch, department, subsidiary, division, unit.
at arm's length aloof, unfriendly, distant, remote, haughty.
with open arms warmly, cordially, affectionately, joyously friendly.

arm *v.* equip, outfit, furnish, supply, gird, provide, accoutre, fit out.

armaments *n.* weaponry, ammunition, arms, artillery, ordnance, guns.

armed *adj.* protected, armored, equipped, steeled, primed, strengthened, fitted out, fortified, forearmed, guarded.

armor *n.* **1.** shell, chain mail, steel plating, garniture, iron-cladding. **2.** protection, defense, shield.

armored *adj.* armor-plated, ironclad, protected, mail-clad, steel-plated, bulletproof, bombproof.

armory *n.* arsenal, ammunition dump, repository, stockpile, depot.

arms *n.* weapons, guns, instruments of war, armaments, firearms, ordnance.
up in arms agitated, alarmed, aroused, excited, riotous.

army *n.* **1.** armed force, military troops, soldiers, militia, land forces. **2.** gang, mob, swarm, pack, throng, horde, array, multitude.

aroma *adj.* smell, scent, odor, fragrance, bouquet, perfume.

aromatic *adj.* fragrant, pungent, perfumed, sweet-smelling, odoriferous, balmy, redolent; *ant.* acrid.

around *adv.* **1.** nearby, close, at hand, nigh. **2.** all over, here and there, everywhere, in all directions, in the air, to and fro.

around *prep.* **1.** approximately, about, more or less, roughly, almost, close to. **2.** encircling, encompassing, on all sides of, on every side of, surrounding, enclosing, circum[a]jacent to.

arouse *v.* **1.** stimulate, excite, stir up, rouse, move, prompt, goad, spark, incite, instigate, spur, whip up, agitate. **2.** wake up, waken, awaken, rouse, startle.

arraign *v.* accuse, charge, incriminate, indict, prosecute, call to account, denounce, impugn.

arrange *v.* **1.** align, lay out, tidy, file, order, organize, position, adjust, regulate, systemize, classify, order, distribute, group, method-ize. **2.** plan, prepare for, coordinate, determine, devise, scheme, construct, contrive, design, schedule, organize, stage-manage, swing (*slang*). **3.** orchestrate, score, harmonize, instrument, adapt.

arrangement *n.* **1.** organization, grouping, classification, ordering. **2.** agreement, settlement, compromise, deal, adjustment, contract, pact.

arrant *adj.* notorious, outright, out-and-out, atrocious, brazen, blatant, flagrant, barefaced, downright, utter, extreme, unmitigated, infamous.

array *n.* **1.** design, arrangement, order, pattern. **2.** formal dress, apparel, attire, finery, garb, garments, raiment, regalia. **3.** throng, assemblage, multitude, host, crowd.

arrears *n.* unpaid *or* outstanding debt, deficit, balance due, back payments, unfinished work, obligations.

arrest *n.* incarceration, imprisonment, appropriation, apprehension, confinement, captivity, protective custody, seizure, detention, duress; **under arrest** taken into custody, seized, apprehended, jailed, imprisoned, detained, arrested, caught, busted; *slang*: snagged, collared, nabbed, booked, sent up the river.

arrest *v.* **1.** apprehend, capture, incarcerate, imprison, jail, detain, take into custody; *slang*: bust, nab, collar, run in; *ant.* free, liberate, parole. **2.** stop, restrain, prevent, restrict, check, abort, limit, control.

arresting *adj.* noticeable, stunning, striking, attention-getting, charming, surprising, extraordinary, engaging, noteworthy, remarkable, conspicuous; *ant.* unremarkable, inconspicuous.

arrival *n.* **1.** appearance, approach, entrance, advent, coming, influx, landing, reaching one's destination; *ant.* departure, leaving. **2.** visitor, newcomer, entrant, immigrant.

arrive *v.* **1.** appear, come, show up, turn up, alight, happen, occur, materialize, land. **2.** succeed, make it (*slang*), get to the top; *ant.* fail, stagnate.

arrogance *n.* conceit, haughtiness, vanity, hubris, condescension, insolence, scorn, contempt, disdain, highhandedness, pretension, lordliness, superciliousness, airs; *ant.* humility.

arrogant *adj.* conceited, haughty, condescending, insolent, contemptuous, disdainful, high and mighty, lordly, patronizing, imperious, supercilious, superior; *ant.* humble.

arrogate *v.* misappropriate, seize, usurp, commandeer, confiscate, demand, presume.

arsenal *n.* supply, stockpile, storehouse, warehouse, armory, repository, ammunition dump, ordnance depot.

art *n.* **1.** masterpiece, painting, picture, sculpture, statue, literature, music, dance. **2.** creativity, imagination, ability, inventiveness, ingenuity, skill.

artful *adj.* **1.** crafty, shrewd, sly, cunning, wily, tricky, canny. **2.** skillful, able, clever, ingenious, adroit, resourceful.

article *n.* **1.** thing, object, substance, commodity. **2.** essay, paper, editorial, commentary, exposition.

articulate *v.* enunciate, verbalize, vocalize, pronounce, say, state, talk, speak, utter, voice; express, spell out, explain, expand *or* enlarge on, elucidate.

articulation *n.* enunciation, diction, pronunciation, elocution, delivery, verbalization, vocalization, saying, speaking, voicing; explanation, elucidation, expression.

artifice *n.* **1.** maneuver, stratagem, trick, wile, ruse. **2.** trickery, guile, cunning, deceit, dishonesty. **3.** skill, ability, know-how, facility.

artificial *adj.* **1.** simulated, unreal, synthetic, bogus, ersatz, imitation, pseudo, sham, spurious, manufactured, pretend, counterfeit, fake, phony (*slang*); *ant.* natural, genuine, real. **2.** feigned, affected, unnatural, insincere, specious, mannered, factitious, stagy, plastic, phony (*slang*); *ant.* sincere.

artillery *n.* guns, battery, cannon, ordnance, fieldpieces.

artisan *n.* expert, technician, craftsperson, workman, journeyman, expert, mechanic.

artist *n.* **1.** craftsperson, painter, sculptor. **2.** expert, master, maestro.

artiste *n.* actor, performer, entertainer, comic, player, trouper, vaudevillian.

artistic *adj.* **1.** creative, talented, inventive, skillful, artful, crafty, imaginative, discriminating, sensitive, sublime, well-executed. **2.** aesthetic, decorative, picturesque, musical, pictorial, rhythmical, poetic, dramatic, patterned, studied, belletristic.

artistry *n.* workmanship, skill, proficiency, creativity, talent, craft, sensibility, brilliance, genius, art, style.

artless *adj.* **1.** natural, simple, genuine, primitive, pure, true, unadorned, unartificial, uncontrived. **2.** guileless, naive, open, sincere, straightforward, unaffected, unpretentious, innocent, candid, frank, honest, humble, ingenuous, green, simple.

as *conj.* because, since, considering that, seeing that, in that, for instance, while, for example, when.

as for with regard to, with respect to, with relation to, in reference to, on the subject of, as regards.

as it were so to say, so to speak, in a way, in a manner of speaking, in some way.

ascend *v.* rise, go up, fly up, soar, take off, climb, mount, move up, slope upwards.

ascendancy *n.* supremacy, dominance, rule, reign, sway, influence, dominion, control, power, preeminence, sovereignty, upper hand, superiority.

ascendant *adj.* **1.** rising, climbing, mounting, uphill. **2.** dominant, authoritative, controlling, prevailing, influential, preeminent, ruling, superior, commanding, powerful.

ascent *n.* **1.** rise, climb, ascendance, climbing, mounting, ascension, levitation. **2.** upgrade, incline, slope, acclivity.

ascertain *v.* learn, find out, discover, determine, make certain, verify, establish, confirm, identify.

ascetic *n.* puritan, abstainer, celibate, flagellant, monk, nun; *ant.* voluptuary.

ascetic *adj.* austere, abstinent, continent, self-denying, severe, spartan, puritanical, temperate, strict, self-disciplined, celibate, abstemious.

asceticism n. self-denial, continence, self-abnegation, puritanism, temperance, absti-nence, celibacy, austerity, harshness; ant. self-indulgence.

ascribe v. credit, attribute, assign, charge, im-pute, chalk up to.

ashamed adj. sorry, guilt-ridden, disgraced, humiliated, embarrassed, humbled, chagrined, shamefaced, sheepish, guilty, abashed, remorse-ful, redfaced, mortified, apologetic; ant. defi-ant, shameless, remorseless.

ashen adj. wan, pallid, pasty, pale, anemic, blanched, ghastly, leaden, gray, white; ant. ruddy.

ashes n. 1. cinders, embers, dust, powder, slag, charcoal, volcanic ash, soot. 2. ruins, remains, vestiges, destruction, remnants.

aside adv. to one side, out of the way, away, in reserve, apart, out of sight.

aside from besides, leaving out, excluding, except for, save.

asinine adj. senseless, stupid, imbecilic, idiotic, moronic, witless, absurd, cretinous, doltish, half-witted, brainless, inane; ant. sensible, in-telligent.

ask v. 1. inquire, question, query, interrogate, quiz, catechize. 2. beg, appeal, plead, entreat, implore, supplicate, beseech, importune, pray, press, request. 3. demand, require, solicit, seek, bid, order.

askance adv. disapprovingly, disdainfully, scornfully, obliquely, sideways, suspiciously, doubtfully, skeptically, distrustfully, contemp-tuously.

askew adj., adv. crooked, off-center, awry, lop-sided, aslant, out of line, oblique.

asleep adj. sleeping, slumbering, dozing, nap-ping, snoozing, reposing, inert, dormant, un-conscious, fast asleep, comatose, dead to the world (slang).

aspect n. 1. appearance, looks, countenance, face, mien, features. 2. viewpoint, point of view, outlook, position, perspective, regard, slant, spin (slang).

asperity n. 1. roughness, harshness, uneven-ness, ruggedness. 2. hardship, trouble, misfor-tune, difficulty, impediment. 3. acrimony, rudeness, bitterness, sharpness, ill temper.

aspersion n. criticism, defamation, slander, slur, vilification, vituperation, denigration, dis-paragement, calumny, censure, smear, mud-slinging.

asphyxiate v. suffocate, smother, choke, stifle, strangle, throttle.

aspirant n. candidate, competitor, applicant, contestant, seeker, suitor, hopeful, striver, wannabe (slang).

aspiration n. goal, dream, aim, hope, objective, endeavor, wish, intent, ambition, ideal, desire, purpose.

aspire v. aim, intend, dream, wish, hope, seek, pursue, yearn, purpose, long.

aspiring adj. ambitious, enterprising, striving, endeavoring, eager, would-be, hopeful, opti-mistic, longing, wishful.

ass n. idiot, simpleton, fool, dunce, numskull, dolt, cretin, half-wit, nitwit, nincompoop, ninny, blockhead, bonehead (slang).

assail v. 1. assault, attack, fall upon, abuse, maltreat, impugn, strike, pelt. 2. berate, ma-lign, revile, criticize, vilify, bombard, belabor, impugn, lay into (slang).

assailable adj. vulnerable, defenseless, ex-posed, weak.

assailant n. attacker, assaulter, perpetrator, mugger, aggressor, abuser.

assassin n. killer, murderer, slayer, execu-tioner, thug, slang; hit man, enforcer.

assassinate v. murder, kill, dispatch, execute, eliminate, slay, slaughter, do away with, slang; hit, rub out, take out, waste.

assassination n. murder, killing, shooting, slay-ing, homicide, hit (slang).

assault n. attack, aggression, invasion, on-slaught, charge, offensive, raid, storm, charge, strike.

assay v. test, measure, examine, assess, ana-lyze, inspect, evaluate, weigh, estimate, ap-praise, investigate.

assemblage n. group, gathering, association, crowd, multitude, assembly, array, body, throng, mass.

assemble v. 1. gather, meet, get together, congregate, group, collect, join up, rally, flock, marshal, muster. 2. construct, com-pose, build, manufacture, erect, set up, piece together, make.

assembly n. 1. gathering, congregation,

throng, assemblage, meeting, association. **2.** construction, manufacture, building, piecing together, joining; *ant.* separation, dismantling, wrecking.

assent *n.* acceptance, approval, OK, agreement, compliance, acquiescence, concurrence, consent, permission, sanction.

assent *v.* consent, approve, allow, permit, grant, sanction, comply, submit, acquiesce, accede, agree, concede, yield, concur; *ant.* refuse.

assert *v.* state, affirm, say, declare, aver, pronounce, proclaim, avow; *ant.* deny.

assertion *n.* affirmation, declaration, statement, word, contention, claim, allegation, pronouncement, vindication, avowal.

assertive *adj.* aggressive, self-assured, domineering, dogmatic, bold, emphatic, insistent, forceful, strong-willed, confident, assuming, pushy (*slang*); *ant.* timid, shy, self-effacing.

assess *v.* appraise, estimate, evaluate, review, value, weigh, consider, determine, judge, rate.

assessment *n.* appraisal, estimation, evaluation, opinion, determination, judgment, review, calculation.

asset *n.* benefit, advantage, strength, aid, virtue, help, plus, resource, service; *ant.* liability.

assets *n.* capital, funds, holdings, means, wealth, property, resources, reserves, possessions, wherewithal, goods, estate.

asseverate *v.* assert, maintain, declare, swear, profess, affirm, avouch, testify, protest, pronounce, certify, avow.

assiduous *adj.* diligent, persevering, conscientious, attentive, industrious, dedicated, indefatigable, unflagging, hard-working, devoted; *ant.* negligent.

assign *v.* **1.** appoint, commission, select, delegate, authorize, ordain, charge, elect, relegate. **2.** distribute, give out, consign, allot. **3.** set apart, earmark, designate, specify, allocate, indicate.

assignation *n.* **1.** allocation, allotment, allowance, ration. **2.** rendezvous, tryst, date, affair, tête-à-tête.

assignment *n.* duty, job, task, responsibility, mission, goal, objective.

assimilate *v.* **1.** absorb, take in *or* up, soak up, digest. **2.** understand, grasp, take in, learn, sense. **3.** adjust, adapt, acclimatize, accustom, conform.

assimilation *n.* **1.** absorption, digestion, inhalation, integration, incorporation. **2.** adjustment, adaptation, agreement, conformity, acclimatization.

assist *v.* help, aid, support, abet, succor, boost, lend a hand to, enable, facilitate, rally around; *ant.* hinder.

assistance *n.* help, aid, support, collaboration, cooperation, succor, reinforcement; *ant.* hindrance.

assistant *n.* aide, associate, helper, partner, collaborator, adjutant, right hand, helpmate, accessory, abettor.

associate *v.* **1.** keep company with, have relations with, be intimate with, work with, fraternize with, join with, get along with, consort with, be friendly with, run *or* hang around with (*slang*). **2.** relate, correlate, compare, link, connect, join. **3.** incorporate, organize, affiliate, unite, federate, ally, amalgamate; *ant.* disband, dissolve, break up.

association *n.* **1.** friendship, fraternization, affiliation, companionship, camaraderie, fellowship, intimacy, union. **2.** organization, federation, corporation, union. **3.** connection, relationship, linkage, correlation, tie-in.

assort *v.* sort, classify, arrange, group.

assorted *adj.* different, various, diverse, mixed, miscellaneous, motley, sundry, manifold, variegated, differing, multifarious.

assortment *n.* mixture, variety, diversity, medley, array. mishmash, mélange, potpourri, jumble, hodgepodge.

assuage *v.* **1.** (as pain) alleviate, lessen, relieve, soothe, mitigate, palliate, modify. **2.** (as thirst or hunger) satisfy, appease, fill, surfeit. **3.** calm, pacify, quiet, still, mollify, settle down; *ant.* agitate.

assume *v.* **1.** take for granted, suppose, presume, posit, presuppose, postulate, theorize, ascertain, speculate, infer, expect. **2.** pretend, feign, affect, put on. **3.** take, seize, appropriate, confiscate.

assumed *adj.* **1.** taken for granted, presumed, understood, presupposed, conjectured, postulated, supposed, accepted, given, granted, hypothesized. 2. fictitious, pretended, false, counterfeit, spurious; *ant.* genuine, bona fide.

assuming *adj.* presumptuous, arrogant, important, audacious, brazen, pretentious, impudent, impertinent, pushy (*slang*), self-forward, bold; *ant.* diffident, deferential.

assumption *n.* presumption, supposition, conjecture, surmise, suspicion, theorization.

assurance *n.* **1.** guarantee, insurance, pledge, certainty, promise, security. **2.** confidence, conviction, trust, certainty, faith; *ant.* doubt, misgivings.

assure *v.* **1.** guarantee, attest, vouch for, aver. **2.** convince, prove, persuade, induce. **3.** promise, pledge, affirm, swear. **4.** encourage, reassure, hearten, inspire.

assured *adj.* **1.** certain, sure, undoubted, guaranteed. **2.** confident, self-possessed, unhesitating, bold; *ant.* insecure, self-doubting.

assuredly *adv.* certainly, surely, positively, definitely.

astir *adj., adv.* in the air, in motion, circulating, about, afoot, roused, up, awake.

astonish *v.* amaze, flabbergast, stun, astound, stupefy, floor, surprise, nonplus, dumbfound, wow (*slang*).

astonishing *adj.* amazing, surprising, astounding, incredible, striking, impressive, prodigious, stunning, breathtaking, staggering, stupefying.

astonishment *n.* surprise, amazement, wonder, awe, shock, dismay, bewilderment, consternation.

astound *v.* amaze, astonish, overwhelm, flabbergast, shock, stagger, shake, dumbfound, surprise, wow (*slang*).

astounding *adj.* amazing, astonishing, overwhelming, incredible, unbelievable, sensational, shocking, staggering, surprising, stunning, electrifying, breathtaking, wonderful, impressive.

astray *adv.* adrift, off course, awry, amiss, off the mark, wrong.

astride *prep.* straddling, on the back of, sitting on.

astringent *adj.* acerbic, harsh, biting, stringent, trenchant, caustic, acid, scathing, severe; *ant.* bland.

astronaut *n.* space traveler, cosmonaut, spaceman *or* spacewoman, space pilot, rocketeer.

astronomical *adj.* **1.** cosmological, celestial, astrophysical. **2.** huge, enormous, high, uncountable, incalculable, out of sight (*slang*).

astronomy *n.* stargazing, cosmology, astrophysics, astrography, uranology.

astute *adj.* shrewd, clever, sharp, adroit, keen, perceptive, wily, discerning, perspicacious, intelligent, crafty, deft, able, canny.

astuteness *n.* shrewdness, acuteness, acumen, insight, discernment, perceptiveness, sagacity, wiliness, penetration, craftiness, cleverness, keenness.

asunder *adv.* apart, in pieces, to bits, in two, in half, in twain.

asylum *n.* **1.** mental institution *or* hospital, madhouse, *slang:* funny farm, loony bin, nuthouse. **2.** refuge, haven, sanctuary, shelter, safety, retreat.

asymmetrical *adj.* dissymmetrical, unbalanced, uneven, crooked, awry, irregular, disproportionate, unequal.

asymmetry *n.* dissymmetry, imbalance, unevenness, irregularity, misproportion, disproportion, inequality.

at *prep.* **1.** in the vicinity of, by, near, on, in, about. **2.** toward, in the direction of, to, through.

atheism *n.* heathenism, impiety, paganism, rationalism, freethinking, nonbelief, skepticism, godlessness.

atheist *n.* nonbeliever, heathen, infidel, pagan, freethinker, agnostic.

atheistic *adj.* irreligious, unbelieving, impious, skeptical, rationalistic, freethinking, ungodly; *ant.* religious.

athlete *n.* sportsman, sportswoman, competitor, contender, contestant, jock (*slang*).

athletic *adj.* active, energetic, fit, muscular, strong, powerful, sinewy, robust, healthy; *ant.* puny, scrawny, flabby.

athletics *n.* sports, games, exercises, calisthenics, events, contests.

atmosphere *n.* surroundings, environment, ambiance, climate, tenor, mood, tone, feeling, air, spirit, vibrations.

atmospheric *adj.* meteorological, climatic, aerial.

atom *n.* speck, particle, bit, iota, grain, crumb, morsel, scrap, mite.

atom bomb atomic bomb, nuclear device *or* bomb, nuclear weapon, thermonuclear device *or* weapon, neutron bomb, hydrogen bomb, A-bomb.

atomic *adj.* 1. minute, microscopic, tiny, diminutive. 2. nuclear, thermonuclear, fissionable, atom-powered.

atone *v.* make amends, compensate for, expiate, do penance, pay for.

atonement *n.* penance, amends, reparation, restitution, compensation, restoration.

atrocious *adj.* heinous, vicious, abominable, vile, hideous, inhuman, barbaric, cruel, savage, monstrous, execrable.

atrocity *n.* crime, brutality, horror, evil, heinousness, viciousness, abomination, hideousness, inhumanity, barbarity, cruelty, savagery, monstrosity, villainy.

atrophy *n.* wasting, shriveling, shrinking, deterioration, emaciation, degeneration, withering, decline.

attach *v.* connect, affix, bind, join, fasten, couple, link, tie, unite, weld, adhere; *ant.* remove, detach.

attachable *adj.* appendable, annexable, separable, adjustable, movable; *ant.* whole, inseparable.

attached *adj.* 1. connected, associated, affiliated. 2. affectionate, devoted, fond, loving.

attachment *n.* 1. accessory, extension, supplement, addition, annex, adjunct. 2. fondness, love, affection, liking, devotion, affinity.

attack *n.* 1. aggression, charge, onslaught, assault, raid, advance, offense, bombardment, invasion; *ant.* withdrawal, retreat. 2. spell, seizure, bout, fit, outburst, paroxysm, relapse.

attack *v.* 1. assault, assail, strike, charge, besiege, invade, storm, bear *or* swoop down on *or* upon; *ant.* retreat, recoil, fall back. 2. berate, malign, revile, refute, censure, inveigh against, pillory, castigate, denounce.

attacker *n.* assailant, abuser, assaulter, aggressor, persecutor, mugger, raider, perpetrator, criminal, felon.

attain *v.* achieve, accomplish, earn, reach, realize, get, acquire, win, obtain; *ant.* lose, miss.

attainable *adj.* achievable, reachable, feasible, available, winnable.

attempt *n.* effort, try, undertaking, essay, trial, go (*slang*), struggle, venture, *slang:* crack, shot, stab.

attend *v.* 1. accompany, escort, chaperon. 2. be present at, make an appearance, show up, visit, be a guest, frequent, haunt; *ant.* leave, be absent.

attend to deal with, see to, look after, concentrate on, take care of, manage.

attendance *n.* audience, crowd, turnout, house, gate, door.

attendant *n.* aide, assistant, helper, guide, guard, servant.

attention *n.* 1. (state of mind) attentiveness, concentration, alertness, intentness, *ant.* neglect, disregard. 2. (act of taking notice) observation, notice, mindfulness, awareness, heed; respect, politeness, courtesy, deference, consideration.

attentive *adj.* 1. alert, concentrating, observant, heedful, conscientious, intent. 2. considerate, helpful, caring, mindful, devoted, deferential.

attenuate *v.* weaken, dilute, thin out, adulterate, debase, water down, reduce; *ant.* intensify, thicken.

attest *v.* declare, certify, maintain, testify, confirm, corroborate, endorse, authenticate, substantiate, vouch, verify, witness.

attire *n.* clothing, outfit, dress, costume, garments, apparel, gear, wear, get-up.

attitude *n.* disposition, demeanor, outlook, perspective, aspect, air, posture, bearing, manner, affectation, pose, mien.

attorney *n.* lawyer, counsel, counselor, attorney-at-law.

attract *v.* appeal to, entice, captivate, interest, charm, draw to, engage, invite, lure, seduce, tempt; *ant.* repel.

attraction *n.* 1. (property of attracting) magnetism, drawing power, pull, affinity, gravitation, inclination, enticement, temptation, fascination; *ant.* revulsion, alienation. 2. (something that attracts) magnet, charm, appeal, spectacle, lure, bait, sex appeal.

attractive *adj.* appealing, tempting, enticing, fetching, alluring, enchanting, beautiful, gorgeous, handsome, pretty, good-looking; *ant.* repulsive.

attribute *n.* characteristic, property, quality, trait, feature, mark, sign, condition.

attribute *v.* credit, ascribe, accredit, impute, charge, blame, assign.

attribution *n.* accreditation, ascription, imputation, charge, assignment.

attrition *n.* abrasion, wearing away, erosion, friction, grinding, chafing, rubbing, scraping, weakening.

attune *v.* 1. tune, adjust the pitch, put in tune. 2. adjust, harmonize, regulate, accustom, adapt, acclimatize, assimilate, familiarize.

attuned *adj.* sensitive, perceptive, sympathetic, receptive, in harmony with, in synch with (*slang*).

atypical *adj.* abnormal, unusual, deviant, exceptional, odd, peculiar, extraordinary, aberrant, divergent, anomalous, freakish, exotic, eccentric; *ant.* ordinary.

audacious *adj.* 1. brave, bold, daring, brazen, courageous, unabashed, dauntless, venturesome; *ant.* cautious, timid, reserved. 2. presumptuous, rude, disrespectful, impertinent, forward, assuming, insolent; *ant.* polite, deferential.

audacity *n.* 1. courage, daring, boldness, bravery, assurance, fearlessness, valor, guts. 2. impudence, insolence, impertinence, gall, brazenness, chutzpah, rudeness.

audible *adj.* hearable, discernible, perceptible, clear, detectable, distinct, recognizable.

audience *n.* viewers, listeners, onlookers, spectators, crowd, assemblage, turnout, fans, devotees, assemblage, reception, ratings.

audit *n.* inspection, scrutiny, examination, statement, balancing, checking, review, investigation, verification.

audit *v.* check, balance, review, investigate, scrutinize, examine, inspect, analyze.

audition *n.* test, trial, hearing, tryout.

auditor *n.* accountant, actuary, inspector, examiner, analyst.

auditorium *n.* hall, theater, playhouse, movie house, amphitheater, assembly hall, opera house, concert hall, assembly room.

auditory *adj.* auditive, auricular, acoustic, aural, audible.

aura *n.* emanation, quality, vibrations, vibes (*slang*), air, feeling, mood, spirit, ambiance, climate, atmosphere, forewarning, prodrome.

auspices *n.* approval, support, sponsorship, patronage, aegis, guidance, charge, supervision, authority, tutelage.

auspicious *adj.* favorable, encouraging, optimistic, promising, opportune, fortunate, hopeful, lucky, felicitous; *ant.* unfavorable, ominous.

austere *adj.* 1. (said of one's manner or appearance) harsh, severe, hard, rigid, solemn, strict, stern, serious, cold. 2. ascetic, puritanical, self-denying, sober, abstemious, abstinent; *ant.* self-indulgent. 3. stark, plain, spare, unadorned, unembellished, simple, economical; *ant.* fancy, ornate.

austerity *n.* 1. severity, sternness, strictness, harshness, rigidity. 2. asceticism, abstemiousness, restraint, reserve, self-denial, self-discipline.

authentic *adj.* genuine, real, actual, legitimate, valid, original, proper, true, bona fide; *ant.* bogus, artificial.

authenticate *v.* guarantee, verify, validate, certify, endorse, vouch for, warrant, authorize, confirm, corroborate.

authenticity *n.* 1. genuineness, realness, purity, validity, legitimacy, actuality. 2. trustworthiness, fidelity, faithfulness, reliability, truthfulness, dependability, honesty.

author *n.* 1. writer, literary artist, littérateur, wordsmith, scribe, penman, penwoman, novelist, playwright. 2. initiator, originator, founder, planner, prime mover, producer, creator, inventor, architect.

authoritarian *adj.* tyrannical, dictatorial, despotic, autocratic, dogmatic, imperious, absolute, oppressive, repressive, domineering, disciplinarian, strict, rigid.

authoritarianism *n.* tyranny, dictatorship, despotism, fascism, autocracy, totalitarianism, absolutism.

authoritative *adj.* **1.** well-documented, well-supported, accepted, sound, valid, authentic, proven, tested. **2.** authorized, official, ruling, sovereign, weighty, imperial, dominant, legal, lawful. **3.** authoritarian, dominating, dictatorial, imperious.

authority *n.* **1.** authorization, jurisdiction, power, right. **2.** expert, specialist, veteran, professional.

authorization *n.* approval, certification, permission, sanction, imprimatur, leave, license, permit, warrant, credentials, *slang:* go-ahead, green light.

authorize *v.* approve, permit, sanction, consent, enable, allow, OK, empower, legalize, license, warrant; *ant.* prohibit.

authorship *n.* invention, creation, instigation, making, doing.

auto *n.* car, automobile, vehicle, passenger car.

autocracy *n.* dictatorship, despotism, tyranny, authoritarianism, totalitarianism, absolutism, fascism; *ant.* democracy.

autocrat *n.* dictator, despot, tyrant, authoritarian, absolutist, fascist.

autocratic *adj.* dictatorial, despotic, tyrannical, authoritarian, imperious, totalitarian, absolute, all-powerful, domineering; *ant.* democratic, liberal.

autograph *n.* signature, seal, token, memento, John Hancock (*slang*).

automated *adj.* mechanical, automatic, motorized, computerized, electronic, programmed, cybernetic.

automatic *adj.* **1.** self-starting, mechanical, motorized, automated, mechanized, electronic, self-acting, self-regulating, computerized, programmed. **2.** involuntary, mechanical, spontaneous, unthinking, reflex, habitual, unconscious; *ant.* deliberate, willed, premeditated.

automation *n.* industrialization, mechanization, motorization, computerization, cybernetics, self-regulation.

automaton *n.* machine, robot, android, cyborg.

automobile *n.* car, vehicle, passenger car, auto, motor car.

autonomous *adj.* independent, autarkic, self-determining, self-governing, sovereign.

autonomy *n.* independence, autarky, freedom, free will, self-government, self-rule, self-determination, sovereignty, home rule; *ant.* subjection.

auxiliary *n.* assistant, helper, supporter, partner, confederate, associate, ally, accessory, reserve.

auxiliary *adj.* assisting, supportive, helping, supplementary, aiding, accessory, subsidiary, secondary, substitute, backup.

avail *n.* usefulness, effectiveness, advantage, worth, benefit.

to no avail in vain, for nought, fruitlessly, unsuccessfully.

avail *v.* help, benefit, profit, serve, aid, assist.
avail oneself of take advantage of, utilize, exploit, profit from, make the most of.

available *adj.* obtainable, procurable, attainable, accessible; free, disengaged, convenient, ready, at hand, within reach.

avalanche *n.* landslide, cascade, deluge, torrent, inundation, barrage, cataclysm.

avant-garde *adj.* progressive, experimental, innovative, forward-looking, advanced, unconventional, inventive, *slang:* far-out, way-out; *ant.* conservative, dyed-in-the-wool.

avarice *n.* greed, miserliness, parsimony, stinginess, tightfistedness, covetousness, predatoriness, acquisitiveness, rapacity, cupidity, penny-pinching; *ant.* generosity.

avaricious *adj.* greedy, miserly, parsimonious, stingy, tightfisted, covetous, predatory, acquisitive, grasping, rapacious, penny-pinching; *ant.* generous.

avenge *v.* take revenge for, take vengeance for, vindicate, repay for, punish for, retaliate for, get even for.

avenging *adj.* vengeful, vindictive, retaliatory, retributive.

avenue *n.* **1.** street, road, boulevard, route, drive, thoroughfare, walk. **2.** entry, entrance, means, way, channel, access, passage.

aver *v.* assert, affirm, attest, allege, profess, declare, insist, protest, avouch, state, swear, testify; *ant.* deny.

award *n.* **1.** prize, reward, grant, gift, trophy, medal. **2.** (legal settlement) payment, restitu-tion, damages, recompense, compensation, reparation, indemnity.

award *v.* grant, give, bestow, present, endow, assign, confer, determine.

aware *adj.* cognizant, observant, conscious, en-lightened, knowledgeable, informed, apprised, on to, clued-in, familiar, sharp, *slang:* on the ball, hip; *ant.* insensitive.

awareness *n.* knowledge, recognition, cogni-zance, consciousness, realization, attention, un-derstanding, sensibility, enlightenment, obser-vation; *ant.* ignorance.

away *adj.* removed, absent, not present, dis-tant, not here, out, remote, far off, off; *ant.* here, present, at hand.

do away with eliminate, get rid of, reject, discard, end.

away *adv.* **1.** (from this place) out, off, forth, hence. **2.** continuously, on and on, without stopping, constantly, endlessly, continually, without rest *or* end *or* break; *ant.* briefly, momentarily, for a while.

awe *n.* wonder, amazement, reverence, venera-tion, respect, admiration, astonishment, appre-hension, fear, dread; *ant.* contempt.

awe-inspiring *adj.* formidable, impressive, in-timidating, overwhelming, astonishing, won-drous, amazing, daunting, breathtaking; *ant.* contemptible.

awesome *adj.* magnificent, impressive, over-whelming, stupendous, wondrous, breathtak-ing, formidable, stunning, astonishing, amaz-ing, august.

awe-struck *adj.* amazed, daunted, stunned, wonder-struck, struck dumb, astonished, im-pressed, intimidated, fearful, cowed, fright-ened.

awful *adj.* **1.** frightful, horrible, terrible, dread-ful, wretched, abysmal, shocking, appalling, offensive, disgusting, repulsive. **2.** impres-sive, lofty, grand, majestic, large, gigantic, colossal, stupendous; *ant.* paltry.

awfully *adv.* **1.** poorly, badly, incompletely, clumsily. **2.** very, very much, indeed, truly, exceedingly, terribly, dreadfully.

awhile *adv.* for the moment, briefly, momen-tarily, for a short time, for a brief respite, not

average *n.* norm, mean, standard, medium, par, rule, mediocrity, midpoint.

average *adj.* **1.** mean, middle, medium, center; overall, general, balanced out. **2.** ordinary, un-exceptional, typical, standard, so-so, mediocre, run-of-the-mill; *ant.* exceptional, outstanding.

averse *adj.* reluctant, unwilling, disinclined, ill-disposed, opposed, loath, antipathetic, unfavor-able, inimical, antagonistic, hostile; *ant.* will-ing, sympathetic.

aversion *n.* repugnance, dislike, abhorrence, repulsion, revulsion, anathema, antipathy, dis-gust, hate, opposition, detestation, disgust; *ant.* liking, sympathy.

avert *v.* prevent, deflect, turn away, turn, evade, avoid, ward off, fend off, forestall, stave off.

aviator *n.* pilot, flier, airman, aeronaut.

avid *adj.* enthusiastic, eager, intense, voracious, fervent, ardent, passionate, devoted, dedi-cated, fanatical, insatiable; *ant.* indifferent.

avocation *n.* hobby, recreation, sideline, pas-time, diversion, distraction, relaxation.

avoid *v.* evade, abstain from, elude, avert, circumvent, eschew, dodge, shirk, get out of *or* around, prevent, sidestep, steer clear of, duck (*slang*).

avoidable *adj.* evadable, evitable, escapable, unnecessary, preventable; *ant.* inevitable, exi-gent.

avow *v.* assert, profess, swear, testify, attest, declare, maintain, proclaim, affirm, own, state.

avowal *n.* assertion, declaration, oath, testi-mony, affirmation, profession, proclamation, acknowledgment, recognition, admission.

avowed *adj.* overt, open, declared, professed, self-confessed, self-proclaimed, admitted, ac-knowledged.

avowedly *adv.* overtly, openly, frankly, can-didly, admittedly, professedly; *ant.* secretly.

await *v.* expect, wait for, anticipate, look for-ward to, hope for, lie in wait, be in store for, look for.

awake *adj.* wakeful, alert, observant, aware, attentive, conscious, aroused, wide-awake, astir, vigilant, heedful.

awaken *v.* **1.** wake, rouse, awake, get up. **2.** excite, arouse, stimulate, provoke, stir up, call forth, prompt, enliven, activate, animate, viv-ify.

for long, temporarily, for a little while, for a spell; *ant.* forever, permanently, for a long time.

awkward *adj.* **1.** (as in performing a task) inept, unskillful, uncoordinated, clumsy, blundering, bungling, maladroit. **2.** (as in behavior) gawky, graceless, ungainly, embarrassed, gauche; ill at ease, uncomfortable, touchy. **3.** (as of a situation) inconvenient, inopportune, difficult, disobliging, thorny, intractable, troublesome, uncomfortable, unsettling.

awry *adv., adj.* crooked, uneven, out of kilter, askew, misaligned, off-center, asymmetrical, cockeyed (*slang*); *ant.* straight, symmetrical.

ax *v.* cut down, get rid of, remove, throw out, dismiss, discharge, discontinue, cut, cancel, terminate, withdraw.

axiom *n.* maxim, adage, dictum, precept, principle, aphorism, postulate, truism, byword.

axiomatic *adj.* obvious, indubitable, absolute, given, self-evident, understood, accepted, assumed, fundamental, presupposed, unquestioned.

axis *n.* axle, pivot, spindle, longitude, center line.

axle *n.* axis, pivot, shaft, pin, hinge, spindle.

azure *adj.* blue, pale blue, sky blue, cerulean.

babble *n.* chatter, gibberish, nonsense, prattle, jabber, blab.

babble *v.* chatter, rant, rave, blather, run on, gossip, run at the mouth (*slang*), drivel, palaver.

babbling *adj.* rambling, incoherent, unintelligible, chattering, prattling.

babel *n.* bedlam, din, clamor, disorder, pandemonium, uproar, chaos, tumult, turmoil, hullabaloo, commotion; *ant.* calm, order.

baby *n.* child, infant, toddler, babe, cherub, brat, *slang:* rugrat, little shaver.

baby *v.* spoil, pamper, coddle, indulge, cosset, pander to, spoon-feed.

babyish *adj.* childish, immature, infantile, spoiled, juvenile, naive, foolish, silly, jejune, puerile; *ant.* mature, precocious.

babysit *v.* watch, oversee, care for, protect, guard, mind, tend.

back *n.* backside, hindquarters, rear end, butt (*slang*), tail, ass (*slang*), posterior, hiney (*slang*). **behind one's back** secretively, covertly, slyly. **flat on one's back** helpless, sick, ill, defeated. **turn one's back on** abandon, desert, fail, reject, betray, let down.

back *v.* **1.** support, endorse, advocate, stand behind, champion, uphold, second, encourage; *ant.* oppose. **2.** finance, subsidize, under-write. **back down** retreat, withdraw, recoil, renege, give way, back out.

back *adj.* posterior, hindmost, rear, end, tail; *ant.* front.

backbite *v.* slander, libel, malign, revile, disparage, vilify, traduce, badmouth (*slang*); *ant.* praise.

backbiting *n.* detraction, aspersion, calumny, vituperation, scandalmongering, spitefulness.

backbone *n.* **1.** spine, vertebrae, chine. **2.** determination, resolve, tenacity, guts (*slang*), will, fortitude, nerve, spirit, heart, mettle, character, grit; *ant.* weakness, cowardice.

backbreaking *adj.* arduous, grueling, strenuous, tiring, toilsome, exhausting, laborious, punishing, wearisome; *ant.* easy.

backer *n.* benefactor, supporter, sponsor, advocate, patron, champion, angel.

backfire *v.* **1.** explode, detonate, burst, erupt. **2.** boomerang, recoil, rebound, ricochet, come home to roost; miscarry, fail, go awry, abort.

background *n.* **1.** setting, environment, environs, ambiance, scene, backdrop, surroundings, milieu, framework. **2.** experience, upbringing, history, past, education, breeding, circumstances, accomplishments, achievements.

backhanded *adj.* ambiguous, double-edged, equivocal, ironic, oblique, dubious, sarcastic, tongue-in-cheek, sardonic; *ant.* sincere, whole-hearted.

backing *n.* assistance, aid, support, endorsement, advocacy, sponsorship, sanction, encouragement, reinforcement.

backlash *n.* response, reaction, repercussion, backfire, boomerang, resentment, opposition, reprisal.

backlog *n.* reserve, accumulation, supply, excess, stock, hoard, savings, quantity.

backslide *v.* relapse, regress, slip, revert, weaken, renege, fall from grace, apostatize, stray.

backward *adj.* **1.** retarded, stupid, slow-witted, dense, dull, unsophisticated, illiterate, provincial underdeveloped, hick (*slang*), underprivileged, underbred, subnormal; *ant.* smart, advanced. **2.** reticent, shy, bashful, hesitant, retiring, withdrawn, shrinking; *ant.* outgoing.

backward *adv.* **1.** rearward, astern, back, behind; *ant.* forward, onward.

backwash *n.* result, wake, aftermath, repercussion, reaction, ramifications.

backwoods *n.* woodlands, forest, country, out-

B

back, bush, *slang:* the sticks, boondocks, boonies.

bad *adj.* 1. wicked, evil, vile, wrong, corrupt, base, mean, immoral, naughty, offensive, sinful; *ant.* virtuous. 2. rotten, rancid, decayed, putrid, spoiled, moldy, noxious, sour, diseased. 3. faulty, poor, defective, inferior, imperfect, inadequate, shoddy; *ant.* high-quality. 4. harmful, injurious, hurtful, damaging, detrimental, dangerous, deleterious, unhealthy; *ant.* beneficial.

not bad average, passable, reasonable, satisfactory, not half bad, tolerable, fair, moderate, respectable, fair to middling, all right, OK, so-so.

badge *n.* seal, trademark, emblem, insignia, shield, medallion, signet, identification, escutcheon.

badger *v.* bother, harass, annoy, pester, hassle, plague, torment, goad, bully, importune.

badly *adv.* 1. inefficiently, crudely, unskillfully, negligently, ineptly, shoddily, haphazardly, clumsily, maladroitly, carelessly. 2. severely, seriously, very, greatly, intensely, acutely, painfully; *ant.* mildly.

bad-tempered *adj.* testy, irritable, cranky, irascible, cantankerous, crotchety, cross, peevish, moody, dyspeptic, querulous, splenetic; *ant.* equable, genial.

baffle *v.* 1. confuse, puzzle, perplex, bewilder, confound, disconcert, mystify, flummox; *ant.* enlighten. 2. hinder, impede, block, thwart, frustrate, obstruct, stump; *ant.* help.

bag *n.* purse, pocketbook, pouch, sack, satchel, knapsack, rucksack, saddlebag, suitcase, briefcase, valise, haversack.

in the bag certain, absolute, sure, definite, sewed up.

left holding the bag framed, set up, deceived, tricked, abandoned, deserted, left in the lurch.

bag *v.* catch, trap, seize, capture, nab, commandeer, appropriate, acquire.

baggage *n.* luggage, gear, bags, suitcases, accoutrements, impedimenta, belongings, effects.

baggy *adj.* slack, loose, flowing, billowing; ill-fitting, oversized, flaccid; *ant.* firm, tight.

bail *n.* bond, surety, warrant, guarantee, pledge, security, collateral, recognizance.

bail *v.* 1. dip, scoop, dredge, spoon out. 2. empty, drain, deplete, clear.

bail out 1. release, guarantee, warrant, assist, finance, relieve, help. 2. retreat, withdraw, flee, escape, quit.

bait *n.* attraction, lure, inducement, enticement, temptation, carrot.

bait *v.* 1. torment, tease, bother, nag, annoy, goad, harass, anger, irritate, provoke, irk. 2. lure, entice, attract, draw, fascinate, engage.

bake *v.* 1. cook, roast, toast, warm. 2. harden, temper, fire, anneal.

balance *n.* 1. excess, surplus, remainder, rest, residue. 2. equilibrium, symmetry, equivalence, parity, stability, counterbalance; *ant.* asymmetry, instability.

off balance 1. unsteady, tipsy, irregular, askew. 2. crazy, insane, eccentric, daft, odd, unpredictable.

balance *v.* 1. (of weights or forces) offset, oppose, steady, stabilize, neutralize, level, even, square, countervail, correspond; *ant.* topple, upset. 2. (of debts and credits) settle, square, compute, adjust, audit, calculate, tally, reckon.

balanced *adj.* 1. equalized, poised, offset, equivalent, on an even keel; *ant.* topheavy. 2. fair, impartial, unbiased, disinterested, unprejudiced, evenhanded; *ant.* prejudiced, erratic.

balcony *n.* gallery, terrace, veranda, catwalk, mezzanine, stoop, portico, porch.

bald *adj.* 1. hairless, shaven, clean-shaven, bare, depilated, shiny, smooth, naked, glabrous. *ant.* hairy, covered. 2. direct, simple, straightforward, forthright, unadorned, plain, severe, unvarnished, blunt.

balderdash *n.* nonsense, gibberish, rubbish, drivel, *slang:* bunk, poppycock; claptrap, tripe, bombast.

bale *n.* package, bundle, parcel, fardel, truss.

baleful *adj.* harmful, deadly, noxious, malevolent, evil, ominous, menacing, pernicious, ruinous, fell; *ant.* auspicious, favorable.

balk *v.* 1. refuse, turn down, demur, desist, resist, shirk. 2. frustrate, thwart, hinder, prevent, defeat, foil, forestall, obstruct, stall, check.

balky *adj.* stubborn, obstinate, contrary, perverse, uncontrollable, refractory.

ball *n.* 1. globe, balloon, orb, marble, pellet, globule, perisphere. 2. dance, prom, party, soiree, masquerade, promenade, reception.

get the ball rolling (*slang*) begin, start, initiate, commence, get things under way.

having something on the ball (*slang*) able, skilled, alert, responsible, clever, capable, resourceful; *ant.* inept.

ballad *n.* song, carol, chant, ditty, folk song, story, shanty.

ballast *n.* weight, counterbalance, counterweight, sandbags.

balloon *v.* bloat, swell, expand, inflate, billow, bulge, distend.

ballot *n.* vote, tally, ticket, poll, election, referendum.

balm *n.* 1. solace, consolation, comfort, relief, alleviation, assuagement; *ant.* irritation, vexation. 2. salve, ointment, lotion, unguent, emollient, balsam, bromide.

balmy *adj.* 1. temperate, mild, tropical, clement, pleasant, summery; *ant.* inclement. 2. (*slang*) crazy, insane, daft, weird, eccentric, *slang:* loony, kooky, off one's rocker.

bamboozle *v.* 1. cheat, fool, swindle, hoodwink, deceive, trick, dupe, con, cozen, hoax. 2. confuse, confound, perplex, baffle, befuddle, mystify, puzzle, stump.

ban *n.* prohibition, limitation, boycott, proscription, stoppage, suppression, refusal; *ant.* permission, dispensation.

ban *v.* forbid, halt, outlaw, prohibit, proscribe, banish, bar, exclude, ostracize, restrict, prevent, suppress; *ant.* permit, allow.

banal *adj.* trite, stale, old, tired, hackneyed, clichéd, dull, jejune, insipid, pedestrian, platitudinous, stock, vapid, threadbare; *ant.* original, creative, fresh.

banality *n.* cliché, platitude, bromide, old saw, truism.

band *n.* 1. ribbon, belt, strap, line, sash, scarf, bandage, thong, strip, ferrule, cincture. 2. binding, chain, cord, fetter, manacle, shackle, stay, truss, harness, hawser. 3. group, association, body, clique, ensemble, company, coterie, party, troop, herd.

bandage *n.* dressing, compress, gauze, swathe, truss.

bandage *v.* dress, bind, fasten, tie, swathe, tourniquet.

bandit *n.* robber, thief, gangster, desperado, hijacker, marauder, pirate, racketeer, brigand.

bane *n.* affliction, blight, calamity, curse, evil, plague, scourge, vexation, torment, pestilence; *ant.* blessing.

baneful *adj.* deadly, deleterious, venomous, harmful, injurious, noxious, ruinous, pestilential, fell; *ant.* beneficial.

bang *n.* detonation, blast, explosion, roar, shot, crash, peal, smack, thud, thump, wallop, boom, report, peal.

bang *v.* hit, strike, pound, slam, drum, hammer, thump, rap.

banish *v.* expel, evict, expatriate, ostracize, excommunicate, deport, extradite, sequester, exile, proscribe; *ant.* receive, welcome.

bank *n.* 1. levee, slope, embankment, ridge, ledge, cliff, rampart, acclivity. 2. accumulation, cache, depository, hoard, reserve, savings, stock, store, treasury. 3. series, group, sequence, succession, tier, train, row, file, array, echelon.

bank *v.* 1. save, deposit, accumulate, stockpile, store, keep. 2. lean, pitch, tilt, slope, incline, grade, bend, slant, cant.

bank on trust, rely *or* depend on, believe in, count on.

bankrupt *adj.* 1. insolvent, destitute, impoverished, penurious, broke (*slang*), out of business, wiped out (*slang*), failed; *ant.* solvent, wealthy. 2. (of ideas) barren, sterile, empty, vacant, destitute, exhausted; *ant.* fecund.

bankruptcy *n.* failure, ruin, insolvency, liquidation, indebtedness, defaulting, chapter 11; *ant.* prosperity.

banner *n.* flag, pennant, emblem, colors, standard, streamer.

banquet *n.* feast, meal, dinner, repast, festivity, revel, binge.

banter *n.* teasing, joking, kidding, play, badinage, chaff, jesting, mockery, repartee, fun, raillery.

banter *v.* joke, tease, josh, kid, jest with.

baptism *n.* christening, beginning, dedication, initiation, introduction, debut.

baptize *v.* 1. cleanse, immerse, purify, regenerate, asperse. 2. name, christen, denominate, call, dub, title, style, term.

bar *n.* 1. strip, pole, rod, lever, shaft, stake, rail. 2. saloon, tavern, inn, bistro, cocktail lounge, *slang:* dive, watering hole; pub, cabaret, hostel, road house. **3.** barrier, hindrance, obstacle, hurdle, impediment, barricade, deterrent. **4.** lawyers, counselors, barristers, judiciary, solicitors, the legal profession.

bar *v.* **1.** (physically obstruct) barricade, fence, wall, dam, dike, bolt, latch, lock, jam. **2.** (obstruct by refusal) ban, disallow, deny, refuse, debar, boycott, ostracize, exclude, discourage, prohibit, forbid, interdict, outlaw, proscribe.

barb *n.* **1.** thorn, spike, spur, quill, bristle, arrow. **2.** insult, affront, gibe, dig (*slang*), cut, sarcasm, sneer, slur, aspersion.

barbarian *n.* savage, brute, cannibal; yahoo, Hun, philistine, troglodyte, vulgarian, lout.

barbaric *adj.* **1.** savage, cruel, brutal, fierce, wild, feral, untamed, brutish; *ant.* humane. **2.** primitive, coarse, uncouth, vulgar, rude uncivil; *ant.* civilized.

barbarous *adj.* **1.** barbaric, brutal, fierce, cruel, inhumane, vicious, genocidal. **2.** uncivilized, unsophisticated, heathenish, philistine, uncultured, unlettered, unrefined; *ant.* cultured, educated.

barbecue *v.* cook, grill, sear, broil.

barbed *adj.* **1.** sharp, pointed, spiked, jagged, thorny, pronged, toothed, hooked. **2.** (of language) caustic, critical, stinging, acerbic, snide, acidic, sarcastic, loaded (*slang*).

bard *n.* poet, minstrel, troubadour, versifier.

bare *v.* disclose, divulge, expose, reveal, publish, uncover, show.

bare *adj.* **1.** naked, uncovered, stripped, denuded, exposed, unclothed, unclad, bald, open. **2.** plain, modest, simple, humble, unadorned, unornamented, austere, essential, severe, spare, unembellished. **3.** void, empty, barren, lacking.

barefaced *adj.* **1.** shameless, unabashed, audacious, bold, brazen, impudent, brash, insolent. **2.** obvious, unconcealed, apparent, clear, palpable, glaring, manifest.

barely *adv.* hardly, just, scarcely, by the skin of one's teeth; sparingly, sparsely.

bargain *n.* **1.** agreement, pact, contract, compact, arrangement, deal, pact, treaty, understanding, settlement, pledge. **2.** discount, value, *slang:* buy, steal; reduction, deal, markdown, giveaway.

bargain *v.* buy, sell, trade, barter, traffic, transact; negotiate, haggle, deal, wheel and deal (*slang*), dicker, confer, make terms.

bargain for expect, anticipate, foresee, imagine, plan on.

bargaining *n.* haggling, trafficking, dealing, wheeling and dealing (*slang*).

barge in interfere, interrupt, intrude, encroach, impinge, push, shove, *slang:* muscle in, gatecrash.

bark *n.* **1.** shell, case, crust, husk, rind, cortex, skin, hide, pelt, coat. **2.** yelp, yap, bay, snap, snarl, growl.

bark *v.* bay, snap, yap, yelp, yell, shout, bawl, bluster.

bark up the wrong tree (*slang*) mistake, misjudge, miscalculate, misconstrue.

baroque *adj.* ornate, elaborate, rococo, extravagant, florid, overwrought; convoluted, fantastic, bizarre, whimsical; *ant.* plain.

barracks *n.* lodging, quarters, camp, bivouac, prefabs (*slang*), billet.

barrage *n.* gunfire, bombardment, shelling, volley, broadside, cannonade, fusillade.

barred *adj.* prohibited, forbidden, banned, illegal, outlawed, proscribed, taboo, excluded, blackballed; *ant.* permissible.

barrel *n.* cask, keg, vat, tub, hogshead, firkin.
over a barrel (*slang*) in trouble, against the wall, at one's mercy.

barren *adj.* sterile, infertile, unproductive, fruitless, fallow, arid, dry; *ant.* fertile, productive, fecund.

barricade *n.* barrier, obstacle, obstruction, bulwark, fence, palisade, screen, rampart.

barricade *v.* bar, block, obstruct, fortify, defend, protect.

barrier *n.* bar, hindrance, hurdle, fortification, impediment, stumbling block, check; *ant.* entry, gateway, access.

barter *v.* trade, bargain, negotiate, haggle, deal, dicker, swap (*slang*).

base *n.* **1.** headquarters, camp, station, terminal, garrison, billet, center, depot, dock, harbor, anchorage, site. **2.** foundation, groundwork, bed, pedestal, substructure, support, underpinning, infrastructure, root, footing. **3.** basis, principle, source, heart, core, authority, evidence.

base adj. vulgar, low, foul, sordid, contemptible, depraved, mean, servile, wretched, wicked, worthless, abject; ant. noble.
off base wrong, mistaken, incorrect, erroneous, faulty, in error.

baseless adj. unconfirmed, unfounded, unjustified, groundless, unsubstantiated, unsupported, gratuitous; ant. justifiable.

bashful adj. shy, humble, timid, reticent, inhibited, timorous, diffident, shrinking, modest, reserved, abashed, sheepish; ant. confident.

basic adj. fundamental, inherent, intrinsic, essential, central, core, vital, key, central; ant. peripheral, marginal.

basics n. necessities, fundamentals, essentials, rudiments, ABC's, slang: nitty-gritty, brass tacks, nuts and bolts; practicalities.

basis n. 1. foundation, base, ground, root, cornerstone. 2. justification, proof, evidence, reason, source, authority, premise, sanction, raison d'être, postulate, antecedent.

bask v. revel, relish, savor, luxuriate, lounge, relax, loll, wallow, laze.

bass adj. deep, low, sonorous, resonant, sepulchral; ant. high-pitched.

bastard n. 1. love child, natural child, Sunday's child (slang). 2. rascal, scoundrel, cheat, slang: son of a bitch, SOB.

bastardize v. corrupt, debase, pervert, degrade, cheapen, adulterate, depreciate, devalue, vitiate.

bastion n. fortress, citadel, stronghold, bulwark, pillar, redoubt.

bat n. club, stick, racket, pole, mallet.
go to bat for defend, intervene, back, support.
having bats in one's belfry (slang) crazy, mad, insane, batty, daft, eccentric, peculiar, nutty, flaky (slang).
right off the bat immediately, at once, instantly.
bat v. hit, strike, whack, sock (slang).

batch n. lot, bunch, group, shipment, load, increment.

bathe v. wash, clean, scour, scrub, cleanse, rinse, soak, dip, immerse.

bathos n. sentimentality, melodrama, slang: mush, schmaltz, sappiness; triteness.

bathroom n. toilet, lavatory, shower, water closet, w.c., slang: john, head, can.

battalion n. mass, throng, horde, multitude, army, legion, host, contingent.

batten v. secure, fasten, tighten, tie, board up, nail down.

batter v. beat, punish, assault, maul, wreck, smash, injure, damage, bruise, thrash, pummel.

battered adj. abused, beaten, dilapidated, ramshackle.

battery n. 1. assault, attack, thumping, thrashing, mugging, mayhem. 2. cannon, gunnery unit, artillery corps.

battle n. fight, combat, conflict, war, struggle, assault, skirmish, sortie, blitzkrieg, engagement.

batty adj. crazy, mad, insane, demented, daft, eccentric, lunatic, loony (slang), queer, slang: screwy, off one's rocker, dippy; ant. sane.

bauble n. trinket, knickknack, toy, trifle, bagatelle, gewgaw, gimcrack, trifle, plaything.

bawdy adj. ribald, risqué, salacious, lascivious, lecherous, lewd, licentious, obscene, libidinous, erotic; ant. chaste.

bawl v. 1. cry, weep, sob, blubber, wail, caterwaul, squall. 2. shout, yell, roar, howl, call, vociferate, halloo.

bawl out scold, chide, berate, upbraid, admonish, tongue-lash, chew out (slang).

bay n. harbor, lagoon, inlet, gulf, cove, bayou, sound, fiord, estuary.

bazaar n. market, fair, mart, agora, exchange, alcazar.

be v. 1. live, exist, endure, persist, subsist, breathe, abide, survive; ant. die, stop, disappear. 2. happen, occur, transpire, take place, come about. 3. equal, comprise, amount to, consist of. 4. mean, signify, denote, explain.

beach n. shore, coast, seashore, the sand, strand, littoral, shingle.

beacon n. guide, lamp, flare, lantern, rocket, sign, lighthouse, beam, radar, watch fire.

bead n. 1. jewel, gem, stone, pearl. 2. drop, droplet, globule, pellet, grain, speck, dab, pill, bubble, spherule.

beak n. bill, snout, nozzle, proboscis, prow, nose, nozzle.

beaked adj. bent, curved, hooked, angled, pointed, sharp, rostrate; ant. straight.

beam n. 1. plank, two-by-four, rafter, timber,

brace, stud, strut, stay, crosspiece, support, trestle, spar, stanchion, joist. **2.** streak, shaft, flicker, gleam, glare, glint, glow, emission, dartle.

beam *v.* **1.** send, emit, transmit, broadcast. **2.** shine, radiate, glitter, glimmer, glare, effulge. **3.** smile, grin, laugh, smirk, glow, radiate.

beaming *adj.* **1.** bright, radiant, glowing, brilliant, sparkling, effulgent, lambent, refulgent. **2.** happy, grinning, animated, cheerful, joyful, sunny, radiant, exuberant; *ant.* sullen.

bear *v.* **1.** carry, transport, convey, transfer, tote. **2.** tolerate, endure, sustain, suffer, support, abide, stomach, stand, weather, brook. **3.** produce, yield, give birth, bring forth, breed, engender, generate, propagate.

bear down 1. approach, close in, advance on, converge on, near. **2.** oppress, compress, weigh down, encumber, strain.

bear on affect, concern, pertain to, touch on, relate to.

bear with forbear, tolerate, put up with, be patient, make allowances for.

beard *n.* goatee, whiskers, muttonchops, sideburns.

bearded *adj.* shaggy, unshaven, hairy, hirsute, bewhiskered; *ant.* smooth, bald.

bearer *n.* **1.** carrier, courier, conveyor, messenger, runner, porter. **2.** payee, beneficiary, consignee, collector, holder.

bearing *n.* **1.** relevance, significance, pertinence, import, application. **2.** demeanor, manner, attitude, deportment, mien, air, carriage, posture, presence.

bearings *n.* orientation, direction, inclination, position, tack, way, aim, course.

beast *n.* brute, degenerate, fiend, animal, swine, lout, hun, satyr, libertine, lecher; *ant.* angel, saint.

beastly *adj.* bestial, coarse, carnal, depraved, disgusting, gross, vulgar, gluttonous, swinish; *ant.* refined, sweet, nice.

beat *n.* **1.** cadence, pulsation, throbbing, pounding, palpitation, flutter, oscillation, undulation. **2.** stress, accent, division, measure, rhythm, meter, time.

beat *v.* **1.** batter, hammer, whip, flog, whale (*slang*), drub, trounce, *slang:* lay into, lick, work

over; smite, lash, lambaste, cane. **2.** pulsate, throb, flutter, palpitate, tremble, quiver, heave, oscillate, quaver, writhe, thrill. **3.** defeat, overcome, conquer, best, vanquish, surpass, worst; *ant.* succumb to, lose to.

beat (*slang*) *adj.* tired, weary, worn out, exhausted, fatigued, bushed, pooped (*slang*).

beaten *adj.* **1.** defeated, conquered, thwarted, vanquished, subjugated, trounced, worsted, humbled, *slang:* whipped, licked; cowed, mastered, routed; *ant.* victorious, successful. **2.** hammered, forged, tramped, milled, rolled, trodden, tamped. **3.** blended, frothy, foamy, whipped, whisked, creamy, bubbly, meringued.

beatific *adj.* angelic, blissful, divine, heavenly, rapturous, serene, sublime, seraphic.

beatify *v.* bless, glorify, sanctify, consecrate, exalt.

beatitude *n.* bliss, joy, delight, ecstasy, felicity, exaltation.

beatnik *n.* Bohemian, rebel, radical, dropout, maverick, iconoclast, beat, *slang:* hippie, longhair.

beau *n.* boyfriend, sweetheart, fiancé, escort, suitor, admirer, swain.

beautiful *adj.* pretty, lovely, stunning, attractive, gorgeous, ravishing, alluring, appealing, charming, graceful, radiant, comely; *ant.* plain, ugly.

beautify *v.* decorate, adorn, array, ornament, embellish, enhance, grace, glamorize.

beauty *n.* **1.** loveliness, allure, attractiveness, delicacy, shapeliness, grace, pulchritude, bloom, comeliness; *ant.* ugliness, homeliness. **2.** belle, goddess, fox (*slang*), siren, looker (*slang*), stunner, Venus, femme fatale.

becalm *v.* calm, quiet, soothe, pacify, still.

becalmed *adj.* motionless, idle, still, stranded, stuck, at a standstill.

beckon *v.* call, summon, signal, motion, sign, bid, invite, lure.

become *v.* **1.** grow, metamorphose, emerge, progress, shift, be transformed into, convert, mature, incline to. **2.** flatter, suit, enhance, set off, befit, behoove, embellish, grace, match; *ant.* spoil, distort, distract.

becoming *adj.* **1.** proper, fitting, appropriate, suitable, seemly, tasteful, congruous. **2.** flat-

bed *n.* 1. sack (*slang*), cot, mattress, bunk, pallet, couch, chaise, berth, hay (*slang*). 2. garden, patch, strip, area, plot, row.

bed *v.* embed, implant, plant, insert, ground, fasten, fix, root, settle.

bedding *n.* sheets, linen, blankets, covers, quilts, spreads, comforters, coverlets, bedclothes, pillows.

bedeck *v.* decorate, adorn, festoon, ornament, embellish, garnish, trim, beautify; *ant.* strip.

bedraggled *adj.* messy, disheveled, unkempt, scruffy, frumpy, tattered, disordered, dirty, slovenly, sullied; *ant.* tidy.

bedevil *v.* afflict, annoy, confound, distress, fret, harass, irk, irritate, plague, torment, vex, beset, beleaguer.

bedlam *n.* pandemonium, chaos, turmoil, furor, uproar, confusion, madhouse, clamor, babel, tumult; *ant.* calm, order.

beef *n.* 1. cow, bull, steer, bovine. 2. (*slang*) complaint, grievance, *slang;* gripe, bitch; objection, protest, protestation.

beefy *adj.* brawny, burly, hulking, fleshy, muscular, stalwart, stocky, strapping, sturdy, strong; *ant.* weak, slight.

befall *v.* happen, occur, take place, ensue, supervene, betide, arrive.

before *adv.* previously, up to now, up until now, earlier, sooner, since, heretofore, formerly, sooner, antecedently, ere; *ant.* now, in the future.

before *prep.* preceding, prior to, antecedent to, in front of, ahead of; *ant.* after, behind.

beforehand *adv.* before, previously, already, in anticipation, sooner.

befriend *v.* make friends with, take a liking to, embrace, take under one's wing, aid, assist, advise, encourage, favor, stand by, support, sustain; *ant.* neglect, oppose.

befuddle *v.* bewilder, confuse, daze, puzzle, muddle, stupefy, disorient, befog, baffle.

beg *v.* 1. plead, entreat, implore, beseech, supplicate, urge, request; *ant.* grant, accede, concede. 2. cadge, *slang:* mooch, bum, sponge, scrounge, panhandle, chisel, leech; *ant.* give, bestow.

beg the question avoid, dodge, shirk, shun, sidestep, hedge, evade, equivocate, tergiversate; hem and haw.

beget *v.* propagate, father, sire, generate, breed, procreate, produce, spawn, create, engender.

beggar *n.* mendicant, supplicant, moocher (*slang*), panhandler, cadger; pauper, street person, bag lady (*slang*), indigent.

begin *v.* 1. start, inaugurate, launch, initiate, induce, activate, cause, introduce, originate, found; *ant.* end, terminate. 2. (come into existence) commence, arise, proceed, sprout, spring *or* crop up, emanate, occur, bud, stem, blossom; *ant.* expire, vanish.

beginner *n.* novice, amateur, apprentice, fledgling, neophyte, greenhorn, rookie (*slang*), student, tenderfoot, freshman, tyro; *ant.* veteran, old hand, professional.

beginning *n.* 1. source, basis, root, origin, germ, kernel, core, heart, antecedent, embryo, seed, fountainhead. 2. (act or process of commencing) introduction, inception, starting, commencement, initiation, origination; *ant.* establishment; *ant.* end, finish.

begrudge *v.* 1. resent, envy, be jealous of, covet, mind, grudge. 2. stint, pinch, be stingy with, skimp, hold back; *ant.* lavish.

beguile *v.* 1. deceive, trick, cheat, mislead, delude, hoodwink, cozen. 2. entertain, charm, delight, amuse, divert, engross.

beguiling *adj.* alluring, bewitching, captivating, enchanting, charming, appealing, winning, enticing, intriguing; *ant.* offensive, repulsive.

begun *adj.* started, initiated, inaugurated, proceeding, active, kinetic, operative, working; *ant.* potential, latent.

behalf *n.* interest, welfare, sake, benefit, advantage, stead, furtherance; *ant.* opposition, detraction.

behave *v.* act, perform, comport, conduct, deport, perform, react, respond.

behavior *n.* 1. (manner of acting socially) conduct, deportment, comportment, demeanor, mien, carriage, decorum, manners, propriety. 2. (the way something works) execution, operation, function, adaptation, adjustment, conduct, response, reflex.

behest *n.* command, direction, order, precept, injunction, bidding, decree, mandate, ordinance, fiat.

behind *n.* backside, rear end, rump, buttocks, butt (*slang*), derrière.

behind *adj.* 1. late, slow, tardy, dilatory. 3. sluggish, retarded, belated, laggard, delayed, backward, underdeveloped; *ant.* rapid, fast.

behind *adv.* following, back, after, in back, to the rear, backward, astern; *ant.* ahead, forward.

behold *v.* see, observe, look at, view, discern, espy, perceive, scan, descry.

beholden *adj.* indebted, bound, obligated, obliged, owing.

behoove *v.* become, suit, beseem, benefit, profit, advance.

being *n.* 1. existence, presence, actuality, animation, essence, soul, spirit, substance, quiddity. 2. creature, beast, thing, animal, body, mortal, sentient.

belabor *v.* harp on, dwell on, run into the ground (*slang*), overdo.

belated *adj.* late, tardy, overdue, delayed, remiss, retarded; *ant.* punctual, timely.

beleaguered *adj.* plagued, beset, vexed, worried, persecuted, harassed, badgered, besieged.

belie *v.* 1. mislead, deceive, misrepresent, disguise, conceal, falsify. 2. contradict, disagree, repudiate, deny, oppose, gainsay, refute, repudiate; *ant.* attest.

belief *n.* 1. faith, credence, acceptance, trust, confidence, persuasion, impression, notion, conception. 2. creed, dogma, credo, position, axiom, tenet, doctrine, ideology, ism.

believable *adj.* credible, convincing, persuasive, compelling, trustworthy, likely, plausible, reliable, acceptable; *ant.* unconvincing.

believe *v.* think, consider, maintain, suppose, conclude, reckon, swear by, trust; *ant.* doubt.

make believe pretend, imagine, act, feign, dream, fantasize, play.

believer *n.* adherent, disciple, devotee, convert, follower, proselyte, zealot; *ant.* skeptic.

belittle *v.* deprecate, disparage, deride, scorn, ridicule, depreciate, disdain, minimize, vilipend; *ant.* exaggerate.

bellicose *adj.* belligerent, hostile, antagonistic, contentious, pugnacious, warlike, violent, warmongering, hawkish; *ant.* peaceable.

belligerent *adj.* hostile, antagonistic, bellicose, contentious, aggressive, combative, militant, pugnacious, spoiling for a fight; *ant.* timid.

bellow *v.* shout, scream, yell, cry, shriek, clamor, howl, cry, roar, yowl, thunder.

bellyache (*slang*) *v.* complain, whine, grumble, gripe (*slang*), protest.

belong *v.* 1. appertain, relate, pertain, bear upon. 2. fit in, be one of, be a member of, be counted among, be a part of, be associated *or* affiliated with, be linked to, be one of the family.

belonging *n.* affinity, association, attachment, inclusion, link, kinship, rapport, compatibility, fellowship; *ant.* antipathy.

belongings *n.* property, possessions, things, goods, effects, accoutrements, paraphernalia, traps, chattels.

beloved *adj.* adored, worshiped, cherished, prized, treasured, venerated; *ant.* hated, abhorred.

below *prep.* under, beneath, underneath, lower than.

belt *n.* waistband, girdle, sash, cincture.

below the belt unscrupulous, unfair, dirty, dishonest, cowardly.

bemoan *v.* mourn, grieve, lament, rue, weep for, bewail, regret; *ant.* celebrate.

bemuse *v.* confuse, bewilder, puzzle, perplex, daze, muddle, distract; *ant.* enlighten, illuminate.

bench *n.* 1. pew, settee, bleacher, seat. 2. court, judges, magistrates, judiciary, tribunal.

benchmark *n.* standard, norm, level, model, reference point, touchstone, yardstick, criterion, example.

bend *n.* curve, bow, arch, arc, elbow, hook, loop, twist, crook, curvature.

bend *v.* 1. (change the shape of) twist, shape, curve, crimp, spiral, coil, crinkle, curl, wind, twine; *ant.* straighten, extend. 2. (change posture or direction) fold, bow, wilt, buckle; deviate, waver, careen, meander, swerve. 3. persuade, mold, direct, compel, influence, shape, modify.

benediction *n.* blessing, sanctification, invocation, consecration, prayer, benison, orison; *ant.* curse, anathema, execration.

benefaction *n.* donation, grant, gift, charity,

favor; benevolence, endowment, alms-giving, munificence, philanthropy.

benefactor *n.* patron, backer, helper, protector, promoter, provider, sponsor, subsidizer.

beneficence *n.* bounty, charity, altruism, generosity, largesse, succor; *ant.* meanness.

beneficent *adj.* helpful, kind, benign, compassionate, benevolent, generous, well-meaning, good-hearted; *ant.* mean.

beneficial *adj.* helpful, useful, advantageous, profitable, rewarding, salutary, salubrious, propitious; *ant.* harmful.

beneficiary *n.* recipient, heir, heiress, inheritor, stipendiary, successor, legatee, pensioner; *ant.* donor, giver.

benefit *n.* advantage, gain, profit, help, good, avail, boon, blessing, asset, assistance; *ant.* harm, detriment.

benefit *v.* aid, advance, profit, avail, enhance, further, promote, ameliorate; *ant.* harm, hinder.

benefits *n.* advantages, bonuses, perquisites, fringe benefits, *slang:* perks, freebies, fringes.

benevolence *n.* kindness, charity, altruism, generosity, good-heartedness, goodwill, sympathy; *ant.* meanness, stinginess.

benevolent *adj.* kind, considerate, humane, solicitous, philanthropic, benign, generous, caring.

benign *adj.* 1. gentle, mild, genial, amiable, benevolent, temperate, complaisant; *ant.* hostile. 2. salutary, beneficial, harmless; *ant.* malignant.

bent *n.* inclination, leaning, tendency, proclivity, penchant, propensity, aptitude, gift, flair, forte.

bent *adj.* curved, twisted, beaked, hooked, crooked, bowed, sinuous, hunched; *ant.* rigid, straight.

bent on determined, resolved, set on, fixed, insistent, hellbent (*slang*).

benumbed *adj.* 1. stupefied, dazed, stunned, confounded, confused. 2. deadened, numbed, paralyzed, frozen, anaesthetized, desensitized, insensible, unfeeling.

bequeath *v.* give, grant, hand down, pass on, will, bestow, endow, entrust, impart, transmit.

bequest *n.* gift, legacy, inheritance, endowment, bestowal, dower, patrimony.

berate *v.* scold, chide, reprimand, rebuke, castigate, upbraid, censure, lambaste, attack, vilify, vituperate; *ant.* praise.

bereavement *n.* deprivation, affliction, loss, dispossession, misfortune; *ant.* addition, increase.

bereft *adj.* bereaved, deprived, divested, destitute, impoverished, lacking, devoid, wanting.

berserk *adj.* crazy, mad, demented, deranged, frenzied, insane, maniacal, rabid, raving, enraged, gone amok; *ant.* calm, sane.

berth *n.* 1. bunk, hammock, cot, bedroom, roomette, billet, transom berth. 2. place, situation, employment, job, profession, post, sinecure.

beseech *v.* beg, plead, implore, entreat, importune, petition, supplicate.

beset *v.* attack, plague, besiege, assail, encircle, surround, pester, harass, badger.

beside *prep.* by, next to, adjacent to, contiguous with, parallel to, adjoining, alongside, abreast of, neighboring, overlooking, near, juxtaposed with.

besides *adv.* too, additionally, as well, also, further, moreover, to boot, likewise, secondly.

besiege *v.* harass, harry, beleaguer, confine, beset, encircle, surround, blockade.

best *n.* choice, finest, flower, cream, crème de la crème, elite, top, utmost.

get the best of defeat, surpass, outdo, best, overcome.

make the best of endure, suffer, tolerate, get by, make do.

best *v.* defeat, beat, overcome, get the better of, worst, conquer, thrash, trounce, vanquish.

best *adj.* finest, prime, supreme, optimum, paramount, nonpareil, inimitable, peerless, transcendent; *ant.* worst, poorest.

bestial *adj.* cruel, brutal, savage, animal, barbaric, brutish, carnal, feral, depraved, sordid, swinish, vile; *ant.* civilized, humane.

bestir *v.* excite, rouse, agitate, animate, incite; *ant.* calm, quell.

bestow *v.* give, grant, impart, bequeath, present, offer, apportion, lavish, dower; *ant.* deprive.

bet *n.* wager, gamble, venture, hazard, ante, stake, chance, risk, speculation.

bet *v.* wager, gamble, stake, venture, hazard, speculate, risk, chance, ante.

43

betoken *v.* signify, foreshadow, bode, denote, augur, import, indicate, portend, presage, promise.

betray *v.* **1.** double-cross, delude, dupe, ensnare, entrap, mislead, stab in the back, *slang:* rat on, send *or* sell down the river, sell out. **2.** reveal, divulge, expose, show, disclose, uncover, give away, spill the beans (*slang*). **3.** abandon, desert, forsake, jilt, strand.

betrayal *n.* deception, treason, treachery, disloyalty, duplicity, perfidy, apostasy; *ant.* loyalty, faithfulness.

betrayer *n.* deceiver, conspirator, informer, traitor, apostate, Judas, Benedict Arnold, quisling; *ant.* protector, supporter.

betrothal *n.* engagement, espousal, promise, troth, vow, plight.

better *v.* **1.** improve, revamp, refine, further, ameliorate; *ant.* deteriorate, worsen. **2.** excel, surpass, transcend, outdo, outstrip.

better *adj.* **1.** superior, greater, finer, preferred, stronger, surpassing, worthier. **2.** convalescent, recovering, improving, mending, progressing, restored, cured; *ant.* worse, failing.

for better or for worse regardless, in any event, no matter what happens, anyhow.

betterment *n.* improvement, upgrading, edification, enhancement, amelioration; *ant.* deterioration.

between *prep.* betwixt, amid, amidst, among.

between you and me secretly, privately, confidentially, entre nous, personally.

bevel *n.* slant, slope, angle, bias, diagonal, oblique.

bevy *n.* gathering, flock, pack, group, band, collection, crowd, gaggle, throng, troupe.

bewail *v.* regret, lament, mourn, bemoan, rue, deplore, keen; *ant.* gloat, glory.

beware *v.* take care, be careful, watch out.

bewilder *v.* confuse, confound, disconcert, baffle, mystify, perplex, disorient, bemuse.

bewildered *adj.* disoriented, confused, puzzled, nonplussed, lost, lost in a fog (*slang*), in a dither, dazed, giddy, dizzy, at a loss, punch-drunk, addled, befuddled, agog, astonished, dumbfounded; *ant.* clearheaded, lucid.

bewitch *v.* fascinate, enthrall, beguile, enchant, charm, allure, enrapture, spellbind, transfix, mesmerize.

beyond *adv.* on the other side, over there, out of range, a good way off, further, yonder.

beyond *prep.* past, further than, in advance of.

bias *n.* **1.** inclination, tendency, bent, leaning, proclivity, predilection, propensity, penchant. **2.** unfairness, prejudice, favoritism, one-sidedness; *ant.* impartiality.

bias *v.* influence, prejudice, sway, predispose, slant, weight, warp, distort, load the dice (*slang*).

bicker *v.* quarrel, wrangle, squabble, dispute, feud, scrap; *ant.* agree.

bid *n.* offer, proposal, proposition, suggestion, venture.

bid *v.* **1.** offer, ante, venture, proffer, tender, propose, request, solicit. **2.** order, demand, command, charge, direct, instruct, require, proclaim.

bidding *n.* **1.** order, command, direction, demand, charge, behest, dictate. **2.** invitation, request, summons.

do someone's bidding serve, obey, follow, carry out orders.

big *adj.* **1.** huge, mammoth, large, long, high, elephantine, enormous, gigantic, immense, massive, titanic, vast; *ant.* little, small. **2.** mature, grown, adult, elder. **3.** important, prominent, major, grand, powerful, leading, significant, influential, considerable, eminent, weighty. **4.** pompous, presumptuous, pretentious, imperious, egoistic, bombastic, flamboyant, ostentatious; *ant.* modest. **5.** generous, magnanimous, liberal, benevolent, benign, unselfish, generous, altruistic; *ant.* petty.

bigot *n.* chauvinist, redneck (*slang*), dogmatist, partisan, fanatic, extremist; racist, sexist, hater; *ant.* humanitarian, liberal.

bigoted *adj.* biased, prejudiced, chauvinistic, dogmatic, intolerant, closed-minded, narrow-minded, opinionated, prejudiced, intolerant, illiberal; *ant.* enlightened, progressive, open-minded, tolerant.

bigotry *n.* intolerance, injustice, bias, discrimination, racism, sexism, sectarianism, jingoism.

bilious *adj.* grouchy, grumpy, cross, choleric, crotchety, irritable, peevish, testy, dyspeptic.

bill *n.* **1.** statement, invoice, tally, account. **2.** law, draft, measure, proposal, legislation. **3.** handbill, poster, circular, advertisement, fold-

billet *v.* accommodate, berth, lodge, quarter, station.

billow *v.* heave, surge, swell, seethe, roll, balloon, belly, undulate.

billowy *adj.* surging, swelling, rising, rolling, heaving, rippling, bouncing.

bin *n.* storeroom, crib, granary, silo, bunker, locker.

binary *adj.* double, twofold, paired.

bind (*slang*) *n.* predicament, dilemma, jam (*slang*), quandary, difficulty, impasse, hole.

bind *v.* **1.** secure, fasten, tie, shackle, fetter, cinch, clamp, manacle, handcuff, hitch, tether, yoke, truss. **2.** obligate, oblige, require, necessitate, compel, force, indenture. **3.** dress, wrap, bandage, treat.

binding *n.* **1.** cover, case, wrapper, jacket, book cover. **2.** tie, adhesive, fastener, band, rope, wire. **3.** union, merging, juncture, tying, coupling, junction, synthesis.

binding *adj.* **1.** restraining, confining, limiting, constraining, tying. **2.** mandatory, necessary, essential, obligatory, requisite, required, compulsory; *ant.* optional.

binge *n.* spree, fling, orgy, bout.

biography *n.* account, chronicle, memoir, confessions, history, life, adventures, recollections.

birth *n.* **1.** delivery, nativity, blessed event, parturition, visit from the stork, act of God. **2.** beginning, source, start, origin, genesis, commencement, derivation. **3.** lineage, heritage, ancestry, extraction, genealogy, family, blood, stock, breeding, strain, rank, status, position, station.

bisect *v.* halve, divide, intersect, separate, split, bifurcate.

bisexual *adj.* androgynous, hermaphroditic, epicene, gynandrous, monoclinous.

bit *n.* fragment, crumb, particle, jot, mite, trifle, scintilla, modicum, speck, pinch, moiety; *ant.* excess, lot.

bit by bit gradually, piecemeal, step by step, insidiously; *ant.* wholesale.

bite *v.* **1.** snap, gnaw, nip, lacerate, chew, masticate, tear, rend, champ, munch, chaw, ruminate. **2.** sting, slash, smart, cut. **3.** strike, take the bait, nibble; swallow hook, line, and sinker (*slang*).

biting *adj.* **1.** (of taste) acidic, sour, tangy, sharp, keen, bitter, tart, lemony; *ant.* bland, mild. **2.** (physically penetrating) piercing, puncturing, incising, lacerating, masticating. **3.** (as a comment) sarcastic, caustic, scathing, withering, trenchant, cynical, mordant, acidulous.

bitter *adj.* **1.** acrid, tart, sour, astringent, vinegary; *ant.* sweet. **2.** (as an experience) harsh, sharp, severe, painful, intense. **3.** (as a comment) sarcastic, acid, biting, acerbic; caustic, galling, hostile, resentful, rancorous; *ant.* genial.

bitterness *n.* **1.** tartness, acidity, piquancy, pungency, brackishness, brininess; *ant.* blandness, sweetness. **2.** painfulness, anguish, resentment, rancor, mordancy, venom, acrimony, virulence.

bizarre *adj.* odd, strange, weird, abnormal, queer, deviant, freakish, fantastic, surreal, eerie, eldritch; *ant.* normal.

black *adj.* **1.** dark, raven, jet, sable, dusky, murky, inky. **2.** threatening, forbidding, sinister, ominous, sullen, menacing, unpropitious. **3.** angry, fierce, enraged, furious. **4.** evil, villainous, mean, diabolical, wicked, nefarious, hostile.

blackball *v.* ostracize, exclude, repudiate, bar, ban, expel, snub, veto, blacklist.

blacken *v.* **1.** dirty, sully, tarnish, slander, defame, calumniate, defile, denigrate, malign, traduce, vilify, besmirch; *ant.* enhance, praise.

blackguard *n.* rascal, villain, scoundrel, rogue, miscreant, wretch.

blacklist *v.* blackball, ostracize, bar, exclude, repudiate, expel.

blackmail *n.* extortion, intimidation, bribe, protection, hush money, ransom.

blackmail *v.* extort, coerce, compel, demand, threaten, force.

black out **1.** erase, eradicate, delete, rub out, cancel, censor, extinguish. **2.** darken, shade, obfuscate, conceal, cover up, eclipse. **3.** faint, collapse, lose consciousness.

black sheep outcast, prodigal, reprobate, pariah, reject, wastrel, dropout.

blamable *adj.* guilty, culpable, accountable, answerable, liable, responsible; *ant.* innocent.

blame *n.* **1.** censure, condemnation, castigation, remonstrance, opprobrium, stricture, criticism, reprimand, rebuke; *ant.* praise, appreciation. **2.** responsibility, culpability, liability, accountability.

blame *v.* censure, condemn, rebuke, criticize, admonish, chide, take to task, reproach, reprove, upbraid; *ant.* exonerate. **2.** accuse, charge, indict, impute.

blameless *adj.* innocent, faultless, upright, virtuous, impeccable, inculpable, sinless, unblemished, unsullied; *ant.* guilty.

blameworthy *adj.* guilty, reprehensible, shameful, unworthy.

blanch *v.* whiten, drain, fade, pale, bleach, etiolate; *ant.* blush, color, redden.

bland *adv.* **1.** flavorless, flat, dull, tasteless, insipid, characterless, vapid, weak; *ant.* piquant, spicy. **2.** mild, soothing, soft, smooth, mollifying, suave, gentle, agreeable, affable, pleasant, congenial; *ant.* harsh, provocative.

blank *n.* **1.** void, cavity, abyss, emptiness, nothingness, space, gap, vacuity, tabula rasa. **2.** form, questionnaire, data sheet.

blank *adj.* **1.** white, clear, fresh, unused, virgin, plain, empty, unmarked, untouched, spotless; *ant.* used, inscribed, printed. **2.** (said of a facial expression) void, barren, vacant, expressionless, enigmatic, poker-faced, vacuous, hollow, meaningless, inscrutable; *ant.* expressive.

blanket *v.* envelop, cover, conceal, cloak, cloud, hide, mask, obscure, eclipse, adumbrate.

blanket *adj.* comprehensive, absolute, all-inclusive, unconditional, sweeping, all-embracing.

blare *v.* boom, trumpet, blast, clamor, clang, peal, resound, ring, shriek.

blarney *n.* flattery, cajolery, blandishment, adulation.

blasé *adj.* indifferent, apathetic, bored, weary, unexcited, jaded, unconcerned, sated, glutted; *ant.* enthusiastic.

blaspheme *v.* curse, swear, revile, desecrate, damn, execrate, abuse.

blasphemous *adj.* profane, sacrilegious, impious, irreverent, irreligious, godless, hubristic; *ant.* reverent, respectful.

blasphemy *n.* profanity, impiety, swearing, cursing, expletive, desecration, profanation; *ant.* piety, prayer.

blast *n.* **1.** explosion, eruption, detonation, discharge, burst, salvo, volley. **2.** bang, roar, din, clap, crash, blare, hoot, peal, scream, shriek, wail. **3.** (*slang*) a good time, fun, excitement, amusement, party, ball (*slang*).

blast *v.* blow up, shatter, annihilate, detonate, wreck, ruin, destroy.

blatant *adj.* obvious, arrant, brazen, conspicuous, flagrant, glaring, pronounced, bald; *ant.* subtle.

blaze *n.* **1.** fire, flames, combustion, eruption, flare-up, conflagration. **2.** burst, gleam, flash, flare, glitter.

blaze *v.* burn, flame, flash, flare, seethe, glare, explode, burst.

blazon *v.* announce, broadcast, proclaim, publicize, trumpet, flaunt, flourish; *ant.* downplay.

bleach *v.* blanch, fade, whiten, lighten, pale, etiolate, peroxide.

bleak *adj.* **1.** dreary, desolate, bare, lonely, somber, gloomy, dismal, blighted; *ant.* verdant, green, fruitful. **2.** chilly, windy, stormy, cold, cutting, wintry, biting, bitter, inclement, misty, foggy; *ant.* mild, pleasant.

blear *v.* shade, dim, blur, obscure.

bleary *adj.* blurred, cloudy, foggy, hazy, misty, indistinct, murky, fuzzy, obscured, dim.

bleed *v.* **1.** hemorrhage, exude, flow, gush, ooze, run, sap, spurt, trickle. **2.** blackmail, extort, strong-arm, put the screws to, *slang:* put the squeeze on, fleece; impoverish, pauperize, confiscate. **3.** suffer, ache, agonize. **4.** drain, exhaust, reduce, deplete.

blemish *n.* imperfection, flaw, defect, taint, tarnish, stigma, birthmark, disfigurement, wart, scar, spot, stain; *ant.* perfection, purity.

blench *v.* wince, flinch, quail, cower, shrink, balk, falter.

blend *n.* mixture, combination, compound, amalgam, alloy, composite.

blend *v.* mix, combine, mingle, fuse, meld, synthesize, unite, amalgamate, coalesce; *ant.* separate.

bless *v.* **1.** baptize, canonize, glorify, honor, dedicate, exalt, anoint, ordain, consecrate, sanctify. **2.** give, endow, bestow, grant, provide, grace.

block n. 1. mass, chunk, slab, piece, hunk (slang), ingot, square, brick, cake, cube, slice, loaf, clod. 2. obstruction, barrier, hindrance, bar, obstacle, blockage, jam (slang), impediment.

block v. 1. impede, hinder, prevent, arrest, bar, check, deter, halt, thwart, stonewall (slang), plug. 2. shape, form, press, reshape, steam.

block out 1. hide, obscure, conceal, screen. 2. plan, outline, sketch, chart.

blockade n. barrier, barricade, bar, encirclement, seige, beleaguerment.

blockage n. clot, embolism, occlusion, stoppage, logjam.

blockhead n. fool, imbecile, dolt, dullard, idiot, ignoramus, bonehead (slang), numskull, slang: pinhead, chump; ant. genius.

blonde adj. fair, pale, light, flaxen, bleached, towheaded, yellow-haired, sandy-haired.

blood n. lineage, stock, ancestry, descent, family, birth, extraction.

bad blood animosity, malice, hard feelings, rancor.

in cold blood deliberately, cruelly, intentionally, indifferently.

bloodcurdling adj. chilling, dreadful, appalling, horrendous, horrid, terrifying, spine-chilling.

blooded adj. thoroughbred, pedigreed, aristocratic, patrician, royal, registered; ant. bastard, mongrel.

bloodless adj. 1. pale, pallid, wan, anemic, ashen, chalky, pasty, sallow; ant. ruddy, vigorous. 2. coldhearted, indifferent, unemotional, unfeeling, spiritless; ant. passionate. 3. listless, indolent, sluggish, lazy, languid, torpid.

bloodshed n. slaughter, carnage, butchery, massacre, gore, murder, slaying.

bloodthirsty adj. savage, vicious, warlike, ferocious, barbaric, brutal, cruel, ruthless, sanguinary.

bloody adj. 1. wounded, bleeding, bloodstained, unstanched, gaping, raw, grisly; ant. unhurt, uninjured. 2. savage, sanguinary, murderous, hand-to-hand, decimating, ferocious, fierce.

bloom n. flower, blossom, bud, efflorescence.

bloom v. flower, open, bud, sprout, burgeon, flourish, thrive, germinate.

blessed adj. 1. happy, joyful, joyous, glad, contented. 2. redeemed, saved, sanctified, dedicated, consecrated, sacred, hallowed, revered; ant. doomed, accursed.

blessing n. 1. benediction, benison, commendation, sanctification, absolution, baptism, unction, consecration; ant. curse, anathema. 2. boon, benefit, advantage, asset, stroke of luck, good fortune, godsend, windfall; ant. obstacle.

blight n. disease, affliction, bane, evil, pestilence, plague, scourge, contamination, decay; ant. blessing, boon.

blind n. 1. curtain, veil, blindfold, cloak. 2. front, façade, cover, camouflage, mask, screen, feint, distraction.

blind v. 1. shade, obscure, darken, shadow, dim. 2. deceive, conceal, mislead, delude.

blind adj. 1. sightless, unseeing, visionless, purblind, blind as a bat, stone blind, in darkness, eyeless; ant. sighted. 2. insensitive, inconsiderate, thoughtless, heedless, careless, unaware, hasty, impetuous, boorish, oblivious, rash, obtuse; ant. aware. 3. obstructed, blocked, closed, dead-end, without egress. 4. concealed, hidden, obscured, disguised, dark, dim; ant. conspicuous. 5. random, chance, incidental, accidental, unplanned, fortuitous; ant. calculated, purposeful.

blink v. 1. flicker, wink, flutter, twinkle, glimmer, sparkle, glitter, shimmer. 2. squint, peep, peek, glimpse, screw one's eyes at.

bliss n. happiness, felicity, delight, rapture, joy, ecstasy, euphoria, elation, cloud nine (slang); ant. damnation, misery.

blister n. boil, cyst, canker, swelling, welt, ulcer, abscess, carbuncle.

blister v. burn, scald, irritate, boil, mark.

blistering adj. hot, scorching, intense, excoriating, scathing, virulent, withering, vicious; ant. mild.

blithe adj. happy, jaunty, lighthearted, lively, buoyant, merry, nonchalant, sprightly, vivacious; ant. morose.

blizzard n. snowstorm, tempest, gale, squall.

bloated adj. enlarged, distended, inflated, swollen, tumid, tumescent, dropsical; ant. shrivelled, shrunken.

bloc n. faction, cabal, ring, group, alliance, axis, cartel, clique, coalition, league, entente.

blossom *n.* flower, bloom, bud.

blossom *v.* bloom, flower, mature, ripen.

blot *n.* blemish, spot, stain, smudge, defect, fault, flaw, smear, taint.

blot *v.* dirty, stain, spot, soil, blotch, disgrace, sully, tarnish, mar, besmirch, dishonor.

blot out 1. cancel, delete, efface, deface, expunge, scratch *or* mark out. **2.** shade, darken, blur, shroud, eclipse, obscure.

blotch *n.* blemish, blot, stain, smudge.

blotchy *adj.* patchy, spotted, uneven, reddened, macular.

blow *n.* **1.** stroke, hit, buffet, wallop, rap, whack, slam, swat, slap. **2.** catastrophe, disaster, setback, calamity, tragedy, affliction, misfortune, reverse.

blowout *n.* **1.** explosion, blast, detonation, eruption. **2.** flat tire, tear, break, puncture, rupture, leak, gap. **3.** (*slang*) party, riot, spree, binge.

blow *v.* **1.** puff, pant, exhale, breathe, whistle, blast, toot. **2.** waft, flutter, whisk, fling, whirl, flap, wave, buffet. **3.** brag, swagger, bluster, boast. **4.** spend, waste, squander, lay *or* pay out.

blow a fuse (*slang*) rage, rant, throw a tantrum, become enraged *or* irate, boil, blow up, lose one's cool.

blow out 1. extinguish, snuff, put out, dampen. **2.** explode, burst, shatter, erupt, rupture.

blow up 1. (*slang*) rage, lose one's cool, *slang:* hit the roof, blow one's top *or* stack, go off the deep end, go off. **2.** inflate, swell, puff *or* pump up, distend, enlarge.

bludgeon *v.* beat, club, batter, strike, cudgel.

blue *adj.* **1.** aquamarine, azure, indigo, sapphire, turquoise, navy, cerulean, cobalt, teal. **2.** sad, depressed, down, low, moody, melancholy, despondent, out of sorts, miserable, gloomy, morose; *ant.* cheerful. **3.** bawdy, lewd, risqué, vulgar, coarse, suggestive, provocative, pornographic, off-color, smutty, obscene; *ant.* decent.

blueprint *n.* draft, design, model, outline, plan, prototype, sketch.

blues *n.* depression, gloom, melancholy, dejection, doldrums; *ant.* euphoria.

bluff *n.* **1.** bank, cliff, ridge, precipice, headland, height, knoll, promontory, escarpment. **2.** trick, ruse, lie, deception, pretense, subterfuge.

bluff *v.* deceive, mislead, trick, fool, feign, hoodwink, bamboozle, sham.

blunder *n.* mistake, lapse, oversight, error, impropriety, indiscretion, faux pas, solecism.

blunt *v.* weaken, deaden, dampen, soften, abate, allay, alleviate; *ant.* intensify.

blunt *adj.* **1.** dull, unsharpened, unpointed, rounded, round; *ant.* sharp. **2.** abrupt, brusque, curt, short, direct, forthright, candid, plain-spoken, rude, insensitive, tactless; *ant.* courteous, tactful.

blur *v.* dim, obscure, blear, cloud, fog, darken, mask, obfuscate.

blurt *v.* exclaim, ejaculate, spout, leak, spill, let the cat out of the bag, spill the beans (*slang*), disclose, divulge.

blush *v.* flush, redden, color, crimson, glow, mantle.

bluster *v.* rant, rave, brag, show off, gloat, shoot off one's mouth (*slang*), crow, swagger, strut, ride the high horse (*slang*), roister.

blustery *adj.* gusty, squally, stormy, tempestuous, wild, windy, tumultuous; *ant.* calm.

board *n.* **1.** plank, beam, slat, strip, lath, panel, sheet. **2.** food, provisions, mess, fare, grub (*slang*), keep, victuals, rations, repasts. **3.** committee, council, cabinet, conclave, commission, jury, trustees.

across the board impartially, fairly, equitably, equally, universally.

board *v.* **1.** embark, catch, mount, emplane, entrain, climb, leave; *ant.* disembark. **2.** accommodate, lodge, room, put up, house, quarter, feed, billet.

boast *n.* brag, claim, bravado, bluster, gasconade, avowal, braggadocio, rodomontade.

boast *v.* gloat, exult, brag, crow, show off, blow one's own horn (*slang*), pat oneself on the back, bluster, flaunt, trumpet.

boastful *adj.* egotistic, pretentious, bombastic, bragging, conceited, cocky, vainglorious, immodest, narcissistic; *ant.* modest.

bob *v.* duck, weave, wobble, jerk, jolt, quiver, falter, swing, oscillate.

bobbed *adj.* clipped, cut, shortened, curtailed, coiffed.

bode *v.* indicate, warn, import, intimate, portend, prophesy, presage, threaten, betoken, augur.

bodily *adj.* fleshly, physical, corporeal, material, tangible, organic, substantial, solid, carnal; *ant.* spiritual.

bodily *adv.* completely, entirely, totally, absolutely, fully, wholly, in toto, en masse; *ant.* piecemeal.

body *n.* 1. physique, frame, form, shape, build, torso, trunk. 2. corpse, cadaver, remains, carcass. 3. chassis, groundwork, fuselage, assembly, hull, skeleton, substructure, scaffold. 4. collection, corpus, compilation. 5. society, group, association, cartel, bloc, confederation, congress.

over one's dead body never, by no means, not if one can help it.

bog *n.* swamp, marsh, lowland, mire, quagmire, wetlands, fen.

bog down delay, hinder, impede, retard, stall, stick.

bogus *adj.* artificial, fake, imitation, pseudo, ersatz, spurious, counterfeit, forged, fraudulent; *ant.* genuine.

bohemian *n.* beatnik, hippie, nonconformist, iconoclast; *ant.* bourgeois.

bohemian *adj.* unconventional, unorthodox, eccentric, irregular, offbeat, nonconformist, exotic, artistic, outré.

boil *v.* 1. cook, seethe, stew, simmer, steam, percolate, brew. 2. rage, fume, sputter, rave.

boil down summarize, abridge, distill, synopsize, condense, decrease.

boiling *adj.* 1. bubbling, simmering, cooking, stewing, bubbling, steaming, percolating. 2. angry, irate, furious, infuriated, fuming, incensed, indignant.

boisterous *adj.* rambunctious, uproarious, clamorous, exuberant, rollicking, unruly, tumultuous, noisy, vociferous; *ant.* quiet, restrained.

bold *adj.* 1. brave, fearless, courageous, intrepid, valiant, heroic, gallant, valorous; *ant.* timid. 2. impertinent, rude, brazen, audacious, presumptuous, cheeky, shameless, saucy, insolent, impudent, forward; *ant.* diffident. 3. prominent, strong, clear, plain, definite, vivid, bright, pronounced, striking; *ant.* bland.

bolster *v.* support, reinforce, prop, boost, brace, buttress, stiffen, strengthen; *ant.* undermine.

bolt *n.* 1. screw, pin, staple, rivet, nut, peg, spike, stud, dowel, rod, stud, coupling. 2. lightning, flash, stroke, shock, thunderbolt.

bolt *v.* 1. secure, lock, latch, fasten, fetter, bar. 2. flee, escape, run, dash, sprint, fly, abscond. 3. devour, gobble, gorge, gulp, wolf, guzzle, stuff, cram.

bomb *v.* attack, shell, bombard, blast, torpedo, napalm, strafe.

bombard *v.* assail, barrage, batter, cannonade, blitz, pelt, pound.

bombast *n.* bluster, braggadocio, grandiloquence, pomposity, pretentiousness, rant, fustian, drivel, nonsense; *ant.* reserve, restraint.

bombastic *adj.* pompous, grandiose, highflown, inflated, turgid, verbose, ostentatious, declamatory.

bona fide authentic, legitimate, genuine, real, valid, kosher, true; *ant.* bogus, false.

bond *n.* 1. fastening, fetters, restraint, shackle, chain, rope, wire. 2. (strong feeling for a person or institution) affinity, tie, attachment, connection, linkage, union, affiliation, relation, duty, obligation. 3. debenture, security, certificate, warranty, surety, guarantee.

bond *v.* bind, connect, fix, fasten, unite, fuse, seal, paste, glue.

bondage *n.* captivity, imprisonment, incarceration, confinement, servitude, enslavement, thralldom, vassalage; *ant.* freedom, independence.

bonus *n.* gratuity, reward, gift, tip, perquisite, commission, benefit.

bony *adj.* thin, emaciated, skinny, angular, scrawny, drawn, gaunt, lanky, lean, gangly; *ant.* plump.

book *n.* volume, tome, paperback, manuscript, tract, work, text.

by the book properly, correctly, legitimately.

know like a book be familiar with, understand, know intimately *or* minutely, comprehend, be on to, have someone's number.

book *v.* 1. reserve, engage, charter, procure, schedule, program, arrange, organize; *ant.* cancel. 2. arrest, charge, take into custody.

bookish *adj.* learned, scholarly, academic, cultured, literary, studious, lettered, pedantic, erudite.

boom *n.* **1.** roar, blast, blare, clap, crash, explosion, noise, reverberation. **2.** increase, growth, rush, inflation, escalation, spurt, upsurge, upturn; *ant.* collapse, failure.

boom *v.* **1.** roar, reverberate, thunder, resound, blare, crash. **2.** prosper, succeed, thrive, expand, grow, flourish, swell; *ant.* fail.

boon *n.* benefit, blessing, gift, godsend, grant, gratuity, windfall; *ant.* blight, disadvantage.

boor *n.* peasant, yokel, hick, rustic, bumpkin, clodhopper, clown, churl, lout, oaf, hayseed (*slang*), vulgarian.

boorish *adj.* vulgar, churlish, coarse, crude, uncouth, clumsy, oafish, churlish; *ant.* cultured, polished, refined.

boost *n.* **1.** increase, addition, enhancement, expansion, supplement; *ant.* setback. **2.** aid, assistance, help.

boost *v.* **1.** raise, hoist, heave, elevate, heighten, lift. **2.** promote, encourage, support, advance, advertise, praise, foster, beat the drum for; *ant.* hinder, undermine.

boot *v.* eject, expel, fire, dismiss, oust, cashier, let go, *slang:* sack, give the bum's rush, bounce.

bootleg *adj.* illegal, unlawful, contraband.

booty *n.* spoils, takings, winnings, pillage, haul, loot, pickings, plunder.

border *n.* **1.** edge, fringe, trimming, rim, hem, end, skirt. **2.** boundary, frontier, outpost, perimeter, periphery, borderline, limit.

borderline *adj.* marginal, uncertain, doubtful, ambivalent, indeterminate, problematic; *ant.* certain, definite.

bore *n.* nuisance, pest, annoyance, bother, vexation; *ant.* pleasure.

bore *v.* drill, penetrate, pierce, gouge, perforate, tunnel, countermine, burrow, sap, sink, ream.

bored *adj.* wearied, fatigued, jaded, blasé, in a rut, sick and tired; *ant.* interested, excited.

boredom *n.* apathy, listlessness, tedium, ennui, indifference, monotony, doldrums; *ant.* excitement.

boring *adj.* unexciting, wearisome, tiresome, tedious, long-winded, stale, routine, dreary, dull, trite, vapid; *ant.* interesting, original.

borrow *v.* **1.** *slang:* bum, beg, sponge, mooch; hire, rent, cadge, *slang:* chisel, hit up for; *ant.* lend, return. **2.** adopt, appropriate, assume, copy, imitate, pirate, plagiarize, usurp.

boss *n.* administrator, foreman, manager, executive, supervisor, superintendent, director, honcho (*slang*).

bossy *adj.* demanding, insistent, overbearing, autocratic, highhanded, domineering, imperious, despotic; *ant.* unassertive.

botch *v.* bungle, blunder, mishandle, fumble, *slang:* screw up, goof, flub, fudge; spoil, mar, ruin, wreck, muff (*slang*); *ant.* accomplish, succeed.

bother *n.* problem, concern, care, worry, vexation, distress, anxiety, trouble.

bother *v.* **1.** (be a nuisance), plague, torment, vex, annoy, pester, irritate, irk, harass, heckle, badger, goad, exasperate, bedevil, *slang:* bug, get on one's nerves; *ant.* please, delight. **2.** (cause discomfort, as by news or circumstances) distress, upset; embarrass, pain, grieve, put out, disconcert, perturb, go against one's grain.

bothersome *adj.* disturbing, irritating, vexatious, troublesome, exasperating, annoying, worrisome, aggravating.

bottleneck *n.* blockage, hindrance, obstacle, obstruction, congestion, jam.

bottle up contain, restrict, restrain, check, curb, suppress, hold in.

bottom *n.* **1.** (lowest part) foundation, base, support, seat, substructure, pedestal, bed; foot, underside; nadir, depths. **2.** (hind part) rear, behind, tail, backside, posterior.

bottomless *adj.* infinite, boundless, unfathomable, limitless, abysmal, profound, deep; *ant.* shallow.

bough *n.* branch, limb, arm, fork.

bought *adj.* acquired, purchased, procured, paid for, requisitioned, contracted for; *ant.* sold, pawned.

boulevard *n.* avenue, street, road, highway, pike, thoroughfare, promenade, terrace.

bounce *v.* **1.** rebound, ricochet, recoil, glance, boomerang, carom, bump. **2.** spring, hop, jump, leap, vault, bound, start. **3.** (*slang*) oust, throw out, eject, fire, dismiss.

bouncing *adj.* healthy, thriving, lively, vigorous, robust.

bound v. 1. leap, jump, vault, spring, caper, frisk, gambol, prance. 2. limit, restrict, confine, circumscribe, define.

bound adj. 1. tied up, chained, fettered, shackled, manacled, handcuffed, pinioned, tethered, secured, roped, hogtied, trussed up. 2. obligated, obliged, impelled, beholden, committed, compelled, constrained, liable, duty-bound, required; ant. free, independent.

boundary n. border, verge, edge, fringe, frontier, limit, perimeter, demarcation, circumference, periphery; ant. center, core.

bounded adj. limited, enclosed, defined, circumscribed, rimmed, hedged, ringed, fenced, skirted, girdled, ant. unlimited, unbounded.

boundless adj. 1. immense, vast, large, tremendous, prodigious. 2. infinite, limitless, endless, immeasurable, incalculable, interminable, unbounded, unending; ant. limited.

bountiful adj. plentiful, abundant, teeming, luxuriant, plenteous, ample, generous, lavish, munificent, overflowing, profuse, unstinting; ant. meager, sparse.

bounty n. 1. recompense, pay, prize, premium, bonus, reward. 2. liberality, generosity, hospitality, beneficence, largesse, philanthropy.

bouquet n. 1. arrangement, spray, garland, wreath, corsage, nosegay, boutonnière. 2. fragrance, aroma, scent, odor, redolence, perfume, savor.

bourgeois adj. common, conventional, conformist, middle-class, conservative, dull, trite, trivial, unimaginative, circumscribed; ant. unconventional, bohemian.

bout n. match, competition, contest, fight, encounter, engagement, competition, heat.

bovine adj. dull, slow, stupid, dense, obtuse; ant. quick.

bow n. 1. prow, head, stem, fore, bowsprit. 2. nod, bend, curtsy, genuflection, salutation, salaam.

bow v. 1. bend, stoop, dip, drop, incline, bob, duck, kowtow, salaam. 2. surrender, submit, capitulate, concede, acquiesce, yield; ant. resist.

bowels n. intestines, guts, entrails, innards (slang), viscera, vitals.

bower n. alcove, arbor, bay, grotto, hideaway, retreat, sanctuary, shelter, summer house.

bowl n. vessel, saucer, basin, pot, pitcher, tureen, stoup.

box n. crate, carton, case, coffer, trunk.

box v. 1. pack, package, crate, confine, encase. 2. spar, slang: scrap, duke; cuff, clout.

boy n. lad, youth, kid, youngster, small fry, urchin, stripling, puppy.

boycott v. reject, ban, bar, embargo, exclude, ostracize, outlaw, prohibit, blacklist; ant. encourage, support.

boyfriend n. beau, admirer, escort, suitor, flame, paramour, date.

boyish adj. puerile, childish, immature, juvenile, innocent.

brace n. support, prop, bolster, stay, beam, truss, girder, strut, buttress, stanchion.

brace v. prop, bolster, fortify, support, shore up, reinforce, hearten, uphold, encourage.

bracing adj. stimulating, invigorating, rousing, brisk, crisp, exhilarating, refreshing; ant. debilitating.

brackish adj. salty, briny, saline, bitter.

brag v. swagger, exult, gloat, boast, bluster, trumpet, vaunt, blow or toot one's own horn.

braggart n. boaster, blowhard, windbag, bigmouth (slang), blusterer, braggadocio, self-promoter.

braid v. plait, weave, interlace, twist, wind, twine, mesh; ant. loosen, undo.

brain (slang) n. genius, scholar, intellectual, egghead (slang), sage, savant, pundit, polymath.

brainless adj. stupid, dumb, daft, thoughtless, witless, empty-headed, idiotic, half-witted.

brains n. intelligence, intellect, mind, gray matter, wits, faculties, common sense, mother wit.

brain-teaser n. puzzle, riddle, conundrum, mind-bender (slang).

brainwash v. indoctrinate, reeducate, instill, teach, convince, catechize.

brake n. restriction, check, damper, constraint, curb, hurdle, rein, deterrent.

brake v. slow, decelerate, slacken, pull up, retard, drag, stop.

branch n. 1. tributary, outpost, chapter, office, bureau, department, subsidiary. 2. bough, limb, sprig, twig, offshoot, bud.

branch out v. diversify, expand, develop, proliferate, ramify.

brand *n.* **1.** trademark, seal, mark, name, emblem, logo, stamp, symbol. **2.** coal, ember, spark, torch.

brand *v.* **1.** stamp, imprint, blaze, burn, scar, label. **2.** stigmatize, label, censure, denounce, discredit, disgrace.

brandish *v.* wield, shake, flourish, gesture, flaunt, raise.

brash *adj.* audacious, bold, brazen, cocky, impertinent, froward, impudent, fresh, cheeky, insolent, precipitate, rash, rude; *ant.* cautious, reserved.

brass *n.* **1.** (*slang*) officers, executives, managers, higher-ups. **2.** impudence, impertinence, audacity, effrontery, *slang:* gall, nerve; insolence, temerity; *ant.* circumspection, timidity.

brassy *adj.* brazen, saucy, flirtatious, pert, forward, meretricious, strident.

bravado *n.* bombast, pretense, pomposity, swagger, hot air (*slang*), bluster, braggadocio, gasconade; *ant.* modesty, restraint.

brave *adj.* courageous, fearless, dauntless, valiant, bold, heroic, intrepid, daring, audacious; *ant.* timid, cowardly.

brave *v.* confront, face, encounter, risk, court, suffer, endure, withstand; *ant.* capitulate.

bravery *n.* courage, valor, intrepidity, fortitude, hardihood, guts, spunk (*slang*), indomitability, resolve, mettle, spirit, grit, resolve.

brawl *n.* fight, riot, fracas, fray, melee, tumult, uproar.

brawn *n.* muscle, bulk, robustness, beefiness, strength, muscularity, power, might, vigor, energy.

brawny *adj.* strong, powerful, muscular, sturdy, strapping, well-built, husky, solid, sinewy, burly; *ant.* frail, slight.

bray *v.* bawl, whinny, neigh, hoot, screech.

brazen *adj.* impudent, impertinent, bold, brassy, defiant, unabashed, saucy, shameless, barefaced, insolent, malapert; *ant.* timid, shamefaced.

breach *n.* **1.** break, gap, rupture, fissure, aperture, rent, rift. **2.** violation, infraction, transgression, trespass, offense, contravention.

bread *n.* **1.** food, sustenance, nourishment, provisions, substinence, victuals, aliment. **2.** (*slang*) money, coin, cash, dollars, *slang:* dough, moolah, greenbacks.

breadth *n.* **1.** (measurement along one dimension) width, broadness, diameter, wideness, thickness. **2.** scope, reach, scale, sweep, extent, compass, magnitude, amplitude, dimension.

break *n.* **1.** rift, fracture, split, schism, breach, rupture, crack, tear, cleft, fissure. **2.** pause, intermission, interim, recess, hiatus, interlude, respite, suspension. **3.** (*slang*) opportunity, chance, fortune, advantage, opening, accident.

break *v.* **1.** burst, split, crack, rend, sunder, sever, fracture, cleave, rive, shatter, splinter, rupture. **2.** demolish, destroy, batter, disintegrate, dilapidate, reduce, undermine, collapse.

break away separate, secede, split, leave, flee, detach, depart.

break down 1. analyze, examine, investigate, dissect. **2.** malfunction, fail, falter, misfire, *slang:* conk *or* peter *or* fizzle out, go kaput, go on the fritz.

break in 1. train, condition, prepare, educate, instruct, teach. **2.** intrude, encroach, invade, burglarize, trespass, rob, steal.

break through penetrate, progress, make headway, intrude, gain ground.

break up *v.* **1.** (cause to come apart) dismantle, disassemble, separate, divide. **2.** crumble, disintegrate, fall apart, dissipate.

breakable *adj.* fragile, delicate, brittle, flimsy, frail, weak, friable; *ant.* durable, sturdy.

breakaway *adj.* dissenting, secessionist, schismatic, rebel, renegade, heretical, apostate.

breakdown *n.* failure, stoppage, collapse, rupture, disruption.

breakthrough *n.* discovery, finding, invention.

breast *n.* **1.** bosom, chest, bust, thorax. **2.** teat, nipple, udder, mamilla.

beat one's breast repent, apologize, regret, be penitent *or* sorry *or* remorseful.

make a clean breast of admit, confess, reveal, expose.

breath *n.* **1.** inhalation, gasp, sigh, respiration, expiration, suspiration. **2.** whiff, flutter, puff, waft.

take one's breath away excite, thrill, stimulate, invigorate, exhilarate, enrapture.

breather (*slang*) *n.* respite, recess, pause, hiatus, halt, break, suspension.

breathless | brisk

breathless adj. 1. exhausted, spent, panting, gasping, wheezing, winded, blown, used up. 2. agog, anxious, excited, expectant, impatient, avid, wondrous; ant. bored, jaded.

breathtaking adj. awe-inspiring, astonishing, exciting, overwhelming, stirring, stunning, thrilling, riveting, sensational.

breed n. variety, kind, class, ilk, family, lineage, race, species, stock, strain, type.

breed v. 1. reproduce, beget, bring forth, create, generate, propagate, spawn, procreate. 2. produce, cause, promote, engender, cultivate, develop, foster. 3. nurture, train, raise, discipline.

breeding n. 1. ancestry, background, lineage, stock, strain. 2. education, cultivation, civility, gentility, manners, refinement, politeness; ant. vulgarity.

breezy adj. 1. windy, gusty, blowing, blustery. 2. jaunty, sprightly, blithe, carefree, casual, nonchalant, cheerful, vivacious; ant. staid, reserved.

brevity n. shortness, conciseness, pithiness, economy; ant. verbosity.

brew v. 1. cook, ferment, boil, seethe, stew, steep. 2. contrive, devise, scheme, plot, concoct, foment, prepare.

bribe n. graft, payola (slang), gratuity, blackmail, hush money, payoff (slang), slush fund, tribute, protection, kickback, enticement, grease (slang).

bribe v. corrupt, coax, lure, entice, tempt, influence, slang; grease one's palms, fix.

bridge v. span, connect, link, join, couple, traverse, unite, yoke.

bridle v. check, curb, control, restrain, govern, subdue.

brief n. summary, abstract, outline, précis, digest.

brief v. 1. summarize, recapitulate, abridge, epitomize. 2. inform, prime, advise, instruct, explain, guide, prepare.

brief adj. 1. concise, compressed, cursory, terse, pithy, succinct, laconic, capsular, aphoristic; ant. verbose. 2. transient, passing, ephemeral, fleeting, fast, momentary, short-lived, temporary; ant. permanent, prolonged. 3. abrupt, blunt, brusque, curt, crisp, hasty, sharp, surly.

briefing n. 1. instruction, preparation, advice, directions, guidance, orders. 2. conference, meeting, colloquium.

brigand n. robber, thief, bandit, highwayman, outlaw, gunman.

bright adj. 1. shining, gleaming, glittering, blazing, sparkling, effulgent, illuminated, dazzling, phosphorescent; ant. dull, clouded. 2. intelligent, clever, astute, keen, lucid, observant, perceptive, perspicacious, quick-witted. 3. (as an outlook) promising, auspicious, propitious, hopeful, encouraging, rosy, favorable; excellent.

brighten v. 1. clear up, gleam, glow, lighten, improve. 2. polish, burnish, shine, kindle, intensify, enliven, illuminate.

brightness n. shine, illumination, luster, glitter, sparkle, luminosity, effulgence; ant. darkness, dullness.

brilliant adj. 1. shining, dazzling, sparkling, gleaming, effulgent, lambent, scintillating, resplendent, vivid; ant. dull. 2. ingenious, adroit, expert, gifted, talented, multitalented, skillful, inventive, intellectual; ant. stupid. 3. illustrious, eminent, extraordinary, superb, splendid, excellent, exceptional, remarkable; ant. ordinary.

brim n. rim, edge, lip, verge, brink, border, perimeter.

bring v. 1. transport, convey, carry, conduct, bear, transfer. 2. cause, produce, effect, begin, make, generate, beget, institute, initiate, engender, create.

bring around 1. convince, persuade, convert, prove, induce. 2. revive, resuscitate, restore, refresh.

bring on cause, provoke, generate, induce, precipitate, instigate, prompt; ant. inhibit.

bring out 1. excite, elicit, arouse, evoke, draw out. 2. intensify, enhance, emphasize, highlight, heighten.

bring up 1. raise, rear, foster, nurture, educate, teach, train. 2. discuss, broach, tender, submit, advance, propose.

brink n. brim, edge, border, threshold.

brisk adj. 1. active, lively, energetic, bustling, busy, quick, sprightly, vigorous; ant. sluggish. 2. stimulating, invigorating, exhilarating, sharp, crisp, bracing.

bristle *v.* **1.** swarm, abound, teem, be thick *or* alive *or* crawl with. **2.** bridle, swell, seethe, prickle, ruffle.

brittle *adj.* delicate, fragile, frail, breakable, friable, crumbly.

broach *v.* mention, propose, suggest, introduce, raise, utter.

broad *adj.* **1.** wide, expansive, vast, ample, spacious, capacious, voluminous; *ant.* narrow, slender. **2.** extensive, comprehensive, general, all-inclusive, widespread. **3.** liberal, tolerant, open, open-minded, progressive; *ant.* narrow-minded, biased. **4.** cultivated, cultured, experienced, cosmopolitan.

broadcast *n.* show, telecast, program.

broadcast *v.* **1.** air, beam, televise, transmit, radio, cable. **2.** announce, circulate, publish, report, publicize, relay, disseminate, spread, proclaim.

broaden *v.* expand, develop, enlarge, widen, stretch, increase, extend, diversify, supplement, augment, thicken; *ant.* constrict.

broad-minded *adj.* liberal, enlightened, cosmopolitan, receptive, tolerant, catholic, flexible, indulgent, permissive; *ant.* biased, prejudiced.

brochure *n.* leaflet, pamphlet, handout, circular, advertisement, booklet, folder, handbill.

broil *n.* sear, bake, roast, cook.

broiler *n.* oven, roaster-oven, grill, hibachi, griddle, barbecue.

broke (*slang*) *adj.* bankrupt, destitute, impecunious, short of funds, impoverished, insolvent, penniless, penurious, ruined, strapped; *ant.* solvent, affluent.

go for broke (*slang*) gamble, wager, risk everything.

broken *adj.* **1.** rent, split, riven, fragmentary, defective; *ant.* sound, whole, intact. **2.** defective, inoperable, disabled, faulty, shot (*slang*), unsatisfactory, *slang:* on the fritz, busted; *ant.* usable, working. **3.** infirm, decrepit, frail, tottering, weak. **4.** discontinuous, spasmodic, erratic, intermittent, irregular.

brokenhearted *adj.* sad, crestfallen, dejected, despondent, devastated, mournful, disappointed, disconsolate, grief-stricken, inconsolable, miserable, sorrowful, wretched.

broker *n.* agent, dealer, factor, handler, intermediary, middleman, negotiator, stockbroker.

bromide *n.* anodyne, banality, cliché, commonplace, platitude, truism, stereotype.

brooch *n.* pin, clip, clasp, badge, breastpin.

brood *n.* children, offspring, young, litter, issue, family, progeny, hatch.

brood *v.* agonize, dwell on, meditate, mope, muse, ponder, ruminate, rehearse, repine.

brook *n.* channel, inlet, rivulet, stream, creek.

brook *v.* abide, accept, allow, bear, countenance, endure, permit, stand, suffer, support, tolerate, withstand.

broom *n.* sweeper, besom, brush, wisp.

broth *n.* brew, distillation, concoction, soup, potage, consommé, puree, bouillon, stock.

brother *n.* **1.** sibling, relative, kinsman. **2.** associate, colleague, companion, comrade, fellow, chum, friend, mate, partner, pal.

brotherhood *n.* fraternity, guild, league, society, union, affiliation, alliance, clan, clique, coterie.

brotherly *adj.* fraternal, affectionate, sympathetic, benevolent, concerned, neighborly, philanthropic; *ant.* aloof, uncaring.

browbeat *v.* bully, coerce, cow, domineer, dragoon, hound, intimidate, oppress, threaten, tyrannize.

brown *v.* toast, scorch, sauté, cook, fry.

browse *v.* look, peruse, scan, skim, survey, leaf through.

bruise *n.* contusion, blemish, discoloration, injury, mark, shiner (*slang*), swelling.

bruise *v.* **1.** blacken, discolor, blemish, wound, hurt. **2.** grieve, insult, offend, wound.

brunt *n.* burden, weight, thrust, stress, force, impact, impetus, pressure, shock.

brush *n.* **1.** broom, whisk, sweeper, besom. **2.** encounter, clash, conflict, confrontation, fracas, incident, skirmish, tussle. **3.** undergrowth, scrub, shrubs, thicket, groundcover, brushwood, bushes.

brush *v.* **1.** cleanse, buff, burnish, clean, polish, rub, shine. **2.** touch, caress, graze, kiss, contact, sweep.

brush aside disregard, ignore, forget about, dismiss.

brush off (*slang*) reject, repulse, scorn, slight, dismiss, snub, spurn, repudiate, cold-shoulder, stand up.

brush up study, cram, read up, relearn, refresh, improve.

brusque *adj.* abrupt, curt, gruff, hasty, surly, terse, blunt; *ant.* tactful, courteous, polite, civil.

brutal *adj.* bloodthirsty, callous, ferocious, harsh, remorseless, vicious, severe, pitiless, cruel, savage; *ant.* humane, sensitive, civil, merciful.

brute *n.* 1. animal, beast, creature. 2. barbarian, devil, fiend, lout, monster, ogre, sadist, savage; *ant.* humanitarian.

brute *adj.* mindless, instinctive, physical, carnal, bestial.

brutish *adj.* barbaric, swinish, uncouth, vulgar, gross, coarse, depraved; *ant.* refined.

bubble *n.* blister, bead, effervescence, foam, froth, fizz, head, lather, suds, spume, drop, globule, droplet.

bubble *v.* boil, burble, gurgle, murmur, percolate, seethe.

bubbly *adj.* 1. carbonated, fizzy, sudsy, effervescent. 2. animated, excited, lively, merry, sprightly, energetic, bouncy, spirited.

buccaneer *n.* corsair, pirate, privateer, searover, sea-wolf.

buck up (*slang*) *v.* cheer up, rally, take heart, take comfort; hearten, encourage, gratify, inspirit.

bucket *n.* pail, basin, can, cask, pan, pitcher, barrel, vessel, bail.

kick the bucket (*slang*) expire, pass away, die, croak (*slang*).

buckle *n.* hasp, catch, clip, fastener.

buckle *v.* 1. catch, clasp, close, connect, fasten, hitch, hook, secure. 2. bend, contort, crumple, distort, fold, warp, wrinkle, collapse, twist.

bucolic *adj.* rustic, rural, pastoral, agrarian, agricultural, countrified; *ant.* industrial, urban.

budding *adj.* burgeoning, developing, fledgling, flowering, growing, incipient, nascent, potential, promising, germinal, embryonic; *ant.* full-blown, mature.

buddy *n.* friend, pal, chum, intimate, mate; fellow, peer, companion, confidant, associate, sidekick (*slang*), crony; *ant.* stranger, enemy.

budge *v.* move, dislodge, give way, roll, shift, slide, yield.

budget *n.* allotment, allowance, finances, funds, means, resources.

budget *v.* allocate, apportion, cost, estimate, plan, ration.

buff *n.* fan, addict, admirer, aficionado, freak (*slang*), connoisseur, devotee, enthusiast, expert.

buff *v.* polish, shine, burnish, rub, smooth, brush.

buff *adj.* tan, fawn, khaki, sandy, straw, tan, fulvous.

in the buff nude, naked, bare; *ant.* clothed.

buffer *n.* cushion, shield, safeguard, pad, screen, bulwark, fender, shock-absorber.

buffet *v.* bang, batter, beat, box, clobber, cuff, hit, knock, pound, pummel, strike, wallop.

buffoon *n.* fool, clown, jester, joker, comedian, comic, goliard, harlequin, mountebank, scaramouch, wag.

buffoonery *n.* nonsense, pantomime, silliness, drollery, waggishness, high jinks.

bug *n.* 1. insect, beetle, vermin, gnat, pest. 2. (*slang*) flaw, defect, fault, imperfection, blemish, virus. 3. (*slang*) enthusiast, fan, devotee, zealot, fanatic. 4. (*slang*) microorganism, bacillus, germ, virus, microbe; disease, illness, malady, sickness.

bug (*slang*) *v.* 1. annoy, irritate, plague, pester, bother, harass, disturb, get on one's case (*slang*). 2. spy, overhear, wiretap, eavesdrop, listen in on.

bugbear *n.* hobgoblin, bogy, anathema, bane, devil, fiend, dread, horror, nightmare.

build *n.* body, figure, form, frame, physique, shape, size, structure.

build *v.* 1. construct, erect, frame, raise, manufacture, assemble, model, sculpture, fashion produce, forge, devise; *ant.* destroy, demolish, wreck. 2. found, formulate, institute, constitute, establish, organize.

build up 1. develop, enhance, expand, extend, improve, increase, amplify, intensify. 2. advertise, hype, promote, publicize, plug (*slang*). 3. fortify, bolster, reinforce, strengthen.

building *n.* structure, edifice, dwelling, construction, domicile, pile.

built (*slang*) *adj.* buxom, well-proportioned, shapely.

bulbous *adj.* bulging, distended, swollen, rounded, convex.

bulge *n.* protuberance, rise, swelling, projection, surge.

bulge *v.* distend, protrude, sag, swell, expand, dilate.

bulk *n.* **1.** size, magnitude, mass, extent, quantity, dimensions. **2.** majority, plurality, weight, preponderance; *ant.* bit, remnant, fraction.

bulky *adj.* cumbersome, hulking, immense, massive, ponderous, unwieldy, voluminous, weighty; *ant.* manageable, handy.

bulldoze *v.* **1.** clear, demolish, flatten, level, raze. **2.** browbeat, bully, coerce, force, intimidate, ride roughshod over.

bullet *n.* shot, slug, projectile, pellet, ball, missile, plumb, sinker, weight, ball.

bulletin *n.* announcement, report, dispatch, news flash, communication, communiqué, message, notification, statement.

bully *n.* ruffian, tough, tyrant.

bully *v.* browbeat, coerce, intimidate, bluster.

bulwark *n.* bastion, buttress, fortification, partition, rampart, security, support, embankment, defense, buffer.

bum *n.* hobo, transient, vagrant, beggar, tramp, ne'er-do-well.

bumbling *adj.* awkward, blundering, clumsy, inept, maladroit; *ant.* competent, efficient.

bump *n.* **1.** jolt, shock, clash, impact, buffet, jerk. **2.** lump, swelling, projection, protuberance, knob, bulge.

bump *v.* hit, collide, strike, crash, sideswipe, jar, bang, knock, shove, slam.

bumpkin *n.* rustic, hick, yokel, peasant, rube (*slang*), boor.

bumptious *adj.* conceited, vain, egotistic, arrogant, presumptuous.

bumpy *adj.* rough, bouncy, choppy, irregular, jarring, jerky, jolting, knobby, lumpy, rutted; *ant.* even, smooth.

bun *n.* muffin, scone, bread, roll, pastry.

bunch *n.* **1.** cluster, clump, quantity, number, batch, assortment. **2.** group, crowd, gang, gathering, party, multitude, troop.

bunch *v.* pack, group, collect, heap.

bundle *n.* parcel, package, collection.

bundle up bale, bind, fasten, pack, tie, wrap, gather; *ant.* loose, scatter.

bunk *n.* **1.** bed, berth, cot, pallet. **2.** (*slang*) nonsense, rubbish, hogwash, twaddle, bosh, rot (*slang*).

buoy *n.* beacon, float, marker, signal.

buoy *v.* keep afloat, sustain, uphold, support.

buoy up boost, cheer, encourage, hearten, lift, raise, support, sustain; *ant.* depress.

buoyant *adj.* **1.** lightweight, weightless, airy, unsinkable, floatable. **2.** cheerful, gay, jovial, lighthearted, elated, walking on air; *ant.* despondent, glum.

burden *n.* **1.** affliction, anxiety, care, grievance, obligation, responsibility, sorrow, stress, trial, trouble. **2.** cargo, load, obstruction, weight.

burden *v.* encumber, load, oppress, overload, overwhelm, strain, tax, worry, bother, handicap; *ant.* lighten, relieve.

burdensome *adj.* difficult, distressing, heavy, irksome, onerous; *ant.* easy.

bureau *n.* **1.** chest of drawers, dresser, desk, chest, highboy, chiffonier. **2.** agency, branch, department, division, office, service, board, committee, commission.

bureaucracy *n.* **1.** administration, government, officialdom, the system, the power structure, apparatus, apparat. **2.** red tape, routine, regulations, officialism.

bureaucrat *n.* civil servant, functionary, minister, officeholder, official, apparatchik.

burglar *n.* cat-burglar, picklock, thief, robber, pickpocket.

burglary *n.* break-in, larceny, robbery, theft, heist.

burial *n.* funeral, entombment, interment, obsequies.

burial ground *n.* graveyard, cemetery, memorial, necropolis, mausoleum, gravesite.

burlesque *n.* caricature, mockery, parody, ridicule, satire, send-up, spoof, travesty.

burlesque *adj.* comic, derisive, droll, farcical; *ant.* serious.

burly *adj.* brawny, hefty, husky, muscular, stout, strapping, sturdy, well-built, athletic; *ant.* puny, small, thin.

burn *v.* **1.** blaze, flame, oxidize, consume, incinerate, flash, flare, cremate, conflagrate, sear, brand, char, cauterize, fire; *ant.* extinguish, put out, quench. **2.** scorch, char, sear, roast, toast, parch, singe, scald, wither. **3.**

(slang) cheat, swindle, defraud, trick, deceive, hornswoggle (slang).

burned up (slang) angered, enraged, infuriated, angry.

burning adj. 1. ablaze, afire, smoking, in flames, smoldering, aflame, kindled, ignited, red hot, incandescent, aglow. 2. fervent, intense, ardent, impassioned, passionate, eager, zealous, fervid, rapt, glowing, enthusiastic; ant. apathetic.

burnish v. polish, buff, shine, glaze, brighten, rub; ant. tarnish.

burrow n. den, hole, lair, retreat, shelter.

burrow v. dig, mine, tunnel, delve, excavate.

bursar n. treasurer, cashier, accountant, comptroller, purser.

burst n. blast, torrent, surge, spurt, rush, outbreak, discharge.

burst v. 1. blow up, explode, erupt, fragment, shatter, split, tear apart, come to pieces, disintegrate. 2. break, crack, rupture, spring a leak.

burst in invade, rush or break in, intrude, enter, meddle.

bury v. 1. inter, conceal, cover, embed, enclose, entomb, inhume, lay to rest, sepulchre, shroud, sink, submerge. 2. defeat, overcome, conquer, beat, win over, vanquish, demolish. 3. engage, engross, immerse, interest, occupy.

bus v. transport, convey, haul, ship.

bush n. 1. shrub, hedge, plant, thicket. 2. backwoods, woodland, brush, wilds, outback, wilderness.

beat around the bush evade, avoid, skirt, hedge, waffle, straddle, tergiversate.

bushy adj. bristly, shaggy, thick, unruly, wiry; ant. neat, well-kept.

business n. 1. commerce, industry, trade, manufacturing, merchandising, selling, transactions, bargaining, exchange. 2. company, corporation, enterprise, establishment, firm, organization, partnership. 3. profession, occupation, career, craft, employment, job, line, function, metier, pursuit, vocation, work. 4. concern, affair, duty, issue, matter, point, problem, question, task, responsibility, subject, topic, assignment.

do business with patronize, deal with, employ, buy from, sell to.

mean business be serious, mean it, stress, impress, emphasize.

businesslike adj. 1. efficient, methodical, orderly, organized, practical, precise, routine, systematic, thorough, well-ordered. 2. formal, impersonal, matter-of-fact, perfunctory, correct, professional.

businessperson n. capitalist, employer, entrepreneur, businessman, businesswoman, executive, financier, personne d'affaires, industrialist, merchant, tradesperson, tycoon.

bust n. 1. breast, bosom, chest. 2. statuette, figurehead, carving, head, torso. 3. (slang) failure, flop, disaster, dud, slang; turkey, washout.

bustle n. activity, ado, agitation, commotion, excitement, flurry, fuss, haste, hurry, stir, to-do (slang), tumult.

bustle v. dash, flutter, fuss, hasten, hurry, rush, scamper, scramble, scurry, stir, tear.

bustling adj. astir, busy, crowded, energetic, lively, restless; ant. quiet.

busy adj. active, assiduous, hectic, diligent, energetic, employed, full, industrious, inquisitive, intent, restless, strenuous; ant. idle, quiet.

busy v. employ, engage, engross, immerse, occupy, interest, absorb, bother, concern.

busybody n. gossip, intruder, meddler, pry, snoop, troublemaker.

but adv. merely, simply, barely, solely, purely, just, no more, exactly, no other than, without, only.

but conj., prep. 1. however, nevertheless, still, yet, though, although, on the contrary. 2. save, disregarding, without, let alone, aside from, not to mention, except, barring.

butcher v. 1. carve, clean, skin, bone, process, cut, dress, prepare, cure, smoke, salt. 2. assassinate, destroy, exterminate, kill, mutilate, slay, slaughter, massacre. 3. ruin, spoil, wreck, botch, destroy, manhandle.

butchery n. bloodshed, carnage, mass destruction, massacre, murder, slaughter.

butt n. 1. base, stump, stub, remainder, hilt; ant. point, peak. 2. laughingstock, sap (slang), dupe, fool, sucker (slang). 3. buttocks, bottom, behind, posterior, buns (slang).

butt *v.* **1.** ram, clash, collide, knock, smack, batter, buffet, strike, gore, horn, buck. **2.** abut, adjoin, touch, bound, join.

butt in (*slang*) interfere, interpose, interrupt, intrude, meddle, horn in (*slang*).

butter up (*slang*) *v.* cajole, flatter, wheedle, suck up to (*slang*).

buttocks *n.* backside, rear, behind, bottom, derrière, butt, haunches, hindquarters, posterior, rump, seat, *slang:* fanny, ass.

button *n.* catch, clasp, frog, knot.

on the button correctly, precisely, accurately, exactly, on target.

button *v.* close, clasp, fasten.

buttress *n.* support, mainstay, abutment, pier, prop, stanchion, stay, strut.

buttress *v.* bolster, brace, reinforce, strengthen, shore up, support, sustain, uphold; *ant.* weaken, undermine.

buxom *adj.* ample, bosomy, busty, chesty, plump, robust, curvaceous, voluptuous; *ant.* petite, slim, small.

buy (*slang*) *n.* value, bargain, steal (*slang*).

buy *v.* **1.** purchase, procure, acquire, get, obtain, square; *ant.* sell. **2.** bribe, corrupt, influence, fix (*slang*).

buyer *n.* customer, consumer, patron, shopper, client, prospect, representative; *ant.* salesman, vendor, dealer.

buzz *n.* **1.** hum, murmur, whisper. **2.** gossip, hearsay, news, scandal, rumor, report.

buzz *v.* reverberate, hum, murmur, ring, whirr.

by *adv.* **1.** near, close, at hand, handy. **2.** aside, away, out of the way, past.

bygone *adj.* past, previous, ancient, antiquated, departed, erstwhile, forgotten, former, lost, olden; *ant.* modern, recent.

by-law *n.* ordinance, local law, municipal regulation.

bypass *v.* avoid, circumvent, ignore, neglect, get around.

by-product *n.* consequence, aftereffect, fallout, repercussion, result, side-effect, aftermath, residue.

bystander *n.* witness, eyewitness, observer, onlooker.

byword *n.* adage, aphorism, epithet, maxim, motto, precept.

cab n. taxi, taxicab, shuttle.

cabal n. 1. clique, league, faction, party, junta, coterie, conclave. 2. conspiracy, intrigue, plot, scheme, machination.

cabin n. cottage, lodge, shack, hut, hovel, shanty, shed, bungalow, chalet.

cabinet n. cupboard, locker, dresser, case, closet, chest, repository, escritoire.

cache n. accumulation, stockpile, hoard, reserve, fund, repository, store, supply.

cache v. bury, stash, conceal, hide, store, stow, secrete, squirrel away.

cacophonous adj. discordant, strident, raucous, jarring, dissonant, grating, harsh; ant. soothing.

cacophony n. dissonance, discord, disharmony; ant. euphony.

cad n. knave, churl, blackguard, caitiff, cur; slang: rat, heel, skunk, swine, worm; ant. gentleman.

cadence n. meter, beat, tempo, measure, pattern, rate; accent, stress, inflection, rhythm.

cadre n. core, nucleus, framework, basis, hierarchy, infrastructure.

café n. coffee shop, coffee bar, cafeteria, snack bar, restaurant, greasy spoon (slang).

cage n. pen, enclosure, coop, aviary, corral, pound.

cagey adj. shrewd, wily, sly, cunning, secretive, discreet, wary, careful, circumspect, guarded; ant. frank, open.

cajole v. coax, wheedle, sweet-talk, flatter, entice, beguile, mislead, dupe, tempt, lure, wheedle.

calamitous adj. disastrous, ruinous, cataclysmic, catastrophic, devastating, tragic, dire, grievous, woeful, fatal, deadly; ant. fortunate, happy.

calamity n. catastrophe, disaster, tragedy, devastation, holocaust.

calculate v. 1. compute, count, figure, tally, crunch numbers (slang), gauge, ascertain, value, weigh, work out. 2. anticipate, intend, plan, consider, determine, surmise, judge, guess, reckon, estimate.

calculated adj. intentional, deliberate, designed, intended, premeditated, planned, managed, stage-managed, rehearsed, purposed, willful; ant. unintentional, impromptu.

calculating adj. contriving, scheming, devious, cunning, crafty, designing, politic, shrewd, deep, subtle, sly, Machiavellian; ant. artless, naïve, open.

caliber n. 1. measurement, bore, diameter, gauge, measure, scope, size. 2. character, ability, gifts, talent, endowment, worth, merit, quality, distinction, stature.

calisthenics n. exercises, workout, gymnastics, aerobics.

call n. 1. appeal, request, invitation, summons, urge, supplication, plea; command, order, signal. 2. shout, cry, whoop, yell, trumpet.

on call ready, prepared, available, at hand, usable.

call v. 1. cry, shout, yell, halloo. 2. summon, hail, contact, get in touch with, telephone, page. 3. name, label, term, declare, dub, christen. 4. (authorize an activity, as a meeting) announce, decree, declare, proclaim, convoke, convene, assemble, gather, bid, rally, rouse.

call for demand, require, necessitate, need, entail, involve, occasion, suggest.

call off discontinue, break off, cancel, desist, drop.

call on 1. appeal to, request, ask, bid, entreat, invoke, summon, supplicate. 2. visit, see, drop in on.

call up 1. call, telephone, ring (up). 2. summon, bid, send for, order. 3. recall, recollect, remember, summon up, call to mind.

calling *n.* occupation, vocation, work, mission, pursuit, profession, business, career, job, trade, field.

callous *adj.* cold, indifferent, heartless, uncaring, hard-boiled, hardened, unmoved, remote, hard-hearted, inured, obdurate, unresponsive; *ant.* kind, sympathetic, sensitive.

callow *adj.* naive, guileless, immature, juvenile, fledgling, puerile, untried, green, raw; *ant.* experienced.

calm *adj.* **1.** balmy, still, halcyon, peaceful, windless, smooth; *ant.* rough, stormy, wild. **2.** (as in manner) serene, placid, composed, collected, confident, impassive, stolid, unruffled, relaxed, tranquil, unhurried, unflappable; *ant.* apprehensive, flustered, perturbed.

calm *v.* soothe, quiet, pacify, compose, hush, still, settle (down), mollify, placate; *ant.* excite, irritate, agitate.

calm down calm *or* compose *or* control *or* restrain oneself, rest, take it easy, keep cool, simmer *or* settle down, *slang:* chill, cool it, keep one's shirt on.

calmness *n.* poise, equability, self-possession, serenity, tranquillity, placidity, evenness, coolness; *ant.* excitement, agitation.

calumniate *v.* malign, slander, denigrate, disparage, asperse, lampoon, libel, stigmatize, vilify.

calumny *n.* slander, aspersion, insult, abuse, smear, revilement, obloquy, vituperation.

camaraderie *n.* brotherhood, sisterhood, fellowship, companionship, comradeship, esprit de corps, fraternization, bonhomie, solidarity.

camouflage *n.* disguise, masquerade, blind, cover, front, guise, mask, subterfuge.

camouflage *v.* conceal, disguise, hide, obscure, obfuscate, screen, cover, veil, cloak; *ant.* reveal.

camp *n.* **1.** bivouac, campground, campsite, barracks, fort, installation, post, encampment. **2.** caucus, faction, party, clique, crowd, group, section, set, side.

camp *v.* quarter, lodge, station, locate, bivouac, camp out, rough it, sleep under the stars; *ant.* leave, depart.

camp (*slang*) *adj.* affected, theatrical, posturing, exaggerated, artificial, mannered, ostentatious.

campaign *n.* operation, movement, promotion, offensive, attack, crusade, drive, excursion, expedition, jihad, push.

campaign *v.* run, throw one's hat in the ring, stump, electioneer.

can *n.* **1.** container, jar, receptacle, canister, pail, tin. **2.** (*slang*) toilet, restroom, lavatory, washroom. **3.** (*slang*) buttocks, backside, seat, posterior.

canal *n.* waterway, trench, channel, conduit, fistula, ditch.

cancel *v.* abort, repeal, nullify, strike, delete, annul, eliminate, erase, abolish, neutralize, revoke, scrub (*slang*).

cancer *n.* malignancy, canker, blight, corruption, pestilence, rot, infection, tumor.

cancerous *adj.* carcinogenic, virulent, malignant, mortal.

candid *adj.* frank, plain-spoken, guileless, blunt, forthright, ingenuous, open, aboveboard, outspoken, straightforward, truthful, sincere, unequivocal; *ant.* contrived, evasive, devious, cagey.

candidate *n.* nominee, contender, competitor, applicant, claimant, contestant, suitor, aspirant.

candor *n.* **1.** frankness, directness, artlessness, forthrightness, openness, plain-dealing, simplicity, straightforwardness, honesty, sincerity, veracity, truthfulness. **2.** fairness, impartiality, evenhandedness; *ant.* prejudice, bias.

candy *n.* sweets, bonbons, confections, sweetmeats.

cane *n.* stick, walking-stick, staff, cudgel, rod, shillelagh, ferule.

canny *adj.* shrewd, astute, perspicacious, knowing, wise, sagacious, clever, smart, aware, sly, circumspect; *ant.* simple, naive.

canon *n.* rule, law, standard, precept, criterion, principle, regulation, statute.

canonical *adj.* sanctioned, authoritative, prescribed, orthodox, accepted, standard, received, recognized, approved, regular, kosher.

canopy *n.* awning, covering, shade, dais.

cant *n.* **1.** hypocrisy, show, pomposity, pretense, deceit. **2.** dialect, vernacular, slang, jargon, lingo, argot.

cantankerous *adj.* irritable, difficult, disagreeable, irascible, quarrelsome, contrary, feisty,

canvass

peevish, choleric, cranky, crotchety; *ant.* pleasant, good-natured.

canvass *v.* poll, review, sound out, test, consult, check, survey, analyze, examine, test the waters.

canyon *n.* ravine, gully, gorge.

cap *n.* hat, beret, yarmulke, bonnet, fez, skullcap, beanie.

cap *v.* 1. surpass, outdo, beat, better, exceed. 2. (put a lid on) cover, stop up, eclipse, top. top, crown.

capability *n.* ability, capacity, competence, wherewithal, potential, skill, qualification, proficiency, faculty, resources, talent.

capable *adj.* able, qualified, experienced, competent, skillful, suited, adept, accomplished, resourceful, talented, reliable, sound; *ant.* useless, inept, incompetent.

capacious *adj.* spacious, expansive, roomy, vast, extensive, ample, generous, substantial, comfortable, liberal, sizable; *ant.* cramped, small.

capacity *n.* 1. volume, limit, space, size, extent, magnitude, expanse, scope, dimensions, measure, range, reach. 2. ability, competency, aptitude, capability, talent, skill, knack, know-how.

cape *n.* 1. peninsula, promontory, jetty, point, spit. 2. cloak, mantle, shawl, wrap, poncho, pelisse.

caper *n.* mischief, prank, antic, escapade, lark, high jinks, stunt, jest, revel.

caper *v.* cavort, frolic, skip, leap, romp, bounce, dance.

capital *n.* assets, resources, wealth, savings, interests, cash.

capital *adj.* 1. principal, primary, foremost, dominant, chief, central. 2. excellent, splendid, delightful, superb, fine, perfect.

capitulate *v.* yield, submit, surrender, give in, throw in the towel, acquiesce, succumb, relent; *ant.* hold one's ground, stand firm.

caprice *n.* notion, whim, fancy, vagary, impulse.

capricious *adj.* fickle, erratic, impulsive, changeable, unpredictable, of two minds, uncertain, volatile, temperamental, fitful, variable, wayward; *ant.* steady, reliable.

capsize *v.* upset, overturn, roll, keel over, invert.

care

captain *n.* commander, leader, head, boss, chief, manager, master, patron, pilot, skipper.

caption *n.* heading, title, superscription, subtitle, inscription, legend.

captious *adj.* 1. hypercritical, critical, faultfinding, cavilling, carping, querulous. 2. subtle, wily, sophistical.

captivate *v.* seduce, mesmerize, enchant, enthrall, attract, beguile, charm, enrapture, win over, fascinate; *ant.* repel, appall.

captive *n.* hostage, detainee, convict, prisoner, POW, slave.

captive *adj.* 1. restricted, confined, imprisoned, subjugated, incarcerated, ensnared, enslaved, under arrest, detained. 2. fascinated, captured, captivated, delighted, enchanted, enraptured, spellbound.

captivity *n.* detention, bondage, internment, custody, restraint, servitude, slavery, thralldom.

capture *v.* 1. arrest, apprehend, detain, hold, take into custody, seize, conquer, overwhelm. 2. (as an honor or promotion) win, attain, achieve, gain, procure, secure, earn.

captured *adj.* 1. caught, taken, seized, arrested, apprehended, detained, kidnaped, abducted, nabbed. 2. occupied, possessed, mastered, won, confiscated, usurped, taken (over), appropriated; *ant.* freed, liberated.

car *n.* automobile, vehicle, auto, *slang:* wheels, hot rod, jalopy.

carafe *n.* decanter, pitcher, flask, flagon, bottle, jug.

caravan *n.* procession, cavalcade, train, motorcade, column, troop.

carcass *n.* corpse, cadaver, body, remains, skeleton.

cardinal *adj.* fundamental, principal, primary, key, vital, core, basic, essential, elementary, central, leading, main, paramount.

care *n.* 1. concern, anxiety, worry, apprehension, distress, solicitude. 2. attention, regard, consideration, interest, vigilance, concentration, prudence, caution, discrimination. 3. custody, guardianship, management, protection, supervision, keeping.

take care beware, be careful *or* cautious, heed.

take care of protect, guard, attend to, be

responsible for, look after, supervise; nurse, rear, bring up.

care *v.* attend, heed, mind, regard, take pains.
care about cherish, love, hold dear, feel for, sympathize with.
care for 1. attend, nurse, protect, foster, tend, mind, watch over, baby-sit. **2.** like, want, desire, have a penchant *or* weakness for.
care to desire to, wish to, like to, prefer to, want to.

careen *v.* hurtle, shoot, run, tear, bolt, rush, speed, dash, race, gallop, career.

career *n.* employment, occupation, calling, vocation, job, livelihood, pursuit, path.

carefree *adj.* cheerful, easygoing, insouciant, breezy, blithe, jaunty, happy-go-lucky, light-hearted, buoyant, sunny, gay; *ant.* troubled, anxious, worried, sober.

careful *adj.* **1.** cautious, wary, judicious, protective; guarded, alert, vigilant, anxious, circumspect, uptight (*slang*); *ant.* imprudent, foolish, heedless, thoughtless. **2.** accurate, precise, strict, exact, thorough, meticulous, attentive, particular, rigorous, fastidious, scrupulous; *ant.* inattentive, haphazard, neglectful.

careless *adj.* **1.** inattentive, irresponsible, absent-minded, heedless, forgetful, lax, lackadaisical, nonchalant, unconcerned. **2.** slipshod, inaccurate, remiss, perfunctory, cursory, slapdash, offhand, negligent; *ant.* meticulous, accurate, careful.

caress *v.* pet, stroke, fondle, pat, squeeze, embrace, cuddle, hug, touch, kiss.

caretaker *n.* **1.** (one who takes care of people) nurse, caregiver, guardian, foster parent, baby-sitter. **2.** (one who tends property) custodian, janitor, superintendent, curator, warden, keeper, watchman.

careworn *adj.* exhausted, weary, fatigued, tired, haggard, gaunt; *ant.* lively, sprightly.

cargo *n.* freight, baggage, merchandise, lading, goods, payload, consignment, haul.

caricature *n.* cartoon, parody, satire, burlesque, lampoon, farce, travesty.

caricature *v.* mimic, satirize, mock, ridicule, distort, lampoon.

carnage *n.* bloodshed, slaughter, butchery, murder, havoc, holocaust, massacre, bloodbath, shambles.

carnal *adj.* **1.** sensual, erotic, salacious, voluptuous, lecherous, sexual, lascivious, lewd, licentious, wanton; *ant.* chaste, pure. **2.** corporeal, physical, earthly, animal, bodily, human, natural; temporal, worldly, secular; *ant.* spiritual.

carnival *n.* fair, festival, fete, fiesta, celebration, revelry, gala, holiday, jamboree, jubilee.

carnivorous *adj.* meat-eating, flesh-eating, predatory, voracious.

carol *n.* song, hymn, ditty, strain, chorus.

carouse *v.* party, revel, roister; drink, imbibe, quaff, tipple.

carousing *n.* celebrating, partying, drinking, raising the roof (*slang*).

carp *v.* complain, criticize, reproach, cavil, fault, censure, quibble, nag, scold; *ant.* praise.

carpet *v.* cover, blanket, pad, overlay, put on, superimpose.

carriage *n.* **1.** demeanor, mien, attitude, air, presence, comportment, gait, bearing, posture, stance. **2.** vehicle, buggy, surrey, coach, cart, hansom, chaise, hack, chariot.

carrier *n.* messenger, delivery person, bearer, runner, porter, transmitter, transporter.

carry *v.* **1.** transport, convey, move, transfer, transplant, cart, take, bring, haul, lug, tote. **2.** (said of a stationary structure) bear, sustain, support, stand, maintain, undergird. **3.** win, prevail, succeed.
carry on 1. misbehave, carouse, raise Cain, get into mischief, make sport. **2.** continue, last, maintain, proceed, persevere, endure, perpetuate, persist. **3.** conduct, practice, manage, administer.
carry out execute, accomplish, perform, achieve, do, effect, discharge, fulfill, implement, realize.
carry over continue, survive, persist, last, extend.
carry off do, triumph, accomplish, handle.
get carried away overreact, become zealous *or* exuberant, be aroused, let go (*slang*).

cart *n.* wheelbarrow, wagon, truck, dray.

cart *v.* carry, move, haul, transport, truck, bear, convey, tote, lug.

carton *n.* box, case, parcel, package, container.

cartoon *n.* caricature, sketch, drawing; satire, joke, lampoon.

cartridge *n.* container, cassette, magazine, canis-

carve

carve v. cut, slice, sculpt, form, chisel, engrave, etch, fashion, hew, tool, whittle.

carving n. sculpture, bust, statue, statuette.

cascade n. waterfall, waterworks, shower, fountain, deluge, flood, rush, torrent, cataract; ant. trickle.

cascade v. plunge, tumble, flood, descend, rush, shower, overflow, pitch, pour, spill, surge.

case n. 1. box, carton, crate, chest, bin, cabinet, casket. 2. example, instance, illustration, sample, exemplification, specimen. 3. (statement to support or refute something) argument, position, reason, evidence, facts. 4. lawsuit, suit, litigation, petition, proceeding.
in case of supposing, in the event that, provided that.

cash n. currency, legal tender, money, hard cash, note, green stuff (slang).

cashier n. clerk, teller, banker, bursar, treasurer, accountant.

cask n. barrel, vat, tub, keg, hogshead.

casket n. coffin, sarcophagus, box, coffer, chest, case.

cast n. 1. mold, impression, replica, reproduction, facsimile, duplicate. 2. players, company, parts, roles, dramatis personae, troupe. 3. tinge, shade, aspect, complexion, color, appearance, face, looks. 4. toss, throw, pitch, lob, hurl, put, propulsion, projection, ejection.

cast v. 1. throw, hurl, put, fling, pitch, heave, toss. 2. choose, pick, appoint, designate, determine, detail, name. 3. formulate, frame, devise, organize, arrange, systematize, marshal, present.

cast aside throw away, reject, jettison, discard, jilt.

cast away throw out, dispose of, reject, get rid of, discard.

cast down 1. overthrow, wipe out, demolish, raze. 2. discourage, dishearten, dismay, dispirit.

cast out evict, expel, ostracize, blackball, outlaw, ban, banish, remove.

caste n. class, rank, station, position, order, estate, grade, lineage, station, status, stratum.

catch

castigate v. chastise, rebuke, scold, berate, chide, reprimand, censure, punish, discipline, correct; slang: chew out, give what-for.

castle n. palace, tower, fortress, mansion, chateau, citadel, stronghold.

castrate v. emasculate, neuter, geld, unsex, unman, caponize.

casual adj. 1. chance, accidental, fortuitous, unexpected, unplanned, offhand, involuntary, unexpected, random. 2. occasional, sometime, now-and-then, indifferent, erratic, unreliable, haphazard. 3. relaxed, informal, easygoing; nonchalant, apathetic, blasé, unconcerned, laid-back (slang).

casualty n. victim, sufferer, death, fatality, loss.

casuistry n. equivocation, sophism, speciousness, chicanery, sophistry.

cat n. feline, tomcat, kitten, kitty, pussycat.
let the cat out of the bag (slang) expose, let slip, reveal, leak, tell a secret, divulge, spill the beans (slang).

cataclysm n. catastrophe, disaster, calamity, destruction, devastation.

catalog n. inventory, list, directory, index, record, register, schedule, roster, table, roll.

catalog v. list, index, classify, record, codify, alphabetize, enumerate, file, inventory, register.

catalyst n. spur, trigger, stimulus, impetus, engine, mover, activator, propellant, incitement.

catastrophe n. cataclysm, calamity, devastation, disaster, fiasco, ruin, tragedy, adversity, blow, upheaval, scourge; ant. blessing, godsend.

catcall n. heckling, hiss, jeer, boo, hoot, Bronx cheer (slang).

catch n. 1. capture, seizure, apprehension, grasp, grab, collar (slang). 2. proviso, fine print, condition, caveat, stipulation; trap, gimmick, trick. 3. prize, treasure, cache, gem, find, jewel, pride and joy; reward, booty, spoils, haul, plunder.

catch v. 1. seize, take, apprehend, snatch, snag, grab, snare, entrap, nab, net; ant. miss, free, unleash. 2. (as a disease) contract, incur, get, acquire, develop, come down with, succumb to; ant. ward off, get over. 3. see, perceive, grasp, understand, follow, apprehend.

catch on 1. understand, grasp, comprehend, perceive, fathom, take in, get the point. **2.** spread, become popular *or* fashionable, find favor, become the rage (*slang*).

catch up with overtake, gain on, draw level with, reach, join.

catching *adj.* **1.** contagious, infectious, communicable, infective, transferable, transmittable. **2.** attractive, winning, captivating, charming, enchanting, fascinating, winsome; *ant.* ugly, boring.

catchword *n.* slogan, password, catch phrase, motto, refrain, watchword, tag, cliché.

catchy *adj.* memorable, infectious, haunting, obsessive, unforgettable, beguiling, captivating, provocative, attractive; *ant.* boring, dull.

categorical *adj.* unequivocal, absolute, unmitigated, explicit, clear, direct, express, positive, total, unquestionable, ineluctable; *ant.* qualified, tentative, vague, ambiguous.

categorize *v.* group, classify, rank, class, pigeonhole, catalog, grade, list, order, sort.

category *n.* classification, division, type, grouping, sort, section, chapter, class, grade, order, rank, genus, species.

cater *v.* **1.** provide, supply, furnish, provision, outfit, victual. **2.** indulge, humor, pander to, coddle, pamper.

catharsis *n.* purgation, purification, cleansing, purging, renewal, release, outlet.

cathartic *adj.* purging, purifying, cleansing.

catholic *adj.* **1.** cosmopolitan, universal, general, worldly, comprehensive, eclectic. **2.** liberal, open-minded, receptive, wide-ranging, broad-minded, tolerant, indulgent; *ant.* prejudiced, narrow.

catty *adj.* backbiting, snide, treacherous, spiteful, malicious, mean, malevolent, rancorous, venomous, vicious; *ant.* kind.

caucus *n.* assembly, meeting, session, convention, conclave, council, parley, synod, powwow.

cause *n.* **1.** motive, foundation, root, antecedent, mainspring, agent, basis, wellspring, source, origin, determinant; *ant.* result, effect, outcome. **2.** aim, object, goal, intention, purpose, target. **3.** belief, principles, conviction, creed.

cause *v.* effect, generate, produce, incite, create, begin, compel, provoke, induce, occasion, bring about, originate, start.

caustic *adj.* **1.** corrosive, burning, erosive, acrid, alkaline, gnawing, destructive. **2.** sarcastic, biting, scathing, sharp, sardonic, stinging, withering, vitriolic, incisive, pungent.

caution *n.* **1.** prudence, care, heed, wariness, discretion, circumspection. **2.** warning, admonition, alarm, tip-off, premonition.

caution *v.* warn, advise, alert, urge, admonish, forewarn.

cautious *adj.* careful, tentative, wary, guarded, alert, vigilant, discreet, prudent, circumspect; *ant.* reckless, headstrong, precipitate.

cavalcade *n.* procession, parade, troop, spectacle, train, array, retinue.

cavalier *adj.* informal, offhand, unconcerned, casual; haughty, condescending, arrogant, swaggering, disdainful, scornful, supercilious.

cave *n.* hollow, den, cavern, cavity, grotto.

caveat *n.* caution, warning, admonition, alarm.

cavernous *adj.* hollow, sunken, deep, yawning, large, huge, spacious, wide, abyssal.

cavil *v.* complain, carp, object, censure, nitpick, quibble, nag.

cavity *n.* hollow, womb, crater, pit, burrow, hole, void, dent, well.

cavort *v.* frolic, sport, romp, caper, dance, frisk, gambol, hop, prance, skip.

cease *v.* desist, finish, discontinue, end, conclude, terminate, stop, die, halt; *ant.* start, persist.

ceaseless *adj.* persistent, incessant, unremitting, nonstop, continuous, endless, unending, eternal, everlasting, interminable, ad infinitum; *ant.* occasional, irregular.

cede *v.* concede, yield, surrender, relinquish, abdicate, abandon, resign, give up, transfer, vouchsafe.

ceiling *n.* roof, canopy, dome.

hit the ceiling (*slang*) lose one's temper, become angry, fume, blow a fuse (*slang*).

celebrate *v.* **1.** rejoice, party, carouse, live it up (*slang*). **2.** (said of a person) praise, honor, toast, laud, extol, glorify, eulogize, publicize. **3.** (as a holiday) observe, perform, keep, commemorate.

celebrated *adj.* famous, well-known, promi-

chagrin   **celebration**

distant, median, focal, pivotal, intermediate; *ant.* outer. **2.** fundamental, basic, principal, chief, main, prime, primary, essential, crucial; *ant.* peripheral, marginal, incidental.

centralize *v.* concentrate, consolidate, merge, compact, condense, coalesce, unify, amalgamate, incorporate, focus; *ant.* disperse, decentralize.

ceremonial *adj.* ritual, formal, liturgical, solemn, stately, lofty, stereotyped, routine; *ant.* informal.

ceremonious *adj.* **1.** formal, exact, precise, deferential, polite, punctilious, stiff, prim; *ant.* relaxed, informal. **2.** dignified, grand, solemn, courtly, ritual, stately.

ceremony *n.* **1.** celebration, event, observance, commemoration, parade, pomp, service, ritual, rite. **2.** etiquette, decorum, protocol, civility, propriety, nicety.

certain *adj.* **1.** confident, assured, positive, convinced, secure, unconcerned; assertive, cocksure; *ant.* troubled. **2.** sure, conclusive, definite, true, irrefutable, incontestable, absolute, unequivocal, undeniable, indubitable; *ant.* doubtful, uncertain, dubious.

for certain without doubt, absolutely, certainly, for sure.

certainly *adj.* doubtlessly, naturally, of course, indeed.

certainty *n.* **1.** conviction, certitude, confidence, faith, assurance, belief. **2.** reality, fact, verity, validity, truth.

certificate *n.* document, credentials, testimonial, warrant, attestation, authorization, guarantee, license, qualification, validation.

certify *v.* guarantee, assure, endorse, attest, approve, sanction, accredit, testify, swear, notarize.

certitude *n.* conviction, certainty, belief, faith, assurance, sureness, definiteness, confidence; *ant.* doubt.

cessation *n.* suspension, discontinuance, abeyance, pause, stay, intermission, recess, hiatus, letup, respite, standstill, termination; *ant.* commencement, renewal.

chafe *v.* rub, abrade, scrape, grate.

chaff *n.* shell, husk, shard, crust, pod.

chagrin *n.* mortification, dismay, embarrassment, discomposure, humiliation, exaspera-

nent, acclaimed, exalted, eminent, illustrious, notable, renowned, revered; *ant.* obscure.

celebration *n.* **1.** recognition, commemoration, observance, remembrance, anniversary, keeping. **2.** ceremony, pageant, festivities; revelry, conviviality, jubilation, mirth, hilarity; *ant.* sadness, solemnity, sorrow.

celebrity *n.* **1.** renown, fame, distinction, glory, notoriety; *ant.* obscurity, disgrace. **2.** star, superstar, VIP, dignitary, notable, luminary, big shot (*slang*).

celerity *n.* haste, speed, rapidity, dispatch, expedition, alacrity, promptness, quickness, velocity; *ant.* sloth.

celestial *adj.* heavenly, divine, elysian, angelic, immortal, seraphic, sublime; *ant.* earthly, mundane.

celibacy *n.* chastity, virginity, abstinence, continence, singleness, bachelorhood, spinsterhood.

cell *n.* chamber, vault, crypt, pen, cage, coop, stall, closet, lockup.

cellar *n.* basement, wine cellar, vault, storeroom, crypt.

cement *n.* concrete, adhesive, plaster, mortar.

cement *v.* attach, weld, bond, fuse, join, combine, unite, bind, glue, seal, plaster.

cemetery *n.* graveyard, gravesite, burial ground, churchyard, catacomb, necropolis.

censor *v.* edit, cut, amend, expurgate, excise, suppress, bowdlerize.

censorious *adj.* querulous, condemnatory, critical, disapproving, disparaging, minatory, captious, severe, faultfinding, hypercritical; *ant.* complimentary, approving, laudatory.

censure *n.* criticism, disapproval, reproach, admonition, blame, castigation, rebuke, remonstrance, reprobation, reprimand, denunciation; *ant.* approval, praise, compliments.

censure *v.* condemn, rebuke, scold, chide, blame, upbraid, reprimand, berate, denounce, castigate, tell off; *ant.* approve, compliment, praise.

center *n.* core, middle, nucleus, heart, hub, nub, pivot; *ant.* periphery, edge, outskirts.

off center irregular, unsteady, crooked, off kilter.

center *v.* revolve, pivot, hinge; focus, converge, cluster, concentrate, gravitate.

central *adj.* **1.** middle, interior, midway, equition, irritation, annoyance, indignation, vexation, bother, unhappiness, mortification, despair; *ant.* delight, pleasure.

chain *n.* **1.** shackle, manacle, link, string, cable, leash, bracelet. **2.** sequence, succession, series, progression, continuity.

chain *v.* fasten, restrain, bind, secure, manacle, fetter, handcuff, shackle, tether, yoke, harness; *ant.* release, free.

chairman *n.* chair, chairwoman, chairperson, director, president, speaker, moderator, administrator, master of ceremonies, MC.

chalk up **1.** credit, attribute, ascribe, charge. **2.** enter, log, tally, mark, record, register, score.

chalky *adj.* pale, ashen, pallid, wan, cretaceous, white.

challenge *n.* **1.** dare, defiance, provocation, confrontation, ultimatum, summons, gauntlet. **2.** hurdle, obstacle, test, trial, barrier.

challenge *v.* **1.** dare, defy, confront, threaten, denounce. **2.** question, dispute, contest, inquire, search, impugn.

chamber *n.* **1.** room, bedroom, hall, boudoir, apartment, closet, compartment, cubicle. **2.** council, legislature, parliament, assembly.

champion *n.* **1.** winner, victor, vanquisher, conqueror. **2.** defender, upholder, guardian, backer, sponsor, booster, supporter.

chance *n.* **1.** fortune, fate, luck, providence, destiny, kismet, the way the cookie crumbles. **2.** accident, happenstance, fortuity, contingency. **3.** probability, likelihood, odds, tendency, indications. **4.** opportunity, possibility, opening, occasion, prospect.

by chance by accident, unexpectedly, as it happens, serendipitously.

on the off chance in case, supposing, in the event that.

chance *v.* **1.** happen, occur, come to pass, come about, transpire, result, befall. **2.** venture, hazard, bet, risk, gamble, wager, take a shot in the dark, go out on a limb, skate on thin ice, run the risk, stick one's neck out.

chancy *adj.* risky, speculative, uncertain, dangerous, dicey, shaky, hazardous, problematical, tricky; *ant.* secure, safe.

change *n.* **1.** alteration, transformation, modification, metamorphosis, variation, move, in-

novation, revision, shift; *ant.* constancy, permanence, consistency. **2.** (departure from something customary) variety, diversity, variance, novelty, surprise.

change *v.* **1.** transform, modify, alter, vary, remodel, renovate, evolve, adapt, revise, amend; *ant.* preserve. **2.** exchange, replace, substitute, trade, swap.

changeable *adj.* capricious, erratic, fickle, variable, mercurial, mutable, protean, volatile, unstable, vacillating; *ant.* reliable, predictable.

channel *n.* conduit, strait, tunnel, tube, canal, furrow, sluice, sewer, artery, ditch, course.

channel *v.* direct, transmit, guide, send, conduct, convey, steer, siphon, funnel.

chant *n.* song, mantra, incantation, slogan, war cry, chorus.

chant *v.* sing, recite, intone, croon, descant.

chaos *n.* confusion, pandemonium, anarchy, tumult, bedlam, disorder, lawlessness; *ant.* order, reason, organization.

chaotic *adj.* tumultuous, anarchic, uncontrolled, riotous, tempestuous, confused, disorganized, lawless, purposeless, topsy-turvy; *ant.* organized, orderly.

chaperon *n.* guardian, escort, companion, governess.

chaperon *v.* watch over, guard, protect, accompany, escort, shepherd, attend.

chapter *n.* part, section, episode, division, sequence, stage, topic.

char *v.* burn, scorch, singe, sear, blacken, carbonize.

character *n.* **1.** makeup, constitution, flavor, quality, substance, composition; temperament, nature, personality, individuality, type, humor. **2.** eccentric, wag, original, *slang:* nut, oddball, weirdo. **3.** symbol, sign, figure, emblem, insignia, logo.

in character true to form, consistent, predictable, usual.

out of character inconsistent, unusual, untypical.

characteristic *n.* trait, attribute, feature, mannerism, quality, idiosyncrasy, singularity, peculiarity, mark, property, sign, element.

characteristic *adj.* **1.** representative, typical, standard, normal, paradigmatic, usual, expected, symbolic, operative; *ant.* unusual,

cheap

charter v. 1. license, authorize, permit, sanction. 2. contract, lease, hire, use.

chary adj. 1. reluctant, cautious, wary, guarded, suspicious, circumspect, uneasy, leery, unwilling; ant. heedless. 2. thrifty, prudent, parsimonious, stingy, frugal, close-fisted.

chase n. hunt, pursuit, race.

chase v. 1. pursue, hunt, give chase, follow, track. 2. expel, repulse, repel, evict, scatter, dispel.

chasm n. gap, fissure, ravine, gulf, canyon, gorge, crevasse, abyss, cleft, crater, hollow.

chassis n. framework, fuselage, frame, substructure, skeleton.

chaste adj. 1. virtuous, moral, subdued, simple, severe, disciplined, proper; ant. sinful, immoral. 2. virgin, celibate, abstinent, continent, vestal; ant. promiscuous, abandoned. 3. pure, innocent, virginal, unsullied, unblemished, unstained, uncontaminated; ant. corruptible, weak, frail.

chasten v. 1. discipline, punish, take to task, chastise, rebuke, rake over the coals, roast (*slang*). 2. purify, refine, clarify, correct, amend.

chastise v. discipline, punish, castigate, scold, reprove, reprimand, censure, berate, scourge, upbraid, chide, admonish, reproach. 2. beat, whip, smack, spank, flog, lash.

chastity n. virtue, modesty, purity, virginity, abstinence, maidenhood, innocence, celibacy, continence, restraint; ant. lechery.

chat n. talk, conversation, tête-à-tête, heart-to-heart, rap or bull session (*slang*), prattle, gossip, palaver.

chat v. converse, talk, visit, gossip, chew the fat (*slang*).

chateau n. mansion, palace, manor house.

chatter n. small talk, gossip, chitchat, babbling.

chatter v. gab, gossip, chat, babble, blather, jabber, prate, pratle, natter.

chatty adj. talkative, gossipy, informal, familiar, friendly, prattling; ant. reticent.

cheap adj. 1. inexpensive, moderate, low-priced, reduced, low-cost, reasonable, half-priced, dirt-cheap; ant. expensive, dear, costly. 2. inferior, ordinary, shoddy, imitation, spurious, sham, meretricious. 3. vulgar, dirty, low, sordid, contemptible, tawdry. 4. stingy, mi-

characterize

atypical. 2. singular, distinctive, specific, idiosyncratic, individual, special, peculiar; ant. general; nonspecific.

characterize v. 1. describe, portray, delineate, depict, represent, label, name, dub, tag. 2. distinguish, identify, mark, specify, single out, discriminate.

charade n. farce, mockery, travesty, parody, fake, pantomime, pretense.

charge n. 1. care, custody, responsibility, brief, management, concern. 2. instruction, order, bidding, direction, command, directive. 3. accusation, indictment, blame, demand, complaint. 4. price, cost, expense, amount, value.

in charge (of) responsible (for), managing, controlling, supervising.

charge v. 1. accuse, indict, censure, impute. 2. command, order, direct, instruct. 3. attack, invade, assault, assail.

charitable adj. generous, benevolent, philanthropic, humane, liberal, compassionate, kind, sympathetic, forgiving; ant. mean, unkind.

charity n. altruism, philanthropy, benevolence, generosity, assistance, endowment, alms, relief, clemency, compassion, tolerance, mercy.

charlatan n. impostor, fake, swindler, cheat, fraud, mountebank, pretender, phony, sham, quack, con man, con artist.

charm n. 1. grace, attraction, desirability, allure, charisma, appeal, attractiveness. 2. talisman, fetish, mascot, good-luck piece, amulet. 3. enchantment, incantation, sorcery, magic.

charm v. entertain, please, delight, beguile, enchant, captivate, possess, enthrall, transport, mesmerize, entrance, bewitch, dazzle, win over, vanquish.

charming adj. delightful, pleasant, appealing, attractive, charismatic, lovely, irresistible, sweet, eye-catching, engaging, captivating, bewitching, winning.

chart n. map, plan, blueprint, graph, diagram, tabulation, table.

chart v. plot, map out, sketch, draw, outline, delineate, draft, place.

charter n. 1. grant, endowment, allotment, concession. 2. treaty, contract, settlement, pact.

serly, grudging, tightfisted, parsimonious, riggling; *ant.* expansive, generous.

cheapen *v.* devalue, depreciate, discredit, lower; degrade, demean, belittle, denigrate, derogate, disparage; *ant.* enhance.

cheapskate (*slang*) *n.* tightwad, penny pincher, skinflint, miser, Scrooge.

cheat *v.* swindle, con, fool, rook, fleece, short-change, double-cross, trick, hoodwink, defraud, gyp, rip off, screw (*slang*).

check *n.* **1.** block, barrier, hindrance, obstacle, hurdle, delay, halt. **2.** control, restraint, damper, rein, harness. **3.** examination, investigation, inquiry, analysis, audit, test, review.
in check restrained, curbed, reined in, controlled, under control.

check *v.* **1.** discourage, curb, impede, hinder; restrain, inhibit, stay, bridle, repress; *ant.* urge, hasten, liberate. **2.** review, investigate, take stock, examine, verify. **3.** mark, tally, score, notch.
check in sign in, register, come, appear.
check out 1. depart, settle up, pay one's bill. **2.** inspect, examine, look at, see.

cheeky *adj.* forward, impudent, saucy, impertinent, insolent, brazen, audacious, disrespectful, insulting; *ant.* polite, respectful.

cheer *n.* **1.** merriment, delight, mirth, glee; geniality, gaiety, vivacity. **2.** encouragement, applause, hurrah, huzzah, approval, approbation.

cheer *v.* **1.** applaud, salute, acclaim, laud. **2.** comfort, solace, gladden, encourage.

cheerful *adj.* pleasant, jovial, optimistic, genial, animated, buoyant, blithe, sunny, merry, light-hearted, exuberant; *ant.* sad, downcast, unhappy.

cheering *adj.* encouraging, comforting, reassuring, auspicious, propitious, heartening, promising; *ant.* disheartening, depressing.

cheerless *adj.* **1.** melancholy, despondent, mournful, forlorn, depressed, disconsolate, sad; *ant.* cheerful, happy. **2.** gloomy, desolate, somber, bleak, austere, desolate, dark, dismal; *ant.* bright.

cherish *v.* treasure, adore, revere, esteem, prize, value, worship, idolize; *ant.* abandon, ill-treat.

cherubic *adj.* **1.** adorable, sweet, lovable, inno-

cent, appealing, cute. **2.** angelic, heavenly, seraphic.

chest *n.* **1.** box, case, crate, coffer, cabinet, locker, bureau, coffin. **2.** thorax, breast, trunk, rib cage, bosom, heart.

chew *v.* masticate, munch, crunch, gnaw, chomp, grind.

chic *adj.* fashionable, trendy, stylish, elegant, à la mode, smart, mod; *ant.* outmoded, dowdy, frumpish.

chicanery *n.* duplicity, deception, intrigue, double-dealing, subterfuge, sophistry, trickery, artifice.

chide *v.* rebuke, scold, reprimand, castigate, admonish, berate, blame, reprove, upbraid; *ant.* praise.

chief *n.* superior, leader, head, boss, master, ringleader, captain, commander, director, manager, ruler.

chief *adj.* principal, predominant, main, paramount, central, essential, vital, primary, supreme, foremost, key; *ant.* minor, secondary, junior.

child *n.* infant, baby, tyke, toddler, youngster, kid, tot, juvenile, minor, offspring, progeny, issue.

childbirth *n.* delivery, child-bearing, lying-in, parturition, confinement.

childhood *n.* youth, adolescence, schooldays, immaturity, boyhood, girlhood, minority.

childish *adj.* puerile, infantile, immature, juvenile, babyish, silly, petty, foolish, trifling; *ant.* adult, sensible.

childlike *adj.* naive, innocent, credulous, simple, artless, guileless, natural, trusting.

children *n.* offspring, progeny, line, issue.

chill *n.* coldness, iciness, frigidity, crispness.

chill *v.* **1.** refrigerate, cool, freeze, ice. **2.** discourage, stifle, dispirit, weaken.

chilly *adj.* **1.** brisk, cold, crisp, frigid, cool, wintry, drafty, nippy. **2.** (said of a manner) aloof, cold, frigid, indifferent, stony, unfriendly, hostile, haughty; *ant.* friendly, warm, responsive.

chime *v.* sound, ring, toll, tell, peal, strike, clang, dong, tinkle, tintinnabulate.

chimera *n.* delusion, illusion, figment, hallucination, fancy, dream, fantasy, phantasmagoria, vagary, snare, specter.

chimeric *adj.* illusory, imaginary, visionary, fabulous, fantastic, whimsical, illusive, quixotic, unfounded; *ant.* real.

china *n.* porcelain, ceramic, earthenware, pottery.

chink *n.* crack, crevice, slot, cut, cleft, aperture, rift, fissure, gap, space.

chip *n.* fragment, shard, flake, sliver, slice, wedge.

having a chip on one's shoulder hostile, spoiling for a fight, pugnacious, belligerent, combative, truculent, scrappy.

when the chips are down in a crisis, in bad times, in adversity.

chip *v.* nick, crack, break, fracture, splinter, flake, sliver, notch, whittle, split, slice.

chip in contribute, share, donate, go Dutch, pitch in, ante up.

chisel *v.* 1. carve, hew, incise, cut; engrave, sculpt, form, fashion, contrive, tool. 2. defraud, cheat, cadge, fleece, rook, gyp (*slang*).

chivalrous *adj.* gallant, heroic, bold, brave, valiant, courageous, honorable, knightly, courtly, courteous, polite; *ant.* cowardly.

chivalry *n.* gallantry, courtesy, politeness.

choice *n.* selection, decision, pick, option, election, alternative, preference, say.

choice *adj.* superior, prime, rare, special, elite, select, elect, exquisite, preferred; *ant.* inferior, common.

choke *v.* asphyxiate, strangle, suffocate, smother, gag, garrote, throttle, stifle.

choke up 1. hold back tears, gasp, falter, stammer, weep, sob. 2. clog, occlude, constrict, block, close, congest, obstruct.

choose *v.* select, pick, take, opt for, adopt; prefer, desire, want, wish, fancy.

chop *v.* divide, sever, hack, cut, cleave, slash, slice, truncate, fell, lop, shear, hew.

choppy *adj.* rough, tempestuous, stormy, blustery, windswept, squally, wavy, white, broken; *ant.* calm.

chore *n.* task, duty, errand, job, nuisance, bother, burden.

chorus *n.* choir, glee club, chorale, ensemble, vocalists.

chosen *adj.* select, elite, elect, preferred, favored.

christen *v.* baptize, inaugurate, launch, dedicate; call, name, designate, title, term, dub, style.

chronic *adj.* persistent, incessant, protracted, incurable, habitual, ingrained, long-lasting, inveterate; *ant.* temporary, acute, occasional.

chronicle *n.* account, record, narrative, history, epic, register, diary, story, annals, journal, saga.

chronicle *v.* 1. record, register, enter, log, list. 2. narrate, relate, recount, tell, report.

chronicler *n.* historian, reporter, recorder, scribe, narrator.

chronological *adj.* sequential, consecutive, serial, progressive, ordered.

chubby *adj.* plump, portly, buxom, rotund, stout, tubby, paunchy, round; *ant.* skinny, slim.

chuckle *v.* laugh, giggle, titter, snicker, chortle, snort, simper.

chunk *n.* piece, hunk, portion, block, mass, slab, wad.

chunky *adj.* stocky, brawny, thick, beefy, fat, square, stubby, thickset; *ant.* slim.

church *n.* 1. temple, chapel, cathedral, meeting-house, basilica, mission, tabernacle. 2. clergy, ministry, priesthood, the pulpit. 3. denomination, sect, religion, affiliation, congregation.

churlish *adj.* surly, rude, harsh, sullen, brusque, morose, unmannerly, impertinent, unfriendly, uncommunicative, vulgar, oafish, boorish; *ant.* civil, polite, urbane.

churn *v.* stir, swirl, agitate, whip, whisk, shake, toss, surge, convulse, froth, writhe, foam.

chute *n.* funnel, trough, shaft, sluice, duct, channel, ramp, passageway, jetway.

cipher *n.* character, symbol, logo, figure, mark, code, monogram.

cipher *v.* compute, figure, estimate, reckon.

circle *n.* 1. ring, wheel, disk, halo, band, loop, coil, orb, globe, sphere. 2. coterie, set, clique, group, party. 3. series, cycle, succession, course, round, continuation, revolution, epicycle.

come full circle go through a cycle or series, come around or back, revert.

circle *v.* 1. encircle, circumscribe, ring, gird, enclose, surround, hem in, belt, envelop, loop. **2.** circumnavigate, tour, compass; orbit, revolve.

circuit *n.* **1.** course, orbit, ambit, revolution, perambulation, journey, tour, route, compass, round, track. **2.** boundary, area, circumference, bounds, limit, perimeter, range, region, district.

circuitous *adj.* indirect, meandering, winding, serpentine, labyrinthine, oblique, rambling, digressive, roundabout, periphrastic; *ant.* direct, straight.

circular *n.* pamphlet, leaflet, notice, announcement, handbill, flier, letter.

circulate *v.* **1.** distribute, disseminate, publicize, broadcast, promulgate. **2.** travel, wander, meander, peregrinate, perambulate, journey.

circulation *n.* **1.** flow, current, rotation. **2.** distribution, dissemination, apportionment, transmission.

circumference *n.* perimeter, girth, boundary, border, edge, margin, periphery, fringe, rim.

circumlocution *n.* discursiveness, digression, redundancy, verbiage, wordiness, prolixity, periphrasis.

circumscribe *v.* **1.** surround, encompass, encircle, girdle. **2.** restrict, limit, outline, confine, corset.

circumspect *adj.* cautious, prudent, leery, wary, observant, vigilant, discreet, politic, sagacious, discriminating, deliberate; *ant.* careless.

circumstance *n.* condition, occurrence, event, situation, incident, particular, detail, factor, contingency, element, fact.

circumstances *n.* status, standing, position, class, condition, prospects, outlook; resources, means, capital, income.

under no circumstances never, absolutely not, under no conditions, by no means, noway (*slang*).

under the circumstances for this reason, conditions being what they are, all things considered, as matters stand.

circumstantial *adj.* tentative, uncertain, conjectural, contingent, hearsay, provisional, presumptive, inconclusive, conditional.

circumvent *v.* **1.** avoid, elude, escape, evade, lose, bypass, dodge, shun, eschew. **2.** outwit, outflank, trick, dupe, entrap.

cistern *n.* basin, tank, sink, reservoir, vat, pool.

citadel *n.* fortress, stronghold, tower, fortification, castle, keep, bastion, acropolis.

citation *n.* **1.** summons, bidding, charge, writ. **2.** reference, extract, excerpt, reference, allusion, mention, quote.

cite *v.* **1.** summon, call, arraign, order. **2.** quote, mention, refer *or* allude to, excerpt, illustrate, evidence, adduce.

citizen *n.* resident, native, national, inhabitant, subject, denizen.

city *n.* metropolis, megalopolis, municipality, town.

civic *adj.* community, municipal, public, local, urban, communal, borough, city.

civil *adj.* **1.** civic, municipal, public, political, secular, communal. **2.** polite, courteous, refined, formal, cordial, mannerly, proper.

civilian *adj.* nonmilitary, noncombative, nonmilitant, noncombatant; private.

civility *n.* courtesy, tact, politeness, breeding, cultivation, refinement, graciousness, urbanity; *ant.* vulgarity.

civilize *v.* educate, enlighten, refine, polish, cultivate, sophisticate, improve, ameliorate, perfect.

civilized *adj.* advanced, sophisticated, refined, cultured, polite, urbane, humane, tolerant; *ant.* primitive, barbarous.

claim *n.* right, title, petition, privilege, pretension, protestation.

claim *v.* **1.** believe, maintain, hold, affirm, assert, state, insist, allege, profess. **2.** demand, request, clamor, exact, compel.

claimant *n.* petitioner, applicant, supplicant.

clairvoyant *n.* prophet, seer, fortuneteller, visionary, diviner, oracle, soothsayer, telepath.

clairvoyant *adj.* psychic, prophetic, telepathic, oracular, prescient, second-sighted.

clamber *v.* scramble, climb, scale, ascend, claw, scrabble.

clammy *adj.* moist, damp, sweaty, slimy, pasty, sticky, viscid; dank, close, muggy, humid; *ant.* dry.

clamor *n.* **1.** uproar, outcry, din, racket, tumult, discord, hubbub, bedlam. **2.** protest, dissent, complaint, remonstrance, lament.

clamorous *adj.* noisy, riotous, tumultuous, blaring, deafening, uproarious, insistent, vehement, vociferous; *ant.* silent.

clamp *n.* vise, press, grip, bracket, clasp, fastener.

clamp *v.* fasten, secure, brace, fix, clinch.

clan *n.* group, tribe, family, house, band, brotherhood, faction, fraternity, sect, clique.

clandestine *adj.* covert, secret, concealed, surreptitious, hidden, furtive, stealthy, conspiratorial, underhanded, on the q.t. (*slang*); *ant.* open.

clang *v.* reverberate, resound, ring, toll, chime, peal, bong, clank, clash, jangle.

clannish *adj.* insular, exclusive, close, select, narrow, private, parochial, sectarian, intolerant; *ant.* open, friendly.

clap *v.* 1. applaud, cheer, acclaim, approve, support. 2. hit, strike, bang, slap, slam.

claptrap *n.* nonsense, jargon, bombast, drivel, balderdash, rubbish, blarney, bunk, hot air.

clarification *n.* illumination, explanation, definition, elucidation, simplification, exposition, gloss, interpretation; *ant.* obfuscation.

clarify *v.* 1. purify, filter, refine, cleanse. 2. explain, interpret, elucidate, explicate, define, simplify, decipher.

clarity *n.* intelligibility, lucidity, distinctness, precision, explicitness, delineation, keenness; *ant.* obscurity, vagueness.

clash *n.* 1. collision, impact, crash. 2. disagreement, encounter, conflict, opposition, argument, confrontation, dispute.

clasp *n.* 1. fastener, snap, pin, clip, buckle, hook, brooch, catch. 2. clutch, hold, embrace, grasp, hug, grip.

clasp *v.* 1. clutch, grasp, grip, squeeze, grapple, seize; embrace, hug, press, enfold. 2. attach, fasten, connect.

class *n.* 1. category, group, type, kind, genre, family, sort, species, order, division, rank. 2. (place in a social order) caste, status, position, standing, lineage, station, sphere, degree, hierarchy, stock. 3. lecture, recitation, seminar, colloquium, lesson.

in a class by itself unique, unusual, different, one of a kind, sui generis.

class *v.* categorize, classify, rank, grade, rate, assort, brand, codify, designate.

classic *n.* masterpiece, model, pièce de résistance, paradigm, standard, chef d'oeuvre, exemplar, masterwork, prototype.

classic *adj.* enduring, ageless, time-honored, standard traditional, established; ideal, exemplary, consummate, quintessential, characteristic.

classical *adj.* established, distinguished, standard, ranking, first-rate, superior, paramount; *ant.* transitory, popular.

classification *n.* 1. arrangement, organization, systematization, taxonomy, codification, categorization, gradation, designation, assignment. 2. kind, order, group, category.

classify *v.* catalog, categorize, systematize, pigeonhole, codify, tag.

classy (*slang*) *adj.* elegant, stylish, fine, select, exclusive, chic, posh, high-class, swanky; *ant.* dowdy, plain.

clause *n.* condition, requirement, codicil, ultimatum.

claw *n.* talon, nail, hook, pincer.

claw *v.* maul, rip, mangle; tear, lacerate, scratch, graze, scrape.

clean *v.* bathe, disinfect, wash, launder, scrub, scour, purify, rinse, disinfect; *ant.* soil.

clean *adj.* 1. spotless, unsullied, unblemished, immaculate, scrubbed, sanitized, laundered; tidy, neat, orderly, spruce, well-kept; *ant.* soiled, stained, messy. 2. (as a sporting event or contest) fair, sportsmanlike, lawful, evenhanded, impartial. 3. thorough, complete, entire, total, absolute, final, irreversible. 4. guiltless, aboveboard, sinless, pure, wholesome, virtuous, unblemished.

come clean confess, admit, acknowledge, own up, purge, reveal, expose, spill the beans (*slang*).

cleanse *v.* 1. disinfect, purify, refine. 2. absolve, purge, excuse, restore.

clear *v.* 1. brighten, lighten, shine, illuminate. 2. empty, clean, unload, unpack. 3. acquit, discharge, exonerate, pardon, exculpate, get off the hook (*slang*). 4. profit, realize, net, make.

clear out 1. empty, clean out, evacuate, vacate. 2. leave, depart, push off, decamp, scram; beat it, split, take off.

clear up 1. clarify, explain, elucidate, delineate, resolve, answer, solve, make sense of, demystify. 2. order, tidy, rearrange, sort, remove, fix.

clear *adj.* **1.** explicit, precise, apparent, manifest, plain, patent; *ant.* fuzzy, ambiguous. **2.** lucid, transparent, translucent, crystal clear; *ant.* opaque, dark, muddy. **3.** unobstructed, unhampered, unfettered, free, disentangled, divested.

in the clear 1. guiltless, blameless, innocent; exonerated, absolved, exculpated. **2.** unencumbered, free, out of the woods.

clear-cut *adj.* precise, straightforward, clear, plain, evident; *ant.* vague, ambiguous.

cleared *adj.* **1.** emptied, cleaned, vacated, cleared away. **2.** freed, vindicated, exonerated, exculpated, set right.

clearheaded *adj.* sensible, rational, lucid, alert, wide awake, attentive, bright, perceptive; *ant.* confused, befuddled.

clearing *n.* opening, open *or* empty space, margin.

clearsighted *adj.* perceiving, discerning, understanding, farsighted, prophetic.

cleave *v.* **1.** adhere, cling, stick, cohere, hold, remain, attach, unite. **2.** split, rend, sever, divide, hew, chop, halve, splinter, slice, crack.

cleft *n.* gap, chasm, fissure, split, crack, break, chink, fracture, crevice, breach, cranny.

cleft *adj.* cloven, divided, separated, rent, split, riven, sundered, torn; *ant.* solid.

clemency *n.* forbearance, lenience, mercy, tolerance, indulgence, forgiveness, amnesty, humanity, sympathy, compassion, kindness; *ant.* severity, ruthlessness, rigor.

clement *adj.* **1.** mild, calm, balmy, pacific, temperate. **2.** merciful, indulgent, gentle, tender; *ant.* harsh, ruthless.

clench *v.* clasp, grip, clutch, grasp; tense, constrict, grip.

clergy *n.* clerics, ministry, priesthood, the church, clergymen, the cloth, preachers, pastors, prelates, ecclesiastics.

clergyman *n.* priest, minister, pastor, rabbi, chaplain, father, cleric, reverend, deacon, parson.

clerical *adj.* ecclesiastical, priestly, pastoral.

clever *adj.* **1.** apt, skillful, deft, adroit, expert, able, handy. **2.** shrewd, smart, bright, keen, inventive, original, quick-witted, resourceful, intelligent, canny.

cliché *n.* stereotype, platitude, tag, banality, truism, bromide, chestnut.

client *n.* customer, patient, patron, consumer, buyer, shopper.

clientele *n.* patronage, business, customers, patrons, market, following, clients, regulars.

cliff *n.* precipice, bluff, overhang, crag, face, escarpment.

climactic *adj.* decisive, critical, crucial; crowning, supreme, central, main, paramount; *ant.* trivial, bathetic.

climate *n.* **1.** mood, feeling, ambiance, temper, trend, tendency, setting. **2.** weather, temperature, clime, atmosphere.

climax *n.* **1.** culmination, high point, peak, summit, apogee, zenith, top, acme, head; *ant.* nadir. **2.** orgasm, fulfillment.

climax *v.* culminate, finish, conclude, accomplish, fulfill.

climb *v.* ascend, scale, mount, clamber, shinny, rise.

clinch *v.* confirm, secure, seal, settle, conclude, decide, determine.

cling *v.* clutch, cleave, adhere, hug, stick, grip, embrace, grasp.

clinical *adj.* **1.** scientific, analytic, experimental, objective, empathetic, unbiased; *ant.* subjective. **2.** disinterested, detached, removed, aloof, impersonal, cold, unemotional; *ant.* passionate.

clip *v.* **1.** cut, shorten, trim, snip, shear, prune, crop, pare. **2.** attach, fasten, clamp, bind, staple, pin, fix. **3.** hit, cuff, slap, box, smack, knock, sock.

clique *n.* group, circle, gang, crowd, cabal, set, faction, coterie, crew, pack, clan.

cloak *n.* **1.** coat, cape, mantle, shield, wrap. **2.** disguise, blind, front, mask, pretext, artifice, dodge, subterfuge.

cloak *v.* conceal, obscure, screen, disguise, camouflage, veil, hide, mask; *ant.* bare, reveal.

clock *n.* timepiece, timer, timekeeper.

around the clock night and day, continuously, twenty-four hours a day, continually, nonstop.

clod *n.* **1.** clot, wad, lump, hunk, gob, nugget. **2.** oaf, lout, yokel, dolt, simpleton, imbecile.

clog *v.* **1.** obstruct, congest, stop *or* dam up, jam, occlude, stuff. **2.** hinder, impede, encumber, hamper, shackle.

| clutch | cloister |

in the clouds fanciful, fantastic, romantic.

under a cloud 1. suspect, dubious, uncertain. **2.** depressed, worried, sad, troubled, distressed, despondent.

cloud *v.* **1.** dim, obscure, eclipse, obfuscate, overshadow, dull, shadow, darken, shade, veil; *ant.* clear. **2.** distort, confuse, muddy, disorient, muddle. **3.** depress, deject, sadden, discourage, mar, sully, taint, stain, smirch.

cloudburst *n.* deluge, torrent, downpour, rainfall, shower.

cloudy *adj.* **1.** overcast, gray, foggy, hazy, leaden, sunless; *ant.* sunny. **2.** obscure, vague, indistinct, faint, nebulous, indefinite, murky; *ant.* clear.

clout (*slang*) *n.* authority, influence, pull, standing, prestige, power, weight.

cloven *adj.* split, divided, cleft, bisected; *ant.* solid.

clown *n.* jester, comedian, harlequin, buffoon, joker, prankster, mountebank, fool, yokel.

clowning *n.* joking, pranks, jesting, buffoonery, fooling around.

clownish *adj.* comic, slapstick, foolish, amusing, zany, witty, droll, antic, waggish.

cloy *v.* glut, satiate, choke, gorge, sate, overeat, overindulge, surfeit; *ant.* whet.

club *n.* **1.** cudgel, stick, bat, baton, nightstick, mace, staff, shillelagh, billy club. **2.** organization, society, guild, union, association, society, order, company, fraternity, lodge, clique.

club *v.* strike, pummel, beat, bludgeon, clobber, bash, hammer.

clue *n.* hint, lead, tip, suspicion, intimation, inkling, sign, evidence, indication, pointer.

clump *n.* bunch, thicket, cluster, tuft, bundle, mass, shock.

clumsy *adj.* awkward, gawky, maladroit, ungainly, uncoordinated, heavy-handed, fumbling, all thumbs; ponderous, unwieldy, heavy, lumbering, gauche; *ant.* coordinated, graceful, nimble, skillful.

cluster *n.* bunch, batch, clump, assemblage, group, collection, clutch, coterie, bouquet, gathering, knot.

cluster *v.* flock, group, assemble, gather, bunch.

clutch *n.* **1.** grip, hold, clasp, grasp. **2.** cluster, clump, bunch.

cloister *n.* monastery, hermitage, order, abbey, convent, retreat, friary, priory, nunnery.

cloistered *adj.* reclusive, withdrawn, sequestered, secluded, insulated, confined, sheltered, protected, shielded.

close *n.* end, termination, adjournment, finish, settlement.

close *v.* **1.** shut, lock, slam, shutter, bolt, fasten, bar. **2.** block, stuff, clog, dam, choke, cork, retard, seal, caulk; *ant.* open, clear. **3.** end, terminate, cease, stop, conclude, finish, wind up, finalize. **4.** (bring together two parts or things) meet, unite, agree, connect, tie, bind, couple, coalesce, federate; *ant.* separate.

close *adj.* **1.** nearby, near, proximal, neighboring, adjoining. **2.** intimate, familiar, cherished, loving, confidential, related. **3.** tight, congested, crowded, packed, jammed; stifling, stuffy, musty, airless, stagnant, suffocating, stale, oppressive, sultry; *ant.* fresh, brisk, refreshing.

closefisted *adj.* tight, miserly, niggardly, cheap, stingy.

closemouthed *adj.* silent, reticent, secretive, laconic, taciturn; *ant.* chatty, talkative.

closet *n.* cabinet, cupboard, sideboard, locker, wardrobe, larder, armoire.

closure *n.* **1.** cessation, conclusion, finish, end, closing, termination; *ant.* beginning. **2.** blockage, clog, seal, occlusion, stricture, anastomosis; *ant.* opening, fistula.

clot *n.* coagulation, consolidation, occlusion, embolism, mass, bulk, thrombus.

clot *v.* coagulate, congeal, curdle, jell, thicken, coalesce.

cloth *n.* rag, towel, textiles, material, fabric, dry goods.

clothe *v.* dress, accoutre, garb, outfit, robe, deck, drape, swathe, don, adorn, endow; *ant.* take off, uncover.

clothed *adj.* clad, costumed, shod, decked out; *ant.* naked, stripped.

clothes *n.* apparel, attire, habiliments, wardrobe, vestments, garb, outfit, raiment, duds, threads (*slang*).

clothing *n.* attire, raiment, garb, clothes.

cloud *n.* **1.** fog, mist, haze, puff, vapor, nebulosity, smoke, veil, film. **2.** spot, shadow, flaw, blemish, fault, obscurity, blotch, stain.

clutch *v.* grasp, snatch, seize, grab, grapple; clasp, embrace, cling, cleave, fasten.

clutches *n.* control, power, dominion, custody, sway, keeping, possession, grip, embrace, hands, claws.

clutter *n.* mess, litter, disorder, untidiness, disarray, muddle, dishevelment, jumble.

clutter *v.* strew, litter, scatter, cover, fill.

coach *n.* instructor, trainer, tutor, teacher, mentor, guide.

coach *v.* drill, exercise, train, instruct, tutor, prepare, teach.

coagulate *v.* congeal, clot, jell, thicken, solidify, curdle; *ant.* melt.

coalesce *v.* blend, merge, mix, combine, commingle, integrate, amalgamate, consolidate, fuse, unite, weld.

coalition *n.* alliance, union, league, bloc, faction, entente, confederation, federation, merger, cooperative.

coarse *adj.* **1.** rough, crude, unrefined, rude; *ant.* smooth, polished. **2.** vulgar, low, uncouth, common, base; *ant.* genteel, polite.

coarseness *n.* indelicacy, offensiveness, earthiness, bawdiness, boorishness, ribaldry, smut; *ant.* subtlety, politeness.

coast *n.* coastline, beach, shore, seaside, seaboard, littoral.

coast *v.* cruise, glide, sail, drift, float.

coat *n.* **1.** jacket, tunic, blazer, cloak, wrap, slicker, mantle, mackintosh. **2.** covering, hide, pelt, fur, fleece, shell, scale, skin, epidermis, pellicle, husk, rind, bark.

coat *v.* cover, spread, apply, smear, paint, plaster.

coating *n.* layer, glaze, crust, dusting, film, finish, patina, lamination, veneer, varnish.

coat of arms *n.* crest, ensign, pennant, escutcheon, pennon.

coax *v.* entice, wheedle, cajole, inveigle, wile, beguile, lure, allure, flatter, encourage, sweet-talk.

cockeyed *adj.* **1.** crooked, askew, asymmetrical, awry, lopsided. **2.** nonsensical, preposterous, silly, daft, ludicrous, cockamamie, crazy; *ant.* sensible, sober.

cocksure *adj.* overconfident, brash, self-confident, cocky, arrogant, presumptuous; *ant.* modest.

cocky *adj.* arrogant, conceited, vain, egotistical, swell-headed, strutting, swaggering, smug, opinionated, supercilious.

coddle *v.* pamper, favor, baby, cosset, indulge, spoil, mollycoddle.

code *n.* system, rules, regulations, convention, etiquette, custom, manners, mores.

codify *v.* classify, organize, catalog, systematize, methodize, regularize, tabulate, digest, summarize.

coerce *v.* force, compel, bully, intimidate, constrain, browbeat, impel, strong-arm, twist someone's arm, put the screws on.

coercion *n.* compulsion, force, constraint, pressure, duress, threats, exaction, intimidation.

coexistence *n.* accord, harmony, order, peacefulness.

coexistent *adj.* synchronous, coexisting, contemporaneous, concomitant, coeval.

coffin *n.* casket, box, sarcophagus, catafalque, burial *or* funerary urn *or* vase, mummy case, pall.

cogency *n.* force, soundness, persuasiveness, potency, strength, power; *ant.* weakness.

cogent *adj.* compelling, effective, forceful, persuasive, convincing, trenchant, weighty, influential, sound, rational, conclusive, solid, potent, powerful; *ant.* ineffective, unsound.

cogitate *v.* think, deliberate, reflect, cerebrate, muse, ponder, ruminate, meditate, consider.

cognate *adj.* alike, similar, related, kindred, analogous, allied, associated, affiliated, matching, parallel; *ant.* disparate, unconnected.

cognition *n.* perception, comprehension, intelligence, awareness, understanding, insight, discernment, reasoning.

cognizance *n.* awareness, apprehension, sentience, grasp, insight, knowledge, comprehension, intelligence, imagination.

cognizant *adj.* aware, familiar, acquainted, knowledgeable, versed, informed, conversant; *ant.* oblivious, unaware.

cohere *v.* **1.** cling, adhere, stick, cleave. **2.** harmonize, correspond, relate, hang together, make sense, fit, jibe.

coherence *n.* intelligibility, rationality, logic, consistency, congruity, clarity.

coherent *adj.* **1.** adhering, cohesive, cleaving; integrated, consistent, combined, connected.

cohesion *n.* adhesion, stickiness, tenacity, agglutination.

cohort *n.* **1.** colleague, companion, partner, accomplice, ally, friend, associate. **2.** gathering, band, company, group, set.

coil *n.* spiral, loop, twist, curl, convolution, helix, whorl.

coil *v.* twist, wind, spiral, loop, snake, curl, convolute, twine, wreathe, writhe.

coincide *v.* **1.** correspond, accord, harmonize, match, tally, agree. **2.** happen, eventuate, befall, come about.

coincidence *n.* agreement, correspondence, congruence, concord, parallelism, correlation, unison, conformity, collaboration.

coincidental *adj.* **1.** simultaneous, concurrent, synchronous, contemporaneous, concomitant. **2.** chance, accidental, casual, unplanned, fortuitous, serendipitous, lucky, important; *ant.* deliberate.

coitus *n.* sexual intercourse, copulation, fornication, lovemaking, mating, coupling, union, coition.

cold *n.* chill, frigidity, frostiness, refrigeration, freeze, draft, glaciation, gelidity; *ant.* warmth, heat.

out in the cold forgotten, ignored, rejected, abandoned, left to rot (*slang*).

cold *adj.* **1.** chilly, inclement, frozen, frigid, arctic, biting, raw, wintry, glacial, icy; *ant.* warm. **2.** distant, reserved, cool, indifferent, aloof, chill, unmoved, standoffish, stony; *ant.* friendly, sympathetic, passionate.

coldblooded *adj.* cruel, merciless, savage, ruthless, implacable, grim, pitiless, inhuman, obdurate, barbaric; *ant.* compassionate, merciful, emotional.

coldhearted *adj.* insensitive, indifferent, callous, unsympathetic, detached, unkind, heartless, frigid; *ant.* caring, compassionate.

collaborate *v.* assist, help out, join in, cooperate, coproduce, conspire, collude, fraternize, participate, coact, team up.

collaboration *n.* cooperation, partnership, teamwork, alliance, association, concert, coactivity, synergism.

collaborator *n.* partner, colleague, associate, co-worker, assistant, teammate, confederate.

collapse *n.* **1.** breakdown, failure, disintegration, ruin, downfall, fiasco, debacle. **2.** exhaustion, prostration, seizure, stroke, burnout.

collapse *v.* crash, fall, fold, tumble, fail, founder, crumple, sink, cave in.

collar *v.* seize, apprehend, catch, arrest, capture, grab, appropriate, nab.

collate *v.* **1.** arrange, group, order, sort, compose. **2.** cross-check, match up, index, cross-refer, analogize, compare.

collateral *n.* guarantee, pledge, security, bond, surety, deposit, funds.

collateral *adj.* **1.** secondary, subordinate, ancillary, complementary, concomitant. **2.** substantiating, corroborating, supporting, validating. **3.** secured, guaranteed, endorsed, bonded.

colleague *n.* associate, collaborator, partner, comrade, ally, cohort, compeer.

collect *v.* **1.** accumulate, amass, assemble, acquire, consolidate. **2.** solicit, raise, secure. **3.** congregate, assemble, gather, flock.

collected *adj.* **1.** accumulated, compiled, assembled, amassed. **2.** composed, poised, self-possessed, cool.

collection *n.* **1.** gathering, concentration, assemblage, accumulation, convocation, muster. **2.** assortment, medley, treasury, anthology, compilation, aggregation, miscellany, selection, arrangement, agglomeration, corpus.

collective *n.* aggregate, group, corporation, association.

collective *adj.* joint, cooperative, shared, common, mutual, cumulative, composite, aggregated, total, concerted, comprehensive; *ant.* separate, individual.

college *n.* institute, seminary, lyceum, university, organization, association.

collide *v.* **1.** crash, hit, strike, smash, sideswipe, knock, slam. **2.** disagree, clash, conflict, interfere.

collision *n.* **1.** crash, accident, contact, impact, concussion, shock, jolt, blow; fenderbender (*slang*). **2.** conflict, contention, struggle, discord, interference.

colloquial *adj.* conversational, informal, casual, vernacular, idiomatic, familiar, everyday; *ant.* formal.

collude *v.* conspire, collaborate, contrive, scheme, intrigue, machinate, plot, connive.

collusion *n.* conspiracy, complicity, intrigue, deceit, craft, artifice, fraudulence.

color *n.* **1.** pigmentation, hue, shade, iridescence, tone, wash, tint, tinge, cast, blush, tincture; **2.** brilliance, intensity, vividness, brightness, colorfulness, richness, glow; *ant.* drabness, dimness. **3.** pretense, guise, cloak, pretext, deception.

color *v.* **1.** dye, stain, fresco, variegate, imbue, emblazon, tone, embellish, illuminate, tint, rouge; *ant.* bleach, fade. **2.** blush, flush, redden, mantle, bloom, glow; *ant.* whiten. **3.** misrepresent, distort, pervert, disguise, stage-manage, give a spin to (*slang*).

colorful *adj.* vibrant, kaleidoscopic, multicolored, brilliant, rich, psychedelic, vivid, jazzy (*slang*); *ant.* colorless, drab, plain. **2.** interesting, lively, stimulating, intense, exciting, engaging, charming.

colorless *adj.* neutral, pale, bleached, drab, anemic, ashen, dreary, lackluster, wan, washed out; *ant.* colorful. **2.** insipid, characterless, tame, vacuous, vapid; *ant.* memorable, interesting.

colors *n.* flag, banner, color, emblem, ensign, standard, bunting.

colossal *adj.* enormous, immense, massive, leviathan, herculean, monumental, prodigious, mammoth, gargantuan; *ant.* tiny.

column *n.* **1.** pillar, support, monument, pylon, minaret, totem, obelisk, mast, monolith, upright, pedestal, shaft. **2.** article, editorial, comment. **3.** single file, line, string, platoon, company.

columnist *n.* writer, journalist, correspondent, reporter, reviewer, critic, editor.

coma *n.* unconsciousness, catalepsy, insensibility, stupor, lethargy, oblivion, somnolence, torpor.

comatose *adj.* insensible, unconscious, torpid.

comb *v.* **1.** straighten, smooth, arrange, disentangle; *ant.* tangle. **2.** search, ransack, scour, hunt, rummage, sift, sweep.

combat *n.* warfare, conflict, action, hostilities, strife, duel, bout, clash, contest.

combat *v.* struggle, battle, fight, contend, strive, engage, oppose, resist, defy, contest, withstand.

combatant *n.* belligerent, foe, enemy, adversary, antagonist, soldier, serviceman, servicewoman, warrior.

combative *adj.* belligerent, contentious, pugnacious, quarrelsome, truculent, scrappy, antagonistic, militant, aggressive, bellicose; *ant.* pacific, peaceful.

combination *n.* **1.** compound, aggregate, mixture, blend. **2.** union, alliance, federation, amalgamation. **3.** order, sequence, succession, key, code.

combine *v.* synthesize, mix, integrate, fuse, amalgamate, merge, unite, incorporate, connect, pool, cooperate; *ant.* separate.

combustible *adj.* **1.** flammable, inflammable, burnable, ignitable. **2.** excitable, passionate, fiery, volatile.

combustion *n.* **1.** burning, fire, oxidization, kindling. **2.** excitement, tumult, agitation, turmoil.

come *v.* **1.** approach, advance, near, appear. **2.** become, develop, arrive, attain, mature, get. **3.** result, emerge, ensue, happen, arise, proceed.

as good as they come choice, superior, best, finest, top drawer.

come about happen, result, occur, transpire, take place, come to pass.

come across discover, uncover, happen *or* stumble upon, find, notice.

come again repeat, reiterate, restate, retell.

come along **1.** accompany, attend, go with. **2.** progress, recover, improve, prosper.

come apart break, collapse, crumble, disintegrate, fall to bits; separate, split, tear.

come around **1.** recover, improve, recuperate, rally. **2.** visit, call on, stop by, drop in on.

come back **1.** return, reappear, reenter. **2.** reply, retort, rejoin, respond. **3.** recover, improve, triumph, win, gain.

come between divide, part, estrange, alienate, separate, split up.

come by **1.** pass, go by, overtake, move past. **2.** acquire, procure, get, win.

come down on reprimand, rebuke, scold.

come into **1.** inherit, acquire, obtain, receive, succeed to. **2.** join, align, associate with.

come off succeed, happen, occur, come about, befall.

comeback

come out 1. conclude, result, be resolved, turn out, end up. **2.** transpire, come to light, be revealed, get out.

come through 1. succeed, accomplish, triumph, achieve, score, perform. **2.** survive, endure, withstand, persist, pull through.

come to 1. revive, recover, rally, recuperate. **2.** result in, end in, terminate, come around.

come up occur, happen, arise, appear. by, conclude by.

come up to 1. equal, match, rival, rank with. **2.** reach, near, approach.

come up with 1. propose, suggest, offer, recommend. **2.** originate, create, invent, propose, suggest, devise.

comeback *n.* **1.** rally, revival, triumph, rebound, recovery, return, resurgence. **2.** rejoinder, retort, crack, witticism, retaliation, repartee, riposte.

comedian *n.* comic, humorist, comedienne, wit, clown, jester, funnyman, wag, cutup, joker, card.

comedown *n.* reversal, blow, disappointment, letdown, decline, deflation, degradation, humiliation.

comedy *n.* humor, drollery, farce, hilarity, wisecracking, facetiousness, witticism.

comely *adj.* attractive, pretty, becoming, lovely, graceful, fair, handsome, pulchritudinous, winsome, buxom.

comeuppance *n.* deserts, dues, recompense, chastening, punishment, rebuke, retribution.

comfort *n.* **1.** contentment, ease, satisfaction, well-being. **2.** encouragement, cheer, support, relief, aid, help, consolation, solace; *ant.* distress, torment.

comfort *v.* **1.** solace, commiserate, reassure, succor, hearten, inspirit; *ant.* discourage, depress. **2.** alleviate, soothe, calm, salve, allay, mitigate.

comfortable *adj.* **1.** contented, cheerful, relaxed, serene, complacent; *ant.* uneasy, disturbed. **2.** adequate, appropriate, sufficient, pleasant, agreeable, satisfying.

comforter *n.* bedspread, quilt, bedcover, throw, coverlet.

comic *n.* comedian, wit, clown.

comic *adj.* comical, funny, facetious.

comical *adj.* humorous, entertaining, farcical,

comment

coming *n.* arrival, approach, accession, advent, birth.

coming *adj.* **1.** approaching, forthcoming, impending, imminent, prospective, anticipated, predestined, eventual, fated, written. **2.** (likely to be popular or successful) ambitious, promising, up-and-coming, probable, brilliant, encouraging; *ant.* hopeless, discouraging.

command *n.* **1.** order, edict, decree, fiat, mandate, commandment, summons, proclamation, ultimatum, warrant. **2.** (power to issue orders) authority, leadership, sovereignty, rule, control, jurisdiction, supremacy, tyranny, dominion, authorization.

command *v.* **1.** compel, charge, authorize, direct, impose, dictate, exact, proclaim, subpoena; *ant.* obey, comply. **2.** dominate, tyrannize, coerce, subdue; conduct, supervise, control, direct.

commandeer *v.* seize, confiscate, appropriate, hijack, usurp, shanghai.

commander *n.* leader, commander-in-chief, boss, director, chief, general.

commanding *adj.* governing, authoritative, dominant, assertive, decisive, autocratic; impressive, eminent, dignified.

commemorate *v.* celebrate, honor, memorialize, salute, immortalize, observe, remember, solemnize.

commence *v.* start, begin, embark, initiate, inaugurate, open, broach; *ant.* cease, finish.

commend *v.* **1.** praise, compliment, extol, eulogize. **2.** entrust, confide, yield, deliver.

commendable *adj.* admirable, meritorious, noble, exemplary, worthy, laudable, praiseworthy; *ant.* blameworthy.

commendation *n.* acclamation, praise, accolade, applause, approval, encouragement, panegyric; *ant.* criticism, blame.

commensurate *adj.* consistent, sufficient, comparable, adequate, equivalent, compatible, meet, proportionate, corresponding, due, just; *ant.* inappropriate.

comment *n.* statement, remark, observation, note, commentary, exposition, footnote, illustration, marginalia.

comment *v.* **1.** observe, remark, note, mention, interject, conclude, assert, opine, criticize. **2.** explain, illustrate, clarify, annotate.

commentary *n.* analysis, critique, review, interpretation, treatise, exegesis; description, elucidation, clarification, example.

commentator *n.* reporter, critic, interpreter, pundit.

commerce *n.* **1.** business, trade, merchandising, traffic. **2.** communication, intercourse, sociability.

commercial *adj.* **1.** mercantile, monetary, economic, financial, pecuniary, profitable. **2.** venal, materialistic, profiteering, exploitive.

commiserate *v.* sympathize, console, pity, condole.

commission *n.* **1.** authorization, order, command, assignment, duty, work, function. **2.** committee, representatives, board, council. **3.** payment, royalty, fee, remuneration, salary, stipend, indemnity.

out of commission damaged, broken, out of order, inoperative, on the blink (*slang*).

commission *v.* hire, charter, engage, contract; authorize, appoint, assign, nominate.

commit *v.* **1.** perpetrate, perform, do, practice. **2.** entrust, confide, consign, charge, allocate. **3.** devote, promise, vow, obligate, bind.

commitment *n.* pledge, vow, guarantee, obligation, assurance, dedication, devotion, duty, loyalty, responsibility.

committed *adj.* active, engaged, fervent, devoted, dyed-in-the-wool, card-carrying; *ant.* apathetic.

committee *n.* board, panel, advisory group, commission, council, cabinet, task force.

commodity *n.* merchandise, wares, goods, vendibles, product, stock.

common *adj.* **1.** ordinary, average, conventional, plain, quotidian, mediocre; *ant.* unique, distinguished. **2.** habitual, regular, inveterate; customary, characteristic. **3.** inferior, base, mean, cheap, shoddy, low. **4.** general, widespread, well-known, familiar, prevalent; *ant.* secret. **5.** communal, public, shared, joint, mutual; *ant.* private.

commoner *n.* peasant, common man, plebeian, citizen; *ant.* noble.

commonplace *n.* cliché, platitude, banality, truism, bromide.

commonplace *adj.* ordinary, everyday, familiar, widespread, customary; pedestrian, quotidian, trite, stale; *ant.* exceptional, rare.

common sense judgment, practicality, prudence, wisdom, sense, moderation, levelheadedness, horse sense, mother wit, smarts (*slang*).

common-sense *adj.* sensible, practical, judicious, realistic, reasonable, sound; *ant.* foolish.

commotion *n.* agitation, excitement, disturbance, fuss, perturbation, uproar, turmoil, racket, ferment, brouhaha; *ant.* order, calm.

communal *adj.* community, shared, public, open; *ant.* private.

commune *n.* cooperative, collective, kibbutz, settlement, colony.

commune *v.* communicate, converse, discourse, confer; muse, contemplate, ponder.

communicable *adj.* contagious, infectious, transmittable, infective, catching.

communicate *v.* **1.** convey, impart, transmit, relate; acquaint, announce, report, inform, reveal. **2.** join, connect, link, touch.

communication *n.* utterance, articulation, transmission, conveyance, dissemination, disclosure, account, report, elucidation.

communicative *adj.* open, candid, forthcoming, frank, articulate, informative, loquacious, conversational, voluble; *ant.* reticent, reserved.

communion *n.* association, fellowship, accord, sympathy, harmony, agreement.

communism *n.* socialism, Marxism, Leninism, Stalinism, collectivism, Bolshevism, Trotskyism.

communist *n.* Marxist, party member, comrade, Bolshevik, Leninist, Stalinist, Maoist; *ant.* capitalist.

community *n.* **1.** town, city, village, society, public, people, nation, body politic. **2.** fellowship, brotherhood, fraternity. **3.** identity, similarity, likeness, affinity, rapport.

commute *v.* reduce, alleviate, decrease, mitigate; reverse, remit.

compact *n.* contract, agreement, deal, treaty, settlement, arrangement.

compact *v.* compress, squeeze, condense, pack, cram, tamp.

compact *adj.* **1.** dense, solid, impenetrable, thick, stocky, firm; *ant.* diffuse. **2.** concise, brief, succinct, terse, laconic, to the point; *ant.* rambling, wordy.

companion *n.* **1.** friend, comrade, mate. **2.** associate, partner, colleague, co-worker. **3.** counterpart, analog, mate, twin, double.

company *n.* **1.** business organization, partnership, firm, corporation, outfit. **2.** guests, visitors, callers, boarders. **3.** companionship, society, presence, fellowship; associates, group, assembly.

keep someone company visit with, entertain, amuse.

part company separate, leave, stop associating with; disagree, fall out, be estranged.

comparable *adj.* **1.** equivalent, tantamount, equal, commensurate. **2.** akin, similar, relative, analogous, parallel, related, correspondent, kindred.

compare *n.* **1.** equate, relate, associate, parallel, contrast, weigh, oppose, correlate. **2.** match, rival, equal, vie.

comparison *n.* analogy, simile, correlation, parallel, distinction, similitude, juxtaposition; resemblance, similarity, likeness.

compartment *n.* stall, booth, niche, cubicle, alcove; section, division, category.

compass *n.* **1.** range, scope, reach, extent, expanse, area. **2.** boundary, perimeter, circumference, limit.

compassion *n.* mercy, pity, clemency, sympathy, understanding, concern, condolence, humanity, fellow feeling, charity; *ant.* indifference.

compassionate *adj.* benevolent, supportive, charitable, sympathetic, tender, humane, caring, feeling, indulgent, lenient; *ant.* coldhearted.

compatibility *n.* accord, harmony, concord, rapport, affinity, correspondence; *ant.* antipathy, antagonism.

compatible *adj.* suitable, congenial, likeminded, kindred, sympathetic, congruent, harmonious, accordant, reconcilable; *ant.* antagonistic, divergent.

compel *v.* **1.** urge, insist, pressure, impel, drive, coerce, force, extort, twist one's arm, overpower, bully, exact. **2.** (cause to feel compelled) oblige, drive, impel, require, constrain.

compelling *adj.* **1.** convincing, persuasive, cogent, valid, sound, irrefutable, conclusive, unarguable, powerful; *ant.* answerable. **2.** urgent, weighty, important, exigent, crying, desperate.

compendium *n.* abbreviation, condensation, abridgment, summary, synopsis, abstract, brief, précis.

compensate *v.* **1.** reimburse, pay, remunerate, requite, indemnify. **2.** offset, counterbalance, cancel, counterveil, neutralize.

compensation *n.* amends, reparation, redress, restitution, damages, atonement, indemnity; *ant.* loss, confiscation.

compete *v.* contend, oppose, struggle, rival, challenge, vie, battle, contest, duel, fight, strive.

competence *n.* proficiency, capability, skill, facility, sufficiency, adequacy, suitability, skill, expertise.

competent *adj.* **1.** qualified, able, capable, proficient, fit. **2.** sufficient, satisfactory, adequate, enough, plenty.

competition *n.* **1.** foe, competitor, rival, opponent, adversary, contestant. **2.** rivalry, contention, struggle, opposition. **3.** contest, match, championship, challenge, event, tournament.

competitive *adj.* aggressive, hard-fought, contentious, antagonistic, combative, emulative; cutthroat, dog-eat-dog.

competitor *n.* opponent, rival, competition, contestant, adversary, antagonist, challenger, contender, opposition; *ant.* ally, teammate.

compilation *n.* assortment, collection, accumulation, anthology.

compile *v.* amass, assemble, collect, gather, garner; organize, compose, select, cull, marshal.

complacency *n.* **1.** smugness, self-satisfaction, gratification, conceit; *ant.* discontent. **2.** composure, serenity, unconcern, repose, equanimity.

complacent *adj.* **1.** proud, egotistic, smug, pleased, self-assured. **2.** content, affable, complaisant, serene.

complain *v.* **1.** criticize, denounce, dissent, oppose, protest, object; cavil, grumble, bellyache (*slang*), whine; *ant.* praise, thank. **2.** lament, grieve, mourn, bemoan, bewail, cry.

complaint *n.* **1.** objection, criticism, reproach, accusation, charge, gripe. **2.** malady, illness, ailment, infirmity, disease.

complaisant *adj.* compliant, deferential, obedient, docile, amenable, tractable, amiable, agreeable, solicitous, gracious; *ant.* obstinate, perverse.

complement *n.* 1. remainder, balance, supplement, rest. 2. wholeness, totality, entirety, whole. 3. counterpart, parallel, equivalent, match.

complementary *adj.* companion, correlative, corresponding, interrelated, interdependent, reciprocal, interwoven, matched.

complete *v.* 1. finish, conclude, terminate, close, end; *ant.* commence. 2. perfect, refine, consummate, crown. 3. achieve, realize, effect, accomplish, fulfill; *ant.* fall short of.

complete *adj.* 1. entire, total, replete, absolute, plenary, whole, full. 2. perfect, flawless, unblemished, impeccable, consummate.

completion *n.* 1. culmination, fruition, settlement, discharge. 2. expiration, termination, conclusion, finalization, end.

complex *n.* 1. obsession, phobia, syndrome, mania. 2. composite, conglomerate, system, association, collection, aggregation, group, entanglement, totality.

complex *adj.* 1. heterogeneous, multiple, motley, aggregate, compound, miscellaneous, multifarious; *ant.* homogeneous, single. 2. intricate, complicated, elaborate, labyrinthine, irreducible, convoluted, inscrutable, puzzling, circuitous; *ant.* apparent, understandable.

complexion *n.* 1. aspect, countenance, semblance, appearance, look, seeming. 2. cast, color, composition, hue, pigmentation, skin. 3. character, disposition, nature, temperament, mien, type.

complexity *n.* intricacy, complication, entanglement, elaboration, difficulty; diversity, variety, multiplicity, variation; *ant.* simplicity.

compliance *n.* acquiescence, obedience, deference, concession, submission, yielding, cooperation; complaisance, tractability, meekness, passivity; *ant.* defiance.

compliant *adj.* docile, deferential, submissive, obedient, tractable; amenable, accommodating, obliging, agreeable, complaisant.

complicate *v.* confuse, involve, compound, entangle, elaborate, embroil, muddle, snarl, knot; *ant.* simplify.

complicated *adj.* 1. complex, intricate, elaborate, involved, manifold, convoluted. 2. problematic, difficult, perplexing, puzzling, tortuous, troublesome.

complication *n.* difficulty, obstacle, problem, snag, confusion, entanglement, puzzlement, drawback, embarrassment.

complicity *n.* collaboration, collusion, involvement, concurrence, approval, connivance, abetment; *ant.* ignorance, innocence.

compliment *n.* accolade, honor, congratulations, kudos, tribute, encomium, plaudit, bouquet; *ant.* criticism.

compliment *v.* applaud, praise, flatter, admire, commend, congratulate, salute, extol, laud; *ant.* condemn, insult.

complimentary *adj.* 1. appreciative, flattering, laudatory, panegyrical, approving; *ant.* critical. 2. free, gratis, gratuitous.

comply *v.* observe, respect, oblige, satisfy; accommodate, conform, toe the line, acquiesce, defer, accede, submit, yield; *ant.* disobey, resist.

component *n.* element, factor, piece, ingredient, part, item.

component *adj.* constituent, integral, fundamental, basic.

comport *v.* conduct, behave, acquit, carry, act, perform, bear, deport.

compose *v.* 1. make up, constitute, form, fashion. 2. create, score, orchestrate, author, design, conceive, forge, invent; *ant.* cancel, erase. 3. calm, soothe, pacify, placate.

composed *adj.* poised, confident, relaxed, sensible, self-possessed, self-assured, levelheaded, clearheaded, imperturbable, sedate, tranquil, cool; *ant.* upset, agitated.

composite *n.* compound, combination, blend, mixture, mélange, hybrid.

composite *adj.* synthesized, mixed, compound, manifold, heterogenous, multiple, complex, conglomerate; *ant.* homogeneous, uniform.

composition *n.* 1. organization, arrangement, balance, symmetry, proportion, distribution, relation. 2. creation, conception, production, invention, fashioning, formation, shaping, sculpturing, forging. 3. essay, article, exposition, writing; opus, work, étude.

composure *n.* poise, calm, serenity, aplomb,

compound

composure *n.* self-confidence, equanimity, tranquillity, self-assurance, savoir-faire; *ant.* passion, agitation.

compound *n.* medley, composite, synthesis, conglomerate, fusion, alloy, pastiche, mélange.

compound *v.* 1. combine, blend, mix, coalesce, join, unite. 2. complicate, intensify, confound, confuse.

compound *adj.* composite, synthesized, intermingled.

comprehend *v.* 1. understand, discern, perceive, grasp, know. 2. involve, include, contain, comprise, embrace.

comprehensible *adj.* intelligible, understandable, conceivable, lucid, distinct, plain.

comprehension *n.* 1. knowledge, understanding, perception, cognizance, awareness. 2. inclusion, incorporation, embodiment.

comprehensive *adj.* inclusive, thorough, extensive, exhaustive, complete, broad, encyclopedic; *ant.* selective.

compress *v.* condense, compact, concentrate, crowd, wedge, press, constrict, squeeze; *ant.* diffuse, expand.

comprise *v.* consist of, incorporate, include, involve, contain, cover, encompass, embrace, embody, subsume.

compromise *n.* concession, trade-off, bargain, accommodation, accord, cooperation, settlement; *ant.* disagreement, intransigence.

compromise *v.* 1. negotiate, conciliate, arbitrate, meet halfway, settle, agree. 2. endanger, jeopardize, imperil, hazard.

compulsion *n.* 1. obligation, urgency, demand, pressure, duty; force, drive, necessity, need. 2. obsession, preoccupation, urge, impulse, prepossession.

compulsive *adj.* compelling, passionate, overwhelming, incorrigible, irresistible, overpowering; *ant.* controllable.

compulsory *adj.* obligatory, mandatory, required, stipulated, forced, imperative, binding, de rigueur, requisite; *ant.* optional, voluntary.

compunction *n.* hesitance, reluctance, misgiving, qualm, regret, scruple, remorse, guilt, repentance, contrition.

compute *v.* calculate, total, tally, count, assess, figure, reckon, sum, enumerate.

conception

comrade *n.* ally, partner, colleague, associate, companion, compeer, co-worker, confederate, chum.

con *n.* (*slang*) fraud, deception, grift, scam (*slang*).

con *v.* (*slang*) deceive, mislead, dupe, beguile; cheat, swindle, defraud, bilk, gull, rook, cozen, inveigle, rip off (*slang*).

concave *adj.* curved, hollow, indented, depressed, cupped, sunken, excavated; *ant.* convex.

concavity *n.* cavity, impression, basin, pit, vacuity, recess; *ant.* protuberance, mound.

conceal *v.* cover, obscure, screen, hide, camouflage; *ant.* reveal.

concede *v.* 1. acknowledge, admit, grant, allow, confess, accept; *ant.* dispute, deny. 2. yield, cede, relinquish, surrender, forfeit.

conceit *n.* 1. arrogance, vanity, narcissism, egotism, self-importance, swagger, smugness, complacency, self-satisfaction; *ant.* modesty, diffidence. 2. caprice, fancy, whim, vagary, fantasy.

conceivable *adj.* tenable, credible, likely, possible, probable.

conceive *v.* 1. formulate, originate, start, begin, create, imagine, envision, speculate. 2. comprehend, perceive, understand.

concentrate *n.* extract, essence, distillation.

concentrate *v.* 1. condense, focus, intensify, strengthen, consolidate, agglomerate, center, mass, gather, collect; *ant.* disperse, extend. 2. study, ruminate, scrutinize, examine, focus, attend, heed; *ant.* drift, ignore.

concentration *n.* 1. convergence, focus, centralization, density, solidity, congestion. 2. attention, thought, application, intentness, absorption, engrossment. 3. collection, assemblage, congregation, array, heap, pile, swarm, horde, congeries.

concept *n.* idea, hypothesis, theory, opinion, notion, construct, conception, visualization.

conception *n.* 1. comprehension, perception, apprehension, cognition, knowledge, consideration, meditation, realization, speculation. 2. fertilization, insemination, impregnation, inception. 3. (something conceived) impression, representation, mental image, fancy. 4. (product of thought) interpretation, version, rendition, explanation, exposition, elaboration, plan, scheme, program.

concern *n.* **1.** affair, matter, responsibility, business. **2.** care, interest, regard, consideration, attention, solicitude. **3.** anxiety, distress, apprehension, worry.

concern *v.* **1.** involve, affect, interest, touch, relate to. **2.** disturb, trouble, perturb, distress, upset, bother, disquiet, worry.

concerning *prep.* about, regarding, apropos, with reference to.

concert *n.* **1.** harmony, accord, concord, agreement, unity. **2.** performance, show, recital.

concerted *adj.* collective, joint, collaborative, united, coordinated, shared; *ant.* separate.

concession *n.* yielding, permission, authorization, permit, warrant.

conciliate *v.* appease, pacify, placate, mollify, propitiate, soften; *ant.* antagonize.

concise *adj.* succinct, terse, brief, condensed, compact, pithy, laconic; *ant.* diffuse, expansive.

conclave *n.* session, meeting, conference, confabulation, powwow.

conclude *v.* **1.** end, finish, terminate, complete, close, cease, desist. **2.** judge, presume, assume; deduce, reason, gather. **3.** determine, resolve, confirm, decide, settle.

concluding *adj.* final, ultimate, terminal, last; *ant.* introductory.

conclusive *adj.* irrefutable, incontrovertible, decisive, undeniable, clear, manifest; final, ultimate, concluding; *ant.* arguable.

concoct *v.* contrive, invent, devise, formulate, fabricate, plan, develop.

concoction *n.* **1.** mixture, brew, potion, blend, solution, combination, compound, potpourri, medley.

concomitant *adj.* concurrent, attendant, accompanying, simultaneous, contemporaneous, joint, synchronous, concordant.

concord *n.* **1.** harmony, rapport, accord, consensus, agreement, unity. **2.** contract, pact, treaty, covenant.

concourse *n.* gathering, assembly, meeting, congregation, confluence; multitude, press, collection, crowd.

concrete *adj.* **1.** tangible, substantial, palpable, solid, physical, material. **2.** explicit, spe-

cific, definite, precise, particular, accurate, detailed; *ant.* abstract. **3.** solid, massive, stony, dense.

concupiscence *n.* lust, desire, libido, appetite, lechery, lubricity.

concupiscent *adj.* lecherous, lustful, lascivious, lewd, lubricious, horny (*slang*).

concur *v.* **1.** synchronize, coincide, harmonize, cooperate. **2.** consent, agree, approve, accede.

concurrence *n.* convergence, association, conjunction, concomitance, coexistence, community; *ant.* difference.

concurrent *adj.* **1.** simultaneous, synchronous, concomitant, coexistent, conjoined, parallel, confluent. **2.** allied, harmonious, joint, unified, mutual, concerted, unanimous.

condemn *v.* **1.** sentence, convict, proscribe, adjudge. **2.** reprove, censure, castigate, upbraid, disparage, denounce, pillory, animadvert, vilify, revile; *ant.* laud, praise.

condemnation *n.* judgment, blame, reproach, damnation, stricture; *ant.* approval.

condense *v.* **1.** consolidate, reduce, compress, compact, thicken, solidify, concentrate; *ant.* diffuse. **2.** abbreviate, abridge, summarize, abstract, encapsulate; *ant.* expand, elaborate on.

condescend *v.* patronize, deign, stoop, descend.

condescending *adj.* superior, haughty, patronizing, imperious, pretentious, supercilious, snobbish, airy; *ant.* humble, approachable.

condescension *n.* disdain, haughtiness, airs, noblesse oblige; *ant.* humility.

condition *n.* **1.** position, status, situation, state. **2.** limitation, qualification, requirement, restriction, caveat, proviso, stipulation, provision; prohibition, restraint. **3.** fitness, tone, form, shape, health; illness, ailment, infirmity, disease, malady, complaint.

condition *v.* train, ready, prepare; season, indoctrinate, accustom, habituate, temper, familiarize, inure.

conditional *adj.* relative, dependent, tied, linked, restricted, contingent; uncertain, tentative, iffy; *ant.* absolute, certain.

condolences *n.* sympathy, support, commiseration, pity, compassion.

condone *v.* tolerate, allow, indulge, excuse,

conducive

conducive *adj.* favorable, expeditious, beneficial, advantageous, promotive, stimulative; *ant.* adverse.

conduct *n.* 1. behavior, manner, demeanor, deportment, way. 2. control, care, direction, superintendence, management.

conduct *v.* 1. guide, lead, escort, usher, pilot. 2. transmit, convey, pass on, transfer, carry, send. 3. manage, administer, supervise, govern, direct, regulate, handle.

conduit *n.* passage, channel, artery, canal, pipe, duct, tube.

confederacy *n.* 1. alliance, union, federation, coalition, league, partnership. 2. conspiracy, cabal, ring.

confederate *n.* conspirator, accomplice, accessory, partisan, ally, colleague, supporter.

confederate *v.* unite, incorporate, merge, bind, federate.

confer *v.* 1. bestow, present, award, give. 2. deliberate, talk, discuss, consider, converse, parley.

conference *n.* 1. meeting, symposium, colloquium, seminar, talk, parley. 2. league, association, organization, synod, ring.

confess *v.* admit, concede, acknowledge, declare, own up, fess up (*slang*), profess, avow, disclose; *ant.* conceal, withhold.

confession *n.* 1. revelation, disclosure, avowal, divulgence, revelation; *ant.* denial, disclaimer. 2. sacrament, absolution, penance, repentance, contrition.

confidant *n.* companion, intimate, friend, crony.

confide *v.* 1. confess, reveal, divulge, unburden, disclose, impart. 2. entrust, commit, consign.

confidence *n.* 1. faith, reliance, trust, assurance, belief, conviction; *ant.* doubt. 2. boldness, aplomb, self-assurance; fortitude, resolution, tenacity, mettle, backbone; *ant.* self-doubt.

confident *adj.* 1. (as a position) certain, sure, positive, convinced, secure, reliable. 2. said of a person) self-assured, fearless, unafraid, bold, dauntless, presumptuous.

confidential *adj.* private, classified, secret, hush-hush, privileged; *ant.* public, common.

conformation

configuration *n.* arrangement, structure, disposition, Gestalt, deployment.

confine *v.* incarcerate, imprison, cage, circumscribe, inhibit, detain, limit, restrict, place under house arrest; bind, truss, straitjacket; *ant.* free.

confinement *n.* incarceration, captivity, detention, custody, house arrest; constraint, circumspection; *ant.* independence, release.

confines *n.* 1. borders, bounds, limits, periphery, boundary. 2. dimension, range, proportions, scope.

confirm *v.* 1. ratify, approve, sanction, affirm, endorse. 2. prove, verify, substantiate, validate, authenticate; strengthen, support, augment, corroborate.

confirmation *n.* 1. verification, authentication, proof, evidence, testimony. 2. authorization, consent, assent, ratification, passage, approval.

confirmed *adj.* chronic, incurable, habitual, dyed-in-the-wool, incorrigible, inveterate, irredeemable, gung-ho (*slang*).

confiscate *v.* seize, impound, appropriate, sequester, commandeer, expropriate; *ant.* restore.

confiscation *n.* seizure, takeover, forfeiture, forfeit.

conflagration *n.* inferno, firestorm, wildfire, holocaust, blaze.

conflict *n.* struggle, strife, feud, quarrel, battle, engagement, confrontation, encounter, warfare, antagonism, discord, dissension, dispute, argument, hostility, friction; *ant.* concord.

conflict *v.* clash, struggle, contend, contest, combat, oppose, differ, dissent, dispute, collide, contradict, lock horns; *ant.* agree.

conflicting *adj.* inconsistent, contrary, contradictory, opposite, antagonistic, paradoxical, discordant, turbulent, ambivalent.

confluence *n.* 1. junction, convergence, meeting, concurrence, conjunction, conflux. 2. assemblage, host, throng, multitude.

conform *v.* 1. comply, adjust, follow, adapt, obey, toe the line, accommodate, yield; *ant.* differ. 2. correspond, harmonize, accord, synchronize, parallel, match, resemble.

conformation *n.* 1. concord, consonance, congruity, affinity, compatibility, similarity, unison. 2. structure, arrangement, formation, shape, symmetry, pattern, mold.

conformist *n.* conventionalist, traditionalist, bourgeois, yes-man; *ant.* bohemian.

conformity *n.* **1.** obedience, allegiance, yielding, submission, compliance, acquiescence, observance, orthodoxy. **2.** harmony, conformation, agreement, congruity, consonance.

confound *v.* **1.** mix, blend, jumble, entangle, commingle. **2.** perplex, puzzle, flabbergast, dumbfound, confuse, flummox, stun, put at a loss.

confounded *adj.* insufferable, arrant, notorious, egregious, consummate, outrageous.

confront *v.* **1.** encounter, face, meet. **2.** challenge, oppose, defy, brave, resist.

confrontation *n.* encounter, meeting, challenge, contest, face-off, showdown, opposition, collision, conflict, disagreement, battle, quarrel, fight, counteraction.

confuse *v.* disconcert, perplex, baffle, confound, puzzle, mystify, bewilder, frustrate, rattle, fluster, disarm; *ant.* clarify, enlighten.

confused *adj.* disoriented, bewildered, lost, misguided, mixed up; upset, disconcerted, at a loss.

confusing *adj.* obscure, ambiguous, inconclusive, inconsistent, contradictory, cryptic, difficult, incoherent, jumbled, unfathomable, incomprehensible; *ant.* clear.

confusion *n.* **1.** bafflement, mystification, puzzlement, perplexity. **2.** chaos, commotion, turmoil, distraction; *ant.* order, organization.

confute *v.* invalidate, nullify, refute, disprove, rebut, controvert, vitiate, overturn, challenge, impugn; *ant.* confirm, prove.

congeal *v.* solidify, thicken, gel, coagulate, set, clot, coalesce, curdle; *ant.* separate, dissolve.

congenial *adj.* **1.** pleasant, agreeable, welcoming, warm, genial, affable, outgoing, cordial, amenable, kindly. **2.** well-suited, compatible, suitable, kindred, sympathetic.

congenital *adj.* inborn, inherited, hereditary, natural, inherent, innate; *ant.* acquired, learned.

congested *adj.* overcrowded, full, crammed, packed, jammed, overflowing; clogged, blocked, swollen; *ant.* clear.

conglomerate *n.* aggregate, medley, combination, agglomerate.

conglomerate *v.* collect, accumulate, mass, assemble, gather, congregate, agglutinate, clump; *ant.* separate.

conglomerate *adj.* bunched, clustered; heterogeneous, composite.

congregate *v.* assemble, convene, gather, rally, converge, convoke, cluster, concentrate; *ant.* disperse, dismiss.

congregation *n.* **1.** assembly, parishioners, flock, parish, laity. **2.** assemblage, multitude, crowd, throng, host.

congress *n.* legislature, parliament, senate, assembly, government, committee, caucus.

congruent *adj.* harmonious, corresponding, consonant, similar, parallel.

congruity *n.* congruence, concurrence, harmony, agreement, correspondence, compatibility, conformity, match, parallelism.

congruous *adj.* suitable, appropriate, fitting, consistent.

conical *adj.* tapered, cone-shaped, pointed, pyramidal.

conjectural *adj.* hypothetical, theoretical, speculative, suppositional; tentative, uncertain, doubtful, problematic, iffy; *ant.* factual, real.

conjecture *n.* inference, guess, hypothesis, opinion, supposition, guesstimate.

conjecture *v.* postulate, speculate, suppose, posit, surmise, estimate, imagine, reckon.

conjugal *adj.* matrimonial, marital, wedded, connubial, spousal.

conjunction *n.* **1.** union, association, connection, combination. **2.** concurrence, coincidence, congruency, parallelism.

conjure *v.* **1.** enchant, charm, entrance, hex, jinx, fascinate. **2.** entreat, implore, beg, beseech, adjure, plead.

conjure up **1.** summon, invoke, call, materialize. **2.** recollect, recall, remember, recognize, review, call to mind.

conjurer *n.* sorcerer, magician, wizard, illusionist, miracle worker, prestidigitator.

connect *v.* unite, join, link, fasten, combine, couple, affix, ally, associate, relate, bind.

connection *n.* **1.** friend, associate, relative; relationship, association, kinship. **2.** junction, nexus, union, splice, link, bond, attachment, fastening, consolidation, combination.

connivance *n.* complicity, collusion, abetment, consent.

connive *v.* scheme, conspire, plot, intrigue, collude, cabal, coact.

connoisseur *n.* aficionado, devotee, buff; authority, expert, specialist, judge.

connotation *n.* implication, suggestion, import, drift, intent, nuance, undertone, hint.

connote *v.* suggest, imply, insinuate, allude, mean, purport, indicate, betoken, suggest.

connubial *adj.* conjugal, married, wedded.

conquer *v.* **1.** master, triumph, achieve, win, prevail, succeed. **2.** defeat, overcome, vanquish, subdue, crush, subjugate; *ant.* yield, surrender.

conqueror *n.* victor, hero, champion, conquistador, vanquisher, winner, champ.

conquest *n.* victory, win, ascendancy; invasion, occupation, subjection, takeover, acquisition, annexation.

conscience *n.* morals, principles, ethics, scruples, standards.

in all conscience rightly, justly, fairly, properly.

conscience-stricken *adj.* penitent, repentant, ashamed, contrite, troubled, guilt-ridden, guilty, remorseful, compunctious.

conscientious *adj.* **1.** honorable, pious, honest, principled, ethical, moral, upright. **2.** scrupulous, meticulous, thorough, dedicated, exact, fastidious, painstaking; *ant.* indifferent, nonchalant.

conscious *adj.* **1.** cognizant, sentient, responsive, alert, apprehending, perceiving. **2.** intentional, deliberate, willful, calculated, premeditated, studied; *ant.* inadvertent, unwitting.

consciousness *n.* awareness, sentience, apprehension, recognition, knowledge, intuition, realization, sensibility.

conscript *v.* draft, recruit, enlist, enroll, call up.

consecrate *v.* **1.** sanctify, bless, ordain, anoint, hallow. **2.** dedicate, devote, destine, surrender, commit.

consecutive *adj.* successive, sequential, serial, ensuing, chronological; continuous, uninterrupted; *ant.* simultaneous, broken.

consensus *n.* harmony, concord, agreement, unanimity, unity; *ant.* discord, dissent.

consent *n.* approval, agreement, sanction, accordance, concession, yielding.

consent *v.* allow, permit, grant, assent, acquiesce, comply, accede, concede, yield; *ant.* oppose, refuse.

consequence *n.* **1.** effect, result, outcome, end, upshot, aftermath, repercussion; *ant.* cause. **2.** significance, importance, moment, portent, weight, value.

consequent *adj.* resultant, subsequent, ensuing, following.

consequential *adj.* important, serious, momentous, impressive, noteworthy, eventful, grave, weighty, substantive, significant, far-reaching.

consequently *adv.* thus, therefore, subsequently, accordingly, ergo, hence, necessarily.

conservation *n.* preservation, safekeeping, upkeep, maintenance, support; *ant.* destruction, waste.

conservative *adj.* traditional, conventional, orthodox, moderate, cautious, guarded, prudent, sober; reactionary, right-wing; *ant.* progressive, radical.

conserve *v.* maintain, keep, save, protect, guard; *ant.* squander.

consider *v.* **1.** contemplate, deliberate, reflect, muse, meditate, ponder, ruminate, cogitate, examine, study; *ant.* ignore. **2.** deem, regard, heed, weigh, rate, remember, bear in mind.

considerable *adj.* **1.** significant, important, noteworthy, influential. **2.** large, ample, substantial, abundant, plentiful, bountiful, lavish; *ant.* slight.

considerate *adj.* **1.** thoughtful, attentive, gracious, kind, obliging, patient, charitable, solicitous; *ant.* selfish. **2.** careful, mindful, circumspect, discreet, tactful.

consideration *n.* **1.** attention, study, reflection, thought, forethought. **2.** courtesy, thoughtfulness, tact, kindliness, favor, philanthropy, benefaction. **3.** factor, concern, reason, motive, cause, ground, score.

consign *v.* **1.** transfer, deliver, dispatch, distribute, ship, transmit, send. **2.** entrust, confide, delegate, assign, commission, authorize, relegate.

consistency *n.* agreement, correspondence, concordance, accord, congruity.

consistent *adj.* **1.** compatible, harmonious, consonant, logical, coherent. **2.** regular, steady, uniform, persistent, constant, dependable; *ant.* erratic.

consist of include, comprise, involve, contain, embody, incorporate, amount to, embrace.

consolation *n.* solace, relief, support, aid, help, succor; *ant.* discouragement.

console *v.* comfort, assuage, calm, alleviate, soothe, ease, cheer, hearten, encourage; *ant.* upset, agitate.

consolidate *v.* 1. combine, unify, federate, unite, amalgamate, affiliate, solidify. 2. fortify, secure, reinforce, strengthen.

consonance *n.* agreement, accord, harmony, conformity.

consonant *adj.* compatible, harmonious, consistent, congruous, correspondent, concordant, suitable; *ant.* dissonant.

consort *n.* partner, companion, associate, spouse, lover, helpmeet.

consort *v.* fraternize, associate, mingle.

conspicuous *adj.* blatant, flagrant, glaring, obvious, apparent, noticeable, evident, salient, manifest, patent, remarked, egregious, sticking out like a sore thumb; *ant.* imperceptible.

conspiracy *n.* intrigue, scheme, plot, machination, treason, confederacy, cabal, collusion.

conspire *v.* 1. plot, scheme, plan, contrive. 2. cooperate, consort (with), unite, join.

constancy *n.* determination, perseverance, devotion, fidelity, tenacity, regularity.

constant *adj.* 1. permanent, immutable, unalterable, uniform, even, stable, resolute, firm, steady, staunch; *ant.* variable, irregular. 2. interminable, endless, eternal, continuous, incessant, relentless, perpetual, persistent, sustained; *ant.* fitful, occasional. 3. faithful, loyal, devoted, true, dependable, trustworthy; *ant.* fickle.

constituent *adj.* component, fundamental, intrinsic, integral.

constitute *v.* 1. establish, found, create, organize, develop; delegate, appoint, authorize, commission, empower. 2. consist of, compose, comprise, aggregate, compound, make up.

constitution *n.* 1. makeup, nature, disposition, character, essence, structure, organization. 2. health, vitality, physique.

constitutional *adj.* 1. representative, democratic, republican. 2. legal, ensured, lawful, approved. 3. inherent, natural, vital, physical, inborn, built-in.

constrain *v.* 1. constrict, bind, tighten, restrain, confine. 2. impel, oblige, urge, necessitate, drive.

constraint *n.* 1. compulsion, necessity, pressure, force, coercion, duress. 2. reserve, modesty, timidity, humility, hesitancy, recalcitrance, shyness, bashfulness. 3. curb, rein, obstacle, hindrance, check, impediment, roadblock.

constrict *v.* 1. narrow, contract, shrink, bind, squeeze, choke, strangle; *ant.* expand. 2. restrict, limit, inhibit, constrain, impede, check, curb.

construct *v.* build, raise, erect, assemble, manufacture, engineer; create, shape, formulate, design, invent.

construction *n.* structure, building, edifice, formation, model.

constructive *adj.* useful, helpful, productive, advantageous, valuable, beneficial, positive, affirmative; *ant.* negative, counterproductive.

construe *v.* interpret, read, explain, infer, render, deduce, translate.

consult *v.* discuss, confer, consider, deliberate, parley; ask, question, inquire.

consultant *n.* adviser, specialist, expert, authority.

consultation *n.* appointment, session, examination, meeting.

consume *v.* 1. destroy, devastate, ravage. 2. use, spend, exhaust, squander, waste, eat up. 3. preoccupy, engross, compel, dominate, spellbind, overwhelm, monopolize.

consumer *n.* buyer, customer, purchaser, shopper, user.

consummate *v.* complete, finish, accomplish, achieve, actualize, realize, fulfill, perfect, crown.

consummate *adj.* perfect, ultimate, transcendent, superior, nonpareil, matchless, unequaled, supreme, absolute, total; *ant.* qualified, imperfect.

consumption *n.* dissipation, depletion, diminution, dispersion, expenditure, use; *ant.* preservation.

contact *n.* connection, association, communication, junction, meeting, union, impact, collision.

contact *v.* 1. touch, graze, impinge, brush,

contagious

phone, get in touch with.

kiss, meet, scrape. **2.** notify, call, reach,

contagious *adj.* infectious, communicable, epidemic, catching, transmissible, pestilential.

contain *v.* **1.** include, comprise, embody, subsume, hold, carry, accommodate. **2.** restrain, restrict, check, inhibit, keep back.

contaminate *v.* pollute, defile, poison, vitiate, taint, adulterate, deprave, debase, tarnish; *ant.* purify.

contamination *n.* corruption, pollution, infection, decay, contagion, impurity, rottenness.

contemplate *v.* **1.** ruminate, deliberate, ponder, reflect, consider, muse, mull over, cogitate. **2.** examine, inspect, scrutinize, study, observe, regard, survey, behold, view. **3.** expect, intend, plan, envisage, foresee.

contemplation *n.* meditation, thought, reverie, rumination, lucubrations.

contemplative *adj.* introspective, pensive, reflective, rapt, cerebral, thoughtful, ruminative, dreamy, nostalgic, absorbed, intent; *ant.* impulsive.

contemporary *adj.* **1.** modern, current, present, recent, à la mode, newfangled, up-to-date; *ant.* ancient, historical. **2.** concurrent, contemporaneous, simultaneous, coexistent, synchronous, coterminous, coeval.

contempt *n.* **1.** disdain, scorn, mockery, condescension, derision, disrespect, neglect, slight; *ant.* regard, admiration. **2.** humiliation, dishonor, shame, disgrace.

contemptible *adj.* base, abject, degenerate, despicable, vile, wretched, detestable, loathsome, worthless; *ant.* honorable, admirable.

contemptuous *adj.* insolent, haughty, arrogant, derisive, cynical, sneering, insulting, supercilious; *ant.* humble, polite.

contend *v.* **1.** compete, vie, strive, struggle, wrestle, grapple, argue, dispute, debate, contest, litigate. **2.** allege, maintain, assert, declare, hold, affirm, avow, aver.

content *n.* **1.** meaning, significance, gist, intent, purport, heart, essence. **2.** size, capacity, volume.

content *v.* satisfy, please, pacify, appease, humor, placate, mollify, gratify.

content *adj.* contented, comfortable, happy, serene, at peace, gratified, appeased, relaxed,

continue

satisfied.

contented *adj.* content, serene, pleased, happy, satisfied.

contention *n.* **1.** quarrel, strife, struggle, dissension, dispute, enmity. **2.** allegation, charge, assertion, claim, argument, position, point.

contentious *adj.* argumentative, hostile, antagonistic, quarrelsome, belligerent, captious, factious, pugnacious, querulous; *ant.* cooperative.

contentment *n.* satisfaction, ease, serenity, equanimity, complacency, peace, pleasure, fulfillment, gratification, happiness.

contents *n.* ingredients, parts, elements, components.

contest *v.* challenge, dispute, question, oppose, refute, debate, deny, doubt, vie, litigate.

contestant *n.* candidate, participant, contender, competitor, athlete, entrant, player, aspirant.

context *n.* circumstances, situation, frame of reference, conditions, background, setting, ambiance.

contiguous *adj.* adjacent, touching, abutting, adjoining, propinquant, proximate; *ant.* separate.

continence *n.* temperance, moderation, self-restraint, sobriety, abstinence, virtue, celibacy, chastity.

contingency *n.* likelihood, probability, chance, possibility, exigency, eventuality.

contingent *adj.* **1.** conditional, dependent, uncertain, unpredictable. **2.** unforeseen, unexpected, fortuitous, accidental.

continual *adj.* **1.** constant, uninterrupted, unbroken, connected, consecutive, recurrent, frequent, regular; *ant.* intermittent, sporadic. **2.** endless, incessant, perpetual, eternal, continuous, interminable, everlasting, ceaseless, unremitting.

continually *adv.* forever, nonstop, always, constantly.

continuance *n.* continuation, duration, protraction, prolongation.

continuation *n.* **1.** prolongation, perpetuation, furtherance; *ant.* termination, cessation. **2.** addition, extension, supplement, appendix, sequel, postscript, epilogue.

continue *v.* **1.** (extend in time) persist, persevere, endure, remain, maintain, sustain, progress; *ant.* cease, discontinue, halt. **2.** (extend in space) protract, project, abut, advance, stick out. **3.** resume, recommence, reinstate, recapitulate, renew.

continuing *adj.* lasting, ongoing, abiding.

continuity *n.* extension, progression, succession, cohesion, sequence, connection, interrelationship, linkage, flow.

continuous *adj.* continual, undivided, unbroken, prolonged.

contort *v.* distort, misshape, disfigure, convolute, deform, warp, writhe, twist, gnarl, knot, wrench, bend.

contour *n.* outline, profile, form, curve, relief, silhouette.

contour *v.* shape, carve, mold.

contract *n.* agreement, deal, commitment, guarantee, promise, covenant, compact, settlement, understanding, treaty.

contract *v.* **1.** agree, pledge, engage, bargain, undertake, stipulate. **2.** narrow, shrink, reduce, constrict, diminish, recede, abate, subside, dwindle; *ant.* stretch, expand.

contradict *v.* counter, dispute, challenge, controvert, impugn, contravene, negate, belie; *ant.* confirm, agree.

contradiction *n.* **1.** disagreement, dissension, defiance, denial. **2.** discrepancy, inconsistency, incongruity, opposition.

contradictory *adj.* conflicting, contrary, irreconcilable, antithetical, dissident, antagonistic, paradoxical; *ant.* consistent, compatible.

contraption *n.* contrivance, gizmo, gadget, gimmick, rig, invention.

contrary *adj.* **1.** opposed, hostile, antagonistic, counter, antithetical. **2.** obstinate, headstrong, perverse, ornery, balky, cantankerous, refractory, difficult.

contrast *n.* **1.** divergence, incompatibility, disparity, variation, distinction, heterogeneity, diversity; *ant.* agreement, uniformity. **2.** antithesis, reverse, converse, inverse.

contrast *v.* **1.** compare, differentiate, distinguish, discriminate. **2.** differ, vary, set off, diverge, mismatch, oppose.

contrasting *adj.* contradictory, divergent, dissimilar.

contravene *v.* **1.** violate, transgress, break,

cross, trespass, infringe, infract; *ant.* uphold, obey. **2.** contradict, deny, refute, gainsay, impugn.

contribute *v.* donate, furnish, give, share, endow, supply, bequeath, confer, will, aid; *ant.* receive, accept.

contribution *n.* donation, grant, gift, present, bestowal, increase, supplement, addition, augmentation.

contributor *n.* **1.** correspondent, reporter, journalist, freelancer. **2.** backer, patron, donor, subscriber, benefactor.

contributory *adj.* additional, ancillary, secondary, subordinate.

contrite *adj.* repentant, penitent, humble, rueful, chastened, sorry, guilt-ridden.

contrition *n.* remorse, regret, sorrow, penitence.

contrivance *n.* **1.** plan, stratagem, ploy, artifice, ruse. **2.** mechanism, gadget, device, contraption, apparatus, implement, invention.

contrive *v.* invent, devise, improvise, create; conspire, intrigue, hatch, plot.

contrived *adj.* artificial, labored, false, forced, overdone, strained, mannered; *ant.* natural.

control *n.* power, dominion, government, sway, rule, force; management, guidance, supervision.

control *v.* **1.** restrain, master, repress, command, constrain. **2.** direct, manage, guide, lead, instruct, advise.

controller *n.* administrator, executive, executor.

controversial *adj.* debatable, suspect, dubious, disputable, questionable, arguable, problematic, doubtful, controvertible; *ant.* certain.

controversy *n.* debate, argument, strife, dissension, polemic, quarrel, wrangling; *ant.* accord, agreement.

controvert *v.* deny, dispute, contradict, counter, oppose, argue against, refute, gainsay; *ant.* affirm.

contumely *n.* invective, derision, insult, affront, indignity, humiliation, insolence, contempt, scorn, disdain, abuse, obloquy; *ant.* civility.

conundrum *n.* puzzle, enigma, riddle, paradox.

convalescence *n.* recuperation, recovery, rehabilitation, healing, improvement, restoration.

convene *v.* assemble, gather, muster, convoke, summon, meet, congregate, rally, get together.

convenience *n.* serviceability, ease, accommodation, benefit, comfort, amenity; enjoyment, satisfaction, leisure; *ant.* hindrance.

convenient *adj.* **1.** serviceable, favorable, conducive, useful, adaptable, ready, opportune, available, commodious, appropriate; *ant.* inconvenient, awkward. **2.** accessible, central, handy, nearby, nigh, proximate, adjacent, adjoining; *ant.* distant, far.

convention *n.* **1.** assembly, gathering, meeting, convocation. **2.** tradition, custom, practice, habit, usage, fashion, precept.

conventional *adj.* **1.** accepted, customary, standard, routine, commonplace, prevalent, predominant, established, sanctioned; *ant.* atypical, unusual. **2.** trite, banal, commonplace, pedestrian.

converge *v.* meet, coincide, join, merge, funnel, combine; focus, concur, agree; *ant.* disperse.

convergence *n.* concurrence, conjunction, union, concentration, confluence, intersection; *ant.* divergence.

conversant *adj.* informed, learned, acquainted, familiar, versed, knowledgeable, practiced, proficient; *ant.* ignorant.

conversation *n.* talk, dialogue, chat, exchange, communication, discourse, tête-à-tête, discussion, powwow, colloquy, intercourse, interlocution.

converse *v.* speak, talk, chat, confabulate, discuss, confer, parley.

converse *n.* antithesis, opposite, reverse, contrary.

converse *adj.* transposed, reversed, contrary, antipodal.

conversion *n.* change, metamorphosis, transformation, rebirth, transfiguration, permutation, reconstruction.

convert *n.* disciple, proselyte, neophyte.

convert *v.* adapt, appropriate, change, modify, remodel, reorganize, restyle, revise, transmogrify.

convertible *adj.* adjustable, adaptable, exchangeable.

convex *adj.* rounded, protuberant, tumid, bulging; *ant.* concave.

convey *v.* **1.** transport, carry, bear, bring, fetch, dispatch. **2.** transmit, communicate, forward, disclose, impart, relate, send.

convict *n.* criminal, prisoner, felon, malefactor, culprit, *slang:* con, jailbird.

convict *v.* condemn, sentence, consign.

conviction *n.* belief, persuasion, faith, doctrine, holding, contention.

convince *v.* persuade, sway, influence, satisfy, reassure, confirm, win over.

convincing *adj.* **1.** plausible, cogent, likely, presumable, rational, reasonable. **2.** reliable, credible, dependable, trustworthy, believable.

convivial *adj.* genial, cheerful, festive, jovial, merry, cordial, friendly, lively, sociable; *ant.* taciturn.

convocation *n.* congress, assembly, congregation, council, synod, meeting, conclave, concourse.

convoluted *adj.* complicated, involved, intricate, complex, tangled, twisted, winding; *ant.* straightforward.

convoy *n.* fleet, escort, train, guard, protection.

convulsion *n.* seizure, paroxysm, spasm, tremor, fit, contortion, throe, contraction, cramp.

cook *v.* bake, heat, boil, steam, grill, roast, brew, broil, fry, sauté, stew.

cook up *v.* concoct, devise, contrive, invent, plan, improvise, fabricate.

cool *(slang) n.* poise, composure, control, discipline, self-possession.

cool *v.* **1.** chill, freeze, refrigerate; *ant.* heat, thaw. **2.** calm, temper, mitigate, allay, moderate, abate; *ant.* instigate, anger.

cool *adj.* **1.** cold, chilly, frosty, refrigerated, wintry, biting; *ant.* tepid. **2.** calm, imperturbable, composed, unruffled, unflappable. **3.** aloof, detached, distant, frigid, indifferent, standoffish, reserved, uninvolved.

coop *n.* pen, cage, enclosure, box, hutch, pound, paddock.

coop *v.* confine, impound, cage, jail, incarcerate, imprison.

cooperate *v.* **1.** combine, unite, pool, join, collaborate, conspire; *ant.* diverge, differ. **2.** share, contribute, assist, reinforce, sustain, encourage; *ant.* hinder, hamper.

cooperation *n.* **1.** collaboration, interaction, teamwork, pulling together, alliance, partnership, association, confederacy, fusion, coalition, federation; *ant.* discord, separation. **2.** assistance, support, participation, aid, service.

cooperative *n.* commune, kibbutz, collective, association, organization, co-op.

cooperative *adj.* **1.** helpful, supportive, useful, assisting, pitching in. **2.** collective, joint, shared, united, unified, synergetic; *ant.* independent.

coordinate *v.* organize, harmonize, integrate, synchronize, correlate, match, relate, arrange, codify, grade, graduate.

coordinate *adj.* correspondent, parallel, equivalent, correlative, coequal, equal.

cope *v.* manage, control, handle; survive, carry on, get by, make do.

copious *adj.* abundant, ample, bountiful, plentiful, profuse, lavish, liberal, luxuriant, overflowing; *ant.* meager, scarce.

copulate *v.* mate, couple, have sex, make love, fornicate, sleep together.

copulation *n.* sexual intercourse, fornication, coitus, sex, congress.

copy *n.* reproduction, replica, likeness, facsimile, duplicate, clone, carbon, photocopy; forgery, counterfeit; *ant.* original.

copy *v.* **1.** imitate, model, pattern, mimic, emulate, mirror, echo, ape, parrot. **2.** duplicate, counterfeit, plagiarize, replicate, simulate, transcribe, repeat, borrow.

coquettish *adj.* coy, flirtatious, wanton, dallying, teasing.

cord *n.* **1.** rope, twine, string, fiber, cordage. **2.** bond, tie, link, union, nexus, yoke, coupling.

cordial *adj.* affable, genial, pleasant, sociable, warm, friendly, inviting, welcoming, cheerful, hospitable; *ant.* cool, aloof, hostile.

cordon *n.* fence, barrier, chain, line, ring.

cordon *v.* enclose, surround, encircle, fence, pen, hem, separate, isolate.

core *n.* essence, heart, kernel, gist, pith; center, hub, focus, pivot.

corner *n.* **1.** bend, curve, angle. **2.** recess, niche, nook, indentation.

around the corner impending, immediate, near, nearby, close.

cut corners reduce, cut down *or* back, decrease, economize, tighten one's belt.

corny *adj.* banal, clichéd, sentimental, hackneyed, trite, commonplace, stale, feeble, maudlin, old-fashioned, platitudinous; *ant.* original, fresh, new.

corollary *n.* **1.** inference, deduction, conclusion, derivation, implication, analogy, judgment. **2.** consequence, upshot, derivative, development, result, by-product, culmination.

corporal *adj.* corporeal, bodily, fleshly, carnal.

corporate *adj.* collective, collaborative, communal, joint, shared, united, allied.

corporation *n.* association, conglomerate, body, society, council.

corporeal *adj.* material, physical, substantial, embodied, actual, concrete, tangible, somatic, bodily, carnal, mortal; *ant.* spiritual.

corps *n.* company, unit, regiment, division, contingent, troop, detachment, squad, brigade, crew, team, squadron.

corpse *n.* cadaver, remains, body, skeleton, carcass.

corpulent *adj.* overweight, portly, stout, obese, bulky, rotund, plump, fleshy, adipose; *ant.* slim, svelte, trim.

corpus *n.* compilation, collection, body, oeuvre, whole, aggregation, entirety.

corral *n.* enclosure, stall, pound, coop.

correct *v.* **1.** remedy, repair, rectify, mend, redress, amend, reconstruct, edit, reform, ameliorate. **2.** reprimand, discipline, admonish, chastise, punish, reprove, castigate, chide.

correct *adj.* **1.** accurate, exact, true, factual, right. **2.** proper, appropriate, suitable, fitting, becoming; *ant.* unseemly.

correction *n.* revision, adjustment, modification, alteration, emendation.

corrective *adj.* therapeutic, medicinal, rehabilitative, curative, restorative, palliative, remedial; educative, disciplinary, punitive.

correctness *n.* **1.** accuracy, precision, exactitude, truth. **2.** propriety, decorum, decency.

correlate *v.* connect, associate, equate, correspond, compare.

correlation *n.* reciprocity, interdependence, interchange, alternation, mutuality, quid pro quo.

correspond *v.* **1.** agree, harmonize, match, tally, concur, coincide. **2.** (be a counterpart) compare, match, resemble, be equivalent to.

correspondence *n.* accord, conformity, agreement, equivalence, harmony, consonance.

correspondent *n.* **1.** pen pal, letter writer, friend. **2.** journalist, contributor, reporter, writer, freelancer.

correspondent *adj.* analogous, comparable, parallel, like, equivalent, correlative, reciprocal, coterminous.

corridor *n.* hallway, aisle, passage, passageway, lobby, foyer, vestibule.

corroborate *v.* authenticate, confirm, substantiate, validate, support, endorse, sustain, ratify, establish, prove; *ant.* contradict.

corrode *v.* decay, rust, deteriorate, oxidize, erode, crumble, eat away, degenerate; consume, waste, destroy.

corrosive *adj.* 1. acidic, eroding, caustic, destructive. 2. sarcastic, scathing, caustic, incisive, cutting, biting, trenchant, vitriolic.

corrugated *adj.* grooved, creased, channeled, ribbed, folded, ridged, fluted, wrinkled, furrowed, scored, crenelated; *ant.* flat, even.

corrupt *v.* 1. disgrace, vitiate, demean, deprave, defile, abuse, pervert, violate, ravage; *ant.* purify, restore. 2. falsify, misrepresent, fabricate, color, counterfeit, adulterate, forge, fix, doctor.

corrupt *adj.* 1. immoral, debased, low, degraded, evil, wicked, reprobate, wanton; fraudulent, unscrupulous, dishonest, venal, mercenary, nefarious. 2. (said of language, documents, etc.) inaccurate, fallacious, deceptive, misleading, adulterated, expurgated, bowdlerized.

corruption *n.* 1. immorality, decadence, debauchery, vice, depravity, iniquity, turpitude. 2. dishonesty, fraud, distortion.

cosmetic *adj.* superficial, nonessential, surface; *ant.* necessary, important.

cosmic *adj.* immense, vast, boundless, infinite, illimitable, limitless, measureless; sweeping, global.

cosmopolitan *adj.* international, worldly, urbane, sophisticated, well-traveled, universal, catholic; *ant.* parochial, insular.

cosmos *n.* galaxy, universe, creation.

cost *n.* 1. price, expense, expenditure, outlay, payment, disbursement, figure, charge, amount, value, worth. 2. loss, penalty, harm, damage, sacrifice, hurt, detriment, deprivation.

cost *v.* require, necessitate, obligate.

costly *adj.* 1. expensive, valuable, dear, precious, lavish, opulent, splendid, excessive,

steep, exorbitant; *ant.* cheap. 2. disastrous, catastrophic, ruinous, harmful, damaging.

costs *n.* expenses, overhead, budget.

costume *n.* attire, ensemble, vestment, apparel, raiment, garb, livery, robes, uniform, get-up.

costume *v.* dress, outfit, clothe, garb, attire, don, array.

coterie *n.* group, circle, clique, camp, set, caucus, gang.

cottage *n.* bungalow, cabin, shack, lodge, chalet, hut, croft.

couch *n.* sofa, divan, davenport, settee, chaise longue *or* lounge, ottoman, daybed.

couch *v.* 1. cradle, support, bear. 2. express, phrase, word, voice, utter, frame.

cough *v.* convulse, choke, hack, bark.

cough up deliver, pay, surrender, hand over, shell out.

council *n.* assembly, meeting, conclave, conference, congress, synod, colloquy.

counsel *v.* advise, advocate, recommend, suggest, exhort, direct; confer, consult, deliberate, parley.

counselor *n.* 1. adviser, guide, mentor, instructor, teacher. 2. attorney, counsel, lawyer, advocate, solicitor, barrister.

count *n.* sum, total, result, outcome, aggregate, tally.

count *v.* 1. calculate, compute, tally, reckon, enumerate, estimate, add, score, include, weigh. 2. consider, judge, deem, hold, regard, esteem, rate, ascribe, impute.

count off number, check, total.

count on trust, heed, rely *or* depend on, expect from.

count out remove, eliminate, ignore, pass over.

countenance *n.* 1. appearance, aspect, demeanor, mien, expression, look, air, face, features, physiognomy, visage. 2. approval, sanction, encouragement, assistance, favor.

countenance *v.* endorse, sanction, approve, condone, tolerate, endure, support, encourage, champion, abet, back.

counter *v.* answer, respond, retort, meet, return, offset, parry, thwart, resist, retaliate, conflict, contrast.

counter *adj.* adverse, contrary, antithetical, opposed, contradictory, reverse, opposite.

counteract *v.* annul, negate, frustrate, hinder, invalidate, foil, resist, oppose, defeat.

counterbalance *v.* neutralize, offset, equalize, counterpoise, countervail.

counterfeit *n.* copy, fake, fraud, imitation, reproduction, sham, phony.

counterfeit *v.* forge, imitate, feign, copy, falsify, simulate, cheat, deceive, dissemble, feign.

counterfeit *adj.* **1.** forged, false, fictitious, spurious, ersatz, bogus, fake, pseudo. **2.** insincere, assumed, pretended, affected, sham, mock, artificial, staged, put-on.

countermand *v.* annul, reverse, repeal, cancel, abrogate, override, rescind, revoke.

counterpart *n.* complement, supplement, correlative, duplicate, clone, equal, fellow, mate, match, twin, doppelgänger.

countless *adj.* infinite, endless, immeasurable, untold, innumerable, incalculable, multitudinous, myriad; *ant.* limited, numbered.

country *n.* **1.** backwoods, back country, range, bush, *slang:* sticks, boondocks, boonies; *ant.* city. **2.** nation, land, sovereign state.

country *adj.* agrarian, rural, pastoral, rustic, bucolic, arcadian; *ant.* urban.

county *n.* district, province, region.

coup *n.* **1.** achievement, accomplishment, masterstroke, maneuver, plot, stratagem. **2.** revolution, overthrow, revolt, coup d'état.

couple *n.* pair, due, two, set, brace.

couple *v.* connect, link, yoke, marry, pair, attach, fasten, unite, conjoin.

courage *n.* **1.** bravery, fearlessness, valor, heroism, daring, intrepidity, heart, audacity, guts; *ant.* cowardice, timidity. **2.** resolution, fortitude, firmness, mettle, endurance, determination, sufferance.

courageous *adj.* brave, daring, bold, heroic, gallant, dauntless, intrepid, hardy, valiant, audacious, resolute, indomitable; *ant.* cowardly, fearful.

courier *n.* envoy, carrier, emissary, messenger, herald, runner, representative, bearer.

course *n.* **1.** route, passage, path, trajectory, way, road, channel, artery. **2.** program, curriculum, subject, education, studies, matriculation.

in due course properly, appropriately, conveniently.

in the course of while, during, when.

as a matter of course ordinarily, commonly, regularly, customarily.

of course certainly, definitely, naturally, no doubt, undoubtedly, obviously, surely, indeed.

off course misdirected, erratic, wrong.

on course on target, correct, accurate.

court *n.* **1.** patio, square, quadrangle, plaza, piazza. **2.** tribunal, bench, magistrate, bar, session.

court *v.* **1.** woo, entice, attract, flirt, pursue, follow, make time with, chase, date. **2.** flatter, please, grovel, fawn, kowtow, ingratiate, toady, pander, praise, supplicate. **3.** (risk bringing on something unpleasant) tempt, lure, provoke, incite.

courteous *adj.* considerate, gracious, polite, civil, mannerly, refined, affable, urbane, genteel; *ant.* rude, ill-mannered.

courtesy *n.* kindness, consideration, compassion, generosity, respect, deference, attention, favor; *ant.* selfishness.

courtly *adv.* **1.** chivalric, gallant, flattering, obsequious, obliging. **2.** ceremonious, elegant, refined, decorous, dignified, polite, formal, polished; *ant.* provincial, rough.

cove *n.* **1.** lagoon, bay, inlet, sound. **2.** cave, cavern, hole, nook.

covenant *n.* contract, pact, promise, commitment, bond, agreement, compact, concordat, deed, treaty.

covenant *v.* pledge, agree, stipulate, engage, undertake.

cover *n.* **1.** canopy, lid, awning, tarpaulin, canvas, tent. **2.** shelter, protection, refuge, asylum, camouflage, defense, umbrella, shield.

cover *v.* **1.** envelop, wrap, hide, protect, screen, shield, submerge, disguise, encase. **2.** (extend, as to meet certain conditions) satisfy, meet, suffice, reach, embrace. **3.** deal with, treat, include, incorporate, comprise, contain, explore, record, note.

coverage *n.* **1.** insurance, protection, assurance. **2.** treatment, attention, analysis, reporting, description.

covering *n.* blanket, layer, wrap, cocoon, casing, sheath, clothing.

covert *adj.* secret, clandestine, surreptitious, hidden, ulterior, sneaky, stealthy, dissembled, veiled; *ant.* open, public.

coverup n. pretext, cloak, front, whitewash, smoke screen.

covert v. crave, desire, fancy, want, lust, yearn, thirst, hunger.

covetous adj. greedy, rapacious, avaricious, acquisitive, venal, insatiable, mercenary; ant. generous.

covey n. flock, bevy, cluster, flight, skein.

coward n. caitiff, recreant, dastard, poltroon, sissy, slang: wimp, chicken, yellow-belly.

cowardice n. fearfulness, timidity, pusillanimity; ant. bravery, valor.

cowardly adv. fearful, craven, trembling, yellow, lily-livered, timorous, irresolute, spineless, gutless, wimpy (slang); ant. brave, heroic, intrepid.

cower v. cringe, grovel, quail, skulk, tremble, shrink, flinch, shake, shiver.

coy adj. 1. coquettish, flirtatious, affected, cutesy; ant. sober. 2. prim, demure, prudish, reserved, timid, virginal, modest, diffident; ant. forward, impudent.

cozy adj. comfortable, snug, secure, safe, sheltered, warm, intimate; ant. cold, desolate.

crack n. 1. crevice, fissure, cleft, rift, break, split, cut, chink. 2. blow, hit, thwack, stroke. 3. joke, wisecrack, remark, return, witticism, jest.

crack v. 1. split, sever, break, cleave, rend, burst. 2. strike, punch, clip, slap, clap, clout, pop. 3. solve, decode, answer, figure out.

crack down on suppress, crush, subdue, check, stop, end.

crack up 1. collide, smash, crash, break up. 2. (slang) laugh, roar, howl.

crackdown n. repression, suppression, clampdown, end.

crackpot n. eccentric, crank, screwball, nut, loon, oddball, weirdo (slang).

cradle n. 1. crib, bassinet, trundle bed. 2. origin, spring, source, fountain, well.

craft n. 1. skill, art, ability, aptitude, proficiency, competence, adeptness, ingenuity, artisanship. 2. artifice, guile, cunning, deceit, duplicity, trickery; ant. naiveté. 3. trade, occupation, career, vocation, metier.

craftsman n. artisan, smith, wright, maker, technician.

craftsmanship n. skill, artistry, workmanship, mastery, expertise, technique, artisanship.

crafty adj. shrewd, devious, insidious, sly, subtle, canny, sharp, wily, deep; ant. naive, open.

crag n. cliff, tor, peak, bluff, pinnacle, palisade.

craggy adj. jagged, rugged, precipitous, broken, rough, rocky, stony; ant. even, smooth.

cram v. 1. stuff, jam, press, compact. 2. gorge, satiate, devour. 3. study, read, review.

cramp n. spasm, stitch, contraction, twinge, kink, convulsion, crick, pang.

cramp v. hinder, restrict, obstruct, inhibit.

cramped adj. 1. narrow, restricted, confining; ant. comfortable, roomy. 2. crowded, packed, jammed, congested.

cranky adj. irritable, surly, cross, testy, splenetic, crotchety, peevish, cantankerous, choleric, ill-tempered; ant. pleasant, sensible.

crash n. 1. clash, bang, clatter, din, clap, boom. 2. collision, wreck, accident, crackup, pileup, fender-bender.

crash v. 1. smash, shatter, break, splinter, demolish. 2. collide, wreck, rear-end, jar, hit, jolt, bang. 3. overturn, plunge, tumble, pitch, dive, hurtle, spill, drop.

crass adj. coarse, crude, rough, vulgar, indelicate, obtuse, boorish, insensitive, ungracious, ill-mannered, brusque; ant. tactful, subtle.

crave v. 1. need, desire, want, hanker, covet, lust for, demand. 2. beg, plead, ask, entreat, implore.

craven adj. cowardly, fearful, scared, lily-livered, yellow, timorous, spineless, wimpy (slang); ant. courageous, fearless.

craving n. desire, yearning, urge, longing, appetite, hunger, hankering, lust, thirst, yen; ant. dislike, distaste.

crawl v. 1. creep, squirm, slither, writhe, wriggle. 2. plod, lag, hang back, poke. 3. grovel, fawn, cringe.

crawling adj. swarming, teeming, crowded, overrun.

craze n. infatuation, rage, fad, trend, fashion, vogue; passion, mania, obsession, preoccupation, frenzy.

crazy adj. 1. insane, demented, deranged, mad, touched, delirious, hysterical, raving, *slang:* nuts, loony, loco, bananas, bonkers, out to lunch; *ant.* sane, rational. **2.** peculiar, bizarre, outrageous, eccentric, fatuous, ludicrous; *ant.* sensible, prudent. **3.** zealous, enthusiastic, wild, eager, ardent, smitten, devoted.

creak *v.* screech, scratch, grate, squeak, grind, rasp, scratch.

cream *n.* best, finest, elite, choice, pick, favorite, top drawer.

creamy *adj.* smooth, oily, buttery, luscious, velvety, rich.

crease *n.* line, wrinkle, tuck, groove, ridge, rumple, fold.

crease *v.* fold, crinkle, corrugate, crimp, crumple, ply.

create *v.* produce, engender, beget, generate, originate, initiate, start, develop, spawn, mother, father, formulate, invent; *ant.* destroy.

creation *n.* **1.** universe, cosmos, nature. **2.** birth, conception, genesis, formation, formulation.

creative *adj.* **1.** imaginative, artistic, aesthetic, gifted, talented, endowed, inventive, original. **2.** productive, fertile, fruitful, propagative, prolific, fecund.

creativity *n.* imagination, inventiveness, originality, artistry, talent, ingenuity, originality, vision.

creator *n.* maker, inventor, author, designer, framer, originator, architect, father, mother.

creature *n.* **1.** animal, brute, beast. **2.** being, individual, mortal, person, soul, wretch, wight.

credence *n.* confidence, belief, faith, support, trust, assurance, reliance; *ant.* distrust.

credentials *n.* accreditation, authorization, qualifications, endorsement, testament, attestation.

credibility *n.* **1.** reliability, integrity, veracity, trustworthiness. **2.** likelihood, chance, prospect, probability, possibility, tenability; *ant.* implausibility.

credible *adj.* **1.** likely, feasible, probable, conceivable, seeming. **2.** sincere, honest, trustworthy, reliable, dependable, believable.

credit *n.* **1.** faith, trust, belief, confidence, reliance, credence. **2.** reputation, repute, honor, prestige, esteem.

give one credit for recognize, congratulate, praise.

credit *v.* **1.** believe, trust, have faith in, rely

on. **2.** attribute, ascribe, accredit, impute, charge to, trace to, saddle with, blame.

creditable *adj.* admirable, honorable, respectable, commendable, deserving, worthy, laudable, exemplary, praiseworthy; *ant.* shameful, blameworthy.

creditor *n.* lender, banker, lessor, debtee.

credulity *n.* naiveté, gullibility, simplicity, innocence, ignorance; *ant.* skepticism.

credulous *adj.* naive, unsuspecting, gullible, trusting, innocent, green, born yesterday, wide-eyed, unwary; *ant.* skeptical, suspicious.

creed *n.* belief, doctrine, credo, dogma, principles, conviction, tenets, persuasion, faith.

creek *n.* stream, brook, inlet, tributary, rivulet, branch, rill.

creep *v.* **1.** cower, cringe, wince, shrink, flinch, grovel, fawn, skulk, quail. **2.** (move slowly) crawl, inch, dawdle, drag, edge. **3.** (move stealthily) sneak, steal, slink, slither, writhe, tiptoe.

creepy *adj.* disturbing, eerie, weird, sinister, frightening, menacing, ominous, gruesome, macabre, scary, hair-raising; *ant.* pleasant.

crest *n.* **1.** tuft, plume, feather. **2.** top, peak, summit, culmination, pinnacle, apex.

crestfallen *adj.* dejected, depressed, despondent, disconsolate, dispirited, downcast, morose, melancholy, woebegone; *ant.* elated, encouraged.

crevice *n.* cleft, fissure, split, rift, crack, chink, cranny, slit, breach, gap.

crew *n.* company, team, assemblage, corps, band, gang, crowd, clique, troupe.

crick *n.* cramp, spasm, twinge, stiffness, sprain.

crime *n.* offense, violation, iniquity, trespass, misconduct, wrong, vice, villainy, outrage, felony, misdemeanor.

criminal *n.* convict, offender, felon, culprit, delinquent, malefactor, sinner, transgressor, perpetrator, crook, *slang:* perp, con.

criminal *adj.* illegal, felonious, corrupt, lawless, indictable, immoral, iniquitous, culpable, deplorable, nefarious, vicious; *ant.* lawful, righteous, upright.

crimp *v.* **1.** crease, wrinkle, coil, fold, pleat. **2.** curl, wave, set, undulate, flow. **3.** hinder, impede, thwart, check, encumber, retard.

cringe *v.* **1.** wince, quail, flinch, recoil, quiver,

cripple

cripple *v.* **1.** damage, impair, sabotage, inca-
paciate, halt, ruin, destroy. **2.** paralyze, disable, maim, debilitate, enfeeble.

crisis *n.* **1.** emergency, plight, exigency, catastrophe, predicament, quandary, disaster, dilemma, strait. **2.** climax, culmination, height.

crisp *adj.* **1.** neat, tidy, spruce, orderly, clean.
2. brisk, invigorating, bracing, stimulating,
refreshing.

criterion *n.* standard, measure, gauge, yardstick, rule, guideline, principle, parameter.

critic *n.* **1.** censor, detractor, slanderer, defamer, mudslinger (*slang*); *ant.* supporter, believer. **2.** connoisseur, dilettante, arbiter, expert, judge, reviewer.

critical *adj.* **1.** discerning, perceptive, observant, penetrating, judicious, perspicacious.
2. faultfinding, cynical, disparaging, censorious, carping, cavilling, sharp, captious,
choleric, trenchant; *ant.* flattering, encouraging. **3.** important, decisive, significant, crucial, deciding, climactic. **4.** dangerous, perilous, risky, hazardous.

criticism *n.* **1.** judgment, evaluation, appraisal,
analysis, study, examination. **2.** objection,
faultfinding, censure, cavilling, carping. **3.** review, critique, exposition, treatise, dissertation.

criticize *v.* **1.** analyze, examine, study, scrutinize, probe. **2.** reprimand, chastise, censure,
find fault, reprove, pillory, flay, pan, bad-
mouth (*slang*), rake.

critique *n.* analysis, evaluation, review, commentary, examination, assessment.

croak (*slang*) *v.* die, pass away, perish, expire,
kick the bucket (*slang*).

crony *adj.* friend, colleague, associate, companion, sidekick, accomplice, ally, follower, henchman, pal, buddy.

crook *n.* **1.** bend, curve, arc, hook, bow, notch,
angle. **2.** criminal, thief, swindler, rogue.

crooked *adj.* **1.** curved, bowed, bent, sinuous,
serpentine, tortuous, hooked, twisted; *ant.*
straight, direct. **2.** dishonest, corrupt, iniquitous, nefarious.

crop *n.* harvest, yield, produce, growth, gathering, vintage.

cruel

crop *v.* cut, clip, lop, snip, mow, pare, prune,
shear.

crop up arrive, happen, occur, arise, emerge.

cross *n.* **1.** ordeal, difficulty, tribulation, affliction, adversity, trial, misfortune. **2.** hybrid,
mongrel, half-breed, mixture, crossbreed.

cross *v.* **1.** traverse, pass, span, ford. **2.** oppose, thwart, frustrate, foil, hinder, check,
interfere. **3.** mix, hybridize, pollinate, inter-
breed, blend, mingle.

cross-examine *v.* interrogate, question, quiz,
catechize, pump, grill.

crotchety *adj.* irritable, grumpy, curmud-
geonly, peevish, cantankerous, difficult, contrary, crabby, surly, fractious, testy; *ant.* pleasant, agreeable.

crouch *v.* **1.** bend, squat, kneel, stoop, bow,
duck, hunch. **2.** cower, grovel, quail, cringe,
wince, flinch.

crow *v.* **1.** boast, brag, exalt, gloat, cry. **2.**
squawk, caw, cackle.

crowd *n.* **1.** multitude, throng, mob, pack,
host, legion, assembly, confluence. **2.** clique,
set, circle, coterie.

crowd *v.* **1.** mass, cram, pack, huddle, pile,
press, squeeze. **2.** elbow, shove, push, jostle,
shoulder, butt. **3.** congregate, gather, assemble, muster, flock.

crowded *adj.* busy, populous, congested,
packed, full, jammed, cramped, overflowing;
ant. empty.

crown *n.* **1.** top, apex, summit, crest. **2.** royalty, monarch, sovereign, queen, king, potentate, emperor.

crown *v.* perfect, fulfil, consummate, cap,
complete, finish, terminate.

crowning *adj.* ultimate, consummate, supreme,
culminating, climactic.

crucial *adj.* vital, urgent, critical, key, pressing,
central, momentous, pivotal, decisive; *ant.* superfluous, marginal.

crucify *v.* torment, torture, persecute, harrow,
brutalize, execute, kill.

crude *adj.* **1.** rude, rough, coarse, rudimentary, sketchy, homemade, makeshift, rough-
hewn, raw; *ant.* refined. **2.** vulgar, coarse,
uncouth, gross, churlish, crass; suggestive, provocative, insulting.

cruel *adj.* ruthless, brutal, sadistic, ferocious,

vicious, fierce, harsh, callous, bitter, malevolent, remorseless, psychopathic; *ant.* gentle, kind, humane.

cruelty *n.* barbarity, severity, depravity, savagery, inhumanity, tyranny, bestiality, sadism, spite, venom; *ant.* compassion, pity, mercy.

crumb *n.* morsel, scrap, bit, speck, grain, particle, iota, jot, sliver, atom, dab, soupçon.

crumble *v.* 1. collapse, deteriorate, break up, fragment, come *or* fall apart, disintegrate, degenerate, decay, go to pieces. 2. granulate, crush, powder, pulverize, pound.

crummy *adj.* rotten, cheap, shoddy, inferior, trashy, crude, worthless, miserable, useless, meretricious, second-rate; *ant.* excellent.

crumpled *v.* crinkled, creased, wrinkled, crushed, puckered, rumpled.

crunch (*slang*) *n.* crisis, emergency, pinch, bind, spot, hot spot (*slang*).

crusade *n.* campaign, expedition, undertaking, cause, movement, holy war, jihad.

crusader *n.* reformer, campaigner, missionary, champion, zealot, enthusiast, advocate, fighter.

crush *v.* 1. smash, crumple, pulverize, granulate, powder. 2. defeat, overwhelm, annihilate, subdue, quell, vanquish; oppress, persecute, subjugate.

crust *n.* coating, exterior, rind, shell, hull, scab, surface, film, patina.

crusty *adj.* 1. crisp, hard, brittle; *ant.* soft, soggy. 2. brusque, gruff, cantankerous, surly, short-tempered, irritable, peevish, captious, curt, choleric, testy; *ant.* calm, pleasant.

crux *n.* core, heart, essence, gist, pith, sine qua non.

cry *n.* 1. exclamation, outcry, clamor, shout, call, whoop, scream, holler, cheer, squall, uproar, yelp; *ant.* whisper, murmur. 2. weeping, sobbing, lamentation, tears.

a far cry unlike, dissimilar, opposed (to), different.

cry *v.* 1. weep, sob, grieve, lament, whimper, fret, groan, wail, bawl, whine, snivel, bemoan; *ant.* laugh, rejoice, exult. 2. yell, shout, scream, shriek, howl, bellow, roar, hoot.

crypt *n.* tomb, vault, catacomb, mausoleum.

cryptic *adj.* puzzling, obscure, ambiguous, vague, hidden, arcane, abstruse, secret, enigmatic, covert, recondite, apocryphal; *ant.* clear, obvious.

crystallize *v.* form, take shape, materialize, appear, emerge; solidify, coalesce, harden.

cub *n.* whelp, babe, fledgling, lad, pup, youngster; beginner, learner, tyro, novice, recruit, greenhorn, whippersnapper, tenderfoot; *ant.* adult, veteran.

cubbyhole *n.* compartment, niche, pigeonhole, slot, hole, recess.

cuddle *v.* snuggle, hug, embrace, fondle, pet, nestle, clasp, cosset.

cuddly *adj.* huggable, lovable, cozy.

cudgel *n.* club, bludgeon, baton, shillelagh, truncheon.

cudgel *v.* beat, pummel, clobber, bludgeon, pound, maul, cane, drub, thrash.

cue *n.* 1. prompt, signal, sign, tip-off. 2. hint, lead, clue, intimation, innuendo, suggestion.

cuff *n.* blow, hit, slap, punch.

off the cuff extemporaneously, impromptu, ad hoc, on the spur of the moment, spontaneously, impulsively, offhand, unrehearsed.

cuff *v.* buffet, smack, box, strike, knock, whack, belt.

cul-de-sac *n.* dead end, blind alley, impasse, enclosure.

cull *v.* 1. choose, select, elect, pick out, winnow. 2. collect, gather, garner, glean, amass.

culminate *v.* climax, peak, consummate, finish, conclude, close, terminate, end; *ant.* begin, start.

culmination *n.* 1. conclusion, finale, finish. 2. peak, summit, acme, zenith, apogee.

culpability *n.* fault, guilt, blame, blot, lapse, peccability.

culprit *n.* criminal, offender, miscreant, felon, delinquent, lawbreaker, transgressor, malefactor, perpetrator, rascal.

cult *n.* sect, religion, denomination, school, faith, following.

cultivate *v.* 1. plant, till, garden, raise, grow, seed. 2. educate, refine, nurture, train, develop, improve, teach, civilize, enrich. 3. encourage, foster, advance, further, bolster.

cultivation *n.* 1. farming, agriculture, horticulture, gardening. 2. refinement, breeding, civility, culture, erudition; enhancement, enrichment, progress, advancement.

cultural *adj.* aesthetic, enlightening, edifying, artistic, educational, developmental, enriching.

culture *n.* **1.** civilization, society, custom, habit, convention, religion, history, human- ism, lore, arts, sciences. **2.** sophistication, re- finement, discrimination, savoir-faire, urban- ity, polish, finish, grace, breeding, gentility; *ant.* vulgarity, ignorance.

cultured *adj.* erudite, versed, accomplished, educated, urbane, well-bred, well-read; *ant.* ignorant.

cumbersome *adj.* burdensome, awkward, un- wieldy, bulky, clumsy, ponderous, hefty, in- commodious, onerous; *ant.* manageable, con- venient.

cunning *n.* **1.** guile, artifice, cleverness, trick- ery, slyness, duplicity. **2.** skill, proficiency, dexterity, craft, adroitness, finesse.

cunning *adj.* shrewd, devious, subtle, wily, deft, shifty, clever, ingenious, foxy, sharp; *ant.* naive, gullible.

cup *n.* mug, goblet, chalice, stein, tankard, vessel, grail, tumbler.

cupidity *n.* avarice, greed, covetousness, ac- quisitiveness, voracity, rapacity, craving, avid- ity, yearning.

curative *adj.* corrective, medicinal, restora- tive, therapeutic, alleviative, healing, reme- dial, salutary.

curator *n.* keeper, custodian, guardian.

curb *n.* **1.** barrier, restraint, hindrance, check, chain. **2.** edge, border, ledge, lip.

curb *v.* restrain, suppress, check, control, mod- erate, restrict, inhibit, retard, contain, subdue, impede; *ant.* encourage, foster.

curdle *v.* clot, sour, coagulate, congeal, thicken, condense, ferment, turn.

cure *n.* antidote, remedy, medication, nostrum, restorative.

cure *v.* **1.** heal, restore, mend, correct, re- lieve. **2.** preserve, salt, pickle, keep. **3.** harden, temper, fire, steel.

curio *n.* antique, curiosity, knickknack, trinket, bibelot.

curiosity *n.* **1.** inquisitiveness, concern, inter- est, questioning, investigation, prying, intru- siveness, nosiness. **2.** (an unusual thing) exoti- cism, rarity, wonder, phenomenon, marvel, spectacle.

curious *adj.* **1.** unusual, strange, odd, rare, exotic, queer, peculiar, remarkable, notable, extraordinary, signal, unique, novel. **2.** in- quisitive, interested, inquiring, playful, ques- tioning, prying, inquisitorial; *ant.* indifferent, apathetic.

curl *n.* ringlet, coil, spiral, wave, twist, helix, scroll.

curl *v.* **1.** twist, curve, bend, wind, loop, crimp, wreathe, meander, zigzag, entwine, twirl; *ant.* straighten.

curly *adj.* curled, kinky, wavy, coiled, wound.

currency *n.* money, coin, bank notes, cash, tender.

current *n.* drift, tidal motion, ebb and flow.

current *adj.* prevailing, general, widespread, common, rife, ubiquitous, popular, contempo- rary, fashionable, voguish, stylish, trendy, au courant.

curse *n.* oath, profanity, expletive, obscenity, execration, invective, malediction, vilification, cuss.

curse *v.* blaspheme, swear, profane, damn, excoriate, denounce, fulminate, revile, vituper- ate, imprecate.

cursed *adj.* **1.** damned, hexed, doomed, ill- fated, blighted, confounded, bewitched, ac- cursed. **2.** detestable, pernicious, villainous, infamous, abominable, odious, vile, disgust- ing, hateful, infernal, loathsome.

cursory *adj.* perfunctory, hasty, brief, careless, hurried, offhand, casual, summary, fleeting, superficial; *ant.* painstaking, thorough.

curt *adj.* abrupt, brusque, terse, blunt, laconic, gruff, short; *ant.* gracious.

curtail *v.* abbreviate, cut, lessen, pare, re- duce, truncate, circumscribe, restrict, de- crease, prune; *ant.* extend, prolong.

curtain *n.* drape, hanging, tapestry, arras, drap- ery, backdrop.

draw the curtain on finish, stop, halt.

lift the curtain on **1.** start, commence, ini- tiate. **2.** expose, uncover, disclose.

curtain *v.* hide, conceal, veil, screen, drape, shield, shroud, shutter.

curvaceous *adj.* shapely, voluptuous, slinky, buxom, comely, well-proportioned.

curve *n.* arc, bend, curvature, trajectory.

curve *v.* arch, twist, wind, spiral, swerve, hook, turn.

curved *adj.* rounded, bent, serpentine, bowed; *ant.* straight.

cushion *n.* pillow, buffer, pad, shock absorber.

cushion *v.* protect, dampen, soften, allay, absorb, support, buttress, cradle.

custodian *n.* superintendent, watchman, overseer, warden, guardian, protector, keeper, concierge.

custody *n.* **1.** guardianship, charge, protection, care, supervision, watch, tutelage, auspices, aegis, ward, keeping. **2.** detention, jail, confinement, house arrest.

take into custody apprehend, arrest, seize, capture.

custom *n.* tradition, observance, convention, manner, etiquette, ritual, habit, practice, rite, ceremony, wont, rule; *ant.* departure.

customary *adj.* wonted, habitual, usual, established, normal, ordinary, familiar, prevailing, routine, traditional, accepted; *ant.* rare, unusual.

customer *n.* patron, shopper, client, buyer, consumer, purchaser.

cut *n.* **1.** incision, severance, cleft, hack, slash, notch, slit. **2.** reduction, decrease, diminution, elision, omission. **3.** section, portion, slice, segment. **4.** (*slang*) insult, indignity, offense, abuse, snub.

a cut above superior, higher, better, more efficient *or* capable *or* competent.

cut *v.* **1.** sever, cleave, quarter, dissect, shear, behead, bisect, amputate, truncate, rive, hew. **2.** pierce, puncture, gash, wound, gouge, incise, perforate. **3.** curtail, delete, edit, condense, abridge, lessen, shorten. **4.** weaken, dilute, impair, undermine.

cut back **1.** decrease, reduce, curb, economize, lower, slash, lessen. **2.** prune, crop, trim.

cut down **1.** decrease, reduce, lower, diminish. **2.** fell, hew, level, lop, raze, **3.** kill, slaughter, slay, massacre.

cut off interrupt, break in, intrude, intervene.

cut out for suitable, fit, adequate, good for.

cut short **1.** terminate, stop, quit, halt, finish. **2.** interrupt, check, intercept. **3.** diminish, abbreviate, abridge, shorten.

cut-and-dried *adj.* fixed, settled, routine, prearranged, predetermined, sewn up.

cutback *n.* reduction, decrease, curtailment, shortening.

cute *adj.* delightful, dainty, pretty, charming, adorable.

cutthroat *adj.* vicious, savage, violent, harsh, ferocious, murderous; ruthless, merciless, unrelenting, unprincipled.

cycle *n.* succession, period, age, eon, epic, era.

cyclone *n.* hurricane, tornado, typhoon, twister, tempest, monsoon.

cynic *n.* skeptic, pessimist, misanthrope, critic, carper, satirist, doubting Thomas; *ant.* optimist, believer.

cynical *adj.* skeptical, distrustful, pessimistic, ridiculing, sardonic, sarcastic, scoffing, mocking, sneering.

cynicism *n.* acerbity, asperity, acrimony, despair, mordancy.

czar *n.* emperor, autocrat, despot, overlord, potentate.

dab n. bit, drop, trace, pat, speck, dollop, smidgen, fleck, touch.

dab v. blot, pat, daub, swab, wipe, touch.

dabble v. dally, toy, tinker, trifle, flirt, slang: dip into, fool with or around, putter around.

dabbler n. amateur, novice, beginner, tinkerer, dilettante; ant. expert, professional.

dad n. father, sire, papa, pop, progenitor, forebear, daddy, the old man (slang).

daft adj. 1. silly, foolish, stupid, ridiculous, idiotic, asinine, absurd, inane, simple; ant. bright. 2. insane, crazy, mad, demented, deranged, hysterical, lunatic, berserk, touched, slang: nuts, screwy; ant. sane.

dagger n. knife, blade, stiletto, bayonet.

daily adj. 1. diurnal, quotidian, per diem, circadian, periodic, cyclic. 2. commonplace, regular, routine, ordinary, normal, everyday, customary.

daily adv. every day, once a day, per diem, quotidian.

dainty adj. 1. delicious, tasty, choice, rare. 2. pretty, lovely, delicate, exquisite, petite, fine, charming, refined, cultured, tasteful, graceful, elegant, ladylike; ant. gross, rough. 3. finicky, fastidious, meticulous.

dairy n. dairy farm, creamery, pasteurizing plant.

dale n. valley, lowland, vale, glen, dell.

dalliance n. 1. flirting, toying, seduction, playing, trifling, puttering. 2. idling, dawdling, loitering, delay, loafing, procrastination, tarrying; ant. haste.

dally v. 1. dabble, toy, play, trifle (with), putter, flirt, sport. 2. dawdle, idle, loiter, procrastinate, linger, tarry, delay, dilly-dally.

dam n. dike, ditch, wall, bank, embankment, gate, levee, barrier, blockage, hindrance, obstruction.

dam v. obstruct, block, bar, barricade, confine, hold (back), check, retard, impede, hinder, clog.

damage n. 1. injury, harm, hurt, wrong, destruction, ruin, mutilation, devastation. 2. (consequences of being damaged) suffering, loss, misfortune; ant. repair, boon.

damage v. wreck, hurt, ruin, spoil, harm, injure, mar, deface, mutilate, tamper with, play havoc with, play hell with; ant. fix, repair.

damages n. compensation, costs, expenses, fine, reparation, reimbursement, indemnity, amercement.

damaging adj. harmful, hurtful, injurious, detrimental, ruinous, deleterious, pernicious; ant. advantageous, favorable, helpful.

damn v. 1. condemn, doom. 2. curse, blaspheme, revile; ant. bless. 3. criticize, denounce, censure, castigate; ant. praise.
not give a damn (slang) not care, be indifferent, reject, neglect.
not worth a damn worthless, valueless, useless, incorrigible.

damnable adj. sinful, abominable, wicked, despicable, cursed, accursed, hateful, atrocious, horrible, execrable, culpable, depraved.

damnation n. doom, condemnation, perdition, excommunication, ban, anathema, proscription, denunciation.

damned adj. 1. doomed, condemned, accursed; ant. blessed, saved. 2. bad, undesirable, lousy, reprobate, despicable, hateful, loathsome, detestable, infernal.

damning adj. incriminating, accusatorial, condemnatory, inculpatory, implicative, dooming, ruinous, serious, fatal.

damp n. wetness, moisture, humidity, fog, drizzle, mist, vapor, dew, clamminess, dankness; ant. dryness.

damp adj. 1. moist, wet, sodden, soggy, sopping, clammy, dank, dripping, dewy; ant.

D

dry. **2.** rainy, drizzly, cloudy, humid, wet, muggy, misty; *ant.* arid.

dampen *v.* **1.** wet, moisten, sprinkle, water, rinse, spray; *ant.* dry. **2.** discourage, dishearten, dispirit, dismay, depress, deter, stifle, dull, diminish, moderate; *ant.* encourage.

damper *n.* hindrance, depressant, restraint, bridle.

damsel *n.* maiden, maid, nymph, girl, lady, woman.

dance *v.* **1.** waltz, step, jig, hop, skip, jump, leap, bob, caper, bounce, cavort, sway. **2.** prom, dress ball, party, reception, social, hop.

dance to another tune change one's mind, backtrack, reverse oneself, do an about-face, shift gears, reconsider.

dander *n.* wrath, anger, temper, animosity, ire, spleen.

get one's dander up enrage, infuriate, anger, annoy.

dandy *n.* fop, coxcomb, dude, cavalier, man-about-town, buck.

dandy *adj.* great, excellent, fine, first-rate, splendid.

danger *n.* hazard, trouble, peril, menace, threat, jeopardy; *ant.* safety, security.

in danger vulnerable, threatened, exposed, in harm's way, endangered, imperiled, on thin ice.

dangerous *adj.* hazardous, treacherous, menacing, perilous, risky, precarious; *ant.* safe, secure.

dangle *v.* **1.** hang, drop, swing, sway, flap, wave. **2.** tempt, lure, tantalize, flaunt, flourish.

dank *adj.* damp, moist, clammy, wet, chilly, soggy, dripping, humid, close, slimy; *ant.* dry.

dapper *adj.* **1.** stylish, smart, neat, chic, spruce, well-dressed, well-groomed, spiffy (*slang*); *ant.* disheveled, scruffy, shabby, sloppy. **2.** spry, nimble, brisk, active, chipper.

dappled *adj.* spotted, speckled, dotted, flecked, mottled, piebald, freckled, variegated, stippled.

dare *v.* **1.** take a chance, chance, risk, venture, gamble, stake, try, attempt, endeavor, hazard, have the nerve (*slang*). **2.** defy, confront, oppose, challenge, brave.

daredevil *n.* adventurer, desperado, stuntman, stuntwoman.

daring *n.* spunk, courage, pluck, nerve, audacity, temerity, bravery, bravura, grit, guts, fearlessness, boldness, defiance; *ant.* cowardice, timidity.

daring *adj.* **1.** brave, fearless, bold, courageous, dauntless, adventurous, valiant, intrepid, plucky, game, venturesome; *ant.* afraid. **2.** impudent, forward, obtrusive, audacious, brazen; *ant.* timid.

dark *n.* **1.** darkness, gloom, murk, dimness, murkiness; *ant.* brightness. **2.** night, nighttime, nightfall, evening, dusk, twilight; *ant.* light, daytime.

in the dark ignorant, uninformed, unaware, naive.

dark *adj.* **1.** dim, shadowy, cloudy, foggy, gloomy, faint, vague, obscure; *ant.* bright, light, sunny, illuminated. **2.** secret, cryptic, hidden, mysterious, mystic, obscure, puzzling; *ant.* obvious, clear. **3.** evil, bad, immoral, corrupt, wicked, vile, sinister, satanic, occult, infernal, nefarious; *ant.* good.

keep dark hide, conceal, keep secret, obscure.

darken *v.* **1.** blacken, shade, shadow, cloud (over), eclipse, dim, obscure, overshadow, deepen; *ant.* brighten, lighten. **2.** deject, depress, sadden, dispirit.

darkness *n.* **1.** gloom, dark, dusk, murk, blackness, murkiness; *ant.* brightness, daylight. **2.** evil, wickedness, sin, corruption.

darling *n.* dear, dearest, sweetheart, beloved, love, pet, favorite, *slang:* sugar, honeybunch.

darling *adj.* dear, beloved, treasured, precious, adored, cherished.

darn *v.* **1.** curse, damn, abuse, blame, swear at. **2.** repair, patch (up), mend.

dart *n.* arrow, shaft, bolt, barb.

dart *v.* **1.** run, sprint, rush, bound, race, fly, dash. **2.** shoot, hurl, spring.

dash *n.* **1.** sprint, race, run. **2.** sprinkle, pinch, bit, taste, soupçon, little, hint, touch, trace, suggestion.

dash *v.* **1.** bludgeon, hit, beat, cudgel, smash, slam. **2.** discourage, dampen, dismay, dispirit, disappoint, frustrate, dishearten. **3.** sprint, race, speed, hurry, run, bound, dart, rush, fly, hasten, bolt, tear. **4.** shatter, ruin, break, destroy, splinter.

dash off rush, hurry, hasten.

dashing adv. 1. debonair, dapper, stylish, elegant, gallant, flamboyant, jaunty; ant. drab. 2. bold, lively, daring, spirited, plucky.

dastardly adj. despicable, mean, vile, contemptible, base, craven, low, sneaking, recreant, underhand; ant. noble.

data n. information, facts, figures, details, info (slang), statistics, input.

date n. 1. time, point in time, age, era, epoch, period, stage. 2. tryst, rendezvous; engagement, appointment, meeting.

out of date passé, old, obsolete, old-fashioned, outmoded, archaic, disused, ancient.

to date until now, as yet, so far.

up to date modern, contemporary, current, fashionable, à la mode.

date v. escort, accompany, attend, take out, keep company (with), consort with, go (out) with; go together, go steady.

dated adj. outdated, obsolete, outmoded, out-of-date, old-fashioned, passé, démodé, archaic, antiquated, obsolescent, out, superseded; ant. fashionable, up-to-the-minute.

daub n. spot, blotch, splotch, blot, stain, smear.

daub v. 1. paint, cover, coat, plaster. 2. smear, dirty, smudge, stain, sully, splatter, spatter.

daunt v. scare, frighten, intimidate, cow, terrify, unnerve, demoralize, discourage, dishearten, deter, dismay, dispirit; ant. encourage, hearten.

dauntless adj. courageous, fearless, brave, bold, gallant, heroic, resolute, intrepid, valiant, lionhearted, stouthearted, indomitable.

dawdle v. dally, loaf, idle, lag, loiter, fritter, dilly-dally; ant. hurry.

dawdler n. laggard, loiterer, loafer, lingerer.

dawn n. 1. morning, sunrise, daybreak, daylight, sunup, aurora; ant. dusk, sundown, sunset. 2. beginning, outset, onset, origin, birth, genesis, inception, start, rise, advent, emergence, dawning.

dawn v. start, begin, initiate, develop, emerge, appear, occur, originate, open, unfold, rise.

day n. era, epoch, time, period, age, generation.

call it a day finish, quit (working), end, stop, knock off (slang).

day after day continually, regularly, steadily, endlessly, perpetually, relentlessly, persistently, monotonously.

day by day gradually, steadily, progressively, little by little, slowly but surely.

day in and day out consistently, steadily, regularly, daily, every day.

daybreak n. dawn, sunrise, sunup, morning, first light, crack of dawn, dayspring; ant. sundown, sunset.

daydream n. reverie, fantasy, dream, pipe dream, musing, woolgathering; vision, phantasm, figment.

daydream v. fantasize, dream, imagine, muse, stargaze, fancy.

daze n. stupor, trance, confusion, bewilderment, shock, distraction.

daze v. dumbfound, shock, stun, paralyze, flabbergast, confuse, stupefy, astound, astonish, amaze, perplex, bewilder, stagger.

dazzle v. 1. fascinate, awe, amaze, astonish. 2. confuse, overwhelm, blind, daze, stupefy.

dazzling adj. 1. brilliant, shining, sparkling, scintillating, stunning, glittering, radiant, refulgent. 2. sensational, superb, splendid, sublime, virtuoso.

dead adj. 1. deceased, perished, expired, lifeless, late, defunct, cadaverous, no more (slang), mortified; ant. alive, animate. 2. numb, insensible, anesthetized, deadened, unconscious, unresponsive. 3. (slang) exhausted, tired, wearied, worn, spent.

deadbeat n. debtor, freeloader, sponger, bum, schmorrer (slang).

deaden v. muffle, repress, suppress, soften, alleviate, allay, abate, dim, dampen, mute, dull, quiet; ant. revitalize, invigorate, enliven.

deadlock n. impasse, stalemate, standstill.

deadly adv. 1. fatal, lethal, murderous, mortal, homicidal, destructive, deleterious, malignant, baneful, injurious; ant. healthful, reviving, beneficial. 2. tiresome, boring, tedious, dull, uninteresting, monotonous, wearisome.

deadpan adj. expressionless, impassive, blank, straight-faced, poker-faced, inscrutable, enigmatic.

deaf adj. oblivious, heedless, indifferent, unmoved, stubborn, obstinate; ant. concerned.

deafening adj. resounding, thunderous, piercinging, ear-piercing, ear-splitting, ringing, roaring, booming, fortissimo; *ant.* pianissimo, quiet.

deal *n.* 1. agreement, pledge, pact, bargain, contract, compromise, understanding. 2. opportunity, chance, fresh start.
a good deal a lot, quite a bit, a considerable amount, much.
make a big deal out of exaggerate, expand, magnify, blow up, *slang:* hype, puff.
deal *v.* 1. distribute, dispense, apportion, give, dole out, allot, divide, share, mete out. 2. trade, bargain, barter, buy, sell, negotiate, traffic.
deal in handle, trade in, specialize in, buy, sell.
deal with handle, cope with, manage, attend to, oversee, see to.

dealer *n.* merchant, vendor, businessperson, trader, wholesaler, marketer, bursar, merchandiser, monger.

dealings *n.* business, commerce, trade, traffic, transactions, intercourse, sales.

dear *adj.* 1. beloved, loved, precious, favorite, cherished, darling, treasured, familiar. 2. expensive, costly, high-priced, overpriced, pricey; *ant.* cheap.
dearly *adv.* 1. lovingly, affectionately, fondly, devotedly, tenderly, yearningly. 2. very, greatly, extremely, profoundly.

dearth *n.* shortage, lack, need, poverty, scarcity, inadequacy, deficiency, want, paucity, insufficiency; *ant.* abundance, excess.

death *n.* annihilation, obliteration, ruin, ruination, passing, demise, end, expiration, extinction, finish, fatality, departure, cessation; *ant.* birth, life.
at death's door dying, moribund, failing, wasting away.
to death much, very much, extremely, to the extreme.

deathless *adj.* eternal, never-ending, everlasting, timeless, undying, immortal, constant, imperishable.

debacle *n.* disaster, fiasco, collapse, defeat, rout, ruin, downfall, catastrophe, devastation, cataclysm.

debar *v.* 1. exclude, shut out, deny, segregate, expel, blackball; *ant.* admit. 2. obstruct, prohibit, prevent, stop, restrain, hamper.

debase *v.* lower, demean, shame, degrade, defile, depreciate, humiliate, humble, cheapen, bastardize, taint, pollute; *ant.* elevate, upgrade.

debased *adj.* corrupt, debauched, depraved, perverted, sordid, vile, degenerate, adulterated, degraded, polluted, devalued; *ant.* elevated, pure.

debatable *adj.* 1. (subject to disagreement) arguable, questionable, controversial, disputable, controvertible. 2. (not established as factual or genuine) unsettled, doubtful, uncertain, dubious, borderline, questionable.

debate *v.* 1. argue, discuss, deliberate, contest, contend, dispute, controvert, question; *ant.* agree. 2. ponder, ruminate, cogitate, consider, question.

debauch *v.* seduce, ravish, corrupt, violate, demoralize, pervert, deprave, pollute, ruin, subvert, vitiate; *ant.* purify.

debauched *adj.* perverted, wanton, licentious, corrupt, lewd, immoral, degenerate, profligate, depraved, debased, dissipated, dissolute; *ant.* decent, pure, virtuous.

debauchery *n.* 1. lust, excess, gluttony, overindulgence, immorality, licentiousness, depravity, wantonness. 2. orgy, riot, revel.

debilitate *v.* weaken, impair, wear out, exhaust, sap, prostrate, undermine, enervate, incapacitate, enfeeble, devitalize, unman; *ant.* strengthen.

debility *n.* infirmity, malaise, weakness, sickliness, frailty, feebleness, decrepitude, enervation, incapacity; *ant.* strength, vigor.

debonair *adj.* urbane, suave, dashing, elegant, charming, refined, courteous.

debris *n.* wreckage, remains, rubble, ruins, fragments, waste, litter, trash, rubbish, wreckage.

debt *n.* debit, liability, arrears, red ink, obligation, bill, commitment, due; *ant.* asset, credit.

debtor *n.* borrower, insolvent, mortgagor, defaulter, welsher (*slang*); *ant.* creditor, lender.

debunk *v.* ridicule, mock, lampoon, expose, puncture, deflate.

debut *n.* introduction, beginning, entrance, premiere, initiation, launching, inauguration.

decadence *n.* corruption, decline, degeneration, deterioration, fall, retrogression, decay, dissipation, dissolution; *ant.* wholesomeness.

decadent *adj.* immoral, self-indulgent, corrupt, debauched, depraved, debased, degenerate, dissolute, degraded; *ant.* moral.

decay *n.* **1.** decline, deterioration, spoilage, collapse, degeneracy, downfall, decadence, corruption, degeneration; *ant.* improvement. **2.** wasting away, depreciation, corrosion, disintegration; rotting, decomposition, putrefaction, spoilage; *ant.* preservation, germination.

decay *v.* **1.** deteriorate, degenerate, disintegrate, atrophy; *ant.* grow, ripen. **2.** waste away, rot, decompose, putrefy, spoil, corrode, molder; *ant.* flourish.

deceased *adj.* dead, gone, late, lost, departed, expired, defunct, extinct, lifeless, finished.

deceit *n.* deception, misrepresentation, artifice, fraud, fraudulence, fakery, sham, trickery, underhandedness, duplicity, cunning, cheating; *ant.* honesty, openness.

deceitful *adj.* deceptive, treacherous, dishonest, insincere, underhand, two-faced, sneaky, tricky, crafty, designing, collusive, duplicitous, fallacious; *ant.* honest, open, trustworthy.

deceive *v.* fool, dupe, mislead, outwit, hoax, hoodwink, delude, cheat, con, betray, doublecross, dissimulate.

decency *n.* decorum, civility, good manners, courtesy, etiquette, propriety, good form, seemliness.

decent *adj.* **1.** proper, decorous, fitting, seemly, appropriate, respectable, conventional, approved, suitable; *ant.* unconventional, unusual. **2.** modest, chaste, moral, decorous, pure, prudent, mannerly, virtuous. **3.** satisfactory, adequate, sufficient, standard, passable.

deception *n.* deceit, hoax, swindle, fraud, trick, lie, bluff, feint, sham, wile, ruse.

deceptive *adj.* dishonest, fraudulent, misleading, false, fake, tricky, specious, spurious, delusory, illusive, illusory; *ant.* artless, genuine, open.

decide *v.* **1.** (make a choice) choose, select, pick, opt, elect. **2.** (come to a conclusion) conclude, establish, determine, resolve, make up one's mind, settle.

decided *adj.* **1.** determined, settled, certain, definite, clear, clear-cut. **2.** resolute, unhesitating, determined, emphatic, assertive, decisive, deliberate, unequivocal, forthright.

deciding *adj.* crucial, determining, conclusive, pivotal, important.

decipher *v.* decode, solve, read, unscramble, translate, interpret, understand, deduce, construe, reveal, unravel, crack; *ant.* encode.

decision *n.* **1.** (the act of deciding) determination, arbitration, deliberation. **2.** (the result of deciding) conclusion, settlement, end, outcome, judgment, finding, resolution, result, verdict, ruling, declaration.

decisive *adj.* **1.** (substantially greater) conclusive, definite, final, determinate, unquestionable, definitive. **2.** (of great importance) crucial, critical, influential, pivotal, key, fateful; *ant.* insignificant. **3.** determined, forthright, incisive, forceful, firm.

deck *v.* **1.** decorate, ornament, adorn, garland, garnish, embellish, trim, festoon, bedeck, dress, clothe, apparel. **2.** (*slang*) floor, hit, punch, smack, slap, beat, knock down.

hit the deck (*slang*) **1.** duck, fall down, throw oneself down, lay down. **2.** get up, get out of bed, rise and shine, get ready, get moving, act.

declaim *v.* rant, spout, orate, recite, hold forth, lecture, preach, harangue, orate.

declamation *n.* **1.** lecture, speech, address, discourse, oration, recitation, rhetoric. **2.** tirade, ranting, harangue, spouting.

declamatory *adj.* pompous, bombastic, verbose, discursive, rhetorical, overblown, windy, grandiose, grandiloquent, theatrical, stagy, high-flown, turgid, fustian.

declaration *n.* **1.** affirmation, attestation, proclamation, profession, notification, publication, statement, manifesto, (public) announcement, bulletin, promulgation. **2.** (legal statement) allegation, testimony, affidavit, deposition.

declaratory *adj.* demonstrative, descriptive, explanatory.

declare *v.* **1.** state, announce, proclaim, claim. **2.** confirm, aver, assert, maintain. **3.** certify, validate, pronounce.

decline *n.* **1.** lessening, recession, falling off, abatement, diminution; deterioration, downturn, decay, slump, worsening, failing, weakening, decrepitude. **2.** hill, incline, slope, descent, dip, divergence.

decline *v.* **1.** decrease, lessen, degenerate, deteriorate, backslide, decay, ebb, fade, fail, wane,

declivity *n.* slope, decline, incline, slant, descent; *ant.* acclivity.

decode *v.* decipher, unscramble, translate, interpret; *ant.* encode.

decompose *v.* decay, disintegrate, break down, rot, spoil, degrade, putrefy, dissolve.

decomposable *adj.* biodegradable, degradable.

decor *n.* decoration, ornamentation, furnishings, color scheme.

decorate *v.* **1.** adorn, ornament, embellish, trim, deck, grace, furbish, beautify, renovate. **2.** honor, crown, cite, garland.

decoration *n.* citation, award, mention, medal, laurel wreath, badge, emblem, crown.

decorative *adj.* ornamental, fancy, ornate, baroque, rococo; superfluous, nonfunctional; *ant.* plain, functional.

decorous *adj.* mannerly, proper, polite, well-behaved, refined, appropriate, decent, seemly, dignified, befitting, sedate.

decorum *n.* decency, politeness, etiquette, propriety, protocol, grace, breeding, good manners, gentility, courtliness, politesse, deportment; *ant.* bad manners.

decoy *n.* lure, trap, bait, imitation, fake, trick, inducement, enticement, camouflage, pretense.

decrease *n.* reduction, decline, lessening, dwindling, ebb, downturn, abatement, curtback, discount, subsidence, diminution; *ant.* increase.

decrease *v.* lessen, wane, taper, diminish, dwindle, decline, abate, subside, slacken, drop; reduce, curtail; *ant.* increase.

decree *n.* law, regulation, statute, ruling, proclamation, ordinance, order, command, act, edict, dictum, mandate, enactment.

decree *v.* declare, command, order, announce, pronounce, proclaim, ordain, enact, dictate, rule, prescribe.

decrepit *adj.* broken-down, ramshackle, deteriorated, dilapidated, rickety, wasted, tumble-down, superannuated, antiquated, debilitated; aged, frail, weak, infirm; *ant.* well-cared-for, youthful.

decrepitude *n.* deterioration, decay, dilapidation, old age, weakness, debility, infirmity,

104

weaken, dwindle. **2.** turn down, forgo, send regrets, refuse.

disability, feebleness, degeneration, incapacity, senescence; *ant.* good repair, youth.

decry *v.* **1.** denounce, disparage, criticize, blame, rail against, censure, belittle, discredit, detract, condemn, inveigh against, traduce; *ant.* praise. **2.** depreciate, devalue, undervalue; *ant.* value.

dedicate *v.* **1.** consecrate, bless, sanctify, hallow, anoint. **2.** appropriate, set aside, allot, consign, apportion, assign; devote, commit, apply, give, donate, offer.

dedication *n.* **1.** allegiance, loyalty, devotion, attachment, faithfulness, commitment, self-sacrifice, adherence, devotedness, single-mindedness. **2.** consecration, hallowing, sanctification, presentation, donation, address, inscription.

deduce *v.* surmise, conclude, infer, assume, gather, reason, glean, derive, draw, understand.

deducible *adj.* consequent, following, provable, inferable, derivable, traceable.

deduct *v.* subtract, take away, reduce by, decrease by, remove, withdraw, diminish by; *ant.* add.

deduction *n.* **1.** reduction, discount, subtraction, withdrawal, decrease, abatement, diminution; *ant.* addition, increase. **2.** conclusion, finding, result, assumption, inference, reasoning, judgment, opinion, corollary.

deed *n.* **1.** act, action, accomplishment, feat, achievement, exploit, performance. **2.** title, contract, agreement, lease, document, certificate, voucher.

deem *v.* regard, esteem, think, imagine, believe, consider, hold, reckon, suppose, judge.

deep *adj.* **1.** low, submerged, subterranean, abysmal, fathomless, submarine, immersed; *ant.* shallow, surface. **2.** profound, acute, penetrating, incisive, wise, sagacious, canny, astute, shrewd, esoteric, recondite, intense. **go off the deep end 1.** go to extremes *or* too far, lose one's good sense; rant, exaggerate, rage. **2.** collapse, lose control, break down, *slang:* crack up, lose one's cool, go bonkers, flip out.

deepen *v.* intensify, magnify, strengthen, grow, reinforce; *ant.* weaken.

deep-seated *adj.* settled, entrenched, ingrained,

deep-rooted, ineradicable, inveterate; subconscious, unconscious.

deface v. vandalize, damage, tarnish, mar, disfigure, sully, spoil, mutilate, blemish, deform, injure; *ant.* repair.

de facto actual, existing, real, tangible.

defamation n. libel, slander, slur, denigration, opprobrium, disparagement, vilification, mudslinging, smear, aspersion, traducement; *ant.* praise.

defamatory *adj.* libelous, slanderous, derogatory, denigrating, pejorative, vituperative, disparaging, insulting, injurious, vilifying, opprobrious; *ant.* complimentary.

default n. failure, neglect, omission, absence, nonpayment, dereliction, lapse.

defeat n. failure, loss, rout, trouncing, vanquishment, debacle, conquest, overthrow; *ant.* victory.

defeat v. conquer, beat, overthrow, repulse, rout, vanquish, overpower, quell, subdue, battle, trounce, clobber (*slang*); *ant.* lose.

defeatist n. pessimist, prophet of doom, doom sayer, futilitarian; *ant.* optimist.

defeatist *adj.* pessimistic, cynical, fatalistic, despairing, melancholy, resigned, despondent, dour, gloomy, hopeless; *ant.* optimistic.

defecate v. excrete, void, discharge, pass.

defecation n. excretion, elimination, expurgation, movement, voiding, excrement, evacuation.

defect n. 1. inadequacy, lack, shortcoming, deficiency. 2. imperfection, flaw, fault, blemish.

defect v. desert, forsake, abandon, revolt, rebel, apostatize.

defective *adj.* faulty, flawed, imperfect, broken, deficient, incomplete, marred; *ant.* operative.

defector n. deserter, renegade, turncoat, apostate, recreant, tergiversator.

defend v. 1. protect, guard, shield, shelter, safeguard, screen, fortify, garrison; *ant.* yield, surrender, give up. 2. plead for, justify, second, exonerate, support, back, vindicate, advocate, endorse, warrant.

defendant *adj.* accused, offender, litigant, appellant, respondent.

defender n. 1. guardian, guard, shield, protec-

tor; *ant.* attacker. 2. vindicator, patron, sponsor, supporter, advocate, champion.

defense n. 1. (act of defending) protection, safeguarding, preservation, security, guardianship, inoculation; *ant.* offense, aggression. 2. justification, vindication, apology, excuse, explanation, extenuation. 3. (arguments in behalf of defendant in a law case) testimony, alibi, plea, rejoinder, rebuttal.

defenseless *adj.* vulnerable, endangered, exposed, helpless, naked, wide open, powerless, unarmed; *ant.* protected.

defensible *adj.* 1. safe, secure, impregnable, unassailable. 2. justifiable, plausible, logical, valid, tenable, vindicable.

defensive *adj.* 1. protective, shielding, safeguarding, watchful, preventive, averting; *ant.* offensive. 2. contentious, combative, bellicose, competitive, argumentative, prickly.

defer v. 1. postpone, delay, suspend, procrastinate, put off, adjourn, shelve, protract. 2. yield, submit, obey, accede, acquiesce, concede, waive, comply, give way, bow, kowtow.

deference n. 1. honor, acclaim, esteem, respect, veneration, homage, reverence, regard. 2. obedience, submission, yielding, compliance, complaisance, acquiescence, obsequiousness, docility, capitulation, obeisance.

deferential *adj.* 1. polite, civil, courteous, considerate, respectful; *ant.* arrogant. 2. submissive, dutiful, complaisant, ingratiating, obsequious.

deferment n. delay, stay, postponement, moratorium, suspension, deferral, putting off, procrastination.

defiance n. disobedience, insubordination, contempt, obstinacy, recalcitrance, opposition, insolence, rebelliousness, spite; *ant.* acquiescence, submissiveness.

defiant *adj.* insubordinate, insolent, uncooperative, audacious, rebellious, recalcitrant, disobedient, challenging, mutinous, truculent; *ant.* acquiescent, submissive.

deficiency n. 1. lack, deficit, dearth, paucity, want, shortage, scarcity, insufficiency, inadequacy, scantiness, absence; *ant.* superfluity. 2. flaw, fault, imperfection, failing, defect, shortcoming, weakness.

deficient *adj.* 1. insufficient, inadequate, lacking, wanting, short, meager, scanty, slight, exiguous; *ant.* excessive, superfluous. **2.** im- perfect, incomplete, defective, flawed, inferior, poor.

deficit *n.* lack, deficiency, default, arrears, loss, shortage; *ant.* excess.

defile *v.* **1.** dirty, pollute, contaminate, stain, taint, tarnish. **2.** corrupt, molest, ravish, rape, seduce, deflower. **3.** dishonor, disgrace, sully, taint, tarnish.

definable *adj.* describable, determinable, expli- cable, ascertainable, definite, specific, percepti- ble.

define *v.* **1.** (name or describe) label, entitle, designate, individualize, formalize, character- ize; determine, interpret, elucidate, expound. **2.** limit, bound, confine, outline, circum- scribe, encompass, mark, settle, establish, dis- tinguish, delineate, demarcate.

definite *adj.* **1.** (having set limits or standards) fixed, exact, specific, set, well-defined, circum- scribed, limited, bounded, strict, certain; posi- tive, absolute; *ant.* ill-defined, vague. **2.** (not subject to doubt) explicit, precise, clear, deci- sive; *ant.* ambiguous, imprecise.

definitive *adj.* **1.** conclusive, decisive, final, complete, ultimate, absolute, exhaustive, au- thoritative. **2.** precise, correct, exact, abso- lute, plain, standard.

deflate *v.* **1.** collapse, puncture, flatten, shrink, empty, contract, squash, squeeze, press, void; *ant.* inflate. **2.** humiliate, humble, dispirit. **3.** decrease, lessen, diminish, re- duce, lower, depreciate, devalue, depress; *ant.* increase.

deflect *v.* ricochet, glance off, avert, veer, di- verge, swerve, curve, twist, bend, deviate.

deflower *v.* defile, molest, rape, seduce, ravish, violate, corrupt, spoil.

deform *v.* distort, disfigure, mangle, warp, twist, mar, pervert, ruin, corrupt, spoil.

deformed *adj.* misshapen, malformed, con- torted, maimed, crippled, crooked, distorted, mangled, mutilated, gnarled, perverted.

deformity *n.* defect, abnormality, disfigure- ment, distortion, irregularity, malformation.

defraud *v.* deceive, cheat, embezzle, swindle, trick, dupe, bilk, fleece, *slang:* con, sting, rip off.

defray *v.* refund, repay, pay, cover, meet, settle; *ant.* incur.

deft *adj.* dexterous, proficient, adept, adroit, agile, skillful, handy, nimble; *ant.* clumsy.

defunct *adj.* dead, expired, departed, deceased, obsolete, nonexistent, extinct; invalid, passé; *ant.* alive, operative.

defy *v.* **1.** resist, oppose, rebel against, brave, stand up to, confront, face; *ant.* yield, quail. **2.** (frustrate completely) baffle, puzzle, foil, thwart. **3.** dare, challenge, goad, throw down the gauntlet.

degenerate *adj.* **1.** deteriorated, decayed, aged. **2.** depraved, debauched, decadent, perverted, immoral, dissolute, low, profligate, aban- doned, mean, corrupt, base, fallen; *ant.* up- right, virtuous.

degenerate *v.* **1.** regress, decay, rot, deterio- rate, age, decline, retrogress, worsen, slip, lapse, fall off, sink; *ant.* improve. **2.** back- slide, sink into despair, drop out (*slang*).

degrade *v.* **1.** (to lower, as in status or value) devalue, depreciate, disgrace, degradate, hum- ble, demote, discredit, demean, cheapen. **2.** corrupt, deprave, debase, pervert, sully, ruin, defile. **3.** degenerate, deteriorate, disinte- grate, pollute, adulterate.

degradation *n.* **1.** deterioration, decline, desti- tution. **2.** disgrace, dishonor, shame, mortifi- cation, humiliation, debasement, ignominy.

degree *n.* **1.** (unit of measurement) interval, space, grade, step, mark, gradation, size, di- mension, point, line, plane. **2.** (relative condi- tion or placement) level, status, rank, station, order, quality, standard, height, length, ex- panse, range, proportion, quantity, amplitude. **by degrees** gradually, step by step, slowly but surely, inch by inch. **to a degree** somewhat, partially, to an extent, partly.

dehydrate *v.* dry out, dry up, drain, evaporate, parch, desiccate, exsiccate, effloresce.

deification *n.* glorification, exaltation, en- noblement, elevation, apotheosis, idolization, divinification.

deify *v.* glorify, idolize, venerate, worship, ideal- ize, immortalize, apotheosize, exalt, extol.

deign *v.* stoop, lower *or* demean oneself, conde- scend, vouchsafe.

deity *n.* divinity, god, goddess, demigod, demigoddess, idol, godhead.

dejected *adj.* despondent, disconsolate, crestfallen, melancholy, downcast, miserable, wretched, gloomy, disheartened, morose, depressed, blue; *ant.* bright, happy, high-spirited.

dejection *n.* despair, despondency, melancholy, sadness, depression, doldrums, dumps, gloom, low spirits, blues; *ant.* happiness.

de jure legally, rightfully, by right, by law.

delay *n.* **1.** postponement, suspension, moratorium, reprieve, deferment, adjournment, stay, stop, procrastination. **2.** hindrance, problem, obstacle, obstruction, impediment, holdup, setback, interruption.

delay *v.* **1.** postpone, prolong, suspend, table, procrastinate; *ant.* expedite. **2.** detain, stall, arrest, impede, hold up, stave off; *ant.* accelerate, hurry.

delectable *adj.* delicious, tasty, appetizing, enjoyable, enticing, scrumptious, luscious, yummy (*slang*).

delectation *n.* delight, enjoyment, entertainment, pleasure, amusement, diversion, gratification, refreshment, contentment.

delegate *n.* representative, envoy, emissary, proxy, agent, substitute, deputy, ambassador, commissioner, consul.

delegate *v.* assign, relegate, designate, appoint, authorize, empower, entrust, commission, mandate, nominate, charge.

delegation *n.* **1.** committee, contingent, organization, envoys, embassy, legation, deputation. **2.** appointment, nomination, ordination, assignment; commissioning, trust, mandate, authorization, charge, investiture, conveyance.

delete *v.* erase, strike *or* cross *or* blot out, cancel, edit, blue-pencil, remove, expunge, obliterate, efface.

deleterious *adj.* harmful, damaging, injurious, noxious, destructive, detrimental, hurtful, prejudicial; *ant.* helpful.

deliberate *v.* think, ruminate, consider, meditate, cogitate, mull over, weigh, ponder, reflect, discuss, debate.

deliberate *adj.* **1.** careful, thought out, predetermined, conscious, prearranged, studied, intentional, willful, planned, calculated, weighed, premeditated; *ant.* incidental, chance, accidental. **2.** slow, stolid, leisurely, measured; *ant.* hurried.

delicate *adj.* **1.** (said of flavor or other quality) light, mild, subtle. **2.** (as of a person's nature) fine, elegant, dainty, refined; cultured, graceful. **3.** (as of a person's constitution) fragile, frail, sensitive, susceptible; sickly, weak, feeble, debilitated; *ant.* robust, healthy. **4.** tactful, diplomatic, considerate, gentle; *ant.* cross, bluff.

delicious *adj.* tasty, appetizing, scrumptious, savory, delectable, mouthwatering, luscious, flavorsome, yummy (*slang*).

delight *n.* joy, ecstasy, bliss, jubilation, happiness, rapture, enjoyment, pleasure, felicity, gratification; *ant.* dismay.

delight *v.* gladden, cheer, please, ravish, tickle, amuse, thrill, enchant, charm, divert, gratify; *ant.* dismay.

delight in love, relish, savor, revel *or* glory in, gloat over, like, enjoy, take pride in.

delightful *adj.* congenial, engaging, captivating, charming, entertaining, pleasant, amusing, refreshing, pleasing; *ant.* horrible.

delimit *v.* define, bound, fix, mark, demarcate, establish, determine.

delineate *v.* **1.** draw, design, outline, trace, sketch. **2.** depict, represent, portray, render, describe, characterize.

delineation *n.* **1.** diagram, design, chart, outline, drawing, sketch. **2.** picture, portrait, drawing, sketch, representation, depiction, portrayal, characterization, description, account.

delinquency *n.* misconduct, misdeed, wrongdoing, offense, crime, misbehavior, misdemeanor.

delinquent *n.* wrongdoer, miscreant, criminal, lawbreaker, derelict, (juvenile) offender, hoodlum, hooligan, tough, punk (*slang*).

delinquent *adj.* **1.** lax, slack, remiss, negligent, procrastinating, careless; *ant.* punctual, scrupulous. **2.** unpaid, overdue, due, owed.

delirious *adj.* **1.** manic, hysterical, incoherent, wild, raving, deranged, demented, mad, frenzied. **2.** excited, enthused, ecstatic.

delirium *n.* madness, lunacy, hysteria, ecstasy, frenzy, insanity, rage, passion, fury, fever.

deliver *v.* **1.** transport, carry, transfer, convey, bear, bring, cart. **2.** set free, release, emancipate, liberate, acquit; save, rescue, redeem. **3.**

deliverance announce, address, present, read, declare, pronounce. **4.** (give birth) yield, produce, bring *or* give forth.

deliverance *n.* liberation, emancipation, release, salvation, redemption, rescue, extrication, forgiveness, pardon.

delivery *n.* **1.** transportation, distribution, consignment, shipment, carting, transfer, freighting, dispatch, conveyance, mailing. **2.** release, liberation, pardon; rescue, salvation. **3.** elocution, intonation, articulation, enunciation, eloquence, speech, accent, pronunciation, emphasis, diction, presentation. **4.** childbirth, parturition, labor; midwifery, obstetrics.

dell *n.* valley, hollow, vale.

delude *v.* fool, mislead, misinform, trick, deceive, con, hoax, hoodwink, dupe, bamboozle, take in, snow (*slang*).

deluge *n.* torrent, avalanche, barrage, inundation, cataclysm, flood, downpour.

delusion *n.* **1.** illusion, hallucination, phantasm, mirage, fancy. **2.** mistake, blunder, lapse, oversight, error, deception, misconception, fallacy, misapprehension.

deluxe *adj.* exclusive, choice, select, elegant, luxurious, rich, sumptuous, opulent, posh, palatial.

delve *v.* investigate, probe, search, research, dig into, explore, examine, root, rummage.

demagogue *n.* agitator, rabble-rouser, firebrand, haranguer, revolutionary, radical, rebel.

demand *n.* **1.** command, order, call, charge, request, bid. **2.** need, desire, requirement, interest, vogue, call; *ant.* indifference, disinterest. **in demand** wanted, sought after, needed, requested.

on demand available, ready, prepared, usable.

demand *v.* **1.** insist on, command, order, charge, enjoin, adjure, importune. **2.** require, need, call for, necessitate, expect.

demanding *adj.* difficult, challenging, tough, taxing, exhausting, trying; fussy, exacting, querulous; pressing, insistent, urgent, exigent; *ant.* easy.

demarcate *v.* define, fix, delimit, establish, determine, differentiate, distinguish, separate.

demarcation *n.* **1.** boundary, limit, margin, division, line. **2.** distinction, differentiation, bound, separation.

108

demean *v.* lower, debase, degrade, humble; descend, deign, stoop, condescend; *ant.* enhance.

demeanor *n.* conduct, behavior, manner, bearing, carriage, deportment, air, mien, comportment.

demented *adj.* crazy, mad, deranged, insane, lunatic, maniacal, frenzied, unbalanced, manic, unhinged.

demise *n.* **1.** death, dying, expiration, end, termination, decease, passing, departure. **2.** downfall, ruin, failure, collapse, dissolution.

democracy *n.* self-government, autonomy, populism; commonwealth, republic.

democratic *adj.* **1.** republican, self-governing, autonomous, representative, populist, egalitarian, popular. **2.** tolerant, liberal, open-minded, broad-minded; *ant.* snobbish.

demolish *v.* **1.** level, flatten, tear *or* knock down, dismantle, wreck, bulldoze. **2.** devastate, obliterate, overthrow, destroy, defeat, pulverize, annihilate.

demon *n.* **1.** devil, evil spirit, goblin, monster, incubus, succubus. **2.** villain, fiend, brute, rogue, rascal, beast.

demoniac *adj.* **1.** devilish, demonic, satanic, wicked, fiendish, diabolical, impious, hellish, infernal, possessed. **2.** frenzied, crazed, insane, frantic, violent, furious, mad, maniacal, manic.

demonstrable *adj.* verifiable, provable, attestable, arguable, substantiable, palpable, self-evident, evident, clear, incontrovertible, irrefutable.

demonstrate *v.* **1.** (make evident) prove, show, exhibit, manifest, display, establish, confirm, substantiate, evince, testify to. **2.** (show by citing examples) explain, illustrate, describe, teach, expound. **3.** protest, parade, march, rally, picket, sit in.

demonstration *n.* **1.** exhibition, display, show, showing, presentation, exhibit, exposition. **2.** protest, rally, picket line, march, sit-in (*slang*). **3.** explanation, proof, testimony, illustration, induction, description, test, evidence, substantiation, validation.

demonstrative *adj.* expressive, effusive, unreserved, affectionate, open, communicative, expansive; *ant.* cold.

demoralize *v.* **1.** discourage, dishearten, daunt, unnerve, weaken, dispirit, depress, lose heart, disconcert, rattle, crush; *ant.* encourage, buoy. **2.** corrupt, deprave, debase, pervert, debauch, vitiate.

demote *v.* downgrade, degrade, reduce, relegate, dismiss; *ant.* promote, upgrade.

demur *v.* refuse, object, challenge, dissent, dispute, protest, balk, disagree.

demure *adj.* modest, reserved, retiring, sober, staid, reticent, strait-laced, decorous, shy; prudish, prissy.

den *n.* **1.** lair, cavern, cave, shelter, hole. **2.** study, hideout, hideaway, sanctuary, recreation room.

denial *n.* **1.** (a statement of opposition) contradiction, negation, veto, rebuff, dissent; refusal, rejection. **2.** (act of disowning) repudiation, abjuration, renouncement; disclaimer, retraction, disavowal; *ant.* adoption, embrace.

denigrate *v.* disparage, slander, malign, revile, belittle, defame, decry, impugn, vilify, blacken; *ant.* praise.

denizen *n.* inhabitant, resident, occupant, dweller, citizen.

denominate *v.* designate, name, title, term, call, christen, baptize, dub.

denomination *n.* **1.** class, category, classification, group, body, grade, school, unit. **2.** sect, church, faith, belief, creed, religious persuasion. **3.** name, title, identification, label, term, designation, appellation.

denote *v.* mean, show, signify, stand for, symbolize, indicate, imply, express, import.

denouement *n.* finish, finale, outcome, close, culmination, resolution, upshot, conclusion, climax, solution.

denounce *v.* condemn, accuse, castigate, attack, impugn, revile, vilify, decry, declaim *or* inveigh against; *ant.* praise.

dense *adj.* **1.** solid, compact, condensed, compressed, thick, crowded, close-knit, jampacked; *ant.* sparse. **2.** impenetrable, impermeable, impassable. **3.** stupid, obtuse, half-witted, slow-witted, imbecilic, dull, ignorant; *ant.* clever.

density *n.* mass, weight, solidity, thickness,

massiveness, quantity, bulk, substantiality, heaviness, body; *ant.* lightness, thinness.

dent *n.* indentation, depression, impression, dimple, hollow, pit, crater, cavity.

dent *v.* depress, indent, push in, gouge, hollow, imprint, dimple, furrow.

denude *v.* bare, strip, defoliate, deforest; *ant.* cover.

denunciation *n.* indictment, incrimination, accusation, condemnation, criticism, castigation, censure, obloquy, diatribe; *ant.* compliment, praise.

deny *v.* **1.** (not accept the truth of) contradict, gainsay, negate; refute, disavow, recant; *ant.* agree, admit. **2.** refuse, withhold, reject, veto; *ant.* allow, grant. **3.** disown, repudiate, renounce, abjure, turn one's back on; *ant.* accept.

deodorant *n.* antiperspirant, deodorizer, air-freshener, disinfectant, fumigant.

deodorize *v.* fumigate, ventilate, freshen, refresh, aerate, disinfect, clean, purify, sweeten.

depart *v.* **1.** leave, go, quit, decamp, retreat, withdraw, retire, exit; *ant.* arrive. **2.** die, perish, expire, pass on.

departed *adj.* **1.** dead, defunct, expired, deceased, late. **2.** gone, left, disappeared, moved.

department *n.* **1.** part, division, branch, section, area. **2.** specialty, vocation, avocation, occupation, interest, walk of life. **3.** office, bureau, quarter, agency, commission, administration; dominion, jurisdiction, station, precinct, territory.

department store variety store, notions store, dry-goods store, emporium, bargain store.

departure *n.* **1.** leaving, going, departing, withdrawal, passage, exit, exodus, leave-taking, getaway (*slang*); *ant.* arrival. **2.** deviation, variation, change, divergence, branching out, difference, novelty, innovation.

depend *v.* **1.** trust, rely on, put faith in, believe in, count on, expect, bank on, lean on, believe in. **2.** require, need, hinge on, be at the mercy of, ride on, revolve around.

dependable *adj.* trustworthy, reliable, sure, faithful, unfailing, responsible, conscientious, steady.

dependence *n.* **1.** contingency, influence, connection, interdependence, need, attachment. **2.** subordination, yoke, servility, subservience; *ant.* independence, faith, trust, belief, credence, hope.

dependent *adj.* **1.** contingent, conditional, depending, relative. **2.** indigent, poor, helpless, defenseless. **3.** subordinate, subservient, inferior, secondary, lesser; parasitic, addicted, clinging.

depict *v.* **1.** picture, draw, illustrate, reproduce, detail, portray; render, sketch. **2.** describe, characterize, portray, narrate.

depiction *n.* **1.** picture, drawing, illustration, image, likeness, sketch, delineation, description. **2.** portrayal, representation, caricature.

deplete *v.* consume, expend, use up, exhaust, empty, evacuate, impoverish; decrease, lessen, attenuate, reduce.

deplorable *adj.* **1.** sad, heartbreaking, melancholy; regrettable, unfortunate, wretched, grievous, calamitous, dire, execrable, pitiable. **2.** disgraceful, shameful, opprobrious.

deplore *v.* **1.** lament, mourn, grieve for, lament, bewail, bemoan; regret, rue, repent of. **2.** condemn, denounce, disapprove, censure, abhor.

deploy *v.* extend, expand, fan out; position, station, arrange, distribute, utilize.

depopulate *v.* **1.** kill, massacre, slaughter, eliminate, wipe out. **2.** evict, oust, banish, exile.

deport *v.* banish, ostracize, oust, exile, expel, extradite, expatriate.

deportment *n.* bearing, manner, conduct, demeanor, posture, stance, behavior, air, aspect, carriage, mien.

depose *v.* oust, dethrone, demote, topple, impeach, displace.

deposit *n.* **1.** security, retainer, pledge, down or partial payment, installment. **2.** accumulation, sediment, silt.

deposit *v.* **1.** place, put, drop, settle, sit, lay, dump. **2.** amass, save, store, hoard, lodge, bank.

deposition *n.* **1.** affidavit, statement, testimony, allegation, affirmation, announcement, evidence. **2.** discharge, ousting, displacement, removal, dethronement, toppling.

depository *n.* warehouse, storehouse, repository, depot, cache, mint, (savings) bank.

depot *n.* **1.** warehouse, storehouse, annex, depository, repository, arsenal, magazine, garage. **2.** (railway) station, terminal, junction.

deprave *v.* corrupt, contaminate, debauch, pervert, seduce, debase, demoralize, subvert, vitiate, degrade; *ant.* improve.

depravity *n.* evil, vice, wickedness, corruption, debasement, lewdness, immorality, sinfulness, baseness, degeneracy; debauchery; *ant.* uprightness.

deprecate *v.* **1.** disapprove, disparage, condemn, deplore, censure, object to; *ant.* approve, commend. **2.** belittle, depreciate.

depreciate *v.* **1.** deteriorate, decrease, lessen, drop, reduce, worsen, decay, deflate; *ant.* appreciate. **2.** belittle, lower, run down, decry, underrate, undervalue, disparage, ridicule, trivialize, put down (*slang*). **3.** condemn, denounce, denigrate, attack; *ant.* praise.

depredation *n.* theft, robbery, pillage, raiding, marauding, looting, plunder, ransacking, destruction, devastation, laying waste, despoliation.

depress *v.* **1.** discourage, dishearten, dispirit, dampen, deject, daunt; *ant.* cheer. **2.** lower, flatten, squash, level, settle.

depressant *n.* sedative, relaxer, tranquilizer, calmant, downer (*slang*); *ant.* stimulant.

depressed *adj.* **1.** saddened, downcast, despondent, disheartened, discouraged, glum, melancholy, miserable, crestfallen, down in the dumps, blue; *ant.* cheerful. **2.** indented, dented, concave, sunken, recessed; *ant.* convex, prominent, protuberant.

depression *n.* **1.** despondency, melancholy, hopelessness, low spirits, dejection, despair, gloominess, dumps, doldrums, blues; *ant.* cheerfulness. **2.** recession, hard times, downturn, stagflation, slump; *ant.* prosperity, boom. **3.** cavity, dent, dimple, pit, indentation, impression, valley, bowl, basin, hollow, excavation; *ant.* prominence, protuberance.

deprivation *n.* **1.** need, want, destitution, hardship. **2.** withdrawal, dispossession, divestment; *ant.* bestowal.

deprive *v.* deny, rob, strip, bereave, seize,

divest, expropriate, dispossess, denude; *ant.* bestow.

depth *n.* **1.** declination, pitch, remoteness. **2.** profundity, wisdom, acumen, insight, sagacity, weight, perspicacity, shrewdness, recondite-ness; *ant.* shallowness, superficiality.

deputation *n.* **1.** representatives, delegates, embassy, commission. **2.** appointment, designation, assignment, nomination.

depute *v.* nominate, appoint, authorize, delegate, commission, mandate, empower, entrust, accredit.

deputy *n.* assistant, second-in-command, alternate, substitute, surrogate, subordinate, proxy, representative, agent.

deranged *adj.* crazy, demented, mad, crazed, unbalanced; *ant.* sane.

derelict *n.* tramp, vagrant, drifter, hobo, bum.

derelict *adj.* **1.** abandoned, forsaken, deserted, forlorn, desolate, neglected, dilapidated. **2.** careless, delinquent, lax, remiss, negligent.

deride *v.* ridicule, mock, scorn, condemn, disparage, belittle, scoff, jeer, satirize, gibe, sneer, contemn; *ant.* praise.

derision *n.* disdain, contempt, mockery, ridicule, scorn, disparagement, disrespect, insult, satire, raillery, contumely; *ant.* praise.

derisive *adj.* insulting, rude, sarcastic, mocking, jeering, taunting; disdainful, scornful, contemptuous; *ant.* appreciative.

derisory *adj.* laughable, outrageous, ridiculous, absurd, ludicrous, preposterous, risible, contemptible.

derivation *n.* origin, source, root, beginning, foundation, basis, extraction, descent, ancestry, genealogy, etymology.

derivative *adj.* imitative, plagiarized, procured, regurgitated, copied, rehashed, borrowed, second-hand, unoriginal, daughter; *ant.* original.

derive *v.* **1.** get, receive, acquire, obtain, procure, collect, extract, draw, borrow, elicit. **2.** deduce, infer, conclude, assume, determine, glean.

derogatory *adj.* detracting, belittling, damaging, pejorative, defamatory, aspersive, insulting, disparaging, snide, critical; *ant.* complimentary, favorable.

descend *v.* **1.** slide, dive, drop, slip, topple, plunge, sink, slump, pitch, tumble. **2.** condescend, patronize, stoop, deign, concede, humble *or* lower oneself.

descendants *n.* children, offspring, family, issue, lineage, progeny, successors, seed, posterity.

descent *n.* **1.** dip, drop, incline, slope, slant, decline; *ant.* ascent. **2.** fall, plunge, degradation, debasement, deterioration, decadence; *ant.* improvement. **3.** family tree, parentage, lineage, origin, genealogy, heredity, ancestry.

describe *v.* **1.** relate, tell, narrate, detail, explain, recount, depict. **2.** illustrate, draw, sketch, limn. **3.** trace, outline, delineate.

description *n.* narrative, explanation, presentation, chronicle, account, report, exposition, delineation, profile.

descriptive *adj.* vivid, graphic, colorful, expressive, illustrative, blow-by-blow, detailed, specific; *ant.* cursory, laconic.

descry *v.* **1.** (catch sight of) discern, see, notice, glimpse, perceive, observe. **2.** (look for and discover) detect, spy, spot, recognize, distinguish.

desecrate *v.* profane, blaspheme, defile, violate, contaminate, vandalize, pollute, pervert, debase, dishonor, insult.

desecration *n.* blasphemy, sacrilege, profanation, violation, impiety, irreverence, defilement, insult, debasement.

desert *n.* comeuppance, retribution, recompense, reward, due, requital, right.

desert *v.* **1.** forsake, abandon, repudiate, renounce, strand, maroon. **2.** run away, leave, flee, defect, resign, vacate, quit, take off (*slang*).

deserter *n.* defector, traitor, fugitive, apostate, truant.

deserve *v.* merit, warrant, justify, earn, gain, incur, procure.

deserved *adj.* due, fair, fitting, just, justifiable, legitimate, warranted, appropriate, apt, well-earned, apposite, condign, merited; *ant.* unfair, unwarranted.

deserving *adj.* admirable, exemplary, praiseworthy, laudable, righteous, commendable, estimable, creditable.

desiccated *adj.* dry, dehydrated, dried, drained; dead, spiritless, lifeless, passionless, sterile.

desideratum *n.* want, aspiration, wish, aim, goal, objective, purpose, hope, desire, ideal, dream.

design *n.* **1.** diagram, drawing, sketch, draft, blueprint, outline, chart, plan, layout, model. **2.** scheme, intrigue, machination, plot, plan; undertaking, enterprise. **3.** purpose, intention, aim, object, goal, end.

design *v.* **1.** plan, scheme, outline, block out, sketch, draw up. **2.** intend, purpose, aim, undertake. **3.** contrive, compose, create, devise, invent, originate, make up, develop, fashion, model, conceive, construct, form.

designate *v.* **1.** point out, indicate, specify, stipulate. **2.** name, dub, christen, name, deem, earmark, term. **3.** appoint, nominate, elect, choose, assign, authorize, name.

designer *n.* creator, maker, inventor, author, stylist, originator, deviser; contriver, artificer.

designing *adj.* scheming, plotting, crafty, tricky, deceitful, cunning, devious, Machiavellian, conniving; *ant.* artless.

desirability *n.* value, worth, merit, advantage, benefit, usefulness; *ant.* inadvisability.

desirable *adj.* **1.** beneficial, worthwhile, advantageous, profitable, helpful, useful, expedient, advisable. **2.** seductive, charming, fascinating, alluring, captivating, tempting, attractive, fetching, sexy.

desire *n.* **1.** aspiration, wish; craving, urge, propensity, predilection, fancy, avidity, mania. **2.** lust, passion, libido, longing, attraction.

desire *v.* **1.** crave, covet, wish for, long for, yearn for, hunger for, want, covet, fancy, need, lack. **2.** request, ask for, beg, seek, solicit, petition, entreat, importune. **3.** (desire sexually) lust for, long for, want.

desirous *adj.* hopeful, hoping, longing, yearning, wishing, ambitious, avid, burning, keen, eager, anxious, aspiring; *ant.* reluctant, unenthusiastic.

desist *v.* stop, abstain, halt, refrain, cease, end, pause, suspend; *ant.* continue.

desolate *adj.* **1.** (said of places) deserted, uninhabited, depopulated; laid waste, bereft, barren. **2.** (said of persons) lonely, solitary, isolated, abandoned, forsaken; wretched, forlorn, despondent, disheartened, hopeless, inconsolable, depressed, melancholy; *ant.* cheerful.

desolation *n.* **1.** barrenness, bareness, devastation, ruin, ravages, dissolution, demolition, annihilation, extinction, desert, waste. **2.** hopelessness, distress, dejection, despondency, despair, sadness, sorrow, wretchedness, gloom, misery, loneliness, anguish, woe.

despair *n.* hopelessness, misery, pain, trial, depression, anguish, wretchedness, desperation, despondency, tribulation; *ant.* cheerfulness, resilience.

despairing *adj.* distraught, depressed, brokenhearted, dejected, disheartened, desperate, hopeless, at the end of one's rope, suicidal; *ant.* cheerful, resilient.

desperado *n.* outlaw, gunman, criminal, bandit, hoodlum, gangster, ruffian, thug.

desperate *adj.* **1.** (said of persons) reckless, rash, heedless, frantic, headlong, foolhardy, imprudent. **2.** (said of actions or circumstances) extreme, drastic, severe, acute, dire, urgent, exigent, pressing, serious, crucial, critical.

despicable *adj.* hateful, abhorrent, contemptible, reprehensible, disgraceful, ignoble, low, mean, vile, base; *ant.* laudable.

despise *v.* **1.** scorn, spurn, slight, condemn, revile, deride, vilipend, contemn. **2.** hate, loathe, detest, abhor.

despite *prep.* regardless of, even with, notwithstanding, in spite of, in the face of, heedless of.

despoil *v.* rob, plunder, ravage, maraud, pillage, sack, vandalize.

despot *n.* tyrant, dictator, oppressor, autocrat, absolutist.

despondency *n.* despair, depression, dejection, melancholy, sadness, sorrow, misery, hopelessness; *ant.* cheerfulness.

despondent *adj.* hopeless, dejected, despairing, discouraged, disheartened, low-spirited, depressed, downcast; *ant.* cheerful, hopeful.

despotic *adj.* tyrannical, oppressive, authoritarian, autocratic, dictatorial, absolutist, imperious, monocratic, overbearing, domineering; *ant.* democratic, egalitarian.

despotism *n.* tyranny, oppression, dictatorship, totalitarianism, repression, autocracy, absolutism, monocracy, autarchy; *ant.* democracy, liberalism.

destination *n.* **1.** stop, station, terminal, haven. **2.** goal, objective, object, end, ambition, aim, intention, aspiration, purpose, design.

destine *v.* **1.** predetermine, preordain, fate, decide, doom. **2.** intend, mean, design; designate, allot, assign.

destiny *n.* fate, fortune, doom, karma, lot.

destitute *adj.* **1.** poor, impoverished, poverty-stricken, needy, penniless, bankrupt, indigent, insolvent; *ant.* prosperous, wealthy. **2.** lacking, wanting, bereft, devoid, depleted.

destroy *v.* **1.** annihilate, exterminate, wipe out, kill, waste, eliminate. **2.** wreck, demolish, tear down, destruct, eradicate, level, ruin, raze; *ant.* create.

destroyer *n.* annihilator, iconoclast, nihilist, assassin, executioner, slayer, slaughterer, terrorist, lyncher, anarchist, firebrand, incendiary; *ant.* creator.

destruction *n.* **1.** (action of destroying) demolition, liquidation, ruin; overthrow, downfall, slaughter, elimination; *ant.* creation. **2.** (result of destroying) devastation, wreckage, defeat, desolation, extinction.

destructive *adj.* **1.** catastrophic, cataclysmic, pernicious, vicious, ruinous, deleterious, lethal, noxious; *ant.* harmless. **2.** damaging, negative, adverse, hostile, injurious; *ant.* positive, constructive.

desultory *adj.* aimless, haphazard, random, discursive, incidental, irregular, hit-or-miss, inconsistent, cursory; *ant.* organized, concerted, methodical, systematic.

detach *v.* remove, sever, cut off, disconnect, divide, separate, disengage, uncouple; *ant.* attach.

detached *adj.* **1.** separated, divided, disconnected, disjoined, severed, unattached, free-standing, loosened; *ant.* connected. **2.** indifferent, disinterested, impassive, neutral, impartial, unbiased, apathetic, aloof, dispassionate; *ant.* concerned, involved.

detachment *n.* **1.** indifference, unconcern, impartiality, neutrality, objectivity, nonpartisanship, disinterestedness, fairness, separation. **2.** patrol, squad, brigade, corps, detail, unit, body, party, task force.

detail *n.* **1.** part, item, portion, particular, trait, element, feature, datum, aspect; minutia, intricacy, singularity. **2.** squad, detachment, patrol, brigade, corps, unit, body, party, task force.

detail *v.* **1.** itemize, particularize, catalog, enumerate, show, report, tell, recount, recapitulate. **2.** appoint, assign, dispatch, delegate, charge, commission.

detailed *adj.* specific, exact, thorough, comprehensive, exhaustive, elaborate, particular, blow-by-blow, intricate, meticulous, itemized; *ant.* sketchy, general, cursory.

details *n.* trivialities, particulars, complexities, intricacies, specifics, minutiae.

detain *v.* **1.** (hold in custody temporarily) keep, confine, hold, restrict, restrain, arrest, place under house arrest; *ant.* release. **2.** delay, hinder, slow, retard, check, impede, prevent.

detect *v.* perceive, notice, observe, recognize; spot, spy, discern, identify, ascertain, expose, uncover.

detection *n.* exposure, discovery, disclosure, unmasking, unearthing, exposé, uncovering, revelation.

detective *n.* investigator, sleuth, private eye, constable, *slang:* gumshoe, flatfoot, dick.

detention *n.* **1.** imprisonment, incarceration, house arrest, restraint, confinement, duress, constraint; *ant.* release. **2.** hindrance, delay, detainment.

deter *v.* discourage, dissuade, daunt, intimidate, frighten, repel, warn, caution, inhibit, put off; *ant.* encourage.

deteriorate *v.* decline, degenerate, lapse, worsen, decay, decompose, depreciate, fade, ebb, weaken, crumble; *ant.* improve.

deterioration *n.* degeneration, decline, slump, retrogression, atrophy, dilapidation, drop, descent, downturn, degradation, debasement; *ant.* improvement.

determinate *adj.* **1.** (having exact limits) definite, distinct, fixed, precise, specific, clear-cut, defined, express. **2.** conclusive, decisive, final, determined, definitive, certain, established; *ant.* tentative.

determination *n.* tenacity, resolve, fortitude,

determine persistence, resolution, perseverance, heart, willpower, steadfastness, grit, drive, ambition, conviction; single-mindedness, stubbornness, obstinacy; toughness, tenacity.

determine *v.* **1.** (set limits) bound, define, restrict, limit, check, control, regulate, circumscribe. **2.** (decide following an inquiry) settle, decide, establish, conclude; find out, discover, ascertain, detect, learn. **3.** (give direction) dictate, govern, arbitrate, ordain, direct, rule, shape, guide.

determined *adj.* persevering, steadfast, persistent, intent, resolute, purposeful, tenacious, strong-willed, decided; bent, obstinate; *ant.* irresolute.

determining *adj.* conclusive, deciding, pivotal, critical, crucial, decisive, definitive.

deterrent *n.* obstacle, barrier, restraint, obstruction, hindrance, repellent, discouragement, turnoff (*slang*); disincentive; *ant.* incentive.

detest *v.* hate, loathe, abhor, despise, abominate, deplore, execrate; *ant.* adore.

detestable *adj.* hateful, abhorrent, loathsome, despicable, heinous, abominable, repugnant, disgusting, repulsive, rotten; *ant.* admirable, adorable.

dethrone *v.* oust, depose, topple, unseat.

detonate *v.* explode, blow up, blast, set off, ignite, discharge, go off.

detonation *n.* explosion, discharge, blast, bang, boom, blowup, report.

detour *n.* digression, diversion, byway, bypass, alternate route.

detract *v.* **1.** lessen, reduce, diminish, devaluate, depreciate, lower, negate, nullify. **2.** belittle, deprecate, depreciate, vilipend, vitiate, disparage, bad-mouth (*slang*); *ant.* praise.

detraction *n.* slander, defamation, aspersion, revilement, muckraking, belitlement, disparagement, traducement, derogation, vituperation, calumny; *ant.* appreciation, praise.

detractor *n.* slanderer, critic, scandalmonger, defamer, backbiter, muckraker, traducer, reviler, vilifier; *ant.* flatterer, supporter.

detriment *n.* **1.** harm, loss, hurt, injury, impairment, damage; *ant.* advantage. **2.** evil, mischief, disservice, prejudice.

detrimental *adj.* harmful, pernicious, hurtful, damaging, destructive, adverse, injurious, dele-

terious, inimical, untoward, baleful, prejudicial; *ant.* advantageous.

detritus *n.* wreckage, remains, debris, junk, litter, fragments, waste, scum.

devastate *v.* destroy, ravage, lay waste, ruin, wreck, demolish, level, raze, ransack, sack; overwhelm, floor, crush.

develop *v.* **1.** enlarge, expand, extend, advance, build up, cultivate; grow, bloom, mature, ripen, sprout. **2.** (grow in power or influence) strengthen, improve, enrich, augment. **3.** (change over time) evolve, progress, advance. **4.** (discuss in speech or writing) enlarge upon, expand, explicate, explain, work out, detail; unfold, disclose, uncover.

deviant *n.* pervert, misfit, *slang:* weirdo, kook, oddball.

deviant *adj.* irregular, abnormal, bizarre, aberrant, perverse, eccentric, anomalous, heretical, heterotypic.

deviate *v.* diverge, differ, vary, aberrate, veer, digress.

deviation *n.* departure, variation, alteration, fluctuation, divergence, inconsistency, disparity; aberration, anomaly, eccentricity, quirk; *ant.* conformity.

device *n.* **1.** instrument, invention, machine, tool, mechanism, contraption, utensil; means, medium. **2.** scheme, artifice, contrivance, wherewithal, design, machination, trick, trap, stratagem, ruse, subterfuge.

devil *n.* **1.** Satan, demon, fiend, Beelzebub, fallen angel, Lucifer, Mephistopheles, Prince of Darkness. **2.** villain, renegade, beast, rascal, brute, swine, rogue, scoundrel, savage, bastard, terror. **between the devil and the deep blue sea** in trouble, desperate, stopped, in difficulty, between a rock and a hard place. **go to the devil** fail, degenerate, fall into bad habits, backslide, decay, go to pot (*slang*).

devilish *adj.* hellish, fiendish, wicked, monstrous, diabolical, damnable, accursed, infernal, satanic, impious, demoniac, nefarious; mischievous, impish.

devil-may-care *adj.* easygoing, happy-go-lucky, jaunty, frivolous, nonchalant, casual, cavalier, flippant, flip (*slang*); reckless, heedless; *ant.* careful, concerned, worried.

devilry *n.* viciousness, villainy, wickedness, sorcery, evil, diabolism, black magic; chicanery, monkey business, mischief.

devious *adj.* scheming, crafty, deceitful, dishonest, sly, deep, subtle, calculating, tricky, surreptitious, wily, underhand, double-dealing, two-faced; *ant.* artless.

devise *v.* contrive, formulate, design, plot, plan, invent, conceive, concoct, forge.

devoid *adj.* empty, void, vacant, wanting, without, needed, lacking, deficient, bereft, free, sans; *ant.* endowed.

devolution *n.* distribution, delegation, dispersal, transference; *ant.* centralization.

devolve *v.* transfer, convey, delegate, commission, entrust, consign.

devote *v.* reserve, allocate, allot, dedicate, pledge, give, sacrifice, commit.

devoted *adj.* dedicated, committed, steadfast, constant, devout, ardent, staunch, faithful, true, loyal, loving; *ant.* negligent.

devotee *n.* fan, disciple, follower, supporter, aficionado, adherent, zealot, enthusiast, fanatic, buff, addict, fiend; *ant.* adversary, skeptic.

devotion *n.* love, steadfastness, loyalty, faith, dedication, fidelity, commitment, support; *ant.* inconstancy, negligence.

devotional *adj.* holy, sacred, divine, religious, pious, spiritual, devout, solemn, reverential, dutiful.

devour *v.* eat, consume, gulp, guzzle, stuff, gobble, bolt, gormandize, cram, polish off, wolf.

devout *adj.* faithful, devoted, staunch, ardent, zealous, fervent, steadfast, orthodox.

dexterity *n.* ability, facility, skill, proficiency, expertise, aptitude, finesse, knack, mastery, adroitness, handiness, deftness; *ant.* clumsiness, ineptitude.

dexterous *adj.* skillful, proficient, adept, adroit, expert, deft, able, handy, facile, agile; *ant.* clumsy, inept.

diabolical *adj.* devilish, fiendish, wicked, hellish, infernal, damnable, villainous, tricky.

diagnosis *n.* analysis, determination, conclusion, pronouncement, verdict, findings, interpretation, opinion.

diagnostic *adj.* indicative, symptomatic, distin-

guishing, characteristic, demonstrative, distinctive, idiosyncratic, particular, peculiar; analytical, interpretive.

diagonal *adj.* oblique, slanting, angled, crooked, sloping, crosswise, crossways, inclining, askew, cater-cornered.

diagram *n.* drawing, sketch, outline, plan, chart, graph, layout, table, illustration, figure, schema.

dial *n.* face, front, gauge, index, circle, control, indicator, meter, register.

dial *v.* telephone, phone, call, ring.

dialect *n.* accent, pronunciation, diction, tongue, vernacular, regionalism, localism, provincialism, lingo, idiom, jargon.

dialectic *n.* logic, reasoning, rationale, discussion, debate, deduction, polemics, analysis, argumentation, casuistry, contention, sophistry.

dialectic *adj.* **1.** (said of a speech variety) regional, provincial, local; colloquial, informal, idiomatic, vernacular. **2.** (said of a kind of reasoning) analytic, persuasive, logical, rational, polemical, inductive, deductive.

dialogue *n.* conversation, talk, discussion, exchange, debate, discourse, communication, interaction, interchange, interlocution, conference.

diametric *adj.* opposite, opposed, contrary, contrasting, counter, adverse, facing, antithetical, antipodal.

diaphanous *adj.* transparent, see-through, delicate, translucent, fine, gossamer, filmy, sheer, thin, gauzy; *ant.* heavy, opaque.

diary *n.* journal, log, record, chronicle, appointment *or* engagement book, daybook, diurnal.

diatribe *n.* tirade, castigation, upbraiding, denunciation, harangue, vituperation, onslaught, broadside, philippic; *ant.* praise.

dictate *n.* decree, edict, fiat, command, injunction, order, ultimatum, mandate, precept, rule, law, statute, ordinance.

dictate *v.* **1.** orate, speak, deliver, announce, pronounce, compose, formulate, verbalize, record. **2.** order, command, instruct, direct, rule, manage, decree, prescribe, ordain, impose, enjoin.

dictation *n.* **1.** account, record, correspondence, notes, transcription. **2.** shorthand, stenography, dictography.

dictator *n.* tyrant, despot, autocrat, fascist, sultan, rajah, czar, emir, khan.

dictatorial *adj.* tyrannical, despotic, oppressive, totalitarian, autocratic, authoritarian, domineering, dogmatic, magisterial, imperious; *ant.* democratic, egalitarian, liberal, tolerant.

diction *n.* 1. articulation, enunciation, pronunciation, delivery, style, inflection, elocution, intonation, speech. 2. phrasing, wording, idiom, style, terminology, vocabulary.

dictionary *n.* lexicon, thesaurus, wordbook, encyclopedia, glossary, vocabulary, concordance.

dictum *n.* 1. pronouncement, announcement, declaration, dictate, affirmation, assertion, command, order, decree, edict, fiat, ruling. 2. proverb, saying, maxim, adage, axiom, precept, motto, saw.

didactic *adj.* educational, instructive, pedantic, prescriptive, pedagogic.

die *v.* expire, pass away *or* on, depart, perish, be no more, decease, *slang:* buy the farm, kick the bucket, bite the dust, croak.

die away decline, go away, stop.

die down decrease, decline, disappear, recede, diminish, lessen.

die off *or* **out** disappear, go, cease to exist, vanish.

die-hard *n.* fanatic, hard-liner, zealot, ultraconservative, intransigent, reactionary, extremist.

die-hard *adj.* zealot, reactionary, extremist, hardcore, incorrigible, entrenched, intransigent, dyed-in-the-wool, ultraconservative, hard-line.

diet *n.* 1. menu, food, victuals, fare, rations, sustenance, nourishment, provisions, foodstuffs, edibles. 2. fast, regimen, weight-reduction plan.

diet *v.* fast, reduce, slim, weight-watch.

differ *v.* 1. vary, change, diverge, digress; *ant.* conform. 2. oppose, disagree, object, argue, fight, dissent, quarrel, dispute, contradict, conflict; *ant.* agree.

difference *n.* 1. dissimilarity, contrast, nonconformity, antithesis, inequality, diversity, variance; deviation, divergence, discrepancy; *ant.* uniformity, conformity. 2. dispute, quarrel, conflict, dissent, dissension, debate, discord, argument, altercation, clash, controversy, contretemps; *ant.* agreement.

different *adj.* 1. unlike, distinct, separate, divergent, variant, dissonant, incongruous, devi-ating, varying, diverse; *ant.* same, similar, uniform. 2. unusual, original, rare, unique, singular, individual, peculiar, distinctive, bizarre, eccentric, strange, queer, weird, alien, startling, extraordinary; *ant.* conventional, normal, common.

differentiate *v.* distinguish, contrast, discern, discriminate, individualize, demarcate, dis-ambiguate; *ant.* assimilate, associate.

difficult *adj.* 1. laborious, hard, strenuous, exacting, arduous, labored, trying, troublesome, demanding, onerous, wearisome, back-breaking; *ant.* easy, light. 2. puzzling, perplexing, intricate, involved, abstruse, complex, complicated, knotty, thorny, trouble-some, mystifying, confusing, bewildering; *ant.* simple, straightforward, clear, obvious. 3. rude, impolite, boorish, irritable, uncoopera-tive, disruptive, refractory, enigmatical, frac-tious, recalcitrant, obstinate, stubborn, hard to handle; *ant.* polite, civil, amenable.

difficulty *n.* 1. trouble, plight, hardship, dis-tress, tribulation, straits, fix, spot. 2. prob-lem, dilemma, quandary, predicament; obsta-cle, impediment.

diffidence *n.* hesitation, reluctance, timidity, fear, insecurity, reserve, self-doubt, modesty, constraint, inhibition, shyness, bashfulness, self-consciousness, self-effacement; *ant.* confi-dence.

diffident *adj.* self-conscious, shy, meek, timid, withdrawn, unsure, tentative, reluctant, hesi-tant; *ant.* confident.

diffuse *v.* spread, dissipate, scatter, dissemi-nate, circulate, distribute, winnow.

diffuse *adj.* 1. scattered, separated, dispersed, spread out, thin, diluted; *ant.* concentra-ted. 2. wordy, verbose, discursive, prolix, long-winded, copious, digressive, rambling, circumlocutory; *ant.* succinct.

dig *n.* insult, gibe, slur, taunt, insinuation, aspersion, barb, jeer, poke, wisecrack (*slang*); *ant.* compliment.

dig *v.* 1. shovel, excavate, burrow, graft, tun-nel, till, mine, grub. 2. prod, probe, thrust, gouge, penetrate.

dig in 1. begin, commence, rise, spring. **2.** entrench, delve, burrow. **3.** eat, consume, chew.

digest *n.* **1.** summary, synopsis, abbreviation, abridgment, condensation, epitome, abstract, précis. **2.** compendium, collection, reader.

digest *v.* **1.** eat, consume, ingest, stomach, macerate. **2.** understand, think, ponder, consider, analyze, contemplate, grasp, assimilate, study. **3.** summarize, abridge, condense, shorten, abstract, survey, abbreviate, compress.

digestion *n.* ingestion, absorption, assimilation, disintegration, conversion, transformation.

dignified *adj.* reserved, stately, majestic, distinguished, formal, august, upright, noble, honorable.

dignify *v.* honor, distinguish, glorify, ennoble, elevate, raise, promote, exalt, aggrandize, apotheosize; *ant.* degrade, demean.

dignity *n.* **1.** worthiness, respectability, honor, rank, standing, status, eminence, importance, station; self-respect, self-possession. **2.** stateliness, propriety, decorum.

digress *v.* ramble, wander, stray, deviate, diverge, drift, go off on a tangent.

dilapidated *adj.* decrepit, ramshackle, tumbledown, decayed, rickety, shabby, broken-down, run-down, neglected.

dilate *v.* enlarge, extend, swell, increase, widen, distend, broaden, expand, amplify, develop, stretch, increase; *ant.* constrict, contract.

dilatory *adj.* slow, sluggish, indolent, lackadaisical, slothful, tardy, laggard, dallying, delaying, tarrying.

dilemma *n.* problem, plight, quandary, strait, difficulty, mess, predicament, fix, jam, bind, pickle.

dilettante *n.* amateur, dabbler, trifler.

diligence *n.* industry, attention, care, activity, pertinacity, earnestness, assiduousness; *ant.* laziness.

diligent *adj.* hard-working, industrious, steady, reliable, conscientious, painstaking, assiduous, meticulous, compunctious; *ant.* dilatory, lazy.

dilly-dally *v.* hesitate, procrastinate, tarry, trifle, vacillate, waver; linger, loiter, dawdle, delay.

dilute *v.* water down, diffuse, attenuate, cut, adulterate, reduce, weaken; decrease, mitigate, temper; *ant.* concentrate.

dilute *adj.* watered down, weak, diluted, thin, adulterated, attenuated, cut; *ant.* concentrated.

dim *adj.* **1.** muted, dark, gloomy, obscured, opaque, overcast, somber, hazy, cloudy, shadowy, dusky; *ant.* bright, distinct. **2.** stupid, dumb, dull, thick, confused, dense, obtuse; *ant.* smart, bright, intelligent.

take a dim view doubt, suspect, be skeptical, disapprove.

dimensions *n.* size, scope, magnitude, bulk, scale, measurements, amplitude, range.

diminish *v.* lessen, decrease, reduce, lower, abate, curtail, dwindle, ebb, depreciate, subside; *ant.* enhance, enlarge, increase.

diminution *n.* reduction, deduction, decrease, shortening, lessening, cutback, contraction, abatement, decline, ebb, subsidence, shrinkage; *ant.* enlargement, increase.

diminutive *adj.* tiny, short, miniature, petite, undersized, pygmy, wee, midget, bantam, lilliputian, dinky (*slang*); *ant.* enormous, oversize.

dimple *n.* hollow, depression, dint, concavity.

dimwit *n.* nitwit, dullard, ignoramus, numskull, blockhead, dunce, bonehead (*slang*).

din *n.* noise, racket, clatter, commotion, pandemonium, confusion, clamor, outcry, hubbub, hullabaloo; *ant.* calm, quiet.

dine *v.* eat, feast, feed, lunch, sup, break bread, banquet.

diner *n.* **1.** patron, guest, eater, gourmet, gourmand. **2.** café, restaurant, coffee shop, luncheonette, dining room.

dingy *adj.* dirty, soiled, drab, grimy, discolored, shabby, run-down; *ant.* bright, clean.

dinner *n.* meal, supper, repast; feast, banquet.

dint *n.* **1.** effort, labor, struggle, force, application. **2.** dent, impression, depression, hollow, indentation.

dip *n.* **1.** bath, soaking, plunge, immersion, douche, drenching; swim, plunge, dive. **2.** infusion, solution, dilution, suffusion, saturation, bath. **3.** hole, depression, slope, inclination; drop, fall, slump, sag, slip, decline.

dip *v.* **1.** submerge, plunge, wet, douse, moisten, bathe, baptize, dunk. **2.** scoop, shovel, ladle, spoon, decant, dredge, draw, dish. **3.** fall, slope, incline, recede, tilt, swoop, sink, plunge.

117

dip into dabble, sample, try, browse, skim; peruse, flip through, scan.

diplomacy *n.* statesmanship, tact, skill, delicacy, savior-faire, finesse, maneuvering, subtlety, discretion.

diplomat *n.* **1.** statesman, stateswoman, representative, ambassador, consul, minister, legate, nuncio, emissary, envoy, attaché, agent. **2.** public speaker, orator, strategist, negotiator, Machiavelli, propagandist.

diplomatic *adj.* sensitive, tactful, polite, prudent, discreet, judicious, sagacious, politic; *ant.* rude, thoughtless.

dire *adj.* **1.** terrible, dreadful, horrible, ominous, grim, grave, catastrophic. **2.** urgent, pressing, exigent, drastic, desperate, crucial, critical, extreme.

direct *v.* **1.** show, guide, govern, rule, command, order, control, supervise, teach, advise, inform, instruct. **2.** aim, sight, train, level, fix, focus. **3.** (to convey, as a message) address, mean, intend, point.

direct *adj.* **1.** straight, uninterrupted, unswerving, straightaway, nonstop; *ant.* crooked, devious. **2.** (immediately resulting) immediate, succeeding, plain, certain, sure, quick, unavoidable.

direction *n.* **1.** (as when consulting a map) position, bearing, region, area, road, route, way. **2.** supervision, management, leadership, control, administration, government, superintendence, guidance. **3.** (issuance of a rule) order, command, charge, regulation, injunction.

directions *n.* instructions, guidelines, recommendations, plan, recipe, guidance, orders, regulations.

directive *n.* order, command, instruction, ruling, edict, decree, injunction, mandate, ordinance, fiat, imperative.

directly *adv.* instantly, quickly, immediately, right away, promptly, forthwith, pronto (*slang*).

directness *n.* honesty, sincerity, straightforwardness, plain-speaking, candor, forthrightness, frankness, bluntness, bluffness, outspokenness; *ant.* deviousness, indirection, subtlety.

director *n.* manager, leader, organizer, controller, head, chief, conductor, producer, supervisor, chairperson, administrator.

dirge *n.* lament, elegy, requiem, hymn, song.

dirt *n.* **1.** earth, soil, loam, clay, mud, dust, mire, muck. **2.** filth, stain, tarnish, grime, impurity; smut, obscenity, indecency; *ant.* cleanliness.

dirty *v.* stain, foul, pollute, spoil, tarnish, soil, mess, defile, sully; *ant.* clean, cleanse.

dirty *adj.* **1.** soiled, filthy, nasty, slovenly, messy, squalid, sloppy, polluted, unhygienic; *ant.* clean, spotless, sanitary. **2.** obscene, indecent, pornographic, smutty, lewd, ribald, salacious, risqué, off-color, vulgar, blue.

disability *n.* handicap, infirmity, weakness, ailment, defect, disorder, impairment, incapacity, malady, affliction, inability.

disable *v.* handicap, impair, cripple, prostrate, paralyze, damage, incapacitate, debilitate, enfeeble, put out of action (*slang*).

disabled *adj.* handicapped, physically challenged, impaired, incapacitated; crippled, maimed, lame, infirm; *ant.* able-bodied.

disadvantage *n.* **1.** loss, damage, injury, hurt, harm, deprivation, privation, detriment, liability, debit, minus, weakness; *ant.* benefit. **2.** impediment, handicap, hardship, obstacle, hindrance, inconvenience, drawback, snag, restraint, nuisance; *ant.* advantage.

disadvantaged *adj.* underprivileged, deprived, handicapped, impoverished, struggling, impeded, hindered; *ant.* privileged.

disadvantageous *adj.* harmful, damaging, detrimental, injurious, hurtful, unfavorable, adverse, deleterious, inconvenient, inopportune, ill-timed, inexpedient; *ant.* advantageous.

disaffected *adj.* estranged, alienated, hostile, mutinous, disloyal, antagonistic, disgruntled, rebellious, discontented, antipathetic; *ant.* contented, loyal.

disagree *v.* differ, vary, deviate, oppose, conflict, counter, object, challenge, argue, protest, dissent, squabble, wrangle; *ant.* agree.

disagree with nauseate, sicken, upset one's stomach, make one ill.

disagreeable *adj.* rude, contrary, surly, irritable, churlish, cross, difficult, bad-tempered, ill-natured, unfriendly, unpleasant, brusque, repellent; *ant.* amiable.

disagreement *n.* **1.** discord, contention, conflict, cross-purposes, opposition, hostility, dissension, animosity, strife, vendetta, ill will. 2. dissimilarity, difference, inconsistency, discrepancy, diversity, disparity, incongruity, divergence, variance; *ant.* similarity.

disallow *v.* forbid, prohibit, refuse, veto, ban, proscribe, censor, cancel, abjure, embargo, dismiss; *ant.* allow, permit.

disappear *v.* **1.** (cease being seen) vanish, fade, wane, ebb, recede, withdraw, depart, evanesce. **2.** (cease being) cease, go, pass, perish, dissolve, evaporate, dematerialize.

disappoint *v.* let down, dismay, dishearten, disgruntle, frustrate, dash, miff; *ant.* delight, please, satisfy.

disappointment *n.* **1.** discouragement, frustration, distress, disenchantment, mortification, disillusionment, regret, discontent; *ant.* delight, pleasure, satisfaction. **2.** failure, setback, letdown, misfortune, disaster, blow, calamity, fiasco; *ant.* boost, success.

disapprobation *n.* censure, disapproval, condemnation, denunciation, reproach, disfavor, reproof, blame, displeasure, dissatisfaction, objection; *ant.* approval, favor.

disapproval *n.* rejection, censure, condemnation, deprecation, disfavor, objection, denunciation, reproach, criticism, disparagement, dissatisfaction, displeasure, disapprobation.

disapprove *v.* reject, oppose, refuse, spurn, disallow.

disapprove of oppose, object to, dislike, deplore, disparage, deprecate, take exception to, censure, reject, disallow.

disarm *v.* **1.** demobilize, disable, demilitarize, debilitate, incapacitate, invalidate, deaden, subdue, muzzle, disband, defeat. **2.** persuade, win over, seduce, coax, convince, urge, appease.

disarming *n.* charming, persuasive, winning, irresistible, convincing, seductive, likable, inveigling.

disarrange *v.* muss, disarray, jumble, disorganize, unsettle, confuse, discompose, disturb; *ant.* neaten, tidy up.

disarray *n.* chaos, jumble, mess, muddle, disorganization, clutter, tangle, confusion, disorder, discomposure, upset; *ant.* array, order.

disaster *n.* tragedy, calamity, accident, catastrophe, cataclysm; debacle, mischance, blow, stroke, misfortune; *ant.* success, triumph.

disastrous *adj.* devastating, terrible, tragic, dreadful, catastrophic, cataclysmic, unfortunate, destructive, dire, fatal, grievous, ill-fated; *ant.* successful, triumphant.

disband *v.* separate, break up, scatter, dissolve, disperse, demobilize, dismiss; *ant.* assemble, combine.

disbelief *n.* skepticism, distrust, rejection, incredulity, suspicion, mistrust, doubt, dubiety; *ant.* belief.

disbelieve *v.* discount, mistrust, reject, repudiate, discredit, suspect; *ant.* believe, trust, credit.

disbeliever *n.* skeptic, doubter, atheist, agnostic, unbeliever, doubting Thomas, scoffer.

disbursement *n.* spending, paying, outlay, expenditure, disposal.

discard *v.* throw away, dispose of, abandon, dispense with, jettison, cast aside, scrap, dump, ditch (*slang*); *ant.* adopt, embrace.

discern *v.* **1.** differentiate, discriminate, determine, judge, ascertain. **2.** perceive, see, make out, detect, notice, observe, espy, discover, behold.

discernible *adj.* perceptible, visible, apparent, obvious, noticeable, recognizable, clear, patent, manifest, distinct, distinguishable, detectable; *ant.* invisible.

discerning *adj.* discriminating, perceptive, astute, shrewd, perspicacious, sharp, clever, keen, critical, insightful, sagacious, wise, intelligent, judicious; *ant.* obtuse.

discharge *n.* **1.** firing, dismissal, *slang:* the sack, the boot. **2.** release, liberation, emancipation, acquittal, pardon. **3.** detonation, explosion, shot, blast, burst, report. **4.** ejection, voiding, discharging; secretion, emission, seepage, ooze.

discharge *v.* **1.** fire, dismiss, let go, lay off, make redundant (*Brit.*), cashier, *slang:* sack, can. **2.** release, free, emancipate, liberate, let go. **3.** shoot, fire, detonate, blast, set off, explode.

disciple *n.* believer, follower, devotee, supporter, adherent, student, pupil, acolyte, votary.

disciplinarian *n.* martinet, tyrant, authoritarian, despot, autocrat.

discipline *n.* **1.** course, curriculum, branch,

subject, specialty. **2.** self-control, restraint, character, conduct, orderliness; strictness, toughness. **3.** rules, regulations, practices, regimen, bylaws, code of conduct. **4.** punishment, penalty, chastisement, castigation.

discipline *v.* **1.** regulate, train, control, govern, drill, toughen, inure. **2.** punish, reprimand, penalize, chastise, chasten, reprove; restrain, limit.

disclaim *v.* **1.** deny, repudiate, retract, refuse, decline, negate, contradict, disavow, disallow, abjure; *ant.* acknowledge. **2.** disown, revoke, renounce, reject, abandon, forswear, discard; *ant.* accept.

disclose *v.* reveal, expose, divulge, confess, broadcast, publish, lay bare, exhibit, leak, let slip; *ant.* conceal, hide.

disclosure *n.* announcement, admission, declaration, confession, revelation, publication, acknowledgment, broadcast, leak, discovery, exposé, divulgence.

discolor *v.* stain, soil, tarnish, fade, streak, tinge, rust.

discoloration *n.* stain, blemish, spot, splotch, mark, blotch, blot.

discomfit *v.* **1.** thwart, frustrate, prevent, stall, hold back, checkmate. **2.** disconcert, confuse, perplex, confound, discompose, fluster, faze, rattle; embarrass, humble, humiliate, demoralize.

discomfort *n.* **1.** unpleasantness, irritation, disquiet, distress; *ant.* comfort, ease. **2.** malaise, trouble, annoyance, hardship, irritant, ache, hurt.

discompose *v.* **1.** disconcert, fluster, unsettle, upset, agitate, perturb, bewilder, faze, ruffle, embarrass; *ant.* compose. **2.** dishevel, tousle, rumple.

disconcert *v.* **1.** upset, worry, unsettle, embarrass, perplex, confuse, disturb, nonplus, bewilder, rattle. **2.** frustrate, thwart, hinder.

disconcerted *adj.* upset, flustered, confused, fazed, embarrassed, thrown, ruffled, nonplussed, discombobulated.

disconcerting *adj.* alarming, bewildering, dismaying, distracting, disturbing, off-putting, awkward, embarrassing, upsetting, confusing, perplexing, baffling.

disconnect *v.* separate, sever, disengage, part,

120

detach, divide, unhook, unplug, unhitch, uncouple, unyoke.

disconnected *adj.* **1.** separated, detached, loose, free; *ant.* attached. **2.** incoherent, unintelligible, garbled, jumbled, confused, rambling, illogical, irrational, disjointed, loose; *ant.* coherent.

disconsolate *adj.* **1.** dejected, inconsolable, despairing, dispirited, miserable, hopeless, melancholy, forlorn, crushed, heavy-hearted; *ant.* cheerful. **2.** (causing dejection) dismal, cheerless, gloomy, dreary, dark, desolate; *ant.* cheery.

discontented *adj.* dissatisfied, unhappy, disgruntled, displeased, miserable, exasperated, complaining, disaffected; *ant.* happy, satisfied.

discontinue *v.* stop, end, terminate, finish, quit, cease, cancel, break off, drop, suspend, abandon.

discord *n.* **1.** disagreement, dissension, conflict, difference, friction, opposition, disunity, variance, dispute, division; *ant.* agreement, concord. **2.** clash, din, dissonance, disharmony, cacophony; *ant.* harmony.

discordant *adj.* **1.** inharmonious, cacophonous, dissonant, strident, harsh, grating, shrill, jarring, jangling; *ant.* melodious. **2.** contradictory, contrary, opposite, incongruous, inconsistent, different, disagreeing, at odds, conflicting; *ant.* concordant.

discount *n.* reduction, deduction, markdown, cut.

discount *v.* **1.** reduce, decrease, deduct, redeem, diminish, depreciate, lower, mark down. **2.** disregard, question, disbelieve, doubt; forgive, overlook, ignore, forget about.

discountenance *v.* **1.** shame, humiliate, embarrass, abash, humble, disconcert, dampen, daunt, age, demoralize, dishearten, dampen, daunt, dispirit.

discourage *v.* **1.** dishearten, dispirit, intimidate, deject, prostrate, unnerve, dampen, dismay, daunt, demoralize, set back; *ant.* encourage, hearten. **2.** warn, dissuade, alarm, scare, deter. **3.** restrain, obstruct, impede, check, inhibit, repress, curb.

discouraging *adj.* disheartening, dampening, daunting, disappointing, dispiriting, dissuasive, off-putting; *ant.* encouraging.

discourse *n.* lecture, speech, address, oration,

discourse dissertation, sermon, treatise, homily, talk, conversation.

discourse *v.* talk, lecture, converse, debate, confer, dissent, expatiate.

discourteous *adj.* rude, impolite, uncivil, illmannered, disrespectful, curt, brusque, insolent, boorish, ill-bred; *ant.* civil, gracious.

discover *v.* find out, ascertain, detect, uncover, unearth, discern, recognize, distinguish, determine, observe.

discovery *n.* finding, results, revelation, disclosure, invention, coup, breakthrough; *ant.* concealment.

discredit *v.* **1.** blame, censure, disparage, reproach, disgrace, degrade, slur, slander, smear, defame, dishonor, vilify. **2.** doubt, question, disbelieve, distrust, mistrust, dispute, discount; *ant.* believe.

discreditable *adj.* unworthy, dishonorable, infamous, ignoble, ignominious, improper, scandalous, shameful, blameworthy, unprincipled, disgraceful; *ant.* worthy.

discredited *adj.* exposed, debunked, rejected, discarded, refuted, disgraced, dishonored.

discreet *adj.* cautious, prudent, sensible, wary, careful; diplomatic, tactful, circumspect, politic, guarded, reserved; *ant.* careless; tactless.

discrepancy *n.* inconsistency, disparity, difference, incongruity, variation, dissimilarity, divergence; conflict, disagreement.

discrete *adj.* distinct, separate, individual, finite, discontinuous, particular.

discriminate *v.* **1.** differentiate, distinguish, discern. **2.** be prejudiced *or* biased, disfavor, segregate, separate, victimize.

discriminating *adj.* discerning, astute, particular, cultivated, selective, critical; particular, fastidious, finicky, fussy.

discrimination *n.* **1.** acumen, insight, judgment, keenness, perception, sagacity, tact, wisdom; discernment, refinement, subtlety, taste. **2.** prejudice, bias, bigotry, inequity, favoritism, unfairness, intolerance.

discriminatory *adj.* prejudiced, prejudicial, inequitable, partisan, unjust, biased, partial, one-sided, weighted, preferential, favoring; *ant.* fair, impartial.

discursive *adj.* rambling, meandering, erratic, circuitous, long-winded, digressive, prolix, desultory, diffuse; *ant.* brief, short.

discuss *v.* debate, confer, converse, consider, deliberate, talk over, thrash out, palaver.

discussion *n.* conversation, argument, dialogue, chat, talk, discourse, exchange, debate, review, consultation, conference, colloquy, meeting, symposium, colloquium, palaver, powwow.

disdain *n.* dislike, derision, contempt, scorn, sneering, superciliousness, deprecation; *ant.* admiration, respect.

disdain *v.* scorn, reject, deride, despise, spurn, contemn, belittle, look down one's nose at, slight, rebuff, pooh-pooh, disregard; *ant.* admire, respect.

disdainful *adj.* haughty, superior, scornful, arrogant, elitist, derisive, insolent, supercilious, aloof, contemptuous, sneering, snobbish; *ant.* admiring, respectful.

disease *n.* illness, sickness, ailment, malady, disorder, complaint, malaise, infirmity; infection, contamination, plague, germ, virus; *ant.* health, wellness.

diseased *adj.* sickly, ailing, infected, contaminated, tainted, poisoned, rotten, unsound, unwholesome; *ant.* healthy, well.

disembark *v.* arrive, land, anchor, alight, detrain.

disembodied *adj.* spiritual, bodiless, intangible, spectral, immaterial, ghostly, incorporeal.

disembowel *v.* gut, eviscerate, kill, draw.

disenchanted *adj.* cynical, embittered, jaundiced, soured, bitter, disillusioned, disenthralled, indifferent, blasé, disappointed.

disenchantment *n.* disillusionment, disappointment, cynicism, bitterness, alienation.

disengage *v.* separate, divide, withdraw, untie, disconnect, disentangle, detach, disjoin, uncouple, release, liberate, free, extricate; *ant.* attach, connect.

disentangle *v.* free, loose, extricate, detach, disconnect, separate, sever, disengage, unfold, unravel; simplify, clarify.

disfavor *v.* disapprove, discredit, disapprobate, dislike; *ant.* esteem.

disfigure v. deform, distort, damage, maim, mutilate, scar, deface, injure, mar, spoil, blemish.

disgorge v. vomit, throw up, expel, regurgitate, eject, spew, spout, belch, effuse, empty, discharge.

disgrace n. disfavor, infamy, disrepute, dishonor, stigma, shame, scandal, contempt, ignominy, defamation; *ant.* esteem, honor, respect.

disgrace v. scandalize, shame, humiliate, dishonor, stain, sully, defame, discredit, disparage, reproach, slur, stigmatize; *ant.* honor, respect.

disgraceful *adj.* shameful, dreadful, shocking, appalling, low, mean, ignominious, infamous, detestable, contemptible, blameworthy, scandalous; *ant.* honorable, respectable.

disgruntled *adj.* petulant, testy, sullen, malcontent, irritated, annoyed, vexed, grumpy, discontented, sulky, peevish; *ant.* pleased, satisfied.

disguise v. hide, mask, conceal, cover, camouflage, veil, shroud, screen; fake, deceive, dissemble, misrepresent, falsify; *ant.* expose, reveal.

disguise n. 1. mask, camouflage, costume, masquerade, cloak, cover. 2. travesty, semblance, pretense, façade, deception, dissimulation, trickery.

disguised *adj.* cloaked, masked, camouflaged; incognito, covert, undercover, false, fake, feigned.

disgust n. loathing, abomination, abhorrence, antipathy, hatred, odium, detestation, revulsion, aversion, repugnance, distaste; *ant.* admiration, liking.

disgust v. revolt, offend, repel, sicken, nauseate; *ant.* delight, gratify, tempt.

disgusted *adj.* appalled, repulsed, repelled, offended, nauseated, sickened; *ant.* attracted, delighted.

disgusting *adj.* offensive, revolting, gross, foul, vile, vulgar, objectionable, obnoxious, abominable, repellent, sickening, nauseating; *ant.* attractive, delightful, pleasant.

dish n. 1. plate, platter, bowl, vessel. 2. meal, food, course, entree, serving, helping, recipe, fare.

dish v. serve, give, offer, proffer, hand out.

disharmony n. 1. (unpleasant sound) disso-

122

nance, cacophony, discordance, discord. 2. (failure to agree) disaccord, incompatibility, friction, conflict, clash.

dishearten v. daunt, dampen, deter, discourage, depress, dash, dispirit, dismay, depress, deject, crush; *ant.* encourage.

disheartened *adj.* disappointed, dismayed, downcast, discouraged, dejected, crestfallen, dispirited, downhearted, crushed; *ant.* encouraged, heartened.

disheveled *adj.* unkempt, messy, disordered, disarranged, tousled, rumpled, slovenly, bedraggled, ruffled, uncombed; *ant.* neat, spruce, tidy.

dishonest *adj.* deceitful, deceptive, fraudulent, lying, crooked, false, mendacious, immoral, untrustworthy, perfidious; *ant.* fair, honest, scrupulous, ethical, trustworthy.

dishonesty n. deceit, duplicity, cheating, fraudulence, insincerity, falsehood, immorality, mendacity, perfidy, trickery; *ant.* truthfulness.

dishonor n. infamy, disgrace, shame, disfavor, offense, abasement, ignominy, odium, opprobrium; *ant.* honor.

dishonor v. 1. disgrace, shame, discredit, degrade, demean, blacken. 2. corrupt, debase, ravish, seduce, defile, sully, debauch.

dishonorable *adj.* corrupt, shameful, contemptible, ignoble, disgraceful, scandalous, infamous, ignominious, despicable, base, shameless, unscrupulous; *ant.* ethical, reputable, trustworthy.

disillusioned *adj.* disappointed, disenchanted, disenthralled, embittered.

disinfect v. clean, decontaminate, sterilize, purify, sanitize, deodorize, fumigate, purge; *ant.* contaminate.

disinfectant n. antiseptic, germicide, sanitizer, sterilizer.

disingenuous *adj.* dishonest, insincere, shifty, two-faced, duplicitous, deceitful, cunning, artful, devious, wily, guileful; *ant.* artless, frank.

disintegrate v. crumble, decompose, decay, rot, molder.

disinterest n. 1. indifference, apathy, ennui; *ant.* concern. 2. impartiality, disinterestedness, neutrality, dispassionateness, fairness, justice; *ant.* bias.

disinterested *adj.* 1. neutral, impartial, equitable, fair, just, evenhanded; *ant.* biased, prejudiced. **2.** indifferent, apathetic, dispassionate, aloof; *ant.* concerned.

disjoin *v.* separate, sever, split, disconnect, divide, detach, disengage, partition, dissociate, uncouple, segregate, divorce; *ant.* connect.

disjointed *adj.* incoherent, rambling, disconnected, confused, irrational, broken, spasmodic, fitful; *ant.* coherent.

dislike *n.* hatred, loathing, enmity, antipathy, animosity, aversion, repugnance, distaste, disgust; *ant.* predilection.

dislike *v.* hate, despise, detest, abhor; *ant.* favor.

dislocated *adj.* displaced, misplaced; disconnected, disjointed, disengaged, disunited; *ant.* together.

dislodge *v.* move, remove, displace, extricate, uproot.

disloyal *adj.* false, two-faced, traitorous, treacherous, perfidious, apostate; *ant.* faithful, trustworthy.

disloyalty *n.* infidelity, betrayal, double-dealing, treason, inconstancy, treachery, sedition, perfidy, falseness, falsity, apostasy.

dismal *adj.* **1.** (said of surroundings, conditions, or prospects) dreary, gloomy, dark, somber, bleak; *ant.* bright. **2.** (said of feelings) sad, melancholy, depressing, despondent, cheerless, hopeless, sorrowful, discouraging, doleful, forlorn; *ant.* cheerful.

dismantle *v.* take apart, demolish, disassemble, rend, amputate, disjoint, anatomize; *ant.* assemble, join.

dismay *n.* anxiety, upset, consternation, dread, fear, panic, apprehension, alarm, trepidation, fright, horror, terror.

dismay *v.* depress, dishearten, daunt, frighten, scare, terrify, horrify, unsettle, unnerve, distress, appall; *ant.* encourage.

dismember *v.* dissect, divide, mutilate, sever, rend, amputate, disjoint, anatomize; *ant.* assemble, join.

dismiss *v.* discharge, fire, banish, expel, cashier, repudiate, reject, spurn; release, free, let go.

dismissal *n.* discharge, removal, expulsion, walking papers, *slang:* the boot, the sack, the bum's rush; *ant.* appointment.

dismissive *adj.* contemptuous, disdainful, short, abrupt, brusque, scornful; *ant.* concerned, interested.

dismount *v.* descend, light, alight; *ant.* mount, climb on.

disobedience *n.* revolt, insubordination, recalcitrance, infraction, mutiny, waywardness, unruliness; *ant.* obedience.

disobedient *adj.* defiant, insubordinate, intractable, refractory, contrary; mischievous, naughty, wayward, unruly, willful, obstreperous; *ant.* obedient.

disobey *v.* rebel, defy, flout, disregard, violate, transgress, contravene.

disoblige *v.* **1.** offend, insult, affront. **2.** disturb, upset, annoy.

disobliging *adj.* disagreeable, rude, discourteous, uncivil, uncooperative, unaccommodating, unhelpful, surly, churlish.

disorder *n.* **1.** confusion, chaos, jumble, disorganization, disarray, shambles, clutter. **2.** (instance of public unrest) riot, commotion, tumult, uproar, disturbance, turbulence. **3.** illness, disease, sickness, affliction, ailment, malady, complaint.

disorder *v.* mix *or* mess up, jumble, disturb, upset; confuse, confound; *ant.* arrange.

disorderly *adv.* **1.** confused, disorganized, messy, jumbled, scattered, cluttered, unkempt, scrambled, heterogeneous, indiscriminate; *ant.* tidy. **2.** unruly, rebellious, intemperate, rowdy, lawless, undisciplined, refractory, disruptive, riotous; *ant.* well-behaved.

disorganized *adj.* confused, haphazard, jumbled, unmethodical, disordered, unsystematic, unregulated, muddled; *ant.* organized, tidy.

disorient *v.* confuse, puzzle, perplex, mislead, muddle, upset, faze.

disparage *v.* slander, denigrate, criticize, put down (*slang*), belittle, malign, vilify, vilipend, deride, pooh-pooh, ridicule, depreciate, scorn; *ant.* praise.

disparagement *n.* slander, ridicule, scorn, criticism, denunciation, debasement, disdain, aspersion, contempt, degradation, derision, derogation; *ant.* praise.

disparate *adj.* different, contrasting, diverse, contrary, distinct; *ant.* equal, similar.

disparity *n.* difference, incongruity, contrast, distinction, unevenness, discrepancy, disproportion; *ant.* equality, similarity.

dispassionate *adj.* unexcited, indifferent, cool,

detached, disinterested, unmoved, composed, collected, objective; *ant.* biased, emotional.

dispatch *n.* speed, quickness, rapidity, swiftness, haste, alacrity, promptness, expedition; *ant.* slowness.

dispatch *v.* 1. send, transmit, express, forward, consign, remit; *ant.* impede. 2. murder, kill, assassinate, bump off (*slang*), execute, slay, slaughter, destroy.

dispel *v.* 1. scatter, distribute, disperse, deploy, dissipate. 2. repel, dismiss, oust, banish, cancel, eliminate, expel, rout.

dispensable *adj.* superfluous, expendable, inessential, unnecessary, disposable, replaceable, trivial, useless; *ant.* indispensable.

dispensation *n.* 1. distribution, allocation, allotment, award, endowment, bestowal, apportionment. 2. supervision, management, direction, administration, regulation, appointment. 3. (release from a religious obligation) exemption, exception, waiver, pardon, forgiveness.

dispense *v.* 1. distribute, supply, give, apportion, assign, allocate, allot, mete out, dole out, disburse. 2. administer, manage, command, undertake, enforce, direct, operate, execute, implement.

dispense with forgo, dispose of, waive, omit, ignore, cancel, abolish; *ant.* accept, use.

disperse *v.* 1. scatter, distribute, strew, spread, disseminate, separate. 2. dispel, diffuse, dissolve, evanesce, disappear.

dispirited *adj.* disheartened, discouraged, crestfallen, despondent, downcast, dejected, depressed; *ant.* buoyant.

displace *v.* remove, move, replace, dislodge, depose, supplant, oust, eject, dismiss.

display *n.* 1. affectation, ostentation, vanity, pretension. 2. spectacle, exhibit, show, exhibition, presentation, exposition, demonstration, performance. 3. advertisement, sample, layout, spread.

display *v.* show, showcase, demonstrate, exhibit, present, parade, blazon, flaunt; *ant.* hide.

displease *v.* upset, vex, anger, annoy, disgust, incense, offend.

displeasure *n.* annoyance, offense, disfavor, indignation, irritation, anger, pique; *ant.* gratification.

disposal *n.* control, ordering, discretion, bequest, authority, direction, government, management, determination.

dispose *v.* lead, motivate, tempt, bias, condition, induce, influence, prompt, actuate.

dispose of discard, dump, unload, jettison, cast off.

disposed *adj.* inclined, prone, liable, likely, minded, given, apt, ready, willing; *ant.* disinclined.

disposition *n.* 1. arrangement, placement, organization, plan, method, management, direction, constitution, control. 2. temperament, temper, nature, character, mood, spirit.

dispossess *v.* deprive, divest, rob, strip, eject, expel, oust, evict, dislodge; *ant.* give, provide.

dispossession *n.* eviction, expulsion, ousting, ejection.

disprove *v.* discredit, negate, refute, rebut, expose, contradict, invalidate, controvert.

disproportion *n.* imbalance, asymmetry, disparity, inequality, lopsidedness, unevenness; *ant.* balance.

disproportionate *adj.* unbalanced, unequal, uneven, excessive, inappropriate, inordinate; *ant.* appropriate, balanced.

disputable *adj.* debatable, questionable, controversial, arguable, dubious, doubtful.

disputatious *adj.* quarrelsome, argumentative, tendentious, contentious, opinionated, litigious, pugnacious.

dispute *n.* quarrel, feud, debate, spar, squabble, brawl, disagreement, discord, altercation, controversy; *ant.* agreement.

dispute *v.* contest, debate, contradict, gainsay, litigate, argue, quarrel; *ant.* agree.

disqualify *v.* invalidate, disable, incapacitate, prohibit, rule out, preclude, disbar; *ant.* accept, allow.

disquiet *n.* distress, anxiety, worry, uneasiness, nervousness, fretfulness, angst, restlessness; *ant.* calmness.

disquiet *v.* upset, worry, disturb, bother, perturb, plague, annoy, agitate, trouble, unsettle; *ant.* calm.

disquisition *n.* thesis, treatise, discourse, paper, dissertation, essay, exposition.

disregard *v.* 1. ignore, overlook, miss, skip, neglect; *ant.* note. 2. slight, snub, disparage, disdain; disobey, defy, transgress.

disrepair *n.* ruin, deterioration, decay, collapse, dilapidation, shabbiness; *ant.* restoration.

disreputable *adj.* notorious, infamous, discreditable, scandalous, base, seedy, shady, low; *ant.* decent, honorable.

disrespectful *adj.* rude, discourteous, insulting, impolite, impudent, sassy, indolent, insolent, impertinent; *ant.* civil, polite.

disrobe *v.* undress, strip, shed *or* remove one's clothing; bare, uncover.

disrupt *v.* interrupt, intrude, upset, unsettle, agitate, confuse.

disruption *n.* **1.** division, separation, interruption, splitting, severance, dissolution. **2.** turmoil, upheaval, cataclysm, disturbance, interference, agitation, confusion.

disruptive *adj.* unruly, uncontrollable, troublesome, boisterous, disorderly, refractory, intractable, overactive, mischievous; upsetting, disturbing, distracting, unsettling; *ant.* well-behaved, disciplined.

dissatisfied *adj.* unhappy, displeased, discontented, disgruntled, disappointed, frustrated; *ant.* pleased, fulfilled.

dissect *v.* **1.** divide, cut, dismember, quarter, operate. **2.** examine, analyze, take apart, scrutinize, study, investigate, inspect, explore.

dissection *n.* **1.** dismemberment, operation, vivisection. **2.** examination, investigation, study, inquest, analysis, scrutiny, inspection.

dissemble *v.* pretend, feign, disguise, camouflage, hide, mask, simulate, dissimulate, fake, conceal, counterfeit.

dissembler *n.* pretender, fraud, deceiver, impostor, trickster, fake, charlatan.

disseminate *v.* distribute, sow, scatter, spread; circulate, propagate, publicize, broadcast, promulgate, publish, evangelize.

dissension *n.* disagreement, discord, quarreling, dispute, friction, conflict, discordance, contention; *ant.* agreement, peace.

dissent *n.* difference, disagreement, discord, refusal, challenge, demurral, resistance, opposition, nonconformity; *ant.* accord, harmony.

dissent *v.* disagree, object, differ, decline, refuse, quibble, protest, challenge, argue, demur; *ant.* agree, consent.

dissenter *n.* protester, objector, nonconformist.

dissertation *n.* thesis, treatise, paper, essay, discourse, exposition.

disservice *n.* injustice, wrong, harm, injury, disfavor.

dissidence *n.* dispute, feud, disagreement, schism, rupture, discordance; *ant.* agreement, peace.

dissident *n.* rebel, protester, agitater, maverick, gadfly, schismatic; *ant.* conformist.

dissident *adj.* differing, disagreeing, nonconformist, heretical, maverick, schismatic, discordant; *ant.* acquiescent.

dissimilar *adj.* different, unlike, diverse, divergent, mismatched, heterogeneous, incongruous; *ant.* alike.

dissimulate *v.* pretend, fake, feign, conceal, hide, mask, cloak, disguise, camouflage, dissemble.

dissimulation *n.* pretense, act, affectation, deception, deceit, duplicity, hypocrisy, sham, feigning, concealment; *ant.* openness.

dissipate *v.* **1.** scatter, disperse, dispel, strew, disseminate, diffuse, spread. **2.** disappear, vanish, dissolve; deplete, exhaust, waste, squander; spill, leak.

dissipation *n.* debauchery, indulgence, intemperance, wantonness, excess, extravagance, prodigality, license, abandonment, excess.

dissociate *v.* separate, divorce, disconnect, detach, break off, segregate, sever; *ant.* attach.

dissolute *adj.* immoral, depraved, corrupt, degenerate, wild, abandoned, licentious, wanton, lewd, libertine, loose; *ant.* virtuous, straitlaced.

dissolution *n.* **1.** disintegration, decay, destruction, ruin, disassembly, overthrow; *ant.* unification. **2.** termination, end, finish, culmination, conclusion, adjournment, discontinuation, dismissal, suspension; *ant.* beginning.

dissolve *v.* **1.** liquefy, melt, thaw, soften, evaporate, run. **2.** disintegrate, break up, crumble, decompose, diffuse. **3.** dismiss, adjourn, postpone, terminate, discontinue, end.

dissonance *n.* **1.** discord, disharmony, cacophony, discordance, harshness. **2.** dissension, disagreement, difference, incongruity, disparity, discrepancy, inconsistency.

dissonant *adj.* **1.** harsh, discordant, strident, raucous, grating, jarring, cacophonous; *ant.* harmonious. **2.** different, inconsistent, incongruous, incompatible, irreconcilable, irregular, anomalous.

dissuade *v.* deter, discourage, warn, divert, remonstrate, expostulate; *ant.* persuade.

distance *n.* **1.** expanse, extent, reach, span, range, length, width. **2.** background, horizon. **3.** aloofness, coldness, remoteness, diffidence, reserve, restraint, standoffishness, stiffness.

go the distance finish, complete, bring to an end, see through.

keep one's distance avoid, be aloof *or* indifferent, shun, ignore.

distant *adj.* **1.** far, faraway, remote, outlying, far-flung, far-off; *ant.* close. **2.** aloof, indifferent, cold, cool, standoffish, stiff, formal, reserved, restrained, diffident, reticent, withdrawn; *ant.* friendly, approachable, outgoing.

distaste *n.* aversion, repugnance, revulsion, dislike, disgust, disfavor, detestation, displeasure; *ant.* penchant, liking.

distasteful *adj.* repulsive, uninviting, unpleasant, unpalatable, undesirable, loathesome, objectionable, obnoxious, offensive, abhorrent, repugnant; *ant.* pleasing.

distend *v.* inflate, swell, enlarge, dilate, balloon, bloat, puff, bulge; *ant.* deflate.

distill *v.* refine, extract, express, clarify, purify, sublimate.

distinct *adj.* **1.** (clearly seen) definite, clear, clear-cut, lucid, plain, evident, obvious, apparent, well-defined, manifest, noticeable, conspicuous, palpable, marked; *ant.* obscure, indistinct. **2.** separated, separate, different, discrete, individual, dissimilar, detached. **3.** audible, clear, sharp, enunciated.

distinction *n.* **1.** discrimination, discretion, discernment, perception, sensitivity, acuteness, judgment; *ant.* dullness, obtuseness. **2.** prominence, fame, repute, honor, eminence, renown, consequence, greatness, celebrity, excellence, importance, prestige; *ant.* insignificance.

distinctive *adj.* different, unique, special, peculiar, extraordinary, original, individual, singular, inimitable, characteristic, distinguishing; *ant.* common.

distinguish *v.* **1.** (make distinctions) classify, identify, define, differentiate, discriminate, characterize, categorize, specify, separate, divide. **2.** (perceive clearly) discern, discover, see, detect, notice, know, recognize. **3.** label, identify, tag, mark, name.

distinguishable *adj.* obvious, plain, clear, noticeable, conspicuous, evident, manifest, recognizable, observable, appreciable, discernible, perceptible.

distinguished *adj.* illustrious, eminent, venerable, renowned, honored, celebrated, well-known, notable, noteworthy, reputable, foremost, famed; *ant.* obscure, insignificant, unimportant.

distort *v.* disfigure, warp, twist, deform, contort, pervert, skew; falsify, slant, bias, misrepresent.

distorted *adj.* **1.** deformed, misshapen, warped, twisted, skewed, awry. **2.** biased, false, misleading, slanted, propagandistic, one-sided, untrustworthy, unfair; *ant.* honest, fair, disinterested.

distract *v.* **1.** divert, amuse, entertain, beguile, engross. **2.** puzzle, confuse, confound, trouble, torment, disconcert, sidetrack, mislead, bewilder, madden, disturb, perplex, discompose, faze, harass.

distracted *adj.* **1.** troubled, confused, confounded, perplexed, puzzled, flustered, anxious, distressed, distraught, overwrought, hassled, frazzled; *ant.* calm. **2.** deranged, insane, maddened, crazed, raving, lunatic.

distraction *n.* **1.** confusion, complication, disturbance, commotion, perplexity, interference, agitation. **2.** diversion, amusement, recreation, pastime, game; preoccupation, compulsion, idée fixe.

distraught *adj.* overwrought, mad, frantic, wild, anxious, distressed, upset, crazed, agitated, shook up (*slang*); distracted, hysterical, worked up; *ant.* calm.

distress *n.* **1.** worry, trouble, grief, anxiety, pain, suffering, misery, suffering, anguish, sorrow, wretchedness; *ant.* ease. **2.** misfortune, catastrophe, disaster, calamity, adversity, trouble, trial.

distress *v.* trouble, pain, torment, upset, disturb, bother, harass, grieve, sadden, afflict, agonize, worry, wound; *ant.* assist, comfort.

distribute *v.* **1.** give, dispense, share, endow, disperse, dole out, mete out, pass out, allo-

distribution

cate, ration; *ant.* collect. **2.** scatter, circulate, spread, diffuse, disseminate, disperse, strew.

distribution *n.* circulation, delivery, transportation, handling, marketing, arrangement, placement; *ant.* collection.

district *n.* area, locale, sector, region, vicinity, ward, precinct, community, neighborhood, quarter, parish.

distrust *v.* doubt, disbelieve, question, suspect; *ant.* believe.

distrustful *adj.* suspicious, doubting, disbelieving, skeptical, wary, cynical; *ant.* unsuspecting.

disturb *v.* upset, trouble, unsettle, worry, distress, annoy, nettle, bother, pester, agitate, perturb, harass; *ant.* calm, quiet.

disturbance *n.* **1.** fight, quarrel, brawl. **2.** turmoil, tumult, turbulence, clamor, uproar, stir, racket; *ant.* peace, quiet.

disturbed *adj.* upset, troubled, worried, confused, unbalanced, anxious, apprehensive, concerned; maladjusted, neurotic, psychopathic; *ant.* calm, normal.

disturbing *adj.* unsettling, worrying, worrisome, distressing, disconcerting, startling, frightening, dismaying, alarming; *ant.* reassuring.

disuse *n.* neglect, idleness, decay, abandonment.

ditch *n.* channel, gully, canal, trench, moat, furrow, drain, dike.

ditch *v.* discard, jettison, scrap, dump, drop, desert, abandon, forsake, leave.

dither *v.* waver, vacillate, falter, hesitate, teeter, oscillate, shilly-shally; *ant.* decide.

divan *n.* couch, sofa, settee, chaise longue *or* lounge.

dive *n.* **1.** fall, jump, plunge, leap, spring, pitch. **2.** saloon, pub, cafe, tavern, club, pool hall, beer garden; inn, hotel, motel, *slang:* fleabag, flophouse.

dive *v.* jump, fall, leap, plummet, plunge, descend, pitch, submerge, dip, swoop.

diverge *v.* **1.** split, part, fork, deviate, divide. **2.** disagree, part company, conflict, dissent, differ, vary; *ant.* agree, compromise.

divergence *n.* **1.** parting, separation, forking, departure; *ant.* convergence. **2.** (as of views) difference, parting of the ways, dissension, variation, disparity, deviation, digression.

divergent *adj.* separate, diverse, differing, con-

flicting, disagreeing, dissimilar, varying, deviating; *ant.* convergent.

diverse *adj.* different, differing, varying, varying, dissimilar, distinct, disparate, varied, sundry, assorted, numerous; *ant.* identical.

diversify *v.* change, vary, expand, branch out, mix, variegate.

diversion *n.* **1.** change, detour, alteration, deviation, departure, digression, variation. **2.** entertainment, amusement, recreation, pastime, sport, relaxation, distraction.

diversity *n.* variety, difference, assortment, medley, multiplicity, variance, distinctiveness; *ant.* sameness, similarity.

divert *v.* **1.** deflect, turn, avert, veer, redirect. **2.** amuse, entertain, delight, beguile, regale, relax, gratify, tickle.

divest *v.* **1.** undress, remove, doff, uncover, strip, take off, disrobe, undress; *ant.* don, clothe. **2.** deprive, seize, expropriate, dispossess, strip.

divide *v.* **1.** disconnect, detach, part, break, separate, cut, disengage, sever, disjoin; *ant.* unite, combine, connect. **2.** distribute, dole, apportion, allot, share, parcel out, allocate.

dividend *n.* surplus, extra, bonus, gratuity, gain, share, cut, portion.

divination *n.* prediction, fortunetelling, clairvoyance, prophecy, soothsaying, second sight, palmistry.

divine *n.* clergy, priest, reverend, pastor, minister, parson, cleric, prelate, ecclesiastic.

divine *adj.* **1.** religious, sacred, spiritual, holy, heavenly, sanctified, consecrated, exalted, transcendent, supernatural, mystical, celestial. **2.** wonderful, perfect, marvelous, excellent, splendid.

diviner *n.* prophet, oracle, seer, soothsayer, augur, sibyl.

divinity *n.* god, goddess, deity, godhead, higher power.

divisible *adj.* separable, dividable, fractional.

division *n.* **1.** separation, detachment, severance, cutting, disconnection, partitioning, apportionment, distribution; *ant.* union, joining. **2.** dispute, feud, disagreement, discord, schism, breach. **3.** army, troops, military unit. **4.** territory, province, country, state, district, county, municipality, city, town, village.

divisive *adj.* disruptive, factional, discordant, alienating; *ant.* harmonious, unifying.

divorce *n.* breakup, separation, split-up, dissolution, annulment.

divorce *v.* separate, part, annul, dissolve, divide, sever, split up, dissociate; *ant.* marry, unify.

divulge *v.* reveal, confess, tell, disclose, leak, spill, expose, uncover, broadcast, publish.

dizzy *adj.* **1.** lightheaded, vertiginous, dazed, faint, shaky, woozy, reeling. **2.** flighty, scatterbrained, capricious, silly, giddy, frivolous; *ant.* sober.

do *v.* **1.** (perform an action), carry out, fulfill, obey, serve; execute, implement, effect, finish, conclude, complete, achieve, accomplish, fulfill, satisfy. **2.** (create a new condition) bring about, cause, begin, create, make, produce, effect, launch, initiate, inaugurate.

do away with (*slang*) **1.** kill, murder, eliminate, exterminate, slay. **2.** abolish, discontinue, discard.

do in (*slang*) **1.** kill, murder, slaughter, eliminate, execute, slay, *slang:* waste, rub out. **2.** tire, exhaust, wear out, weary, fatigue.

dos and don'ts rules, standards, regulations, customs, etiquette, p's and q's, niceties, code.

do without give up, forgo, relinquish, waive, abstain from, dispense with, get along without.

make do get by *or* along, manage, survive, endure.

docile *adj.* meek, submissive, obedient, compliant, complaisant, mild, obliging, tractable, pliant; *ant.* truculent.

dock *n.* wharf, pier, marina, quay, waterfront, harbor, boatyard.

dock *v.* **1.** moor, (drop) anchor, land, berth. **2.** reduce, subtract, lessen, diminish, cut, crop, clip, deduct, decrease, withhold, shorten, truncate, curtail.

docket *n.* receipt, tab, tally, bill, chit.

doctor *n.* physician, MD, medic, clinician; general practitioner, GP, internist, gynecologist, primary-care physician.

doctor *v.* change, forge, falsify, adulterate, alter, misrepresent, fake, fudge, tamper with, fix.

doctrinaire *adj.* inflexible, dogmatic, insistent, ideological, fanatical, rigid, biased.

doctrine *n.* belief, concept, tenet, conviction, principle, teaching, dogma, creed, precept, canon.

document *n.* paper, deed, form, certificate, record.

document *v.* substantiate, verify, authenticate, certify, corroborate, validate, support, detail, enumerate, list.

dodge *n.* maneuver, ruse, subterfuge, feint, wile, stratagem, ploy, machination, contrivance, trick, scheme, device.

dodge *v.* avoid, parry, hedge, shirk, evade, duck, elude, shuffle, sidestep, equivocate, fudge.

doer *n.* activist, organizer, achiever, go-getter, dynamo, powerhouse, live wire.

dog *n.* **1.** hound, puppy, canine, mongrel, stray, cur, pooch, mutt. **2.** rascal, villain, swine, scamp, heel, blackguard.

a dog's life misery, wretchedness, bad luck, trouble, poverty.

go to the dogs deteriorate, degenerate, decay.

let sleeping dogs lie leave well enough alone, pass over, overlook, ignore, forgive.

dogged *adj.* relentless, persistent, tenacious, unyielding, gritty, indefatigable, unshakable, dogmatic, stubborn, mulish; *ant.* irresolute.

dogma *n.* belief, creed, conviction, principle, teaching, credo, doctrine, precept, tenet.

dogmatic *adj.* **1.** (relating to a dogma) authoritative, peremptory, categorical, ideological, doctrinal, canonical. **2.** (said of persons or attitudes) arrogant, overbearing, imperious, pontifical, opinionated, doctrinaire, magisterial.

doings *n.* actions, acts, deeds, exploits, happenings, events, proceedings, affairs, handiwork, transactions, dealings.

dole *n.* share, pittance, allowance, allotment, dispensation, benefit, grant.

dole *v.* distribute, share, parcel, mete, allot, allocate, ration, divide, apportion.

doleful *adj.* sad, mournful, melancholy, forlorn, gloomy, saturnine, funereal, dolorous, sorrowful, pathetic; *ant.* cheerful.

dollar *n.* greenback, currency, bank note, buck, smacker (*slang*).

dollop *n.* blob, glob, gob, lump, ball, clump.

doll up (*slang*) dress up, primp, preen, deck out.

dolor *n.* sadness, suffering, sorrow, anguish,

dolorous *adj.* sad, miserable, melancholy, wretched, mournful, sorrowful, anguished; distressing, heart-rending, painful; *ant.* happy.

dolt *n.* dullard, cretin, idiot, ignoramus, fool, simpleton, clod, dunce, dimwit, half-wit, blockhead, dope.

doltish *adj.* idiotic, stupid, dumb, obtuse, foolish, dimwitted, half-witted, mindless, dopey, boneheaded (*slang*); *ant.* smart, clever.

domain *n.* **1.** work, discipline, area, field, forte, province, sphere, realm, realty, job, branch, department. **2.** property, real estate, land, empire, scope, realm, region, territory.

domestic *adj.* **1.** tame, house-trained, household, pet, family. **2.** indigenous, native, homebred, internal.

domesticate *v.* tame, train, break, housetrain, familiarize, habituate, accustom, domesticize, acclimatize, naturalize.

domesticated *adj.* tame, tamed, domestic, broken in, naturalized; *ant.* feral, wild.

domicile *n.* house, home, residence, dwelling, abode, lodgings, quarters, mansion.

dominant *adj.* prevailing, prevalent, main, leading, chief, leading, preeminent, outstanding, principal, superior, ruling, presiding, assertive, commanding; *ant.* subordinate.

dominate *v.* **1.** control, rule, prevail, lead, tyrannize, master, lord it over. **2.** monopolize, eclipse, outshine, dwarf.

domination *n.* control, leadership, mastery, authority, rule, dictatorship, despotism, supremacy, tyranny, sway; *ant.* subjection, subordination.

domineering *adj.* overbearing, tyrannical, dictatorial, despotic, autocratic, authoritarian, imperious, iron-handed, oppressive, bossy, magisterial; *ant.* meek, obsequious.

dominion *n.* **1.** power, authority, jurisdiction, control, rule, sway, reign, sovereignty, supremacy. **2.** government, administration, management, control, leadership.

donate *v.* give, present, bestow, bequeath, contribute, proffer, impart.

donation *n.* grant, gift, contribution, alms, gratuity, boon, benefaction, offering, present, bequest.

done *adj.* **1.** accomplished, finished, completed, over, through, realized, consummated, effected, executed, performed, rendered. **2.** cooked, baked, brewed, stewed, broiled, boiled, fried, browned.

done for defeated, beaten, vanquished, doomed, finished, foiled, ruined, lost, undone.

done in tired, exhausted, weary, worn out, dog-tired, *slang:* bushed, pooped, zonked.

done up prepared, packaged, finished, wrapped.

donor *n.* contributor, giver, benefactor, donator, sponsor, philanthropist; *ant.* beneficiary.

do-nothing *n.* loafer, idler, ne'er-do-well, *slang:* deadbeat, goof-off, shirker, sluggard.

do-nothing *adj.* lazy, idle, indolent, passive, indifferent.

doom *n.* **1.** fate, destiny, lot, predestination, foreordination, fortune, kismet, ruin, downfall. **2.** verdict, sentence, condemnation, decision, judgment, decree.

doomed *adj.* cursed, accursed, star-crossed, ill-fated, ill-starred, damned, condemned.

door *n.* doorway, entrance, exit, entry, opening, egress, ingress, portal.

dope (*slang*) *n.* **1.** drugs, narcotic, opiate. **2.** fool, dunce, dolt, simpleton, idiot, dullard, dimwit, half-wit, blockhead, bonehead (*slang*). **3.** news, facts, information, knowledge, details, lowdown (*slang*), account, tip, inside information.

dope *v.* drug, anesthetize, deaden, stupefy.

dopey *adj.* **1.** drugged, groggy, woozy, dazed, drowsy; *ant.* alert. **2.** thick, slow, dumb, idiotic, simple, silly, stupid, dense; *ant.* bright.

dormant *adj.* inactive, inert, suspended, fallow, torpid, latent, inchoate, undeveloped; *ant.* active.

dose *n.* **1.** measure, draft, shot, prescription. **2.** (*slang*) social disease, sexually transmitted disease, STD, venereal disease.

dose *v.* medicate, administer, treat, dispense.

dot *n.* mark, mite, speck, spot, jot, iota, dab, atom, mote.

dot *v.* spot, punctuate, stipple, fleck, dab.

dotage *n.* old age, senility, weakness, feebleness, decrepitude, senescence, second childhood; *ant.* youth.

dote *v.* spoil, indulge, pamper, prize, treasure, adore, idolize.

doting *adj.* fond, devoted, indulgent, soft, adoring.

double *adj.* twice, twin, duplicate, doubled, coupled, paired, dual, twofold, duplex.

double back backtrack, retrace one's steps, reverse, return, circle, loop.

double up unite, combine, join.

double-cross *v.* betray, two-time, swindle, hoodwink, trick, con, cheat, cozen, mislead, defraud.

double-dealer *n.* traitor, betrayer, fraud, swindler, rogue, dissembler, cozener.

double-dealing *n.* dishonesty, betrayal, deception, deceit, treachery, trickery, duplicity, cheating, perfidy.

double-dealing *adj.* crooked, cheating, deceitful, dishonest, fraudulent, duplicious, underhanded, treacherous, scheming, wily, perfidious.

double-entendre *n.* pun, double meaning, innuendo.

doubt *v.* distrust, mistrust, suspect, question, be skeptical; hesitate, vacillate, waver; *ant.* believe, trust.

no doubt doubtless, doubtlessly, presumably, surely, admittedly, assuredly, certainly, probably, unquestionably.

doubter *n.* disbeliever, cynic, skeptic, scoffer, agnostic; *ant.* believer.

doubtful *adj.* 1. ambiguous, uncertain, indeterminate, dubious, unlikely, improbable, inconclusive, indefinite, obscure, vague, indistinct, unclear; *ant.* certain, definite. 2. (said of character) disreputable, questionable, unreliable, unsound, suspicious, dubious, suspect, weak.

doubting *adj.* suspicious, questioning, dubious, skeptical.

doubtless *adv.* undoubtedly, no doubt, indisputably, surely, assuredly, certainly, probably, ostensibly, presumably, supposedly, apparently, seemingly.

dough *n.* 1. batter, mixture, paste, pulp. 2. money, dollars, moola (*slang*), wealth.

dour *adj.* grim, melancholy, pessimistic, sour, sullen; austere, strict, severe, inflexible; *ant.* bright, cheery, easygoing.

douse *v.* dunk, submerge, immerse, plunge, soak, saturate, dip, steep, drench, smother.

dowdy *adj.* shabby, unfashionable, out-of-fashion, out-of-style, frumpish, frumpy, drab, unattractive.

down *n.* fluff, pile, shag, nap, fuzz.

down *v.* 1. drink, gulp, swallow, imbibe. 2. fell, floor, defeat, beat, topple, tackle, overthrow, vanquish, nail.

down and out impoverished, destitute, penniless, penurious; derelict, defeated, beaten, finished, ruined.

down at the heel impoverished, run-down, shabby, seedy, worn, dowdy, slovenly.

down in the mouth depressed, dispirited, crestfallen, melancholy, sad, unhappy, disheartened, dejected.

down the drain gone, lost, ruined, wasted.

down-to-earth *adj.* sensible, practical, rational, no-nonsense, commonsense, reasonable, honest, frank.

downcast *adj.* cheerless, depressed, sad, disheartened, dispirited, discouraged, despondent, crestfallen, miserable, dejected, disconsolate; *ant.* cheerful, elated, happy.

downfall *n.* destruction, ruin, debacle, failure, collapse, undoing.

downgrade *v.* lower, demote, humble, degrade, belittle, disparage, denigrate; *ant.* improve, upgrade.

downhearted *adj.* depressed, sad, downcast, gloomy, glum, despondent, discouraged, dispirited, sorrowful, dejected, crestfallen, blue; *ant.* cheerful, happy.

downpour *n.* deluge, flood, torrent, cloudburst, rainstorm, inundation.

downright *adj.* 1. utter, absolute, outright, explicit, total, unequivocal, complete. 2. honest, frank, open, forthright, straightforward, blunt, blatant.

downtown *adj.* metropolitan, urban, central.

downtrodden *adj.* victimized, oppressed, afflicted, subjugated, subservient, exploited, abused, tyrannized.

downy *adj.* soft, fluffy, woolly, velvety, silky, feathery, fleecy, nappy.

dowry *n.* legacy, endowment, inheritance, portion, provision, share, gift.

doze *n.* nap, catnap, shut-eye (*slang*), snooze, forty winks.

doze *v.* sleep, slumber, nap, nod off, catnap, drowse, snooze.

drab *adj.* somber, gray, mousy, colorless, gloomy, dreary, uninspired, vapid, dingy, dismal; *ant.* bright.

draft *n.* **1.** design, plans, blueprint, sketch, outline, abstract, schema, delineation. **2.** drink, glass, swallow, quaff. **3.** breeze, wind, gust, puff

draft *v.* **1.** sketch, outline, draw, design, delineate, plan, formulate, compose. **2.** recruit, enlist, conscript, select, choose.

drag *n.* **1.** net, dragnet, anchor, harrow, scraper, bar, clog, brake, shoe, floater. **2.** suction, resistance, pull, friction, tow, curb. **3.** restraint, impediment, hindrance, burden, encumbrance. **4.** (*slang*) nuisance, trouble, pain, bother, annoyance, pest, bore.

drag *v.* **1.** lag, straggle, loiter, dawdle, creep, crawl, linger, suffer delays, extend. **2.** transport, haul, move, tow, tug, yank, pull, lug. **3.** smoke, puff, inhale.

drag out prolong, extend, protract, lengthen, persist.

drag one's feet (*slang*) stall, delay, procrastinate.

drain *n.* **1.** duct, culvert, sewer, drainpipe, sink, ditch, pipe, outlet, trench, conduit, channel. **2.** expenditure, exhaustion, reduction, drag, depletion.

drain *v.* deplete, consume, exhaust, weary, bleed, dry, finish, swallow, sap; *ant.* fill.

drainage *n.* waste, sewage, bilge, seepage.

drama *n.* acting, theater, theatricals, melodrama, play, dramatization, scene, histrionics, spectacle.

dramatic *adj.* melodramatic, effective, affecting, climactic, suspenseful, thrilling, emotional, impressive, exciting, electrifying, powerful, sensational; *ant.* normal, ordinary.

dramatize *v.* **1.** perform, enact, produce, stage. **2.** exaggerate, overstate, overdo, amplify.

drape *v.* fold, hang, dangle, drop, suspend, droop, swathe, adorn, wrap, cover, cloak.

drastic *adj.* radical, extreme, dire, severe, desperate, strong; *ant.* mild, temperate.

draw *n.* **1.** appeal, lure, enticement, bait, attraction, pull, interest. **2.** stalemate, tie, impasse, deadlock.

draw *v.* **1.** pull, drag, bring, tug, lug, tow, carry, jerk, wrench, yank, trawl, haul. **2.** sketch, draft, outline, form, etch, depict, portray, describe, caricature. **3.** lure, attract, allure, entice, persuade, influence, fascinate.

draw back withdraw, retreat, recoil, shrink.

draw out **1.** elongate, prolong, extend, lengthen, drag out, protract, stretch. **2.** elicit, evoke, wrest, bring out.

draw the line say no, set a limit, lay down the law, put one's foot down.

draw up **1.** prepare, draft, formulate, compose. **2.** stop, stop short, halt, pull up.

draw upon use, make use of, rely on, employ.

drawback *n.* impediment, obstacle, difficulty, detriment, imperfection, defect, nuisance, trouble, hindrance, snag, deficiency, disability; *ant.* advantage.

drawing *n.* illustration, outline, depiction, delineation, sketch, study, representation, picture, portrait.

drawn *adj.* tense, strained, tired, worn, haggard, stressed, taut, sapped, pinched, fatigued.

dread *n.* trepidation, awe, worry, apprehension, aversion, phobia, horror, misgiving, fear, fright, terror, alarm, dismay; *ant.* confidence, security.

dread *v.* fear, tremble, shudder, flinch, shrink from, quail, cringe at.

dreadful *adj.* frightful, horrendous, horrible, tragic, distressing, monstrous, grievous, terrible, alarming, dire, awful; *ant.* comforting.

dream *n.* **1.** ambition, aspiration, goal, hope, wish, desire, design. **2.** fantasy, illusion, reverie, vision, imagination, hallucination, delusion, phantasm, vagary.

dream *v.* fantasize, imagine, visualize, envisage, stargaze, muse, conjure, fancy, hallucinate.

dream up devise, create, invent, concoct, conceive, contrive, imagine, hatch.

dreamer *n.* visionary, utopian, woolgatherer, idealist, fantasizer, romancer, theorizer, stargazer; *ant.* pragmatist, realist.

dreamlike *adj.* surreal, insubstantial, illusory, chimerical, visionary, phantasmagorical, hallucinatory, trancelike; *ant.* real.

dreary *adj.* **1.** bleak, downcast, drab, sad, gloomy, dismal, depressing, melancholy, sombre, mournful, cheerless; *ant.* bright. **2.** routine, commonplace, monotonous, boring, tedious, trite, dull, humdrum; *ant.* interesting.

dredge *v.* dig up, drag up, raise, uncover, unearth, expose, discover.

dregs *n.* **1.** residue, sediment, grounds, deposit. **2.** debris, trash, waste, refuse, scum, excrement, feces, leftovers.

drench *v.* saturate, soak, wet, steep, immerse, douse, drown, flood, inundate, imbue.

dress *n.* apparel, clothing, clothes, ensemble, attire, garments, garb, costume, wardrobe, raiment, accoutrements.

dress *v.* **1.** clothe, don, wear, garb, robe, attire, drape, accouter, array, cover; *ant.* disrobe, strip. **2.** prepare, groom, ornament, embellish, trim, decorate, garnish, furbish, deck. **3.** attend, heal, treat, bandage, cleanse, sterilize, cauterize.

dress down scold, upbraid, reprove, reprimand, berate, chew out (*slang*), chide, castigate, rebuke.

dress up beautify, improve, embellish, dandify, gild, adorn, deck.

dressy *adj.* stylish, smart, elaborate, ornate, elegant, formal, swanky, *slang:* classy, ritzy; *ant.* dowdy, scruffy.

dribble *n.* sprinkling, droplet, drip, leak, seepage, trickle.

dribble *v.* drivel, salivate, slobber, drool, drip, leak, seep, trickle.

dried *adj.* dehydrated, parched, withered, mummified, arid, drained, desiccated, wilted, wizened, shriveled.

drift *n.* **1.** (progressive movement in space or time) inclination, trend, tendency, bent, effort, movement, push. **2.** (implicit meaning or tone) intention, tenor, object, thrust, end, design, gist, implication, significance, import. **3.** bank, mass, pile, dune, heap.

drift *v.* wander, stray, meander, float, coast, waft.

drifter *n.* vagrant, wanderer, tramp, vagabond, hobo, wastrel, itinerant.

drill *n.* practice, training, coaching, exercise, preparation, repetition, instruction.

drill *v.* **1.** bore, pierce, penetrate, puncture,

perforate. **2.** train, rehearse, practice, exercise, teach, instruct, discipline, coach, tutor.

drink *v.* swallow, gulp, quaff, sip, guzzle, toss off, imbibe, knock back, tipple, swill, swig.

drink in absorb, soak up, assimilate.

drink like a fish imbibe, get drunk, become inebriated, tipple, drink.

drink to toast, praise, honor, salute.

drinker *n.* alcoholic, drunkard, inebriate, drunk, wino (*slang*); lush; *ant.* teetotaler.

drip *v.* drop, trickle, sprinkle, splash, drizzle, dribble.

drive *n.* **1.** ride, trip, journey, outing, ramble, tour, expedition, excursion, jaunt, spin. **2.** road, street, avenue, boulevard, turnpike. **3.** ambition, push, aggressiveness, get-up-and-go, verve, energy, will power. **4.** impulse, instinct, urge, appetite.

drive *v.* **1.** impel, propel, instigate, hasten, urge, compel, induce, press, force, hurry, incite, motivate. **2.** control, steer, guide, direct, manage, lead, operate. **3.** attack, hit, strike, thrust.

drive at mean, suggest, imply, allude to, intimate, insinuate, indicate.

drive crazy exasperate, infuriate, bother, annoy, irritate, aggravate, madden, drive up the wall (*slang*).

drivel *n.* nonsense, mumbo-jumbo, gibberish, blathering, rubbish, balderdash.

driven *adj.* ambitious, energetic, dynamic, vigorous, forceful, aggressive, motivated, compulsive, type A; *ant.* laid-back.

drizzle *v.* spray, mist, shower, sprinkle, rain.

drizzle *v.* spray, sprinkle, shower, rain, spit, dribble.

droll *adj.* funny, humorous, amusing, comical, witty, entertaining, farcical, laughable, risible.

drollery *n.* fun, humor, wit, farce, banter, absurdity, buffoonery, jocularity, waggery.

drone *n.* hum, buzz, purr, whir, murmuring.

drone *v.* **1.** hum, buzz, purr, murmur, whir. **2.** drawl, intone, chant.

drool *v.* slobber, drivel, slaver, salivate, spit, dribble.

droop *v.* sag, sink, hang, dangle, wilt, wither, slouch, slump, drop, diminish, languish; *ant.* rise, straighten.

drooping *adj.* floppy, limp, wilting, sagging, droopy, pendulous, flaccid, flabby; languid, languorous; *ant.* stiff, straight.

drop *n.* **1.** bit, speck, dab, dash, pinch, spot, shot, nip, trace, droplet. **2.** fall, tumble, reduction, decrease, descent, slump, lapse, slip, decline, downfall, declivity, precipitation.

drop *v.* **1.** drip, fall, dribble, trickle, leak, distill. **2.** forsake, part with, cast off, abandon, desert, leave, divorce, separate from.

drop a line write, correspond with; mail, send, post.

drop back lag, fall back, recede, retreat.

drop in visit, call, stop in.

drop off 1. fall asleep, doze, drowse, catnap, nod off, sleep, snooze. **2.** deliver, give, leave, present.

drop out quit, leave, back out, renege, withdraw, resign.

dropout *n.* truant, quitter, failure, rebel, dissident, deviant, renegade, malcontent, loner, nonconformist, bohemian.

droppings *n.* manure, excrement, feces, dung, guano, stools.

dross *n.* waste, trash, remains, refuse, dregs, debris, rubbish, scum.

drought *n.* **1.** dearth, scarcity, lack, need, want, shortage, deficiency, insufficiency. **2.** dryness, aridity, dehydration, desiccation, parchedness.

drove *n.* herd, horde, swarm, throng, mob, multitude, crowd, flock, gathering.

drown *v.* **1.** sink, submerge, drench, immerse, flood, engulf. **2.** stifle, muffle, overpower, overcome, inundate, obliterate, silence, deaden.

drowsy *adj.* tired, sleepy, drugged, lethargic, torpid, dreamy, dazed, dopey; restful, lulling, somnolent, soporific; *ant.* alert, awake.

drubbing *n.* defeat, beating, thrashing, trouncing, pounding, clobbering, flogging, pummeling, whipping, walloping, hammering, licking.

drudge *n.* slave, servant, menial, worker, toiler, lackey, scullion.

drudge *v.* work, slave, toil, labor, plod, grind.

drudgery *n.* toil, labor, slavery, chore, grind, sweat.

drug *n.* medicine, medication, remedy, narcotic.

drug *v.* anesthetize, medicate, treat, dose, numb, dope, deaden, knock out, put to sleep.

drugged *adj.* comatose, unconscious, doped up, *slang:* stoned, high, spaced-out, looped.

drum into instill, harp on, reiterate, drive home, hammer, expound.

drum up solicit, round up, attract, petition, gather, collect, canvass, obtain.

drunk *adj.* intoxicated, inebriated, tipsy, *slang:* lit up, tanked up, plastered, sloshed; *ant.* sober.

drunkard *n.* alcoholic, drinker, tippler, boozer, *slang:* lush, wino, barfly.

drunken *adj.* intoxicated, inebriate, debauched, Bacchanalian, Dionysian; *ant.* sober.

dry *v.* dehydrate, desiccate, drain, harden, mummify, parch, shrivel, wilt, wizen; *ant.* soak, wet.

dry *adj.* **1.** parched, arid, evaporated, desiccated, barren, dehydrated, drained, thirsty, shriveled; *ant.* wet, moist, damp. **2.** dull, boring, tedious, monotonous, pedantic, longwinded, interminable, dreary, tiresome; *ant.* lively, spicy. **3.** droll, tongue-in-cheek, satirical, subtle, sarcastic, sly, ironic, sardonic, oblique, witty; *ant.* obvious, broad.

dual *adj.* paired, twin, combined, double, coupled, binary, duplicate, matched, twofold, duplex.

dub *v.* **1.** hit, strike, poke, push. **2.** entitle, name, nickname, label, denominate, christen, call, designate, tag, term.

dubious *adj.* (said of a person's character or an attitude) doubtful, suspicious, shady, fishy; skeptical, wavering. **2.** (as of a proposal) questionable, debatable, specious, risky, uncertain, suspect; *ant.* sound, surefire.

duck *v.* **1.** immerse, submerge, dunk, wet, douse, dive, plunge, dip. **2.** avoid, evade, sidestep, dodge, shirk. **3.** stoop, crouch, bow, bob, drop.

ductile *adj.* yielding, pliable, pliant, malleable, flexible, amenable, plastic, tractable, compliant, manipulatable, docile; *ant.* intractable, refractory.

dud *n.* failure, flop, *slang:* lemon, turkey, washout.

duds *n.* clothes, clothing, garb, garments, gear.

due *adj.* **1.** owed, expected, outstanding, unpaid, payable, requisite, in arrears, obligatory. **2.** deserved, rightful, fitting, ample, appropriate, proper, merited, justified.

duel *n.* fight, contest, rivalry, combat, competition.

dues *n.* fee, charges, subscription, levy.

duffer *n.* oaf, dolt, clod, bungler, lummox.

dull *adj.* **1.** blunt, flat; *ant.* sharp, sharpened, keen. **2.** (said of a color) drab, gloomy, sober, somber, matte, dismal, dark, dingy, dim, dusky, lackluster; *ant.* bright, colorful, gleaming. **3.** stupid, stolid, sluggish, slow, retarded, backward, dense, obtuse, ignorant, feeble-minded; *ant.* witty, intelligent. **4.** monotonous, tedious, prosaic, lackluster, wearisome, insipid, trite, hackneyed, humdrum, dreary, dismal, boring, vapid; *ant.* exciting, fascinating, exhilarating.

dull *v.* **1.** fade, obscure, tarnish, sully, cloud, darken; *ant.* brighten. **2.** moderate, lessen, subdue, muffle, depress; *ant.* sharpen, stimulate.

dullard *n.* idiot, ignoramus, moron, nitwit, simpleton, imbecile, dolt, dunce, dope, blockhead, dimwit, dummy (*slang*).

duly *adj.* rightfully, appropriately, accordingly, correctly, decorously, deservedly, properly, fittingly, suitably.

dumb *adj.* **1.** mute, quiet, silent, speechless, wordless. **2.** stupid, dull, simpleminded, feebleminded, dense, moronic, foolish, thick; *ant.* intelligent.

dumbbell (*slang*) *n.* fool, dunce, blockhead.

dumbfound *v.* surprise, amaze, astonish, awe, flabbergast, confuse, puzzle.

dumbfounded *adj.* stunned, flabbergasted, nonplussed, astonished, thunderstruck, astounded, overwhelmed, speechless, bowled over, floored, thrown.

dummy *n.* **1.** (*slang*) fool, dolt, simpleton, dullard, dunce, numskull, blockhead, dimwit. **2.** imitation, substitute, sham, counterfeit, duplicate, copy. **3.** mannequin, model, figure.

dummy *adj.* phony, fake, false, imitation, sham, artificial, bogus, mock, practice, simulated, trial.

dump *n.* **1.** rubbish pile, landfill, junkyard. **2.** hole, hovel, slum, shack, shanty. **down in the dumps** sad, despondent, dejected, depressed, despairing, gloomy; *ant.* happy.

dump *v.* unload, jettison, throw away, get rid of, scrap, drop, dispose of, *slang:* deep-six, ditch.

dunce *n.* ignoramus, nincompoop, ass, dolt, half-wit, loon, simpleton, moron, numskull, blockhead, dullard, dimwit, bonehead (*slang*); *ant.* intellectual.

dungeon *n.* cell, prison, pit, cage, lockup.

dupe *n.* victim, pawn, puppet, gull, stooge, *slang:* sucker, pushover, easy mark, sap, fall guy.

dupe *v.* delude, hoodwink, hoax, swindle, trick, deceive, cheat, bamboozle, defraud, *slang:* rip off, con.

duplicate *n.* reproduction, replica, facsimile, clone, carbon copy, photocopy, Xerox (Tm), Photostat (Tm).

duplicate *v.* copy, ditto, clone, reproduce, replicate, double, photocopy, Xerox (Tm), Photostat (Tm).

duplicate *adj.* twin, matching, identical, corresponding.

duplicity *n.* dishonesty, deception, deceit, fraud, mendacity, guile, double-dealing, perfidy, treachery.

durability *n.* stability, endurance, constancy, persistence, strength, longevity, imperishability, durableness; *ant.* fragility, impermanence.

durable *adj.* tough, enduring, constant, permanent, strong, sturdy, sound, lasting, dependable, persistent; *ant.* fragile, impermanent, perishable.

duration *n.* length, span, period, stretch, spell, extent, continuation, perpetuation; *ant.* shortening.

duress *n.* **1.** coercion, pressure, force, compulsion, bullying, control, restraint. **2.** imprisonment, bondage, captivity, confinement, detention, arrest, incarceration, slavery, constraint.

dusk *n.* evening, twilight, sunset, darkness, nightfall, sundown, gloom, eventide; *ant.* dawn.

dusky *adj.* **1.** dark, sooty, swarthy, black. **2.** overcast, shadowy, twilight, dim, murky, cloudy, veiled, obscure.

dust *n.* particles, dirt, grime, grit.

dust *v.* **1.** clean, polish, wipe, burnish. **2.** sprinkle, powder, scatter, sift, spread, spray.

dusty *adj.* **1.** dirty, filthy, chalky, sooty, unswept; *ant.* clean, polished. **2.** crumbly, powdery, granular, friable, pulverized, sandy; *ant.* hard, solid.

dutiful *adj.* respectful, obedient, acquiescent,

deferential, devoted, submissive, docile, compliant, complaisant, filial; *ant.* fractious.

duty *n.* **1.** obligation, work, office, task, function, part, calling, charge, service, mission. **2.** tax, charge, tariff, toll, revenue, custom, levy, excise.

dwarf *n.* midget, pygmy, Lilliputian, Tom Thumb.

dwarf *v.* stunt, diminish, minimize, check, retard, overshadow, dim, dominate.

dwarfish *adj.* small, miniature, mini, tiny, undersized, baby, diminutive, dwarfed, petite, pint-sized, Lilliputian, pocket; *ant.* large.

dwell *v.* live, reside, stay, abide, inhabit, lodge, settle, tenant, quarter, populate, people.

dweller *n.* resident, inhabitant, occupant, denizen.

dwelling *n.* house, home, residence, domicile, lodging, lodge, abode, quarters.

dwindle *v.* decrease, diminish, subside, shrink, taper off, waste away, die out, decline, ebb, fade, abate, peter out; *ant.* increase.

dye *n.* color, tint, stain, pigmentation, tinge.

dye *v.* color, tint, stain, tinge, imbue, tincture.

dyed-in-the-wool *adj.* hard-core, deep-rooted, die-hard, inveterate, established, inflexible, long-standing, unchangeable, complete, entrenched, card-carrying; *ant.* superficial.

dying *adj.* **1.** perishing, final, mortal, passing, final, failing, expiring, being on one's deathbed, declining, moribund. **2.** obsolescent, vanishing, fading, archaic, disappearing, dwindling, passé, diminishing, on the way out; *ant.* coming, reviving.

dynamic *adj.* vigorous, spirited, active, electric, driving, go-getting, high-powered, lively, powerful, forceful, self-starting, vital; *ant.* apathetic, inactive, slow.

dynamism *n.* initiative, drive, vim, vigor, liveliness, enterprise, energy, forcefulness, get-up-and-go; *ant.* apathy, inactivity.

dynamite *n.* trinitrotoluene, TNT, blasting powder, detonator, explosive.

dynasty *n.* regime, authority, dominion, rule, government, empire, sovereignty, succession, ascendancy.

dyspeptic *adj.* short-tempered, grouchy, crabby, testy, crotchety, touchy, peevish, bad-tempered.

each *adv.* apiece, individually, singly, separately, per person.

eager *adj.* enthusiastic, earnest, longing, yearning, fervent, impatient, hungry, raring; *ant.* apathetic.

ear *n.* appreciation, regard, discrimination, sensitivity, taste.

all ears attentive, listening, hearing.

in one ear and out the other ignored, unnoticed, neglected, forgotten.

lend an ear listen, give attention, heed, take notice.

play it by ear improvise, concoct, ad-lib.

early *adj.* 1. young, undeveloped, prehistoric, primitive, primordial, primeval. 2. forward, advanced, premature, precocious.

early *adv.* in advance, ahead of time, prematurely, too soon, beforehand; *ant.* late.

earmark *v.* reserve, put *or* set aside, allocate, designate; tag, label.

earn *v.* 1. deserve, win, merit, warrant. 2. acquire, obtain, attain, get, gain, procure, profit, net, draw, gather, secure, reap; *ant.* lose, spend.

earnest *adj.* 1. enthusiastic, eager, ardent, zealous, passionate, impassioned, heartfelt, vehement, fervent, fervid; *ant.* apathetic. 2. solemn, serious, grave, sober, staid, sincere; *ant.* flippant.

earnings *n.* 1. salary, wages, income, pay, stipend; *ant.* expenses, outgoings. 2. revenue, profits, proceeds, return, receipts, remuneration, gain, reward; *ant.* investment.

earth *n.* 1. planet, world, globe, orb, geosphere. 2. dirt, soil, clay, ground, land, loam, topsoil, sod.

down to earth 1. realistic, mundane, practical, earthy. 2. sincere, unaffected, casual, homely, plain, unpretentious.

earthly *adj.* 1. worldly, terrestrial, sublunar; *ant.* heavenly. 2. physical, sensual, fleshly, carnal, base, human; *ant.* spiritual.

earthy *adj.* unrefined, crude, coarse, unsophisticated, ribald, vulgar, lusty; down-to-earth, uninhibited, simple, hearty; *ant.* cultured.

ease *n.* 1. comfort, rest, peace of mind, leisure, repose, calm, tranquillity, solace, consolation. 2. facility, expertness, efficiency, adroitness, aplomb; *ant.* difficulty, clumsiness.

ease *v.* 1. alleviate, allay, mitigate, comfort, soothe, relieve, assuage, palliate, ameliorate, tranquilize; *ant.* aggravate, hurt, injure. 2. extricate, disentangle, remove; guide, maneuver, slide, handle, manipulate. 3. facilitate, expedite, smooth the way for.

ease off abate, moderate, decrease, relent, die down, wane, slacken, subside; *ant.* build up, increase.

easily *adv.* 1. effortlessly, readily, efficiently, smoothly, quickly; *ant.* laboriously. 2. definitely, surely, certainly, doubtlessly, probably, undoubtedly, undeniably, indubitably, clearly, far and away, by far, unequivocally.

easy *adj.* 1. simple, effortless, facile, light, manageable, tractable; *ant.* difficult, arduous. 2. leisurely, relaxed, calm, peaceful, tranquil, content, carefree. 3. fluent, flowing, unaffected, effortless, natural; *ant.* awkward, stiff.

easygoing *adj.* carefree, happy-go-lucky, relaxed, laid-back (*slang*), insouciant; amenable, lenient, complaisant, permissive; *ant.* worried, intolerant.

eat *v.* 1. consume, devour, dine, feed on, chew, bite, swallow, gobble, ingest. 2. leisurely, corrode, erode, wear away, dissolve, dissipate, squander.

eats *n.* food, victuals, comestibles, grub (*slang*).

eavesdrop *v.* overhear, listen in, spy, tap, monitor, wire, snoop, bug (*slang*).

ebb *v.* decline, recede, withdraw, subside, retreat, abate, lessen, deteriorate, diminish, flag, slacken, wane, fade away; *ant.* increase.

ebullient *adj.* enthusiastic, elated, excited, exuberant, exhilarated, irrepressible, vivacious, effusive, buoyant; *ant.* apathetic, dull, lifeless.

eccentric *n.* nonconformist, character, freak, *slang:* weirdo, oddball, flake.

eccentric *adj.* unconventional, offbeat, idiosyncratic, peculiar, abnormal, bizarre, quirky, erratic, flaky (*slang*), strange, weird, freakish, outlandish; *ant.* normal.

eccentricity *n.* idiosyncrasy, peculiarity, foible, nonconformity, aberration, anomaly, abnormality, oddity, quiddity, singularity; *ant.* normalcy.

ecclesiastic *n.* priest, minister, parson, pastor, cleric, abbey, man *or* woman of the cloth, member of clergy.

ecclesiastical *adj.* religious, holy, spiritual, divine, priestly, pastoral, clerical.

echelon *n.* status, rank, degree, grade, level, position, place, step, tier.

echo *n.* **1.** reverberation, reiteration, repetition, reproduction. **2.** imitation, reflection, parallel.

echo *v.* **1.** resound, reverberate, rebound, return, bounce back. **2.** imitate, reiterate, repeat, mimic, ape, copy, parrot; reflect, mirror, match, agree with.

éclat *n.* **1.** celebrity, fame, glory, success, distinction. **2.** acclaim, applause, approval, pomp.

eclectic *adj.* **1.** diverse, multifarious, varied, divers, many-sided. **2.** general, wide-ranging, broad, comprehensive, liberal, catholic, all-embracing; *ant.* narrow.

eclipse *n.* overshadowing, darkening, shading, obscuration, adumbration.

eclipse *v.* obscure, shroud, veil, cloud, dim, darken, adumbrate, overshadow, surpass, transcend, exceed, outdo.

ecology *n.* conservation, bionomics, environmental sciences *or* studies, ecological engineering, survival studies.

economic *adj.* **1.** financial, fiscal, budgetary. **2.** cost-effective, cheap, low-priced, reasonable, sensible, budget-conscious, profitable; *ant.* expensive.

economical *adj.* **1.** cheap, sound, low-priced, reasonable, fair, moderate, inexpensive, on sale, cost-effective. **2.** thrifty, sparing, saving, economizing, frugal, provident, niggardly, mi-

serly, stingy, tightfisted, avaricious; *ant.* liberal, generous, wasteful. **3.** efficient, practical, time-saving, labor-saving, methodical.

economics *n.* commerce, finance, social science, commercial theory.

economize *v.* save, scrimp, cut back, cut corners, tighten one's belt, husband, retrench; *ant.* squander.

ecstasy *n.* rapture, joy, exaltation, rhapsody, delight, bliss, seventh heaven, elation; *ant.* torment.

ecstatic *adj.* elated, delirious, euphoric, blissful, rhapsodic, overjoyed, joyful, enraptured; *ant.* downcast.

eddy *n.* whirlpool, vortex, swirl, countercurrent.

edge *n.* **1.** border, frontier, extremity, brink, boundary, end, limit, brim, rim, margin. **2.** advantage, upper hand, handicap, head start, lead.

on edge apprehensive, anxious, ill at ease, keyed up, nervous, tense, edgy; *ant.* relaxed.

edge *v.* decorate, trim, border, fringe, bind, stitch, hem, hone, rim.

edgy *adj.* nervous, touchy, irritable, tense, testy, anxious, on edge, ill at ease, uptight (*slang*); *ant.* calm.

edible *adj.* eatable, palatable, digestible, comestible.

edict *n.* law, act, fiat, decree, command, order, ruling, regulation, dictum, mandate, statute, injunction.

edification *n.* guidance, instruction, enlightenment, education, improvement.

edifice *n.* building, structure, construction, erection.

edify *v.* teach, instruct, educate, train, school, inform, tutor, guide, enlighten; improve, nurture, elevate.

edit *v.* correct, emend, censor, revise, rewrite, check, blue-pencil, polish, condense, rephrase, annotate.

edition *n.* version, printing, copy, issue, volume, number.

educate *v.* teach, school, train, tutor, instruct, enlighten, catechize, edify, indoctrinate, rear.

educated *adj.* **1.** trained, skilled, scholarly, schooled, learned, well-read, well-versed, erudite, instructed, well-informed, developed;

ant. illiterate, ignorant, unlettered. **2.** cultured, cultivated, refined, polished, sophisticated, well-bred; *ant.* crude, coarse.

education *n.* **1.** (process of educating) schooling, teaching, training, instruction, coaching, indoctrination, tutelage, tutoring. **2.** (quality or result of being educated) scholarship, knowledge, enlightenment, development, edification, improvement.

educational *adj.* enlightening, informative, edifying, enriching, heuristic, improving, cultural.

educator *n.* teacher, tutor, instructor, trainer, pedagogue, coach.

eerie *adj.* **1.** scary, frightening, creepy, spine-chilling. **2.** spooky, strange, weird, mysterious, eldrich, unearthly, uncanny, ghostly; *ant.* natural, ordinary.

efface *v.* erase, eradicate, obliterate, remove, cross *or* rub out, delete, eliminate, expunge, raze, extirpate.

effect *n.* **1.** conclusion, consequence, outcome, result, upshot, aftermath, fruit. **2.** meaning, drift, substance, neat, heart, core, pith, essence, import, impression. **for effect** insincerely, artificially, ostentatiously, demonstratively, purposely, deliberately. **in effect** in fact, actually, really; virtually, to all intents and purposes.

effect *v.* **1.** cause, produce, create, make, begin, bring about, initiate, actuate, wreak. **2.** accomplish, achieve, fulfill, complete, execute, perform, consummate.

effective *adj.* efficient, capable, powerful, forceful, effectual, cogent, compelling, moving, potent, striking, productive; *ant.* useless.

effects *n.* trappings, belongings, goods, possessions, property, things, belongings, paraphernalia.

effectual *adj.* successful, influential, efficient, productive, useful, valid, legal, licit, potent, powerful.

effeminate *adj.* womanish, epicene, delicate, feminine, womanly; *ant.* manly.

effervesce *v.* bubble, fizz, foam, froth, ferment, boil.

effervescence *n.* **1.** vitality, vivacity, animation, enthusiasm, ebullience, liveliness, exuberance, high spirits, vim. **2.** foam, bubbles, froth, fizz, buoyancy, ebullition.

effervescent *adj.* **1.** foaming, bubbly, fizzy, frothy, carbonated, sparkling, fermenting, boiling; *ant.* crude, coarse. vivacious, excited, exhilarated, ebullient, enthusiastic, exuberant, vital, animated; *ant.* apathetic, dull.

effete *adj.* **1.** sterile, infertile, barren, unproductive, incapable; *ant.* fecund, prolific, teeming, fruitful. **2.** weak, exhausted, spent, decrepit, wasted, tired out, used up, ineffectual, degenerate, enervated, dissipated; *ant.* vigorous.

efficiency *n.* effectiveness, efficacy, productivity, economy, proficiency, skill, power, capability, ability, competence, competency.

efficient *adj.* **1.** effective, competent, capable, able, adept, productive, skillful. **2.** economic, powerful, streamlined, well-organized, well-regulated, businesslike.

effigy *n.* likeness, image, representation; portrait, dummy, statue, icon, carving, idol.

effluent *adj.* flowing, emanating, issuing forth.

effort *n.* **1.** work, travail, labor, exertion, toil, pains, job, energy, strain, struggle, stress, ordeal, stretch. **2.** try, attempt, endeavor, shot, stab, essay, application, go. **3.** accomplishment, feat, achievement, deed, product.

effortless *adj.* easy, simple, facile, uncomplicated, smooth, painless; *ant.* difficult.

effrontery *n.* insolence, rudeness, arrogance, impudence, impertinence, brashness, presumption, temerity, boldness, brazenness, nerve, gall.

effusion *n.* outflow, flow, outpouring, stream, emission, discharge, gush, shedding, emanation.

effusive *adj.* talkative, profuse, gushing, wordy, demonstrative, enthusiastic, expansive, exuberant; *ant.* quiet, restrained, reserved.

egalitarian *adj.* fair, impartial, equal, just.

egg *n.* ovum, seed, germ, spawn, roe, embryo, nucleus, cell.

egghead *n.* brain (*slang*), scholar, intellectual, genius, intellect, Einstein.

egg on *v.* encourage, prompt, push, urge, spur, prod, exhort, coax, incite, goad; *ant.* discourage.

egoism *n.* narcissism, selfishness, egomania, egocentricity, self-centeredness, self-love, self-importance, self-absorption, self-interest, self-regard; *ant.* altruism.

egoist *n.* egomaniac, narcissist, self-seeker.

egoistic *adj.* egocentric, egomaniacal, narcissistic, self-centered, self-absorbed, self-involved, self-seeking, self-important; *ant.* altruistic.

egotism *n.* egomania, egocentricity, narcissism, conceit, vanity, vainglory, egoism, self-importance, superiority, self-love, self-centeredness, self-esteem, bigheadedness; *ant.* humility.

egotist *n.* egomaniac, egoist, braggart, boaster, braggadocio.

egotistic *adj.* conceited, self-centered, vain, vainglorious, narcissistic, egomaniacal, superior, egocentric, self-important, pompous, swellheaded, bigheaded; *ant.* humble.

egregious *adj.* flagrant, heinous, notorious, scandalous, glaring, gross, arrant, intolerable, insufferable, monstrous, rank, infamous; *ant.* slight.

egress *n.* exit, escape, vent, outlet, exodus.

ejaculate *v.* **1.** spurt, discharge, emit, eject. **2.** yell, shout, scream, exclaim, cry, call, blurt, utter.

ejaculation *n.* **1.** orgasm, climax, secretion, discharge, emission. **2.** cry, exclamation, yell, scream, shout, call.

eject *v.* **1.** spout, emit, discharge, spew, vomit, disgorge, dispossess. **2.** exile, evict, remove, oust, expel, banish, deport, throw *or* drive *or* kick out.

eke out stretch, economize on, make do with, husband.

elaborate *adj.* **1.** extravagant, fancy, ornate, ornamental, decorative, detailed; showy, ostentatious, fussy; *ant.* plain. **2.** complicated, complex, involved, detailed, convoluted, intricate; *ant.* simple. **3.** painstaking, labored, thorough, detailed, exact, careful, minute, precise.

elaborate *v.* explain, detail, expand, develop, flesh out, enlarge upon, refine, develop, amplify; *ant.* simplify.

élan *n.* flair, dash, verve, flourish, animation, vigor, liveliness, style, panache, vivacity, zip, esprit, pizazz; *ant.* apathy, lifelessness.

elapse *v.* lapse, go by, pass, slip away.

elastic *adj.* **1.** supple, plastic, rubbery, stretchy, springy, bouncy, resilient, flexible; *ant.* rigid.

2. (said of persons) adaptable, resilient, flexible, buoyant.

elated *adj.* jubilant, joyous, ecstatic, euphoric, overjoyed, exultant, delighted, blissful, gleeful, pleased, exhilarated; *ant.* downcast.

elation *n.* joy, rapture, ecstasy, euphoria, glee, high spirits, jubilation, exaltation, exultation, delight, bliss, exhilaration; *ant.* depression.

elbow *n.* bend, turn, crook, joint, angle, curve, fork.

elbow *v.* nudge, bump, push, shove, jostle, knock.

elbowroom *n.* space, freedom, latitude, scope, leeway, play.

elder *n.* senior, deacon, presbyter.

elder *adj.* senior, older, first-born; *ant.* younger.

elderly *adj.* old, aged, hoary, long in the tooth, retired, ancient, venerable; *ant.* young, youthful.

elect *v.* pick, select, choose, vote, designate, appoint, opt for.

election *n.* vote, selection, choice, judgment, decision, appointment, determination.

elective *adj.* optional, voluntary, selective.

electric *adj.* charged, exciting, rousing, stirring, thrilling, electrifying, dynamic, stimulating, tense; *ant.* tedious, unexciting.

electrify *v.* stir, stimulate, excite, fire, rouse, jolt, invigorate, galvanize, thrill, astound, amaze; *ant.* bore.

elegance *n.* refinement, culture, taste, cultivation, polish, style, grace, gentility, breeding, class (*slang*).

elegant *adj.* refined, cultivated, genteel, graceful, polished, tasteful, comely, beautiful, exquisite, fashionable, debonair.

elegiac *adj.* sad, melancholy, funereal, lamenting, mournful, plaintive, doleful; *ant.* happy.

elegy *n.* lament, dirge, requiem.

element *n.* part, piece, portion, particle, factor, ingredient, component, module, section, unit, constituent, subdivision, feature.

elementary *adj.* basic, fundamental, primary, principal, initial, rudimentary, introductory; simple, easy, clear, facile; *ant.* advanced, complex.

elements *adj.* fundamentals, basics, essentials, rudiments, foundations, principles.

elephantine *adj.* **1.** large, immense, huge,

monstrous, gigantic, enormous. 2. awkward, clumsy, ungainly; *ant.* graceful.

elevate *v.* 1. raise, heighten, lift, uplift, hoist, heave, boost; *ant.* lower. 2. promote, advance, upgrade, further, sublimate, augment, exalt; *ant.* lessen.

elevated *adj.* 1. raised, high, aerial, towering, tall, lofty. 2. noble, sublime, dignified, eminent, exalted, grand, high-flown, high-minded; *ant.* base, informal, lowly.

elevation *n.* altitude, rise, uplift, acclivity, height.

elfin *adj.* 1. small, petite, elflike, elfish, delicate, impish, puckish. 2. mischievous, playful, frolicsome, arch, charming.

elicit *v.* extract, draw out, evoke, wrest, exact, derive, extort, wring.

eligible *adj.* suitable, appropriate, acceptable, fit, worthy, proper, qualified, desirable, available.

eliminate *v.* get rid of, remove, take out, dispense with, eject, expunge, delete, erase, eradicate, terminate, extinguish, annihilate, kill, liquidate; omit, leave out.

elite *n.* aristocracy, gentry, society, nobility, establishment, high society, elect, crème de la crème.

elixir *n.* cure-all, remedy, panacea, solution, tonic, potion, tincture.

elliptical *adj.* 1. oval, egg-shaped, ovoid, oviform. 2. (said of a manner of expression) ambiguous, oblique, roundabout, obscure, recondite, incomprehensible, abstruse, cryptic; *ant.* clear, lucid. 3. (said of speech) succinct, laconic, terse, curt, pithy.

elocution *n.* 1. diction, enunciation, pronunciation, articulation, delivery. 2. speech, rhetoric, oratory, utterance, declamation.

elongated *adj.* stretched, extended, long, lengthened, prolonged, protracted.

elope *v.* run off, leave, escape, disappear, run *or* slip *or* steal away, decamp, bolt.

eloquent *adj.* fluent, articulate, expressive, persuasive, stirring, silver-tongued; moving, meaningful, pregnant, revealing; *ant.* tongue-tied.

elucidate *v.* explain, clarify, explicate, gloss, illustrate, expound, annotate, spell out, interpret, illuminate; *ant.* confuse, obscure.

elude *v.* evade, escape, flee, circumvent, dodge, thwart, foil, stump, frustrate, baffle, confound, puzzle.

elusive *adj.* 1. evasive, fleeting, temporary, slippery, shifty, transient, fugitive. 2. mysterious, baffling, indefinable, intangible, tricky.

emaciated *adj.* gaunt, thin, haggard, pinched, lank, lean, skeletal, scrawny, cadaverous, atrophied, wasted; *ant.* plump, well-fed.

emanate *v.* give off, emit, radiate, send out, exude, discharge, issue, exhale.

emanation *n.* 1. generation, emergence, beginning, origin, flowing, outpour, arising, issuance, outflow, escape, effusion. 2. emission, effluvium, discharge, drainage, exhalation, leakage, vapor, steam, radiation, ejaculation.

emancipate *v.* set free, free, liberate, release, deliver, discharge, unchain, unfetter, unshackle, disencumber, enfranchise; *ant.* enslave.

emancipation *n.* freedom, liberty, release, deliverance, discharge, enfranchisement; *ant.* enslavement.

emasculate *v.* 1. castrate, neuter, spay, geld, sterilize, mutilate. 2. weaken, soften, enervate, cripple, debilitate, impoverish.

embalm *v.* preserve, mummify, enshrine, consecrate, immortalize.

embankment *n.* dike, breakwater, pier, dam, levee, causeway, earthwork, rampart.

embargo *n.* ban, bar, prohibition, stoppage, blockage, restriction, restraint, impediment, barrier, proscription.

embark *v.* leave, set out, set sail, leave port, board ship, enplane, entrain.

embark on begin, start, launch, initiate, commence, undertake, broach, enter, engage; *ant.* finish.

embarrass *v.* mortify, shame, humiliate, disconcert, abash, chagrin, fluster, distress, discomfit, discompose, discountenance.

embassy *n.* consulate, delegation, mission, committee.

embed *v.* insert, put in, set, root, implant, plant, deposit, bury, enclose, inlay.

embellish *v.* 1. decorate, adorn, trim, ornament, gild, embroider, festoon, enhance, dress up, garnish, beautify, deck. 2. elaborate, exaggerate, embroider, build up.

emergency *n.* danger, crisis, exigency, predicament, quandary, strait, scrape, difficulty, crunch, plight, pinch.
emergent *adj.* 1. budding, developing, emerging, emanating, rising, coming; *ant.* declining, disappearing. 2. urgent, pressing, sudden, immediate, important.
emigrant *n.* exile, expatriate, refugee, fugitive, defector, wayfarer, pilgrim, wanderer, outcast, foreigner, alien.
emigrate *v.* leave, quit, defect; *ant.* immigrate.
eminence *n.* 1. importance, greatness, standing, prestige, preeminence, distinction, illustriousness, esteem, rank, celebrity, fame. 2. hill, rise, peak, ridge, summit, elevation, height, knoll, highland, projection.
eminent *adj.* 1. distinguished, renowned, famous, celebrated, illustrious, esteemed, prominent, important, notable, high-ranking, august; *ant.* unknown. 2. tall, high, raised, elevated, lofty.
emissary *n.* messenger, envoy, representative, deputy, scout, ambassador, agent, courier, delegate, spy, nuncio, herald.
emit *v.* discharge, give off, eject, gush, secrete, spurt, expel, vomit, belch, void, vent; *ant.* absorb.
emollient *n.* moisturizer, oil, ointment, cream, balm, lotion, salve, liniment, poultice.
emollient *adj.* soothing, balsamic, softening, mollifying, mitigative.
emolument *n.* earnings, fee, salary, wages, pay, payment, profits, return, recompense, benefit, compensation, allowance, stipend.
emotion *n.* feeling, sentiment, reaction, ardor, affect, fervor, passion.
emotional *adj.* 1. sentimental, fervent, ardent, passionate, gushing, hysterical, demonstrative, excitable, impulsive, irrational, histrionic, hypersensitive; *ant.* calm, apathetic. 2. moving, touching, affecting, stirring, thrilling, heartwarming, poignant, tear-jerking (*slang*).
emotionless *adj.* cold, indifferent, unfeeling, frigid, detached, impassive, remote, undemonstrative, distant, cold-blooded, phlegmatic; *ant.* emotional.
emotive *adj.* touching, moving, stirring, impassioned, exciting, inflaming, affecting, poi-

embers *n.* ashes, coals, cinders.
embezzle *v.* steal, appropriate, pilfer, misuse, filch, pinch, purloin.
embezzler *n.* thief, cheat, fraud.
embittered *adj.* resentful, sour, cynical, bitter.
emblazon *v.* decorate, adorn, embellish, ornament, illuminate, beautify, paint, color.
emblem *n.* 1. symbol, sign, mark, image, representation, design. 2. badge, insignia, crest, token, medal.
emblematic *adj.* symbolic, representative, figurative.
embodiment *n.* personification, symbol, incarnation, essence, representation, example, exemplar, image.
embody *v.* personify, represent, stand for, symbolize, typify, incarnate, actualize.
emboss *v.* decorate, design, raise.
embrace *v.* 1. clasp, hug, hold, squeeze, cuddle, grasp, encircle, enclose, encompass, enfold. 2. adopt, accept, hold, endorse, support, incorporate, include, involve, welcome, espouse; *ant.* recant, reject.
embroider *v.* 1. stitch, knit, quilt, braid, weave, decorate, ornament, beautify, embellish, garnish, deck, gild. 2. exaggerate, lie, falsify, embellish.
embroidery *n.* 1. needlepoint, needlework, sewing, brocade, decoration, patterning, adornment, edging, fringing. 2. exaggeration, embellishment, fabrication, hyperbole, hype (*slang*).
embroil *v.* 1. involve, implicate, entangle, ensnare, enmesh. 2. perplex, confound, confuse, muddle, disturb, trouble, distract.
embryo *n.* nucleus, root, germ, beginning, rudiment.
embryonic *adj.* underdeveloped, immature, early, incipient, beginning, primary, inchoate, rudimentary, seminal, germinal; *ant.* advanced, developed.
emend *v.* correct, rectify, improve, revise, edit, rewrite, alter; *ant.* stet.
emerge *v.* develop, appear, surface, materialize, rise, transpire, crop up, issue, emanate, proceed; *ant.* disappear, fade.
emergence *n.* appearance, rise, evolution, development, arrival, materialization, coming, visibility, apparition; *ant.* decline, disappearance.

gnant, heartwarming, thrilling, passionate, tear-jerking (*slang*).

emperor *n.* ruler, monarch, dictator, sovereign, tsar, caesar, shogun, kaiser, mikado.

empathy *n.* understanding, compassion, sympathy.

emphasis *n.* importance, stress, weight, urgency, significance, underscoring, import, accent, priority, intensity.

emphasize *v.* stress, accentuate, highlight, underline, underscore, spotlight, play up, point out, punctuate, feature, intensify; *ant.* depreciate, understate.

emphatic *adj.* insistent, forceful, resounding, definite, strong, decided, graphic, pronounced, unequivocal, trenchant, powerful, striking; *ant.* quiet, understated.

empire *n.* kingdom, territory, domain, dominion, commonwealth, realm, jurisdiction.

empirical *adj.* practical, pragmatic, experimental, observed, experiential; *ant.* conjectural, speculative, theoretical.

employ *v.* 1. use, utilize, operate, spend, take up, manipulate, apply, exercise, exert, occupy, ply. 2. hire, engage, contract, enlist, indenture, retain, take on, apprentice, commission.

employee *n.* worker, laborer, staffer, servant, wage-earner, hand, hireling, lackey, flunky.

employer *n.* boss, owner, proprietor, patron, taskmaster; company, business, firm, establishment, outfit, organization.

employment *n.* 1. job, work, vocation, profession, occupation, trade, line, business, avocation, calling, craft. 2. use, utilization, application, engagement, enlistment.

emporium *n.* store, shop, bazaar, market, mart, establishment.

empower *v.* license, permit, authorize, allow, warrant, sanction, delegate, commission, enfranchise, qualify, accredit, enable.

emptiness *n.* 1. void, vacuum, blank, vacuity, vacancy, gap, chasm, barrenness, exhaustion, depletedness, absence; *ant.* plenum, fullness. 2. banality, senselessness, futility, meaninglessness, insincerity, insubstantiality, triviality, silliness, frivolity, purposelessness, aimlessness, ineffectiveness.

empty *v.* void, unload, drain, clear, deplete, dump, discharge, evacuate, exhaust, vacate; *ant.* fill.

empty *adj.* 1. void, vacant, vacuous, unoccupied, bare, blank, deserted, uninhabited, untenanted, stark, wanting; *ant.* filled, full, replete. 2. futile, worthless, ineffective, purposeless, fruitless, aimless, idle, vain, inane, silly, superficial, insincere.

empty-headed *adj.* silly, vacuous, flighty, giddy, brainless, inane, harebrained, scatterbrained, frivolous, dizzy.

emulate *v.* imitate, copy, mimic, echo, follow, follow in someone's footsteps, challenge.

enable *v.* allow, permit, authorize, license, commission, sanction, accredit, qualify, empower, capacitate, prepare, facilitate; *ant.* inhibit, prevent.

enact *v.* 1. decree, sanction, ordain, order, dictate, legislate, pass, establish, ratify, vote in, authorize, appoint, institute; *ant.* repeal. 2. act, play, portray, personify, impersonate, act out.

enamored *adj.* captivated, infatuated, smitten, taken, bewitched, enraptured, fascinated, charmed.

encampment *n.* campsite, quarters, tents, base, campground, bivouac.

encapsulate *v.* 1. summarize, sum up, condense, abridge, compress, précis. 2. epitomize, typify, represent, exemplify.

enchant *v.* charm, spellbind, mesmerize, fascinate, captivate, bewitch, enrapture, enamor, hypnotize, beguile, enthrall; *ant.* bore.

enchantment *n.* 1. spell, sorcery, hypnotism, incantation, magic, witchcraft, wizardry. 2. allure, charm, bliss, beguilement, rapture, transport, delight.

encircle *v.* envelop, enclose, surround, ring, gird, encompass, enfold, circumscribe, hem in.

enclose *v.* encircle, confine, encompass, wrap, embrace, circumscribe, hem in, hold, contain, shut in, pen, fence.

enclosure *n.* pen, sty, yard, stockade, corral, compound, cage, pound, paddock, cell.

encompass *v.* 1. surround, ring, circle, encircle, envelop, enclose, circumscribe, gird, girdle, hem in, hold. 2. include, involve, embrace, comprise, contain, embody, incorporate.

encore *n.* repeat performance, repetition, reprisal.

encounter *n.* confrontation, fight, conflict, dispute, collision, brush, meeting, skirmish, clash, battle, combat, run-in, set-to.

encounter *v.* meet, face, come upon, run into, run across, engage, fight, grapple with, combat, clash with, struggle with, experience, chance upon, happen upon.

encourage *v.* **1.** hearten, rally, strengthen, cheer, reassure, support, foster; *ant.* discourage, depress, dissuade. **2.** incite, inspire, stimulate, urge; *ant.* deter.

encouraging *adj.* reassuring, heartening, uplifting, promising, hopeful, cheering, auspicious, comforting.

encroach *v.* intrude, invade, overstep, trespass, infringe, usurp, appropriate.

encumber *v.* handicap, hamper, burden, saddle, obstruct, overload, retard, weigh down.

encumbrance *n.* impediment, hindrance, obstruction, burden, liability, obstacle, onus, handicap; *ant.* aid.

encyclopedic *adj.* complete, comprehensive, thorough, universal, all-encompassing, all-inclusive, exhaustive, wide-ranging, all-embracing; *ant.* narrow.

end *n.* **1.** conclusion, outcome, result, resolution, upshot, consequence, effect, payoff. **2.** expiration, completion, termination, adjournment, close, denouement, finish, conclusion, finis, finale; *ant.* beginning, opening, start. **3.** purpose, goal, aim, objective, object, intention, reason, aspiration.

make ends meet survive, subsist, budget, estimate, manage.

end *v.* finish, stop, quit, close, halt, conclude, discontinue, cease, abort, drop, call it a day; *ant.* begin, start.

endanger *v.* jeopardize, threaten, risk, hazard, imperil, compromise, expose; *ant.* protect, shelter, shield.

endearing *adj.* charming, engaging, winsome, enchanting, captivating, lovable, adorable, delightful, winning, sweet.

endeavor *n.* effort, try, trial, attempt, undertaking, venture, enterprise, shot, stab, essay, go, crack.

endeavor *v.* try, attempt, aim, aspire, undertake, strive, venture, essay.

ending *n.* conclusion, finish, close, completion, resolution, cessation, culmination, termination, consummation, finale, epilogue, denouement; *ant.* beginning, start.

endless *adj.* constant, incessant, ceaseless, interminable, continual, uninterrupted, limitless, everlasting, unending, undying, eternal, perpetual.

endorse *v.* **1.** sign, legalize, ratify. **2.** support, back, advocate, champion, recommend, approve, subscribe to; *ant.* denounce.

endow *v.* fund, donate, give, grant, award, bestow, finance, furnish, provide; leave, will; *ant.* divest.

endowment *n.* **1.** gift, grant, fund, donation, award; bequest, benefaction, dowry, provision, legacy. **2.** gift, talent, aptitude, ability, flair, capacity, capability, genius, attribute.

endurable *adj.* bearable, tolerable, sufferable, sustainable.

endurance *n.* **1.** stamina, fortitude, resolution, strength, tenacity. **2.** durability, staying power, immutability, longevity, permanence.

endure *v.* **1.** undergo, bear, survive, withstand, suffer, sustain, weather, brave. **2.** tolerate, put up *or* cope with, abide, stand, stomach.

enduring *adj.* long-lasting, durable, permanent, imperishable, eternal, firm, steady, persistent, steadfast, unwavering, prevailing; *ant.* changeable, fleeting.

enema *n.* douche, purgative, clyster.

enemy *n.* adversary, foe, opponent, rival, competitor, antagonist, opposer; *ant.* ally, friend.

energetic *adj.* vigorous, active, lively, spirited, animated, dynamic, brisk, strong, forceful, indefatigable, tireless; *ant.* idle, lazy, sluggish.

energize *v.* stimulate, animate, electrify, invigorate, motivate, inspirit, activate, enliven, vitalize, galvanize; *ant.* daunt.

energy *n.* vitality, liveliness, spirit, vigor, zeal, zest, vim, pep, strength, intensity, get-up-and-go; *ant.* inertia, lethargy, weakness.

enervate *v.* tire, exhaust, fatigue, wear out, weaken, enfeeble, sap, debilitate, incapacitate, paralyze, prostrate, deplete; *ant.* vitalize, activate, energize.

enfeeble *v.* exhaust, enervate, weaken, under-

enfold mine, deplete, sap, wear out, debilitate, diminish, geld, emasculate, devitalize; *ant.* strengthen.

enfold *v.* enclose, shroud, swathe, wrap up, encircle, encompass, envelop, clasp, embrace, hug, hold.

enforce *v.* **1.** strengthen, reinforce, fortify, support. **2.** compel, urge, drive, demand, dictate, exact, commandeer, require, oblige, insist upon, necessitate, impel.

enfranchise *v.* free, release, emancipate.

engage *v.* **1.** hire, employ, contract, commission, appoint, enlist, take on, retain; *ant.* dismiss, discharge. **2.** lease, charter, book, reserve, retain. **3.** (involve one's interest or attention) involve, draw into, engross, absorb, captivate, fascinate; attract, charm, enchant, bewitch, allure, win. **4.** attack, fight, assault, strike, combat, assail, fall upon.

engaged *adj.* **1.** betrothed, pledged, promised, spoken for, unavailable, committed, bound. **2.** (said of one's use of time or one's attention) busy, working, occupied, employed, preoccupied, tied up; interested, engrossed, involved, absorbed, immersed; *ant.* free, uninvolved. **3.** employed, practicing, performing, dealing in, at work, working; *ant.* idle, out-of-work.

engagement *n.* **1.** appointment, meeting, rendezvous, encounter, date, gig (*slang*). **2.** betrothal, commitment, vow, pact, pledge, espousal. **3.** skirmish, battle, fight, action, combat, conflict, confrontation, contest.

engaging *adj.* charming, likable, pleasant, appealing, attractive, winning, enchanting, possessing, captivating, fascinating, beguiling, winsome, pleasing; *ant.* boring, loathesome.

engender *v.* **1.** cause, create, make, produce, incite, instigate, propagate. **2.** beget, generate, propagate, procreate, father, hatch, spawn, sire.

engine *n.* **1.** motor, generator, turbine, transformer, dynamo, apparatus, mechanism, contraption. **2.** locomotive, motor, steam engine.

engineer *n.* inventor, designer, originator, planner, architect, contriver, deviser.

engineer *v.* create, concoct, cause, originate, mastermind, plot, plan, devise, contrive, machinate, manipulate, finagle, wangle.

engrave *v.* inscribe, etch, carve, chisel, cut, embed, imprint, impress, ingrain, print, mark, blaze.

engraving *n.* **1.** etching, carving, inscribing, cutting, chiseling. **2.** print, design, etching, illustration, inscription, impression, copy, print, plate, proof.

engross *v.* fixate, rivet, arrest, absorb, hold, monopolize, engage, immerse, occupy, preoccupy, involve.

engrossing *adj.* intriguing, gripping, compelling, enthralling, fascinating, absorbing, captivating, interesting, riveting, suspenseful; *ant.* boring, tiresome.

engulf *v.* immerse, envelop, inundate, consume, swamp, submerge, swallow up, deluge, flood, bury, overrun, overwhelm.

enhance *v.* **1.** (to make more desirable) improve, embellish, better, enrich. **2.** expand, augment, enlarge, lift, raise, magnify, intensify, elevate, augment, boost, escalate, heighten, amplify; *ant.* decrease, minimize.

enigma *n.* puzzle, riddle, mystery, poser, problem, conundrum.

enigmatic *adj.* mysterious, unfathomable, cryptic, impenetrable, inscrutable, obscure, unintelligible, perplexing, baffling, ambiguous, inexplicable, recondite; *ant.* simple, straightforward.

enjoin *v.* **1.** urge, order, demand, charge, command, instruct, require. **2.** forbid, prohibit, disallow, proscribe, bar, ban, interdict, restrain.

enjoy *v.* **1.** like, relish, savor, luxuriate in revel in, delight in, take pleasure in, appreciate; *ant.* abhor, detest. **2.** use, have, own, possess, hold, command.

enjoyable *adj.* entertaining, pleasant, delightful, amusing, fun, agreeable, pleasurable, satisfying, gratifying.

enjoyment *n.* fun, delight, joy, happiness, pleasure, satisfaction, relish, amusement, diversion, entertainment, gratification.

enlarge *v.* grow, heighten, expand, amplify, broaden, lengthen, extend, develop, increase, swell, widen; *ant.* decrease, diminish, shrink.

enlighten *v.* instruct, teach, educate, advise, illuminate, inform, indoctrinate, counsel, edify; *ant.* confuse, puzzle.

enlightened *adj.* educated, literate, cultivated,

aware, knowledgeable, wise, informed, sophisticated; liberal, open-minded; *ant.* confused, ignorant.

enlightenment *n.* education, awareness, understanding, literacy, knowledge, information, wisdom, erudition, learning, insight, civilization, refinement; *ant.* confusion, ignorance.

enlist *v.* recruit, muster, conscript, enroll, gather, employ, engage; join up, volunteer, sign up, register.

enliven *v.* stimulate, invigorate, exhilarate, animate, brighten, kindle, rouse, excite, inspire, inspirit, perk up, gladden, hearten; *ant.* subdue.

enmesh *v.* trap, entrap, catch, snare.

enmity *n.* hatred, hostility, animosity, acrimony, antagonism, rancor, bitterness, malice, malevolence, spite, ill will, bad blood; *ant.* amity, friendship.

ennoble *v.* honor, raise, glorify, elevate, exalt, aggrandize, dignify.

ennui *n.* boredom, tedium, listlessness, lassitude, apathy, languor, the doldrums.

enormity *n.* 1. size, bulk, magnitude, immensity, enormousness; *ant.* triviality, unimportance. 2. injustice, iniquity, crime, evil, atrocity, horror, wickedness, heinousness, outrage, abomination, monstrosity, depravity, nefariousness.

enormous *adj.* gigantic, immense, mammoth, huge, gargantuan, jumbo, vast, tremendous, titanic, leviathan, hulking, colossal, herculean; *ant.* small, tiny.

enough *adj.* sufficient, adequate, ample, plenty.

enough *adv.* fairly, sufficiently, adequately, satisfactorily, tolerably, passably, reasonably, amply.

enrage *v.* anger, infuriate, madden, exasperate, incense, inflame, incite, provoke, acerbate; *ant.* calm, placate, soothe.

enrapture *v.* delight, charm, beguile, captivate, bewitch, enchant, enthrall, entrance, fascinate, thrill.

enrich *v.* improve, supplement, augment, enhance, fortify; refine, cultivate; adorn, decorate, embellish; *ant.* impoverish.

enroll *v.* register, join, enter, sign up, enlist; *ant.* leave.

enrollment *n.* registration, enlistment, admission, acceptance, matriculation, recruitment.

en route on the way, in transit, flying, driving, traveling, midway, in passage, on the road heading toward.

ensconce *v.* settle, establish, install, entrench, lodge, place, nestle, shelter, protect.

ensemble *n.* 1. group, collection, gathering, assemblage, troupe, organization, company. 2. outfit, clothes, suit, garb, costume, coordinates, getup.

enshrine *v.* 1. consecrate, sanctify, embalm. 2. exalt, idolize, revere, cherish, hallow, treasure, apotheosize, dedicate.

enshroud *v.* veil, cover, hide, conceal, wrap, envelop, enclose, enfold, cloak, obscure, cloud, pall.

ensign *n.* 1. cadet, officer, subaltern. 2. title, insignia, badge, colors. 3. flag, banner, pennant, streamer.

enslave *v.* dominate, conquer, overcome, subjugate, subject, bind, yoke, enchain; *ant.* emancipate, free, liberate, release.

enslavement *n.* bondage, servitude, repression, oppression, subjection, subjugation, vassalage, serfdom; *ant.* emancipation, freedom, liberation, release.

ensnare *v.* 1. capture, catch, entrap, trap, entangle, enmesh, embroil. 2. deceive, mislead, cheat, trick, dupe.

ensure *v.* confirm, warrant, guarantee, protect, guard, safeguard, secure.

ensue *v.* 1. follow, succeed, happen, befall, turn out *or* up; *ant.* precede. 2. result, stem, eventuate, arise, derive.

entail *v.* involve, necessitate, require, cause, impose, demand, occasion, imply.

entangle *v.* 1. ensnare, entrap, catch. 2. involve, compromise, implicate, embroil.

entanglement *n.* 1. predicament, complication, difficulty, embarrassment. 2. involvement, affair, liaison. 3. mix-up, confusion, imbroglio, jumble, muddle, mess.

entente *n.* treaty, deal, understanding, pact, agreement, arrangement, compact.

enter *v.* 1. penetrate, invade, intrude, insert, pierce; *ant.* leave. 2. enroll, enlist, sign up, register, join, participate.

enterprise *n.* 1. initiative, drive, effort, energy, spirit, resourcefulness, enthusiasm, eagerness, get-up-and-go, gumption, boldness; *ant.*

apathy, inertia. 2. undertaking, venture, operation, project, concern, effort, establishment, company, firm, program, endeavor.

enterprising *adj.* ambitious, eager, resourceful, spirited, self-reliant, energetic, aspiring, up-and-coming; *ant.* lethargic.

entertain *v.* 1. amuse, cheer, please, interest, delight, divert, distract, engross, enthrall, captivate, stimulate; *ant.* bore. 2. host, receive, invite, treat. 3. (accept mentally) support, harbor, foster, consider, conceive, maintain, hold; *ant.* reject.

entertainer *n.* performer, player, artist, actor, actress, troubadour, trouper.

entertaining *adj.* amusing, diverting, delightful, pleasing, funny, fun, droll, humorous, pleasant, cheering, pleasurable, interesting; *ant.* boring.

entertainment *n.* amusement, enjoyment, merriment, fun, pleasure, delight, play, pastime, diversion, recreation, revelry, distraction.

enthrall *v.* charm, fascinate, intrigue, mesmerize, spellbind, rivet, captivate, entrance, enchant, beguile, enrapture, thrill, grip; *ant.* bore, weary.

enthused *adj.* enthusiastic, excited, approving, eager, impassioned, ecstatic, effervescent.

enthusiasm *n.* 1. excitement, fervor, zeal, zest, spirit, passion, devotion, avidity, vehemence, relish; *ant.* apathy. 2. craze, rage, fad.

enthusiast *n.* fan, fanatic, supporter, devotee, follower, zealot, lover, admirer, aficionado, fiend, buff, freak (*slang*); *ant.* detractor.

enthusiastic *adj.* keen, passionate, excited, fervent, fervid, devoted, eager, exuberant, hearty, wholehearted, gung-ho; *ant.* apathetic, reluctant, lukewarm.

entice *v.* tempt, lure, allure, draw, lead on, seduce, coax, persuade, wheedle, cajole, inveigle, sweet-talk.

entire *adj.* whole, total, complete, full, intact, absolute, unabridged, unified, unmitigated, uncut; *ant.* incomplete, partial, divided.

entirely *adv.* fully, wholly, thoroughly, totally, in toto, completely; absolutely, without reservation, utterly; *ant.* partially.

entirety *n.* 1. totality, unity, completeness, wholeness, fullness, absoluteness. 2. whole, total, aggregate, sum; *ant.* element, part.

entitle *v.* 1. allow, permit, authorize, enable,

empower, license, warrant, qualify, enfranchise. 2. name, call, designate, label, christen, dub, term, denominate.

entity *n.* 1. being, essence, presence, quintessence. 2. thing, creature, organism, body, individual, object.

entomb *v.* bury, intern, inter.

entourage *n.* retinue, companions, followers, court, escort, company, associates.

entrails *n.* bowels, guts, intestines, offal, viscera, insides, innards.

entrance *n.* 1. arrival, ingress, incoming, entry, start, induction, initiation, entrée, debut; *ant.* departure, exit. 2. access, admission, admittance. 3. doorway, gateway, entry, inlet, opening, passage, vestibule, archway, portal; *ant.* exit.

entrance *v.* spellbind, captivate, enchant, charm, enthrall, enrapture, fascinate, hypnotize, ravish, transport, mesmerize, bewitch; *ant.* bore, repel.

entrant *n.* 1. candidate, player, suitor, petitioner, solicitor, aspirant, entry. 2. opponent, competitor, rival, contender, contestant, participant.

entrap *v.* 1. capture, ensnare, catch, net. 2. involve, entangle, embroil, implicate. 3. beguile, lure, seduce, trick.

entrapment *n.* snare, ambush, ruse.

entreat *v.* beg, ask, beseech, plead with, implore, enjoin, importune, supplicate, appeal to, petition, invoke, pray.

entreaty *n.* plea, appeal, request, petition, solicitation, invocation, prayer, supplication, importunity, suit.

entrée *n.* 1. main dish, main course, meal. 2. admittance, entrance, introduction, admission, initiation, entry, induction.

entrench *v.* surround, fortify, fence, protect, lodge, fix, ensconce; *ant.* dislodge.

entrenched *adj.* well-established, deep-rooted, deep-seated, firm, set, fixed, ineradicable, unshakable, ingrained, implanted, inbred.

entrepreneur *n.* businessperson, businesswoman, financier, impresario, industrialist, tycoon, magnate, contractor.

entrust *v.* authorize, consign, assign, turn over, delegate, commend, commit, confide, invest, depute.

entry *n.* **1.** entrance, doorway, threshold, opening, passageway, gateway, portal, inlet, ingress; *ant.* exit. **2.** admission, introduction, initiation, access, entrance, admittance, entree, passage.

entwine *v.* braid, plait, interweave, thatch, interlace, wind, knit, twist, interlink; *ant.* unravel.

enumerate *v.* **1.** number, count, tally, calculate. **2.** name, itemize, list, specify, detail, cite.

enunciate *v.* **1.** speak, say, state, voice, utter, declare, proclaim, broadcast, propound. **2.** pronounce, articulate, sound.

envelop *v.* **1.** wrap up *or* around, surround, engulf, enclose, encircle, encase, embrace. **2.** obscure, hide, conceal, cover, veil, cloak, shroud.

envelope *n.* pouch, pocket, wrapper, wrapping, case, casing, coating, sheath, jacket, shell, covering.

enviable *adj.* **1.** desirable, covetable, favored. **2.** privileged, fortunate, blessed, lucky, advantageous.

envious *adj.* jealous, covetous, green-eyed, green, resentful, grudging, malicious, spiteful.

environment *n.* surroundings, milieu, ambiance, atmosphere, territory, domain, medium, locale, habitat, conditions, background, setting, situation, context.

environs *n.* surroundings, neighborhood, district, locality, vicinity, precincts.

envisage *v.* imagine, picture, envision, visualize, see, realize, conceive of, foresee, conceptualize, preconceive.

envoy *n.* agent, messenger, emissary, intermediary, representative, delegate, legate, deputy, ambassador, minister, nuncio, plenipotentiary, courier.

envy *n.* jealousy, covetousness, resentment, resentfulness, spite, malice, ill will.

envy *v.* covet, begrudge, grudge, crave, resent.

enwrap *v.* envelop, enclose, encase, sheathe, enshroud, swathe, enfold, wind.

ephemeral *adj.* passing, momentary, transient, fleeting, brief, temporary, short-lived, fugitive, impermanent; *ant.* enduring, lasting, perpetual.

epic *n.* legend, saga, narrative, heroic poem *or* story.

epic *adj.* vast, great, colossal, grand, majestic, imposing, exalted, lofty, sublime, grandiloquent; heroic, Homeric; *ant.* ordinary.

epicure *n.* **1.** gourmet, connoisseur, gourmand, gastronome. **2.** sensualist, hedonist, voluptuary, glutton, bon vivant.

epicurean *adj.* self-indulgent, libertine, sensual, voluptuous, luscious, lush, luxurious, hedonistic, gluttonous, gormandizing.

epidemic *n.* plague, rash, spread, wave, outbreak, upsurge, growth.

epigram *n.* witticism, quip, bon mot, aphorism, gnome.

epigrammatic *adj.* witty, sharp, laconic, piquant, aphoristic, pithy; short, concise, pointed, succinct, terse.

epilogue *n.* afterword, postscript, coda, conclusion; *ant.* foreword, preface, prologue.

episode *n.* **1.** installment, section, scene, chapter, part, passage. **2.** occurrence, event, happening, incident, experience, circumstance.

episodic *adj.* intermittent, occasional, irregular, disconnected, disjointed, digressive.

epistle *n.* letter, message, note, line, communication, missive.

epithet *n.* name, nickname, title, tag, appellation, designation, description, denomination.

epitome *n.* **1.** essence, embodiment, exemplar, quintessence, personification, representation, archetype. **2.** summary, synopsis, abridgment, compendium.

epitomize *v.* **1.** exemplify, represent, personify, embody, symbolize, typify, illustrate. **2.** encapsulate, summarize, condense, abridge, shorten, contract, compress; *ant.* elaborate, expand.

epoch *n.* era, time, period, age, date.

equable *adj.* **1.** steady, uniform, constant, regular; *ant.* variable. **2.** tranquil, serene, easygoing, calm, levelheaded, imperturbable, composed, even-tempered, unflappable, laid-back (*slang*); *ant.* excitable.

equal *n.* equivalent, mate, match, peer, rival, counterpart, parallel, twin, brother, fellow.

equal *v.* equate, parallel, match, balance, square with, even, correspond to.

equal *adj.* **1.** identical, same, tantamount, matched, alike, even, commensurate, symmetrical, proportionate, corresponding; *ant.* differ-

equality ent. 2. fair, just, impartial, unbiased, egalitarian, evenhanded; *ant.* inequitable.

equality *n.* 1. fairness, justice, equitability, egalitarianism. 2. similarity, sameness, uniformity, likeness, par, evenness, balance.

equalize *v.* balance, level, even up, match, standardize, square.

equanimity *n.* composure, poise, placidity, calm, self-possession, tranquillity, serenity, sang-froid, levelheadedness, imperturbability; *ant.* alarm, anxiety.

equate *v.* 1. (to be equivalent) balance, square, match, parallel, agree, correspond. 2. (to judge equivalence or similarity) compare, liken, associate, pair, relate, offset.

equation *n.* comparison, balancing, correspondence, match, pairing, parallel, likeness, agreement.

equilibrium *n.* balance, stability, steadiness, poise, calm, cool (*slang*), collectedness, composure, serenity.

equip *v.* supply, provide, stock, furnish, outfit, arm, prepare, implement.

equipment *n.* supplies, furnishings, accessories, accoutrements, equipage, material, gear, things, stuff, implements, appurtenances.

equitable *adj.* objective, unbiased, fair, just, ethical, dispassionate, impartial, evenhanded, fair and square; *ant.* prejudiced.

equity *n.* justice, integrity, fairness, fair play, evenhandedness, objectivity, impartiality, disinterest, righteousness, uprightness, fair-mindedness.

equivalent *n.* match, peer, parallel, twin, counterpart, correspondent, correlative, homotype, homologue.

equivalent *adj.* same, alike, similar, equal, twin, corresponding, comparable, commensurate, interchangeable, synonymous, correspondent, homotypic; *ant.* dissimilar.

equivocal *adj.* 1. obscure, ambiguous, vague, oblique, misleading, evasive, ambivalent; *ant.* clear. 2. uncertain, undecided, indefinite, doubtful. 3. suspicious, questionable.

equivocate *v.* evade, dodge, parry, mislead, hedge, fudge, waffle, sidestep, fence, deceive, mislead.

era *n.* age, period, time, day, generation, epoch, date, eon, stage, century.

eradicate *v.* destroy, erase, eliminate, annihilate, obliterate, expunge, remove, abolish; root *or* weed out, uproot.

erase *v.* 1. obliterate, remove, efface, delete, cancel, eliminate, expunge, eradicate, blot out. 2. kill, murder, slay, rub out (*slang*).

erect *v.* 1. build, construct, raise, form, fabricate. 2. raise, elevate, lift *or* set *or* put up, pitch.

erect *adj.* 1. raised, elevated, perpendicular, vertical, upright. 2. stiff, straight, tense, rigid, hard, firm, engorged; *ant.* limp, relaxed.

erection *n.* building, structure, edifice, construction; raising, assembly, elevation.

erode *v.* corrode, eat *or* wear away, deteriorate, consume, disintegrate, abrade, wear down.

erotic *adj.* sexy, sensual, seductive, carnal, stimulating, suggestive, rousing, erogenous, amorous, libidinous, titillating, lustful, voluptuous.

err *v.* 1. mistake, slip up, misjudge, lapse, fail, blunder; sin, trespass, offend, transgress. 2. go astray, deviate, wander.

errand *n.* assignment, task, job, duty, charge.

errant *adj.* 1. roaming, itinerant, vagrant, roving, nomadic, wandering. 2. straying, aberrant, wayward; wrong, erring.

erratic *adj.* 1. wandering, nomadic, rambling, meandering, roving, directionless, wayward, desultory; *ant.* straight. 2. unusual, strange, abnormal, eccentric, aberrant, queer, irregular. 3. variable, inconsistent, changeable, fitful, capricious, unpredictable, inconstant, fluctuating, shifting; *ant.* consistent, reliable, stable.

erroneous *adj.* mistaken, wrong, incorrect, false, fallacious, invalid, inaccurate, faulty, inexact, specious, spurious; *ant.* correct, true.

error *n.* mistake, blunder, fault, lapse, misjudgment, inaccuracy, slip, slip-up, false step, gaffe, gaucherie, wrongdoing, misdeed, offense, transgression.

ersatz *adj.* artificial, synthetic, false, imitation, fake.

erstwhile *adj.* former, once, late, old, previous, past, bygone, ex-; onetime.

erudite *adj.* learned, scholarly, educated, knowledgeable, recondite, literate, academic, cultured, wise, well-read, lettered, highbrow; *ant.* ignorant.

erupt *v.* **1.** explode, burst, spew, spout, gush, discharge, vomit, belch. **2.** emerge, break through, break out.

eruption *n.* **1.** explosion, outburst, discharge, venting, ejection. **2.** outbreak, rash, inflammation.

escalate *v.* **1.** increase, enlarge, grow, extend, expand, magnify, amplify, accelerate; *ant.* diminish. **2.** rise, raise, ascend, climb, step up.

escapade *n.* **1.** trick, caper, prank, joke, lark, romp, antic, spree, stunt, exploit. **2.** impropriety, indiscretion, fling.

escape *n.* flight, breakout, getaway, jailbreak; evasion, circumvention, elusion.

escape *v.* flee, break out *or* loose *or* free, get *or* slip away, dodge, elude, bolt, skedaddle, vamoose (*slang*).

escapist *n.* daydreamer, dreamer, fantasizer, wishful thinker, Walter Mitty; *ant.* realist.

eschew *v.* renounce, repudiate, abjure; shun, spurn, disdain; avoid, abstain from, give up, forgo, forswear, swear off, refrain from; *ant.* embrace.

escort *n.* chaperon, guide, squire, protector, guard, companion, attendant, aide, convoy, guardian, protection.

escort *v.* chaperon, guide, guard, protect, shepherd, usher, squire, accompany.

esoteric *adj.* **1.** confidential, inside, private, secret, recondite, inner; *ant.* popular. **2.** mysterious, mystical, arcane, cryptic, inscrutable, hermetic.

especial *adj.* special, particular, individual, specific, singular, exclusive; striking, marked, outstanding, remarkable, preeminent.

espionage *n.* spying, surveillance, intelligence, counterintelligence, undercover operations, infiltration; reconnaissance, investigation.

espousal *n.* **1.** support, adoption, advocacy, defense, championing, aid, backing. **2.** marriage, wedding, nuptials, engagement, betrothal, matrimony.

espouse *v.* **1.** support, advocate, defend, adopt, patronize, embrace, back, champion. **2.** marry, wed, betroth.

espy *v.* see, spot, glimpse, detect, discern, notice, observe, distinguish, perceive, sight, discover.

essay *n.* **1.** composition, commentary, paper, dissertation, thesis, treatise, tract, article, critique, discourse, exposition. **2.** effort, attempt, endeavor, try, stab, shot, venture, undertaking, trial, experiment, go, whirl.

essay *v.* try, attempt, endeavor, undertake, tackle, go for, take on, have a go, take a crack, struggle, strive.

essence *n.* **1.** fundamentals, gist, substance, core, center, kernel, heart, pith, soul, spirit, lifeblood, principle, quintessence. **2.** perfume, fragrance, scent; distillation, extract, elixir, concentrate, tincture, spirits.

essential *adj.* **1.** necessary, vital, crucial, needed, required, requisite, indispensable. **2.** innate, inherent, basic, core, central, fundamental, cardinal.

establish *v.* **1.** organize, create, start, institute, found, form, inaugurate, constitute, enact. **2.** (be the first to uncover) determine, discover, ascertain, learn, find out, fix. **3.** (show conclusively) prove, verify, validate, substantiate, authenticate, certify, confirm, affirm, corroborate, attest to, show, demonstrate.

established *adj.* **1.** settled, secure, fixed, stable, steadfast. **2.** demonstrated, proven, attested, accepted, confirmed. **3.** traditional, orthodox, standard, conventional, experienced.

establishment *n.* **1.** company, organization, foundation, office, system, institution, concern, business, enterprise. **2.** inauguration, ordination, founding, introduction, formation, creation, inception.

estate *n.* **1.** domain, holdings, land, property, manor, grounds, plantation, territory, realty, dominion, lot. **2.** inheritance, bequest, fortune, endowment, legacy, heritage, effects, earthly possessions, wealth, assets, goods, chattels.

the fourth estate the press, the media, mass media, journalists, reporters.

esteem *n.* respect, regard, good opinion, honor, veneration, reverence, estimation, admiration, credit.

esteem *v.* **1.** appreciate, admire, honor, venerate, value, treasure, prize, cherish, hold, respect, revere. **2.** consider, account, rate, estimate, view, judge, reckon, count, calculate, deem.

esthetic *adj.* See aesthetic.

estimable *adj.* 1. calculable, appreciable, considerable, computable, appraisable. 2. worthy, good, deserving, admirable, respectable, honorable, commendable, noteworthy, venerable, praiseworthy, distinguished, laudable; *ant.* despicable.

estimate *n.* 1. evaluation, judgment, assessment, appraisal, valuation, appraisement, calculation, gauging, survey, rating, reckoning, approximation. 2. impression, conceit, belief, conception, calculation, opinion, surmise, conjecture, guess, guestimate.

estimate *v.* 1. guess, rate, value, evaluate, count, number, reckon, judge, figure, assess, outline, appraise. 2. surmise, determine, decide, consider, reckon, suspect, suppose, reason, compute, regard, judge.

strange *v.* 1. divide, part, separate, sever, sunder, drive apart; *ant.* unite, bind. 2. alienate, antagonize, withdraw, put a barrier between, drive a wedge between; *ant.* reconcile.

estrangement *n.* 1. separation, split, breakup, division, parting. 2. dissociation, disaffection, hostility, antipathy, alienation, antagonism, breach.

estuary *n.* inlet, mouth, creek, fjord, firth.

et cetera etc., and so on, and so forth, and the rest, et al., and the like.

etch *v.* imprint, ingrain, groove, carve, cut, inscribe, dig, impress, stamp, engrave.

etching *n.* carving, cut, sketch, print, imprint, engraving, impression.

eternal *adj.* everlasting, perpetual, limitless, unending, undying, never-ending, interminable, constant, ceaseless, timeless, perennial, enduring; *ant.* changeable, ephemeral, temporary.

eternity *n.* endlessness, ages, eons, infinity, perpetuity, timelessness, world without end, all eternity.

ethereal *adj.* 1. delicate, subtle, airy, fragile, tenuous, fine, gossamer, light, insubstantial, dainty, diaphanous, exquisite; *ant.* solid. 2. celestial, divine, heavenly, spiritual, supernal, empyreal; *ant.* earthly, worldly.

ethical *adj.* fair, just, righteous, seemly, honest, good, virtuous, upright, commendable, conscientious, noble, principled.

ethics *n.* values, morality, conscience, moral values, principles, code, standards, rules, propriety, seemliness.

ethnic *adj.* racial, cultural, national, tribal, ancestral, aboriginal, folk, native, indigenous.

ethos *n.* morality, principles, manners, code, character, standards, ethic, beliefs, mores, attitudes, tenor, spirit.

etiquette *n.* manners, protocol, courtesy, civility, rules, code, conventionalities, politeness, decorum, propriety, formalities, ceremony.

etymology *n.* word history *or* derivation *or* origin, lexicology, philology, linguistics.

eulogize *v.* glorify, honor, praise, acclaim, adulate, extol, commend, celebrate, compliment, exalt, flatter, applaud; *ant.* condemn.

eulogy *n.* tribute, paean, praise, accolade, compliment, applause, acclaim, commendation, exaltation, glorification, laud; *ant.* condemnation.

euphemism *n.* polite term, fig leaf, evasion, genteelism; *ant.* dysphemism.

euphonious *adj.* melodious, sweet, musical, tuneful, harmonious, soft, silvery, sugared, mellifluous, sweet-sounding, consonant; *ant.* cacophonous.

euphony *n.* mellifluousness, consonance, harmoniousness, mellowness, melodiousness, harmony, musicality; *ant.* cacophony.

euphoria *n.* ecstasy, elation, rapture, joy, high spirits, jubilation, intoxication, bliss, transport, joyousness, exaltation, buoyancy, cloud nine; *ant.* depression.

euphoric *adj.* happy, joyous, jubilant, cheerful, ecstatic, enthusiastic, high, intoxicated, elated, enraptured, exhilarated, exultant; *ant.* depressed.

evacuate *v.* 1. leave, vacate, withdraw, depart, clear out, decamp, quit; abandon, forsake, desert. 2. empty, void, expel, purge, eject, eliminate, excrete, discharge, defecate.

evade *v.* 1. avoid, avert, put off, parry, hedge, dodge, beg, beat around the bush, sidestep, give the runaround, prevaricate, lie, dissemble. 2. escape, elude, slip out, sneak away from; *ant.* face.

evaluate *v.* assess, value, weigh, estimate, appraise, gauge, size up, judge.

evanescent *adj.* transitory, vanishing, fading, fleeting, brief, fugacious, ephemeral, disappearing, short-lived; *ant.* permanent.

evangelical *adj.* zealous, proselytizing, propagandistic, crusading, missionary, campaigning.

evangelize *v.* proselytize, preach, convert, crusade, campaign, propagandize.

evaporate *v.* **1.** dry, dehydrate, condense, distil, concentrate. **2.** disappear, evanesce, fade, melt away, vanish. **3.** dissipate, vaporize, dispel, disperse, dissolve.

evaporation *n.* **1.** drying, dehydration, condensation, distillation. **2.** disappearance, evanescence, fading, melting, vanishing, dematerialization. **3.** dissipation, vaporization, dispersal, dissolution.

evade *v.* elude, dodge, avoid, circumvent, escape, steer clear of, sidestep, duck.

evasion *n.* subterfuge, avoidance, dodge, escape, circumvention, euphemism, sophism, cop-out (*slang*).

evasive *adj.* elusive, devious, misleading, slippery, cagey, disingenuous, sophistical, secretive, ambiguous, indirect, dissembling; *ant.* direct, frank.

eve *n.* verge, threshold, brink, edge.

even *v.* stabilize, steady, balance, equalize, regulate, level, align.

even *adj.* **1.** flat, smooth, level. **2.** uniform, similar, alike, regular, equal, homogeneous, equivalent, commensurate.

even *adv.* still, yet; moreover.

evenhanded *adj.* fair, just, impartial, equitable, disinterested.

evening *n.* twilight, dusk, sunset, sundown, nightfall.

event *n.* occurrence, experience, happening, incident, circumstance, situation, occasion, development, episode, case.

even-tempered *adj.* levelheaded, composed, imperturbable, coolheaded, stable, impassive; *ant.* excitable.

eventful *adj.* momentous, important, consequential, noteworthy, significant, memorable, epochal, fateful, exciting, historic; *ant.* dull.

eventual *adj.* final, inevitable, last, consequent, ultimate.

eventuality *n.* outcome, possibility, probability, likelihood, contingency, chance.

ever *adv.* **1.** always, at all times, eternally, perpetually, constantly, continually, endlessly, unceasingly, unendingly, everlastingly, cease-

lessly, evermore, forever. **2.** at any time, in any circumstances. **3.** (used with a negative statement) at all, in any way, in any case, on any account.

everlasting *adj.* **1.** eternal, infinite, endless, timeless, never-ending, immortal, perpetual, constant, unchanging, undying. **2.** durable, enduring, indestructible, lasting.

evermore *adv.* always, to the end of time, eternally, forever, for ever and a day, henceforth, hereafter, in perpetuum.

every *adj.* each one, all, without exception.

every now and then sometimes, occasionally, once in a while, from time to time, every so often.

everybody *pron.* everyone, the whole world, tout le monde, one and all, each one, all and sundry.

everyday *adj.* **1.** ordinary, commonplace, routine, daily, usual, habitual, run-of-the-mill, workaday, quotidian. **2.** mundane, dull, banal, monotonous; *ant.* special, exceptional.

everyone *pron.* everybody, one and all, each one, the whole world, all and sundry.

everything *pron.* all, the entirety, the total, the whole lot, the aggregate, the whole kit and caboodle, lock, stock and barrel.

everywhere *adv.* all over, far and wide, all around, far and near, omnipresent, ubiquitous.

evict *v.* eject, expel, remove, dispossess, expropriate, cast *or* put *or* kick out, oust, show the door, *slang:* give the bum's rush, give the boot.

eviction *n.* ejection, expulsion, removal, dispossession, expropriation, dislodgment, the bum's rush (*slang*).

evidence *n.* proof, confirmation, documentation, substantiation, smoking gun, testimony, witness, deposition, indication, grounds.

evident *adj.* clear, apparent, obvious, plain, manifest, patent, undeniable, distinct, incontrovertible, ostensible, indisputable; *ant.* uncertain.

evil *n.* **1.** wickedness, sin, immorality, heinousness, viciousness, depravity, crime, corruption, licentiousness. **2.** harm, ill, misfortune, mischief, disaster, plague, catastrophe, outrage.

evil *adj.* **1.** wicked, immoral, sinful, corrupt, cruel, vile, nefarious, vicious, depraved. **2.** un-

evince propitious, unlucky, unfortunate, catastrophic, dire, calamitous, disastrous.

evince *v.* manifest, display, exhibit, reveal, show, demonstrate, indicate, attest, bespeak, declare; *ant.* conceal.

eviscerate *v.* disembowel, gut, exenterate, draw, declare; *ant.* conceal.

evoke *v.* **1.** call *or* summon forth, call out, invoke. **2.** arouse, excite, provoke, elicit; *ant.* quell, suppress.

evolution *n.* progression, development, derivation, descent, growth, maturation, gyration, provoke, exasperate.

evolve *v.* progress, develop, descend, derive, mature, grow, expand, increase.

exacerbate *v.* **1.** worsen, aggravate, intensify, increase, heighten. **2.** bother, irritate, annoy, provoke, exasperate.

exact *v.* **1** extort, force, compel, wrest, extract. **2.** demand, insist upon, require.

exact *adj.* **1.** accurate, correct, precise, perfect; *ant.* rough, inexact, approximate. **2.** well-defined, clear, distinct, sharp, definite, specific, clear-cut; *ant.* vague, fuzzy. **3.** strict, scrupulous, demanding, rigorous; *ant.* lax, loose.

exacting *adj.* **1.** (said of a person) strict, demanding, tyrannical, rigid, severe, harsh, unsparing, tough. **2.** (said of an undertaking) painstaking, stringent, arduous, difficult, laborious, taxing, toilsome.

exactly *adv.* precisely, accurately, specifically, explicitly, correctly, expressly, unequivocally, literally, to the letter.

exactly *interj.* right, of course, certainly, absolutely, precisely, indeed, agreed, true.

exaggerate *v.* inflate, embellish, magnify, overstate, overdo, make a mountain out of a molehill, embroider, hyperbolize, stretch the truth; *ant.* understate, minimize.

exaggeration *n.* **1.** overestimation, elaboration, embellishment, hyperbole, overstatement, overkill. **2.** lie, falsehood, fabrication, untruth, falsification, misrepresentation, tall story, whopper.

exalt *v.* **1.** glorify, venerate, laud, worship, adore, praise, extol, honor, acclaim, idolize, put on a pedestal; *ant.* denigrate. **2.** elevate, aggrandize, raise up; *ant.* debase.

exaltation *n.* **1.** praise, adulation, glory, worship, deification, idolization, adoration. **2.** ec-

152

stasy, elation, happiness, joyfulness, rapture, enthusiasm.

exalted *adj.* **1.** noble, illustrious, magnificent, august, glorified, eminent. **2.** rapturous, elated, happy, rhapsodic, joyful, blissful, ecstatic, exhilarated.

examination *n.* **1.** investigation, research, exploration, inquiry, analysis, study; inquisition, questioning. **2.** test, quiz, review, questionnaire.

examine *v.* **1.** inspect, analyze, appraise, review, scrutinize, vet, investigate, go into, inquire into, delve into, study, survey, probe, go over with a fine-toothed comb. **2.** test, question, catechize, interrogate, grill, quiz.

examiner *n.* inspector, reviewer, analyst, tester, assessor, scrutinizer, censor, critic, judge, interviewer, questioner, auditor.

example *n.* standard, model, type, sample, archetype, case, precedent, paradigm, exemplar, paragon, parallel, stereotype. **for example** for instance, e.g., such as, as a model, to illustrate, like.

exasperate *v.* irk, provoke, bother, aggravate, irritate, annoy, rankle, vex, goad, bug (*slang*), get on one's nerves.

excavate *v.* dig, burrow, mine, unearth, exhume, tunnel, hollow, quarry.

excavation *n.* mine, shaft, tunnel, burrow, hollow, trough, ditch, pit, quarry, trench.

exceed *v.* outdo, better, surpass, overtake, outshine, top, beat, transcend, eclipse, excel, outrival.

exceedingly *adv.* exceptionally, extraordinarily, astonishingly, superlatively, amazingly, excessively, extremely, greatly, inordinately, hugely, vastly.

excel *v.* surpass, outshine, overshadow, beat, outdo, transcend, top, better, eclipse, outrival, exceed, stand out.

excellence *n.* distinction, perfection, superiority, greatness, eminence, supremacy, worth, merit, virtue, quality.

excellent *adj.* great, superb, superior, terrific, wonderful, exemplary, nonpareil, splendid, superlative, choice; *ant.* inferior.

except *v.* ban, exclude, bar, omit, leave *or* rule out, reject, eliminate, disallow.

except *prep.* barring, not counting, excluding,

other than, besides, apart from, except for, but, omitting, save.

exception *n.* irregularity, anomaly, abnormality, deviation, peculiarity, rarity, oddity, quirk, special case, exemption, deviation.

take exception 1. disagree, object, differ. 2. be offended, resent, take umbrage.

exceptional *adj.* 1. excellent, marvelous, superlative, superior, prodigious, remarkable, outstanding, phenomenal, extraordinary; *ant.* mediocre. 2. unusual, rare, strange, unexpected, uncommon, extraordinary, atypical, odd, singular, irregular, anomalous, aberrant; *ant.* conventional.

excerpt *n.* passage, section, quotation, fragment, part, selection.

excerpt *v.* quote, cite, borrow.

excess *n.* 1. abundance, plethora, surplus, superfluity, surfeit, profusion, inundation, lavishness; *ant.* deficiency, lack. 2. intemperance, indulgence, prodigality, dissipation. 3. remainder, rest, surplus, balance, residue, waste, leftovers, leavings.

excess *adj.* extra, superfluous, surplus, additional, spare, residual, remaining, leftover.

excessive *adj.* inordinate, immoderate, extreme, exorbitant, disproportionate, overmuch, intemperate, superfluous.

exchange *n.* 1. substitution, replacement, reciprocity, switch. 2. barter, trade, bargain, swap, dealing, market, commerce, traffic.

exchange *v.* bargain, trade, barter, swap, substitute, reciprocate, switch.

excise *v.* cut, extract, remove, expunge, eradicate, delete, rescind.

excitable *adj.* emotional, high-strung, mercurial, temperamental, sensitive, passionate, edgy, unstable, volatile, feisty.

excite *v.* stimulate, rouse, inspire, titillate, affect, incite, galvanize, provoke, kindle, induce, motivate; *ant.* quell, bore.

excited *adj.* 1. enthusiastic, eager, elated, thrilled, enthused. 2. agitated, aroused, impassioned, frenzied, worked up, discomposed, nervous, frantic, wrought-up, overwrought.

excitement *n.* 1. stimulation, excitation, delirium; *ant.* apathy. 2. activity, commotion, tumult, clamor, furor, agitation, ado, discomposure; *ant.* calm.

exciting *adj.* exhilarating, stimulating, thrilling, electrifying, intoxicating, moving, stirring, suspenseful; *ant.* boring.

exclaim *v.* call, shout, cry, blurt, interject, vociferate, declare.

exclude *v.* 1. bar, ban, prohibit, disallow, forbid, ostracize, blacklist, blackball. 2. expel, remove, eliminate, eject, evict, excommunicate.

exclusive *adj.* 1. restricted, selective, discriminating, esoteric, snobbish, elitist, cliquish. 2. choice, posh, classy, chic, fashionable, elite.

excommunicate *v.* banish, bar, execrate, exclude, remove, eject.

excoriate *v.* 1. denounce, condemn, criticize, attack, savage. 2. abrade, chafe, flay, remove, skin.

excrement *n.* fecal matter, feces, manure, stool, offal, dung, droppings, evacuation, secretion, discharge.

excrete *v.* secrete, exude, eliminate, discharge, void, evacuate, defecate, urinate.

excretion *n.* discharge, evacuation, defecation, urination, perspiration, dung, excrement, stool.

excruciating *adj.* agonizing, intense, painful, unbearable, intolerable, extreme, severe, acute, sharp, insufferable, searing, torturous.

exculpate *v.* absolve, exonerate, vindicate, acquit, clear, free, pardon, forgive, let off, excuse; *ant.* indict, convict.

excursion *n.* outing, trip, expedition, journey, tour, walk, ride, jaunt, ramble.

excursive *adj.* rambling, desultory, digressive, discursive.

excusable *adj.* understandable, warrantable, allowable, permissible, defensible, explicable, forgivable, justifiable.

excuse *n.* 1. explanation, apology, reason, defense, justification, vindication, alibi. 2. pretense, subterfuge, trick, evasion.

excuse *v.* 1. absolve, acquit, pardon, vindicate, exonerate, exculpate; liberate, free, release, discharge, exempt. 2. explain, apologize for, justify, defend.

excuse me pardon me, forgive me, I'm sorry, beg your pardon.

execrable *adj.* 1. offensive, abhorrent, revolting, disgusting, vile, detestable, heinous, abominable. 2. inferior, poor, defective, bad.

execrate *v.* 1. curse, damn, condemn, denounce, revile, vilify; 2. detest, abhor, loathe, hate, despise, deplore.

execute *v.* 1. perform, act, do, effect, accomplish, achieve, fulfill, realize, finish, complete. 2. kill, put to death, dispatch.

execution *n.* 1. performance, achievement, accomplishment, completion, consummation. 2. death penalty, capital punishment.

executioner *n.* exterminator, hangman, assassin, killer, murderer, slayer, hit man.

executive *n.* directors, directorate, administration, management, government, hierarchy, leadership, brass; official, CEO, president, higher-up.

executive *adj.* directorial, managerial, administrative, governing, supervisory, regulating, guiding, organizational, gubernatorial.

exemplar *n.* example, model, pattern, prototype, standard, criterion, archetype, paradigm, epitome, ideal.

exemplify *v.* illustrate, represent, show, typify, demonstrate, depict, epitomize.

exempt *v.* excuse, exonerate, free, clear, absolve, dismiss, release, spare, let off, make an exception for.

exempt *adj.* excepted, excluded, excused, absolved, clear, free, spared, released, liberated, favored, immune.

exemption *n.* exoneration, absolution, immunity, dispensation, freedom, release, discharge.

exert *v.* expend, apply, use, utilize, employ, exercise, wield.

exercise *n.* 1. practice, drill, training, workout. 2. test, examination, lesson, theme, study, activity, task. 3. use, application, employment, implementation, utilization.

exercise *v.* 1. train, drill, work out. 2. use, employ, utilize, apply, execute, put in practice.

exertion *n.* endeavor, attempt, travail, struggle, effort, perseverance, assiduity, toil, labor, work, application, utilization.

exhale *v.* breathe out, expel, emanate, emit, respire.

exhaust *n.* emission, emanation, fumes, discharge, exhalation.

exhaust *v.* 1. wear out, deplete, expend, consume, use up, finish, spend, drain, dry, empty, bankrupt; *ant.* supply. 2. fatigue, weaken, tax, tire out, overwork, weary; *ant.* refresh.

exhaustible *adj.* limited, inadequate, insufficient, expendable.

exhaustion *n.* 1. fatigue, weariness, tiredness, prostration, lassitude, debilitation; *ant.* freshness. 2. depletion, emptying, consumption.

exhaustive *adj.* comprehensive, complete, all-inclusive, thorough, definitive, extensive, in-depth, full-scale, sweeping.

exhibit *v.* display, show, present, demonstrate, showcase, parade, flaunt.

exhibit *n.* display, model, illustration, demonstration, show.

exhibition *n.* 1. display, presentation, showing, advertisement. 2. show, performance, exposition, fair, carnival.

exhibitionist *n.* showoff, self-advertiser, extrovert; pervert, flasher.

exhilarating *adj.* stimulating, invigorating, cheering, gladdening, exciting, thrilling, vitalizing; *ant.* boring.

exhilaration *n.* excitement, gladness, gaiety, joy, delight, elation, high spirits, vivacity, zeal.

exhort *v.* 1. urge, persuade, beseech, entreat, implore, press, encourage. 2. warn, caution, admonish, advise, counsel.

exigency *n.* 1. urgency, emergency, crisis, plight, quandary, difficulty, predicament, bind, jam, scrape, fix. 2. requirement, need, demand, necessity, essentiality.

exigent *adj.* 1. urgent, pressing, critical, crucial, imperative. 2. demanding, exacting, strict, rigorous, stringent, difficult, tough.

exile *n.* 1. banishment, expulsion, deportation, ostracism, displacement, expatriation, separation. 2. outcast, expatriate, deportee, refugee, fugitive, outlaw.

exile *v.* deport, ostracize, expel, expatriate, oust, banish.

exist *v.* 1. (be present) be, breathe, happen, occur. 2. (to continue life) live, be extant, survive, subsist, endure, abide, last, prevail, stand.

existence *n.* 1. being, actuality, life, reality, presence, permanence, continuation, sustenance, duration, endurance, survival. 2. creation, life, the world, reality.

existent *adj.* real, actual, living, enduring, remaining, standing, surviving, extant, present, current.

exit *n.* **1.** egress, opening, way *or* passage out, outlet, door. **2.** departure, going, leaving, egress, exodus, evacuation.

exit *v.* leave, depart, retreat, withdraw, retire.

exodus *n.* departure, leaving, evacuation, emigration, retreat, withdrawal, flight; *ant.* influx.

exonerate *v.* acquit, vindicate, clear, absolve, exculpate, dismiss, excuse, pardon, grant amnesty, release, free, liberate; *ant.* incriminate.

exorbitant *adj.* excessive, extreme, inordinate, undue, unwarranted, immoderate, extravagant, outrageous, preposterous; *ant.* reasonable.

exotic *adj.* **1.** bizarre, peculiar, unusual, strange, curious, different, outlandish, mysterious. **2.** foreign, alien, imported, extrinsic.

expand *v.* grow, increase, multiply, enlarge, amplify, widen, heighten, lengthen, magnify, inflate, elaborate, embellish.

expanse *n.* breadth, extent, vastness, area, space, stretch, range.

expansive *adj.* **1.** broad, extensive, comprehensive, far-reaching, thorough, inclusive, widespread. **2.** generous, open, sympathetic, demonstrative, friendly, garrulous, sociable, unreserved, affable, effusive, loquacious.

expatiate *v.* elaborate, embellish, expound, enlarge, amplify, descant.

expatriate *n.* exile, refugee, emigrant, displaced person.

expect *v.* **1.** anticipate, await, wait for, hope for, look for, look forward to, envisage. **2.** require, insist upon, demand. **3.** assume, presume, suppose, think, trust, count on, bank on.

expectant *adj.* eager, ready, anticipating, waiting, in suspense, watchful, apprehensive, anxious.

expectation *n.* anticipation, hope, eagerness; supposition, presumption, conjecture, possibility, likelihood.

expected *adj.* **1.** conventional, familiar, normal, habitual, predictable. **2.** anticipated, looked for, longed for, hoped for, planned for, prepared for, counted on.

expecting *adj.* pregnant, with child, in the family way.

expedient *adj.* **1.** appropriate, fitting, judicious, prudent, pragmatic, suitable, advantageous, beneficial, helpful, practical, useful, convenient. **2.** self-serving, self-seeking, politic.

expedite *v.* facilitate, advance, hasten, speed, rush, quicken, accelerate, hurry, aid, assist; *ant.* delay.

expedition *n.* **1.** excursion, journey, voyage, trip, exploration, quest, mission. **2.** alacrity, haste, speed, readiness, promptness, dispatch.

expeditious *adj.* speedy, prompt, fast, swift, rapid, ready, immediate, efficient, diligent; *ant.* slow.

expel *v.* ban, exclude, dismiss, banish, exile, evict, drive out, drum out, cast out, throw out, oust, send packing.

expend *v.* **1.** spend, pay, shell out, dish out, fork out; *ant.* save. **2.** exhaust, use up, consume.

expendable *adj.* nonessential, dispensable, unimportant, unnecessary, replaceable.

expenditure *n.* expense, outlay, charge, cost, payment.

expense *n.* fee, charge, cost, outlay, payment.

expenses *n.* costs, overhead, outlay, incidentals.

expensive *adj.* high-priced, overpriced, costly, extravagant, lavish, exorbitant, inordinate, dear, steep, stiff.

experience *n.* **1.** knowledge, wisdom, judgment, maturity, seasoning, sense. **2.** occurrences, happenings, episodes, encounters, adventures.

experience *v.* undergo, live through, endure, face, feel.

experienced *adj.* **1.** practiced, adept, skilled, accomplished, expert, qualified, professional, knowledgeable. **2.** seasoned, worldly, well-versed, sophisticated, traveled, mature, veteran.

experiment *n.* **1.** analysis, research, examination, investigation, scrutiny, inspection, test. **2.** trial, attempt, try, assay, undertaking, venture.

experiment *v.* try, test, attempt, assay, investigate.

experimental *adj.* empirical, heuristic, exploratory, speculative, tentative, preliminary.

expert *n.* professional, master, ace, virtuoso, authority, wizard.

expert *adj.* skilled, trained, professional, experienced, practiced, facile, adept, adroit, masterly, proficient.

expertise *n.* proficiency, skill, facility, mastery, knack, know-how, deftness, cleverness.

expiate *v.* atone, appease, compensate, reconcile, redeem.

expiation *n.* amends, atonement, penance, redress, shrift, redemption.

expiration *n.* 1. end, finish, close, closing. 2. dying, death, demise, passing.

expire *v.* 1. end, finish, stop, quit, terminate. 2. die, perish, breathe one's last, depart, pass on.

explain *v.* 1. explicate, elucidate, illustrate, demonstrate, clarify, define, interpret, translate. 2. account for, justify, excuse.

explanation *n.* 1. clarification, elucidation, explication, exposition, definition, description, demonstration, illustration, interpretation, exegesis, gloss. 2. answer, solution; justification, vindication, excuse, account, cause, motive, reason.

explanatory *adj.* illuminative, expository, elucidatory, descriptive, illustrative, demonstrative.

explicable *adj.* explainable, understandable, justifiable, warranted, accountable, intelligible, resolvable, solvable.

explicate *v.* clarify, elucidate, explain, expound.

explication *n.* clarification, explanation, elucidation, interpretation, exegesis.

explicit *adj.* 1. (said of language) clear, definite, unequivocal, distinct, exact, specific, precise, absolute, plain. 2. (said of a person or of one's manner) frank, outspoken, open, straightforward, direct, bluff.

explode *v.* burst, erupt, rupture, shatter, blow up, detonate, discharge.

exploit *v.* capitalize on, take advantage of, misuse, profit by, use, abuse, manipulate, cash in on.

exploit *n.* accomplishment, achievement, feat, deed, adventure, stunt.

exploration *n.* 1. research, inquiry, analysis, examination, investigation, scrutiny, study, probe. 2. expedition, travel, trip, tour, voyage, safari.

exploratory *adj.* investigative, analytical, probing, searching, fact-finding, experimental, tentative.

explore *v.* 1. investigate, research, analyze, examine, scrutinize, inspect, probe, search. 2. travel, tour, traverse.

explosion *n.* blast, detonation, bang, burst, discharge, eruption, paroxysm, report, crack.

explosive *adj.* hazardous, dangerous, perilous, volcanic; volatile, violent, unstable.

exponent *n.* 1. advocate, supporter, backer, proponent; expounder, interpreter. 2. representative, sample, example, type, model, index.

export *v.* ship, transport, send out, sell *or* trade abroad.

expose *v.* 1. uncover, divulge, disclose, reveal, unmask, bring to light, lay open, lay bare, air. 2. endanger, jeopardize, imperil, lay open to, subject to.

exposé *n.* disclosure, revelation, account, article.

exposition *n.* 1. display, presentation, exhibition, show, fair. 2. elucidation, explication, illustration, description, interpretation, exegesis, thesis, discourse, study.

expository *adj.* descriptive, illustrative, explanatory, explicative, interpretive.

expostulate *v.* object, argue, protest, dissuade, reason, plead.

expound *v.* elucidate, explain, explicate, describe, interpret, preach, sermonize, set forth.

express *v.* declare, tell, state, say, speak, voice, verbalize, put into words.

express *adj.* 1. nonstop, direct, fast, rapid, swift, quick, high-speed. 2. explicit, specific, exact, definite, clear, precise; *ant.* vague.

expression *n.* 1. countenance, cast, look, appearance, air, mien, aspect, character. 2. idiom, phrase, turn of phrase, locution, phraseology, wording, term. 3. representation, exposition, interpretation, elucidation, explanation, articulation.

expressionless *adj.* inscrutable, impassive, deadpan, straight-faced, poker-faced, phlegmatic, blank, vacuous, wooden, empty, glassy.

expressive *adj.* 1. demonstrative, effusive, emotional, showing. 2. meaningful, telling, moving, poignant, pregnant.

expressly *adv.* particularly, specifically, especially, explicitly, unequivocally, precisely, exactly, definitely, absolutely, categorically, distinctly, pointedly.

expropriate *v.* usurp, take, dispossess, seize, commandeer, appropriate, confiscate, requisition, impound, sequester.

expulsion *n.* banishment, disbarment, dismissal, exclusion, exile, eviction, dislodgment, removal, ejection.

expunge *v.* erase, delete, cancel, annul, eradicate, abolish, extinguish, obliterate, annihilate, exterminate, blot out, wipe out.

expurgate *v.* censor, clean up, purify, sanitize, bowdlerize, purge.

exquisite *adj.* perfect, impeccable, superlative, outstanding, excellent, choice, rare, delicate, beautiful, meticulous; *ant.* flawed, ugly.

extant *adj.* alive, living, existent, surviving, subsisting, remaining; *ant.* extinct.

extemporaneous *adj.* impromptu, spontaneous, unplanned; improvised, unprepared, unrehearsed, ad-lib.

extemporaneously *adv.* on impulse, spontaneously, ad lib, by ear, off the cuff (slang).

extend *v.* 1. increase, enlarge, augment, expand, stretch, protract, lengthen, prolong. 2. reach, go as far as, spread, continue.

extensive *adj.* 1. large, huge, great, vast, wide, broad, long, extended, expanded, capacious, widespread, boundless. 2. comprehensive, inclusive, thorough, sweeping, universal.

extent *n.* scope, range, reach, expanse, measure, magnitude, volume, sweep, limits, bounds.

extenuate *v.* lessen, minimize, reduce, temper, diminish, decrease.

extenuation *n.* 1. excuse, explanation, justification, vindication, apology. 2. reduction, abatement, diminution, mitigation, moderation.

exterior *n.* surface, façade, outside, appearance, externals, covering, finish; *ant.* interior.

exterior *adj.* outer, external, superficial, surface.

exterminate *v.* eliminate, abolish, destroy, annihilate, wipe out.

external *adj.* exterior, outer, surface, superficial, visible, apparent; *ant.* internal.

extinct *adj.* obsolete, gone, lost, dead, vanished, defunct, exterminated, extinguished, terminated.

extinguish *v.* 1. put out, smother, stifle, douse, quench, snuff out, drown out. 2. destroy, annihilate, wipe out, exterminate.

extirpate *v.* exterminate, abolish, annihilate, eliminate, eradicate, expunge, remove, root out, wipe out.

extol *v.* praise, laud, exalt, glorify, celebrate, applaud, commend; *ant.* denigrate.

extort *v.* blackmail, extract, coerce, force, wring, bully, twist someone's arm (*slang*), bleed, squeeze, milk.

extortionate *adj.* 1. oppressive, avaricious, rapacious, severe, exacting, rigorous, harsh. 2. excessive, wasteful, exorbitant, extravagant, unreasonable.

extra *n.* addition, supplement, bonus, accessory, adjunct.

extra *adj.* additional, supplemental, surplus, reserve, spare, leftover, extraneous, superfluous, inessential; *ant.* integral.

extract *n.* 1. essence, distillation, concentrate, infusion. 2. excerpt, selection, passage, citation, quotation, abstract.

extract *v.* 1. extort, extricate, eradicate, remove, wrest, wring, uproot. 2. elicit, derive, obtain, get, secure, draw. 3. cite, excerpt, quote, cull, glean.

extraction *n.* 1. ancestry, lineage, parentage, origin, descent, blood, race, family. 2. drawing, removal, uprooting, wrenching.

extradite *v.* 1. surrender, give up, abandon, release, turn over. 2. obtain, bring to justice *or* trial, apprehend, arrest.

extraneous *adj.* 1. irrelevant, inessential, superfluous, unnecessary, incidental, accidental, tangential, extra. 2. foreign, alien, strange, exotic, extrinsic, external.

extraordinary *adj.* 1. phenomenal, fantastic, amazing, strange, unimaginable, peculiar, odd, bizarre, curious, unusual. 2. wonderful, marvelous, exceptional, unique, rare.

extravagance *n.* exorbitance, lavishness, excess, outrageousness, preposterousness, immoderation, waste, squandering.

extravagant *adj.* 1. immoderate, inordinate, excessive, exorbitant, wasteful, costly, overpriced, expensive. 2. ostentatious, lavish, flamboyant, grandiose, gaudy, garish; *ant.* modest.

extravaganza *n.* spectacle, pageant, show, display.

extreme *n.* limit, ultimate, utmost, climax, extremity, top, edge, end.

go to extremes be excessive or immoderate, go too far, overdo things, go overboard.

extreme *adj.* **1.** ultimate, final, last, utmost, remote, outermost, farthest. **2.** intemperate, immoderate, imprudent, excessive, inordinate, unreasonable, radical.

extremism *n.* radicalism, zeal, fanaticism, terrorism; *ant.* moderation.

extremist *n.* radical, fanatic, zealot, militant, diehard, terrorist; *ant.* moderate.

extremist *adj.* radical, zealous, fanatical, diehard.

extremity *n.* end, limit, terminus, tip.

extricate *v.* free, release, disentangle, disengage, liberate, remove, withdraw, clear; *ant.* involve.

extrinsic *adj.* outside, external, exterior, foreign; inessential, superficial, extraneous; *ant.* intrinsic, inherent.

extrovert *n.* socializer, joiner, mixer, life of the party; *ant.* introvert.

exuberance *n.* enthusiasm, fervor, exhilaration, high spirits, liveliness, vitality, zest.

exuberant *adj.* enthusiastic, passionate, ex-

cited, exhilarated, high-spirited, vivacious, cheerful, ebullient, effervescent.

exude *v.* **1.** discharge, excrete, secrete, emanate, issue. **2.** emit, radiate, display, show, manifest.

exult *v.* **1.** celebrate, rejoice, revel, glory, delight, make merry. **2.** boast, crow, brag, gloat.

exultant *adj.* elated, jubilant, joyous, overjoyed, gleeful, delighted, triumphant, reveling, rejoicing; *ant.* depressed.

eye *n.* **1.** appreciation, taste, discrimination, discernment, perception, opinion, judgment. **2.** center, focus, core, heart.

all eyes observant, attentive, aware, perceptive.

keep an eye on look after, watch over, guard, protect.

make eyes at flirt, leer, ogle, tease, come on to.

open one's eyes inform, tell, apprise, make aware.

set eyes on notice, behold, observe, encounter.

shut one's eyes to ignore, refuse, reject, shun.

eyesight *n.* vision, perception, view, observation.

eyesore *n.* blight, blemish, disfigurement, monstrosity, atrocity, ugliness.

eyewitness *n.* observer, onlooker, spectator, viewer, watcher.

F

fable *n.* story, fairy tale, allegory, parable, yarn, myth, old wives' tale, fantasy, fiction.

fabled *adj.* renowned, mythical, legendary, famous; *ant.* unknown.

fabric *n.* 1. material, textile, cloth. 2. structure, framework, substance, makeup, constitution; foundations, organization, infrastructure, construction.

fabricate *v.* 1. misrepresent, make up, feign, falsify, fake, invent. 2. construct, make, form, forge, create, build, manufacture, fashion, concoct, devise, shape.

fabrication *n.* 1. falsehood, lie, cock-and-bull story, forgery, invention. 2. fairy tale, myth, fable, fiction; *ant.* truth.

fabulous *adj.* 1. fantastic, phenomenal, unbelievable, legendary, amazing, breathtaking, superb, wonderful, marvelous, spectacular, astounding. 2. imaginary, fictitious, unbelievable, invented, apocryphal, mythical, fabled; *ant.* real.

façade *n.* 1. front, exterior, face. 2. guise, mask, veneer, disguise, cloak, pretense, semblance, show.

face *n.* 1. countenance, visage, expression, *slang:* mug, puss; feature, image, look, physiognomy, appearance, front. 2. surface, front, finish, façade, outside, exterior. 3. reputation, status, standing, honor, dignity.

face to face eye to eye, vis-à-vis, confronting, tête-à-tête, à deux.

fly in the face of defy, rebel against, disobey, dare.

wear a long face scowl, pout, frown.

show one's face be seen, show up, come, appear.

to one's face candidly, openly, frankly, brazenly, boldly; *ant.* behind one's back.

face *v.* 1. (meet face-to-face) confront, defy, dare, challenge. 2. (expose oneself to danger or hardship) risk, brave, hazard; withstand, endure, sustain. 3. refinish, coat, front, redecorate, polish. 4. trim, bind, hem, back, pipe, tuck, overlay, bias.

face up to 1. deal with, accept, cope with, acknowledge, recognize, come to terms with. 2. confront, meet head-on, stand up to.

facet *n.* 1. angle, side, aspect, plane. 2. characteristic, feature, side, face, aspect.

facetious *adj.* jesting, droll, tongue-in-cheek, witty, funny, humorous, comical, jocular, amusing; *ant.* serious, solemn.

facile *adj.* 1. easy, simple, effortless; *ant.* complicated, hard. 2. skilled, adept, adroit, proficient, practiced, able, dexterous, fluent; *ant.* clumsy, awkward. 3. superficial, glib, simplistic; *ant.* profound.

facilitate *v.* promote, help, ease, assist, expedite, further, forward.

facility *n.* office, agency, department, bureau, company.

facing *n.* surface, veneer, skin, façade, overlay, coating, trimming.

facsimile *n.* 1. replica, reproduction, print; *ant.* original. 2. duplicate, carbon copy, copy, Xerox (Tm), photocopy, Photostat (Tm), mimeograph; *ant.* original.

fact *n.* 1. certainty, reality, truth, actuality, palpability. 2. item, detail, datum, particular, specific.

as a matter of fact actually, really, truthfully, in point of fact.

faction *n.* 1. cabal, conclave, party, lobby, inner circle, sect, side; conspiracy, intrigue. 2. dissension, discord, conflict, disunity, division, strife, friction, disharmony, divisiveness; *ant.* agreement, peace.

factious *adj.* rebellious, refractory, troublemaking, dissident, seditious, insurrectionary, malcontent, mutinous, partisan; *ant.* cooperative.

159

factitious *adj.* imitation, artificial, simulated, false, fake, contrived, fabricated, synthetic, forced, unnatural; *ant.* genuine.

factor *n.* **1.** part, element, point, aspect, constituent, parameter. **2.** representative, manager, agent, deputy, administrator.

factory *n.* works, mill, plant, industry, shop, machine shop, forge, foundry, sweatshop.

factotum *n.* handyman, jack-of-all-trades, man or girl Friday, gofer (*slang*).

facts *n.* **1.** information, data, details, *slang*: info, the lowdown. **2.** reality, certainty, actuality, the score (*slang*).

factual *adj.* true, sure, correct, real, authentic, genuine, accurate, faithful, credible, veritable, exact, precise; *ant.* false, fictitious.

faculties *n.* senses, wits, reason, intelligence, powers, capabilities, functions.

faculty *n.* **1.** staff, personnel, teachers, instructors, academics, literati; university, college, institute, organization. **2.** ability, propensity, capacity, aptitude, dexterity, talent, forte, knack, gift, strength, skill.

fad *n.* trend, craze, rage, mania, vogue, style, whim, fashion.

fade *v.* **1.** bleach, tone down, wash out, blanch, etiolate, neutralize; tarnish, discolor. **2.** decrease, diminish, dwindle, ebb, shrivel, wane.

faded *adj.* pale, dull, washed-out, bleached, etiolated, discolored, dim, indistinct; *ant.* bright, intense.

fail *v.* **1.** miscarry, fall short, miss, lose, neglect, slip, abort, fall flat, go up in smoke; *ant.* succeed, win, triumph. **2.** decay, lessen, worsen, sink, decline, dwindle, fade, founder, weaken, wane, droop, peter out; *ant.* gain, improve. **3.** default, go bankrupt, fold, go out of business, go under, *slang*: go belly up, go down the tubes, lose one's shirt, bite the dust; *ant.* prosper.
without fail constantly, dependably, reliably, regularly.

failing *n.* shortcoming, foible, weakness, deficiency, frailty, fault; *ant.* advantage, strength.

fail-safe *adj.* foolproof, safeguarding, protective.

failure *n.* loss, ruin, downfall, collapse, defeat, folding, breakdown, abortion, fiasco; *ant.* success.

160

faint *v.* lose consciousness, swoon, collapse, pass out, black out.

faint *adj.* **1.** (said of a feeling) weak, faltering, enervated, dizzy, lethargic, languid, woozy; *ant.* strong. **2.** (said of a sound, image, etc.) muffled, muted; dull, thin; indistinct, hazy, vague, ill-defined; *ant.* clear.

fair *n.* carnival, fête, bazaar, exposition, show, festival, exhibition, gala, bourse, market.

fair *adj.* **1.** just, impartial, upright, righteous, legitimate, dispassionate, disinterested, honest, evenhanded, aboveboard, fair and square; *ant.* prejudiced, biased. **2.** clear, pleasant, sunny, bright, clement, placid, tranquil, balmy, mild; *ant.* stormy, threatening, overcast, cloudy. **3.** light-complexioned, blonde, white-skinned, milky, flaxen, chalky, pallid, sallow, pale, wheyfaced; *ant.* swarthy, brunette. **4.** attractive, lovely, beautiful, handsome, pretty, beauteous, comely; *ant.* ugly.
fair to middling fair, moderately good, so-so, ordinary, average.

fairly *adv.* **1.** reasonably, somewhat, adequately, quite, rather. **2.** impartially, objectively, equitably, justly.

fairy *n.* elf, sprite, pixie, brownie, fay, nymph, will-o'-the-wisp, leprechaun, succubus, demon, goblin, hobgoblin.

fairy tale *n.* children's story, folk-tale, myth, Mother Goose story, fantasy, fiction, fabrication.

faith *n.* **1.** confidence, trust, credence, credit, assurance, acceptance, dependence, conviction; *ant.* doubt, suspicion. **2.** fidelity, loyalty, allegiance, troth. **3.** creed, doctrine, dogma, tenet, credo, gospel, canon, principle, piety, orthodoxy.
break faith abandon, betray, be disloyal, fail.
good faith sincerity, honor, trustworthiness, honesty.
keep faith adhere, follow, support, be loyal.

faithful *adj.* **1.** loyal, constant, dependable, reliable, steadfast, devoted, true, trustworthy, unwavering, unswerving; *ant.* treacherous. **2.** accurate, reliable, exact.
the faithful followers, supporters, believers,

congregation, brethren, adherents, communicants.

faithless *adj.* **1.** inconstant, untrustworthy, unreliable, traitorous, adulterous, falsehearted, perfidious, recreant; *ant.* true. **2.** doubting, distrustful, skeptical, questioning; *ant.* believing.

fake *n.* **1.** imitation, hoax, sham, phony, forgery. **2.** fraud, imposter, charlatan, mountebank.

fake *v.* pretend, put on, affect, simulate, feign, fabricate, counterfeit, copy, forge.

fake *adj.* false, phony, artificial, imitation, simulated, mock, ersatz, affected, spurious, pseudo, bogus; *ant.* genuine.

fall *n.* **1.** tumble, slip, spill, plunge, plummet, nose dive. **2.** (a going downward) decline, descent, drop; *ant.* rise, elevation, ascent. **3.** (a decrease in size or value) lessening, reduction, diminution, miniaturization; loss, collapse, decrease, decline, downward spiral. **4.** capture, overthrow, ruin, destruction, resignation, capitulation, surrender. **5.** sin, transgression, lapse, breakdown; degradation, abasement, humiliation, shame.

fall *v.* **1.** topple, stumble, trip, tumble, slip. **2.** plunge, descend, sink, drop, decline, subside, collapse, cave in; *ant.* rise, ascend, climb. **3.** surrender, submit, yield, succumb, resign, capitulate; *ant.* prevail, endure, resist. **4.** happen, occur, arrive, take place, come about, come to pass.

fall asleep nod off, doze, drop off.

fall back on turn to, revert to, rely on.

fall for **1.** be tricked, be duped, be deceived. **2.** become infatuated with, desire, fall in love with, have a crush on.

fall in with **1.** go along with, support, acquiesce in, agree with, cooperate with, comply with, assent to. **2.** become friendly with, associate with, hang out *or* around with, mingle with, meet.

fall off wane, slow, drop, decrease, slacken, decline, slump, worsen, decelerate; *ant.* pick up, wax.

fall out quarrel, fight, argue, squabble, bicker, clash, differ, disagree.

fall short fail, be deficient, be lacking, need, come up short.

fall through fail, come to nothing *or* nought, collapse, founder, miscarry.

fallacious *adj.* **1.** false, incorrect, untrue, mistaken, wrong, fictitious, erroneous; *ant.* correct, true. **2.** misleading, deceptive, delusive, delusory.

fallacy *n.* **1.** error, flaw, mistake, inconsistency, delusion. **2.** deception, illusion, deceit, sophistry, sophism.

fall guy (*slang*) *n.* victim, scapegoat, dupe, patsy (*slang*).

fallible *adj.* erring, faulty, errant, imperfect, human, mortal, frail, weak, uncertain; *ant.* infallible.

fallow *adj.* idle, undeveloped, unused, inert, dormant, inactive, uncultivated.

false *adj.* **1.** wrong, mistaken, incorrect, inaccurate, erroneous, faulty, invalid, inexact, fallacious; *ant.* true. **2.** artificial, simulated, mock, synthetic, imitation, ersatz, forged, fraudulent, counterfeit, bogus; *ant.* genuine, real. **3.** unfaithful, two-faced, untrustworthy, treacherous, disloyal, double-dealing; lying, deceptive, dishonest, deceitful, mendacious; *ant.* honest, reliable.

falsehood *n.* lie, fabrication, story, tall story, deception, fib, deceit, dishonesty, perjury, mendacity.

falsify *v.* forge, tamper with, alter, adulterate, distort, pervert, garble, counterfeit, doctor, take liberties with.

falter *v.* stumble, waver, flag, vacillate, hesitate, hem and haw, fail, flinch, stammer.

faltering *adj.* **1.** irresolute, uncertain, hesitant, tentative, stumbling, stammering. **2.** weak, timid, flagging, failing; *ant.* firm, strong.

fame *n.* renown, prominence, eminence, repute, esteem, glory, illustriousness, reputation, kudos, honor, credit, stardom, celebrity.

famed *adj.* renowned, famous, celebrated, acclaimed, well-known, noted; *ant.* unknown.

familiar *adj.* **1.** common, everyday, well-known, usual, ordinary, habitual, customary, accustomed, humble, old hat (*slang*); *ant.* unusual, exotic, strange. **2.** intimate, friendly, gracious, cordial, amicable, relaxed, casual; *ant.* formal, reserved.

familiarize *v.* acquaint, accustom, habituate, enlighten, brief, prime, inure, become aware of.

family *n.* **1.** kin, folk, clan, relatives, tribe, breed, blood tie, progeny, offspring, race, ancestry, forebears, dynasty, house. **2.** order, class, genus, species, subdivision.

family *adj.* kindred, tribal, familial.

family tree ancestry, line, lineage, genealogy, pedigree, extraction.

famine *n.* starvation, hunger, dearth, want, scarcity, destitution; *ant.* plenty.

famished *adj.* starving, hungry, ravenous, voracious; *ant.* sated.

famous *adj.* renowned, celebrated, acclaimed, well-known, prominent, legendary, notable, great, honored, famed, eminent, illustrious, lionized, notorious; *ant.* unknown, obscure.

fan *n.* **1.** admirer, enthusiast, follower, devotee, adherent, lover, addict, aficionado, zealot, groupie, buff, freak (*slang*). **2.** blower, ventilator, agitator, propeller.

fan *v.* **1.** excite, arouse, stir up, whip up, work up, stimulate, impassion, rouse, provoke, aggravate, agitate, enkindle. **2.** cool, air-condition, ventilate, winnow, blow.

fanatic *n.* enthusiast, devotee, zealot, addict, *slang:* freak, fiend; extremist, activist.

fanatical *adj.* passionate, fervent, enthusiastic, obsessive, wild, mad, zealous, frenzied, extreme, rabid, fervid; *ant.* moderate.

fanciful *adj.* whimsical, imaginary, visionary, mythical, romantic, fantastic, imaginative, metaphysical, chimerical, wild, extravagant; *ant.* ordinary.

fancy *n.* **1.** desire, wishes, preference, liking, fondness, urge, hankering, inclination, impulse, caprice, partiality, penchant, predilection; *ant.* dislike. **2.** imagination, thought, idea, conception, notion, visualization, creation; *ant.* fact, reality.

fancy *v.* **1.** like, be attracted to, desire, yearn for, long for, lust after, prefer, crave, hanker after, go for; *ant.* dislike. **2.** guess, suppose, surmise, infer, think, believe, reckon, conjecture.

fancy *adj.* **1.** ornamental, elaborate, ornate, embellished, intricate, rococo, baroque, adorned, florid, ostentatious, gaudy, showy; *ant.* plain. **2.** capricious, whimsical, fanciful.

fanfare *n.* flourish, display, show, parade.

fang *n.* tooth, tusk, canine tooth, venom-tooth.

fantasize *v.* imagine, dream, daydream, hallucinate, invent, live in a dream world, build castles in the air.

fantastic *adj.* **1.** first-rate, incredible, great, wonderful, excellent, marvelous, sensational, superb, out of this world; *ant.* ordinary, poor. **2.** far-fetched, implausible, preposterous, absurd, irrational, ludicrous, ridiculous; whimsical, imaginative, fanciful, phantasmagorical.

fantasy *n.* dream, mirage, reverie, pipe-dream, vision, whimsy, apparition, hallucination, illusion, delusion, fancy, flight of fancy, imagination; *ant.* reality.

far *adj.* faraway, far-off, remote, removed, distant, far-flung, out-of-the-way, far-removed, outlying; *ant.* close, nearby.

far *adv.* **1.** at a distance, faraway, afar; *ant.* near. **2.** extremely, very, much, greatly, considerably, decidedly, incomparably, notably.

by far by a long shot, easily, far and away, immeasurably, incomparably, much.

far and wide worldwide, everywhere, widely, extensively, far and near, broadly.

so far thus far, until now, up to this point.

faraway *adj.* distant, remote, outlying, far-off, far-flung; *ant.* nearby.

farce *n.* satire, parody, sendup, mockery, burlesque, joke, low comedy, slapstick, buffoonery, sham, travesty.

farcical *adj.* funny, silly, amusing, droll, comic, facetious, nonsensical, laughable, ridiculous, preposterous, ludicrous, absurd; *ant.* sensible.

fare *n.* **1.** fee, cost, charge, price, toll, passage, ticket, token, tariff. **2.** menu, meals, provisions, rations, diet, victuals, eatables.

fare *v.* do, manage, get along, go, happen, proceed, go on, prosper.

farewell *n.* departure, good-bye, adieu, valediction; sendoff, leave-taking, parting; *ant.* hello.

farfetched *adj.* implausible, improbable, unlikely, doubtful, dubious, unrealistic, preposterous, fantastic, incredible.

farm *n.* farmstead, plantation, ranch, grange, homestead, smallholding, croft.

farm *v.* plant, cultivate, till, work the land.

farm out lease, rent, allot, distribute.

farmer *n.* planter, grower, agriculturist, agronomer, rancher, sharecropper, harvester.

far-reaching *adj.* sweeping, extensive, widespread, broad, pervasive; momentous, significant.

farsighted *adj.* **1.** long-sighted, hypermetropic, presbyopic. **2.** provident, perceptive, prophetic, farseeing, percipient, discerning, acute, canny; circumspect, cautious; judicious, politic, sage; *ant.* imprudent.

farther *adv.* at a greater distance, beyond, further, more remote, longer.

farthest *adv.* furthest, remotest, ultimate, last.

fascinate *v.* mesmerize, spellbind, bewitch, enchant, intrigue, engross, beguile, captivate, transfix, rivet, enthrall, enrapture, infatuate.

fascination *n.* enchantment, allure, attraction, interest; spell, magic, sorcery, witchery.

fascist *n.* authoritarian, autocrat, totalitarian, absolutist, Nazi, Hitlerite, skinhead (*slang*).

fascist *adj.* authoritarian, autocratic, totalitarian, dictatorial, absolutist, despotic, Nazi, Hitlerite.

fashion *n.* fad, craze, rage, vogue, trend, mode. **after a fashion** somewhat, to some extent, in a way, moderately.

fashion *v.* make, create, design, shape, mold, manufacture, form, construct, tailor, forge, fit.

fashionable *adj.* stylish, trendy, in (*slang*), up-to-date, trendsetting, all the rage, chic, up-to-the-minute, modern, contemporary; *ant.* unfashionable.

fast *adj.* **1.** rapid, swift, fleet, quick, speedy, accelerated, hasty, winged, *slang:* like a bat out of hell, like a house on fire; *ant.* slow, sluggish. **2.** firm, adherent, attached, stuck, immovable, secure, steadfast; *ant.* impermanent, loose. **3.** promiscuous, loose, whorish, wanton, wild; licentious, profligate, immoral; *ant.* chaste. **4.** permanent, colorfast, durable, lasting, washable, indelible, waterproof, vat-dyed. **play fast and loose** behave recklessly, run wild, be careless, misbehave.

fast *adv.* **1.** rapidly, speedily, quickly, swiftly, hurriedly, hastily, apace, posthaste, lickety-split, like a shot, like a flash, presto; *ant.* slow. **2.** securely, firmly, tightly, fixedly; *ant.* loosely.

fasten *v.* **1.** secure, lock, fix, close, bind, batten, tighten, clasp, clamp, bolt, rivet, cinch; *ant.* release, loosen. **2.** join, combine, connect, unite, link, interlock, interlink, interdigitate; *ant.* separate, untie.

fastener *n.* buckle, hook, lock, clamp, tie, vise, grip, clasp, snap, bolt.

fastidious *adj.* **1.** (hard to please) picky, choosy, finicky, fussy, particular, discriminating, difficult, hypercritical, captious. **2.** meticulous, exacting, precise, punctilious. **3.** (having delicate feelings) dainty, squeamish, oversensitive, hypersensitive.

fat *adj.* **1.** (said of a person) obese, portly, stout, corpulent, fleshy, potbellied, beefy, brawny, rotund, plump, husky, porcine; *ant.* thin, lean, skinny. **2.** (said of a thing) thick, large, plump, big. **3.** fertile, productive, fruitful, rich, prosperous, affluent, flourishing, lucrative, remunerative, thriving, profitable.

fatal *adj.* deadly, lethal, mortal, terminal, incurable, destructive, malignant, catastrophic, pernicious, calamitous; *ant.* harmless.

fatalism *n.* **1.** (shaping of events by fate alone) determinism, inexorability, inevitability, predestination. **2.** (fatalistic attitude) acceptance, passivity, resignation.

fatality *n.* death, casualty, mortality, loss.

fate *n.* **1.** providence, predestination, fortune, chance, divine will, karma, lot, stars, future. **2.** ruin, doom, end, downfall, nemesis.

fated *adj.* destined, predestined, preordained, foreordained, inescapable, inevitable; *ant.* avoidable.

fateful *adj.* **1.** momentous, important, ominous, portentous, critical, decisive, crucial, significant. **2.** deadly, fatal, lethal, destructive, ruinous, disastrous.

fathead (*slang*) *n.* imbecile, fool, nitwit, nincompoop, ass, dolt, idiot, numskull, goose, jackass, dope.

father *n.* **1.** sire, forefather, procreator, progenitor, parent, forebear, ancestor, paterfamilias, dad, daddy, papa, pa, pop. **2.** originator, creator, architect, founder, inventor, sponsor, patron, promoter, supporter, author, promulgator. **3.** leader, patriarch, governor, senator, administrator. **4.** priest, pastor, ecclesiastic, parson.

fatherland *n.* homeland, native land, motherland, old country, mother country.

fatherly *adj.* paternal, patriarchal, forbearing,

protective, supportive, benevolent, avuncular.

fathom *v.* understand, comprehend, deduce, interpret, grasp, divine, see, work out, get to the bottom of.

fatigue *n.* exhaustion, tiredness, weariness, lethargy, listlessness, ennui, languor; *ant.* energy, freshness.

fatigued *adj.* tired, exhausted, spent, weary, *slang:* bushed, beat, zonked, out of gas.

fatten *v.* feed; stuff, plump, build up, round out, bloat, distend, swell, thicken, broaden.

fatty *adj.* greasy, oily, blubbery, oleaginous.

fatuous *adj.* stupid, inane, moronic, idiotic, asinine, silly, brainless, witless, mindless, vacuous, silly, foolish, absurd; *ant.* sensible, sober.

fault *n.* **1.** blemish, flaw, defect, mar. **2.** handicap, disability, drawback, lack, deficiency, shortcoming, weakness, frailty, failing, infirmity; *ant.* advantage, strength. **3.** error, mistake, blunder, slip, defect, peccadillo, oversight. **4.** blame, responsibility, liability, accountability, culpability. **5.** misdemeanor, offense, wrongdoing, transgression, crime, sin, impropriety, moral shortcoming, evildoing, delinquency, trespass, fall from virtue *or* grace. **at fault** guilty, responsible, accountable, culpable, blameworthy, answerable. **find fault** criticize, complain, reprove, disparage, carp, censure, nag, nitpick, quibble, cavil; *ant.* praise.

to a fault too much, excessively, to excess, very.

fault *v.* **1.** blame, charge, accuse, criticize, censure, impugn; *ant.* praise. **2.** err, fail, blunder, bungle.

faultfinder *n.* hypercritic, nitpicker, hairsplitter, niggler, carper, nagger, caviler, grumbler, kvetch (*slang*).

faultless *adj.* **1.** innocent, blameless, sinless, pure, irreproachable, spotless, unblemished, untainted, unsullied, exemplary. **2.** accurate, correct, perfect.

faulty *adj.* defective, impaired, damaged, flawed, imperfect; weak, unsound; incorrect, inaccurate, wrong, invalid.

faux pas *n.* blunder, gaffe, goof, indiscretion, impropriety, gaucherie.

favor *n.* **1.** kindness, courtesy, indulgence,

164

goodwill, good turn. **2.** gift, present, keepsake, memento, token, souvenir. **3.** preference, patronage, approval, acceptance, backing, esteem, regard, approbation, partiality, favoritism, bias.

find favor criticize, complain, reprove, disparage, carp, censure, nag, nitpick, quibble, cavil; *ant.* praise.

find favor be appreciated, win praise, gain credit, rank.

in favor of approving, endorsing, condoning, supporting.

in one's favor to one's advantage or credit, on one's side, creditable.

favor *v.* **1.** prefer, like, take to, be fond of, fancy, approve, sanction. **2.** praise, esteem, be sweet on, have in one's good graces; *ant.* dislike, misprise. **3.** (give preferred treatment to) be partial to, indulge, promote, advance, encourage, assist, back, champion, stick up for, commend, patronize, pull strings for; *ant.* hinder, bear a grudge against. **4.** resemble, take after, look like.

favorable *adj.* **1.** beneficial, good, advantageous, promising, propitious, opportune, auspicious, encouraging, hopeful, helpful. **2.** commendatory, approving, affirmative, positive, approbative, assenting, complimentary, well-disposed. **3.** friendly, amicable, kind, understanding, sympathetic, well-intentioned, benign.

favorite *n.* beloved, choice, dear, darling, idol, preference, pick, pet, teacher's pet, apple of one's eye.

favorite *adj.* preferred, choice, favored, dearest, esteemed, pet; *ant.* hated.

favoritism *n.* bias, partiality, one-sidedness, partisanship, preferential treatment, preference, nepotism, biasedness; *ant.* impartiality.

fawn *v.* ingratiate oneself, flatter, grovel, kowtow, curry favor, court, bootlick.

fawn *adj.* beige, tan, buff, sandy, khaki.

fawning *adj.* groveling, flattering, obsequious, servile, unctuous, sycophantic, deferential, cringing, slavish, bootlicking; *ant.* proud.

faze *v.* bother, intimidate, worry, disturb.

fear *n.* fright, phobia, dread, horror, terror, panic, trepidation, apprehension, foreboding; *ant.* courage, fortitude.

fear *v.* **1.** worry, dread, tremble, take fright, shudder at. **2.** suspect, anticipate, foresee.

fearful *adj.* **1.** cowardly, afraid, frightened, timid, timorous, fainthearted, jumpy, jittery, shy, hesitant, apprehensive, anxious, intimidated; *ant.* courageous. **2.** shocking, strange, grim, frightful, terrible, hideous, appalling, horrendous, horrible, atrocious, dreadful, hair-raising, monstrous.

fearless *adj.* courageous, unafraid, intrepid, valiant, indomitable, bold, heroic, lionhearted, plucky, unflinching, game, gutsy; *ant.* afraid, timid.

fearsome *adj.* horrible, horrifying, frightening, appalling, terrible, horrendous, terrible, horrific, frightful, hair-raising, hideous, menacing; *ant.* delightful.

feasible *adj.* **1.** likely, possible, available, practical, reasonable, doable, practicable, viable, achievable, attainable, workable; *ant.* impossible, impracticable. **2.** suitable, fit, expedient, practical, worthwhile, convenient; *ant.* unworkable, unsuitable.

feast *n.* banquet, dinner, spread, repast, holiday, binge, festivity, fête.

feast *v.* eat, overindulge, gorge, gormandize, regale, gratify.

feat *n.* achievement, accomplishment, exploit, deed, act, performance.

feather *n.* plume, quill, plumage, down.

feathery *adj.* plumed, fluffy, downy, light, wispy, featherlike.

feature *n.* **1.** characteristic, character, aspect, attribute, facet, trait, factor, quality, peculiarity, aspect. **2.** attraction, highlight, main event, drawing card, specialty. **3.** article, story, editorial, column, serial.

feature *v.* spotlight, star, accentuate, play up, headline, highlight, promote, push, emphasize, recommend.

features *n.* face, looks, countenance, physiognomy, lineaments.

febrile *adj.* feverish, flushed, inflamed, burning, fiery, pyretic, delirious.

feces *n.* excrement, excretion, waste, dung.

feckless *adj.* **1.** ineffectual, incompetent, futile, worthless, useless, hopeless, weak, feeble, aimless, shiftless; *ant.* efficient. **2.** careless, thoughtless, irresponsible.

fecund *adj.* productive, fruitful, fertile, prolific, teeming, fructuous; *ant.* infertile.

federal *adj.* national, general, central, governmental.

federate *v.* combine, unite, join together, unify, amalgamate, integrate, confederate, associate, league, syndicate; *ant.* separate.

federation *n.* union, association, coalition, league, confederation, alliance, combination, amalgamation, syndicate.

fed up *v.* aggravated, dissatisfied, sick and tired; *ant.* contented.

fee *n.* charge, bill, toll, payment, compensation, remuneration, salary, pay, recompense, reward.

feeble *adj.* weak, powerless, enervated, ineffective, frail, delicate, lame, sickly, faint, puny; *ant.* strong, worthy.

feebleminded *adj.* stupid, slow-witted, retarded, half-witted, imbecilic, idiotic, moronic, simple, vacant, cretinous, slow.

feed *n.* provisions, supplies, fodder, forage, provender, pastorage, roughage.

feed *v.* **1.** eat, dine, graze; provide for, nourish, sustain, supply, fare, cater. **2.** encourage, foster, fuel, nurture, strengthen, augment, bolster.

feed in inject, supply, key in, input.

feed on eat, devour, consume, partake of, live on, live off of, exist on, feast upon, prey on.

feel *n.* feeling, texture, quality, sense, touch, gift, knack.

feel *v.* **1.** handle, touch, hold, caress, finger, explore, stroke, fondle, grip, clutch, clasp, grope. **2.** experience, go through, undergo, sense, perceive, be aware of. **3.** believe, sense, know, think, reckon, deem, have a hunch, judge. **4.** be perceived as, seem, appear.

feel for sympathize with, empathize with, understand, pity, have compassion for.

feeler *n.* (tactile organ) **1.** antenna, finger, claw, hand, vibrissa. **2.** probe, hint, overture, advance, approach, proposal, prospectus, intimation, suggestion, tender.

feeling *n.* **1.** opinion, thought, outlook, attitude, point of view. **2.** sensitivity, taste, emotion, passion, tenderness, discernment, sentiment, refinement, capacity, faculty, intelligence.

feelings *n.* ego, self-esteem, emotions, passions, sensitivities, affections, susceptibilities.

feign *v.* pretend, act, fake, simulate, put on, counterfeit, imitate, fabricate, affect, make a show of, dissemble, assume.

feigned *adj.* pretended, artificial, imitation, fabricated, counterfeit, simulated, affected, false, fake, sham, pseudo, spurious; *ant.* genuine, sincere.

feint *n.* ruse, pretense, dodge, bluff, deception, distraction, artifice, subterfuge, maneuver, stratagem.

felicitations *n.* congratulations, good *or* best wishes, compliments, salutations.

felicitous *adj.* timely, appropriate, fitting, suitable, apt, opportune, well-chosen, apropos; *ant.* inappropriate, inept.

felicity *n.* **1.** happiness, delight, joy, bliss, delectation. **2.** aptness, appropriateness, eloquence, applicability.

feline *adj.* catlike, sensual, seductive, sinuous, sleek, graceful, stealthy, smooth, leonine, slinky.

fell *v.* knock down, raze, level, prostrate, floor, flatten, demolish.

fellow *n.* **1.** youth, lad, boy, adolescent, cadet, juvenile, youngster, teenager, chap, guy. **2.** associate, peer, colleague, comrade, brother, co-worker, equal, partner, counterpart. **3.** scholar, graduate, academician, master, tutor, don, instructor, professor, lecturer.

fellowship *n.* **1.** conviviality, sociability, familiarity, brotherhood, sisterhood, camaraderie, fraternity, amity, affability, communion, fraternization, society, alliance, comradeship. **2.** organization, association, corporation, club, gang, league, fraternity, guild, order. **3.** grant, stipend, scholarship, endowment, honorarium, subsidy, assistantship.

felon *n.* criminal, outlaw, delinquent, convict.

felony *n.* crime, offense, misconduct, transgression.

female *adj.* feminine, womanly, ladylike, distaff; *ant.* male.

feminine *adj.* ladylike, womanly, soft, tender, girlish, graceful, delicate, effeminate; *ant.* mannish, masculine.

femininity *n.* femaleness, womanliness, womanhood, muliebrity, yin; delicacy, softness, gentleness; *ant.* masculinity.

femme fatale *n.* siren, temptress, vamp, seductress, vixen, minx, charmer, enchantress.

fen *n.* swamp, marsh, bog, quagmire, morass, slough.

fence *n.* barrier, paling, balustrade, backstop, railing, barricade, wall, dike, hedge. **on the fence** undecided, uncertain, uncommitted, indifferent, irresolute, of two minds.
fence *v.* **1.** confine, pen, guard, surround, restrict, secure, enclose, encircle, coop, circumscribe, guard, defend. **2.** dodge, evade, parry, hedge, equivocate, cavil, tergiversate, beat around the bush, stonewall, pussyfoot.

fencing *n.* evasiveness, equivocation, prevarication, hedging, parrying, quibbling, beating around the bush, doubletalk, weasel-words, stonewalling, pussyfooting.

fend *v.* parry, repel, resist, oppose.
fend off repel, repulse, stave off, ward off, hold at bay, parry, shut out, deflect, resist, avert, defend.
fend for oneself take care of oneself, stay alive, make a living, eke out an existence, subsist, survive.

feral *adj.* savage, fierce, bestial, wild, vicious, untamed, ferocious, brutal, fell, brutish, undomesticated, unbroken, uncultivated; *ant.* tame.

ferment *v.* **1.** brew, froth, effervesce, foam, leaven. **2.** incite, rouse, provoke, work *or* stir up, agitate, inflame; seethe, fester, smolder.
ferment *n.* turbulence, tumult, agitation, commotion, frenzy, disruption, turmoil, stir, uproar, stew, furor, unrest; *ant.* calm.

ferocious *adj.* savage, vicious, wild, barbaric, brutal, fearsome, predatory, merciless, pitiless, relentless, sadistic, murderous, inhuman; *ant.* gentle, mild.

ferret *v.* hunt, search, seek.
ferret out unearth, search out, track, hunt down, root out, find, discover, elicit, extract, disclose, dig up.

ferry *n.* barge, ferryboat, packet boat.
ferry *v.* transport, shuttle, taxi, chauffeur, convey, ship, drive, carry, run, move.

fertile *adj.* productive, prolific, teeming, fruitful, flowering, lush, generative, abundant, fecund, fructuous, rich, virile; *ant.* arid, barren.

fertility *n.* **1.** fruitfulness, fecundity, richness, prolificity, potency, virility, pregnancy, productivity, *ant.* barrenness, sterility, infecundity. **2.** ingenuity, creativity, resourcefulness, imagination, inventiveness.

fertilization *n.* **1.** insemination, impregnation, pollination, implantation, breeding, fecundation, propagation, generation, procreation, conjugation, begetting. **2.** enriching, manuring, dressing, top-dressing, preparation, covering, liming, mulching, spreading.

fertilize *v.* **1.** impregnate, breed, generate, fecundate, germinate, pollinate, inseminate, propagate, procreate, beget. **2.** manure, compost, dress, top-dress, spread, lime, prepare, mulch, cover, treat, enrich.

fertilizer *n.* manure, compost, mulch, plant food, top dressing, humus.

fervent *adj.* passionate, impassioned, devout, zealous, intense, vehement, spirited, wholehearted, vigorous, enthusiastic, excited, energetic.

fervor *n.* enthusiasm, passion, excitement, ardor, zeal, intensity, eagerness, unction, spirit, verve, vehemence, animation; *ant.* apathy.

fester *v.* **1.** vex, irk, gall, rankle, chafe, smolder. **2.** decay, putrefy, rot, suppurate, maturate, discharge, ulcerate; *ant.* dissipate, heal.

festival *n.* jubilee, celebration, carnival, festivities, fiesta, fête, holiday, merrymaking, junketing, gala, commemoration.

festive *adj.* jubilant, happy, merry, gleeful, gay, rollicking, sportive, joyful, uproarious, celebratory, mirthful; *ant.* gloomy, sober, somber.

festivities *n.* party, festival, celebration, revelries, bacchanalia, carousal, feasting, banqueting, rejoicings.

festivity *n.* fun, merriment, pleasure, sport, enjoyment, amusement, mirth, gaiety, revelry, junketing, jollity, joviality, wassail.

festoon *n.* decoration, frill, garland, swag, lei, wreath, molding.

festoon *v.* adorn, decorate, garnish, swag, wreathe, array, garland, beribbon, bedizen, swathe.

fetch *v.* **1.** bring, get, obtain, carry, transport, convey. **2.** produce, make, yield, earn, elicit, sell for.

fetching *adj.* attractive, charming, alluring, cap-

tivating, disarming, pretty, enchanting, beguiling, winsome, enticing, winning, taking; *ant.* repellent.

fête *n.* gala, carnival, celebration, festival, fair, bazaar, feast, holiday.

fête *v.* entertain, regale, wine and dine, make much of, roll out the red carpet for.

fetid *adj.* rank, rancid, smelly, stinking, foul, disgusting, offensive, noxious, nauseating, odorous, reeking, sickly; *ant.* fragrant.

fetish *n.* obsession, fixation, craze, mania, idée fixe.

fetter *v.* bind, chain, restrict, confine, tie, encumber, hamper, manacle, hobble, shackle, pinion, curb, truss; *ant.* free.

fetters *n.* bondage, restraint, constraint, hindrance, obstruction, captivity, curb, check, shackles, chains, handcuffs, manacles.

feud *n.* dispute, quarrel, grudge, argument, rivalry, dissension, row, discord, hostility, antagonism, bad blood, estrangement; *ant.* agreement, peace.

fever *n.* **1.** febricula, pyrexia, delirium, temperature. **2.** unrest, turmoil, agitation, frenzy, excitement, passion, fervor, restlessness, intensity, ferment.

fevered *adj.* hot, flushed, burning, fiery, febrile, pyretic, pyrexic, pyrexial; *ant.* cool.

few *pron.* not many, one or two, scarcely any, some, small number, a couple, handful, small quantity, scattering.

few *adj.* scarce, sparse, infrequent, scant, rare, sporadic, negligible, scattered.

few and far between rare, scarce, sparse.

fiancé *n.* bridegroom-to-be, husband-to-be, intended, betrothed.

fiancée *n.* bride-to-be, wife-to-be, intended, betrothed.

fiasco *n.* mess, calamity, debacle, failure, disaster, catastrophe, collapse, breakdown, blunder, farce, flop, washout; *ant.* success.

fiat *n.* **1.** decree, proclamation, dictate, order, mandate, command, edict, ordinance. **2.** permission, sanction, OK, authorization, warrant.

fib *n.* lie, untruth, story, tale, concoction, falsehood, white lie, misrepresentation, fabrication, invention, prevarication, yarn, whopper.

fiber *n.* **1.** thread, cord, string, strand, filament, vein, hair. **2.** quality, texture, grain, tissue, nap, grit, feel, surface.

fibrous *adj.* sinewy, wiry, stringy, woody, pulpy, veined, hairy, coarse, stalky, ropy, tissued, threadlike, fibroid.

fickle *adj.* changeable, capricious, mutable, unfaithful, vacillating, erratic, irresolute, mercurial, disloyal, treacherous; *ant.* constant.

fiction *n.* **1.** lie, falsehood, fabrication, fib, invention, concoction, tall or cock-and-bull story, fancy, figment, whopper; *ant.* truth. **2.** novel, tale, romance, story, legend, myth, parable, yarn, fantasy, fable.

fictitious *adj.* make-up, invented, imaginary, artificial, counterfeit, false, mythical, bogus, non-existent, fraudulent; *ant.* genuine, real.

fiddle *v.* tamper, toy, tinker, fidget, play, interfere, trifle, cheat, swindle, racketeer, mess around, finagle.

fidelity *n.* faithfulness, constancy, loyalty, devotion, dedication, allegiance, adherence, trustworthiness, steadfastness, true-heartedness; *ant.* inconstancy, treachery.

fidget *v.* fret, play around, toy, stir, fiddle, twitch, squirm, worry.

fidgety *adj.* nervous, uneasy, edgy, on edge, restless, jumpy, skittish, jittery; *ant.* still.

fiduciary *n.* trustee, guardian, curator, depositary.

field *n.* **1.** range, meadow, pasture, acreage, plot, garden, mead, grassland, green, moor, tract. **2.** range, territory, province, domain, sphere, reach, area, scope, jurisdiction. **3.** entrants, entries, participants, competitors, contestants, opponents, contenders, competition, opposition, nominees, runners.

field *v.* answer, cope *or* deal with, deflect, return, handle, retrieve, catch, receive.

field day *n.* success, victory, triumph, opportunity, holiday.

fiend *n.* **1.** devil, demon, Satan, evil spirit, ghoul, goblin, hobgoblin, ogre, succubus, incubus. **2.** (evil person) monster, barbarian, savage, brute, beast, degenerate. **3.** (*slang*) fan, aficionado, devotee, addict, fanatic, maniac, enthusiast, *slang:* freak, nut.

fiendish *adj.* inhuman, diabolic, atrocious, ungodly, wicked, cruel, hellish, malevolent, devilish, infernal, nefarious, Mephistophelian.

fierce *adj.* **1.** brutal, savage, wild, murderous, cruel, barbarous, ferocious, menacing, cutthroat, terrible, bloodthirsty, fearsome; *ant.* calm, kind. **2.** strong, violent, tempestuous, intense, howling, blustery, relentless, raging, tumultuous; *ant.* gentle.

fiery *adj.* **1.** hot, burning, blazing, heated, inflamed, afire, flaming, red-hot, fevered, sultry, torrid, volcanic; *ant.* cold. **2.** violent, impetuous, impulsive, ardent, excitable, passionate, tempestuous, fierce, volatile, high-strung, hotheaded; *ant.* impassive.

fight *n.* altercation, dissension, skirmish, scuffle, hostilities, fracas, conflict, combat, brawl, duel, battle, bout, scrap.

fight *v.* **1.** wage war, squabble, altercate, grapple, lock horns, argue, assault, clash, exchange blows, dispute, quarrel, spar. **2.** (try hard to bring about) campaign, argue, work, petition, proselytize, pull strings, lobby.

fight back retaliate, resist, defend oneself, retort, reply.

fight off repel, rout, repulse, rebuff, resist, hold off, stave off, ward off, beat off, keep at bay, repress.

fighter *n.* contender, warrior, soldier, competitor, combatant, aggressor, antagonist, rival, opponent, champion, swashbuckler, fire-eater.

fighting *n.* combat, battle, bloodshed, quarreling, warfare, war, fisticuffs, conflict, clash, hostilities, melee, scuffling, fray.

fighting *adj.* warfaring, warlike, aggressive, militant, pugnacious, quarrelsome, combative, fierce, argumentative, belligerent, contentious, martial, bellicose, militaristic.

figment *n.* illusion, creation, delusion, fiction, concoction, fable, fabrication, improvisation, fancy.

figurative *adj.* metaphorical, symbolic, emblematic, allegorical, representative, analogous; descriptive, flowery, poetical, picturesque, ornate; *ant.* literal.

figure *n.* **1.** form, shape, configuration, mass, structure. **2.** torso, body, physique, frame, shape, form, build, appearance, outline. 3. design, sketch, pattern, composition, drawing, illustration, depiction, diagram. 4. sum, total, number, amount; numeral, digit.

figure of speech turn of phrase, rhetorical device, conceit, trope.

figure v. 1. decide, suppose, think, surmise, judge, infer, believe, opine. 2. comprehend, understand, figure out, master, reason, discover, get to the bottom of. 3. compute, calculate, add, work out, reckon, number, count, sum, tally.

figure out understand, fathom, comprehend, make out, decipher, resolve, puzzle out, work out, make out, reckon, get to the bottom of, make sense of.

figurehead n. leader, front man, puppet, nonentity, mouthpiece, token.

filament n. thread, fiber, string, wire, hair, whisker, strand.

filch v. steal, thieve, pilfer, pinch, purloin, finger, palm, misappropriate, embezzle, plagiarize, *slang:* rip off, lift.

file n. 1. repository, folder, portfolio, binder, dossier. 2. sharpener, rasp, steel. 3. line, rank, row, column, list, procession, queue, cortege, string, trail, stream.

file v. 1. classify, index, categorize, catalog, record, register, list, arrange, pigeonhole, docket. 2. hone, sand, abrade, rasp, scrape, grate, smooth, rub down, level off, finish, burnish, sharpen, grind, shave.

filial adj. dutiful, loyal, devoted, affectionate, fond, respectful, loving.

filibuster n. hindrance, interference, impediment, opposition, peroration, stonewalling, postponement, delay, procrastination.

filibuster v. block, hinder, impede, prevent, obstruct, procrastinate, delay, put off; ant. expedite.

filigree n. scrollwork, latticework, lacework, interlace, fretwork, wirework.

fill n. enough, plenty, abundance.

fill v. 1. pack, stuff, lade, supply, satisfy, sate, ram, cram, crowd, saturate; ant. empty, clear. 2. overflow, swell, distend, blow up, bulge out, brim over, permeate, take up, pervade. 3. elect, appoint, choose, assign.

fill in 1. fill out, complete, answer. 2. inform, brief, acquaint, bring up to date, advise, apprise. 3. substitute, replace, stand in, understudy, act for, deputize.

fill out v. 1. enlarge, swell out, expand, grow. 2. insert, write or fill in, sign, answer.

filler n. stuffing, padding, packing, caulking, waste material.

filling n. stuffing, insides, innards, contents, filler, padding, wadding, grouting.

fillip v. 1. hit, rap, tap, slap, pat. 2. stimulate, spur, arouse, goad, excite.

film n. 1. movie, video, motion picture, movie, cinema, photoplay, flick (*slang*). 2. gauze, tissue, membrane, transparency, haze, partition, onionskin, veil, screen, cobweb, mist, cloud.

film v. 1. cloud, blur, mist, veil, dull, haze, screen, glaze, blear. 2. photograph, record, take, shoot.

filmy adj. sheer, gossamer, translucent, delicate, diaphanous, thin, insubstantial, seethrough, flimsy, fragile, fine, cobwebby; ant. opaque.

filter n. strainer, sieve, colander, sifter, mesh, membrane.

filter v. 1. strain, purify, refine, screen, clarify, sieve, sift. 2. leak, trickle, ooze, seep, penetrate, exude.

filth n. 1. dirt, refuse, sewage, garbage, slime, scum, grime, excrement, pollution, muck, sludge, bilge, crud (*slang*). 2. vulgarity, obscenity, coarseness, indecency, vileness, impurity, defilement, smuttiness; ant. decency, purity.

filthy adj. 1. dirty, unclean, unwashed, squalid, grimy, grubby, muddy, mucky, polluted, slimy, sooty; ant. clean. 2. indecent, obscene, gross, lewd, licentious, blue, coarse, base, suggestive, vulgar, foul-mouthed; ant. inoffensive, pure.

final adj. last, latest, end, ultimate, closing, conclusive, dying, last-minute, definitive, irrevocable.

finale n. close, climax, final curtain, last act, swan song, epilogue, finis, denouement, conclusion, culmination, crowning glory.

finalize v. finish, complete, resolve, settle, conclude, clinch, wind up, tie up, wrap up.

finally *adv.* at length, at last, in *or* at the end, subsequently, in conclusion, after all, eventually, ultimately, at long last, at the last moment, belatedly, when all is said and done.

finance *n.* economics, money management, business, commerce, banking, accounting, stock market, trade, investment.

finance *v.* fund, pay for, back, underwrite, support, subsidize, set up, bail out, bankroll, guarantee, capitalize.

finances *n.* money, cash, budget, revenue, resources, assets, funds, income, wealth, capital.

financial *adj.* monetary, economic, budgetary, fiscal, commercial, pecuniary.

financier *n.* investor, banker, broker, stock-broker, speculator, moneymaker, financialist, cambist.

find *n.* bargain, acquisition, coup, bonanza, catch, discovery.

find *v.* **1.** discover, detect, notice, observe, perceive, arrive at, discern, hit upon, uncover, expose, run across *or* into, stumble upon, happen upon, come upon *or* across. **2.** judge, determine, decide.

find out discover, observe, note, realize, learn, uncover, ascertain, detect, dig up, expose, unmask.

finding *n.* judgment, decision, verdict, recommendation, pronouncement, conclusion; discovery, breakthrough.

findings *n.* data, discoveries, conclusions, summary.

fine *adj.* **1.** light, powdery, granular, dainty, delicate, fragile, gossamer. **2.** well-made, supreme, exquisite, select, elegant, tasteful, fashionable, exceptional, excellent, first-rate, masterly.

fine *n.* penalty, punishment, damages, amercement.

fine *v.* penalize, punish, sting, mulct, amerce.

finery *n.* apparel, clothes, Sunday best; trappings, trimmings, jewelry, gear, ornaments; splendor, showiness, glad rags (*slang*).

finesse *n.* discretion, diplomacy, adroitness, savoir-faire, delicacy, subtlety, tact, artifice; expertise, deftness, craft.

finger *n.* claw, talon, digit, index, phalanges, digital.

have one's fingers crossed hope, wish, anticipate.

lift a finger try, make an effort, attempt, endeavor

put one's finger on identify, isolate, locate, pinpoint, place, recall, remember, ascertain, detect, discover.

finger *v.* **1.** feel, handle, touch, manipulate, caress, fondle, stroke, paw, maul, toy with. **2.** specify, point out, name, designate.

finical *adj.* choosy, finicky, particular, fussy, persnickety.

finicky *adj.* choosy, particular, fussy, finical, persnickety, difficult; *ant.* easygoing.

finis *n.* end, close, finale, conclusion.

finish *v.* **1.** end, complete, accomplish, consummate, culminate, conclude, finalize, perfect. **2.** defeat, beat, overpower, overcome, rout, ruin, destroy, kill, dispose of, execute, annihilate. **3.** polish, wax, stain, buff, burnish, coat, lacquer, hone, gild, veneer.

finish *n.* **1.** end, close, termination, completion, culmination, windup, cessation; annihilation, defeat, denouement, coup de grace. **2.** polish, shine, gloss, luster, patina, glaze, burnish.

finite *adj.* measurable, calculable, limited, restricted, terminable, fixed, bounded, circumscribed, demarcated, definable; *ant.* endless, bottomless.

fire *n.* **1.** blaze, flames, burning, inferno, pyre, incandescence, sparks, heat, glow, warmth, luminosity, scintillation, combustion. **2.** enthusiasm, dash, sparkle, verve, life, intensity, vivacity, passion, animation, excitement, drive, zip, fervor, spirit. **3.** bombardment, artillery attack, rounds, barrage, bombings, shelling, volley, fusillade, sniping, mortar attack, salvos, cross-fire.

go through fire and water undergo difficulty *or* danger, survive, suffer, endure.

on fire excited, impassioned, full of ardor, enthusiastic, zealous.

open fire start shooting, shoot, attack.

play with fire gamble, run a risk, tempt fate.

set the world on fire achieve, become famous, excel, succeed.

under fire criticized, censured, under attack,

slang: in the hot seat, on the spot, getting heat or flak; embattled.

fire *v.* **1.** ignite, kindle, light, burn, inflame. **2.** shoot *or* set off, discharge, shell, hurl, detonate, launch. **3.** dismiss, discharge, let go, depose, show the door. **4.** excite, stimulate, animate, arouse, rouse, inspire, incite, impassion, stir, inflame.

firearm *n.* gun, weapon, shooter.

firebrand *n.* **1.** torch, coal, flame, spill. **2.** agitator, incendiary, rabble-rouser, demagogue, mischief-maker.

fired *adj.* discharged, dismissed, terminated, laid-off, given one's walking papers.

fireproof *adj.* incombustible, nonflammable, fire-resistant, noncombustible; *ant.* flammable, inflammable, combustible, incandescent.

fireworks *n.* **1.** pyrotechnics, rockets, firecrackers, sparklers, illuminations, feux d'artifice. **2.** uproar, temper, rage, anger, hysterics.

firm *n.* company, business, corporation, association, organization, enterprise, outfit, establishment, conglomerate, concern, syndicate, institution.

firm *adj.* **1.** stable, fixed, solid, rooted, immovable, secured, steady, rigid; *ant.* unsound, loose, mobile. **2.** determined, steadfast, constant, resolute, obdurate, staunch, definite, adamant, committed, reliable, dogged, unwavering.

firmament *n.* heaven, sky, atmosphere, welkin.

first *adj.* **1.** initial, original, leading, head, opening, introductory. **2.** uppermost, primary, principal, paramount, highest.

first *adv.* in the beginning, at the outset, early on, to start with, to begin with, before all else, originally, beforehand, initially.

first aid *n.* emergency medical aid, emergency relief, roadside treatment, field dressing.

first-born *adj.* oldest, eldest, elder, senior.

first-class *adj.* excellent, superior, supreme, choice, top drawer, grade A.

firsthand *adj.* direct, personal, immediate, straight from the horse's mouth; *ant.* hearsay.

first-rate *adj.* exceptional, excellent, superlative, outstanding, leading, superior, first-class, prime, nonpareil, A-1; *ant.* inferior.

fiscal *adj.* monetary, financial, economic, budgetary, bursal, pecuniary.

fish *n.* seafood, panfish, denizen of the deep.

like a fish out of water displaced, alien, unfamiliar, freakish, like a square peg in a round hole.

neither fish nor fowl unrecognizable, unknown, amorphous, anamalous, strange.

fish *v.* **1.** cast, angle, trawl, troll. **2.** seek, hunt, search.

fish for solicit, invite, angle for, bid for.

fish out find, come up with, extricate, produce, extract, dredge *or* haul up, uncover, expose.

fisherman *n.* angler, piscator, harpooner, trawler, caster, whaler.

fishy *adj.* suspect, suspicious, questionable, shady, funny, odd, implausible, unlikely, dubious; *ant.* honest, legitimate.

fissile *adj.* divisible, separable, cleavable, fissionable, severable.

fission *n.* splitting, breaking, parting, division, rupture, severance, rending, cleavage, schism, scission.

fissure *n.* break, breach, chasm, rupture, split, crevice, fault, crack, cleft, fracture, gap.

fist *n.* clutch, grasp, clasp, grip, hold.

fit *n.* **1.** convulsion, spasm, seizure, stroke, paroxysm. **2.** outburst, caprice, outbreak, torrent, tantrum, mood, huff, miff, rage.

by fits and starts sporadically, periodically, unevenly, irregularly, erratically, intermittently; *ant.* regularly, continuously.

throw a fit lose one's temper, rage, blow one's top *or* stack (*slang*).

fit *v.* **1.** agree, accord, concur, harmonize, belong, conform, be in keeping, parallel, relate, suit, apply, match; *ant.* oppose, clash. **2.** equip, provide, supply, outfit, furnish, implement.

fit *adj.* **1.** healthy, able-bodied, trim, strong, robust, strapping, hale and hearty, in good shape, fit as a fiddle, in the pink. **2.** appropriate, suitable, proper, apt, meet, convenient, timely, opportune; *ant.* unseemly.

fitful *adj.* erratic, uneven, sporadic, spasmodic, intermittent, variable, irregular, discontinuous, interrupted; on-again, off-again. disturbed; *ant.* regular, steady.

fitting *n.* part, attachment, piece, component, accessory, unit, fixture, connection, assemblage.

171

fitting *adj.* correct, appropriate, proper, right, apt, meet, suitable, apposite, becoming, seemly, decorous, deserved, comme il faut; *ant.* uncalled-for, unseemly.

fittings *n.* trimmings, accessories, extras, conveniences, furnishings, fixtures, appointments, accoutrements, equipment, appurtenances.

fix *n.* **1.** difficulty, predicament, mess, plight, dilemma, quandary, scrape, jam, *slang:* pickle (*slang*). **2.** (*slang*) injection, dose, shot, *slang:* hit, score.

fix *v.* **1.** repair, mend, correct, restore. **2.** secure, fasten, attach, install, bind, implant, embed, anchor, inculcate. **3.** (arrange for a predetermined outcome) prearrange, preplan, stack the deck, frame, set up, rig. **4.** (*slang*) get even, avenge, pay back, get, even the score.

fixation *n.* infatuation, obsession, fetish, preoccupation, monomania, complex, compulsion, idée fixe, hangup (*slang*).

fixture *n.* attachment, appliance, fittings, installation.

fizzle *v.* hiss, sputter, bubble.

fizzle out subside, dissipate, taper off, peter out; come to nothing, fall through, fail, stop, collapse.

fizzy *adj.* effervescent, frothy, gassy, bubbly, carbonated, sparkling, aerated.

flabbergasted *adj.* dumbfounded, astonished, astounded, amazed, speechless, stupefied, overwhelmed, nonplussed, stunned, bowled over.

flabby *adj.* pendulous, toneless, slack, drooping, flaccid, fleshy, plump; *ant.* firm, lean, strong.

flaccid *adj.* slack, soft, relaxed, limp, inert, lax, sagging, toneless, drooping, weak, loose, floppy; *ant.* firm.

flag *n.* banner, pennant, standard, streamer, colors, emblem, ensign.

flagstone *n.* rock, paving stone *or* block, flag, pavement.

flag *v.* wane, tire, abate, deteriorate, diminish, weaken, subside, taper off, fade, ebb, falter; *ant.* revive.

flagellate *v.* beat, whip, flog, thrash, flay.

flagellation *n.* beating, whipping, thrashing, lashing, flaying, flogging, castigation, whaling, chastisement, scourging.

flagrant *adj.* blatant, glaring, overt, brazen,

audacious, open, shameless, undisguised, flaunting, barefaced; *ant.* covert, secret.

flail *v.* beat, whip, thrash.

flair *n.* **1.** gift, ability, skill, talent, knack, feel, acumen, aptitude; *ant.* ineptitude. **2.** dash, panache, style, chic.

flak *n.* criticism, censure, faultfinding, hostility, condemnation, bad press, brickbats, disparagement, disapprobation, aspersions.

flake *n.* scale, shaving, sliver, chip, layer, peeling, disk, paring.

flake *v.* peel, chip, scale, exfoliate, blister.

flaky *adj.* **1.** scaly, dry, exfoliative, peeling. **2.** (*slang*) eccentric, odd, quirky.

flamboyant *adj.* flashy, ostentatious, gaudy, showy, theatrical, elaborate, dazzling, extravagant, ornate, baroque; *ant.* modest, restrained.

flame *n.* **1.** fire, blaze. **2.** enthusiasm, zeal, affection, passion, fervor, keenness, ardor. **3.** lover, sweetheart, beau, heartthrob.

flame *v.* burn, blaze, shine, glow, radiate.

flaming *adj.* **1.** burning, blazing, afire, fiery, ablaze, glowing, red, hot, fiery, smoldering; brilliant, vivid. **2.** impassioned, intense, aroused, ardent, angry, raging, vehement, frenzied, fervid.

flammable *adj.* inflammable, combustible, ignitable, combustive; *ant.* fire-resistant, flameproof, nonflammable.

flange *n.* rim, lip, splay, skirt, flare.

flank *n.* side, loin, quarter, thigh, wing, edge, haunch, ham, hip.

flap *n.* **1.** cover, tab, tag, overlap, skirt, lapel, apron, fly. **2.** commotion, fuss, agitation, twitter, fluster, dither, tizzy.

flap *v.* beat, flutter, vibrate, flail, thrash, swish, agitate, wave, thresh.

flare *n.* **1.** flash, flame, glare, flicker, blaze, burst, dazzle. **2.** widening, broadening, splay, bell-bottom.

flare *v.* burn, flash, blaze, burst, glare, flame, explode, erupt, flicker.

flare up fly off the handle, lose one's cool, blow one's top.

flash *n.* **1.** glimmer, sparkle, glitter, dazzle, shimmer, shine, gleam, beam. **2.** blaze, flicker, flame, glare, burst. **3.** bulletin, dispatch, report, news.

flash in the pan failure, fiasco, dud, disappointment.

flash v. **1.** glimmer, sparkle, glitter, glisten, scintillate, gleam, dazzle, shimmer, shine, glow, twinkle. **2.** flare up, blaze, flame, glare. **3.** speed, fly, flit, shoot, run, race, bolt, dash, dart, streak, sprint.

flashy adj. garish, ostentatious, brassy, gaudy, showy, tasteless, cheap, loud, tacky, tawdry, meretricious; ant. plain, simple, tasteful.

flask n. bottle, decanter, flagon, container, jar, ewer, carafe, canteen, beaker.

flat n. marsh, swamp, lowland, morass, mud flat, shoal, shallow, strand, moss, plain.

flat adj. **1.** level, even, smooth, spread out, extended, horizontal. **2.** tasteless, unseasoned, insipid, flavorless, stale, unpalatable, weak, watery.

flat-footed adj. **1.** forthright, unwavering, resolute, firm, intransigent. **2.** unprepared, not ready, surprised.

flatten v. crush, squash, compress, raze, level, trample, floor, demolish, knock down, prostrate, fell, smooth.

flatter v. **1.** adulate, cajole, fawn, laud, glorify, praise, inveigh, wheedle, sycophantize, sweet-talk, butter up, play up to; ant. criticize. **2.** enhance, become, suit, grace, beautify, embellish, adorn, enrich, go with, compliment, set off, show to advantage.

flatterer n. adulator, groveler, sycophant, fawner, bootlicker, brown-noser (slang), toady; ant. critic, opponent.

flattering adj. **1.** ingratiating, obsequious, honey-tongued, servile, fawning, sycophantic, unctuous, effusive, laudatory. **2.** becoming, enhancing, favorable, complimentary.

flatulence n. **1.** gas, gassiness, eructation, borborygmus. **2.** pomposity, windiness, turgidity.

flatulent adj. **1.** gassy, swollen, distended. **2.** pompous, prolix, windy, turgid.

flaunt v. exhibit, display, show off, flourish, parade, boast, brandish, flash, sport.

flavor n. **1.** taste, savoriness, tang, relish, smack, piquancy, soupçon. **2.** characteristic, character, quality, property, feel, essence, touch, style, tone, tinge.

flavor v. season, spice, leaven, lace, imbue, infuse, taint, contaminate.

flavorful adj. delicious, tasty, savory, palatable, toothsome; ant. insipid, tasteless.

flavoring n. seasoning, extract, essence, tincture, zest.

flavorless adj. tasteless, bland, insipid, vapid, mawkish.

flaw n. **1.** (of a person or thing) defect, imperfection, blemish, disfigurement, break, tear, rent. **2.** (a characteristic of a person) weakness, fault, failing, shortcoming. **3.** (as in thought) error, mistake, fallacy.

flawed adj. imperfect, blemished, damaged, defective, broken, marred, disfigured, chipped, marked, cracked; erroneous, faulty, unsound; ant. perfect.

flawless adj. perfect, unblemished, intact, whole, unsullied, impeccable, sound, spotless, immaculate, faultless, irreproachable; ant. imperfect.

flay v. **1.** skin, scalp, peel, excoriate, flog. **2.** criticize, reprove, castigate, censure, rebuke, lambaste, revile, upbraid, scourge.

flea-bitten adj. wretched, decrepit, seedy, shabby.

fleck n. speck, dot, spot, point, mark, speckle.

fledgling n. novice, neophyte, newcomer, beginner, apprentice, trainee, recruit, greenhorn, novitiate, tenderfoot, rookie.

flea-ridden adj. infested, decrepit, scruffy, grubby, run-down, squalid, sordid, unhygienic, mangy, scabby, moth-eaten, tatty; ant. salubrious.

flee v. get away, escape, bolt, take flight, withdraw, leave, depart, abscond, take off, decamp, make oneself scarce; ant. stand, stay.

fleece n. wool, fell, hide, pelt.

fleecy adj. fluffy, woolly, soft, downy, hairy, shaggy, nappy.

fleet n. navy, squadron, armada, flotilla, task force.

fleeting adj. brief, momentary, transient, flitting, passing, ephemeral, temporary, vanishing, short-lived, fugitive, transitory; ant. lasting, permanent.

flesh n. **1.** tissue, body, brawn, fat, substance, pulp; corporeality, physicality. **2.** relatives, family, relations, kin, kinsfolk, kindred, flesh and blood.

fleshly adj. **1.** corporeal, corporal, bodily,

173

flex *v.* physical, human, animal, mundane, earthly, material, secular, terrestrial, worldly; *ant.* spiritual. **2.** lewd, erotic, sensuous, sensual, carnal, lascivious, lecherous, lustful, bestial, earthy, brutish.

flex *v.* bend, contract, tighten, angle, crook, curve, bow, ply.

flexibility *n.* pliancy, adaptability, pliability, resilience, suppleness, elasticity, give, adjustability; complaisance, agreeability.

flexible *adj.* **1.** supple, lithe, limber, springy, elastic, pliable, willowy, loose-limbed, adaptable, yielding. **2.** (said of persons) accommodating, complaisant, tractable, amenable.

flick *v.* hit, strike, tap, whip, touch, dab, flip, jab, rap, fillip.

flick through scan, thumb, skim, flip, glance, riffle.

flicker *n.* **1.** trace, iota, atom, breath, drop, indication, vestige, inkling. **2.** gleam, glimmer, scintillation, flash, flare.

flicker *v.* shimmer, sparkle, twinkle, glimmer, flare, flash, scintillate, waver, quiver, vibrate, flutter.

flight *n.* **1.** flying, soaring, winging, gliding, aviation. **2.** departure, breakaway, escape, exit, fleeing, getaway, running away, retreat, exodus. **3.** staircase, stairs, steps, ascent.

flightiness *n.* changeability, inconstancy, capriciousness, mercurialness; fickleness, flippancy, irresponsibility; *ant.* steadiness.

flighty *adj.* impetuous, impulsive, changeable, capricious, skittish, volatile, unstable, fickle, silly; *ant.* steady.

flimflam *n.* **1.** deception, trickery, craft. **2.** nonsense, trifling, drivel, foolishness.

flimsy *adj.* **1.** thin, sheer, transparent, gossamer, delicate, ephemeral, diaphanous, superficial, ethereal. **2.** insubstantial, shaky, makeshift; *ant.* sturdy.

flinch *v.* shrink, cringe, withdraw, cower, recoil, duck, start, blanch, wince, shudder.

fling *n.* **1.** celebration, indulgence, party, good time, spree, bash. **2.** affair, romance, liaison, one-night stand.

fling *v.* cast, sling, throw, toss, heave, chuck, catapult, pitch, lob, hurl, let fly.

flinty *adj.* hard, cruel, unmerciful, obdurate,

---

flip *v.* throw, pitch, cast, jerk, spin, twirl, twist, flick, toss, turn.

flippant *adj.* disrespectful, cocky, impudent, saucy, rude, cheeky, brash, offhand, impertinent, irreverent; *ant.* earnest.

flirt *n.* philanderer, wanton, coquette, heartbreaker, tease, siren, vamp, vixen, minx.

flirt *v.* ogle, philander, tease, coquet, dally, wink at, toy with.

flirt with try, play with, toy with, dabble in, consider, entertain, trifle with.

flirtation *n.* affair, dalliance, fling, philandering, trifling, toying, coquetry, dallying.

flirtatious *adj.* provocative, teasing, wanton, loose, promiscuous, coy, coquettish, comehither, amorous.

flit *v.* flutter, dart, fly, skim, bob, speed, flash.

float *n.* **1.** buoy, pontoon, air cushion, lifesaver, outrigger, bobber, cork, raft, life preserver. **2.** exhibit, entry, platform.

float *v.* bob, drift, swim, hover, sail, waft, glide; *ant.* sink.

floating *adj.* uncommitted, unfixed, wandering, fluctuating.

flock *n.* **1.** herd, group, pack, litter, bevy, gaggle, swarm, colony. **2.** gathering, assembly, throng, congregation, crowd, mass, multitude, convoy, horde, company, host.

flock *v.* swarm, crowd, converge, herd, gather, gravitate, group, cluster, throng, bunch, congregate.

flog *v.* beat, whip, lash, flay, punish, whack, welt, thrash, trounce, chastise, flagellate.

flogging *n.* whipping, whaling, beating, lashing, horsewhipping, caning, trouncing, thrashing, scourging, flagellation.

flood *n.* **1.** deluge, surge, overflow, torrent, inundation, cataclysm, wave, high tide, flood tide, tidal flood *or* flow; *ant.* drought, trickle. **2.** abundance, plenty, bounty, multitude, glut, profusion, plethora, superfluity; *ant.* dearth.

flood *v.* drown, drench, immerse, soak, deluge, submerge, overflow, engulf, gush, overwhelm, inundate.

floor *n.* **1.** floorboards, deck, flagstones, tiles, planking, carpet, rug, linoleum. **2.** story, level, deck, tier.

floor *v.* stun, dumbfound, baffle, bewilder,

perplex, puzzle, stump, confound, disconcert, nonplus, knock *or* throw for a loop (*slang*).

flop *n.* failure, disaster, fiasco, debacle, loser, washout.

flop *v.* **1.** wobble, teeter, stagger, flounder, wriggle, squirm, tumble, totter. **2.** dangle, hang, sag, droop, flap. **3.** fail, misfire, miscarry, founder, fall short, fall flat, fold, bomb (*slang*).

floppy *adj.* loose, droopy, sagging, pendulous, baggy, dangling, limp, flaccid, flabby, hanging, flapping; *ant.* firm.

flora *n.* plants, vegetation, vegetable kingdom, botany, herbage.

floral *adj.* flowery, blossoming, blooming, verdant, botanic, sylvan, herbaceous, dendritic.

florescence *n.* **1.** blooming, flowering, blossoming, flourishing. **2.** prosperity, development, production, outgrowth.

florid *adj.* **1.** overelaborate, ornate, busy, fussy, flamboyant, baroque, rococo, embellished, flowery; grandiloquent, bombastic, fustian; *ant.* plain. **2.** red, ruddy, flushed, rubicund, high-colored, purple; *ant.* pale.

flotsam *n.* debris, wreckage, junk, trash, refuse, jetsam, scum.

flounce *n.* ruffle, frill, furbelow, trimming, fringe, decoration, valance.

flounce *v.* storm, stamp, bounce, toss, fling, spring, throw, jerk, bob, twist.

flounder *v.* thrash, fumble, flail, grope, muddle, bungle, falter, stumble, stagger, plunge, welter.

flourish *v.* **1.** prosper, advance, progress, thrive, succeed, burgeon, blossom, flower, increase, develop, boom, mushroom; *ant.* fail, languish. **2.** wave, display, flaunt, brandish, parade, wield, vaunt.

flout *v.* mock, insult, ridicule, taunt, deride, mock, spurn, jeer at, scorn; *ant.* respect.

flow *n.* flood, cascade, tide, stream, gush, wash, course, current, outpouring, plenty, plethora, deluge.

flow *v.* pour out, spurt, squirt, flood, jet, spout, gush, well, spew, stream, cascade.

flower *n.* blossom, bloom, bud, pompon, efflorescence, spray, floret, shoot, cone.

flower *v.* blossom, bloom, mature, open, unfold, flourish, burgeon, effloresce.

flowery *adj.* floral, fancy, ornate, figurative,

rococo, baroque; overelaborate, affected, overwrought, high-flown; *ant.* plain.

flowing *adj.* surging, streaming, cascading, teeming, prolific, gushing, brimming, abounding, continuous, uninterrupted, fluent; *ant.* hesitant, interrupted.

fluctuate *v.* hesitate, vacillate, waver, sway, change, alternate, seesaw, shift, vary, pendulate.

fluent *adj.* articulate, eloquent, glib, smooth-talking, well-versed, voluble, mellifluous.

fluffy *adj.* fleecy, downy, feathery, soft, woolly, shaggy, fuzzy, nappy.

fluid *adj.* **1.** flowing, liquid, melted, molten, runny, watery; *ant.* solid. **2.** adaptable, changeable, flexible, mutable, unstable. **3.** (as in movement) graceful, feline, smooth, sinuous, nimble.

fluid *n.* liquid, vapor, solution.

fluke *n.* windfall, accident, coincidence, freak, lucky break, serendipity, chance, break, blessing, fortuity, quirk, stroke.

fluky *adj.* lucky, fortunate, fortuitous, accidental, coincidental, freakish, chance, serendipitous.

flummoxed *adj.* confused, bewildered, befuddled, puzzled, perplexed, mystified, confounded, baffled, nonplussed, at a loss, stumped, stymied.

flunk *v.* fail, miss, have to repeat.

flunky *n.* slave, underling, manservant, minion, menial, drudge; hanger-on, yes man, cringer, toady, bootlicker, brown-noser (*slang*).

flurry *n.* disturbance, fuss, agitation, tumult, stir, to-do, upset, furor, commotion, ado, hubbub.

flush *v.* **1.** redden, blush, color; *ant.* pale. **2.** cleanse, wash, rinse, hose, drench, douche, expel, purge, evacuate, empty, eject. **3.** uncover, discover, drive *or* force out.

flush *adj.* abundant, overflowing, lavish, prosperous, rich, wealthy, moneyed, well-off, affluent, well-to-do, prodigal.

fluster *n.* commotion, turmoil, agitation, state, ruffle, discomposure, dither, flurry, tizzy, flap; *ant.* calm.

fluster *v.* upset, unsettle, unnerve, disconcert, discombobulate, rattle, confuse, hassle, agitate, excite, embarrass; *ant.* calm.

fluted *adj.* corrugated, grooved, furrowed, ribbed, channeled, rutted, ridged.

flutter *v.* beat, vibrate, flicker, flap, flit, tremble, quiver, agitate, ruffle, fluctuate, ripple, palpitate.

flux *n.* fluctuation, change, alteration, motion, movement, transition, mutability, fluidity; instability, chaos, unrest; *ant.* stability.

fly *v.* **1.** soar, wing, float, glide, hover, sail, flit, flutter, take wing. **2.** speed, rush, sprint, tear, bolt, dart, scoot, take to one's heels, vamoose (*slang*), hightail it (*slang*), clear out. **3.** escape, retreat, abscond, get away, withdraw, disappear, run for it. **4.** pilot, navigate, aviate, jet, maneuver.

fly at attack, assault, assail, have at, fall upon, light into, lay into (*slang*).

fly-by-night *adj.* unreliable, undependable, disreputable, shady, untrustworthy; impermanent, short-lived, ephemeral, brief; *ant.* reliable; permanent.

flyer *n.* pilot, aviator, navigator.

flying *adj.* **1.** fast, speedy, rapid, rushed, fleeting, hurried. **2.** airborne, winged, soaring, streaming.

foam *n.* froth, bubbles, head, lather, frothiness, suds, effervescence, spume.

focus *n.* crux, center, core, nucleus, hub, heart, axis, focal point, center of attraction, linchpin, target, pivot.

in focus clear, distinct, obvious, sharply defined.

out of focus indistinct, unclear, blurry, obscure.

focus *v.* concentrate, zero *or* home in, converge, spotlight, aim, center, direct, rivet, fix.

fodder *n.* feed, food, forage, foodstuff, rations, provender, fuel, nourishment.

foe *n.* enemy, adversary, opponent, rival, antagonist, competitor; *ant.* friend.

fog *n.* **1.** mist, haze, murk, cloud, nebula, film, steam, wisp, effluvium, smoke, smog. **2.** confusion, perplexity, uncertainty, bewilderment, trance, stupor, daze, muddle.

foggy *adj.* **1.** hazy, murky, shadowy, cloudy, blurry, misty, gray, dim, vaporous; *ant.* clear. **2.** muddled, obscure, indistinct, vague.

fogy *n.* stick-in-the-mud, fuddy-duddy, relic, fossil, antique, anachronism.

foible *n.* **1.** idiosyncrasy, oddity, eccentricity, peculiarity, crotchet, quirk, quiddity. **2.** weakness, defect, failing, shortcoming, fault, limitation, infirmity.

foil *v.* thwart, obstruct, outsmart, outwit, frustrate, baffle, elude, counter, stop, stump, check, circumvent; *ant.* abet.

foist *v.* impose, unload, pass *or* palm off, thrust, insinuate, insert, interpolate, force.

fold *n.* crease, bend, wrinkle, crimp, corrugation, furrow, pleat, overlap, layer, ply.

fold *v.* **1.** crease, crimp, wrinkle, ruffle, corrugate, pucker, gather, double over, overlap. **2.** fail, become insolvent, go bankrupt, close, shut down, collapse, go bust.

folder *n.* binder, folio, portfolio, file, holder, envelope.

foliage *n.* greenery, leafage, foliature, verdure.

folk *n.* people, society, tribe, clan, race.

folklore *n.* legends, lore, myths, mythology, superstitions, folk tales, tradition, fables.

folks *n.* family, relatives, relations, kin, kinsmen, kinfolk.

follow *v.* **1.** come next, come after, ensue, succeed. **2.** conform, imitate, copy, take after, walk in the footsteps of, mirror, reflect, follow the example of, mimic, follow suit, emulate. **3.** pursue, chase, seek, track, hunt, dog, hound, shadow, stalk, tail, trail. **4.** understand, comprehend, see, catch on, fathom, grasp, get, get the picture. **5.** (to occur as a consequence) result, spring from, come from, happen, develop, ensue.

follow through see through, complete, conclude, consummate, fulfill, finish, pursue, implement.

follow up continue, investigate, pursue, check out, consolidate, substantiate.

follower *n.* fan, buff, admirer, fancier, aficionado, devotee; adherent, disciple, acolyte, supporter, emulator; *ant.* leader, opponent.

following *n.* fans, followers, audience, entourage, supporters, patronage, circle, public, backing, clientele, constituency.

foil *n.* contrast, complement, counterpart, antithesis.

following *adj.* next, coming, succeeding, subsequent, ensuing, later, successive, consecutive; resulting, consequent.

folly *n.* foolishness, stupidity, idiocy, imbecility, nonsense, senselessness, silliness, irresponsibility, recklessness; *ant.* prudence.

foment *v.* goad, foster, incite, prompt, stimulate, rouse, encourage, excite, instigate, spur, activate, stir up; *ant.* quell.

fomenter *n.* troublemaker, instigator, agitator, rabble-rouser, demagogue, abettor, incendiary, firebrand.

fond *adj.* loving, doting, devoted, affectionate, adoring, warm, tender, amorous, caring, sanguine; *ant.* hostile.

fond of partial to, predisposed toward, enamored of, attached to, addicted to, stuck on, keen on, sweet on.

fondle *v.* caress, stroke, pet, cuddle.

food *n.* edibles, fare, provisions, victuals, comestibles, nourishment, cuisine, foodstuffs, larder, nutrition, *slang:* grub, chow.

fool *n.* idiot, jackass, dolt, imbecile, dupe, ignoramus, dunce, buffoon, stooge, *slang:* sap, schmuck, sucker.

play the fool joke, be silly, show off, clown.

fool *v.* **1.** joke, kid, put one over on, con, dupe, delude, deceive, swindle, hoodwink, mislead, string along. **2.** play, toy, cavort, frolic, be silly, clown, mess, lark, mess *or* horse around (*slang*).

foolery *n.* horseplay, childishness, mischief, carryings-on, practical jokes, monkey business, high jinks, tomfoolery, clowning, buffoonery, antics, shenanigans.

foolhardy *adj.* reckless, rash, irresponsible, ill-considered, impetuous, precipitate, brash, headstrong; *ant.* cautious, prudent.

fooling *n.* nonsense, joking, tricks, buffoonery, trifling, jesting, clownishness, kidding, pretense, farce.

foolish *adj.* idiotic, imbecilic, senseless, stupid, moronic, ludicrous, absurd, mad, illconsidered, short-sighted, simple-minded, witless; *ant.* wise.

foolproof *adj.* safe, fail-safe, infallible, guaranteed, sure-fire, certain; *ant.* unreliable.

foot *n.* **1.** pedal extremity, pad, hoof, *slang:*

tootsie, dog. **2.** foundation, base, bottom. **3.** (unit used in verse) measure, accent, stress, interval.

footing *n.* relationship, relations, state, standing, base, foundation, position, terms, ground, establishment, rank, status.

footprint *n.* track, trail, trace, vestige.

fop *n.* dandy, fashion plate, dasher, silk stocking, blade, man about town, coxcomb.

foppish *adj.* overdressed, preening, dandified.

forage *v.* search, seek, ransack, explore, scavenge, scour, raid, plunder, rummage, hunt, scrounge.

foray *n.* raid, invasion, offensive, excursion, descent, inroad, sally, swoop, depredation.

forbear *v.* abstain, refrain, keep from, restrain, withhold, avoid, stop, desist, cease.

forbearance *n.* moderation, abstinence, temperance, self-control, restraint; tolerance, endurance, patience.

forbid *v.* ban, rule out, block, veto, prevent, hinder, exclude, refuse, deny, outlaw, preclude, proscribe; *ant.* allow.

forbidding *adj.* ominous, threatening, daunting, menacing, frightening, inhospitable, hostile, unfriendly, off-putting; *ant.* approachable, congenial.

force *n.* **1.** strength, power, might, energy, vitality, potency. **2.** determination, persistence, willpower, drive, competence, energy, ability, capability, dominance, authority. **3.** army, battalion, corps, regiment, legion, troop, detail, division, patrol, unit.

in force in full strength, totally, all together.

force *v.* **1.** compel, coerce, press, drive, make, impel, obligate, necessitate, require, enforce, demand, order. **2.** break open, pry, crack, prize, break into, undo, jimmy.

forced *adj.* unnatural, affected, contrived, insincere, false, feigned, artificial; strained, labored; mandatory, compulsory, involuntary; *ant.* spontaneous.

forceful *adj.* strong, powerful, domineering, vigorous, dynamic, potent, effective, persuasive, convincing; *ant.* feeble, puny.

forcible *adj.* strong, powerful, brutal, compelling, weighty, potent, mighty, aggressive; *ant.* voluntary.

forcibly *adv.* against one's will, under duress, under compulsion, compulsorily; violently, vehemently.

forebear *n.* ancestor, predecessor, forerunner, progenitor, forefather, antecedent; *ant.* descendant.

forebode *v.* predict, foreshadow, foretell, warn, forewarn, presage, portend, import, indicate, promise.

foreboding *adj.* foreshadowing, premonition, prediction, sign, warning, fear, dread, omen, misgiving, augury, chill.

forecast *n.* prediction, prognostication, augury, prophecy, projection, outlook, foresight, prognosis, conjecture, guess.

forecast *v.* predict, foretell, prophesy, prognosticate, estimate, divine, conjecture, foresee, expect, augur.

foreclose *v.* bar, exclude, shut out, deprive.

forefather *n.* ancestor, predecessor, forerunner, forebear, procreator, progenitor, primogenitor, antecedent, antecessor; *ant.* descendant.

forefront *n.* front line, prominence, foreground, center, lead, vanguard, spearhead, avant-garde, firing line; *ant.* rear.

foregoing *adj.* preceding, earlier, prior, former, previous, aforementioned, above, antecedent.

foregone *adj.* predetermined, inevitable, predictable, foreseen, anticipated, open-and-shut, cut-and-dried.

foreground *n.* forefront, center, limelight, prominence; *ant.* background.

forehead *n.* brow, temples, visage, countenance, front.

foreign *adj.* **1.** exotic, strange, unaccustomed, different, unknown, unfamiliar; remote, faraway, distant, far-off; *ant.* local, indigenous. **2.** imported, alien, immigrant, adopted; *ant.* native, homemade.

foreigner *n.* immigrant, alien, outlander, newcomer; *ant.* native.

foreknowledge *n.* premonition, foresight, second sight, clairvoyance, prescience, precognition, forewarning.

foreman *n.* supervisor, overseer, manager, superintendent, taskmaker, head, boss, straw boss, slavedriver.

foremost *adj.* first, leading, supreme, cardinal, paramount, highest, uppermost, chief; primary, central, main.

forensic *adj.* **1.** judicial, legal, juristic. **2.** argumentative, controversial, debatable, rhetorical.

forerunner *n.* **1.** ancestor, forebear, antecedent, predecessor; prototype, precursor. **2.** herald, harbinger, envoy.

foresee *v.* envisage, anticipate, expect, predict, forecast, divine, augur, prophesy, foretell.

foreshadow *v.* portend, predict, presage, signal, bode, forebode, promise, omen, augur.

foresight *n.* vision, perspicacity, prescience, preparedness, caution, farsightedness, readiness; *ant.* improvidence.

forest *n.* woods, woodland, timberland, backwoods, stand of trees, grove, copse.

forestall *v.* hinder, thwart, prevent, preclude, intercept, ward or head off, obstruct, frustrate, circumvent, avert, balk; *ant.* encourage, facilitate.

foretell *v.* predict, prognosticate, prophesy, forecast, augur, soothsay, presage, forebode, foreshadow, portend, forewarn.

forethought *n.* precaution, prudence, preparation, foresight, farsightedness, circumspection, providence.

forever *adv.* eternally, always, endlessly, permanently, perpetually; everlastingly, constantly, unremittingly, interminably, persistently.

forewarn *v.* alert, caution, advise, dissuade, admonish, apprise, tip off.

foreword *n.* introduction, preamble, preface, prologue, preliminary; *ant.* epilogue, postscript.

forfeit *v.* lose, give up, relinquish, forgo, renounce, abandon, surrender, sacrifice.

forfeiture *n.* loss, sacrifice, surrender, relinquishment, abandonment, confiscation, forgoing.

forge *v.* **1.** make, construct, create, devise, shape, hammer out, fashion, form, mold. **2.** progress, proceed, advance, gain ground, make headway, make great strides, press or push on.

forger *n.* counterfeiter, falsifier, faker, coiner, framer, fabricator, contriver.

forgery *n.* counterfeit, fraud, imitation, sham, fake, phony, falsification, fraudulence, coining; *ant.* original.

forget *v.* ignore, lose sight of, overlook, dismiss, neglect; *ant.* remember.

forget about omit, let slip one's memory, miss, neglect.

forget oneself 1. offend, trespass, misbehave. **2.** daydream, lose oneself, be distracted.

forgetful *adj.* **1.** absent-minded, preoccupied, oblivious, dreamy, distracted, amnesiac. **2.** careless, inattentive, neglectful, lax, heedless; *ant.* mindful.

forgivable *adj.* excusable, pardonable, venial; innocent.

forgive *v.* excuse, pardon, absolve, exonerate, condone, acquit, overlook, remit, let off the hook; *ant.* hold to account.

forgiveness *n.* pardon, mercy, absolution, amnesty, acquittal, exoneration, remission, condonation, shrift, exculpation; *ant.* blame, censure.

forgiving *adj.* sparing, tolerant, humane, compassionate, indulgent, lenient, mild, merciful, softhearted, clement, forbearing, magnanimous; *ant.* censorious.

forgo *v.* give up, do without, surrender, relinquish, sacrifice, forfeit, yield, abjure, abstain from, eschew, waive; *ant.* claim, insist on.

forgotten *adj.* neglected, overlooked, ignored, omitted, disregarded, blotted out, lost, bygone, past, out of mind; *ant.* remembered.

fork *n.* **1.** trident, prong, spear, scepter. **2.** junction, intersection, crossroad, divergence, separation, split, confluence, branch, division.

forked *adj.* split, divided, branched, pronged.

forlorn *adj.* destitute, unhappy, forgotten, desolate, abandoned, miserable, wretched, abject, bereft, woebegone, disconsolate; *ant.* hopeful.

form *n.* **1.** shape, figure, arrangement, outline, configuration, formation, structure, construction, framework. **2.** method, plan, way, manner, mode, custom, format, style, procedure. **3.** chart, card, application, copy.

form *v.* **1.** mold, pattern, model, arrange, make, fashion, construct, devise, design, contrive, invent, erect. **2.** teach, nurture, instruct, educate, rear, bring up, discipline, breed, school, cultivate. **3.** constitute, compose, make up, figure in, serve as, act as.

formal *adj.* **1.** conventional, traditional, orthodox, approved, received, correct; impersonal, stiff, rigid, polite, prim, perfunctory. **2.** official, confirmed, directed, bureaucratic, legal. **3.** dress, full-dress, black tie.

formality *n.* **1.** propriety, decorum, etiquette, protocol, correctness, politeness. **2.** custom, ritual, rite, ceremony, convention.

format *n.* layout, structure, shape, plan, form, arrangement, style, look, pattern, construction, makeup.

formation *n.* **1.** development, generation, evolution, establishment, organization, genesis, compilation, emergence, crystallization. **2.** configuration, arrangement, pattern, shaping, format, grouping, structure, design.

formative *adj.* **1.** developmental, impressionable, malleable, pliant, moldable, determining. **2.** influential, guiding, dominant, controlling.

former *adj.* erstwhile, preceding, past, above, earlier, prior, old, late, previous, aforementioned, antecedent, pristine; *ant.* current, present, future, prospective, subsequent.

formerly *adv.* previously, at one time, before, hitherto, once, earlier, already, heretofore, lately; *ant.* currently, later, now, presently, subsequently.

formidable *adj.* awesome, challenging, intimidating, terrible, daunting, difficult, arduous; great, powerful; *ant.* weak, unimposing.

formless *adj.* shapeless, vague, indefinite, inchoate, indeterminate, nebulous, amorphous, chaotic; *ant.* definite, orderly.

formula *n.* **1.** specifications, direction, description, method, recipe, blueprint. **2.** custom, principal, ritual, code, credo, way, precept, method, modus operandi, rubric, rule of thumb.

formulate *v.* invent, originate, create, develop, plan, work out, devise, detail, specify, particularize, systematize.

fornication *n.* sexual intercourse, coitus, copulation; promiscuity, carnality, licentiousness.

forsake *v.* **1.** abandon, reject, forswear, cast off, renounce, turn one's back on. **2.** surrender, relinquish, give up, quit.

forsaken *adj.* outcast, rejected, abandoned, desolate, forlorn, disowned, jilted, shunned, deserted, discarded, isolated.

179

forswear *v.* **1.** renounce, repudiate, disown, forsake, forgo, abandon. **2.** deny, repudiate, retract, recant, abjure; lie, perjure oneself.

fort *n.* fortress, stronghold, camp, citadel, garrison, tower, fortification.

forte *n.* strength, strong point, gift, bent, specialty, aptitude, talent, skill, metier; *ant.* inadequacy.

forth *adv.* first, out, into, ahead.

forthcoming *adj.* **1.** impending, imminent, approaching, at hand, expected, prospective, future, projected. **2.** sociable, conversational, communicative, chatty, open, accessible, frank, talkative, loquacious, unreserved, informative; *ant.* distant, reserved.

forthright *adj.* candid, straightforward, sincere, blunt, frank, bold, direct, open, plain-spoken, outspoken; *ant.* reticent, reserved.

forthrightly *adv.* frankly, truthfully, honestly, candidly, unreservedly, bluntly, plainly, straight from the shoulder.

forthwith *adv.* immediately, instantly, at once, posthaste, right away, without delay, straightaway, directly, tout de suite, pronto (*slang*).

fortification *n.* fort, fortress, citadel, stockade, entrenchment, bastion, defense, bulwark, stronghold, buttressing, rampart.

fortify *v.* strengthen, reinforce, brace, protect, steel, secure, entrench, buttress, boost, invigorate, hearten; *ant.* weaken.

fortitude *n.* strength, courage, bravery, guts, valor, grit, staying power, determination, dauntlessness, endurance; *ant.* cowardice, weakness.

fortress *n.* fortification, citadel, stronghold, bastion.

fortuitous *adj.* **1.** lucky, fortunate, adventitious, felicitous, serendipitous, providential; *ant.* unfortunate, unhappy. **2.** chance, arbitrary, accidental, coincidental, random, unexpected, unplanned, unforeseen; *ant.* intentional, planned.

fortunate *adj.* lucky, opportune, timely, auspicious, favorable, fortuitous, providential, advantageous.

fortune *n.* **1.** chance, fate, happenstance, providence, destiny, luck, circumstance, lot. **2.** wealth, riches, affluence, prosperity, income, assets, means, treasure.

fortuneteller *n.* seer, crystal gazer, soothsayer, augur, oracle, prophet, tea-leaf reader, mind-reader, clairvoyant.

fortunetelling *n.* prediction, prognostication, prophecy, divination, second sight, augury, chiromancy, crystal-gazing, palmistry.

forward *adj.* **1.** first, advance, leading, ahead, foremost; progressive, advanced, enterprising; *ant.* backward, retreating, regressive. **2.** bold, presumptuous, impertinent, rude, cheeky, audacious, impudent, brazen, pushy, brash, fresh (*slang*).

forward *adv.* ahead, forth, onward, outward, to the fore; *ant.* backward.

forward *v.* **1.** facilitate, aid, assist, expedite, further, help, foster, hasten, advance, back, favor, promote; *ant.* impede, obstruct. **2.** send, post, ship, dispatch, transmit, freight, route.

forward-looking *adj.* progressive, liberal, innovative, enterprising, avant-garde, farsighted, enlightened; *ant.* conservative, retrograde.

forwarded *adj.* shipped, expressed, dispatched, delivered.

foster *v.* **1.** raise, rear, bring up, care for, nurture, nurse, feed, nourish. **2.** promote, support, sustain, cultivate; *ant.* neglect, discourage.

fossilized *adj.* **1.** archaic, prehistoric, extinct, stony, petrified, antediluvian. **2.** old-fashioned, out-of-date, inflexible, outmoded, obsolete, passé, antiquated, anachronistic; *ant.* up-to-date.

foul *adj.* **1.** soiled, dirty, filthy, fetid, contaminated, nasty, putrid, polluted, tainted; *ant.* clean, pure. **2.** lewd, obscene, offensive, vulgar.

foul *v.* **1.** dirty, contaminate, pollute, taint, sully, defile; *ant.* clean. **2.** clog, choke, snarl, entangle, jam.

foul-mouthed *adj.* profane, obscene, coarse, offensive, blasphemous, abusive.

foul play *n.* treachery, fraud, duplicity, deception, roguery, villainy, double-dealing, funny business, crime, perfidy; *ant.* fair play.

found *v.* start, create, establish, originate, inaugurate, organize, set up, initiate, settle.

foundation *n.* **1.** basis, base, reason, justification. **2.** organization, institution, endowment, institute, society, company, guild, trusteeship, corporation, association, charity.

founder *n.* inventor, organizer, initiator, originator, father, mother, patriarch, matriarch, benefactor, designer, author, architect.

foundling *n.* orphan, outcast, waif, urchin, stray.

fountain *n.* **1.** source, origin, cause, spring, font, fountainhead, inspiration. **2.** spray, jet, stream, spout, geyser, pump, spurt.

foursquare *adj.* **1.** firm, stable, solid, hard, immovable, steady, resolute, strong, unyielding; *ant.* uncertain, wavering. **2.** frank, direct, honest, forthright. **3.** geometrical, quadrangular, rectangular.

foursquare *adv.* resolutely, firmly, frankly, squarely, honestly.

fox *n.* rascal, Volpone, artful dodger, sly one, cunning devil, cheat, con man (*slang*).

foxy *adj.* **1.** crafty, canny, shrewd, cunning, wily, sly, devious, tricky, sharp, vulpine. **2.** (*slang*) sexy, attractive, desirable, appealing.

foyer *n.* entrance hall, lobby, anteroom, antechamber, vestibule, reception area.

fracas *n.* fight, disturbance, quarrel, scuffle, brawl, riot, melee, free-for-all, uproar, row, ruckus, rumpus.

fraction *n.* section, portion, part, division.

fractional *adj.* partial, constituent, sectional, fragmentary, incomplete, divided, segmented, compartmented, parceled, dispersed, piecemeal; *ant.* whole, total, complete.

fractious *adj.* **1.** unruly, rebellious, refractory, recalcitrant; *ant.* placid. **2.** cross, touchy, testy, grouchy, petulant, irritable, peevish, choleric, crabby, crotchety; *ant.* complaisant.

fracture *n.* crack, break, rent, rift, split, breach, opening, gap, fissure, rupture, cleft.

fragile *adj.* breakable, brittle, delicate, dainty, fine, flimsy, frail, weak, feeble; *ant.* durable, tough, robust.

fragment *n.* part, shred, particle, chip, fraction, bit, piece, portion, remnant, shard.

fragmentary *adj.* sketchy, incomplete, disjointed, incoherent, piecemeal, broken, partial, separate; *ant.* complete.

fragrance *n.* **1.** odor, scent, smell, aroma, bouquet, redolence, balminess. **2.** balm, perfume, cologne.

fragrant *adj.* aromatic, perfumed, sweet-smelling, redolent, balmy, odorous, odoriferous; *ant.* smelly, unscented.

frail *adj.* feeble, fragile, delicate, infirm, weak, vulnerable, brittle, breakable, unsound, flimsy; *ant.* firm, robust, strong, tough.

frailty *n.* weakness, shortcoming, fault, defect, failing, vice, foible, peccadillo, deficiency, susceptibility, infirmity; *ant.* strength.

frame *n.* **1.** scaffold, truss, scaffolding, casing, support, stage, groundwork, organization, architecture, skeleton, anatomy. **2.** border, fringe, hem, valance, flounce, trim, wreath, outline, mounting, molding, frieze.

frame *v.* **1.** surround, border, enclose, encase; mount, back, mat. **2.** (give shape to) construct, erect, build, make, form, forge, fashion, assemble, mold, fabricate, model, shape. **3.** draft, write, devise, sketch, plan, concoct, map out, formulate, hatch, cook *or* draw up. **4.** conspire against, leave holding the bag, victimize, trap; double-cross, set up, *slang:* plant, fix.

framed *adj.* bordered, enclosed, mounted, encircled, fringed, enveloped, outlined, confined, wreathed, wrapped, girdled, compassed.

frame of mind outlook, disposition, temper, humor, morale, attitude, spirit, mood, state, vein.

frame-up *n.* trap, fabrication, trumped-up charge, fix (*slang*).

framework *n.* skeleton, structure, core, shell, foundation, plan, schema, bare bones, groundwork, fabric.

franchise *n.* immunity, freedom, liberty, exemption, suffrage, charter, concession, prerogative, right, privilege.

frank *adj.* forthright, straightforward, honest, direct, candid, downright, plain-spoken, blunt, truthful; *ant.* evasive, insincere.

frantic *adj.* distraught, overwrought, frenzied, fraught, desperate, frenetic, hectic, berserk, furious; *ant.* calm.

fraternal *adj.* friendly, intimate, congenial, brotherly.

fraternity *n.* brotherhood, fellowship, kinship, camaraderie, association, guild, union, society, league, clan, club.

fraternize *v.* socialize, mingle, associate, consort, mix, hobnob, affiliate; *ant.* ignore, shun.

fraud *n.* **1.** deception, deceit, trickery, guile, artifice, duplicity, double-dealing, swindling, chicanery, treachery. **2.** fake, forgery, sham, hoax. **3.** impostor, cheat, pretender, charlatan, quack, counterfeiter, mountebank, swindler, malingerer, phony.

fraudulent *adj.* false, dishonest, deceptive, deceitful, duplicitous, crooked; spurious, phony, sham, specious, counterfeit, bogus; *ant.* genuine, calm.

fray *n.* fight, battle, brawl, riot, scuffle, row, ruckus, combat, quarrel, melee, free-for-all, rumble.

frayed *adj.* worn, tattered, threadbare, ragged; on edge, frazzled.

frazzle *n.* exhaustion, enervation, prostration, collapse, lassitude.

freak *n.* abnormality, monstrosity, monster, rarity, anomaly, malformation, mutation, oddity, aberration, curiosity, hybrid, changeling.

freakish *adj.* malformed, monstrous, weird, odd, outlandish, fantastic, aberrant, strange, anomalous, unusual, unconventional, outré, abnormal, preternatural; *ant.* ordinary.

freckle *n.* pigmentation, blemish, blotch, macula, nevus, lentigo.

free *adj.* **1.** sovereign, independent, autonomous, liberated, self-governing, democratic, self-ruling; *ant.* restricted, enslaved, subject. **2.** unimpeded, unobstructed, unhampered, loose, unentangled, clear, disengaged, extricated; *ant.* fixed, fastened, rooted. **3.** gratuitous, gratis, for nothing, without charge, complimentary, on the house; *ant.* paid for, charged for.

with a free hand liberally, generously, abundantly.

free *v.* liberate, release, rescue, extricate, disengage, let loose; *ant.* seize, capture, incarcerate.

freedom *n.* **1.** liberty, independence, sovereignty, autonomy, democracy, self-government, franchise. **2.** prerogative, option, license, discretion, latitude, carte blanche, right, privilege, free hand.

182

free-for-all *n.* fight, riot, battle, knock-down, drag-out fight.

freehand *adj.* drawn, sketched, unrestrained.

freelance *adj.* self-employed, unattached, independent.

freely *adv.* liberally, lavishly, abundantly, openhandedly, generously, willingly, of one's own accord; *ant.* reluctantly.

free-spoken *adj.* frank, candid, direct, open, blunt, outspoken.

freethinker *n.* atheist, agnostic, skeptic, humanist, rationalist, nihilist, dissenter, radical; *ant.* believer, sectarian.

freeway *n.* superhighway, turnpike, expressway, thruway, toll road.

free will *n.* volition, choice, free choice, discretion, willingness.

freeze *v.* **1.** harden, ice over, congeal, solidify. **2.** (to cause to suffer from extreme cold) chill, nip, bite, cool, pierce.

freezing *adj.* raw, icy, cold, biting, bitter, arctic, wintry, numbing, glacial, polar, frosty, penetrating; *ant.* hot, warm.

freight *n.* **1.** burden, load, contents, weight, bulk, ballast, cargo, shipping, consignment, goods, wares. **2.** carrying *or* handling charges, shipping *or* transportation costs, rates, fee, bill.

frenetic *adj.* frantic, hyperactive, overwrought, frenzied, distraught, wild, unbalanced, demented, maniacal, excited, beside oneself, obsessive; *ant.* calm, placid.

frenzied *adj.* hysterical, feverish, frantic, rabid, excited, agitated, wild, frenetic, furious, distraught, maniacal; *ant.* calm, placid.

frenzy *n.* turmoil, hysteria, delirium, rage, outburst, spasm, mania, fit, seizure, passion, fury; *ant.* calm.

frequency *n.* **1.** regularity, recurrence, prevalence, repetition, reiteration. **2.** wavelength, beat, pulse, cycle, pulsation, scillation, rhythm, meter, rotation, rate.

frequent *adj.* often, usual, commonplace, recurring, familiar, habitual, everyday, repeated, reiterated, regular, customary, numerous.

frequent *v.* visit, patronize, attend, haunt, hang out at.

fresh *adj.* **1.** (said of food) green, crisp, raw, new; recent, current, late, garden-fresh, farm-fresh; *ant.* old, stale, musty. **2.** original, unusual, novel, unconventional, innovative, radical, different, inventive; *ant.* trite, used, imitative, tired. **3.** unspoiled, green, well-preserved, virgin, new; *ant.* despoiled, exhausted. **4.** (*slang*) impudent, rude, insolent, disrespectful, impertinent, presumptuous, flip (*slang*); *ant.* polite.

freshen *v.* **1.** clean, cleanse, purify, ventilate, air, spruce up. **2.** revive, resuscitate, invigorate, revitalize, enliven, restore.

freshman *n.* underclassman, lowerclassman, beginner, first-year student, novice, recruit, tenderfoot, greenhorn, apprentice.

fret *v.* worry, agonize, brood, anguish.

fretful *adj.* touchy, testy, edgy, uneasy, irritable, agitated, upset, short-tempered, fractious, petulant.

friar *n.* monk, brother, mendicant, abbot, father, padre, abbé, prior, pilgrim, penitent, palmer.

friction *n.* **1.** rubbing, chafing, irritation, grating, rasping, scraping. **2.** conflict, disharmony, rivalry, opposition, antagonism, dissagreement, discord, bad blood, dissension, resentment, hostility.

friend *n.* pal, companion, buddy, crony, confidant, ally, partner, associate, benefactor, supporter; *ant.* foe, enemy.

friendless *adj.* shunned, forsaken, alone, alienated, deserted, ostracized, solitary, lonesome, isolated.

friendly *adj.* sociable, amiable, affable, convivial, approachable, neighborly, helpful, welcoming, genial, receptive, benevolent, chummy; *ant.* cold.

friendship *n.* fellowship, amity, alliance, harmony, affinity, rapport, affection, closeness, love, intimacy; *ant.* enmity.

fright *n.* **1.** alarm, panic, terror, shock, dread, horror, fear, apprehension, trepidation, scare. **2.** ugliness, monstrosity, eyesore, sight.

frighten *v.* scare, terrify, terrorize, shock, petrify, alarm, startle, spook; intimidate, unnerve, daunt; *ant.* calm.

frightful *adj.* horrid, terrible, terrifying, horren-dous, dreadful, ghastly, harrowing, horrible, hideous, macabre.

frigid *adj.* **1.** cold, freezing, frozen, icy, frosty, arctic, glacial; *ant.* warm. **2.** unresponsive, undersexed, passionless, cold, cool; aloof, standoffish, forbidding, formal, stiff; *ant.* loving, feeling.

frill *n.* ruffle, flounce, trimming, gathering, tuck, valance.

frills *n.* embellishment, ornamentation, fanciness, finery, froth; ostentation, affectations, superfluities, frippery.

frilly *adj.* ruffled, fancy, lacy, ornate, flouncy, frothy; *ant.* plain, unadorned.

fringe *n.* **1.** flounce, hem, trimming, rickrack, edging, lace, tatting, border, binding, bias, pinking. **2.** border, outside, edge, limits, outskirts, margin, perimeter, periphery.

frippery *n.* trinkets, trifles, finery, frilliness, gaudiness, foppery, frills, frothery; *ant.* plainness.

frisk *v.* **1.** inspect, search, shake down, check. **2.** caper, dance, gambol, cavort, frolic, jump, hop, prance, skip, romp, play, rollick.

frisky *adj.* playful, lively, high-spirited, sportive, kittenish, romping, rollicking, bouncy, frolicsome, coltish, skittish; *ant.* quiet.

fritter *n.* pancake, hotcake, fried *or* batter cake.

fritter *v.* waste, squander, idle, misspend, blow.

frivolity *n.* nonsense, superficiality, triviality, flippancy, childishness, folly; jest, levity, lightheartedness, whimsy, silliness, giddiness; *ant.* seriousness.

frivolous *adj.* foolish, giddy, childish, flighty, juvenile, silly, flippant, shallow, empty-headed, ill-considered, light-headed; *ant.* serious, solemn.

frizzy *adj.* wiry, crimped, curly, corrugated; *ant.* straight.

frock *n.* clothes, dress, gown, habit, apron.

frog *n.* **1.** amphibian, batrachian; tadpole, polliwog. **2.** hoarseness, catch, obstruction.

frolic *n.* fun, romp, spree, gambol, amusement, game, escapade, merriment, lark, high jinx, antic, revel.

frolic *v.* play, romp, make merry, cavort, caper, gambol, frisk, sport, rollick, lark.

front *n.* **1.** foreground, exterior, frontage, anterior, façade, face, head, breast, obverse, bow;

front *ant.* posterior, back, rear. 2. front line, no man's land, advance position *or* guard, line of battle, vanguard, outpost. 3. demeanor, expression, face, countenance, bearing, mien, carriage, port, aspect, presence, figure, exterior. 4. false front, mask, disguise, coverup, window dressing; façade, exterior, facing, display.

in front of before, preceding, leading, ahead of.

front *v.* face, border, overlook.

front *adj.* leading, head, first, foremost, anterior; *ant.* back, last, least, posterior.

frontier *n.* 1. edge, boundary, verge, limit, borderline, confines, perimeter. 2. backwoods, country, outskirts, hinterland, borderland.

frost *n.* ice, hoar, rime.

frosty *adj.* 1. cold, chilly, wintry, icy, frigid, frozen, ice-capped, icicled, rimy, hoar; *ant.* warm. 2. unfriendly, unwelcoming, discouraging, standoffish, off-putting, stiff; *ant.* warm.

froth *n.* foam, bubbles, suds, lather, effervescence, spume, head.

frothy *adj.* 1. bubbly, foaming, soapy, sudsy, fizzy, foamy, spumescent, having a head; *ant.* flat. 2. trivial, insubstantial, unsubstantial, trite, frivolous, light, empty, slight.

frown *n.* scowl, grimace, glower, dirty look.

frown *v.* scowl, glare, grimace, glower, pout, sulk; *ant.* smile, laugh, grin.

frown on disapprove of, object to, take a dim view of, discourage, dislike, look askance at, deprecate.

frowzy *adj.* dirty, slovenly, disorderly, unkempt, unwashed, slatternly, disheveled, messy, sloppy; *ant.* well-groomed, tidy.

frozen *adj.* 1. icy, ice-cold, ice-covered, numb, frigid, gelid, chilled, arctic, frosted; *ant.* warm. 2. solidified, petrified, rooted, stopped, stock-still, suspended.

frugal *adj.* thrifty, economical, sparing, abstemious, Spartan, prudent, provident, meager, parsimonious, niggardly, penny-wise; *ant.* generous, wasteful.

fruit *n.* 1. berry, vegetable, grain, nut, root, tuber; crop, harvest, produce, product, yield. 2. result, outcome, consequences, aftermath, effect, profits, pay, benefit, return, yield, harvest.

fruitful *adj.* 1. fertile, prolific, productive, fecund, abundant, copious, spawning, teeming, profuse, flush, plenteous, fructuous; *ant.* barren. 2. profitable, productive, conducive, useful, worthwhile, advantageous, beneficial, effective, rewarding.

fruition *n.* completion, success, maturation, realization, fulfillment, accomplishment, attainment, materialization, maturity, actualization, consummation, ripeness; *ant.* failure.

fruitless *adj.* futile, vain, useless, pointless, ineffectual, unproductive, hopeless, unavailing, barren, abortive, idle, profitless; *ant.* successful.

frump *n.* slob, slattern, dowd, drab woman, slovenly person, old bag (*slang*).

frustrate *v.* 1. disappoint, discourage, dishearten, let down; *ant.* encourage. 2. (prevent from happening) impede, stall, circumvent, neutralize, nullify, countermine, inhibit, block, check, forestall, baffle, stymie; *ant.* fulfill, abet, further, promote. 3. (stop from advancing) defeat, foil, turn back; *ant.* push ahead, stimulate.

fry *v.* cook, sauté, sear, singe, brown, grill, fricassee, sizzle.

frying pan *n.* skillet, griddle.

fuddled *adj.* confused, stupefied, muddled, befuddled, groggy, hazy, woozy; *ant.* clear.

fuddy-duddy *n.* conservative, carper, fossil, museum piece, old fogy, stick-in-the-mud, stuffed shirt (*slang*).

fudge *v.* falsify, misrepresent, hedge, evade, fake, avoid, dodge, stall, equivocate.

fuel *n.* 1. food, fodder, means, nourishment. 2. encouragement, incitement, provocation.

fuel *v.* fire, feed, sustain, inflame, charge, nourish, incite, fan, encourage, stoke up; *ant.* discourage.

fugitive *n.* refugee, runaway, deserter, escapee, truant, outlaw, outcast.

fugitive *adj.* elusive, transitory, flitting, fleeting, momentary, evanescent; *ant.* fixed.

fulfill *v.* finish, complete, conclude, realize, execute, consummate, implement, satisfy, achieve, accomplish, carry out, effect; *ant.* fail.

fulfillment *n.* completion, end, achievement, consummation, realization, attainment, crowning, success, accomplishment, perfection; *ant.* failure, frustration.

full *adj.* **1.** sated, replete, abundant, satisfied, saturated, glutted, cloyed, stuffed to the gills, jam-packed; *ant.* empty, void. **2.** occupied, assigned, reserved, taken, engaged, in use; *ant.* available, vacant. **3.** (said of clothes) baggy, flowing, loose, flapping; *ant.* tight. **4.** mature, grown, entire, complete; *ant.* partial. **5.** deep, resonant, rounded, throaty, loud.

in full for the entire amount *or* value, thoroughly, completely.

full blast 1. full throttle, wide open, to the hilt, fast. **2.** loudly, noisily, deafeningly.

full-grown *adj.* adult, of age, mature, prime, grown-up, developed, nubile, ripe.

full-scale *adj.* all-out, wide-ranging, thorough, intensive, comprehensive, extensive, exhaustive, all-encompassing, in-depth, sweeping; *ant.* partial.

fully *adv.* completely, totally, utterly, entirely, altogether, thoroughly, absolutely, wholly, positively, without reserve; *ant.* partly, partially.

fulminate *v.* rage, criticize, denounce, fume, protest, rail, thunder, fume, inveigh, vituperate, curse; *ant.* praise.

fulsome *adj.* excessive, effusive, offensive, smarmy, fawning, unctuous, sycophantic.

fumble *n.* error, mistake, blunder, faux pas, mixup, dropped ball.

fumble *v.* **1.** grope, paw, flounder. **2.** botch, bungle, bumble.

fume *v.* rage, boil, seethe, chafe, storm, rave, rant, smoke.

fumes *n.* exhaust, pollution, smoke, smog, haze, gas, vapor, effluvium, reek, stench.

fumigate *v.* cleanse, sanitize, deodorize, disinfect, sterilize, purify.

fun *n.* amusement, mirth, pleasure, merriment, merrymaking; play, playfulness, jesting; buffoonery, tomfoolery; high jinks, sport; *ant.* tedium.

for fun for no reason, for kicks, for laughs, for thrills.

in fun for amusement, not seriously, playfully.

make fun of tease, deride, ridicule, taunt, poke fun at, rag (slang), mock, parody, lampoon, satirize.

fun *adj.* enjoyable, pleasant, lively, happy, merry.

function *n.* **1.** use, employment, capacity, faculty. **2.** party, social gathering, celebration, reception, get-together, affair, gathering, junket, meeting, shindig.

function *v.* work, operate, run, go, be in running order, perform, serve, officiate, act, behave.

functional *adj.* operational, useful, working, serviceable, operative, utilitarian, plain; *ant.* inoperative, useless.

functionary *n.* official, officeholder, deputy, representative, dignitary, bureaucrat, agent, officer, apparatchik.

fund *n.* treasury, kitty, reserve, well, repository, cache, hoard, store, supply, pool, capital.

fund *v.* back, finance, endow, support, subsidize, underwrite, stake, capitalize.

fundamental *adj.* basic, vital, necessary, rudimentary, elementary, essential, first, important, crucial, principal, key, central, primary.

fundamentally *adv.* basically, essentially, primarily, at heart, intrinsically, centrally, radically.

fundamentals *n.* basics, essentials, first principles, elements, foundation, cornerstone, rudiments; practicalities, brass tacks, nitty-gritty (*slang*).

funds *n.* money, cash, capital, backing, savings, resources, finance, wherewithal, ready money, *slang:* bread, dough.

funeral *n.* burial, interment, obsequies, last rites, entombment, requiem, cremation, inhumation.

funk *n.* depression, despondency, gloom, misery.

funnel *n.* pipe, duct, shaft, conduit.

funny *adj.* **1.** amusing, laughable, droll, comical, whimsical, entertaining, humorous, witty, capricious, jocular, absurd, ridiculous; *ant.* serious. **2.** suspicious, unusual, odd, peculiar, strange, weird, curious, mysterious, puzzling, perplexing, queer.

fur *n.* coat, pelt, hide, down, fleece, skin, wool, hair, brush, fluff.

make the fur fly 1. fight, bicker, argue; stir up trouble, excite. **2.** hurry, hasten, act hastily, rush.

furbish v. 1. restore, refurbish, renovate, improve, renew. 2. shine, polish, clean, brighten, burnish.

furious adj. 1. angry, infuriated, livid, enraged, vehement, wrathful, incensed, fuming, maddened; ant. pleased. 2. (as of a manner or pace) intense, extreme, excessive, intensified, all-out, flat-out (slang). 3. turbulent, violent, fierce, tumultuous, stormy, savage, tempestuous, raging, wild; ant. calm.

furl v. fold, wrap up, curl, roll.

furlough n. leave of absence, leave, vacation.

furnace n. heater, heating system, boiler, stove, forge, smithy.

furnish v. 1. provide, supply, fit out, stock, equip, rig, provision, endow, bestow, grant; ant. divest. 2. decorate, appoint, make habitable.

furnishings n. household goods, furniture, decorations, things.

furniture n. furnishings, goods, household goods, effects, possessions, appointments, chattels, fittings, appurtenances, things.

furor n. 1. fury, rage, frenzy. 2. disturbance, tumult, uproar, commotion, frenzy, fuss, to-do, stir, excitement, enthusiasm, craze, mania; ant. calm.

furrow n. rut, channel, groove, trench, hollow; crease, wrinkle, line, fluting, crow's foot.

furrow v. wrinkle, crease, knit, draw together, corrugate, seam, flute.

further v. back, champion, advance, advocate, boost.

further adj. 1. distant, far, faraway. 2. additional, extra, more.

furthermore adv. also, too, in addition, moreover, additionally, besides, likewise, what's more, to boot, as well.

furthest adj. farthest, outermost, furthermost, ultimate, extreme, most remote, uttermost, outmost; ant. nearest.

furtive adj. 1. secret, clandestine, covert, hidden, surreptitious, stealthy, conspiratorial, cloaked; ant. open. 2. sly, sneaky, evasive, elusive, shifty, underhand, back-door, backstairs, slinking; ant. open.

fury n. 1. anger, rage, wrath, ire, ferocity,

vehemence. 2. violence, frenzy, passion, intensity, severity.

fuse n. wick, tinder, kindling, igniter, brand.

blow a fuse become angry, lose one's temper, rage.

fuse v. unite, merge, combine, intermingle, intermix, join, weld, amalgamate, commingle, meld, federate, coalesce.

fusillade n. outburst, volley, barrage, hail, crossfire, discharge, burst, firing, salvo.

fusion n. 1. union, unification, amalgamation, blend, coalition, synthesis, federation, integration, merger, commingling, mixture, alloy. 2. melting, liquefaction, liquefying, heating, smelting, separation.

fuss n. unrest, to-do, trouble, difficulty, agitation, upset, row.

fuss-budget n. perfectionist, hypercritic, worrier, nit-picker.

fussy adj. nit-picking, difficult, overparticular, fastidious, meticulous, punctilious.

fustiness n. stuffiness, staleness, closeness, dampness, moldiness, mustiness; ant. airiness.

fusty adj. 1. musty, stuffy, stale, dank, damp, rank, moldy, close, mildewy, mildewed, moldering; ant. airy. 2. old-fashioned, outdated, out-of-date, passé, antiquated, archaic, antediluvian; ant. chic, up-to-date.

futile adj. 1. fruitless, barren, useless, worthless, vain, unsuccessful, unavailing, hopeless, sterile, pointless, unproductive, abortive; ant. fruitful, profitable. 2. frivolous, trifling, petty, small, trivial, unimportant.

future n. 1. eternity, events to come, prospect, tomorrow, hereafter, by-and-by; ant. past. 2. destiny, fate, expectation, outlook, doom.

future adj. forthcoming, approaching, prospective, subsequent, fated, destined, later, expected, impending, eventual, to come, in the offing, to be; ant. past.

fuzz n. 1. down, hair, fluff, nap, fur, pile, fiber, lint. 2. (slang) police, patrol, cops.

fuzzy adj. 1. hairy, woolly, furry, fluffy, downy, napped, frizzy. 2. indistinct, blurry, vague, distorted, hazy, foggy, bleary, obscure, faint, ill-defined, misty, out of focus.

G

gab *n.* gossip, prattle, small talk, drivel, chatter, chitchat, tête-à-tête, palaver.

gab *v.* gossip, talk, prattle, chatter, blather, buzz, jabber, yak.

gadabout *n.* wanderer, rover, gallivanter, rambler, idler, itinerant, traveler, gypsy.

gadget *n.* contrivance, contraption, gimmick, novelty, invention, doodad, gizmo (*slang*).

gaffe *n.* indiscretion, blunder, mistake, slip, faux pas, solecism, gaucherie, *slang:* goof, booboo, boner.

gag *n.* joke, wisecrack, quip, witticism, pun, jest, one-liner.

gag *v.* **1.** quiet, silence, muzzle, stifle, throttle, suppress, curb, obstruct, garrote, deaden. **2.** retch, vomit, throw up, disgorge, heave, spew, puke.

gage *v.* See gauge.

gaiety *n.* **1.** joviality, vivacity, effervescence, animation, joie de vivre, exhilaration, jollity, cheerfulness, conviviality; *ant.* sadness. **2.** celebration, festivity, merrymaking, revelry.

gaily *adv.* **1.** happily, joyously, merrily, light-heartedly, gleefully, blithely, cheerfully; *ant.* sadly. **2.** flamboyantly, flashily, colorfully, showily, brightly, gaudily, brilliantly; *ant.* dully, drably.

gain *n.* **1.** profit, return, winnings, proceeds, dividend, yield; *ant.* losses. **2.** progress, advancement, improvement, growth, headway, advance, advantage; *ant.* decline, regression.

gain *v.* **1.** increase, grow, augment, expand, enlarge. **2.** advance, progress, improve, better, develop, thrive, flourish, blossom. **3.** win, earn, get, acquire, make, profit, net, collect, procure, yield, bag, reap, harvest; *ant.* lose.

gainful *adj.* profitable, advantageous, beneficial, rewarding, lucrative, productive, fruitful, remunerative; *ant.* useless.

gainsay *v.* oppose, contradict, dispute, disaffirm, controvert, nay-say, contravene, repudiate, deny; *ant.* agree.

gait *n.* walk, stride, pace, step, tread, manner, bearing, carriage.

gala *n.* party, fete, affair, function, celebration, festivity, jamboree, pageant, fiesta, shindig (*slang*).

gale *n.* storm, tempest, squall, blast, eruption, outbreak, outburst.

gall *n.* **1.** rancor, spleen, bitterness, venom, malice, spite, hostility, enmity, acrimony, antipathy. **2.** rudeness, impudence, effrontery, insolence, impertinence, nerve, sauciness, cheek, chutzpah.

gall *v.* **1.** rile, rankle, provoke, exasperate, annoy, pester, harass, irritate. **2.** chafe, abrade, excoriate, scuff, skin, nick.

gallant *n.* suitor, admirer, beau, escort, lover, paramour, ladies' man, buck, lady-killer.

gallant *adj.* brave, heroic, courageous, valiant, intrepid, dauntless; *ant.* cowardly, craven. **2.** courteous, polite, chivalrous, courtly, honorable, magnanimous.

gallantry *n.* valor, daring, bravery, heroism, boldness, nerve, mettle, pluck; *ant.* cowardice.

gallery *n.* **1.** balcony, arcade, grandstand, walk, passage, veranda, porch, portico. **2.** spectators, onlookers, audience, public, attendance.

galling *adj.* annoying, vexing, exasperating, bothersome, irritating, infuriating, plaguing, rankling, irksome, bitter, vexatious; *ant.* pleasing.

gallivant *v.* traipse, ramble, meander, junket, travel, wander, roam, stray, rove, gad about, range.

gallop *v.* hurry, sprint, dash, tear, bolt, race, hasten, rush, dart, speed, run, hie.

galore *adj.* abundant, plentiful, copious, teeming, replete, lush, overflowing; *ant.* sparse, meager.

galvanize v. 1. excite, electrify, incite, provoke, stimulate, vitalize, rally, foment, startle, astonish. 2. coat, protect, plate, electroplate, cover.

gambit n. ploy, stratagem, trick, scheme, machination, maneuver, artifice, device.

gamble n. risk, venture, bet, wager, chance, hazard.

gamble v. bet, wager, stake, hazard, risk, speculate, prospect.

gambol v. frolic, cavort, romp, prance, rollick, caper, frisk, jump, skip, bound, hop, bounce.

game n. 1. contest, competition, tournament, match, rivalry, conflict. 2. entertainment, amusement, festivity, fun, sport, pastime, recreation, diversion.

game adj. 1. plucky, brave, spirited, hardy, resolute, courageous, spunky, willing, dauntless, intrepid, gutsy (slang); ant. cowardly. 2. lame, disabled, bad, ailing, weak, crippled, deformed, incapacitated, injured, maimed.

gamut n. spectrum, range, scope, compass, scale, sweep, ken, extent, purview.

gang n. group, crowd, pack, circle, clique, ring, coterie, mob, club, party.

gangling adj; tall, lanky, lean, skinny, angular, rangy, spindly, awkward, ungainly, gawky.

gangster n. mobster, racketeer, hoodlum, mafioso, bandit, crook, thug, hood (slang).

gap n. 1. opening, aperture, space, interval, chink, break, rift, breach, cleft, fissure. 2. hiatus, pause, interruption, intermission, stoppage, recess, lacuna, caesura.

gape v. 1. stare, ogle, goggle, gaze, peer, gawk, wonder. 2. split, part, crack, cleave, divide, yawn.

gaping adj. wide, broad, yawning, vast, great, cavernous; ant. tiny.

garb n. outfit, clothes, clothing, attire, dress, apparel, duds, threads (slang), vestments, habiliment, raiment, livery.

garb v. clothe, dress, attire, array, habilitate, apparel, robe, rig out.

garbage n. trash, waste, refuse, rubbish, litter, detritus, debris, offal, filth, swill.

garble v. jumble, confuse, mix up, pervert, distort, corrupt, mangle, mistranslate, misrepresent, tamper with, falsify; doctor; ant. decipher.

gargantuan adj; big, huge, large, colossal, gigan-

tic, mammoth, immense, enormous, tremendous, titanic, leviathan, monumental, prodigious; ant. small.

garish adj. showy, tasteless, vulgar, gaudy, cheap, tawdry, brassy, loud, glitzy, glaring, raffish, meretricious; ant. modest, plain, quiet.

garland n. wreath, crown, festoon, laurel, coronal, chaplet, swag, lei, bays.

garment n. clothing, dress, attire, apparel, costume, vestments, garb, gear, habiliment, wear, array, duds.

garner v. gather, assemble, save, stockpile, collect, store, hoard, accumulate, reserve, amass, husband, cull; ant. dissipate.

garnish n. trimming, decoration, embellishment, relish, adornment, enhancement, ornamentation.

garnish v. decorate, enhance, embellish, ornament, trim, spruce, adorn, deck, beautify, grace; ant. divest.

garrison n. 1. troops, militia, defenders, picket, guard, watch, detachment. 2. fortress, fort, post, stronghold, blockhouse, redoubt, bastion, base, barracks, encampment.

garrison v. station, man, place, position, assign, occupy, post, entrench.

garrulity n. wordiness, verbosity, chattiness, long-windedness, loquacity, logorrhea, effusiveness, prolixity, prattle, chattering; ant. terseness.

garrulous adj. verbose, wordy, gossiping, chatty, effusive, long-winded, voluble, mouthy, loquacious, prolix; ant. taciturn, terse.

gas n. 1. vapor, air, fumes, ether. 2. bombast, exaggeration, claptrap, fustian, braggadocio.

step on the gas (slang) hurry, rush, hasten, move fast.

gash n. wound, cut, gouge, slash, laceration, slit, tear, rent, incision, notch, nick, split.

gash v. gouge, wound, cut, tear, split, lacerate, rend, cleave, incise, nick, slash, slit, score, notch.

gasp v. choke, pant, puff, breathe, gulp, heave, blow.

gate n. gateway, entrance, opening, door, passage, port, portal, entrance, exit, ingress, egress, portcullis.

gather v. 1. assemble, meet, congregate, flock,

rally, crowd, throng, convene, collect, unite, associate, swarm; *ant.* scatter, disperse. **2.** conclude, infer, deduce, reckon, assume, find, learn, surmise, understand. **3.** choose, pick, select, cull, glean, garner.

gathering *n.* assembly, meeting, convocation, assemblage, conclave, convention, rally; concentration, heap, collection, procurement, aggregate, roundup, stockpile; *ant.* scattering.

gauche *adj.* uncouth, unsophisticated, graceless, maladroit, rough, uncultured, inelegant, ill-mannered, gawky, clumsy, wooden, bungling, ungainly; *ant.* graceful.

gaucherie *n.* **1.** awkwardness, oafishness, ineptness, gracelessness, tactlessness, indiscretion, clumsiness, bad taste, ill-breeding, maladroitness; *ant.* elegance. **2.** mistake, slip, faux pas, gaffe, blunder, solecism, *slang:* goof, boner.

gaudy *adj.* ostentatious, showy, tawdry, glitzy, garish, tasteless, vulgar, chintzy, flashy, loud, meretricious; *ant.* drab, plain, quiet.

gauge *n.* **1.** criterion, standard, rule, yardstick, exemplar, guideline, indicator, measure, pattern, model, touchstone. **2.** size, magnitude, dimensions, measure, scope, degree, caliber, width, capacity, height, depth, thickness, bore.

gauge *v.* evaluate, check, determine, value, figure, compute, measure, judge, assess, estimate, appraise, ascertain, reckon, calibrate.

gaunt *adj.* skeletal, emaciated, hollow-eyed, cadaverous, pinched, thin, skinny, wasted, angular, haggard, lean, spare; grim, dismal, bleak, forlorn; *ant.* hale, plump.

gauzy *adj.* transparent, sheer, thin, insubstantial, flimsy, see-through, gossamer, diaphanous, delicate, filmy; *ant.* heavy, thick.

gawk *v.* stare, look, ogle, gape, gaze, goggle.

gawky *adj.* clumsy, ungainly, awkward, gangling, maladroit, lumbering, oafish; loutish, gauche, uncouth; *ant.* graceful, lithe.

gay *adj.* **1.** happy, cheerful, festive, merry, vivacious, animated, playful, frivolous, sunny, carefree, frolicsome; *ant.* sad, gloomy. **2.** bright, brilliant, vivid, intense, rich, garish, flashy, gaudy, colorful, showy; *ant.* drab.

gaze *n.* stare, look, gawp, gape.

gaze *v.* stare, watch, look, regard, view, contemplate, scrutinize, ogle, glare.

gazette *n.* newspaper, paper, periodical, magazine, journal, notice, dispatch.

gear *n.* **1.** equipment, material, tackle, accessories, trappings, accoutrements, instruments, machinery, rigging, apparatus. **2.** cog, pinion, spurwheel, sprocket, ragwheel, lanternwheel.

gear *v.* **1.** prepare, organize, harness, ready, equip, fit, rig, suit, tailor. **2.** regulate, adjust, match, blend, adapt.

gelatinous *adj.* congealed, viscous, glutinous, gummy, sticky, jellified, viscid, mucilaginous, gooey (*slang*).

gem *n.* **1.** jewel, bauble, ornament, bijou, brilliant, rock (*slang*). **2.** paragon, masterpiece, pièce de résistance, nonpareil, prize, treasure, flower, pearl.

genealogy *n.* ancestry, descent, lineage, extraction, bloodline, family tree, pedigree, stock, strain, derivation, progeniture.

general *adj.* **1.** universal, inclusive, comprehensive, across-the-board, global, broad, far-reaching, catholic; widespread, prevalent, ubiquitous, ecumenical; *ant.* particular, limited. **2.** vague, indefinite, uncertain, imprecise, approximate, ill-defined, inaccurate, inexact, loose; *ant.* exact. **3.** normal, common, everyday, customary, prevailing, popular, accepted, conventional, ordinary, typical; *ant.* novel, rare.

generality *n.* **1.** breadth, universality, prevalence, extensiveness, catholicity, ecumenicity. **2.** vagueness, inexactness; generalization, sweeping statement, truism, platitude.

generally *adv.* usually, commonly, ordinarily, regularly, normally, for the most part, typically, on the whole, characteristically; *ant.* rarely.

generate *v.* make, create, form, originate, cause, initiate, bring about, produce, engender, propagate, father, beget, spawn; *ant.* prevent.

generation *n.* creation, production, genesis, formation, origination, procreation, propagation, begetting, breeding, engendering, progeniture.

generic *adj.* universal, general, common, wide, inclusive, collective, sweeping, blanket, comprehensive; bland, faceless; *ant.* particular, specific.

generosity *n.* liberality, benevolence, munificence, bounty, charity, kindness, magnanimity,

generous goodness, softheartedness, beneficence, unselfishness, largesse, expansiveness; *ant.* meanness, selfishness.

generous *adj.* **1.** bountiful, liberal, munificent, charitable, openhanded, altruistic, beneficent, lavish, profuse, copious, prodigal, unstinting; *ant.* stingy, tightfisted. **2.** noble, honorable, chivalrous, unselfish, humane, bighearted; *ant.* petty, mean-spirited.

genesis *n.* start, origin, inception, birth, beginning, creation, formation, root, source, commencement, outset, dawn; *ant.* end.

genetic *adj.* hereditary, ancestral, causal, evolutionary, basic, underlying.

genial *adj.* **1.** friendly, cordial, congenial, kind, affable, outgoing, amiable, easygoing, warmhearted, jovial, glad, merry, good-natured, convivial; *ant.* mean. **2.** (said of climate or surroundings) pleasant, favorable, warm, cheerful, fair, mild, sunny; *ant.* cold.

geniality *n.* friendliness, kindness, mirth, amiability, cordiality, warmth, cheerfulness, congeniality, conviviality, gemütlichkeit; *ant.* coldness, aloofness.

genius *n.* **1.** brilliance, originality, creativity, inventiveness, discernment, intelligence, sagacity, wisdom, intuition, subtlety. **2.** propensity, flair, bent, penchant, proclivity, predilection, aptitude, faculty, talent, knack, ability, gift.

genocide *n.* slaughter, massacre, extermination, mass killing, ethnocide.

genre *n.* variety, type, sort, group, kind, style, category, class, genus, species, strain.

genteel *adj.* polite, refined, well-mannered, civil, courteous, aristocratic, urbane, cultured, elegant, formal, polished; *ant.* boorish, crude.

gentility *n.* **1.** refinement, civility, cultivation, elegance, polish, decorum, courtesy, propriety. **2.** rank, high birth, aristocracy, nobility, gentry, elite, upper classes, blue bloods.

gentle *adj.* **1.** (said of weather or its effects) soft, smooth, moderate, balmy, clement, pacific, peaceful, placid, serene, soothing, temperate; *ant.* rough. **2.** (said of a person's or people's disposition, manners, etc.) kindly, tender, considerate, benign, amiable, compassionate, humane, lenient, sweet-tempered. **3.** (applied to animals) tame, domesticated, obedient, easygoing, sweet-natured, well-trained,

tractable, accommodating, playful, pliable; *ant.* wild, feral. **4.** well-born, highbred, blueblooded, aristocratic, noble; refined, courteous, civilized, cultured, educated, elegant, genteel, polished; *ant.* crude.

gentlemanly *adj.* refined, cultivated, genteel, urbane, suave, polite, honorable, civilized, reputable, mannerly; *ant.* impolite, boorish.

gentry *n.* upper class, aristocracy, nobility, nobles, gentility, gentlefolk, elite, high society.

genuine *adj.* **1.** authentic, real, true, actual, original, veritable, unadulterated, unmixed, unalloyed, official, certified; *ant.* spurious, sham. **2.** sincere, honest, frank, candid, straightforward, ingenuous.

genus *n.* type, category, group, kind, class, division, genre, breed, species, order, set, taxon.

germ *n.* **1.** origin, beginning, inception, source, root, cause, rudiment, spark. **2.** embryo, seed, egg, nucleus, bud, sprig, ovum, ovule, spore, sprout. **3.** bacillus, microbe, antibody, bacteria, bacterium, bug, virus.

germane *adj.* pertinent, relevant, material, appropriate, proper, fitting, applicable, apropos, suitable, apposite; *ant.* irrelevant.

germinate *v.* bud, sprout, grow, generate, develop, shoot, swell, vegetate.

gestation *n.* **1.** development, incubation, maturation, growth, metamorphosis, planning, drafting, ripening. **2.** pregnancy, reproduction, parturition, propagation, fecundation.

gesticulate *v.* gesture, sign, signal, motion, pantomime, wave, point, indicate.

gesture *n.* **1.** sign, action, motion, gesticulation, intimation, sign, signal, act, wave, indication. **2.** pose, posture, attitude, appearance. *v.* gesticulate, motion, signal, sign, indicate, point, wave.

get *v.* **1.** obtain, gain, procure, acquire, achieve, attain, earn, reap, receive, secure, seize. **2.** (force or influence someone to do something) urge, persuade, coax, induce, enjoin, influence, excite, egg on, prevail upon, stimulate. **3.** catch, contract, succumb to, come down with, fall victim to. **4.** understand, comprehend, grasp, perceive, know, fathom, realize, see.

get across 1. (*slang*) communicate, convey, transmit, impart, pass on, bring home to someone. 2. ford, cross, negotiate, traverse.

get ahead succeed, prosper, thrive, progress, flourish, make it, get there; *ant.* fail.

get along 1. succeed, thrive, prosper, flourish, make a living. 2. advance, progress, proceed, move on, push ahead. 3. age, wane, decline.

get at 1. arrive, achieve, reach, ascertain, attain. 2. intend, suggest, mean, aim, purpose, hint, imply.

get away *v.* escape, leave, flee, get out, break out, depart, decamp, elude, disappear.

get back 1. regain, retrieve, reclaim, salvage, recover, repossess, recoup. 2. revenge, retaliate, strike back, give tit for tat.

get by survive, exist, subsist, cope, manage, fare, make ends meet, make do, shift, contrive.

get it (*slang*) 1. understand, comprehend, get the message *or* picture, catch on, perceive, know. 2. suffer, get one's just deserts, be scolded, catch it, catch hell, be punished, suffer the consequences.

get off 1. depart, go, leave, exit, shove off; *ant.* arrive. 2. dismount, alight, disembark, descend; *ant.* board.

get on 1. dress, attire, don, wear. 2. mount, go up, ascend, scale, climb, board, embark; *ant.* alight. 3. succeed, manage, prosper, get along, cope, fare, make out, progress, proceed.

get out of 1. gain from, get from, obtain from, secure from. 2. evade, dodge, avoid, shirk, shun. 3. leave, exit, depart, go away, withdraw.

get over overcome, surmount, survive, shake off, recuperate, recover, mend, heal, convalesce.

get to 1. arrive, reach, approach, land at. 2. (*slang*) influence, reach, have an effect, hit home, make its point, talk to, approach.

get through 1. complete, achieve, discharge, enact, finish. 2. endure, survive, subsist, bear, tolerate.

get together meet, join, assemble, convene, converge, congregate, unite, rally, gather, accumulate, muster.

get-together *n.* gathering, function, party, social, reception, soiree, do.

gewgaw *n.* toy, trinket, novelty, knickknack, bauble, trifle, bijou, bagatelle, chachka (*slang*).

ghastly *adj.* 1. ghostly, spectral, wan, wraithlike, pallid, ashen, grim, funereal, cadaverous, unearthly, weird, unnatural; *ant.* natural, real, substantial. 2. frightful, terrifying, hideous, horrible, horrid, loathsome, lurid, repellent, shocking; *ant.* delightful.

ghost *n.* apparition, vision, specter, spirit, soul, demon, shade, phantom, spook, phantasm, wraith.

ghostly *adj.* pale, wan, frightful, eerie, spectral, wraithlike, supernatural, spooky, weird, unearthly, phantasmal.

ghoulish *adj.* morbid, gruesome, gothic, macabre, sinister, hair-raising, fiendish, grisly, revolting.

giant *n.* monster, behemoth, titan, leviathan, colossus, Goliath, Hercules.

giant *adj.* large, huge, colossal, gigantic, gargantuan, jumbo, monstrous, vast, enormous, immense, mammoth, leviathan, prodigious, titanic, elephantine; *ant.* tiny, minuscule.

gibberish *n.* nonsense, blather, drivel, jargon, lingo, prattle, balderdash, *slang:* gobbledegook, mumbo jumbo; *ant.* sense.

gibe *v.* ridicule, scoff, sneer, flout, deride, tease.

giddy *adj.* 1. fickle, unsettled, capricious, changeable, inconstant, vacillating, careless, frivolous, silly, flighty, irresponsible, erratic; *ant.* sensible, sober. 2. dizzy, reeling, faint, lightheaded, vertiginous, unbalanced, unstable.

gift *n.* 1. present, donation, benefaction, grant, gratuity, boon, alms, endowment, bequest, bounty, charity, provision. 2. ability, aptitude, knack, talent, faculty, capacity, genius.

gifted *adj.* talented, endowed, clever, capable, adroit, accomplished, expert, masterly, ingenious, intelligent.

gigantic *adj.* giant, enormous, colossal, immense, tremendous, stupendous, mammoth, huge, vast, titanic, herculean, prodigious, elephantine; *ant.* small.

giggle *n.* laugh, chuckle, tee-hee, snicker, chortle, titter, snigger.

giggle *v.* laugh, chuckle, tee-hee, snicker, snigger, chortle, titter.

gild v. 1. overlay, plate, wash, tinsel, electroplate, coat. 2. array, embellish, enhance, festoon, enrich, garnish, ornament, beautify, dress up, trim.

gilt adj. glittering, showy, gaudy, specious, meretricious, painted, gleaming, lustrous, golden.

gimcrack adj. cheap, trashy, tawdry, shoddy, tacky; ant. well-made.

gimmick n. 1. gadget, apparatus, fixture, device, contrivance; gizmo (slang). 2. stratagem, gambit, trick, stunt, ploy; scheme; means, method.

gingerly adv. carefully, gently, cautiously, delicately, hesitantly, daintily, timidly, warily, charily; ant. carelessly, roughly.

gird v. 1. encircle, girdle, surround, belt, enclose, encompass, ring, hem in, enfold, pen. 2. support, brace, fortify, strengthen, steel, ready, prepare.

girdle n. corset, belt, sash, cummerbund, waistband, cincture, fillet.

girdle v. surround, encircle, hem, ring, bind, enclose, encompass, environ, circumscribe.

gist n. substance, pith, essence, marrow, heart, core, crux, meaning, import, drift, significance.

give v. 1. grant, bestow, confer, impart, endow, bequeath, donate, award, dispense, subsidize, contribute. 2. concede, grant, allow, cede, relinquish.

give away 1. give, bestow, award, dispense, present, donate. 2. reveal, betray, divulge, disclose, expose, leak, tattle, let slip, uncover.

give back restore, return, refund, remit, repay, reimburse.

give in submit, surrender, concede, capitulate, yield, recant, cede; ant. hold out.

give off emit, release, effuse, emanate, discharge, exude, vent, produce, exhale.

give out 1. emit, emanate, exude, discharge, exhale, give off, release, vent, generate. 2. deliver, deal, dole, pass or hand out, distribute, disseminate, scatter, strew. 3. proclaim, publish, make known, announce, advertise, broadcast, transmit, utter. 4. weaken, fail, malfunction, break down, tire, collapse, run down.

give up surrender, cede, hand over, yield, capitulate, relinquish, quit, forswear, renounce, waive, desist, resign, throw in the towel (slang); ant. hold out.

give way 1. collapse, fall, crumble, crumple, break, cave in, sag, crack; ant. withstand. 2. give ground, retreat, back up or away, flinch, move aside.

given adj. 1. inclined, liable, prone, apt, likely, disposed. 2. granted, admitted, agreed, specified.

glacial adj. 1. cold, icy, frozen, freezing, frigid, polar, arctic, frosty, biting, chilly, bitter, gelid; ant. warm. 2. antagonistic, hostile, inimical, haughty, cool; ant. friendly.

glad adj. 1. happy, joyous, delighted, gratified, pleased, jovial, blithe, gay, jocund. 2. willing, inclined, amenable, eager, disposed.

gladden v. cheer, brighten, hearten, encourage, exhilarate, please, elate, enliven, gratify; ant. sadden.

gladness n. happiness, mirth, delight, joy, glee, blitheness, gaiety, brightness; ant. sadness.

glamorous adj. captivating, bewitching, alluring, enchanting, fascinating, dazzling, entrancing, resplendent; ant. boring, drab, plain.

glamour n. allure, magnetism, appeal, charm, magic, fascination, attraction, enchantment.

glance v. 1. look, glimpse, once-over, sight, peek, peep, look-see, view, squint.

glance v. 1. look, view, gaze, browse, leaf, scan, glimpse, peek, peep. 2. ricochet, bounce, rebound, graze, skim; reflect, shine, flash, shimmer, glint, glitter, glisten, twinkle.

glare v. 1. shine, beam, glow, radiate, blaze, dazzle, flame, flare. 2. stare, gaze, glower, scowl, frown, fix, wither.

glaring adj. 1. shining, blinding, dazzling, bright, brilliant, vivid, fulgent, garish, flashy; ant. dull, dim. 2. staring, gazing, searching, intent, penetrating; scowling, frowning, glowering. 3. obvious, visible, evident, conspicuous, manifest, blatant, flagrant, gross, egregious; ant. hidden, subtle.

glassy adj. glazed, expressionless, blank, empty, dull, vacant, lifeless, transparent, fixed.

glaze n. varnish, lacquer, polish, enamel, finish, shine, patina, topcoat, gloss, luster.

glaze v. polish, varnish, lacquer, gloss, burnish, enamel, shellac, furbish.

gleam n. sparkle, glimmer, shimmer, luster, sheen, flicker, flash, glint.

gleam v. glimmer, shine, glow, shimmer, glitter,

glean glint, scintillate, glisten, flash, flare, glance, coruscate.

glean *v.* cull, harvest, reap, gather, garner, amass, collect; learn, pick up.

glee *n.* exuberance, exhilaration, hilarity, elation, delight, joy, exultation, jollity, verve, merriment, jocularity.

gleeful *adj.* delighted, overjoyed, jubilant, elated, exuberant, jovial, gratified, triumphant, exultant; *ant.* sad, morose.

glib *adj.* 1. talkative, talky, voluble, talky, loquacious, fluent, articulate, gabby. 2. facile, suave, insincere, fast-talking, slick, slippery, artful, ingratiating.

glide *v.* skim, slide, drift, coast, float, slip, fly, skate, sail, glissade, volplane.

glimmer *n.* glow, twinkle, shimmer, sparkle, ray, hint, inkling, trace, gleam, glint.

glimmer *v.* twinkle, shine, sparkle, glow, shimmer, glitter, flicker, glisten, glint, scintillate.

glimpse *n.* look, view, peek, glance.

glimpse *v.* sight, spot, espy, peek, glance.

glint *n.* twinkle, gleam, glimmer, shine, sparkle, flash, glitter.

glisten *v.* shine, sparkle, twinkle, gleam, glimmer, scintillate, glint, flash, shimmer.

glitter *n.* sparkle, shimmer, shine, flash; radiance, brightness, luster, splendor, tinsel, pageantry.

glitter *v.* sparkle, twinkle, flash, shine, spangle, glimmer, shimmer, glisten, gleam, scintillate, glint, glare, flare.

gloat *v.* relish, exult, rejoice, crow, glory, triumph, vaunt, bask, revel.

global *adj.* universal, international, comprehensive, thorough, sweeping, general, pandemic, planetary; *ant.* limited, parochial.

globe *n.* 1. sphere, orb, balloon, bubble, ball. 2. earth, planet, world.

globe-trotter *n.* jet-setter, world traveler, voyager, wanderer, tourist.

globular *adj.* round, spherical, spheroid, orbicular, globoid, globate.

gloom *n.* 1. darkness, twilight, murk, obscurity, dimness, dusk, shade; *ant.* brightness. 2. sadness, depression, woe, melancholy, despondency, misery, sorrow, dolor, grief, foreboding; *ant.* happiness, optimism, gaiety.

gloomy *adj.* 1. dark, clouded, unlit, dim, shadowy, dusky, murky, obscure, sepulchral, stygian; *ant.* bright. 2. melancholy, sad, downhearted, depressed, joyless, morose, pessimistic, sullen, sepulchral, saturnine, *slang:* down in the dumps, down at the mouth; *ant.* happy, joyful.

glorify *v.* 1. praise, laud, extol, acclaim, eulogize, dignify, exalt, honor, venerate, idolize, illuminate, aggrandize; *ant.* denounce, vilify. 2. worship, deify, immortalize, sanctify, revere, bless, canonize, beatify, enshrine.

glorious *adj.* splendid, marvelous, grand, fine, magnificent, majestic, radiant, resplendent, shining, dazzling; *ant.* plain, inglorious.

glory *n.* 1. fame, renown, honor, distinction, prestige, celebrity, eminence, illustriousness; *ant.* obscurity. 2. splendor, radiance, effulgence, majesty, brilliance, sumptuousness, richness, beauty. 3. worship, adoration, blessing, benediction.

glory *v.* delight, revel, rejoice, relish, exult, gloat, crow, pride oneself, boast.

gloss *n.* 1. brightness, sheen, shine, varnish, veneer, luster, polish, gleam, burnish. 2. mask, semblance, façade, veneer, pretense, front, sham. 3. commentary, explanation, annotation, footnote, interpretation, elucidation, note.

gloss *v.* explain, annotate, interpret, comment, elucidate.

gloss over disguise, hide, camouflage, whitewash, conceal, gild, mask, smooth over.

glossy *adj.* shining, silken, lustrous, polished, sleek, smooth, glassy, enameled, bright, burnished; *ant.* matte.

glow *n.* 1. phosphorescence, radiance, luminosity, effulgence, incandescence, glimmer, brightness, lambency. 2. enthusiasm, passion, vehemence, intensity, ardor, gusto.

glow *v.* 1. radiate, brighten, gleam, shine, glimmer, coruscate. 2. color, redden, flush, blush, flare up; burn, flame, kindle, smolder.

glower *v.* glare, scowl, frown, sulk.

glowing *adj.* 1. bright, gleaming, lustrous, phosphorescent, luminous, beaming, lambent, vibrant, aglow, flushed, vivid; *ant.* dull. 2. (full of praise) enthusiastic, laudatory, complimentary, rhapsodic. 3. ardent, zealous, fervent, impassioned; *ant.* restrained.

glue *n.* adhesive, cement, paste, mucilage, gum, isinglass.

glue *v.* stick, fix, cement, paste, seal, agglutinate, gum.

glum *adj.* morose, sullen, doleful, pessimistic, grumpy, sour, surly, gruff, saturnine; *ant.* ecstatic, happy.

glut *n.* surplus, excess, overabundance, surfeit, plethora, saturation, superfluity; *ant.* lack, scarcity.

glut *v.* 1. oversupply, flood, overwhelm, inundate, deluge, congest, saturate, clog, cloy. 2. gorge, satiate, stuff, cram, hog, feast, wolf, devour; *ant.* starve, diet.

glutinous *adj.* adhesive, sticky, viscous, gluey, cohesive, mucilaginous, viscid.

glutton *n.* gourmand, pig, hog, cormorant, gorger, guzzler, gobbler, epicure, sensualist; *ant.* ascetic.

gnarled *adj.* twisted, contorted, knotted, knobby, wrinkled, rough, weather-beaten, rugged, leathery, knarred, knurled.

gnaw *v.* 1. chew, nibble, bite, munch, masticate, champ. 2. erode, wear, eat away, corrode, consume. 3. worry, fret, chafe, plague, trouble, rankle.

go *v.* 1. move, proceed, progress, advance, hie, wend. 2. depart, leave, quit, withdraw, decamp, retreat, run away, scram (*slang*). 3. function, work, run, perform, operate. 4. (be appropriate) belong, match, mesh, correspond, suit, fit in, harmonize, accord, agree, complement.

go along with 1. cooperate, agree, concur, assent. 2. accompany, escort, squire, go with.

go back forsake, renege, repudiate, retract, revert, return, backslide, desert, retreat.

go between intervene, mediate, arbitrate, meddle, reconcile.

go by 1. pass, overshoot, exceed, outstrip, lap (*slang*), beat. 2. follow, adopt, heed, conform to, respect.

go hard with hinder, plague, oppress, torment, burden.

go in for 1. participate in, practice, take up, pursue. 2. advocate, endorse, espouse, favor, back, promote, adopt, embrace; like, enjoy, be fond of, fancy; *ant.* frown on, dislike.

go off 1. leave, quit, depart, part, abscond,

decamp, vanish, vamoose. 2. explode, blow up, detonate, discharge, fire.

go on 1. act, execute, behave, conduct oneself. 2. happen, occur, come about, take place, proceed. 3. endure, persevere, persist, continue, bear, last, stay. 4. talk, chatter, converse, speak, blather, prattle, ramble on, natter.

go over 1. rehearse, repeat, practice, review, rehash. 2. examine, inspect, investigate, analyze, study, peruse, scan.

goad *v.* incite, provoke, spur, instigate, impel, push, propel.

goal *n.* aim, target, aspiration, ambition, objective, intention, purpose, design, end, destination, mark.

gobble *v.* cram, devour, stuff, gorge, bolt, gulp, eat, consume, guzzle, hog, wolf, put away, shovel.

go-between *n.* middleman, referee, mediator, agent, messenger.

goblin *n.* demon, gremlin, hobgoblin, imp, sprite, spirit, troll.

godforsaken *adj.* desolate, wretched, dismal, bleak, forlorn, abandoned, lonely, deserted, miserable, backward; *ant.* blessed.

godless *adj.* 1. sacrilegious, wicked, profane, blasphemous, impious, evil, irreverent. 2. atheistic, pagan, heathen, irreligious, freethinking, agnostic.

godlike *adj.* heavenly, saintly, superhuman, celestial, divine, transcendent, sublime, exalted, reverent, righteous, moral, good; *ant.* impious.

godly *adj.* pious, holy, God-fearing, devout, reverent, righteous, moral, good; *ant.* impious.

godsend *n.* miracle, blessing, boon, windfall, gift, manna.

going *adj.* continuing, extant, viable, flourishing, thriving, successful, profitable; *ant.* failing, bankrupt.

golden *adj.* 1. precious, priceless, invaluable, rich. 2. opportune, favorable, promising, auspicious, timely, propitious, advantageous, excellent, glorious. 3. yellow, flaxen, fair.

gone *adj.* 1. (no longer at a given place) moved, transferred, displaced, shifted, withdrawn, retired, departed, disappeared; *ant.* dead, demolished, vanished, passed, dissipated, nonextant, extinct, finished, dissolved, burned up, disintegrated.

goo *n.* sludge, mud, mire, ooze, slime, slush, *slang*; gunk, grunge.

good *n.* **1.** benefit, welfare, advantage, gain, asset, boon, profit. **2.** goodness, virtue, ethic, ideal, morality, righteousness, uprightness, rectitude, rightness, merit.

good *adj.* **1.** moral, upright, virtuous, honorable, righteous, ethical, honest, humane, noble; *ant.* evil, wicked. **2.** kind, considerate, tolerant, benign, generous, amiable, congenial, friendly, polite; *ant.* mean, unkind. **3.** proper, suitable, becoming, desirable, fit, appropriate, seemly, satisfactory; *ant.* wrong. **4.** qualified, suited, competent, able, adequate, capable, efficient, sufficient; *ant.* inept. **5.** favorable, approving, commendatory, commending; advantageous, positive, auspicious; *ant.* poor, inauspicious.

for good permanently, forever, for all time, irrevocably, henceforth, finally, irreversibly, irreparably, once and for all.

make good 1. repay, reimburse, pay back, compensate. **2.** succeed, prove oneself, accomplish, achieve, arrive. **3.** justify, support, uphold, maintain.

good-for-nothing *n.* loafer, vagabond, bum, tramp, wastrel, ne'er-do-well, reprobate, profligate, idler; *ant.* achiever, winner.

good-hearted *adj.* charitable, gracious, benevolent, kind.

good-humored *adj.* genial, amiable, cheerful, merry, happy, affable, jovial, pleasant, blithe, jocund; *ant.* crabby, churlish, cross.

good-looking *adj.* attractive, handsome, beautiful, pretty, comely, fair, well-proportioned, clean-cut; *ant.* plain, ugly.

good-natured *adj.* kindly, amiable, friendly, affable, agreeable, tolerant, sympathetic, indulgent, benevolent.

goodness *n.* **1.** virtue, justness, integrity, morality, uprightness, righteousness, fairness, piety. **2.** excellence, value, merit, worth. **3.** kindness, benevolence, charity, altruism.

goods *n.* **1.** commodities, merchandise, wares, stock, vendibles, appurtenances, chattels. **2.** (items belonging to an individual) property, effects, possessions, belongings, equipment, baggage, furnishings, furniture, traps.

gooey *adj.* **1.** sticky, thick, gluey, gummy, tacky, viscid, viscous, glutinous, mucilaginous, soft. **2.** sentimental, maudlin, syrupy, cloying, mawkish.

gore *v.* stab, impale, pierce, spear, stick, spit, puncture, gouge, transfix, rend.

gorge *n.* gulch, fissure, gap, gully, canyon, ravine, pass, chasm, abyss, cleft, defile.

gorge *v.* devour, stuff, gulp, satiate, sate, wolf, hog, cram, glut, gormandize; *ant.* abstain.

gorgeous *adj.* **1.** attractive, pretty, beautiful, glamorous, lovely, exquisite, ravishing. **2.** rich, showy, brilliant, luxurious, magnificent, resplendent, opulent, splendiferous; *ant.* dull, plain, seedy.

gory *adj.* bloody, bloodstained, sanguinary; brutal, murderous.

gospel *n.* doctrine, creed, credo, dogma, faith, truth, certainty, verity.

gossamer *adj.* thin, gauzy, sheer, insubstantial, diaphanous, flimsy, silky, airy, delicate, fine, light; *ant.* opaque, thick.

gossip *n.* **1.** rumor, heresay, scandal, earful, chit-chat, chatter. **2.** snoop, tattler, scandalmonger, backbiter, magpie, chatterbox, blabbermouth (*slang*).

gossip *v.* chat, prattle, tattle, jaw, blather, rumor, report, blab.

gouge *n.* cut, slash, groove, hollow, trench, furrow, gash, score, scoop, hack.

gouge *v.* **1.** channel, dig, hollow out, chisel, cut, scoop, claw, groove, gash, incise, slash, scratch, hack, score. **2.** cheat, steal, chisel, blackmail, extort.

gourmet *n.* connoisseur, epicure, bon vivant, critic, epicurean, gastronome.

govern *v.* rule, command, oversee, preside, control, reign, supervise, guide, administer, manage, regulate.

government *n.* authority, command, control, direction, dominion, administration, management, guidance, rule, sovereignty, ministry.

governor *n.* administrator, controller, head, leader, supervisor, director, overseer.

gown *n.* dress, frock, garment, robe, habit, negligee.

grab *v.* clutch, grasp, grip, seize, snatch, capture, nab, pluck, usurp, commandeer, expropriate, confiscate.

grace *n.* **1.** agility, dexterity, balance, supple-

grace v. **1.** embellish, adorn, beautify, decorate, trim. **2.** honor, dignify, ennoble, distinguish.

graceful adj. **1.** supple, lissome, limber, agile, lithe, pliant, nimble, elastic, dexterous; ant. awkward, stiff. **2.** balanced, symmetrical, comely, handsome, statuesque, beautiful, fair, pretty; ant. ugly, shapeless. **3.** polite, cultured, charming, gracious, elegant; ant. crude, graceless.

graceless adj. **1.** ungainly, awkward, clumsy, gawky; ant. graceful. **2.** crude, boorish, coarse, barbarous, vulgar, rude, unsophisticated, rough, loutish, brazen, shameless; ant. gracious.

gracious adj. **1.** friendly, affable, genial, amiable, courteous, polite, accommodating, cordial, pleasant, courtly, refined. **2.** merciful, tender, charitable, compassionate, lenient, indulgent, mild.

gradation n. **1.** arrangement, grouping, ordering, sequence, classification, series, stage. **2.** measurement, level, mark, notch, tier, step.

grade n. **1.** incline, slope, gradient, slant, pitch, ascent, descent, declivity. **2.** (measurement on a scale) degree, increment, mark, gradation, step.

grade v. evaluate, rate, value, classify, brand, categorize, rank, type, sort.

gradient n. slope, grade, incline, slant, bank, downgrade, upgrade, cant, tilt.

gradual adj. slow, leisurely, moderate, regular, deliberate, measured, incremental, steady, cautious, piecemeal; ant. precipitate, sudden.

graduate v. **1.** (assign to dirrerent levels) rank, classify, grade, group, arrange, order, sort. **2.** (mark in specified units) measure, calibrate, standardize.

graft n. **1.** scion, splice, transplant, slip, shoot, transplant, implant, insert. **2.** fraud, peculation, thievery, corruption.

graft v. **1.** unite, join, splice, implant, insert, transplant. **2.** cheat, thieve, swindle, steal.

grain n. **1.** seed, kernel, cereal, maize. **2.**

particle, mite, speck, fragment, bit, modicum, crumb, iota, jot, morsel, granule, scintilla. **3.** texture, striation, pattern, weft, tooth, nap, weave, warp and woof.

against the grain disturbing, irritating, bothersome, offensive.

grand adj. **1.** sumptuous, rich, splendid, magnificent, luxurious, marvelous, opulent, ostentatious, palatial; ant. modest. **2.** exalted, imposing, impressive, majestic, lofty, stately, regal, noble, illustrious, sublime, august; formal, dignified, eloquent, classical; ant. lowly, vulgar. **3.** first-class, good, superb, excellent, great, supreme; ant. poor, mediocre.

grandeur n. magnificence, majesty, splendor, pomp, stateliness, loftiness, imperiousness, graciousness, sublimity, hauteur; ant. lowliness, simplicity.

grandiloquent adj. pompous, pretentious, bombastic, inflated, flowery, turgid, high-flown, florid, stilted, magniloquent, fustian; ant. simple, understated.

grandiose adj. ostentatious, pompous, pretentious, showy, affected, bombastic; imposing, majestic, impressive, monumental, ambitious, grand; ant. modest.

grant n. donation, award, endowment, gift, scholarship, subsidy, benefaction, annuity, honorarium.

grant v. **1.** admit, concede, accede, acknowledge, acquiesce, consent, accord; ant. deny. **2.** bestow, give, confer, award, donate, provide, allocate, apportion, vouchsafe; ant. withhold.

granular adj. rough, grainy, gritty, grainy, sandy, crumbly, granulated.

granule n. grain, speck, seed, iota, jot, fragment, crumb, particle, scrap.

graph n. diagram, chart, grid, table, histogram.

graphic adj. **1.** detailed, specific, explicit, vivid, lucid, telling, striking, emphatic; ant. impressionistic, vague. **2.** visual, descriptive, expressive, illustrative, pictorial, representational, symbolic.

grapple v. **1.** fasten, hook, catch, close, join, grip, clasp, clinch, make fast. **2.** wrestle, engage, fight, battle, struggle, tussle, contend; ant. avoid, evade.

grasp n. **1.** grip, clutches, hold, clasp, embrace, possession, reach. **2.** understanding, perception, ken, comprehension, scope, capacity, awareness, insight.

grasp *v.* **1.** clutch, grip, enclose, clasp, clinch, grab, catch, seize, snatch, nab. **2.** comprehend, understand, get, perceive, apprehend, realize, see, envisage, imagine.

grasping *adj.* greedy, selfish, acquisitive, avaricious, covetous, mean, venal, miserly, mercenary, penny-pinching, rapacious; *ant.* generous.

grate *v.* **1.** (make a harsh sound) grind, rasp, rub, scrape, scratch, creak. **2.** irritate, aggravate, annoy, irk, rankle, exasperate, vex, fret, chafe, peeve, *slang:* get on one's nerves, set one's teeth on edge. **3.** shred, mince, granulate, grind, pulverize.

grateful *adj.* **1.** thankful, appreciative, indebted, obliged, beholden. **2.** agreeable, delectable, welcome, pleasing, pleasant, satisfying, soothing.

gratification *n.* satisfaction, enjoyment, contentment, pleasure, delight. **2.** payment, indulgence, reward, recompense, fruition.

gratify *v.* **1.** please, charm, delight, gladden, content, cheer, amuse. **2.** (meet a demand) appease, cater to, indulge, humor, satisfy, pamper, coddle, comply.

grating *adj.* **1.** discordant, cacophonous, grinding, strident, harsh, jarring, raucous, rasping; *ant.* harmonious. **2.** irritating, annoying, vexatious, irksome, disagreeable, exasperating; *ant.* pleasing.

gratis *adj.* free, complimentary, gratuitous.

gratitude *n.* thankfulness, appreciation, indebtedness, mindfulness, recognition, acknowledgedness, awareness; *ant.* ingratitude, indifference, thanklessness.

gratuitous *adj.* **1.** free, voluntary, gratis, complimentary, donated. **2.** unwarranted, unjustified, groundless, unmerited, uncalled-for, unnecessary, superfluous, wanton; *ant.* justified, reasonable.

gratuity *n.* tip, bonus, gift, present, donation, largesse, recompense, perquisite, benefaction.

grave *n.* crypt, tomb, vault, mausoleum, sepulcher, catacomb, charnel, barrow, cairn.

grave *adj.* **1.** important, momentous, pressing, urgent, vital, weighty, crucial, significant, imperative, exigent; *ant.* trivial, unimportant. **2.** life-threatening, dangerous, critical, serious, perilous, hazardous, acute; *ant.* mild. **3.** solemn, serious, sober, quiet, earnest, dour, dull, grim, restrained, leaden, sedate; *ant.* cheerful.

gravel *n.* sand, pebbles, shale, macadam, alluvium, marl.

gravelly *adj.* **1.** granular, grainy, pebbly, gritty, sabulose, sabulose; *ant.* fine, powdery. **2.** throaty, hoarse, gruff, guttural, harsh; *ant.* clear, bell-like.

gravitate *v.* **1.** drift, be attracted, incline, tend, lean, move toward. **2.** precipitate, drop, descend, fall, sink, settle.

gravity *n.* **1.** attraction, pull, weight, heaviness, pressure, force, gravitation. **2.** importance, seriousness, weight, moment, urgency, exigency, magnitude, consequence, momentousness; *ant.* levity, triviality. **3.** dignity, composure, calm, reserve, solemnity; *ant.* frivolity.

gray *adj.* **1.** dusky, neutral, somber, dingy, drab, shaded, sere, leaden, ashen; dismal, cheerless. **2.** aged, old, venerable, grizzled, hoary, decrepit.

graze *n.* scratch, abrasion, scrape, score.

graze *v.* **1.** touch, skim, brush, glance; scrape, rub, chafe, abrade, skin, shave. **2.** pasture, feed, eat, gnaw, nibble, bite, uproot, forage, ruminate, batten, crop, masticate; munch, nosh (*slang*), snack.

grease *n.* oil, ointment, unction, wax, salve, tallow, unguent, fat, lard.

grease *v.* oil, lubricate, anoint, smear, swab, salve, daub, pomade.

greasy *adj.* **1.** oily, slimy, slippery, slick, sebaceous, waxy, fatty, smeary, tallowy. **2.** ingratiating, glib, fawning, smooth, unctuous, smarmy, sycophantic, toadying.

great *adj.* **1.** remarkable, eminent, exalted, renowned, celebrated, august, majestic, dignified; *ant.* obscure, anonymous. **2.** large, huge, immense, enormous, gigantic, tremendous, vast, bulky, massive, colossal, mammoth; *ant.* small. **3.** excellent, exceptional, superb, fabulous, fantastic, marvelous, stupendous, good, fine, first-rate, outstanding; *ant.* mediocre.

greatness *n.* **1.** eminence, prominence, renown, importance, import, fame, celebrity, distinction, illustriousness; *ant.* insignificance, pettiness. **2.** largeness, size, bulk, weight, extent, heaviness, immensity, amplitude, hugeness, vastness; *ant.* smallness. **3.** merit, worth, virtue, character, magnanimity, nobleness, morality, idealism; *ant.* littleness.

greed *n.* avarice, rapacity, gluttony, voracity, selfishness, desire, cupidity, avidity, covetousness, hunger.

greedy *adj.* **1.** avaricious, avid, grasping, rapacious, selfish, miserly, parsimonious, tightfisted, grudging; *ant.* generous, munificent. **2.** gluttonous, swinish, voracious, devouring, hoggish, ravenous, insatiate, gorging, surfeiting, gormandizing; *ant.* ascetic, abstemious.

green *n.* lawn, grass, field, park, turf, common, greensward, sward.

green *adj.* **1.** growing, verdant, lush, leafy, sprouting, luxuriant, blooming, thriving, budding, foliate, flourishing; *ant.* withered, sere, yellow. **2.** immature, young, growing, unripe, unseasoned, half-baked, callow, naive, unskilled; *ant.* mature, ripe. **3.** pale, pallid, peaked, wan, ill, nauseated, sick, unhealthy.

greenery *n.* vegetation, foliage, verdure, verdancy.

greenhorn *n.* beginner, novice, ingenue, tyro, neophyte, tenderfoot, amateur, fledgling, initiate, rookie, learner; *ant.* veteran.

greet *v.* meet, welcome, hail, receive, address, salute, compliment; *ant.* ignore.

greeting *n.* reception, welcome, address, hail, acknowledgment, salutation, salute, obeisance, congratulations, felicitations.

gregarious *adj.* outgoing, genial, affable, social, friendly, convivial, companionable, warm, cordial; *ant.* unsociable.

grief *n.* **1.** sorrow, anguish, misery, distress, bereavement, woe, pain, lamentation. **2.** tribulation, affliction, trouble, difficulty, hardship.

grief-stricken *adj.* stricken, crushed, grieving, inconsolable, devastated, desolate, forlorn, afflicted, despairing, mourning; *ant.* overjoyed.

grievance *n.* complaint, gripe, beef (*slang*); hardship, injury, distress, injustice, wrong, tribulation, trial, affliction.

grieve *v.* **1.** (to feel grief) mourn, lament, sorrow, bemoan, pine, rue, regret, agonize, suffer. **2.** (to cause grief) sadden, hurt, harrow, pain, wound, hurt.

grievous *adj.* **1.** (causing grief) distressing, disquieting, upsetting, troublesome, disturb-

ing, burdensome, overwhelming. **2.** (marked by grief) painful, dismal, tragic, pathetic, sad, deplorable, heart-rending, pitiful, lamentable. **3.** flagrant, atrocious, villainous, heinous, outrageous, appalling, glaring, offensive, shocking, shameful, calamitous, monstrous.

grill *v.* **1.** broil, roast, sauté, barbecue, cook. **2.** question, cross-examine, interrogate, catechize, pump, give the third degree.

grim *adj.* **1.** harsh, stern, merciless, severe, ferocious, fierce, savage. **2.** unyielding, relentless, implacable, inexorable, resolute, firm, adamant. **3.** sullen, sour, crabbed, gloomy, morose, sulky, somber, dour, sullen, glum, scowling; *ant.* happy, cheerful.

grimace *v.* pout, frown, scowl, sneer, smirk, grin, make a face, mug.

grime *n.* dirt, filth, soil, soot, muck, smut, squalor, smudge.

grimy *adj.* dirty, filthy, soiled, sooty, foul, besmirched, smutty, squalid, grubby, begrimed; *ant.* clean, pure.

grin *v.* smile, beam, smirk, simper.

grind *n.* drudgery, toil, labor, work, sweat, exertion.

grind *v.* **1.** pulverize, crush, powder, mill, grate, granulate, pound, pestle. **2.** sharpen, whet, hone, polish, smooth, scour, abrade. **3.** oppress, persecute, harass, torment, worry.

grind out create, manufacture, compose, produce, churn out.

grip *n.* **1.** grasp, hold, clutch, clasp, cinch, vise, clench, clinch, embrace, handshake. **2.** understanding, perception, ken, comprehension. **3.** control, dominance, power, influence. **4.** suitcase, valise, satchel, bag.

grip *v.* **1.** clasp, seize, clutch, grasp, catch, hold, latch on to. **2.** enthrall, fascinate, engross, entrance, mesmerize, rivet, spellbind, involve, absorb, thrill, compel.

gripe *n.* objection, complaint, grievance, protest, grumble, beef (*slang*), whine.

gripe *v.* **1.** disturb, annoy, vex, irritate, bother, irk, aggravate. **2.** complain, grumble, mutter, fuss, carp, whine, moan, groan, grouch, grouse, *slang;* bellyache, bitch, kvetch.

gripping *adj.* absorbing, suspenseful, riveting,

spellbinding, engrossing, fascinating, enthralling, compelling.

grisly *adj.* ghastly, terrible, sickening, hairraising, awful, shocking, macabre, gruesome, terrible, abominable, appalling, horrid, dreadful; *ant.* delightful.

grit *n.* **1.** gravel, sand, dust, dirt. **2.** courage, pluck, determination, tenacity, mettle, nerve, perseverance, guts, stamina, spunk, spine, staying power.

gritty *adj.* **1.** abrasive, rough, sandy, rasping, lumpy, gravelly, dusty, powdery, granular, raspy, scratchy; *ant.* fine, smooth. **2.** brave, plucky, determined, resolute, courageous, tough, tenacious, dogged, game, hardy, spirited, steadfast; *ant.* spineless.

grizzled *adj.* gray, graying, salt-and-pepper, hoary, hoar, canescent, griseous.

groan *n.* moan, cry, wail, sigh, lament, sob, whimper, bleat.

groan *v.* cry, moan, murmur, lament, wail, sigh, complain, object, protest, keen.

groggy *adj.* dazed, stunned, befuddled, confused, reeling, stupefied, punch-drunk, wobbly, shaky, weak, woozy; *ant.* lucid.

groom *n.* **1.** servant, hostler, stable boy, equerry. **2.** bridegroom, spouse, benedict, consort.

groom *v.* **1.** clean, neaten, preen, primp, tidy, spruce, brush. **2.** train, school, prepare, ready, drill, initiate.

groove *n.* rut, channel, gutter, trench, canal, furrow, flute, hollow, valley; *ant.* ridge.
in the groove (*slang*) efficient, skillful, operative, working.

grope *v.* fumble, founder, cast about, feel around, flounder, search, fish, probe.

gross *n.* total, aggregate, whole, totality, entirety, bulk, sum.

gross *v.* earn, make, take in, rake, accumulate, total, aggregate.

gross *adj.* **1.** flagrant, egregious, glaring, grievous, deplorable, bald. **2.** rude, coarse, crude, tasteless, indelicate, improper, indecent, obscene, foul, vulgar, lewd, ribald, bawdy, blue; *ant.* delicate. **3.** obese, corpulent, heavy, porcine, hulking, bulky; corporeal, fleshly, sensual, bestial.

grotesque *adj.* deformed, misshapen, hideous,

ugly, monstrous, unnatural, gruesome, freakish, macabre, gothic, strange, bizarre.

grotto *n.* cave, cavern, chamber, hollow, hole, catacomb, subterrene.

grouch *n.* curmudgeon, churl, grumbler, malcontent, crank, crab, complainer, bellyacher, whiner.

grouch *v.* complain, mutter, grumble, gripe, carp, grouse, whine, moan, *slang:* bellyache, beef.

grouchy *adj.* irritable, testy, petulant, churlish, discontented, irascible, cantankerous, cross, crotchety, peevish, surly, out of sorts, captious; *ant.* contented.

ground *n.* **1.** soil, sand, dirt, earth, clay, sod, turf, terra firma, dust, loam, pitch. **2.** area, spot, field, tract, terrain, territory, region.

from the ground up thoroughly, wholly, entirely, completely.

give ground withdraw, yield, retire, retreat.

on firm ground reliable, secure, supported, safe.

ground *v.* **1.** establish, base, anchor, install, rest, settle. **2.** teach, train, indoctrinate, educate, tutor, coach, drill, prepare.

groundless *adj.* unjustified, unsubstantiated, unfounded, unwarranted, absurd, illusory, unproven, unreasonable, idle, absurd; *ant.* justified, reasonable.

grounds *n.* **1.** property, lot, territory, domain, tract, habitat, park, surroundings, environs. **2.** basis, premise, motive, rationale, foundation, justification, cause, reason, argument, proof, vindication.

groundwork *n.* **1.** foundation, basis, footing, cornerstone, underpinning. **2.** preliminaries, preparation, arrangements, homework, research.

group *n.* **1.** gathering, assemblage, congregation, crowd, gang, team, squadron, clique, circle, faction, coterie. **2.** category, class, division, set, branch.

group *v.* **1.** mass, assemble, collect, band, marshal, get together, fraternize, congregate; *ant.* disperse. **2.** classify, categorize, sort, order, cluster, arrange, assort.

grouse *n.* complaint, grievance, objection, gripe, peeve, lament.

grouse *v.* gripe, grouch, grumble, complain, carp, fret, bellyache, beef, moan.

grove *n.* thicket, wood, woodland, copse, arbor, plantation, forest, stand, orchard.

grovel *v.* defer, cringe, kowtow, bootlick, flatter, fawn, backscratch, cower, creep, crawl.

grow *v.* **1.** increase, expand, swell, enlarge, dilate, stretch, spread, burgeon; *ant.* shrink, wither. **2.** develop, evolve, mature, sprout, germinate, flower, shoot up, blossom. **3.** cultivate, raise, nurture, foster, plant, farm. **4.** flourish, prosper, breed, thrive, advance, progress; *ant.* decline.

growl *n.* snarl, grumble, rumble, bellow, gnarl, gnarr, bark, grunt, snap.

growl *v.* **1.** snarl, gnarr, gnarl, grumble. **2.** scold, upbraid, castigate, carp.

grown-up *adj.* of age, adult, mature, ripe, full-grown; *ant.* childish, immature.

growth *n.* **1.** increase, expansion, growing, burgeoning, stretching, widening, proliferation, multiplication; *ant.* shrinkage, stagnation. **2.** development, ripening, completion, adulthood, fullness, maturation, flower, prime, harvest.

grub *v.* **1.** dig, delve, burrow, excavate, forage, rummage, ferret, root, probe, investigate, explore, hunt, scour, uproot. **2.** work, drudge, toil, labor, slave.

grub *n.* **1.** larva, worm, maggot, caterpillar, pupa, nymph, chrysalis, entozoon. **2.** (*slang*) food, rations, provisions, sustenance, edibles, fodder, victuals, comestibles, *slang:* chow, eats.

grubby *adj.* dirty, sloppy, slovenly, shabby, untidy, soiled, squalid, unkempt, grimy, filthy, unwashed, seedy, sordid; *ant.* clean, smart.

grudge *n.* resentment, spite, bitterness, enmity, animosity, hard feelings, malice, rancor, jealousy, aversion, pique.

grudge *v.* resent, object to, begrudge, stint, pinch, covet, withhold, repine.

grudging *adj.* reluctant, unwilling, half-hearted, unenthusiastic, hesitant, guarded.

grueling *adj.* arduous, severe, hard, punishing, grinding, demanding, taxing, trying, wearying, backbreaking, laborious, strenuous, uphill; *ant.* easy.

gruesome *adj.* ghastly, grisly, horrific, spine-chilling, monstrous, repulsive, fearsome, shocking, loathsome, hideous, abominable, repellent; *ant.* charming, congenial.

gruff *adj.* **1.** hoarse, husky, throaty, grating, gravelly, rough, guttural, rasping, strident; *ant.* clear, sweet. **2.** brusque, blunt, curt, abrupt, rude, crude, impolite, unmannerly, uncivil, discourteous; *ant.* courteous.

grumble *n.* **1.** muttering, growl, murmur, rumble, gurgle, moan. **2.** complaint, grievance, objection, lament, gripe, beef.

grumble *v.* **1.** complain, carp, fuss, gripe, grouch, bellyache (*slang*), repine, deplore. **2.** growl, snarl, gnarl, bark, grunt, mutter, rumble, splutter, snuffle.

grumpy *adj.* surly, testy, petulant, cantankerous, cross, irritable, grouchy, peevish, crotchety, truculent; *ant.* civil, contented.

grunt *v.* snort, squawk, squeak, cry.

guarantee *n.* warranty, promise, pledge, assurance, word of honor, covenant, insurance, security, assurance, oath, voucher, surety, endorsement.

guarantee *v.* assure, ensure, insure, promise, swear, warrant, certify, vouch for, secure, protect, underwrite.

guarantor *n.* sponsor, supporter, underwriter, backer, voucher, bondsman, guarantee, warrantor, covenantor.

guaranty *n.* **1.** promise, assurance, pledge, attestation, certification, covenant. **2.** contract, warrant, bond, recognizance, certificate, charter, stake, collateral, security.

guard *n.* **1.** sentry, escort, protector, lookout, custodian, sentinel, patrol, watch; bulwark, shield, screen. **2.** precaution, vigilance, care, watchfulness, heed, wariness, attention.

guard *v.* watch, protect, secure, defend, safeguard, supervise, tend, mind, oversee, patrol, police.

guarded *adj.* **1.** protected, safeguarded, secured, defended. **2.** cautious, circumspect, careful, prudent, reticent, wary, watchful, reserved, discreet, noncommittal; *ant.* frank, open.

guardian *n.* guard, keeper, warden, attendant, custodian, protector, conservator, preserver, trustee.

guess *n.* conjecture, supposition, theory, hypothesis, estimate, prediction, speculation, opinion, judgment, belief, surmise.

guess v. speculate, suppose, surmise, estimate, conjecture, hypothesize, predict, imagine, suspect, think, judge, dare say.

guest n. 1. visitor, caller, company, visitant. 2. tenant, boarder, patron, customer, habitué, sojourner, frequenter, lodger, regular, renter.

guidance n. 1. direction, leadership, management, government, supervision, navigation, control, auspices, aegis. 2. counsel, advice, help, recommendation, caution, warning.

guide n. 1. pathfinder, pilot, scout, escort, pioneer, usher, docent, tutor, vanguard, chaperon. 2. model, pattern, example, standard, exemplar, ideal, inspiration, polestar, beacon, signpost.

guide v. 1. (have charge of) direct, supervise, oversee, control, rule, manage, command, govern, regulate, handle. 2. (take in a desired direction) lead, conduct, pilot, steer, point, counsel, teach, educate, train, head, sway, shepherd.

guild n. association, league, fellowship, brotherhood, organization, corporation, fraternity, order, society, union, club, lodge.

guile n. deceit, cunning, craft, treachery, slyness, duplicity, cleverness, artifice, ruse, trickery; ant. innocence, candor.

guileful adj. deceitful, devious, clever, crafty, tricky, cunning, sneaky, sly, foxy, underhanded, artful, wily, duplicitous, disingenuous; ant. sincere, naive.

guileless adj. open, candid, simple, sincere, truthful, honest, frank, direct, innocent, naive, trusting, straightforward, transparent; ant. artful, guileful.

guilt n. (bad feeling) shame, blame, selfreproach, remorse, contrition; ant. shamelessness. 2. culpability, delinquency, blameworthiness, criminality; ant. innocence.

guiltless adj. innocent, blameless, irreproachable, sinless, unsullied, spotless, untarnished, pure, unimpeachable; ant. guilty, tainted.

guilty adj. 1. convicted, condemned, sentenced, incriminated, indicted, damned, doomed, censured; ant. vindicated, absolved. 2. culpable, responsible, delinquent, wrong, blameworthy, reproachable, derelict; ant. blameless, innocent.

guise n. 1. disguise, mask, façade, pretense, masquerade. 2. likeness, semblance, appearance, form, manner, custom, aspect, mien.

gulch n. gully, ditch, gorge, ravine.

gulf n. 1. chasm, abyss, void, opening, gap, gorge, cleft, breach, rift, rent, split. 2. inlet, sound, cove, bay, basin.

gullible adj. trusting, naive, born yesterday, credulous, foolish, green, unsuspecting; ant. suspicious, wary.

gully n. ravine, ditch, gulch, gutter, crevasse, watercourse.

gulp v. guzzle, knock back, quaff, swig, swill, devour, bolt, gobble, gormandize, wolf, stuff; ant. sip, nibble.

gum n. glue, adhesive, paste, mucilage, resin, cement, sap, pitch, tar.

gummy adj. sticky, tacky, adhesive, viscid, viscous, gluey.

gumption n. boldness, nerve, spunk, daring, guts (slang), aggressiveness, initiative, enterprise; ant. timidity.

gunman n. assassin, murderer, sniper, killer, gangster, bandit, terrorist, hit man (slang), desperado.

gurgle v. babble, murmur, bubble, trill, purl, burble, lap.

guru n. mentor, teacher, instructor, master, authority, sage, eminence grise, swami, Svengali.

gush n. spout, torrent, cascade, eruption, spurt, burst, jet, flood, rush, tide, flow, stream, effusion.

gush v. 1. spout, pour, well, jet, spew, spurt, burst; cascade, surge, flow, stream, rush, run. 2. sentimentalize, maunder, babble, blather, slobber, effuse, drivel, prate, prattle.

gushing adj. 1. flowing, spouting, pouring out, emitting. 2. sentimental, maudlin, mushy, emotional, effusive, cloying, fulsome, mawkish; ant. restrained, sincere.

gust n. blast, squall, rush, gale, breeze, blow, flurry.

gusto n. fervor, enjoyment, delight, relish, pleasure, zeal, zest, vigor, exhilaration, verve, exuberance; ant. apathy, distaste.

gusty adj. shifting, fitful, variable, tempestu-

gut ous, windy, blustery, breezy, stormy, squally, blustering; *ant.* calm.

gut *v.* ravage, ransack, pillage, rifle, plunder, loot, clean out, sack, despoil.

gut *adj.* instinctive, innate, visceral, intuitive, natural, spontaneous, unthinking, involuntary, deep-seated, heartfelt.

gutless (*slang*) *adj.* cowardly, submissive, spineless, weak, abject, chicken-livered, timid, craven, feeble, irresolute, lily-livered, chicken (*slang*); *ant.* courageous.

guts *n.* **1.** bowels, insides, intestines, entrails, innards, viscera. **2.** (*slang*) courage, daring, audacity, boldness, spunk, moxie (*slang*), endurance, stamina, backbone, mettle, grit, pluck, fortitude; *ant.* spinelessness.

gutsy (*slang*) *adj.* spirited, courageous, gallant, plucky, brave, bold, staunch, game, resolute; *ant.* quiet, timid.

gutter *n.* ditch, canal, runnel, gully, trench, channel, trough, sluice.

guttural *adj.* hoarse, husky, gruff, rasping, throaty, rough, gravelly, harsh, low, deep, thick, gargling; *ant.* dulcet.

guy *n.* **1.** cable, truss, sling, hawser, tackle, cinch, bond, line. **2.** fellow, chap, lad, man, individual, person.

guzzle *v.* imbibe, swill, tipple, quaff, gulp, chug (*slang*).

gyp *n.* cheat, fraud, trick, swindle, hoax, *slang:* scam, rip-off.

gyp *v.* cheat, defraud, swindle, cozen, bamboozle, gull, hoodwink.

gypsy *n.* nomad, vagabond, vagrant, tramp, Bohemian, wanderer, roamer, migrant, gadabout.

gyrate *v.* twirl, whirl, pirouette, spin, spiral, gyre, rotate, coil, swirl.

gyrating *adj.* spinning, twirling, revolving, rotating, whirling, corkscrewing.

gyration *n.* spinning, rotation, twirl, pirouette, whirling, convolution, spiral, eddy, turn, roll.

H

habit *n.* **1.** custom, practice, convention, routine, manner, way, fashion; bent, propensity, proclivity, inclination, nature, tendency, wont, penchant, disposition. **2.** dress, costume, clothing, apparel, attire, garb.

habitable *adj.* livable, inhabitable, comfortable, fit for habitation.

habitat *n.* surroundings, domain, environment, element, locality, terrain, territory; abode, home, turf (*slang*).

habitation *n.* dwelling, abode, domicile, home, residence, lodging, living quarters, inhabitance.

habitual *adj.* customary, routine, everyday, established, fixed, frequent, recurrent, continual; chronic, inveterate; *ant.* exceptional, unusual.

habituate *v.* acclimatize, accustom, condition, break in, familiarize, inure, school, season.

habitué *n.* devotee, regular, customer, patron, frequenter.

hack *v.* cut, chop, hew, cleave, gash, slice, lacerate; whack, kick; mangle, mutilate.

hackneyed *adj.* trite, banal, pedestrian, stale, clichéd, stock, commonplace, threadbare, overworked, tired, bromidic.

haggard *adj.* cadaverous, careworn, gaunt, drawn, emaciated, thin, wan, wasted, hollow-eyed, pinched; *ant.* robust.

haggle *v.* bargain, barter, dicker, wrangle, bicker, cavil, palter, squabble, argue.

hail *v.* greet, salute, wave, signal, address, flag down, acknowledge, welcome; honor, acclaim, applaud, exalt.

hair *n.* locks, tresses, mane, mop, shock.

get in one's hair (*slang*) irritate, annoy, disturb, bother, bug (*slang*).

make one's hair stand on end frighten, terrify, scare, horrify.

split hairs quibble, cavil, nag, nit-pick, pettifog.

to a hair precisely, perfectly, exactly.

hairdo *n.* haircut, hairstyle, coiffure, perm.

hairless *adj.* bald, beardless, clean-shaven, depilated, shorn, shaven, glabrous.

hair-raising *adj.* alarming, frightening, bloodcurdling, eerie, ghastly, petrifying, spine-chilling; exciting, thrilling; *ant.* calming, boring.

hair-splitting *adj.* finicky, minute, nit-picking, fussy, quibbling, captious, carping, caviling, faultfinding, pettifogging; *ant.* tolerant, accepting.

hairy *adj.* **1.** shaggy, bushy, unshorn, bearded, furry, bristly, hirsute, tufted; *ant.* bald, smooth, clean-shaven. **2.** (*slang*) difficult, perilous, risky, tricky, hazardous, dicey, nerve-racking.

halcyon *adj.* balmy, mild, golden, calm, care-free, gentle, happy, pacific, placid, quiet, serene, tranquil; *ant.* stormy, turbulent.

hale *adj.* robust, strong, vigorous, hearty, healthy, ablebodied, athletic, fit, sound; *ant.* ill, sickly.

half *n.* bisection, division, fifty percent, half-share, hemisphere, fraction, portion, section.

half *adj.* bisected, divided, fractional, halved, incomplete, limited, part, partial; *ant.* all, full, whole.

half-baked *adj.* premature, immature, shallow, superficial; brainless, foolish, harebrained, ill-conceived, short-sighted, silly, stupid.

halfhearted *adj.* apathetic, listless, lackluster, lackadaisical, perfunctory, lukewarm, cool, indifferent, ambivalent, blasé; *ant.* enthusiastic.

halfway *adj.* **1.** intermediate, mid, middle, midway, central, equidistant. **2.** incomplete, partial, unsatisfactory; *ant.* complete.

half-wit *n.* cretin, dimwit, dolt, dullard, dunce, dunderhead, imbecile, moron, nitwit, simpleton.

half-witted *adj.* addlebrained, batty, feeble-minded, cretinous, simple.

hall *n.* **1.** arena, auditorium, gym, concert hall, lyceum, rotunda, chamber, armory, assembly room. **2.** entrance, foyer, anteroom, gallery, lobby, vestibule, concourse, corridor.

hallmark *n.* badge, emblem, seal, stamp, sign, trademark, symbol, signet.

hallowed *adj.* consecrated, sanctified, blessed, dedicated, established; holy, honored, revered, sacred.

hallucinate *v.* imagine, fantasize, hear voices, daydream, *slang:* freak out, trip.

hallucination *n.* illusion, fantasy, vision, phantasm, apparition, mirage, figment, delusion, phantasmagoria.

halo *n.* radiance, nimbus, corona, aurora, aura, gloria, glory, halation.

halt *n.* stop, break, pause, impasse, interruption, recess, standstill, stoppage, arrest, termination, close; *ant.* continuation, start.

halt *v.* **1.** cease, desist, end, pack it in (*slang*), terminate, quit, rest, wait, pause, stay. **2.** (bring to a halt) arrest, check, impede, interrupt, hamper, hinder, frustrate, quell.

halting *adj.* labored, awkward, broken, faltering, stammering, uncertain, hesitant, indecisive, wavering, vacillating; *ant.* confident, fluent, graceful.

halve *v.* bisect, divide, split, lessen, reduce; share, go Dutch (*slang*).

hammer *n.* mallet, gavel, club, peen, mace, ram.

hammer *v.* beat, hit, strike, clobber, knock, whack, bang, pound, drive, cudgel, batter, drum, maleate.

hammer out accomplish, complete, produce, forge, shape, settle, work out.

hamper *v.* impede, hinder, thwart, restrain, inhibit, hamstring, fetter, restrict, curb, curtail; *ant.* aid, expedite.

hamstring *v.* disable, cripple, injure, lessen.

hamstrung *adj.* crippled, disabled, foiled, frustrated, handicapped, helpless, incapacitated, paralyzed, stymied.

hand *n.* **1.** fist, flipper, mitt, paw, palm, grip. **2.** role, responsibility, part, share, complicity. **3.** worker, helper, employee, hired man, hireling, laborer. **4.** aid, guidance, help, instruction, assistance, influence, participation.

at first hand directly, originally, from the horse's mouth.

at hand 1. nearby, close by, within reach, approximate, immediate, ready, available, convenient. **2.** imminent, impending, approaching, coming.

by hand homemade, handcrafted, manual.

eat out of one's hand serve, obey, comply, be subordinated.

from hand to mouth from day to day, in poverty, insecurely, precariously, uncertainly, improvidently, on the breadline.

hands down easily, effortlessly, in a canter, handily; completely, totally; *ant.* with difficulty.

hand in glove together, in collusion, in league, intimately, in cahoots (*slang*).

in hand managed, in order, under control, keep one's hand in continue, carry on, make a practice of.

off one's hands rid of, not responsible for, free, released from.

on hand present, available, stocked, at hand, within reach, at one's fingertips.

out of hand unmanageable, wild, chaotic, unchecked, out of control.

show one's hand reveal, divulge, disclose.

throw up one's hands resign, give up, quit, throw in the towel.

wash one's hands of reject, deny, refuse, spurn.

with a heavy hand harshly, oppressively, coercively.

hand *v.* transfer, transmit, deliver, conduct, convey, give, pass, present, provide, return.

hand down bequeath, give, pass on, will, grant.

hand in submit, deliver, return.

hand out distribute, disseminate, disburse, dispense, mete.

hand over surrender, relinquish, deliver, give up, yield, present, turn over, release.

handbook *n.* manual, guide, textbook, companion, vade mecum, directory.

handcuff *v.* fasten, fetter, manacle, secure, shackle, tie.

handcuffs *n.* manacles, shackles, fetters, cuffs.

handful *n.* few, some, scattering, smattering, sprinkling.

handicap *n.* **1.** disadvantage, barrier, obstacle, defect, penalty, drawback, hindrance, block,

handicap impediment, encumbrance, stumbling-block; *ant.* privilege, headstart. **2.** affliction, disability, impairment, loss. **3.** (advantage in a sports competition) edge, advantage, headstart.

handicap *v.* disable, disadvantage, hamper, limit, cripple, deter; *ant.* aid, support, help.

handily *adv.* easily, deftly, skillfully, adroitly, smoothly, cleverly, intelligently.

handiwork *n.* creation, product, achievement, doing, design, invention, production.

handle *n.* arm, handgrip, crank, knob, grasp, grip, haft, heft, hilt.

handle *v.* **1.** touch, check, finger, prod, probe, feel, fondle, grasp, clutch, paw. **2.** direct, control, supervise, manage, run, operate, administer, conduct, oversee. **3.** deal in, retail, sell, trade, traffic, market.

handling *n.* administration, approach, conduct, management, treatment, direction, manipulation, operation.

hand-me-down *adj.* inherited, used, secondhand, worn, threadbare; *ant.* new.

handout *n.* **1.** alms, charity, contribution, dole, donation, freebie, free meal. **2.** bulletin, circular, leaflet, handbill, notice, statement.

hand-picked *adj.* choice, chosen, elect, elite, picked, screened, select.

hands *n.* authority, care, command, control, custody, guardianship, guidance, jurisdiction, keeping, possession, power, supervision, tutelage.

handsome *adj.* **1.** attractive, becoming, comely, elegant, beautiful, fine, good-looking, smart, dapper, graceful, virile. **2.** abundant, ample, bountiful, considerable, generous, large, liberal, plentiful, sizable, full.

handsomely *adv.* lavishly, magnanimously, munificently, plentifully, richly, unsparingly, unstintingly; *ant.* stingily.

handwriting *n.* penmanship, script, calligraphy, chirography, holograph, hand, longhand, manuscript, scrawl.

handy *adj.* **1.** near, accessible, proximate, at hand, available, convenient, nearby, ready; *ant.* far, distal. **2.** useful, beneficial, helpful, manageable, gainful, advantageous; *ant.* inconvenient. **3.** skillful, dexterous, adept, adroit, deft, apt, ingenious, nimble, proficient; *ant.* clumsy, unwieldy.

handyman *n.* helper, hired man, Jack-of-all-trades, factotum.

hang *v.* **1.** suspend, dangle, drape, sag, droop, loll, sling; attach, stick, nail, hook. **2.** lynch, execute, gibbet, string up.

hang about dally, frequent, haunt, linger, loiter, tarry, hang around.

hang back demur, hesitate, recoil, shy away.

hang fire delay, procrastinate, stall, stop, vacillate, be on hold, wait, hang back; *ant.* press on.

hang on 1. carry on, continue, persevere, endure, persist, hold fast, remain, hold the line; *ant.* give up. **2.** cling, clutch, depend on, grasp, grip.

hang over impend, loom, menace, threaten.

hangdog *adj.* abject, browbeaten, cowed, cringing, pathetic, sorry, downcast, furtive, miserable, shamefaced; sneaking, wretched.

hanger-on *n.* follower, lackey, minion, sycophant; leech, sponge, parasite, freeloader; nuisance, dependent.

hanging *adj.* **1.** dangling, drooping, floppy, swinging, loose, pendent, suspended. **2.** pending, undecided, unresolved, unsettled, up in the air.

hangout (*slang*), *n.* resort, bar, *slang:* den, dive, haunt, home, joint, watering-hole, hole.

hang-up (*slang*), *n.* block, inhibition, difficulty, problem, predicament, disturbance; obsession, preoccupation, idée fixe, thing (*slang*).

hank *n.* coil, knot, length, loop, piece, portion, roll, skein.

hanker *v.* desire, covet, crave, want, wish, lust, hunger, itch, thirst, yearn.

hankering *n.* thirst, urge, wish, craving, yearning, yen.

hanky-panky *n.* cheating, chicanery, deception, devilry, funny business, knavery, subterfuge, machinations, mischief, monkey business, nonsense, shenanigans, trickery.

haphazard *adj.* **1.** random, arbitrary, aimless, indiscriminate, hit-or-miss; *ant.* ordered, structured. **2.** careless, disorderly, disorganized, slipshod, reckless, uncoordinated, unmethodical; *ant.* deliberate, planned, careful.

hapless *adj.* unlucky, unfortunate, cursed, luckless, ill-fated, jinxed, star-crossed; miserable, unhappy, wretched; *ant.* lucky, fortunate.

happen *v.* occur, arise, develop, transpire,

happening befall, chance, result, ensue, issue, proceed, supervene.

happen on discover, find, light on, chance on, come on, hit on.

happening n. occurrence, event, incident, episode, affair, circumstance, experience, occasion, proceeding, scene.

happiness n. bliss, contentment, delight, joy, elation, exuberance, jubilation, gaiety, pleasure, satisfaction; ant. depression, melancholy, dejection.

happy adj. **1.** gay, delighted, cheerful, joyful, joyous, elated, ecstatic, contented; ant. sad, melancholy. **2.** apt, appropriate, fit, propitious; seasonable, timely.

happy-go-lucky adj. blithe, carefree, nonchalant, heedless, unconcerned, casual, cheerful, improvident, insouciant, irresponsible; ant. anxious, wary.

harangue n. tirade, diatribe, lecture, peroration, sermon, declamation, exhortation, oration, philippic, spiel.

harangue v. lecture, preach, rant, sermonize, declaim, descant, exhort, hold forth, orate, perorate.

harass v. annoy, badger, pester, hassle, torment, vex, harry, beleaguer, exasperate, irritate.

harassment n. aggravation, annoyance, bother, trouble, molestation, persecution, vexation.

harbinger n. sign, omen, portent, signal, foretoken, herald, indication, precursor, warning.

harbor n. **1.** anchorage, inlet, pier, wharf, jetty, marina, roadstead. **2.** refuge, haven, retreat, sanctuary, asylum, shelter.

harbor v. **1.** protect, provide, secure, shelter, refuge, conceal, hide, lodge, nurture, shield. **2.** (said of thoughts, beliefs, etc.) consider, cherish, entertain, regard, hold.

hard adj. **1.** compact, solid, tough, impenetrable, rigid, unyielding, inflexible, dense; ant. soft, porous, flexible. **2.** difficult, arduous, formidable, complex, intricate, laborious, rigorous, uphill. **3.** severe, demanding, cruel, antagonistic, callous, implacable, harsh, pitiless, exacting, grim, unrelenting; ant. indulgent.

hard and fast binding, fixed, rigid, inflexible, set, immutable, unalterable, stringent, incontrovertible, invariable; ant. flexible, variable, optional, voluntary.

hard up broke, bankrupt, in the red, busted (slang), insolvent, impoverished, penniless, impecunious, penurious; ant. rich.

hard-bitten adj. callous, hard-boiled, tough, unsentimental, cynical, matter-of-fact, practical, ruthless, shrewd; ant. tenderhearted, idealistic.

hard-core adj. absolute, steadfast, dedicated, determined, devoted, die-hard, dyed-in-the-wool, intransigent, obstinate, staunch, uncompromising, unwavering; ant. moderate.

harden v. **1.** solidify, crystallize, bake, cement, consolidate, concentrate, fossilize, freeze, ossify, petrify, vitrify, vulcanize; ant. soften, melt. **2.** brace, buttress, fortify, gird, reinforce. **3.** toughen, acclimate, accustom, habituate, inure, season, indurate, develop, nerve; ant. weaken, debilitate.

hardheaded adj. **1.** obstinate, willful, stubborn, headstrong, tough. **2.** shrewd, astute, cool, pragmatic, rational, realistic, sensible, no-nonsense, hard-nosed (slang).

hardhearted adj. cold, indifferent, insensitive, unsympathetic, uncaring, callous, cruel, heartless, inhuman, merciless, pitiless; ant. kind, merciful.

hard-hitting adj. aggressive, forceful, tough, unsparing, vigorous; critical, condemnatory; ant. mild.

hardihood n. fortitude, courage, determination, mettle, resolution, firmness, grit, assurance; strength, power; ant. weakness, timidity.

hardiness n. resilience, resolution, ruggedness, stamina, sturdiness, valor, courage, fortitude; ant. timidity.

hardline adj. uncompromising, intransigent, unyielding, dogmatic, militant, inflexible, undeviating; ant. moderate.

hardly adv. barely, not quite, scarcely, just, only, faintly, imperceptibly, infinitesimally, infrequently; ant. readily, easily.

hard-pressed adj. harassed, pressured, beset, beleaguered, put-upon, stressed-out, harried, overworked; ant. untroubled.

hardship n. adversity, suffering, privation, affliction, tribulation, burden, calamity, misfortune, trial; ant. ease, luxury.

hard-working adj. diligent, energetic, industrious, assiduous, indefatigable, sedulous, zealous; ant. lazy.

hardy *adj.* **1.** durable, sturdy, rugged, stalwart, strong, vigorous, firm, tough, rigorous, robust; *ant.* unhealthy, weak. **2.** brave, resolute, dauntless, bold, intrepid, valiant; rash, audacious, presumptuous, brazen, reckless.

harebrained *adj.* foolish, asinine, daft, flighty, scatterbrained, dizzy, irresponsible, rash, reckless, wild; *ant.* sensible.

harlot *n.* call girl, prostitute, streetwalker, whore, trollop, strumpet, hooker (*slang*).

harm *n.* **1.** injury, damage, hurt, ill, impairment, detriment, infliction, misfortune; *ant.* benefit, service. **2.** evil, wickedness, vice, iniquity, immorality, mischief, abuse, outrage; *ant.* virtue.

harm *v.* damage, hurt, injure, wound, impair, cripple, maltreat, mar, ruin, scathe, spoil; *ant.* benefit, improve.

harmful *adj.* damaging, injurious, hurtful, destructive, deleterious, detrimental, noxious, pernicious, toxic; *ant.* harmless, beneficial.

harmless *adj.* safe, benign, inoffensive, gentle, innocent, innocuous, nontoxic; *ant.* harmful.

harmonious *adj.* **1.** melodious, musical, sonorous, tuneful, euphonic, harmonic, euphonious, mellifluous, symphonious; *ant.* shrill, dissonant, jangling. **2.** amicable, congenial, cordial, peaceful, agreeable, compatible; concordant, consonant, congruous, accordant, symmetrical; *ant.* opposed, incompatible.

harmonize *v.* blend, match, coordinate, correspond, reconcile, jibe, accommodate, adapt, conform, arrange, attune, reconcile; *ant.* clash.

harmony *n.* concord, accord, unity, agreement, amicability, amity, balance, symmetry, compatibility; friendship, peace, rapport, sympathy.

harness *v.* channel, control, employ, use, utilize, yoke, apply, manage; bridle, tame, domesticate, secure, constrain.

harp on *v.* dwell on, press, belabor, repeat, reiterate, renew, nag about.

harpoon *n.* arrow, barb, dart, javelin, lance, spear.

harried *adj.* harassed, hassled, pressured, put-upon, troubled, worried, agitated, anxious, bothered, distressed; *ant.* untroubled.

harrow *v.* **1.** plow, drag, dig, cultivate. **2.** torment, torture, vex, harass, perturb, daunt, dismay, distress; *ant.* assuage, hearten.

harrowing *adj.* frightening, terrifying, traumatic, wrenching, alarming, heart-rending, nerve-racking, trying; *ant.* calming, reassuring.

harry *v.* **1.** raid, lay waste, pillage, plunder, ravage, rob, maraud, molest, sack, devastate; *ant.* aid. **2.** harass, pester, badger, disturb, annoy, fret, hassle, tease, trouble, vex, worry, depredate; *ant.* calm.

harsh *adj.* **1.** discordant, cacophonous, grating, jarring, squawky, dissonant, strident, caterwauling, assonant. **2.** discourteous, gruff, uncivil, ungracious, insensitive, boorish; *ant.* gentle, sensitive. **3.** severe, unrelenting, hard, austere, brutal, ruthless, scabrous, abusive, punitive, Draconian; *ant.* mild, smooth, soft.

harum-scarum *adj.* careless, reckless, irresponsible, rash, impetuous, haphazard, helter-skelter, hasty, ill-considered, imprudent, wild; *ant.* sensible.

harvest *n.* crop, yield, produce, product, reaping, fruit, consequence, fruition, result, return, vendage.

harvest *v.* collect, reap, mow, glean, gather, garner, cull, cut, pick, pluck, accumulate, acquire, collect; *ant.* plant, sow, seed.

hash *n.* **1.** goulash, ragout, stew, casserole, leftovers, olio. **2.** mixture, mess, hodgepodge, mishmash, jumble, shambles.

hashish *n.* bhang, cannabis, dope, ganja, hash, hemp, marijuana, *slang:* pot, grass, weed.

hash out conclude, settle, resolve, work out.

hash over debate, discuss, ponder, review.

hassle (*slang*) *n.* argument, quarrel, squabble, dispute, altercation; bother, difficulty, inconvenience, nuisance, trial; *ant.* agreement, peace.

hassle (*slang*) *v.* annoy, harass, bother, pester, badger, bug, harry, hound; *ant.* assist, let be.

haste *n.* speed, swiftness, alacrity, celerity, dispatch, expedition, rapidity, urgency; *ant.* caution, slowness.

hasten *v.* hurry, rush, speed, dash, scurry, hie, hightail it (*slang*), accelerate, expedite, quicken, dispatch, goad, precipitate; *ant.* dawdle, delay.

hastily *adv.* **1.** quickly, rapidly, fast, apace, promptly, straightaway; *ant.* slowly, gradually. **2.** heedlessly, impetuously, impulsively, precipitately, recklessly; *ant.* carefully, deliberately.

hasty *adj.* **1.** quick, prompt, expeditious,

rapid, fast. **2.** foolhardy, precipitate, impulsive, indiscreet; cursory, hurried, fleeting, perfunctory; *ant.* careful, deliberate, placid.

hatch *v.* bear, breed, brood, incubate, conceive, concoct, contrive, design, develop, devise, originate, plan, plot, scheme.

hate *n.* animosity, enmity, hostility, loathing, execration, antipathy, detestation, disgust, malignity, rancor; *ant.* desire, favor, love.

hate *v.* abhor, detest, despise, execrate, loathe, scorn; *ant.* enjoy, like, adore.

hateful *adj.* odious, abominable, repugnant, detestable, heinous, repellent, revolting, vile; *ant.* pleasing.

hatred *n.* malice, misanthropy, prejudice, animosity, antagonism, enmity, rancor; *ant.* devotion, attraction, affection.

haughtiness *n.* arrogance, disdain, condescension, contempt, insolence, hauteur, imperiousness; airs, pomposity, snobbishness, elitism, aloofness, loftiness; *ant.* friendliness, humility.

haughty *adj.* arrogant, vain, conceited, fatuous, high, high-and-mighty, scornful, imperious, proud, elitist, disdainful, stiffnecked, supercilious; *ant.* friendly, humble.

haul *n.* **1.** pull, wrench, tug, lift, drag, heave. **2.** loot, booty, catch, find, gain, harvest, spoils, takings, yield.

haul *v.* drag, pull, tug, lug, draw, heave; carry, cart, convey, move, tow, transport.

haunches *n.* buttocks, thighs, hindquarters, backside, rump.

haunt *n.* den, hangout, lair, retreat, headquarters, rendezvous, resort, stamping ground, turf (*slang*).

haunt *v.* **1.** habituate, frequent, occupy, hang around. **2.** prey upon, torment, possess, trouble, plague, harass, terrify, harrow.

haunted *adj.* possessed, plagued, jinxed, cursed, tormented, troubled, worried, preoccupied.

haunting *adj.* unforgettable, poignant, memorable, indelible, seductive, evocative, disturbing, eerie, persistent, recurrent.

have *v.* **1.** possess, hold, get, procure, acquire, obtain, secure, own, accept; comprise, contain, include. **2.** bear, beget, bring forth, deliver. **3.** deceive, cheat, dupe, fool, outwit, swindle, trick.

have at strike, thrust, attack.

have done with cease, desist, finish with, give up, leave, quit, stop, throw over, wash one's hands of.

have to be obliged, must, ought, should, be compelled, be forced, be obliged, be required.

haven *n.* sanctuary, shelter, refuge, retreat, asylum, harbor, port, hideaway, haunt.

havoc *n.* **1.** carnage, destruction, devastation, ruin, plunder, despoliation. **2.** chaos, confusion, mayhem, uproar.

hawk *n.* warmonger, militarist, belligerent, chauvinist, jingoist; *ant.* dove, pacifist.

hawk *v.* peddle, sell, vend, tout, market, bark, cry.

hawker *n.* peddler, huckster, vendor, seller, costermonger (*Brit.*).

haywire *adj.* chaotic, confused, crazy, topsyturvy, tangled; inoperative, amiss, erratic, kaput; *ant.* correct, in order.

hazard *n.* **1.** danger, jeopardy, menace, threat, peril, risk; misfortune, mischance, mishap; *ant.* safety. **2.** luck, accident, chance, possibility.

hazard *v.* **1.** venture, risk, gamble, speculate, dare, presume, attempt, chance. **2.** endanger, jeopardize, imperil.

hazardous *adj.* risky, dangerous, perilous, precarious, unpredictable, insecure, chancy, dicey, hairy, ticklish, uncertain; *ant.* safe, secure.

haze *n.* mist, cloud, film, fog, smokiness, smog, fume, vapor, steam, miasma, nebulosity.

hazy *adj.* cloudy, misty, murky, smoky, crepuscular, veiled; vague, dull, faint, blurry, indistinct, nebulous, obscure; *ant.* clear, definite, bright.

head *n.* **1.** skull, brain, cranium, crown, pate, scalp; intelligence, aptitude, mentality, mind, *slang:* noggin, noodle, bean. **2.** ruler, leader, boss, supervisor, commander, director, manager; *ant.* subordinate. **3.** top, crest, peak, summit, apex, acme, height, promontory, vertex. **4.** beginning, start, source, fore, front, origin. **5.** climax, crisis, turning point, culmination, end, conclusion.

get it through one's head apprehend, comprehend, learn, understand, grasp, follow, make heads or tails of, get the picture, get it (*slang*).

hang one's head be sorry, repent, be contrite, regret.

head over heels 1. completely, entirely, unreservedly, thoroughly, utterly, wholeheartedly. **2.** recklessly, wildly, uncontrollably, precipitately.

lose one's head take leave of one's senses, go mad, become angry *or* excited, rave, lose one's cool (*slang*).

head *v.* lead, command, direct, govern, guide, point, manage, oversee, supervise.

head for aim for, direct toward, gravitate toward, make for, point to, steer for, turn for, zero in on.

head off avert, deflect, intercept, divert, interpose, parry, fend off, forestall, prevent, stop, ward off.

head *adj.* chief, dominant, first, foremost, leading, main, top, preeminent, premier, principal, supreme.

headache *n.* **1.** cephalalgia, hemicrania, migraine, neuralgia, megrim. **2.** vexation, bother, hassle, bane, inconvenience, nuisance, pain in the neck.

headed *adj.* en route, going, started, in transit; directed, aimed.

headfirst *adv.* hastily, rashly, recklessly, impetuously, precipitately; pell-mell, helter-skelter.

heading *n.* banner, caption, legend; title, name, category, designation, division, rubric, specification.

headlong *adj.* breakneck, hasty, headfirst, impetuous, impulsive, precipitate, reckless, thoughtless.

headstrong *adj.* stubborn, contrary, determined, fractious, intractable, obdurate, refractory, pigheaded, dogged; heedless, imprudent, impulsive, rash, unruly; *ant.* docile, obedient.

headway *n.* progress, advance, improvement, increase, inroads, furtherance, promotion.

heady *adj.* **1.** exciting, exhilarating, intoxicating, stimulating, potent, thrilling. **2.** hasty, impetuous, impulsive, precipitate, rash, reckless.

heal *v.* cure, restore, treat, remedy, mend, rejuvenate, medicate, physic, salve, rehabilitate, resuscitate, ameliorate; *ant.* infect, injure.

healing *adj.* restorative, comforting, curative, soothing, assuaging, therapeutic, analeptic, palliative, remedial.

health *n.* **1.** fitness, soundness, well-being, wellness, vigor, robustness, strength, salubrity;

ant. disease, infirmity. **2.** condition, constitution, form, shape, tone, weal.

healthful *adj.* salubrious, beneficial, advantageous, innocuous; invigorating, restorative, curative, tonic, cathartic; nourishing, sustentative; hygienic, sanative, aseptic; *ant.* unwholesome, noxious, sickly.

healthy *adj.* active, hardy, hale, robust, sound, sturdy, vigorous, fit as a fiddle (*slang*); *ant.* diseased, ill, infirm.

heaps *n.* profusion, abundance, accumulation, mass, mound, pile, store, hoard, aggregation; *ant.* handful, bit.

heap *v.* pile, gather, amass, hoard, collect, stack, stockpile.

hear *v.* listen, heed, attend, hearken, eavesdrop; examine, judge, try.

not hear of reject, refuse, disallow, decline, turn a deaf ear.

hearing *n.* **1.** inquiry, inquest, council, trial; audition, interview, tryout, performance, presentation. **2.** ear, audition, auditory sense, perception. **3.** earshot, range, reach, sound.

hearsay *n.* rumor, gossip, report, talk of the town, scandal, grapevine, say-so, buzz, canard.

heart *n.* **1.** feeling, affection, love, sympathy, sensitivity, compassion, concern, benevolence. **2.** root, quintessence, core, center, essence, hub, kernel, nucleus. **3.** courage, fortitude, nerve, mettle, stamina, character, boldness, bravery, grit, guts (*slang*).

after one's own heart pleasing, suitable, lovable.

at heart fundamentally, inherently, basically, privately.

break one's heart pain, disappoint, hurt, crush, dismay.

by heart by rote, pat, word for word.

from the bottom of one's heart honestly, deeply, frankly, sincerely.

heart and soul absolutely, completely, devotedly, entirely, unreservedly, wholeheartedly.

set one's heart on need, long for, desire, covet, prize.

with half a heart apathetically, listlessly, lukewarmly.

heartache *n.* grief, sorrow, heartbreak, heartsickness, misery, pain, remorse, anguish, bitter-

heartbreaking ness, dejection, despair, despondency; *ant.* elation, joy, relief.

heartbreaking *adj.* pitiful, poignant, sad, tragic, harrowing, heart-rending; agonizing, bitter, distressing, grievous; *ant.* heartening, heart-warming, comforting.

heartbroken *adj.* crushed, desolate, forlorn, grieved, heartsick, despondent, disappointed, downcast, miserable, woebegone; *ant.* delighted, elated.

hearten *v.* encourage, assure, embolden, inspire, rouse, stimulate, buck up; cheer, comfort, console, gladden; *ant.* dishearten.

heartfelt *adj.* sincere, earnest, genuine, honest, devout, fervent, ardent, deep, impassioned, profound; *ant.* false, insincere.

heartily *adv.* 1. enthusiastically, earnestly, vigorously, energetically, keenly, zealously, eagerly, warmly. 2. completely, absolutely, thoroughly, totally, wholly; genuinely, sincerely, profoundly, resolutely.

heartless *adj.* brutal, callous, cruel, merciless, pitiless, coldblooded, harsh, inhuman, insensitive; *ant.* considerate, merciful, sympathetic.

heart-rending *adj.* affecting, moving, touching, distressing, poignant, pitiful, sad, tragic, harrowing, heartbreaking.

heartwarming *adj.* cheering, encouraging, gratifying, pleasing, rewarding, satisfying; *ant.* discouraging, depressing.

hearty *adj.* 1. genial, cordial, cheery, jovial, friendly, effusive, warm; *ant.* cold, emotionless, false. 2. vigorous, healthy, robust, hardy, hale.

heat *n.* 1. warmth, fever, incandescence, sultriness, swelter, tepidity, torridness; *ant.* cold, frigidity, frost. 2. passion, ardor, fervor, intensity, agitation, excitement, vehemence, violence, zeal.

heat *v.* 1. warm up, toast, melt, oxidize, sear, chafe, incinerate; *ant.* chill, cool, freeze. 2. inflame, kindle, excite, animate, impassion, inspirit, rouse, stimulate; *ant.* dampen.

heated *adj.* acrimonious, angry, bitter, loud, violent, vehement; impassioned, charged, intense, raging, stormy, tempestuous, violent; *ant.* cordial, dispassionate.

heathen *n.* barbarian, savage, philistine, gentile, idolater, idolatress, infidel, pagan, unbeliever; *ant.* believer.

heathen *adj.* pagan, idolatrous, godless, unconverted, unenlightened, polytheistic, agnostic, amoral, atheistic; barbaric, uncivilized, savage; *ant.* Christian, godly, religious.

heating *n.* baking, boiling, broiling, cooking, grilling, steaming, scalding, roasting, melting, warming; *ant.* freezing, cooling, refrigeration.

heave *v.* cast, fling, hurl, throw, toss, wing, raise, hoist, hurl, bob, pitch, lurch, reel, sway, swell, palpitate, breathe, swirl, ebb and flow, undulate; *ant.* rest, lie still

heaven *n.* 1. paradise, Arcadia, Elysium, Elysian Fields, Olympus, Valhalla, afterworld, heavenly city, Holy City, New Jerusalem, Zion, nirvana, the hereafter; *ant.* hell, inferno, underworld.

heavenly *adj.* 1. angelic, beatific, blessed, celestial, divine, glorious, holy, immortal, seraphic, sublime, supernal. 2. exquisite, blissful, sweet, alluring, ambrosial, delightful, entrancing, rapturous; *ant.* hellish.

heavily *adv.* 1. awkwardly, ponderously, laboriously; *ant.* easily, gently, lightly. 2. considerably, decisively, thoroughly, massively, strongly, profoundly.

heaviness *n.* 1. weightiness, heftiness, ponderousness, gravity, bulkiness; ballast, burden. 2. oppression, despondency, languor, melancholy, numbness, somnolence, torpor; *ant.* sprightliness, liveliness.

heavy *adj.* 1. weighty, considerable, ample, copious, cumbersome, unwieldy, dense, laden; portly, stout, corpulent, *slang:* beefy, chunky; *ant.* light, buoyant. 2. oppressive, vexatious, hard, arduous, taxsome, onerous, vexatious, hard, arduous, taxing, exhausting. 3. grave, serious, solemn, dull, depressing, melancholy; complex, difficult, dense, hard-going; *ant.* trivial, light.

heavy-handed *adj.* 1. strict, harsh, coercive, autocratic, domineering, oppressive, overbearing. 2. awkward, bungling, inept, clumsy, maladroit; thoughtless, tactless, insensitive, inconsiderate; *ant.* adroit, tactful.

heavy-hearted *adj.* sad, discouraged, downcast, forlorn, glum, heartsick, miserable, morose, mournful, sorrowful; *ant.* lighthearted.

heckle *v.* taunt, provoke, bait, gibe, jeer, needle, pester, snipe at, shout down.

hectic *adj.* boisterous, chaotic, frantic, frenetic,

riotous, tumultuous, turbulent, excited, rapid, wild; *ant.* leisurely.

hector *v.* badger, browbeat, harass, intimidate, bully, menace, nag, tease, harry, pester.

hedge *n.* shrubbery, thicket, hedgerow, windbreak, barrier, boundary, enclosure, obstacle, fence.

hedge *v.* **1.** circumscribe, confine, cover, hem in, hinder, obstruct, restrict, safeguard, fortify, shield. **2.** sidestep, dodge, evade, equivocate, stall, temporize, waffle.

hedonist *n.* libertine, profligate, bon vivant, epicure, gourmand, sensualist, sybarite, voluptuary, swinger (*slang*); *ant.* ascetic.

hedonistic *adj.* self-indulgent, voluptuous, luxurious, epicurean, sybaritic; *ant.* austere.

heed *n.* attention, care, caution, consideration, mind, note, notice, regard; *ant.* inattention, indifference, unconcern.

heed *v.* attend, beware, consider, follow, listen, mark, mind, note, regard, pay attention; *ant.* disregard, ignore.

heedful *adj.* attentive, mindful, observant, vigilant, wary; careful, cautious, circumspect, discreet, prudent; *ant.* heedless.

cool one's heels wait, linger, loiter, hang around.

heedless *adj.* careless, rash, reckless, foolhardy, imprudent, oblivious, precipitate, headstrong, thoughtless, unconcerned; *ant.* cautious.

heel *n.* scoundrel, rascal, bounder, cad, blackguard, scamp, chiseler.

hefty *adj.* heavy, brawny, bulky, massive, powerful, solid, robust, husky, stout, beefy, strapping.

height *n.* **1.** elevation, altitude, eminence, stature, loftiness, tallness. **2.** peak, pinnacle, summit, top, zenith, acme, apex, climax, culmination; *ant.* bottom.

heighten *v.* intensify, amplify, augment, sharpen, elevate, emphasize, enhance, exalt, improve, increase, strengthen; *ant.* decrease, diminish.

heinous *adj.* abhorrent, abominable, execrable, revolting, shocking, nefarious, iniquitous, hideous, vicious, odious.

heir *n.* beneficiary, inheritor, heiress, legatee, successor, descendant, scion.

held *adj.* clutched, grasped, gripped, con-

trolled, occupied, taken, defended, guarded; *ant.* freed, lost, released.

held up **1.** robbed, assaulted, beaten, mugged, jumped. **2.** postponed, delayed, put off, withheld.

hell *n.* **1.** abyss, Hades, inferno, nether world, Tophet, pandemonium, underworld, Gehenna, Styx, Acheron. **2.** torment, affliction, agony, anguish, misery, ordeal, suffering, torture, trial.

catch hell (*slang*) be scolded, get into trouble, be in hot water, get hell.

for the hell of it (*slang*) playfully, whimsically, for the fun of it.

hell-bent *adj.* determined, intent, resolved, settled, fixed, intransigent, obdurate, set, tenacious, unhesitating, unwavering.

hellish *adj.* brutal, savage, barbarous, vicious, damnable, detestable, diabolical, execrable, infernal, nefarious, Stygian, wicked; *ant.* pleasant, heavenly.

helm *n.* command, control, direction, reins, rudder, saddle, steerage, tiller, wheel.

help *n.* **1.** assistance, support, aid, advice, cooperation, guidance, backing, maintenance, nourishment, relief; *ant.* hindrance. **2.** assistant, employee, aide, hand, helper, hired help.

help *v.* **1.** aid, assist, cooperate, accommodate, support, stand by, back up, succor, sustain, nourish, promote, lend a hand, second, *slang:* take under one's wing, go to bat for; *ant.* hinder, oppose, rival. **2.** ease, ameliorate, allay, alleviate, mitigate; improve, better, correct. **cannot help but** have to, must, will, cannot fail to, be obliged or compelled to.

helper *n.* adjutant, aide, assistant, apprentice, factotum, attendant, auxiliary, right-hand man; collaborator, ally, colleague, partner, mainstay, second, supporter.

helpful *adj.* **1.** useful, advantageous, beneficial, efficacious, practical, pragmatic, profitable, utilitarian, serendipitous, timely, valuable; *ant.* futile, useless, worthless. **2.** benevolent, sympathetic, caring, accommodating, considerate, constructive, neighborly, supportive; *ant.* malicious.

helping *n.* serving, share, allowance, plateful, portion, amount, dollop, piece, ration.

helpless *adj.* defenseless, powerless, impotent, unable, feeble, infirm, paralyzed, dependent, vulnerable, exposed, forlorn, abandoned, friendless; *ant.* protected, competent, self-reliant.

helpmate *n.* companion, consort, spouse, better half, other half, partner, helper, support, aide, assistant, associate.

helter-skelter *adj.* confused, cluttered, haphazard, hit-or-miss, jumbled, muddled, random, topsy-turvy, unsystematic, tumultuous.

helter-skelter *adv.* hastily, headlong, hurriedly, impulsively, pell-mell, rashly, recklessly, wildly, higgledy-piggledy.

hem *n.* border, edge, fringe, margin, piping, skirt, trimming.

hem *v.* border, circumscribe, confine, edge, enclose, beset, gird, environ, hedge, skirt, surround.

hem and haw falter, hesitate, stutter.

hence *adv.* **1.** therefore, consequently, thus, for that reason, on that account. **2.** away, forward, onward.

henceforth *adv.* consequently, hence, henceforward, hereafter, hereinafter.

henchman *n.* minion, jackal, heavy, bodyguard, right-hand man, sidekick; cohort, crony, supporter, partner.

henpeck *v.* browbeat, badger, carp, cavil, chide, harass, hector, nag, pester, scold.

herald *n.* forbearer, harbinger, omen, precursor, portent, signal, token; courier, crier, messenger, advance man, ambassador.

herald *v.* advertise, announce, broadcast, proclaim, trumpet; precede, forebode, portend, promise, prognosticate.

heraldry *n.* **1.** badge, crest, arms, emblem, ensign, escutcheon, insignia. **2.** ceremony, pageantry, pomp, regalia.

herculean *adj.* **1.** laborious, arduous, exacting, exhausting, daunting, onerous, strenuous, toilsome, tough. **2.** gigantic, colossal, prodigious, mammoth, strapping, titanic, muscular, powerful.

herd *n.* **1.** bevy, drove, pack, flock, covey, gaggle, troop, swarm. **2.** crowd, crush, horde, mass, mob, multitude, press, rabble, riff-raff, swarm, throng.

herd *v.* gather, assemble, collect, congregate,

212

huddle, rally; drive, flock, guide, guard, lead, protect, shepherd, watch.

hereafter *adv.* hence, from now on, henceforth, henceforward, hereupon, in the future, later.

hereditary *adj.* congenital, genetic, handed down, transmitted, inbred, inherited, ancestral, maternal, paternal.

heredity *n.* **1.** ancestry, inheritance, genealogy, pedigree, family tree. **2.** genetics, eugenics, Mendelism.

heresy *n.* dissent, apostasy, dissidence, heterodoxy, iconoclasm, nonconformity, protestantism, revisionism; *ant.* orthodoxy.

heretic *n.* dissident, freethinker, renegade, schismatic, separatist, apostate; *ant.* conformist.

heretical *adj.* unorthodox, impious, irreverent, iconoclastic, rationalistic, freethinking, heterodox; *ant.* conventional, orthodox.

heritage *n.* inheritance, bequest, birthright, endowment, lot, portion, share, inheritance, legacy, past.

hermetic *adj.* **1.** closed, sealed, shut, airtight, watertight. **2.** magical, alchemical, mystical, occult.

hermit *n.* ascetic, recluse, monk, anchoress, anchorite, troglodyte, eremite, holy man.

hermitage *n.* **1.** isolation, seclusion, self-exile, withdrawal. **2.** retreat, asylum, monastery, shelter.

hero *n.* champion, celebrity, paragon, idol, heroine, star, protagonist, model, exemplar, paladin.

hero-worship *n.* admiration, adoration, adulation, deification, idealization, idolization, veneration.

heroic *adj.* **1.** brave, courageous, daring, intrepid, valiant, dauntless; *ant.* cowardly, timid. **2.** epic, exaggerated, grandiose, Homeric, legendary, mythological.

hesitancy *n.* doubt, dubiousness, indecision, misgiving, qualm, reservation, skepticism, uncertainty, wavering.

hesitant *adj.* doubtful, irresolute, shy, skeptical, timid, uncertain, slow, dawdling, half-hearted, halting, reluctant, vacillating.

hesitate *v.* pause, balk, falter, lag, tarry, vacillate, flounder, think twice, debate, ponder, scruple, demur, *slang*: drag one's feet *or* heels.

hesitating *adj.* doubtful, irresolute, doubtful, skeptical, unsure, slow, dawdling, wavering; *ant.* certain.

hesitation *n.* **1.** doubt, skepticism, uncertainty, circumspection, stammering, vacillation, misgivings, qualms, reluctance; delay, demurral, faltering; *ant.* assurance, alacrity, eagerness.

heterodox *adj.* dissident, freethinking, heretical, iconoclastic, revisionist, schismatic, skeptical; *ant.* orthodox.

heterogeneous *adj.* diverse, assorted, varied, disparate, divergent, motley, variegated, miscellaneous, multiform, polymorphic; *ant.* homogeneous.

hew *v.* ax, carve, chop, hack, lop, slash, split; form, make, model, sculpt, smooth, shape.

heyday *n.* prime of life, golden age, flower, bloom, florescence, boom time.

hiatus *n.* aperture, breach, break, rift, chasm, gap, discontinuance, interruption, interval, lacuna, lapse, blank, void.

hidden *adj.* concealed, veiled, latent, obscure, dark, secret, covert, clandestine, surreptitious, ulterior; *ant.* apparent, obvious, open.

hide *n.* pelt, skin, fleece, husk, epidermis, rind, coat, leather.

hide *v.* conceal, bury, camouflage, disguise, mask, shelter, shroud, cloak, stash, withhold; *ant.* display, reveal, show.

hidebound *adj.* conventional, entrenched, narrow-minded, rigid, straitlaced, traditional, conservative, unprogressive; *ant.* liberal, unconventional.

hideous *adj.* abominable, appalling, ghastly, grotesque, horrid, loathsome, macabre, monstrous, odious, repulsive, shocking; *ant.* beautiful.

hideout *n.* hideaway, cloister, den, hermitage, lair, refuge, shelter.

hideaway *n.* haven, nest, retreat, sanctuary.

hiding *n.* **1.** beating, drubbing, flogging, hammering, licking, spanking, tanning, thrashing, walloping, whaling, whipping. **2.** camouflage, concealment, disguise, screening, veiling.

hierarchy *n.* **1.** ranking, grading, scale, strata, pecking order. **2.** regime, ministry, administration, top brass, the authorities, the power structure, top echelon.

higgledy-piggledy *adj.* confused, disorderly, disorganized, haphazard, indiscriminate, jumbled, muddled, topsy-turvy.

high *n.* **1.** apex, apogee, height, peak, summit, top, zenith. **2.** delirium, ecstasy, euphoria, intoxication, trip (*slang*); *ant.* low, nadir.

high *adj.* **1.** tall, towering, lofty, steep, skyscraping, sky-high, colossal, gigantic, huge, immense; *ant.* short, diminutive, undersized. **2.** elevated, upraised, uplifted, aerial, cloudswept, flying, hovering, soaring; *ant.* depressed, low, underground. **3.** important, chief, crucial, essential, eminent, leading, powerful, distinguished, prominent, significant, superior; *ant.* insignificant, petty. **4.** costly, exorbitant, lavish, dear, extravagant, inflated; *ant.* cheap. **5.** (*slang*) drugged, inebriated, intoxicated, tipsy, *slang:* chewing sawdust, hammered, stoned, smashed, trashed, tripping, walking sideways, wasted, whacked.

high and dry abandoned, marooned, stranded, bereft, helpless.

high and low everywhere, exhaustively, in all possible places, in every nook and corner.

high and mighty haughty, conceited, pompous, vain.

highborn *adj.* aristocratic, blue-blooded, genteel, lordly, noble, patrician, pedigreed, thoroughbred.

highbrow *n.* intellectual, scholar, savant, classicist, aesthete, mastermind, brain, egghead (*slang*); *ant.* lowbrow.

highbrow *adj.* bookish, brainy, cultivated, erudite, deep, intellectual, sophisticated.

high-class *adj.* superior, A one, choice, deluxe, elite, exclusive, first-rate, posh, select, tiptop, top-flight; *ant.* mediocre, ordinary.

high-falutin *adj.* affected, pompous, grandiose, high-flown, magniloquent, pretentious, supercilious; bombastic, florid.

high-flown *adj.* elaborate, overblown, extravagant; haughty, pretentious, turgid; *ant.* modest, down-to-earth.

highhanded *adj.* arbitrary, autocratic, bossy, overbearing, peremptory, imperious, tyrannical, willful, despotic, domineering, arrogant, oppressive.

highjack *v.* See hijack.

213

highlight *n.* climax, feature, focal point, attraction, high point, peak, zenith.

highlight *v.* accent, accentuate, emphasize, feature, illuminate, underline, stress, play up, set off, spotlight.

highly *adv.* **1.** very, considerably, extremely, profoundly, immensely, decidedly, eminently, vastly. **2.** appreciatively, approvingly, favorably, warmly, enthusiastically, sanguinely.

high-minded *adj.* idealistic, magnanimous, conscientious, altruistic, ethical, honorable.

high-powered *adj.* aggressive, driving, dynamic, forceful, go-getting, industrious, energetic, enterprising, proactive.

high-pressure *adj.* compelling, forceful, potent, coercive.

high-priced *adj.* costly, expensive, dear, exorbitant, high, precious, pricy, steep, stiff, unreasonable; *ant.* cheap.

high-quality *adj.* select, superior, choice, blue-chip, quality, classy, deluxe, gilt-edged.

high society *n.* aristocracy, gentry, nobility, the four hundred, upper crust, crème de la crème, haut monde, jet set; *ant.* hoi polloi.

high-sounding *adj.* pretentious, grandiose, magniloquent, high-flown, bombastic, pompous, orotund, affected, artificial, stilted, strained.

high-spirited *adj.* animated, vivacious, vibrant, enthusiastic, avid, bold, daring, spunky, feisty, ebullient, effervescent; *ant.* downcast, glum.

high spirits *n.* boisterousness, exhilaration, exuberance, good cheer, hilarity, joie de vivre, liveliness, sparkle, vivacity.

high-strung *adj.* impatient, nervous, tense, edgy, skittish, hyper (*slang*).

high-toned *adj.* **1.** high-pitched, shrill, piercing, raucous, sharp. **2.** dignified, grand, noble, lofty, stately, righteous.

highway *n.* freeway, thruway, expressway, parkway, superhighway, toll road, turnpike.

hijack *v.* steal, commandeer, expropriate, kidnap, privateer, pirate, capture, seize, skyjack, snatch. Also highjack.

hike *v.* **1.** walk, trudge, tramp, hoof it (*slang*), plod, trek, backpack, explore. **2.** raise, lift, hitch, pull up.

hilarious *adj.* comical, humorous, hysterical, uproarious, jolly, jovial, killing, sidesplitting, rollicking, witty; *ant.* grave, serious.

hilarity *n.* glee, merriment, exhilaration, mirth, levity, gaiety, jollity, frivolity, levity, play; *ant.* gravity, seriousness.

hill *n.* acclivity, bluff, rise, mound, hillock, mount, knoll, butte, kopje, mesa, promontory, rise, tor.

over the hill 1. old, departed, dead, gone. **2.** supernnuated, declining, washed up.

hilly *adj.* sloping, undulating, uneven, broken, bumpy.

hilt *n.* grip, handle, haft, handgrip, heft, helve.

hind *adj.* back, caudal, hindmost, posterior, rear, after, tail; *ant.* fore.

hinder *v.* burden, check, frustrate, impede, hamper, interfere with, interrupt, obstruct, prevent, foil, retard, stymie, thwart; *ant.* assist, facilitate, expedite.

hindmost *adj.* concluding, endmost, final, furthest, last, rearmost, remotest, tail, terminal, ultimate; *ant.* foremost.

hindrance *n.* difficulty, drag (*slang*), drawback, encumbrance, restriction, hitch, impediment, obstacle, snag, stumbling block, trammel, remora; *ant.* aid, assistance, help.

hinge *v.* depend, rest, revolve, pivot, turn, hang, be contingent, center, connect.

hint *n.* clue, tip, help, advice, inkling, sign, notice, intimation, innuendo, insinuation, suspicion.

hint *v.* allude, imply, suggest, intimate, mention, prompt, tip off (*slang*).

hip (*slang*) *adj.* aware, enlightened, informed, au courant; wise, percipient, astute, shrewd.

hippie (*slang*) *n.* beatnik, bohemian, dropout, flower child, nonconformist.

hire *n.* charge, cost, fare, fee, price, rental, toll.

hire *v.* **1.** employ, engage, commission, appoint, sign up, enlist, book; let, charter, rent, lease; *ant.* discharge, dismiss, fire.

hirsute *adj.* hairy, bearded, whiskered, bristly, shaggy, woolly, furry, crinite, hispid; *ant.* bald, hairless.

hiss *n.* catcall, hoot, boo, mockery, raspberry, Bronx cheer; sibilance, whistle.

hiss *v.* boo, condemn, damn, decry, deride, jeer, mock, revile, ridicule; *ant.* applaud.

historic *adj.* significant, notable, outstanding, remarkable, extraordinary, memorable, famed, momentous, renowned.

historical *adj.* recorded, archival, attested, verifiable, chronicled, commemorated, documented, factual, real, authentic.

history *n.* record, account, annals, archives, chronicle, genealogy, memoir, narrative, saga.

histrionic *adj.* melodramatic, sensational, theatrical, fustian, ranting, affected, artificial, forced, insincere.

histrionics *n.* 1. acting, dramatics, performance, showmanship. theatricality. 2. affectation, deceit, pretension, overacting, staginess, ranting and raving, tirade, tantrum.

hit *n.* 1. impact, collision, blow, bump, knock, punch, smack, stroke, swipe, wallop. 2. success, triumph, achievement, masterstroke, winner, knockout (*slang*), sellout, smash, sensation; *ant.* flop, dud.

hit *v.* strike, belt, cudgel, cuff, club, flail, pelt, rap, slap, smite, *slang:* pop, let have it, whack.

hit back reciprocate, retaliate, get back at, get even.

hit on discover, guess, invent, light on, realize, stumble on, contrive, chance on.

hitch *n.* 1. knot, loop, noose, yoke. 2. difficulty, snag, tangle, block, catch, hindrance, holdup, problem, impediment, obstacle.

hitch *v.* harness, attach, couple, chain, bind, fasten, hook, join, lash, moor, tether, yoke; *ant.* sever, loosen.

hitherto *adv.* beforehand, previously, heretofore; so far, thus far, until now, up to now.

hit-or-miss *adj.* random, haphazard, indiscriminate; perfunctory, cursory, casual, disorganized, uncertain.

hoard *n.* accumulation, cache, reserve, reservoir, stockpile, store, fund, heap, mass, pile, profusion.

hoard *v.* save, gather, amass, cache, coffer, garner, husband, lay up, stash, stockpile, store; *ant.* spend, squander, use.

hoarder *n.* collector, gatherer, magpie, miser, niggard, squirrel, pack rat.

hoarse *adj.* gruff, guttural, harsh, gravelly, husky, rough, strident, raspy, throaty, dry, grating; *ant.* clear, mellifluous, smooth.

hoary *adj.* old, ancient, aged, venerable, grizzled, antique, gray-haired, white-haired.

hoax *n.* trick, swindle, fraud, scam (*slang*), ruse, imposture, deception, sham, subterfuge, fabrication, fast one, joke, prank, put-on.

hoax *v.* bamboozle, bluff, con, delude, dupe, cozen, fool, gull, hoodwink, hornswoggle, string, swindle, take for a ride, flimflam.

hoaxer *n.* trickster, prankster, shyster, cheat, swindler.

hobble *v.* 1. restrict, clog, fetter, shackle, tie. 2. limp, falter, stagger, stumble, totter.

hobby *n.* amusement, pastime, recreation, relaxation, sideline, avocation, sport, diversion.

hobgoblin *n.* fairy, ghost, goblin, imp, ogre, specter, spirit, sprite.

hobnob *v.* fraternize, associate, consort, mingle, mix, socialize.

hobo *n.* vagabond, vagrant, tramp, wanderer, bum.

hocus-pocus *n.* chicanery, hoax, trickery, sleight of hand, deception, artifice, sham, dodge, subterfuge.

hodgepodge *n.* combination, medley, melange, olio, miscellany, jumble, mess.

hog *n.* pig, boar, razorback, swine, sow, warthog.

high on the hog extravagantly, luxuriously, sumptuously, lavishly, expensively.

hoggish *adj.* 1. squalid, foul, smelly, unclean. 2. greedy, gluttonous, grasping, rapacious.

hogwash *n.* 1. garbage, debris, refuse, swill, scum. 2. nonsense, absurdity, foolishness, balderdash, rubbish, drivel, tripe, baloney (*slang*).

hoi polloi masses, proletariat, rabble, riffraff, crowd, multitude, herd, mob, third estate; *ant.* aristocracy, elite, nobility.

hoist *n.* crane, davit, derrick, elevator, jack, lift, tackle, winch.

hoist *v.* elevate, erect, heave, jack, lift, raise, rear.

hold *n.* authority, influence, sway, grasp, leverage, control, mastery, pull, weight, footing, clout (*slang*).

no holds barred unrestrained, unrestricted, without rules.

hold *v.* 1. grasp, clutch, embrace, clench, squeeze, press, secure, handle, cling to; *ant.* let go, release. 2. possess, keep, retain, have, own; *ant.* divest, deaccession. 3. support, sustain, brace, prop, stay, shoulder, uphold. 4. believe, adhere to, maintain, accept, presume, regard, judge; *ant.* deny. **5.** persist, endure, continue, persevere, last; *ant.* expire.

hold back 1. control, curb, inhibit, restrain. **2.** desist, forbear, refrain.

hold forth lecture, orate, harangue, preach, spiel, spout, declaim, descant, sermonize, soliloquize.

hold off 1. wait, defer, delay, postpone, refrain, put off. **2.** fend off, stave off, avoid, keep aloof from, rebuff, repel, repulse.

hold out 1. grant, offer, proffer, tempt with. **2.** endure, hold on, suffer, withstand.

hold up 1. show, elevate, exhibit, raise high. **2.** delay, interfere with, stop, pause. **3.** rob, steal, waylay, mug. **4.** support, brace, prop, shoulder.

hold water bear scrutiny, convince, make sense, pass the test, ring true, wash, work.

hold with accept, agree to, approve of, countenance, go along with, subscribe to, support.

holder *n.* **1.** case, container, cover, cradle, receptacle. **2.** keeper, owner, possessor, bearer, proprietor, purchaser, custodian.

holdings *n.* assets, resources, wealth, lands, possessions, security.

holdout *n.* objector, obstructionist, resister, damper, wet blanket, spoilsport.

holdup *n.* **1.** delay, bottleneck, difficulty, gridlock, hitch, obstruction, setback, snag, stoppage, traffic jam. **2.** heist, theft, robbery, stickup.

hole *n.* **1.** aperture, opening, window, eyelet, perforation, puncture, tear, cleft, fissure, rift; cave, cavity, den, burrow, hollow, orifice, pore. **2.** difficulty, impasse, predicament, quandary, scrape, tangle, imbroglio, quagmire, pickle. **in the hole** in debt, owing, in the red, in hock (*slang*).

make a hole in consume, expend, use up.

pick holes in criticize, disprove, refute, rebut, controvert, expose.

hole up (*slang*) retire, hibernate, lie low, wait out, take cover, shelter.

holiday *n.* **1.** celebration, festival, fête, fiesta, jubilee; vacation, sabbatical, leave, recess, time off.

holier-than-thou *adj.* sanctimonious, self-righteous, self-satisfied, smug, complacent, pious, priggish, unctuous.

holiness *n.* faith, devoutness, reverence, humility, grace, asceticism, piety, righteousness, purity, sanctity, divinity; *ant.* impiety, wickedness.

holler *n.* bawl, bellow, cry, shout, yell, howl, shriek, roar, bray.

hollow *n.* cavity, cave, channel, crater, depression, excavation, indentation, pit, womb.

hollow *v.* burrow, dig, furrow, scoop, excavate, indent.

hollow *adj.* **1.** coreless, empty, vacant, void, excavated, reamed, concave, sunken. **2.** false, artificial, meaningless, flimsy, worthless, unreliable, unsound. **3.** echoing, resonant, reverberating; deep, muffled, dull, mute.

holocaust *n.* annihilation, devastation, extermination, extinction, genocide, massacre, slaughter, carnage, inferno.

holy *adj.* sacred, blessed, sanctified, hallowed, venerable, revered; devout, pious, believing, chaste, moral, spiritual; *ant.* evil, sinful, wicked.

home *n.* **1.** residence, dwelling, abode, domicile, household, lodging, residence. **2.** asylum, clinic, hospice, hospital, institution. **at home** at ease, familiar, relaxed, comfortable. **bring home to** convince, impress upon, make clear to.

homage *n.* deference, admiration, adulation, devotion, duty, esteem, fealty, honor, loyalty, respect, service, tribute, worship.

homeless *adj.* displaced, abandoned, estranged, forsaken, outcast, exiled, itinerant, wandering, poor, destitute; *ant.* established, settled.

homely *adj.* **1.** simple, unpretentious, artless, unassuming, informal, everyday; *ant.* exotic. **2.** ugly, plain, modest, drab, unattractive; *ant.* comely.

Homeric *adj.* epic, grand, heroic, sweeping, impressive.

homespun *adj.* **1.** domestic, homemade, handcrafted, handspun. **2.** amateurish, plain, folksy, plain, unaffected, coarse, crude, rough, rude, rustic; *ant.* sophisticated.

homestead *n.* estate, manor, plantation, ranch, farm, grange.

homey *adj.* cozy, comfortable, familiar, intimate, cheerful, enjoyable, genial, homespun, unassuming.

homicidal *adj.* murderous, bloodthirsty, sanguinary, maniacal, violent, deadly, destructive, lethal.

homicide *n.* assassination, bloodshed, death, killing, manslaughter, murder, slaying.

homily *n.* sermon, spiel, talk, address, discourse, harangue, lecture.

homogeneous *adj.* akin, alike, kindred, similar, analogous, harmonious; identical, uniform, standardized, monolithic; *ant.* different, varying.

homologous *adj.* analogous, comparable, correspondent, equivalent, like, matching, related, similar; *ant.* different, dissimilar.

homosexual *adj.* homoerotic, homophile, gay, lesbian; *ant.* heterosexual, straight.

hone *v.* sharpen, edge, file, grind, strop, whet, point, polish, smooth.

honest *adj.* **1.** true, genuine, real, legitimate, sound, valid; *ant.* fraudulent. **2.** ethical, honorable, law-abiding, respectable, trustworthy, upright; *ant.* crooked. **3.** frank, candid, direct, forthright, guileless, straightforward, aboveboard; *ant.* deceitful, lying. **4.** fair, equitable, just, impartial, disinterested, unbiased; *ant.* biased, unfair, prejudiced.

honesty *n.* integrity, morality, fidelity, equity, fairness, probity, objectivity, candor, sincerity, artlessness, bluntness; *ant.* deviousness, dishonesty.

honk *v.* trumpet, bellow, blare, croak.

honor *v.* **1.** acclaim, notice, recognition, renown; aggrandizement, esteem, deference, homage, praise, veneration; *ant.* opprobrium, disgrace. **2.** integrity, character, equity, fairness, nobleness.
upon one's honor by one's faith, on one's word, staking one's good name.

honor *v.* **1.** revere, esteem, value, venerate, adore, glorify, hallow. **2.** praise, acclaim, applaud, celebrate, compliment, credit, laud, acknowledge, recognize; *ant.* disgrace, dishonor.

honorable *adj.* **1.** ethical, virtuous, upright, conscientious, scrupulous, worthy, sincere; *ant.* dishonest, unworthy. **2.** distinguished, eminent, illustrious, prestigious, renowned.

honorary *adj.* nominal, titular, honorific, complimentary, gratuitous; *ant.* paid, salaried.

honors *n.* **1.** courtesies, ceremony, privilege, duties. **2.** award, decorations, distinctions, fa-

vor, feather in one's cap (*slang*), garland, medal, prize, laurels, rewards, titles, trophies; *ant.* aspersions, indignities.

hood *n.* bonnet, shawl, kerchief, cowl, mantle, veil, babushka.

hoodlum *n.* thug, criminal, crook, gangster, ruffian, hooligan, *slang:* punk, hood.

hoodwink *v.* cheat, con, cozen, swindle, trick; deceive, dupe, fool, mislead, outwit.

hook *n.* **1.** (something that grabs or fastens) lock, catch, clasp, claw, talon, link, snag. **2.** (curved cutting implement) sickle, scythe, machete, adze.

hook *v.* catch, clasp, grab, snare, nab, gaff, hasp, hitch, collar, entrap, capture.
hook up attach, connect, link, yoke, join.

hooked *adj.* **1.** angled, arched, beaked, bent, curved, sickle-shaped. **2.** (*slang*) addicted, devoted, enamored, obsessed, enraptured.

hooligan *n.* delinquent, hood, hoodlum, lout, roughneck, rowdy, ruffian, thug, tough, vandal.

hoop *n.* band, circlet, gird, girdle, loop, ring, wheel.

hoot *n.* catcall, hiss, jeer, raspberry (*slang*); scream, shout, shriek, toot, whistle, whoop, yell.

hoot *v.* boo, jeer, ridicule, condemn, decry, deride, howl down; clamor, scream, shout, shriek, whistle, whoop, yell at.

hop *n.* jump, bounce, bound, leap, skip, spring, step.

hop *v.* bound, caper, dance, frisk, jump, leap, limp, nip, prance, skip, spring, vault.

hope *n.* **1.** faith, assurance, belief, expectation, confidence, optimism; *ant.* despair, pessimism. **2.** ambition, anticipation, aspiration, desire, dream, goal, wish, promise. **3.** mainstay, support, prop, strength, investment.

hope *v.* trust, reckon on, rely on, expect, anticipate, await, desire, contemplate, foresee, desire, long, dream, pray; *ant.* despair.

hopeful *adj.* **1.** optimistic, expectant, blithe, buoyant, enthusiastic, faithful, cheerful, sanguine, serene, trustful. **2.** encouraging, attractive, auspicious, bright, favorable, rosy, promising, heartening, reassuring, propitious; *ant.* discouraging, unfortunate, unfavorable.

hopeless *adj.* **1.** despairing, demoralized, abject, despondent, down in the mouth; pessimistic, cynical. **2.** impossible, futile, vain, lost, incurable, irrevocable, to no avail, disastrous, tragic; *ant.* favorable, heartening, cheering.

horde *n.* multitude, drove, swarm, throng, bevy, gang, herd, host, mob, pack, press, troop.

horizon *n.* purview, vista, skyline, range, scope, verge, ken, limit, perspective, prospect, realm.

horizontal *adj.* level, even, flush, aligned, flat, parallel, plane; prostrate, recumbent.

horn *n.* tusk, antler, point, quill, spine, spike.
blow one's own horn (*slang*) brag, boast, gloat, swagger, congratulate oneself.
on the horns of a dilemma conflicted, torn, in a quandary, between a rock and a hard place, between the devil and the deep blue sea.

horn in intrude, impose, encroach, interlope, barge in, butt in, gate-crash.

horny *adj.* **1.** callous, tough, firm, hard, keratoid. **2.** (*slang*) lustful, aroused, lascivious, lecherous, libidinous, randy, sensual, priapic, concupiscent; *ant.* cold, frigid.

horrendous *adj.* catastrophic, frightful, horrible, terrible.

horrible *adj.* offensive, appalling, heinous, disgusting, repulsive, shameful; fearsome, frightening, bloodcurdling, ghastly, gruesome, macabre, shocking.

horrid *adj.* beastly, cruel, mean, odious, despicable; disturbing, frightful, harrowing, hideous, ghastly, revolting, terrifying; *ant.* agreeable, lovely, pleasant.

horrific *adj.* awful, horrendous, appalling, dreadful, frightening, grisly, shocking, spine-chilling, terrifying.

horrify *v.* appall, disgust, harrow, shock, unnerve, terrify, petrify, sicken, repel; *ant.* delight, gratify, please.

horror *n.* **1.** dread, apprehension, terror, fright, fear, panic, shock, alarm, terror. **2.** aversion, dislike, abhorrence, antipathy, detestation, disgust, loathing, repugnance, revulsion.

hors d'oeuvre *n.* appetizer, canapé, tidbit, relishes.

horse *n.* steed, stallion, pony, nag, mount, equine.

beat a dead horse harp on, nag, argue, persist.
on one's high horse arrogant, disdainful, haughty.

horse around cavort, clown, fool around, misbehave, romp, roister, roughhouse.

horseman *n.* equestrian, gaucho, jockey, rider, cavalier, cowboy.

horseplay *n.* buffoonery, high jinks, capers, clowning, pranks, romping, tomfoolery, roughhousing, skylarking.

horticulture *n.* agriculture, cultivation, floriculture, gardening.

hose *n.* **1.** stockings, pantyhose, tights, nylons. **2.** conduit, fire hose, line, garden hose, tubing.

hospitable *adj.* receptive, open, accessible, kind, gracious, cordial, welcoming; congenial, convivial, gemütlich; *ant.* hostile, inhospitable.

hospital *n.* clinic, dispensary, infirmary, sanitarium, sick bay.

hospitality *n.* conviviality, affability, geniality, heartiness, good cheer, amiability; consideration, cordiality, accommodation, generosity, liberality, graciousness.

host *n.* **1.** announcer, anchor, emcee, entertainer, master of ceremonies, MC, presenter, toastmaster. **2.** army, array, drove, horde, legion, multitude, myriad, pack, swarm, throng.

host *v.* introduce, present, receive, treat, wine and dine.

hostage *n.* prisoner, captive, guaranty, security, pawn.

hostel *n.* boarding house, dormitory, hospice, hotel, inn.

hostile *adj.* antagonistic, belligerent, bellicose, warlike, contrary, opposed, malevolent, rancorous, inimical, adverse, ill-disposed; *ant.* friendly, sympathetic.

hostilities *n.* war, battle, bloodshed, conflict, fighting, strife.

hostility *n.* animosity, malice, ill will, enmity, hate, contempt, bitterness, animus, resentment; *ant.* affection, friendliness, sympathy.

hot *adj.* **1.** heated, torrid, burning, fiery, blazing, feverish, scorching, blistering, searing, tropical, scalding; *ant.* cold, chilly, frigid. **2.** close, humid, stuffy, sultry. **3.** eager, ardent, distracted, passionate; aroused, furious, indignant, irascible; *ant.* calm. **4.** erotic, sexy, carnal, salacious, sensual, spicy, voluptuous. **make it hot for** discomfit, vex, fluster, frustrate.

hot air (*slang*) *n.* balderdash, blather, bombast, bluster, drivel, folderol, cant, claptrap, nonsense, bunk; *ant.* wisdom.

hotbed *n.* breeding ground, cradle, den, hive, nest, nursery, school, seedbed.

hotblooded *adj.* ardent, bold, fervent, eager, excitable, impetuous, impulsive, rash, lustful, passionate, wild; *ant.* cool, dispassionate.

hotel *n.* boarding house, inn, motel, lodge, hostelry, bed-and-breakfast, resort, spa.

hotheaded *adj.* **1.** foolhardy, hasty, impetuous, impulsive, precipitate, unmanageable, reckless, wild; *ant.* cautious. **2.** irritable, crabby, touchy, quick-tempered, volatile; *ant.* placid, even-tempered.

hothouse *n.* conservatory, glasshouse, greenhouse, nursery.

hot-tempered *adj.* explosive, fiery, choleric, irascible, irritable, petulant, testy, violent, volcanic; *ant.* cool, imperturbable.

hound *v.* annoy, badger, goad, harass, nag, pester, prod, provoke, persecute, pursue, rag (*slang*).

house *n.* **1.** habitation, abode, domicile, dwelling, residence. **2.** business, corporation, establishment, firm, partnership, company. **3.** family, ancestry, blood, clan, line, lineage, descent, race, tradition. **4.** congress, council, assembly, legislature, senate, parliament. **like a house on fire** quickly, actively, energetically, vigorously.

on the house free, complimentary, gratis, gratuitous.

house *v.* accommodate, bed, board, quarter, lodge, harbor, hold; keep, protect, shelter, store, sheathe.

household *adj.* domestic, domiciliary, common, everyday, familiar, ordinary, plain, well-known, established.

householder *n.* owner, landlord, occupant, resident, proprietor, tenant.

house-trained *adj.* domesticated, tamed, housebroken.

housewife *n.* homemaker, family manager, lady

or mistress of the house, wife and mother, hausfrau.

housing *n.* **1.** lodging, accommodations, quarters, residence, habitation, protection, roof, shelter, digs (*Brit. slang*). **2.** casing, bracket, cabinet, enclosure.

hovel *n.* shack, cabin, shed, shanty, hut, den, hutch, lean-to, dump.

hover *v.* **1.** float, fly, levitate, glide, sway. **2.** dally, linger, hesitate, pause, vacillate, waver, seesaw, fluctuate, alternate. **3.** (be nearby constantly or annoyingly) follow, cling to, hang about *or* around, attend, breathe down one's neck, be on one's back.

however *conj., adv.* but, nevertheless, still, though, all the same, nonetheless.

howl *n.* bay, clamor, hoot, cry out, wail, yelp, roar, scream, ululation.

howl *v.* bawl, bellow, cry, holler, shout, shriek, ululate, yawl, yell.

hub *n.* axis, center, core, nub, nucleus, focal point, heart, middle, kernel, crux, linchpin, nave, pivot.

hubbub *n.* turbulence, uproar, bedlam, chaos, din, clamor, pandemonium, racket, tumult, brouhaha, to-do, disturbance, fuss, riot; *ant.* peacefulness, order.

huckster *n.* salesman, vendor, peddler, hawker, haggler, hustler, promoter, dealer, pitcher.

huddle *n.* assemblage, cluster, conference, group, clump, clot, jumble, crowd, heap, muddle.

huddle *v.* **1.** bunch, congregate, converge, crowd, gather, press, throng; *ant.* disperse. **2.** cuddle, curl up, nestle, snuggle.

hue *n.* color, shade, tincture, tone, cast, character, tinge, complexion, dye, nuance, chroma.

hue and cry clamor, furor, hullabaloo, shout, outcry, din, rumpus, uproar, fanfare, ado.

huff *n.* pique, anger, annoyance, snit, perturbation, tiff.

huffy *adj.* angry, cross, disgruntled, grumpy, offended, surly; touchy, sensitive, irritable, miffed, moody, peevish, petulant, choleric, irascible; *ant.* cheery, happy.

hug *n.* embrace, squeeze, caress, clasp, clinch, cuddle.

hug *v.* hold, squeeze, embrace, cuddle, cling to, enfold, nestle, snuggle.

huge *adj.* colossal, enormous, gigantic, jumbo, mammoth, grand, immense, great, leviathan, massive, stupendous, titanic, vast; *ant.* dainty, tiny.

hulk *n.* **1.** wreck, shambles, shell, skeleton, ruins, remains, frame, hull. **2.** lout, oaf, clod, ox.

hulking *adj.* awkward, bulky, clumsy, ponderous, cumbersome, lumbering, massive, ungainly, unwieldy, cloddish, oafish; *ant.* delicate, small.

hull *n.* body, husk, casing, capsule, covering, peeling, pod, rind, shell.

hullabaloo *n.* furor, uproar, tumult, brouhaha, clamor, din, racket, commotion, panic, ruckus, to-do.

hum *n.* whir, murmur, buzz, drone, purr, throb, vibration.

hum *v.* buzz, croon, mumble, murmur, purr, trill, sing.

human *adj.* **1.** mortal, anthropoid, hominid, anthropomorphic, fleshly, biped; *ant.* divine. **2.** compassionate, humane, considerate, kindly, reasonable. **3.** natural, fallible, susceptible, vulnerable.

humane *adj.* altruistic, benevolent, benign, charitable, philanthropic; clement, gentle, kindly, merciful, tolerant, tenderhearted; *ant.* barbaric, cruel, inhuman.

humanitarian *n.* altruist, benefactor, Good Samaritan, helper, philanthropist; *ant.* egoist, self-seeker.

humanitarianism *n.* benevolence, charity, compassion, generosity, goodwill, humanism, philanthropy; *ant.* egoism.

humanity *n.* **1.** Homo sapiens, mankind, humankind, people, man, woman, mortals. **2.** kindness, tolerance, mercy, sympathy, understanding, charity, benignity, brotherly love.

humble *v.* humiliate, abase, break, bring down, chasten, debase, degrade, discredit, reduce, shame, cut down to size, take down a peg; *ant.* exalt, glorify, raise.

humble *adj.* **1.** meek, modest, shy, bashful, blushing, mild, reserved, sheepish, self-conscious, submissive, withdrawn; *ant.* assertive, haughty, pretentious. **2.** lowly, common, homespun, mean, menial, ignoble, low-born, plebeian, vulgar; *ant.* noble, refined.

humbly *adv.* deferentially, meekly, submissively, respectfully, docilely, obsequiously, simply, unassumingly; *ant.* boastfully, haughtily, proudly.

humbug *n.* nonsense, drivel, folderol, balderdash, doublespeak; bluff, cant, deception, pretense, trick, lie; *slang:* baloney, bullshit, bunk.

humdrum *adj.* boring, common, dull, everyday, tedious, monotonous, dreary, pedestrian, mundane, routine, uneventful; *ant.* exceptional, interesting, unusual.

humid *adj.* clammy, damp, dank, muggy, soggy, moist, sticky, sultry, stuffy, vaporous; *ant.* dry.

humiliate *v.* shame, embarrass, abash, mortify, insult, chagrin, disgrace, debase, degrade, humble, chasten; *ant.* dignify, exalt, vindicate.

humiliation *n.* mortification, embarrassment, shame, chagrin, ignominy, disgrace; dishonor, denigration, condescension, affront, snub, indignity, put-down; *ant.* gratification, triumph.

humility *n.* deference, modesty, humbleness, self-abasement, timidity, submissiveness, obedience, subjection, servility, obsequiousness; *ant.* conceit, pride, vainglory.

humor *n.* **1.** comedy, amusement, clowning, facetiousness, farce, jesting, jocularity, merriment, raillery, wit. **2.** mood, bent, disposition, fancy, frame of mind, propensity, temper. **humor** *v.* accommodate, appease, indulge, pamper, spoil, mollify, cosset, placate, flatter, gratify, baby; *ant.* enrage, provoke, thwart.

humorist *n.* joker, parodist, satirist, wit, clown, comedian, zany, funnyman, jester, wisecracker.

humorless *adj.* morose, glum, dour, crass, dull, tedious; *ant.* witty.

humorous *adj.* amusing, comic, farcical, funny, hilarious, whimsical, jocose, satirical, sidesplitting, witty, zany, droll.

hump *n.* bulge, knob, hummock, mound, knoll, projection, prominence, protuberance, swelling.

humped *adj.* arched, bent, crooked, curved, gibbous, hunched; *ant.* flat, straight.

hunch *n.* **1.** hump, bump, protuberance, swelling. 2. inkling, premonition, presentiment, intuition, hint, clue, feeling, impression, notion, qualm, suspicion, foreboding.

hunch v. arch, bend, stoop, huddle, squat, crouch, cower, hump.

hung adj. dangling, suspended, swaying.

hung up (slang) 1. obsessed, fixated, absorbed, engrossed, preoccupied, intent, haunted, fascinated, troubled, disturbed. 2. delayed, stuck, stalled, impeded, obstructed, checked.

hunger n. 1. appetite, desire, yen, itch, lust, slang: the munchies, sweet tooth; gluttony, greed, rapacity, voracity; ant. glut, satisfaction, satiety. 2. famine, drought, starvation, malnutrition, want, emptiness.

hunger v. ache, crave, hanker, long, pine, wish, yearn; starve, thirst, wish.

hungry adj. ravenous, craving, covetous, avid, eager; empty, famished, hollow, lean, undernourished; ant. replete, satisfied.

hunk n. block, chunk, clod, gob, lump, nugget, slab, wedge.

hunt v. chase, pursue, stalk, track, trail, follow; investigate, seek, look for, rummage, scour, search.

hunted adj. chased, followed, hounded, harried, trailed, stalked, tracked, pursued, searched for, wanted.

hurdle n. 1. barricade, barrier, impediment, obstruction, blockade, earthwork, fence, hedge, wall. 2. complication, difficulty, problem, snag, stumbling block.

hurdle v. vault, leap, clear, jump, scale, overcome, surmount.

hurl v. fling, propel, heave, cast, catapult, launch, pitch, project, sling, throw.

hurly-burly n. commotion, disorder, turmoil, upheaval, furor, hubbub.

hurried adj. hasty, rushed, quick, swift, breakneck, headlong, precipitate; perfunctory, careless, cursory, hectic, superficial; ant. leisurely, thorough.

hurry n. rush, urgency, haste, dispatch, celerity, alacrity, expedition; ant. leisureliness

hurry v. accelerate, hasten, spur, expedite, push, urge, goad, rush, speed, scurry, bustle, dash, slang: floor it, step on it, shake a leg; ant. delay, procrastinate.

hurt v. 1. injure, abuse, afflict, harm, torment,

try, bruise, wound, maul, impair, cripple; ant. comfort, ease, soothe. 2. offend, insult, spite, abuse, distress, victimize.

hurt adj. aching, aggrieved, sad, pained, stricken, suffering, scarred, maimed.

hurtful adj. damaging, destructive, harmful, noxious, injurious; cruel, malicious, mean, nasty, scathing, spiteful, vicious, pernicious, prejudicial; ant. helpful, kind.

hurtle v. 1. charge, rush, scramble, dash, chase, shoot, speed, spin, tear. 2. crash, collide, slam into, smash into.

husband n. spouse, mate, consort, groom, breadwinner, married man.

husband v. economize, budget, conserve, hoard, ration, save, store, reserve; ant. squander, waste.

husbandry n. 1. farming, agriculture, land management, tillage. 2. thrift, conservation, frugality, providence.

hush n. silence, calm, peace, repose, serenity, stillness, tranquillity.

hush v. silence, quiet, soothe, allay, mollify, still, stop, settle, shush, compose; ant. disturb, rouse.

hush up conceal, cover up, smother, stifle, suppress, gag, soft-pedal; ant. publicize.

hush-hush adj. classified, confidential, secret, restricted, under wraps; ant. open, public.

husk n. case, covering, bark, rind, shell, pod, bran, chaff, hull, shuck.

husky adj. 1. hoarse, gruff, guttural, low, harsh, rasping, strident, croaking, growling, raucous, throaty. 2. strong, muscular, powerful, sturdy, sinewy, strapping, thickset, beefy, brawny, burly.

hustle v. hurry, hasten, pressure, push, goad, spur, incite, drive, prod, elbow, jostle, buffet, shoulder.

hut n. shack, cabin, bungalow, hovel, shanty, lean-to, shed.

hutch n. 1. pen, cage, coop, kennel, corral. 2. cupboard, buffet, cabinet, sideboard.

hybrid n. amalgam, combination, pastiche, compound, mixture; crossbreed, mongrel, mutt (slang).

hygiene n. cleanliness, sanitation, sterility, disinfection, hygienics, purity, salubrity.

hygienic adj. clean, disinfected, germ-free,

aseptic, pure, sanitary, sterile, healthy, whole-some, salutary, salubrious; *ant.* filthy, contaminated.

hymn *n.* anthem, chorale, evensong, litany, ode, paean, psalm.

hype (*slang*) *n.* hoopla, puffery, ballyhoo, buildup, advertising, publicity.

hyperbole *n.* exaggeration, embellishment, overstatement, distortion, enlargement, extravagance, magnification, overkill; *ant.* meiosis, understatement.

hypercritical *adj.* captious, carping, nit-picking, pedantic, hair-splitting, cavilling, fault-finding, finicky, fussy, persnickety, quibbling; *ant.* tolerant, uncritical.

hypnotic *adj.* 1. sleep-inducing, sedative, anesthetic, narcotic, opiate, soothing, somnolent, soporific. 2. compelling, dazzling, fascinating, magnetic, mesmerizing, spellbinding, enchanting, irresistible.

hypnotize *v.* bewitch, entrance, induce, mesmerize, spellbind, stupefy, charm, captivate, dazzle, fascinate, enthrall.

222

hypocrisy *n.* affectation, pretense, insincerity, cant, deceit, duplicity, dissimulation, fraud, imposture, Tartuffery; *ant.* candor, sincerity.

hypocrite *n.* charlatan, dissimulator, impostor, pretender, fake, pharisee, sham, sophist.

hypocritical *adj.* false, duplicitous, phony, specious, artificial, fraudulent, spurious, unctuous, sanctimonious, self-righteous, two-faced; *ant.* genuine, sincere.

hypothesis *n.* assumption, conjecture, guess, postulate, premise, presumption, proposition, proposal, supposition, theory, thesis.

hypothetical *adj.* conjectural, speculative, theoretical, postulated, proposed; contingent, equivocal, debatable, suspect; *ant.* factual, proven, real.

hysteria *n.* agitation, frenzy, madness, panic, delirium; *ant.* calm, composure, reason.

hysterical *adj.* 1. frantic, overwrought, distraught, frenzied, crazed, delirious, mad, neurotic, raving, berserk, violent; *ant.* calm, composed. 2. comical, farcical, hilarious, side-splitting.

I

ice *n.* **1.** coldness, frost, chill, frigidity; hoar, rime, glacier. **2.** formality, reserve, distance, stiffness.

break the ice initiate, commence, make a start, get the ball rolling.

on ice (*slang*) in reserve, held, in abeyance.

on thin ice imperiled, insecure, in danger, out on a limb.

icon *n.* idol, image, symbol, figure, portrait.

iconoclasm *n.* skepticism, irreverence, radicalism, opposition, subversion, dissent, criticism, heresy, denunciation, disabusing, dissidence, questioning; *ant.* credulity, trustfulness.

iconoclast *n.* heretic, skeptic; dissenter, nonconformist, critic, dissident, opponent, radical, rebel, maverick.

icy *adj.* **1.** frozen, arctic, bitter, chilly, cold, freezing, frigid, glacial, gelid, ice-cold, raw. **2.** formal, distant, cold, aloof, unmoved, indifferent, reserved, stiff; *ant.* friendly, warm.

idea *n.* **1.** thought, concept, notion, conception, brainstorm; opinion, belief, conviction. **2.** (a plan of action) intention, plan, doctrine, design, approach, program. **3.** gist, meaning, sense, import, purport, heart, substance, meat, pith.

ideal *n.* archetype, standard, model, example, prototype, epitome, exemplar, image, paradigm, paragon.

ideal *adj.* **1.** typical, model, archetypical, prototypical. **2.** perfect, supreme, exemplary, fitting. **3.** utopian, imaginary, abstract, theoretical, unattainable, chimerical, fanciful; *ant.* practical, earthly, real.

idealism *n.* romanticism, utopianism, perfectionism, principles, conscience, aspirations, sense of duty, humanitarianism.

idealist *n.* dreamer, perfectionist, romantic, visionary; *ant.* realist, pragmatist.

idealistic *adj.* impractical, optimistic, unrealis-

tic, quixotic, romantic, utopian, visionary, starry-eyed; *ant.* realistic, pragmatic.

idealization *n.* glorification, magnification, ennoblement.

idealize *v.* romanticize, exalt, worship, apotheosize, deify, ennoble, glorify, put on a pedestal; *ant.* caricature.

ideals *n.* principles, standards, goals.

idée fixe obsession, complex, fixation, fixed idea, compulsion, monomania, leitmotif, hang-up (*slang*).

identical *adj.* alike, synonymous, equivalent, indistinguishable, duplicate, same, corresponding, equal, interchangeable, like, matching, twin; *ant.* different.

identifiable *adj.* recognizable, discernible, detectable, ascertainable, distinguishable, unmistakable, known; noticeable, perceptible; *ant.* unfamiliar, unknown.

identification *n.* **1.** classifying, naming, cataloging. **2.** credentials, letter of introduction, papers, testimony, letter of credit, badge, ID.

identify *v.* **1.** classify, name, label, catalog, distinguish, specify, tag, diagnose. **2.** detect, recognize, know, make out, name, pick *or* point out, pinpoint, single out, spot.

identity *n.* individuality, uniqueness, self, personality, ego, integrity.

ideology *n.* philosophy, doctrine, beliefs, convictions, ideas, principles, ethics, creed, metaphysics, worldview, tenets.

idiocy *n.* **1.** folly, madness, lunacy, foolishness, stupidity, insipidity. **2.** imbecility, cretinism, feeblemindedness.

idiom *n.* colloquialism, expression, locution, regionalism, turn of phrase; dialect, idiolect, jargon, language, style, usage, vernacular.

idiomatic *adj.* **1.** colloquial, vernacular, dialect. **2.** (used of a style of language use) grammatical, appropriate, correct, sensitive.

idiosyncrasy *n.* eccentricity, peculiarity, quirk, oddity, singularity, habit, mannerism, characteristic, feature, trait.

idiot *n.* imbecile, dummy (*slang*), moron, fool, *slang*: ass, schmuck, nincompoop, blockhead; simpleton, cretin, dimwit, half-wit, mental incompetent.

idle *v.* **1.** close, close *or* shut down, discontinue, cease operation. **2.** lay off, discharge, dismiss, put out of work.

idle *adj.* **1.** inactive, still, inert, dormant, motionless, out of action, unemployed, jobless; unused, unoccupied, abandoned, vacant, deserted; *ant.* active, busy, engaged. **2.** useless, pointless, vain, rambling.

idleness *n.* laziness, sloth, torpor, ease, inactivity, indolence, inertia, loafing, shiftlessness, sluggishness, leisure; *ant.* industriousness, activity.

idler *n.* dawdler, good-for-nothing, do-nothing, *slang*: slouch, lazybones; slacker, drone, dodger, loafer, malingerer, shirker, lounger, laggard.

idol *n.* **1.** deity, icon, image, fetish, god, graven image. **2.** hero, beloved, favorite, superstar.

idolatry *n.* adoration, hero-worship, idolism, adulation, deification, exaltation, glorification; *ant.* vilification.

idolize *v.* worship, adore, reverence, venerate, deify, admire, dote on, exalt, glorify, lionize, love, revere; *ant.* vilify.

idyllic *adj.* idealized, pastoral, peaceful, rustic, delightful, happy, heavenly, innocent, picturesque, unspoiled; *ant.* disagreeable.

iffy *adj.* doubtful, dubious, improbable, contingent, unsettled, uncertain, up in the air.

ignite *v.* combust, inflame, light, burn, catch fire, fire, flare up, kindle, set fire to, touch off; *ant.* quench.

ignoble *adj.* **1.** shameful, degenerate, disgraceful, dishonorable; *ant.* honorable. **2.** lowborn, common, vulgar, lowly, mean, abject, base; *ant.* noble, elegant.

ignominious *adj.* **1.** (deserving of shame) offensive, vile, despicable, shameful, sordid, base, vicious, nasty. **2.** (producing feelings of shame, as from a defeat) humiliating, outrageous, shocking, mortifying.

ignoramus *n.* dunce, dullard, numskull, idiot, bonehead (*slang*), illiterate, know-nothing; *ant.* intellectual, highbrow, scholar.

ignorance *n.* stupidity, obtuseness, unenlightenment, insensitivity, bewilderment, mental incapacity, simplicity; *ant.* learning, erudition.

ignorant *adj.* **1.** unaware, unconscious, uninformed, in the dark, green, misguided, inexperienced, unwitting, innocent, naive, misinformed, benighted; *ant.* cognizant. **2.** untrained, illiterate, uneducated, superstitious, vulgar, crude; *ant.* learned, tutored.

ignore *v.* neglect, overlook, slight, disregard, pass over, pay no attention to, set aside, shut one's eyes to, take no notice of, turn a blind eye to, turn a deaf ear to, turn one's back on; *ant.* note, heed.

ilk *n.* character, class, sort, brand, breed, cast, cut, kind, stamp, style, type, variety.

ill *adj.* **1.** sick, ailing, unhealthy, unwell, under the weather. **2.** harmful, noxious, bad, evil. **take ill 1.** get sick, become sick, fall ill. **2.** take offense, resent, be offended, take umbrage, be annoyed.

ill-advised *adj.* imprudent, hasty, impolitic, foolish, inappropriate, hazardous, misguided, rash, reckless, shortsighted, thoughtless; *ant.* sensible.

ill at ease uneasy, uncomfortable, anxious, discomfited.

ill-bred *adj.* ill-mannered, rude, uncouth, vulgar, coarse, impolite, crude, indelicate, unmannerly, crass; *ant.* urbane, refined.

ill-considered *adj.* heedless, ill-advised, precipitate, imprudent, hasty, reckless, rash, shortsighted.

ill-defined *adj.* vague, imprecise, indistinct, nebulous, unclear, shadowy, blurred, blurry, dim, hazy; *ant.* clear.

ill-disposed *adj.* averse, opposed, inimical, unsympathetic, antipathetic, hostile, antagonistic.

illegal *adj.* forbidden, criminal, banned, felonious, illicit, outlawed, prohibited, proscribed, unconstitutional.

illegible *adj.* unreadable, indecipherable, obscure, scrawled, faint, hieroglyphic.

illegitimate *adj.* **1.** unlawful, contraband, illicit, illegal, wrong. **2.** (born out of wedlock)

ill-fated *adj.* luckless, star-crossed, ill-omened, unfortunate, doomed, blighted, forlorn, hapless, ill-starred; *ant.* lucky.

ill-favored *adj.* unattractive, homely, plain, ugly, repulsive, hideous; *ant.* beautiful.

ill-humored *adj.* disagreeable, irritable, moody, testy, cantankerous, irascible, choleric, impatient, bitter, petulant, morose, peevish, sullen; *ant.* amiable.

illiberal *adj.* **1.** miserly, selfish, niggardly. **2.** prejudiced, intolerant, bigoted, partial, reactionary, parsimonious, narrow-minded.

illicit *adj.* clandestine, forbidden, prohibited, criminal, illegal, felonious, contraband, illegitimate, immoral, improper, inadmissible; *ant.* legal, authorized.

illiterate *adj.* uneducated, ignorant, untaught, untutored, unread, uncultured.

ill-mannered *adj.* rude, ill-behaved, impolite, coarse, discourteous, unmannerly, insensitive, insolent, uncivil, uncouth, crude, boorish; *ant.* polite.

ill-natured *adj.* disagreeable, surly, petulant, mean, sullen, vindictive, malevolent, nasty.

illness *n.* sickness, ailment, malady, affliction, disease, disorder, infirmity, indisposition.

illogical *adj.* absurd, faulty, inconsistent, senseless, fallacious, inconclusive, incorrect, invalid, illegitimate, specious, spurious; *ant.* sound, rational.

ill-proportioned *adj.* distorted, disfigured, grotesque.

ill-suited *adj.* inappropriate, mismatched, unsuitable.

ill temper petulance, temper, peevishness, irascibility, spleen, cholera, animosity.

ill-tempered *adj.* ill-humored, petulant, indignant, disagreeable, irritable, choleric, testy, peevish, irascible; *ant.* amiable.

ill-timed *adj.* inopportune, inconvenient, inappropriate, tactless, untimely, awkward; *ant.* well-timed.

ill-treat *v.* abuse, mistreat, misuse, injure, wrong, harm, damage, neglect; *ant.* care for.

illuminate *v.* **1.** lighten, irradiate, brighten. **2.** clarify, enlighten, explain, reveal, elucidate, instruct, inform, edify, educate, interpret.

illusion *n.* **1.** hallucination, apparition, delusion, deception, image, figment of the imagination, ghost, chimera. **2.** misconception, false impression, confusion.

illusory *adj.* illusive, misleading, beguiling; *ant.* real.

illustrate *v.* **1.** picture, depict, portray, represent, exemplify, delineate, allegorize, imitate. **2.** adorn, embellish, illuminate, decorate.

illustration *n.* **1.** example, sample, model, instance. **2.** picture, engraving, etching, cartoon, frontispiece, vignette.

illustrative *adj.* explanatory, descriptive, expository, representative, graphic, delineative.

illustrious *adj.* distinguished, eminent, celebrated, exalted, great, brilliant, notable, prominent, renowned; *ant.* inglorious, shameful.

ill will hostility, enmity, animosity, grudge, hard feelings, antagonism, bitterness, frustration, resentment, bad blood; *ant.* cordiality, friendship.

image *n.* **1.** impression, perception, conception, concept. **2.** representation, likeness, model, photograph, reproduction, reflection, copy, facsimile, *slang:* dead ringer, spitting image; effigy, idol, icon.

imagery *n.* representation, depiction, illustration, metaphor.

imaginable *adj.* conceivable, plausible, possible, believable, comprehensible, likely, predictable.

imaginary *adj.* fictional, invented, fanciful, hypothetical, ideal, visionary, imagined, legendary, supposed; *ant.* real.

imagination *n.* creativity, mental agility, inventiveness, artistry, ingenuity, insight, visualization, fancy.

imaginative *adj.* creative, clever, original, inventive, inspired, ingenious, innovative, resourceful.

imagine *v.* **1.** visualize, conceive, envision, invent, picture, conceptualize, create, formulate, devise, dream. **2.** suppose, think, presume, guess, gather.

imbalance *n.* disparity, inequality, disproportion, unevenness, lopsidedness; *ant.* parity.

imbecile *n.* idiot, dummy (*slang*), moron, fool, *slang:* ass, schmuck, nincompoop, blockhead; simpleton, cretin, dullard, dolt, dimwit, halfwit, mental incompetent.

imbecile *adj.* moronic, imbecilic, inane, ludicrous, simple, asinine, fatuous, feebleminded, thick, stupid; *ant.* sensible, intelligent.

imbibe *v.* **1.** drink, ingest, gorge, guzzle. **2.** absorb, take in, soak up, suck up.

imbue *v.* **1.** color, dye, tint, stain, tinge. **2.** fill, permeate, saturate, pervade, impregnate, infuse, inculcate.

imitate *v.* **1.** mimic, impersonate, mirror, mime, echo, caricature, parody, mock, ape. **2.** resemble, emulate, look *or* be like, copy, follow, parallel, match.

imitation *n.* **1.** (act of imitating) simulation, duplication, mimicry; impersonation, impression. **2.** replica, reproduction, copy, substitution, reflection, animation; counterfeit, forgery.

immaculate *adj.* **1.** clean, spotless, stainless. **2.** innocent, morally pure, sinless, undefiled, unsullied.

immanent *adj.* intrinsic, native, indwelling, inborn, innate, natural.

immaterial *adj.* **1.** insignificant, inconsequential, meaningless, unimportant. **2.** insubstantial, incorporeal, intangible, spiritual, bodiless, ethereal, metaphysical, impalpable, incorporate; *ant.* physical, substantial, real.

immature *adj.* inexperienced, green, juvenile, adolescent, childish, infantile, undeveloped, unripe, young, wet behind the ears; *ant.* mature, adult.

immaturity *n.* **1.** inexperience, imperfection, incompleteness, callowness. **2.** childhood, adolescence, youth, infancy.

immeasurable *adj.* limitless, infinite, boundless, endless, inestimable, inexhaustible, unfathomable, vast; *ant.* limited.

immediacy *n.* imminence, promptness, directness, swiftness, spontaneity; *ant.* remoteness.

immediate *adj.* **1.** urgent, pressing, critical, exigent, necessary, paramount. **2.** direct, firsthand, prompt, instant; *ant.* delayed, distant.

immediately *adv.* instantly, directly, now, promptly, right away, straightaway, right off the bat, tout de suite, without delay, pronto.

immemorial *adj.* age-old, ancient, time-

imbecile *adj.* moronic, imbecilic, inane, ludicrous, simple, asinine, fatuous, feebleminded, thick, stupid; *ant.* sensible, intelligent.

imbibe *v.* **1.** drink, ingest, gorge, guzzle. **2.** absorb, take in, soak up, suck up.

honored, traditional, ancestral, fixed, long-standing; *ant.* recent.

immense *adj.* **1.** huge, gigantic, tremendous, vast, great, grand, sprawling, enormous. **2.** limitless, boundless, eternal, endless.

immensity *n.* magnitude, bulk, expanse, size, extent, scope, sweep, vastness; *ant.* minuteness.

immerse *v.* **1.** submerge, dip, plunge, dunk, drown, bathe, steep, soak, drench, souse; *ant.* raise up, uncover. **2.** engross, engage, involve, absorb, preoccupy, consume, interest.

immersion *n.* absorption, preoccupation, involvement, concentration.

immigrant *n.* settler, newcomer, foreigner, wetback (*slang*); *ant.* emigrant, native.

immigrate *v.* migrate, resettle, settle, colonize, move in; *ant.* emigrate.

imminence *n.* immediacy, nearness, threat, menace, approach; *ant.* remoteness.

imminent *adj.* impending, approaching, threatening, at hand, near, close, forthcoming, looming, menacing, in the air; *ant.* far-off.

immobile *adj.* **1.** stable, fixed, stationary, constant, still. **2.** inflexible, rigid, stiff.

immobilize *v.* disable, halt, paralyze, stop, cripple, transfix.

immoderate *adj.* excessive, extreme, inordinate, intemperate, unreasonable, profligate, unrestrained, unjustified, egregious, unwarranted, exaggerated, over-the-top.

immoderation *n.* extravagance, overindulgence, prodigality, license; *ant.* control.

immodest *adj.* brazen, audacious, forward, indecent, impudent, obscene, shameless, lewd, revealing, titillating, bawdy; *ant.* decorous, delicate.

immodesty *n.* **1.** indecency, shamelessness, impropriety, indecorum; boldness, temerity, gall. **2.** vanity, boastfulness, conceit; *ant.* humility.

immoral *adj.* unethical, wanton, sinful, corrupt, degenerate, indecent, licentious, reprobate, lecherous, loose, wicked; *ant.* righteous, decent.

immorality *n.* depravity, debauchery, vice, turpitude; *ant.* rectitude.

immortal *adj.* **1.** deathless, eternal, endless, enduring, constant, perpetual, abiding, undying, timeless, lasting, perennial. **2.** illustrious, eminent, renowned, glorious, heroic, divine, famous, celebrated, great; *ant.* unsung.

immortalize v. eternalize, memorialize, apotheosize, celebrate, glorify, deify, enshrine, exalt, commemorate, perpetuate, canonize.

immovable adj. **1.** resolute, inflexible, adamant, determined, obstinate, firm, constant, steadfast, unyielding, set, unwavering. **2.** entrenched, rooted, stationary, stuck, jammed, fixed, stable, set.

immunity n. **1.** exemption, favor, privilege, license. **2.** resistance, protection, immunization; ant. vulnerability, susceptibility.

immunize v. vaccinate, inoculate, inject, safeguard, protect.

immure v. confine, imprison, incarcerate, cage, cloister, jail, shut up; ant. free.

immutable adj. unalterable, constant, fixed, perpetual, steadfast, durable, lasting, enduring, permanent, sacrosanct, stable, invariable; ant. changeable.

imp n. sprite, demon, prankster, trickster, rascal, urchin, brat.

impact n. **1.** contact, collision, concussion, blow, crash. **2.** effect, significance, meaning, consequences, impression, repercussions, influence, aftermath.

impair v. **1.** damage, injure, spoil, hurt, harm. **2.** weaken, undermine, lessen, diminish, deteriorate, reduce.

impaired adj. **1.** flawed, defective, imperfect, faulty; drunk, intoxicated. **2.** handicapped, physically challenged, challenged, disabled.

impalatable adj. unsavory, inedible, nauseating, sickening, loathsome, uneatable.

impale v. lance, pierce, skewer, perforate, puncture, spear, transfix, spit, run through, spike.

impalpable adj. indistinct, insubstantial, intangible, tenuous, slight, imperceptible, incorporeal, disembodied, elusive, insensible, shadowy; ant. perceptible.

impart v. **1.** give, grant, present, bestow. **2.** inform, tell, divulge, announce.

impartial adj. disinterested, neutral, objective, just, fair, nonpartisan, nondiscriminating, open-minded, detached, equal; ant. biased, passionate.

impassable adj. impenetrable, obstructed, blocked, closed.

impasse n. **1.** stalemate, deadlock, standoff, standstill. **2.** dead end, cul-de-sac, blind alley, halt.

impassible adj. **1.** invulnerable, invincible, strong, secure. **2.** unfeeling, unconcerned, insensible, passionless.

impassioned adj. excited, passionate, enthusiastic, animated, vehement, fervent, spirited, furious, heated, inspired, stirring, violent; ant. apathetic, mild.

impassive adj. indifferent, apathetic, inscrutable, unemotional, callous, stoic, phlegmatic, composed, laid back (slang); ant. moved, responsive, compassionate.

impatient adj. **1.** anxious, restless, chafing at the bit, agitated, eager, feverish. **2.** irritable, hasty, excitable, quick-tempered, fretful.

impeach v. indict, charge, arraign, accuse, censure, challenge, denounce, disparage, impugn.

impeccable adj. flawless, unblemished, precise, blameless, exact, immaculate, incorrupt, scrupulous, stainless, unimpeachable; ant. flawed.

impecunious adj. poor, insolvent, destitute, impoverished, penniless, poverty-stricken, slang: broke, cleaned out; ant. rich.

impede v. hinder, disrupt, block, delay, hamper, thwart, obstruct, hold up, restrain, bar, check, curb, slow; ant. expedite, facilitate.

impediment n. obstacle, detriment, setback, prohibition, barricade, shackle, disadvantage, burden, drawback, fault; ant. help, assistance, aid.

impel v. compel, incite, motivate, instigate, prompt, stimulate, drive, influence, move, urge, prod; ant. dissuade.

impending adj. imminent, looming, threatening, approaching, menacing, coming, brewing, close, in store.

impenetrable adj. **1.** dense, impervious, compact, hard. **2.** incomprehensible, unintelligible, unfathomable, inscrutable.

impenitent adj. defiant, hardened, incorrigible, remorseless, unabashed, stubborn, unashamed, obdurate, unreformed, unremorseful, unrepentant.

imperative n. duty, obligation, commandment, order, requirement, necessity.

imperative *adj.* 1. necessary, requisite, mandatory, immediate, inescapable, urgent, crucial; *ant.* optional. 2. authoritative, commanding, dominant, masterful.

imperceptible *adj.* undetectable, unobtrusive, inappreciable, faint, subtle, subliminal, inaudible, impalpable, invisible, microscopic, fine, unnoticeable, slow; *ant.* discernible, apparent, distinguishable.

imperceptive *adj.* insensitive, obtuse, superficial, unappreciative, undiscerning, unaware, crass, dim, dull; *ant.* observant.

imperfection *n.* defect, flaw, inadequacy, weakness, deficiency, blemish, insufficiency, failing.

imperfect *adj.* impaired, faulty, marred, defective, incomplete, limited, unfinished, broken, damaged.

imperial *adj.* supreme, sovereign, august; regal, magnificent, princely.

imperil *v.* endanger, hazard, compromise, threaten, put at risk, expose, jeopardize; *ant.* protect, secure.

imperious *adj.* 1. domineering, overbearing, oppressive, tyrannical, autocratic, dictatorial. 2. urgent, critical, pressing, imperative.

imperishable *adj.* enduring, immortal, permanent, abiding, perpetual, undying, perennial, eternal, deathless, indestructible; *ant.* extinguishable.

impermanent *adj.* temporary, passing, brief, elusive, fleeting, fugitive, ephemeral, momentary, transient, perishable, transitory.

impermeable *adj.* impenetrable, impervious, resistant, impassable, waterproof.

impersonal *adj.* formal, neutral, aloof, detached, dispassionate, cold, official, remote, unsympathetic; *ant.* friendly.

impersonate *v.* imitate, mimic, parody, caricature, mock, ape, masquerade as, personate, pose as.

impersonation *n.* imitation, enactment, portrayal, role, performance.

impertinent *adj.* 1. inappropriate, incongruous, inapplicable, unsuitable, pointless. 2. disrespectful, insolent, impudent, saucy, cheeky, forward, brash.

imperturbable *adj.* composed, complacent, self-possessed, tranquil, sedate, calm, immovable, unflappable, stoical, cool, cool as a cucumber; *ant.* excitable.

impervious *adj.* 1. unreceptive, unaffected, unmoved, invulnerable, untouched; *ant.* responsive. 2. impenetrable, impermeable, resistant, sealed, impassable.

impetuous *adj.* impulsive, spontaneous, hasty, rash, precipitate, reckless; eager, impassioned, vehement, unrestrained; *ant.* prudent, circumspect.

impetus *n.* incentive, motivation, stimulus, motive, drive, catalyst.

impiety *n.* 1. godlessness, irreverence, wickedness, sinfulness. 2. (an impious act) sacrilege, error, profanity, blasphemy, iniquity.

impinge *v.* 1. encroach, invade, intrude. 2. strike, hit, crash against, ricochet.

impious *adj.* irreverent, sacrilegious, blasphemous, profane, sinful, iniquitous, wicked, ungodly; *ant.* righteous.

impish *adj.* mischievous, frolicsome, playful, waggish, naughty, devilish, wanton, sportive, wicked.

implacable *adj.* merciless, relentless, uncompromising, cruel, immovable, inexorable, pitiless, remorseless, ruthless, unyielding, intractable, rancorous; *ant.* flexible, forgiving.

implant *v.* inseminate, plant, instill, insert, root, graft, place, embed.

implausible *adj.* suspect, dubious, improbable, far-fetched, unlikely, weak, transparent, unbelievable, incredible, unreasonable; *ant.* believable, credible.

implement *n.* instrument, utensil, device, apparatus, tool, appliance, agent, gadget.

implement *v.* effect, execute, perform, bring about, discharge, accomplish, enforce, complete, realize, fulfil.

implicate *v.* 1. involve, associate, connect, relate, link, charge, incriminate, cite. 2. imply, suggest, insinuate, indicate, assume.

implicated *adj.* incriminated, suspected, entangled, embroiled, compromised; *ant.* exonerated.

implication *n.* meaning, import, suggestion, insinuation, hint, indication, inference, assumption; ramification, consequence, effect.

implicit *adj.* 1. implied, inherent, presupposed, understood, latent, unspoken; *ant.* ex plicit. **2.** complete, absolute, firm, fixed, wholehearted, without stint, unqualified; *ant.* measured.

implicitly *adv.* utterly, completely, absolutely, unconditionally, unhesitatingly, unreservedly; *ant.* with reservations.

implied *adj.* suggested, insinuated, inherent, assumed, hinted, unspoken, implicit, understood, indirect, undeclared, tacit, unstated; *ant.* stated, explicit.

implore *v.* plead, supplicate, beseech, entreat, beg, ask, solicit, pray, importune.

imply *v.* indicate, suggest, intimate, hint at.

impolite *adj.* disrespectful, bad-mannered, discourteous, rude, uncivil, crass, insolent, unmannerly, abrupt, course; *ant.* refined, delicate.

impolitic *adj.* imprudent, misguided, indiscreet, ill-advised, foolish, undiplomatic, unwise; *ant.* wise, judicious.

imponderable *adj.* inestimable, incomputable, incalculable.

import *n.* importance, implication, meaning, essence, intention, substance, gist.

import *v.* **1.** introduce, bring in, ship; *ant.* export. **2.** indicate, signify, imply, mean, purport.

importance *n.* **1.** import, emphasis, point, force, sense, consequence, purport, bearing, stress, concern. **2.** prominence, consequence, moment, greatness; *ant.* triviality, insignificance, emptiness.

important *adj.* **1.** significant, relevant, essential, serious, considerable, critical, paramount, primary, crucial, substantial, vital; *ant.* inconsequential, trivial. **2.** eminent, illustrious, wellknown, influential, distinguished, prominent, noted, aristocratic, honored, four-star, highlevel; *ant.* obscure, unrecognized, unknown.

imported *adj.* (produced abroad) alien, shipped in, exotic, foreign-made; *ant.* domestic, native.

importune *v.* harass, entreat, plead with, solicit, urge, plague, press, pester, badger, hound, beg, enjoin.

importunity *n.* insistence, solicitation, persistence, urgency, tenacity, entreaties, impatience.

impose *v.* compel, force upon, burden, command.

impose upon disturb, interrupt, intrude, presume.

imposing *adj.* impressive, striking, dignified, effective, grand, pompous, stately, majestic.

imposition *n.* constraint, encumbrance, demand, restraint.

impossibility *n.* inability, impracticability, hopelessness, unattainableness.

impossible *adj.* **1.** inconceivable, vain, unattainable, insurmountable, inaccessible, preposterous, infeasible, out of the question; *ant.* likely, reasonable. **2.** improbable, unlikely, doubtful.

impostor *n.* fraud, hypocrite, grifter, cheat, charlatan, pretender, rogue, swindler, sham, *slang:* phony, con man; quack.

impotent *adj.* **1.** sterile, infertile, barren, unproductive, frigid; *ant.* fecund. **2.** weak, inept, powerless, infirm, feeble.

impound *v.* **1.** imprison, incarcerate, confine. **2.** seize, appropriate, confiscate, usurp, take, keep.

impoverished *adj.* destitute, bankrupt, depleted, ruined, distressed, drained, indigent, poor, needy; *ant.* rich.

impractical *adj.* idealistic, unrealistic, romantic, visionary, academic; impossible, nonviable, infeasible, hopeless, inoperable; *ant.* doable, feasible, workable.

imprecation *n.* denunciation, blasphemy, abuse, profanity, vilification, curse, vituperation.

imprecise *adj.* indefinite, ambiguous, estimated, inaccurate, loose, unprecise, fluctuating, ill-defined, indeterminate, inexact, unscientific, vague; *ant.* exact, explicit, unequivocal.

impregnable *adj.* impenetrable, invulnerable, fortified, invincible, secure, unconquerable, indestructible, strong; *ant.* vulnerable.

impregnate *v.* **1.** beget, conceive, reproduce, procreate. **2.** permeate, pervade, fill up, overflow, saturate.

impress *v.* **1.** affect, strike, sway, influence, inspire; stand out, excite notice, arouse comment, make a hit (*slang*). **2.** indent, imprint, emboss, stamp.

impressed *adj.* **1.** influenced, affected, moved, excited, stirred, struck, taken, touched, turned on (*slang*). **2.** imprinted, stamped, indented, marked.

impression *n.* **1.** awareness, opinion, recollection, belief, sense, conviction, suspicion, idea, hunch. 2. dent, indentation, imprint, mark, stamp. 3. imitation, impersonation, parody, burlesque, take-off (*slang*).

impressionable *adj.* gullible, naive, impressible, suggestible, vulnerable, susceptible, receptive.

impressive *adj.* effective, striking, imposing, exciting, powerful, memorable, forcible.

imprint *n.* 1. identification, trademark, heading, sponsorship. 2. impression, indentation, dent, print.

imprint *v.* impress, mark, brand, engrave, stamp, print, etch, fix.

imprison *v.* incarcerate, lock up, detain, confine, jail, put away (*slang*), cage, constrain, encage, immure; *ant.* free.

imprisonment *n.* detention, custody, internment, captivity, house arrest; *ant.* freedom.

improbable *adj.* unlikely, doubtful, implausible, dubious, uncertain, questionable, preposterous.

impromptu *adv.* extempore, off the top of one's head, on the spur of the moment, spontaneously, ad hoc.

impromptu *adj.* spontaneous, improvised, ad hoc, ad-lib, off-the-cuff; extemporaneous, unrehearsed, unprepared; *ant.* planned, rehearsed.

improper *adj.* 1. unsuitable, incorrect, imprudent, unseemly, inappropriate, irregular, untimely, inadvisable, inopportune, unfit, awkward, discordant, clumsy. 2. immoral, suggestive, untoward, naughty, smutty.

impropriety *n.* blunder, faux pas, gaffe, slip, lapse, mistake; indecency, immodesty, indecorum, vulgarity.

improve *v.* 1. upgrade, develop, enhance, reorganize, gentrify, refine, progress; *ant.* downgrade. 2. mend, recuperate, ameliorate, recover, rectify, turn over a new leaf, perk up; *ant.* decline.

improvement *n.* 1. correction, repair, recovery, reform; *ant.* deterioration, decay. 2. development, modernization, progress, growth, promotion, increase, regeneration, revision, enhancement, supplement, addition, attachment; *ant.* retrogression.

improvident *adj.* extravagant, spendthrift, free-spending, lavish, wasteful, profligate, slack; impulsive, unwise, shortsighted.

improvisation *n.* spontaneity, impromptu, ad-lib, extemporizing.

improvise *v.* extemporize, contrive, invent, devise, concoct, play it by ear (*slang*), make do, ad-lib.

improvised *adj.* unrehearsed, improvisational, makeshift.

imprudence *n.* indiscretion, irresponsibility, carelessness, foolishness, heedlessness, improvidence, folly, inadvisability, temerity.

imprudent *adj.* irresponsible, careless, injudicious, hasty, rash, heedless, ill-considered, indiscreet, ill-advised, foolish, reckless, shortsighted; *ant.* cautious, careful.

impudent *adj.* insolent, brazen, audacious, forward, assured, rude, cocky (*slang*), saucy, shameless, impertinent, pert, presumptuous, fresh, bold; *ant.* polite, modest.

impugn *v.* challenge, attack, criticize, oppose, assail, dispute, question, vilify; *ant.* praise.

impulse *n.* urge, wish, inclination, caprice, fancy, thought, motivation, drive, appeal, notion.

impulsive *adj.* 1. spontaneous, offhand, extemporaneous, unpremeditated. 2. impetuous, sudden, hasty, precipitate, reactionary, reckless, rash, violent; *ant.* cautious.

impunity *n.* exemption, immunity, amnesty, freedom, license, dispensation, liberty, permission, security; *ant.* liability.

impure *adj.* 1. adulterated, diluted, contaminated, mixed, polluted, amalgamated, tainted, tampered with, doctored; *ant.* pure, unalloyed. 2. unchaste, corrupt, defiled, obscene, licentious, salacious; *ant.* virginal, chaste.

impurity *n.* 1. lewdness, indecency, pornography, profligacy. 2. filth, dirt, excrement, defilement, contamination.

imputation *n.* insinuation, suggestion, reproach, slander, aspersion, censure, slur.

impute *v.* 1. accuse, charge, blame, stigmatize, brand. 2. attribute, assign, credit, ascribe.

in *adj.* 1. here, at home, present, attending, available. 2. popular, fashionable, trendy, modish.

in *adv.* inward, inside, toward the center, into, within.

inability *n.* incompetence, inadequacy, disability, weakness, handicap, impotence, incapacity, ineptitude, ineptness.

inaccessible *adj.* unapproachable, unattainable, remote, isolated, solitary, unfrequented, unreachable.

inaccuracy *n.* error, miscalculation, blunder, defect, fault, mistake, slip.

inaccurate *adj.* incorrect, erroneous, mistaken, wrong, inexact, imprecise.

inactive *adj.* 1. idle, immobile, inoperative, latent, out of service, stagnant, dormant, sedentary, inert, stabilized; *ant.* operative. 2. dull, lethargic, low-key, quiet, passive. 3. unemployed, jobless, out of work.

inactivity *n.* abeyance, hibernation, sloth, indolence, languor, lassitude, quiescence, torpor, rest; *ant.* activeness.

inadequacy *n.* 1. inferiority, ineptitude, insufficiency, incompetence. 2. flaw, shortcoming, drawback, defect, lapse.

inadequate *adj.* 1. deficient, lacking, incomplete, insufficient, depleted, inappreciable, sparse, defective; *ant.* sufficient, substantial, productive. 2. incompetent, impotent, unequal, falling short.

inadmissible *adj.* immaterial, inappropriate, irrelevant, unacceptable, improper, unqualified, prohibited, disallowed.

inadvertent *adj.* unintended, accidental, negligent, unintentional, heedless, inattentive, unplanned, unwitting, thoughtless, careless; *ant.* deliberate, guarded.

inadvisable *adj.* imprudent, indiscreet, foolish, ill-advised, misguided, ill-judged, impolitic, unwise, impulsive, regrettable; *ant.* judicious, expedient, cautious.

inalienable *adj.* inviolable, inherent, basic, natural, absolute, sacrosanct, inbred, nonnegotiable, permanent, unassailable.

inane *adj.* senseless, futile, idiotic, asinine, vain, fatuous, foolish, puerile, stupid, trifling, worthless; *ant.* sensible, intelligent.

inanimate *adj.* 1. inorganic, mineral, lifeless, nonanimal, nonvegetable; *ant.* living. 2. inert, inactive, dull, inoperative.

inapplicable *adj.* inappropriate, unrelated, irrelevant, beside the point, unsuited, inapt, inconsequent, unsuitable.

inappropriate *adj.* 1. incongruous, untimely, unseemly, malapropos, out of place, unfitting, ill-suited, unfit. 2. improper, tasteless, tactless, unbecoming, unseemly.

inapt *adj.* crass, awkward, incompetent, gauche, maladroit, tactless, dull, inept, inappropriate, inopportune, unsuitable.

inarticulate *adj.* 1. incomprehensible, unintelligible, uncommunicative, incoherent, indistinct, faltering, mumbled, unspoken. 2. silent, mute, speechless, dumb, voiceless.

inattentive *adj.* absent-minded, distracted, heedless, preoccupied, negligent, careless, remiss, unmindful; *ant.* observant.

inaudible *adj.* imperceptible, faint, indistinct, low, muted, silent, muffled, mumbled, out of earshot.

inaugural *adj.* first, initial, maiden, introductory.

inaugurate *v.* 1. install, ordain, christen, commission, consecrate, dedicate, enthrone, introduce, invest, usher in. 2. launch, debut, begin, start off, commence, set up.

inauguration *n.* induction, initiation, consecration, installation, institution; startup, commissioning, beginning, commencement.

inauspicious *adj.* discouraging, ominous, ill-omened, unfortunate, ill-boding, ominous, threatening, unfavorable, unlucky, unpromising, untoward.

inborn *adj.* inherent, innate, essential, congenital, hereditary, native, instinctive, natural, intuitive, ingrained, inherited, inbred; *ant.* learned, acquired.

incalculable *adj.* 1. immense, inestimable, immeasurable, limitless, boundless; *ant.* limited. 2. unpredictable, unforeseen, unfixed.

incandescence *n.* radiance, brilliance, luster, glow, shine.

incandescent *adj.* radiant, glowing, brilliant, intense.

incantation *n.* 1. chant, mantra, invocation, charm. 2. spell, black magic, witchcraft, sorcery, enchantment.

incapability *n.* inability, incompetence, inadequacy, impotence, disability, ineffectiveness, insufficiency.

incapable *adj.* incompetent, impotent, unqualified, inadequate, unfit, ineffective, unable, ineffectual, inept, insufficient, powerless; *ant.* able.

incapacitate *v.* disable, immobilize, paralyze, cripple, maim; *ant.* facilitate, set up.

incapacitated *adj.* indisposed, laid up, prostrate, unfit, out of commission; *ant.* operative, well.

incapacity *n.* inability, incapability, inadequacy, disability, disqualification, insufficiency, incompetence, impotence, ineffectiveness, weakness; *ant.* capability.

incarcerate *v.* detain, imprison, impound, commit, jail, confine, cage, restrain, restrict, lock up, put away (*slang*); *ant.* free.

incarceration *n.* detention, captivity, bondage, internment, custody; *ant.* freedom.

incarnate *adj.* made flesh, typified, embodied.

incarnation *n.* 1. manifestation, embodiment, personification. 2. matter, flesh-and-blood, substance, body.

incendiary *n.* 1. arsonist, pyromaniac, firebug. 2. agitator, insurgent, revolutionary, rabble-rouser.

incendiary *adj.* 1. combustible, flammable, inflammable. 2. nonflammable. 2. inciting, provocative, inflammatory, arousing, controversial; *ant.* calming, bland.

incense *n.* scent, frankincense, myrrh, essence, punk, balm, fragrance, aroma, odor.

incense *v.* infuriate, anger, rile, provoke, exasperate, excite, inflame, irritate, madden, make one's blood boil, make one see red (*slang*), raise one's hackles; *ant.* placate, calm, serene.

incensed *adj.* furious, irate, outraged, enraged, indignant, angry, fuming, mad, steamed (*slang*), on the warpath, up in arms; *ant.* calm, serene.

incentive *n.* motivation, lure, inducement, bait, reward, enticement, stimulus, cause, encouragement, impetus, reason, spur.

inception *n.* beginning, origin, start, initiation, birth, commencement, inauguration, installation, outset, rise, kickoff; *ant.* conclusion, completion, end.

incertitude *n.* perplexity, hesitation, misgiving, doubt.

incessant *adj.* interminable, persistent, relentless, monotonous, ceaseless, unrelenting, continuous, constant, endless, continual, nonstop; *ant.* intermittent, ceasing.

inch *n.* small degree, iota, jot. **by inches** slowly, by degrees, step by step. **every inch** thoroughly, entirely, in all respects.

incidence *n.* occurrence, rate, frequency, extent, prevalence, tendency, range, degree, trend.

incident *n.* occurrence, event, episode, circumstance; disturbance, mishap, confrontation, commotion, scene, adventure.

incidental *adj.* 1. accidental, chance, random, occasional, casual, fortuitous, odd. 2. inconsequential, irrelevant, nonessential, trivial, slight, minor; *ant.* essential. 3. contingent, attendant, subordinate, secondary, accompanying, related.

incidentally *adv.* by the way, parenthetically, casually, by chance, by the by, en passant, in passing.

incidentals *n.* odds and ends, extras, accessories; *ant.* essentials.

incinerate *v.* burn, cremate, char, parch, reduce.

incipient *adj.* nascent, embryonic, inchoate, inceptive, originating, beginning, commencing, developing, rudimentary, starting; *ant.* developed.

incise *v.* 1. cut, dissect, split, chop. 2. engrave, etch, chisel, carve, mold.

incision *n.* cut, slit, discission, gash, notch, opening, slash.

incisive *adj.* astute, perceptive, perspicacious, acute, penetrating, keen, trenchant. 2. caustic, severe, sarcastic, sardonic, biting, satirical, mordant.

incite *v.* instigate, provoke, agitate, encourage, urge, prompt, impel, motivate, inflame, solicit, stir up, egg on; *ant.* restrain, discourage, check.

inciting *adj.* inflammatory, exciting, incendiary, rabble-rousing; *ant.* calming.

inclement *adj.* 1. (said of weather) severe, wintry, raw. 2. (as of a judgment) ruthless, unkind, severe, harsh, savage; *ant.* merciful.

inclination *n.* **1.** tendency, bias, propensity, predilection, penchant, predisposition, attraction, preference, proclivity, trend, idiosyncrasy, persuasion. **2.** bank, incline, slant, angle.

incline *n.* bank, hill, slope, rise, ramp, gradient, acclivity, ascent, declivity, descent, dip.

inclined *adj.* disposed, willing, prone, apt, likely, liable, leaning.

include *v.* **1.** (have as parts or contents) contain, entail, accommodate, involve, hold, cover, embrace, admit, embody, implicate, carry, be composed of; *ant.* omit. **2.** (cause to become a part) introduce, enter, incorporate, append, interject, merge, add on, insert, combine, reject, discard.

including *prep.* as well as, not to mention, in addition to, in conjunction with, to say nothing of; *ant.* exclusive of, except for, aside from.

inclusive *adj.* comprehensive, sweeping, across-the-board, all-embracing, general, overall; *ant.* narrow, exclusive.

incognito *adj.* disguised, masked, unrecognized, unknown, veiled; *ant.* open, recognizable.

incoherent *adj.* inarticulate, confused, illogical, incomprehensible, unintelligible, inconsistent, disconnected, rambling, disjointed, tongue-tied, indistinct, puzzling; *ant.* clear, eloquent, distinct, communicative.

incoherently *adv.* frantically, chaotically, randomly, spasmodically, ineptly, unsystematically, aimlessly, casually, sloppily, by fits and starts.

incombustible *adj.* fireproof, flame-resistant, nonflammable.

income *n.* earnings, salary, interest, pay, profits, receipts, wages, yield, means; *ant.* expenses.

incoming *adj.* approaching, ensuing, arriving, landing, entering, returning, succeeding.

incommensurate *adj.* disproportionate, inordinate, excessive, extreme, extravagant, inadequate, inequitable, insufficient, unequal; *ant.* appropriate.

incommunicado *adj.* silenced, gagged, under wraps, cut off, hidden.

incomparable *adj.* inimitable, unequaled, peerless, unparalleled, unmatched, unrivaled; paramount, superlative, brilliant, superb, supreme, transcendent; *ant.* poor, run-of-the-mill.

incompatible *adj.* antipathetic, contradictory, antagonistic, discordant, mismatched, irreconcilable, ill-assorted, incongruous, unsuited, disparate; *ant.* consistent, harmonious, congenial.

incompetent *adj.* incapable, inadequate, incapacitated, ineffective, inefficient, inept, inexpert, insufficient, unfit, useless; *ant.* skillful, able.

incomplete *adj.* unfinished, rough, half-done, under construction.

incomprehensible *adj.* inconceivable, arcane, enigmatic, unfathomable, obscure, mysterious, perplexing, impenetrable, inscrutable, all Greek (*slang*); *ant.* intelligible, imaginable.

inconceivable *adj.* unimaginable, implausible, incredible, mind-boggling, unknowable, staggering, unheard-of, unthinkable, out of the question; *ant.* believable.

inconclusive *adj.* unsettled, ambiguous, indeterminate, uncertain, up in the air, open to question, indecisive, unconvincing, vague, *ant.* definite, certain.

incongruous *adj.* inconsistent, unconnected, discrepant, inapt, contradictory, divergent, incompatible, unrelated, divergent, disparate, discordant, conflicting; *ant.* coordinated, harmonious, coherent, related.

inconsequential *adj.* insignificant, negligible, minor, immaterial, trivial, inconsequent, inconsiderable, slight, paltry, petty, small-time, trifling; *ant.* important, considerable.

inconsiderate *adj.* rude, selfish, imprudent, insensitive, careless, intolerant, rash, self-centered, tactless, thoughtless, unkind, unthinking; *ant.* gracious, delicate, concerned.

inconsistent *adj.* contradictory, incoherent, erratic, illogical, irreconcilable, eccentric, capricious, discrepant, fickle, random, incongruous, varying; *ant.* dependable, compatible, reliable, predictable.

inconsolable *adj.* despairing, disconsolate, heartbroken, desolate, devastated, wretched.

inconspicuous *adj.* unobtrusive, camouflaged, hidden, insignificant, quiet, unassuming, low-key, low-profile, modest, ordinary, plain; *ant.* ostentatious, noticeable.

inconstant *adj.* inconsistent, fickle, capricious, varying, random, contradictory, eccentric.

incontestable *adj.* obvious, self-evident, irrefutable, clear, undeniable, indubitable, positive, indisputable.

incontinent *adj.* lecherous, profligate, unbridled, promiscuous, debauched, dissipated, ungovernable, dissolute, lascivious, lewd, licentious, wanton; *ant.* restrained, chaste, controlled, checked.

incontrovertible *adj.* incontestable, indisputable, established, irrefutable, clear, evident, undeniable, indubitable, positive, self-evident, sure; *ant.* questionable, uncertain.

inconvenience *n.* nuisance, drawback, hindrance, discomfort, vexation; *ant.* advantage.

inconvenience *v.* bother, disrupt, disturb, trouble, put out, upset, annoy, irk, put out, embarrass; *ant.* accommodate.

inconvenient *adj.* awkward, cumbersome, difficult, tiresome, unmanageable, vexatious, unwieldy, unseasonable, unsuitable, untimely, untoward, unhandy; *ant.* opportune, advantageous.

incorporate *v.* **1.** include, add, enter, combine, fuse, assimilate, place. **2.** (form a company) organize, charter, consolidate, found, set up; *ant.* dissolve.

incorporation *n.* amalgamation, federation, alliance, establishment, confederation, affiliation, merger, unification; *ant.* dissolution, division, disbanding.

incorporeal *adj.* insubstantial, spiritual, ethereal, bodiless; ghostly, spectral, wraithlike, celestial, angelic.

incorrect *adj.* wrong, inaccurate, erroneous, false, untrue, unfactual, mistaken.

incorrigible *adj.* irremediable, irredeemable, incurable, uncorrectable, unreformable, intractable, beyond the pale.

incorruptible *adj.* honest, loyal, honorable, stalwart, upright, scrupulous, just.

increase *n.* growth, expansion, amplification, extension, addition, increment, annex, appreciation, accession, accretion.

increase *v.* augment, intensify, supplement,

amplify, exaggerate, extend, enlarge, expand, escalate, multiply, boost, up the ante (*slang*).

incredible *adj.* unbelievable, implausible, unlikely, improbable, ridiculous, preposterous.

incredulity *n.* disbelief, skepticism, suspicion, doubt, amazement.

incredulous *adj.* doubting, dubious, skeptical, leery, suspicious; *ant.* trusting.

increment *n.* accretion, supplement, gain.

incriminate *v.* implicate, accuse, blame, charge, inculpate, condemn, convict, damage, damn.

inculcate *v.* instill, impress, indoctrinate, infuse, implant, engrain.

inculpate *v.* involve, accuse, implicate, blame, charge, incriminate, censure, connect, impeach; *ant.* exonerate, exculpate.

incumbent *adj.* necessary, mandatory, compulsory, obligatory, binding, prescribed.

incur *v.* bring upon, provoke, earn, expose oneself to, arouse, suffer, induce, meet with, contract, draw, gain, run up.

incurable *adj.* **1.** fatal, terminal, inoperable; *ant.* treatable. **2.** hopeless, inveterate, irrecoverable, irremediable, incorrigible.

incursion *n.* foray, raid, infiltration, penetration, invasion, attack, inroads, irruption.

indebted *adj.* beholden, grateful, obliged, in debt, obligated.

indecency *n.* immodesty, impropriety, obscenity, vulgarity, indecorum, indelicacy, impurity, lewdness, pornography, smut, bawdiness; *ant.* modesty.

indecipherable *adj.* illegible, unintelligible, indistinguishable, indistinct, unreadable.

indecisive *adj.* hesitant, irresolute, ambivalent, indeterminate, doubtful, inconclusive, indefinite, tentative, undecided, vacillating, hung up (*slang*); *ant.* certain, sure.

indecorous *adj.* indelicate, undignified, insensitive, rude, unseemly, unmannerly, uncivil, uncouth.

indeed *adv.* certainly, surely, definitely, of course, naturally.

indefatigable *adj.* inexhaustible, relentless, diligent, persevering, unremitting, pertinacious, patient, tireless, undying; *ant.* slothful, flagging.

indefensible *adj.* **1.** inexcusable, unpardonable, bad, inexpiable. **2.** submissive, defenseless, vulnerable, yielding.

indefinable *adj.* obscure, indescribable, vague, impalpable, inexpressible, subtle, unclear, unrealized, nameless, dim; *ant.* distinct.

indefinitely *adv.* **1.** endlessly, interminably, continually, continuously, inexhaustibly. **2.** vaguely, indecisively, loosely, inexactly, ambiguously, irresolutely, indistinctly, obscurely, equivocally, amorphously, generally; *ant.* positively, exactly, clearly.

indelible *adj.* enduring, indestructible, permanent, ineradicable, ineffaceable, lasting, ingrained, written in stone, inerasable, inexpungible; *ant.* erasable.

indelicate *adj.* rude, embarrassing, crude, offensive, vulgar, indecent, obscene, suggestive, tasteless, unbecoming, unseemly; *ant.* proper, polite.

indemnify *v.* **1.** repay, return, remit, reimburse. **2.** assure, register, answer for.

indemnity *n.* immunity, exemption, guarantee, amnesty, impunity, insurance, protection, satisfaction, security, privilege. **2.** reparation, compensation, requital, restitution, remuneration, redress.

indent *v.* mark, space inward, serrate, cut, dent, nick.

indentation *n.* imprint, depression, impression, gouge.

independence *n.* liberty, sovereignty, autonomy, freedom, self-rule, license.

independently *adv.* alone, individually, solo, unaided; *ant.* together.

indescribable *adj.* inexpressible, indefinable, incommunicable, ineffable, unutterable.

indestructible *adj.* imperishable, durable, unbreakable, permanent, immortal, abiding, enduring, eternal, everlasting, lasting, unfading; *ant.* dissoluble, corruptible.

indeterminate *adj.* imprecise, unspecified, inconclusive, undefined, uncertain, undecided, unfixed, unstated, unstipulated, vague, openended; *ant.* exact, definite.

index *n.* **1.** bibliography, appendix, directory, dictionary. **2.** indicator, indicant, pointer, guide, token, symbol; formula, ratio, rule.

index *v.* alphabetize, file, tabulate, itemize, categorize, arrange.

indicate *v.* **1.** signify, mean, represent, be, symbolize, intimate. **2.** designate, show, point out *or* to, register.

indicated *adj.* recommended, suggested, advisable, needed, called-for, required.

indication *n.* sign, mark, evidence, suggestion, explanation, forewarning, clue, hint, warning.

indicative *adj.* suggestive, denotive, significant, symptomatic.

indicator *n.* guide, gauge, dial, index, sign, pointer, marker, meter, display.

indict *v.* accuse, charge, impugn, incriminate, prosecute, impeach, arraign.

indictment *n.* **1.** charge, accusation, incrimination, censure, blame, findings, presentment. **2.** document, citation, summons, warrant, bill, statement.

indifference *n.* apathy, unconcern, nonchalance, impassivity, insensitivity, disinterest, neutrality, aloofness, coldness, callousness; *ant.* concern.

indifferent *adj.* **1.** apathetic, impassive, unconcerned, listless, unsympathetic, cold, nonchalant, detached, unresponsive, aloof, distant, neutral, uncaring; *ant.* excited, warm, sympathetic. **2.** ordinary, mediocre, so-so, common, conventional, usual, dull, average, fair; *ant.* excellent.

indigence *n.* poverty, destitution, need, deprivation, distress, want; *ant.* affluence.

indigenous *adj.* native, domestic, primitive, autochthonous, original, aboriginal.

indigent *adj.* poor, destitute, needy, impoverished, poverty-stricken, penniless; *ant.* affluent.

indigestible *adj.* inedible, unpalatable, uneatable, unhealthy, unwholesome, undercooked, raw, moldy, rotten, putrid, moldy, poisonous, toxic; *ant.* appetizing, tasty, delicious.

indigestion *n.* dyspepsia, heartburn, flatulence, cardialgia.

indignant *adj.* resentful, incensed, upset, disgruntled, huffy, provoked, riled, scornful, angry, mad, annoyed, *slang:* peeved, miffed, put out; *ant.* pleased.

235

indignation *n.* anger, scorn, resentment, exasperation, ire, pique, fury, rage.

indignity *n.* affront, outrage, insult, snub, slight, disrespect, incivility, humiliation, abuse, contempt.

indirect *adj.* 1. circuitous, deviating, rambling, meandering, crooked, wandering. 2. roundabout, periphrastic, long-winded; back-handed, oblique, slanted, unintended.

indirectly *adv.* second-hand, obliquely, periphrastically; *ant.* directly.

indiscernible *adj.* indistinct, imperceptible, indistinguishable, undiscernible, unapparent, minuscule, minute, hidden.

indiscreet *adj.* imprudent, rash, heedless, reckless, tactless, unthinking, injudicious, unwise, careless, ill-advised, impolitic.

indiscretion *n.* 1. recklessness, foolishness, imprudence, heedlessness, indiscreetness, tactlessness, thoughtlessness, rashness, carelessness, temerity; *ant.* prudence, caution, thoughtfulness. 2. blunder, error, faux pas, folly, gaffe, mistake, slip of the tongue.

indiscriminate *adj.* random, desultory, undiscriminating, chaotic, confused, haphazard, aimless; *ant.* selective.

indiscriminately *adv.* randomly, haphazardly, unsystematically.

indispensable *adj.* essential, required, necessary, requisite, imperative, key, crucial, vital, needed; *ant.* unnecessary.

indisposed *adj.* 1. ailing, sick, ill, infirm, under the weather. 2. averse, unwilling, hesitant, hostile, reluctant, uncaring.

indisposition *n.* 1. ailment, illness, sickness, fever. 2. aversion, dislike, unwillingness, hesitancy, resentment, hatred, malice.

indisputable *adj.* unquestionable, undeniable, plain, uncontrovertible, obvious, self-evident, doubtless; *ant.* debatable, arguable.

indistinct *adj.* ill-defined, obscure, indefinite, indistinguishable, unclear, indiscernible, vague, ambiguous, unintelligible, faint; *ant.* clear, sharp.

indistinguishable *adj.* 1. identical, alike, like, same, interchangeable, equivalent, equal. 2. indistinct, vague, obscure, uncertain, invisible, indiscernible, being, character, creature, body, soul, mortal.

individual *n.* person, being, character, creature, body, soul, mortal.

236

individual *adj.* 1. separate, specific, personal, discrete, particular, singular, peculiar, definite, own, lone, distinctive, exclusive, separate, sole; *ant.* collective, public, general. 2. unusual, different, unique, singular, uncommon, peculiar.

individualism *n.* egoism, libertarianism, free-thinking, independence, self-direction; *ant.* conformity, conventionality.

individualist *n.* nonconformist, freethinker, independent, libertarian, original, lone wolf, maverick.

individualistic *adj.* unconventional, nonconformist, idiosyncratic, original, distinctive, libertarian, egocentric.

individuality *n.* 1. (quality of being distinct) distinctiveness, originality, particularity, separateness, dissimilarity, singularity. 2. personality, selfhood, character, idiosyncrasy, eccentricity, peculiarity; attitude, air, manner, habit, behavior.

individually *adv.* separately, independently, singly, particularly; *ant.* together.

indivisible *adj.* inseparable, undividable, unified, unitary, one, unbreakable.

indoctrinate *v.* imbue, instruct, train, teach, school, drill, propagandize, initiate.

indoctrinated *adj.* convinced, persuaded, trained, educated, brainwashed.

indoctrination *n.* training, schooling, instruction, inculcation.

indolence *n.* laziness, sloth, idleness, torpor, inertia, lethargy, inactivity, languor; *ant.* industriousness, activity, enthusiasm.

indolent *adj.* lazy, slothful, lackadaisical, idle, torpid, inert, inactive, sluggish, lethargic, listless, languid; *ant.* industrious, active, energetic.

indomitable *adj.* invincible, unyielding, steadfast, unbeatable, unconquerable, undaunted, unflinching, untamable, staunch, resolute; *ant.* compliant.

indoors *adj.* inside, in the house, under a roof, within; *ant.* outdoors.

indorse *v.* endorse, sign, support, underwrite, approve.

indubitable *adj.* unquestionable, incontrovertible, undeniable, unarguable, indisputable, irrefutable, obvious, certain, evident, sure; *ant.* arguable.

inedible *adj.* uneatable, rotten, decayed, contaminated, spoiled.

ineducable *adj.* unteachable, slow, dull; incorrigible, indocile; intractable.

ineffable *adj.* inexpressible, indescribable, incommunicable, unspeakable, unutterable; *ant.* describable.

ineffective *adj.* ineffectual, useless, impotent, inefficient, unproductive, fruitless, barren, weak, worthless; *ant.* effective, effectual.

inefficacy *n.* ineffectiveness, uselessness, unproductiveness, inadequacy, futility; *ant.* efficiency.

inefficiency *n.* incompetence, disorganization, carelessness, sloppiness, slackness, waste.

inefficient *adj.* 1. wasteful, extravagant, prodigal, disorganized, disorderly, unsystematic, improvident. 2. incapable, incompetent, unfit, faulty.

inelegant *adj.* graceless, gauche, crude, unrefined, uncouth, unpolished, coarse, rough.

ineligible *adj.* unqualified, unsuitable, disqualified, unfit, unacceptable, inappropriate, objectionable, improper.

inept *adj.* 1. awkward, clumsy, gauche, ungraceful. 2. unsuitable, inappropriate, out of place, unfit, unadapted.

ineptitude *n.* 1. inability, incapacity, disability. 2. awkwardness, clumsiness, gracelessness.

inequality *n.* disparity, difference, disproportion, unevenness, prejudice, bias, preferentiality.

inequitable *adj.* partisan, discriminatory, biased, partial, prejudiced, unjust, unfair, one-sided; *ant.* fair, evenhanded.

inequity *n.* discrimination, prejudice, bias, partiality, injustice, one-sidedness; *ant.* fairness.

inert *adj.* dormant, inactive, idle, inanimate, slothful, torpid, still, slack, lifeless; *ant.* alive, animated.

inertia *n.* inactivity, stillness, deadness, lethargy, indolence, idleness, sluggishness, torpor, laziness; *ant.* activity, liveliness.

inescapable *adj.* destined, fated, unavoidable, unpreventable, ineluctable, inevitable, inexorable, unalterable, irrevocable, certain.

inessential *n.* unnecessary, extraneous, expendable, superfluous, dispensable, extrinsic, irrelevant.

induce *v.* 1. cause, produce, initiate, begin, make, effect. 2. persuade, convince, influence, urge, wheedle.

inducement *n.* incentive, encouragement, attraction, influence, lure, motive, bait, spur, consideration, motive, reason; *ant.* deterrent.

induct *v.* initiate, inaugurate, install, ordain, consecrate, swear in.

inducted *adj.* drafted, called up, initiated, conscripted.

induction *n.* initiation, introduction, ordination, consecration, instatement, installation.

indulge *v.* 1. take part in, go in for, revel, wallow, join, give way to. 2. humor, entertain, coddle. 3. tolerate, endure, bear, allow to pass, oblige.

indulgence *n.* 1. humoring, coddling, pampering, spoiling, placating, babying, kowtowing. 2. forbearance, tolerance, lenience, allowance, patience; *ant.* sternness. 3. revelry, hedonism, self-indulgence, overindulgence, prodigality, dissipation, intemperance, luxury; *ant.* self-denial.

indulgent *adj.* kind, lenient, yielding, tolerant, liberal, complaisant, easygoing, permissive, understanding; *ant.* strict.

industrial *adj.* mechanized, automated, industrialized, modern, technical.

industrialist *n.* captain of industry, manufacturer, producer, magnate, tycoon, baron, financier.

industrious *adj.* hard-working, diligent, productive, conscientious, energetic, zealous, purposeful, laborious, busy, tireless; *ant.* slothful.

industry *n.* 1. diligence, enterprise, zeal, attention, application, assiduity, persistence, intentness; *ant.* laziness, lethargy, idleness. 2. organization, business, trade, monopoly. 3. big business, management, corporation officers, monopolists, shareholders, entrepreneurs, private enterprise, capital, stockholders.

inebriate *v.* exhilarate, stimulate, intoxicate, animate, excite, fire, carry away; *ant.* dampen, sober up.

inebriated *adj.* drunk, intoxicated, under the influence, tipsy, *slang:* plastered, smashed, sloshed, high, bombed; *ant.* sober.

inebriation *n.* drunkenness, intoxication, insobriety, intemperance, tipsiness; *ant.* sobriety.

inestimable *adj.* immeasurable, unfathomable, infinite, immense, untold, incalculable, prodigious, vast; *ant.* insignificant.

inevitable *adj.* destined, fated, fixed, unalterable, ineluctable, unavoidable, unpreventable, inescapable, inexorable, sure, certain, ordained; *ant.* avoidable, uncertain, alterable.

inexact *adj.* imprecise, indistinct, indeterminate, indefinite, lax, erroneous, inaccurate, incorrect.

inexcusable *adj.* unforgivable, unjustifiable, indefensible, intolerable, reprehensible, unpardonable; *ant.* venial.

inexhaustible *adj.* 1. tireless, never-ending, indefatigable, unwearied, unflagging, unsleeping. 2. unlimited, endless, vast, infinite, limitless, boundless, bottomless; *ant.* finite.

inexorable *adj.* 1. unyielding, immovable, intransigent, inflexible, uncompromising, obstinate, unrelenting, adamant. 2. inescapable, unavertable, irresistible, ineluctable.

inexpensive *adj.* economical, cheap, lowpriced, bargain, modest, reasonable, budget.

inexperience *n.* ignorance, newness, unfamiliarity, greenness, verdancy, nescience, callowness, innocence, naiveté.

inexperienced *adj.* unpracticed, unskilled, untrained, amateur, inexpert, verdant, nascent, callow, green, unversed, unseasoned, innocent; *ant.* veteran.

inexpert *adj.* amateurish, unprofessional, untrained, unskilled, inept, incompetent, maladroit, bungling, awkward.

inexplicable *adj.* unexplainable, incomprehensible, inscrutable, enigmatic, intractable, mystifying, baffling, puzzling, mysterious.

inexplicably *adv.* unexplainably, unaccountably, without cause *or* reason, incomprehensibly, incredibly, mysteriously, miraculously, strangely.

inexpressible *adj.* indescribable, ineffable, incommunicable, unspeakable, unutterable, nameless, indefinable.

inexpressive *adj.* impassive, expressionless, emotionless, inscrutable, blank, dead-pan, stolid, stony, poker-faced.

inextinguishable *adj.* unquenchable, unsuppressible, indestructible, irrepressible, enduring, eternal, everlasting, undying, immortal; *ant.* perishable, impermanent.

inextricable *adj.* complicated, involved, tangled, intricate, complex.

infallibility *n.* 1. reliability, dependability, faithfulness, safety. 2. perfection, supremacy, impeccability, consummation.

infallible *adj.* unerring, reliable, exact, perfect, unfailing, dependable, incontrovertible, unquestionable, sure, true, irrefutable.

infamous *adj.* scandalous, offensive, shameful, disgraceful, heinous, bad, wicked, vile, disreputable, notorious, base, foul.

infamy *n.* 1. notoriety, ignominy, dishonor, stigma, stain, shame, disrepute, disgrace; *ant.* glory. 2. wickedness, crime, villainy, atrocity, depravity, turpitude.

infancy *n.* 1. early childhood, babyhood. 2. onset, outset, origin, start, opening, beginning, early stages.

infant *n.* baby, child, tot, toddler, neonate.

infantile *adj.* immature, juvenile, babyish, childish, puerile, young, tender, adolescent; *ant.* adult, mature.

infantry *n.* army, soldiers, foot soldiers.

infatuated *adj.* enamored, enraptured, smitten, captivated, bewitched, beguiled, fascinated, spellbound, obsessed, fixated; *ant.* indifferent, disenchanted.

infatuation *n.* fascination, obsession, passion, love, devotion, fixation, fondness, intoxication, crush (*slang*).

infect *v.* contaminate, taint, pollute, affect, influence, corrupt, defile, blight.

infection *n.* contamination, illness, disease, epidemic, inflammation, virus, pestilence, influence, taint, contagion.

infectious *adj.* contagious, transmittable, infective, communicable, catching, contaminating, virulent, pestilential.

infer *v.* 1. conclude, deduce, come to *or* reach a conclusion, gather, conjecture, assume, presume, presuppose, suppose, arrive at, construe, reckon, read between the lines. 2. imply, insinuate, mean to say, suggest, hint, indicate.

inference *n.* 1. supposition, assumption, presumption, conjecture, surmise. 2. judgment, deduction, conclusion, answer, result.

inferior *n.* subordinate, underling, junior, minion, menial; *ant.* superior.

inferior *adj.* **1.** low-quality, mediocre, low-grade, poor, substandard, worse, lesser, bad. **2.** low-ranking, subordinate, humble, unworthy, menial, secondary, minor; *ant.* superior.

inferiority *n.* **1.** deficiency, inadequacy, shoddiness, worthlessness, imperfection, mediocrity. **2.** subordination, lowliness, subservience, unworthiness, humbleness; *ant.* superiority.

infernal *adj.* hellish, diabolic, fiendish, inhuman, damned, demonic, accursed, satanic, devilish.

infertile *adj.* barren, sterile, unproductive, unfruitful, infecund, arid; *ant.* fecund.

infertility *n.* sterility, barrenness, unproductiveness, infecundity, unfruitfulness, aridity.

infest *v.* **1.** contaminate, pollute, corrupt, dirty, defile, infect. **2.** swarm, overrun, overwhelm, flood, flock, crowd, press, beset, teem, abound.

infested *adj.* **1.** overrun, beset, overwhelmed, jammed, crowded, full. **2.** diseased, ravaged, ratty, wormy, lousy, pediculous, grubby.

infidel *n.* atheist, heathen, pagan, skeptic, disbeliever, heretic, iconoclast; *ant.* believer.

infidelity *n.* disloyalty, treachery, betrayal, apostasy, adultery.

infiltrate *v.* permeate, filter, insinuate, penetrate, sift, creep into, pervade.

infiltration *n.* permeation, penetration, insinuation, intrusion, interpenetration.

infiltrator *n.* penetrator, intruder, spy, plant, subversive, insinuator, subverter, counterspy, double agent.

infinite *adj.* endless, never-ending, unending, eternal, perpetual, unlimited, unbounded, unconfined, boundless, countless, incalculable, interminable, inexhaustible, immeasurable, without end, incessant, constant.

infinitesimal *adj.* minuscule, negligible, insignificant, imperceptible, exiguous, minute, paltry, tiny.

infinity *n.* endlessness, everlastingness, immeasurableness, limitlessness, boundlessness, perpetuity, eternity, infinite space, ubiquity, vastness.

infirm *adj.* sick, decrepit, ill, anemic, weak, frail, debilitated, feeble, delicate, faint, decrepit.

infirmary *n.* hospital, clinic, sickroom, sick bay.

infirmity *n.* **1.** weakness, frailty, deficiency, debility. **2.** illness, sickness, ailment, affliction.

inflame *v.* **1.** irritate, anger, incense, aggravate, vex, annoy, bother, disturb, madden. **2.** excite, ignite, incite, stir up, provoke, fire up. **3.** (break or cause to break into a rash) redden, swell, chafe, erupt, infect, irritate.

inflamed *adj.* congested, sore, fevered, irritated, chafed, infected, festering, raw, swollen, red, hurt.

inflammable *adj.* **1.** flammable, combustible, burnable, pyrophorous; *ant.* fireproof, nonflammable. **2.** short-tempered, irascible, volatile, choleric.

inflammation *n.* infection, abscess, sore, rash, redness, tenderness, painfulness, burning.

inflammatory *adj.* provocative, incendiary, inflaming, instigative, rabble-rousing, rebellious, insurgent, fiery, riotous; *ant.* calming, appeasing.

inflate *v.* **1.** amplify, expand, increase, swell, enlarge, balloon, bloat, blow out. **2.** exaggerate, aggrandize, bombast, boost, puff up.

inflated *adj.* exaggerated, overblown, grandiloquent, pompous, turgid, ostentatious, bombastic, puffed up.

inflation *n.* increase, expansion, extension, buildup.

inflect *v.* turn, bend, curve, arch, crook.

inflection *n.* modulation, pitch variation, pronunciation, enunciation, accent, pitch, intonation, articulation, stress, emphasis.

inflexibility *n.* **1.** solidity, stability, rigidity, toughness, stiffness, firmness. **2.** stubbornness, tenacity, obstinacy, determination.

inflexible *adj.* **1.** stiff, rigid, taut, hardened, firm, solid. **2.** adamant, resolute, determined, stubborn, stiff-necked, relentless.

inflict *v.* deal, wreak, lay on, deliver, mete *or* deal out, do to, dispense, give, bring down upon; impose, force upon, apply.

infliction *n.* punishment, retribution, chastisement, castigation, penalty.

influence *n.* **1.** attraction, sway, magnetism, spell, charisma, appeal. **2.** control, authority, power, clout (*slang*), domination, weight, command, supremacy, prerogative, esteem, prestige, importance, pull (*slang*).

influence *v.* sway, affect, manipulate, persuade,

instigate, impress, guide, motivate, incite, impel, rouse.

influential *adj.* persuasive, compelling, powerful, significant, instrumental, important, guiding, leading, dominant, strong, telling, authoritative; *ant.* ineffectual.

influx *n.* flood, rush, inundation, convergence, inflow, instreaming, invasion, arrival.

inform *v.* tell, relate, instruct, teach, notify.

inform on tell on, *slang:* rat on, put the finger on, squeal on.

informal *adj.* casual, relaxed, natural, familiar, simple, colloquial, homey, unceremonious, unofficial.

informality *n.* casualness, familiarity, ease, congeniality, simplicity, unceremoniousness, unpretentiousness.

informally *adv.* casually, simply, easily, colloquially, unofficially, privately, unceremoniously.

informant *n.* source, informer, tipster, insider, double agent, plant, *slang:* rat, stool pigeon.

information *n.* 1. knowledge, facts, input, data, learning. 2. news, report, notice, message.

informative *adj.* educational, enlightening, instructive, newsy, useful, valuable, constructive, illuminating, revelatory.

informed *adj.* knowledgeable, versed, briefed, abreast, filled in, up-to-date, posted, erudite, well-read, au courant, authoritative, learned; *ant.* unaware, ignorant.

informer (*slang*) *n.* snitch, stool pigeon, stoolie, fink; betrayer, denouncer, *slang:* rat, narc, canary.

infrastructure *n.* foundation, base, underpinnings, basic structure.

infrequent *adj.* occasional, sporadic, intermittent, rare, sparse, scanty, unusual, exceptional.

infrequently *adv.* seldom, rarely, sporadically, occasionally, sometimes, once in a while; *ant.* often.

infringe *v.* encroach, intrude, infract, transgress, overstep, trespass, violate, break, defy.

infringement *n.* encroachment, violation, trespass, transgression, noncompliance, breach, infraction, nonobservance.

infuriate *v.* enrage, incense, anger, madden, rile, vex, provoke, antagonize, irritate; *ant.* calm, mollify.

infuriated *adj.* furious, enraged, mad, incensed, angry, maddened, agitated, boiling, irate, vexed, beside oneself, in a rage.

infuriating *adj.* irritating, aggravating, annoying, maddening, galling, intolerable, vexatious, pestilential; *ant.* soothing.

infuse *v.* instill, imbue, inculcate, breathe into, saturate, steep, brew.

ingenious *adj.* clever, original, skillful, intelligent, inventive, innovative, creative, artistic, imaginative, original, resourceful.

ingenuity *n.* cleverness, originality, inventiveness, resourcefulness, innovativeness, flair, genius, gift.

ingenuous *adj.* 1. frank, outspoken, candid, straightforward, blunt, direct; *ant.* devious. 2. simple, unsophisticated, artless, plain, naive, innocent; *ant.* worldly wise.

inglorious *adj.* 1. ignoble, dishonorable, undignified, shameful, offensive. 2. obscure, unknown, unsung, unhonored.

ingrain *v.* embed, engrain, imbue, entrench, imprint, instill, root, fix.

ingrained *adj.* intrinsic, inborn, congenital, hereditary, indelible, deep-seated, rooted, fundamental, ineradicable, fixed, entrenched; *ant.* superficial.

ingratiate *v.* fawn, get in with, flatter, grovel, blandish, *slang:* brown-nose, suck up.

ingratiating *adj.* fawning, flattering, obsequious, unctuous, sycophantic, servile, bootlicking (*slang*).

ingratitude *n.* ungratefulness, thanklessness, unappreciativeness, ungraciousness.

ingredient *n.* part, element, component, factor, constituent.

ingredients *n.* parts, elements, components, pieces, additives, fixings (*slang*), makings.

inhabit *v.* occupy, reside, live, dwell, lodge, take up one's abode in, tenant, stay, populate, people.

inhabitant *n.* occupant, resident, tenant, dweller, lodger, citizen, native.

inhabited *adj.* populated, occupied, peopled, settled, colonized; *ant.* deserted.

inhalation *n.* respiration, breath, suction, toke (*slang*).

inhale *v.* breathe in, inspire, draw in, suck in; *ant.* exhale, expire.

inharmonious *adj.* **1.** atonal, unmelodious, discordant, cacophonous, tuneless, unmusical. **2.** conflicting, clashing, incompatible, dissonant, antipathetic, strident.

inherent *adj.* innate, inborn, fundamental, intrinsic, congenital, instinctive, inherited, basic, natural, hereditary.

inherit *v.* assume, fall heir to, be bequeathed, come into, succeed to, accede to.

inheritance *n.* legacy, bequest, birthright, heritage, accession, succession.

inhibit *v.* impede, hinder, restrain, suppress, prohibit, curb, arrest, check, discourage, stop; *ant.* encourage, promote.

inhibited *adj.* reserved, reticent, scrupulous, hesitant, self-conscious, withdrawn, bashful, guarded, shy, repressed, subdued; uptight (*slang*).

inhibition *n.* reserve, reticence, self-consciousness, shyness, hang-up (*slang*).

inhospitable *adj.* unfriendly, unreceptive, unsociable, unwelcoming, inimical, uncivil, cold, brusque, unkind, forbidding; *ant.* receptive.

inhuman *adj.* savage, brutal, fiendish, barbaric, cruel, cold-blooded, diabolical, merciless, pitiless, vicious, inhumane; *ant.* kind.

inhumane *adj.* cruel, brutal, coldhearted, uncompassionate, unfeeling, heartless, callous, uncaring; *ant.* kind, merciful.

inhumanity *n.* cruelty, brutality, coldheartedness, brutishness, ruthlessness, sadism, callousness, atrocity, viciousness.

inimical *adj.* hostile, unfriendly, adverse, antagonistic, contrary, ill-disposed, intolerant, hurtful.

inimitable *adj.* unparalleled, matchless, unequaled, nonpareil, unsurpassable, superlative, distinctive, unrivaled, incomparable, peerless, exceptional.

iniquitous *adj.* wicked, unjust, heinous, reprehensible, vicious, nefarious, evil, atrocious, abominable; *ant.* virtuous.

iniquity *n.* wickedness, injustice, viciousness, evil, offense, sin, wrongdoing, impiety, infamy, crime.

initial *adj.* basic, primary, first, fundamental, original, introductory, inaugural, beginning, commencing; *ant.* final.

initially *adv.* at first, originally, to start with, at the outset, in the beginning, introductorily, prefatorily; *ant.* finally.

initiate *n.* beginner, newcomer, apprentice, freshman.

initiate *v.* **1.** start, launch, begin, cause, commence, prompt, actuate. **2.** indoctrinate, teach, train, instruct, coach, introduce, haze.

initiated *adj.* **1.** begun, established, started, introduced, proposed, originated, instituted, inaugurated. **2.** (admitted as a member of an organization) installed, inducted, instated, passed, admitted, approved, accepted.

initiation *n.* **1.** beginning, start, origin, institution, introduction, launch, preliminaries, grounding. **2.** (formal acceptance into an organization) introduction, indoctrination, induction, inauguration, investment, investiture.

initiative *n.* **1.** eagerness, enthusiasm, energy, push, vigor, enterprise, ambition, get-up-and-go (*slang*), inventiveness. **2.** first step *or* move, start, lead, opening, responsibility.

inject *v.* **1.** vaccinate, inoculate, shoot. **2.** interject, insert, force into, instill, include, add, stick *or* throw in, add, interpolate.

injection *n.* inoculation, vaccination, dose, infusion, vaccine, fix (*slang*).

injunction *n.* command, directive, mandate, order, instruction, exhortation, direction, dictate.

injure *v.* hurt, harm, wound, maim, damage, abuse, disable, cripple; *ant.* heal.

injured *adj.* hurt, harmed, wounded, damaged, maltreated, abused, disabled.

injurious *adj.* **1.** harmful, hurtful, dangerous, poisonous, detrimental, painful, damaging, bad, deadly; *ant.* beneficial. **2.** slanderous, insulting, libeling, abusive; *ant.* flattering.

injury *n.* **1.** wound, hurt, trauma, damage, ill, lesion. **2.** injustice, prejudice, wrong, grievance, detriment, hurt, insult.

injustice *n.* **1.** unfairness, prejudice, favoritism, inequality, discrimination, partisanship, partiality, oppression. **2.** (an unjust act) iniquity, miscarriage, infringement, wrong, breach, offense, infraction, hurt.

inkling *n.* hint, clue, intimation, notion, suggestion, indication, faint *or* foggy idea, glimmering, suspicion.

inland *adj.* interior, inner, central, domestic, up-country.

inlet *n.* fjord, bay, ingress, passage, opening, cove.

inmate *n.* prisoner, convict, patient.

inmost *adj.* 1. deep, deepest, innermost. 2. inherent, intrinsic, ingrained, individual, private, intimate.

inn *n.* hotel, roadhouse, hostelry, public house, tavern, saloon, alehouse.

innards *n.* intestines, entrails, viscera, organs, vitals, insides, guts.

innate *adj.* instinctive, ingrained, inherent, intuitive, natural, basic, fundamental, inborn, congenital; *ant.* acquired.

inner *adj.* 1. interior, inside, internal, inward, central, middle. 2. personal, private, secret, intimate, emotional, spiritual.

innermost *adj.* deep, ingrained, personal, private, inherent.

innocence *n.* 1. guiltlessness, blamelessness, integrity, impeccability, inculpability, faultlessness; *ant.* guilt, culpability, dishonesty. 2. guilelessness, artlessness, naïveté, frankness, candidness, simplemindedness, unaffectedness, ingenuousness, sincerity; *ant.* wiliness, shrewdness. 3. inexperience, naïveté, ignorance, virginity, purity, chastity, virtue; *ant.* worldliness.

innocent *n.* naif, beginner, baby, child, ingenue, neophyte, greenhorn, tenderfoot, babe in the woods; *ant.* sophisticate.

innocent *adj.* 1. guiltless, blameless, inculpable, impeccable, faultless, safe, uninvolved, above suspicion; *ant.* guilty, blameworthy, culpable. 2. guileless, ingenuous, open, fresh, frank, confiding, trusting, childish, naive, simple. 3. inexperienced, youthful, young, raw, ignorant, untried, green; *ant.* experienced, worldly-wise. 4. (morally pure) chaste, undefiled, unstained, pure, immaculate, incorrupt, virtuous, impeccable, wholesome, angelic, moral; *ant.* dishonest, sinful, corrupt. 5. well-intended, harmless, innocuous, inoffensive; *ant.* malicious.

innocuous *adj.* 1. harmless, inoffensive, safe, nonirritant, innoxious, unobjectionable. 2. dull, uninspiring, bland, boring.

innovation *n.* modernization, progress, alteration, change, newness, reform, variation.

innovative *adj.* creative, inventive, imaginative, progressive, revolutionary, enterprising, bold, resourceful, adventurous, new; *ant.* conservative, unimaginative.

innuendo *n.* hint, implication, intimation, insinuation, whisper, suggestion, aspersion, slant.

innumerable *adj.* countless, numerous, infinite, multitudinous, untold, incalculable, many, myriad.

inoculate *v.* immunize, vaccinate, inject.

inoculation *n.* immunization, vaccination, injection, shot, protection.

inoperable *adj.* intractable, nonviable, unworkable, impractical; irremovable; *ant.* practicable.

inoperative *adj.* broken, defective, useless, out of order, out of service, out of commission, ineffective, unworkable.

inopportune *adj.* inconvenient, untimely, unfavorable, inappropriate, ill-timed, unsuitable, malapropos, inauspicious.

inordinate *adj.* disproportionate, unwarranted, immoderate, excessive, exorbitant, undue, unreasonable, intemperate, preposterous; *ant.* moderate, reasonable.

inorganic *adj.* artificial, mineral, inanimate; *ant.* organic, vegetable, animal.

input *v.* insert, feed in, key in, store, process, code.

inquest *n.* investigation, hearing, inquiry, trial, examination.

inquire *v.* 1. interrogate, question, probe, ask, make an inquiry. 2. investigate, analyze, study, examine.

inquirer *n.* questioner, investigator, interrogator, researcher, seeker, explorer.

inquiring *adj.* inquisitive, questioning, analytical, interested, curious, probing, skeptical, wondering, quizzical.

inquiry *n.* 1. question, interrogation, query, questioning. 2. investigation, probe, hearing, examination, analysis.

inquisition *n.* interrogation, questioning, investigation, cross-examination, inquest, witch hunt, third degree (*slang*), grilling.

inquisitive *adj.* questioning, curious, probing, prying, snooping, intrusive, meddlesome, nosy (*slang*); *ant.* incurious.

inroad *n.* **1.** encroachment, invasion, incursion, intrusion, foray, raid. **2.** advance, progress, revolution.

insane *adj.* **1.** deranged, crazy, lunatic, wild, crazed, frenzied, maniacal, nuts (*slang*), demented, raving, mentally unsound *or* disturbed, psychotic, schizophrenic, paranoid, wacko (*slang*). **2.** foolish, stupid, idiotic, madcap.

insanitary *adj.* unhygienic, contaminated, impure, polluted, unclean, infested, disease-ridden, filthy, unhealthy.

insanity *n.* **1.** mental illness, derangement, mental aberration, madness, dementia, lunacy, psychosis, neurosis, phobia, mania, alienation. **2.** folly, oddity, idiosyncrasy, eccentricity.

insatiable *adj.* ravenous, voracious, gluttonous, greedy, rapacious, unappeasable, unquenchable, unsatisfiable, immoderate; *ant.* moderate.

inscribe *v.* write, engrave, sign, dedicate.

inscription *n.* dedication, epigraph, label, caption, saying, legend, signature, autograph, holograph.

inscrutable *adj.* incomprehensible, mysterious, secret, enigmatic, inexplicable, esoteric, impassive, sphinxlike, cryptic, deadpan, poker-faced.

insect *n.* bug, beetle, arthropod, mite, vermin, pest.

insecure *adj.* apprehensive, anxious, worried, troubled, vague, uncertain; *ant.* confident.

insecurity *n.* anxiety, uncertainty, doubt, vacillation, indecision, instability.

insensible *adj.* **1.** unconscious, swooning, torpid, lethargic. **2.** indifferent, impassive, apathetic, unmoved, cold.

insensitive *adj.* unfeeling, uncaring, callous, indifferent, boorish, crass, unaffected, unsympathetic, tactless, impervious, imperceptive.

insensitivity *n.* indifference, unconcern, callousness, imperviousness, bluntness, boorishness, crassness, tactlessness; numbness, imperceptiveness.

inseparable *adj.* **1.** indivisible, as one, tied up, joined, entwined, integrated, whole, connected, attached, conjoined, united, unified. **2.** congenial, friendly, loving, close, intimate.

insert *n.* enclosure, addition, advertisement, notice.

insert *v.* put in, imbed, stick *or* place in, root.

inside *adj.* **1.** esoteric, exclusive, confidential, classified, private, secret, innermost. **2.** inner, interior, central, inward, internal, close-up.

inside *adv.* inward, in, indoors, internally.

inside *prep.* within, within the boundaries *or* circumference of, bounded, surrounded by; *ant.* outside, beyond, after.

insides (*slang*) *n.* stomach, belly, viscera, entrails, intestines, organs, bowels, innards, vitals, guts.

insidious *adj.* deceptive, dishonest, sly, tricky, cunning, duplicitous, wily, crooked, devious.

insight *n.* perception, discernment, perspicacity, acumen, shrewdness, awareness, intuition, sensitivity, understanding, judgment.

insightful *adj.* perceptive, sage, astute, perspicacious, clever, keen, smart, discerning, penetrating, shrewd, understanding, intelligent.

insignia *n.* crest, ensign, emblem, regalia, brand, symbol, trademark, mark, badge.

insignificance *n.* irrelevance, meaninglessness, unimportance, triviality, inconsequentiality, negligibility, immateriality.

insignificant *adj.* irrelevant, meaningless, negligible, unimportant, trivial, immaterial, inconsequential, nondescript, meager, petty, piddling, trifling; *ant.* momentous.

insincere *adj.* dishonest, duplicitous, deceitful, dissembling, false, hollow, two-faced, artificial, hypocritical, phony (*slang*).

insincerity *n.* dishonesty, duplicity, pretense, falseness, deceitfulness, hypocrisy, artificiality, lip service, phoniness (*slang*).

insinuate *v.* **1.** imply, hint, suggest, refer, purport, mention, propose. **2.** infiltrate, infuse, introduce, ingratiate, force through, horn in.

insinuation *n.* implication, innuendo, intimation, suggestion, allusion, hint, aspersion, slur, slant.

insipid *adj.* **1.** tasteless, flat, stale, vapid. **2.** uninteresting, dull, weak, lifeless, characterless.

insist *v.* **1.** maintain, assert, contend, emphasize, stress, claim, stand firm, swear. **2.** demand, require, order, urge, exhort.

insistence *n.* urging, persuasion, persistence, determination, exhortation, demand, entreaty, emphasis, stress.

insistent *adj.* persistent, demanding, relentless, forceful, persevering, emphatic, dogged, unremitting, urgent.

insolence *n.* audacity, rudeness, impertinence, presumptuousness, impudence, defiance, effrontery, gall, disrespect, insubordination, sauciness, *slang:* lip, cheekiness; *ant.* respect, politeness.

insolent *adj.* impertinent, rude, disrespectful, impudent, insubordinate, defiant, presumptuous, forward, brazen, saucy, fresh, cheeky; *ant.* respect, politeness.

insoluble *adj.* unsolvable, inexplicable, indecipherable, baffling, perplexing, intractable, indecipherable, mystifying, obscure; *ant.* explicable.

insolvent *adj.* destitute, bankrupt, defaulting, out of funds, failed, ruined, *slang:* flat broke, busted.

insomnia *n.* sleeplessness, restlessness, wakefulness; *ant.* sleep.

insouciance *n.* carefreeness, lightheartedness, flippancy, nonchalance, jauntiness, breeziness, ease, indifference, unconcern; *ant.* anxiety, care.

insouciant *adj.* carefree, lighthearted, happy-go-lucky, jaunty, flippant, breezy, easygoing, unconcerned, nonchalant, untroubled, unworried; *ant.* anxious, careworn.

inspect *v.* examine, scrutinize, look over, check, oversee, supervise, investigate, pursue.

inspection *n.* examination, investigation, inquiry, inventory.

inspector *n.* controller, tester, examiner, checker, investigator, overseer, supervisor, superintendent, reviewer, censor, critic.

inspiration *n.* **1.** stimulus, motivation, incentive, influence, spur. **2.** idea, thought, notion, hunch, whim, fancy, impulse.

inspire *v.* encourage, spur, invigorate, inspirit, stimulate, spark, motivate, urge, fire, provoke, cause, underlie; *ant.* dampen, discourage.

inspired *adj.* **1.** stimulated, roused, motivated, energized, stirred, encouraged, galvanized, moved, exhilarated, influenced. **2.** possessed, in a frenzy, carried away, fired, elated, uplifted, transported, ecstatic.

inspiring *adj.* affecting, moving, stirring, exhilarating, stimulating, exciting, encouraging, uplifting, heartening, invigorating; *ant.* dull.

inspirit *v.* exhilarate, inspire, cheer, galvanize, invigorate, rouse, stimulate, encourage, embolden, hearten, enliven, animate.

instability *n.* inconstancy, changeability, uncertainty, variability, unreliability, impermanence, vacillation, oscillation, fluctuation, capriciousness, fickleness, undependableness, unpredictability.

install *v.* set up, establish, situate, place, plant, institute, instate, induct, ensconce, station.

installation *n.* **1.** induction, ordination, placing, investiture, inauguration, establishment, accession, coronation. **2.** fort, bunker, fortification, munitions.

installment *n.* portion, part, division; episode, chapter, section; repayment, partial payment.

instance *n.* case, situation, example, occurrence.

instant *n.* moment, split second, twinkling, jiffy, flash, minute.

instant *adj.* immediate, instantaneous, quick, rapid, fast, split-second, direct.

instantaneous *adj.* immediate, instant, rapid, prompt, unhesitating, on-the-spot; *ant.* delayed, gradual.

instantaneously *adv.* immediately, instantly, rapidly, at once, on the spot, straight away, there and then, unhesitatingly, promptly.

instantly *adv.* immediately, instantaneously, at once, now, without delay, on the spot, straightaway, pronto, directly, tout de suite.

instead *adv.* alternatively, as a substitute, in lieu, rather, preferably.
instead of in place of, in lieu of, rather than, as proxy for, on behalf of, in default of.

instigate *v.* stimulate, prompt, encourage, incite, excite, initiate, provoke, arouse, start, stir up, impel, inspire, spur.

instigation *n.* prompting, urging, incitement, insistence, encouragement, incentive, provocation.

instigator *n.* agitator, inciter, leader, troublemaker, provocateur, ringleader, firebrand, mischief-maker.

instill *v.* imbue, impress, inculcate, engender, infuse, introduce, implant.

instinct *n.* intuition, proclivity, predisposition, tendency, sixth sense, gut feeling.

instinctive *adj.* **1.** automatic, intuitive, reflex, mechanical, involuntary. **2.** natural, spontaneous, accustomed, normal, habitual.

instinctively *adv.* intuitively, unthinkingly, naturally, automatically, mechanically, spontaneously; *ant.* deliberately, consciously.

institute *n.* academy, school, university.

institute *v.* **1.** organize, found, establish, launch, set up. **2.** begin, initiate, start, open.

institution *n.* **1.** organization, system, association, company, business, foundation, university. **2.** academy, orphanage, reformatory.

institutionalize *v.* standardize, formalize, incorporate, make official, regulate, systemize.

instruct *v.* **1.** teach, educate, give lessons, guide, tutor, coach. **2.** order, command, tell, direct, bid.

instruction *n.* guidance, direction, preparation, education, tutelage, coaching.

instructions *n.* directions, rules, guidance, handbook, manual, information, key.

instructive *adj.* informative, educational, didactic, edifying, illuminating, useful, helpful, enlightening, heuristic; *ant.* unenlightening.

instructor *n.* teacher, adviser, guide, tutor, trainer, coach, mentor.

instrument *n.* implement, device, apparatus, contraption, tool, means, agent, vehicle, way, medium, force, factor.

instrumental *adj.* helpful, useful, contributory, assisting, influential, involved; contingent, accessory; *ant.* obstructive, unhelpful.

insubordinate *adj.* impudent, impertinent, defiant, unruly, rude, rebellious, mutinous, disobedient, disorderly, refractory; *ant.* obedient, docile.

insubordination *n.* impudence, impertinence, rebellion, disobedience, defiance, mutiny, revolt, riotousness; *ant.* obedience, docility.

insubstantial *adj.* **1.** imaginary, unreal, ephemeral, illusory, intangible, fanciful. **2.** flimsy, slight, poor, decrepit, petty.

insufferable *adj.* intolerable, unbearable, unendurable, difficult, impossible, hateful, dreadful, detestable, hard to live with; *ant.* pleasant, tolerable.

insufficiency *n.* inadequacy, deficiency, want,

need, scarcity, dearth, shortage, lack, sparsity; *ant.* excess.

insufficient *adj.* inadequate, deficient, scarce, short, sparse, lacking, wanting; *ant.* excessive.

insular *adj.* **1.** isolated, detached, alone, separate. **2.** biased, prejudiced, narrow-minded, bigoted, parochial, provincial; *ant.* broad-minded, cosmopolitan.

insulate *v.* shield, cushion, sequester, protect, isolate, cut off, cocoon, quarantine.

insulation *n.* cushioning, padding, protection, stuffing.

insult *n.* aspersion, snub, libel, offense, slander, slight, indignity, insolence, abuse, slap in the face; *ant.* compliment, honor.

insult *v.* vilify, abuse, give offense to, libel, revile, offend, snub, call names, slander, slight.

insulting *adj.* offensive, rude, disparaging, slanderous, hurtful, libelous, abusive, scurrilous, contemptuous, insolent.

insuperable *adj.* insurmountable, overwhelming, formidable, invincible, impassable, unconquerable; *ant.* surmountable.

insupportable *adj.* indefensible, unjustifiable, untenable, intolerable, insufferable, unbearable, invalid.

insuppressible *adj.* irrepressible, lively, incorrigible, unstoppable, unsubduable, unruly, uncontrollable, ungovernable, energetic.

insurance *n.* protection, assurance, safeguard, security, indemnity, guarantee, coverage, policy, provision, warranty.

insure *v.* **1.** protect, cover, guarantee, warrant, assure, safeguard, underwrite, indemnify. **2.** confirm, make sure, ascertain, guarantee, warrant.

insurgent *n.* agitator, rebel, radical, rioter, revolter, revolutionary, resister.

insurgent *adj.* rebellious, revolutionary, riotous, partisan, mutinous.

insurmountable *adj.* unconquerable, invincible, overwhelming, impossible, unsurmountable, hopeless, impassable.

insurrection *n.* mutiny, riot, insurgence, revolt, rebellion.

insusceptible *adj.* impassive, indifferent, callous, unfeeling, unemotional.

intact *adj.* whole, one, unitary, complete, all in

one piece, sound, together, entire, undamaged, unbroken, unscathed, untouched, unharmed, unviolated; *ant.* broken, damaged, harmed.

intangible *adj.* 1. ethereal, ephemeral, impalpable, immaterial, airy; *ant.* material. 2. uncertain, indefinite, unsure, vague, hypothetical.

integral *adj.* essential, requisite, indispensable, intrinsic, fundamental, basic, elemental.

integrate *v.* 1. unify, mix, blend, combine, merge, incorporate. 2. (remove barriers to minorities) desegregate, include, assimilate, open, bus.

integrated *adj.* 1. joined, combined, interspersed, unified, mingled. 2. nonsegregated, interracial, multicultural, nonsectarian, free, open.

integration *n.* unification, combination, co-operation, alliance.

integrity *n.* honor, uprightness, honesty, virtue, righteousness, principle, goodness.

intellect *n.* 1. sense, intelligence, reason, judgment, understanding, comprehension, brain power, brains (*slang*). 2. intellectual, genius, thinker, highbrow, *slang:* brain, egghead.

intellectual *n.* thinker, highbrow, scholar, academic, *slang:* brain, egghead.

intellectual *adj.* intelligent, cerebral, rational, scholarly, studious, discursive, bookish.

intelligence *n.* 1. intellect, understanding, comprehension, acumen, judgment, perspicacity, discernment. 2. ability, capacity, skill, aptitude. 3. information, news, report, facts, inside information, knowledge, *slang:* info, the dope.

intelligent *adj.* smart, bright, clever, thinking, rational, well-informed, enlightened, perspicacious, discerning, knowing, brainy (*slang*); *ant.* foolish.

intelligentsia *n.* intellectuals, literati, academics, illuminati, highbrows.

intelligible *adj.* comprehensible, understandable, fathomable, decipherable, clear, distinct, plain, lucid; *ant.* confusing.

intemperate *adj.* 1. drunken, inebriated, intoxicated, soused (*slang*), dissipated, crapulent. 2. excessive, immoderate, inordinate, unrestrained, extreme.

intend *v.* 1. propose, plan, aim, expect, purpose, be resolved *or* determined, aspire to, have

246

in mind, hope *or* resolve to, contemplate. 2. mean, indicate, signify, denote.

intense *adj.* powerful, strong, concentrated, great, fierce, impassioned, profound, deep, fervent, ardent, vehement, consuming, severe.

intensification *n.* buildup, increase, escalation, acceleration, heightening, deepening, worsening, exacerbation; *ant.* lessening.

intensify *v.* increase, deepen, emphasize, enhance, heighten, strengthen, boost, concentrate, exacerbate, escalate, add to, reinforce; *ant.* lessen, die down.

intensive *adj.* concentrated, detailed, comprehensive, deep, thorough, exhaustive, in-depth; *ant.* superficial.

intensity *n.* 1. forcefulness, concentration, power, vehemence, violence, passion, fervor, ardor, extremity, severity, deepness, emphasis. 2. ferociousness, wildness, fury, anger.

intent *n.* intention, objective, goal, aim, purpose, plan, meaning, end.

to all intents and purposes in almost every respect, virtually, practically, almost.

intent *adj.* engrossed, attentive, rapt, preoccupied, absorbed, concentrating; determined, committed, earnest, fixed, steadfast, resolved, hell-bent (*slang*).

intention *n.* 1. goal, objective, purpose, plan, aim, intent, point, meaning, idea, end.

intentional *adj.* deliberate, intended, premeditated, planned, concerted, willful, studied, calculated, meant, prearranged; *ant.* accidental.

intentionally *adv.* deliberately, on purpose, willfully, by design, with malice aforethought.

intently *adv.* attentively, carefully, closely, watchfully, keenly, steadily, hard; *ant.* absent-mindedly.

inter *v.* bury, lay to rest, entomb, sepulchre; *ant.* exhume.

intercede *v.* mediate, arbitrate, intervene, advocate, plead, speak.

intercept *v.* obstruct, interrupt, frustrate, impede, thwart, arrest, seize, block, deflect, cut off, check, head off, stop.

intercession *n.* mediation, intervention, advocacy, entreaty, supplication, plea, beseeching, solicitation.

intercessor *n.* mediator, negotiator, arbitrator, judge.

interchange *n.* **1.** barter, trade, exchange, reciprocation. **2.** alternation, variation, change of places, transposition, exchange, shift. **3.** intersection, cloverleaf.

interchangeable *adj.* transposable, synonymous, exchangeable, equivalent, reciprocal, similar, identical; *ant.* different.

intercourse *n.* **1.** association, communication, dealings, interchange, contact. **2.** copulation, fornication, sex, sexual relations, coitus.

interdependence *n.* reliance, dependence, mutuality.

interdict *n.* ban, injunction, prohibition, proscription, veto, disallowance, taboo; *ant.* permission.

interdict *v.* forbid, prohibit, enjoin, ban, disallow, outlaw, bar, rule out, veto, prevent; *ant.* permit.

interest *n.* **1.** concern, care, attention, curiosity, excitement. **2.** premium, credit, due, discount, profit, percentage, gain, bonus, earnings. **3.** (vested interests) lobby, interest group, constituency.

in the interest of for the sake of, on behalf of, in order to promote.

interest *v.* involve, engage, attract, intrigue, concern, fascinate, move, touch, affect.

interested *adj.* **1.** curious, stimulated, attentive, enticed, lured, drawn, affected, moved, touched, sympathetic, inspired, roused, stirred. **2.** concerned, occupied, engrossed, involved, absorbed in; partial, prejudiced, biased; *ant.* indifferent, impartial.

interesting *adj.* intriguing, engrossing, thought-provoking, compelling, fascinating, engaging, absorbing, stimulating, gripping, appealing, provocative; *ant.* boring.

interfere *v.* **1.** meddle, intervene, interpose, interlope, butt in (*slang*). **2.** prevent, hinder, stop, oppose, conflict.

interference *n.* **1.** intervention, resistance, impedance, checking, blocking, barring, hampering, hindrance, clashing. **2.** meddling, prying, interposition, interruption, trespassing, tampering, butting in (*slang*). **3.** barrier, obstacle, obstruction, impediment, restraint.

interim *n.* meantime, meanwhile, pause, interlude, interval.

interim *adj.* temporary, acting, provisional, stand-in, stopgap, improvised, makeshift; *ant.* permanent.

interior *n.* inside, center, core, heart.

interior *adj.* inner, inside, internal, central, inward, private, personal, secret.

interject *v.* interrupt, interpolate, interpose, introduce, cry, call, exclaim, shout.

interjection *n.* **1.** insertion, interpolation, insinuation, inclusion. **2.** exclamation, cry, utterance, ejaculation.

interlock *v.* intertwine, engage, mesh, lock together.

interlocutor *n.* spokesperson, speaker, orator, conversationalist, press agent, host, interviewer.

interloper *n.* intruder, trespasser, meddler, uninvited guest, gate-crasher (*slang*).

interlude *n.* recess, pause, delay, hiatus, interruption, wait.

intermediary *n.* mediator, go-between, agent, broker, middleman.

intermediate *adj.* middle, median, mean, halfway, midway, mid; *ant.* extreme.

interment *n.* funeral, burial, entombment, sepulture, obsequy.

interminable *adj.* perpetual, ceaseless, unlimited, immeasurable, endless, infinite, long, protracted, unbounded, wearisome; *ant.* limited.

intermingle *v.* commingle, combine, mix, amalgamate, merge, blend, fuse; *ant.* separate.

intermission *n.* interval, suspension, pause, recess, interlude, break, recess, respite, rest, lull, breather (*slang*).

intermittent *adj.* periodic, sporadic, occasional, irregular, recurrent, discontinuous; *ant.* continuous.

internal *adj.* **1.** within, inside, inward, inner, interior, private, intrinsic, innate, inherent, intimate, circumscribed; *ant.* outer, outward. **2.** indigenous, native, domestic, centralized.

international *adj.* worldwide, intercontinental, global, universal, cosmopolitan; *ant.* parochial.

internecine *adj.* **1.** (denoting conflict within a group) civil, domestic, fratricidal. **2.** exterminatory, destructive, murderous, dangerous, deadly.

interplay *n.* interaction, exchange, interchange, reciprocation, give-and-take.

interpolate *v.* interject, interjaculate, introduce, insert, add, incorporate.

interpose *v.* **1.** intrude, interrupt, interfere, intervene. **2.** insert, introduce, include, add.

interpret *v.* translate, explicate, clarify, explain, decipher, elucidate, paraphrase, define, expound.

interpretation *n.* **1.** explanation, description, exposition, paraphrase, translation, exegesis, annotation, statement, account. **2.** conception, version, reading, rendition, point of view, commentary, idea, analysis, spin (*slang*).

interpreter *n.* translator, elucidator, annotator, commentator, expositor.

interrogate *v.* cross-examine, question, investigate, inquire, grill, *slang:* pump, give (someone) the third degree.

interrogation *n.* inquisition, questioning, cross-examination, inquiry, grilling, third degree (*slang*).

interrogative *adj.* questioning, interrogatory, inquisitive, curious, quizzical.

interrupt *v.* **1.** impede, hinder, prevent, obstruct, get in the way of. **2.** intrude, intervene, cut in on, break in *or* into, interfere, infringe, chime in, cut off, come between.

interruption *n.* disruption, disturbance, break, cessation, pause, halt, hiatus.

intersect *v.* **1.** divide, cut across, separate, bisect. **2.** meet, join, converge, cross, touch.

intersection *n.* crossroads, junction, interchange, division, bisection.

intersperse *v.* scatter, dot, pepper, sprinkle, distribute.

intertwine *v.* entwine, interlace, interweave, braid, link, twist.

interval *n.* interim, pause, interlude, break, period, gap, space, hiatus, intermission, term, wait.

intervene *v.* **1.** settle, intercede, mediate, negotiate, step in, reconcile. **2.** meddle, interrupt, intrude, interpose, come between.

intervention *n.* mediation, intercession, interruption, interposition, stepping in.

interview *n.* **1.** meeting, conference, audience, conversation, communication. **2.** statement, record, account, case history. *v.* question, interrogate, examine, evaluate.

interviewer *n.* questioner, inquisitor, examiner, interrogator, investigator, reporter, host, talk-show host.

interweave *v.* interlace, intertwine, braid, crisscross, blend, splice.

interwoven *adj.* entwined, intermingled, interworked, interwrought, blended, knit.

intestines *n.* entrails, bowels, viscera, vitals, digestive organs, guts, insides, innards, offal.

intimacy *n.* **1.** closeness, familiarity, friendship, affection, fraternization, brotherliness, sisterliness. **2.** sexual intercourse, copulation, fornication, coitus.

intimate *v.* imply, hint, suggest, allude, insinuate, infer.

intimate *adj.* **1.** personal, close, guarded, near, familiar, trusted, confidential, innermost, private, secret. **2.** devoted, fond, friendly, fast, loyal, close.

intimately *adv.* thoroughly, inside out, in detail, exhaustively, familiarly, tenderly, affectionately, closely, personally.

intimation *n.* implication, hint, suggestion, allusion, insinuation, indication, inkling, clue.

intimidate *v.* daunt, threaten, bully, scare, frighten, dishearten, dismay, lean on (*slang*).

intimidation *n.* terrorizing, bullying, pressure, threats, coercion, fear, browbeating, arm-twisting (*slang*).

intolerable *adj.* unbearable, unendurable, impossible, insufferable.

intolerance *n.* prejudice, discrimination, bigotry, chauvinism, racism, narrow-mindedness, jingoism; *ant.* acceptance.

intolerant *adj.* prejudiced, discriminatory, bigoted, chauvinistic, racist, narrow-minded, impatient, small-minded, opinionated.

intonation *n.* inflection, cadence, modulation, tone, accentuation.

intone *v.* pronounce, intonate, recite, utter, declaim.

intoxicate *v.* **1.** drug, muddle, befuddle, dope up, confuse. **2.** excite, exhilarate, stimulate, turn on (*slang*), arouse, stir.

intoxicated *adj.* **1.** drunk, inebriated, under the influence, tipsy, *slang:* soused, wasted, plastered, smashed, trashed, blotto. **2.** elated, stimulated, captivated, absorbed.

intoxicating *adj.* **1.** alcoholic, intoxicant, inebriant. **2.** stimulating, exciting, heady, thrilling, euphoric, dizzy.

intoxication *n.* **1.** drunkenness, inebriation, insobriety, tipsiness; *ant.* sobriety. **2.** excitement, euphoria, elation, exhilaration, infatuation.

intractable *adj.* unruly, unmanageable, difficult, stubborn, refractory, obstinate, contrary, headstrong, uncooperative, willful, strong-willed, unyielding; *ant.* docile.

intransigent *adj.* uncompromising, irreconcilable, hardline, stubborn, intractable, unyielding, unbending, unpersuadable, obstinate, immovable, unamenable; *ant.* flexible, yielding.

intrepid *adj.* dauntless, bold, brave, courageous, stouthearted, stalwart, unflinching, fearless, valiant, heroic, gutsy (*slang*); *ant.* timid, cowardly.

intricacy *n.* complexity, elaborateness, intricateness, entanglement, knottiness; *ant.* simplicity.

intricate *adj.* complex, elaborate, involved, fancy, ornate, labyrinthine, convoluted, complicated, rococo, daedal; *ant.* simple.

intrigue *n.* **1.** plot, scheme, conspiracy, plan, complication, ruse, artifice, contrivance, maneuver. **2.** intimacy, love affair, liaison, interlude, infatuation, flirtation, romance.

intrigue *v.* attract, fascinate, entertain, charm, delight, please.

intriguing *adj.* fascinating, engaging, enchanting, alluring, appealing, bewitching, attractive, delightful, charming, pleasant, winning.

intrinsic *adj.* essential, fundamental, central, inherent, natural, basic, constitutional, elemental, inborn, inbred; *ant.* extrinsic.

introduce *v.* **1.** present, set forth, submit, advance, offer, proffer, propose. **2.** set up, found, institute, organize, launch, create, plan. **3.** put in, insert, include, add, enter.

introduction *n.* **1.** admittance, initiation, entrance, inception, installation, induction, influx. **2.** initiation, debut, baptism, start, beginning, onset. **3.** preface, preamble, prefatory note, foreword, prologue, prelude, overture.

introductory *adj.* **1.** preliminary, prefatory, initial, opening, first, prior, starting, beginning, original, precursory. **2.** elementary, rudimentary, preparatory, fundamental, basic, beginning.

introspection *n.* self-examination, self-analysis, soul-searching, self-observation.

introspective *adj.* inward-looking, meditative, ruminative, contemplative, pensive, reflective, introverted, brooding; *ant.* outward-looking.

introverted *adj.* withdrawn, self-centered, introspective, inward-looking; *ant.* gregarious.

intrude *v.* interfere, encroach, infringe, meddle, violate, trespass, butt in (*slang*).

intruder *n.* trespasser, prowler, burglar, interloper, infiltrator, gate-crasher (*slang*).

intrusion *n.* encroachment, violation, infringement, interruption, interference, trespass, invasion; *ant.* withdrawal.

intrusive *adj.* interfering, meddlesome, *slang:* nosy, pushy; invasive, unwanted, unwelcome, disturbing, obtrusive; *ant.* welcome.

intuition *n.* instinct, insight, feeling, sixth sense, presentiment, perception, discernment, gut feeling (*slang*); *ant.* reasoning.

intuitive *adj.* instinctive, innate, involuntary, untaught, spontaneous; *ant.* learned.

inundate *v.* deluge, bombard, glut, overwhelm, flood, overflow, fill, swamp, immerse, submerge, bury.

inundation *n.* deluge, bombardment, glut, overflow, torrent, tidal wave; *ant.* trickle.

inure *v.* accustom, familiarize, habituate, temper, desensitize, strengthen, toughen, harden.

invade *v.* raid, assail, seize, swarm over, attack, penetrate, overrun, descend upon, assault, infest, encroach.

invader *n.* trespasser, raider, intruder, attacker, aggressor.

invalid *n.* convalescent, valetudinary, patient.

invalid *adj.* **1.** baseless, null and void, irrational, unreasonable, illogical, wrong, unfounded, worthless, fallacious. **2.** ailing, disabled, bedridden, frail, ill, infirm, sickly, weak.

invalidate *v.* nullify, undo, annul, rescind, cancel, overrule, quash, vitiate.

invaluable *adj.* valuable, precious, priceless, costly, inestimable; *ant.* worthless.

invariable *adj.* immutable, fixed, constant, unchanging, rigid, set, inflexible, unwavering; *ant.* changeable, fluid.

invariably *adv.* consistently, without exception, unfailingly, always, regularly, habitually, customarily.

invasion n. intrusion, violation, assault, attack, infraction, usurpation, infiltration, encroachment, foray, raid, seizure.

invective n. insult, vituperation, curse, abuse, vilification, diatribe, tirade, denunciation, castigation, tongue lashing (*slang*).

inveigh v. castigate, lambaste, rail, vituperate, recriminate, denounce, berate, reproach, upbraid, expostulate.

inveigle v. lure, entice, beguile, seduce, entrap, wheedle, maneuver, manipulate, wile, coax, bamboozle.

invent v. 1. create, originate, devise, design, contrive, fashion, form, find, coin, discover, conceive, think *or* make up. 2. fabricate, lie, fake, feign, misrepresent, falsify, concoct, create out of thin air, make believe, conjure *or* think up.

invention n. 1. contrivance, contraption, design, discovery. 2. ingenuity, imagination, creativeness, originality, inventiveness.

inventive adj. creative, imaginative, innovative, original, ingenious, inspired, resourceful.

inventor n. creator, designer, originator, maker, author, architect, father, mother.

inventory n. 1. list, itemization, register, record, index, table, file, catalog. 2. inspection, review, examination, counting, checking, accounting, tabulation, summary.

inverse adj. opposite, contrary, reverse, inverted, transposed, upside down.

inversion n. opposite, reversal, antithesis, contraposition, transposition.

invert v. 1. upset, overturn, turn upside-down, tip. 2. reverse, transpose, exchange, rearrange, change; alter, modify, convert.

invest v. 1. spend, devote, put in, lay out. 2. authorize, license, ordain, empower, sanction, install.

investigate v. examine, scrutinize, look into, probe, study, consider, explore, inspect, search.

investigation n. probe, exploration, examination, inquiry, study, research, inquest, analysis, scrutiny.

investigator n. detective, researcher, sleuth, inspector, private eye, *slang*: gumshoe, dick.

investiture n. induction, installation, instatement, inauguration, ordination, coronation, admission.

investment n. venture, speculation, stake, gamble.

inveterate adj. confirmed, chronic, habitual, established, deep-rooted, incurable, incorrigible, entrenched, diehard, dyed-in-the-wool, hard-core.

invidious adj. 1. offensive, objectionable, odious, repugnant, undesirable, hateful, obnoxious. 2. unfair, unfavorable, discriminatory, prejudiced, bigoted, narrow-minded, biased.

invigorate v. exhilarate, stimulate, galvanize, energize, enliven, rejuvenate, vitalize, liven up, freshen, brace; ant. weary, dishearten.

invigorating adj. exhilarating, stimulating, energizing, refreshing, rejuvenating, vivifying, uplifting, bracing; ant. wearying.

invincible adj. indestructible, invulnerable, unconquerable, unassailable, indomitable, unsurmountable, unbeatable, impenetrable; ant. weak, vulnerable, beatable.

inviolability n. 1. sacredness, holiness, sanctity, sacrosanctness. 2. invulnerability, inviolableness, inalienability.

inviolable adj. 1. divine, sacred, holy, hallowed, sacrosanct. 2. indestructible, unalterable, inalienable.

inviolate adj. unbroken, pure, sacred, undefiled, unprofaned, intact, unsullied, untouched, entire, virgin.

invisible adj. unseen, hidden, transparent, out of sight, unseeable, unviewable, microscopic, ethereal, supernatural, ghostly, wraithlike, impalpable, unreal, intangible; ant. real, substantial, material.

invitation n. solicitation, asking, bidding, request, overture, summons, allurement, inducement, enticement, come-on (*slang*).

invite v. ask, summon, welcome, bid, beckon, solicit, call, entice, encourage, draw, request; ant. turn away.

inviting adj. welcoming, enticing, tempting, alluring, intriguing, engaging, attractive, magnetic, captivating, beguiling, seductive, winning.

invocation n. supplication, entreaty, petition, appeal, prayer, beseeching.

invoice n. 1. bill, statement, receipt, bill of shipment. 2. inventory, manifest, itemized account, checklist.

invoke v. **1.** appeal to, call upon, request, entreat, beg. **2.** send for, summon, bid.

involuntary adj. unintentional, instinctive, automatic, spontaneous, unthinking, unconscious, uncontrolled, reflex, conditioned; ant. deliberate.

involve v. include, draw in, incorporate, connect, take in, engage, concern, bind, commit, compromise, associate, incriminate.

involved adj. **1.** participating, caught up or in, mixed up in or with, implicated. **2.** complex, intricate, elaborate, tangled, concerned, knotty, labyrinthine, convoluted; ant. simple.

involvement n. relation, relatedness, materiality, purchase, connection.

invulnerability n. inviolability, safety, impenetrability, unassailability, strength, security; ant. susceptibility.

invulnerable adj. invincible, indestructible, safe, impenetrable, unassailable, secure, insusceptible; ant. susceptible.

inward adj. **1.** inside, internal, interior. **2.** penetrating, through, incoming, ingoing, entering, infiltrating.

inwardly adv. within, deep down, inside, at heart, privately, secretly, to oneself.

iota n. bit, hint, scintilla, speck, trace, atom, jot, particle, scrap, whit, smidgeon (slang).

irate adj. furious, enraged, infuriated, livid, indignant, riled, provoked, incensed, hot under the collar, exasperated, fuming; ant. calm.

ire n. fury, wrath, rage, passion, anger, displeasure, indignation, annoyance.

iridescent adj. opalescent, pearly, prismatic, glittering, opaline, polychromatic, rainbow-colored, shimmering.

irk v. irritate, provoke, bother, annoy, aggravate, peeve, vex, perturb, weary, tire, rile, bug (slang), rub the wrong way; ant. please.

irksome adj. tedious, vexatious, boring, disagreeable, burdensome, troublesome; ant. pleasing.

iron v. press, flatten, smooth; ant. crease.

iron adj. hard, strong-willed, steely, unyielding, inflexible, adamant, stubborn, implacable, dense, cruel, insensible, robust, strong.

ironic adj. incongruous, paradoxical, sardonic, satirical, wry.

irons n. manacles, shackles, fetters, bonds, chains, trammels.

irony n. incongruity, paradox, contrariness, satire.

irradiate v. brighten, lighten, expose, illuminate, reflect, illumine, enlighten.

irrational adj. **1.** illogical, invalid, specious, incoherent, unreasonable, fallacious; ant. cogent. **2.** stupid, senseless, ridiculous, absurd, insane, idiotic; ant. reasonable, sensible.

irreconcilable adj. **1.** incompatible, inconsistent, incongruous, conflicting, opposed, clashing. **2.** inflexible, uncompromising, inexorable, implacable, hardline, intransigent; ant. accommodating.

irrefutable adj. incontestable, incontrovertible, undeniable, certain, unquestionable, unassailable, impregnable, unanswerable, indubitable, invincible, sure; ant. disputable, resistible.

irregular adj. **1.** inconstant, erratic, uneven, spasmodic, occasional, intermittent, discontinuous, sporadic, random, capricious, haphazard, casual; ant. constant, steady, systematic, methodical. **2.** amorphous, shapeless, jagged, distorted, lumpy, eccentric, elliptical, devious, aberrant, variable; ant. symmetrical, aligned. **3.** questionable, strange, debatable; ant. proper.

irregularity n. **1.** aberration, shift, break, imperfection, variability, deviation, distortion, spasm; ant. consistency, certainty. **2.** peculiarity, singularity, anomaly, abnormality, exception, deviation, excess, allowance, privilege, rarity, oddity; ant. custom, rule, conformity.

irrelevant adj. inapplicable, tangential, unrelated, extraneous, impertinent, beside the point, immaterial, inconsequent, inessential; ant. apt, appropriate, related.

irreplaceable adj. invaluable, priceless, unique, unmatched, inimitable, peerless, sublime, vital; ant. dispensable, inessential.

irrepressible adj. uninhibited, insuppressible, resilient, uncontrollable, inextinguishable, uncontainable, unmanageable, boisterous, ebullient, buoyant, effervescent; ant. stoppable, depressed, despondent.

irreproachable adj. faultless, unblemished, innocent, pure, irreprovable, immaculate, impeccable, squeaky-clean, perfect; ant. tainted, blameworthy, reprehensible.

irresistible *adj.* **1.** overwhelming, compelling, overpowering, invincible. **2.** fascinating, alluring, enchanting, lovable.

irresolute *adj.* indecisive, tentative, hesitant, undecided, weak, vacillating, doubtful, fickle, infirm, variable, wavering; *ant.* determined, settled, stable.

irresponsible *adj.* negligent, immature, heedless, careless, rash, reckless, scatterbrained, thoughtless, footloose, wild; *ant.* reliable, dependable, trustworthy.

irreverent *adj.* **1.** blasphemous, impious, iconoclastic, profane. **2.** discourteous, disrespectful, impudent, impertinent, flippant, contemptuous, derisive.

irreversible *adj.* irrevocable, incurable, inoperable, permanent.

irrevocable *adj.* settled, fixed, hopeless, invariable, irremediable, inexorable, irretrievable, fated, predetermined, predestined; *ant.* reversible, alterable, mutable, flexible.

irrigate *v.* water, flood, inundate, wet, dampen, moisten.

irritable *adj.* cantankerous, hypersensitive, impatient, petulant, captious, irascible, tense, peevish, choleric, edgy, crotchety, testy; *ant.* cheerful, complacent.

irritant *n.* annoyance, nuisance, vexation, provocation, bother, menace, pain, plague, trouble, pest.

irritate *v.* **1.** bother, provoke, exasperate, pester, aggravate, annoy, harass. **2.** inflame, swell, pain, chafe, sting, redden; *ant.* soothe.

irritated *adj.* **1.** swollen, red, infected. **2.** irritable, exasperated, flustered, impatient, irked, angry, put out, riled, uptight, piqued, peeved; *ant.* composed, pleased, gratified.

irritating *adj.* disturbing, abrasive, aggravating, galling, trying, vexatious, infuriating, maddening, nagging; *ant.* pleasing, pleasant.

irritation *n.* **1.** soreness, tenderness, rawness, irritability, hypersensitivity, susceptibility. **2.** provocation, excitement, upset.

island *n.* **1.** isle, islet, archipelago, key, bar. **2.** retreat, sanctuary, haven, refuge.

isolate *v.* **1.** seclude, sequester, quarantine, divorce, insulate, detach, exclude, separate, dissociate, ostracize, remove, segregate; *ant.* incorporate, assimilate, connect. **2.** identify, pinpoint, discover.

isolated *adj.* **1.** deserted, outlying, remote, secluded; *ant.* populous, trodden. **2.** atypical, random, unique, abnormal, exceptional, single, anomalous; *ant.* usual, related.

isolation *n.* withdrawal, exile, detachment, aloofness, disassociation, insulation, retirement.

issue *n.* **1.** (a subject of discussion) concern, problem, question, point, subject, argument, matter, problem. **2.** progeny, heirs, descendants, young, children, brood. **3.** outcome, result, aftermath, resolution, conclusion, end.

issue *v.* **1.** come forth, emerge, proceed, flow out; originate, rise from, spring, stem. **2.** (produce for public dissemination, as a statement) release, circulate, announce, send out; distribute, allot, dispense, assign. **3.** (produce a sound or smell) emit, send forth, exude, give off.

itch *n.* **1.** itchiness, prickling, rawness, psoriasis. **2.** desire, craving, hankering, yearning, yen.

itch *v.* **1.** tickle, prick, prickle. **2.** yearn, long for, hanker for, desire.

itchy *adj.* eager, fidgety, restless, impatient, unsettled, edgy, restive, inquisitive, roving.

item *n.* element, particular, detail, factor, feature, component, article, ingredient, entry, piece, object, point.

itemize *v.* list, tabulate, count, document, inventory, catalog, record, detail, number, enumerate, particularize, index, specify.

itinerant *n.* wanderer, pilgrim, vagabond, wayfarer, traveler, gypsy, nomad, hobo, tramp.

itinerant *adj.* migratory, nomadic, ambulatory, vagrant, peripatetic, rootless; *ant.* settled, stationary.

itinerary *n.* schedule, program, plan, route, course, journey, tour, circuit, line.

J

jab *v.* dig, elbow, nudge, poke, prod, punch, stab.

jabber *v.* babble, blather, chatter, jaw (*slang*), prate, ramble, rattle, yap.

jackass *n.* dolt, blockhead, fool, ingrate, moron.

jacket *n.* **1.** coat, tunic, parka, mackinaw. **2.** sheath, shell, envelope, wrap.

jack-of-all-trades *n.* handyman, factotum, do-all.

jackpot *n.* prize, award, bonanza, pot (*slang*), stakes, winnings.

jaded *adj.* **1.** insensitive, cold, nonchalant, impassive, blunted, bored, cloyed; *ant.* fresh, refreshed. **2.** exhausted, spent, fatigued, worn, satiated, dulled, played out, tired, weary.

jagged *adj.* barbed, serrated, ragged, notched, saw-edged, spiky, broken, craggy, rough, pointed, ridged, snaggy; *ant.* smooth

jail *n.* cage, cell, penitentiary, slammer (*slang*), dungeon, lockup (*slang*), bastille, *slang:* brig, clink, pen, stir, hoosegow, reformatory, stockade, cooler (*slang*), detention camp.

jail *v.* confine, incarcerate, detain, impound, imprison, lock up, put behind bars, *slang:* send down, throw away the keys, send uptown, send up the river.

jailbird (*slang*) *n.* convict, inmate, felon, criminal, con (*slang*) culprit.

jailer *n.* keeper, warden, guard, captor, turnkey.

jam *n.* **1.** preserves, jelly, marmalade, conserve, spread. **2.** (*slang*) dilemma, bind, difficulty, impasse, fix (*slang*) imbroglio, predicament, quandary, scrape, *slang:* spot, hot water.

jam *v.* **1.** compress, compact, confine, cram, crush, pack, bind, block, clog, press, sandwich, squash, squeeze. **2.** garble, scramble, drown out, muddle, confuse.

jamboree *n.* carnival, celebration, festival, jubilee, party, spree, convention, junket, festivity, field day.

jammed *adj.* **1.** stuck, obstructed, barred, blocked, caught, fast, fixed, frozen, immovable; *ant.* working. **2.** thronged, crowded, crammed, populous, packed, mobbed, teeming, congested, multitudinous; *ant.* empty, vacant.

jangle *n.* clang, clangor, din, cacophony, jingle, dissonance, rattle, stridency; *ant.* euphony, harmony.

jangle *v.* chime, clank, clink, jar, jingle, rattle, vibrate.

janitor *n.* custodian, cleaning person, caretaker, porter.

jar *n.* crock, pot, can, container, flagon, vase, vessel, jug, urn, mug, bottle, amphora, ewer.

jar *v.* discompose, rattle, shake, upset, rock, agitate, disturb, bounce, jounce, jiggle, bang, slam.

jargon *n.* shoptalk, argot, slang, colloquialism, localism; doublespeak, gobbledygook, doubletalk, bureaucratese.

jarring *adj.* **1.** discordant, unharmonious, dissonant, grating, irritating, rasping, jangling, strident. **2.** jolting, unsettling, bumpy, rough, shaking, jouncy; *ant.* firm, steadying.

jaundiced *adj.* cynical, bitter, resentful, misanthropic, hostile, jealous, envious, pessimistic, biased, opprobrious; *ant.* fresh, naive, optimistic.

jaunt *n.* sally, trip, excursion, tour, saunter, amble, trek, gallop, canter, constitutional, walk.

jaunty *adj.* cocky, bold, rakish, chipper, insouciant, sprightly, dapper, natty, swashbuckling, scampish, waggish, insolent, cheeky, cavalier; *ant.* anxious, depressed, dowdy.

jaw *n.* muzzle, mandible, maw, mouth, chops, proboscis, trap (*slang*).

jaw (*slang*) *v.* talk, gossip, converse, chatter, yak, prate, patter, palaver.

jazzy (*slang*) *adj.* animated, fancy, flashy, vivacious, sexy, snazzy (*slang*), gaudy, wild.

jealous *adj.* possessive, covetous, envious, monopolizing, guarded, resentful, begrudging, jaundiced.

jealousy *n.* covetousness, possessiveness, envy, resentment, spite, suspicion.

jeer *n.* catcall, derision, gibe, aspersion, abuse, dig (*slang*), raillery, raspberry (*slang*), taunt, ridicule.

jeer *v.* mock, scoff, razz (*slang*) ridicule, knock (*slang*), taunt, gibe.

jejune *adj.* banal, callow, prosaic, puerile, trite, spiritless, vapid, inane, colorless, unsophisticated, dull, empty, foolish; *ant.* mature, meaningful.

jell *v.* coagulate, congeal, crystallize, condense, set, solidify, thicken, stiffen; *ant.* disintegrate.

jeopardize *v.* imperil, endanger, expose, chance, venture, risk, stake, hazard; *ant.* protect, safeguard.

jeopardy *n.* risk, peril, hazard, danger, exposure, endangerment, imperilment; *ant.* safety, security.

jerk *n.* **1.** tic, twitch, shrug, flick, shake, shiver, tug, pull, lurch, jolt, bounce. **2.** (*slang*) fool, chump, *slang*: creep, schmuck, drip, nerd, dork.

jerk *v.* **1.** quiver, convulse, shake, quake, shake, twitch. **2.** snatch, grab, pull, pluck, whisk, snag, hook, wrench, yank.

jerky *adj.* spasmodic, convulsive, tremulous, twitchy, fitful, spastic, incoherent, shaky, disconnected, jolting, uncoordinated, bouncy, bumpy; *ant.* smooth.

jerry-built *adj.* flimsy, cheap, insubstantial, ramshackle, tacky, ticky-tacky, rickety, shoddy, slipshod, defective, faulty; *ant.* firm, stable, substantial.

jersey *n.* pullover, sweater, turtleneck, T-shirt, sweatshirt.

jest *n.* bon mot, foolery, gag, quip, sally, waggery, wisecrack, witticism, trick, prank, hoax.

jest *v.* joke, josh, kid, tease, fool, trifle.

jester *n.* buffoon, clown, joker, fool, harlequin, juggler, mummer, prankster.

jet *n.* **1.** spray, flow, gush, issue, rush, spout, stream, spurt, squirt, surge, fountain, nozzle,

sprayer, sprinkler. **2.** airplane, plane, aircraft, jumbo jet.

jet *adj.* ebony, raven, black, inky, sable, sloe.

jettison *v.* eject, abandon, discard, expel, heave, dump, unload, ditch; *ant.* load, take on.

jetty *n.* dock, pier, wharf, breakwater, quay.

jewel *n.* **1.** gem, bauble, brilliant, sparkler, stone, trinket. **2.** genius, prodigy, humdinger (*slang*), paragon, pearl, pride, treasure, wonder.

jewelry *n.* gems, jewels, bangles (*slang*), regalia, adornments, frippery, *slang*: gewgaws, gimcrackery.

jibe *n.* barb, crack, dig (*slang*), jeer, derision, poke, quip, raillery, taunt.

jibe *v.* **1.** deride, mock, rail, flout, ridicule, scorn, taunt. **2.** (*slang*) match, agree, correspond, fit.

jiffy *n.* instant, *slang*: flash, no time; minute, moment, second; two shakes (*slang*).

jig *v.* dance, bob, bobble, bounce, caper, hop, jerk, jiggle, jounce, jump, prance, shake, skip, wiggle, wobble.

jiggery-pokery (*slang*) *n.* chicanery, subterfuge, trickery, funny business, deceit, deception, fraud; *ant.* honesty.

jiggle *v.* wiggle, shake, twitch, agitate, bounce, jerk, jog, shift, shimmy, waggle.

jilt *v.* betray, forsake, abandon, brush off (*slang*), deceive, desert, discard, spurn, throw over; *ant.* cleave to.

jingle *n.* **1.** ringing, tinkle, jangle, clank, rattle, tintinnabulation. **2.** ditty, chant, chorus, couplet, doggerel, limerick, melody, rhyme, song, tune, verse.

jingle *v.* tinkle, clink, rattle, chime, chink, ring, jangle.

jingoism *n.* chauvinism, flag-waving, nationalism, parochialism, xenophobia, insularity.

jinx *v.* bedevil, bewitch, curse, doom, hex, plague.

jinx *n.* hex, spell, charm, curse, hoodoo, spell, voodoo.

jitters *n.* nerves, fidgets, tenseness, anxiety, *slang*: the creeps, the shakes, the shivers, the willies.

jittery *adj.* nervous, panicky, perturbed, agitated, anxious, edgy, flustered, jumpy, shaky, uneasy; *ant.* calm, composed, confident.

job *n.* **1.** vocation, place, post, position, assign-

ment, calling, career, pursuit, profession, metier, situation, chore, consignment, livelihood. **2.** task, duty, responsibility, mission, burden, assignment, brief, undertaking, project, errand, deed, tour of duty.

jobless *adj.* unemployed, out of work, laid off, on the street, on the dole; workless, inactive, idle; *ant.* employed, busy.

jockey *v.* maneuver, cajole, coax, engineer, finagle, induce, inveigle, manipulate, negotiate, wheedle.

jocose *adj.* blithe, jocular, jovial, merry, mirthful, mischievous, jesting, facetious, droll, waggish, witty; *ant.* morose.

jocular *adj.* jovial, roguish, amusing, arch, droll, facetious, teasing, waggish, whimsical, witty, jesting; *ant.* serious.

jocularity *n.* gaiety, hilarity, drollery, facetiousness, joviality, mirth, waggishness, whimsicality, laughter, whimsy, absurdity, jolliness.

jog *n.* **1.** trot, amble, saunter, canter, gallop, lope, lumber, pad, run. **2.** nudge, poke, push, prod, whack (*slang*), bump, shove, shake, jolt. **jog** *v.* activate, arouse, bounce, jar, jerk, jolt, jounce, stimulate, stir, shake, shove, poke, prod, motivate, instigate, push.

joie de vivre *n.* ebullience, buoyancy, enthusiasm, gaiety, merriment, mirth, pleasure, blitheness, zest, brio, gusto, relish; *ant.* depression.

join *v.* unite, blend, combine, juxtapose, splice, yoke; *ant.* separate.

joined *adj.* linked, allied, intertwined, connected, united, fixed, cemented, welded, confederated, incorporated, federated; *ant.* separated, disparate, apart.

joint *n.* **1.** juncture, nexus, junction, intersection, link, confluence, seam, articulation, connection, seam, hinge, copula, bridge. **2.** (*slang*) hangout, *slang:* hole in the wall, dump, haunt, dive.

out of joint dislocated, disjointed, fractured.

jointly *adv.* mutually, conjointly, together, in combination, concomitantly, concurrently; *ant.* singly, separately.

joke *n.* **1.** prank, sport, gag, practical joke, shenanigan, lark, monkeyshine (*slang*); jest, pun, bon mot, conceit, rejoinder, quip, witticism, wisecrack. **2.** laughing-stock, buffoon, butt, clown, simpleton, jackass.

joke *v.* banter, jest, raise laughter, trifle, poke fun, quip, kid, fool, tease, ridicule, deride.

joker (*slang*) *n.* buffoon, jester, character, clown, comic, fool, prankster, wag, wit, kidder.

jollity *n.* vivacity, sport, merriment.

jolly *adj.* cheerful, happy, merry, pleasant, gay, convivial, exuberant, frisky, gladsome, festive, jaunty, jocund, jovial, jubilant, sprightly, sunny; *ant.* sad.

jolt *n.* **1.** blow, bump, hit, impact, jar, jerk, jog, lurch, quiver, thunderbolt. **2.** surprise, start, shock.

jolt *v.* **1.** bounce, bump, discompose, disturb, jar, jerk, jostle, jounce, knock, push, shake, shove. **2.** astonish, disconcert, dismay, disturb, nonplus, perturb, shock, startle, stun, surprise.

jostle *v.* nudge, bump, jog, joggle, jolt, elbow, shoulder, shove, force, hustle, push.

jot *n.* scrap, trace, trifle, bit, detail, fraction, grain, iota, mite, morsel, particle, atom, scintilla, smidgen, speck.

jot *v.* record, scribble down, write, take down.

jounce *v.* bounce, bump, jerk.

journal *n.* **1.** diary, memoir, chronicle, log, reminiscence, daybook, record. **2.** publication, magazine, newspaper, review, periodical, weekly, monthly, annual.

journalism *n.* reporting, writing, correspondence, copywriting, feature-writing, news, press, the fourth estate.

journalist *n.* reporter, commentator, correspondent, scribe, stringer, *slang:* hack, newshound; member of the fourth estate.

journey *n.* excursion, tour, passage, pilgrimage, voyage, expedition, odyssey, outing, trek, trip, quest, junket, peregrination.

journey *v.* roam, rove, gallivant, tour, travel, wander, jaunt, traverse, trek.

joust *n.* engagement, contest, encounter, tournament, skirmish, passage d'armes.

jovial *adj.* jocular, affable, animated, buoyant, cheery, convivial, ebullient, happy.

joviality *n.* merriment, affability, cheerfulness, gaiety, high spirits.

jowl *n.* jaw, dewlap, cheek.

joy *n.* **1.** (feeling of happiness) rapture, ecstacy, bliss, ravishment, wonder, delight, gladness, gratification, contentment, happiness, pleasure; *ant.* sorrow. **2.** (expression of happiness) hilarity, mirth, revelry, geniality, gaiety, merriment, frolic, animation; *ant.* lamentation, mourning.

joyful *adj.* delighted, ecstatic, elated, glad, happy, jubilant, merry, satisfied, blithe, gratified, cheery, lighthearted; *ant.* mournful, sorrowful.

joyless *adj.* doleful, dreary, bleak, cheerless, dejected, dour, gloomy, glum, miserable, somber, unhappy, dismal, grim.

joyous *adj.* joyful, gleeful, happy, glad, ebullient, exuberant, elated, ecstatic.

jubilant *adj.* euphoric, overjoyed, celebratory, excited, exuberant, exultant, flushed, gratified, rejoicing, thrilled, triumphal; *ant.* defeated, depressed.

jubilation *n.* delight, joy, ecstacy, elation, exultation, excitement, euphoria, jollification, triumph; *ant.* depression, lamentation.

jubilee *n.* carnival, festival, celebration, commemoration, gala, festivity, fête.

judge *n.* **1.** magistrate, justice, chancellor, justice of the peace. **2.** moderator, umpire, referee, arbitrator, adjudicator, mediator, negotiator, go-between (*slang*); intercessor.

judge *v.* **1.** adjudge, adjudicate, try, consider, decree, rule, sentence, condemn, doom. **2.** conclude, decide, resolve, appraise, arbitrate, ascertain, assess, determine, estimate, evaluate, mediate, gauge, find, reckon.

judgment *n.* **1.** (ability to judge well) discernment, discrimination, shrewdness, sapience, percipience, sagacity, understanding, taste, common sense, knowledge, wit, keenness, perception, incisiveness, prudence, wisdom; *ant.* stupidity, simplicity. **2.** (act of judging) deliberation, decision, consideration, appraisal, assaying, weighing, probing, contemplation, study, research, inquiry, scrutiny, inquest, analysis. **3.** verdict, finding, conclusion, assessment, diagnosis, dictum, decree; sentence, retribution, punishment.

judiciary *n.* judges, justices, bench, tribunal, bar, legal profession, judicial branch.

judicious *adj.* prudent, sensible, sagacious, careful, canny, efficacious, acute, discriminating, practical, expedient, perspicacious, circumspect, politic, calculating; *ant.* hasty, ill-advised.

jug *n.* flask, jar, pot, demijohn.

juggle *v.* alter, delude, change, disguise, fake, *slang*; rig, doctor; falsify, fix (*slang*), misrepresent, modify.

juice *n.* liquid, nectar, sap, secretion, fluid, sauce, essence, extract, serum, syrup.

juicy *adj.* **1.** succulent, lush, moist, wet, watery, dewy, humid, viscid, dank, oozy, sodden, soaked, saturated; *ant.* dry, arid. **2.** (*slang*) intriguing, colorful, interesting, titillating, naughty, provocative, racy, spicy, piquant, tantalizing, risqué, salacious, suggestive, sexy (*slang*); *ant.* bland, boring.

jumble *n.* confusion, clutter, mess, miscellany, hodge-podge.

jumble *v.* tangle, tumble, muddle, mix, mix up (*slang*); confuse, disarrange, disarray, disorder; *ant.* order.

jumbo *adj.* large, immense, gigantic, mammoth.

jump *v.* **1.** skip, hop, rise, pounce, spring, bound, lunge, leap, vault; plunge, fall, nose-dive, plummet. **2.** hurdle, bar, fence, barrier, impediment, gate, hedge, obstacle, rail. **3.** (an advantage, as in a sporting competition) (*slang*) advantage, upper hand, head start, edge, handicap. **4.** (a sudden rise, as in prices) ascent, advance, augmentation, boost, escalation, increase, rise, upsurge.

jump *n.* **1.** vault, leap, spring, surge, lurch, lunge, pop up *or* out, bound, skip; drop, plummet, plunge, dive; skip across, traverse, avoid, bypass, evade, miss. **2.** flinch, jerk, quail, quiver, waver, rattle, recoil, shrink, start, wince. **3.** (*slang*) rob, attack, accost, hold up, mug; spring upon, tackle.

jumpy *adj.* fidgety, jittery, restless, tense, discomposed, agitated, apprehensive, uneasy, sensitive, nervous, edgy, anxious; *ant.* calm, composed.

junction *n.* confluence, intersection, connection, coupling, juncture, joint, linking, seam, union, abutment, combination, interstice.

juncture *n.* conjunction, connection, convergence, link, nexus, point, weld.

jungle *n.* wilderness, wood, bush, undergrowth, forest, primeval forest, boscage; *ant.* clearing, cultivation.

junior *adj.* subordinate, lesser, inferior, minor, secondary, subsidiary, puisne; *ant.* senior.

junk *n.* **1.** rubbish, garbage, dregs, litter, refuse, waste, filth, trash. **2.** salvage, debris, detritus, scraps, miscellany, oddments, rummage, wreckage, odds and ends.

junk *v.* discard, dump, wreck, scrap.

junket *n.* excursion, outing, trip, voyage, celebration, ceremony, feast, political tour.

junta *n.* **1.** council, conclave, assembly, meeting, confederacy, convocation, league, committee, gathering. **2.** cabal, cartel, camarilla, clique, coterie, faction, gang, oligarchy, party, ring.

jurisdiction *n.* authority, control, dominion, judicature, prerogative, province, sovereignty, sphere, sway, bailiwick, cognizance, orbit, reach.

jury *n.* tribunal, panel, judges, peers.

just *adj.* fair, appropriate, correct, deserved, equitable, even-handed, good, honest, impartial, justified, legitimate, merited, lawful, right, true, unbiased, virtuous; *ant.* biased, unscrupulous, dishonest.

just *adv.* **1.** precisely, exactly, accurately, correctly, perfectly, rightly. **2.** barely, hardly, scarcely, by very little. **3.** presently, now, at this moment, right *or* just now.

justice *n.* **1.** fairness, impartiality, equity, honesty, integrity, rightfulness, truth, appropriateness. **2.** validity, legitimacy, lawfulness, authority, constitutionality, legality, sanction, statutory *or* established right, legalization; *ant.* lawlessness, disorder, despotism. **3.** (judicial action) adjudication, settlement, arbitration, hearing, legal process, due process, litigation, prosecution, judgment, trial, regulation, re-

view. **4.** magistrate, judge, umpire, chancellor, justice of the peace, justiciar.

do justice to honor, pay tribute to, respect, esteem.

justifiable *adj.* acceptable, allowable, explainable, defensible, justified, proper, suitable, right, sound, valid, warranted, well-founded; *ant.* culpable, illicit.

justification *n.* excuse, defense, apology, explanation, foundation, grounds, plea, rebuttal, mitigation, reason, validation, rationalization, exculpation, raison d'être, apologia; *ant.* blame, incrimination, conviction.

justify *v.* **1.** support, plead, argue for, defend, explain, sustain, advocate, palliate, stand up for, speak in favor of, countenance, condone, vindicate; *ant.* convict, implicate. **2.** warrant, verify, confirm, validate, substantiate, legitimize, prove.

justly *adv.* **1.** honorably, impartially, honestly, conscientiously, frankly, candidly, equitably, even-handedly, uprightly, reasonably, fairly, objectively, properly, rightly, morally. **2.** exactly, judiciously, fittingly, precisely, clearly, lucidly, rigorously, unerringly, severely, painstakingly, factually, accurately.

jut *v.* extend, project, bulge, overhang, stick out, protrude, poke, impend, beetle; *ant.* recede.

juvenile *n.* adolescent, boy, girl, child, infant, minor, youngster, youth, kid, halfling; *ant.* adult.

juvenile *adj.* adolescent, immature, pubescent, babyish, callow, infantile, impressionable, beardless, undeveloped, unsophisticated, jejune, puerile, untested, naive; *ant.* mature.

juxtaposition *n.* contiguity, adjacency, immediacy, nearness, proximity, vicinity, contact, closeness; *ant.* separation, disassociation.

257

K

kaleidoscopic *adj.* **1.** colorful, multicolored, vivid, motley, many-splendored, multifarious, variegated, polychrome; *ant.* dull, mono-chrome. **2.** changing, protean, fluid, fluctuating, mobile, plastic, ever-changing, liquid; *ant.* fixed, frozen.

kaput (*slang*) *adj.* broken, dead, defunct, destroyed, finished, out of order, ruined, undone, smashed, wrecked, fini; *ant.* operational.

keel over overturn, capsize, fall, faint, founder, pass out, swoon, black out, crumple.

keen *adj.* **1.** sharp, acute, pointed, edged, cutting, piercing, razorlike; *ant.* blunt. **2.** clever, biting, astute, bright, shrewd, canny, caustic, incisive, perceptive, penetrating, perspicacious, quick, sagacious, sardonic, satirical; *ant.* dull, stupid, slow. **3.** ardent, eager, interested, intent, anxious, assiduous, devoted, diligent, earnest, enthusiastic, fervid, impassioned, industrious, zealous; *ant.* apathetic, lackluster.

keep *v.* **1.** accumulate, amass, preserve, retain, grasp, hold, collect, conserve, maintain, heap, hold on to, pile, stock, store. **2.** care for, minister to, attend, run, direct, look after, manage, operate, safeguard, shelter, support, sustain, tend. **3.** arrest, stop, block, avert, curb, constrain, detain, deter, hinder, impede, obstruct, prevent, retard, stall, hamper, inhibit, hold up. **4.** adhere to, comply with, fulfill, hold, honor, obey, observe, respect.

keep from 1. abstain, desist, avoid, refrain. **2.** prevent, prohibit, impede, hinder, restrain, forestall.

keep in bottle up, stop up, inhibit, suppress, keep back; *ant.* declare, release.

keep on keep at, stay the course, hold on, continue.

keep up 1. maintain, care for, preserve, support, continue. **2.** keep pace, compete, contend, equal, match, rival, vie.

keeper *n.* **1.** guard, jailer, custodian, overseer, attendant, governor, warden, caretaker, conservator, defender, warder. **2.** manager, superintendent, owner, entrepreneur, supervisor, custodian, administrator.

keeping *n.* custody, guardianship, patronage, aegis, protection, safekeeping, supervision, tutelage, wardship.

keepsake *n.* memento, remembrance, token, reminder, souvenir, emblem, pledge, relic.

keg *n.* cask, drum, barrel, hogshead, tun, vat, firkin.

ken *n.* cognizance, comprehension, compass, field, perception, range, reach, scope, understanding, vision, acquaintance, awareness.

kept *adj.* **1.** preserved, maintained, put up, stored, held, guarded, clutched, watched over, retained, saved, at hand, reserved; *ant.* abandoned. **2.** observed, obeyed, honored, regarded, maintained, held inviolate, commemorated, continued; *ant.* dishonored, forgotten.

kerchief *n.* handkerchief, bandanna, headscarf, babushka, cravat.

kernel *n.* **1.** center, heart, essence, core, germ, gist, marrow, pith, substance; *ant.* chaff. **2.** piece, bit, morsel, part, atom.

kettle *n.* pot, cauldron, saucepan.

key *n.* clue, guide, indicator, answer, explanation, interpretation, pointer, sign, secret, tip-off, lead, earmark, cipher.

key *adj.* basic, cardinal, central, essential, fundamental, important, pivotal, principal, salient, leading, chief, crucial, decisive; *ant.* marginal.

keynote *n.* standard, basic idea, stress, motif, theme, marrow, kernel, heart, essence, gist, core, emphasis, accent.

keystone *n.* buttress, prop, base, basis, cornerstone, foundation, root, linchpin, mainspring, crux, source, core.

kick *n.* **1.** boot, blow, punt, fillip. **2.** (*slang*)

kick joy, refreshment, enjoyment, fun, gratification, pleasure, stimulation, thrill, *slang*: buzz.

kick *v.* **1.** boot, beat, jolt, punt, dropkick. **2.** (*slang*) give up, abandon, break, desist from, drop, leave, quit, spurn, stop, forsake.

kick off commence, inaugurate, launch, initiate, open, start, get under way.

kickback (*slang*) *n.* refund, payment, bribe, payola (*slang*), percentage.

kid *n.* juvenile, youngster, youth, boy, girl, whippersnapper, stripling, *slang*: kiddie, shaver; tot, baby, infant, babe.

kid *v.* tease, pretend, joke, pull someone's leg (*slang*), hoax, hoodwink, jest, delude, dupe, trick, put one over on (*slang*), josh, ridicule, gull, con.

kidnap *v.* abduct, capture, hijack, skyjack, seize, steal, waylay, shanghai, impress, spirit away, ravish, hold for ransom, pirate, snatch (*slang*); *ant.* rescue, ransom, release.

kill *v.* **1.** slay, murder, assassinate, do away with, eliminate, execute, exterminate, lynch, extinguish, finish off, massacre, *slang*: rub out, bump off, hit; slaughter, butcher; sacrifice, put to sleep. **2.** cancel, annul, nullify, counteract, recant, turn off, halt, shut off, stop, veto, prohibit, refuse, forbid; *ant.* initiate, renew.

killer *n.* murderer, assassin, butcher, hitman, gunman, slayer, sniper, liquidator, shootist, executioner, exterminator, hatchet man (*slang*), terminator.

killing *n.* **1.** slaying, homicide, assassination, slaughter, bloodshed, carnage, liquidation, fatality, manslaughter, massacre, murder, fratricide, extermination. **2.** (*slang*) success, coup, bonanza, hit, windfall, cleanup (*slang*).

killing *adj.* **1.** mortal, lethal, fatal, destructive, deadly, murderous, deathly, final. **2.** exhausting, fatiguing, punishing, prostrating, tiring, debilitating, enervating, vital.

killjoy *n.* pessimist, skeptic, complainer, cynic, spoilsport, wet blanket, whiner, grouch; *ant.* enthusiast, optimist.

kiln *n.* furnace, hearth, oven.

kin *n.* relatives, relations, cousins, family, people, blood, flesh and blood, kindred, kinsfolk, kinsmen, kith, lineage, extraction, stock, consanguinity.

kin *adj.* akin, allied, close, connected, kindred, linked, related, similar, cognate.

kind *n.* sort, brand, category, breed, ilk, description, stamp, family, genus, set, tribe, denomination, type, variety.

in kind similarly, in a similar fashion, in the same way.

kind *adj.* tender, considerate, affectionate, altruistic, amicable, benign, loving, pleasant, gracious, motherly, softhearted, compassionate, genial, warm, sympathetic, understanding; *ant.* callous, crass.

kindhearted *adj.* amiable, generous, compassionate, philanthropic, sympathetic, warmhearted, kind, bighearted, generous, helpful; *ant.* cold-hearted.

kindle *v.* **1.** light, ignite, burn, set fire to, enkindle, fire, foment, inflame. **2.** arouse, excite, inspire, animate, agitate, activate, awaken, incite, initiate, provoke, rouse, stimulate, stir; *ant.* douse.

kindliness *n.* generosity, charity, sympathy, warmth, goodwill, benevolence, compassion, friendliness, amiability; *ant.* cruelty, meanness.

kindling *n.* tinder, firewood, coals, fuel, wood; ignition, burning, combustion.

kindly *adj.* generous, helpful, gentle, benefic, giving, caring, sympathetic, compassionate, cordial, good-natured, helpful, indulgent, genial.

kindly *adv.* cordially, considerately, graciously, tenderly, gently, generously, genially, thoughtfully, patiently, humanely, politely, agreeably.

kindness *n.* **1.** consideration, tenderness, sweetness, sympathy, courtesy, cordiality, bonhomie, gentilesse, mildness, affection, forbearance, goodness, charity, altruism, philanthropy, succor, grace, clemency, understanding; benefaction, hospitality, munificence. *ant.* cruelty, inhumanity. **2.** (a kind act) favor, help, service, aid, assistance.

kind of (*slang*) moderately, somewhat, sort of (*slang*), having the nature of.

kindred *n.* family, people, clan, kin, kinsmen, kinswomen, folk, relations, relatives, flesh and blood.

kindred *adj.* similar, like, affiliated, affined, akin, allied, common, congenial, germane, corresponding, matching, related.

king *n.* monarch, sovereign, ruler, majesty, emperor, despot, potentate, tyrant, boss, chieftain, patriarch, autocrat, sultan, caliph, khan, master; *ant.* subject.

kingdom *n.* realm, domain, dominion, principality, province, sphere, suzerainty, commonwealth, territory, tract, sway, dynasty, sovereignty.

kingly *adj.* majestic, regal, royal, august, grand, imperious, imposing, splendid, sublime, stately, imperial, lordly; *ant.* low, commonplace, trashy.

kink *n.* **1.** twist, tangle, crinkle, cramp, crimp, bend, coil, corkscrew, wrinkle, knot, loop, curl, crick. **2.** eccentricity, fetish, idiosyncrasy, oddity, quirk, vagary, whim, peculiarity, caprice, foible, singularity, crotchet. **3.** difficulty, complication, hitch, snag, impediment, defect, entanglement, flaw, imperfection.

kink *v.* bend, coil, crimp, curl, tangle, twist, wrinkle; *ant.* straighten.

kinky *adj.* **1.** curled, frizzled, coiled, crimped, knotted, twisted, wrinkled, crumpled; *ant.* straight. **2.** (*slang*) bizarre, weird, odd, degenerate, depraved, deviant, freakish, licentious, perverted, peculiar, strange, warped, unconventional, capricious, sick (*slang*).

kinship *n.* affiliation, connection, bond, relationship, affinity, alliance, correspondence, similarity; lineage, consanguinity.

kiosk *n.* pavilion, newsstand, booth, box, stall, stand, bookstall, counter, cabin.

kismet *n.* destiny, fate, fortune, doom, karma; providence, portion, lot.

kiss *n.* osculation, caress, *slang:* smooch, peck; embrace, endearment.

kiss *v.* graze, brush, touch, scrape, caress, glance, fan.

kit *n.* set, equipment, stock, assortment, accoutrements, effects, gear, instruments, material, paraphernalia, tackle, tools, utensils, apparatus.

kitchen *n.* galley, cook's room, scullery, gallery, canteen, kitchenette, mess.

kittenish *adj.* playful, mischievous, flirtatious, arch, coquettish, coy, cute, pert, frisky, frolicsome; *ant.* staid.

knack *n.* aptitude, ability, skill, faculty, bent, capacity, gift, propensity, talent, flair, adroitness, dexterity, facility, forte.

knapsack *n.* backpack, rucksack, bag, haversack, dufflebag, musette.

knave *n.* scamp, fraud, villain, rascal, stinker (*slang*), cheat, rapscallion, rogue, reprobate, bastard (*slang*), scoundrel, blackguard, swindler, swine.

knavish *adj.* felonious, fraudulent, corrupt, damnable, devilish, deceptive, fiendish, wicked, villainous, roguish, reprobate, contemptible, rascally; *ant.* honest, scrupulous.

knead *v.* ply, shape, alter, work, mix, form, massage, manipulate, aerate, blend, press, rub, knuckle.

kneel *v.* genuflect, bend, stoop, curtsy, bow down, fall to one's knees, bend the knee, do obeisance.

knell *n.* ring, signal, chime, toll, peel, death bell.

knick-knack *n.* curio, gadget, ornament, trifle, bauble, trinket, conversation piece, bric-a-brac, objet d'art, gewgaw, gimcrack, gizmo (*slang*).

knife *n.* blade, cutter, sword, bayonet, dagger, stiletto, lance, machete, poniard, scalpel, sickle, scythe, bodkin.

knife *v.* stab, cut, lacerate, pierce, slash, impale, rip, spit, lance, thrust through.

knight *n.* cavalier, champion, chevalier, gallant, gentleman, thane, Templar, knight-at-arms, knight-errant.

knit *v.* **1.** intermingle, affiliate, connect, purl, web, cable, net, sew, weave, join, ally, bind, fasten, interlace, link. **2.** heal, mend, repair, bind.

knob *n.* hump, protruberance, bump, doorknob, handle, bulge, knot, nub, stud, swelling.

knobby *adj.* lumpy, bumpy, knobbed, bent, crooked, irregular.

knock *n.* **1.** rap, thump, whack, beat, blow, slap, smack, thump, punch, cuff, box, clip, clout. **2.** (*slang*) setback, reversal, rejection, failure, defeat, criticism, condemnation, censure; *ant.* boost, praise.

knock *v.* **1.** rap, thump, buffet, clap, cuff, hit, punch, slap, smite, strike, beat, hit. **2.** (*slang*) abuse, belittle, disparage, carp, cavil, censure, deprecate, condemn, lambaste, criticize, put down (*slang*), vilify.

knock off (*slang*) **1.** kill, assassinate, murder. **2.** accomplish, complete, finish, conclude. **3.** (end a period of working) finish, stop, clock out, pack it in (*slang*), call it a day.

knock out *v.* **1.** anesthetize, drug, etherize, put to sleep. **2.** strike down, strike senseless, KO (*slang*), render unconscious, make one see stars (*slang*).

knockout *n.* **1.** knockout blow, coup de grace, finishing *or* final blow, technical knockout, KO, TKO. **2.** (*slang*) success, sensation, triumph, hit, smash, winner.

knoll *n.* rise, mound, hill, barrow, hillock.

knot *n.* **1.** snarl, gnarl, snag, clump, tuft, coil, spiral, contortion, tie, entanglement, tangle, twist, twirl, whirl, whorl, hitch. **2.** cluster, bunch, assortment, gathering, aggregation, collection, heap, mass, pile.

knot *v.* bind, tie, secure, tether, tie, weave, entangle, entwine, knit, tangle.

knotty *adj.* **1.** gnarled, bumpy, hard, knobby, knotted, nodular, rough, rugged. **2.** (said of a problem) difficult, complex, troublesome, complicated, unresolvable, hard.

know *v.* comprehend, understand, perceive, discern, distinguish, experience, fathom, identify, intuit, ken, learn, make out, realize, recognize. **in the know** aware, informed, educated, knowing, cognizant.

knowable *adj.* understandable, graspable, visible, distinct, obvious, plain.

know-how (*slang*) *n.* skill, ability, aptitude, savvy (*slang*), faculty, proficiency, talent, knack, flair, adroitness, capability, knowledge, savoir-faire.

knowing *adj.* acute, sharp, clever, astute, aware, discerning, intelligent, perceptive, qualified, sagacious, well-informed, judicious, reasonable, competent, experienced; *ant.* ignorant, obtuse.

knowingly *adv.* purposely, intentionally, deliberately, consciously, willfully, wittingly, designedly, on purpose; *ant.* unwittingly.

knowledge *n.* learning, lore, erudition, scholarship, education, book-learning, wisdom, cognizance, enlightenment, apprehension, comprehension, discernment, judgment, insight; *ant.* ignorance, pretension.

knowledgeable *adj.* aware, bright, cognizant, educated, erudite, intelligent, experienced, learned, lettered, scholarly, well-informed, au courant, au fait, conversant; *ant.* ignorant.

known *adj.* acknowledged, admitted, avowed, revealed, discovered, open, published, recognized, notorious, familiar, confessed, manifest, noted, obvious, certified.

know-nothing *n.* ignoramus, illiterate, moron, imbecile, clod, dolt, fool, dunce.

knuckle under give in, give up, acquiesce, accede, capitulate, defer, succumb, submit, yield, abandon, surrender, give way.

kook (*slang*) *n.* eccentric, *slang:* loony, screwball, ding-a-ling, flake, fruitcake, dingbat, weirdo, oddball, crackpot.

kosher *adj.* conventional, genuine, proper, official, orthodox, safe, on the up and up (*slang*).

kowtow *v.* stoop, fawn, prostrate, cringe, defer, grovel, pander, suck up (*slang*), bow, court, flatter, toady, genuflect, kneel.

kudos *n.* praise, credit, glory, acclaim, applause, honor, prestige, regard, renown, repute, distinction, esteem, laurels, plaudits.

label n. 1. badge, marker, tag, sticker, stamp, insignia. 2. characterization, classification, description, epithet, brand.

label v. 1. stamp, tag, identify, mark, brand. 2. classify, categorize, designate, describe, name, dub, style, christen, specify, define.

labor n. 1. work, chore, job, task; toil, drudgery, effort, exertion; ant. ease, leisure, relaxation, rest. 2. laborers, labor force, workers, work force, hands, employees, operatives; ant. employers, management, capitalists. 3. childbirth, parturition, contractions, delivery.

labor v. 1. work, toil, endeavor, plod, slave, strive, struggle, suffer, sweat, travail; ant. idle, laze, loaf, lounge. 2. belabor, dwell on, elaborate, overdo, overemphasize, overstress, strain.

labored adj. forced, strained, unnatural, difficult, awkward, stilted, complicated, contrived, overdone, overwrought; ant. easy, natural.

laborer n. worker, hireling, hired hand.

laborious adj. 1. arduous, difficult, painstaking, backbreaking, strenuous, herculean, tiresome, ponderous, burdensome; ant. easy, effortless, relaxing, simple. 2. diligent, hardworking, assiduous, industrious, indefatigable, persevering, tireless.

labyrinth n. maze, puzzle, riddle, circumvolution, coil, complexity, convolution, entanglement, intricacy, complication.

labyrinthine adj. Byzantine, complex, convoluted, puzzling, knotty, winding, tortuous, twisted, complicated, confused, kafkaesque.

lace n. 1. filigree, meshwork, netting, tatting, edging, trimming, border, decoration. 2. cord, tie, thong.

lace v. 1. bind, attach, fasten, close, strap. 2. (add an alcoholic beverage to) fortify, strengthen, spike (slang).

lacerate v. 1. slash, rip, tear, gash, rend, slash, maim, wound, harm, hurt. 2. (hurt emotionally) wound, distress, upset, pain, offend, savage.

laceration n. cut, lesion, gash, wound, injury, mutilation, rent, rip, slash, tear.

lachrymose adj. 1. tearful, weepy, crying, sobbing, teary; ant. smiling, laughing. 2. mournful, sad, woeful, dolorous, lugubrious; ant. cheerful, happy.

lack v. need, require, want, miss.

lack n. deficiency, need, want, dearth, insufficiency, deprivation, privation, scarcity, shortage, vacancy, absence, void; ant. abundance, profusion.

lacking adj. deficient, inadequate, wanting, needing, flawed, impaired, missing.

lackadaisical adj. apathetic, listless, lazy, lethargic, halfhearted, indifferent, indolent, languid.

lackey n. sycophant, minion, parasite, flunky, gofer (slang); attendant, valet.

lackluster adj. boring, dull, unimaginative, uninspired, mundane, prosaic, lifeless, spiritless, tired, flat, dry, leaden; ant. brilliant.

laconic adj. brief, terse, concise, succinct, pithy, curt, short; ant. wordy, garrulous, verbose.

lacquer n. stain, veneer, finish, varnish.

lad n. boy, juvenile, kid, youngster, youth, chap, fellow.

laden adj. burdened, encumbered, loaded, packed, fraught, full, jammed, stuffed, weighed down.

ladle v. spoon, dip, scoop.

lady n. woman, madam, matron, dame, damsel.

lady-killer n. womanizer, ladies' man, heartbreaker, libertine, philanderer, rake, skirtchaser, Casanova, Don Juan, Lothario.

ladylike adj. proper, respectable, polite, refined, cultured, decorous, genteel, matronly, modest, well-bred.

lag v. dawdle, tarry, linger, loiter, idle, straggle, trail; ant. lead.

L

laggard *n.* dawdler, loafer, idler, loiterer, slowpoke (*slang*), straggler; *ant.* dynamo.

lagoon *n.* lake, pond, pool, marsh, bog, shoal.

laid-back (*slang*) *adj.* easygoing, relaxed, calm, untroubled, unflappable, casual, unworried; *ant.* tense, uptight (*slang*).

laid up disabled, incapacitated, immobilized, housebound, bedridden, injured, sick, ill, out of action (*slang*).

lair *n.* burrow, den, nest, refuge, hideout, retreat, sanctuary.

lake *n.* pond, creek, loch.

lambaste *v.* **1.** beat, thrash, whip, strike, flay. **2.** berate, castigate, excoriate, reprimand, rebuke, censure, upbraid, scold.

lambent *adj.* flickering, sparkling, twinkling, shimmering, glistening, glowing, incandescent, luminous, lustrous, radiant, brilliant, dancing.

lame *adj.* **1.** disabled, handicapped, hobbling, limping, crippled. **2.** inadequate, feeble, defective, insufficient, poor, weak, half-baked, pitiful.

lament *v.* weep, grieve, moan, sorrow, wail, bemoan; rue, regret, deplore; *ant.* celebrate, rejoice.

laminate *v.* cover, coat, face, veneer, exfoliate, stratify.

lamp *n.* light, beacon, torch.

lampoon *n.* satire, parody, caricature, sendup, takeoff, spoof, burlesque.

lampoon *v.* satirize, parody, caricature, ridicule.

lance *v.* pierce, lacerate, cut.

land *n.* **1.** dirt, soil, terra firma, earth, ground, property, real estate, realty, tract. **2.** country, nation, province, territory.

land *v.* **1.** alight, arrive, dock, end up, touch down. **2.** (*slang*) get, achieve, obtain, win, secure, nail down (*slang*).

landed *adj.* rich, wealthy, secure.

landlord *n.* landowner, lessor, property owner, host, innkeeper, proprietor.

landmark *n.* **1.** historic structure, vestige, remnant, ruins, memorial. **2.** milestone, turning point, watershed, signpost, beacon.

lands *n.* acreage, grounds, estates, spread.

landscape *n.* view, scenery, vista, panorama, scene, prospect, outlook.

landslide *adj.* conclusive, overwhelming, decisive, emphatic.

lane *n.* alley, alleyway, avenue, path, passage, road, towpath.

language *n.* speech, vocabulary, discourse, conversation, wording, parlance, idiom, terminology; vernacular, jargon, argot, cant.

languid *adj.* lethargic, lackadaisical, drooping, weak; listless, indifferent, spiritless, unenthusiastic, uninterested; sluggish, slow, torpid, dull; *ant.* lively, vivacious, alert.

languish *v.* **1.** droop, fade, wilt, wither, waste away, decline, sicken, faint. **2.** pine, grieve, sorrow, sigh, brood.

languor *n.* lassitude, drowsiness, inertia, lethargy, torpor, listlessness, indolence, fatigue, heaviness, calm, lull, stillness, dreaminess; *ant.* alacrity, gusto.

lanky *adj.* attenuated, thin, gaunt, lean, emaciated, scrawny, slender, slim, meager, spare; *ant.* burly.

lap *n.* **1.** legs, thighs, front, seat. **2.** circuit, round, course, distance.

lap *v.* drink, lick, sip, tongue.

lapse *n.* **1.** fault, mistake, error, failing, negligence, oversight, indiscretion, slip, fall, gaffe, blunder. **2.** interruption, break, gap, hiatus, interval, interlude, pause, intermission.

lapse *v.* **1.** backslide, decline, slip, degenerate, deteriorate, worsen, fail. **2.** end, expire, stop, terminate, cease, quit.

larceny *n.* robbery, burglary, thievery, heist, expropriation, stealing, misappropriation, pilfering, piracy, purloining.

large *adj.* **1.** big, enormous, huge, giant, gigantic, immense, jumbo, massive, capacious, substantial; *ant.* small, tiny, diminutive. **2.** generous, liberal, magnanimous, openhearted; *ant.* petty.

at large liberated, on the loose, free, on the run.

largely *adv.* **1.** primarily, mostly, mainly, chiefly, principally. **2.** abundantly, considerably, broadly, magnificently, extensively, extravagantly, prodigiously.

largeness *n.* bigness, magnitude, bulk, size, heft, volume, enormity, enormousness, expanse, extent, greatness, heftiness, immensity.

largesse *n.* generosity, munificence, philanthropy, benefaction, charity; donation, endowment, gift, bequest, aid.

lark n. escapade, spree, caper, antic, fling, mischief, prank, revel, romp.

lascivious adj. lewd, lustful, wanton, vulgar, bawdy, coarse, crude, lecherous, licentious, obscene, prurient, salacious.

lash v. 1. beat, flay, flog, thrash, whip, hit, smack, strike. 2. berate, lambaste, castigate, chastise, criticize, scold; ridicule, satirize, lampoon.

lass n. girl, maid, maiden, damsel.

lassitude n. exhaustion, fatigue, drowsiness, languor, prostration, enervation, listlessness, apathy, ennui.

last n. close, finish, end, completion, conclusion, ending, windup, finale, termination; ant. beginning, start.

last adj. concluding, final, closing, definitive, terminal; ant. first, initial.

at last finally, in the end, at length, at long last, in conclusion, in due course, eventually.

lasting adj. permanent, enduring, immutable, durable, indelible, indestructible, continuing, perennial; ant. ephemeral, fleeting.

lastly adv. finally, in conclusion, in the end, ultimately; ant. firstly.

latch n. lock, bolt, fastening, catch, hook.

late adj. 1. overdue, belated, delayed, tardy, behind, slow; ant. early, punctual. 2. dead, deceased, defunct, departed. 3. recent, up-to-the-minute, last-minute, fresh.

late adv. belatedly, slowly, tardily; ant. early, punctually.

lately adv. recently, these days, of late.

latent adj. dormant, hidden, quiescent, underlying, potential, undeveloped, unrealized, secret, concealed, veiled; ant. overt, patent.

later adj. after, afterwards, thereafter; ant. earlier.

latest adj. current, fashionable, in, modern, newest, up-to-date, up-to-the-minute.

lather n. suds, bubbles, foam, froth.

lather v. suds up, foam, froth, shampoo.

latitude n. 1. leeway, range, scope, independence. 2. distance, degree, measure.

latrine n. toilet, bathroom, commode, outhouse, slang: john, can, head.

latter adj. succeeding, successive, latest, last, ensuing, recent; ant. former.

lattice n. mesh, grid, grate, grill, trellis, grating, fretwork, espalier, network, web.

laud v. praise, honor, hail, acclaim, applaud, celebrate, extol, glorify; ant. condemn, damn.

laudable adj. exemplary, praiseworthy, admirable, estimable, commendable, creditable, excellent, meritorious; ant. damnable, execrable.

laudatory adj. glorifying, celebratory, admiring, championing, acclamatory, adulatory, eulogistic, panegyrical; ant. damning.

laugh v. chuckle, giggle, guffaw, chortle, snicker, snigger.

laugh n. chuckle, chortle, giggle, snicker, titter, guffaw, hoot.

laughable adj. amusing, comical, humorous, hilarious, funny, droll, farcical; absurd, ludicrous, preposterous, ridiculous, pitiful, derisory.

laughingstock n. butt, target, victim.

laughter n. chuckling, giggling, tittering, chortling; merriment, mirth, amusement.

launch v. 1. originate, initiate, inaugurate, introduce, start, commence. 2. propel, thrust, fire off, set in motion, send forth, eject.

launder v. wash, scrub, clean.

lavatory n. bathroom, restroom, washroom, WC, water closet, toilet, commode, outhouse, latrine, urinal; slang: john, can, head.

lavish adj. extravagant, opulent, bountiful, effusive, fulsome, gorgeous, prodigal, excessive, immoderate, copious; ant. sparing, parsimonious.

lavish v. shower, heap, pour, deluge, expend, lavish, bestow.

law n. 1. jurisprudence, legal science, equity, legal practice, judicature. 2. rule, principle, precept, theorem, maxim, axiom, reason, assumption. 3. code, constitution, ordinance, statute, edict, regulation.

lawful adj. legal, legitimate, statutory, decreed, authorized, within the law, constitutional, enacted, vested, licit, canonical; ant. illegal.

lawless adj. 1. uncivilized, savage, barbarous, violent, outlaw, uncontrolled, wild. 2. insurgent, ungovernable, anarchistic, tyrannous, despotic, revolutionary, mutinous, riotous.

lawlessness *n.* irresponsibility, disorder, anarchy, chaos, disturbance.

lawn *n.* yard, grass, park, garden.

lawsuit *n.* litigation, action, suit, prosecution, claim.

lawyer *n.* attorney, counsel, solicitor, attorney at law, barrister, *slang:* ambulance-chaser, mouthpiece, legal eagle.

lax *adj.* **1.** slack, flaccid, loose, flabby; *ant.* taut. **2.** careless, derelict; casual, easygoing; lenient, permissive; *ant.* strict, punctilious. **3.** inaccurate, indefinite, inexact.

laxative *n.* purgative, cathartic, loosener.

lay *v.* **1.** put, place, set, deposit. **2.** order, arrange, organize, systematize. **3.** (bring forth eggs) deposit, yield, generate, have, bear. **lay off** fire, dismiss, discharge, let go, oust.

lay *adj.* amateur, nonprofessional, secular, civilian.

layer *n.* stratum, tier, coating, cover, covering, film, mantle.

layman *n.* amateur, layperson, outsider.

layoff *n.* discharge, dismissal, unemployment; furlough, lockout.

layout *n.* outline, plan, blueprint, draft, sketch, map, geography.

laze *v.* lounge, lie around, sit around, idle, loaf, loll.

laziness *n.* sloth, indolence, idleness, sluggishness, inactivity.

lazy *adj.* idle, inactive, indolent, shiftless, slow, languid, languorous, lethargic, sluggish, torpid; *ant.* energetic, industrious.

leach *v.* extract, drain, filter, seep, strain.

lead *n.* clue, hint, suggestion, direction, example.

lead *v.* **1.** guide, conduct, escort, usher, pilot, steer. **2.** direct, govern, command, preside over, supervise, manage, chair, run. **3.** influence, induce, prompt, sway, incline, cause. **4.** (be first) exceed, excel, surpass, outperform; *ant.* lag.

leaden *adj.* **1.** heavy, burdensome, oppressive, crushing. **2.** sluggish, listless, lifeless, dead.

leader *n.* chief, boss, director, head, superior, captain, commander, conductor; *ant.* follower.

leadership *n.* direction, guidance, authority, command, management, supremacy, control.

leading *adj.* dominant, main, chief, first, foremost, preeminent, governing, greatest, highest, outstanding; *ant.* subordinate.

leaf *n.* **1.** sheet, folio, page. **2.** needle, blade, cotyledon. **turn over a new leaf** reform, go straight, mend one's ways, repent.

leaf *v.* skim, glance, browse, riffle, thumb through.

leaflet *n.* pamphlet, bill, booklet, brochure, circular, handbill, handout.

league *n.* alliance, association, class, category, coalition, confederation, federation, fraternity, union, syndicate, cartel.

leak *n.* **1.** fissure, hole, opening, aperture, crack, crevice, perforation, puncture. **2.** divulgence, disclosure, slip (*slang*). **3.** drip, seepage, oozing.

leak *v.* **1.** drip, spill, exude, seep, trickle, ooze. **2.** divulge, disclose, reveal, let slip, make known, *slang:* let the cat out of the bag, spill the beans.

leaky *adj.* porous, permeable, perforated, holey, punctured.

lean *adj.* slender, slim, thin, angular, wiry, emaciated, gaunt, scrawny, skinny, bony.

lean *v.* slant, tilt, bend, slope, tip, recline, repose.

leaning *n.* penchant, predilection, inclination, proclivity, propensity, tendency, bias, liking, partiality, taste.

leap *v.* jump, hop, skip, vault, cavort, caper, gambol.

learn *v.* understand, discern, assimilate, master, determine, discover, memorize.

learned *adj.* wise, scholarly, adept, erudite, knowledgeable, informed, sage, lettered, well-read, academic; *ant.* untutored.

learning *n.* education, knowledge, enlightenment, erudition, information, letters, research, scholarship, study, attainments, culture.

lease *v.* let, loan, rent, sublet, charter, hire.

leash *n.* hold, check, discipline, control, restraint, rein, tether.

least *adj.* fewest, smallest, lowest, last, merest, poorest, slightest.

leathery *adj.* rugged, tough, durable, hardened.

leave n. 1. consent, concession, authorization, allowance, dispensation. 2. liberty, vacation, holiday.

leave v. 1. depart, exit, move, move out or away, go away, relocate, set out, decamp. 2. abandon, quit, walk out on, jilt, desert, forsake. 3. bequeath, allot, assign, entrust, will.

leaven v. elevate, raise, ferment, lighten, inspire, expand.

leavings n. leftovers, refuse, remains, scraps, spoil, waste, residue.

lecher n. debaucher, libertine, profligate, fornicator, rake, womanizer, Don Juan.

lecherous adj. lascivious, lewd, wanton, carnal, licentious, lustful, prurient, salacious, raunchy (slang).

lechery n. lewdness, licentiousness, lust, profligacy, prurience, libertinism, lubricity, lasciviousness.

lecture n. 1. address, speech, discourse, talk, instruction. 2. scolding, reprimand, rebuke, castigation, chiding, reproof, talking-to.

lecture v. 1. address, speak, talk, discourse, expound. 2. scold, castigate, admonish, berate, harangue, reprove, reprimand.

ledge n. ridge, shelf, sill, mantle, step, projection.

leech n. freeloader, parasite, sycophant.

leer n. grin, smirk, smile, wink.

leer v. ogle, smirk, stare, wink, eye, gloat.

leery adj. suspicious, skeptical, wary, mistrustful, dubious, careful, cautious, guarded, worried.

leeward adj. sheltered, protected, safe, peaceful, still, secure, screened.

leeway n. play, room, scope, space, latitude.

left adj. liberal, progressive, radical, communist, socialist.

leftovers n. leavings, remains, remnants, scraps, refuse, residue.

leg n. 1. limb, appendage, member, part. 2. brace, prop, upright. 3. (a part of a race or other competition) lap, portion, segment, stretch.

on one's last legs exhausted, failing, worn out, dying, moribund, at death's door, with one foot in the grave, fading fast.

pull someone's leg (slang) tease, kid, fool, trick, deceive.

legacy n. inheritance, bequest, endowment, estate, heirloom, heritage, birthright.

legal adj. lawful, licit, authorized, constitutional, legitimate, permissible, allowable, aboveboard, proper, correct; ant. illegal.

legalize v. sanction, permit, allow, legitimize, license, approve, authorize, warrant, validate; outlaw, prohibit.

legate n. envoy, deputy, delegate, emissary, ambassador.

legatee n. beneficiary, heir, inheritor, recipient.

legation n. delegation, consulate, embassy, commission, ministry, mission, representation.

legend n. 1. myth, fable, fiction, folk tale, saga, story, tale, narrative. 2. luminary, marvel, prodigy, household name. 3. caption, inscription, key, cipher, code.

legendary adj. 1. famed, fabled, famous, renowned, world-renowned, illustrious, well-known. 2. fictional, fictitious, mythical, immortal, romantic.

legerdemain n. sleight of hand, magic; trickery, artifice, deception, contrivance, manipulation, subterfuge, craftiness.

legible adj. decipherable, intelligible, readable, clear, distinct, large-type.

legion adj. countless, innumerable, myriad, numerous, numberless, multitudinous.

legion n. 1. army, regiment, company, division, battalion, brigade. 2. multitude, swarm, throng, mass, army.

legislate v. enact, pass, make laws, deliberate.

legislation n. act, ruling, law, regulation, statute, authorization, bill, charter.

legislative adj. congressional, judicial, lawmaking, ordaining, parliamentary, deliberative.

legislator n. lawmaker, congressman, congresswoman, senator, representative, parliamentarian.

legislature n. senate, assembly, chamber, congress, law-making body, legislative body, house.

legitimate adj. 1. legal, licit, lawful, sanctioned, valid, warranted, justifiable, proper, rightful, correct. 2. (not fake) authentic, real, genuine, rightful, authenticated, vouched-for, attested.

legitimize v. legalize, sanction, license, permit, authorize, entitle.

legume *n.* bean, pea, pod.

leisure *n.* spare time, ease, freedom, quiet, relaxation, respite, time off.

leisurely *adj.* slow, relaxed, unhurried, carefree, comfortable.

lend *v.* **1.** advance, loan, let out. **2.** impart, contribute, bestow, add, furnish, grant.

length *n.* distance, extent, longitude, stretch, reach, section, segment, span, term, duration, period.

at length exhaustively, in detail, in depth, thoroughly, fully, completely.

lengthen *v.* elongate, extend, stretch, protract, prolong, increase, expand.

lengthwise *adj.* lengthways, horizontally, vertically.

lengthy *adj.* drawn-out, long, protracted, prolonged, interminable, rambling.

leniency *n.* permissiveness, indulgence, clemency, compassion, forbearance, tolerance, mercy, softheartedness.

lenient *adj.* clement, forgiving, merciful, forbearing, compassionate, indulgent, softhearted, tolerant; *ant.* stern, harsh, exacting.

lenitive *adj.* soothing, assuaging, alleviating, palliative, mitigating, calming, easing.

lens *n.* eye, eyepiece, eyeglass, glass.

leper *n.* outcast, pariah, undesirable, untouchable.

leprechaun *n.* elf, gnome, goblin, brownie, fairy.

lesion *n.* abrasion, wound, cut, gash, scrape, injury.

lessen *v.* reduce, decrease, minimize, shrink; abate, ease, diminish, weaken, lighten, moderate; *ant.* increase.

lessening *n.* dwindling, ebbing, abatement, diminution, deadening, contraction.

lesser *adj.* smaller, inferior, lower, minor, subordinate, secondary.

lesson *n.* instruction, lecture, reading, message, class, exercise, drill, assignment.

let *v.* **1.** allow, sanction, permit, authorize, OK, agree to, consent to, enable, empower, delegate, give leave, give the go-ahead to, give the green light to; *ant.* forbid, prohibit. **2.** lease, rent, hire out.

let down betray, desert, fail, disappoint, disillusion; *ant.* come through.

let go relinquish, part with, release, dismiss, abandon; *ant.* keep, hold on to.

let on suggest, hint, imply, indicate.

let up stop, cease, abate, subside, slow down.

letdown *n.* anticlimax, disappointment, disillusionment, blow, frustration.

lethal *adj.* deadly, fatal, mortal, virulent, dangerous, destructive, devastating, murderous.

lethargic *adj.* listless, sluggish, slow, torpid, languid, apathetic, drowsy, sleepy, indifferent, lazy, inactive; *ant.* alert, energetic.

lethargy *n.* lassitude, languor, torpor, drowsiness, sloth, inertia, apathy, indifference.

letter *n.* **1.** character, symbol, sign. **2.** note, message, communication, missive, epistle, dispatch, line.

lettered *adj.* educated, scholarly, scholarly, erudite, informed, accomplished, cultivated, cultured, versed, well-read.

letup *n.* pause, recess, breather, cessation, abatement, lessening, slackening.

level *n.* **1.** altitude, elevation, position, degree, height, stratum. **2.** class, rank, echelon, position, standing, status.

on the level candid, straightforward, honest, frank, aboveboard; *ant.* devious.

level *v.* **1.** straighten, balance, align, even out. **2.** demolish, destroy, flatten, bulldoze, raze, wreck, tear down.

level *adj.* horizontal, smooth, straight, comparable, equal, even, flush, stable.

levelheaded *adj.* even-tempered, composed, calm, unflappable, collected, cool, dependable, sensible, steady, balanced.

lever *n.* handle, bar, joystick (*slang*).

leverage *n.* influence, pull, clout (*slang*), advantage, authority, rank.

leviathan *n.* colossus, mammoth, giant, hulk; monster, sea-monster, serpent, whale.

levity *n.* frivolity, giddiness, silliness, gaiety, merriment, facetiousness, hilarity, lightheartedness, flippancy, playfulness, irreverence; *ant.* solemnity.

levy *n.* tax, tariff, toll, duty, collection, contribution, assessment, exaction, excise.

levy *v.* **1.** tax, collect, demand, conscript, assess, exact, raise. **2.** summon, assemble, call, muster.

lewd *adj.* lascivious, vulgar, wanton, licen-

lewdness *n.* tious, bawdy, impure, libidinous, salacious, profligate, wicked, obscene, pornographic, indecent.

lewdness *n.* bawdiness, lasciviousness, salaciousness, debauchery, depravity, obscenity, lechery, licentiousness.

lexicographer *n.* dictionary-maker, glossarist, lexicologist, linguist.

lexicon *n.* dictionary, wordbook, glossary, vocabulary, word-list, thesaurus.

liability *n.* 1. accountability, responsibility, obligation, debt, culpability. 2. disadvantage, drawback, inconvenience, detriment, handicap, debit, encumbrance, burden; *ant.* asset.

liable *adj.* 1. accountable, responsible, obligated, answerable, susceptible, vulnerable. 2. inclined, likely, predisposed, tending.

liaison *n.* 1. affair, romance, entanglement, amour. 2. contact, connection, link, communication, interchange, intrigue.

liar *n.* fabricator, deceiver, fibber, falsifier, perjurer, prevaricator, storyteller.

libation *n.* gift, offering, drink.

libel *n.* defamation, aspersion, slander, vilification, slur, smear, denigration.

libelous *adj.* defamatory, slanderous, vilifying, scurrilous, derogatory, malicious, injurious.

liberal *n.* reformist, progressive, libertarian, individualist, freethinker, leftist, left-winger; *ant.* conservative, right-winger.

liberal *adj.* 1. lavish, bounteous, abundant, ample, copious. 2. humanistic, tolerant, broad-minded, progressive; beneficent, charitable, altruistic; magnanimous, generous, munificent.

liberalism *n.* freethinking, humanitarianism, libertarianism, progressivism, radicalism; *ant.* conservatism, narrow-mindedness.

liberality *n.* beneficence, benevolence, largesse, philanthropy, charity, kindness, broad-mindedness, altruism, catholicity.

liberate *v.* emancipate, free, release, discharge, let go, enfranchise, unchain, unfetter, rescue; *ant.* enslave.

liberation *n.* freedom, emancipation, liberty, redemption, release, deliverance, enfranchisement.

liberator *n.* emancipator, redeemer, rescuer, savior, deliverer; *ant.* enslaver, jailer.

libertine *n.* rake, reprobate, womanizer, seducer, debaucher, profligate, lecher.

liberty *n.* 1. freedom, emancipation, release, autonomy, independence, license. 2. sanction, authorization, dispensation, immunity, rights, leave, prerogative, privilege. **at liberty** free, on the loose, at large, unconstrained, unrestricted.

libidinous *adj.* lewd, lascivious, salacious, wanton, debauched, impure, lecherous, lustful, prurient, wicked, carnal; *ant.* chaste.

license *v.* warrant, permit, sanction, allow, authorize, certify, empower, entitle.

license *n.* 1. permit, permission, authorization, latitude, carte blanche, leave. 2. license, authority, entitlement, dispensation, exemption, licentiousness, debauchery, excess, irresponsibility, immorality, abandonment, profligacy, wantonness.

licentious *adj.* lascivious, immoral, wanton, promiscuous, impure, lustful, profligate.

lick *v.* 1. taste, tongue. 2. (as a light or flame) dart, play over, touch. 3. (*slang*) vanquish, win, beat, overwhelm, wallop, smash, whip, thrash, beat, subdue, conquer.

licking *n.* whipping, beating, spanking, thrashing, trouncing, defeat.

lid *n.* cover, cap, top, roof.

lie *n.* falsehood, untruth, fib, fabrication, deceit, white lie, whopper (*slang*).

lie *v.* 1. fabricate, misrepresent, equivocate, falsify, fib, perjure, prevaricate, dissimulate. 2. recline, loll, lounge, repose, rest, sprawl, stretch out.

liege *n.* master, lord, sovereign, owner.

life *n.* 1. existence, living, being, presence, animation, growth, consciousness, viability. 2. lifetime, career, history, biography, background, experience, conduct, attainment. **for dear life** desperately, urgently, for all one is worth, intensely, vigorously, with might and main, energetically.

lifeless *adj.* 1. spiritless, apathetic, torpid, insipid, lackluster, sterile, wooden, cold, colorless, empty, inert; *ant.* lively, animated. 2. dead, deceased, defunct, extinct, inanimate, unconscious; *ant.* alive.

lifelike *adj.* realistic, authentic, exact, faithful, true, graphic, natural, photographic, pictorial.

lifelong *adj.* constant, loyal, enduring, inveterate, lasting, long-standing, entrenched, perennial, abiding.

lifetime *n.* life span, course, days, period, time, career, existence.

lift *v.* hoist, raise, boost, elevate, upraise.

ligature *n.* **1.** tying, binding, connection. **2.** (something used in tying together) tie, bond, rope, bandage, strap, string, thong, tourniquet.

light *n.* **1.** illumination, radiance, brightness, luminosity, brilliance; dawn, day, daybreak, morning. **2.** lamp, light bulb, lantern, flame, candle, beacon, flare, torch. **3.** point of view, standpoint, aspect, angle, slant, frame of reference.

light *v.* **1.** illuminate, make visible, irradiate. **2.** ignite, inflame, spark, kindle.

light *adj.* **1.** airy, feathery, fluffy, floating, buoyant, thin, gaseous, effervescent; *ant.* dense, heavy. **2.** radiant, illuminated, bright; *ant.* dark. **3.** (not serious or profound) superficial, slight, mean, frivolous, trivial, unimportant; *ant.* serious. **4.** jaunty, lively, merry, animated, gay.

lighten *v.* mitigate, alleviate, ease, reduce, cut down, decrease.

light-footed *adj.* spry, agile, nimble, graceful, lithe, sprightly, tripping, winged; *ant.* clumsy.

lightheaded *adj.* **1.** dizzy, faint, delirious, giddy, confused, vertiginous. **2.** flighty, vacuous, shallow, superficial, inane, foolish, thoughtless, flippant.

lighthearted *adj.* gay, carefree, untroubled, jovial, joyous, blithe, elated, glad, gleeful, merry, playful, upbeat; *ant.* gloomy, despondent.

lightly *adv.* **1.** gently, gingerly, delicately. **2.** nimbly, deftly, easily, effortlessly. **3.** cheerfully, merrily, gaily, airily, breezily. **4.** carelessly, thoughtlessly, offhandedly, frivolously.

lightweight *adj.* unimportant, trivial, inconsequential, insignificant, trifling, negligible, petty, paltry; *ant.* weighty, serious.

likable *adj.* congenial, amiable, friendly, warm, charming, winning, engaging, agreeable, appealing, attractive.

like *v.* admire, appreciate, delight in, choose, enjoy, esteem, prefer, approve.

like *adj.* similar, alike, resembling, analogous, corresponding, homologous, parallel, relating, akin.

likelihood *n.* chance, possibility, probability, prospect, plausibility.

likely *adj.* **1.** probable, expected, anticipated; believable, plausible. **2.** liable, apt, prone.

like-minded *adj.* agreeing, harmonious, in accord, in agreement, of the same mind, unanimous, compatible.

liken *v.* equate, juxtapose, associate, compare, relate, link, match, parallel.

likeness *n.* representation, reproduction, image, appearance, affinity, copy, depiction, semblance, similitude.

likewise *adv.* also, similarly, besides, further, in addition, moreover, by the same token.

liking *n.* **1.** fondness, affection, attraction, affinity, appreciation. **2.** preference, predilection, partiality, penchant, desire, favor, inclination, bent, bias, taste, soft spot.

lilt *n.* cadence, rhythm, beat, song, measure, sway.

limb *n.* appendage, member, extremity, branch, extension, part, offshoot, projection.

limber *adj.* agile, lissome, lithe, flexible, pliable, pliant, nimble, supple, elastic, plastic; *ant.* stiff.

limbo *n.* purgatory, oblivion, nothingness, neither here nor there.

limelight *n.* fame, celebrity, stardom, spotlight, prominence, renown, big time (*slang*).

limit *n.* **1.** border, boundary, perimeter, periphery, rim; confines, bounds, boundary lines. **3.** threshold, extent, saturation point. **4.** maximum, quota, ceiling, limitation; curb.

limit *v.* restrain, restrict, bound, confine, constrain, curb, circumscribe, demarcate, specify.

limitation *n.* restriction, qualification, condition, constraint, control, check, curb; disadvantage, drawback.

limited *adj.* restricted, hampered, constrained, circumscribed, confined, defined, finite, fixed.

limitless *adj.* infinite, boundless, countless, endless, never-ending, unending, vast, measureless, untold.

limp *n.* lameness, hobble, falter, hitch.

limp *v.* hobble, falter, shamble, shuffle.

limp *adj.* **1.** flaccid, drooping, wilted, flabby,

floppy, flexible, pliable; *ant.* rigid. 2. enervated, exhausted, lifeless, weak.

limpid *adj.* bright, pure, translucent, transparent, clear; comprehensible, lucid.

line *n.* 1. length, list, rank, file, border, outline, tracing, channel, demarcation, row, sequence. 2. lineage, family, descent, ancestry, race, stock, strain, breed, bloodline, pedigree.

line *v.* 1. fill, reinforce, strengthen, panel, overlay, sheathe. 2. trace, delineate, outline, draw.

lineage *n.* genealogy, race, ancestry, descendants, ancestors, family, stock, strain, breed, birth.

lineal *adj.* inherited, transmitted, descended, ancestral.

lineament *n.* appearance, form, aspect, characteristic, detail, quality, face, features.

linear *adj.* one-dimensional, sequential, lineal; long, elongated, outstretched, extended.

lined *adj.* 1. furrowed, ruled, lineate, worn, wrinkled. 2. coated, faced, sheathed, wainscoted.

linesman *n.* arbiter, judge, official, umpire, referee.

lineup *n.* list, roster, program, agenda, schedule, slate, card.

linger *v.* tarry, dally, remain, delay, hang around, idle, lag, loiter, dawdle, procrastinate.

lingering *adj.* protracted, drawn-out, long, dragging.

lingo *n.* jargon, vernacular, vocabulary, argot, cant, dialect, parlance, terminology, idiom.

linguist *n.* philologist, grammarian, etymologist, lexicologist, verbalist, vocabularian, structuralist.

linguistics *n.* philology, grammar, semantics, phonology, syntax, etymology; sociolinguistics, psycholinguistics, computational linguistics.

liniment *n.* ointment, cream, lotion, balm, emollient, salve.

lining *n.* backing, inlay, interfacing, padding, encasement.

link *n.* 1. section, member, part, component, element. 2. bond, connection, attachment, joint, knot, tie; union, liaison, relationship, association, communication.

link *v.* associate, relate, connect, couple, fasten, join, tie, bind, yoke, unite; *ant.* sever.

lionhearted *adj.* brave, courageous, heroic, intrepid, valiant, bold, dauntless, daring; *ant.* fearful, timid.

lionize *v.* praise, acclaim, honor, celebrate, idolize, adulate, eulogize, exalt, worship.

lip *n.* 1. edge, border, rim, verge, margin. 2. insolence, cheek, impudence, impertinence, effrontery, rudeness, sauciness; sass, back talk.

liquefaction *n.* dissolution, dissolving, melting, thawing, fusion; *ant.* solidifying.

liquefy *v.* dissolve, melt, thaw.

liqueur *n.* cordial, cocktail, aperitif, after-dinner drink.

liquid *n.* fluid, solution, potation, drink, lotion, sap, secretion.

liquidate *v.* 1. dissolve, abolish, dispatch, sell off, annul. 2. kill, annihilate, assassinate, exterminate, *slang:* bump off, rub out, knock off.

liquor *n.* alcohol, drink, intoxicant, booze, *slang:* juice, hard stuff, rotgut.

lissome *adj.* lithesome, lithe, agile, limber, flexible, graceful, nimble, pliable, pliant, supple, willowy.

list *n.* catalog, directory, enumeration, file, index, tally, roster, tabulation, roll, inventory.

list *v.* 1. tabulate, catalog, itemize, file, index, alphabetize, record, register, note. 2. lean, tilt, tip, incline, slope, cant, heel.

listen *v.* 1. hear, overhear, monitor, prick up one's ears. 2. obey, heed, mind, take note, pay attention.

listless *adj.* lethargic, enervated, apathetic, languishing, limp, vacant, bored, depressed, heavy; *ant.* lively, energetic.

listlessness *n.* lethargy, torpor, ennui, lifelessness, sluggishness, apathy, indifference.

litany *n.* 1. invocation, refrain, recitation. 2. list, repetition, account, catalog, enumeration.

literacy *n.* education, erudition, knowledge, learning, intelligence, ability, proficiency.

literal *adj.* 1. actual, real, simple, direct, strict, word-for-word, verbatim; *ant.* figurative, metaphorical, loose. 2. prosaic, matter-of-fact, colorless, down-to-earth.

literally *adv.* actually, really, exactly, verbatim, faithfully, precisely, strictly, plainly.

literary *adj.* literate, erudite, learned, lettered, scholarly, cultivated, cultured, formal, refined, well-read, bookish.

literature *n.* writings, belles-lettres, lore, information, letters.

lithe *adj.* lissome, limber, flexible, supple, pliant; *ant.* stiff.

litigant *n.* disputant, contestant, party, claimant, contender, plaintiff.

litigation *n.* case, lawsuit, suit, contention, action.

litigious *adj.* argumentative, contentious, belligerent, quarrelsome, disputatious; *ant.* easygoing.

litter *n.* 1. trash, rubbish, refuse, debris, mess; clutter, disarray, disorder, jumble, confusion. 2. family, offspring, brood, progeny, young.

litter *v.* strew, clutter, derange, disarrange, disorder.

little *adj.* 1. small, diminutive, tiny, miniature, dwarfish, elfin; infinitesimal, minuscule, imperceptible. 2. (of space or extent) limited, slight, insufficient, cramped. 2. insignificant, petty, unimportant, trivial.

liturgy *n.* service, ceremony, ritual, form, rite, sacrament, celebration, worship.

live *adj.* alive, animate, sentient, alert, existent, breathing, dynamic, active; *ant.* dead, inert.

live *v.* exist, abide, breathe, draw breath, endure, last, fare.

livelihood *n.* employment, income, job, work, career, occupation, living, maintenance, means, subsistence, support.

liveliness *n.* vivacity, energy, vitality, animation, gaiety, verve, spirit, boisterousness, activity, briskness.

lively *adj.* vivacious, active, alert, animated, dynamic, busy, bustling, cheerful, frisky, exciting, spirited; *ant.* listless, lethargic.

liven up *v.* vitalize, enliven, vivify, energize, animate, rouse, stir up, brighten.

live wire (*slang*) go-getter, dynamo, self-starter, hustler.

livid *adj.* 1. angry, enraged, incensed, fuming, furious, exasperated, beside oneself. 2. bruised, contused, discolored.

living *adj.* alive, animated, breathing, existing, vital, vigorous, active; *ant.* dead, deceased.

load *n.* 1. burden, encumbrance, cargo, freight, goods, haul, contents. 2. charge, responsibility, obligation.

load *v.* 1. place, store, stuff, stow, pile, heap, cram, fill, encumber, pack, pile, stack. 2. burden, weigh down, oppress, strain, overwhelm, pressure.

loaded (*slang*) *adj.* 1. wealthy, rich, affluent, moneyed, well-heeled, well-off, well-to-do. 2. intoxicated, drunk, tipsy, under the influence, drugged.

loads (*slang*) *adj.* a lot, many, much, numerous, heaps (*slang*), lots.

loaf *v.* idle, laze, lounge, loiter, loll, take it easy.

loafer *n.* idler, bum, shirker, ne'er-do-well, lazybones, beachcomber, goldbricker (*slang*).

loan *n.* advance, credit, allowance.

loan *v.* lend, advance, entrust, allow.

loath *adj.* averse, indisposed, remiss, disinclined, unwilling, resistant, reluctant; *ant.* eager, willing.

loathe *v.* hate, despise, detest, abhor, abominate, dislike, execrate; *ant.* like, appreciate.

loathing *n.* hatred, revulsion, detestation, repulsion, disgust, abhorrence, aversion, repugnance, execration, horror, antipathy.

loathsome *adj.* abhorrent, detestable, execrable, hateful, horrible, vile, abominable, obnoxious, disgusting, nauseating, offensive, repellent; *ant.* attractive, pleasant.

lob *v.* toss, fling, loft, pitch, throw, heave, chuck.

lobby *n.* anteroom, vestibule, entrance way, hall, hallway, passage, porch.

lobby *v.* campaign for, promote, persuade, press for, pressure, demand, influence, pull strings, call for.

local *n.* native, resident, inhabitant, yokel, denizen, aborigine.

local *adj.* regional, nearby, neighborhood, community, confined, limited, restricted, autochthonous.

locale *n.* area, location, locality, position, scene, spot, zone, place.

locality *n.* district, section, sector, position, place, site.

localize *v.* pinpoint, assign, ascribe, circumscribe, concentrate, confine, contain, limit, restrain, restrict.

locate *v.* 1. find, detect, discover, pinpoint, place, track down, fix, identify, establish. 2. settle, establish oneself, inhabit.

location *n.* locale, locus, site, place, bearings, spot, venue.

lock *n.* **1.** bolt, clasp, fastening, padlock, catch, hook, clamp. **2.** (piece of hair) ringlet, tuft, tress, twist, plait, braid.

lock *v.* bolt, bar, clasp, fasten, join, link, enmesh, engage.

lockup *n.* prison, jail, holding area, penitentiary, *slang:* pen, can, brig, pokey.

locomotion *n.* movement, motion, action, ambulation, progress, travel.

locution *n.* accent, inflection, intonation, articulation, diction, expression, idiom, phrasing, term.

lodge *n.* inn, hotel, motel, abode, dormitory.

lodge *v.* **1.** catch, stick, abide, stay. **2.** board, quarter, put up, billet.

lodger *n.* boarder, tenant, resident, guest, renter, inmate.

lodging *n.* quarters, accommodation, billet, residence, rooms, shelter, abode, dwelling.

lofty *adj.* **1.** high, exalted, elevated, sublime, dignified, distinguished, esteemed, grand, noble; *ant.* base, lofty. **2.** arrogant, disdainful, condescending, supercilious.

log *n.* **1.** timber, trunk, stump. **2.** record, diary, journal, account, chart, daybook, tally.

logic *n.* reasoning, rationale, argumentation, deduction, dialectic, reason, sense.

logical *adj.* rational, cogent, coherent, well-founded, plausible, reasonable, sensible, sound, valid; *ant.* irrational.

logistics *n.* organization, planning, orchestration, management, engineering, masterminding, strategy.

loiter *v.* loaf, idle, loll, hang out (*slang*), dally, dawdle, delay, lag, linger.

loll *v.* **1.** lounge, loaf, recline, hang around. **2.** droop, hang, dangle, drop, lean.

lollipop *n.* sucker, sweet, confection, candy.

lone *adj.* alone, solitary, single; lonesome, deserted.

loneliness *n.* aloneness, isolation, seclusion, solitude, segregation, desolation, friendlessness.

lonely *adj.* lonesome, forlorn, forsaken, alone, companionless, deserted, desolate, secluded, isolated.

loner *n.* individualist, maverick, lone wolf, outsider, hermit, pariah, recluse.

lonesome *adj.* lonely, forlorn, forsaken, alone, companionless, deserted, desolate, secluded, isolated.

long *v.* desire, pine, wish, hanker, yearn.

long *adj.* elongated, extended, protracted, stretched, extensive, sustained; interminable, dragging, prolonged; *ant.* short, fleeting.

as long as assuming, provided, supposing, on condition that, with the provision that.

longevity *n.* endurance, perpetuity, durability, persistence, continuance, survival.

long-drawn-out *adj.* interminable, protracted, tedious, prolix, lengthy, marathon, overextended, prolonged.

longing *n.* yearning, wish, desire, hungering, ambition, craving, coveting, hankering, yen.

longing *adj.* wanting, desirous, ravenous, ardent, avid.

long-lasting *adj.* enduring, entrenched, established, long-lived, durable, abiding, continuing, unchanging; *ant.* brief, transient, fleeting.

long-lived *adj.* durable, enduring, lasting.

long-standing *adj.* established, fixed, time-honored, traditional.

long-suffering *adj.* forbearing, tolerant, patient, stoic, resigned.

long-winded *adj.* verbose, wordy, garrulous, discursive, lengthy, prolix, prolonged, tedious, repetitive; *ant.* terse.

look *v.* **1.** (have the appearance of) appear, display, seem, resemble. **2.** observe, survey, behold, peer, stare, eyeball (*slang*), gawk, scrutinize, study, take a gander (*slang*).

look down on disparage, belittle, despise, disdain, scorn; dismiss, patronize.

look into investigate, examine, study, probe.

look out watch out, be careful, pay attention, notice, take care, take heed, heads up (*slang*).

look *n.* **1.** appearance, aspect, bearing, countenance, air, presence, mien, semblance. **2.** stare, survey, glimpse, examination.

look-alike *n.* replica, clone, double, dead ringer (*slang*), spitting image, doppelgänger.

lookout *n.* **1.** observation tower, lighthouse, observatory, post, watchtower. **2.** view, panorama, outlook, prospect.

loom *v.* overshadow, threaten, menace, hang over, hover, impend, rise, tower, take shape, appear.

loop *n.* curve, hoop, coil, ring, arc, bend, circle, spiral, convolution, turn, whorl, twirl.

loop *v.* bend, twist, braid, circle, connect, curl, curve round, encircle, spiral, turn.

loophole *n.* **1.** excuse, pretense, pretext, evasion, subterfuge, escape. **2.** aperture, opening, slot, avenue, gap.

loose *adj.* **1.** unbound, unfettered, free, floating, movable, released, unconfined, unrestricted. **2.** (as of language or reasoning) vague, diffuse, imprecise, ill-defined, indefinite, inaccurate, sloppy; *ant.* strict, exact. **3.** wanton, promiscuous, lax, debauched, imprudent, lewd; *ant.* chaste. **4.** (said of an action or behavior) careless, thoughtless, rash, ill-considered, precipitate, hasty. **on the loose** free, wild, unrestricted, unconfined, running free.

loosen *v.* **1.** (become loose) slacken, relax, unravel, separate. **2.** (cause to be loose or free) detach, set free, let go, let out, liberate, untie, slacken, unfasten.

loot *n.* booty, spoils, goods, haul, prize, cache.

loot *v.* ransack, pillage, plunder, maraud, raid, despoil, ravage, burglarize, rob.

lop *v.* shorten, trim, clip, cut, prune, chop, truncate, curtail.

lope *v.* gallop, run, bound, canter, stride, spring.

lopsided *adj.* tilted, uneven, off balance, askew, crooked, awry, cockeyed, disproportionate, asymmetrical, warped.

loquacious *adj.* chatty, garrulous, talkative, verbose, long-minded, prolix, wordy, babbling.

loquacity *n.* garrulity, talkativeness, effusiveness, chattiness.

lore *n.* teachings, beliefs, doctrine, erudition, knowledge, wisdom, myths, traditions, sayings, letters.

lose *v.* **1.** misplace, mislay, forget; miss, be deprived of, forfeit; *ant.* find. **2.** be defeated, fail, capitulate, give up, succumb; *ant.* win.

loser *n.* failure, flop, sufferer, underdog.

loss *n.* defeat, forfeiture, failure, debt, deficiency, misfortune, bereavement, privation, damage.

at a loss unsure, confused, puzzled, undecided, perplexed, baffled, stumped, stuck.

lost *adj.* **1.** misplaced, mislaid, missing, hidden, obscured, forfeited. **2.** perplexed, baffled, bewildered, confused. **3.** demolished, destroyed, devastated, wasted, ruined.

lot *n.* **1.** parcel, part, division, patch, clearing, plot, acreage. **2.** group, batch, set, order. **3.** fate, destiny, accident, doom, fortune.

lotion *n.* emollient, balm, cream, liniment, salve, solution.

lots *adj.* a lot, many, much, an abundance, a great deal, oodles (*slang*).

lottery *n.* drawing, raffle, sweepstake, gamble, venture.

loud *adj.* **1.** blaring, deafening, ear-piercing, ear-splitting, resounding, raucous, stentorian, noisy, vocal, strident. **2.** flashy, brazen, ostentatious, showy, tawdry.

loudspeaker *n.* amplifier, public address system, tweeter, woofer, bullhorn.

lounge *n.* **1.** couch, divan, davenport. **2.** parlor, lobby, reception room, club, bar.

lounge *v.* relax, take it easy, loaf, loll, idle.

lousy *adj.* poor, awful, bad, miserable, shoddy, inferior, terrible, base, contemptible, despicable, mean, rotten.

lout *n.* boor, clod, dolt, yahoo, churl.

lovable *adj.* endearing, adorable, amiable, attractive, captivating, enchanting, winning, charming, delightful, engaging, fetching.

love *n.* adoration, adulation, devotion, fondness, affection, attachment, delight; *ant.* hatred, aversion.

for love or money under any circumstances, by any means, for anything, ever.

make love copulate, sleep with, go to bed with, screw (*slang*).

love *v.* adore, cherish, delight in, dote on, prize, adulate, idolize, worship, treasure; *ant.* dislike.

loveless *adj.* **1.** unloved, forsaken, lovelorn. **2.** hard, insensitive, frigid, coldhearted, unfeeling; *ant.* warm, loving.

loveliness *n.* beauty, appeal, charm, grace, attractiveness.

lovely *adj.* beautiful, exquisite, comely, pretty, attractive; pleasing, charming, captivating, engaging, delightful, graceful.

lover *n.* paramour, boyfriend, girlfriend, beau, admirer, beloved, suitor, swain, significant other.

lovesick *adj.* longing, languishing, pining, yearning, desiring, infatuated.

loving *adj.* affectionate, solicitous, amorous, passionate, demonstrative, warmhearted, devoted, friendly, fond; *ant.* cold, indifferent.

low *adj.* **1.** flat, squat, level, low-lying, prostrate, crouched, knee-high; *ant.* raised. **2.** muffled, soft, hushed, quiet; *ant.* loud, blaring. **3.** dejected, unhappy, dispirited, moody, downcast, down, blue; *ant.* cheerful, upbeat. **4.** vulgar, base, mean, cheap, coarse, contemptible, crude, degraded, scurvy; *ant.* noble, lofty.

lowbrow *adj.* crude, ignorant, plebeian, uncultured, rude, uneducated, unlearned, unrefined, philistine; *ant.* highbrow, intellectual.

lowdown (*slang*) *n.* information, facts, inside story, scoop, dope, info (*slang*).

lower *v.* **1.** scale down, decrease, downgrade, curtail; *ant.* increase. **2.** (reduce in esteem, respect, etc.) belittle, condescend, humiliate, degrade, devalue, debase, demote.

lower *adj.* inferior, lesser, minor, subordinate, subservient, junior, secondary.

lowering *adj.* threatening, menacing, ominous.

lowest *adj.* shortest, littlest, smallest, slightest, base, ground.

low-grade *adj.* inferior, substandard, second-rate, cheap, poor, second-class.

low-key *adj.* muffled, quiet, soft, muted, subdued, understated, restrained.

lowly *adj.* **1.** (low in status) ignoble, inferior, subordinate, proletarian. **2.** humble, meek, mild, submissive; *ant.* haughty, proud. **3.** or dinary, commonplace, average, plebeian, mean, plain, unpretentious; *ant.* superior.

loyal *adj.* faithful, trustworthy, true, staunch, steadfast, honest, constant, dependable, devoted, true-blue, unwavering.

loyalty *n.* allegiance, fidelity, faithfulness, dependability, devotion, honesty, reliability, steadfastness, constancy, patriotism.

lubricant *n.* ointment, grease, oil, lotion, salve.

lubricate *v.* grease, oil, smear, wax.

lucid *adj.* **1.** clear, comprehensible, understandable, accessible, plain, intelligible, distinct, clear-cut, transparent, manifest. **2.** sane, clearheaded, rational. **3.** bright, shining, brilliant, radiant, resplendent.

luck *n.* fate, destiny, chance, fortune, prosperity, happenstance, accident, fluke.

luckless *adj.* cursed, hapless, jinxed, doomed, star-crossed, calamitous, catastrophic; *ant.* fortunate.

lucky *adj.* happy, fortuitous, serendipitous, opportune, propitious, advantageous, auspicious; charmed, favored, blessed.

lucrative *adj.* profitable, productive, gainful, fruitful, worthwhile, money-making.

ludicrous *adj.* ridiculous, absurd, crazy, farcical, laughable, outlandish, silly, comic, droll.

lug *v.* carry, tote, tow, drag, heave, pull.

luggage *n.* baggage, bags, suitcases, gear, impediments, things.

lugubrious *adj.* morose, funereal, woeful, melancholy, somber, saturnine, dreary, gloomy, glum.

lukewarm *adj.* indifferent, apathetic, cool, ambivalent, aloof, phlegmatic, unenthusiastic, halfhearted, unresponsive; *ant.* enthusiastic.

lull *n.* pause, respite, letup, calm, silence, hush, quiet, peace, tranquillity, stillness.

lumber *n.* timber, wood, logs, boards, hardwood.

lumber *v.* plod, trudge, waddle, shuffle.

luminary *n.* star, celebrity, dignitary, leader, notable, personage, superstar, VIP.

luminescent *adj.* radiant, shining, luminous, glowing, bright.

luminous *adj.* radiant, lustrous, brilliant, resplendent, bright, glowing, lit; *ant.* dim.

lump *n.* growth, protuberance, protrusion, swelling, mass, bump, cyst.

lumpy *adj.* bumpy, nodulous, clotted; *ant.* smooth.

lunacy *n.* craziness, dementia, insanity, madness, mania, psychosis, idiocy, imbecility, absurdity, folly, foolishness.

lunatic *n.* madman, maniac, psychopath, nut (*slang*).

lunge *n.* pass, swipe, jab, cut.

lunge *v.* charge, bound, plunge, strike, poke, stab at, thrust, pounce, set upon.

lurch *v.* pitch, stagger, stumble, reel, totter, weave, lean, list, tilt.

lure *n.* trap, snare, bait, decoy, fake.

lure *v.* entice, allure, seduce, tempt, lead on, draw, invite, beckon; *ant.* repel.

lurid *adj.* graphic, startling, shocking, sensational, bloody, gory.

lurk *v.* prowl, sneak, crouch, skulk, slink, hide.

luscious *adj.* delicious, appetizing, delectable, sumptuous, succulent, juicy, rich, tasty.

lush *adj.* luxuriant, opulent, abundant, dense, elaborate, flourishing, overgrown, sumptuous; *ant.* sparse.

lust *n.* appetite, desire, craving, avidity, carnality, greed, passion, lasciviousness, licentiousness, prurience.

lust *v.* desire, want, crave, thirst for, yearn for, have a yen for.

luster *n.* radiance, glow, brilliance, luminosity, brightness; *ant.* dullness.

lustful *adj.* passionate, sensual, libidinous, carnal, craving, licentious; *ant.* cold, frigid.

lustrous *adj.* burnished, gleaming, luminous, radiant, bright, glossy.

lusty *adj.* robust, vigorous, hearty, red-blooded, blooming, brawny, energetic, hale, rugged, stalwart; *ant.* feeble.

luxuriant *adj.* lavish, baroque, profuse, fecund, abundant, rich, copious, ample.

luxuriate *v.* delight, enjoy, relish, indulge, bask, revel; flourish, abound, bloom, grow, thrive.

luxurious *adj.* lavish, opulent, deluxe, plush, sensual, rich, expensive; *ant.* spare, austere.

luxury *n.* opulence, comfort, affluence, richness, extra, frill, hedonism.

lynch *v.* hang, string up, kill, murder.

lyric *n.* 1. text, words, verse. 2. ode, sonnet, poem, hymn, poetry, song, verse.

lyrical *adj.* melodious, musical, rhythmical, poetic, expressive, emotional.

macabre *adj.* grim, horrible, morbid, ghastly, grisly, sick, eerie, gruesome, ghoulish.

macerate *v.* soften, mash, tear, chop, chew, pulp, soak.

machinate *v.* plot, scheme, design, conspire, devise, plan, maneuver, contrive.

machine *n.* **1.** apparatus, device, implement, contraption, gadget, mechanism, tool, gizmo (*slang*). **2.** organization, institution, bureaucracy, administration, movement, agency, party, *slang:* ring, setup.

machinery *n.* **1.** appliances, equipment, tools, gear, instruments. **2.** means, devices, contrivances, mechanism, organization, system.

macrocosm *n.* universe, cosmos, whole, totality, nature.

mad *adj.* **1.** insane, demented, deranged, psychotic, crazed, delirious, raving, unbalanced, unstable, daft, *slang:* nuts, bonkers, bananas, batty, having bats in the belfry, off one's rocker, around the bend; *ant.* rational, sane. **2.** incensed, furious, enraged, livid, wrathful, fuming, angry, irate. **3.** distraught, frenetic, frantic, agitated; *ant.* calm, clearheaded.

madcap *adj.* foolish, foolhardy, imprudent, impulsive, rash, reckless, *slang:* birdbrained, harebrained.

madden *v.* infuriate, enrage, incense, inflame, provoke, anger, vex, craze, upset; *ant.* calm, pacify.

made-up *adj.* fictitious, fabricated, staged, imaginary, false, concocted, untrue, trumped-up.

madhouse *n.* **1.** mental hospital, asylum, sanitarium, bedlam, *slang:* nut house, loony bin, funny farm. **2.** chaos, pandemonium, bedlam, commotion, uproar, disorder.

madly *adv.* **1.** irrationally, insanely, crazily, psychotically, deliriously, dementedly, nonsensically, rabidly. **2.** (without control) wildly, furiously, fanatically, frantically, desperately, passionately, rashly, hastily, violently.

madman *n.* lunatic, maniac, mental case, psychopath, psychotic, *slang:* nut, loony, schizo, screwball, psycho, cuckoo.

madness *n.* insanity, lunacy, derangement, delusion, craziness, aberration, raving.

maelstrom *n.* **1.** whirlpool, vortex, Charybdis. **2.** commotion, pandemonium, chaos, bedlam, turmoil, confusion, disorder, tumult, uproar.

maestro *n.* master, virtuoso, conductor, composer, teacher.

magazine *n.* **1.** armory, arsenal, ammunition storehouse, cache, depot, ordnance. **2.** periodical, serial, journal, review, monthly, weekly, quarterly, manual, brochure, pamphlet, circular, mag (*slang*).

magic *n.* sorcery, witchcraft, black magic, alchemy, hocus-pocus, enchantment, incantation, necromancy, wizardry, occultism, black art, voodooism.

magical *adj.* **1.** sorcerous, wizardly, witchlike, necromantic, diabolic, satanic, demonic, mystic, occult. **2.** enchanting, miraculous, fantastic, wondrous, beguiling, bewitching, mysterious, transcendent.

magician *n.* illusionist, enchanter, necromancer, conjurer, sorcerer, wizard, seer, soothsayer, diviner, warlock, witch doctor, shaman.

magisterial *adj.* **1.** authoritative, official, judicial, masterful, lordly, impressive, regal, commanding. **2.** domineering, imperious, overbearing, arrogant, highhanded.

magistrate *n.* justice, judge, official, tribune, justice of the peace, JP.

magnanimity *n.* benevolence, generosity, altruism, unselfishness, charity, munificence, open-handedness, largesse; *ant.* meanness.

magnanimous *adj.* generous, kind, unselfish,

altruistic, beneficent, charitable, philanthropic; *ant.* mean, paltry, petty.

magnate *n.* industrialist, tycoon, mogul, businessman, financier, capitalist, captain of industry, big cheese (*slang*), bigwig, fat cat (*slang*), VIP.

magnetic *adj.* charismatic, captivating, alluring, charming, enchanting, entrancing, irresistible, seductive; *ant.* repellent, repugnant.

magnetism *n.* charisma, attraction, charm, lure, power, pull, seductiveness, draw, influence.

magnification *n.* enlargement, amplification, enhancement, expansion, augmentation, intensification, exaggeration, inflation; *ant.* reduction, diminution.

magnificence *n.* grandeur, majesty, glory, radiance, pomp, splendor, ostentation, lavishness, resplendence, impressiveness; sublimity, stateliness; *ant.* modesty, plainness.

magnificent *adj.* **1.** exalted, elevated, noble, stately, august, grand, great, sublime; *ant.* humble, modest. **2.** gorgeous, radiant, glittering, elegant, lavish, luxurious, opulent, resplendent, rich; *ant.* plain, simple.

magnify *v.* **1.** (make larger) amplify, enlarge, expand, increase, augment, boost, enhance, inflate, blow up; *ant.* diminish. **2.** overstate, exaggerate, embroider, aggrandize, dramatize, overdo; *ant.* belittle, play down.

magniloquent *adj.* pompous, grandiose, pretentious, bombastic, overblown, turgid, lofty, high-sounding; *ant.* simple, straightforward.

magnitude *n.* **1.** dimension, extent, size, breadth, measure, amplitude, bulk, capacity, expanse, mass, volume, weight, proportion. **2.** importance, consequence, significance, moment, degree, greatness, eminence, grandeur.

magnum opus masterpiece, master work, piece de résistance, chef d'oeuvre.

maid *n.* **1.** domestic, housekeeper, housemaid, cleaning woman, chambermaid, barmaid, maidservant, dresser, femme de chambre, handmaiden. **2.** girl, maiden, child, lass.

maiden *n.* virgin, girl, damsel, lass, miss, nymph.

maiden *adj.* **1.** earliest, beginning, virgin, first, inaugural, initial, new. **2.** pure, chaste, undefiled, virginal, unmarried; untapped, untried, unused; *ant.* defiled, deflowered.

maidenhood *n.* innocence, purity, virginity, chastity.

maidenly *adj.* feminine, girlish; chaste, demure, vestal, virtuous, reserved, proper; *ant.* immodest.

mail *n.* letter, post, communication, correspondence, parcel.

mail *v.* send, post, dispatch, forward.

maim *v.* mutilate, mangle, cripple, dismember, disfigure, deface; *ant.* heal, repair.

main *n.* pipe, conduit, trough, channel, duct, line.

main *adj.* principal, chief, foremost, leading, cardinal, central, preeminent, primary, essential, vital, crucial; *ant.* minor.

mainly *adv.* chiefly, largely, essentially, as a rule, for the most part, generally, predominantly.

mainspring *n.* heart, root, driving force, motive, source, wellspring.

mainstay *n.* pillar, support, anchor, bulwark, linchpin, backbone, strength.

mainstream *adj.* conventional, orthodox, accepted, established, normal, standard, average; *ant.* heterodox, peripheral.

maintain *v.* **1.** (be a proponent of) uphold, sustain, support, champion, vindicate, stand by, fight for, defend; *ant.* oppose. **2.** assert, attest, declare, avow, hold, contend, allege, claim, insist, profess; *ant.* deny. **3.** (keep in good condition) care for, nurture, preserve, keep, conserve; *ant.* neglect. **4.** (keep in safekeeping) reserve, cache, husband, store, put away. **5.** (keep observing as a tradition) continue, preserve, persevere, carry on, perpetuate; *ant.* abandon, discontinue.

maintenance *n.* **1.** preservation, upkeep, support; *ant.* neglect. **2.** subsistence, sustenance, livelihood, resources, upkeep.

majestic *adj.* grand, lofty, dignified, exalted, august, magisterial, noble, lofty, regal, sublime; *ant.* mean.

majesty *n.* **1.** grandeur, nobility, greatness, augustness, dignity, glory, loftiness, resplendence, splendor. **2.** sovereignty, divine right, supremacy, power, pomp, regalness, royalty.

major *adj.* **1.** greater, higher, larger, superior, primary, main, leading, preeminent, principal, chief, supreme, uppermost. **2.** important, critical, crucial, grave, key, vital; *ant.* minor.

majority *n.* preponderance, bulk, mass, plurality, greater number; *ant.* minority.

make *n.* brand, kind, manufacture, model, style, type, sort, variety, build, composition, shape.

make *v.* **1.** manufacture, construct, produce, build, assemble, compose, fabricate, create, fashion, forge, mold, conceive; *ant.* dismantle. **2.** add up to, total, amount to, come to, equal. **3.** force, coerce, impel, compel, prevail upon, require. **4.** (arrive at a goal) reach, accomplish, attain, do, carry out, execute, get, obtain, gain, secure, acquire, win; *ant.* lose, fail.

make do cope, survive, endure, manage, muddle through, scrape by, get by.

make for head toward, aim for, approach.

make it prosper, succeed, arrive, reach, pull through.

make like pretend, feign, simulate, fake (*slang*).

make off leave, depart, run, go, abscond, bolt, decamp, flee, run away, run for it, run off, clear out, beat a hasty retreat, take to one's heels.

make out **1.** understand, comprehend, recognize, decipher, discern, distinguish, fathom, grasp, realize, see, perceive. **2.** succeed, achieve, accomplish, prosper, thrive, fare well; *ant.* fail. **3.** discern, espy, perceive, detect, see, distinguish.

make up **1.** create, coin, devise, fabricate, invent, formulate, concoct, imagine, feign, dream up, cook up, trump up, hatch. **2.** make peace, come to terms, settle, bury the hatchet, forgive and forget, mend one's fences, shake hands.

make up for offset, compensate, balance, atone for, expiate, recompense, redeem, redress, requite.

make-believe *n.* fantasy, charade, pretense, sham, fairy tale, dream, fancy; *ant.* reality.

maker *n.* creator, God, producer, author, inventor, architect, begetter, contriver, manufacturer, producer, constructor.

makeshift *adj.* temporary, stopgap, improvised, provisional, band-aid, jerry-rigged.

makeup *n.* **1.** cosmetics, paint, grease paint. **2.** composition, arrangement, structure, substance, layout, configuration, construction,

style; nature, disposition, constitution, character.

makings *n.* capability, potential, capacity, possibilities, qualities, promise, beginnings; ingredients, materials.

maladjusted *adj.* disturbed, unstable, confused, neurotic, estranged, alienated, hung-up (*slang*).

maladroit *adj.* awkward, inept, bungling, graceless, clumsy, inelegant, ham-handed; *ant.* graceful.

malady *n.* ailment, sickness, illness, disease, affliction, disorder, infirmity, malaise, affection.

malaise *n.* despair, depression, angst, anguish, anxiety, doldrums, melancholy, uneasiness; *ant.* happiness.

malcontent *adj.* rebellious, unruly, factious, disgruntled, unhappy, resentful, bellyaching.

malcontent *n.* complainer, bellyacher, grouser, agitator, dissenter, whistle-blower, rebel, troublemaker, mischief-maker.

malediction *n.* **1.** curse, damnation, imprecation, execration, anathema; *ant.* blessing. **2.** slander, denunciation; *ant.* praise.

malefactor *n.* wrongdoer, evildoer, transgressor, villain, delinquent, miscreant, offender.

maleficent *adj.* harmful, hurtful, evil, pernicious, injurious, detrimental, destructive; *ant.* beneficent, harmless.

malevolence *n.* enmity, ill will, malice, resentment, bitterness, hatred, hate, rancor, spite, venom, viciousness.

malevolent *adj.* malicious, evil, wicked, vicious, rancorous, spiteful, bitter, vindictive, venomous; *ant.* benevolent.

malfunction *v.* fail, break down, go wrong.

malfunction *n.* failure, breakdown, defect, fault, flaw, glitch.

malice *n.* spite, rancor, animosity, animus, hostility, bitterness, umbrage, acerbity, venom, spleen, vindictiveness; *ant.* kindness.

malicious *adj.* spiteful, vengeful, vindictive, pernicious, hateful, vicious, baleful, catty; *ant.* benevolent, well-meaning.

malign *v.* slander, insult, defame, denigrate, disparage, vilify, smear, badmouth, libel, scandalize, blacken the name of; *ant.* praise.

malign *adj.* hurtful, noxious, baneful, sinister, evil, hostile, malevolent, pernicious, vicious; *ant.* benign.

malignant *adj.* **1.** diseased, cancerous, fatal, lethal, poisonous, deadly, mortal, pestilential, cankered, virulent, corrupt; *ant.* benign. **2.** hostile, malicious, vicious, evil; *ant.* kind, harmless.

malingerer *n.* loafer, slacker, shirker, dodger.

malleable *adj.* pliant, flexible, soft, workable, adaptable, impressionable, tractable, ductile; manageable, compliant, docile.

malnutrition *n.* hunger, starvation, undernourishment; *ant.* nourishment.

malodorous *adj.* stinking, rancid, rank, fetid, mephitic, noisome, putrid, reeking, smelly, miasmal, offensive, nauseating.

malpractice *n.* negligence, neglect, carelessness, misconduct, mismanagement, transgression, misbehavior.

maltreat *v.* abuse, hurt, injure, damage, harm, bully ; *ant.* care for.

mammoth *adj.* gigantic, immense, enormous, colossal, formidable, massive, monumental, prodigious, stupendous, leviathan, elephantine, titanic; *ant.* small, diminutive.

man *n.* Homo sapiens, mankind, humankind, humanity, human beings, mortals.
be one's own man be free, be independent, stand alone.

man in the street John Doe, average Joe, Everyman, John Q. Public.
to a man everybody, all, everyone, with no exception.

manacle *v.* bind, chain, fetter, handcuff, shackle, restrain; check, hamper, inhibit; *ant.* unshackle.

manacles *n.* handcuffs, irons, fetters, chains, shackles, bonds.

manage *v.* **1.** direct, lead, oversee, rule, run, handle, supervise, administer, superintend, officiate, govern. **2.** contrive, accomplish, effect, bring about, achieve, succeed, engineer; *ant.* fail. **3.** survive, endure, scrape by, carry on, cope, make do, muddle through.

manageable *adj.* docile, controllable, governable, tractable, obedient, amenable, submissive, pliant, yielding, malleable.

management *n.* **1.** supervision, direction, con-

trol, charge, care, command, governance, administration, operation. **2.** administrators, directors, executives, superintendents, board, bosses, employers, managers, supervisors.

manager *n.* administrator, supervisor, director, superintendent, boss, comptroller, executive, overseer.

mandate *n.* decree, command, order, directive, edict, injunction, precept, behest, sanction, warrant.

mandatory *adj.* compulsory, imperative, obligatory, binding, requisite, necessary, required; *ant.* optional.

maneuver *n.* stratagem, plan, tactics, ploy, subterfuge, trick, ruse; procedure, movement.

maneuver *v.* plot, contrive, devise, design, scheme, trick, cheat, conspire.

mangle *v.* mutilate, maul, twist, maim, deform, disfigure, distort, crush.

mangy *adj.* scabby, rash-ridden; dirty, motheaten, shabby, squalid, seedy, scruffy, mean, ratty (*slang*).

manhandle *v.* mistreat, push, shove, rough up, maul, paw.

man-hater *n.* misanthropist, misanthrope, eremite.

manhood *n.* **1.** adulthood, maturity, postpubescence, majority, coming of age. **2.** virility, machismo, valor, honor, bravery, courage, gallantry, chivalry.

mania *n.* craziness, lunacy, madness, derangement, delirium, dementia, fetish, fixation, obsession, compulsion.

maniac *n.* madman, lunatic, psychopath, fiend.

maniacal *adj.* insane, raving, mad, deranged.

manic *adj.* **1.** overexcited, agitated, hyperactive, overactive; berserk, crazed, deranged, demented, lunatic, mad, psychotic, raving, unbalanced, unhinged. **2.** excited, exhilarated, elated, high (*slang*); *ant.* depressed.

manifest *v.* display, show, exhibit, disclose, reveal, demonstrate, prove, establish, illustrate; *ant.* hide.

manifest *adj.* clear, visible, apparent, patent, plain, conspicuous, distinct, evident, glaring, salient, obvious, palpable, unmistakable, noticeable; *ant.* unclear, obscure.

manifestation *n.* indication, sign, symptom,

display, expression, materialization, revelation, exhibition, phenomenon.

manifesto *n.* decree, proclamation, announcement, platform, policy, pronunciamento.

manifold *adj.* various, numerous, diverse, assorted, multifarious, multiple, multitudinous.

manipulate *v.* form, shape, mold, ply; maneuver, control, guide, direct, engineer; influence.

mankind *n.* humanity, human race, Homo sapiens, society, people, fellowmen.

manliness *n.* masculinity, virility, machismo, valor, chivalry, bravery, fearlessness.

manly *adj.* masculine, stalwart, valiant, strong, strapping, powerful, robust; *ant.* timid.

man-made *adj.* manufactured, fabricated, synthetic, artificial, imitation, simulated; *ant.* natural.

manna *n.* bread, food, nourishment, sustenance, subsistence.

manner *n.* 1. mien, behavior, deportment, demeanor, style, air, appearance, bearing, conduct, deportment, presence. 2. method, practice, custom, habit, way, procedure, process, means.

mannered *adj.* affected, self-conscious, posed, posturing, pretentious, pseudo, stilted, put-on; *ant.* natural.

mannerism *n.* characteristic, quirk, idiosyncrasy, peculiarity, foible, habit, trait, pretension, peccadillo, oddity.

mannerly *adj.* polite, civilized, considerate, civil, courteous, deferential, gracious, genteel, ladylike, refined, well-bred; *ant.* rude, vulgar.

manners *n.* etiquette, social graces, politeness, proprieties, protocol, mores, urbanities, courtesy, decorum, formalities; *ant.* impoliteness.

mannish *adj.* masculine, unfeminine, unladylike, unwomanly, virilescent, butch (*slang*); *ant.* feminine.

man-of-war *n.* warship, battleship, destroyer, naval vessel.

manor *n.* estate, mansion, hotel, hall.

manservant *n.* valet, steward, attendant, butler, valet-de-chambre.

mansion *n.* estate, villa, hall, castle, chateau, manor house.

mantle *n.* veil, wrap, cloak, shawl, cape, shroud, pall, pelisse.

manual *n.* guidebook, reference book, handbook, instructions, primer, companion, bible (*slang*).

manufacture *n.* making, creation, assembly, fashioning, forming, construction, formation, mass production.

manufacture *v.* fabricate, produce, turn out, construct, form, fashion, assemble, build, create, forge, concoct, turn out, put together.

manufacturer *n.* producer, fabricator, constructor, builder, industrialist, maker, craftsman.

manure *n.* dung, fertilizer, compost, droppings.

manuscript *n.* text, composition, original, typescript, hard copy.

many *adj.* abundant, countless, numerous, sundry, plentiful, divers, multifarious, multitudinous, *slang:* galore, umpteen; *ant.* few, meager, scanty.

map *n.* delineation, atlas; chart, graph, plan, plot.

put on the map establish, bring fame to, make famous, glorify, make (*slang*).

map *v.* plan, outline, draft, plot, chart.

mar *v.* harm, hurt, injure, damage, deform, disfigure, ruin, spoil, scar, sully, taint, tarnish; *ant.* enhance.

maraud *v.* plunder, pillage, loot, raid, ransack, ravage, sack, depredate, despoil.

marauder *n.* raider, pillager, plunderer, ravager, brigand, robber, thief, bandit, outlaw, pirate, buccaneer.

march *n.* progression, movement, advance, walk, trek, hike, stride, step; procession, parade, demonstration.

march *v.* move, advance, proceed, forge ahead, patrol, walk, promenade, strut, stride, tramp, tread, parade; *ant.* halt, retreat.

margin *n.* 1. boundary, edge, border, limit, perimeter, periphery, brim, rim, brink, confine; *ant.* center, core. 2. allowance, latitude, leeway, play, room, space, surplus.

marginal *adj.* bordering, peripheral, rimming, edging, verging, borderline; doubtful.

marijuana *n.* cannabis, hemp, hashish, ganja, THC, *slang:* dope, grass, pot, weed, tea, maryjane, hash.

marina *n.* dock, harbor, mooring, port.

marine *adj.* maritime, nautical, naval, oceanic, oceangoing, seafaring, seagoing.

mariner *n.* sailor, seaman, seafarer, navigator, deckhand, sea dog, salt, bluejacket.

marital *adj.* conjugal, married, wedded, matrimonial, nuptial, connubial.

maritime *adj.* **1.** seaside, seashore, oceanic, coastal; *ant.* inland, hinterland. **2.** naval, nautical, marine, seagoing, seafaring, aquatic, pelagic, Neptunian, hydrographic.

mark *n.* **1.** spot, blemish, nick, pock, scar, bruise, scratch, blotch, splotch, stain; stamp, brand, imprint, impression, check. **2.** target, bull's eye, aim, goal, objective, prey. **3.** (a graphic representation) symbol, emblem, sign, token, distinction, earmark, label, seal, stamp. **4.** trait, characteristic, character, idiosyncrasy, indication, hallmark, particularity.

hit the mark succeed, achieve, accomplish, do well.

make one's mark prosper, succeed, make good, make the big time, be somebody; *ant.* fail.

miss the mark fail, err, be mistaken, be unsuccessful, be off base (*slang*).

mark *v.* **1.** brand, stamp, imprint, blaze, label, inscribe, seal, check off. **2.** (be a sign of) characterize, distinguish, qualify, indicate, earmark, signify, denote, designate.

marked *adj.* clear, conspicuous, distinct, evident, glaring, manifest, obvious, prominent, pronounced; *ant.* slight, unnoticeable.

market *v.* sell, vend, exchange, retail, barter, peddle, hawk.

marketable *adj.* sellable, sought after, wanted, in demand; commercial, retail, wholesale.

marksman *n.* sharpshooter, crack shot, sniper, rifleman.

markup *n.* increase, profit, margin, gross profit.

maroon *v.* abandon, desert, forsake, strand, cast away, put ashore.

marriage *n.* wedding, espousal, nuptials, sacrament, matrimony, conjugality, wedlock, wedded bliss, union, alliance, coupling; *ant.* divorce.

married *adj.* wedded, mated, espoused, united, hitched (*slang*); *ant.* single.

marrow *n.* essence, quintessence, heart, core, kernel, pith, quick, soul, nucleus.

marry *v.* **1.** wed, espouse, mate, tie the knot,

get hitched (*slang*); *ant.* divorce. **2.** unite, bond, join, link, merge, ally, unify.

marsh *n.* swamp, morass, bog, quagmire, bayou.

marshal *v.* lead, guide, direct, order, align, assemble, deploy, muster, shepherd.

marshy *adj.* swampy, boggy, moory, miry, quaggy, spongy, waterlogged, wet, damp; *ant.* solid.

martial *adj.* warlike, military, heroic, combative, bellicose; *ant.* pacific.

martyrdom *n.* sacrifice, suffering, persecution, torment, torture, agony, ordeal; *ant.* self-gratification, indulgence.

marvel *n.* wonder, miracle, phenomenon, spectacle; prodigy, whiz (*slang*).

marvel *v.* wonder, gape, stare, stand in awe, goggle.

marvelous *adj.* **1.** fabulous, wonderful, terrific, glorious, out of this world, spectacular, astonishing, amazing, incredible, phenomenal, beyond belief, miraculous, magical, extraordinary, fantastic; *ant.* ordinary.

mascot *n.* lucky charm, talisman, amulet.

masculine *adj.* virile, potent, hardy, macho, manly; *ant.* effeminate.

masculinity *n.* manhood, manliness, virility, potency.

mash *v.* crush, pulverize, squash, masticate, macerate, grind, pummel, beat.

mask *n.* disguise, cover, façade, front, guise, pretense, semblance, veneer, costume.

mask *v.* disguise, hide, conceal, cloak, cover, screen, shield, camouflage, veil, obscure.

masquerade *n.* **1.** costume ball, mask, mummery, Mardi Gras. **2.** pretense, deception, dissimulation, pose, disguise, imposture, screen, coverup, counterfeit.

masquerade *v.* disguise, mask, impersonate, pose, pretend, dissemble, dissimulate.

mass *n.* **1.** bulk, lump, chunk, heap, hunk, accumulation, aggregate. **2.** majority, plurality, crowd, entirety, group, horde, throng.

the masses *n.* the common people, the majority, the multitude, the people, the proletariat, the rank and file, the crowd.

mass *v.* assemble, congregate, crowd, muster, come together, rally, gather; *ant.* separate, disperse.

mass *adj.* comprehensive, general, sweeping, extensive, widespread, popular, blanket, across-the-board; *ant.* limited.

massacre *n.* carnage, killing, slaughter, butchery, murder, extermination, decimation, annihilation, blood bath.

massacre *v.* kill, murder, exterminate, annihilate, decimate, slaughter, slay, wipe out.

massage *n.* rubdown, rubbing, manipulation.

massage *v.* stimulate, caress, knead, manipulate, rub down.

massive *adj.* huge, colossal, immense, gargantuan, hulking, titanic, imposing, extensive, substantial, vast, whopping; *ant.* slight, small.

master *n.* 1. chief, leader, governor, ruler, director, lord, overseer, boss, commander; *ant.* servant, underling, subject. 2. instructor, teacher, mentor, guide, guru, swami; *ant.* disciple. 3. genius, maestro, savant, sage, expert, pro, virtuoso, wizard; *ant.* second-rater, amateur.

master *v.* 1. control, govern, rule, manage, regulate; defeat, conquer, vanquish; subdue, tame. 2. understand, comprehend, rule, learn, grasp, get the hang of.

master *adj.* 1. chief, main, major, controlling, leading, principal, foremost. 2. adept, skilled, professional, expert.

masterful *adj.* 1. commanding, authoritative, dictatorial, autocratic, domineering, despotic, peremptory; *ant.* humble. 2. adept, adroit, consummate, deft, expert, skillful.

mastermind *n.* leader, expert, genius, architect, creator, brains, originator, planner, prime mover.

mastermind *v.* devise, create, engineer, design, originate, plan, hatch, dream up.

masterpiece *n.* masterwork, magnum opus, pièce de résistance, classic, treasure.

mastery *n.* comprehension, understanding, control, knowledge, proficiency, prowess, preeminence, know-how.

masticate *v.* chew, bite, gnaw, nibble, munch, chomp.

masturbation *n.* self-stimulation, autoeroticism, onanism, self-abuse.

mat *n.* carpet, rug, floor covering, pad, underlay, place setting, table runner.

match *n.* 1. equivalent, counterpart, analog,

equal, peer, replica, duplicate, copy. 2. (one of a pair) mate, partner, twin, double. 3. contest, competition, event, sport, game, race, bout.

match *v.* 1. liken, equate, correspond; coordinate, pair, mate, unite, go with, go together; agree, accord; *ant.* separate, clash. 2. rival, compete, contend, oppose, vie, pit against, be on a level with.

matching *adj.* comparable, analogous, parallel, equal, corresponding, duplicate, equivalent, identical, same, similar, twin; *ant.* clashing, different.

matchless *adj.* incomparable, unparalleled, unequaled, nonpareil, unrivaled, unsurpassed, consummate, exquisite, supreme, unique; *ant.* commonplace.

mate *n.* match, analog, counterpart, complement. 2. partner, comrade, associate, colleague, friend, chum, crony, pal, helper, side-kick (*slang*).

mate *v.* 1. couple, pair, match, join, yoke, marry, wed. 2. breed, copulate, reproduce.

material *n.* 1. substance, corporeality, element, matter, stuff, body. 2. fabric, cloth, textile. 3. material, supplies, stock, stuff, accoutrements.

material *adj.* 1. palpable, corporeal, tangible, physical, real, actual, substantial, concrete, bodily, fleshly, worldly; *ant.* ethereal. 2. considerable, appreciable, much, notable, substantial; *ant.* slight. 3. (said of an argument, as in legal contexts) essential, important, grave, germane, key, meaningful, pertinent, relevant, vital; *ant.* immaterial, irrelevant.

materialist *n.* capitalist, money-grubber, self-seeker, opportunist.

materialistic *adj.* acquisitive, possessive, greedy, secular, capitalistic, opportunistic; *ant.* spiritual, ascetic.

materialize *v.* 1. appear, emerge, show up; actualize, become real; *ant.* dissolve, disintegrate. 2. develop, grow, evolve, arise, unfold, come to pass.

maternal *adj.* motherly, parental, protective, loving.

matriculate *v.* join, register, sign up, enroll, enter.

matrimonial *adj.* conjugal, connubial, wedded, marital, nuptial, bridal, spousal.

matrimony *n.* marriage, wedlock, union, conjugality, nuptials.

matron *n.* matriarch, dame, dowager, lady.

matted *adj.* tangled, twisted, gnarled, uncombed, disordered.

matter *n.* **1.** substance, material, corporeality, body, stuff. **2.** difficulty, trouble, distress, complication, concern, problem, upset; episode, incident. **3.** subject, issue, business, topic, question.

matter *v.* make a difference, carry weight, have influence, be of consequence, be worthy of notice.

matter-of-fact *adj.* direct, plain, literal, objective, prosaic, unembellished, unvarnished, deadpan, dry; *ant.* emotional.

mattress *n.* bed, pallet, box spring, bedding.

mature *adj.* **1.** adult, full-grown, grown-up, of age, womanly, manly. **2.** developed, prepared, ready, prime, ripe, seasoned. **3.** considered, well-thought-out, reasoned.

mature *v.* grow up, come of age, develop, cut one's eye teeth, accrue, evolve, bloom, ripen, season.

maturity *n.* **1.** development, advancement, cultivation, sophistication, wisdom; civilization. **2.** ripeness, readiness, adulthood, nubility, full growth, prime of life; *ant.* adolescence.

maudlin *adj.* mawkish, gushing, emotional, sentimental, sappy, weepy; *ant.* matter-of-fact.

maul *v.* beat, pummel, hit, batter, manhandle, pound, rough up.

maw *n.* jaws, mouth, throat, craw, gorge, gullet.

mawkish *adj.* **1.** nauseating, disgusting, insipid, vapid, tasteless. **2.** maudlin, emotional, sentimental, schmaltzy (*slang*), jejune.

maxim *n.* proverb, saying, adage, axiom, aphorism, epithet, motto, precept, saw.

maximum *n.* utmost, apogee, supremacy, nonpareil, pinnacle, zenith, crest, peak, summit, apex; *ant.* minimum.

maximum *adj.* supreme, greatest, paramount, uppermost, highest, biggest, largest; *ant.* minimum.

maybe *adv.* perhaps, possibly, perchance, conceivably, feasibly; *ant.* definitely.

maze *n.* labyrinth, intricacy, entanglement, convolution, puzzle, snarl, web, imbroglio.

meadow *n.* grass, pasture, field, plain, mead, lea, upland, bottom land, heath.

meager *adj.* **1.** thin, gaunt, lean, starved, emaciated, bony, slim, puny, scrawny, skinny; *ant.* fat, plump, stout. **2.** scanty, inadequate, deficient, wanting, insubstantial, insufficient, negligible, slight, forgettable, exiguous; *ant.* substantial, plentiful.

meal *n.* **1.** grain, flour, farina, bran, feed, fodder, forage. **2.** repast, fare, refreshment, snack, nosh (*slang*).

mealy-mouthed *adj.* indirect, mincing, euphemistic, equivocal.

mean *n.* average, center, median, norm, middle; compromise; *ant.* extreme.

mean *v.* **1.** denote, indicate, express, signify, designate, stand for, import, symbolize, represent, imply, suggest. **2.** propose, intend, anticipate, expect, plan, design.

mean *adj.* **1.** (of low quality) base, low, inferior, poor, sorry, debased. **2.** (of humble origin or quality) humble, base-born, ignoble, pitiful, shabby, abject, squalid, tawdry, sordid, servile, wretched; *ant.* noble. **3.** stingy, miserly, niggardly, rapacious, closefisted, tightfisted, greedy, mercenary, selfish, cheese-paring, penny-pinching; *ant.* generous. **4.** cruel, unkind, malicious, vicious, despicable, unscrupulous; petty, mean-spirited, narrow-minded, intolerant. **5.** (being of average value) average, common, halfway, conventional, ordinary, middling, mediocre, undistinguished; *ant.* superior.

meander *v.* **1.** turn, wind, twine, recoil, curve, snake, twist, zigzag. **2.** wander, ramble, roam, drift, amble, stroll.

meandering *adj.* **1.** serpentine, circuitous, sinuous, tortuous, winding, roundabout; convoluted, indirect; *ant.* straight. **2.** wandering, traveling, nomadic, rambling.

meaning *n.* **1.** sense, implication, import, definition, intent, significance, drift, gist, upshot. **2.** object, aim, point, purpose, message.

meaningless *adj.* insignificant, trivial, unimportant, negligible, inconsequential, trivial, trifling, futile, inane, absurd, nonsensical, pointless, aimless.

means *n.* **1.** ability, capacity, wherewithal;

283

funds, wealth, assets, resources. **2.** method, way, mechanism, agency, system, machinery.
by all means surely, yes, of course, certainly, positively, absolutely.
by any means in any way, somehow, anyhow, by hook or by crook.
by no means never, no, in no way, definitely not, on no account.

meanwhile *adv.* at the same time, concurrently, simultaneously; in the interim, for now; for the moment, in the interval, until.

measly *adj.* paltry, piddling, petty, meager, poor, puny, scanty, miserly, niggardly, mean, pathetic.

measurable *adj.* **1.** estimable, calculable, assessable, weighable, computable, determinable, quantifiable. **2.** restricted, limited, moderate, prescribed, measured.

measure *n.* **1.** dimension, capacity, degree, quantity, intensity, mass, frequency, density, viscosity, scope, magnitude, amplitude. **2.** standard, criterion, yardstick, benchmark, norm, example, model, pattern, rule, scale. **3.** (a legislative proposal) bill, action, enactment, law, resolution, statute, proposal. **4.** (a way of working toward a goal) stratagem, device, means, procedure, course.
for good measure extra, added, as a bonus, to boot, additionally.
made to measure tailored, made to order, custom-made.

measure *v.* assess, evaluate, estimate, judge, determine, calculate, appraise, gauge, quantify, weigh.

measure up pass muster, make the grade, succeed, fill the bill.

measured *adj.* **1.** steady, regular, uniform, systematic, deliberate, cautious, temperate, constant. **2.** restricted, limited, rationed, restrained, confined, predetermined, quantified.

measureless *adj.* endless, infinite, unlimited, indefinite, boundless, inestimable, immense, vast.

measurement *n.* **1.** (act of measuring) estimation, judgment, determination, computation, appraisal, assessment, calibration. **2.** dimension, degree, volume, size, amount, magnitude.

meanwhile *adv.* at the same time, concurrently, simultaneously; in the interim, for now; for the moment, in the interval, until.

mechanic *n.* machinist, repairer, technician.

mechanical *adj.* **1.** automatic, involuntary, programmed, power-driven, automated. **2.** cursory, emotionless, impersonal, unanimated, unconscious, habitual, automatic, unfeeling, unthinking.

mechanism *n.* machine, machinery, contrivance, instrument, appliance, device, tool, apparatus.

mechanize *v.* equip, automate, motorize, computerize.

medal *n.* badge, award, honor, trophy, decoration.

meddle *v.* interfere, pry, stick one's nose in, snoop, infringe, encroach, intervene, interpose, chime in, butt in, horn in, trespass; *ant.* mind one's own business.

meddlesome *adj.* interfering, meddling, intrusive, prying, snoopy, nosy, kibitzing; interrupting, obtrusive, bothersome, impeding.

median *adj.* middle, center, halfway, medial.

mediate *v.* negotiate, arbitrate, intercede, interpose, intervene, moderate, reconcile, resolve, settle, referee, umpire.

mediation *n.* intervention, arbitration, intercession, parley, negotiation, interposition.

mediator *n.* arbitrator, intermediary, intercessor, negotiator, arbiter, middleman, medium, moderator, judge, peacemaker, umpire.

medical *adj.* healing, medicinal, curative, therapeutic, restorative, corrective, cathartic, Hippocratic.

medicinal *adj.* curative, therapeutic, healing.

medicine *n.* **1.** (the healing profession) physicians, practitioners, doctors, healers, American Medical Association, AMA. **2.** drug, dose, prescription, remedy, cure.

medicine man *n.* shaman, witch doctor, sorcerer.

medieval *adj.* old, antiquated, archaic, oldworld, primitive, unenlightened.

meat *n.* essence, substance, gist, point; marrow, core, crux, kernel, heart.

meaty *adj.* **1.** beefy, brawny, fleshy, fat, burly, husky, hefty, strapping, solid. **2.** significant, important, weighty, meaningful, pithy, substantial.

mediocre *adj.* common, average, ordinary, conventional, dull, commonplace, middling, pedestrian, run-of-the-mill, unexceptional, uninspired; *ant.* excellent; exceptional.

meditate *v.* ponder, contemplate, ruminate, reflect, consider, cogitate, deliberate, mull over, brood over, chew the cud.

meditation *n.* reflection, study, examination, contemplation, concentration, reverie, rumination.

medium *n.* **1.** means, mode, way, avenue, agency, channel, vehicle. **2.** fortuneteller, clairvoyant, psychic, seer, prophet, oracle. **3.** average, center, mean, middle, middle-of-the-road, midpoint.

medium *adj.* median, middling, midway, standard, average, fair.

medley *n.* mixture, variety, assortment, conglomeration, mélange, potpourri, miscellany, pastiche, melee, hodge-podge, jumble.

meek *adj.* **1.** humble, modest, unassuming, mild, gentle, tame, subdued; *ant.* haughty. **2.** passive, submissive, compliant, docile, timid, acquiescent, deferential, slavish, spineless, spiritless, weak, yielding; *ant.* self-assertive.

meet *v.* **1.** be introduced, be presented to, encounter, come across, bump into, run into; face, grapple with, jostle. **2.** converge, gather, convene, congregate, assemble; *ant.* disperse. **3.** join, abut, adjoin, connect, unite.

meet *adj.* proper, fitting, seemly, appropriate, correct, fit, traditional.

meeting *n.* **1.** juncture, conjunction, intersection, abutment, connection; *ant.* separation, dispersal. **2.** conference, gathering, rally, assembly, convention, forum, reunion, conclave, tryst.

meeting of minds *n.* agreement, assent, accord.

meeting-point *n.* crossroads, intersection, junction, confluence, convergence, interface.

megalomania *n.* delusions of grandeur, self-importance, egomania, conceitedness, narcissism, vanity.

melancholy *n.* sadness, despair, wistfulness, dejection, depression, gloom, pensiveness, woe, glumness, blues, low spirits; *ant.* exhilaration.

melancholy *adj.* sad, depressed, dejected, despondent, crestfallen, dispirited, downhearted,
somber, downcast, heavy-hearted; *ant.* cheerful, happy, joyful.

mélange *n.* mixture, medley, assortment, pastiche, miscellany, potpourri.

meld *v.* unite, blend, merge, mix, fuse.

melee *n.* fracas, fray, rumpus, scuffle, skirmish, brawl, fight, tussle.

mellifluous *adj.* resonant, melodious, musical, euphonious, honeyed, mellow, smooth, soothing, sweet; *ant.* discordant, harsh.

mellow *v.* mature, ripen, season, sweeten, temper.

mellow *adj.* **1.** ripe, mature, seasoned, aged, cured, sweet, full-flavored, juicy, perfected; *ant.* green, hard, unripe. **2.** relaxed, serene, placid, tranquil, laid-back (*slang*), content, jovial, genial; *ant.* uptight, tense.

melodious *adj.* euphonic, harmonious, musical, sonorous, resonant, symphonic, pleasant, sweet, silvery; *ant.* discordant, harsh.

melodramatic *adj.* histrionic, theatrical, overdramatized, exaggerated, overdone, overwrought, stagy, sensational, artificial, hammy (*slang*).

melody *n.* song, tune, air, strain, theme, music; harmony, musicality, melodiousness, euphony.

melt *v.* **1.** liquefy, thaw, soften, dissolve, disintegrate, flow; *ant.* solidify, coagulate, freeze, harden. **2.** relent, yield, become lenient, forgive, be mollified.

member *n.* **1.** constituent, affiliate, associate, colleague, fellow, initiate, brother, sister, comrade; chapter, post, branch, division. **2.** part, portion, segment, component, fragment. **3.** appendage, organ, extremity, limb, arm.

membership *n.* participation, affiliation, enrollment, association, fellowship, brotherhood, club, society, company, group.

membrane *n.* layer, sheath, film, veil, lamina, velum, tissue.

memento *n.* keepsake, souvenir, remembrance, token, relic, trophy.

memoir *n.* biography, autobiography, account, narrative, journal, life story.

memoirs *n.* reminiscences, recollections, chronicles, annals, journals, experiences.

memorable *adj.* **1.** (worthy of being remembered) historic, momentous, unforgettable,

memorial monumental, eventful, notable, significant, important; famous, illustrious, celebrated; *ant.* forgettable. **2.** (making a strong mental impression) remarkable, exceptional, singular, unusual, striking.

memorial *n.* testimonial, remembrance; tombstone, monument, mausoleum, statue, inscription, plaque.

memorial *adj.* dedicatory, commemorative, consecrating, canonizing, celebratory.

memorize *v.* record, retain, learn by rote, learn by heart, learn verbatim; *ant.* forget.

memory *n.* recollection, reminiscence, retrospection, retention, consciousness, subconsciousness.

menace *n.* threat, hazard, peril, danger, jeopardy; annoyance, nuisance, plague, pest.

menace *v.* threaten, intimidate, browbeat, bully, alarm, frighten, terrorize, threaten; portend, loom.

menacing *adj.* threatening, alarming, dangerous, frightening, intimidating, harassing.

menagerie *n.* zoo, zoological garden, terrarium, vivarium.

mend *v.* repair, fix, patch, remedy, cure, heal, recover, amend, rectify; *ant.* break, destroy. **on the mend** improving, recuperating, healing, recovering, getting better, convalescent.

mendacious *adj.* false, lying, dishonest, spurious, deceitful, deceptive, fallacious, perjured, perfidious, fraudulent, duplicitous; *ant.* honest, truthful.

mendacity *n.* lying, falsification, fraudulence, misrepresentation, prevarication, insincerity, perfidy, distortion; *ant.* honesty, truthfulness.

mendicant *n.* beggar, tramp, hobo, vagabond, pauper, bum, panhandler, vagrant.

mendicant *adj.* begging, scrounging, bumming (*slang*).

menial *n.* servant, domestic, maid, attendant, lackey, underling, peon, serf, flunky.

menial *adj.* servile, abject, base, ignoble, ignominious, low, mean, slavish, subservient, demeaning, degrading.

menstruation *n.* period, the menses, catamenia, the curse (*slang*).

mental *adj.* **1.** (of or using the mind) cerebral, reasoning, rational, thinking, cognitive, intellectual, theoretical, conceptual; *ant.* physical.

2. (taking place in the mind) subjective, subliminal, subconscious, imaginary; *ant.* objective.

mentality *n.* **1.** mind, intellect, brains, intelligence quotient, IQ, comprehension, reasoning, understanding, rationality. **2.** attitude, character, disposition, frame of mind, outlook, personality.

mentally *adv.* rationally, intellectually, subjectively, introspectively, psychologically.

mention *n.* allusion, remark, citation, acknowledgment, reference, tribute, observation.

mention *v.* cite, quote, refer to, intimate, reveal, state, tell.

mentor *n.* teacher, instructor, guide, coach, adviser, counselor, tutor, guru, swami.

menu *n.* bill of fare, cuisine, carte du jour; list, selection, choices.

mercantile *adj.* commercial, industrial, trade, business, marketing.

mercenary *adj.* greedy, avaricious, acquisitive, selfish, grasping, materialistic, money-grubbing, venal.

mercenary *n.* legionnaire, professional soldier, soldier of fortune, hired gun.

merchandise *n.* commodities, wares, goods, products, vendibles.

merchandise *v.* sell, market, promote, peddle, retail, trade, traffic in, deal in, vend.

merchant *n.* storekeeper, retailer, shopkeeper, wholesaler, salesman, trafficker.

merciful *adj.* lenient, clement, compassionate, tolerant, forbearing, forgiving, humane, kind, sympathetic, gracious; *ant.* cruel, pitiless, unsparing.

merciless *adj.* cruel, ruthless, pitiless, unsparing, barbarous, inexorable, harsh, severe, callous, hardhearted; *ant.* clement.

mercurial *adj.* changeable, erratic, fluctuating, inconstant, moody, capricious, fickle, flighty, unpredictable, volatile, impetuous, temperamental; *ant.* steady, stable, stolid.

mercy *n.* leniency, clemency, compassion, generosity, tolerance, forbearance, pity, sympathy, grace, humanitarianism, kindness, benevolence.

mere *adj.* small, insignificant, minor, little, poor, paltry, petty, simple, common.

meretricious *adj.* gaudy, flashy, tawdry, cheap, showy, fake, specious, loud.

merge v. join, meet, synthesize, amalgamate, blend, combine, meld, mix, unite, coalesce, marry, consolidate.

merger n. consolidation, incorporation, fusion, confederation, alliance, amalgamation, coalition, pool; ant. separation, divestment.

merit n. worth, value, quality, credit, asset, virtue, excellence, honor, due, right.

merit v. deserve, warrant, justify, earn, rate.

meritorious adj. praiseworthy, commendable, honorable, noble, admirable, deserving, laudable.

merriment n. gaiety, joy, jollity, amusement, levity, frolic, conviviality, revelry, merrymaking; ant. gloom, gravity.

merry adj. happy, festive, gay, joyous, mirthful, amusing, blithe, jocular, fun-loving; ant. gloomy, somber, sober.

merry-go-round n. carousel, whirligig.

mesh n. net, lattice, web, screen, snare.

mesh v. coincide, agree, connect, fit, engage, interlock, interdigitate, knit.

mesmerize v. entrance, captivate, enthrall, fascinate, benumb, stupefy, spellbind, hypnotize.

mess n. 1. jumble, disorder, disarray, disorganization, clutter, confusion, chaos; ant. order, tidiness. 2. imbroglio, muddle, plight, predicament, turmoil, pickle, jam.

mess v. dishevel, muss, dirty, litter, pollute; ant. clean.

mess up botch, bungle, spoil, muddle, muck up, screw up (slang).

mess with 1. tinker with, play with, fiddle with, tamper with. 2. provoke, incite, anger, arouse, tangle with.

message n. 1. note, letter, report, bulletin, cable, word, news, information. 2. idea, import, intimation, meaning, moral, point, theme.

messenger n. courier, carrier, emissary, envoy, herald, crier, go-between, internuncio, mercury.

messy adj. dirty, disordered, rumpled, untidy, slovenly, disheveled, cluttered, littered, unkempt, untidy, sloppy; ant. neat, ordered, tidy.

metallic adj. 1. hard, iron, steely, leaden, silvery, golden, tinny. 2. clanging, rasping, grating, ringing, resonant, resounding, plangent.

metamorphosis n. change, transformation, evolution, modification, alteration, conversion, mutation, rebirth, transfiguration, recasting.

metaphor n. comparison, trope, simile, analogy, figure of speech.

metaphorical adj. symbolic, figurative, allegorical, emblematic.

metaphysical adj. spiritual, transcendental, mystical, abstract, esoteric, incorporeal, insubstantial, intangible.

mete v. distribute, give, allot, dispense, parcel out, ration, administer, assign.

meteor n. meteorite, meteoroid, comet, falling star, shooting star.

meteoric adj. brief, fast, transient, fleeting, momentary; brilliant, dazzling, spectacular, bright.

meter n. measure, beat, rhythm, metrical feet.

method n. procedure, mode, way, approach, modus operandi, manner, plan, practice, routine, system, technique, style.

methodical adj. orderly, exact, scrupulous, precise, punctilious, painstaking, meticulous, deliberate, disciplined, systematic, regular, planned, organized; ant. irregular, random, disorderly.

meticulous adj. scrupulous, fastidious, precise, careful, fussy, particular, perfectionist, thorough; ant. careless, slapdash.

metier n. trade, profession, occupation, vocation, calling, craft, field, forte, pursuit, specialty.

metropolis n. city, capital, megalopolis, municipality.

metropolitan adj. urban, cosmopolitan, municipal, civic.

mettle n. spirit, spunk, pluck, vitality, energy, vigor; boldness, daring, bravery, courage, nerve, grit, fortitude; resolve.

mettlesome adj. spunky, spirited, plucky, ardent, brave.

mew v. meow, caterwaul, mewl, pule, whine.

mewl v. whimper, whine, cry, snivel, blubber.

miasma n. 1. gas, vapor, steam, fume, haze.

miasmal adj. fetid, foul, noxious, putrid, malodorous.

microbe n. microorganism, germ, bacterium, bacillus, virus.

microscopic adj. minuscule, minute, diminutive, infinitesimal, imperceptible, indiscernible, negligible; *ant.* huge, vast.

middle *adj.* between, midway, medial, equidistant, intermediate; average, mean.

middle *n.* **1.** center, heart, inside; mean, middle way, midpoint, halfway point; *ant.* end, border, periphery. **2.** midriff, midsection, waist.

middle-class *adj.* bourgeois, conventional, suburban, white-collar.

middleman *n.* broker, distributor, representative, agent, negotiator, retailer.

middling *adj.* mediocre, ordinary, average, common, modest, passable, run-of-the-mill, unexceptional, unremarkable.

midget *n.* dwarf, pygmy, homunculus, shrimp (*slang*), runt.

midget *adj.* small, tiny, little, miniature, dwarf, pocket-sized, Lilliputian; *ant.* giant.

midst *n.* center, middle, heart, hub, nucleus. **in the midst of** in the middle of, while engaged in, during.

midway *adv.* halfway, intermediate, betwixt and between.

mien *n.* manner, bearing, carriage, demeanor, deportment; semblance, appearance, aspect, look.

miffed *adj.* irked, irritated, vexed, offended, in a huff, nettled, displeased, annoyed, disgruntled, piqued.

might *n.* power, strength, force, potency, capacity, ability, puissance, sway, clout (*slang*).

mightily *adv.* powerfully, strongly, forcefully, strenuously; intensely, decidedly, exceedingly.

mighty *adj.* **1.** strong, powerful, muscular, omnipotent, puissant, forceful, lusty, stalwart, stout, strapping; *ant.* frail, weak. **2.** great, immense, imposing, magnificent, towering, colossal, grand, indomitable, monumental, stupendous, titanic.

migrant *n.* immigrant, nomad, drifter, itinerant, wanderer, transient, vagrant, gypsy.

migrant *adj.* migratory, nomadic, transient, drifting, roving, vagrant, wandering.

migrate *v.* immigrate, journey, travel, trek, wander, roam.

migration *n.* emigration, departure, wandering, dispersal, diaspora.

migratory *adj.* **1.** (moving with the seasons, as certain animals) emigrating, immigrating, seasonal, transient, impermanent; *ant.* local, hibernating. **2.** wandering, nomadic, vagrant, roaming, itinerant; *ant.* permanent, settled.

mild *adj.* **1.** gentle, kind, meek, amiable, serene, easygoing, moderate; soothing, smooth, mellow, delicate; *ant.* fierce, harsh. **2.** temperate, summery, pacific, tropical, balmy, clement, clear, sunny, warm, calm, fair; *ant.* rough, cold, stormy.

milieu *n.* environment, setting, surroundings, ambiance, scene, place, locale, location, element, sphere, arena, medium.

militant *n.* activist, rioter, demonstrator, protestor.

militant *adj.* aggressive, assertive, pugnacious, belligerent, offensive, hawkish, combative, warring, contending; *ant.* peaceable, pacific.

militaristic *adj.* aggressive, antagonistic, warlike, sabre-rattling, jingoistic.

military *n.* armed forces, army, troops, soldiers.

military *adj.* armed, martial, militant, soldierly, combatant, warlike, aggressive.

militia *n.* minutemen, civilian army, National Guard, weekend warriors (*slang*).

milk *v.* squeeze, draw out, drain, siphon, bleed, extract; exploit.

milky *adj.* white, pearly, alabaster, chalky, opaque, cloudy.

mill *n.* **1.** factory, plant, foundry, shop, works, manufactory. **2.** grinder, grater, crusher. **through the mill** tested, tried, experienced.

mill *v.* **1.** grind, crush, pulverize, granulate, grate. **2.** crowd, seethe, throng, swarm; wander.

millennium *n.* utopia, kingdom come, golden age, heaven on earth, thousand years of peace.

millstone *n.* burden, load, responsibility, encumbrance, weight, impedance, difficulty.

mime *n.* **1.** mimic, imitator, impersonator, comedian, actor. **2.** mockery, imitation, caricature, mimicry, parody, mummery, pantomime, dumb show.

mime *v.* impersonate, mimic, parody, imitate, pretend, act out, represent, simulate.

mimic *n.* mime, caricaturist, imitator, impersonator, impressionist, parodist, comedian.

mimic *v.* **1.** imitate, impersonate, copy, ape, simulate, mirror, resemble. **2.** mock, ape, caricature, burlesque, ridicule, parody, take off.

mimicry *n.* imitation, parody, mockery, burlesque, caricature.

mince *v.* **1.** chop, dice, hash, cut, grind. **2.** euphemize, soften, lessen, minimize, mitigate, moderate, palliate, tone down.

mincing *adj.* affected, artificial, pretentious, foppish, sissyish, effeminate, dainty.

mind *n.* **1.** intellect, brain, consciousness, thought, mentality, perception, conception, understanding, wisdom, intuition, gray matter, marbles (*slang*), brainpower. **2.** purpose, intention, inclination, bent, fancy, leaning, outlook, disposition, tendency, view.

bear in mind remember, consider, note, heed, be mindful of, be cognizant of.

call to mind remember, recall, recollect, be reminded of.

make up one's mind decide, determine, resolve, choose, pick, elect, settle; *ant.* waver.

out of one's mind insane, raving, mad, crazy, deranged, lunatic, *slang:* loony, nuts.

mind *v.* **1.** heed, obey, behave, regard, adhere to; mark, note, pay attention to. **2.** tend, watch out for, have charge of, guard, keep an eye on, look after, take care of, baby-sit; *ant.* neglect. **3.** object, complain, be opposed to, disapprove, resent, take offense; *ant.* agree, concur.

mindful *adj.* heedful, attentive, watchful, alert, aware, knowing, sensible, cognizant, wary; *ant.* heedless, inattentive.

mindless *adj.* **1.** careless, inattentive, thoughtless, unthinking, oblivious, neglectful, gratuitous, heedless; *ant.* mindful, attentive. **2.** stupid, foolish, senseless, asinine, brutish, idiotic, imbecilic, moronic, obtuse, witless; *ant.* intelligent.

mine *n.* **1.** shaft, pit, well, excavation, quarry, vein, lode, deposit. **2.** land mine, bomb, explosive, booby trap.

mine *v.* excavate, dig for, dig up, quarry, burrow, drill, delve, tunnel, unearth.

miner *n.* excavator, digger, driller, dredger, prospector, forty-niner, sourdough.

mingle *v.* **1.** combine, blend, coalesce, compound, merge, mix. **2.** hobnob, socialize, fraternize, associate.

miniature *adj.* little, minute, diminutive, small, tiny, midget, pygmy, reduced, toy, scaled-down, dwarf, Lilliputian; *ant.* giant.

minimal *adj.* least, minimum, smallest, nominal, slightest, nominal, token; *ant.* maximal.

minimize *v.* decrease, lessen, reduce, curtail, diminish, abbreviate, depreciate; *ant.* maximize.

minimum *n.* jot, iota, whit, soupçon, trace, scintilla; *ant.* maximum.

minimum *adj.* least, smallest, tiniest, merest, slightest.

mining *v.* excavating, prospecting, delving, tunneling, boring, drilling.

minion *n.* follower, lackey, flunky, underling, pet; parasite, hanger-on; sycophant, toady, flatterer, bootlicker, yes man (*slang*).

minister *n.* **1.** pastor, parson, preacher, priest, cleric, ecclesiastic, clergyman, rector, vicar, monk, abbot, curate, missionary; *ant.* layman. **2.** ambassador, diplomat, representative, statesman, consul, delegate, envoy, executive, official.

minister *v.* tend, mind, help, nurse, serve, take care of.

ministration *n.* assistance, aid, help, support, relief, succor, supervision, patronage.

ministry *n.* **1.** vicarage, holy orders, the church, the priesthood, the cloth, the pulpit. **2.** bureau, office, department, administration, council.

minor *adj.* trivial, unimportant, secondary, lesser, insignificant, inconsequential, negligible, paltry, piddling, slight, trifling; junior; *ant.* major.

minstrel *n.* troubadour, balladeer, street singer, songsmith, bard, poet.

mint *v.* coin, mold, cast, forge, stamp, print; devise, create, invent.

mint *adj.* immaculate, perfect, undamaged, untarnished, excellent, brand-new.

minuscule *adj.* little, diminutive, tiny, infinitesimal, microscopic, minute, Lilliputian; *ant.* gigantic, huge.

minute *n.* instant, moment, second, flash, jiffy, bat of an eye, twinkling, shake.

up to the minute modern, contemporary, current, recent, fashionable, à la mode.

minute *adj.* **1.** microscopic, infinitesimal, miniature, minuscule, little, tiny, teeny; *ant.* large, huge, immense. 2. trivial, trifling, negligible, paltry, picayune, piddling. 3. exact, precise, meticulous, painstaking.

minutely *adv.* meticulously, precisely, exactly, exhaustively, scrupulously, systematically, with a fine-toothed comb.

minutes *n.* notes, records, transcript, transactions, memorandum.

minutiae *n.* details, particulars, subtleties, trivialities; niceties, trifles.

minx *n.* coquette, flirt, wench, hussy.

miracle *n.* marvel, wonder, phenomenon, revelation.

miraculous *adj.* astonishing, astounding, wondrous, amazing, extraordinary, marvelous, supernatural, preternatural, inexplicable; *ant.* natural, normal.

mirage *n.* illusion, hallucination, delusion, fantasy.

mire *n.* bog, marsh, swamp, morass, quagmire, fen, mud, ooze.

mirror *n.* copy, double, replica, spitting image, likeness, representation, twin.

mirror *v.* copy, emulate, imitate, mimic, reflect, represent.

mirth *n.* merriment, joyfulness, gaiety, revelry, glee, hilarity, levity, jocularity; *ant.* gloom, melancholy.

mirthful *adj.* blithe, merry, happy, jovial, light-hearted, amused, uproarious, hilarious; *ant.* glum, mirthless.

misadventure *n.* accident, mishap, setback, misfortune, debacle, tragedy, calamity.

misanthrope *n.* cynic, pessimist, skeptic, doubter, loner; hater, man-hater, woman-hater; misogynist.

misanthropic *adj.* antisocial, cynical, malevolent, inhumane; *ant.* philanthropic.

misapprehend *v.* misunderstand, mistake, be confused about.

misapprehension *n.* fallacy, delusion, error, misunderstanding, mistake, misconception.

misappropriate *v.* embezzle, steal, filch, cheat, swindle, rob; misuse, abuse, pervert.

misbegotten *adj.* illicit, illegal, illegitimate, unlawful, ill-gotten, shady, purloined.

misbehave *v.* offend, transgress, err, lapse, be delinquent, sin; be bad, be reprehensible; *ant.* behave, be good.

misbehavior *n.* mischief, transgression, disobedience, insubordination, misconduct, shenanigans, naughtiness; impropriety, incivility.

miscalculate *v.* mistake, err, blunder, miscount, misjudge, miss the mark.

miscarriage *n.* 1. failure, fiasco, breakdown, malfunction, error, mistake, mishap, defeat, collapse; *ant.* success. 2. stillbirth, abortion.

miscarry *v.* fail, abort, misfire, fall through, lose.

miscellaneous *adj.* multifarious, sundry, motley, various, assorted, diverse, disparate.

miscellany *n.* 1. medley, mélange, potpourri, motley, hodge-podge, jumble, mixture, assortment. 2. anthology, compilation, collection, extracts.

mischance *n.* 1. accident, misadventure, mishap, misfortune, bad break, calamity, disaster, tragedy. 2. bad luck, ill fortune, misfortune, infelicity.

mischief *n.* 1. damage, harm, injury, hurt, trouble. 2. prankishness, devilment, impishness, roguery, waggishness, naughtiness, rascality, monkey business, shenanigans; *ant.* sedateness.

mischievous *adj.* naughty, wayward, roguish, playful, frolicsome, impish, puckish; exasperating, vexatious; *ant.* good, well-behaved.

misconceive *v.* misunderstand, mistake, err, misinterpret, misapprehend, misconstrue.

misconception *n.* misunderstanding, error, blunder, delusion, fallacy, misreading.

misconduct *n.* mischief, wrongdoing, dereliction, impropriety, misdemeanor, transgression, offense.

misconstrue *v.* misunderstand, take the wrong way, mistake, distort, exaggerate, pervert.

miscreant *n.* wretch, villain, reprobate, profligate, malefactor, scoundrel, knave, rogue, blackguard, scallywag.

misdeed *n.* crime, transgression, trespass, wrong, delinquency, misconduct, peccadillo, sin.

misdemeanor *n.* indiscretion, lapse, misconduct, misbehavior, misdeed, fault.

miser *n.* penny pincher, cheapskate, tightwad, skinflint, Scrooge, money-grubber; *ant.* spendthrift.

miserable *adj.* **1.** (feeling misery) abject, discontented, anguished, crestfallen, forlorn, despondent, disconsolate, melancholy; suffering, sick, ailing, afflicted; *ant.* happy, well. **2.** poor, inferior, sorry, worthless, shoddy; *ant.* worthy, good. **3.** (denoting substandard conditions) pitiable, wretched, unfortunate, hard, shameful, disgraceful; *ant.* comfortable, well-appointed.

miserliness *n.* avarice, stinginess, parsimony, covetousness, tightfistedness, closefistedness, greed; *ant.* generosity, lavishness.

miserly *adj.* stingy, tight, covetous, parsimonious, mercenary, penny-pinching, penurious; *ant.* generous, prodigal.

misery *n.* **1.** distress, agony, suffering, affliction, anguish, despair, pain, sorrow, woe, grief, torment, torture. **2.** (difficult circumstances) trouble, adversity, hardship, trial; poverty, squalor.

misfire *v.* fail, miscarry, bomb, fall short, fall through, flop; *ant.* succeed.

misfit *n.* nonconformist, individualist, maverick, loner, lone wolf, fish out of water, odd man out, square peg in a round hole, oddball; *ant.* conformist.

misfortune *n.* **1.** bad luck, infelicity, ill luck, trouble, adversity; *ant.* luck, success. **2.** (an unfortunate event) mishap, accident, misadventure, affliction, setback, calamity, catastrophe, tragedy.

misgiving *n.* doubt, uncertainty, trepidation, hesitation, apprehension, qualm, reservation, fear; distrust, suspicion, unease; *ant.* confidence.

misguided *adj.* misled, ill-advised, deceived, deluded, mistaken, rash, unwise, unwarranted; *ant.* sensible.

mishandle *v.* **1.** mismanage, botch, mess up, screw up (*slang*), bungle. **2.** abuse, mistreat, harm.

mishap *n.* accident, misfortune, setback, misstep, misadventure, ill fortune, ill luck.

mishmash *n.* mixture, hodgepodge, jumble, pastiche, potpourri, conglomeration, medley.

misinform *v.* mislead, misdirect, lie, deceive, hoodwink, *slang:* snow, take for a ride; lead up the garden path, give a bum steer.

misinformation *n.* propaganda, distortion, lies, misdirection, *slang:* hype, bum steer, baloney; eyewash, bluff.

misinterpret *v.* misconstrue, misunderstand, misapprehend, misread; distort, garble, warp, pervert, falsify, misrepresent.

misjudge *v.* **1.** presume, prejudge, presuppose, be unfair, be one-sided, jump to conclusions. **2.** miscalculate, miscount, overestimate, underestimate.

misjudgment *n.* mistake, error, misinterpretation, misconception; prejudice, bias, partiality, unfairness.

mislead *v.* deceive, delude, fool, dupe, lead astray, trick, gull, bamboozle, put on (*slang*), snow (*slang*), pull the wool over someone's eyes, take in.

misleading *adj.* **1.** (tending to mislead) disingenuous, confusing, evasive, ambiguous, specious, perplexing; *ant.* plain, unequivocal. **2.** (intending to mislead) deceitful, deceptive, dissimulating, fallacious, false, mendacious.

mismanage *v.* mishandle, misgovern, bungle, blunder, mess up, botch, *slang:* screw up, louse up; squander, waste.

mismatched *adj.* incongruent, disparate, clashing, discordant, misallied, incompatible, unsuitable, irreconcilable.

misogynist *n.* woman-hater, male chauvinist, sexist, male supremacist.

misplace *v.* lose, mislay; *ant.* find.

misquote *v.* exaggerate, misrepresent, distort, overstate.

misrepresent *v.* deceive, lie, mislead, distort, falsify.

misrule *n.* **1.** misgovernment, mismanagement. **2.** anarchy, riot, chaos, tumult, turbulence.

miss *n.* **1.** failure, blunder, error, mishap, mistake, omission, oversight. **2.** lass, girl, female, damsel, maid, nymphet, schoolgirl.

miss *v.* **1.** long for, pine for, wish for, desire, crave, yearn for, need, want; lament, grieve for. **2.** overshoot, undershoot, fall short, fall wide of the mark; *ant.* be on target. **3.** neglect, overlook, leave out, pass by, skip, avoid.

missal *n.* prayer book, hymnal, psalter, breviary.

misshapen *adj.* deformed, disfigured, crippled, ungainly, twisted, contorted, warped; *ant.* shapely.

missing *adj.* absent, gone, lost, mislaid, misplaced, disappeared, strayed, unaccounted for; *ant.* found, present.

mission *n.* purpose, object, goal, quest, job, assignment, delegation, duty, task, undertaking, operation.

missionary *n.* apostle, evangelist, preacher, pastor, minister, padre, ambassador, champion, emissary, envoy, propagandist.

missive *n.* letter, word, note, message, bulletin, communication, dispatch, epistle.

misspent *adj.* dissipated, frittered away, wasted, prodigal, squandered; unprofitable; *ant.* profitable.

misstep *n.* slip, error, stumble, trip, blunder.

mist *n.* fog, cloud, haze, film, condensation, dew, drizzle, steam, spray, vapor, smog.

mist *v.* **1.** shower, drizzle, rain, spray, dampen. **2.** fog, cloud, veil, glaze, film, blur, obscure; *ant.* clear.

mistake *n.* **1.** error, blunder, faux pas, gaffe, indiscretion, lapse, slip. **2.** misunderstanding, misconception, misapprehension, delusion, confusion, misreading.

mistake *v.* **1.** err, blunder, slip, bungle, botch, lapse, miss the boat, *slang:* goof, screw up. **2.** misconstrue, misapprehend, confuse, misinterpret, be wrong about; *ant.* be accurate, get right.

mistaken *adj.* **1.** confused, deluded, misguided, having the wrong impression, misinformed, ill-advised, duped, fooled, misled, tricked; *ant.* correct. **2.** erroneous, unfounded, invalid, false, wrong.

mistaken for confused with, taken for, mixed up with.

mistakenly *adv.* erroneously, inaccurately, incorrectly, wrongly, falsely, fallaciously; unjustly, unfairly; *ant.* appropriately, justly, correctly.

mistimed *adj.* inopportune, inappropriate, malapropos, unsuitable, infelicitous, unsynchronized, unseasonable; *ant.* opportune.

mistreat *v.* abuse, harm, injure, brutalize, manhandle, maul, molest, bully, rough up.

mistreatment *n.* abuse, cruelty, violation, battery, assault.

mistress *n.* **1.** proprietress, housekeeper, caretaker, schoolmistress, chaperon, matron, manager. **2.** lover, the other woman, kept woman, paramour, concubine, courtesan.

mistrust *n.* distrust, doubt, suspicion, misgiving, skepticism, uncertainty, wariness, apprehension, caution, reservations.

mistrust *v.* doubt, suspect, distrust, disbelieve, question, beware.

mistrustful *adj.* dubious, unsure, cynical, fearful, suspicious, leery, wary, hesitant; *ant.* trustful.

misty *adj.* foggy, hazy, cloudy, nebulous, indistinct, obscure, vague, veiled, shrouded, opaque, murky; *ant.* bright, clear.

misunderstand *v.* misconceive, misinterpret, misapprehend, misconstrue, mistake, confuse, confound, have the wrong impression, be perplexed, be bewildered, be at cross-purposes, not register, miss the point; *ant.* grasp, understand, get it.

misunderstanding *n.* **1.** misapprehension, error, mistake, delusion, miscalculation, confusion, misinterpretation. **2.** debate, dissension, conflict, dispute, disagreement, quarrel, argument, clash, rift, squabble; *ant.* agreement.

misunderstood *adj.* underestimated, unappreciated, unacknowledged, unrecognized, disregarded, rejected, scorned.

misuse *v.* abuse, maltreat, corrupt, desecrate, molest, profane.

mite *n.* **1.** vermin, parasite, bug, tick. **2.** iota, jot, modicum, morsel, scrap, smidgen, trace, whit.

mitigate *v.* relieve, lessen, moderate, allay, assuage, ease, dull, mollify, palliate, slake, subdue; *ant.* aggravate, exacerbate, increase.

mitigating *adj.* extenuating, vindicating, palliating, qualifying.

mitigation *n.* moderation, relief, alleviation, reduction, remission, abatement, diminution; *ant.* aggravation, increase.

mix *n.* alloy, blend, mixture, combination, composite, compound, fusion, synthesis, pastiche.

mix *v.* **1.** blend, fuse, merge, coalesce, unite,

combine, amalgamate, incorporate, commingle, merge, synthesize, adulterate; *ant.* separate. **2.** confuse, jumble, tangle, shuffle. **3.** associate, fraternize, mingle, hobnob, consort with, socialize.

mix up confuse, confound, perplex, puzzle, bewilder, complicate.

mixed *adj.* **1.** commingled, blended, fused, composite, compounded, assimilated, married; *ant.* separated, severed. **2.** various, assorted, miscellaneous, diverse; mongrel, heterogenous, motley. **3.** confused, disordered, jumbled.

mixer *n.* **1.** blender, beater, Osterizer (Tm). **2.** party, fraternity *or* sorority party, cocktail party, tea, gathering, social.

mixture *n.* combination, composite, amalgam, fusion, adulteration, hybrid, medley, miscellany, melange, pastiche, stew, hodgepodge.

mix-up *n.* commotion, turmoil, chaos, muddle, complication, confusion, snafu.

moan *n.* groan, wail, cry, sob, whimper, whine.

moan *v.* complain, carp, grumble, gripe, grouse, *slang:* bellyache, bitch, kvetch, beef; grieve, lament, mourn.

mob *n.* **1.** throng, gang, pack, horde, multitude, assemblage, populace, crowd, gathering. **2.** plebeians, proletariat, common herd, the great unwashed, masses, hoi polloi, riff-raff.

mob *v.* crowd, swarm, attack, descend on, besiege, overrun, overwhelm, storm.

mobile *adj.* active, agile, ambulatory; movable, roaming, roving, itinerant; locomotive, motorized; *ant.* fixed, stationary.

mobility *n.* portability; flexibility, changeability, versatility, flux, plasticity, mutability; *ant.* rigidity.

mobilize *v.* ready, galvanize, rally, muster, marshal, assemble, prepare, activate, summon.

mob rule *n.* anarchy, mobocracy, lawlessness, disorder.

mock *v.* **1.** ridicule, deride, scorn, taunt, disparage, insult, jeer, scoff, sneer, tease; *ant.* flatter, praise. **2.** mimic, parody, imitate, mime, burlesque, parrot, caricature, ape, lampoon, satirize, send up.

mock *adj.* imitation, artificial, fake, counterfeit, false, forged, ersatz, pseudo, simulated, spurious, synthetic.

mockery *n.* **1.** ridicule, disparagement, con-

tempt, derision, disdain, sarcasm, jeering, disrespect. **2.** farce, satire, burlesque, caricature, takeoff.

mocking *adj.* derisive, sardonic, sarcastic, contemptuous, disdainful, scornful, rude, insulting; *ant.* respectful.

mode *n.* **1.** method, manner, form, style, approach, plan, practice, procedure, system, technique, vein, way. **2.** fashion, vogue, convention, rage, craze, trend, fad.

model *n.* **1.** (one to be emulated) ideal, archetype, paradigm, exemplar, hero, paragon, epitome. **2.** (one to be copied or used as a guide) original, prototype, yardstick, mold, basis, standard, precedent, guide, pattern, image. **3.** (an altered version) miniature, replica, reduction, representation, mock-up. **4.** mannequin, poser, clotheshorse.

model *v.* **1.** shape, work, create, fashion, mold, carve, cast, design, pattern, sculpt. **2.** (make a copy of) duplicate, imitate, simulate, represent. **3.** display, demonstrate, sport, wear, exhibit, show, parade *or* pose in.

model *adj.* ideal, exemplary, consummate, prototypical; representative, standard, typical.

moderate *v.* temper, modulate, abate, allay, lessen, mitigate, regulate, curb, calm, quiet, assuage, tone down.

moderate *adj.* **1.** (said of price) reasonable, modest, nominal; inexpensive, cheap, low-priced; average, usual, middling; *ant.* expensive, exorbitant. **2.** (avoiding extreme positions) nonpartisan, middle-of-the-road, neutral, impartial; tolerant, judicious, equable, reserved, calm, temperate, restrained, sober; *ant.* radical, partial. **3.** (of weather) pleasant, gentle, soft, balmy, clement, calm, temperate, pacific, mild; *ant.* severe, bitter.

moderately *adv.* tolerantly, temperately, somewhat, slightly, to a degree, in moderation, sparingly, within limits, within reason, frugally, soberly.

moderation *n.* temperance, discipline, restraint, self-restraint, tolerance, forbearance, abstemiousness, golden mean; *ant.* excess, overindulgence.

moderator *n.* judge, arbitrator, mediator, head.

modern *adj.* **1.** contemporary, recent, current, present-day, twentieth-century. **2.** chic, stylish, swank, fashionable, current, avant-garde, modish, trendy, upscale, progressive, novel; *ant.* old-fashioned, out-of-date, out-of-style.

modernize *v.* update, remodel, renovate, redesign, renew, revamp, streamline; *ant.* regress.

modest *adj.* **1.** humble, unassuming, self-effacing, unpretentious, diffident; unaffected, plain, simple, natural. **2.** shy, reserved, meek, timid, bashful, diffident; *ant.* conceited. **3.** (as in price) moderate, reasonable, fair, economical, inexpensive, cheap, unexceptional; *ant.* exorbitant, costly. **4.** proper, decent, chaste, decorous, seemly, demure; *ant.* indecent.

modesty *n.* **1.** humility, unpretentiousness, self-effacement, diffidence; *ant.* vanity, conceit. **2.** shyness, timidity, diffidence, bashfulness, meekness, inhibition. **3.** constraint, reserve, decorum, discreetness, seemliness, decency; chastity, purity, virtue.

modicum *n.* bit, iota, speck, particle, fragment, fraction, scrap, shred, touch, trace.

modification *n.* adjustment, alteration, change, modulation, revision, variation, refinement.

modified *adj.* **1.** changed, varied, adjusted, mutated. **2.** reduced, limited, diminished.

modify *v.* **1.** alter, change, vary, transform, adapt, adjust, convert, revise, remodel. **2.** moderate, temper, mitigate, curb, allay, lessen, reduce, restrict, tone down.

modish *adj.* fashionable, stylish, chic, smart, trendy, voguish, modern, contemporary, all the rage, *slang:* with it, hip; *ant.* dowdy, old-fashioned.

modulate *v.* adjust, alter, attune, balance, inflect, moderate, accentuate, regulate, tune, vary, lower, soften; *ant.* increase, raise.

modulation *n.* **1.** shade, shift, intonation, inflection, accent, adjustment, alteration. **2.** pitch, sound, timbre, tuning.

modus operandi *n.* method, system, procedure, manner, technique, operation, way, plan, process, practice.

mogul *n.* notable, magnate, potentate, tycoon, bigwig, royalty, *slang:* big cheese, big shot, big gun.

moist *adj.* damp, wet, watery, soggy, dank, clammy, marshy, swampy; *ant.* dry.

moisten *v.* dampen, moisturize, saturate, water, wet, dip, irrigate, soak, mist; *ant.* dry.

moisture *n.* wetness, dampness, precipitation, mist, drizzle, dew, mugginess, dankness; *ant.* dryness.

mold *n.* **1.** form, cast, frame, shape, pattern, design, image, template, impression, depression, matrix. **2.** mildew, fungus, rust, smut, lichen.

mold *v.* **1.** form, fashion, create, make. **2.** molder, mildew, rust, decay.

moldy *adj.* mildewed, rotten, musty, dank.

mole *n.* birthmark, flaw, blemish, blotch.

molest *v.* harass, hassle, plague, torment, vex, disturb; abuse, attack, accost, assail, harm, injure, ill-treat, maltreat, persecute.

mollify *v.* **1.** appease, pacify, soothe, calm, quiet, allay, assuage, placate; *ant.* anger. **2.** lessen, abate, alleviate, diminish, decrease, ameliorate, moderate; *ant.* aggravate.

mollycoddle *v.* pamper, spoil, baby, indulge, mother, overprotect, spoon-feed; *ant.* neglect, ill-treat.

molt *v.* shed, cast off, lose.

molten *adj.* hot, heated, melted, fused, liquefied, fluid, seething.

moment *n.* instant, minute, flash, second, twinkling, jiffy, three winks.

momentarily *adv.* briefly, fleetingly, for an instant, temporarily, for a moment.

momentary *adj.* fleeting, passing, transient, brief, quick, hasty; *ant.* lasting, permanent.

momentous *adj.* important, significant, crucial, serious, signal, critical, decisive, grave, historic, major, pivotal, weighty, apocalyptic.

momentum *n.* impetus, force, drive, propulsion, impulse, energy, incentive, urge, push, thrust, velocity.

monarch *n.* sovereign, ruler, despot, potentate, tyrant, king, emperor, empress.

monarchial *adj.* noble, autocratic, eminent, royal.

monarchy *n.* sovereignty, rule, despotism, realm, command, tyranny, kingdom, majesty.

monastery *n.* abbey, priory, cloister, convent, friary, nunnery.

monastic *adj.* sequestered, cloistered, reclusive, secluded, monkish, hermetical, celibate; *ant.* worldly.

monetary *adj.* fiscal, financial, pecuniary, economic, budgetary, capital.

money *n.* **1.** currency, banknotes, cash, bills, coinage, legal tender, scrip, *slang:* dough, bread, bucks, moola. **2.** wealth, capital, funds, property. **3.** pay, payment, salary, wages. **put one's money on** bet, speculate, gamble, wager.

money-grubber *n.* penny pincher, Scrooge, miser, materialist.

money-grubbing *adj.* grasping, miserly, acquisitive, mercenary.

mongrel *n.* hybrid, crossbreed, half-breed, mutt, mule; *ant.* purebred, pedigree.

monied *adj.* affluent, prosperous, rich, wealthy, well-off, well-heeled, well-to-do, loaded (*slang*); *ant.* impoverished.

monitor *n.* counselor, adviser, guide, overseer, supervisor.

monitor *v.* watch, observe, keep an eye on, keep track of, follow, note, oversee, supervise, check, survey.

monk *n.* brother, friar, abbot, priest, prior; eremite, ascetic, monastic; hermit, recluse.

monkey *n.* **1.** ape, simian, primate. **2.** fool, buffoon, clown, goofball (*slang*), scamp, rascal. **monkey business 1.** deception, deceit, conniving. **2.** horseplay, mischief, tomfoolery, shenanigans, high jinks.

monkey *v.* fiddle, tamper with, pry, meddle, interfere, tinker, trifle.

monochrome *adj.* unicolored, black-and-white, monotone; *ant.* multicolored.

monolithic *adj.* colossal, huge, gigantic, monumental, vast; solid, undifferentiated, unvaried.

monologue *n.* lecture, speech, oration, sermon, soliloquy, harangue, talk, discourse; *ant.* dialogue, conversation.

monomania *n.* fixation, obsession, compulsion, fetish, fanaticism, mania, neurosis.

monopolize *v.* dominate, control, take over, appropriate, corner, exclude; *ant.* share, include.

monopoly *n.* control, domination, sole right, corner, copyright; *ant.* open market.

monotonous *adj.* **1.** tiresome, tedious, boring, plodding, dull, wearying, wearisome, prosaic; *ant.* colorful, lively. **2.** unvarying, repetitious, monochrome, unchanging, uniform; *ant.* varied, kaleidoscopic.

monotony *n.* sameness, tediousness, flatness, repetitiveness, boredom, routine; *ant.* colorfulness, liveliness.

monster *n.* **1.** chimera, demon, fiend, bogeyman, behemoth, nightmare. **2.** abnormality, mutant, aberration, freak, sport.

monstrous *adj.* **1.** enormous, colossal, elephantine, gargantuan, gigantic, hulking, immense, mammoth, towering, tremendous. **2.** deformed, freakish, grotesque, malformed, misshapen, cyclopean, unnatural, abnormal. **3.** (said of an act or of behavior) shocking, frightful, terrible, horrible, egregious, gruesome, hideous, odious, atrocious, evil, abhorrent, heinous, loathsome, horrible, inhuman.

monument *n.* **1.** shrine, statue, column, pillar, monolith, tomb, headstone, memorial. **2.** magnum opus, masterpiece, work of art, achievement.

monumental *adj.* **1.** grand, great, majestic, imposing, magnificent, prodigious, tremendous, vast. **2.** historic, important, impressive; *ant.* insignificant.

mood *n.* state, humor, frame of mind, temper, bent, propensity, disposition, inclination, pique, fancy, whim, caprice.

moody *adj.* capricious, changeable, choleric, fickle, flighty, inconstant, irascible, mercurial, volatile, temperamental, splenetic, touchy, unstable; *ant.* equable. **2.** unhappy, low-spirited, cranky, gloomy, sullen, morose, cantankerous, cross, dour, downcast, glum, saturnine, sulky, miserable; *ant.* cheerful.

moon *v.* brood, mope, languish, pine, daydream, fantasize.

moonshine *n.* **1.** light, effulgence, radiance, luminosity, glint, scintillation, lambency. **2.** (illegal whiskey) (*slang*), *slang:* hootch, swamp root, mountain dew, white lightning. **3.** (*slang*) nonsense, tripe, claptrap, crap, hogwash, *slang:* bunk, baloney, hot air.

moonstruck *adj.* lovesick, infatuated; crazed, insane, lunatic.

moor *n.* heath, upland, fell, downs.

moor *v.* anchor, berth, dock, fasten, fix, hitch, lash, secure, bind; *ant.* loose.

moot *adj.* **1.** arguable, debatable, disputable, controvertible, questionable. **2.** unresolvable, academic, hypothetical, theoretical, conjectural, suppositional; *ant.* pragmatic.

mop *v.* wipe, swab, clean, wash, rub, sponge.

mop the floor with (*slang*) defeat, beat, thrash, trounce.

mope *v.* sulk, brood, be in a funk, be in the doldrums, lose heart, repine, despair, languish; moon, pine; *ant.* cheer up.

moral *n.* message, meaning, dictum, point, precept, lesson, maxim, adage, teaching, aphorism, saying.

moral *adj.* virtuous, decent, good, ethical, just, principled, exemplary; respectable, proper, chaste, pure.

morale *n.* resolve, spirit, mettle, heart, mood, esprit de corps.

morality *n.* 1. virtue, righteousness, decency, goodness, integrity, honesty, standards, principle. 2. (social norms) propriety, mores, respectability, chastity, purity.

moralize *v.* lecture, scold, admonish, pontificate, preach, sermonize, edify.

morals *n.* standards, ideals, beliefs, mores, principles, scruples, ethics.

morass *n.* 1. swamp, marsh, bog, quagmire. 2. confusion, mix-up, mess, muddle, mire, jam, can of worms.

moratorium *n.* suspension, delay, halt, cessation, ban, embargo, freeze, standstill, stay; *ant.* go-ahead, green light.

morbid *adj.* 1. gruesome, grisly, horrible, grim, horrid, hideous, ghastly, macabre, dreadful. 2. morose, sullen, brooding, gloomy, somber, pessimistic, neurotic; *ant.* cheerful, sane. 3. diseased, sickly, ailing, unhealthy, pathological, infected, malignant; *ant.* healthy.

mordant *adj.* caustic, sarcastic, acerbic, acid, biting, cutting, stringent, trenchant, scathing, stinging, venomous; *ant.* gentle, sparing.

more *adj.* 1. (being an added amount) additional, further, extra, other, over and above; *ant.* less. 2. expanded, increased, augmented, enhanced, added to; *ant.* lessened, decreased.

more *adv.* in addition, increasingly, also, likewise.

moreover *adv.* additionally, also, furthermore, likewise, what is more.

moribund *adj.* 1. dying, incurable, wasting away, at death's door, with one foot in the grave, on one's last legs, doomed. 2. fading, failing, waning, doomed, ebbing, collapsing,

crumbling, stagnating, on the way out; *ant.* nascent, flourishing.

moron *n.* imbecile, simpleton, dullard, dunce, cretin, idiot, dolt, dimwit, halfwit, *slang:* boob, ass, bonehead; *ant.* philosopher, sage, genius.

moronic *adj.* asinine, foolish, mindless, simple, thick, stupid, unintelligent.

morose *adj.* sullen, gloomy, depressed, dolorous, melancholy, dour, splenetic, moody, saturnine, sulky; *ant.* cheerful.

morsel *n.* bit, piece, fragment, tidbit, taste.

mortal *adj.* 1. fatal, deadly, malignant, lethal. 2. human, transient, impermanent, frail, passing, ephemeral, evanescent, corporeal, earthly, temporal, sublunary; *ant.* immortal. 3. extreme, implacable, unrelenting, remorseless.

mortal *n.* human, earthling, man, woman, being, body, creature, animal, sublunary; *ant.* god, immortal.

mortality *n.* 1. transience, impermanence, temporality, extinction, fatality, dying, death; *ant.* immortality. 2. death, bloodshed, killing, carnage, destruction. 3. humanity, mankind, human race, mortals.

mortgage *n.* contract, lease, title, debt, lien, loan, bond, pledge, security.

mortgage *v.* put up, stake, pawn, put in hock.

mortgaged *adj.* promised, pledged, liable, tied, bound, obligated, guaranteed.

mortified *adj.* humiliated, embarrassed, humbled, shamed, chagrined, chastened, abashed.

mortify *v.* disgrace, humiliate, ridicule, shame, belittle, embarrass, distress.

mortuary *n.* morgue, funeral parlor *or* home, charnel house.

mossback *n.* conservative, right-winger, reactionary, stick-in-the-mud.

mossy *adj.* soft, covered, overgrown, velvety, tufted, plushy, downy; *ant.* bare, prickly.

mostly *adv.* 1. often, frequently, regularly, usually, many times; *ant.* seldom. 2. primarily, chiefly, essentially, characteristically, customarily, generally, mainly, on the whole, predominantly, principally.

mote *n.* bit, iota, jot, mite, speck, atom, particle, trace.

moth-eaten *adj.* 1. worn-out, threadbare, ragged, tattered, mangy, moldy, seedy, shabby, dilapidated; *ant.* new. 2. (said of ideas) outdated, old-fashioned, obsolete, antiquated, tired, worn-out, passé.

mother *n.* parent, matriarch, mom, mommy, mama.

mother *v.* care for, nurture, tend, rear, protect, pamper, spoil, cosset, fuss over, baby, cherish; *ant.* neglect.

mother country homeland, native country, motherland.

motherly *adj.* maternal, devoted, caring, comforting, gentle, loving, tender, sympathetic, supporting, protective, indulgent; *ant.* indifferent, neglectful.

mother tongue native language, dialect, local idiom.

motif *n.* theme, subject, topic, concept, idea, leitmotif; figure, form, design, pattern, shape.

motion *n.* 1. change, movement, act, action, passage, flow, flux, transit, travel, mobility. 2. suggestion, proposal, proposition, recommendation, consideration.

motion *v.* gesture, sign, signal, gesticulate, beckon, wave.

motionless *adj.* 1. still, unmoving, dead, inert, stagnant, calm, at rest, inanimate, paralyzed, static, transfixed; *ant.* active. 2. firm, unmovable, fixed, rigid, stationary, frozen; *ant.* moving.

motivate *v.* incite, arouse, spur, goad, induce, instigate, fire, provoke, prompt, stimulate, whet; *ant.* deter, prevent.

motivation *n.* inducement, inspiration, stimulus, incentive, drive, impetus, motive, interest, ambition; *ant.* discouragement, prevention.

motive *n.* reason, cause, purpose, design, desire, impulse, intent.

motley *adj.* 1. mottled, multicolored, kaleidoscopic, varicolored, variegated, patchwork, rainbow. 2. mixed, various, assorted, disparate, mingled, diversified; *ant.* homogeneous.

mottled *adj.* dappled, flecked, speckled, streaked, variegated, spotted, freckled, blotchy; *ant.* uniform.

motto *n.* maxim, adage, saying, axiom, saw, slogan, watchword, byword, precept, proverb, epigram.

mount *v.* 1. ascend, climb, scale, escalate. 2. climb on, straddle, get astride. 3. install, put

on, display, set up, assemble, place, position, frame, exhibit; *ant.* take down.

mountain *n.* 1. elevation, height, peak, steep, palisade, precipice, cliff, butte. 2. pile, mass, mound, heap.

mountainous *adj.* 1. steep, lofty, hilly, alpine, elevated, craggy, rocky, soaring, enormous, hulking, immense; *ant.* flat, small. 2. daunting, formidable, ponderous, prodigious; *ant.* easy.

mounted *adj.* attached, fixed, secured, firm, supported.

mourn *v.* bemoan, bewail, regret, rue, grieve, lament, miss, repine; *ant.* rejoice.

mourner *n.* bereaved, commiserator, condoler.

mournful *adj.* 1. sorrowful, disconsolate, dejected, depressed, gloomy, heartbroken, miserable, somber, woeful; *ant.* cheerful, joyful. 2. distressing, pitiable, pathetic, deplorable, desolate, piteous, tragic.

mousy *adj.* drab, dull, brownish, colorless, plain, indeterminate, characterless, uninteresting, timid, shy; *ant.* vibrant.

mouth *n.* 1. orifice, opening, cavity, aperture, vent, outlet. 2. estuary, delta, harbor, gateway, portal, inlet, sound.

down at the mouth depressed, discouraged, sad, unhappy.

mouth *v.* articulate, enunciate, form, utter, elegize, spout.

mouthful *n.* bite, taste, piece, morsel, sample, forkful, spoonful, swallow, sip.

mouthpiece *n.* spokesperson, press agent, press secretary, publicist, representative, agent, delegate, adviser, counselor, propagandist.

movable *adj.* portable, mobile, transportable, transferable, conveyable; adaptable, alterable, changeable; *ant.* fixed, stationary.

move *n.* 1. movement, transit, progress, maneuver, migration, relocation, removal. 2. action, deed, ruse, stratagem, tactic, tack.

move *v.* 1. go, proceed, progress, travel, traverse, walk, run, stir; *ant.* stay put. 2. relocate, leave, decamp, depart, migrate, transfer, transport. 3. affect, arouse, stir, stir up, influence, urge, push, activate, induce, incite, stimulate, encourage, excite. 4. (make a formal proposal) propose, suggest, submit, recommend, put forward, advocate.

movement *n.* 1. progress, journey, advance, flow, flux, change, shift; immigration, migration; evolution. 2. unrest, groundswell, organization, campaign, crusade.

moving *adj.* 1. going, progressing, advancing, ambulatory, dynamic, mobile, traversing, traveling, changing. 2. affecting, poignant, touching, stirring, emotional, inspirational, pathetic.

mow *v.* scythe, reap, harvest, crop, cut, shear, trim, clip.

mow down massacre, slaughter, decimate, butcher, cut down.

much *adj.* 1. abundant, considerable, voluminous, substantial, ample, plentiful, profuse, lavish, generous; *ant.* inadequate, insufficient, little, limited.

muck *n.* refuse, waste, mud, sewage, trash, dung.

muckraker *n.* gossip, exposer, scandalmonger, meddler.

mucky *adj.* dirty, filthy, foul, muddy, soiled, grimy, messy; *ant.* clean.

mud *n.* dirt, muck, mire, ooze.

muddle *n.* 1. confusion, disorder, disarray, mess. 2. difficulty, quandary, predicament, dilemma, trouble, plight, jam, pickle, complication.

muddle *v.* 1. confound, confuse, entangle, shake up, disturb, perturb, ruffle, disarrange, entangle, complicate. 2. bungle, botch, mess up.

muddle through cope, get by, make it through, succeed.

muddled *adj.* confused, uncertain, unclear, vague, at sea, disoriented, addled, bewildered, dazed.

muddy *adj.* 1. murky, obscure, cloudy, indistinct, dull, dark; *ant.* clear. 2. swampy, sodden, miry, mucky, watery; *ant.* dry.

muddy *v.* dirty, smear, smirch, soil.

muff *v.* blunder, fail, botch, fumble, mismanage.

muffle *v.* stifle, hush, mute, deaden, soften, dull, muzzle, suppress; *ant.* amplify.

muffled *adj.* obscure, indistinct, suppressed, stifled.

mug *n.* 1. cup, tankard, stein, flagon. 2. face, countenance, features, visage.

298

mug *v.* rob, hold up, steal from, attack, jump, set upon.

muggy *adj.* damp, humid, sultry, sweltering, clammy, oppressive, stuffy; *ant.* dry.

mulish *adj.* opinionated, obstinate, stubborn, intransigent, headstrong, willful, pigheaded, inflexible.

mull *v.* contemplate, ponder, think over, deliberate, ruminate, reflect, cogitate, meditate, muse on, study, examine.

multicolored *adj.* varicolored, kaleidoscopic, motley, speckled, flecked, spotted, pied, checkered.

multifarious *adj.* diverse, manifold, various, different, sundry, variegated, legion.

multiple *adj.* 1. various, many, manifold, multifarious, many-sided, compounded. 2. reoccurring, repetitious, repeated, duplicated.

multiplicity *n.* abundance, profusion, heaps, loads, lots, tons; array, myriad, diversity.

multiply *v.* 1. increase, add, augment, expand, double; *ant.* decrease, lessen. 2. propagate, reproduce, breed, proliferate, generate, produce.

multitude *n.* throng, crowd, swarm, mass, mob, assemblage, host, legion, abundance; *ant.* handful, scattering.

multitudinous *adj.* abundant, copious, myriad, numerous, profuse, swarming, teeming, countless, innumerable, infinite.

mum *adj.* reticent, close-lipped, close-mouthed, quiet, hushed, uncommunicative, silent; confidential, secretive, hush-hush.

mumble *v.* mutter, murmur, grumble, whisper, say to oneself, swallow one's words.

mumbo-jumbo *n.* gibberish, doublespeak, cant, claptrap, rigmarole, gobbledygook.

munch *v.* chomp, chew, crunch, eat, bite, masticate, grind.

mundane *adj.* ordinary, commonplace, everyday, banal, prosaic, workaday; *ant.* extraordinary.

municipal *adj.* public, civic, community, metropolitan, urban, self-governing; *ant.* national, worldwide.

munificence *n.* generosity, kindness, benevolence, magnanimity, openhandedness, philanthropy; *ant.* meanness.

munificent *adj.* generous, lavish, unstinting, hospitable, charitable; *ant.* mean.

munitions *n.* weapons, arms, ammunition, armaments, ordnance.

murder *n.* killing, slaying, homicide, manslaughter, bloodshed, carnage.

murder *v.* slay, kill, assassinate, annihilate, slaughter, massacre, eliminate, *slang:* hit, rub out, bump off, waste, do in.

murderer *n.* killer, assassin, hit-man, slayer, butcher.

murderous *adj.* brutal, cruel, savage, ferocious, killing, lethal, barbarous, bloodthirsty; *ant.* placid, kind.

murky *adj.* **1.** obscure, cloudy, foggy, dusky, dark, dim, overcast, veiled; *ant.* bright, clear. **2.** gloomy, dark, dismal, dreary, somber, dull.

murmur *v.* mumble, mutter, whisper, buzz, drone, grumble, hum.

muscle *n.* **1.** sinew, tendon, beef, horseflesh. **2.** strength, power, might, brawn, potency, clout, force.

muscle in strongarm, bully, elbow, force *or* butt in, impose oneself, intervene, crash.

muscular *adj.* strong, brawny, powerful, husky, wiry, strapping, stalwart, sturdy; *ant.* feeble, weak.

muse *v.* ponder, contemplate, reflect, ruminate, meditate, brood, consider, weigh, speculate.

mush *n.* **1.** pulp, mash, slush, paste, swill, hasty pudding. **2.** sentimentalism, mawkishness, romanticism, schmaltz (*slang*).

mushroom *v.* grow, increase, augment, spread, boom, burgeon, escalate, flourish, proliferate, sprout, multiply.

mushy *adj.* **1.** pulpy, doughy, soft, squashy. **2.** romantic, sentimental, maudlin, emotional, schmaltzy (*slang*), mawkish, gushy, sloppy, sugary, weepy.

face the music accept the consequences, take what's coming, pay the piper.

music *n.* melody, harmony, lyricism, melodiousness, strain, air, cadence.

musical *adj.* **1.** tuneful, melodious, harmonious, euphonious, lyric, silvery, pleasing, agreeable; *ant.* discordant, harsh. **2.** (musically inclined) gifted, artistic, talented.

musing *n.* thought, reflection, deliberation, absorption, introspection, dreaming, contemplation, cogitation.

muss *v.* tousle, dishevel, ruffle, disarrange, tangle, mess up.

must *n.* necessity, essential, need, requirement, prerequisite, sine qua non, imperative, obligation, duty, stipulation, provision.

muster *v.* marshal, summon, assemble, gather, convene, mobilize.

musty *adj.* **1.** dusty, airless, stuffy, stale, moldy, putrid, rank, dank, decayed, mildewed, motheaten, threadbare; *ant.* new. **2.** trite, stale, worn-out, ancient, obsolete, antiquated.

mutability *n.* instability, variability, alterability, volatility, vacillation, irresolution, uncertainty.

mutable *adj.* changing, vacillating, wavering, alterable, flexible, fickle, uncertain, doubtful, unstable, unsteady; *ant.* constant, invariable, permanent.

mutation *n.* change, deviation, modification, alteration, metamorphosis, transformation; deviant, anomaly.

mute *v.* silence, muffle, hush, subdue, soften, dampen, moderate, reduce, tone down, deaden.

mute *adj.* silent, speechless, voiceless, dumb, deaf and dumb, inarticulate, aphonic; *ant.* vocal.

muted *adj.* muffled, faint, stifled, suppressed, low-key.

mutilate *v.* maim, disfigure, dismember, mangle, deface, ravage, mar.

mutilated *adj.* deformed, disfigured, maimed, mangled, defaced, dismembered, amputated, castrated, butchered.

mutinous *adj.* insubordinate, rebellious, insurgent, subversive, seditious, ungovernable, unmanageable, unruly; *ant.* compliant, dutiful.

mutiny *n.* revolt, insurrection, revolution, resistance, uprising, defiance, insubordination.

mutiny *v.* rebel, revolt, resist, protest, rise up, take over, disobey.

mutter *v.* mumble, murmur, grumble, rumble, grunt, sputter.

mutual *adj.* reciprocal, requited, shared, returned, common, joint, interchangeable.

muzzle *v.* suppress, restrain, repress, mute, stifle, silence, still, hush, bind, gag, muffle, deaden; *ant.* give free rein to.

myopic *adj.* **1.** nearsighted, shortsighted. **2.** (unable to plan or anticipate the future) undiscerning, obtuse, foolish, shortsighted, blind.

myriad *adj.* infinite, innumerable, immeasurable, incalculable, countless, limitless, untold, endless.

mysterious *adj.* **1.** puzzling, enigmatic, baffling, inscrutable, incomprehensible, perplexing, cryptic, strange, weird; *ant.* straightforward. **2.** mystic, magic, occult, spiritual, supernatural, arcane, esoteric, necromantic.

mystery *n.* enigma, conundrum, riddle, puzzle.

mystical *adj.* **1.** metaphysical, preternatural, supernatural, transcendental, otherworldly. **2.** abstruse, cryptic, arcane, esoteric, hidden, inscrutable, mysterious, occult.

mystify *v.* baffle, perplex, bewilder, confound, puzzle, trick.

mystique *n.* appeal, charm, charisma, magic, spell, fascination, glamour.

myth *n.* fable, legend, lore, allegory, parable, superstition, fairy tale.

mythical *adj.* **1.** fabled, legendary, mythological. **2.** fabricated, fabulous, false, unreal, invented, imaginary, pretended, nonexistent; *ant.* actual, historical, real, true.

mythological *adj.* chimerical, whimsical, fictitious, folkloric.

mythology *n.* **1.** legends, lore, myths, tales, traditions. **2.** faith, religion, belief, conviction.

N

nab (*slang*) *v.* apprehend, arrest, seize, capture, catch, *slang*: collar, grab, snatch, take, nail.

nabob *n.* tycoon, celebrity, magnate, personage, financier, bigwig (*slang*), millionaire, billionaire, VIP, luminary, panjandrum, Croesus.

nadir *n.* depth, bottom, minimum, zero, rock bottom; *ant.* apex, peak, zenith.

nag *n.* 1. horse, hack, mount, plug (*slang*). 2. shrew, scold, harpy, harridan, tartar, virago.

nag *v.* vex, pester, annoy, badger, harass, harry, irritate, plague, henpeck, torment, berate, scold, goad, upbraid.

nagging *adj.* persistent, continuous, distressing, upsetting, worrying, painful, irritating, scolding, critical, tormenting.

nail *n.* peg, stud, pin, rivet, screw, spike, staple, tack.

hard as nails 1. steely, impenetrable, tough, impervious, hard-nosed (*slang*). 2. callous, unfeeling, cruel, remorseless.

nail *v.* 1. hammer, drive, spike, pound, beat, hit. 2. hold, bind, clinch, fasten, fix, tack, pin, secure. 3. (*slang*) capture, detain, apprehend, catch, collar (*slang*).

naive *adj.* ingenuous, unaffected, innocent, artless, candid, childlike, unschooled, jejune, ignorant, callow, gullible, natural, green, guileless, facile; *ant.* experienced, sophisticated.

naiveté *n.* ingenuousness, artlessness, candor, gullibility, simplicity, childishness, inexperience, innocence.

naked *adj.* 1. bared, nude, stripped, unclad, disrobed, divested, threadbare, leafless, exposed, adamic, denuded, stark-naked, in one's birthday suit (*slang*), in the raw, in the buff, in the altogether (*slang*). 2. unadorned, plain, simple, artless, modest, unvarnished, unexaggerated, blatant, manifest, overt.

namby-pamby *adj.* insipid, simpering, feeble, anemic, vapid, wishy-washy, weak, mawkish, prim, prissy, colorless, sentimental, spineless.

name *n.* 1. title, proper name, given name, appellation, designation, denomination, acronym, moniker (*slang*), sobriquet, term, title, epithet, cognomen. 2. reputation, renown, fame, honor, distinction, eminence, esteem, praise, repute, note.

name *v.* 1. christen, baptize, call, designate, nickname, characterize, label, dub, style, term. 2. specify, identify, refer to, point to, cite, mention, single out, mark, index, list, classify, denote, signify, connote. 3. appoint, delegate, elect, select, nominate, commission, choose.

named *adj.* 1. christened, designated, termed, titled, baptized, labeled, dubbed, known as, styled, termed. 2. appointed, chosen, picked, nominated, selected, delegated, commissioned.

name-dropper *n.* braggart, snob, poseur, pseudointellectual.

nameless *adj.* anonymous, incognito, untitled, unnamed, undesignated, unacknowledged, unknown, unheard of, unsung, obscure, undistinguished, inconspicuous.

namely *adv.* to wit, that is to say, particularly, specifically, as much as to say, in other words, in plain English, i.e., id est, viz., videlicet.

nap *n.* 1. siesta, rest, sleep, snooze (*slang*), catnap, *slang*: forty winks, shuteye. 2. down, pile, shag, fiber, woof, warp and woof, grain, weave, roughness, smoothness, texture.

nap *v.* drop off (*slang*), nod off, doze, rest, sleep, snooze.

narcissistic *adj.* egotistic, egocentric, self-centered, conceited, vain, self-loving.

narcotic *n.* opiate, anesthetic, analgesic, sedative, tranquilizer, anodyne, painkiller.

narcotic *adj.* numbing, deadening, calming, dulling, somniferous, hypnotic, sedative, soporific, stupefying, Lethean, analgesic.

narrate *v.* recite, rehearse, enumerate, describe, recount, delineate, portray, chronicle,

narration relate, report, set forth, tell, unfold, spin a yarn *or* tale.

narration *n.* description, narrative, account, explanation, telling, storytelling, recital.

narrative *n.* account, parable, story, tale, chronicle, history, report.

narrator *n.* relator, storyteller, teller of tales, reciter, raconteur, bard, annalist, chronicler, commentator.

narrow *v.* constrict, tighten, circumscribe, diminish, limit, reduce, straiten; *ant.* loosen, broaden, increase.

narrow *adj.* **1.** close, cramped, tight, confined, compressed, contracted, pinched, restricted, tapering, tapered, slim, attenuated, small, meager, incapacious. **2.** dogmatic, intolerant, parochial, narrow-minded, prejudiced, irrational, stupid, bigoted, exclusive, mean, niggardly, illiberal, small-minded; *ant.* liberal, tolerant.

narrowly *adv.* nearly, barely, scarcely, strictly, precisely, only, just, by a hair's breadth, by a whisker.

narrow-minded *adj.* bigoted, provincial, biased, intolerant, reactionary, shortsighted, small-minded, insular, conservative, opinionated, parochial; *ant.* broad-minded.

nascent *adj.* budding, evolving, growing, incipient, rising, young, advancing, developing, embryonic; *ant.* dying.

nastiness *n.* malice, spitefulness, meanness, foulness, squalor, unsavoriness, offensiveness, indecency, defilement, dirtiness, licentiousness, obscenity, pornography, smuttiness.

nasty *adj.* **1.** gross, foul, revolting, offensive, vulgar, base, disgusting, filthy, polluted, impure, lascivious, lewd, loathsome, nauseating, sickening, vile; *ant.* clean, pleasant. **2.** injurious, damaging, dangerous, harmful, painful, severe. **3.** unpleasant, disagreeable, vicious, hateful, abusive.

nation *n.* country, state, commonwealth, republic, kingdom, principality, dominion, realm, domain, community, society, race, populace, people, body politic.

national *n.* citizen, inhabitant, native, indigene, resident, denizen, subject.

national *adj.* **1.** nationwide, internal, country-wide, federal, interstate. **2.** ethnic, societal, cultural, native.

302

nationalism *n.* allegiance, provincialism, chauvinism, jingoism, flag-waving, patriotism, ethnocentricity, fealty, loyalty, xenophobia.

nationalistic *adj.* jingoistic, loyal, patriotic, chauvinistic, ethnocentrist.

nationality *n.* allegiance, native land, ethnic group, nation, race, tribe, society, community, citizen, inhabitant, resident, dweller, countryman, denizen.

native *adj.* **1.** indigenous, aboriginal, primitive, autochthonous, primeval, vernacular, domestic, regional, home-born, home-bred, local, natal, original; *ant.* imported, transplanted. **2.** innate, inherent, inborn, inbred, natural, immanent, ingrained, congenital, endemic, hereditary, inherited, instinctive, inveterate; *ant.* unnatural, foreign, alien.

native *n.* **1.** (original inhabitant) primitive, aborigine, indigene, autochthon. **2.** national, citizen, inhabitant, resident, dweller, countryman, denizen.

nativity *n.* birth, origin, childbirth, delivery, parturition.

natural *adj.* **1.** intrinsic, original, essential, fundamental, inborn, inherent, congenital, essential, innate, incarnate, indigenous, instinctive, intuitive; *ant.* foreign, alien, acquired. **2.** normal, typical, characteristic, usual, habitual, customary, familiar, common, prevalent, general, uniform, constant; *ant.* unknown, unexpected. **3.** ingenuous, artless, candid, frank, genuine, simple, innocent, spontaneous, impulsive, uncontrolled, involuntary, childlike, unaffected, forthright, sincere, unlearned, unrefined, unsophisticated; *ant.* affected, pretentious.

naturalistic *adj.* realistic, representational, life-like, natural, photographic, graphic, true-to-life.

naturalize *v.* adapt, acclimate, accustom, adopt, domesticate, familiarize, adjust, inure, enfranchise, habituate, conform.

naturally *adv.* characteristically, typically, normally, as a matter of course, usually, ordinarily, habitually, intuitively, customarily, normally.

naturally *interj.* of course, certainly, absolutely, surely.

nature *n.* **1.** characteristics, essence, character, quality, constitution, attributes, complexion, disposition, humor, mood, outlook, quality, traits, temperament, description. **2.** out-of-doors, environment, country, countryside, landscape, scenery, outside world, the great outdoors.

by nature inherently, as a matter of course, by birth.

in a state of nature untamed, uncultivated, primitive, feral, wild, naked.

naught *n.* nothing, zero, cipher, nil, not anything, nought, nada, zilch (*slang*).

naughty *adj.* wayward, disobedient, impish, mischievous, fiendish, badly behaved, roguish, exasperating, fractious, playful, remiss, ribald, risqué, perverse, smutty, wicked; *ant.* polite, well-behaved.

nausea *n.* **1.** sickness, illness, queasiness, vomiting, biliousness, motion sickness, qualms, retching, squeamishness. **2.** make ill, disgust, offense, aversion, revulsion, loathing, abhorrence, repugnance, hatred.

nauseate *v.* make ill, disgust, horrify, offend, sicken, repulse, disturb, revolt, turn one's stomach, make sick to the stomach.

nauseating *adj.* offensive, abhorrent, detestable, disgusting.

nauseous *adj.* **1.** (feeling nausea) sick, ill, queasy, squeamish. **2.** (causing nausea) sickening, disgusting, dizzying, disorienting, upsetting.

nautical *adj.* seagoing, seafaring, marine, naval, aquatic, maritime, oceanic, oceangoing, oceanographic.

naval *adj.* seagoing, marine, nautical, maritime.

navel *n.* umbilicus, omphalos, bellybutton (*slang*), abdomen; center, hub, middle.

navigable *adj.* passable, open, safe.

navigate *v.* pilot, steer, direct, drive, guide, sail, voyage, handle, helm, maneuver, plot, skipper, lay the course, operate.

navigation *n.* piloting, navigating, aviation, seamanship, pilotage, steerage, aeronautics.

navigator *n.* flier, helmsman, pilot, mariner, seagoer, sailor.

navy *n.* fleet, flotilla, armada, task force, amphibious force, argosy.

near *adj.* **1.** adjacent, nigh, adjoining, attached, contiguous, proximal, neighboring, proximate, bordering, at close quarters, nearby; *ant.* distant, far. **2.** approaching, at hand, imminent, expected, coming, forthcoming, near-at-hand, close, looming, impending, in the off-ing; *ant.* remote. **3.** akin, dear, familiar, allied, intimate, related, touching.

near *prep.* beside, alongside, next to, close to, a stone's throw away from, by, toward.

nearby *adj.* handy, convenient, neighboring, accessible, adjacent, adjoining, near; *ant.* faraway.

nearing *adj.* approaching, impending, imminent, coming.

nearly *adv.* almost, about, approximately, practically, virtually, all but, as good as, not quite, *slang:* just about, pretty much, pretty well; well-nigh.

nearness *n.* contiguity, closeness, proximity, adjacency, vicinity, propinquity, availability, immediacy, imminence, juxtaposition, handiness, close quarters, vicinage, approximation; *ant.* distance, remoteness, difference.

nearsighted *adj.* myopic, shortsighted, astigmatic.

neat *adj.* **1.** tidy, clean, orderly, immaculate, spotless, meticulous, exact, precise, trim, spruce, natty, dapper, fastidious, dainty, methodical, systematic, uncluttered; *ant.* slovenly, unkempt. **2.** clever, deft, skillful, expert, proficient, handy, apt, adroit, agile, dexterous, graceful, artful, nimble, finished, practiced; *ant.* awkward, clumsy.

neaten *v.* arrange, straighten, groom, clean up, spruce up, tidy, trim, smarten, put to rights (*slang*).

neatly *adv.* **1.** tidily, orderly, systematically, methodically, immaculately, trimly, primly, daintily, elegantly, nicely, stylishly; *ant.* untidily, sloppily. **2.** skillfully, deftly, agilely, cleverly, adroitly, aptly, easily, nimbly, precisely, handily, expertly.

neatness *n.* cleanliness, cleanness, tidiness, clearness, correctness, fastidiousness, grace, niceness, preciseness.

nebulous *adj.* indistinct, dim, vague, ambiguous, cloudy, confused, imprecise, indefinite, misty, obscure, shadowy, uncertain, unclear, unformed, indeterminate; *ant.* clear.

necessarily *adv.* fundamentally, vitally, cardinally, importantly, momentously, unavoidably, inexorably, inevitably, assuredly, automatically, by definition, of necessity, certainly, consequently, perforce.

necessary *adj.* **1.** essential, requisite, needful,

necessitate v. compel, oblige, constrain, demand, entail, impel, require, call for, coerce, involve, oblige.

necessities n. essentials, requirements, needs.

necessity n. 1. (something that must be had) need, want, requisite, requirement, vital part, essential, imperative, fundamental, sine qua non. 2. (the state of being necessary) exigency, urgency, essentiality, needfulness, indispensability, requisiteness, obligation, compulsion. 3. destitution, privation, need, hardship, extremity, indigence, penury, poverty.

neck n. nape, scrag, scruff.

risk one's neck risk, gamble, take a chance, endanger oneself, go out on a limb.

neck of the woods place, locality, area, neighborhood, section.

necromancy n. magic, sorcery, witchcraft, wizardry, conjuration, demonology, enchantment, divination, thaumaturgy, voodoo, black magic, black art, hoodoo (slang).

necrosis n. decay, rot, corruption, putrefaction.

need n. 1. obligation, requirement, compulsion, urgency, necessity, demand, emergency, extremity, want, wish. 2. insufficiency, lack, shortage, inadequacy exigency; ant. sufficiency. 3. indigence, poverty, penury, pennilessness, deprivation, destitution, hardship, indigence, paucity, privation; ant. wealth, abundance.

if need be if necessary, if the occasion demands, if it is required.

need v. lack, require, necessitate, crave, demand, miss, want, be bereft or deprived of, be deficient, go hungry, live from hand to mouth, slang: be hard up, be up against it; ant. own, have, hold.

needed adj. desired, wanted, required, compulsory, essential, lacking, necessary, obligatory, called for; ant. unnecessary.

needful adj. essential, necessary, needed, indispensable, requisite, stipulated, vital.

---

indispensable, expedient, compulsory, imperative, mandatory, obligatory, required, requisite, vital, incumbent upon, cardinal, quintessential, intrinsic, de rigueur; ant. unimportant, unnecessary. 2. inevitable, fated, ineluctable, inescapable, inevitable, inexorable, unavoidable, certain, imminent.

necessitate v. compel, oblige, constrain, demand, entail, impel, require, call for, coerce, involve, oblige.

necessities n. essentials, requirements, exigencies, fundamentals, indispensables, needs.

---

needle n. pin, darner, awl, spike, skewer.
needle (slang) v. goad, spur, taunt, sting, rile ruffle, nag, nettle, irritate, aggravate, annoy, bait, harass, irk, pester, provoke, quiz, question.

needless adj. unwanted, excessive, unnecessary, useless, dispensable, gratuitous, inessential, pointless, superfluous, uncalled-for, redundant; ant. necessary, needful.

needlework n. embroidery, sewing, stitching, fancywork.

needy adj. poor, destitute, indigent, penniless, impoverished, deprived, disadvantaged, penurious, impecunious; ant. affluent, wealthy.

ne'er-do-well n. idler, bum (slang), loafer, wastrel, vagrant, good-for-nothing.

nefarious adj. treacherous, bad, evil, base, vicious, vile, villainous, wicked, heinous, foul, execrable, infamous, infernal, iniquitous, odious, opprobrious; ant. exemplary.

negate v. 1. nullify, cancel, repeal, retract, rescind, abrogate, annul, disallow, invalidate, nullify, void, countermand, quash, reverse. 2. contradict, oppose, refute, gainsay, belie, deny; ant. affirm.

negation n. denial, opposition, contradiction, repudiation, refusal, cancellation, neutralization, nullification, rejection, reverse, veto, repeal; ant. affirmation.

negative n. refusal, denying, contradiction, opposite, disavowal, refutation, thumbs down, nix (slang).

negative adj. 1. contrary, antagonistic, uncooperative, unwilling, unenthusiastic, cynical, dissenting, nay-saying, jaundiced, pessimistic; ant. optimistic, upbeat, positive. 2. negating, nullifying, negatory, annulling, contradicting, neutralizing.

neglect n. 1. (act of neglecting) disregard, slight, thoughtlessness, disrespect, carelessness, scorn, oversight, heedlessness, inattention, dereliction, disdain, forgetfulness, laxity, negligence, slovenliness, unconcern. 2. (instance of being neglected) delay, default, lapse.

neglect v. forget, ignore, overlook, disregard, leave alone; slight, scorn, contemn, disdain, spurn, affront, depreciate, undervalue, gloss over, be remiss, rebuff; ant. consider, appreciate, value.

---

neglected *adj.* slighted, scorned, disregarded, unappreciated, uncared-for, untended, untilled, unweeded, derelict, deteriorated, declined, decayed, out in the cold, dropped, put on a shelf.

neglectful *adj.* negligent, careless, lax, remiss, lazy, uncaring, inconsiderate, indifferent; *ant.* attentive, careful.

negligee *n.* nightgown, robe, kimono, nightdress, pajamas.

negligence *n.* carelessness, oversight, neglect, indifference, inadvertence, laxness, omission, inattention, forgetfulness, shortcoming, default, disregard, slackness, stupidity; *ant.* attentiveness, care, regard.

negligent *adj.* indifferent, inattentive, neglectful, careless, cursory, nonchalant, offhand, thoughtless, uncareful, lax, remiss, slack, unmindful; *ant.* attentive, scrupulous, careful.

negligible *adj.* petty, small, trifling, trivial, minor, insignificant, inconsequential, minute, unimportant; *ant.* significant.

negotiate *v.* arrange, bargain, haggle, dicker, confer, consult, parley, transact, deal, debate, discuss, settle, work out.

negotiation *n.* **1.** conference, consultation, meeting, colloquy, discussion. **2.** compromise, arbitration, intervention, mediation, diplomacy, bargaining, transaction, wheeling and dealing (*slang*).

negotiator *n.* mediator, moderator, broker, intermediary, adjudicator, arbitrator, ambassador, diplomat, delegate, go-between.

neigh *v.* bray, whinny, nicker, hinny.

neighborhood *n.* environs, community, suburb, block, vicinity, locality, district, quarter, precinct, ward, area, section, zone, confines, surroundings.

in the neighborhood of (*slang*) close to, about, in the proximity of, approximately, more or less.

neighboring *adj.* adjacent, contiguous, adjoining, abutting, bordering, near, nearby, nearest, next, surrounding, vicinal; *ant.* distant, remote.

neighborly *adj.* sociable, hospitable, amiable, civil, friendly, genial, obliging, companionable, solicitous, well-disposed, chummy (slang).

nemesis *n.* enemy, foe, opponent, adversary, antagonist, rival, competitor.

neophyte *n.* amateur, novice, student, beginner, rookie (*slang*), greenhorn; *ant.* veteran, old pro.

nerve *n.* **1.** courage, resolution, mettle, spirit, boldness, bravery, determination, energy, fearlessness, fortitude, gameness, grit, guts, resolution, steadfastness; *ant.* cowardice, weakness. **2.** impudence, effrontery, audacity, rudeness, temerity, brazenness, cheek, brass, gall, impertinence, insolence, pluck, *slang:* chutzpah, sauce, spunk.

get on one's nerves bother, exasperate, annoy, vex, irritate, get in one's hair (*slang*).

nerveless *adj.* **1.** weak, feeble, spineless, nervous, afraid, cowardly, inert, slack, timid, weak, unnerved; *ant.* bold, strong. **2.** calm, controlled, impassive, tranquil, intrepid, unfazed, fearless.

nerve-racking *adj.* exhausting, wearisome, horrible, difficult, disquieting, disturbing, harrowing, stressful, tense, trying.

nervous *adj.* **1.** excitable, sensitive, neurotic, high-strung, agitated, anxious, edgy, flustered, hysterical, jittery, jumpy, uptight (*slang*), fidgety; *ant.* calm, cool, relaxed. **2.** timid, apprehensive, afraid, shy, shrinking, fearful, hesitant, shaky, timorous, weak; *ant.* bold, confident.

nervousness *n.* agitation, anxiety, perturbation, disquietude, tension, discomfiture, tremulousness, turbulence, excitability, irascibility, moodiness, hypersensitivity, neuroticism; *ant.* calmness, coolness.

nervy (*slang*) *adj.* rude, crass, pushy, cheeky, bold, brash, inconsiderate, crude.

nescience *n.* ignorance, inexperience, naiveté, rawness.

nest *n.* den, haunt, cradle, burrow, dray, hideaway, refuge, resort, aerie, womb, incubator, breeding-ground, formicary.

nest egg cache, reserves, funds, savings, store, something for a rainy day.

nestle *v.* cuddle, snuggle, huddle, lie against, curl up, ensconce, nuzzle, settle down.

nestling *adj.* fledgling, suckling, infant, baby, chick, weanling.

net *n.* mesh, netting, lattice, network, screen, web, dragnet, driftnet, reticulum, tracery.

net *v.* **1.** apprehend, trap, ensnare, enmesh, capture, catch, *slang:* bag, nab. **2.** (gain

net above expenses) make, profit, clear, accumulate, earn, gain, obtain, realize, reap, secure, bring in.

net *adj*. remaining, excluding, after-tax, clear, irreducible, final, lowest; *ant.* gross.

nether *adj*. beneath, below, lower, under, basal, bottom, inferior, infernal, Stygian, Plutonian.

netted *adj*. caught, captured, arrested, apprehended, seized, enmeshed.

nettle *v*. annoy, chafe, irritate, pester, disturb, fret, exasperate, harass, needle, pique, ruffle, sting, tease, vex.

network *n*. system, labyrinth, artery, chain, weave, mesh, plexus, grillwork, screening, grid, maze, net, nexus, interconnections, reticulation.

neurosis *n*. compulsion, deviation, instability, mental disorder, abnormality, affliction, derangement, disturbance, obsession, phobia, maladjustment.

neurotic *adj*. upset, disoriented, unstable, erratic, disturbed, dysfunctional, aberrant, anxious, compulsive, deviant, manic, nervous, overwrought, unhealthy, obsessive; *ant.* stable, normal.

neuter *v*. geld, spay, emasculate, castrate, fix, caponize.

neuter *adj*. sterile, unfertile, barren, sexless, asexual, impotent, fallow, frigid.

neutral *adj*. **1.** (not taking sides in a conflict) nonpartisan, noncombatant, inactive, disengaged, uninvolved, bystanding, inert, impartial, nonaligned, noncommittal, unprejudiced; *ant.* engaged, involved, active. **2.** (without an opinion) nonchalant, disinterested, indifferent, unconcerned, dispassionate, uninvolved, uncommitted, indeterminate, expressionless. **3.** (said of colors) intermediate, colorless, dull, indistinct, nondescript, drab, vague.

neutrality *n*. aloofness, noninterference, disinterest, nonpartisanship, impartiality, nonalignment.

neutralize *v*. offset, counterbalance, counterpoise, compensate, cancel, frustrate, invalidate, negate, nullify, undo.

never *adv*. not ever, not at any time, not in the least, in no way, not at all, no way, not under any conditions, nevermore, when hell freezes over; *ant.* always, sometimes.

306

never-ending *adj*. timeless, eternal, endless, perpetual, boundless, ceaseless, incessant, interminable, relentless, unremitting, unceasing, unbroken, Sisyphean; *ant.* fleeting, transitory.

nevertheless *adv*. nonetheless, anyhow, but, notwithstanding, anyhow, anyway, even so, regardless, still, yet.

new *adj*. **1.** recent, current, fresh, just out, late, contemporary, modern, renewed, trendy, up-to-date, up-to-the-minute, modish, au courant; *ant.* old, outdated. **2.** novel, unique, unusual, original, bizarre, unlike, dissimilar, distinct, different, newfangled, unfamiliar, unknown; *ant.* usual, common, hackneyed. **3.** additional, further, extra, supplementary, increased, more. **4.** inexperienced, unseasoned, unskilled, unspoiled, uncontaminated, undecayed, fresh, virgin, newborn; *ant.* experienced, seasoned.

newborn *n*. neonate, infant, recent, preemie (*slang*).

newcomer *n*. neophyte, immigrant, outsider, foreigner, beginner, colonist, incomer, rookie, Johnny-come-lately, novice, tenderfoot, parvenu, settler, stranger.

newfangled *adj*. novel, unique, trendy, modernistic, contemporary, fashionable, futuristic, gimmicky.

newly *adv*. lately, recently, afresh, anew, just, latterly.

newness *n*. originality, uniqueness, novelty, oddity, innovation, strangeness, unusualness; *ant.* oldness, ordinariness.

news *n*. intelligence, discovery, account, bulletin, communiqué, dispatch, exposé, report, revelation, statement, update, scandal, broadcast, communication, scoop (*slang*).

newspaper *n*. publication, journal, daily, gazette, periodical, tabloid, *slang:* rag, sheet.

newsworthy *adj*. notable, important, interesting, noteworthy, remarkable, significant, arresting, stimulating.

next *adj*. **1.** succeeding, following, subsequent, ensuing, consequent, sequential; *ant.* preceding, previous. **2.** adjacent, adjoining, closest, nearest, neighboring, meeting, touching, abutting, bordering.

next to beside, near, adjacent to, by.

next *adv*. afterwards, later, subsequently, thereafter, then.

nibble *n.* bit, bite, morsel, peck, crumb, taste, tidbit, piece.

nibble *v.* nip, gnaw, bite, munch, peck, snack.

nice *adj.* **1.** pleasing, likable, admirable, agreeable, winning, winsome, amiable, refined, charming, delightful, cordial, ingratiating, friendly; *ant.* disagreeable, nasty, unpleasant. **2.** (marked by precise distinction) fine, discerning, elegant, precise, exact, refined, careful, particular; *ant.* gross.

nicely *adv.* carefully, delicately, tactfully.

niceness *n.* **1.** kindness, prudence, discretion, discernment, taste, refinement, amiability, charm, courtesy, delightfulness, friendliness, gentility, attractiveness; *ant.* nastiness, disagreeableness. **2.** discernment, fineness, precision, exactitude, refinement, carefulness, particularity, elegance.

nicety *n.* nuance, delicacy, refinement, touch.

niche *n.* **1.** cranny, corner, hole, cubbyhole, hollow, nook, opening, recess, alcove. **2.** calling, place, position, metier, slot, vocation, pigeonhole.

nick *n.* chip, cut, dent, indentation, notch, slit, dint, scar, score, scratch.

nick *v.* cut, indent, notch, slit.

nickname *n.* label, epithet, moniker, pet name, sobriquet, cognomen.

nifty *adj.* adroit, agile, apt, deft, stylish, neat, pleasing, clever, enjoyable, smart, chic, stylish.

niggardly *adj.* greedy, miserly, parsimonious, stingy, avaricious, beggarly, covetous, frugal, grudging, hardfisted, mean, mercenary, miserly, ungenerous, penurious; *ant.* generous, open-handed.

niggling *adj.* trivial, trifling, petty, unimportant, piddling.

nigh *adj.* near, close at hand, close, impending, imminent, approaching.

night *n.* dark, darkness, evening, dead of night, nightfall, twilight, witching hour, gloom, duskiness; *ant.* day, daytime.

nightclothes *n.* nightgown, pajamas, robe, negligee, lingerie, nightshirt.

nightclub *n.* cabaret, tavern, discothèque, club, casino, cafe, roadhouse, nightspot, wateringhole.

nightfall *n.* twilight, dusk, evening, moonrise, sundown, sunset, vespers; *ant.* dawn, sunrise.

nightgown *n.* nightdress, nightrobe, negligee, lingerie, nightwear, nightclothes, pajamas, *slang:* nightie, PJ's.

nightly *adv.* by night, at night, nocturnally, each night, nights, regularly.

nightmare *n.* bad dream, night terrors, horror, hallucination, ordeal, torment, trial, tribulation, succubus.

nightmarish *adj.* terrifying, unreal, alarming, creepy, demonic, dreadful, fell, disturbing, harrowing, frightening, agonizing, alarming.

nihilism *n.* **1.** rejection, denial, refusal, repudiation, atheism, renunciation, abnegation, negation, nullity, emptiness, nothingness, disbelief, pessimism. **2.** anarchy, disorder, lawlessness, mob rule, terrorism.

nihilist *n.* cynic, disbeliever, pessimist, negativist, agnostic, atheist; revolutionary, agitator, insurgent, anarchist, terrorist.

nil *n.* nothing, zero, naught, none, null, cipher, nullity.

nimble *adj.* **1.** agile, spry, active, graceful, deft, dexterous, light-footed, lively, quick, sprightly, swift; *ant.* awkward, clumsy. **2.** quick-witted, alert, bright, clever, intelligent, judicious.

nimbleness *n.* agility, grace, vivacity, skill, adroitness, alacrity, finesse, dexterity, niftiness, smartness, sprightliness, spryness.

nimbly *adv.* swiftly, rapidly, actively, alertly, deftly, easily, fleetly, proficiently, quickly, readily, snappily, speedily, spryly; *ant.* clumsily.

nimbus *n.* halo, light, aura, radiance, glow, nebula, aurora, cloud, nebulous light, aureole, effulgence, emanation.

nincompoop *n.* imbecile, dolt, fool, blockhead, dimwit, idiot, ignoramus, nitwit, numskull, simpleton, *slang:* ninny, sap, dope.

nip *n.* nibble, morsel, bite, pinch, dram, draft, finger, mouthful, portion, sip, slug, snifter, taste.

nip *v.* bite, nibble, snap, munch, snip, clip, compress, grip, pinch, tweak.

nipple *n.* breast, pap, teat, mamilla, papilla, areola, mammary gland, dug, tit, udder.

nippy *adj.* pungent, sharp, stinging, astringent, biting, chilly, cold.

nirvana *n.* bliss, ecstasy, exaltation, joy, rapture, ravishment, paradise, peace, serenity, tranquillity.

nit-picking *adj.* carping, finicky, fussy, hair-splitting, captious, caviling, hypercritical, pedantic, pettifogging, quibbling.

nitwit *n.* fool, simpleton, blockhead, nincompoop, dimwit, *slang:* dummy, half-wit, ninny, numskull.

no *interj.* absolutely not, by no means, nay, nope, nix (*slang*).

nobility *n.* **1.** magnificence, grandeur, majesty, dignity, greatness, honor, illustriousness, loftiness, incorruptibility, integrity, magnanimity, sublimity, stateliness, superiority, virtue; *ant.* baseness. **2.** aristocracy, gentry, ruling class, peerage, royalty, elite, high society, lords, nobles, patricians; *ant.* proletariat.

noble *n.* lord, nobleman, patrician, peer, aristocrat, baron, gentilhomme; *ant.* plebe.

noble *adj.* **1.** meritorious, generous, magnanimous, magnificent, courtly, lofty, elevated, august, reputable, eminent, lordly, dignified, supreme, virtuous, worthy; *ant.* base, ignoble. **2.** aristocratic, titled, patrician, blue-blooded, imperial, lordly, of gentle birth or blood, kingly, born to the purple; *ant.* common, plebeian, lowborn.

nobly *adj.* honorably, justly, fairly, respectably, honestly.

nobody *n.* upstart, cipher, nonentity, jackstraw, parvenu, whippersnapper, lightweight, zero, also-ran (*slang*); *ant.* somebody.

nocturne *n.* song, lullaby, serenade, evening-song.

nocuous *adj.* dangerous, poisonous, toxic, noxious, malignant, injurious, harmful; *ant.* benign.

nod *n.* **1.** bow, dip, inclination, greeting, salute, beck, gesture, cue, greeting, indication, sign, signal. **2.** permission, acceptance, affirmation, yes, OK, go-ahead.

nod *v.* **1.** assent, greet, salute, sign, signal, beckon, bow, gesture, cue, acknowledge, concur, salaam, curtsy, recognize; *ant.* deny, dissent. **2.** drowse, sleep, droop, nap, drift off.

node *n.* bump, bulge, lump, swelling, clot, knob, knot, nodule, protuberance, burl, caruncle.

nodule *n.* bud, knob, protuberance, bulge.

noise *n.* sound, clamor, tumult, racket, fracas, din, pandemonium, turbulence, caterwauling,

---

blare, clatter, commotion, babel, stridency, uproar, ballyhoo, hubbub; *ant.* silence, quiet, lull.

noiseless *adj.* silent, still, hushed, inaudible, wordless, voiceless, muted, quiet; *ant.* loud, noisy.

noisome *adj.* **1.** harmful, pernicious, baneful, unwholesome, dangerous, deadly, deleterious, injurious, mischievous, poisonous; *ant.* wholesome. **2.** putrid, rank, rotten, mephitic, malodorous, fetid, foul, fulsome, noxious, offensive, pestiferous, pestilential, reeking, smelly, stinking; *ant.* fragrant, pleasant.

noisy *adj.* loud, clamorous, vociferous, cacophonous, clangorous, deafening, riotous, uproarious, piercing, boisterous, chattering, rackety, tumultuous, turbulent; *ant.* quiet, silent.

nomad *n.* migrant, wanderer, vagabond, drifter, itinerant, roamer, rambler, traveler.

nomadic *adj.* roaming, drifting, travelling, gypsy, itinerant, migratory, unsettled, peripatetic, peregrinating, vagrant; *ant.* settled, stationary.

nom de plume pen name, pseudonym, alias, nom de guerre, allonym.

nomenclature *n.* vocabulary, locution, terminology, lexicon, classification, codification, phraseology, hosology, taxology.

nominal *adj.* **1.** titular, given, named, formal, professed, ostensible, purported, supposed, symbolic, theoretical; *ant.* actual, genuine, true. **2.** insignificant, trifling, trivial, unnecessary, meaningless, low, inconsiderable, minimal, small, token.

nominate *v.* appoint, assign, choose, elect, recommend, propose, submit, suggest, mention, name, present, commission, call, specify, draft.

nomination *n.* appointment, recommendation, proposal, selection, suggestion, choice, designation.

nominee *n.* aspirant, appointee, candidate, contestant, entrant, runner, solicitor.

nonacceptance *n.* refusal, renunciation, disapproval, rejection.

nonaligned *adj.* neutral, uncommitted, impartial, independent, nonpartisan, undecided.

nonchalance *n.* indifference, apathy, disregard, insouciance, aplomb, composure, calm, equanimity, imperturbability, sang-froid, self-

nonintervention *n.* noninterference, nonalignment, neutrality, dormancy, apathy.

nonjuror *n.* nonconformist, radical, dissenter, eccentric.

no-nonsense *adj.* practical, purposeful, earnest, serious, matter-of-fact, solemn, dedicated, resolute.

nonpareil *n.* paragon, quintessence, nonesuch.

nonpartisan *adj.* unbiased, unprejudiced, neutral, impartial, dispassionate, objective, detached, just, unaffected, unbigoted; *ant.* biased, prejudiced.

nonplus *v.* baffle, take aback, bewilder, confound, confuse, discomfit, disconcert, dumbfound, flabbergast, mystify, perplex, puzzle, stump.

nonprofit *adj.* charitable, philanthropic, generous, altruistic, humane.

nonproliferation *n.* restraint, restriction, limitation, holding down or back or in.

nonsense *n.* balderdash, drivel, trash, inanity, senselessness, palaver, idle chatter, prattle, rant, bombast, claptrap, rubbish, absurdity, bilge, folly, hogwash; *ant.* sense, reason.

nonsensical *adj.* absurd, silly, senseless, daft, fatuous, inane, ludicrous, irrational; *ant.* logical, sensible.

nonstop *adj.* constant, continuous, unbroken, uninterrupted, ceaseless, incessant, interminable, unremitting, ongoing, unfaltering; *ant.* intermittent, sporadic.

nonstop *adv.* ceaselessly, constantly, continuously, incessantly.

nonviolent *adj.* passive, peaceful, quiet, pacifist, irenic.

nook *n.* niche, cranny, recess, hole, cavity, crevice, retreat, shelter.

noose *n.* knot, hitch, running knot, lasso.

norm *n.* average, standard, measure, pattern, criterion, mean, rule, type, yardstick, benchmark.

normal *adj.* usual, ordinary, conventional, typical, accustomed, average, common, habitual, mainstream, regular, routine, standard, run-of-the-mill, par for the course; *ant.* irregular, odd, peculiar.

normality *n.* **1.** ordinariness, averageness, conventionality, routine, usualness, commonality; *ant.* abnormality, irregularity, oddity. **2.** sanity, mental balance, reason, rationality, balance.

possession, unconcern; *ant.* anxiousness, worriedness.

nonchalant *adj.* **1.** casual, unflappable, aloof, blasé, composed, unruffled, easygoing, lackadaisical, uninterested, incurious, offhand, airy, collected, unperturbed, laid-back (*slang*); *ant.* ardent, enthusiastic. **2.** negligent, careless, neglectful, indifferent, unconcerned; *ant.* attentive.

noncommittal *adj.* careful, reserved, wary, ambiguous, circumspect, equivocal, discreet, indefinite, politic, reserved, tactful, tentative, vague, judicious.

noncompliance *n.* refusal, dissent, objection, protest, denial, nonconformity.

nonconformist *n.* rebel, eccentric, iconoclast, maverick, gadfly, dissenter, malcontent, bohemian, deviant, individualist, radical, secessionist; *ant.* conformist.

nonconformity *n.* dissent, deviation, unconventionality, eccentricity, secession, heterodoxy, opposition, heresy, discordance, refusal, originality; *ant.* conformity.

nondescript *adj.* common, dull, indeterminate, ordinary, plain, undistinguished, unexceptional, unremarkable, vague, uninteresting, empty, mousy; *ant.* remarkable, vivacious, outstanding.

none *pron.* no one, not anyone, nobody, zero, nothing.

nonentity *n.* upstart, cipher, mediocrity, nobody, lightweight.

nonessential *adj.* superfluous, dispensable, expendable, extraneous, extrinsic, inessential, peripheral, excessive, supplementary, unnecessary, petty, trivial, unimportant; *ant.* required.

nonesuch *n.* paragon, quintessence, select, nonpareil.

nonetheless *adv.* nevertheless, anyway, anyhow, even so, however, notwithstanding, yet.

nonexistence *n.* oblivion, nonbeing, unreality, insubstantiality, nothingness, fiction.

nonexistent *adj.* chimerical, fictitious, fanciful, illusory, imaginary, incorporeal, mythical, unreal, immaterial, hallucinatory; *ant.* actual, existing, real.

nonflammable *adj.* fireproof, flame-resistant, incombustible, uninflammable; *ant.* flammable, inflammable.

normally *adv.* usually, commonly, frequently, regularly, characteristically, ordinarily, typically, habitually, as a rule.

normative *adv.* standardizing, regulating, normalizing.

northern *adj.* northerly, arctic, boreal, hyperborean, polar.

North Star polestar, Polaris, lodestar.

nose *n.* nostrils, nasal passages, olfactory organ, proboscis, *slang:* beak, snout, schnozzle; muzzle.

by a nose almost, barely, just.

look down one's nose at scorn, disdain, snub.

on the nose exactly, precisely, correctly, to the point.

pay through the nose pay heavily, get taken.

under one's nose obvious, visible, in plain sight, at one's fingertips.

nose *v.* search, inspect, detect, inquire, intrude, meddle, pry, push, snoop.

nosy *adj.* snooping, eavesdropping, interfering, meddlesome, intrusive, officious, prying, inquisitive, interested; *ant.* circumspect.

nostalgia *n.* wistfulness, sentimentality, reminiscence, yearning, remembrance, remorse, loneliness, pining, regret, longing.

nostalgic *adj.* sentimental, longing, homesick, maudlin, regretful, romantic, wistful.

notability *n.* fame, notoriety, esteem, celebrity, distinction, eminence, luminary, magnate, renown, notable, personage; *ant.* nonentity.

notable *n.* celebrity, luminary, dignitary, personage, notability, VIP.

notable *adj.* **1.** remarkable, distinguished, important, striking, unusual, conspicuous, evident, manifest, marked, noticeable, over, pronounced, striking, unusual; *ant.* commonplace, ordinary, usual. **2.** famous, well-known, celebrated, renowned, distinguished, notorious, preeminent, eminent.

notably *adv.* conspicuously, distinctly, eminently, impressively, reputably, prominently, markedly, particularly, remarkably, outstandingly, strikingly, uncommonly.

notation *n.* characters, code, noting, record, script, shorthand, algebra, signs, system.

notch *n.* mark, nick, groove, indent, cut, cleft, incision, score, insection.

notch *v.* mark, nick, scallop, score, scratch, cut, indent, chisel.

note *n.* **1.** reminder, comment, observation, notice, agenda, entry, journal, notation, jotting, mark, scrawl, representation, annotation. **2.** dispatch, announcement, letter, epistle, communication, message, summary, brief, memorandum. **3.** distinction, consequence, celebrity, eminence, fame, heed, prestige, renown, reputation. **4.** (musical sound) tone, key, interval, degree, step, sharp, flat, natural, pitch.

note *v.* **1.** (perceive visually) remark, regard, see, notice, detect, observe, perceive, witness, heed. **2.** (make a written notation) record, enter, transcribe, write down, denote, designate, indicate, mark, register.

compare notes discuss, exchange views, confer, go over.

noted *adj.* acclaimed, celebrated, conspicuous, famous, well-known, notorious, illustrious, prominent, distinguished, notable, eminent; *ant.* obscure, unknown.

notes *n.* observations, impressions, recordings, findings, report, sketch, synopsis, jottings, outline, draft, commentary, interpretation.

noteworthy *adj.* outstanding, remarkable, unique, exceptional, extraordinary, notable, significant, important, unusual, on the map; *ant.* ordinary, usual, commonplace.

nothing *n.* not anything, trifle, nothingness, nonexistence, inexistence, nonbeing, nullity, zero, extinction, oblivion, null, obliteration, annihilation, nought, bagatelle, cipher, *slang:* zip, zilch.

for nothing **1.** gratis, without cost, free, unencumbered. **2.** in vain, for naught, unnecessarily, emptily.

think nothing of minimize, underplay, play down, disregard, ignore, neglect.

nothingness *n.* **1.** void, nihility, nonexistence, nullity, oblivion, vacuum, blank, hollowness. **2.** worthlessness, insignificance, pettiness, unimportance, smallness.

notice *n.* **1.** notification, comments, declaration, report, intimation, announcement, advertisement, communication, news, note, poster, review, sign. **2.** attention, heed, remark, observation.

take notice regard, see, observe, heed, pay attention, become aware.

notice v. observe, detect, descry, discern, distinguish, espy, heed, mark, mind, note, observe, perceive, remark, see, spot.

noticeable adj. observable, appreciable, obvious, conspicuous, clear, distinct, evident, manifest, perceptible, plain, striking, unmistakable; ant. hidden, insignificant.

notification n. announcement, declaration, disclosure, statement, telling, warning, intelligence, message, notice, publication, revelation.

notify v. announce, declare, inform, enlighten, publish, express, apprise, mention, advise, herald, blazon, disseminate, vent, broadcast, circulate.

notion n. idea, opinion, thought, concept, understanding, inkling, intimation, insight, apprehension, belief, conceit, impulse, whim, fancy, inclination.

notoriety n. repute, renown, fame, reputation, name; infamy, opprobrium, dishonor, disrepute.

notorious adj. infamous, disreputable, wicked, arrant, disreputable, egregious, opprobrious, obvious, overt, scandalous; ant. decent.

notwithstanding adv. although, however, nevertheless, nonetheless, though, yet, regardless of, to the contrary.

notwithstanding prep. despite, in spite of, regardless of.

nought n. nothing, naught, cipher, nil, zero, slang: nix, zilch.

nourish v. feed, sustain, supply, provide, support, promote, maintain, nurse, foster, attend, comfort, cultivate, harbor.

nourishing adj. healthy, nutritious, substantial, wholesome, beneficial, good, alimentative, macrobiotic.

nourishment n. food, diet, nutriment, provender, pabulum, aliment, sustenance, victuals.

nouveau riche upstart, newly-rich, parvenu, status-seeker.

novel n. fiction, book, narrative, romance, saga, story, tale, yarn.

novel adj. new, odd, strange, unique, different, fresh, imaginative, original, singular, uncommon, surprising, unconventional; ant. familiar, ordinary.

novelty n. **1.** innovation, originality, modernity, freshness, newness, creativity; peculiarity, surprise, unfamiliarity, uniqueness. **2.** oddity, curiosity, trinket, trifle, knick-knack, gimcrack, gadget, gewgaw, gimmick (slang).

novice n. beginner, learner, neophyte, amateur, apprentice, newcomer, pupil, tyro, cub, rookie, proselyte, convert, probationer.

now adv. **1.** presently, at this time, right now, at this moment, this day, momentarily, just now, here and now, these days, at present. **2.** promptly, soon, in a moment, in a minute, directly, next, straightaway, immediately, instantly, at once, forthwith.

now and then sometimes, seldom, infrequently, occasionally, at times, desultorily, intermittently, now and again, from time to time, periodically, sporadically, spasmodically.

nowadays adv. these days, today, any more, as things are, at the moment, now.

noxious adj. **1.** harmful, dangerous, baneful, pernicious, deleterious, deadly, detrimental, hurtful, injurious, pestilential, unhealthy, unwholesome; ant. innocuous, wholesome. **2.** foul, noisome, spoiled, rotten, putrid, offensive, morbiferous, morbific; ant. clean, inoffensive.

nuance n. subtlety, refinement, nicety, overtone, shade, suggestion, touch, trace, tinge, hint, gradation.

nub n. essence, gist, crux, center, core, heart, kernel, pith, point, nucleus, nitty-gritty (slang).

nubile adj. marriageable; ripe, sexy, voluptuous, erotic, provocative, sensual, shapely, enticing.

nucleus n. **1.** essence, core, gist, kernel, crux, center, hub, pivot, focus, matter, nub. **2.** foundation, basis, premise.

nude adj. naked, stripped, unclothed, bare, au naturel, disrobed, exposed, unattired, unclad, undraped, undressed, slang: in one's birthday suit, in the buff, in the altogether.

nudge v. push, poke, bump, tap, dig, jog, prod, jab, prompt.

nudge n. bump, push, shove, tap, poke, prod, jab.

nudity n. nakedness, nudeness, bareness, nudism, undress, dishabille.

nugget n. chunk, clump, lump, mass, piece, hunk.

nuisance *n.* annoyance, bother, vexation, irritation, drawback, inconvenience, infliction, bore, pest, problem child, gadfly, thorn in one's side, pain in the neck.

null *adj.* 1. invalid, void, unsanctioned, vain, ineffective, powerless; *ant.* valid. 2. nonexistent, absent, nothing, imaginary, negative, incorporeal. 3. useless, worthless, barren, valueless.

nullify *v.* repeal, cancel, revoke, void, invalidate, abolish, abrogate, annul, counteract, rescind, veto, vitiate, neutralize, quash; *ant.* validate.

numb *v.* paralyze, stun, dull, deaden, stupefy, benumb, obtund.

numb *adj.* insensible, insensitive, deadened, dead, insensate, unfeeling, asleep, benumbed, stupefied, anesthetized, senseless, apathetic, lethargic, phlegmatic, listless, torpid, stunned; *ant.* sensitive.

number *n.* amount, sum, total, totality, aggregate, estimate, count, figure, index, integer, quantity, plenty, plenitude, abundance. **have one's number** (*slang*) see through, understand, know, find out about, be on to.

number *v.* count, total, calculate, enumerate, estimate, account, compute, inventory, apportion, reckon.

numbered *adj.* designated, enumerated, marked, specified, indicated, checked.

numberless *adj.* countless, limitless, infinite, endless, innumerable, myriad, multitudinous, untold, unsummed, unnumbered.

numbness *n.* deadness, dullness, stupefaction, insensibility, paralysis, anesthesia, insensitivity, torpor; *ant.* sensitivity.

numeral *n.* character, cipher, digit, figure, number, integer.

numerate *v.* count, number, measure, enumerate.

numerous *adj.* copious, diverse, various, abundant, multitudinous, many, myriad, profuse, several, sundry; *ant.* few, scanty.

numskull *n.* fool, simpleton, jackass, nitwit, buffoon, blockhead, dolt, dullard, dunce, *slang:* bonehead, dope, dummy, dunderhead, fathead, twit.

nun *n.* sister, abbess, prioress, postulant, mother superior, bride of Christ, canoness, anchoress, vestal.

nunnery *n.* convent, abbey, cloister, retreat, priory.

nuptial *adj.* marital, conjugal, connubial, matrimonial, bridal, wedded, epithalamial, hymeneal.

nuptials *n.* wedding, marriage, marriage ceremony, matrimony, espousal.

nurse *n.* attendant, therapist, nanny, nursemaid, caretaker, wet nurse, amah.

nurse *v.* attend, minister, heal, treat, aid, tend, care for, look after, nurture, foster, cherish, cultivate, encourage, feed, succor, suckle, support.

nursery *n.* 1. preschool, nursery school, day nursery, playroom. 2. hothouse, greenhouse, plantation, hotbed.

nurture *n.* upbringing, care, education, training, cultivation, discipline, instruction, rearing; nourishment, food, sustenance, pabulum.

nurture *v.* nourish, care for, sustain, develop, educate, feed, instruct, rear, tend, train.

nut (*slang*) *n.* eccentric, fanatic, maniac, zealot, psychopath, lunatic, madman, *slang:* crackpot, loony, nutcase.

nuts (*slang*) *adj.* crazy, deranged, insane, demented, eccentric, irrational, mad, unbalanced, unhinged, *slang:* bananas, batty, loony, loopy, nutty.

nuts and bolts (*slang*) basics, essentials, fundamentals, elements, components, practicalities, details, bits and pieces.

nutrition *n.* diet, victuals, nourishment, subsistence, eutrophy.

nutritious *adj.* strengthening, substantial, wholesome, invigorating, nourishing, healthful, good, beneficial, alimental; *ant.* bad, unwholesome.

nutriment *n.* nourishment, sustenance, provisions, subsistence, provender, food, aliment, pabulum.

tough nut to crack difficulty, problem, toughie, burden, responsibility.

nuzzle *v.* nestle, burrow, cuddle, fondle, nudge, pet, snuggle.

nymph *n.* sprite, fairy, mermaid, damsel, lass, maid, maiden, sylph, dryad, hamadryad, naiad, oread, undine.

O

oaf *n.* idiot, moron, fool, lout, dolt, bonehead, blockhead.

oafish *adj.* **1.** obtuse, stupid, thick, dumb, dense, dull, moronic, boorish. **2.** clumsy, ungainly, awkward, graceless; *ant.* graceful, deft.

oar *n.* paddle, scull, pole.

oasis *n.* refuge, sanctuary, haven, retreat, resting place, sanctum, watering hole, island, safe house.

oath *n.* **1.** pledge, promise, word, vow, avowal, affirmation, bond. **2.** curse, blasphemy, expletive, profanity, swearword.

obdurate *adj.* stubborn, firm, fixed, adamant, callous, unyielding, immovable, implacable, unrelenting, unshakable; *ant.* reasonable, flexible, accommodating.

obedient *adj.* compliant, passive, docile, deferential, tractable, complaisant, submissive, subservient, well-trained; *ant.* rebellious, disobedient.

obediently *adv.* loyally, willingly, dutifully, submissively.

obeisance *n.* reverence, homage, praise, respect, courtesy, salutation; deference, genuflection, kowtow.

obelisk *n.* column, tower, monolith, pillar, pyramid.

obese *adj.* fat, overweight, heavy, fleshy, bulky, stout, rotund, portly, gross, corpulent, tubby, paunchy, roly-poly; *ant.* skinny, slender, thin.

obey *v.* comply, follow, heed, mind, observe, submit, yield, surrender, abide by, adhere to, execute, toe the line.

obfuscate *v.* muddle, confuse, bewilder, obscure, camouflage, whitewash.

obituary *n.* eulogy, death notice, necrology, obit.

object *n.* **1.** thing, body, article, entity, item. **2.** purpose, aim, design, end, focus, goal, intent, intention, motive, objective, point, reason, raison d'être. **3.** receiver, recipient, target, victim.

object *v.* oppose, take exception to, disagree, repudiate, protest, rebut, argue, complain, refuse, dissent, dispute; *ant.* accede, acquiesce, agree, assent.

objectify *v.* externalize, reify, project, materialize, substantiate, actualize.

objection *n.* exception, opposition, protest, challenge, protestation, criticism, reproach, complaint, counterargument, remonstrance; *ant.* agreement, assent.

objectionable *adj.* disagreeable, insufferable, intolerable, detestable, offensive, deplorable, repugnant, distasteful, obnoxious, undesirable, unpleasant, unseemly; *ant.* acceptable, pleasant, welcome.

objective *n.* goal, intention, aim, purpose, target, ambition, end, aspiration, design.

objective *adj.* detached, dispassionate, impartial, open-minded, disinterested, judicial, equitable, evenhanded, fair, unprejudiced, sober; *ant.* biased, subjective.

objectively *adv.* impartially, justly, indifferently, soberly, dispassionately, without bias *or* prejudice.

obligate *v.* force, bind, constrain, indebt.

obligation *n.* responsibility, duty, agreement, commitment, promise, bond, contract, indebtedness, liability, requirement, stipulation; *ant.* choice, discretion.

obligatory *adj.* compulsory, required, requisite, binding, involuntary, mandatory, imperative, unavoidable, enforced, de rigueur; *ant.* optional, voluntary.

oblige *v.* **1.** accommodate, assist, help, serve, aid, please, contribute. **2.** require, command, bind, coerce, compel, constrain, force, impel, make.

obliging *adj.* amiable, accommodating, agreeable, cooperative, complaisant, helpful, willing, courteous, considerate, polite, civil, friendly; *ant.* disobliging.

oblique *adj.* 1. slanting, sloped, tilted, inclined, transverse, angled. 2. indirect, subtle, vague, evasive, indirect, circuitous, circumlocutory, roundabout; *ant.* straight.

obliterate *v.* destroy, erase, eradicate, expunge, annihilate, extirpate; rub out, wipe out, cancel, delete.

oblivion *n.* 1. nothingness, obscurity, void, limbo, extinction. 2. forgetfulness, disregard, neglect, stupor, lethe; *ant.* awareness, consciousness.

oblivious *adj.* careless, ignorant, forgetful, inattentive, negligent, unaware, unconscious, heedless; *ant.* mindful, aware.

obliviously *adv.* carelessly, thoughtlessly, ignorantly, heedlessly.

obloquy *n.* criticism, vituperation, defamation, aspersion, slander; dishonor, disgrace, humiliation, infamy, ignominy, opprobrium, stigma, shame.

oblong *adj.* elongated, oval, elliptical, ellipsoidal, rectangular, egg-shaped, ovate; *ant.* square, circular.

obnoxious *adj.* offensive, disgusting, insufferable, nasty, repulsive, revolting, loathsome, detestable, odious, nauseating, foul, sickening; *ant.* agreeable, likeable, pleasant.

obscene *adj.* lewd, pornographic, offensive, dirty, smutty, indecent, immoral, loose, bawdy, wanton, lascivious; *ant.* decent, decorous.

obscenity *n.* 1. profanity, pornography, smut, bawdiness, immodesty, indecency, impropriety. 2. expletive, profanity, four-letter word, swearword.

obscure *v.* obfuscate, conceal, cover, disguise, mask, camouflage, cloak, overshadow, veil, blur, dim, screen, cloud, eclipse; *ant.* clarify, illuminate.

obscure *adj.* 1. hidden, vague, ambiguous, indistinct, hazy, cryptic, enigmatic, mysterious; *ant.* definite, explicit. 2. cloudy, hazy, dim, dusky, faint, gloomy, murky, twilight, opaque, unlit; *ant.* clear.

obscurity *n.* 1. ambiguity, vagueness, abstruseness, reconditeness; *ant.* clarity. 2. anonymity, inconspicuousness, insignificance, unimportance, oblivion; *ant.* fame.

obsequious *adj.* flattering, fawning, ingratiating, brown-nosing (*slang*), bootlicking, toadying, groveling; subservient, submissive, abject, deferential, servile, kowtowing; *ant.* insulting, assertive, proud.

observable *adj.* evident, discernible, obvious, noticeable, perceptible, perceivable, visible, recognizable, apparent, appreciable, detectable, measurable; *ant.* hidden, obscure.

observance *n.* 1. custom, ceremony, ritual, practice, rite, tradition, celebration, service, honoring. 2. attention, adherence, compliance, formality, orthodoxy, obedience.

observant *adj.* alert, attentive, perceptive, wide-awake, sharp, sensible, *slang:* on the ball, on one's toes, all ears *or* eyes.

observation *n.* 1. attention, perception; examination, inspection, once-over, research, probe, study, review, investigation, surveillance; cognition, knowledge, experience. 2. remark, note, comment, notice, opinion, reading, reflection, review, thought, utterance.

observatory *n.* tower, lookout, watchtower, observation tower, observation post.

observe *v.* 1. watch, examine, inspect, scrutinize, keep an eye on, monitor, notice, perceive, see, view, witness; *ant.* miss, overlook. 2. commemorate, celebrate, solemnize, dedicate, honor, remember. 3. (do what is expected or customary) follow, heed, keep, mind, obey, abide by, respect, adhere to, comply, conform to, fulfill; *ant.* break, violate. 4. (say about something) comment, note, remark, mention.

observer *n.* spectator, bystander, eyewitness, onlooker, witness, watcher, sentinel, guard, lookout, sentry, policeman, spy, voyeur, peeping Tom.

obsess *v.* consume, possess, grip, dominate, plague, engross, preoccupy, torment, haunt, nag.

obsessed *adj.* infatuated, captivated, preoccupied, dominated, hounded, bedeviled, seized, plagued, haunted, hung up (*slang*); *ant.* detached, indifferent.

obsession *n.* complex, fixation, infatuation, mania, preoccupation, passion, fetish, fascination, compulsion, neurosis, hang-up (*slang*).

obsessive *adj.* compulsive, consuming, haunting, maddening, tormenting, gripping, fixed; *ant.* optional, volitional.

obsolete *adj.* old-fashioned, out-of-date, antiquated, old hat, archaic, ancient, anachronistic, dated, outmoded, passé; *ant.* contemporary, current, modern, new, up-to-date.

obstacle *n.* barrier, impediment, obstruction, restriction, hindrance, hurdle, interference, snag, hitch, catch, check, interruption, stumbling block; *ant.* advantage, help.

obstetrics *n.* Ob., tocology, midwifery.

obstinate *adj.* firm, stubborn, headstrong, inflexible, pigheaded, strong-minded, adamant, resolved, persistent, steadfast, resolute, diehard, set in one's ways, hellbent (*slang*); *ant.* amenable, yielding.

obstinately *adv.* firmly, stubbornly, tenaciously, persistently, resolutely, stolidly, inflexibly, recalcitrantly.

obstreperous *adj.* vociferous, loud, noisy, boisterous, contrary, clamorous, out of hand, raucous, rambunctious, riotous, rowdy; *ant.* quiet, disciplined.

obstruct *v.* hinder, restrain, prevent, impede, stop, interfere, detain, block, occlude, hamper, frustrate, slow down, inhibit, thwart; *ant.* help.

obtain *v.* 1. acquire, get, attain, secure, win, earn, collect, realize, accomplish, drum up, scrape up *or* together, score, corral, get hold of, seize, capture, take, procure. 2. be in effect, be the case, pertain, hold, prevail.

obtainable *adj.* attainable, achievable; ready, accessible, at hand, available, on call, on tap.

obtrusive *adj.* prominent, protruding, jutting, obvious, blatant; meddling, intrusive, nosy, prying, pushy, interfering, forward.

obtuse *adj.* stupid, thick, dumb, slow, unintelligent, insensitive, uncomprehending, dense; *ant.* bright, sharp.

obverse *n.* 1. front, face, main surface. 2. counterpart, complement, match, equivalent, mirror image.

obviate *v.* prevent, hinder, restrain, block, forestall, preclude, counter, counteract, avert, divert.

obvious *adj.* clear, visible, apparent, distinct, evident, patent, manifest, overt, plain; understandable, straightforward, self-explanatory, plain as the nose on one's face, clear as a bell,

clear as day, hitting one on the head; *ant.* obscure.

obviously *adv.* clearly, plainly, undeniably, unmistakably, evidently, distinctly, of course, certainly, palpably, patently, without doubt, unquestionably, indubitably.

occasion *n.* 1. event, happening, occurrence, incident, affair, case, celebration, experience, instance, moment, cause, antecedent. 2. opportunity, chance, excuse, grounds, call, cause, opening, motive, justification, provocation, reason.

on occasion sometimes, once in a while, seldom, hardly.

rise to the occasion succeed, do what is necessary, meet an emergency, come through.

occasion *v.* cause, induce, evoke, create, engender, bring about, generate, provoke, prompt, inspire, elicit, introduce.

occasional *adj.* 1. irregular, odd, sporadic, infrequent, intermittent, fitful, incidental, periodic; *ant.* frequent. 2. exclusive, rare, uncommon, exceptional, unusual, particular.

occasionally *adv.* sometimes, periodically, at times, from time to time, every so often, once in a while, seldom, hardly; *ant.* regularly, frequently.

occlude *v.* clog, close, block, prevent, curb, impede, stop.

occult *v.* conceal, hide, mask, veil, cover up, block, eclipse, screen, obscure; *ant.* reveal.

occult *adj.* secret, hidden, obscure, abstruse, impenetrable, recondite, veiled, esoteric, cabalistic, mysterious, mystical, supernatural, magical.

occultism *n.* magic, black magic, mysticism, spiritualism, supernaturalism, the black arts, witchcraft.

occupancy *n.* ownership, deed, title, claim, possession; inhabitance, habitation, residence, tenancy, tenure, term.

occupant *n.* inhabitant, tenant, lessee, renter, resident, addressee, denizen, incumbent, dweller, inmate, squatter.

occupation *n.* 1. attack, capture, seizure, invasion, takeover, control. 2. ownership, occupancy, holding. 3. vocation, job, trade, profession, work, business, craft, calling, employment, line, pursuit, walk of life.

315

occupational *adj.* vocational, professional, career, technical, official, workaday, industrial.

occupied *adj.* 1. full, leased, rented, taken, inhabited, lived-in, unavailable; employed, utilized, engaged. 2. busy, absorbed, involved, engrossed, engaged, distracted, preoccupied.

occupy *v.* 1. (come to possess) obtain, seize, take over, invade, conquer, capture, overrun. 2. (have as an owner) possess, own, use, utilize, monopolize. 3. reside, tenant, inhabit, live in; pervade, permeate, immerse. 4. (be of consuming interest) absorb, busy, divert, engage, engross, entertain, interest, fascinate, preoccupy.

occur *v.* happen, take place, transpire, come about, arise, come to pass, develop, crop up; befall, exist, manifest itself, materialize.

occurrence *n.* event, incident, happening, episode, development, instance, occasion, manifestation, proceeding, transaction, appearance, case.

ocean *n.* sea, high seas, the deep, the great waters, Neptune, Davy Jones's locker, the big pond, the abyss, briny deep.

oceanic *adj.* maritime, marine, nautical, aquatic, pelagic.

ocular *adj.* beheld, viewed, seen, visual.

oculist *n.* ophthalmologist, eye doctor, optometrist.

odd *adj.* 1. unusual, unique, atypical, abnormal, different, bizarre, queer, curious, singular; *ant.* regular. 2. remaining, exceeding, leftover.

oddity *n.* 1. abnormality, irregularity, anomaly, incongruity, peculiarity, anomaly; idiosyncrasy, eccentricity, kink, quirk. 2. misfit, freak, oddball.

odds *n.* probability, likelihood, advantage, edge, chance.

at odds in conflict, opposed, in dispute, at variance, at loggerheads, quarreling, feuding, at one another's throats, at outs, with daggers drawn.

odds and ends miscellany, bits and pieces, flotsam and jetsam, debris, remnants, scraps.

ode *n.* lyric, canzone, poem.

odious *adj.* vile, heinous, horrible, disgusting, repulsive, hateful, repellent, abhorrent, revolting, repugnant.

316

odium *n.* 1. hostility, hatred, enmity, aversion, malice, contempt. 2. shame, disgrace, dishonor.

odor *n.* scent, smell, aroma, fragrance, bouquet, perfume.

odorless *adj.* unscented, odor-free; *ant.* odorous, fragrant, perfumed.

odorous *adj.* 1. offensive, stinking, smelly, redolent, fetid, putrid, foul, odiferous, malodorous, cloying, moldy, musty, stale, rank, skunky, stinky. 2. sweet, pungent, spicy, savory, aromatic, redolent, odiferous, balmy, fragrant; *ant.* smelly, stinking.

odyssey *n.* journey, travels, wandering, meanderings, junket.

off *adj.* 1. mistaken, wrong, confused, below par, erring; divergent, distant. 2. canceled, postponed, shelved. 3. begun, started, launched, initiated. 4. (*slang*) crazy, odd, queer, peculiar, insane, abnormal. 5. absent, on vacation, on leave, not on duty, unemployed; *ant.* present, here, at hand.

off and on occasionally, now and then, now and again, seldom, sometimes, from time to time, once in a while, periodically, sporadically; *ant.* continuously, without letup.

off *adv.* behind, ahead, beside, aside, beneath, below, afar, above, apart.

offal *n.* trash, refuse, waste, garbage.

offbeat *adj.* unusual, strange, idiosyncratic, unique, odd, individual, peculiar, one-of-a-kind; *ant.* traditional.

off-color *adj.* 1. risqué, racy, bawdy, blue, suggestive, indecent. 2. ill, sick, indisposed, out of sorts, under the weather.

off-duty *adj.* not at work, off, on holiday, on vacation, on break, on *or* at liberty.

offend *v.* annoy, insult, affront, irritate, disgruntle, outrage, anger, pique, provoke, step on someone's toes; *ant.* please.

offended *adj.* angry, insulted, vexed, upset, in a huff, in a snit; *ant.* pleased.

offender *n.* criminal, culprit, guilty party, transgressor, perpetrator, wrongdoer, miscreant.

offense *n.* 1. misdeed, crime, transgression, sin, assault, felony, misdemeanor, attack. 2. (a feeling of hurt at a perceived insult) anger, resentment, indignation, umbrage.

offensive *n.* attack, assault, drive, onslaught, raid.

offensive *adj.* **1.** aggressive, assaulting, invading, incursive. **2.** insulting, impudent, irritating, impertinent, rude; revolting, obnoxious, rank, nasty, indecent, dirty, corrupt, intolerable; *ant.* agreeable, pleasant, likeable.

offer *n.* proposal, suggestion, bid, overture, proposition.

offer *v.* **1.** present, advance, proffer, donate, tender, put forth, extend, grant, allow, volunteer, award. **2.** propose, submit, suggest, try, endeavor, attempt.

offer up sacrifice, present, proffer.

offering *n.* donation, gift, present, sacrifice, contribution.

offhand *adj.* impromptu, informal, casual, ad hoc, spontaneous, extemporaneous, throwaway.

offhand *adv.* ad lib, extemporaneously, spontaneously, off the top of one's head.

offhandedly *adv.* nonchalantly, carelessly, thoughtlessly, indifferently; *ant.* guardedly.

office *n.* **1.** profession, job, employment, occupation, business, duty, function, performance, province, service. **2.** room, agency, bureau, facility, suite.

officer *n.* official, agent, bureaucrat, representative, public servant, dignitary, appointee, administrator.

official *n.* administrator, executive, director, officer, representative, bureaucrat, apparatchik.

official *adj.* **1.** (approved by a government or institution) authorized, formal, sanctioned, endorsed, ordered, ceremonious, proper. **2.** reliable, authentic, trustworthy, true, real, absolute, valid, authenticated, credible, irrefutable.

officially *adv.* formally, ceremoniously, authoritatively; *ant.* informally, casually.

officiate *v.* manage, oversee, direct, preside, chair, adjudicate, umpire, referee.

officious *adj.* meddling, obtrusive, interfering, impertinent; highhanded, self-important.

off-key *adj.* out of tune, discordant, dissonant, jarring; *ant.* harmonious.

off-putting *adj.* daunting, intimidating, unnerving, distressing, disconcerting, discouraging, formidable.

offset *n.* balance; redress, compensation.

offset *v.* make up for, neutralize, balance, compensate, make amends, requite, negate, equalize.

offshoot *n.* **1.** branch, appendage, arm, limb. **2.** byproduct, outgrowth, spinoff, offspring.

offshore *adj.* aquatic, oceanic, marine.

offside *adj.* illegal, faulty, foul, out of bounds.

offspring *n.* children, descendants, progeny, lineage, family, heirs, successors, issue, young, chip off the old block.

often *adv.* frequently, regularly, repeatedly, usually; *ant.* seldom.

ogle *v.* leer, look, eye, stare, gaze, gape.

ogre *n.* monster, demon, fiend, giant.

oil *n.* grease, lubricant, fat, unction, fuel.

oil *v.* lubricate, grease, smear, coat, anoint.

oily *adj.* **1.** fatty, buttery, rich, sebaceous, oleaginous, greasy, smooth; *ant.* dry, gritty, rough. **2.** suave, glib, slick, flattering, ingratiating, fast-talking, unctuous; *ant.* brusque, frank.

ointment *n.* cream, balm, salve, lotion, unction, emollient.

okay *n.* OK, permission, endorsement, approval, affirmation, consent, go-ahead, nod, green light, sanction.

okay *v.* OK, approve, endorse, condone, agree to, permit, allow, pass, validate, sanction.

okay *adj.* OK, good, adequate, acceptable, fair, fine.

okay *interj.* OK, all right, very good, correct, surely, fine, yes, agreed.

old *adj.* **1.** aged, elderly, senior, ancient, antique, classic, ancestral, traditional; *ant.* young, youthful. **2.** decrepit, worn, used, obsolete, gone to seed, with one foot in the grave, old as the hills; *ant.* vigorous, fresh, new. **3.** mature, adult, grown, seasoned, experienced; *ant.* immature.

old age *n.* seniority, retirement, senility, twilight years, autumn of one's life, golden years.

older *adj.* elder, former, preceding, earlier, first, senior; *ant.* newer, younger.

oldest *adj.* first, original, initial, primeval, most aged.

old-fashioned *adj.* antiquated, obsolete, out of date, dated, passé; retro, traditional, quaint.

old hand n. master, veteran, old-timer.

old man n. father, parent, patriarch, head of the house, paterfamilias; husband, lover.

oldster n. veteran, patriarch, dowager, senior citizen, codger, old coot, *slang:* old geezer, codger, old bag.

Old Testament n. the Covenant, Pentateuch, Hebrew Scripture, Jewish Law, the Prophets, the Hebrew Testament, the Torah.

old-time adj. old-fashioned, outmoded, obsolete, ancient.

old-world adj. ancient, classical, Hellenic, European, archaic, traditional; conservative; courtly, formal, gallant, continental.

olive n. greenish yellow, yellowish green, khaki, olive-drab, green.

olympian adj. elevated, exalted, glorious, godlike, majestic, lofty, sublime.

omelet n. fried egg, soufflé, scrambled eggs.

omen n. sign, premonition, warning, portent, augury, indication, writing on the wall.

ominous adj. foreboding, menacing, dark, impending, threatening, grim, sinister; ant. auspicious, favorable, encouraging.

omission n. exclusion, neglect, oversight, disregard, breach, elimination, gap, need, want; ant. addition, inclusion.

omit v. leave out, drop, edit out, exclude, pass over, delete, eliminate, skip, cancel, void, ignore, overlook, disregard.

omnibus n. 1. anthology, readings, selection, collection, compilation. 2. vehicle, streetcar, bus, tram.

omnibus adj. wide-ranging, inclusive, comprehensive, all-embracing; ant. selective.

omnipotence n. power, mastery, dominion, authority, control, invincibility, divine right, supremacy; ant. impotence.

omnipotent adj. all-powerful, almighty, supreme, godlike.

omnipresent adj. pervasive, universal, infinite, everywhere, ubiquitous.

omniscient adj. all-knowing, all-seeing, preeminent, almighty.

omnivorous adj. greedy, rapacious, gluttonous, voracious.

on prep. upon, atop, against, near, above, next to, about, at; in contact with, touching, held by, supported by.

on adj. ongoing, proceeding, moving, operating.

on again, off again intermittently, occasionally, sometimes.

on and off sometimes, infrequently, now and then, from time to time, periodically.

once adv. 1. one or this time, never again, a single time, on one occasion; ant. repeatedly, frequently. 2. formerly, previously, earlier, in the old days, in the past, heretofore, long ago, already, before.

at once directly, now, right away, straightaway, this minute, without delay, instantly, unhesitatingly.

once in a blue moon seldom, rarely, infrequently, hardly ever.

once in a while sometimes, occasionally, from time to time.

once-over n. examination, inspection, checkup.

oncoming adj. approaching, imminent, impending, advancing, forthcoming, looming.

one pron. somebody, someone, person, individual, item, unit, thing, example.

one adj. 1. whole, entire, total, complete; indivisible, integral, united. 2. identical, compatible, equal. 3. peculiar, singular, lone, single, solitary, unique, different.

one-man adj. little, small, single, limited, restricted.

oneness n. unity, harmony, consistency, sameness, totality, entirety, indivisibility, wholeness, completeness; ant. multiplicity.

onerous adj. oppressive, difficult, demanding, laborious, taxing, formidable, arduous, grueling, tedious, heavy, hard, harsh.

one-sided adj. 1. unilateral, uneven, asymmetrical, lopsided. 2. prejudiced, biased, discriminatory, partial, partisan, unfair, unjust, narrow-minded.

one-time adj. previous, past, prior, former, ex-, late, erstwhile.

ongoing adj. current, continuing, developing, evolving, advancing, in progress, unfolding, continuous.

onlooker n. bystander, eyewitness, spectator, observer, sightseer.

only adj. lone, sole, single, exclusive, unique, individual.

only adv. 1. exclusively, solely; individually, singly. 2. just, merely, barely, hardly.

onrush *n.* attack, assault, surge, charge, cascade, flood, flow, onslaught, stampede.

onset *n.* assault, rush, attack, encounter, commencement, onslaught, outbreak, start.

onshore *adj.* inland, aground, ashore.

onslaught *n.* offensive, barrage, assault, attack, charge, bombardment, invasion, rush.

onto *prep.* to, toward, adjacent to, against, upon, above, over.

onus *n.* duty, liability, burden, obligation, responsibility, load.

onward *adv.* forward, ahead, beyond, forth, in front; *ant.* backward.

oodles (*slang*) *n.* loads, lots, masses, heaps (*slang*), scads (*slang*), abundance, much.

ooze *n.* slime, sediment, muck, mire, sludge.

ooze *v.* seep, bleed, leak, flow, exude, discharge, drip, sweat.

oozy *adj.* wet, slimy, sloppy, moist, mucky, sludgy, sweaty, dripping.

opalescent *adj.* prismatic, iridescent, rainbow-colored, bright.

opaque *adj.* **1.** (impossible to see through) dull, blurred, hazy, obscure. **2.** (hard to understand) impenetrable, concealed, enigmatic, abstruse, incomprehensible, vague; *ant.* transparent, translucent, clear.

open *v.* **1.** begin, initiate, start, commence, inaugurate, launch, set in motion, prepare, present. **2.** (free from obstruction) clear, free, loosen, disengage, breach, penetrate, jimmy, expose, reveal; *ant.* close, bar, lock.

open *adj.* **1.** accessible, clear, wide, rent, ajar; *ant.* locked, blocked, obstructed. **2.** public, admissible, permitted, allowed, welcoming; *ant.* restricted. **3.** obvious, apparent, well-known, plain, candid, disclosed, divulged; *ant.* secret.

open-air *adj.* outdoor, outside, alfresco, spacious, airy.

open-and-shut *adj.* obvious, simple, straightforward.

open-door *adj.* unrestricted, free, hospitable, welcoming, unlimited.

open-ended *adj.* unlimited, freewheeling, wide-ranging, ongoing, continuing.

openhanded *adj.* generous, free, benevolent, altruistic, charitable, liberal; *ant.* tightfisted.

openhandedly *adv.* lavishly, freely, unstintingly.

openhearted *adj.* good, true, candid, frank, honest, warm, welcoming, accessible.

opening *n.* **1.** hole, gap, break, crack, aperture, breach, orifice, space, entrance; *ant.* closing. **2.** beginning, start, commencement, debut, launch; *ant.* closure. **3.** chance, opportunity, position, slot, shot, gamble, try.

opening *adj.* first, primary, initial, beginning, introductory, maiden; *ant.* closing.

openly *adv.* frankly, blatantly, candidly, straightforwardly, honestly, publicly; shamelessly, immodestly.

open-minded *adj.* liberal, enlightened, impartial, unbiased, broad-minded, objective, receptive, tolerant, just; *ant.* bigoted, intolerant, prejudiced.

open-mouthed *adj.* spellbound, amazed, astounded, thunderstruck, dumbfounded, aghast, surprised.

open seas high seas, the deep, ocean.

open sesame code, password, key, sign, watchword.

opera *n.* musical, drama, libretto, score.

operate *v.* **1.** manage, handle, maneuver, manipulate, engage, use, utilize; perform, run, function, act, move, work; *ant.* stop, break down, stall. **2.** (perform surgery) treat, administer, serve, excise, cut, explore.

operated *adj.* regulated, maintained, handled, governed, accomplished, worked, guided, executed.

operation *n.* **1.** administration, guidance, superintendence, supervision, management, direction, control, conduct. **2.** (an action) performance, deed, act, enterprise, service, transaction, undertaking. **3.** (military undertaking) exercise, maneuver, campaign, offensive, assault, attack. **4.** (medical procedure) surgery, excision, removal.

operational *adj.* functioning, in service, in working order, prepared, ready, usable, viable.

operative *n.* **1.** employee, worker, artisan, operator. **2.** agent, spy, detective.

operative *adj.* effective, efficient, influential, adequate, functional, key, relevant, workable.

operator *n.* **1.** engineer, laborer, worker, employee, technician, executor, executive, director, administrator. **2.** schemer, conniver, wheeler-dealer (*slang*), manipulator, fraud.

opiate *n.* drug, depressant, narcotic, sedative, tranquilizer, pacifier.

opine *v.* guess, judge, presume, believe, conclude, suppose, surmise, think, venture.

opinion *n.* view, belief, assessment, estimation, conclusion, supposition, assumption, thesis, judgment, verdict, notion, sentiment, idea.

opinionated *adj.* stubborn, willful, adamant, biased, prejudiced, bigoted, single-minded, overbearing; *ant.* open-minded.

opium *n.* opiate, drug, narcotic, soporific.

opponent *n.* rival, adversary, challenger, competitor, contestant, contender, opposition, antagonist, enemy, foe, litigant; *ant.* supporter, defender.

opportune *adj.* appropriate, fitting, convenient, favorable, proper, suitable, fortuitous, timely.

opportunism *n.* timeliness, expediency, pragmatism, striking while the iron is hot, making hay while the sun shines; exploitation, unscrupulousness, taking advantage, Realpolitik.

opportunist *n.* go-getter, self-seeker; carpetbagger, user, exploiter, realpolitiker.

opportunity *n.* chance, break, shot, opening, fortuity, luck, timeliness, moment, occasion, time.

oppose *v.* counter, defy, contradict, object, argue, deny, confront, face, fight, resist, stand up to.

opposed *adj.* against, contrary, conflicting, antagonistic, antithetical, incompatible, hostile, at odds.

opposing *adj.* rival, clashing, warring, combatant, contentious, contrary, crossing; *ant.* friendly, allied.

opposite *n.* inverse, reverse, antithesis, contrary, converse, antistrophe, antonym, contradiction; foil, counterpart; *ant.* same.

opposite *adj.* **1.** (altogether different in nature) dissimilar, contrasting, diametrical, antipodal, poles apart, like day and night; *ant.* same, matched. **2.** (in conflict) adverse, hostile, conflicting, antithetical, contrary, opposing, contradictory. **3.** facing, nose to nose, opposing; *ant.* side by side.

opposition *n.* **1.** hostilities, contention, fight-

ing, conflict, clashing, combat, contest, warfare, skirmish, rivalry; *ant.* peace. **2.** (a negative reaction) antagonism, hostility, protest, resistance, defiance, malice, hate, dislike, defiance, antipathy, aversion, anger; *ant.* support. **3.** rival, the other side, opponent.

oppress *v.* persecute, subjugate, tyrannize, abuse, dispirit, trample, suppress, burden, overwhelm.

oppressed *adj.* enslaved, downtrodden, browbeaten, burdened, maltreated, persecuted, abused, underprivileged; *ant.* free.

oppression *n.* **1.** cruelty, abuse, brutality; injustice, persecution, domination, subjugation, tyranny; suffering, hardship; *ant.* freedom. **2.** melancholy, low spirits, depression, grief, misery.

oppressive *adj.* **1.** overwhelming, difficult, burdensome, troublesome. **2.** (as a regime or ruler) overbearing, tyrannical, inhuman, cruel. **3.** (said of weather) close, sultry, suffocating, confining, unbearable.

oppressor *n.* persecutor, tyrant, tormentor, taskmaster, despot, dictator, bully, intimidator.

opprobrious *adj.* **1.** (showing complete lack of respect) abusive, contemptuous, derogatory, disdainful, offensive, insolent, insulting; *ant.* appreciative, friendly. **2.** (deserving censure) slanderous, infamous, disgraceful, wrong.

opt *v.* choose, elect, decide, select, pick, prefer.

optical *adj.* seeing, visual, visible.

optimism *n.* faith, idealism, hopefulness, cheerfulness, encouragement, enthusiasm; *ant.* pessimism, despair.

optimist *n.* idealist, dreamer, positivist, yea-sayer.

optimistic *adj.* confident, hopeful, assured, positive, heartened, upbeat, looking on the bright side, seeing through rose-colored glasses, sanguine; *ant.* pessimistic.

optimum *adj.* best, choice, ideal, perfect, maximum, highest; *ant.* worst.

option *n.* **1.** choice, selection, discretion, consideration, alternative, opportunity. **2.** right, prerogative, grant, license, privilege, title.

optional *adj.* discretionary, voluntary, elective, arbitrary; possible; *ant.* compulsory.

opulence *n.* abundance, affluence, luxury,

plenty, riches, wealth, prosperity, sumptuousness; *ant.* poverty.

opulent *adj.* lavish, luxuriant, abundant, copious, profuse; prosperous, rich, affluent; *ant.* penurious, poor.

opus *n.* composition, creation, piece, production, work, brainchild.

oracle *n.* 1. revelation, commandment, canon, edict, law. 2. prophet, seer, soothsayer, fortuneteller, Cassandra.

oracular *adj.* 1. vague, enigmatic, obscure, cryptic, mysterious, ambiguous; *ant.* clear, intelligible. 2. prophetic, predicting, portending, foretelling, divining, foreseeing, auguring.

oral *adj.* verbal, vocal, voiced, lingual, phonic, phonetic, spoken, articulate; *ant.* written.

orally *adv.* verbally, literally, by word of mouth.

orange *n.* red-yellow, tangerine, peach, coral, salmon.

orange *adj.* reddish, glowing, ocherous.

orate *v.* talk, speak, sermonize, pontificate, hold forth, discourse.

oration *n.* address, lecture, sermon, speech, discourse, spiel.

orator *n.* speaker, rhetorician, lecturer.

oratorical *adj.* eloquent, rhetorical, fluent, persuasive, elocutionary, dramatic, sonorous, grandiloquent, verbose, bombastic.

oratory *adj.* rhetoric, speech, elocution, eloquence.

orb *n.* sphere, ball, globe, circle, ring, globule.

orbit *n.* 1. path, circuit, course, cycle, lap, apogee, perigee, hold pattern, flight path, revolution. 2. range, field, compass, circle, boundary, limit; province, precinct, circumference, arena, area.

orbit *v.* 1. revolve, ring, encircle, circle, encompass. 2. launch, project, blast off, lift off, fire.

orchard *n.* grove, farm, fruit plantation, fruit trees, nut trees.

orchestra *n.* symphony, musical ensemble, band.

orchestral *adj.* symphonic, instrumental, operatic, vocal, philharmonic, musical.

orchestrate *v.* compose, score, harmonize, arrange; coordinate, organize.

ordain *v.* 1. enact, install, establish, institute, appoint, delegate, decree, dictate, instruct, order. 2. predetermine, fate, predestine, intend. 3. (accept into the clergy) bless, consecrate, frock, invest, anoint.

ordeal *n.* trial, test, tribulation; difficulty, calamity, nightmare, torture, suffering, agony.

order *n.* 1. command, mandate, law, injunction, decree, directive, ordinance, rule. 2. purchase, request, shipment, quantity, amount, bulk. 3. (the way in which things are arranged) series, structure, succession, sequence, placement, symmetry, arrangement, array, classification, permutation, grouping, composition, pattern, layout. 4. organization, group, union, association, brotherhood, society, sect. 5. peace, quiet, calm, tranquility, serenity.
call to order assemble, convene, congregate, start a meeting.
in order operative, efficient, working, effective.
in order to so that, to, with a view to, with the intention of, with the purpose of, intending to.
in short order soon, rapidly, without delay, quickly.
on order sent for, on the way, requested.
on the order of like, similar to, approximately, roughly.

order *v.* 1. command, decree, direct, require, instruct, manage, marshal, require, prescribe. 2. buy, obtain, request, secure, reserve, book, charge. 3. organize, arrange, methodize, classify, index, regulate, standardize, group, settle, fix; *ant.* confuse.

orderly *n.* aide, attendant, valet, steward.

orderly *adj.* 1. organized, neat, shipshape, arranged, tidy, clean; *ant.* messy, cluttered. 2. methodical, correct, formal, systematic, exact, precise, careful, controlled, disciplined; *ant.* inaccurate. 3. peaceful, quiet, calm, tranquil.

ordinance *n.* law, command, mandate, decree, direction, fiat, injunction, regulation, rule.

ordinarily *adv.* generally, commonly, customarily, normally, usually, habitually, as a rule, regularly, frequently.

ordinary *adj.* average, common, usual, customary, everyday, traditional, popular, conventional, normal; *ant.* extraordinary, odd, special, unusual.
out of the ordinary uncommon, special, extraordinary, odd.

ordination *n.* 1. installation, consecration,

coronation. **2.** system, organization, plan, classification.

ordnance *n.* weapons, arms, ammunition, artillery, munitions.

ordure *n.* excrement, dung, filth, dirt.

ore *n.* parent rock, unrefined rock *or* earth, native material, matrix.

or else rather, instead, on the other hand, conversely, in other words, preferentially, as an alternative, on the contrary, in turn, oppositely.

organ *n.* part, means, medium, device, tool, way, agency.

organic *adj.* **1.** fundamental, integral, vital, constitutional, basic, primary, essential, inherent, necessary. **2.** structured, systematic, coordinated, integrated, whole. **3.** biological, physical, systemic, bodily; *ant.* mental.

organism *n.* entity, being, creature, living thing, animal, body, cell.

organization *n.* **1.** classification, formulation, plan, grouping, design, structure, formation, construction, establishment, regulation, coordination, schematization. **2.** association, union, corporation, institute, system, cartel, confederation, society, league, club, fraternity, alliance, party, clique, coterie.

organize *v.* **1.** arrange, systematize, methodize, put in order, coordinate, correlate, group, marshal; *ant.* mess up, randomize. **2.** establish, set up, put together, form, lay out, create, design, build, found, instate, institute, plan; *ant.* eradicate, break up.

organized *adj.* arranged, neat, orderly, planned, composed, regulated, harmonized, interrelated; *ant.* random, chaotic.

orgy *n.* binge, indulgence, debauchery, revelry, bacchanal, celebration, splurge, spree, fling, jag (*slang*).

orient *v.* **1.** get one's bearings, locate, direct, determine, point, steer, lead. **2.** adjust, adapt, conform, familiarize, acquaint, learn the ropes.

Oriental *adj.* Asian, Eastern, Far Eastern, Near Eastern, Asiatic.

orientation *n.* bearings, familiarization, acclimatization, assimilation, adaptation, introduction, adjustment.

orifice *n.* hole, opening, inlet, gap, aperture.

origin *n.* beginning, cause, root, source, de-scent, derivation, etymology, ancestry, parentage, birth, inception; *ant.* end, termination, result.

original *n.* **1.** model, archetype, standard, master, paradigm; *ant.* copy, imitation, replica. **2.** eccentric, nonconformist, maverick, character.

original *adj.* **1.** first, primary, primordial, earliest, initial, introductory, rudimentary, starting, opening, commencing; *ant.* recent, late. **2.** creative, imaginative, innovative, inventive, novel, ingenious, unconventional; *ant.* imitative. **3.** unique, unprecedented, unusual, one-of-a-kind, sole, lone, single; *ant.* common.

originate *v.* emanate, emerge, evolve; create, invent, conceive; launch, pioneer, found, begin, commence, start; *ant.* end, terminate.

originator *n.* creator, architect, author, inventor, founder, mother, father, pioneer.

ornament *n.* embellishment, decoration, adornment, accessory, bauble, frill, trinket.

ornament *v.* adorn, beautify, embellish, deck, decorate, dress up, gild, trim, garnish.

ornamental *adj.* adorning, embellishing, decorative, enhancing, heightening, dressy, accessory; *ant.* plain.

ornate *adj.* elaborate, fancy, busy, florid, showy, lavish, decorated, embroidered, bedecked, baroque, rococo, resplendent, sumptuous; *ant.* plain.

orphan *n.* waif, foundling, ragamuffin, stray.

or so approximately, roughly, practically, about.

orthodox *adj.* conventional, traditional, conservative, customary, conformist, correct, official, approved, doctrinal, kosher.

orthodoxy *n.* authority, conformity, tradition, dogma, doctrine, devotion, faith.

oscillate *v.* swing, vibrate, sway, wave, vacillate, fluctuate, change.

osseous *adj.* bony, ossified, skeletal, calcified, stiff, rigid, firm; *ant.* flexible, yielding.

ossify *v.* fossilize, calcify, petrify, stiffen, congeal, harden.

ossified *adj.* bony, petrified, fossilized, hardened, inflexible, rigid, stiff.

ostensible *adj.* alleged, purported, professed, seeming, apparent, so-called, supposed, plausible, pretended.

ostensibly adv. supposedly, to all intents and purposes, apparently, reputedly, seemingly, purportedly.

ostentatious adj. extravagant, flamboyant, gaudy, garish, pretentious, showy; pompous, vain, egotistic, boastful.

ostracize v. exile, deport, banish, bar, blacklist, blackball, cast out, expatriate, shun, snub, expel; ant. receive, welcome, reinstate.

other adj. alternative, different, separate; added, further, another, extra, spare; new, fresh.

others n. some, a few, a number, a handful, not many, two or three, many, the rest, the remainder, they; ant. none.

otherwise adv. in another way, differently, contrarily, oppositely, on the other hand, in other respects, with this exception, or else, unless.

otherworldly adj. dreamy, ethereal, abstract, metaphysical, supernatural, spectral, mysterious, rapt; ant. mundane, solid, substantial, worldly.

otiose adj. 1. lazy, indolent, idle, listless, slothful. 2. futile, useless, hopeless, vain.

ottoman n. hassock, stool, footstool, footrest.

ought v. should, have to, be required, behooves, be necessary, be fitting, be becoming, be reasonable, must.

ounce n. measure, atom, drop, iota, modicum, particle.

our adj. belonging to us, inherent in us, used by us, owned by us, due to us, a part of us, in our employ.

oust v. eject, evict, cast out, force or drive out, expel, banish, give the boot or sack (slang), send packing; overthrow, supplant, depose, bounce; ant. reinstate, restore.

out (slang) n. escape, way out; excuse, explanation.

out adj. 1. outer, removed, away, distant, external, outside, extraneous, open, exposed; ant. inside. 2. absent, away, busy, elsewhere, gone, left; ant. in. 3. unconscious, insensible, comatose; passed out, blotto (slang), out cold.
all out completely, wholeheartedly, with enthusiasm.
on the outs fighting, opposing, disagreeing, at odds.
out in left field crazy, insane, wild; unlikely, impractical.

out of bounds forbidden, illegal, outlawed, banned, prohibited, off-limits.

out of hand out of control, unchecked, wild.

out of it (slang) behind the times, old-fashioned, uninformed, unhip (slang).

out of the blue sudden, unexpected, unanticipated, unforeseen.

outage n. blackout, brownout, dim-out.

out-and-out adj. complete, outright, total, utter, altogether, arrant.

outbreak n. 1. appearance, eruption, flare-up, outburst, spurt, discharge, epidemic, rash, explosion. 2. violence, fury, brawl, riot, mutiny, revolution, insurrection, uprising, disorder.

outbuilding n. stable, barn, outhouse, storehouse, hut, shed.

outburst n. eruption, explosion, outbreak, gush, surge, upheaval, disturbance.

outcast n. exile, outsider, refugee, persona non grata, fugitive, derelict, bum, pariah, leper; ant. favorite, idol.

outcast adj. exiled, expelled, driven out, ousted, outlawed, hounded, hunted, untouchable.

outclass v. outdo, beat, eclipse, outrank, top, surpass.

outcome n. result, consequence, upshot, aftermath, conclusion, effect, issue, end.

outcry n. clamor, commotion, outburst, protest, uproar; yell, howl, scream.

outdated adj. behind the times, old-fashioned, out-of-style, antiquated, outmoded, ancient, passé; ant. modern, fashionable.

outdistance v. exceed, beat, better, outdo, pass, overtake, leave behind.

outdo v. surpass, defeat, exceed, best, eclipse, top, surpass, transcend.

outdone adj. bettered, surpassed, improved upon; beaten, defeated.

outdoor adj. outside, alfresco, open-air, free, rustic, informal, airy; ant. indoor, interior.

outdoors n. fresh air, garden, Mother Nature, nature, environment; ant. inside.

outdoors adv. outside, in the open, alfresco, without.

outer adj. external, outward, without, extrinsic or extraneous to, outside, foreign or alien to, exterior, peripheral.

outermost adj. surface, external, peripheral.

outfit n. 1. clothes, costume, ensemble, garb,

outfit n. gear, get-up, rig, apparel, equipment. **2.** business, company, corps, organization, team, squad, unit.

outfit v. provide, supply, equip, fit out, stock, attire, furnish.

outfitter n. tailor, clothier, costumer, seamstress.

outflow v. current, tide, ebb, effluence, drainage, gush, jet, emanation, outpouring.

outflowing adj. gushing, leaking, rushing, spurting.

outgo n. costs, expenses, losses.

outgoing adj. friendly, sociable, approachable, cordial, genial, warm, affable; ant. reserved.

outgrow v. give up, abandon, discontinue, relinquish, discard.

outgrowth n. **1.** product, outcome, effect, result, end. **2.** projection, prominence, jut, protuberance, bulge.

outing n. excursion, expedition, jaunt, spin, adventure, airing, ride, vacation.

outlander n. foreigner, immigrant, alien, stranger.

outlandish adj. exotic, bizarre, eccentric, strange, odd, unheard of, weird.

outlast v. outlive, survive, remain.

outlaw n. fugitive, bandit, criminal, outcast, desperado.

outlaw v. ban, banish, condemn, forbid, make illegal, stop, embargo, exclude, prohibit.

outlawed adj. condemned, disallowed, embargoed, stopped, banned; excommunicated, banished.

outlay n. cost, expenditure, expenses, investment, payment, price, charge.

outlet n. opening, hole, break, avenue, channel, exit, duct, way out.

outline n. **1.** plan, sketch, drawing, draft, skeleton, framework. **2.** edge, boundary side, profile, silhouette, shape, figure, configuration, representation.

outline v. **1.** draw, sketch, paint; recapitulate, summarize. **2.** plan, draft, rough out, trace.

outlined adj. bounded, bordered, delineated, edged, marked, zoned, mapped, charted, diagrammed; summarized.

outlive v. outlast, endure, survive, weather.

outlook n. **1.** viewpoint, perspective, standpoint, vision, scope, angle, attitude, slant. **2.**

forecast, prospect, probability, future, likelihood, expectations.

outlying adj. distant, outer, remote, further, far-off, peripheral, external.

outmaneuver v. outwit, outdo, defeat, exceed, excel, beat, outsmart, outthink.

outmoded adj. old, out of date, out-of-style, passé, superannuated, anachronistic, superseded; ant. fashionable, modern, new.

outnumbered adj. bested, overcome, beaten.

out-of-the-way adj. isolated, secluded, far-off, distant, remote, off the beaten path.

outpost n. forward station, advanced position, point of attack, listening post, boundary.

outpouring n. torrent, cascade, overflow, emission, drainage, flow.

output n. production, yield, amount, crop, product.

outrage v. incense, infuriate, affront, offend, insult.

outrageous adj. wanton, notorious, shameless, brazen, immoderate, extreme, excessive, exorbitant.

outrider n. guide, escort, guardian, herald, scout, precursor.

outright adj. absolute, categorical, complete, definite, pure, total, unequivocal, unqualified, straightforward, out-and-out, unmitigated; ant. ambiguous, provisional.

outright adv. absolutely, explicitly, thoroughly, unhesitatingly, completely.

outset n. beginning, commencement, opening, start, inauguration.

outside n. **1.** exterior, surface, covering, façade, topside, face, cover, shell, skin; ant. inside. **2.** limit, border, bounds, boundary, edge, end; ant. inside.

outside adj. **1.** external, outdoor, outer; ant. inside. **2.** superficial, surface, outer. **3.** (said of probability) faint, minute, negligible, marginal.

outsider n. stranger, foreigner, alien, immigrant, newcomer; observer; outcast; ant. inhabitant, native, resident, insider.

outskirts n. border, boundary, limits, edge, periphery, fringes, suburbs; ant. center.

outsmart v. outwit, best; deceive, dupe, trick, outfox.

outspoken adj. blunt, frank, artless, candid, direct, forthright, unequivocal.

outspread *adj.* outstretched, unfolded, unfurled, open, wide, extended, expanded; unrestrained, unrestricted; *ant.* narrow; bounded.

outstanding *adj.* **1.** great, leading, distinguished, notable, important, exceptional, excellent; *ant.* ordinary. **2.** due, pending, remaining, unpaid, unsettled.

outstandingly *adv.* superbly, supremely, notably, well, excellently.

outward *adj.* on the surface, to the eye, obvious, apparent, exterior, outer, public, noticeable.

outward bound going, departing, leaving, traveling.

outwardly *adv.* superficially, on the surface, apparently, evidently, seemingly, ostensibly, supposedly; *ant.* internally, inwardly.

outweigh *v.* exceed, cancel out, eclipse, predominate, tip the scales in favor of, prevail over, take precedence over.

outwit *v.* baffle, deceive, trick, bewilder, cheat, dupe, swindle, con, get the better of.

outworn *adj.* obsolete, extinct, archaic, old, defunct; hackneyed, trite.

oval *adj.* elliptical, ellipsoidal, egg-shaped, oblong.

ovation *n.* acclaim, applause, bravos, cheers, praise, laudation, tribute; *ant.* boos, jeering, catcalls.

oven *n.* stove, furnace, broiler, oil-burner, hot-air chamber.

over *adj.* **1.** accomplished, completed, closed, concluded, ended, finished, settled, up; forgotten, past, bygone. **2.** extra, in excess, remaining, surplus, superfluous.

over *adv.* **1.** above, aloft, yonder, there. **2.** again, another time, afresh. **3.** additionally, in addition, besides.

over *prep.* **1.** above, atop, higher than. **2.** protecting, covering. **3.** superior to, in charge of, in command of.

overabundance *n.* surplus, glut, excess, satiety, profusion, plethora.

overact *v.* exaggerate, overdo, overplay, ham up, emote; *ant.* underplay.

overall *adj.* complete, comprehensive, inclusive, total, thorough, general, broad; *ant.* narrow.

overall *adv.* generally speaking, by and large, in general, in the long run, on the whole.

overalls *n.* coveralls, jump suit, dungarees, work-wear.

overbearing *adj.* egotistic, arrogant, proud, haughty, bossy; domineering, despotic, oppressive, dictatorial, tyrannical, imperious; *ant.* modest, meek.

overblown *adj.* exaggerated, excessive, profuse, fulsome, superfluous, verbose, windy; *ant.* understated.

overcast *adj.* cloudy, dreary, hazy, gray, somber, threatening, darkened, dismal, lowering; *ant.* bright, clear, sunny, fair.

overcharge *v.* cheat, extort, overtax, short-change.

overcoat *n.* greatcoat, raincoat, topcoat.

overcome *v.* subdue, master, overwhelm, defeat, beat, conquer, vanquish.

overcome *adj.* beaten, conquered, overpowered, overwhelmed; speechless, swept off one's feet.

overcrowded *adj.* congested, packed, full, overloaded, overpopulated, chock-full; *ant.* deserted, empty.

overdevelopment *adj.* overexpansion, overbuilding, congestion.

overdo *v.* **1.** overwork, strain, bite off more than one can chew, burn the candle at both ends. **2.** exaggerate, magnify, stretch, do to death, run into the ground.

overdone *adj.* **1.** excessive, exaggerated, undue, unnecessary; *ant.* understated. **2.** overcooked, charred, burnt, dried up; *ant.* underdone, raw.

overdrawn *adj.* depleted, exhausted, paid out, broke.

overdue *adj.* late, tardy, past due, delayed, belated.

overeager *adj.* overzealous, overenthusiastic.

overexcite *v.* provoke, quicken, incite, overstimulate, arouse, tease, titillate.

overexert *v.* strain, exhaust, tire, fatigue, knock oneself out, burn the candle at both ends, drive oneself too hard.

overexpand *v.* overdevelop, overextend, grow or develop too much.

overextended *adj.* spread too thin, overexpanded.

overflow n. surplus, overabundance, inundation, deluge, spillover, flood; ant. scarcity.

overflow v. spill, well over, deluge, brim over, flood, inundate, soak, surge.

overflowing adj. profuse, swarming, teeming, superabundant, abounding, rife, bountiful; ant. scanty.

overgrown adj. excessive, disproportionate, crowded, thick.

overhang n. protrusion, projection, extension, overlap, droop, suspension.

overhang v. 1. protrude, project, jut, bulge, stick out.

overhaul n. examination, check-up, inspection, restoration.

overhaul v. fix, renew, reconstruct, restore, repair, recondition, service.

overhead n. expenses, depreciation, operating costs, running costs; ant. income, profit.

overhead adj. elevated, aerial, upper; ant. ground.

overhead adv. up, upward, above.

overhear v. eavesdrop, listen in on, catch, bug (slang).

overheated adj. impassioned, inflamed, excited, agitated, overwrought; ant. calm, dispassionate, cool.

overheating n. sunstroke, heatstroke, hyperthermia.

overindulge v. binge, gorge, debauch, gormandize.

overindulgence n. immoderation, intemperance, debauchery, excess, overeating, drunkenness; ant. abstention, abstemiousness.

overjoyed adj. delighted, elated, thrilled, happy, ecstatic, charmed, jubilant; ant. disappointed, sad.

overkill n. excess, exaggeration, overabundance, too much.

overland adj. coast-to-coast, transcontinental, cross-country.

overlap n. flap, overhang, projection, addition, extension.

overlapping adj. layered, coincidental, overlying, superimposed.

overlay v. 1. burden, overload, encumber, cram. 2. overlap, superimpose, cover, extend.

overload v. oppress, encumber, weigh down, burden, saddle.

overlook v. 1. survey, inspect, view, look out on, tower over, surmount. 2. neglect, ignore, slight, disdain, make light of, miss, omit, skip; wink at, look the other way; ant. note, notice, record, remember.

overlooked adj. forgotten, omitted, neglected, left out; ant. prized, sought after, valued.

overly adv. exceedingly, inordinately, excessively, too, unreasonably, immoderately; ant. inadequately, insufficiently.

overpower v. overcome, master, overwhelm, subdue, subjugate, vanquish, defeat.

overpowering adj. strong, extreme, compelling, oppressive; sickening, nauseating.

overrate v. overestimate, overvalue, magnify, build up, exaggerate; ant. underrate.

overrated adj. overblown, overvalued, disappointing.

override v. cancel, annul, nullify, overrule, quash, rescind, supersede, thwart, revoke.

overriding adj. main, determining, major, dominant, cardinal, first, prime, overruling, ultimate; ant. insignificant, unimportant.

overrule v. disallow, invalidate, nullify, override, overturn, veto, vote down, rescind, cancel, annul, abrogate.

overrun v. infest, inundate, permeate, ravage, swarm, choke, defeat, invade, overwhelm, occupy, run riot over; ant. evacuate, desert.

overseas adj. exotic, foreign, strange, outland.

overseas adv. abroad, away, in or to foreign lands.

oversee v. superintend, manage, supervise, look after, watch over.

overseer n. foreman, boss, chief, manager, superintendent, supervisor, master, gaffer.

overshadow v. dominate, surpass, eclipse, outweigh; darken, veil, obscure, cloud.

overshoes n. galoshes, rubbers, boots, rubber shoes.

overshoot v. overreach, exceed, overdo.

oversight n. omission, mistake, blunder, error, lapse, slip.

oversimplified adj. simplistic, made easy, simple.

overstate *v.* emphasize, amplify, exaggerate, expand upon.

overstep *v.* violate, cross, encroach, trespass.

overstock *v.* cram, overload, overfill, overstuff.

overt *adj.* clear, open, obvious, visible, manifest, evident; *ant.* covert.

overtake *v.* outdistance, pass, pull ahead of.

overtax *v.* exhaust, trouble, strain, tire.

overthrow *v.* conquer, crush, depose, topple, vanquish, dethrone, destroy, master, overcome, eradicate.

overtime *n.* extra, supplementary, additional, added, late.

overtone *n.* innuendo, hint, flavor, feeling, nuance, sense, suggestion, undercurrent.

overture *n.* **1.** proposition, invitation, advance, approach, suggestion, proposal. **2.** introduction, prelude, preface.

overturn *v.* upset, quash, repeal, rescind, reverse, upend.

overused *adj.* hackneyed, clichéd, stale, tired, trite, worn, unoriginal, stereotyped.

overview *n.* summary, sketch, general outlook, summation.

overweening *adj.* arrogant, haughty, insolent, proud, egotistic.

overweight *adj.* heavy, fat, plump, ample, stout, chubby, chunky, fleshy, flabby, portly, gross, obese; *ant.* emaciated, thin, skinny.

overwhelm *v.* **1.** defeat, overcome, conquer, overthrow, beat, vanquish. **2.** astonish, bowl over, stagger, confound, surprise. **3.** submerge, drown, inundate, deluge, engulf.

overwhelming *adj.* overpowering, devastating, overriding, irresistible, inundating; astonishing, breathtaking; *ant.* insignificant, negligible.

overwork *v.* exhaust, wear out, overdo, fatigue, exploit; work one's finger's to the bone.

overwrought *adj.* emotional, excited, agitated, distracted, tense, hyper (*slang*), uptight, wound up, keyed up, affected.

overzealous *adj.* overeager, overenthusiastic, fanatical.

owe *v.* be indebted, be obligated, be bound, be beholden, be contracted.

owed *adj.* unpaid, outstanding, overdue, unpaid, unsettled, in arrears.

owing *adj.* indebted, obligated, in debt.

owing to because of, as a result of, on account of, thanks to.

owl *n.* night bird, nocturnal bird, bird of prey, owlet.

own *v.* **1.** possess, have, hold, keep, enjoy, retain. **2.** concede, acknowledge, admit, allow, grant, confess, recognize.

own up admit, come clean, face, confess, fess up, tell the truth, spill the beans, put one's cards on the table.

own *adj.* mine, yours, personal, individual, particular, private, idiosyncratic.

on one's own independent, autonomous, self-sufficient, self-supporting.

owner *n.* possessor, proprietor, master, mistress, keeper, purchaser.

ownership *n.* possession, claim, holding, title, deed; tenure, occupancy, dominion.

ox *n.* **1.** buffalo, bison, castrated bull, steer, bullock. **2.** oaf, clod, dolt, lout.

oyster *n.* seafood, mollusk, bivalve.

pace *n.* **1.** speed, velocity, rate, tempo, momentum, time. **2.** walk, step, stride, gait.

put one through the paces try, test, examine, audition, try out.

pace *v.* **1.** walk, stride, tread, trot, canter; gallop. **2.** measure, determine, count.

pacific *adj.* **1.** calm, mild, tranquil, placid, gentle, serene, peaceful. **2.** conciliatory, appeasing, diplomatic, equable; *ant.* aggressive.

pacifist *n.* conscientious objector, passive resister, dove, peace-lover; *ant.* hawk, warmonger.

pacify *v.* **1.** appease, placate, allay, soothe, humor, mollify; *ant.* aggravate, anger. **2.** subdue, silence, quiet, still, tame, lull, tranquilize.

pack *n.* **1.** package, parcel, bundle, load. **2.** group, gang, mob, number.

pack *v.* **1.** prepare, ready, gather, collect, arrange, fasten, bind, tie. **2.** compress, stuff, condense, cram, squeeze, insert; *ant.* scatter. **3.** crowd, mob, press, push, throng.

package *n.* **1.** packet, parcel, pack, container, carton, box. **2.** deal, arrangement, proposal, agreement, proposition, consignment.

packing *n.* stuffing, wadding, filler, padding, waste.

pact *n.* agreement, arrangement, covenant, understanding, alliance, contract, deal, bond, cartel, treaty; *ant.* breach, disagreement.

pad *n.* **1.** tablet, note paper, note pad. **2.** (*slang*) apartment, home, residence, living quarters, room, flat.

pad *v.* **1.** cushion, protect, line, wrap, fill, stuff. **2.** increase, augment, enlarge, amplify, expand, inflate, elaborate.

padding *n.* **1.** filling, stuffing, wadding, waste. **2.** verbosity, wordiness, bombast, redundancy.

paddle *v.* **1.** propel, scull, row, boat, navigate. **2.** punish, spank, swat, thrash, beat.

paean *n.* hymn, psalm, anthem, eulogy, tribute, panegyric; *ant.* denunciation.

pagan *n.* heathen, infidel, idolater, atheist, polytheist.

page *n.* leaf, sheet, folio, side.

page *v.* call, summon, hunt for, seek, bid.

pageant *n.* extravaganza, spectacle, display, parade, procession, play, show, tableau.

pageantry *n.* pomp, spectacle, extravagance, splendor, grandeur, ostentation, melodrama, theatricality, drama, ceremony, display, show.

pail *n.* bucket, tub, container, receptacle.

pain *n.* agony, misery, distress, suffering, anguish, torment, affliction, hurt, discomfort, grief, woe, tribulation, throb, pang.

feeling no pain (*slang*) intoxicated, inebriated, drunk, drugged, stoned (*slang*).

pain *v.* afflict, hurt, wound, torture, torment, irritate, nettle, vex, annoy, distress, grieve.

painful *adj.* **1.** aching, throbbing, sore, tender, raw, inflamed, uncomfortable. **2.** (applied to the mind or feelings) disturbing, worrying, depressing, saddening, troublesome, grievous, disagreeable, distasteful. **3.** (as an experience) harrowing, laborious, trying; *ant.* easy.

painkiller *n.* anesthetic, analgesic, drug, sedative, anodyne, palliative, paregoric.

painless *adj.* easy, simple, effortless, fast, quick, downhill, trouble-free; *ant.* demanding, difficult.

pains *n.* **1.** bother, care, trouble, diligence, assiduity, effort. **2.** (process of childbirth) labor, throes, contractions, cramps.

painstaking *adj.* meticulous, conscientious, assiduous, diligent, sedulous, industrious, punctilious, scrupulous, thorough, careful; *ant.* careless, negligent.

paint *n.* oils, enamel, lacquer, primer, stain, tint, wash, color, dye.

paint *v.* **1.** (make a painting) portray, picture, depict, compose, apply, shade, tint, wash. **2.**

(put paint on) cover, coat, apply, brush, tint, decorate, ornament.

painting *n.* portrait, picture, depiction, representation, illustration, landscape, mural, oil painting, still life, watercolor, fresco.

pair *n.* combination, match, couple, duo, twins, twosome, duet.

pair *v.* couple, join, link, marry, wed, yoke, mate, pair off, put together, match, splice, team; *ant.* sever.

pal (*slang*) *n.* friend, companion, confidant, intimate, comrade, crony, partner, sidekick (*slang*).

palace *n.* castle, royal *or* official residence, palazzo, chateau; *ant.* hovel.

palatable *adj.* appetizing, savory, tasty, attractive, enjoyable, satisfactory, acceptable, agreeable.

palate *n.* taste, appreciation, enjoyment, gusto, relish, zest, appetite.

palatial *adj.* grand, regal, stately, magnificent, luxurious, opulent, plush, posh (*slang*), sumptuous, majestic, spacious, swanky (*slang*).

pale *v.* blanch, whiten, faint, fade, diminish, lessen; *ant.* blush, color.

pale *adj.* pallid, sallow, ashen, wan, pasty, faint, waxy, chalky, bloodless, colorless, bleached, faded, washed-out, weak; *ant.* ruddy.

palisade *n.* barricade, stockade, wall, bulwark, enclosure, fence, fortification, defense.

pall *n.* **1.** gloom, depression, melancholy, dismay, shadow, damper. **2.** shroud, mantle, veil.

pall *v.* satiate, glut, cloy, jade, bore, tire, weary.

palliate *v.* relieve, alleviate, ease, abate, lessen, diminish, mollify, minimize, allay, assuage, soothe, temper; *ant.* exacerbate, intensify.

palliative *n.* easing, assuaging, soothing, analgesic, anodyne, sedative; *ant.* aggravating, irritant.

pallid *adj.* **1.** pale, ashen, bloodless, wan, waxen, pasty, sallow, livid, anemic, cadaverous; *ant.* ruddy, vigorous. **2.** insipid, vapid, uninspired, lifeless, tired.

palm *v.* steal, appropriate, grab, lift (*slang*), conceal, sneak.

palm off unload, impose, foist, pass off.

palpable *adj.* tangible, substantial, manifest, real, unmistakable, obvious, evident, blatant, clear, visible.

palpitate *v.* pulse, throb, beat, pound, pulsate, vibrate, flutter.

palsied *adj.* debilitated, disabled, paralyzed, crippled, arthritic, rheumatic, spastic.

paltry *adj.* small, slight, negligible, piddling, puny, trifling, unimportant, insignificant, petty, trivial; *ant.* substantial.

pamper *v.* indulge, overindulge, coddle, mollycoddle, baby, mother, pet, spoil.

pamphlet *n.* booklet, brochure, leaflet, tract, broadside, folder.

pan *n.* pot, skillet, saucepan, fryer, wok.

pan *v.* denigrate, disparage, criticize, jeer at, censure, lampoon.

pan out work out, turn out, succeed, happen, result, culminate, come to an end, yield.

panache *n.* dash, elan, style, flair, pizazz, verve, enthusiasm, spirit, flamboyance, swagger, ostentation.

pancake *n.* flapjack, hot cake, batter cake, griddlecake, latke, tortilla, crepe.

pandemonium *n.* bedlam, chaos, tumult, ruckus, commotion, confusion, disorder, frenzy, hullabaloo, clamor, din, uproar; *ant.* order, calm, peace.

pander to *v.* cater to, indulge, pamper, please, gratify, satisfy.

panegyric *n.* accolade, praise, compliment, eulogy, homage, tribute, citation, commendation; *ant.* censure.

pang *n.* ache, pain, spasm, stab, twinge, throe, gripe, prick, sting, wrench.

panhandle (*slang*) *v.* beg, solicit, ask alms, bum (*slang*).

panhandler (*slang*) *n.* beggar, vagrant, tramp, bum (*slang*).

panic *n.* alarm, hysteria, fear, fright, scare, horror, terror, consternation, dismay, tizzy.

panic *v.* overreact, *slang:* lose one's cool *or* nerve, go to pieces; *ant.* relax.

panic-stricken *adj.* frightened, fearful, horrified, petrified, frenzied, hysterical, perturbed, agitated, stunned, stupefied, in a cold sweat (*slang*); *ant.* confident, relaxed, laidback.

panoply *n.* **1.** armor, shield, protection, covering. **2.** regalia, raiment, attire, dress, garb, gear, get-up (*slang*), trappings.

panorama *n.* view, scenery, spectacle, vista,

panoramic scene, overview, perspective, bird's-eye view, survey.

panoramic *adj.* comprehensive, sweeping, inclusive, extensive, far-reaching, widespread, universal; *ant.* limited.

pant *v.* gasp, wheeze, huff, puff.

pant *v.* 1. gasp, wheeze, huff, puff, blow, breathe, sigh; throb, palpitate, pulsate. 2. (become excited over) yearn, desire, crave, want, covet, hanker, hunger, thirst, long, pine, ache.

panting *adj.* breathless, out of breath, short-winded, gasping.

pantomime *n.* charade, dumb show, mime.

pantry *n.* larder, cupboard, scullery, storeroom, cooler.

pants *n.* slacks, trousers, jeans, knickers, briefs, drawers, panties, shorts, underpants, undershorts, trunks.

paper *n.* 1. newspaper, journal, gazette, daily. 2. document, exposition, essay, article, theme, writing.

on paper in theory, theoretically, in the abstract; supposedly.

papers *n.* identification, passport, naturalization papers, ID (*slang*).

par *n.* standard, average, norm, level, median, equivalence.

below par inferior, below average, substandard, wanting, second-rate; *ant.* up to snuff.

parable *n.* story, allegory, fable, homily.

parabolic *adj.* figurative, metaphorical, allegorical, illustrative, explanatory.

parade *n.* 1. procession, pageant, march, motorcade, promenade, cavalcade, ceremony, review, show, spectacle, display, exhibition. 2. ostentation, flaunting, pomp.

parade *v.* 1. march, strut, walk, file. 2. flaunt, brandish, exhibit, display, show off, strut, swagger, make a show of.

paradigm *n.* model, example, pattern, prototype, archetype, exemplar, ideal.

paradise *n.* 1. bliss, delight, ecstasy, felicity. 2. heaven, City of God, heavenly kingdom, Promised Land, Zion. 3. Eden, Garden of Eden, utopia, Valhalla, Elysian fields, Elysium, Arcadia, Olympus.

paradox *n.* 1. contradiction, inconsistency, incongruity, absurdity. 2. mystery, anomaly, enigma, puzzle, riddle.

paradoxical *adj.* contradictory, conflicting, incongruous, inconsistent, self-contradictory, absurd, baffling, incomprehensible, confounding, enigmatic, puzzling, illogical.

paragon *n.* model, paradigm, pattern, archetype, prototype, ideal, epitome, exemplar, nonpareil, quintessence, apotheosis.

parallel *n.* equivalent, match, duplicate, likeness, similarity, correlation, analog, analogy, corollary, correlation, counterpart.

parallel *v.* match, duplicate, correlate, equal, resemble, correspond, agree.

parallel *adj.* 1. like, similar, analogous, correspondent, homologous. 2. equidistant, aligned, alongside, collateral; *ant.* convergent, divergent.

paralysis *n.* 1. immobility, torpor, paraplegia, quadriplegia, stroke, palsy, paresis. 2. standstill, halt, shutdown, breakdown, arrest, stagnation, torpor.

paralyze *v.* 1. immobilize, disable, incapacitate, debilitate, anesthetize, numb, cripple. 2. arrest, halt, stun, stupefy, transfix.

parameter *n.* variable, quantity; limit, boundary, restriction, framework, guideline, specification, criterion.

paramount *adj.* dominant, eminent, premier, foremost, superior, highest, supreme; *ant.* inferior, lowest.

paramour *n.* lover, concubine, courtesan, kept woman *or* man, mistress, beau.

paranoia *n.* mental disorder, complex, delusions, megalomania, psychosis.

paranoid *adj.* neurotic, distrustful, suspicious.

parapet *n.* fortification, bulwark, bastion, battlement, rampart.

paraphernalia *n.* gear, equipment, apparatus, accessories, accoutrements, belongings, odds and ends, stuff, things, baggage, trappings.

paraphrase *v.* rephrase, reword, restate, rehash, interpret, translate, recapitulate.

parasite *n.* 1. bloodsucker, leech, sucker, epizoon, endophyte. 2. freeloader (*slang*), hanger-on, *slang:* scrounger, sponger.

parcel *n.* 1. package, carton, bundle, packet. 2. bunch, group, collection, set, pack, batch. 3. lot, plot, tract, property.

parcel out *v.* allocate, portion out, share out, distribute, dispense, allot, mete, dole out.

parch *v.* dry up, dehydrate, shrivel, wither, burn, blister, roast, scorch.

pardon *n.* amnesty, acquittal, exoneration, reprieve, allowance, excuse, forgiveness, mercy.

pardon *v.* acquit, exculpate, emancipate, exonerate, reprieve, liberate, free, let off, release, excuse, forgive, absolve.

pare *v.* **1.** crop, trim, prune, cut, clip, lop, shave. **2.** diminish, decrease, reduce, cut (back).

parent *n.* mother, father, sire, procreator, progenitor; origin, source, architect, originator.

parentage *n.* lineage, descent, ancestry, pedigree, extraction, origin, stock, family.

pariah *n.* outcast, exile, undesirable, untouchable, outlaw, leper, scapegoat, black sheep.

parity *n.* equality, similarity, affinity, par, congruence, likeness, sameness, uniformity.

park *n.* recreational area, woodland, garden, esplanade, playground.

park *v.* station, deposit, leave, position.

parlance *n.* idiom, jargon, lingo, phraseology, speech, argot, dialect.

parley *v.* discuss, negotiate, confer, deliberate, speak, talk.

parliament *n.* council, assembly, congress, house, legislature, senate.

parlor *n.* living room, sitting room, drawing room, lounge.

parochial *adj.* provincial, narrow, limited, insular, small-minded, blinkered; *ant.* catholic.

parody *n.* burlesque, satire, caricature, spoof, lampoon, *slang:* sendup, takeoff, mimicry.

parole *v.* discharge, free, release, liberate, pardon.

parrot *v.* mimic, imitate, ape, copy, echo, repeat.

parry *v.* deflect, circumvent, evade, ward off, dodge, avert, avoid, fend off, stave off, sidestep.

parsimonious *adj.* stingy, miserly, niggardly, tightfisted, penurious, closefisted, cheap, penny-pinching.

part *n.* **1.** portion, piece, section, fragment, fraction, particle, element, bit, slice, scrap, chunk. **2.** duty, share, responsibility, task, work, role.

for the most part mostly, mainly, generally, chiefly, on the whole, usually, largely, principally.

in part partially, somewhat, to some degree, to a certain extent, in some measure, partly, slightly; *ant.* totally, completely.

take someone's part support, side with, stand up for, defend.

part *v.* **1.** divide, separate, split up, break, sever. **2.** leave, depart, part company, go, withdraw, split (*slang*).

part with give up, let go of, relinquish, sacrifice, surrender, lose.

partake *v.* take part, participate, engage, share, enter, be involved.

partial *adj.* **1.** incomplete, unfinished, fragmentary, limited. **2.** (showing favoritism) prejudiced, biased, unfair, influenced.

partial to taken with, crazy about (*slang*), mad about, fond of, keen on.

partiality *n.* **1.** prejudice, bias, favoritism, unfairness, discrimination, intolerance. **2.** liking, fondness, love, taste, penchant, inclination, propensity, proclivity, soft spot, weakness.

participant *n.* contributor, helper, worker, member, associate.

participate *v.* take part, be involved, join, partake, share, cooperate.

particle *n.* bit, iota, smidgen, speck, mite, whit, jot, shred, scrap.

particular *n.* fact, detail, specification, circumstance, point, item, datum.

particular *adj.* **1.** specific, distinct, singular, unique, special, unusual, exceptional; *ant.* general. **2.** exact, precise, accurate, minute; *ant.* vague, approximate. **3.** fastidious, discriminating, exacting, thorough, painstaking, finicky, hard to please, scrupulous.

parting *n.* **1.** departure, good-bye, farewell, leave-taking. **2.** (the end of an association) rift, split, rupture, severance, separation, disjunction, disunion, estrangement, divorce. **3.** divergence, split, separation, division, fork, bifurcation, crossroads.

partisan *n.* follower, supporter, backer, champion, devotee, disciple, factionary, guerrilla.

partisan *adj.* factional, biased, prejudiced, discriminatory, one-sided, predisposed, sectarian, slanted; disinterested, fair.

partition *n.* barrier, wall, room-divider, screen, traverse.

partition *v.* **1.** allocate, allot, parcel out, share, divide, portion. **2.** divide, separate, fence off, bar, screen.

partly *adv.* slightly, partially, somewhat, to a certain extent, to a certain degree, up to a point.

partner *n.* associate, colleague, consort, accomplice, helper, collaborator, ally, spouse, helpmate, husband, wife, roommate.

partnership *n.* alliance, association, corporation, conglomerate, union, fellowship, fraternity.

party *n.* **1.** affair, gathering, celebration, festivity, soiree, reception, bash. **2.** group, body, alliance, faction, coalition, association, caucus, league.

parvenu *n.* nouveau riche, new rich, upstart, climber (*slang*), vulgarian.

pass *n.* **1.** permit, license, authorization, right, admission, ticket, passport, visa. **2.** sexual overture, proposition, suggestion, approach, advance.

pass *v.* **1.** move, go by *or* past, shoot ahead of, go beyond, overtake, outdistance. **2.** be graduated, succeed, matriculate. **3.** give, transfer, exchange, relinquish, hand over. **4.** enact, legislate, establish, vote in, accept, adopt, approve, authorize.

come to pass come about, happen, occur, develop, transpire.

pass by **1.** leave, move past, depart from. **2.** overlook, neglect, abandon, pass over, not choose, omit.

pass off as pretend, pass for, make a pretense of, fake, feign.

pass out faint, lose consciousness, swoon, black out.

pass over reject, ignore, omit, disregard, eliminate, turn down.

pass the buck (*slang*) dodge, evade, avoid, delegate.

passable *adj.* **1.** allowable, admissible, acceptable, adequate, OK. **2.** clear, navigable, traversable, open.

passage *n.* **1.** journey, voyage, trek, tour. **2.** route, avenue, road, crossing, path, thoroughfare; hall, corridor, passageway, access. **3.** (a piece of writing) section, excerpt, paragraph, quotation.

passé *adj.* dated, old-fashioned, out-of-date, out, outmoded, démodé, obsolete, antiquated, old hat; *ant.* in (*slang*), fashionable.

passenger *n.* traveler, commuter, rider, straphanger (*slang*).

passer-by *n.* bystander, onlooker, spectator, witness.

passing *n.* death, demise, end, termination, expiration, loss.

passing *adj.* temporary, fleeting, transitory, transient, momentary, brief, fugitive, short-lived; *ant.* permanent, long-lasting.

passion *n.* **1.** sexual desire, lust, the hots (*slang*), fervor, adoration, craving, fascination, love. **2.** intensity, zeal, enthusiasm, love, excitement, emotion, verve.

passionate *adj.* **1.** excitable, vehement, hot-headed, tempestuous, hot, heated, impetuous, emotional, agitated, hot under the collar (*slang*). **2.** ardent, impassioned, amorous, wanton, torrid, erotic, sexy, sultry, fervid, desirous, fiery.

passive *adj.* **1.** compliant, docile, submissive, receptive, influenced, affected, stirred; *ant.* aggressive. **2.** motionless, inert, inactive, latent, lifeless, indolent; *ant.* vigorous. **3.** patient, resigned, enduring, docile, reactive, forbearing, quiet; *ant.* active.

past *n.* background, history, experience, track record (*slang*), dossier, life.

past *adj.* gone, over, done, finished, former, previous, prior, preceding, early, bygone.

paste *n.* glue, adhesive, putty, mucilage.

paste *v.* glue, fasten, fix, cement.

pastel *adj.* soft-hued, pale, light, muted, delicate, subtle.

pastiche *n.* medley, potpourri, hodgepodge, mélange, miscellany, motley, composition.

pastime *n.* hobby, recreation, amusement, diversion, relaxation, avocation, play, sport, game.

pastor *n.* clergyman, parson, priest, vicar, minister.

pastoral *adj.* rural, bucolic, rustic, country, simple, idyllic.

pasture *n.* meadow, grassland, mead, greensward, green.

pasty *adj.* pale, sallow, wan, waxy, pallid, sickly; *ant.* healthy.

pat *n.* **1.** tap, touch, stroke, caress. **2.** piece, portion, dab, lump.

pat *v.* tap, pet, stroke, touch, caress, fondle.

pat *adj.* **1.** appropriate, fitting, suitable, well-chosen, relevant, right, apt, felicitous. **2.** glib, automatic, neat, slick, easy, facile.

pat *adv.* precisely, perfectly, exactly, faultlessly, flawlessly.

patch *n.* area, plot, lot, tract, parcel, land, ground, spot.

patch *v.* fix, mend, repair, cover, sew up, stitch, reinforce.

patchy *adj.* uneven, irregular, variable, random, sketchy, spotty, erratic, fitful, incongruous.

patent *n.* copyright, registered trademark, certificate, invention.

patent *adj.* **1.** licensed, copyrighted, proprietary, protected, controlled, monopolized, limited. **2.** obvious, open, evident, clear, ostensible, explicit, manifest, plain, undeniable, transparent.

paternal *adj.* fatherly, patrimonial, benevolent, protective, solicitous, concerned.

paternity *n.* **1.** fatherhood, parentage, lineage, descent, extraction, family, origination. **2.** authorship, creation, derivation, origination.

path *n.* trail, walkway, route, road, passage, track, direction, course.

pathetic *adj.* **1.** pitiful, touching, affecting, moving, poignant, plaintive. **2.** miserable, deplorable, contemptible, worthless, pitiable, meager, inadequate, puny, poor.

pathological *adj.* neurotic, mentally ill, disordered, sick, morbid, unhealthy.

pathos *n.* pitifulness, poignancy, plaintiveness, sadness, misery.

patience *n.* forbearance, endurance, perseverance, stoicism, calmness, composure, restraint, cool (*slang*).

patient *n.* invalid, case, client, victim, sufferer.

patient *adj.* **1.** imperturbable, unruffled, calm, composed, tolerant, forebearing, easygoing, passive, mild-tempered. **2.** steady, dependable, reliable, stable, enduring, unwavering.

patio *n.* piazza, courtyard, square, open porch.

patriarch *n.* paterfamilias, father, elder, master, ancestor.

patrician *n.* aristocrat, noble, gentleman, lord.

patrician *adj.* aristocratic, noble, highborn, royal.

patrimony *n.* inheritance, birthright, revenue, share, heritage, legacy, estate.

patriot *n.* loyalist, nationalist, jingoist, flag-waver.

patrol *n.* guard, security, watchman, sentinel; surveillance, protecting, policing, defense.

patrol *v.* guard, police, watch, inspect, stake out.

patron *n.* **1.** supporter, benefactor, advocate, helper, sponsor, philanthropist, defender, protector. **2.** client, customer, frequenter, regular, subscriber.

patronage *n.* **1.** support, assistance, financing, sponsorship, benefaction, backing, aid, subsidy. **2.** business, commerce, trading, shopping.

patronize *v.* condescend, talk down to, snub, disdain, lord over.

patter *n.* tapping, patting, sound.

pattern *n.* **1.** model, example, guide, original, template, paradigm. **2.** design, markings, decoration, ornament.

patterned *adj.* decorated, printed, ornamented.

paucity *n.* insufficiency, lack, deficiency, sparsity, scantiness, scarcity, meagerness, paltriness.

paunch *n.* stomach, belly, *slang:* tummy, beerbelly, potbelly, beer-gut.

pauper *n.* indigent, beggar, insolvent, downand-out, have-not.

paunchy *adj.* portly, chubby, pudgy, fat, rotund, corpulent.

pause *n.* interval, lull, break, caesura, suspension, halt, intermission, abatement, cessation, letup (*slang*).

give one pause cause doubt, create suspicion *or* uncertainty, frighten, alarm.

pause *v.* wait, delay, cease, desist; hesitate, take a break, *slang:* take a breather, take five.

pave *v.* cover, surface, asphalt, tar, macadamize, tile.

pavement *n.* **1.** sidewalk, street, road, thoroughfare, highway. **2.** asphalt, concrete, macadam.

paw *n.* foot, hand, forepaw, pad.

paw *v.* **1.** hit, clutch, grasp, grab, maul, manhandle, molest. **2.** scrape, scratch, dig, rub, rake, claw.

pawn *n.* dupe, stooge (*slang*), tool, toy, puppet, plaything, instrument, hostage, security.

pawn *v.* hock (*slang*), pledge, stake, mortgage, wager, hazard, put up.

pay *n.* income, salary, earnings, wages, stipend, allowance, fee, recompense, remuneration.

pay *v.* **1.** compensate, recompense, make restitution *or* reparation, pay up, settle, reimburse. **2.** retaliate, punish, repay, revenge. **pay the piper** take *or* suffer the consequences, pay, take one's medicine.

payable *adj.* due, owed, receivable, outstanding, unpaid.

payment *n.* **1.** wage, salary, fee, restitution, recompense, subsidy, settlement, remuneration. **2.** installment, advance, deposit, portion, outlay, premium.

payoff *n.* settlement, adjustment, conclusion, payment, reward; bribe.

payroll *n.* **1.** staff, employees, workers, personnel. **2.** salary, payment, wages.

peace *n.* **1.** calm, tranquillity, serenity, placidity, silence, stillness, hush, quiet, repose, relaxation. **2.** truce, ceasefire, agreement, armistice, reconciliation, treaty, unanimity, amity, concord, union, fraternization; *ant.* war. **hold one's peace** be silent, be *or* keep quiet, shut up. **make one's peace with** accept, admit, agree, acquiesce, conciliate, come to terms with.

peaceable *adj.* **1.** tranquil, serene, quiet, calm, placid. **2.** friendly, amicable, pacific, conciliatory, amiable; *ant.* belligerent, offensive; *ant.* warlike, bellicose.

peaceful *adj.* tranquil, serene, restful, calm, still, placid, quiet, undisturbed.

peacemaker *n.* mediator, arbitrator, interceder, conciliator, pacifier, peacemonger.

peace offering *n.* overture, olive branch, placation, appeasement, sacrifice, gift.

peak *n.* **1.** mountain, hill, summit, tip, apex, crest. **2.** maximum, high point, apogee, pinnacle, top, zenith, culmination; *ant.* nadir.

peak *v.* climax, come to a head, culminate, top out, crest, tower.

peaked *adj.* pale, wan, sickly, ill, *slang:* under the weather, washed-out.

peal *n.* ring, chime, clang, reverberation, resounding, sound, noise.

peal *v.* ring out, chime, clang, reverberate, resonate, resound, vibrate, toll.

peanuts (*slang*), *n.* pittance, pennies, next to nothing, chickenfeed (*slang*).

pearl *n.* **1.** jewel, gem, nacre, margarite. **2.** drop, droplet, globule, dewdrop, raindrop.

peasant *n.* rustic, provincial, farmer, farmworker, sharecropper, laborer.

peasantry *n.* **1.** the masses, rank and file, commonality, common people, proletariat, hoi polloi. **2.** vulgarity, crudeness, rudeness, impropriety, indelicacy.

pebble *n.* stone, chip, small rock, gravel, agate.

peccadillo *n.* sin, misdeed, infraction, delinquency, indiscretion, error, fault, slipup.

peck *n.* **1.** kiss, smooch (*slang*), buss. **2.** blow, rap, jab, hit, tap.

peck *v.* hit, rap, jab, blow, tap.

peculiar *adj.* **1.** singular, exceptional, unique, one-of-a-kind, individual, signal, characteristic, distinct. **2.** outlandish, unusual, strange, eccentric, idiosyncratic, bizarre, queer, odd, weird, wonderful, extraordinary.

peculiarity *n.* unusualness, singularity, eccentricity, idiosyncrasy, oddity, characteristic, quirk, foible, trait, whimsicality, quiddity.

pecuniary *adj.* financial, monetary, fiscal.

pedagogue *n.* instructor, teacher, schoolteacher, schoolmarm, educator, preceptor.

pedagogy *n.* instruction, teaching, education, guidance, training, tutelage.

pedal *v.* operate, treadle, drive, accelerate.

pedal *n.* clutch, brake, lever.

pedant *n.* dogmatist, literalist, pedagogue, formalist, doctrinaire, methodologist, quibbler, hair-splitter, nit-picker.

pedantic *adj.* formal, precise, punctilious, pedagogic, didactic, academic, scholastic, pompous, pontificating, nit-picking, hair-splitting, overprecise.

peddle *v.* hawk, sell, trade, vend, market.

peddler *n.* hawker, vender, huckster, seller, salesperson.

pedestal *n.* platform, podium, base, stand, support, dais.

pedestrian *n.* walker, foot-traveler, hiker, stroller, ambler.

pedigree *n.* lineage, ancestry, heritage, genealogy, extraction, descent, parentage, family, blood, stock.

peek *n.* look, glance, glimpse, gander, peep.

peek *v.* look, peer, spy, glance.

peel *n.* skin, rind, zest, epicarp.

peel *v.* skin, scale, pare, strip.

peep *v.* **1.** glance, look, glimpse, peek, gander. **2.** cheep, chirp, squeak, cry, sound.

peer *n.* equal, counterpart, match, rival, companion, fellow, colleague.

peer *v.* scrutinize, examine, inspect, scan, snoop, spy.

peer group equals, one's peers, associates, cohort, gang, age group.

peerless *adj.* nonpareil, unequaled, incomparable, unparalleled, unmatched, paramount, superlative, unsurpassed, beyond compare, second to none.

peeved *adj.* annoyed, irritated, irked, exasperated, miffed, vexed, galled, piqued, put out, sore (*slang*), upset.

peevish *adj.* irritable, cross, cantankerous, acrimonious, querulous, fretful, testy, touchy, sulky, irascible, cranky, splenetic, sullen, petulant.

peg *n.* knob, hook, stake, post.

take down a peg humiliate, humble, criticize, embarrass, mortify.

pejorative *adj.* disparaging, derogatory, deprecatory, debasing, slighting, detractive, belittling, negative; *ant.* complimentary, laudatory.

pell-mell *adj.* haphazard, chaotic, tumultuous, disordered, disorganized, confused, scrambled.

pell-mell *adv.* heedlessly, rashly, recklessly, impetuously, helter-skelter, full tilt, hastily.

pelt *n.* fur, hide, skin, fleece, coat.

pelt *v.* beat, hit, strike, wallop, belt, pummel, assail, bombard.

pen *n.* enclosure, cage, corral, stall, hutch, sty, coop, penitentiary.

pen *v.* **1.** enclose, close *or* fence in, confine, shut up, coop up (*slang*). **2.** write, author, compose, draft, jot down.

penal *adj.* punitive, punishing, reformatory, corrective, chastening, retributive.

penalize *v.* punish, discipline, correct, chasten, castigate; *ant.* reward.

penalty *n.* punishment, retribution, fine, forfeit, amercement; *ant.* reward.

penance *n.* **1.** punishment, penalty, reparation, retribution, mortification, self-flagellation. **2.** contrition, remorse, atonement, repentance, confession.

penchant *n.* fondness, preference, proclivity, inclination, liking, leaning, predilection, bias, affinity, soft spot, taste.

pendant *n.* necklace, locket, medallion, lavaliere.

pending *adj.* impending, imminent, forthcoming, awaiting, on the back burner, unfinished, unsettled, undecided, hanging fire.

pendulous *adj.* hanging, drooping, dangling, swinging, swaying, suspended.

penetrable *adj.* passable, permeable, porous, accessible.

penetrate *v.* **1.** pierce, enter, insert, bore, perforate, go *or* pass through, thrust. **2.** permeate, infiltrate, enter, seep, percolate, filter, pervade. **3.** understand, comprehend, discern, perceive, grasp, fathom.

penetrating *adj.* **1.** piercing, boring, puncturing, passing *or* going through, permeating, infiltrating; *ant.* blunt, rounded. **2.** shrewd, keen, incisive, perceptive, intelligent, sharpwitted, discerning, astute, perspicacious; *ant.* obtuse.

penitence *n.* contrition, repentance, remorse, regret, self-reproach, shame.

penitent *adj.* contrite, remorseful, rueful, repentant, regretful, abject, atoning, in sackcloth and ashes.

penitentiary *n.* jail, prison, penal institution, correctional facility, reformatory, pen (*slang*).

pen name *n.* pseudonym, nom de plume, alias, anonym.

pennant *n.* flag, banner, streamer, emblem.

penniless *adj.* destitute, bankrupt, indigent, poverty-stricken, poor, impoverished, needy, broke (*slang*), ruined; *ant.* rich, wealthy.

penny-ante (*slang*) *adj.* trifling, petty, insignificant, trivial, unimportant, of no account.

penny pincher miser, niggard, Scrooge, skinflint, cheapskate, tightwad.

pension *n.* annuity, benefit, superannuation, stipend, grant, subsidy, allowance.

pensive *adj.* contemplative, ruminative, meditative, musing, reflective, dreamy, wistful, absent-minded, absorbed, thoughtful, preoccupied.

pent-up *adj.* suppressed, repressed, inhibited,

restrained, bridled, checked, curbed, bottled-up, stifled, smothered.

penurious *adj.* **1.** stingy, miserly, niggardly, grudging, tightfisted, penny-pinching, parsimonious; *ant.* generous. **2.** indigent, broke (*slang*), poverty-stricken, penniless, needy, impoverished, destitute; *ant.* wealthy.

people *n.* **1.** humanity, humankind, the human race, mankind. **2.** race, nationality, extraction, tribe, clan, family, community. **3.** citizens, masses, the multitude, the majority, the public, common people, folk, rank and file, the horde, rabble.

people *v.* inhabit, colonize, occupy, settle, tenant, populate.

pep (*slang*) *n.* energy, vigor, vivacity, liveliness, spirit, gusto, exuberance, life, animation, vitality, verve, get-up-and-go (*slang*).

peppy (*slang*) *adj.* lively, energetic, vigorous, high-spirited.

perceive *v.* **1.** see, look, observe, notice, note. **2.** comprehend, grasp, understand, discern, discover, sense, feel, get (*slang*), realize.

percentage *n.* percent, cut (*slang*), rate, division, portion, payoff (*slang*), allotment, commission, winnings; *slang:* split, slice.

perceptible *adj.* perceivable, discernible, distinguishable, recognizable, noticeable, visible, obvious, evident, apparent, clear.

perception *n.* **1.** (act or condition of perceiving) realizing, understanding, awareness, recognition. **2.** (a way of looking at things) opinion, viewpoint, thought, observation, knowledge, insight, idea, sense, notion. **3.** (sensitive understanding) acumen, judgment, discernment, perspicacity, insight, sagacity, sense, taste.

perceptive *adj.* **1.** aware, observant, keen, alert. **2.** sharp, incisive, sagacious, perspicacious, discerning, astute, insightful, sensitive.

perch *n.* roost, landing place, seat, pole.

perch *v.* land, alight, rest, sit, roost.

percolate *v.* filter, permeate, pervade, pass through, penetrate, bubble.

perdition *n.* damnation, condemnation, doom, hell.

peregrinate *v.* travel, trek, wander, roam, ramble, rove, meander, stray.

peregrination *n.* journey, expedition, excursion, exploration, wandering, odyssey, voyage, tour.

peremptory *adj.* **1.** absolute, fixed, firm, authoritative, binding, final, irrefutable, decisive. **2.** dictatorial, tyrannical, imperious, autocratic, domineering, overbearing, intolerant, decisive, assertive.

perennial *adj.* perpetual, continuing, permanent, enduring, unchanging, unceasing, inveterate, lasting, unfailing.

perfect *adj.* **1.** complete, absolute, whole, entire, sound, utter, integral, full; *ant.* partial, unfinished. **2.** flawless, pure, immaculate, unadulterated, impeccable, infallible, excellent, correct, right, ideal, exact; *ant.* defective, flawed.

perfect *v.* consummate, achieve, realize, finish, fulfill, complete, accomplish, effect; fine-tune, polish.

perfectionist *n.* precisionist, formalist, stickler, purist, idealist.

perfidious *adj.* untrustworthy, faithless, treacherous, underhanded, traitorous, disloyal, duplicitous, two-faced, false, deceitful, apostate, dishonest; *ant.* faithful, loyal.

perfidy *n.* betrayal, treason, treachery, disloyalty, duplicity, faithlessness, infidelity, apostasy.

perforate *v.* puncture, pierce, prick, drill, bore, stab, penetrate.

perforation *n.* hole, puncture, prick, slit, cut, dotted line.

perforce *adv.* necessarily, unavoidably, inevitably.

perform *v.* **1.** do, execute, achieve, accomplish, fulfill, complete, finish, bring about, carry out, work. **2.** act, dramatize, play, enact, present, execute, stage, represent, produce.

performance *n.* **1.** completion, fulfillment, fruition, achievement, accomplishment, realization, execution, doing, consummation. **2.** production, play, show, presentation, exhibition.

performer *n.* actor, actress, player, thespian, trouper.

perfume *n.* cologne, fragrance, toilet water, balm; aroma, scent, smell, odor, redolence.

perfumed *adj.* scented, fragrant, aromatic.

perfunctory *adj.* abrupt, cursory, offhand, brusque, indifferent, apathetic, thoughtless, routine, automatic, mechanical, wooden, superficial, brief, hurried; *ant.* painstaking, thoughtful.

peril *n.* danger, pitfall, jeopardy, hazard, risk, menace, uncertainty, vulnerability.

perilous *adj.* dangerous, precarious, hazardous, risky, chancy, unsafe, threatening; *ant.* safe, secure.

perimeter *n.* border, boundary, periphery, circumference, margin, limit, edge, outline; *ant.* center, middle.

period *n.* **1.** time, era, age, epoch, generation, cycle, stage, term, season. **2.** menstruation, menstrual flow, menses, the curse (*slang*).

periodical *n.* journal, magazine, serial, publication, weekly, monthly, quarterly, review, newspaper, gazette.

periodically *adj.* regularly, cyclically, repeatedly, intermittently, seasonally, spasmodically, sporadically.

peripatetic *adj.* itinerant, migrant, nomadic, wandering, roving, roaming, traveling, vagabond, vagrant; *ant.* settled.

peripheral *adj.* **1.** outside, outer, external, surface, outlying, superficial; *ant.* central. **2.** incidental, inessential, tangential, marginal, superficial, unimportant, trivial, unnecessary; *ant.* crucial.

periphery *n.* circumference, border, perimeter, boundary, edge, outskirts, fringe; *ant.* center.

periphrasis *n.* circumlocution, wordiness, verbosity, prolixity, ambiguity, evasion.

perish *v.* die, expire, pass away, fall, collapse, crumble, decay, decline, disintegrate, decompose, rot, waste, wither.

perishable *adj.* short-lived, fast-decaying, biodegradable, decomposable, unstable.

perjure *v.* lie, falsify, prevaricate, swear falsely.

perk (*slang*) *n.* See perquisite.

perk up *v.* cheer up, buck up, pep up, liven up, rally, recover, revive, recuperate.

perky *adj.* lively, vivacious, cheerful, bright, bubbly, bouncy, spirited, animated, energetic, effervescent, sunny; *ant.* gloomy.

permanence *n.* continuity, stability, dependability, longevity, endurance, constancy.

permanent *adj.* unchanging, perpetual, constant, steadfast, fixed, invariable, lasting, long-lasting, stable, durable, indestructible.

permeable *adj.* penetrable, porous, absorbent, spongy.

permeate *v.* saturate, seep through, soak through, fill, filter through, infiltrate, impregnate, imbue.

permissible *adj.* allowable, acceptable, sanctioned, authorized, legitimate, lawful, OK, all right; *ant.* forbidden, outlawed.

permission *n.* approval, authorization, consent, assent, sanction, license, liberty, go-ahead, green light.

permissive *adj.* lenient, complaisant, liberal, open-minded, easygoing, acquiescent, indulgent, lax, tolerant; *ant.* strict, severe.

permit *n.* license, authorization, sanction, liberty, pass, passport, visa, warrant.

permit *v.* allow, grant, give leave, consent, enable, authorize, endorse, warrant.

permutation *n.* transformation, alteration, change, shift, transmutation, shift, transposition.

pernicious *adj.* fatal, deadly, destructive, noxious, poisonous, venomous, malicious, wicked, evil, malevolent, harmful, dangerous.

peroration *n.* summary, conclusion, recapitulation, reiteration, closing remarks.

perpetrate *v.* commit, execute, enact, carry out, do, perform, wreak, inflict.

perpetual *adj.* constant, unceasing, perennial, unchanging, lasting, endless, continuous, undying, infinite, unflagging, interminable, incessant, unremitting; *ant.* transient, intermittent.

perpetuate *v.* sustain, continue, maintain, preserve, keep alive.

perplex *v.* confuse, confound, bewilder, mystify, befuddle, baffle, puzzle, muddle.

perquisite *n.* fringe benefit, bonus, extra, plus, dividend, perk (*slang*).

per se essentially, in essence, intrinsically, virtually, as such.

persecute *v.* **1.** afflict, oppress, tyrannize, illtreat, abuse, castigate, victimize, martyr, crucify. **2.** annoy, bother, badger, harass, pester, vex, hound, tease.

persecution *n.* oppression, suppression, tyranny, subjugation, castigation, discrimination, maltreatment, torture, abuse, molestation.

perseverance *n.* resolution, determination, dedication, diligence, tenacity, assiduity, persis-

persevere tence, steadfastness, doggedness, indefatigability, grit.

persevere *v.* persist, carry on, continue, keep at it, endure, hold on, remain, stand fast *or* firm, last; *ant.* give up, throw in the towel.

persist *v.* persevere, continue, carry on, hold on, endure, remain, stand fast *or* firm, insist, last.

persistence *n.* tenacity, resolution, determination, diligence, assiduousness, perseverance, steadfastness, endurance, stamina, pluck, grit. diligent, tireless, continual, constant, endless, incessant, obstinate, stubborn.

persistent *adj.* tenacious, determined, resolute,

person *n.* **1.** individual, human being, somebody, self, oneself, personality, mortal, soul, spirit. **2.** body, physique, form, frame.

persona *n.* image, public face, façade, mask, role, part, character.

personable *adj.* amiable, affable, friendly, outgoing, warm, winning, likeable, charming, attractive.

personage *n.* public figure, personality, notable, dignitary, celebrity, luminary, star, name, VIP, big shot (*slang*).

personal *adj.* **1.** private, secret, intimate, exclusive. **2.** individual, particular, idiosyncratic, peculiar, subjective. **3.** bodily, corporeal, corporal.

personality *n.* **1.** self, character, identity, nature, makeup, traits, disposition, humor, temperament. **2.** public figure, notable, dignitary, celebrity, luminary, star, name, VIP, big shot (*slang*).

personally *adv.* subjectively, individually, independently, alone, solely.

personification *n.* embodiment, representation, portrayal, semblance, likeness, incarnation, image.

personify *v.* **1.** impersonate, represent, live as, act out, imitate. **2.** symbolize, represent, exemplify, typify, embody, epitomize.

personnel *n.* employees, staff, workers, workforce, human resources, crew.

perspective *n.* viewpoint, outlook, attitude, aspect, context, angle, slant.

perspicacious *adj.* shrewd, sharp, perceptive, astute, sagacious, keen, acute, clear-sighted, clever; *ant.* obtuse.

338

perspire *v.* sweat, swelter, exude, secrete, drip.

persuade *v.* urge, induce, convince, talk into, cajole, coax, harangue, inveigle, entice, incite, compel, sway, sweet-talk (*slang*).

persuasion *n.* **1.** enticement, cajolery, inducement, influence, exhortation, inveiglement, wheedling. **2.** belief, denomination, faith, creed, school of thought, tenet, faction, sect, camp, party.

persuasive *adj.* convincing, influential, effectual, swaying, compelling, powerful, forceful, moving, impressive, sound, valid, pointed, logical, cogent.

pert *adj.* **1.** bold, saucy, cheeky, brash, forward, flippant, insolent, impudent, impertinent. **2.** jaunty, gay, perky, spirited, lively.

pertain *v.* apply, relate, be relevant, bear on, concern, be appropriate, regard, refer, come under.

pertinacious *adj.* **1.** obstinate, stubborn, insistent, willful, headstrong, mulish. **2.** unyielding, persistent, resolute, persevering, dogged, tenacious, gritty, tough, determined.

pertinent *adj.* relevant, applicable, germane, appropriate, apropos, suitable, fitting.

perturb *v.* **1.** annoy, irritate, pester, agitate, vex, bother, disturb, trouble, worry. **2.** confuse, bewilder, confound, perplex, fluster, muddle, ruffle, disconcert, unsettle, upset.

peruse *v.* **1.** inspect, examine, scrutinize, analyze, study, check. **2.** read, scan, browse, skim, look through, pore over.

pervade *v.* permeate, suffuse, imbue, saturate, fill, infest, overrun.

pervasive *adj.* prevalent, immanent, widespread, universal, general, common, ubiquitous, omnipresent, extensive.

perverse *adj.* **1.** abnormal, deviant, miscreant, delinquent, depraved, perverted, wicked, unhealthy. **2.** contrary, contradictory, balky, spiteful, wrongheaded, obstinate, stubborn, mulish, unreasonable, unyielding, willful; *ant.* accommodating, flexible. **3.** intractable, disobedient, rebellious, wayward, refractory, unmanageable, troublesome; *ant.* compliant.

perversion *n.* **1.** distortion, misrepresentation, contortion, untruth, corruption, misapplication, misuse, twisting, falsification, lie. **2.** aberration, anomaly, unnaturalness, abnormality, deviation; sexual deviation, vice, kinkiness, unnaturalness, depravity, immorality, wickedness.

pervert *n.* deviant, degenerate, debauchee, weirdo (*slang*).

pervert *v.* distort, misrepresent, misconstrue, misinterpret, falsify, twist, warp, bend, subvert, vitiate, corrupt, debase, debauch, deprave, degrade.

pesky *adj.* annoying, troublesome, disturbing, provoking, nagging, irritating, bothersome, irksome.

pessimist *n.* cynic, defeatist, melancholic, doomsayer, worrywart (*slang*), killjoy, wet blanket (*slang*), worrier, complainer; *ant.* optimist.

pessimistic *adj.* cynical, defeatist, fatalistic, gloomy, morose, depressed, despondent, dismal, resigned; *ant.* optimistic.

pest *n.* nuisance, annoyance, irritation, vexation, bother, pain in the neck (*slang*), bane, scourge, worry.

pester *v.* annoy, irritate, bother, vex, irk, plague, torment, harass, badger, *slang:* bug, ride, drive up the wall.

pestilence *n.* disease, epidemic, plague, sickness.

pestilent *adj.* **1.** diseased, disease-ridden, plague-ridden, contagious, communicable, infectious, catching, tainted, contaminated. **2.** harmful, dangerous, detrimental, corrupting, destructive.

pet *v.* **1.** touch, caress, pat, stroke, fondle, pamper, baby, coddle. **2.** kiss, *slang:* make out, neck, smooch; embrace, hug, cuddle.

pet *adj.* favorite, preferred, darling, dear, beloved.

petite *adj.* small, little, dainty, delicate, slight, elfin; *ant.* big, large.

petition *n.* entreaty, appeal, solicitation, supplication, request, invocation, plea.

petition *v.* request, entreat, ask, appeal, implore, supplicate, urge, beg, beseech, plead, pray, press.

petrified *adj.* **1.** hardened, calcified, mineralized, ossified, fossilized, set in stone, firm, rigid, inert. **2.** frightened, scared stiff, afraid, terror-stricken, stupefied, shocked, stunned, numb, dumbfounded, aghast, transfixed.

petrify **1.** harden, solidify, fossilize, calcify,

mineralize, set. **2.** frighten, terrify, horrify, scare, startle.

pettish *adj.* petulant, cross, peevish, splenetic, irritable, grumpy, fretful, waspish, touchy, snappish.

petty *adj.* **1.** trivial, insignificant, unimportant, negligible, inessential, trifling, smalltime, secondary; puny, measly, paltry, piddling; *ant.* significant. **2.** shallow, smallminded, ungenerous, mean, contemptible; *ant.* large-minded, generous.

petulant *adj.* peevish, irritable, querulous, irascible, snappish, impatient, cross, testy.

phantasm *n.* apparition, ghost, phantom, specter, wraith, chimera, hallucination, vision, illusion, figment of the imagination.

phantom *n.* apparition, phantasm, specter, spirit, wraith, chimera.

pharmacist *n.* druggist, apothecary, chemist (*Brit.*).

pharmacy *n.* drugstore, apothecary, variety store.

phase *n.* stage, point, juncture, period, state, development, step, time, season, chapter, aspect, condition.

phenomenal *adj.* amazing, stupendous, extraordinary, marvelous, miraculous, wondrous, fantastic, prodigious, sensational, outstanding, unusual, unique.

phenomenon *n.* event, circumstance, experience, occurrence, happening, incident, rarity, curiosity, spectacle, sight, marvel, miracle, wonder, sensation.

philanthropic *adj.* humanitarian, altruistic, charitable, benevolent, alms-giving, gracious, kindhearted, magnanimous, public-spirited, civic-minded; *ant.* misanthropic.

philanthropist *n.* benefactor, patron, contributor, donor, alms-giver, humanitarian, altruist.

philosophical *adj.* **1.** (having the qualities of a philosopher) thoughtful, reflective, cogitative, rational, logical, judicious, erudite, profound, deep, thoughtful, analytical, learned, wise. **2.** (able to accept misfortune) stoical, resigned, serene, tranquil, composed, cool, dispassionate, impassive.

philosophy *n.* **1.** (system of principles) theory, doctrine, tenets, ideology, metaphysics, epistemology, theory of knowledge, logic, wisdom, reasoning. **2.** (personal views) beliefs, values, convictions, opinion, outlook, thinking, attitude, worldview, Weltanschauung, gestalt.

phobia *n.* **1.** (a psychological illness) fear, dread, anxiety, terror, neurosis, obsession, angst, hangup (*slang*). **2.** aversion, avoidance, hatred, repulsion, disgust, revulsion.

phone *v.* call, contact, ring up, buzz, dial.

phonograph *n.* stereo, record player, juke box, gramophone, hi-fi.

phony *n.* fake, fraud, impostor, mountebank, sham, charlatan, cheat, con man (*slang*); forgery, counterfeit.

phony *adj.* affected, fake, artificial, imitation, false, pseudo, bogus, forged, counterfeit, sham, spurious.

photograph *n.* photo, print, snapshot, picture, portrait, likeness, image.

photograph *v.* take a picture, shoot (*slang*), snap, film, record, videotape.

photographic *adj.* detailed, exact, accurate, precise, graphic, realistic, lifelike, faithful, natural-istic, vivid, pictorial, cinematic.

phrase *n.* idiom, expression, maxim, saying, motto, catchword, slogan.

phrase *v.* express, say, word, put, present, formulate, couch.

physical *n.* health checkup, medical examination, exam, work-up.

physical *adj.* **1.** real, actual, tangible, concrete, visible, material, palpable, substantial, corporeal. **2.** bodily, fleshly, carnal, earthly, incarnate, corporeal, corporal, natural; *ant.* spiritual.

physician *n.* doctor, practitioner, doctor of medicine, medic, resident, intern, healer, MD, shape, structure.

physique *n.* build, frame, body, figure, form, shape, structure.

picayune *adj.* trivial, petty, unimportant, small, nit-picking.

pick *n.* **1.** tool, pickax, mattock, rock hammer. **2.** choice, selection, preference, option; candidate, designee.

pick *v.* **1.** choose, select, pick out, decide on, opt for, settle on, elect. **2.** gather, collect, accumulate, pluck, pull, cull.

pick at nibble, play *or* toy with, tease.

pick on (*slang*) needle, nag, carp at, badger, criticize, tease, torment, harass, bully.

pick up **1.** raise, lift, hoist, carry, cuddle. **2.**

receive, get, acquire, buy, purchase. **3.** recover, recuperate, improve, get better, get well, perk up, gain ground. **4.** invite, accompany, bring along, call for, stop for, go to get. **5.** (meet for sexual favors) solicit, proposition.

picket *n.* demonstrator, protestor, striker, dissenter.

picket *v.* protest, demonstrate, boycott, strike, blockade.

pickings (*slang*) *n.* earnings, profits, yield, proceeds, *slang:* take, gravy, booty, loot.

pickle (*slang*) *n.* bind, dilemma, quandary, predicament, jam (*slang*), difficulty, scrape, straits, *slang:* fix, tight spot, hot water.

picnic *n.* **1.** outing, barbecue, cookout, excursion. **2.** (*slang*) lark, *slang:* cinch, pushover, snap, piece of cake; child's play.

pictorial *adj.* **1.** picturesque, scenic, striking, graphic, vivid. **2.** illustrated, embellished, adorned, decorated.

picture *n.* **1.** view, sight, spectacle, panorama. **2.** (somebody or something taken as typical or representative) representation, image, epitome, figure, copy, replica. **3.** portrait, photograph, snapshot, print, painting, drawing, illustration, cartoon; movie, film, cinema, flick (*slang*). **in the picture** (*slang*) involved, part of, concerned. **out of the picture** (*slang*) immaterial, unimportant, irrelevant, not considered.

picture *v.* **1.** depict, illustrate, render, delineate, sketch, draw, paint, portray. **2.** imagine, conceive of, envision, visualize, conjure up.

picturesque *adj.* **1.** pictorial, scenic, striking, vivid, graphic, descriptive. **2.** charming, quaint, pretty, beautiful, attractive, scenic, idyllic.

piece *n.* **1.** part, portion, section, allotment, share, bit, chunk, lump, cut, percentage, component, element, segment. **2.** work of art, creation, composition, study. **3.** role, part, lines. **go to pieces** **1.** come *or* fall apart, break up, fail. **2.** lose control, break down, cry, quit, collapse, have a breakdown, go off the deep end (*slang*).

piece together assemble, fix, mend, repair, restore.

speak one's piece have one's say, air one's opinion, sound off (*slang*), talk, tell, reveal.

pièce de résistance *n.* masterpiece, masterwork, magnum opus, prize, jewel, chef-d'oeuvre.

piecemeal *adj.* fragmentary, partial, patchy, intermittent, unsystematic, scattered, incremental.

piecemeal *adv.* bit by bit, little by little, partially, by degrees, in dribs and drabs, step by step, intermittently, at intervals, gradually, slowly.

pied *adj.* variegated, piebald, multicolored, varicolored, motley, flecked, dappled, spotted, streaked.

pier *n.* dock, wharf, landing, quay, jetty, piling, support.

pierce *v.* 1. stab, barb, prick, spike, stick into, impale, sting, wound, hurt, lancinate. 2. affect, move, touch, excite, rouse, stir. 3. (make a hole in) perforate, puncture, penetrate, bore, drill. 4. (get past a barrier) break through, enter, intrude, penetrate. 5. comprehend, fathom, discern, realize, discover, grasp, see.

piercing *adj.* 1. shrill, earsplitting, earpiercing, high-pitched, deafening, loud. 2. (as of a mind or intelligence) penetrating, discerning, keen, incisive, probing. 3. (as of pain) agonizing, painful, severe, sharp, shattering, shooting, exquisite, acute, intense. 4. wintry, Siberian, biting, bitter, arctic, cold, nippy, numbing, raw.

piety *n.* 1. devotion, loyalty, fealty, faith, piousness, duty, reverence, sanctity, veneration. 2. sermon, lecture, preaching.

pig *n.* 1. piglet, swine, hog, shoat, sow, boar. 2. glutton, gormandizer, gourmand, hog, brute, slob.

pigeonhole *n.* compartment, cubbyhole, section, niche, category, class, place.

pigeonhole *v.* classify, catalog, codify, label, sort, file.

pigheaded *adj.* obstinate, stubborn, inflexible, unyielding, intractable, willful, bullheaded, mulish.

pigment *n.* color, hue, tint, tincture, stain, paint, dye.

pile *n.* 1. mass, quantity, collection, accumulation, heap, stack. 2. wealth, fortune, money, mint, hoard, pot. 3. piling, support, upright, foundation, column, beam, post, stanchion.

pile *v.* 1. hoard, store, amass, gather, accumulate, collect, load up. 2. heap, stack, bunch, pack.

pilfer *v.* steal, appropriate, rob, embezzle, thieve, filch, purloin, *slang:* lift, pinch; shoplift.

pilgrim *n.* traveler, wanderer, wayfarer, crusader, palmer.

pilgrimage *n.* crusade, odyssey, excursion, journey, trip, junket, mission, hadj.

pill *n.* 1. tablet, capsule, pellet. 2. contraceptive drug, oral contraceptive, prophylactic.

pillage *n.* 1. destruction, devastation, depredation, robbery, stealing, marauding, theft. 2. booty, loot, spoils, plunder.

pillage *v.* plunder, ravage, ransack, loot, rob, vandalize, rape, despoil, maraud, raze, depredate.

pillar *n.* 1. column, post, shaft, mast, pedestal, baluster. 2. support, prop, upright, mainstay, bastion, stanchion.

from pillar to post transient, moving about, here today and gone tomorrow.

pillory *v.* denounce, brand, slur, shame, stigmatize, scorn, vilify, ridicule, mock.

pilot *n.* aviator, flier, navigator, helmsman, guide, captain.

pilot *v.* guide, steer, navigate, direct, lead, manage, run.

pimp *n.* panderer, procurer, whoremonger, fleshmonger, flesh-peddler (*slang*).

pimple *n.* pustule, papule, blemish, acne, zit (*slang*).

pin *n.* 1. fastener, clip, catch, clasp, tack, needle, bodkin. 2. jewelry, brooch, stickpin, tiepin. 3. brace, bolt, bar, dowel.

pin *v.* 1. tack, attach, affix, fasten, secure. 2. hold down, restrain, immobilize, pinion.

pin down specify, pinpoint, identify, determine, locate, home in on; force to deal with, put it to, nail to the wall (*slang*).

pincers *n.* tweezers, pinchers, forceps, grippers.

pinch *n.* 1. squeeze, tweak, grasp, nip, contraction, pressure, compression, cramp, hurt. 2. (tiny amount) smidgen, dash, bit, jot, mite,

pinch *n.* nip, taste. **3.** emergency, crisis, difficulty, dilemma, predicament, plight, hot spot (*slang*).

pinch *v.* **1.** squeeze, tweak, press, grasp, nip, stint. **2.** (*slang*) steal, rob, pilfer, filch, snatch, nab.

pinch-hit (*slang*) *v.* substitute for, replace, act *or* stand for, succeed.

pine *v.* **1.** waste, languish, wither, decline, dwindle, decay, wilt, weaken, sicken. **2.** desire, yearn, crave, covet, hunger, ache.

pinnacle *n.* height, top, peak, apex, summit, zenith, acme, apogee.

pioneer *n.* colonist, settler, founder; trailblazer; innovator, leader.

pioneer *v.* **1.** colonize, settle, establish, found, discover, explore. **2.** create, develop, originate, launch, initiate, institute, start.

pious *adj.* devout, religious, spiritual, reverent, righteous, virtuous, moral, churchgoing, God-fearing; sanctimonious, self-righteous, holier-than-thou, goody-goody (*slang*).

pipe *n.* **1.** tube, conduit, channel, passage, duct, pipeline, drainpipe, waterpipe, aqueduct. **2.** wind instrument, flageolet, horn, tooter, whistle.

pipe *v.* play, sound, whistle, trill, warble.

pipe down (*slang*) be quiet, hush, speak lower, stop talking, settle down.

pipe up (*slang*) speak up, say, speak, talk, volunteer, shout, interrupt, exclaim, speak out of turn.

piquancy *n.* seasoning, flavoring, relish, zest, pungency, spiciness, tang, bite, zip (*slang*).

piquant *adj.* **1.** savory, flavored, pungent, spicy, tangy, tart, zesty, sharp, biting. **2.** interesting, exciting, arresting, stimulating, provocative, scintillating.

pique *n.* offense, resentment, umbrage, ire, displeasure, annoyance, anger.

pique *v.* **1.** anger, irritate, annoy, irk, vex, rile, miff, bother, nettle. **2.** excite, stimulate, arouse, galvanize, spur.

piracy *n.* **1.** larceny, robbery, theft, pillage, holdup. **2.** plagiarism, copying, cheating, lifting (*slang*).

pirate *n.* thief, robber, raider, plunderer, marauder, buccaneer, sea-rat, sea-robber, plagiarist.

pirate *v.* steal, appropriate, plagiarize, copy, reproduce, *slang:* lift, crib, nick.

pirouette *v.* twirl, whirl, spin, turn, pivot, gyrate.

pistol *n.* gun, revolver, automatic, six-shooter, *slang:* rod, piece.

pit *n.* hole, cavity, abyss, crater, chasm, gulf, trench, hollow, depression.

pit against oppose, match, set against.

pitch *n.* **1.** throw, toss, hurl, heave, fling, lob, sling, cast. **2.** slope, incline, grade, angle, tilt, drop, steepness, level. **3.** sound, tone, timbre. **4.** tar, gum, resin, rosin.

pitch *v.* **1.** throw, toss, hurl, heave, fling, lob, sling, cast. **2.** fall, dive, plunge, lunge, lurch, topple, tumble, flounder, stagger, flop. **3.** slope, lean, tilt, rise, raise, drop.

pitch in volunteer, cooperate, join in, help, aid, work, lend a hand.

pitcher *n.* container, jug, bottle, urn, crock, jar, vessel.

piteous *adj.* pathetic, plaintive, poignant, lamentable, woeful, bathetic, wretched, miserable, sad, poor.

pitfall *n.* drawback, hazard, snare, snag, trap, difficulty, peril, stumbling block.

pith *n.* center, crux, essence, gist, point, core, kernel, marrow, heart, meat.

pithy *adj.* concise, succinct, pointed, meaningful, trenchant, laconic, cogent, forceful, terse, meat.

pitiable *adj.* pitiful, pitiful, pathetic, piteous, poor, sad, wretched, miserable, sorry.

pitiful *adj.* **1.** lamentable, pathetic, piteous, touching, poignant, heartbreaking, moving, distressing, sorrowful, miserable, comfortless, cheerless. **2.** paltry, measly, inadequate, mean, base, low, wretched, pathetic.

pitiless *adj.* **1.** unfeeling, obdurate, callous, coldhearted, indifferent, uncaring, unsympathetic; *ant.* commiserative. **2.** cruel, brutal, coldblooded, ruthless, unmerciful, inhuman; *ant.* compassionate, humane.

pittance *n.* trifle, modicum, *slang:* slave wages, peanuts, chicken feed, crumbs.

pitted *adj.* pockmarked, nicked, indented, riddled, scarred, gouged, blemished, rough.

pity *n.* **1.** sympathy, compassion, understanding, benevolence, forbearance, tenderness, mercy, charity, condolence. **2.** misfortune, mishap, ill *or* bad luck, crisis, catastrophe, disaster.

pity *v.* **1.** sympathize with, commiserate with, condole with, feel for, understand, cry *or* weep with, bleed for, be sorry for. **2.** pardon, absolve, reprieve, spare, be merciful to.

pivot *n.* axis, axle, fulcrum, linchpin, hub, hinge, swivel, spindle, shaft.

pivot *v.* turn, swivel, spin, whirl, rotate, revolve, hinge.

pivotal *adj.* central, focal, crucial, critical, vital, decisive, determining, climactic.

pixie *n.* fairy, sprite, elf, leprechaun, brownie.

pixilated *adj.* eccentric, daft, frivolous, whimsical, puckish.

placard *n.* advertisement, circular, bulletin, poster, bill.

placate *v.* pacify, appease, assuage, calm, mollify, soothe.

place *n.* **1.** position, location, point, spot, vicinity. **2.** (area meant to be used to seat or house a person) space, room, compass, stead, area, seat, berth, reservation, accommodation. **3.** job, position, office, post, station. **go places** (*slang*) succeed, achieve, advance, get ahead, get somewhere, move up. **put someone in his place** humble, humiliate, reprimand, derogate, take down a peg, give comeuppance.

place *v.* put, plant, assign, lodge, stow, locate, settle, deposit, install, situate.

placid *adj.* calm, tranquil, quiet, still, serene, peaceful, mild, undisturbed, composed; *ant.* agitated, jumpy.

plague *n.* pestilence, bane, blight, affliction, contagion, epidemic, scourge.

plague *v.* disturb, trouble, bother, fret, harry, annoy, afflict, pester, vex, beset, harass.

plain *n.* prairie, grassland, steppe, plateau, flat, mesa, heath.

plain *adj.* **1.** obvious, manifest, clear, understandable, apparent, evident, patent, lucid, legible; *ant.* unclear, abstruse. **2.** modest, ordinary, simple, common, conventional, unadorned, unostentatious, unpretentious, everyday; *ant.* ostentatious, elaborate. **3.** homely, ugly, unattractive. **4.** candid, forthright, artless, blunt, frank, abrupt, outspoken, bluff, rude.

plaintive *adj.* sad, melancholy, mournful, wistful, disconsolate, pitiful, woebegone.

plan *n.* **1.** blueprint, diagram, map, chart, sketch, illustration. **2.** scheme, method, design, plot, strategy, project, intention.

plan *v.* **1.** (organize carefully) plot, prepare, scheme, devise, contrive, engineer, concoct, conspire, organize. **2.** (make a graphic representation) outline, draft, sketch, map, chart, trace, illustrate, delineate, represent, rough out, block out. **3.** have in mind, propose, intend, mean, foresee, envisage, contemplate.

plane *n.* **1.** level, horizontal, flat, surface, face. **2.** aircraft, jet, airliner, bird (*slang*).

plane *v.* flatten, finish, smooth, level.

plant *n.* **1.** bush, shrub, flower, weed. **2.** factory, foundry, mill, shop; apparatus, equipment, machinery.

plaster *v.* cover, coat, smear, spread, bedaub, bind, cement.

plastic *adj.* **1.** pliant, flexible, supple, malleable, ductile, impressionable, tractable; *ant.* inflexible, rigid. **2.** substitute, synthetic, ersatz, fake.

plate *v.* laminate, coat, cover, veneer, gild, overlay, electroplate, galvanize.

plateau *n.* plain, tableland, mesa, highland.

platform *n.* **1.** stage, stand, dais, rostrum, podium, pulpit. **2.** policies, tenets, principles, manifesto, objectives, program, party planks (*slang*).

platitude *n.* banality, cliché, inanity, stereotype, truism, proverb, bromide.

platitudinous *adj.* dull, flat, hackneyed, overworked, stock, trite, truistic, vapid.

platonic *adj.* idealistic, utopian, quixotic, nonphysical, spiritual.

plaudit *n.* praise, approval, acclaim, accolade, commendation, kudos.

plausible *adj.* **1.** likely, probable, believable, credible, reasonable; *ant.* improbable, unlikely. **2.** convincing, persuasive, facile, glib, smooth-talking.

play *n.* **1.** fun, amusement, enjoyment, diversion, pleasure, happiness, entertainment, recreation, relaxation, game, sport. **2.** drama, theatrical performance, show, tragedy, musical. **3.** action, activity, movement, working, employment, motion.

play v. **1.** gambol, frisk, sport, cavort, romp, frolic, caper, revel, *slang:* carry on, play the fool. **2.** (produce music) perform, execute, sound, finger, pedal, bow, pipe, mouth, fiddle, twang. **3.** impersonate, portray, act, perform, present, represent. **4.** participate, compete, contest, rival, engage, contend, challenge, take a part.

playboy n. womanizer, ladies' man, libertine, philanderer, rake, debauchee, lady-killer.

player n. **1.** athlete, competitor, contestant, opponent, jock (*slang*). **2.** actor, actress, performer, entertainer, thespian, ham (*slang*).

playful adj. **1.** humorous, joking, whimsical, comical, jesting, waggish, puckish. **2.** frolicsome, spirited, jaunty, frisky, coquettish, impish, roguish, sprightly, vivacious; *ant.* serious, stern.

plaything n. toy, amusement, bauble, trinket, gadget, gimcrack, gewgaw.

plea n. **1.** appeal, request, supplication, petition, suit, imploration, entreaty. **2.** defense, argument, case, claim, extenuation, invocation, justification, vindication.

plead v. **1.** beg, implore, beseech, crave, entreat. **2.** (enter a plea) declare, allege, cite, maintain, assert. **3.** (discuss in court) defend, advocate, prosecute, argue, debate, examine, cross-examine, question.

pleasant adj. **1.** affable, charming, gracious, agreeable, engaging, genial, amiable, winning, polite, urbane, civil, cordial, convivial, good-natured, jovial; *ant.* disagreeable. **2.** (as of an experience) gratifying, pleasurable, cheering, welcome, refreshing, satisfying, comfortable, enjoyable, festive, relaxing; *ant.* disappointing. **3.** (said of weather) temperate, fair, mild, balmy, bright, sunny.

pleasantry n. joke, banter, bon mot, quip, sally, witticism, persiflage, badinage.

please v. **1.** gratify, satisfy, entertain, amuse, captivate, charm, delight, enchant; *ant.* anger, annoy. **2.** desire, wish, want, demand, indulge, opt, prefer, suit.

pleased adj. gratified, satisfied, contented, elated, thrilled, tickled pink (*slang*); *ant.* annoyed.

pleasure n. **1.** enjoyment, bliss, delight, ease, happiness, contentment, solace; *ant.* pain, sorrow. **2.** will, want, preference, behest, disposition, inclination, wish, desire, command. **3.** indulgence, gratification, revelry, self-indulgence, gluttony.

pleat v. ruffle, fold, crease, plait, crimp, flute, gather.

plebeian adj. vulgar, ordinary, coarse, low, mean, peasant, uncultivated, unrefined, ignoble; *ant.* aristocratic, noble.

pledge n. promise, guarantee, assurance, oath, vow, word of honor.

pledge v. **1.** ensure, mortgage, contract, secure, bind, sign for. **2.** promise, swear, vouch, vow.

plenary adj. whole, entire, complete, inclusive, absolute, unqualified, general.

plenitude n. abundance, excess, profusion, wealth, bounty, luxuriance, copiousness, cornucopia; *ant.* scarcity.

plentiful adj. bountiful, profuse, lavish, liberal, ample, abundant, fruitful, luxuriant, replete; *ant.* scanty, rare.

plenty n. abundance, sufficiency, plentitude, profusion, plethora, wealth, *slang:* oodles, tons; *ant.* lack, scarcity, want.

plethora n. excess, surplus, overabundance, glut, surfeit.

pliability n. **1.** (said of materials) flexibility, elasticity, malleability, tractableness, ductility. **2.** (said of persons) adaptability, amenability, impressionableness, obedience, docility; *ant.* inflexibility, rigidity.

pliable adj. **1.** flexible, limber, supple, lithe, plastic. **2.** tractable, manipulable, docile, responsive, persuadable, malleable.

pliant adj. malleable, limber, flexible, supple, tractable, manipulable, plastic, lithe.

plight n. dilemma, predicament, difficulty, jam (*slang*), impasse, quandary, pickle (*slang*), scrape, straits.

plod v. trudge, drag, clump, lumber, slog, tramp, tread.

plot n. **1.** intrigue, conspiracy, trick, cabal, machination, stratagem. **2.** narrative, outline, story, suspense, structure, unfolding, development, design. **3.** lot, tract, division, parcel.

plot v. contrive, scheme, plan, outline, draft, brew, conceive, concoct, frame, hatch, map, project, collude.

plow v. break, cultivate, furrow, turn, dig, ridge, spade, till.

ploy n. stratagem, trick, subterfuge, ruse, scheme, gambit, artifice, contrivance, maneuver.

pluck v. depilate, deplume, pick, pull, snatch, tug, tweak, yank, jerk.

plucky adj. courageous, bold, brave, intrepid, spirited, spunky, gritty, tenacious, gutsy (slang); ant. feeble, weak.

plug v. stop, obstruct, close, cork, fill, seal, stuff, tamp, occlude.

plumb n. fathom, measure, gauge, sound, probe, search, explore, investigate.

plumb adj. straight, perpendicular, vertical, erect.

plummet v. plunge, fall, nosedive, swoop, tumble, crash; ant. soar.

plump adj. stout, fleshy, buxom, chubby, corpulent, rotund, portly; ant. skinny, thin.

plunder n. loot, booty, winnings, spoils, pillage, rapine.

plunder v. burn, steal, raid, ravage, devastate, ransack, rifle, sack, spoliate, depredate.

plunge v. fall, dive, drop, hurtle, pitch, plummet, sink, swoop, tumble.

plurality n. majority, preponderance, most, multiplicity.

plus n. extra, bonus, credit, benefit, asset, surplus, perk (slang).

plush (slang) adj. rich, elegant, luxurious, sumptuous, lavish, palatial, deluxe, posh.

ply n. thickness, fold, overlay, leaf, sheet, layer.

ply v. 1. practice, pursue, follow, exercise, work at. 2. provide, supply, replenish, equip, furbish.

poach v. steal, pilfer, filch, smuggle, appropriate, plunder, trespass, infringe.

pocket n. 1. hole, cavity, hollow, opening. 2. pouch, receptacle, sac, envelope, bag, pod.

pocket v. steal, conceal, appropriate, lift (slang), pilfer, pinch (slang), purloin, embezzle.

poet n. bard, versifier, minstrel, troubadour, lyrist, rhymester.

poetic adj. lyric, metrical, rhythmical, melodious, sonorous, elegiac, romantic, dramatic, graceful; ant. prosaic.

poignancy n. 1. intensity, concentration, sharpness, piquancy, pungency, keenness, evocativeness. 2. emotion, sentiment, tenderness, plaintiveness, pathos, feeling.

poignant adj. biting, pointed, sharp, piquant, stinging, caustic, bitter, acute, piercing; sad, painful, heartbreaking, touching, moving.

point n. 1. position, location, spot, place, locality, spot, site, station. 2. tip, end, apex, thorn, spike, barb, prick, spur, tine, tooth, nub. 3. purpose, motive, aim, goal, objective, end, object, intention, intent.

beside the point irrelevant, immaterial, not pertinent, not germane.

to the point relevant, pertinent, apt, exact, on target.

point v. 1. indicate, designate, show, name, suggest, draw attention to, signify, signal, denote. 2. direct, guide, lead, steer, train, influence, hint.

point-blank adj. blunt, direct, plain-spoken, straightforward, unreserved, forthright, express, explicit, downright, categorical, abrupt, plain.

point-blank adv. candidly, bluntly, frankly, unequivocally, openly, straightforwardly, directly, plainly, explicitly, forthrightly, brusquely, straight.

pointed adj. cutting, biting, keen, sharp, incisive, caustic, tart, trenchant, barbed, penetrating.

pointer n. hint, advice, suggestion, caution, recommendation, tip, warning, clue, information.

pointless adj. ineffectual, ineffective, vain, worthless, useless, senseless, absurd, irrelevant, futile, inane, unavailing, nonsensical, futile, meaningless, unproductive; ant. meaningful, profitable.

poise n. composure, dignity, aplomb, calmness, collectedness, grace, elegance, equanimity, savoir-faire, sang-froid, presence of mind, cool (slang), coolness, equilibrium, assurance.

poise v. position, balance, hold, hang, float, suspend, support, hover.

poised adj. self-confident, suave, urbane, composed, dignified, self-possessed, nonchalant, unruffled, serene, graceful, collected, calm, cool, ready, prepared, expectant, waiting.

poison n. toxin, venom, contamination, virus, contagion, blight, bane, corruption, canker, malignancy, cancer, miasma, aconite, aconitum.

poison v. taint, corrupt, defile, contaminate, adulterate, envenom, pollute, subvert, pervert, infect, warp, undermine, murder, deprave, vitiate.

poisonous adj. venomous, lethal, toxic, noxious, fatal, deadly, virulent, pestilential, mephitic, pernicious, baneful, mortal, virose, corruptive, baleful.

poke n. nudge, prod, shove, jab, thrust, punch, butt, dig.

poke v. prod, stab, push, shove, nudge, jab, stick, thrust, hit, elbow, dig, butt, hit, punch, interfere.

poke fun at tease, ridicule, mock, parody, rib, make fun of, spoof, send up (*slang*), jeer.

polarity n. duality, dichotomy, paradox, contradiction, opposition, ambivalence, oppositeness, contrariety.

pole n. bar, post, rod, staff, shaft, stick, stake, mast.

polemics n. argument, dispute, debate, controversy, contention, argumentation, disputation, logomachy.

police n. police force, *slang:* cops, the law, the fuzz; constabulary, gendarmerie, the boys in blue (*slang*).

police v. protect, monitor, defend, guard, patrol, watch, supervise, check, keep guard over, keep a check on, oversee, regulate, stand guard over, keep the peace, keep in order.

policy n. rule, practice, custom, course, stance, theory, protocol, plan, program, procedure, line, stratagem, code, guideline.

polish n. **1.** gloss, glaze, veneer, sheen, luster, varnish, finish, sparkle, brightness, brilliance; *ant.* dullness. **2.** cultivation, sophistication, style, breeding, grace, urbanity, class, refinement, elegance, politesse, savoir-faire, suavity, expertise, proficiency, perfectionism; *ant.* clumsiness, gaucherie.

polish v. **1.** wax, buff, burnish, rub, shine, finish, brighten, clean, furbish, slick, touch up, luster, file; *ant.* dull, tarnish. **2.** cultivate, improve, refine, perfect, brush up, enhance.

polish off (*slang*) eat, finish, consume, devour, gobble, wolf, stuff, down, put away (*slang*).

polished adj. **1.** bright, glossy, shining, lustrous, gleaming, burnished, smooth, slippery, glassy, sheeny, finished; *ant.* dull, tarnished. **2.** refined, sophisticated, polite, well-bred, cultured, graceful, civilized, courtly, suave, urbane, gracious, educated, professional, impeccable, elegant; *ant.* clumsy, gauche, inexpert.

polite adj. considerate, courteous, refined, mannerly, well-mannered, respectful, tactful, deferential, civilized, diplomatic, well-bred, cordial, gracious, urbane, thoughtful; *ant.* impolite, rude, uncultivated.

politeness n. consideration, cordiality, gentility, graciousness, refinement, tact, manners, mannerliness, deference, diplomacy, respect, refinement, polish, civility, cultivation; *ant.* rudeness, impoliteness.

politic adj. judicious, sagacious, prudent, wise, sensible, opportune, expedient; crafty, scheming, canny, sly, shrewd, artful, astute, ingenious.

political adj. governmental, legislative, partisan, executive, administrative, civic, state, federal.

politician n. officeholder, office-seeker, statesman, politico, legislator; tactician, manipulator, machinator, opportunist, agitator, stirrer, Machiavellian.

politics n. government, political science, ideology, affairs of state, polity, statesmanship, statecraft, civics, diplomacy; machinations, manipulation, Machiavellianism.

poll n. survey, census, count, sampling, kite-flying, canvass, ballot, returns, tally, figures, vote, voting, plebiscite.

poll v. question, list, examine, register, enroll.

pollute v. dirty, contaminate, corrupt, foul, soil, sully, taint, stain, defile, mar, infect, desecrate, debase, poison.

pollution n. contamination, corruption, defilement, impurity, desecration, stain, taint, dirtying, foulness, infection, profanation, violation, adulteration, befouling; *ant.* purification, purity.

poltergeist n. ghost, spirit, spook, ghoul, goblin.

polyglot adj. multilingual, polyglottal, polyglottic, international, cosmopolitan; *ant.* monoglot, monolingual.

pomp n. grandeur, show, splendor, magnificence, vainglory, display, ceremoniousness, ostentation, pomposity, pageantry, flourish, state, ritual, solemnity, éclat; *ant.* austerity, simplicity.

pomposity *n.* pretension, pretentiousness, affectation, airs, bombast, vanity, vainglory, self-importance, portentousness, presumption, grandiloquence, stuffiness, rhetoric, ranting, fustian; *ant.* modesty, simplicity.

pompous *adj.* self-important, ostentatious, overbearing, arrogant, pretentious, turgid, supercilious, vainglorious, grandiose, high-flown, stilted, windy, affected, bloated, flatulent; *ant.* modest, simple, unaffected, unassuming.

ponder *v.* think, brood, cogitate, deliberate, reflect, meditate, ruminate, consider, contemplate, weigh, study, mull over, muse, give thought to, examine.

ponderous *adj.* cumbersome, weighty, heavy, huge, laborious, pedestrian, heavy-handed, lumbering, massive, bulky, awkward, dull, stilted, pedantic, portentous; *ant.* delicate, light, simple.

pontificate *v.* preach, expound, harangue, sound off (*slang*), lecture, sermonize, hold forth, lay down the law, moralize, dogmatize, pronounce, declaim, perorate.

pooh-pooh *v.* dismiss, deride, ridicule, reject, slight, scorn, minimize, belittle, disdain, scoff, spurn, turn up one's nose at, disparage, disregard, play down; *ant.* consider, exaggerate, magnify, regard.

pool *n.* 1. pond, lake, swimming pool, watering hole, puddle, mudpuddle, fishpond, millpond, tarn, linn. 2. supply, funds, provisions, equipment, reserve, pot (*slang*), kitty, accumulation, combine, collective, bank, purse, stakes. 3. billiards, eight ball, snooker.

pool *v.* combine, merge, put together, amalgamate, chip in, contribute, share.

poor *adj.* 1. wanting, deficient, lacking, needy, penniless, impoverished, broke (*slang*), destitute, pinched, impecunious, hard up, in reduced circumstances; *ant.* affluent, opulent, rich, wealthy. 2. weak, puny, feeble, infirm, exhausted, depleted, trivial, pathetic, pitiful, inferior, faulty, sorry; *ant.* superior.

poorly *adv.* inadequately, unsatisfactorily, insufficiently, inferiorly, incompetently, unsuccessfully, badly, crudely, inexpertly, meanly, shoddily, shabbily, unjustly, faultily, feebly; *ant.* well.

pop *n.* 1. explosion, report, noise, crack, bang, burst, snap. 2. soda pop, soda water, soft drink, drink, beverage.

pop *v.* explode, burst, bang, crack, report, go off, go bang, snap.

poppycock *n.* nonsense, drivel, balderdash, gibberish, rubbish, gobbledygook, *slang:* guff, bunk; trash; *slang:* baloney, hooey; babble; *ant.* sense.

populace *n.* public, general public, multitude, people, masses, hoi polloi, rank and file, inhabitants, rabble, throng, commonality, plebs, proletariat, crowd, common herd; *ant.* aristocracy, elite, nobility.

popular *adj.* 1. liked, well-liked, favorite, favored, celebrated, idolized, feted, approved, accepted, sought-after, fashionable, modish, voguish, lionized, in demand. 2. common, general, standard, universal, ubiquitous, prevailing, prevalent, public, stock, trite, widespread, vernacular, vulgar, conventional, household; *ant.* exclusive, unusual.

popularity *n.* fame, favor, adulation, worship, regard, mass appeal, repute, vogue, acceptance, approval, celebrity, stardom, idolization, glory, recognition, esteem.

popularize *v.* spread, propagate, disseminate, universalize, give currency to, familiarize, simplify, democratize, vulgarize, debase; *ant.* discredit.

popularly *adv.* generally, traditionally, ordinarily, conventionally, usually, universally, widely, regularly, customarily, commonly, in the vernacular, vernacularly, vulgarly.

populate *v.* settle, inhabit, occupy, colonize, people, tenant, put down roots in, live in, establish oneself in, overrun, habit.

population *n.* people, citizens, citizenry, residents, denizens, inhabitants, populace, occupants, natives, society, community, folk.

populous *n.* teeming, swarming, overpopulated, crowded, packed, crawling, overpeopled, populated, thickly populated, frequented, thronged; *ant.* deserted, unfrequented.

porch *n.* piazza, portico, breezeway, veranda, balcony, entrance, doorstep, stoop, gallery, galilee, stoa.

pore v. study, peruse, examine, ponder, dwell on, contemplate, scrutinize, go over, brood, devour, read, scan.

pornographic adj. lewd, indecent, obscene, offensive, filthy, dirty, blue (slang), smutty, bawdy, coarse, prurient, off-color, X-rated, risqué, salacious; ant. innocent, inoffensive.

porous adj. permeable, absorbent, spongy, spongelike, pitted, penetrable, honeycombed, absorptive, foveate, pervious, foraminous, cellular; ant. impermeable, impenetrable.

port n. harbor, seaport, anchorage, haven, roadstead.

port adj. left, lefthand, larboard.

portable adj. movable, transportable, handy, manageable, light, lightweight, convenient, compact, carriageable, portative; ant. fixed, immovable.

portal n. entrance, gate, gateway, opening, ingress.

portend v. omen, herald, indicate, threaten, predict, forebode, forecast, promise, foreshadow, signify, prognosticate, forewarn, warn of, harbinger, betoken.

portent n. precursor, omen, foreshadowing, presentiment, sign, signification, presage, indication, harbinger, augury, threat, warning, premonition, forerunner, prognostication.

portentous adj. 1. ominous, looming, prophetic, forewarning, imminent, sinister, fateful, threatening, crucial, pregnant, prodigious, ponderous, menacing, earth-shaking, momentous; ant. insignificant, unimportant, unimpressive. 2. amazing, extraordinary, significant, remarkable. 3. pompous, grandiose, pretentious, magniloquent, self-important.

portfolio n. 1. briefcase, attaché case, folder, bag. 2. collection, holdings, selection, documents.

portion n. part, piece, fragment, scrap, section, segment, share, fraction, bit, allotment, morsel, measure, ration, helping, division.

portion v. distribute, deal, allot, allocate, divide, apportion, divvy up (slang), dole, parcel, partition, slice up, assign.

portly adj. obese, heavy, large, overweight, corpulent, fat, fleshy, rotund, plump, stout, bulky, beefy, chubby, tubby, paunchy; ant. slight, slim.

portrait n. picture, photograph, painting, image, likeness, depiction, caricature, characterization, representation, miniature, portrayal, thumbnail sketch, vignette.

portray v. impersonate, depict, play, act, personify, represent, characterize, evoke, describe, render, suggest, personate, draw, capture, illustrate.

portrayal n. impersonation, performance, representation, presentation, characterization, depiction, evocation, interpretation, sketch, picture, description, delineation, rendering.

pose n. position, posture, stance, mien, role, bearing, façade, attitude, air, pretense, sham, mask, masquerade, act, affectation.

pose v. 1. model, sit, position, posture. 2. masquerade, pretend, affect, impersonate, feign, put on an act, pass oneself off, sham. 3. advance, present, put forward, submit, state, posit.

poser n. pretender, phony, impostor, mimic, hypocrite, charlatan, con (slang), cheat, mountebank, masquerader, posturist, exhibitionist, quack.

posh (slang) adj. luxurious, sumptuous, lavish, opulent, deluxe, grand, classy, exclusive, select, ritzy, swanky (slang), stylish, smart, high-class, upper-class; ant. cheap, inferior.

posit v. 1. place, set, fix, secure, fasten. 2. state, assert, propound, advance, postulate, put forward, submit, pose, predicate, presume, assume; ant. refute.

position n. 1. place, placement, placing, location, locality, spot, seat, ground, environment, whereabouts, station, point, situation, site, area. 2. opinion, judgment, view, viewpoint, point of view, belief, outlook, attitude, perspective, standpoint, disposition. 3. job, office, responsibility, place, slot, post.

position v. place, put, set, settle, stick, arrange, locate, stand, lay out, pose, array, deploy, dispose, fix, range.

positive adj. 1. certain, definite, sure, undeniable, irrefutable, indisputable, conclusive, clear-cut, unmitigated, incontestable, incontrovertible, real, actual, decisive; ant. indefinite, uncertain. 2. assertive, forceful, emphatic, dogmatic, resolute, confident, uncompromising, peremptory, authoritative, arrant, direct, assured, cocksure; *ant.* indecisive, uncertain. **3.** good, beneficial, helpful, constructive, useful, favorable, advantageous, wholesome, rewarding; *ant.* detrimental, harmful, useless.

positively *adv.* **1.** boldly, firmly, assertively, stubbornly, obstinately, confidently, peremptorily, emphatically, authoritatively, uncompromisingly, dogmatically, decidedly, absolutely, insistently, unhesitatingly. **2.** surely, definitely, certainly, undoubtedly, conclusively, unmistakably, undeniably, unequivocally, unquestionably, expressly, categorically, assuredly, incontestably, incontrovertibly.

possess *v.* own, have, maintain, hold, control, occupy, acquire, dominate, obtain, enjoy, possess oneself of, seize, take, take over, be endowed with.

possessed *adj.* **1.** insane, crazed, demented, berserk, frenzied, haunted, obsessed, infatuated, maddened, raving, bewitched, bedeviled, cursed, enchanted, mesmerized. **2.** owned, held, kept, retained, enjoyed, controlled, dominated, in one's possession.

possession *n.* **1.** ownership, control, hold, custody, dominion, proprietorship, tenure. **2.** territory, province, colony, protectorate, real estate, dependency.

possessions *n.* belongings, assets, things, stuff, effects, property, junk (*slang*), riches, wealth, traps, paraphernalia, estate, goods, movables, chattels.

possessive *adj.* selfish, covetous, jealous, domineering, dominating, clinging, overprotective, proprietorial, acquisitive, grasping; *ant.* generous, sharing, unassertive.

possessor *n.* owner, proprietor, holder, occupant, occupier, retainer, master, buyer, purchaser, landlord, landlady, beneficiary.

possibilities *n.* potential, promise, prospects, capabilities, potentiality.

possibility *n.* chance, hope, prospect, probability, plausibility, likelihood, hazard, conceivability, potentiality, odds, risk, liability, feasibility, practicability, workableness.

possible *adj.* conceivable, probable, imaginable, credible, tenable, plausible, attainable, realizable, viable, workable, achievable, practicable, feasible, doable, accomplishable.

possibly *adv.* perhaps, maybe, at all, by any

means, in any way, perchance, God willing, hopefully, by any chance.

post *n.* **1.** column, pole, pillar, shaft, stake, banister, leg, picket, support, upright, stanchion, strut, newel, pier. **2.** mail, mail or postal service, post office, P.O.

postdate *v.* succeed, replace, ensue, follow; *ant.* antedate.

poster *n.* sign, placard, notice, advertisement, bill, handbill, announcement.

posterior *n.* buttocks, backside, derrière, *slang:* behind, rear end, rear; hindquarters, tail (*slang*), haunches, rump, seat, bottom (*slang*), hind end.

posterior *adj.* **1.** later, following, latter, subsequent, ensuing, succeeding, after; *ant.* previous. **2.** rear, back, behind, hind, dorsal, rearward, hinder, posticous; *ant.* anterior, front.

posterity *n.* descendants, offspring, successors, children, family, heirs, issue, progeny, seed, scions, epigons, future; *ant.* ancestors, antiquity, forebears, past.

posthaste *adv.* quickly, speedily, promptly, at once, presently, immediately, swiftly, straightaway, full tilt, double quick, directly, *slang:* pronto; *ant.* gradually, slowly.

posthumous *adj.* post-mortem, after-death, continuing, future.

postpone *v.* put off, delay, shelve, table, suspend, defer, hold over, waive, put on ice (*slang*), pigeonhole, adjourn, freeze, prorogue; *ant.* advance, forward.

postponement *n.* delay, suspension, stay, moratorium, freeze, respite, deferment, deferral, adjournment, prorogation.

postscript *n.* P.S., afterthought, afterword, appendix, epilogue, addition, addendum, codicil, supplement; *ant.* introduction, prologue.

postulate *v.* **1.** theorize, hypothesize, assume, predicate, suppose, take for granted, presuppose, stipulate, propose, advance, lay down, posit. **2.** implore, beg, request, demand, ask, question.

posture *n.* **1.** stance, pose, position, carriage, bearing, aspect, demeanor, mien, presence, condition. **2.** attitude, disposition, sentiment, feeling, point of view, viewpoint, view, stance.

posture *v.* affect, put on airs, strike attitudes, show off, attitudinize, pose, strut.

pot *n.* **1.** pan, container, basin, crock, vase, urn, jar, receptacle, vessel, samovar, beaker, bowl, flask. **2.** (*slang*) marijuana, *slang:* weed, grass; cannabis.

go to pot deteriorate, decay, go to ruin, fall apart, backslide.

potable *adj.* drinkable, pure, sanitary, fit for drinking, uncontaminated, clean, unpolluted, fresh, potulent.

potency *n.* **1.** strength, power, energy, puissance, force, might, vigor, *slang:* muscle, punch, kick; efficacy, effectiveness, headiness; *ant.* impotence, weakness. **2.** authority, power, influence, control, command, dominion, sway.

potent *adj.* **1.** powerful, mighty, strong, great, influential, dominant, puissant, forceful, formidable, weighty, impressive, persuasive, moving, heady, compelling, convincing, dynamic; *ant.* impotent, weak. **2.** effective, useful, efficient, efficacious.

potential *n.* possibility, potentiality, ability, power, talent, wherewithal, the makings, what it takes, flair.

potential *adj.* possible, imaginable, likely; probable, conceivable, prospective, promising, inherent, budding, embryonic, undeveloped, unrealized, latent, dormant, hidden.

potentiality *n.* potential, capability, aptitude, ability, likelihood, capacity, promise, possibilities, prospect, virtuality.

potion *n.* drink, brew, concoction, elixir, medicine, mixture, tonic, dose, draft, beverage, treacle, electuary.

potpourri *n.* mixture, combination, medley, blend, hodgepodge, patchwork, salad, collection, mélange, jumble, olio, pastiche, miscellany, mixed bag.

pottery *n.* ceramics, earthenware, china, porcelain, stoneware, crockery, terra cotta.

pouch *n.* sack, sac, bag, purse, pocket, container, receptacle, wallet, fanny pack (*slang*).

pounce *v.* jump, attack, fall upon, swoop, strike, leap at, lunge at, ambush, drop, dive at, spring, snatch, dash at, grab.

pound *n.* kennel, coop, doghouse, cage, pen, compound, yard, corral, enclosure.

pound *v.* hammer, pummel, thump, drum, pelt, thud, stomp, thunder, crush, beat, batter, bang, bash, clobber, pulverize.

pour *v.* **1.** (issue in great quantity) flow, run, course, gush, flood, teem, stream, cascade, deluge, tumble, discharge, exude, emit, issue, effuse, drain, spill. **2.** rain, shower, rain cats and dogs (*slang*), drench, flood.

pour out 1. discharge, issue, emit, spew forth, disgorge, lave, decant, disembogue, embogue. **2.** divulge, confess, confide, unburden.

pour it on burden, overwork, overburden, increase, add to.

pout *n.* grimace, scowl, glower, long face, moue; *ant.* grin, smile.

pout *v.* grimace, scowl, glower, sulk, mope, pull a face.

poverty *n.* **1.** poorness, destitution, insolvency, indigence, impoverishment, pennilessness, paucity, penury, hardship, beggary; *ant.* affluence, riches, richness. **2.** want, need, lack, deficiency, insufficiency, shortage, scarcity, dearth, depletion, inadequacy, necessity, necessitousness, privation, barrenness, bareness; *ant.* abundance.

powder *n.* talc, dust, triturate, particles, film, pulverance.

take a powder (*slang*) leave, depart, split (*slang*), run away, abandon, desert.

powder *v.* **1.** crush, pulverize, granulate, grind, pound, pestle, dredge. **2.** dust, cover, sprinkle, scatter, strew.

powdery *adj.* fine, dusty, chalky, granular, grainy, sandy, dry, crumbly, loose, crumbling, friable, pulverized, pulverous.

power *n.* **1.** strength, vigor, might, energy, stamina, force, puissance, muscle (*slang*), forcefulness, weight, intensity, brawn, juice (*slang*). **2.** leadership, authority, control, command, sovereignty, jurisdiction, dominion, sway, ascendancy, dominance, preponderance, supremacy, supreme authority, prestige, warrant. **3.** ability, skill, endowment, capability, capacity, faculty, talent, competency.

powerful *adj.* **1.** strong, robust, mighty, muscular, strapping, sturdy, energetic; *ant.* impotent, weak. **2.** commanding, compelling, persuasive, effectual, effective, winning, sovereign, authoritative, impressive, dominant, prevailing, influential, supreme, omnipotent, ascendant; *ant.* ineffective.

powerless *adj.* impotent, ineffectual, weak, vulnerable, feeble, defenseless, frail, debilitated, dependent, disabled, incapable, infirm, prostrate, unarmed, subject; *ant.* commanding, potent.

practicable *adj.* possible, feasible, workable, viable, attainable, accomplishable, doable, negotiable, achievable, performable, compassable, effectible, passable; *ant.* impracticable.

practical *adj.* functional, feasible, workable, serviceable, proficient, efficient, utilitarian, pragmatic, sensible, commonsense, nuts-and-bolts (*slang*), realistic, working, empirical, workaday, down-to-earth; *ant.* quixotic, impractical.

practicality *n.* **1.** feasibility, serviceability, usefulness, utility, *slang:* nuts and bolts, nitty-gritty; workability, practicability, soundness, basics, practicalness. **2.** (a practical outlook) sense, common sense, realism, pragmatism.

practically *adv.* **1.** almost, just about, nearly, quite, virtually, all but, in effect, essentially, pretty well, very nearly, actually, fundamentally, in practice, in principle. **2.** reasonably, realistically, rationally, sensibly, matter-of-factly, unsentimentally, clearly.

practice *n.* **1.** custom, tradition, convention, habit, routine, way, use. **2.** method, way, procedure, wont, mode, modus operandi, manner, fashion, policy, operation.

practice *v.* **1.** rehearse, prepare, drill, train, run through, repeat, perfect, discipline, exercise, warm up. **2.** function, ply, work at, put into effect, put into practice, carry out, engage in, pursue, perform, undertake, execute, implement.

practiced *adj.* expert, versed, well-trained, knowledgeable, experienced, accomplished, proficient, seasoned, veteran, consummate, knowing, highly developed, finished, qualified, refined; *ant.* inexpert.

pragmatic *adj.* practical, realistic, sensible, utilitarian, unsentimental, unidealistic, factual, hardheaded, efficient, businesslike, opportunistic; *ant.* idealistic, romantic, unrealistic.

pragmatism *n.* realism, practicality, utilitarianism, humanism, opportunism, hardheadedness, practicalism; *ant.* idealism, romanticism.

pragmatist *n.* realist, humanist, opportunist, utilitarian, empiricist, practicalist, Machiavellian; *ant.* idealist, romantic.

praise *n.* compliments, encomium, homage, honor, kudos, recognition, accolade, congratulation, approbation, flattery, ovation, acclaim, cheering, extolment, plaudit; *ant.* criticism, revilement.

praise *v.* acclaim, compliment, flatter, recognize, applaud, rave over, celebrate, congratulate, hail, glorify, cheer, honor, admire, tout, panegyrize; *ant.* criticize, revile.

praiseworthy *adj.* exemplary, commendable, laudable, meritorious, worthy, reputable, honorable, estimable, deserving, fine, excellent, admirable, sterling, creditable; *ant.* discreditable, dishonorable, ignoble.

prance *v.* frolic, dance, gambol, caper, cavort, skip, bound, frisk, romp, parade, swagger, jump, leap, curvet, capriole.

prank *n.* joke, practical joke, trick, antic, escapade, caper, lark, stunt, vagary, frolic, spree, rig, dido.

prate *v.* chatter, blather, gab, jaw (*slang*), babble, ramble, yak (*slang*), drivel, prattle, jabber, brag, maunder, boast, burble, palaver.

prattle *n.* talk, tattle, gossip, gibberish, drivel, chat, chatter, foolishness, maundering, nonsense, prating, gab, hot air (*slang*).

prattle *v.* gossip, chat, blather, drivel, jabber, chatter, babble, gabble, patter, twitter.

pray *v.* implore, beg, beseech, plead, entreat, importune, request, ask, supplicate, petition, invoke, solicit, press, adjure, obsecrate, urge, sue, call on, crave.

prayer *n.* plea, entreaty, appeal, supplication, petition, request, litany, invocation, solicitation, suit, suffrage, communion, paternoster, devotion, Kyrie eleison.

preach *v.* lecture, orate, exhort, harangue, address, sermonize, advocate, admonish, pontificate, evangelize, pontify, urge, preachify, prose, ethicize.

preacher *n.* minister, evangelist, missionary, parson, revivalist, sermonizer, homilist, moralizer, pontificator, predicant, ranter.

preachiness *adj.* pomposity, self-righteousness, sanctimony, sanctimoniousness, dogmatism, didacticism, sermonizing, portentousness, religiosity, cant, pietism, pulpitry, moralizing.

preaching *n.* gospel, doctrine, sermon, teaching, message, instruction, exhortation, homily, dogma, precept, homiletic.

preachy *adj.* self-righteous, holier-than-thou, moralizing, didactic, exhortatory, homiletic, sanctimonious, pompous, bombastic, religiose, pontifical, pontificating, preceptive, canting.

preamble *n.* introduction, preface, prelude, foreword, preliminaries, preparation, lead-in, prologue, overture, exordium; *ant.* epilogue, postscript.

precarious *adj.* shaky, hazardous, dangerous, perilous, risky, insecure, unstable, *slang:* hairy, dicey; unsure, unsafe, uncertain, tricky, dodgy (*slang*), ticklish, unreliable; *ant.* certain, safe, secure.

precaution *n.* safeguard, security, preparation, insurance, caution, provision, care, foresight, forethought, protection, safety measure, prudence, anticipation, buffer, circumspection.

precautionary *adj.* preventive, protective, self-protective, provisional, preparatory, anticipatory, preliminary, judicious, foresighted, cautious, safe, prudent, prophylactic, provident, foresightful; *ant.* reckless.

precede *v.* go before, head, lead, forerun, prelude, herald, come first, antecede, take precedence, preface, introduce, prefix, premise, antedate, anticipate; *ant.* follow.

precedence *n.* lead, priority, first place, seniority, supremacy, superiority, preeminence, primacy, preference, rank.

precedent *n.* standard, guideline, example, model, prototype, pattern, yardstick, paradigm, criterion, exemplar.

preceding *adj.* above, previous, earlier, prior, past, former, aforementioned, aforesaid, antecedent, precedent, foregoing, precursory; *ant.* following, later.

precept *n.* rule, order, law, commandment, mandate, regulation, statute, decree, ordinance, charge, bidding, behest, direction, injunction, rubric.

precinct *n.* district, area, zone, sector, quarter,

section, limit, confine, division, boundary, bound, banlieue.

precious *adj.* 1. valuable, priceless, expensive, costly, choice, dear, irreplaceable, rare, invaluable, high-priced, pricey, inestimable. 2. beloved, loved, adored, favorite, dear, dearest, darling, prized, treasured, idolized, valued. 3. affected, artificial, flowery, fastidious, overnice, overrefined, recherché.

precipice *n.* cliff, brink, bluff, crag, drop, escarpment, height, cliff face.

precipitate *v.* hurry, further, accelerate, advance, quicken, hasten, expedite, launch, induce, press, occasion, cause, project, trigger, speed.

precipitate *adj.* impatient, abrupt, rash, hasty, headlong, reckless, heedless, hotheaded, impulsive, incautious, madcap, pell-mell, frantic, breakneck, precipitous; *ant.* cautious.

precipitation *n.* rain, rainfall, snow, hail, sleet, condensation.

precipitous *adj.* steep, sheer, perpendicular, abrupt, dizzy, giddy, vertiginous, high; *ant.* gradual, sloping.

précis *n.* abbreviation, summary, encapsulation, condensation, synopsis, abstract, digest, epitome, sketch, rundown, compendium, outline, abridgment, contraction.

précis *v.* shorten, condense, abbreviate, summarize, sum up, compress, encapsulate, epitomize, outline, abridge, abstract, contract, digest, synopsize; *ant.* amplify, expand.

precise *adj.* 1. exact, accurate, absolute, specific, authentic, verbatim, minute. 2. punctilious, fastidious, finicky, particular, strict, literal.

precisely *adv.* just, exactly, absolutely, accurately, correctly, literally, word for word, verbatim, blow by blow, dead, just so, smack, square, squarely, bang.

precision *n.* accuracy, exactitude, exactness, meticulousness, fastidiousness, correctness, fidelity, rigor, punctiliousness, explicitness, neatness, preciseness, particularity, definiteness, scrupulosity.

preclude *v.* eliminate, rule out, exclude, prohibit, debar, check, inhibit, obviate, restrain, stop, forestall, prevent, hinder, avoid; *ant.* incur, involve.

precocious *adj.* smart, gifted, bright, clever, advanced, developed, mature, premature, quick, forward, fast, ahead; *ant.* backward.

preconceive *v.* presuppose, presume, assume, conceive, anticipate, conceptualize, project, visualize, picture, imagine, envisage, ideate; prejudge.

preconception *n.* prejudice, bias, assumption, predisposition, presupposition, notion, presumption, conjecture, prepossession, anticipation, prenotion.

precondition *n.* requirement, essential, must, need, stipulation, prerequisite, requisite, necessity, proviso, sine qua non.

precursor *n.* predecessor, forerunner, ancestor, antecedent, parent, forefather, forebear, pioneer, harbinger, indication, usher, way-maker, trailblazer, pathfinder, originator; *ant.* aftereffect, aftermath.

precursory *adj.* prior, preliminary, antecedent, preceding, introductory, preparatory, previous, preambular, preludial, anterior, warning, premonitory, prelusive, precursive, prevenient; *ant.* following, resulting, subsequent.

predatory *adj.* preying, hunting, rapacious, predative, carnivorous, voracious, vulturine, wolfish; marauding, plundering, ravening, thieving, despoiling, avaricious, covetous.

predecessor *n.* ancestor, forefather, forerunner, precursor, antecedent, forebear, progenitor, antecessor; *ant.* descendant, successor.

predestination *n.* predetermination, foreordination, foreordainment, preordination, preordainment, fate, destiny, doom, fortune, karma, lot, portion.

predestine *v.* doom, fate, destine, preordain, predetermine, foreordain, intend, mean, predestinate, foredoom, preelect.

predetermine *v.* destine, predestine, fate, doom, decide.

predetermined *adj.* preplanned, foregone, prearranged, fixed (*slang*), set, set up, settled, agreed, cut and dried, foreordained, preordained, deliberate.

predicament *n.* dilemma, jam (*slang*), mess, situation, plight, quandary, embarrassment, *slang*; pickle, hot water, between a rock and a hard place; impasse, crisis, corner, scrape, kettle of fish (*slang*), emergency.

predicate *v.* maintain, assert, affirm, avow, contend, aver, postulate, state, posit, rest, avouch, proclaim, build, found, establish.

predict *v.* prophesy, forecast, presage, portend, soothsay, second-guess, augur, foretell, prognosticate, project, divine, forebode, foreshow, vaticinate.

predictable *adj.* dependable, reliable, anticipated, certain, expected, probable, foreseeable, foreseen, imaginable, calculable, presumable, likely, foregone, determinate.

prediction *n.* forecast, prognosis, fortunetelling, augury, divination, soothsaying, prophecy, prognostication, crystal gazing, second sight, auspication, vaticination.

predilection *n.* proclivity, preference, fondness, affinity, fancy, liking, love, tendency, propensity, inclination, penchant, bias, bent, leaning, predisposition, soft spot; *ant.* antipathy, disinclination.

predispose *v.* stimulate, prompt, induce, affect, lead, make, animate; prepare, dispose, prime, influence, sway, incline, head, bias.

predisposed *adj.* inclined, liable, biased, amenable, willing, ready, prejudiced, susceptible, favorable, subject, prone, well-disposed, not unwilling, prepared.

predisposition *n.* **1.** tendency, inclination, proclivity, propensity, leaning, bent, penchant, likelihood, proneness, disposition. **2.** preference, bias, prejudice, predilection, mind.

predominance *n.* control, dominance, leadership, mastery, ascendancy, supremacy, superiority, power, prevalence, upper hand, hold, influence, sway, preponderance, paramountcy; *ant.* ineffectiveness, weakness.

predominant *adj.* **1.** powerful, mighty, almighty, supreme, omnipotent, all-powerful, ascendant, ruling, reigning, sovereign, prevailing, controlling, paramount, influential, governing; *ant.* ineffective, weak. **2.** principal, main, leading, chief, primary, preeminent, prime, supreme, capital, transcendent, surpassing, superlative, prominent; *ant.* lesser, minor.

predominate *v.* prevail, override, outweigh, rule, reign, dominate, transcend, overshadow, overrule, outnumber, tell, obtain, preponderate.

preeminence *n.* renown, repute, fame, prestige, predominance, prominence, supremacy, transcendence, superiority, distinction, incomparability, peerlessness, matchlessness, paramountcy, excellence.

preeminent *adj.* leading, chief, foremost, renowned, superior, consummate, outstanding, inimitable, incomparable, exceptional, superlative, surpassing, unequaled, peerless, predominant; *ant.* undistinguished, unknown.

preempt *v.* usurp, seize, acquire, arrogate, assume, secure, appropriate, bag, anticipate, forestall.

preen *v.* groom, primp, dress up, do up, beautify, adorn, array, doll up, spruce up, slick, deck, trim, prettify, titivate.

prefabricate *v.* assemble, preassemble, set up, fabricate, coordinate, perform.

preface *n.* introduction, preamble, foreword, prelude, preliminaries, exordium, prologue, prologomenon, proem, intro (*slang*); *ant.* afterthought, epilogue, postscript.

preface *v.* begin, start, introduce, prefix, open, precede, lead up to, premise, launch, prelude; *ant.* append, complete, finish.

prefatory *adj.* opening, introductory, preparatory, precursory, preliminary, preambulatory, explanatory, antecedent, prefatorial, prolegomenons, preludial, prelusive, exordial; *ant.* closing, final.

prefect *n.* supervisor, administrator, official, consul, regent, monitor, prepositor.

prefer *v.* favor, like better, choose, opt for, pick, back, advocate, endorse, fancy, would rather *or* sooner, single out, incline toward, want, select; *ant.* reject.

preferable *adj.* favored, preferred, better, best, nicer, superior, worthier, chosen, choice, stronger, advantageous, desirable, expedient, advisable, eligible; *ant.* ineligible, inferior, undesirable.

preferably *adv.* rather, first, sooner, by preference, by choice.

preference *n.* 1. inclination, partiality, fancy, liking, predilection; option, choice, first choice, selection, pick, wish, desire, election. 2. special treatment, preferential treatment, favor, precedence, priority, favoritism, special consideration, advantage.

preferential *adj.* favored, partial, partisan, special, privileged, advantaged, preferred, given a leg up; biased, better, favorable, superior, advantageous, prior; *ant.* disadvantaged.

preferment *n.* promotion, advantage, handicap, advancement, elevation, raise, improvement, upgrading, betterment, step *or* leg up, furtherance, exaltation, aggrandizement; *ant.* demotion, disadvantage.

preferred *adj.* choice, chosen, favored, selected, desired, predilect, approved, recommended, sanctioned, authorized; *ant.* rejected, undesirable.

prefix *n.* 1. addition, affix, adjunct, preflex, prefixure. 2. name, title, designation, cognomen.

pregnancy *n.* gestation, impregnation, parturition, fertilization, gravidity, conception, fecundation.

pregnant *adj.* 1. gestating, expecting, impregnated, expectant, gravid, with child, be in the family way (*slang*), parturient, teeming, enceinte. 2. meaningful, charged, pointed, significant, ominous, weighty, full, loaded, pithy, telling, suggestive, heavy, eloquent, expressive; *ant.* jejune.

prehistoric *adj.* early, earliest, ancient, old, primitive, primordial, primeval, antiquated, antediluvian, archaic, hoary, obsolete, outmoded, out-of-date; *ant.* modern.

prejudge *v.* presume, assume, anticipate, predetermine, presuppose, judge, forejudge, prejudicate, preconceive.

prejudice *n.* bias, bigotry, racism, intolerance, discrimination, sexism, unfairness, injustice, partiality, narrow-mindedness, chauvinism, preconception, prejudgment, partisanship; *ant.* fairness, tolerance.

prejudiced *adj.* bigoted, biased, discriminatory, narrow-minded, unfair, sexist, racist, partial, opinionated, conditioned, influenced, intolerant, one-sided, subjective, unenlightened; *ant.* fair, tolerant.

prejudicial *adj.* harmful, hurtful, injurious, noxious, counterproductive, detrimental, ruinous, pernicious, undermining, deleterious, disadvantageous, hostile, inimical, unfavorable, mischievous; *ant.* advantageous, beneficial.

preliminaries *n.* beginning, start, opening, prelude, introduction, formalities, preface, proem, initiation, preparation; basics, foundations, groundwork, rudiments.

preliminary *adj.* first, opening, early, earliest, initial, introductory, primary, pilot, inaugural, trial, embryonic, precursory, exploratory, preparatory, initiative; *ant.* closing, final.

prelude *n.* **1.** introduction, intro (*slang*), start, beginning, commencement, foreword, opener, prologue, preamble, preface, prolegomenon, precursor, preliminary, exordium, preparation, taster; *ant.* aftermath, epilogue, postscript. **2.** (musical introduction) overture, toccata, curtain raiser.

premature *adj.* immature, early, undeveloped, incomplete, embryonic, half-formed, precipitate, raw, unripe, green, precocious, forward, unseasonable, inopportune; preterm, preemie (*slang*); *ant.* late, tardy, term.

premeditated *adj.* intentional, deliberate, premeditated, planned, willful, conscious, calculated, intended, aforethought, plotted, predetermined, studied, contrived, prearranged; *ant.* spontaneous, impromptu.

premeditation *n.* scheming, deliberation, forethought, planning, plotting, willfulness, intention, purpose, design, predetermination, deliberateness, prearrangement; *ant.* impulse, spontaneity.

premier *n.* head of government, prime minister, chancellor, chief minister, secretary of state, first minister.

premiere *n.* debut, opening, opening night, first night.

premise *v.* introduce, begin, commence, start, announce, state, stipulate, propose, proffer, suggest, postulate, suppose, predicate, lay down, assume, presuppose, posit, hypothesize.

premise *n.* ground, supposition, assertion, thesis, hypothesis, presupposition, statement, proposition, stipulation, assumption, postulation, predication, postulate.

premises *n.* property, site, grounds, estate, establishment, building, office, place.

premium *n.* prize, bonus, gift, lagniappe, benefit, extra, dividend, surplus, remuneration.

premonition *n.* feeling, foreboding, warning, presentiment, misgiving, omen, sign, suspicion, intuition, anxiety, fear, apprehension, portent, uneasiness, worry.

preoccupation *n.* fixation, absorption, distraction, oblivion, obsession, hangup (*slang*), inattentiveness, daydreaming, reverie, musing, engrossment, immersion, absent-mindedness, absence of mind, brown study.

preoccupied *adj.* distracted, wrapped up, intent, fixated, daydreaming, engrossed, immersed, obsessed, heedless, absent-minded, absorbed, oblivious, faraway, pensive, unaware.

preordain *v.* doom, fate, destine, predestine, prearrange, predetermine, foreordain.

preparation *n.* **1.** (process of preparing) readying, fitting, development, construction, formation, building, putting in order, adapting, compounding, incubation, rehearsal, *slang:* prep, buildup; foreseeing. **2.** (state of being prepared) readiness, alertness, preparedness, fitness, suitability, capacity, qualification, ripeness, maturity, training, education. **3.** mixture, potion, composition, compound, lotion, medicine, concoction, application, tincture.

preparatory *adj.* opening, primary, initial, basic, elementary, fundamental, preliminary, rudimentary, introductory, prefatory, preparative, exordial; *ant.* conclusive, final.

prepare *v.* make, construct, contrive, develop, form, fashion, compose, assemble, arrange, produce, devise, furnish, supply, plan, accoutre.

prepared *adj.* **1.** (trained or educated to do something) able, fit, ready, fitted, disposed, predisposed, adapted, qualified, adjusted. **2.** (psychologically attuned) ready, combat-ready, briefed, psyched up, all set, programmed, all systems "go"; *ant.* unready, hesitant.

preponderance *n.* majority, weight, bulk, lion's share, prevalence, superiority, supremacy, force, extensiveness, ascendancy, sway, dominance, domination, dominance.

preponderant *adj.* overruling, controlling, prevailing, greater, larger, foremost, superior, significant, important, dominant, ascendant, paramount, predominant, extensive.

preponderate *v.* outnumber, prevail, dominate, overrule, rule, override, predominate, turn the scale, weigh with, tell.

prepossessing *adj.* lovable, likable, disarming, enchanting, winning, engaging, charismatic, beautiful, attractive, handsome, good-looking, appealing, amiable, striking, bewitching, winsome, magnetic; *ant.* unattractive, ugly.

prepossession *n.* **1.** preoccupation, absorption, engrossment. **2.** bias, inclination, partiality, prejudice, predilection, predisposition, leaning, liking.

preposterous *adj.* ridiculous, laughable, absurd, asinine, crazy, bizarre, insane, foolish, unbelievable, extreme, inane, impossible, unthinkable, nonsensical, unconscionable; *ant.* reasonable.

prerequisite *n.* requirement, requisite, condition, precondition, necessity, essential, must, imperative, qualification, proviso, provision, sine qua non.

prerequisite *adj.* required, requisite, necessary, mandatory, essential, imperative, obligatory, indispensable, vital, basic, fundamental, needed, needful; *ant.* unnecessary.

prerogative *n.* liberty, license, choice, right, due, privilege, birthright, claim, immunity, sanction, title, advantage, authority, carte blanche, perquisite.

presage *n.* feeling, foreboding, omen, portent, presentiment, sign, warning, premonition, misgiving, apprehension, harbinger, prophecy, prediction, prognostication, augury, intimation.

presage *v.* predict, forecast, foretell, prognosticate, prophesy, portend, foresee, foreshadow, forewarn, sense, signify, soothsay, augur, divine, warn.

prescience *n.* clairvoyance, foresight, foreknowledge, second sight, precognition, prophecy, farsightedness, prevision, telepathy.

prescient *adj.* clairvoyant, psychic, prophetic, foresighted, telepathic, divining, mantic, farsighted, farseeing, foreknowing, perceptive, discerning, previsional, divinatory; *ant.* imperceptive, obtuse.

prescribe *v.* command, decree, require, dictate, direct, appoint, assign, specify, stipulate, impose, lay down, rule, set, fix, define.

prescription *n.* medicine, remedy, treatment, drug, formula, recipe, mixture, preparation.

prescriptive *adj.* customary, authoritarian, dictatorial, rigid, didactic, dogmatic, preceptive, prescribing, legislating; *ant.* permissive.

presence *n.* **1.** attendance, occupancy, resi-

dence, inhabitance, habitation, ubiquity; *ant.* absence. **2.** appearance, behavior, personality, carriage, port, demeanor, mien, air, comportment; poise, self-assurance, statuesqueness. **3.** spirit, ghost, specter, apparition, shade.

presence of mind composure, level-headedness, self-assurance, self-possession, alertness, aplomb, calmness, coolness, cool (*slang*), gumption, self-command, wits, imperturbability, sang-froid; *ant.* agitation, confusion.

present *n.* **1.** now, right now, present moment, today, instant, this time. **2.** gift, favor, benefaction, gratuity, endowment, bounty, boon, grant, donation, largesse, offering, cadeau, compliment.

present *v.* **1.** give, furnish, grant, award, bestow, confer, hand over, extend, donate, entrust, tender. **2.** (put up an exhibit or produce a performance) display, mount, exhibit, show, stage, demonstrate, manifest, produce, undertake, demonstrate, manifest, produce, write, fund. **3.** (propose ideas) suggest, proffer, put forth, pose, advance, raise, offer.

present *adj.* here, at hand, near, ready, there, available, attending, immediate, current, contemporary, existent, extant; *ant.* absent, out-of-date, past.

presentable *adj.* proper, decent, suitable, tidy, becoming, clean, acceptable, neat, respectable, satisfactory, passable, tolerable; *ant.* untidy.

presentation *n.* **1.** donation, delivery, bestowal, award, giving, offering, submission, conferral, investiture. **2.** show, display, exhibition, pageant, staging, demonstration, exposition, performance.

present-day *adj.* present, modern, contemporary, current, living, existing, up-to-date, fashionable; *ant.* future, past.

presenter *n.* host, master of ceremonies, MC, anchorman, anchorwoman, anchorperson, frontperson, compere (*Brit.*).

presentiment *n.* feeling, fear, foreboding, presage, misgiving, premonition, intuition, hunch, apprehension, bad vibes (*slang*), expectation, forecast, forethought, anticipation.

presently *adv.* soon, shortly, in a minute, before long, by and by, directly, immediately, anon.

dence, inhabitance, habitation, ubiquity; *ant.* absence. **2.** appearance, behavior, personality, carriage, port, demeanor, mien, air, comportment; poise, self-assurance, statuesqueness. **3.** spirit, ghost, specter, apparition, shade.

presence of mind composure, level-headedness, self-assurance, self-possession, alertness, aplomb, calmness, coolness, cool (*slang*), gumption, self-command, wits, imperturbability, sang-froid; *ant.* agitation, confusion.

present *n.* **1.** now, right now, present moment, today, instant, this time. **2.** gift, favor, benefaction, gratuity, endowment, bounty, boon, grant, donation, largesse, offering, cadeau, compliment.

present *v.* **1.** give, furnish, grant, award, bestow, confer, hand over, extend, donate, entrust, tender. **2.** (put up an exhibit or produce a performance) display, mount, exhibit, show, stage, demonstrate, manifest, produce, underwrite, fund. **3.** (propose ideas) suggest, proffer, put forth, pose, advance, raise, offer.

present *adj.* here, at hand, near, ready, there, available, attending, immediate, current, contemporary, existent, extant; *ant.* absent, out-of-date, past.

presentable *adj.* proper, decent, suitable, tidy, becoming, clean, acceptable, neat, respectable, satisfactory, passable, tolerable; *ant.* untidy.

presentation *n.* **1.** donation, delivery, bestowal, award, giving, offering, submission, conferral, investiture. **2.** show, display, exhibition, pageant, staging, demonstration, exposition, performance.

present-day *adj.* present, modern, contemporary, current, living, existing, up-to-date, fashionable; *ant.* future, past.

presenter *n.* host, master of ceremonies, MC, anchorman, anchorwoman, anchorperson, frontperson, compere (*Brit.*).

presentiment *n.* feeling, fear, foreboding, presage, misgiving, premonition, intuition, hunch, apprehension, bad vibes (*slang*), expectation, forecast, forethought, anticipation.

presently *adv.* soon, shortly, in a minute, before long, by and by, directly, immediately, anon.

preservation *n.* conservation, protection, perpetuation, salvation, safety, safeguarding, safekeeping, support, upholding, security, upkeep, retention, defense, maintenance, keeping; *ant.* destruction, ruination.

preserve *n.* sanctuary, reservation, game preserve, safari park; area, field, realm, domain, sphere.

preserve *v.* **1.** guard, safeguard, defend, shelter, shield, secure, protect, save; *ant.* ruin. **2.** maintain, keep, retain, sustain, care for, perpetuate, store, uphold; *ant.* destroy.

preserves *n.* jelly, jam, marmalade, conserve, spread, pectin, pickles.

preside *v.* govern, head, lead, manage, direct, run, supervise, officiate, control, chair, conduct, administer.

press *n.* news media, reporters, journalists, writers, columnists, correspondents, photographers, papers, paparazzi, hacks, fourth estate.

press *v.* **1.** push, thrust, compress, flatten, iron, drive, crush, mash, jam, mill, depress, squeeze, force down, pressurize; *ant.* expand. **2.** hug, embrace, hold, caress, clasp, encircle, enfold.

pressed *adj.* hurried, rushed, pressured, coerced, bullied, enjoined, lobbied, browbeaten, constrained, forced, pushed, harassed, pressurized.

pressing *adj.* important, serious, high-priority, crucial, exigent, vital, urgent, imperative, importunate, burning, essential, constraining, crowding.

pressure *n.* **1.** weight, heaviness, stress, tension, force, power, burden, thrust, mass, load, encumbrance, strength, strain. **2.** influence, coercion, compulsion, arm-twisting (*slang*), persuasion, demands, constraint, obligation.

pressure *v.* force, compel, impel, press, enjoin, lobby, pressurize, coerce, drive, browbeat, persuade, bully, *slang*; lean *or* sit on, arm-twist, bulldoze; squeeze, induce, oblige, constrain, dragoon.

prestige *n.* standing, distinction, esteem, stature, honor, importance, eminence, fame, celebrity, renown, reputation, authority, clout, pull (*slang*), cachet; *ant.* humbleness, unimportance.

prestigious *adj.* great, important, illustrious, impressive, prominent, renowned, respected, celebrated, esteemed, reputable, exalted, influential, eminent, imposing, blue-chip; *ant.* humble, modest.

presumably *adv.* probably, in all probability, most likely, doubtlessly, doubtless, no doubt, in all likelihood, in all probability, apparently, seemingly, as like as not.

presume *v.* suppose, presuppose, think, believe, take for granted, assume, infer, conjecture, take it, surmise, hypothesize, venture; take the liberty, dare, go so far.

presumption *n.* **1.** presupposition, supposition, conjecture, belief, surmise, guess, hypothesis, opinion. **2.** arrogance, audacity, gall, nerve, boldness, effrontery, presumptuousness, forwardness, insolence, cheek, chutzpah (*slang*), impudence, temerity; *ant.* humility, politeness.

presumptive *adj.* believable, reasonable, credible, possible, plausible, conceivable, likely, probable; *ant.* unlikely.

presumptuous *adj.* arrogant, rude, impudent, overconfident, insolent, conceited, bigheaded (*slang*), bold, impertinent, audacious, forward, overfamiliar, pushy, overweening, foolhardy; *ant.* modest, diffident.

presuppose *v.* suppose, presume, assume, take for granted, posit, postulate, premise, accept, imply, consider.

presupposition *n.* supposition, presumption, assumption, belief, theory, preconception, hypothesis, premise.

pretend *v.* make believe, simulate, act, fake, feign, impersonate, assume, purport, allege, dissimulate, sham, pass oneself off, counterfeit, go through the motions, suppose.

pretended *adj.* pretend, fake, false, phony, sham, so-called, counterfeit, bogus, fictitious, spurious, specious, ostensible, imaginary, purported; *ant.* real.

pretender *n.* fraud, hypocrite, cheat, rogue.

pretense *n.* dishonesty, imitation, affectation, misrepresentation, falsification, falsehood, act, deceit, fabrication, trickery, double-dealing, simulation, prevarication, dissimulation, artifice.

pretension *n.* **1.** claim, assertion, aspiration, demand, pretense, assumption. **2.** ostentation, show, showiness, pomposity, hypocrisy,

pretentiousness, snobbery, snobbishness, affectation, airs, self-importance, vanity, vainglory, conceit; *ant.* humility, modesty, simplicity, straightforwardness.

pretentious *adj.* showy, ostentatious, affected, extravagant, pompous, conceited, highfalutin (*slang*), vainglorious, grandiose, bombastic, ambitious, inflated, magniloquent, snobbish, exaggerated; *ant.* humble, modest, simple, straightforward.

pretentiousness *n.* ostentation, show, theatricality, pretension, posturing, posing, flamboyance, floweriness, floridness, attitudinizing, bombast, conceit; *ant.* humbleness, modesty, simplicity, straightforwardness.

pretext *n.* guise, ruse, mask, show, veil, cover, cloak, ploy, semblance, appearance, excuse, pretense, device, simulation, rationale.

prettify *v.* beautify, decorate, adorn, garnish, trim, embellish, ornament, gild, do up, primp, deck, doll *or* tart up, titivate; *ant.* mar, uglify.

pretty *adj.* 1. attractive, beautiful, handsome, good-looking, comely, lovely, cute, fair, fine, elegant, dainty, graceful, personable, nice, tasteful, sightly; *ant.* tasteless, ugly. 2. considerable, much, large, ample, sizeable, notable. **sitting pretty** successful, thriving, prospering.

pretty *adv.* somewhat, moderately, rather, a little, tolerably.

prevail *v.* rule, reign, predominate, succeed, win, triumph, overrule, overcome, abound, obtain, preponderate; *ant.* lose.

prevail upon *v.* influence, persuade, talk into, win over, prompt, incline, convince, dissuade, talk out of, bring round, induce, sway, talk out of, dispose.

prevailing *adj.* prevalent, ruling, widespread, mainstream, popular, controlling, established, current, dominant, customary, fashionable, predominating, principal, ruling, general; *ant.* minor, uncommon.

prevalence *n.* frequency, pervasiveness, popularity, ubiquity, profusion, regularity, omnipresence, predominance, primacy, currency, ascendancy, commonness, universality, rule, acceptance; *ant.* uncommonness.

prevalent *adj.* dominant, successful, governing, ruling, popular, prevailing, established, commonplace, epidemic, frequent, ubiquitous, universal, usual, widespread, habitual; *ant.* subordinate, uncommon.

prevaricate *v.* lie, deceive, evade, dodge, equivocate, fib, hedge, temporize, shift, shuffle, quibble, tergiversate, cavil, palter.

prevarication *n.* lie, untruth, deception, deceit, falsehood, fib, half-truth, falsification, fibbing, misrepresentation, equivocation, pretense, evasion, cavil, caviling.

prevaricator *n.* liar, fibber, deceiver, dissembler, equivocator, evader, hypocrite, sophist, dodger, pettifogger, casuist, caviler, quibbler.

prevent *v.* inhibit, frustrate, stop, restrain, stave off, check, thwart, forestall, frustrate, foil, intercept, obstruct, check, block, hamper, head off, preclude, impede; *ant.* permit.

prevention *n.* obstruction, frustration, stoppage, deterrence, hindrance, avoidance, elimination, preclusion, forestalling, bar, thwarting, safeguarding, check, obviation, precaution.

preventive *n.* obstacle, shield, obstruction, impediment, block, neutralizer, deterrent, protection, safeguard, remedy, prevention, hindrance, prophylactic.

preventive *adj.* obstructive, deterrent, shielding, preventative, prophylactic, impeding, inhibitory, precautionary, counteractive, hampering, hindering, protective; *ant.* causative, fostering.

previous *adj.* prior, former, past, preceding, foregoing, antecedent, onetime, sometime, erstwhile, earlier, precipitate, premature, untimely; *ant.* later, timely.

previously *adv.* before, earlier, beforehand, formerly, once, heretofore, hitherto; *ant.* later.

prey *n.* victim, kill, target, fall guy (*slang*), dupe, quarry, mark (*slang*), game, booty, plunder.

prey on 1. destroy, seize, raid, pillage, waste, terrorize, despoil, victimize, exploit, take advantage of. 2. eat, feed on, devour, consume, gnaw at, hunt, live off.

price *n.* cost, fee, rate, expense, expenditure, worth, value, amount, charge, bill, figure, toll, sum, sacrifice, outlay.

price *v.* assess, rate, value, evaluate, estimate, offer, cost.

priceless *adj.* valuable, precious, invaluable, inestimable, expensive, costly, dear, beyond price, irreplaceable, rare, treasured, without

price, incalculable, prized, rich; *ant.* cheap, run-of-the-mill.

pricey *adj.* expensive, costly, dear, exorbitant, high-priced, excessive, extortionate, *slang:* steep; *ant.* cheap.

prick *n.* pinhole, perforation, puncture, pang, tap, stab, wound, probing.

prick *v.* stab, pierce, puncture, sting, jab, bite, nip, punch, perforate, penetrate; trouble, pain, stimulate.

prickle *n.* **1.** needle, barb, thorn, spike, spur, point, pin, spine. **2.** sensation, feeling, chill, tingling, tickle.

prickly *adj.* **1.** thorny, brambly, spiny, barbed, bristly, sharp, scratchy, jaggy; *ant.* smooth. **2.** complicated, touchy, intricate, tricky, difficult, involved, troublesome; *ant.* simple. **3.** grumpy, cantankerous, peevish, edgy, touchy, short-tempered, petulant; *ant.* easygoing.

pride *n.* **1.** arrogance, haughtiness, pretension, pretentiousness, conceit, egotism, snobbery, hubris, presumption, smugness, superciliousness, vanity, vainglory, self-love, bigheadedness; *ant.* humility. **2.** self-esteem, self-respect, self-satisfaction, amour-propre, satisfaction, gratification, happiness, delight; *ant.* shame. **3.** (collection of lions) herd, pack, group, drove, bunch.

pride oneself crow, exalt, take pride, pat oneself on the back, flatter oneself, congratulate oneself, revel, preen, vaunt, brag, boast, glory; *ant.* belittle, humble.

priest *n.* minister, cleric, father, clergyman, ecclesiastic, abbé, cleric, vicar, man of God, man of the cloth, holy man, curate, lama.

priestly *adj.* ecclesiastic, pastoral, clerical, episcopal, ministerial, canonical.

prig *n.* puritan, prude, *slang:* goody-two-shoes, goody-goody, old maid; formalist.

priggish *adj.* prim, puritanical, stiff, sedate, prudish, starchy, strait-laced, Victorian, goody-goody (*slang*), narrow-minded, holier-than-thou, self-righteous, stuffy, pedantic, self-satisfied; *ant.* broad-minded, informal.

prim *adj.* proper, tidy, demure, sedate, fastidious, formal, particular; prudish, prissy, puritanical, stiff, strait-laced, fussy, old-maidish, priggish, schoolmarmish; *ant.* broad-minded, informal.

---

primacy *n.* supremacy, superiority, seniority, command, ascendancy, dominance, sovereignty, eminence, paramountcy, preeminence, dominion; *ant.* inferiority.

prima donna diva, star, actress, vocalist, singer.

prima facie *adj.* superficially, seemingly, by all appearances, apparently, at first blush.

primal *adj.* primitive, primordial; fundamental, earliest, initial, original, primeval, primary, prime, first, chief, central, major, greatest, principal; *ant.* later, minor.

primarily *adv.* principally, fundamentally, basically, mainly, chiefly, mostly, generally, essentially, especially; at first, initially, originally.

primary *adj.* **1.** earliest, first, original, primal, primitive, primordial, primeval, initial, introductory, leading, basic, beginning, aboriginal. **2.** fundamental, rudimentary, elementary, essential, underlying, cardinal, chief, basic, central; *ant.* secondary.

primate *n.* monkey, ape, gorilla, chimpanzee, orangutang, gibbon, hominid, hominoid.

prime *n.* peak, zenith, heyday, height, flowering, maturity, spring, springtime, opening, maturity, morning, beginning, perfection, springtide.

prime *v.* prepare, groom, train, coach, brief, fill in (*slang*), cram, charge, inform, notify.

prime *adj.* **1.** principal, basic, fundamental, primary, main, chief, ruling, underlying, original, earliest, leading; *ant.* minor, secondary. **2.** excellent, best, top, superior, first-rate, first-class, quality, highest, selected, choice, preeminent; *ant.* second-rate.

primer *n.* reader, speller, introduction, manual, textbook, hornbook.

primeval *adj.* old, ancient, prehistoric, primordial, early, earliest, first, original, primal, primitive, pristine; *ant.* developed, later, modern.

primitive *adj.* **1.** (said of a human group or culture) simple, rudimentary, crude, Neanderthal, uncivilized, naive, undeveloped, untrained, childlike, untutored, rough, rude, unsophisticated, uncultivated, unrefined; *ant.* advanced, civilized, developed. **2.** ancient, earliest, early, old, primeval, archaic, primordial.

primordial *adj.* first, earliest, original, oldest, basic, prehistoric, ancient, fundamental, elemental, primitive, first-formed, first-made, primal, primeval, pristine; *ant.* developed, later, modern.

prince *n.* monarch, sovereign, ruler, potentate, lord, mogul.

princely *adj.* royal, noble, regal, gracious, majestic, dignified, rich, imperial, sovereign, grand, magnificent, august, munificent, lofty, generous; *ant.* humble, mean.

princess *n.* sovereign, monarch, dauphiness, czarina.

principal *n.* chief, director, dean, leader, star, lead, *slang:* prima donna, top dog; headmaster, head teacher (*Brit.*), superintendent, master, boss, rector.

principal *adj.* leading, main, chief, primary, foremost, first, cardinal, capital, dominant, controlling, essential, paramount, preeminent, key, controlling; *ant.* subordinate, least, lesser, minor.

principality *n.* realm, country, state, territory.

principally *adv.* mainly, mostly, primarily, above all, chiefly, especially, particularly, predominantly.

principle *n.* doctrine, dogma, code, golden rule, canon, dictum; attitude, belief.

principles *n.* scruples, morals, honor, ethics, morality, conscience, integrity; *ant.* corruption, wickedness.

principled *adj.* moral, ethical, upright, scrupulous, righteous, virtuous, honorable, decent, correct, conscientious, high-minded, just, logical, rational, sensible; *ant.* unethical, immoral, unscrupulous.

print *n.* engraving, photograph, photo, picture, lithograph, sketch, reproduction, stamp.

print *v.* publish, produce, issue, run off, stamp, write, imprint, impress, reproduce, engrave.

printing *n.* 1. composition, typography, typesetting, presswork. 2. print, reprint, printout, edition, page, sheet.

prior *adj.* previous, preceding, earlier, foregoing, former, aforementioned, antecedent, anterior, preexistent; *ant.* later.

prior to before, previous to, preceding, earlier than, preparatory to; *ant.* after.

priority *n.* preeminence, precedence, seniority, preference, superiority, supremacy, the lead, privilege, right of way, rank, prerogative.

priory *n.* convent, abbey, monastery, nunnery, cloister, beguinage, religious house.

prison *n.* jail, penitentiary, correctional facility; cell, dungeon, gulag, stalag, cage, lockup, confinement, *slang:* cooler, pokey, slammer, brig, tank.

prisoner *n.* convict, con (*slang*), captive, inmate, jailbird (*slang*), hostage, detainee, internee.

prissy *adj.* strait-laced, prudish, prim, prim and proper, fussy, finicky, fastidious, effeminate, old-maidish, schoolmarmish (*slang*), overnice, squeamish, starchy.

pristine *adj.* first, earliest, virgin, unspoiled, undefiled, original, untouched, uncorrupted, primary, initial, former, primal, primary, primeval; *ant.* developed, later, spoiled.

privacy *n.* solitude, retreat, isolation, seclusion, concealment, secrecy, quietness, quietude, confidentiality, clandestinity, retirement, seclusiveness, privateness, separateness, segregation.

private *n.* enlisted man, enlisted woman, conscript, draftee, infantryman, soldier, GI, dogface (*slang*).

private *adj.* secluded, secret, withdrawn, intimate, exclusive, clandestine, concealed, personal, hush-hush (*slang*), separate, sequestered, confidential, isolated, off the record, own; *ant.* open, public.

in private secretly, privately, personally, in camera.

privateer *n.* 1. pirate, buccaneer, freebooter, sea-robber, corsair, sea-wolf.

private parts genitals, genitalia, privates, reproductive organs, pudenda.

privation *n.* poverty, need, want, destitution, suffering, distress, misery, lack, loss, penury, hardship, indigence, austerity, affliction, neediness; *ant.* affluence, wealth.

privilege *n.* right, entitlement, prerogative, licence, freedom, perquisite, concession, liberty, claim, birthright, franchise, due, advantage.

privileged *adj.* advantaged, indulged, empowered, favored, special, vested, elite, exempted, rich, powerful, influential, well-connected; *ant.* disadvantaged.

privy *n.* bathroom, toilet, *slang:* john, can, head; water closet, lavatory, latrine, loo (*Brit. slang*).

privy *adj.* confidential, secret, intimate, top

secret, off the record, personal, hush-hush (*slang*), private, hidden; *ant.* public.

privy to informed about, aware of, wise to, in on, in the know (*slang*), cognizant of, apprised of; *ant.* unaware.

prize *n.* purse, goal, award, winnings, conquest, desire, aim, reward, trophy, haul (*slang*), stakes, hope, honor, windfall, accolade.

prize *v.* treasure, cherish, value, esteem, revere, reverence, appreciate, hold dear; *ant.* despise, undervalue.

probability *n.* likelihood, chance, chances, prospect, liability, odds, expectation, likeliness, assumption, presumption.

probable *adj.* possible, feasible, likely, plausible, reasonable, credible, odds-on, in the cards, verisimilar, apparent, presumed.

probably *adv.* most likely, perhaps, possibly, in all likelihood, maybe, in all probability, doubtless, likely, as likely as not, presumably.

probation *n.* trial, trial period, test, testing, apprenticeship, proof, examination, initiation, noviciate.

probe *n.* investigation, inquiry, exploration, inquest, research, drill, scrutiny, study, detection.

probe *v.* explore, examine, investigate, look into, search, sift, poke, prod, pierce, go into, query, scrutinize, sound, test, verify.

probity *n.* honesty, honor, equity, fairness, integrity, righteousness, rectitude, worth, uprightness, morality, virtue, fidelity, goodness, sincerity, justice.

problem *n.* **1.** predicament, difficulty, dilemma, complication, jam, trouble, quandary, dispute, disagreement, no laughing matter. **2.** puzzle, riddle, brain-teaser, poser, enigma, question.

problem *adj.* difficult, unruly, uncontrollable, delinquent, froward, perverse, intractable, unmanageable, refractory; *ant.* manageable, well-behaved.

problematic *adj.* debatable, unsure, questionable, moot, puzzling, tricky, uncertain, unestablished, dubious, chancy, doubtful, enigmatic, puzzling, unestablished, unsettled; *ant.* certain.

procedure *n.* **1.** (customary way of doing things) method, fashion, style, routine, mode, system, formula, custom, form, conduct, practice, ground rules, modus operandi. **2.** (series of steps to be taken) plan, course of action, plan of action, scheme, idea, strategy, process.

proceed *v.* **1.** continue, carry on, press on, advance, start, go ahead, set out, progress, move on; *ant.* retreat, stop. **2.** issue, spring, stem, derive, originate, flow.

proceedings *n.* matters, transactions, affairs, action, events, doings, dealings, measures, process, business, procedure, annals, minutes, moves, undertaking.

proceeds *n.* product, results, reward, income, profit, revenue, takings, receipts, return, gain, interest, yield; *ant.* losses, outlay.

process *n.* procedure, transaction, method, course, evolution, manner, operation, progression, step, formation, development, advance, performance, practice, measure.

process *v.* deal with, treat, handle, refine, prepare, convert, alter, transform, digitize, dispose of, fulfill.

processing *n.* preparation, refinement, handling, conversion, datamation.

procession *n.* parade, train, cavalcade, column, march, file, sequence, series, string, cortege, succession, motorcade, cycle, course, run.

proclaim *v.* declare, announce, herald, profess, publish, trumpet, testify, make known, promulgate, enunciate, enounce, advertise, affirm, broadcast, blazon, blaze, show.

proclamation *n.* declaration, announcement, pronouncement, publication, edict, decree, manifesto, pronunciamento, interlocution, notification, notice, ukase.

proclivity *n.* tendency, predisposition, weakness, leaning, bent, bias, inclination, penchant, liability, predilection, liableness, propensity, proneness, disposition, facility; *ant.* disinclination.

procrastinate *v.* postpone, stall, retard, protract, delay, defer, dally, dilly-dally, drag one's feet (*slang*), prolong, play for time, put off, stall, temporize, adjourn, gain time; *ant.* advance, proceed.

procrastination *n.* stalling, deferral, delaying, dallying, dilly-dallying, temporizing, tergiversation.

procreate *v.* engender, breed, produce, reproduce, generate, father, sire, mother, propagate, beget, conceive, spawn.

procreation *n.* reproduction, conception, impregnation, generation, breeding, propagation.

procure *v.* **1.** get, obtain, secure, acquire, appropriate, purchase, gain, bag (*slang*), effect, come by, pick up, win, lay hands on; *ant.* lose. **2.** pimp, pander, prostitute.

procurer *n.* pimp, whoremonger, madam, panderer, procuress.

prod *n.* **1.** push, shove, dig, jab, nudge, poke, boost, elbow. **2.** reminder, stimulus, signal, cue, prompt, catalyst.

prod *v.* **1.** jab, shove, poke, dig, elbow, nudge, prick, push. **2.** incite, motivate, drive, egg on, push, propel, impel, goad, prompt, spur, stimulate, rouse.

prodigal *n.* big spender, wastrel, waster, squanderer, philanderer, profligate.

prodigal *adj.* **1.** reckless, squandering, wasteful, excessive, extravagant, wanton, unsparing, lavish, spendthrift, profligate; *ant.* parsimonious, thrifty. **2.** profuse, bountiful, sumptuous, teeming, superabundant; *ant.* modest, skimpy.

prodigality *n.* **1.** affluence, richness, abundance, bounty, bountifulness, amplitude, plenty, plenteousness, copiousness; *ant.* shortage, deficiency. **2.** wastefulness, waste, wantonness, unthrift, unthriftiness, profligacy, intemperance, lavishness, dissipation, extravagance, recklessness, abandon, excess, squandering, immoderation; *ant.* modesty, thrift.

prodigious *adj.* huge, mammoth, immense, enormous, colossal, tremendous, staggering, stupendous, astounding, fantastic, gigantic, massive, monstrous, unusual, vast.

prodigy *n.* genius, boy *or* girl genius, Wunderkind, whiz kid (*slang*); talent, spectacle, marvel, curiosity, rarity, wizard, sensation.

produce *n.* product, yield, crop, harvest.

produce *v.* **1.** (give birth to) yield, bear, deliver, engender, beget, breed, bring forth, generate. **2.** (bring into being) compose, create, invent, originate, conceive, develop, effectuate, write, design, fabricate, imagine, engender, turn out, devise, manufacture. **3.** (lead to a result) cause, effect, occasion, bring about, begin, start. **4.** (put on as a show) display, present, show, stage, exhibit, demonstrate, mount.

producer *n.* maker, grower, farmer, manufacturer; manager, director, impresario, presenter.

product *n.* **1.** result, outcome, offspring, consequence, fruit, legacy, yield, upshot, effect, issue, returns, spinoff, offshoot. **2.** commodity, artifact, merchandise, work.

production *n.* **1.** making, creation, construction, assembly, fabrication, manufacture, manufacturing, originating, producing, formation; *ant.* consumption. **2.** product, crop, result, stock.

make a production out of make a fuss over, elaborate, exaggerate, overdo, make a mountain out of a molehill, make much ado over nothing.

productive *adj.* fertile, rich, teeming, valuable, fruitful, constructive, profitable, inventive, gainful, beneficial, advantageous, dynamic, effective, prolific, rewarding; *ant.* fruitless.

productivity *n.* yield, output, production, work rate, effectiveness, productiveness, abundance, achievement.

profane *v.* degrade, abuse, defile, debase, desecrate, violate, blaspheme, curse, pervert, misuse, pollute, contaminate, prostitute, vitiate, misemploy; *ant.* revere, honor.

profane *adj.* **1.** secular, worldly, temporal, transitory, transient; *ant.* sacred. **2.** irreverent, sinful, wicked, obscene, blasphemous, impious, sacrilegious, disrespectful, heathen, pagan, godless, ungodly, idolatrous, irreligious, crude; *ant.* reverent, pious.

profanity *n.* obscenity, expletive, curse, swearword, four-letter word; abuse, blasphemy, swearing, sacrilege, irreverence, profaneness, execration, impiety, malediction.

profess *v.* confess, claim, assert, state, vouch, avow, avouch, reveal, acknowledge, confirm, declare, maintain, propound, aver, allege, certify, purport; *ant.* deny, disclaim.

professed *adj.* proclaimed, so-called, self-styled, would-be, avowed, ostensible, purported, declared, self-acknowledged, certified, supposed, pretended, surrogate, manqué.

profession *n.* **1.** occupation, job, line of work, career, vocation, employment, calling, position, business, office, sphere, metier, walk of life. **2.** declaration, confession, affirmation, acknowledgment, claim, assertion, statement, testimony, manifesto, attestation, vow, avowal.

professional *n.* master, pro, expert, authority, virtuoso, specialist, wizard, maestro.

professor *n.* teacher, educator, faculty member, schoolmaster, pedagogue, pundit, savant, sage.

proffer *v.* offer, suggest, present, submit, extend, volunteer, propose, advance, tender, propound, hold out, hand.

proficiency *n.* skill, skillfulness, talent, competence, ability, dexterity, expertise, know-how, finesse, facility, aptitude, mastery, knack, virtuosity, accomplishment; *ant.* clumsiness, incompetence.

proficient *adj.* competent, able, skilled, skillful, adept, talented, expert, capable, efficient, gifted, versed, trained, conversant, clever, qualified; *ant.* clumsy, incompetent.

profile *n.* **1.** silhouette, side view, outline, drawing, sketch, form, figure, shape, portrait, contour, thumbnail sketch. **2.** biography, characterization, review, biopic, study, survey, examination, analysis.

profit *n.* **1.** gain, yield, proceeds, earnings, revenue, receipts, gravy (*slang*), surplus, benefit, interest, winnings, takings, returns, percentage, a fast buck (*slang*); *ant.* loss. **2.** (nonmonetary gain) advantage, return, gain, help; *ant.* disadvantage, setback.

profit *v.* gain, benefit, better, improve, help, advance, aid, avail, line one's pockets, promote, contribute, serve, advantage; *ant.* harm, hinder.

profitable *adj.* **1.** lucrative, rewarding, moneymaking, gainful, commercial, remunerative, cost-effective. **2.** worthwhile, useful, serviceable, productive, utile, advantageous, beneficial, helpful.

profiteer *n.* extortionist, exploiter, racketeer, extortioner.

profiteer *v.* extort, exploit, overcharge, fleece, racketeer, *slang:* make a killing, make a fast buck.

profiteering *n.* racketeering, extortion, exploitation.

profligacy *n.* promiscuity, excess, depravity, corruption, abandon, degeneracy, immorality, extravagance, recklessness, fecklessness, wan-

tonness, waste, wastefulness, dissipation, laxity, prodigality; *ant.* morality, parsimony, thrift, uprightness.

profligate *n.* degenerate, wastrel, squanderer, waster, reprobate, prodigal, spendthrift, libertine, rake, debauchee, roué.

profligate *adj.* corrupt, promiscuous, wanton, wild, wicked, licentious, libertine, degenerate, debauched, immoderate, abandoned, loose, shameless, unprincipled, dissolute; *ant.* moral, upright.

profound *adj.* **1.** (hard to understand) deep, complex, subtle, recondite, difficult, many-sided, esoteric, complicated, abstruse; *ant.* shallow. **2.** (said of one's mind or intellect) learned, wise, intellectual, scholarly, erudite, sage, sagacious, philosophical, discerning, keen, skilled. **3.** (deeply felt) heart-rending, heartfelt, great, intense, extreme, total, utter, thoroughgoing, complete, absolute, extensive, exhaustive, consummate; *ant.* mild.

profoundly *adv.* seriously, greatly, extremely, sincerely, deeply, awfully, intensely, thoroughly, heartily, dreadfully, acutely, abjectly, keenly; *ant.* slightly.

profundity *n.* **1.** depth, pitch, deepness, subtlety, complexity; *ant.* shallowness. **2.** perception, intelligence, insight, wisdom, acumen, acuity, learning, sagacity, perceptiveness, perspicacity, erudition, profoundness, seriousness, perspicuity, strength.

profuse *adj.* **1.** (too generous) extravagant, lavish, excessive, fulsome, immoderate, prodigal, liberal, unstinting; *ant.* sparing. **2.** (occurring in large amounts) abundant, ample, bountiful, overflowing, luxuriant, prolific, copious, plentiful, generous, teeming; *ant.* sparse.

profusion *n.* abundance, wealth, surplus, plethora, multitude, excess, glut, quantity, superfluity, cornucopia, bounty, riot, plenitude, luxuriance, prodigality; *ant.* sparingness, sparsity.

progenitor *n.* ancestor, parent, father, mother, forefather, forerunner, predecessor, precursor, procreator, founder, antecedent, architect, begetter, originator, source, instigator, forebear.

progeny *n.* children, young, offspring, descendants, family, posterity, issue, lineage, race, seed, stock, scions, breed.

prognosis *n.* outlook, projection, forecast, pre-

prognosticate v. forecast, predict, prophesy, harbinger, herald, foreshadow, portend, presage, soothsay, augur, betoken, indicate, divine, foretell, forebode.

prognostication n. prediction, forecast, projection, prophecy, prognosis, speculation, expectation, horoscope, surmise, guess.

program n. 1. agenda, schedule, order of events, lineup, list, listing; procedure, plan, curriculum, syllabus, scheme, project. 2. performance, show, production, broadcast, presentation, transmission.

program v. prearrange, plan, arrange, schedule, formulate, design, map out, engage, book, bill, line up, work out, map out, itemize; brainwash (*slang*).

progress n. 1. motion, progression, advancement, advance, way, passage, headway, journey, course, continuation, procession, circuit; *ant.* standstill, regress. 2. improvement, gain, betterment, promotion, amelioration, advancement, breakthrough, step forward, development, growth, increase; *ant.* deterioration, decline.

progress v. 1. advance, move, travel, proceed, come on, make headway, gather momentum, forge ahead, continue, blossom, grow, mature, develop, increase; *ant.* decline. 2. improve, prosper, better, gain, advance, ameliorate, make strides; *ant.* deteriorate.

progression n. 1. advancement, gain, progress, furtherance, advance, headway; *ant.* decline, deterioration. 2. succession, course, cycle, sequence, series, string, chain, concatenation, order.

progressive adj. 1. rising, advancing, ongoing, growing, developing, escalating, increasing, intensifying, dynamic, accelerating, continuing; *ant.* stagnant. 2. liberal, avant-garde, radical, forward-looking, revolutionary, modern, reformist, advanced, enlightened, enterprising, up-and-coming; *ant.* regressive, reactionary.

prohibit v. 1. forbid, disallow, outlaw, rule out, stop, veto, preclude, ban, bar, prevent, constrain, proscribe, interdict. 2. hinder, obstruct, hamper, impede, restrict.

prohibited adj. forbidden, taboo, banned, barred, disallowed, verboten, proscribed, embargoed, interdicted, vetoed; *ant.* permitted.

prohibition n. ban, bar, obstruction, prevention, forbiddance, negation, embargo, exclusion, injunction, disallowance, constraint, interdiction, proscription, taboo; *ant.* permission.

prohibitionist n. abolitionist, abstainer, teetotaler.

prohibitive adj. forbidding, impossible, suppressive, restrictive, prohibitory, steep, sky-high, repressive, exorbitant, extortionate, restraining, preposterous, proscriptive, prohibiting, excessive, out of sight (*slang*); *ant.* encouraging, reasonable.

project n. enterprise, undertaking, plan, design, conception, idea, venture, job, task, plot, idea, scheme, program, assignment, work, proposal.

project v. 1. protrude, extend, jut, overhang, stick out, stand out, bulge, extrude. 2. throw, hurl, propel, launch, fling, shoot, cast, exert, discharge, transmit.

projectile n. bullet, shell, missile, rocket, grenade, ball, shot, mortar-bomb.

projection n. 1. protrusion, protuberance, prominence, ridge, bulge, overhang, jut, jetty, ledge, eaves, jutty, shelf, sill, outjet, outjut. 2. forecast, prediction, estimate, estimation, calculation, computation, extrapolation, reckoning, outline, plan, map, diagram, blueprint, representation.

proletariat n. masses, mob, lower classes, common people, rabble, commoners, working class, hoi polloi, plebeians, herd, peasants, canaille, commonalty.

proliferate v. multiply, increase, expand, escalate, snowball, mushroom, breed, run riot, burgeon, exuberate; *ant.* dwindle.

proliferation n. increase, escalation, multiplication, expansion, buildup, concentration, intensification, spread, luxuriance, snowballing, extension, mushrooming, duplication, metastasis; *ant.* decrease.

prolific adj. fertile, fruitful, productive, abundant, bountiful, profuse, teeming, rich, copious, generative, fecund, luxuriant, abounding, voluminous, rank; *ant.* infertile, scarce.

prolix adj. verbose, wordy, long-winded, rambling, lengthy, tedious, windy, protracted, prosy, discursive, digressive, fustian, diffuse, tiresome, long, prolonged; *ant.* succinct.

prolixity *n.* verbosity, long-windedness, wordiness, windiness, verbiage, discursiveness, diffuseness, circuitry, logorrhea, rambling, wandering, maundering, tediousness, repetitiousness; *ant.* succinctness.

prologue *n.* introduction, prelude, foreword, preamble, preface, preliminary, exordium, proem, prolegomenon.

prolong *v.* extend, lengthen, drag out, draw out, expand, stretch out, elongate, protract, perpetuate, continue, delay, spin out; *ant.* shorten, contract.

promenade *n.* walk, stroll, constitutional, saunter, airing, meandering, turn, walk-about. (*Brit.*)

promenade *v.* walk, stroll, saunter, parade, swagger, strut, sally forth, perambulate, mosey (*slang*).

prominence *n.* **1.** projection, bulge, bump, mound, lump, protrusion, protuberance, rise, jutting, hump, elevation, height, prominency, promontory, crag. **2.** notability, fame, celebrity, greatness, importance, precedence, distinction, eminence, prestige, reputation, standing, visibility, weight, outstandingness, salience; *ant.* inconspicuousness, unimportance.

prominent *adj.* **1.** protruding, protuberant, extended, bulging, salient, jutting, projecting, outstanding, pronounced, protrusive, obtrusive. **2.** famous, celebrated, well-known, renowned, distinguished, respected, popular, preeminent, eminent, important, weighty, foremost, main, noted; *ant.* unimportant. **3.** conspicuous, obvious, eye-catching, noticeable, remarkable, signal, unmistakable; *ant.* inconspicuous.

promiscuity *n.* immorality, lechery, wantonness, licentiousness, libertinism, depravity, profligacy, debauchery, looseness, permissiveness, promiscuousness, abandon, amorality, dissipation, laxity; *ant.* chastity.

promiscuous *adj.* **1.** mixed, miscellaneous, motley, confused, chaotic, diverse, intermingled, intermixed, disordered, casual, haphazard, jumbled, random, mingled, ill-assorted, higgledy-piggledy, heterogeneous; *ant.* controlled, selective. **2.** lewd, wanton, licentious,

libertine, depraved, debauched, dissipated, immoral, of easy virtue, abandoned, loose, wild, unchaste, dissolute, fast; *ant.* chaste.

promise *n.* **1.** pledge, guarantee, oath, vow, word, word of honor, covenant, commitment, assurance, compact, bond, engagement. **2.** hope, potential, talent, aptitude, capability, ability, capacity, flair.

promise *v.* vow, swear, affirm, pledge, guarantee, assure, warrant, take an oath, vouch, contract, engage.

promising *adj.* encouraging, auspicious, hopeful, reassuring, favorable, bright, gifted, good, propitious, rosy, likely, rising, talented, up-and-coming.

promontory *n.* ridge, cape, point, peninsula, projection, spur, mull, foreland, headland, ness.

promote *v.* advance, endorse, support, back, boost, popularize, lobby for, champion, espouse, push, nurture, recommend, assist, aid, help, *slang:* hype, plug; *ant.* demote, disparage, obstruct.

promotion *n.* **1.** advancement, furtherance, rise, boosting, support, preferment; improvement, development, elevation, cultivation, ennoblement, exaltation; *ant.* demotion, obstruction. **2.** publicity, advertising, *slang:* hype, plugging; campaign, fanfare, propaganda, lobbying, ballyhoo (*slang*), trumpeting; *ant.* disparagement.

prompt *n.* cue, prod, reminder, hint, help, instigation, stimulus, jolt, jog, spur.

prompt *v.* **1.** instigate, stimulate, motivate, cause, provoke, evoke, induce, incite, impel, elicit, inspire, give rise to, occasion, call forth. **2.** (to aid the memory) assist, advise, coach, remind, cue.

prompt *adj.* punctual, on time, early, efficient, quick, rapid, speedy, swift, ready, responsive, immediate, alert, expeditious, instant, instantaneous; *ant.* slow.

prompting *n.* encouragement, persuasion, reminder, influence, suggestion, urging, jogging, admonition, incitement, pressing, pressure, prodding, reminding, hint, protreptic; *ant.* dissuasion.

promptly *adv.* on time, immediately, instantly, punctually, quickly, speedily, swiftly, pronto (slang), directly, posthaste, forthwith, unhesitatingly.

promptness *n.* punctuality, alacrity, promptitude, eagerness, readiness, haste, dispatch, speed, expedition, quickness, willingness, swiftness, alertness, briskness; *ant.* tardiness.

promulgate *v.* publicize, announce, broadcast, declare, decree, publish, spread, proclaim, promote, advertise, issue, notify, circulate, communicate, disseminate, preconize.

promulgation *n.* announcement, declaration, proclamation, publication, publicizing, promulgating, dissemination, communication, issuance.

prone *adj.* **1.** likely, apt, bent, predisposed, inclined, liable, susceptible, tending, vulnerable, given, propense, subject; *ant.* unlikely. **2.** face-down, prostrate, flat, horizontal, full-length, recumbent, procumbent, stretched; *ant.* upright.

prong *n.* spike, tine, spur, tip, fork, projection.

pronounce *v.* enunciate, utter, vocalize, sound, articulate, accent, stress, speak; decree, declare, deliver, declaim, judge, say.

pronounced *adj.* distinct, conspicuous, clear, obvious, striking, noticeable, strong, decided, definite, marked, broad, unmistakable, positive; *ant.* unnoticeable, vague.

pronouncement *n.* announcement, notice, declaration, decree, edict, manifesto, judgment, proclamation, statement, pronunciamento, promulgation, assertion, dictum, notification.

pronunciation *n.* enunciation, articulation, elocution, diction, intonation, inflection, speech, stress, modulation, accent, accentuation.

proof *n.* **1.** evidence, authentication, verification, certification, documentation, confirmation, corroboration, substantiation, attestation. **2.** (process of verifying) trial, attempt, test, testimony, ordeal, demonstration, experiment, examination, scrutiny, assay.

proof *adj.* repellent, impervious, resistant, impenetrable, strong, tight, proofed, treated; *ant.* permeable, untreated.

prop *n.* support, brace, buttress, stay, mainstay, strut, truss, stanchion.

prop *v.* bolster, support, sustain, rest, stand, stay, buttress, maintain, uphold, shore, lean, set, strut, underpin, truss.

propagate *v.* **1.** beget, breed, reproduce, procreate, multiply, proliferate, produce, spawn, generate, engender, increase. **2.** spread, publicize, circulate, broadcast, publish, transmit, diffuse, promote, promulgate, disseminate, proclaim.

propagation *n.* **1.** procreation, reproduction, breeding, generation, multiplication, increase, proliferation, spawning, issuance. **2.** spread, spreading, diffusion, distribution, circulation, dissemination, communication, transmission, promotion, promulgation.

propel *v.* drive, force, shove, thrust, push, launch, shoot, impel, waft, start, send; *ant.* slow, stop.

propensity *n.* proclivity, tendency, inclination, predisposition, bent, bias, aptness, liability, leaning, penchant, foible, proneness, weakness, susceptibility, readiness; *ant.* disinclination.

proper *adj.* **1.** suitable, appropriate, apt, decorous, seemly, right, fit, fitting, becoming, befitting, decent, correct, regular, kosher, legitimate, conventional, accepted, established, orthodox; *ant.* unconventional, irregular **2.** formal, sedate, prudish, prim, prissy, polite, mannerly, punctilious, particular, refined. **3.** personal, own, individual, special, respective; *ant.* common.

property *n.* **1.** possessions, belongings, goods, assets, resources, riches, wealth, means, effects, capital, estate, title, chattels; land, real estate, realty, acres, holdings, freehold, buildings, houses. **2.** characteristic, quality, feature, trait, mark, attribute, idiosyncrasy, hallmark, virtue, peculiarity, distinction, affection.

prophecy *n.* prediction, forecast, revelation, augury, divination, second sight, foretelling, soothsaying, prognosis, prescience, prognostication, vaticination.

prophesy *v.* predict, forecast, foretell, forewarn, divine, augur, foresee, presage, prognosticate, soothsay, vaticinate.

prophet *n.* oracle, seer, soothsayer, clairvoyant, sybil, forecaster, diviner, divinator, augur, foreteller, prognosticator, tipster (*slang*), vaticinator.

prophetic *adj.* foreshadowing, predictive, mantic, prognostic, prescient, presaging, augural, divinatory, fey, oracular, fatidical, sibylline, vaticidal.

propinquity *n.* **1.** proximity, adjacency, closeness, nearness, vicinity, neighborhood; *ant.* remoteness. **2.** kinship, relationship, relation, tie, affiliation, affinity, connection, blood, kindredship, kindredness, consanguinity.

propitiate *v.* soothe, placate, pacify, conciliate, appease, satisfy, reconcile, mollify; *ant.* anger, provoke.

propitiation *n.* appeasement, peacemaking, pacification, pacifying, conciliation, placation, reconciliation, mollification; *ant.* angering, provocation.

propitiatory *adj.* appeasing, assuaging, placative, soothing, reconciliatory, conciliatory, mollifying, pacifying, peacemaking, pacificatory, placatory, propitiative; *ant.* provocative.

propitious *adj.* fortunate, lucky, promising, auspicious, advantageous, rosy, happy, prosperous, benevolent, benign, favorable, bright, encouraging, beneficial, well-disposed; *ant.* unauspicious, ominous.

proponent *n.* advocate, supporter, backer, friend, enthusiast, fan, defender, patron, partisan, apologist, exponent, vindicator, champion, subscriber, propounder; *ant.* opponent.

proportion *n.* **1.** ratio, fraction, percentage, quota, part, measure, share, segment, cut, division, amount. **2.** (pleasing relationship among parts) balance, agreement, harmony, symmetry, congruity; *ant.* imbalance.

proportional *adj.* even, equitable, balanced, fair, just, consistent, commensurate, compatible, proportionate, comparable, correspondent, corresponding; *ant.* disproportionate, unjust.

proportionally *adv.* evenly, proportionately, comparably, correspondingly, commensurately, pro rata; *ant.* disproportionately.

proportions *n.* measurements, dimensions, size, bulk, volume, expanse, breadth, magnitude, capacity, amplitude, extent, range, scope.

proposal *n.* **1.** offer, proposition, bid, tender, proffer, suggestion, recommendation, presentation, overture, motion. **2.** plan, scheme, outline, project, design, program, draft, sketch, platform, manifesto.

propose *v.* **1.** suggest, recommend, submit, bring up, introduce, put forward, lay before, propound, tender, move, enunciate, advance, proffer, invite. **2.** mean, intend, plan, purpose, aim, have in mind, scheme, design.

proposition *n.* suggestion, proposal, recommendation, plan, scheme, project, program, motion, manifesto, tender.

proposition *v.* solicit, ask, approach, accost, come on to (*slang*).

propound *v.* suggest, propose, contend, submit, postulate, present, advance, advocate, put forward, move, set forth, lay down, enunciate; *ant.* oppose.

proprietary *adj.* patented, copyrighted, private, vested.

proprieties *n.* etiquette, protocol, decorum, niceties, social graces, civilities, conventions, decencies, p's and q's.

proprietor *n.* owner, landlord, landlady, deed holder, title holder, freeholder, chatelaine, landowner, possessor.

propriety *n.* **1.** suitability, appropriateness, rightness, correctness, rectitude, fitness, aptness, seemliness, decency, becomingness. **2.** (proper behavior) manners, protocol, politeness, etiquette, respectability, decorum, courtesy, modesty, decency, refinement, delicacy, breeding; *ant.* boorishness.

propulsion *n.* power, drive, momentum, push, thrust, pressure, impulse, impetus, impulsion.

prorate *v.* distribute, allocate, allot, divide.

prosaic *adj.* dull, routine, stale, trite, tame, everyday, flat, mundane, boring, commonplace, quotidian, banal, uninspiring, vapid, pedestrian, matter-of-fact; *ant.* imaginative, interesting.

proscribe *v.* prohibit, boycott, embargo, outlaw, condemn, bar, banish, denounce, excommunicate, reject, doom, censure, exclude, exile, expatriate; *ant.* admit, allow.

proscription *n.* prohibition, taboo, ban, deportation, banishment, boycott, eviction, embargo, excommunication, rejection, ejection, denunciation, condemnation, expulsion, bar, expatriation, damning; *ant.* admission, allowing.

prose *n.* writing, literature, story, fiction, nonfiction, composition.

prosecute *v.* **1.** (carry on an activity) pursue,

execute, engage in, practice, continue, persist, work at, conduct, direct, manage, see through, follow through, carry on, persevere; *ant.* desist. 2. sue, try, indict, litigate, summon, bring suit against, take to court, bring to trial, put on trial, arraign, prefer charges.

prosecution *n.* execution, pursuit, pursuance, persistence, conduct, following through.

proselytize *v.* convert, persuade, win over, spread the gospel, make converts, bring to the fold, bring to God, evangelize, propagandize.

prospect *n.* 1. view, vista, panorama, scene, sight, landscape. 2. outlook, forecast, plan, future, prognosis, presumption, promise, hopes, expectation, calculation, contemplation. 3. candidate, bet; potentiality, possibility, probability, likelihood.

prospect *v.* search, seek, explore, survey, quest, nose, fossick (*Australian*).

prospective *adj.* likely, possible, potential, to-be, coming, destined, future, forthcoming, imminent, soon-to-be, designated, eventual, awaited, intended.

prospectus *n.* plan, outline, scheme, program, platform, syllabus, account, manifesto, list, synopsis, catalog, announcement, conspectus, pamphlet.

prosper *v.* succeed, thrive, advance, boom, flourish, make good, fare well, progress, burgeon, bloom, flower, get on; *ant.* fail.

prosperity *n.* riches, wealth, success, luxury, affluence, fortune, the good life, good times, plenty, well-being, good fortune, prosperousness, ease, boom, weal; *ant.* poverty.

prosperous *adj.* successful, thriving, wealthy, rich, flourishing, affluent, burgeoning, opulent, well-off, well-to-do, in the money (*slang*), moneyed, lucky, booming; *ant.* poor.

prostitute *n.* harlot, whore, streetwalker, wench, call girl, trollop, strumpet, courtesan, fallen woman, *slang:* hooker, working girl, tart, moll, floozie.

prostitute *v.* cheapen, demean, degrade, devalue, profane, pervert, misuse, debase, misapply.

prostitution *n.* vice, whoring, whoredom, harlotry, the oldest profession, street-walking; meretriciousness, degradation, misuse, cheapening.

prostrate *v.* 1. submit, yield, give in, obey, surrender. 2. overthrow, crush, ruin, overwhelm, paralyze, disarm, tire, wear out, exhaust, sap, fatigue, drain, weary, poop (*slang*), shatter.

prostrate *adj.* 1. defenseless, helpless, overcome, powerless, brought to one's knees, prone, paralyzed, spent, reduced, impotent, crushed, worn out, exhausted, procumbent. 2. submissive, obedient, subservient, docile, kowtowing, given in.

prostration *n.* 1. submission, surrender, obeisance, downfall, destruction, docility, abasement; bow, genuflection, kneeling. 2. exhaustion, weariness, weakness, paralysis, paresis.

protagonist *n.* hero, heroine, lead, champion, principal, leader, proponent, advocate, supporter, mainstay, exponent, prime mover, standard-bearer.

protean *adj.* changeable, changing, mutable, variable, multiform, polymorphic, polymorphous, mercurial, volatile, inconstant, many-sided, amebic, ever-changing; *ant.* stable, unchanging.

protect *v.* shield, shelter, defend, guard, safeguard, secure, watch over, cover, preserve, look after, stand guard over, care for, chaperon, escort, screen; *ant.* attack, threaten.

protection *n.* 1. (something that protects) shelter, shield, covering, cover, umbrella, barrier, guard, buffer, screen, aegis, bulwark, armor, refuge, safeguard; *ant.* attack, threat. 2. (state of being protected) surety, care, safety, custody, defense, charge, guardianship, guarding, preservation, safekeeping, protecting, wardship; *ant.* abandonment, neglect.

protective *adj.* sheltering, shielding, defensive, covering, safeguarding, maternal, motherly, fatherly, paternal, insulating, careful, jealous, vigilant, warm, custodial; *ant.* aggressive, threatening.

protector *n.* defender, bodyguard, guardian, guard, safeguard, champion, patron, benefactor, counsel, advocate, father-figure; *ant.* attacker, threat.

protégé *n.* student, disciple, pupil, charge, dependent, ward, discovery; *ant.* guardian, tutor.

protest *n.* complaint, dissent, objection, disapproval, outcry, protestation, remonstrance, demurral, demur, declaration; *ant.* acceptance.

protest *v.* **1.** object, disapprove, oppose, complain, demonstrate, remonstrate, squawk (*slang*), disagree, expostulate, take exception, cry out; *ant.* accept. **2.** maintain, insist, testify, contend.

rotestation *n.* **1.** dissent, protest, outcry, objection, complaint, disagreement, remonstrance, remonstration, expostulation. **2.** affirmation, avowal, statement, pledge, oath, assurance.

protestor *n.* dissident, dissenter, rebel, agitator, demonstrator, remonstrator, remonstrant.

protocol *n.* etiquette, manners, decorum, customs, propriety, politesse, conventions, courtesies, formalities, good form, procedure, p's and q's.

prototype *n.* example, model, type, original, paradigm, standard, precedent, archetype, exemplar, mock-up, pattern, basis.

protract *v.* lengthen, stretch out, extend, prolong, draw out, delay, sustain, keep going, continue; *ant.* shorten.

protracted *adj.* lengthy, long, prolonged, drawn-out, long-drawn-out, interminable, extended, extensive, dragged out, overlong, endless, wearisome; *ant.* shortened, compressed.

protrude *v.* bulge, stand out, extend, stick out, jut, project, point, protuberate, obtrude, pop.

protruding *adj.* prominent, jutting, protuberant, sticking out, protrusive, extrusive, extrusory, protrudent; *ant.* flat, flush.

protrusion *n.* projection, outgrowth, protuberance, lump, bump, bulge, swelling, jut, process.

protuberance *n.* outgrowth, knob, lump, bulge, bump, prominence, projection, swelling, protrusion, bulb, wart, welt, tumor, tuber, prominence.

protuberant *adj.* protruding, bulging, swollen, swelling, jutting, popping, bulbous, prominent, protrudent, proud, protrusive, extrusive; *ant.* flat.

proud *adj.* **1.** dignified, august, noble, honored, great, illustrious, stately, majestic, magnificent, distinguished, grand, eminent, lofty, glorious. **2.** egotistic, conceited, arrogant, self-important, snobbish, *slang:* stuck-up, snotty, snooty; vain, haughty, overbearing, over-

weening, presumptuous, prideful, misproud; *ant.* humble.

provable *adj.* evincible, verifiable, demonstrable, establishable, attestable, confirmable, corroborable, testable; *ant.* unprovable.

prove *v.* substantiate, demonstrate, justify, determine, confirm, attest, ascertain, establish, authenticate, verify, show, evidence, corroborate, check, try; *ant.* discredit, disprove, falsify.

proven *adj.* valid, verified, established, accepted, proved, trustworthy, reliable, dependable, definite, authentic, certified, confirmed, corroborated, undoubted, proved.

provenance *n.* source, origin, birthplace, derivation, provenience.

provender *n.* food, feed, fodder, rations, supplies, provisions, sustenance, victuals, edibles, comestibles, forage, groceries, provand, eatables; eats (*slang*).

proverb *n.* saying, saw, maxim, adage, byword, dictum, aphorism, bromide, precept, gnome.

proverbial *adj.* traditional, legendary, famous, famed, well-known, customary, typical, archetypical, notorious, self-evident, accepted, axiomatic, time-honored, acknowledged, current.

provide *v.* **1.** (give something to someone) supply, furnish, equip, accommodate, grant, replenish, outfit, implement, stock, render, bestow, purvey, give, proffer, provision. **2.** (have as a product) yield, produce, furnish, give, present, afford, impart.

providence *n.* **1.** caution, farsightedness, presence of mind, prudence, discretion, foresight, forethought. **2.** God's will, karma, divine intervention, predestination, predetermination, destiny, fate.

provident *adj.* wise, sagacious, farsighted, thrifty, vigilant, shrewd, economical, cautious, careful, discreet, canny, prudent, wary, well-prepared.

providential *adj.* fortunate, lucky, timely, opportune, propitious, foruitous, heaven-sent, convenient, happy, welcome; *ant.* untimely.

provider *n.* source, supplier, supporter, funder, benefactor, breadwinner, mainstay, giver, donor, wage-earner, angel (*slang*).

providing *conj.* as long as, given that, provided, on condition, on the assumption, with the proviso that, on the understanding that.

province *n.* district, domain, county, department, tract, territory, zone, post, field, colony, charge, sphere, section, orbit, role.

provincial *adj.* rural, small-town, country, local, rustic, bucolic, home-grown, narrow-minded, homespun, limited, parochial, unsophisticated, uniformed, narrow, inward-looking; *ant.* sophisticated, urban.

provincialism *n.* 1. (local expression) dialect, vernacular, localism, regionalism. 2. narrow-mindedness, localism, regionalism, parochialism, factionalism, sectionalism, provinciality, insularity; *ant.* sophistication, catholicity.

provision *n.* 1. plan, arrangement, preparation, prearrangement. 2. reserve, accoutrements, equipment, supplies. 3. requirement, condition, prerequisite, demand, proviso, specification, stipulation, term, clause, caveat.

provisional *adj.* temporary, transitional, interim, stopgap, limited, tentative, conditional, contingent, pro tem, provisory, qualified; *ant.* definite, fixed, permanent.

provisionally *adv.* for the time being, meanwhile, interim, pro tempore, pro tem.

provisions *n.* food, supplies, rations, stores, foodstuffs, groceries, fare, sustenance, victuals, edibles, eatables, comestibles, provender, *slang:* eats, grub.

proviso *n.* requirement, condition, stipulation, rider, qualification, restriction, small print, clause, limitation, provision, reservation, caveat.

provisory *adj.* temporary, tentative, interim, provisional, conditional, qualified; *ant.* definite, fixed, permanent.

provocation *n.* instigation, incitement, inducement, grounds, stimulus, motive, cause, reason, justification, dare, challenge; taunt, affront, insult, injury.

provocative *adj.* 1. confrontational, challenging, incensing, offensive, goading, aggravating; *ant.* pacificatory, tactful. 2. stimulating, suggestive, sexy, seductive, arousing, tantalizing, tempting, erotic, exciting, alluring, inviting.

provoke *v.* 1. vex, anger, infuriate, aggravate, madden, annoy, irritate, incense, chafe, insult, offend, irk, rile, affront, *slang:* gall; *ant.* pacify, please. 2. incite, stir, rouse, arouse, inspire, instigate, motivate, promote, induce,

370

elicit, fire, kindle, occasion. 3. cause, begin, make, produce, generate, give rise to, bring about.

prow *n.* front, nose, head, bow, prore, stem, fore, forepart, cutwater; *ant.* stern.

prowess *n.* ability, command, expertise, expertness, dexterity, skill, mastery, excellence, facility, accomplishment, bravery, aptitude, adroitness, genius; *ant.* clumsiness, mediocrity.

prowl *v.* creep, sneak, roam, lurk, skulk, range, slink, scavenge, stalk, steal, hunt, cruise, patrol, nose, rove.

proximity *n.* closeness, nearness, vicinity, adjacency, neighborhood, proximation, contiguity, juxtaposition, propinquity; *ant.* remoteness.

proxy *n.* representative, surrogate, stand-in, substitute, agent, deputy, delegate, attorney, factor.

prude *n.* puritan, priss, Victorian, old maid, goody-goody (*slang*), Mrs. Grundy, bluenose, spoilsport, stick-in-the-mud (*slang*), wet blanket.

prudence *n.* judgment, caution, wisdom, sagacity, common sense, good sense, thrift, precaution, providence, policy.

prudent *adj.* sensible, discreet, judicious, circumspect, cautious, politic, discerning, wary, frugal, vigilant; *ant.* reckless.

prudish *adj.* prissy, puritanical, strait-laced, demure, proper, stuffy, overmodest.

prune *v.* clip, cut, pare, snip, shape, trim, lop.

prurient *adj.* obscene, lascivious, salacious, indecent, erotic, lewd, lecherous, voyeuristic, concupiscent, lubricious.

pry *v.* 1. force, heave, hoist, jimmy, lift, elevate, raise. 2. meddle, inquire, snoop, search, peek, reconnoiter, seek, peer.

prying *adj.* inquisitive, curious, meddlesome, intrusive, officious, interested, nosy (*slang*).

psalm *n.* hymn, praise, canticle, sacred song, paean.

pseudo *adj.* quasi, counterfeit, pretended, bogus, artificial, mock, imitation, false, fake, spurious; *ant.* genuine.

pseudonym *n.* alias, pen name, stage name, nom de plume, assumed name, false name, moniker (*slang*), anonym.

psyche *n.* consciousness, soul, intellect, self,

psychiatrist *n.* therapist, analyst, psychoanalyst, doctor, shrink (*slang*).

psychic *adj.* 1. mental, intellectual, analytic, psychological. 2. spiritual, telepathic, supernatural, mystic, immaterial.

psychological *adj.* 1. (having to do with the mind or its processes) cognitive, mental, cerebral, rational. 2. (being in the mind) subjective, emotional, subconscious, psychosomatic, unconscious.

psychopath *n.* maniac, lunatic, madman, sociopath.

psychotic *adj.* insane, psychopathic, mad, certifiable, deranged, demented; *ant.* balanced.

puberty *n.* adolescence, pubescence, youth, maturity.

public *n.* community, society, population, citizens, audience, constituency, buyers, market, multitude, supporters, voters, nation, masses. **in public** openly, candidly, plainly.

public *adj.* common, accessible, universal, widespread, communal, civic, social, exposed, prominent, notorious; *ant.* private.

publication *n.* announcement, appearance, disclosure; periodical, issue, book, advertisement, brochure, pamphlet.

publicist *n.* publicity agent, promoter, plugger, advertiser, PR agent.

publicity *n.* notice, notoriety, intelligence, news; advertising, release, report.

publicize *v.* publish, broadcast, declare, promote, spread about, bruit about.

publish *v.* advertise, announce, publicize, proclaim, promulgate; print, issue, distribute, write.

pucker *n.* fold, wrinkle, crease, crinkle, furrow, plait, ruck.

pucker *v.* purse, squeeze, condense, compress, contract, gather, shrivel, ruffle, tighten, crumple.

puckish *adj.* mischievous, frolicsome, naughty, waggish.

pudding *n.* custard, mousse, tapioca, junket, dessert.

puddle *n.* pool, plash, rut.

pudgy *adj.* chubby, fat, plump, chunky, stout, flaccid; *ant.* well-muscled.

personality, spirit, mind, awareness, individuality, anima.

puerile *adj.* juvenile, immature, infantile, irresponsible, childish, petty, trivial, foolish, inane, ridiculous, jejune.

puff *n.* gust, wind, blast, whiff.

puff *v.* 1. flatter, praise, commend, congratulate, admire. 2. inflate, swell, distend, enlarge, fill. 3. pant, exhale, blow, expire.

puffed up arrogant, proud, self-righteous, preening, cocky, high and mighty, too big for one's britches (*slang*), full of oneself, bigheaded; *ant.* modest.

puffy *adj.* 1. windy, breezy, airy, gusty. 2. conceited, pompous, egocentric, mettlesome, egotistic. 3. swollen, distended, livid, inflamed; inflated, expanded, blown, full.

pugnacious *adj.* belligerent, contentious, hostile, irascible, aggressive, petulant, quarrelsome, antagonistic, combative, warlike, feisty, choleric, bellicose; *ant.* easygoing.

puke (*slang*) *v.* vomit, retch, heave, throw up, regurgitate, spew, barf (*slang*).

pull *n.* 1. exertion, effort, force; influence, power, advantage, sway, clout (*slang*). 2. attraction, seduction, magnetism, lure.

pull *v.* 1. tug, drag, haul, strain, wrench, yank. 2. draw up or together, pick, gather, rend. **pull a fast one** (*slang*) swindle, cheat, grift, sting, deceive, *slang*: con, take for a ride; hoodwink.

pull oneself together recover, improve, revive, get one's act together (*slang*).

pulp *n.* flesh, marrow, paste, mush, pap, pomace, curd, poultice.

pulpit *n.* 1. ministry, clergy, priesthood, ecclesiastics. 2. platform, lectern, rostrum, dais, soapbox.

pulsate *v.* beat, throb, palpitate, vibrate, oscillate, quiver.

pulse *n.* beat, rhythm, vibration, pulsation.

pulse *v.* pulsate, throb, tick.

pulverize *v.* 1. grind, granulate, hammer, crush, pestle, pound, flatten, mill. 2. destroy, demolish, annihilate, wreck.

pummel *v.* pound, beat, strike.

pump *v.* 1. tap, draw, supply, drive, push, send. 2. (*slang*) interrogate, question, probe, cross-examine, debrief.

pun *n.* joke, double entendre, play on words, witticism, quip, conceit.

punch v. **1.** strike, hit, knock, jab, clobber, box, slap. **2.** perforate, bore, pierce.

punctilious adj. conscientious, meticulous, precise, exact, strict, scrupulous, ceremonious, exacting, particular, fussy.

punctual adj. prompt, on time, early; ant. tardy.

punctuate v. emphasize, accentuate, stress, underline, point, interject, interrupt.

puncture n. leak, slit, break.

puncture v. perforate, pierce, rupture, prick.

pundit n. expert, authority, master, teacher, maestro, guru.

pungent adj. **1.** sharp, piquant, spicy, strong, tangy; ant. mild. **2.** sarcastic, caustic, incisive, trenchant, biting.

punish v. chasten, correct, reprove, sentence, abuse, castigate, oppress, lecture, chastise, admonish, reprimand.

punishing adj. arduous, strenuous, exhausting, difficult, harrowing, laborious.

punishment n. discipline, retribution, penalty, sanction, penance.

punitive adj. vindictive, penal, retributive, retaliative, punitory.

puny adj. **1.** diminutive, feeble, frail, tiny, undeveloped, meager, slight, dwarfish; ant. formidable. **2.** trivial, inferior, minor, insignificant, unimportant, negligible; ant. important, significant.

pupil n. student, disciple, scholar, protegé, novice, beginner; ant. teacher.

puppet n. **1.** marionette, doll, figurine, moppet, manikin. **2.** figurehead, mouthpiece, dupe, instrument, servant.

purchase v. acquire, buy, procure, obtain, secure, ransom, attain; ant. sell.

purchaser n. customer, client, consumer.

pure adj. **1.** genuine, true, straight, classic, lucid, transparent, clear, limpid, simple, whole, unmixed; ant. adulterated, alloyed. **2.** (free from contamination) clean, sanitary, germ-free, spotless; ant. contaminated. **3.** innocent, immaculate, sinless, virginal, chaste, clean; ant. sullied. **4.** (said of a scholarly discipline) theoretical, speculative, tentative, abstract, philosophical; ant. applied, practical. **5.** absolute, utter, complete, sheer.

purebred adj. pedigreed, thoroughbred, pureblooded; ant. hybrid, mongrel, mixed.

purgation n. purge, catharsis, clarification, evacuation, expulsion.

purgative n. physic, laxative, enema, purge, emetic, evacuant.

purge v. **1.** purify, clear, clarify, cleanse. **2.** eliminate, eradicate, dispose of, remove, extinguish, eject, extirpate, assassinate, exterminate, abolish, liquidate. **3.** excrete, defecate, evacuate.

purify v. **1.** cleanse, disinfect, sanitize, wash, deodorize; ant. contaminate. **2.** (make free from sin) absolve, sanctify, shrive, chasten.

purist n. pedant, quibbler, formalist, classicist, vocabularian.

puristic adj. strict, fastidious, austere, captious, finicky, hypercritical; ant. tolerant.

puritan n. moralist, zealot, fanatic, disciplinarian, prude.

puritanical adj. ascetic, narrow, austere, self-denying, fastidious, severe, zealous; ant. liberal, compromising.

puritanism n. abstinence, propriety, self-denial; ant. indulgence, hedonism.

purity n. innocence, sincerity, naturalness, genuineness, simplicity, chastity, virtue, continence, self-command.

purlieu n. **1.** border, fringe, periphery, boundary, edge. **2.** environment, ambiance, vicinity, area, locale, district, neighborhood.

purloin v. steal, remove, rob, thieve, appropriate, take, swipe, filch.

purport n. significance, meaning, implication, tenor, gist, theme, direction, import.

purport v. declare, allege, indicate, assert, suggest.

purpose n. **1.** goal, end, mission, objective, design, target, resolve, intent, proposal, prospect, ambition, destination. **2.** resolution, tenacity, persistence, grit, perseverance, constancy, determination, confidence.

purpose v. intend, aim, propose, plan.

purposeful adj. **1.** determined, resolute, goal-oriented, persistent, obstinate, stubborn. **2.** worthwhile, profitable, deliberate, useful, helpful.

purposely adv. intentionally, designedly, advisedly.

purse n. pocketbook, pouch, billfold, wallet, money belt, coin purse, receptacle.

purse *v.* pucker, tighten, close, compress, wrinkle, contract.

pursuance *n.* accomplishment, achievement, completion, discharge, execution, performance, prosecution.

pursue *v.* 1. chase, seek, stalk, track (down), hound, shadow, follow. 2. (follow a course of action) continue, persevere, proceed, carry on, practice, perform.

pursuit *n.* chase, hunt, race.

purvey *v.* supply, provision, stock, provide, furnish, victual, serve.

push *v.* 1. (press through or against something) force, thrust, shove, crowd, ram, exert, contend, strain. 2. (move something forward) drive, propel, impel, accelerate, launch, actuate. 3. promote, advance, urge, expedite.

pushover (*slang*) *n.* victim, fool, sucker, dupe, easy mark, patsy (*slang*).

pushy *adj.* assertive, forward, offensive, presumptuous, aggressive, obtrusive, ambitious, arrogant, brash, officious; *ant.* restrained.

pusillanimous *adj.* cowardly, feeble, fearful, craven, timid, wimpy (*slang*); *ant.* assertive, courageous, ambitious.

pussyfoot (*slang*) *v.* avoid, evade, equivocate, dodge, sidestep, hedge.

put *v.* place, lay, set, seat, settle; establish, install, quarter, fix; deposit, invest, insert, embed, plant; *ant.* take, remove.

put up 1. build, erect, construct, fabricate. 2. bet, speculate, gamble, wager, put

one's money on. 3. (provide a bed for) house, shelter, entertain, make welcome.

putative *adj.* conjectural, hypothetical, suppositional, presumed, alleged, reputed, assumed, imputed.

put-down (*slang*) *n.* insult, criticism, retort, rejoinder, slur.

put-on (*slang*) *n.* deception, pretense, device, trick, hoax, joke, fake.

put-on *adj.* feigned, simulated, pretended, calculated, staged.

putrid *adj.* rotten, decayed, putrified, corrupt.

putter *v.* loiter, dawdle, poke, fritter.

put-upon *adj.* imposed on, abused, exploited, harassed, harried, henpecked, ill-used, inconvenienced, overworked, persecuted, beset.

puzzle *n.* 1. perplexity, vexation, doubt, disorientation, hardship; *ant.* clarity, certitude, lucidity. 2. problem, dilemma, question, mystery, issue, riddle, conundrum, oracle, secret; *ant.* solution, answer, development.

puzzle *v.* 1. perplex, obscure, confuse, frustrate, mystify, complicate, bewilder. 2. marvel, wonder, be mystified.

puzzlement *n.* puzzle, confusion, doubt, perplexity, wonder.

puzzling *adj.* 1. obscure, mysterious, curious, ambiguous, inexplicable, enigmatic, peculiar, abstruse, bizarre; *ant.* clear, accountable, fathomable. 2. difficult, circuitous, equivocal, intricate, complex, profound.

pylon *n.* 1. arch, entrance, door, span. 2. pillar, post, shaft, column, tower.

quack *n.* fraud, swindler, impostor, charlatan, cheat, mountebank.

quack *adj.* fraudulent, counterfeit, bogus, fake; *ant.* genuine.

quaff *v.* drink, gulp, swig, imbibe, swill, guzzle, *slang:* knock back, toss off.

quagmire *n.* 1. swamp, bog, mire, marsh, quicksand. 2. predicament, dilemma, quandary, plight, impasse, imbroglio.

quail *v.* cower, recoil, blanch, back away, shrink, tremble, flinch.

quaint *adj.* 1. charming, picturesque, old-fashioned. 2. unusual, odd, eccentric, weird, droll, absurd, whimsical.

quake *v.* shake, shudder, tremble, quiver, convulse, vibrate.

qualification *n.* 1. competence, aptitude, capability, suitability, fitness. 2. limitation, condition, criterion, reservation, stipulation, restriction, fine print, proviso, caveat.

qualifications *n.* ability, competence, accomplishment, certification, training, credentials, portfolio, experience, background.

qualified *adj.* 1. limited, conditional, restricted, contingent, with reservations; *ant.* unreserved. 2. competent, capable, accomplished, experienced, trained, proficient, able.

qualify *v.* 1. limit, restrain, reduce, temper. 2. fulfill, fit, suit, measure up, pass muster; *ant.* fail, be unsuited.

quality *n.* 1. characteristic, trait, feature, aspect, attribute, property, peculiarity, distinction. 2. excellence, merit, worth, value, caliber, standing, importance.

qualm *n.* apprehension, fear, doubt, hesitation, misgiving, reluctance, uncertainty, anxiety, twinge, pang.

quandary *n.* problem, predicament, dilemma, entanglement, mess, confusion, impasse, corner, hole, jam; *slang:* kettle of fish, hornet's nest.

quantity *n.* amount, capacity, measure, portion, sum, total, aggregate, volume, weight.

quarantine *v.* isolate, segregate, detain, separate, place apart, restrain, hospitalize.

quarantine *n.* isolation, segregation, detention, separation.

quarrel *n.* argument, dispute, disagreement, contention, spat, bickering, squabbling, fracas, fuss; *ant.* agreement, harmony.

quarrel *v.* argue, fight, bicker, differ, disagree, dispute, object, squabble, fall out, be at loggerheads; *ant.* agree.

quarrelsome *adj.* argumentative, combative, antagonistic, belligerent, cantankerous, petulant, irascible, fractious, cross, peevish, testy; *ant.* peaceable, placid.

quarry *n.* 1. mine, shaft, vein, lode. 2. prey, game, victim, prize, target.

quarter *n.* 1. neighborhood, area, territory, region, sector, section, zone. 2. mercy, compassion, clemency, pity, forbearance.

quarter *v.* 1. divide, cleave, dismember, cut up. 2. lodge, accommodate, shelter, board, house, put up, billet.

quarters *n.* lodgings, accommodation, residence, habitation, billets; apartment, flat, house, pied-à-terre.

quash *v.* 1. annul, cancel, invalidate, nullify, void. 2. (put down an uprising) crush, subdue, quell, suppress.

quasi *adj.* pseudo, would-be, self-styled, imitation, surrogate, counterfeit, mock, manqué.

quaver *n.* quiver, tremor, vibration, shake, warble, tremble.

quaver *v.* quake, quiver, tremble, vibrate, warble, shudder, shake, oscillate.

quay *n.* dock, pier, harbor, wharf, jetty.

queasy *adj.* 1. nauseated, sick, squeamish,

Q

queen   dizzy, faint, ill, woozy. **2.** troubled, uncomfortable, uneasy, restless, edgy.

queen *n.* monarch, empress, goddess, ruler, sovereign, beauty, grande dame, prima donna.

queenly *adj.* dignified, majestic, royal, sovereign, regal, gracious.

queer *adj.* odd, abnormal, atypical, bizarre, deviant, extraordinary, peculiar, curious, strange, weird, mysterious, inexplicable, funny.

quell *v.* **1.** allay, mollify, pacify, assuage, calm, alleviate, soothe. **2.** (put down an uprising) subdue, crush, quash, extinguish, defeat, suppress, vanquish.

quench *v.* **1.** satisfy, sate, slake, appease. **2.** stifle, smother, put out, dampen, douse, extinguish.

querulous *adj.* petulant, cantankerous, fretful, peevish, irritable, ill-tempered, critical, carping, complaining, whining, crabby, grouchy, waspish; *ant.* cheerful, placid.

query *n.* inquiry, question, doubt, suspicion.

query *v.* ask, question, doubt, suspect, challenge, investigate, probe, inspect; *ant.* accept.

quest *n.* mission, expedition, journey, pilgrimage, crusade, pursuit, search.

question *n.* **1.** inquiry, query, interrogation, inquisition, catechism, inquest; *ant.* answer, solution, reply. **2.** topic, subject, theme, problem, thesis.

question *v.* **1.** ask, inquire, interview, probe, interrogate, query, grill, pump. **2.** doubt, challenge, impugn, dispute, suspect.

questionable *adj.* **1.** doubtful, borderline, arguable, debatable, dubious, uncertain, equivocal, iffy (*slang*). **2.** disreputable, suspect, suspicious, unreliable; slang: sleazy, fishy, shady; *ant.* aboveboard.

questioner *n.* inquirer, examiner, inquisitor, interrogator, doubter, skeptic.

quibble *n.* evasion, equivocation, subterfuge, dodge, prevarication, sophism; cavil, hairsplitting, nit-picking.

quibble *v.* equivocate, carp, cavil, split hairs, evade, prevaricate.

quick *adj.* **1.** rapid, swift, fast, brisk, nimble, fleet, precipitate, expeditious, winged, prompt, hurried; *ant.* slow. **2.** clever, shrewd, alert, keen-witted, smart, adroit, astute, per-

ceptive, sharp, discerning, responsive; *ant.* dull, slow.

quicken *v.* **1.** speed, accelerate, pick up speed, expedite, hasten, hurry. **2.** animate, rouse, energize, enliven, excite, revive, stimulate, incite; *ant.* dull, retard.

quickly *adv.* rapidly, swiftly, briskly, expeditiously, fast, hastily, hurriedly, promptly, pronto.

quick-tempered *adj.* volatile, mercurial, irritable, irascible, excitable, petulant, quarrelsome, snappy, testy, touchy; *ant.* dispassionate, cool.

quick-witted *adj.* clever, astute, alert, bright, witty, perceptive, penetrating, intelligent, shrewd; *ant.* dull, slow, stupid.

quiescent *adj.* dormant, inactive, latent, still, abeyant, resting, tranquil, calm, serene, placid, quiet; *ant.* active.

quiet *n.* silence, tranquillity, calm, stillness, peace, repose; *ant.* noise, disturbance.

quiet *v.* calm, subdue, restrain, compose, tranquilize, pacify, placate, appease, hush, lull, allay, mollify; *ant.* excite, agitate.

quiet *adj.* silent, mute, dumb, hushed, inaudible; peaceful, serene, still, tranquil, untroubled, pacific; *ant.* noisy.

quilt *n.* bedspread, bedcover, comforter, coverlet, duvet.

quintessence *n.* essence, embodiment, core, heart, marrow, soul, nub, spirit, kernel, sum and substance.

quintessential *adj.* archetypical, consummate, definitive, ultimate, ideal, prototypical.

quip *n.* jest, witticism, wisecrack, bon mot, one-liner.

quip *v.* jest, retort, wisecrack, ridicule, taunt, jeer.

quirk *n.* idiosyncrasy, mannerism, peculiarity, eccentricity, peccadillo, foible, caprice, vagary, fetish, oddity, turn.

quisling *n.* traitor, betrayer, turncoat, fifth columnist, Judas, collaborator, Benedict Arnold, apostate; *ant.* patriot.

quit *v.* **1.** leave, depart, vacate, go away, retire, decamp. **2.** cease, desist, discontinue, end, stop, renounce, relinquish, abandon.

quite *adv.* **1.** completely, totally, entirely, wholly. **2.** really, truly, positively, actually.

quitter *n.* shirker, dropout, deserter, malingerer, slacker, defeatist.

quiver *n.* tremor, shiver, shake, convulsion, palpitation, vibration, oscillation, shudder, spasm.

quiver *v.* shake, tremble, vibrate, shudder, convulse, flutter, oscillate, palpitate.

quixotic *adj.* chivalrous, romantic, idealistic, utopian, visionary, starry-eyed, fanciful, impractical.

quiz *n.* test, examination, exam, questionnaire, investigation, catechism.

quiz *v.* question, examine, interrogate, investigate, grill, pump, sound out.

quizzical *adj.* 1. teasing, mocking, sardonic, satirical, whimsical, derisive, coy, droll, arch,

elliptical. 2. puzzled, nonplussed, perplexed, baffled, curious, inquiring.

quondam *adj.* preceding, former, erstwhile, past, extinct.

quota *n.* percentage, proportion, allocation, share, allowance, ration, slice, cut.

quotation *n.* excerpt, passage, selection, citation, reference, extract, quote.

quote *v.* cite, refer to, repeat, echo, recite, retell, attest.

quotidian *adj.* daily, commonplace, customary, routine, everyday, habitual, ordinary, regular, mundane.

quotient *n.* result, outcome, remainder, computation.

R

rabble *n.* mob, masses, riffraff, hoi polloi, populace, horde, proletariat, peasantry, commoners; *ant.* elite, aristocracy, nobility.

rabble-rouser *n.* agitator, troublemaker, mischief-maker, gadfly, firebrand, incendiary, fomenter, ringleader, demagogue.

Rabelaisian *adj.* lusty, lewd, indecent, vulgar, coarse, bawdy, blue, risqué, ribald, scabrous.

rabid *adj.* 1. frenzied, hysterical, maniacal, furious, berserk, mad, violent, deranged, raging, wild. 2. zealous, fanatical, dedicated, ardent, flaming.

race *n.* 1. ancestry, descent, lineage, blood, kindred, people, stock, strain, clan, tribe, house, issue, progeny. 2. competition, contest, derby, sprint, scramble, chase, pursuit, quest.

race *v.* run, speed, hurry, dash, tear, chase, sprint, scamper, hasten, fly, hie; contend, vie, compete.

racial *adj.* ethnic, national, tribal, parental, ancestral, genetic, inherited.

raciness *n.* 1. vigor, vitality, liveliness, spirit, excitement, spice. 2. indecency, lewdness, suggestiveness, indelicacy, prurience, pornography.

rack *n.* frame, framework, lattice, scaffold, skeleton, grating, bracket, stand, shelf; holder, receptacle, perch.

rack *v.* torment, agonize, torture, afflict, persecute, oppress.

racket *n.* 1. uproar, din, disturbance, riot, commotion, to-do, pandemonium, clamor, tumult. 2. fraud, swindle, graft, con game, shakedown, scam, deception, trick.

racy *adj.* 1. spirited, zesty, vigorous, animated, saucy, lively, sprightly, playful, witty, exhilarating. 2. risqué, ribald, erotic, bawdy, salacious, lewd, blue, indecent, prurient, suggestive, smutty.

radiance *n.* brilliance, incandescence, splendor, luminosity, shine, luster, refulgence; *ant.* dullness.

radiant *adj.* 1. aglow, shining, sparkling, resplendent, sunny, illuminated, gleaming, lustrous; *ant.* dull, drab. 2. ecstatic, exultant, delighted, overjoyed, elated, blithe, merry, rapturous.

radiate *v.* shine, gleam, illuminate, irradiate, emanate, beam, emit, send out, diffuse, spread, scatter, disseminate, issue, proliferate, ramify.

radical *n.* extremist, leftist, rebel, militant, insurgent, insurrectionist, revolutionary, terrorist.

radical *adj.* fundamental, profound, thorough-going, basic, intrinsic, deep-rooted, extreme.

rag *(slang)* *v.* bother, nag, annoy, scold, upbraid, castigate.

rage *n.* 1. anger, fury, wrath, ire, fury, vehemence; frenzy, conniption *(slang)*, passion, tantrum. 2. *(slang)* style, fad, fashion, vogue, craze, mania.

rage *v.* rant, rave, inveigh, fulminate, storm, explode, rampage, seethe, fume, chafe.

ragged *adj.* tattered, frayed, ripped, rent, shabby, unkempt, threadbare, worn out.

raging *adj.* furious, frenzied, incensed, irate, infuriated, seething, fuming, fulminating.

raid *n.* invasion, attack, onslaught, strike, sortie, foray, bust, seizure, incursion, despoliation.

raid *v.* attack, invade, maraud, pillage, assail, storm, sack, despoil, rifle, forage, loot, plunder, ransack.

rail *v.* rant, rage, fume, thunder.

rail at denounce, castigate, upbraid, harangue, lambaste, chastise, criticize, vituperate, abuse, revile, ridicule, inveigh against.

railing *n.* fence, banister, balustrade, parapet, paling.

raiment *n.* clothing, attire, garb, garments.

rain *n.* shower, cloudburst, deluge, downpour, torrent, squall, drizzle, sprinkle, mist.

rain v. 1. shower, pour, drizzle, sprinkle, mist, drop, fall, teem. 2. (give abundantly) heap, shower, lavish, expend.

raise n. increase, advance, promotion, gain, augmentation, expansion.

raise v. 1. lift, heighten, upraise, hoist, elevate, boost, mount, jack up. 2. build, construct, erect, rear, fabricate, fashion. 3. nurture, rear, nurse, support, suckle, nourish, foster, cultivate, breed, parent, propagate. 4. (acquire funds) collect, gather, procure, accumulate, appropriate, borrow.

rake n. libertine, lecher, playboy, philanderer, gigolo, Don Juan, Casanova, sensualist, roué, profligate, Lothario.

rake up scrape up, scratch together, accumulate, gather, amass.

rakish adj. 1. smart, dashing, chic, debonair, jaunty, flashy, raffish, dapper, natty. 2. dissolute, depraved, loose, immoral, debauched, lecherous.

rally n. 1. gathering, convention, assembly, jamboree, conference, meeting. 2. revival, recovery, rebound, rebirth, renaissance.

rally v. 1. muster, assemble, convene, mobilize, convoke. 2. (improve the spirits of) encourage, urge, inspirit, cheer, buoy, embolden, hearten. 3. make a comeback, surge, recover, revive, rejuvenate, perk up, recuperate, improve, pull oneself together.

ram v. beat, pound, batter, butt, collide, hit; stuff, jam, pack, cram, tamp.

ramble n. tour, trip, walk, excursion, hike, traipse, stroll, peregrination, perambulation.

ramble v. 1. stroll, saunter, roam, meander, straggle, traipse, peregrinate. 2. twist, branch off, fork, stray, turn, wind; digress, babble, maunder, drivel, run off at the mouth.

rambling adj. incoherent, disjointed, confused, disconnected, discursive, wordy, prolix, longwinded, drawn-out; ant. terse, pithy.

rambunctious adj. 1. boisterous, loud, noisy, clamorous; ant. quiet. 2. unruly, stubborn, headstrong, refractory, defiant, intractable, froward, uncontrollable, ornery, mulish, perverse; ant. compliant, obedient, docile.

ramification n. consequence, upshot, result, development, offshoot, outgrowth, subdivision, fork, extension, sequel.

ramp n. rise, incline, slope, grade, hill, inclination, acclivity.

rampage n. uproar, ferment, disturbance, furor, tumult, tempest, rage, fury, storm.

rampant adj. 1. excessive, wild, ungovernable, riotous, unrestrained, egregious, flagrant, unbridled, wanton. 2. widespread, epidemic, rife, prevalent, unchecked, universal.

rampart n. fence, embankment, barricade, wall, bulwark, earthwork, parapet, palisade.

ramshackle adj. dilapidated, broken-down, derelict, unsafe, crumbling, decrepit, rickety, jerry-built, shabby, flimsy, tacky, unsteady; ant. solid, stable.

rancid adj. putrid, rank, rotten, foul, fusty, stale, sour, bad, tainted, gamy; ant. fresh, fragrant, sweet.

rancor n. hostility, resentment, bitterness, hatred, spite, ill will, acrimony, animosity, malice, venom, spleen, enmity.

rancorous adj. vindictive, bitter, hostile, spiteful, resentful, virulent, splenetic.

randy adj. amorous, aroused, lustful, hot, lecherous, lubricious, lascivious, concupiscent, slang: horny, turned-on.

random adj. chance, arbitrary, aimless, indiscriminate, haphazard, fortuitous, purposeless, stray, unplanned, accidental; ant. deliberate, systematic.

at random randomly, arbitrarily, fortuitously, indiscriminately, haphazardly, unsystematically.

range n. distance, reach, limits, expanse, scope, parameters, confines, bounds, radius, breadth, compass.

range v. 1. arrange, rank, order, align, classify, array. 2. traverse, roam, stroll, wander, ramble, explore, scour, cruise, search, reconnoiter.

rangy adj. thin, slender, slim, gangly, lanky, long-legged, leggy, rawboned, angular.

rank n. 1. row, line, column, file, string. 2. standing, caste, status, grade, class, degree, order, sphere, station; eminence, distinction.

rank v. arrange, position, order, sort, class, classify, place, align, marshal, array, range, dispose, locate.

rank adj. 1. lush, wild, dense, tropical, fertile, rich, luxuriant, proliferating, green, thick; ant. arid, sparse. 2. foul, smelly, gamy, putrid,

rankle rancid, stinking, offensive, nauseating, reeking, sour; *ant.* fragrant, sweet, fresh.

rankle *v.* irritate, peeve, rile, irk, bother, mortify, embitter; fester, chafe, gall, gnaw.

ransack *v.* **1.** search, comb, rifle, rummage, scour, strip. **2.** maraud, pillage, ravage, plunder, loot, gut, despoil, raid, sack, depredate.

rant *n.* harangue, rhetoric, bombast, bluster, tirade, storm, swagger, fustian, balderdash, nonsense, cant, rubbish.

rant *v.* rave, fume, bellow, bluster, spout, declaim, babble, holler, clamor, rail, vociferate, let off steam (*slang*).

rap (*slang*) *n.* **1.** blame, responsibility, punishment, reprimand, rebuke, censure, castigation, animadversion. **2.** talk, discussion, bull *or* rap session, parley, dialogue, colloquy.

rap *v.* **1.** tap, knock, strike, hit, cuff, whack. **2.** (*slang*) talk, chat, converse, discuss, commune, confabulate. **3.** (*slang*) criticize, castigate, animadvert, lampoon, assail, ridicule, pillory.

rapacious *adj.* greedy, predatory, avaricious, plundering, grasping, marauding, covetous, usurious, wolfish, ravenous.

rape *n.* violation, ravaging, defilement, desecration, spoliation, molestation, assault, abuse.

rape *v.* violate, assault, molest, debauch, deflower, plunder, despoil, force, ravish.

rapid *adj.* fast, quick, speedy, hurried, prompt, brisk, swift, fleet, headlong, precipitate, mercurial; *ant.* leisurely, sluggish.

rapine *n.* robbery, theft, looting, marauding, plunder, pillage, sacking, spoliation, despoilment, depredation, ransacking.

rapport *n.* compatibility, affinity, bond, link, sympathy, empathy, harmony.

rapprochement *n.* reconciliation, reunion, reconcilement, agreement, detente, démarche.

rapscallion *n.* rogue, knave, cad, cur, scoundrel, scamp, reprobate, ne'er-do-well, scallywag, blackguard.

rapt *adj.* captivated, gripped, held, absorbed, enraptured, enthralled, enchanted, fascinated, engrossed, intent, spellbound.

rapture *n.* ecstasy, delight, bliss, euphoria, happiness, joy, exaltation, rhapsody, cloud nine (*slang*).

rapturous *adj.* rhapsodic, delighted, euphoric, happy, exalted, overjoyed, enthusiastic, ravished, transported, ecstatic, joyful, blissful.

rare *adj.* exceptional, singular, extraordinary, uncommon, unusual, odd, out-of-the-ordinary, remarkable, unique; *ant.* common, usual.

rarefied *adj.* private, exclusive, esoteric, select, refined, high, lofty, sublime, exalted.

rarely *adv.* infrequently, barely, atypically, seldom, occasionally, once in a blue moon, sparingly, now and then; *ant.* frequently, often.

raring *adj.* impatient, eager, willing, ready, keen, itching, longing, avid.

rarity *n.* **1.** scarcity, uncommonness, sparseness, infrequency, dearth, shortage. **2.** curio, treasure, pearl, gem, find, wonder.

rascal *n.* rogue, knave, devil, scoundrel, scamp, rapscallion, miscreant, ne'er-do-well, reprobate.

rash *n.* epidemic, outbreak, plague, succession, spate, wave, eruption, flood.

rash *adj.* unthinking, imprudent, madcap, careless, brash, foolhardy, reckless, precipitate, impetuous, impulsive, hasty, indiscreet; *ant.* cautious, responsible.

rasp *v.* grate, scratch, rub, irritate, grind, scour, abrade, excoriate.

rasping *adj.* croaking, gravelly, rough, hoarse, grating, gruff, scratchy, harsh, husky, croaky, raucous, strident; *ant.* mellifluous.

rate *n.* **1.** class, rank, status, degree, position, standing. **2.** price, cost, value, worth, duty, fee, tariff, tax.

rate *v.* assess, rank, judge, estimate, evaluate, grade, class, determine, appraise, evaluate, consider, reckon, assay.

rather *adv.* **1.** preferably, sooner, more, first, before. **2.** somewhat, slightly, moderately, kind of, a bit, relatively, pretty, tolerably.

ratification *n.* acceptance, confirmation, sanction, approval.

ratify *v.* approve, endorse, sanction, confirm, corroborate, legalize, validate, authorize, affirm, authenticate; *ant.* reject, veto.

rating *n.* classification, position, rank, status, standing, designation, assessment, grade, sort, order.

ratio *n.* proportion, share, percentage, balance, correlation, rate, correspondence, quotient, relationship.

ration n. allowance, allotment, portion, dole, helping, measure, part, share, quota, provision.

ration v. mete, allocate, apportion, allot, distribute, issue, dispense, supply, dole, budget, restrict, conserve, save.

rational adj. 1. intellectual, cognitive, mental, deductive, analytical. 2. sensible, wise, judicious, logical, sagacious, realistic, knowing; lucid, coherent, sober, sane, balanced.

rationale n. basis, grounds, reasons, motivation, explanation, pretext, logic, raison d'être, theory, hypothesis.

rationalize v. excuse, explain away, justify, vindicate, account for, elucidate, reason out, extenuate, resolve, whitewash.

rations n. provisions, supplies, stores, food, groceries, provender, commons.

rattle n. clatter, racket, din, clangor, noise, hubbub.

rattle v. 1. chatter, prattle, prate, babble, gush. 2. disconcert, fluster, unnerve, confuse, disturb, discompose, discomfit, faze, frighten, shake, scare, upset.

rattle off enumerate, list, itemize, recite, reel off.

raucous adj. 1. hoarse, grating, rasping, husky, harsh, rough, rusty, strident, gruff. 2. loud, noisy, boisterous, uproarious, cacophonous, clamorous, rowdy, turbulent.

ravage v. devastate, raze, destroy, lay waste, plunder, ruin, sack, gut, loot, pillage, wreck, spoil, depredate.

rave v. fume, rage, roar, rant, thunder, storm, declaim, harangue, ramble, splutter, fulminate.

rave about praise, extol, boost, enthuse, magnify.

ravenous adj. 1. (extremely hungry) starving, famished, gluttonous, wolfish, insatiable, devouring, voracious. 2. (extremely desirous) greedy, predatory, rapacious, grasping, avid.

ravine n. gully, gorge, canyon, gulch, arroyo, valley, gap, break, crevice, crevasse.

raving adj. crazy, frantic, irrational, berserk, manic, wild, frenzied, delirious, hysterical, furious.

ravish v. 1. enchant, bewitch, captivate, attract, allure, enthrall, draw, mesmerize, hold, magnetize, hypnotize, fascinate. 2. rape, seduce, deflower, abduct.

raw adj. 1. uncooked, rare, bloody, fresh, undone. 2. natural, untreated, rough, crude, uncut, unrefined, unprocessed, unstained, untanned; ant. processed, refined. 3. nasty, cold, bleak, biting, chill, windy. 4. inexperienced, callow, green, immature, unseasoned, untried.

in the raw (slang) naked, nude, bare, unclothed, in the buff (slang).

ray n. beam, flash, glimmer, spark, shaft, flicker, glint; hint, trace, speck, bit, scintilla.

raze v. destroy, ruin, level, obliterate, demolish, flatten, efface, erase, expunge, extirpate.

re prep. regarding, about, in reference to, respecting, concerning, touching, apropos.

reach n. stretch, distance, span, extent, scope, sweep, compass, range, grasp, jurisdiction, dominion, mastery.

reach v. 1. (said of a goal or destination) attain, arrive at, get to, come to, enter, make. 2. join, touch, span, stretch.

react v. respond, reply, reciprocate, answer, counter, requite, offset; behave, function, act.

reaction n. 1. reply, response, answer, acknowledgment, rejoinder, feedback, retort, reciprocation. 2. recoil, reversal, regression, backlash, rebound; repercussion, consequence.

reactionary n. conservative, diehard, rightwinger, archconservative, tory, mossback, Bourbon; ant. progressive, liberal.

read v. interpret, understand, decipher, construe, infer, see, comprehend.

readable adj. clear, comprehensible, understandable, legible, decipherable, intelligible, plain, distinct; ant. illegible.

readily adv. eagerly, willingly, voluntarily, freely; promptly, quickly, speedily.

readiness n. 1. preparation, preparedness, vigilance, alertness, wariness. 2. aptitude, adroitness, proficiency, dexterity, facility, ease.

reading n. 1. interpretation, recital, recitation, rendition, enactment, performance, version, treatment. 2. excerpt, passage, section, installment, quotation, extract, brief, digest.

ready v. prepare, arrange, complete, devise, contrive, provide for.

ready adj. 1. (mentally prepared) prompt, instant, quick, fast, sharp, alert, wide-awake, immediate; willing, eager, inclined, disposed,

set, prepared, keyed up, psyched up (*slang*). **2.** (easily available) accessible, convenient, near, handy.

get ready prepare, arrange, plan, rehearse, gird one's loins (*slang*).

ready-made *adj.* prepared, instant, prefabricated, ready-to-wear, store-bought, off-the-rack.

real *adj.* **1.** physical, objective, actual, material, tangible, sensible, solid; *ant.* imaginary, hypothetical. **2.** genuine, true, authentic, bona fide, original; *ant.* counterfeit, spurious.

realistic *adj.* **1.** (resembling something real) representational, lifelike, true-to-life, photographic, naturalistic. **2.** objective, practical, sober, unsentimental, pragmatic, no-nonsense, unromantic, down-to-earth, level-headed, sensible; *ant.* idealistic, romantic.

reality *n.* actuality, fact, truth, verity, authenticity, realism, verisimilitude, genuineness, palpability, materiality.

realization *n.* comprehension, understanding, awareness, consciousness, recognition, insight, appreciation, cognition.

realize *v.* **1.** complete, bring to fulfillment, perfect, make good, actualize. **2.** understand, recognize, apprehend, recognize, see, perceive, learn, appreciate, discern. **3.** profit, gain, reap, earn, obtain.

really *adv.* absolutely, positively, truly, surely, certainly, undoubtedly, indeed, verily, assuredly, genuinely.

realm *n.* domain, jurisdiction, region, territory, zone, area, department, sphere, kingdom.

reap *v.* collect, gather, acquire, get, secure, obtain, win, gain, realize, harvest, garner, mow, crop, cut.

reapportion *v.* redistribute, divide, allot, distribute, redistrict, resection.

rear *n.* buttocks, derrière, rump, bottom, behind, backside, tail, posterior, hindquarters, *slang;* butt, buns.

rear *v.* **1.** (rise to a higher level) raise, lift, erect, fabricate, build, elevate, hoist, boost. **2.** (take care of and educate children) raise, bring up, foster, parent, nurse, nurture, train, educate, cultivate.

rearrange *v.* alter, reposition, shift, adjust, reset, revamp, reorder, rework, vary.

reason *n.* **1.** motive, purpose, cause, intention, rationale, idea, design, aim, end. **2.** excuse, rationalization, alibi, explanation, defense, apologia. **3.** reasoning, logic, cognition, thought, intellection, ratiocination, conceptualization, cogitation.

reason *v.* **1.** think, contemplate, deliberate, cogitate, reflect, analyze, conclude, deduce, infer, solve, work out, syllogize. **2.** (have a constructive dialogue) discuss, discourse, demonstrate, point out, debate, argue, justify, contend, dispute.

reasonable *adj.* **1.** (said of persons) rational, intelligent, level-headed, equitable, moderate, broad-minded, liberal, temperate, sensible, sober, unbiased, unprejudiced; *ant.* intolerant, biased. **2.** (said of arguments, theories, or ideas) credible, considered, sound, plausible, reasoned, thoughtful, sagacious; *ant.* ill-considered, unwise. **3.** (said of costs) cheap, inexpensive, reduced, fair.

reasoning *n.* thought, logic, analysis, cogitation, deliberation, argument, explication, exposition.

reassure *v.* hearten, comfort, rally, nerve, bolster, encourage, inspirit, brace.

rebel *n.* dissenter, malcontent, nonconformist, heretic, revolutionary, seditionist, insurgent, mutineer, secessionist, maverick, apostate, schismatic.

rebel *v.* defy, disobey, mutiny, revolt, dissent, secede, resist, combat, oppose; *ant.* obey.

rebellion *n.* revolt, revolution, dissent, defiance, insubordination, uprising, mutiny, insurrection, overthrow, coup, putsch.

rebellious *adj.* disobedient, unmanageable, defiant, difficult, unruly, ungovernable, obstinate, refractory, recalcitrant, contrary, insubordinate; *ant.* obedient, submissive.

rebirth *n.* reincarnation, resurrection, rejuvenation, renewal, revival, reactivation, renaissance, resurgence.

rebound *n.* return, ricochet, bounce, recoil, recovery, kick.

rebound *v.* recover, rally, improve, recoup, bounce back, boomerang, return.

rebuff *n.* rejection, refusal, snub, denial, repulse, slight, brushoff, check, cold shoulder.

381

rebuff *v.* discourage, reject, repulse, slight, spurn, snub, refuse, deny, resist, oppose, turn away.

rebuild *v.* renovate, restore, remodel, remake, reconstruct, refurbish.

rebuke *n.* reproach, condemnation, admonition, castigation, blame, censure, chastisement, tongue-lashing, dressing-down, reprimand; *ant.* compliment, praise.

rebuke *v.* scold, reprimand, chide, reprove, admonish, berate, upbraid, reprehend, blame, castigate, censure, chastise; *ant.* compliment, praise.

rebut *v.* counter, retort, refute, discredit, negate, invalidate, overturn, defeat, disprove, explode, quash.

rebuttal *n.* reply, answer, response, comeback; refutation, negation, invalidation, disproof, confutation.

recalcitrant *adj.* uncooperative, defiant, contrary, willful, insubordinate, refractory, stubborn, intractable, disobedient; *ant.* amenable, docile.

recall *n.* memory, recollection, remembrance, reminiscence, retention.

recall *v.* **1.** remember, recollect, recapture, summon, evoke, bring to mind, review, retrace; *ant.* forget. **2.** revoke, countermand, retract, repeal, abjure, rescind.

recant *v.* withdraw, rescind, retract, disavow, forswear, renounce, repudiate, disown, disclaim, abjure, abrogate, deny.

recapitulate *v.* review, summarize, recount, recap, reiterate, repeat, restate, sum up.

recede *v.* fade, dwindle, shrink, withdraw, retreat, ebb, regress, wane, subside, abate, evanesce; *ant.* advance, proceed.

receipt *n.* **1.** acquisition, receiving, taking, acceptance, reception, accession, acquiring, admittance. **2.** voucher, cancellation, slip, stub, chit.

receive *v.* **1.** acquire, gain, procure, get, take, come by, collect, gather, reap, earn; endure, suffer, undergo, experience, bear, sustain. **2.** welcome, greet, accommodate, entertain, host, usher in, shelter.

recent *adj.* late, modern, current, contemporary, up-to-date, new, novel, fresh; *ant.* dated, old.

382

receptacle *n.* holder, container, repository, vessel, reservatory, box, well, bin, basket.

reception *n.* **1.** greeting, welcome, salutation, salute, acknowledgment. **2.** reaction, response, treatment, welcome, acceptance.

receptive *adj.* amenable, interested, responsive, approachable, open, accessible, sympathetic, welcoming, favorable, friendly, available.

recess *n.* **1.** intermission, respite, pause, hiatus, interlude, break; cessation, stoppage, halt. **2.** indentation, dent, niche, embrasure, hollow, nook, cleft, alcove.

recessive *adj.* receding, regressive, retrograde, declining, diminishing, ebbing, shrinking; latent, dormant, idle, passive.

recipe *n.* instructions, directions, prescription, ingredients, procedure, method, system, technique, formula.

reciprocal *adj.* mutual, shared, corresponding, equivalent, complementary, interchangeable, convertible, interdependent, correlative.

reciprocate *v.* respond, reply, retaliate, requite, match, equal; exchange, barter, trade, swap.

recital *n.* **1.** concert, performance, show, musical, presentation, portrayal. **2.** narration, report, story, account, recapitulation, relation, account, history.

recitation *n.* narrating, speaking, elocution, reading, soliloquizing, recounting, recital, discourse, talk, speech, lecture.

recite *v.* **1.** declaim, relate, deliver, perform, speak, rehearse, repeat. **2.** itemize, enumerate, detail, particularize, recount.

reckless *adj.* irresponsible, negligent, imprudent, careless, foolhardy, thoughtless, harebrained, madcap, daredevil, hasty, precipitate, unthinking, headlong; *ant.* calculating, careful.

reckon *v.* **1.** count, calculate, tally, compute, estimate, conjecture. **2.** esteem, assess, appraise, regard, consider, judge, class, rate. **reckon on** trust, rely, depend on, bank on, count on, lean on, expect, hope for.

reckoning *n.* **1.** estimation, appraisal, calculation, evaluation, assessment, computation. **2.** retribution, vengeance, retaliation, requital, satisfaction, atonement.

reclaim *v.* salvage, regain, retrieve, recover, recondition, enhance, remodel, develop, restore, redeem, rescue.

recline *v.* lounge, rest, lie, stretch out, loll, sprawl.

recluse *n.* hermit, monk, solitaire, anchorite, ascetic, eremite.

reclusive *adj.* withdrawn, isolated, cloistered, secluded, solitary, monastic, hermetical, ascetic, sequestered, retiring; *ant.* convivial, social.

recognition *n.* 1. recollection, recall, remembrance, memory, awareness, avowal, perception, enlightenment, identification. 2. acceptance, acknowledgment, notice, appreciation, attention, citation.

recognize *v.* acknowledge, remember, recall, see, understand, notice, know, realize, perceive, accept, concede, appreciate, allow, place, spot.

recoil *v.* shrink, flinch, falter, quail, rebound, boomerang, ricochet, resile.

recollect *v.* recall, remember, reminisce, remind, call up, call to mind, conjure up; *ant.* forget.

recollection *n.* remembrance, memory, recall, reminiscence, impression, retrospection.

recommend *v.* 1. support, sanction, commend, advocate, extol, compliment, applaud, celebrate, praise, acclaim; *ant.* disapprove, veto. 2. suggest, prescribe, urge, counsel, advise.

recommendation *n.* advocacy, endorsement, blessing, praise, approval, sanction, commendation; *ant.* disapproval, veto.

recompense *n.* remuneration, compensation, reparation, restitution, satisfaction, indemnity, amends, requital, payment.

recompense *v.* remunerate, compensate, redress, reward, satisfy, redeem, indemnify, repay, reimburse, requite.

reconcile *v.* conciliate, settle, resolve, square, rectify; harmonize, placate, pacify, propitiate, appease.

reconciliation *n.* settlement, agreement, rapprochement, compromise, conciliation, appeasement, harmony, pacification, detente, understanding, accommodation; *ant.* estrangement.

recondite *adj.* obscure, difficult, involved, complicated, mysterious, esoteric, arcane, occult, mystical, hidden, concealed; *ant.* obvious.

recondition *v.* fix, renovate, overhaul, repair, restore, remodel, refurbish, renew, revamp.

reconnaissance *n.* exploration, investigation, surveillance, patrol, probe, survey, scouting, survey, examination, inspection, scan.

reconnoiter *v.* investigate, examine, scrutinize, explore, probe, survey, inspect, patrol, scout.

reconstruct *v.* recreate, reassemble, rebuild, renovate, restore, remodel, regenerate, refashion, reform.

record *n.* documentation, transcript, file, log, minutes, archives, paper trail.

record *v.* register, write down, put down, mark down, jot down, set down, take down, transcribe, note, file, inscribe, log.

recount *v.* relate, tell, report, describe, recite, enumerate, portray, depict, narrate.

recoup *v.* retrieve, recover, regain; refund, repay, reimburse, remunerate, make good, redeem, requite, satisfy, indemnify.

recourse *n.* alternative, option, resort, choice, remedy, expedient, means.

recover *v.* 1. salvage, rescue, retrieve, reclaim, recoup, recapture, regain, repossess, redeem; *ant.* forfeit, lose. 2. improve, rally, revive, mend, heal, convalesce, come around, pull through, recuperate; *ant.* worsen.

recovery *n.* 1. convalescence, recuperation, revival, rebirth, renaissance, resurgence, rejuvenation, cure, resuscitation. 2. retrieval, restoration, reclamation, indemnification, reparation, compensation, return, recouping, reimbursement.

recreation *n.* amusement, entertainment, sport, pastime, play, leisure activity, diversion, hobby, distraction, relaxation.

recruit *n.* novice, beginner, rookie, apprentice, greenhorn, learner, proselyte, trainee, conscript, neophyte, novitiate.

recruit *v.* draft, muster, impress, induct, enroll, mobilize, proselytize, supply, replenish.

rectify *v.* fix, repair, remedy, amend, correct, redress, right, put to right, straighten, reform, square.

rectitude *n.* righteousness, integrity, decency, probity, honor, equity, morality, scrupulousness, honesty, principle, verity *ant.* fecklessness.

recumbent *adj.* prone, prostrate, supine, flat,

horizontal, lounging, reclining, sprawling; *ant.* erect, upright.

recuperate *v.* recover, convalesce, get better, mend, improve, revive, rally, recoup, regain, retrieve, reclaim, get back on one's feet. *ant.* worsen.

recurrent *adj.* recurring, repetitive, frequent, periodic, regular, habitual, cyclical, chronic.

recycle *v.* reprocess, reconstitute, salvage, reuse, reclaim, save.

red-blooded *adj.* lusty, vigorous, lively, hearty, strong, robust, virile, vital; *ant.* anemic.

redden *v.* blush, color, suffuse, flush, crimson, rubefy.

redeem *v.* **1.** salvage, regain, rescue, ransom, emancipate, free; trade in, convert, claim, swap, exchange. **2.** make good, fulfill, satisfy, succeed, come through; *ant.* renege, forfeit.

redemption *n.* **1.** atonement, salvation, liberation, deliverance, fulfillment. **2.** amends, compensation, reparation, ransom, reclamation, recovery.

red-hot *adj.* **1.** burning, hot, heated, sizzling, scorching. **2.** (*slang*) popular, trendy, successful, voguish, newest, latest, hip (*slang*).

redolent *adj.* aromatic, perfumed, sweet-smelling, scented, fragrant, odorous.

redoubtable *adj.* strong, formidable, mighty, invulnerable, indomitable, impregnable, commanding, fearsome.

redound *v.* lead to, cause, result in, eventuate, contribute to, yield, affect, influence, determine.

redress *n.* compensation, atonement, recompense, amends, restitution, satisfaction, correction, expiation, rectification, payment.

redress *v.* rectify, correct, reform, remedy, mend, amend, repair, square, expiate, avenge, revenge.

reduce *v.* **1.** lessen, diminish, cut down, decrease; curtail, abbreviate, abridge, condense, summarize, truncate; *ant.* boost, increase. **2.** degrade, debase, shame, humiliate, cheapen. **3.** defeat, conquer, overcome, subjugate, subdue, crush, immobilize.

reduction *n.* loss, decrease, cut, diminution, shrinkage, deduction, curtailment, constriction, attenuation; abridgment, condensation, summary; *ant.* increase, augmentation.

redundancy *n.* **1.** repetition, iteration, wordiness, verbosity, circumlocution. **2.** superfluity, surplus, excess, overabundance, profusion, glut, overkill.

redundant *adj.* **1.** repetitious, wordy, verbose, padded, prolix, pleonastic, tautological, windy, diffuse; *ant.* concise. **2.** excessive, unnecessary, superfluous, inordinate, inessential, wasteful; *ant.* essential, necessary.

reel *v.* stagger, lurch, totter, stumble, wheel, roll, pitch, flounder.

refer *v.* **1.** (have as a subject) concern, regard, relate, involve, pertain to, deal with, include. **2.** (use as a source of information) mention, allude, ascribe, attribute, credit, charge, assign, cite. **3.** recommend, direct, send to, transfer, relegate, consign, deliver.

referee *n.* judge, arbiter, arbitrator, umpire, mediator, adjudicator.

referee *v.* judge, arbitrate, adjudicate, mediate, umpire.

reference *n.* **1.** allusion, mention, hint, implication intimation, suggestion, citation, note. **2.** referral, recommendation, direction, consignment, assignment; testimonial, attestation, voucher, good word.

refine *v.* cultivate, civilize, polish, enhance, improve, perfect, hone, temper, purify, rarefy, elevate.

refined *adj.* sophisticated, cultivated, urbane, well-mannered, courtly, gracious, genteel, gentlemanly, ladylike, polite, polished, discriminating; *ant.* coarse, rude, vulgar.

refinement *n.* **1.** purification, cleansing, clarifying, distillation. **2.** sophistication, cultivation, breeding, erudition, scholarship, learning, enlightenment, subtlety, lore.

reflect *v.* **1.** contemplate, think, consider, ruminate, ponder, muse, mediate, deliberate, mull. **2.** mirror, echo, return, bounce, reverberate, resound.

reflection *n.* **1.** thought, consideration, contemplation, introspection, rumination, musing, deliberation, study, meditation, cogitation. **2.** image, impression, appearance, likeness; shadow, picture, echo, reproduction, copy.

reflective *adj.* absorbed, meditative, ruminative, thoughtful, pensive, pondering, introverted, introspective, deliberative, nostalgic.

reflex *adj.* unthinking, mechanical, automatic, spontaneous, knee-jerk (*slang*), habitual.

reform *n.* correction, improvement, rectification, amelioration, amendment, betterment, change.

reform *v.* revise, amend, reorganize, remodel, reconstruct, rearrange, repair, transform, ameliorate, rectify, better, improve, correct, cure.

refractory *adj.* stubborn, obstinate, recalcitrant, intractable, headstrong, mulish, uncooperative, disobedient, willful, unruly; *ant.* cooperative, obedient.

refrain *v.* abstain, forbear, eschew, avoid, renounce, cease, desist, stop, quit, swear off.

refresh *v.* stimulate, invigorate, freshen, revitalize, brace, rejuvenate, revive, restore, inspirit; *ant.* exhaust, tire.

refreshing *adj.* stimulating, invigorating, bracing, rejuvenating, energizing; different, fresh, original, new, novel; *ant.* stale.

refuge *n.* asylum, haven, retreat, sanctuary, shelter, harbor, protection, stronghold, fortress, hideaway.

refugee *n.* emigré, exile, expatriate, displaced person, renegade, defector, fugitive.

refulgent *adj.* radiant, shining, resplendent, bright, beaming, lustrous, lambent, brilliant.

refund *n.* rebate, reimbursement, repayment, remuneration, compensation, settlement, retribution.

refund *v.* rebate, reimburse, return, repay, restore, pay back, indemnify, recoup, compensate, make amends.

refurbish *v.* renovate, overhaul, remodel, refit, recondition, repair, mend, restore, retrofit.

refusal *n.* rejection, denial, veto, rebuff, negation, repudiation, dissent, objection; *ant.* acceptance.

refuse *n.* waste, trash, garbage, rubbish, litter, dross, remains, residue, leavings.

refuse *v.* repudiate, spurn, reject, deny, veto, decline, rebuff, scorn, demur; *ant.* accept.

refute *v.* counter, disprove, confute, rebut, deny, negate, discredit, gainsay, contend.

regal *adj.* kingly, queenly, royal, sovereign, majestic, noble, magnificent, stately, proud.

regard *n.* 1. respect, esteem, honor, favor, veneration, approval, appreciation, fondness, affection, attachment. 2. look, gaze, glance, view, notice, attention, consideration, reflection, thought, judgment.

regard *v.* 1. admire, venerate, respect, esteem, value; *ant.* despise, hate. 2. consider, surmise, suspect, fancy, deem, conceive, think. 3. observe, notice, view, look, watch, stare at, peruse, ogle, attend, mark, note; *ant.* disregard.

regarding *prep.* on the subject of, concerning, about, with reference to, with regard to, in the matter of, touching, apropos, in respect of.

regardless *adj.* indifferent, negligent, heedless, rash, uncaring, remiss, inattentive, nonchalant, unconcerned, careless, lax; *ant.* attentive, heedful.

regardless *adv.* nevertheless, anyhow, anyway, nonetheless, in any case, no matter what.

regenerate *v.* 1. (give new vigor to) revive, invigorate, refresh, rejuvenate, inspirit, renew, restore, reanimate. 2. resurrect, recreate, re-form, rebuild, reconstruct, reconstitute, reproduce.

regime *n.* government, administration, leadership, command, management, system, rule, reign, dynasty, sovereignty.

regiment *v.* systematize, order, classify, rank, standardize, regulate.

region *n.* (geographical place) territory, area, district, province, zone, quarter, section, district, locality. 2. (area of influence or concern) realm, domain, sphere, arena, interest, field, turf (*slang*).

regional *adj.* sectional, areal, localized, provincial, parochial, limited.

register *n.* ledger, file, record, roster, annals, diary, log, list, chronicle, archives, catalog, memorandum, schedule, almanac.

register *v.* 1. record, check in, enroll, enter, enlist, log, list, file, chronicle. 2. show, display, express, disclose, manifest, betray, reveal, exhibit, reflect.

registered *adj.* pedigreed, purebred, thoroughbred, pure-blooded, full-blooded.

registrar *n.* clerk, chronicler, administrator, secretary, recorder, annalist, archivist, cataloguer.

regress *v.* revert, relapse, lapse, degenerate, retrogress, wane, return, backslide, deteriorate; *ant.* progress.

regressive *adj.* reverse, reactionary, backward, retrogressive; *ant.* progressive.

regret *n.* remorse, self-reproach, grief, sorrow, bitterness, disappointment, ruefulness, lamentation, shame, compunction, contrition, penitence, repentance.

regret *v.* be sorry for, have qualms about, lament, mourn, rue, grieve, bemoan, deplore, repent, *slang:* cry over spilt milk, kick oneself.

regretful *adj.* sorry, apologetic, sorrowful, remorseful, rueful, sad, conscience-stricken, mournful, ashamed, repentant, penitent, contrite.

regrettable *adj.* unfortunate, sad, unlucky, distressing, deplorable, shameful, sorry, lamentable, disappointing, unhappy, pitiable, woeful; *ant.* fortunate, happy.

regular *adj.* conventional, customary, usual, routine, standard, ordinary, orthodox, traditional.

regulate *v.* **1.** control, rule, command, manage, direct, legislate, supervise, monitor, govern, oversee, run, superintend. **2.** adjust, arrange, methodize, classify, systematize, put in order, standardize, coordinate.

regulation *n.* requirement, law, statute, rule, control, ordinance, decree, precept, edict.

regurgitate *v.* vomit, throw up, disgorge, regorge, retch, spew, puke, lose one's lunch (*slang*).

rehabilitate *v.* reform, mend, save, recondition, redeem, reintegrate, rebuild, renew, restore, reclaim.

rehash *n.* reworking, rewrite, rearrangement, restatement.

rehash *v.* rework, rewrite, reshuffle, rearrange, refashion, rejig, restate.

rehearsal *n.* practice, dry run, recitation, recital, reading, run-through, dress rehearsal.

rehearse *v.* practice, drill, test, prepare, ready, review, repeat, train.

reign *v.* rule, govern, command, prevail, dominate, be supreme.

reimburse *v.* compensate, repay, refund, remunerate, rebate, indemnify, recompense, requite.

rein *n.* **1.** restraint, hold, brake, control, restriction, check, curb, overcheck, checkrein. **2.** harness, bridle.

draw in the reins slow down, halt, cease, end.

give free rein to allow, authorize, permit, give carte blanche, condone, cut one's apron strings.

386

keep a rein on control, manage, have authority over, check, restrict, keep on a short leash.

reincarnation *n.* rebirth, incarnation, reanimation, transmigration.

reinforce *v.* strengthen, supplement, bolster, steel, augment, fortify, support, buttress; *ant.* undermine, weaken.

reinforcements *n.* support, reserves, backup, auxiliaries.

reinstate *v.* restore, return, reestablish, reappoint, reinstall.

reiterate *v.* restate, reword, resay, recapitulate, retell, repeat, iterate; reaffirm, emphasize, repeat for emphasis.

reiteration *n.* recapitulation, restatement, repetition, reaffirmation, redundancy.

reject *v.* **1.** refuse, repudiate, decline, renounce, deny, disallow, rebuff, spurn, veto, cut (*slang*); *ant.* accept, welcome. **2.** discard, cast off *or* out, throw out, eliminate, cut, exclude, jettison, expel, dump; *ant.* retain.

rejection *n.* dismissal, refusal, repudiation, renunciation, elimination, rebuff, snub, brushoff (*slang*), exclusion, Dear John letter (*slang*).

rejoice *v.* celebrate, revel, make merry, delight, glory, enjoy, joy, exult, jubilate.

rejoicing *n.* celebration, revelry, merrymaking, festivity, jubilation, delight, happiness, joy, cheer, elation, gaiety, gladness, exultation.

rejoin *v.* respond, reply, answer, quip, retort, riposte.

rejoinder *n.* reply, response, answer, retort, repartee, quip, comeback, counterclaim, riposte, countercharge, counter.

rejuvenate *v.* revitalize, reanimate, renew, rekindle, reinvigorate, restore, recharge, refresh, regenerate.

relapse *n.* reversion, recidivism, weakening, retrogression, recurrence, backsliding, setback, lapse, worsening, deterioration.

relapse *v.* regress, deteriorate, retrogress, backslide, degenerate, revert, weaken, lapse, worsen, succumb.

relate *v.* **1.** tell, describe, report, narrate, recount, recite, retell, chronicle, detail, impart. **2.** (have to do with) connect, associate, correlate, coordinate, ally.

relate to be associated with, be connected

with, have a relation to, pertain to, affect, be joined with, concern, bring to bear upon, correspond to, tie in with (*slang*).

related *adj.* interconnected, affiliated, linked, kin, kindred, associated, joint, linked, accompanying, akin, correlated, concomitant; *ant.* different, unconnected.

relation *n.* **1.** relative, kin, kinsman, kinswoman, sibling, cousin. **2.** similarity, connection, affiliation, relationship, bond, bearing, interdependence, propinquity, link, correlation, affinity, consanguinity.

relations *n.* **1.** connections, contact, relationship, intercourse, affairs, interaction, dealings, communications, doings, rapport, associations. **2.** family, relatives, kindred.

relationship *n.* association, bond, connection, similarity, rapport, link, correlation, parallel.

relative *n.* relation, kin, family member, blood relation, next of kin, sibling, kinsman, kinswoman.

relative *adj.* related, associated, connected, dependent, contingent, interrelated, corresponding, reciprocal; relevant, applicable, germane, pertinent, apropos.

relatively *adv.* rather, somewhat, comparatively, quite, fairly.

relativity *n.* dependence, pertinency, relevancy, interdependence, comparability, proportionality, interconnection, contingency.

relax *v.* **1.** (become less formal) rest, loosen up; *slang:* wind down, let one's hair down, let it all hang out. **2.** (control less rigidly) moderate, ease, loosen, mitigate, relieve, remit, diminish, lower, abate, reduce, lessen, slacken; *ant.* intensify, tighten.

relaxation *n.* **1.** leisure, rest, refreshment, amusement, enjoyment, pleasure, distraction, recreation, entertainment, fun; *ant.* tension. **2.** reduction, lessening, easing, loosening, letup; *ant.* intensification.

relaxed *adj.* easygoing, calm, collected, composed, unflappable, nonchalant, cool, tranquil, serene, placid, mild, insouciant; laidback (*slang*); *ant.* edgy, nervous, stiff, tense, uptight.

relay *n.* broadcast, transmission, communication, dispatch.

relay *v.* transmit, communicate, spread, broad-

cast, deliver, transfer, send, send forth, carry, pass on.

release *n.* liberation, discharge, freedom, emancipation, enfranchisement, acquittal, deliverance, exoneration, liberty, absolution, delivery, manumission; *ant.* detention.

release *v.* free, discharge, liberate, loose, disengage, acquit, deliver, extricate, undo, emancipate, enfranchise, dispense, disseminate, unfetter, excuse, exempt; *ant.* check, detain.

released *adj.* announced, stated, broadcast, made public, published.

relegate *v.* **1.** remove, banish, eliminate, expel, dismiss, demote, deport, dispatch, downgrade, eject, exile, expatriate, transfer. **2.** assign, commit, entrust, confide, delegate, refer, consign.

relent *v.* ease, slacken, relax, capitulate, drop, give in, weaken, melt, soften, yield, acquiesce.

relentless *adj.* incessant, unrelenting, persistent, ruthless, cruel, remorseless, unabated, unyielding, pitiless, merciless, uncompromising, fierce, harsh, implacable, unstoppable; *ant.* lenient, sparing.

relevance *n.* connection, significance, pertinence, importance.

relevant *adj.* related, appropriate, fitting, germane, material, admissible, pertinent, congruous, suited, applicable, apposite, apt; *ant.* beside the point.

reliability *n.* dependability, trustworthiness, constancy, loyalty, faithfulness, sincerity, devotion, honesty, steadfastness.

reliable *adj.* sound, trustworthy, dependable, loyal, trusty, faithful, solid, safe, stable, unfailing, staunch, predictable, sure, true; *ant.* doubtful, suspect.

reliance *n.* dependence, credence, faith, trust, belief.

relic *n.* fragment, trace, remnant, vestige, scrap; memento, remembrance, token, keepsake, souvenir.

relief *n.* **1.** aid, help, assistance, support; alleviation, respite, solace, break, a load off one's mind, release, mitigation, remission, remedy, relaxation, ease. **2.** frieze, embossment, projection, high relief, bas-relief, low relief, hollow relief, intaglio.

relieve *v.* **1.** lessen, assuage, alleviate, soothe, comfort, allay, divert, free, ease, soften, dimin-

387

relieved ish, mitigate; *ant.* aggravate, intensify. **2.** take the place of, replace, dismiss, discharge, throw out; substitute for, take over from, stand in for; exempt, release.

relieved *adj.* **1.** comforted, solaced, consoled, reassured, allayed, soothed, relaxed, put at ease, appeased, placated, alleviated, mollified. **2.** replaced, dismissed, released, discharged, supplanted, superseded, succeeded, substituted, interchanged, exchanged.

religion *n.* belief, faith, theology, creed, persuasion, sect, cult, denomination; devotion, spirituality, morality, religiosity, faithfulness, devoutness.

get religion (*slang*) become converted, believe, reform, be born again, change.

religious *adj.* **1.** holy, ethical, spiritual, moral, ecclesiastical, clerical, theological, canonical, divine, sacred, sacrosanct; *ant.* ungodly. **2.** careful, scrupulous, thorough, methodical, minute, conscientious, exact, fastidious, meticulous, punctilious, rigorous, rigid; *ant.* lax.

relinquish *v.* surrender, hand over, cede, abdicate, discard, release, resign, abandon, forgo, renounce, repudiate, desert, forsake, quit; *ant.* keep, retain.

relish *n.* gusto, enjoyment, appetite, love, liking, appreciation, penchant, fancy, partiality, fondness, predilection.

relish *v.* enjoy, savor, like, revel in, lap up, appreciate, fancy, prefer.

reluctance *n.* disinclination, aversion, hesitancy, unwillingness, recalcitrance, dislike, distaste, repugnance; *ant.* eagerness.

reluctant *adj.* unwilling, averse, disinclined, unenthusiastic, indisposed, hesitant, loath, recalcitrant, grudging; *ant.* eager.

rely *v.* depend, trust, lean, count, bank, swear by, bet, bank, reckon, have faith in.

remain *v.* stay, survive, endure, last, prevail, abide, stand, dwell, persist, bide, continue; *ant.* depart, go, leave.

remainder *n.* rest, surplus, balance, residue, excess, dregs, vestiges, leavings, residuum.

remaining *adj.* surviving, outstanding, left, left over, residual, lingering, persisting, unused, abiding, unspent, extant.

remains *n.* remnants, carcass, corpse, body, debris, remainder, pieces, residue, scraps,

traces, fragments, leavings, crumbs, relics, ashes.

remake *v.* change, transform, revise, alter, make over.

remark *n.* comment, mention, statement, assertion, opinion, notice, observation, declaration, utterance.

remark *v.* mention, state, comment, declare, say, mark, note, notice, observe, see, perceive, regard, reflect, speak.

remarkable *adj.* amazing, exceptional, striking, phenomenal, outstanding, rare, wonderful, surprising, extraordinary, singular, distinguished, uncommon, unusual, odd; *ant.* average, commonplace.

remedial *adj.* healing, therapeutic, corrective, invigorating, medicinal, recuperative, tonic, health-giving, antidotal, restorative, purifying, reformative, soothing.

remedy *n.* medicine, antidote, cure, solution, therapy, treatment, panacea, relief, restorative, corrective, countermeasure, nostrum, redress.

remember *v.* recall, recollect, think back, summon up, place, recognize, reminisce, retain, commemorate, dig into the past, think of, be reminded of, look back upon, have memories of; *ant.* forget.

remembrance *n.* **1.** memory, recall, recollection, afterthought, hindsight, retrospection, recognition, reconstruction, mental image, thought. **2.** gift, reward, token, keepsake, memento.

remind *v.* refresh one's memory, call up, cue, jog one's memory, hint, prompt, put in mind, bring to mind, call to mind.

reminder *n.* memorandum, prompt, hint, cue, suggestion, memo, nudge, notice, admonition, keepsake, souvenir.

reminisce *v.* remember, think back, look back, recollect, recall, review.

reminiscence *n.* memoir, account, version, recollection, remembrance, review, anecdote, chronicle; memory, recall, retrospection, reflection.

reminiscent *adj.* suggestive, evocative, redolent, nostalgic, similar.

remiss *adj.* negligent, careless, forgetful, inattentive, at fault, lackadaisical, neglectful, dilatory, delinquent, indifferent, regardless, slipshod, thoughtless, heedless, slack, sloppy; *ant.* careful, scrupulous.

remission *n.* **1.** alleviation, abatement, lessening, release, relief, absolution, exoneration, moderation, slackening, amnesty, pardon, release. **2.** interruption, pause, lull, break, delay, respite, ebb.

remit *v.* **1.** send, make payment, forward, dispatch, pay. **2.** pardon, absolve, exonerate, release, forgive.

remittance *n.* fee, payment, allowance, reimbursement, enclosure.

remnant *n.* scrap, shred, leftovers, trace, residue, piece, vestige, remains, fragment, bit, remainder, rest, balance, residuum.

remonstrance *n.* complaint, objection, grievance, protest, petition, protestation, exception, expostulation, reprimand, reproof.

remonstrate *v.* complain, admonish, scold, challenge, protest, object, argue, dispute, dissent, expostulate, gripe (*slang*).

remorse *n.* regret, sorrow, anguish, guilt, bad conscience, repentance, ruefulness, penitence, contrition, grief, compunction, self-reproach, compassion, ruth.

remorseful *adj.* sorry, regretful, conscience-stricken, guilt-ridden, guilty, ashamed, rueful, sad, sorrowful, apologetic, penitent, repentant, contrite, compunctious; *ant.* impenitent, remorseless.

remorseless *adj.* cruel, callous, harsh, relentless, ruthless, tyrannical, merciless, pitiless, exacting, inflexible, implacable, inexorable; *ant.* merciful, repentant.

remote *adj.* far, distant, out-of-the-way, secluded, outlying, lonely, withdrawn, far-off, removed, inaccessible, faraway; *ant.* adjacent, close, nearby, significant.

removal *n.* withdrawal, abstraction, ejection, elimination, transfer, expulsion, extraction, departure, move, purge, metastasis.

remove *v.* displace, transfer, dislodge, uproot, discharge, get rid of, evacuate, withdraw, separate, extract, take away from, unload, take down; *ant.* install.

remunerate *v.* repay, pay, compensate, recompense, reimburse, reward, requite, indemnify, redress.

remuneration *n.* repayment, reimbursement, compensation, pay, payment, earnings, reparation, stipend, salary, indemnity, remittance, return, wages.

remunerative *adj.* profitable, rewarding, rich, lucrative, fruitful, gainful, moneymaking, worthwhile.

renaissance *n.* resurrection, revival, new dawn, rejuvenation, rebirth, reawakening, reappearance, regeneration, re-emergence, renascence, resurgence.

renascent *adj.* resurrected, revived, born-again, resurgent, reawakened, reborn, re-emergent, reanimated, renewed.

rend *v.* rip, tear, break, hurt, rupture, cleave, separate, split, divide, lacerate.

render *v.* **1.** interpret, play, depict, act, represent, reproduce, transcribe, translate, construe, exhibit, explain, portray. **2.** (do a service) perform, do, act, execute.

rendezvous *n.* meeting, date, engagement, appointment, tryst, tête-à-tête, meeting place, trysting place, assignation.

rendezvous *v.* meet, meet secretly, meet behind closed doors, convene, converge, assemble, collect, gather.

rendition *n.* interpretation, portrayal, arrangement, presentation, reading, version, rendering, performance, depiction, execution.

renegade *n.* rebel, traitor, defector, turncoat, mutineer, outlaw, deserter, dissident, betrayer, apostate, recreant, quisling, runaway, tergiversator.

renegade *adj.* rebellious, dissident, rebel, outlaw, traitorous, unfaithful, mutinous, disloyal, recreant, runaway, apostate, perfidious.

renege *v.* default, back down, back off, welch (*slang*); *ant.* come through.

renew *v.* restore, overhaul, mend, repair, recreate, refurbish, rejuvenate, transform, revitalize, modernize, refashion, refresh, replace.

renewal *n.* renovation, repair, reconditioning, reconstruction, refurbishment, reconstitution, resurrection, resuscitation, revitalization, revivification, kiss of life.

renounce *v.* reject, recant, discard, quit, abandon, forsake, repudiate, spurn, eschew, forgo, abdicate, abjure, relinquish, forswear.

renovate *v.* remodel, repair, modernize, improve, rehabilitate, reform, recreate, refit, re-

renovation *n.* restoration, improvement, reconditioning, repair, modernization, refurbishment, face lift, renewal.

renown *n.* acclaim, reputation, celebrity, illustriousness, fame, eminence, honor, glory, distinction, repute, stardom, kudos; *ant.* anonymity,
obscurity.

renowned *adj.* celebrated, noted, preeminent,
well-known, acclaimed, distinguished, famous,
illustrious, esteemed, famed, eminent, notable;
ant. anonymous, obscure, unknown.

rent *n.* 1. lease, rental, payment, fee, tariff,
hire, gale. 2. break, tear, crack, split, gash,
rip, rupture, hole, chink, perforation; breach,
opening, schism, rift, division.
for rent on the market, for hire, available,
advertised, to let.

rent *v.* 1. (pay for the use of) hire, pay rent for,
charter, contract, engage, borrow. 2. (allow
the use of) lease, let, sublet, make available,
take in roomers, farm out, put on loan.

renunciation *n.* repudiation, rejection, resignation, abandonment, waiver, disclaimer, relinquishment, denial, forgoing, abdication, abstention, disavowal.

repair *v.* 1. improvement, restoration, overhaul, rehabilitation, renovation, replacement.
2. condition, state, shape, form.

repair *v.* 1. fix, mend, adjust, correct, settle,
reform, patch, rejuvenate, refurbish, touch up,
put in order, revamp, rectify, put or set
right. 2. go, retire, withdraw, move, remove.

reparable *adj.* restorable, curable, rectifiable,
recoverable, savable, salvageable, retrievable,
corrigible.

reparation *n.* restitution, compensation, damages, indemnity, satisfaction, amends, recompense, redress, requital, atonement, propitiation, repair.

repartee *n.* wordplay, banter, badinage, riposte,
pleasantry, wit, witticism, jesting, wittiness,
raillery, persiflage.

repast *n.* meal, spread, victuals, food, feed,
nourishment.

repay *v.* 1. remunerate, compensate, reimburse, refund, make restitution, reward, return, recompense, requite, reciprocate. 2. get

constitute, revamp, restore, recondition, overhaul, refurbish, renew.

even, with, avenge, revenge, settle the score,
retaliate.

repayment *n.* 1. reimbursement, retribution,
compensation, rebate, recompense, remuneration, reparation, restitution, retribution,
amends, reciprocation, requital, redress. 2.
vengeance, avengement, retaliation.

repeal *n.* cancellation, withdrawal, invalidation, nullification, reversal, rescinding, abolition, annulment, rescission, revocation, abrogation; *ant.* enactment, establishment.

repeal *v.* abolish, void, withdraw, annul, cancel, nullify, invalidate, revoke, reverse, rescind, recall, countermand, abrogate; *ant.*
enact, establish.

repeat *n.* repetition, rerun, duplicate, rebroad-
cast, reproduction, recapitulation, echo, reiteration, replay, reshowing.

repeat *v.* restate, say again, recite, echo, iterate,
duplicate, rehearse, reproduce, quote, rebroad-
cast, relate, renew, recapitulate, retell, reshow.

repeatedly *adv.* again and again, time after
time, time and time again, over and over,
often, oftentimes, ofttimes, recurrently, frequently, time and again.

repel *v.* repulse, rebuff, fight, ward off, offend,
sicken, disgust, nauseate, oppose, revolt, reject, refuse, check.

repellent *adj.* repulsive, obnoxious, disgusting,
revolting, sickening, offensive, distasteful, nauseating, loathsome, horrid, abominable, repugnant, off-putting, abhorrent, odious.

repent *v.* lament, regret, rue, sorrow, atone,
deplore, bewail, relent.

repentance *n.* regret, remorse, guilt, sorrow,
compunction, grief, self-reproach, contrition,
penitence.

repentant *adj.* sorry, remorseful, apologetic, rueful, ashamed, contrite, penitent, compunctious, regretful, chastened.

repercussion *n.* backlash, aftermath, result,
reverberation, side effect, consequence, rebound, echo.

repertory *n.* repertoire, reserve, reservoir, supply, stock, store, collection, repository.

repetition *n.* recital, repeat, redundancy, rehearsal, reiteration, iteration, recapitulation,
repetitiousness, restatement, rehash, tautology,
recurrence, replication, reappearance.

repetitious *adj.* redundant, wordy, verbose, tedious, long-winded, tautological, prolix, windy, pleonastic.

repetitive *adj.* unchanging, unvaried, monotonous, interminable, boring, tedious, dull, verbose, recurrent.

rephrase *v.* reword, paraphrase, rewrite, recast.

repine *v.* complain, mope, sulk, brood, fret, grieve, lament, whine, moan, grumble, languish, murmur, beef (*slang*).

replace *v.* supersede, follow, oust, substitute, supplant, deputize, reestablish, reinstate, restore, supply.

replacement *n.* successor, substitute, double, fill-in, second, understudy, surrogate, proxy.

replenish *v.* fill, refill, recharge, replace, restock, stock, furnish, reload, recruit, renew, restore, supply.

replete *adj.* filled, full, glutted, gorged, teeming, abounding, brimming, crammed, well-stocked, jammed, jam-packed, chock-full, stuffed, satiated, sated.

repletion *n.* glut, superabundance, fullness, overfullness, plethora, satiation, satiety, superfluity.

replica *n.* copy, reproduction, duplicate, ditto, clone, imitation, facsimile, model.

replicate *v.* copy, clone, recreate, reproduce, duplicate, mimic, ape, follow, repeat.

reply *n.* response, answer, comeback, reaction, rejoinder, counter, acknowledgment, retort, riposte, repartee.

reply *v.* respond, answer, rejoin, retort, counter, acknowledge, reciprocate, react, retaliate, riposte, return, come back with.

report *n.* **1.** story, news, tale, narration, narrative, description, announcement, wire, cable, telegram, broadcast. **2.** noise, detonation, bang, blast, explosion.

report *v.* **1.** summarize, publish, proclaim, announce, enunciate, promulgate, make known, list, itemize, account for, give the facts, write up. **2.** arrive, present oneself, be at hand, come, reach, *slang:* show up, turn up.

reporter *n.* journalist, correspondent, press person, newscaster, newspaperman, newspaperwoman, newshound, writer, stringer, hack.

repose *n.* rest, calmness, inactivity, relaxation, composure, tranquillity, stillness, restfulness,

calm, self-possession, sleep, slumber, serenity, poise, quietude; *ant.* activity, strain, stress.

repose *v.* rest, recline, laze, doze, sleep, relax, slumber, loll, lounge.

repository *n.* depository, warehouse, storehouse, receptacle, store, archive, treasury, depot, emporium, vault, magazine.

reprehend *v.* rebuke, reprove, reprimand, censure, scold.

reprehensible *adj.* bad, disgraceful, shameful, delinquent, blameworthy, errant, ignoble, censurable, objectionable, remiss, condemnable, opprobrious; *ant.* creditable, good.

represent *v.* **1.** (be an agent for) serve for, speak *or* act for, hold office, be deputy for, act *or* stand in place of, be proxy for. **2.** symbolize, stand for, personify, signify, typify, exemplify, substitute, impersonate, copy, imitate, reproduce.

representation *n.* **1.** likeness, image, portrait, show, portrayal, depiction, resemblance, illustration, model, production, delineation, description. **2.** delegation, delegates, committee.

representative *n.* **1.** spokesperson, spokesman, spokeswoman, agent, delegate, member, proxy, deputy, councillor, commissioner, rep. **2.** epitome, exemplar, archetype, embodiment, personification, type, paradigm, standard.

representative *adj.* **1.** normal, illustrative, characteristic, typical, usual, symbolic, archetypal, exemplary, emblematic, evocative; *ant.* atypical. **2.** elected, chosen, delegated, elective.

repress *v.* control, overpower, suppress, silence, restrain, put down, overcome, muffle, subjugate, stifle, subdue, crush; *ant.* let go, release.

repression *n.* tyranny, suppression, domination, control, despotism, coercion, subjugation, authoritarianism, suffocation, constraint, censorship, restraint; *ant.* expression, liberty.

repressive *adj.* tyrannical, severe, authoritarian, dictatorial, autocratic, despotic, oppressive, ironhanded, harsh, tough, absolute, coercive, restrictive, extreme; *ant.* free.

reprieve *n.* pardon, exoneration, amnesty, deferment, redemption, relief, remission, suspension, respite, mitigation, postponement, abatement, abeyance, letup.

reprieve *v.* absolve, forgive, exonerate, redeem, rescue, pardon.

reprimand *n.* reproach, lecture, castigation, reproof, admonition, censure, rebuke, redown, telling-off, talking-to, tongue-lashing, reprehension.

reprimand *v.* scold, admonish, check, chide, reprehend, lecture, castigate, reproach, reprove, upbraid, bawl out (*slang*), censure, rebuke, tongue-lash.

reprint *v.* republish, reproduce, reissue.

reprisal *n.* retaliation, retribution, revenge, vengeance, counterstroke, requital, payback.

reproach *n.* scorn, disapproval, contempt, stigma, blame, condemnation, censure, disrepute, dishonor, disgrace, ignominy, discredit.

reproach *v.* criticize, scold, upbraid, reprimand, berate, reprove, admonish, chide, censure, defame, disparage, condemn, reprehend, blame, animadvert.

reproachful *adj.* critical, fault-finding, opprobrious, scolding, reproving, disapproving, admonitory, monitory, condemnatory, castigatory, censorious; *ant.* complimentary.

reprobate *n.* villain, wrongdoer, rogue, rascal, degenerate, miscreant, evildoer, outcast, pariah, wretch, wastrel, sinner, scoundrel, rake, knave.

reprobate *adj.* sinful, degenerate, corrupt, damned, unprincipled, immoral, depraved, hardened, incorrigible, abandoned, base, bad, shameless, wicked, dissolute; *ant.* upright.

reproduce *v.* **1.** copy, photocopy, Xerox (Tm), duplicate, photograph, photostat, mimeograph, print, type, reprint. **2.** multiply, procreate, engender, breed, generate, propagate, hatch, father, beget, sire.

reproduction *n.* **1.** breeding, propagation, procreation, multiplication, generation, increase, proliferation. **2.** copy, Xerox (Tm), duplicate, facsimile, replica, print, picture, imitation, clone; *ant.* original.

reproductive *adj.* sexual, procreative, genital, generative, progenitive, propagative.

reprove *v.* reprimand, chide, admonish, scold, berate, upbraid, check, rebuke, reprehend, censure, condemn, abuse; *ant.* praise.

repudiate *v.* disclaim, rescind, disavow, di-

vorce, revoke, cast off, deny, disown, forsake, reject, renounce, abandon, abjure; *ant.* admit, own.

repudiation *n.* refusal, denial, disclaimer, renunciation, rejection, disavowal, recantation, renouncement, retraction, abjuration; *ant.* acceptance.

repugnance *n.* disgust, aversion, hatred, repulsion, loathing, abhorrence, antipathy, revulsion, dislike, distaste; *ant.* liking, pleasure.

repugnant *adj.* disgusting, repulsive, distasteful, disagreeable, offensive, revolting, repulsive, horrid, vile, putrid, terrible, foul; *ant.* acceptable, pleasant.

repulse *v.* rebuff, refuse, drive back, beat off, refuse, reject, repel, spurn.

repulsion *n.* disgust, repugnance, aversion, distaste, hatred, revulsion, loathing, abhorrence, resentment, malice; *ant.* liking.

repulsive *adj.* disgusting, revolting, sickening, foul, vile, unpleasant, offensive, odious, repellent, hideous, horrid, objectionable, nauseating, obnoxious; *ant.* friendly.

reputable *adj.* legitimate, trustworthy, honorable, upright, respectable, reliable, dependable, principled, good, creditable, worthy, estimable, irreproachable, unimpeachable, excellent; *ant.* infamous.

repute *n.* standing, stature, name, distinction, renown, reputation, fame, celebrity, esteem, estimation.

reputation *n.* **1.** character, reliability, trustworthiness, respectability, dependability, standing, credit, esteem, estimation, honor, opinion. **2.** fame, prominence, eminence, notoriety, distinction, infamy, name, renown, repute.

reputed *adj.* alleged, believed, regarded, supposed, thought, rumored, estimated, held, said, considered, deemed; *ant.* actual.

request *n.* appeal, solicitation, petition, entreaty, prayer, requisition, supplication, application, suit, imperation.

request *v.* ask for, ask, solicit, pray, seek, beg, beseech, importune, supplicate, requisition, entreat, petition.

require *v.* need, demand, necessitate, force, make, take.

required *adj.* necessary, mandatory, essential,

compulsory, obligatory, requisite, exigent, un-avoidable, vital, crucial, prescribed, demanded, needed, stipulated; *ant.* optional.

requirement *n.* necessity, precondition, need, stipulation, term, demand, essential, qualifica-tion, prerequisite, requisite, must, provision, specification, want, proviso.

requisite *n.* necessity, condition, need, require-ment, essential, prerequisite, must, precondi-tion, desideratum, sine qua non.

requisite *adj.* essential, necessary, mandatory, required, prerequisite, vital, obligatory, im-perative, indispensable, de rigueur, needed; *ant.* inessential, optional.

requisition *n.* seizure, takeover, use, appropria-tion, confiscation, commandeering; demand, request, summons, call, order, request.

requisition *v.* confiscate, commandeer, take, seize, appropriate, demand.

requital *n.* repayment, compensation, repara-tion, recompense, amends, redress, payment, quittance, restitution, indemnification, satisfac-tion, indemnity, pay-off.

requite *v.* return, respond, retaliate, redress, reciprocate, remunerate, reward, satisfy.

rescind *v.* retract, recall, revoke, repeal, re-verse, void, invalidate, annul, cancel, negate, nullify, overturn, countermand, abrogate; *ant.* enforce.

rescission *n.* repeal, annulment, nullification, retraction, reversal, negation, cancellation, in-validation, recall, revocation, abrogation; *ant.* enforcement.

rescue *n.* release, salvation, liberation, delivery, deliverance, salvage, recovery, redemption, re-lief; *ant.* capture.

rescue *v.* save, free, liberate, release, extricate, deliver, redeem, salvage, recover, ransom; *ant.* capture.

research *n.* search, study, inquiry, investiga-tion, analysis, probe, exploration, quest, exami-nation, fact-finding, delving, scrutiny.

research *v.* investigate, explore, analyze, search, study, examine, scrutinize, probe.

researcher *n.* analyst, inspector, investigator.

resemblance *n.* likeness, similarity, affinity, fac-simile, kinship, parallel, similitude, closeness, conformity, semblance, sameness, assonance.

resemble *v.* look like, mirror, favor, duplicate, echo, take after, parallel; *ant.* differ from.

resent *v.* take offense at, begrudge, grudge, take exception to, take umbrage at, object to, chafe at, dislike, be insulted, take amiss; *ant.* accept, like, appreciate.

resentful *adj.* aggrieved, offended, revengeful, piqued, jealous, put out, indignant, embit-tered, bitter, grudging, miffed, incensed, hurt, unforgiving; *ant.* contented.

resentment *n.* bitterness, vexation, umbrage, animosity, vindictiveness, grudge, indignation, ill will, malice, pique, rancor, hurt, disaffec-tion; *ant.* contentment.

reservation *n.* restraint, hesitation, hesitancy, second thought, inhibition.

reserve *n.* **1.** store, provisions, supply, stock-pile, cache, fund, hoard, backlog, nest egg. **2.** calmness, restraint, reticence, formality, cool-ness, secretiveness, modesty, unresponsive-ness, caution, taciturnity, inhibition, coyness, demureness, aloofness; *ant.* friendliness.

reserve *v.* retain, hold, book, save, engage, withhold, secure, keep, hoard, conserve, be-speak, prearrange, set apart; *ant.* use up.

reserved *adj.* **1.** set aside, taken, booked, engaged, earmarked, spoken for, retained, in-tended, meant, restricted, bound, designated. **2.** cool, aloof, formal, unsociable, restrained, shy, diffident, cold, retiring, standoffish; reti-cent, close-mouthed, uncommunicative, taci-turn, demure, unforthcoming, unresponsive; *ant.* friendly, outgoing.

reserves *n.* reinforcements, volunteers, army, troops.

reservoir *n.* store, supply, stock, stockpile, repository, reserves, source.

reshuffle *v.* restructure, reorganize, rearrange, shuffle, shift, redistribute, regroup, revise, shake up, interchange, realign.

reside *v.* live, stay, inhabit, abide, dwell, lodge, remain.

residence *n.* **1.** house, home, household, quar-ters, dwelling, habitat, lodging, place, domi-cile, manor, seat. **2.** tenancy, occupancy, occu-pation, habitation, stay.

resident *n.* denizen, inhabitant, lodger, tenant, occupant, citizen, habitant, local, indweller.

residential *adj.* suburban, private, domestic, exurban.

residual *adj.* remaining, leftover, unused, surplus, extra, lingering, vestigial; *ant.* core.

residue *n.* remains, remainder, leftovers, rest, surplus, dregs, balance, excess, difference, extra; *ant.* core.

resign *v.* abandon, forsake, sacrifice, step down, vacate, yield, renounce, abdicate, cede, forgo, quit, relinquish, leave, surrender, waive; *ant.* join, maintain.

resign oneself submit, yield, accept, bow, comply, acquiesce, reconcile, accede; *ant.* resist.

resignation *n.* retirement, leaving, abdication, departure, surrender, abandonment, relinquishment, forbearing; *ant.* resistance.

resigned *adj.* submissive, compliant, patient, stoical, unresisting, subdued, acquiescent, defeatist, long-suffering, unprotesting.

resilience *n.* flexibility, give, elasticity, spring, springiness, pliability, hardiness, strength, suppleness, bounce, buoyancy, plasticity; *ant.* rigidity.

resilient *adj.* adaptable, flexible, hardy, buoyant, pliable, bouncy, elastic, tough, strong, springy, plastic, irrepressible, supple; *ant.* rigid.

resist *v.* withstand, defy, oppose, combat, repel, ward off, hold back, thwart, fight *or* strike back, battle, avoid, refuse; *ant.* accept, submit.

resistance *n.* defiance, opposition, struggle, withstanding, defense, battle, combat, counteraction, rebuff, obstruction; *ant.* acceptance, submission.

resistant *adj.* antagonistic, hostile, unyielding, combative, defiant, recalcitrant, intractable, impervious, opposed, strong, tough, stiff, unwilling, dissident; *ant.* compliant, yielding.

resolute *adj.* unbending, fixed, firm, steadfast, undaunted, constant, determined, persevering, stubborn, dogged, purposeful, tenacious, set, strong-minded; *ant.* irresolute.

resolution *n.* resolve, willpower, courage, constancy, determination, firmness, dedication, earnestness, perseverance, grit, purpose, steadfastness; *ant.* indecision.

resolve *n.* determination, resolution, sense of purpose, willpower, conviction, courage, firmness; *ant.* indecision.

resolve *v.* settle, solve, unravel, analyze, determine, conclude, dispel, clear, explain, disentangle, elucidate.

resonant *adj.* resounding, reverberating, reverberant, booming, rich, full, echoing, sonorous, ringing; *ant.* faint.

resort *n.* 1. refuge, retreat, watering hole, spa, health resort. 2. alternative, hope, recourse, chance, possibility, course, expedient. **as a last resort** in desperation, in the end, lastly, finally, when push comes to shove (*slang*).

resound *v.* boom, echo, reverberate, sound, thunder, ring, resonate.

resounding *adj.* resonant, reverberating, booming, full, rich, sonorous; *ant.* faint, slight.

resource *n.* reserve, supply, stockpile, source, cache, hoard.

resourceful *adj.* imaginative, talented, quickwitted, sharp, creative, fertile, ingenious, inventive, capable, clever, innovative, able, bright, slick.

resources *n.* money, capital, funds, wealth, assets, means, reserves, riches, holdings, wherewithal.

respect *n.* 1. reverence, homage, admiration, esteem, honor, regard, veneration, deference, estimation, obeisance, adulation. 2. aspect, facet, way, regard, characteristic, detail, point, particular, consideration, feature.
pay one's respects wait upon, show regard, be polite, visit.
in respect to about, concerning, in reference to, regarding, re.

respect *v.* venerate, revere, regard, pay homage to, admire, value, honor, esteem, obey, reverence; *ant.* scorn.

respectability *n.* integrity, decency, propriety, honesty, virtue, probity, righteousness, civility.

respectable *adj.* 1. proper, upright, venerable, admirable, righteous, honorable, upstanding, aboveboard, clean-living, seemly, good; *ant.* disreputable. 2. sizable, substantial, ample, appreciable, considerable, large, goodly; *ant.* small, insignificant.

respectful *adj.* courteous, gracious, civil, humble, well-mannered, self-effacing, submissive, deferential, polite, reverent, subservient, mannerly, solicitous, regardful.

respecting *prep.* regarding, about, concerning, with respect to, with regard to, in relation to, pertaining to, in respect of, anent, in the matter of.

respective *adj.* corresponding, individual, own, personal, particular.

respects *n.* greetings, salutations, compliments, deference, courtesies, best wishes, kind wishes, cordial regards.

respiration *n.* breathing, breath, inhalation, exhalation, expiration.

respite *n.* reprieve, suspension, stay, intermission, breather, postponement, hiatus, lull, moratorium, pause, recess, remission, lapse, adjournment.

resplendent *adj.* radiant, bright, brilliant, luminous, glorious, refulgent, effulgent, lustrous, splendid, shining, gleaming, glittering, dazzling, irradiant; *ant.* dull.

respond *v.* reply, answer, react, reciprocate, answer back, come back, acknowledge, counter, retort, return, rejoin.

response *n.* answer, reply, reaction, feedback, retort, return, riposte, rejoinder, comeback, acknowledgment, counterblast.

responsibility *n.* liability, accountability, duty, obligation, onus, reliability, burden, dependability, guilt; *ant.* irresponsibility.

responsible *adj.* 1. conscientious, accountable, ethical, dependable, reliable, sound, sober, mature, sensible; *ant.* reckless, unreliable. 2. culpable, guilty, to blame; liable, answerable.

responsive *adj.* alert, awake, reactive, receptive, forthcoming, sensitive, respondent, alive.

rest *n.* 1. repose, quiet, tranquillity, slumber, calm, peace, peacefulness, relaxation, siesta. 2. excess, remainder, residue, surplus, remnant, balance, leftover.

at rest resting, dormant, inert, inactive, immobile.

lay to rest bury, inter, entomb.

rest *v.* relax, sleep, doze, repose, lie down, recuperate, settle down, nap.

restaurant *n.* eatery, cafeteria, bistro, grill, diner, cafe, luncheonette, snack bar, buffet.

restful *adj.* calm, tranquil, serene, languid, relaxed, unhurried; peaceful, relaxing, soothing, calming, tranquilizing; *ant.* disturbed, disturbing.

restitution *n.* repayment, compensation, remuneration, damages, reimbursement, refund, indemnity, indemnification, requital, redress, satisfaction.

restive *adj.* restless, nervous, jittery, jumpy, unruly, edgy, fidgety, fretful, agitated, uneasy, impatient, unquiet, antsy (*slang*); *ant.* calm, relaxed.

restless *adj.* anxious, nervous, restive, fitful, transient, wandering, roving, shifting, inconstant, fretful, nomadic, turbulent, unsteady, troubled, footloose; *ant.* calm, relaxed.

restlessness *n.* agitation, edginess, fitfulness, restiveness, wanderlust, inconstancy, uneasiness, anxiety, instability, jumpiness, turmoil; *ant.* calmness, relaxation.

restoration *n.* renovation, repair, reconstruction, refurbishing, rejuvenation, renewal, rehabilitation, revitalization, replacement; *ant.* damage, removal, weakening.

restorative *adj.* corrective, therapeutic, medicinal, healthful, remedial; preservative.

restore *v.* 1. repair, rebuild, alter, rehabilitate, reconstruct, recondition, renew, rejuvenate, retouch; *ant.* damage, weaken. 2. return, give back, make restitution, replace, put back; *ant.* remove.

restrain *v.* 1. hold back, restrict, suppress, bridle, govern, curtail, constrain, inhibit, hinder, hold, subdue, harness; *ant.* encourage, liberate. 2. (show self-control) forgo, desist, curb, discipline, limit, get hold of.

restrained *adj.* moderate, controlled, discreet, understated, temperate, unobtrusive, mild, low-key, reticent, calm, reasonable, self-controlled, temperate, subdued.

restraint *n.* limitation, control, curtailment, inhibition, check, restriction, lid, self-discipline, rein; *ant.* freedom, license.

restrict *v.* restrain, confine, hamper, circumscribe, handicap, demarcate, impede, inhibit, bound, contain, cramp, limit; *ant.* broaden, encourage, free.

restriction *n.* constraint, regulation, limitation, demarcation, handicap, rule, stipulation, condition, control, check, confinement; *ant.* broadening, encouragement, freedom.

result *n.* end, end product, outcome, upshot, effect, conclusion, consequence, issue, fruit;

result aftermath, consequences, aftereffects. *ant.* beginning, cause.

result *v.* happen, follow, ensue, stem, emerge, arise, appear, lead to, derive, develop, culminate, eventuate, spring, emanate, issue; *ant.* begin, cause.

result in end in, effect, achieve.

résumé *n.* **1.** summary, synopsis, rundown, review, overview, recapitulation, abstract, outline, digest, précis, epitome. **2.** curriculum vitae, biography, history, track record, CV.

resume *v.* continue, restart, begin again, recommence, go on with, proceed, keep *or* carry on, renew, take up again; *ant.* cease.

resurgence *n.* revival, return, rebirth, resurrection, reemergence, renaissance, revivification, recrudescence, renascence; *ant.* decrease.

resurrect *v.* revive, restore, renew, bring back to life; *ant.* bury, kill off, quash.

resurrection *n.* rebirth, resuscitation, return, revival, comeback, renaissance, renewal, reactivation, revivification; *ant.* burying, killing off, quashing.

resuscitate *v.* revive, save, bring around, revitalize, rescue, reanimate, revivify, resurrect, reinvigorate.

retail *v.* sell, vend, have for sale.

retain *v.* **1.** hold, cling to, grasp, clutch, grip, keep, save; *ant.* release, spend. **2.** hire, employ, maintain, engage, pay, commission.

retainer *n.* **1.** deposit, advance, fee, retaining fee. **2.** servant, attendant, valet, domestic, menial, flunky.

retaliate *v.* avenge, strike back, take revenge, requite, get even with, fight back, return, repay in kind, get back at, reciprocate; *ant.* forgive, turn the other cheek.

retaliation *n.* counterstroke, retribution, revenge, vengeance, reciprocation, requital, repayment, counterblow, reprisal, retort, tit for tat.

retard *v.* hinder, postpone, delay, impede, handicap, encumber, obstruct, slow, arrest; *ant.* advance.

retardation *n.* mental handicap, deficiency, incapacity, slowness, incapability, impediment, hindrance.

retch *v.* vomit, throw up, regurgitate, dis-

gorge, heave, gag, spew, *slang:* puke, toss one's cookies.

retention *n.* **1.** hold, custody, charge, reservation, arrest. **2.** memory, recall, recognition, remembrance, recollection.

reticence *n.* silence, reserve, taciturnity, restraint, diffidence, quietness, closeness, muteness, shyness; *ant.* forwardness, frankness.

reticent *adj.* closed-mouthed, tight-lipped, close-lipped, silent, taciturn, mute, reserved, restrained, uncommunicative, unforthcoming, quiet, secretive; *ant.* forward, frank.

retinue *n.* following, attendants, personnel, entourage, servants, followers, staff, aides, cortege, escort, train.

retire *v.* **1.** leave, withdraw, depart, recede, retreat, exit, secede, remove, decamp; *ant.* enter, join. **2.** rest, go to bed, lie down, sleep, turn in, hit the sack (*slang*).

retired *adj.* former, past, ex-, emeritus.

retirement *n.* withdrawal, retreat, seclusion, solitude, privacy.

retiring *adj.* reticent, self-effacing, shy, timid, unassuming, diffident, meek, bashful, quiet, reserved, mousy, demure, reclusive, shrinking; *ant.* assertive, forward.

retort *n.* answer, reply, rejoinder, response, quip, comeback, repartee, riposte.

retort *v.* answer, reply, respond, return, rejoin, counter, retaliate.

retract *v.* withdraw, renounce, rescind, recant, repeal, recall, revoke, cancel, abjure, repudiate, reverse; *ant.* maintain.

retreading *n.* updating, improvement, renewal.

retreat *n.* **1.** flight, departure, evacuation, retirement, withdrawal, ebb; *ant.* advance. **2.** sanctuary, refuge, haven, hideaway, shelter, resort.

beat a retreat retreat, pull back, leave, evacuate, abandon, withdraw.

retreat *v.* withdraw, leave, recede, depart, recoil, shrink, quit, retire, turn tail, ebb; *ant.* advance.

retrench *v.* reduce, economize, tighten one's belt, lessen, limit, pare, prune, trim, slim down, decrease, curtail, diminish, cut; *ant.* increase.

retrenchment *n.* cut, cutback, reduction,

shrinkage, curtailment, cost-cutting, pruning, downsizing; *ant.* increase, expansion.

retribution *n.* punishment, revenge, vengeance, an eye for an eye, retaliation, comeuppance, compensation, payment, reprisal, requital, recompense, redress.

retrieve *v.* recover, salvage, save, recoup, rescue, fetch, regain, repossess, recapture; *ant.* lose.

retrograde *adj.* regressive, degenerative, deteriorating, declining, worsening, relapsing, reverse, inverse, backward; *ant.* progressive.

retrogress *v.* revert, backslide, decline, worsen, deteriorate, regress, ebb, relapse, degenerate; *ant.* progress.

retrogression *n.* decline, recidivism, worsening, deterioration, relapse, fall, ebb, drop, regression, retrogradation; *ant.* progress.

retrospect *n.* hindsight, afterthought, review, reexamination, contemplation, remembrance, recollection, reminiscence, recapitulation.

retrospective *adj.* backward-looking, historical, reminiscent, evocative; retroactive.

return *v.* 1. recur, come back, reappear, repeat, come again; *ant.* move, advance, go forward. 2. answer, reply, respond, retort, counter, come back.

reunion *n.* reuniting, reconciliation, rejoining, reconcilement, homecoming, *slang:* get-together.

reuse *v.* recycle, use again, reconstitute.

revamp *v.* renovate, refurbish, restore, overhaul, recondition, reconstruct, rehabilitate, revise, repair, rebuild, do up (*slang*).

reveal *v.* tell, disclose, divulge, bare, expose, leak (*slang*), announce, unmask, uncover; *ant.* hide.

revel *n.* party, celebration, festivity, gala, merry-making, bacchanal, carousal, debauch.

revel *v.* celebrate, carouse, frolic, rejoice, make merry, party, roister, play, *slang:* live it up, paint the town red, raise the roof, whoop it up. **revel in** take pleasure in, luxuriate, relish,

delight, bask, lap up (*slang*), savor, gloat, crow, thrive on, glory; *ant.* dislike.

revelation *n.* discovery, disclosure, exposure, publication, divulgence, broadcasting, apocalypse, display, manifestation, exposition, proclamation, announcement.

reveler *n.* merrymaker, carouser, pleasure-seeker, celebrator, partygoer, roisterer, bacchant, bacchanal.

revelry *n.* fun, festivity, celebration, party, merrymaking, carousal, debauch, debauchery, roistering; *ant.* sobriety.

revenge *n.* vengeance, reprisal, retaliation, retribution, requital, satisfaction.

revenge *v.* avenge, vindicate, retaliate, repay, pay back, requite, even the score, get even, get satisfaction.

revenue *n.* income, profits, yield, returns, gain, proceeds, receipts, take (*slang*), rewards; *ant.* expenditure.

reverberate *v.* echo, resound, vibrate, ring, rebound, recoil, reecho.

reverberation *n.* echo, resonance, resounding, vibration, recoil; consequences, repercussions, effects, results.

revere *v.* venerate, adore, honor, pay homage to, worship, idolize, adulate, respect, exalt, reverence, defer to; *ant.* despise, scorn.

reverence *n.* respect, veneration, esteem, devotion, honor, adoration, adulation, awe, deference; *ant.* scorn.

reverence *v.* revere, venerate, worship, honor, admire, respect; *ant.* despise, scorn.

reverent *adj.* respectful, reverential, pious, humble, devout, awed, dutiful, meek, solemn.

reverie *n.* trance, musing, preoccupation, daydream, distraction, daydreaming, nostalgia; inattention, woolgathering, absent-mindedness.

reversal *n.* turnaround, about-face, turnabout, U-turn, reverse, repeal, rescission, rescinding; setback, mishap, stumbling block, reverse, check. *ant.* advancement, progress.

reverse *n.* 1. contrary, opposite, inverse, converse, reversal, antithesis, contradiction; underside, rear. 2. setback, reversal, mishap, misstep, barrier.

reverse *v.* turn, go back, shift, invert, backtrack.

revert v. relapse, regress, backslide, retrogress, reverse, lapse, return; *ant.* progress.

review n. **1.** study, scrutiny, reexamination, reconsideration, retrospection. **2.** summary, synopsis, abstract, outline, overview.

review v. inspect, scrutinize, study, reexamine, assess, vet, evaluate, analyze.

revile v. slander, libel, defame, vituperate, malign, scorn, denigrate, vilify, reproach, traduce, calumniate; *ant.* praise.

revise v. change, alter, correct, modify, amend, emend, revamp, edit, rewrite, redact, redo, update, reconstruct, recast.

revision n. change, alteration, modification, amendment, redaction, correction, recast, reconstruction, rewriting.

revitalize v. revive, reanimate, refresh, rejuvenate, resurrect, revivify, reactivate, renew; *ant.* dampen, suppress.

revival n. rebirth, resuscitation, reawakening, resurgence, resurrection, renewal, renaissance, restoration, reactivation, reanimation, revitalization, revivification; *ant.* suppression.

revivalist n. missionary, evangelist, preacher, minister, televangelist.

revive v. **1.** wake up, resurrect, resuscitate, bring to *or* around; enliven, reanimate, rejuvenate, exhilarate, refresh, renew, revivify; *ant.* weary. **2.** cheer, comfort, brighten, encourage, console, gladden, delight; *ant.* suppress.

revivify v. revive, resuscitate, refresh, invigorate, reactivate, renew, reanimate; *ant.* dampen, depress.

reviving adj. stimulating, bracing, refreshing, invigorating, exhilarating, regenerating, tonic, revivifying, reanimating, reinvigorating; *ant.* exhausting.

revocation n. abolition, repeal, nullification, cancellation, reversal, revoking, repudiation, withdrawal, retraction, rescission, retraction, countermanding; *ant.* enforcement.

revoke v. repeal, retract, annul, cancel, rescind, nullify, withdraw, reverse, abolish, countermand, disclaim, recant, negate, invalidate; *ant.* enforce.

revolt n. rebellion, revolution, uprising, insurrection, mutiny, insurgency, secession, sedition.

revolt v. **1.** rebel, mutiny, riot, rise up, be up in arms; *ant.* submit. **2.** disgust, nauseate, offend, outrage, sicken, shock, repel, repulse, scandalize; *ant.* please, attract.

revolting adj. disgusting, appalling, repugnant, repulsive, sickening, distasteful, foul, nasty, horrible, obscene, offensive, abominable, noxious; *ant.* pleasant.

revolution n. **1.** uprising, revolt, rebellion, mutiny, insurrection, riot, anarchy, outbreak, coup, overthrow, reversal. **2.** rotation, turn, gyration, pirouette, orbit, cycle, roll, circuit, spin, circumvolution.

revolutionary n. rebel, radical, insurrectionist, anarchist, insurgent, mutineer.

revolutionary adj. **1.** radical, extremist, progressive, subversive, insurgent, insurrectionary; *ant.* conservative. **2.** new, novel, different, radical, experimental; *ant.* commonplace.

revolutionize v. reform, change, remodel, recast, refashion.

revolve v. orbit, rotate, circle, spin, turn, gyrate, whirl.

revolver n. gun, pistol, firearm, handgun, six-shooter, peacemaker (*slang*).

revolving adj. spinning, rotating, turning, gyrating, whirling; *ant.* stationary.

revulsion n. disgust, loathing, distaste, hatred, abomination, abhorrence, repulsion, aversion, dislike, distaste, repugnance; *ant.* pleasure.

reward n. prize, bonus, payment, gain, compensation, remuneration, payoff, benefit, desert; *ant.* punishment.

reward v. honor, compensate, pay, repay, remunerate, require, recompense; *ant.* punish.

rewarding adj. satisfying, worthwhile, fulfilling, enriching, gratifying, pleasing, beneficial, edifying, profitable.

rewording n. rephrasing, paraphrase, revision, metaphrase, metaphrasis.

rewrite v. revise, edit, emend, correct, reword, rework, recast, redraft.

rhapsody n. ecstasy, rapture, delight, effusion.

rhetoric n. **1.** address, oratory, composition, discourse, speech. **2.** bombast, verbosity, wordiness, pomposity, grandiloquence, rant, fustian.

rhetorical adj. **1.** expressive, fluent, articulate, eloquent, articulate. **2.** pretentious, pompous, inflated, exaggerated, overdone, artificial; *ant.* simple, understated.

rhyme *n.* **1.** poem, song, lyric, ballad, epic, ode, sonnet, dithyramb, ditty, limerick, jingle, doggerel. **2.** poetry, verse, poetics, versification, prosody, poesy, rime.

rhythm *n.* pulse, tempo, beat, cadence, meter, time, lilt, accent, measure, pulsation, swing, stress, repetition.

rhythmic *adj.* melodious, musical, harmonious, flowing, metric, metrical, throbbing, periodic.

rib *n.* support, rod, girder, bar, strip.

ribald *adj.* naughty, obscene, risqué, racy, suggestive, prurient, vulgar, smutty, indecent, bawdy, licentious, off-color, blue; *ant.* polite.

ribaldry *n.* smut, filth, indecency, vulgarity, obscenity, prurience, bawdiness, raciness, grossness, licentiousness.

ribbon *n.* strip, sash, band, tatter, shred.

rich *adj.* **1.** wealthy, affluent, moneyed, opulent, well-to-do, well off, *slang:* in the money, well-heeled, loaded; *ant.* poor, poverty-stricken, destitute. **2.** lush, luxurious, magnificent, resplendent, lavish, sumptuous, opulent, deluxe, lavish; *ant.* cheap, plain, simple. **the rich** of be freed, evade, have done with, fat cats (*slang*).

riches *n.* wealth, fortune, assets, money, resources, property.

rickety *adj.* unstable, unsteady, dilapidated, decrepit, shaky, ramshackle, weak, wobbly, infirm, derelict, precarious, broken-down, flimsy; *ant.* stable, strong.

rid *adj.* relieved, delivered, free.
be rid of be freed, evade, have done with, escape, be shut of.
get rid of shed, jettison, dump, ditch (*slang*), expel.

rid *v.* free, unburden, purge, deliver, clear, relieve, disburden, disencumber; *ant.* burden.

riddance *n.* purgation, freedom, release, relief, deliverance; disposal, ejection, expulsion, removal, extermination, clearance, elimination; *ant.* burdening.

riddle *n.* problem, puzzle, mystery, enigma, brain-teaser, poser, conundrum.

riddle *v.* pierce, puncture, pepper, invade, damage, fill, infest, impair, mar, permeate, perforate.

ride *n.* drive, trip, outing, journey, spin.

ride *v.* **1.** motor, drive, travel, journey. **2.** (*slang*) harass, persecute, hound, harry, badger, bait, disparage, revile, reproach, berate.

rider *n.* **1.** passenger, driver, motorist, cyclist, horseman, hitchhiker. **2.** addition, amendment, addendum, appendix, supplement, adjunct, appendage, codicil.

ridge *n.* welt, ripple, arete, hill, escarpment, reef, crinkle.

ridicule *n.* sarcasm, satire, scorn, taunting, derision, jeering, mockery, raillery; *ant.* praise, admiration.

ridicule *v.* mock, lampoon, send up, satirize, caricature, humiliate, parody, rib, taunt, deride, crucify, jeer, mock; *ant.* praise, respect.

ridiculous *adj.* absurd, nonsensical, stupid, preposterous, incredible, outrageous, off the wall (*slang*), unbelievable, beyond belief, ludicrous; hilarious, funny, laughable, silly, comical, foolish; *ant.* sensible.

rife *adj.* abundant, widespread, teeming, common, epidemic, prevalent, abounding, plentiful, rampant; *ant.* scarce.

riffraff *n.* mob, masses, rabble, scum, undesirables, hoi polloi, the great unwashed (*slang*).

rifle *n.* gun, shotgun, firearm, musket.

rifle *v.* rob, ransack, plunder, rummage, sack, loot, maraud, pillage.

rift *n.* **1.** cleft, division, fracture, breach, chink, schism, crevice, cranny. **2.** separation, quarrel, estrangement, divorce, disagreement, disparity, alienation; *ant.* unity.

rig *v.* **1.** equip, supply, outfit, provision, furnish, accoutre. **2.** engineer, arrange, falsify, fix, gerrymander, manipulate, tamper with, doctor, trump up, cook up.
rig out outfit, equip, clothe, accoutre, furnish, fit up, fit out, dress, dress up, costume, attire, array.
rig up erect, build, construct, arrange, assemble; *ant.* dismantle.

rigging *n.* equipment, gear, apparatus, implements.

right *n.* **1.** privilege, prerogative, freedom, license. **2.** conservatives, reactionaries, traditionalists, right wing, Old Guard, Republicans; *ant.* radical, left, liberals.
by rights rightly, justly, properly, suitably.

in one's own right independently, individually, on one's own, by one's own authority.

in the right correct, true, accurate, valid.

right *v.* rectify, fix, vindicate, repair, redress, put to right, correct, set right; *ant.* wrong, damage.

right *adj.* 1. correct, accurate, true, precise, valid, veritable, authentic, factual, exact, genuine, veracious; *ant.* invalid, wrong. 2. fitting, proper, suitable, appropriate, just, ethical, seemly; honorable, fair, virtuous; *ant.* inappropriate, wicked.

right away now, at once, this instant, immediately, presently, instantly, without delay, promptly, without hesitation, straightaway, tout de suite, directly, forthwith; *ant.* eventually, in due course.

righteous *adj.* just, virtuous, blameless, good, guiltless, honest, upright, fair, equitable, incorrupt, saintly, pure, chaste, moral, sinless; *ant.* wicked.

righteousness *n.* 1. holiness, piety, saintliness, devotion, devoutness, reverence, religiousness, godliness, spirituality, zeal, worship; *ant.* blasphemy. 2. justice, honor, fairness, virtue, integrity, rectitude, blamelessness, innocence, probity.

rightful *adj.* true, valid, legal, lawful, bona fide, proper, authorized, legitimate, correct, licit; *ant.* unlawful.

rightfully *adv.* rightly, justly, justifiably, correctly, legally, lawfully, legitimately, properly, de jure.

rightly *adv.* correctly, appropriately, justly, with reason, uprightly, properly, fitly, suitably, exactly, truly, accurately, well; *ant.* wrongly, without reason, erroneously.

rigid *adj.* inflexible, unbending, set, stiff, fixed, fast; uncompromising, unyielding, austere, stern, severe, adamant, harsh, strict; *ant.* pliant, indulgent.

rigmarole *n.* 1. hassle, bother, to-do, fuss, paperwork, red tape (*slang*). 2. nonsense, drivel, inanity, trash, balderdash.

rigor *n.* strictness, rigidity, precision, exactitude, meticulousness; asperity, austerity, firmness, inflexibility, sternness, privation, harshness; *ant.* leniency, mildness.

rigorous *adj.* thorough, severe, tough, strict, unsparing, meticulous, exacting, hard, extreme, painstaking, precise; *ant.* lenient, mild, rough.

rile *v.* anger, annoy, irritate, gall, provoke, pique, upset, vex, irk, peeve, exasperate, put out, *slang:* bug, get; *ant.* soothe.

rim *n.* edge, lip, brink, brim, circumference, border, perimeter, skirt, ledge, margin, verge; *ant.* center.

rime *n.* snow, sleet, icicle, frost, ice.

rind *n.* peel, skin, hull, shell, coating, bark, husk, crust, cortex, zest.

ring *n.* 1. circle, circuit, loop, enclosure, hoop, girdle, rim, halo, brim, collar, knot. 2. group, organization, party, faction, syndicate, bloc, monopoly, cartel, cabal, junta, gang, racket (*slang*).

ring *v.* 1. encircle, surround, circumscribe, encompass, hem in, enclose, loop, gird, belt, confine. 2. sound, resound, thunder, boom, reverberate, peal, chime, tinkle, jingle, vibrate, clang, tintinnabulate.

ringleader *n.* chief, leader, head, brains, spokesperson; rabble rouser, demagogue, bellwether, agent provocateur.

rinse *v.* clean, wash, cleanse, bathe, wet, splash, flush, dip, swill, sluice.

riot *n.* turmoil, uproar, anarchy, disturbance, insurrection, turbulence, commotion, strife, tumult, riotry, excess, revelry; *ant.* calm, order.

riot *v.* revolt, rebel, rise up, fight, run wild, rampage, frolic, carouse, romp, revel, roister.

riotous *adj.* loud, boisterous, rowdy, rambunctious, unruly, restive, insubordinate, mutinous, wild, anarchic, wanton; rollicking, festive; *ant.* orderly, restrained.

rip *n.* tear, hole, slit, rent, gash.

rip *v.* cut, tear, split, lacerate, slash, cleave, shred, rend, separate, claw, rive, rupture.

ripe *adj.* 1. mature, mellow, aged, wise, experienced, seasoned, sweetened. 2. ready, prepared, fit, conditioned, primed, set, all-set.

ripen *v.* develop, mature, age, mellow, season, prepare, burgeon.

rip-off (*slang*) *n.* robbery, theft, con, fraud, *slang:* scam, sting.

rip off (*slang*) *v.* defraud, cheat, dupe, trick, exploit, swindle, rob, steal, overcharge, pilfer, filch, fleece.

riposte *n.* response, answer, reply, comeback, retort, rejoinder, repartee, sally.

riposte *v.* respond, return, reciprocate, reply, rejoin, quip.

ripple *n.* wave, eddy, disturbance, ripplet, undulation, lapping, babble, gurgle.

rise *n.* **1.** increase, growth, acceleration, multiplication, increment, addition, enlargement, advance, accession; *ant.* reduction, decrease, lessening. **2.** (a coming into existence) origin, beginning, commencement, initiation, onset, start, source; *ant.* end, finish.

get a rise out of anger, tease, provoke, bait, annoy.

give rise to cause, initiate, begin, start.

rise *v.* **1.** ascend, mount, climb, scale, surmount, soar, tower, levitate, surge, lift; *ant.* fall, descend, drop. **2.** increase, move up, grow, enlarge, swell, intensify, heighten, spread, inflate, augment; *ant.* decrease, lessen, contract. **3.** wake, get up, arise; *ant.* retire.

risible *adj.* humorous, funny, amusing, comical, laughable, farcical, droll; *ant.* serious.

rising *n.* revolution, revolt, uprising, insurrection, riot.

rising *adj.* advancing, approaching, emerging, assurgent.

risk *n.* danger, peril, jeopardy, hazard, chance, possibility, speculation, venture, adventure, gamble; *ant.* certainty, safety.

at risk endangered, vulnerable, susceptible.

take risks play with fire, hang by a thread, stick one's neck out, be out on a limb, gamble.

risk *v.* hazard, venture, chance, jeopardize, imperil, dare, endanger.

risky *adj.* tricky, precarious, dodgy, touch-and-go, dicey (*slang*); *ant.* safe, certain.

risqué *adj.* suggestive, daring, racy, bawdy, ribald, naughty, crude, off-color, coarse, blue, earthy; *ant.* decent, modest, proper.

rite *n.* practice, custom, ritual, tradition, ceremony, ceremonial, observance, procedure, lit-

urgy, sacrament, service, worship, solemnity, formality, office.

ritual *n.* routine, procedure, practice, ceremony, habit, custom, convention, tradition, rite, observance, sacrament, ceremonial.

ritual *adj.* formal, prescribed, usual, stereotyped.

ritzy (*slang*) *adj.* luxurious, elegant, posh, rich, stylish, upscale.

rival *n.* **1.** adversary, competitor, opponent, challenger, contender, antagonist, contestant, emulator; *ant.* associate, colleague, co-worker. **2.** equal, match, peer, fellow, compeer.

rival *v.* compete, oppose, contend, vie with, match, emulate, equal; *ant.* cooperate.

rivalry *n.* conflict, contest, duel, struggle, antagonism.

river *n.* stream, creek, waterway, tributary, flow, course, estuary, current, rivulet, brook, flood, rush, surge.

sell down the river (*slang*) deceive, betray, abuse, cheat, double-cross, stab in the back (*slang*).

rivet *v.* **1.** fasten, nail, affix, fix. **2.** fascinate, absorb, engross, enthrall, captivate, hypnotize, magnetize, spellbind, grip, arrest; *ant.* bore.

rivulet *n.* brook, stream, creek, river.

road *n.* route, course, street, avenue, boulevard, drive, lane, path, highway, freeway, thoroughfare.

roam *v.* wander, meander, stroll, stray, ramble, drift, rove, range, walk, travel, prowl, gallivant; *ant.* stay.

roar *v.* thunder, rumble, howl, bellow, bawl, cry, holler, bay, guffaw, vociferate; *ant.* whisper.

roast *v.* cook, toast, broil, barbecue.

rob *v.* steal, swindle, rip off (*slang*), hold up, gyp, defraud, cheat, *slang:* sting, skin, fleece; loot, raid, strip, ransack; *ant.* give, provide.

robber *n.* thief, burglar, con man, bandit, pirate, highwayman, brigand, kleptomaniac.

robbery *n.* theft, heist, hold-up, stickup (*slang*), burglary.

robe *n.* bathrobe, housecoat, dressing-gown, wrap, peignoir, vestment, costume.

robe *v.* dress, clothe, attire, drape, vest.

robot *n.* automaton, machine, android, humanoid.

robust *adj.* hardy, sturdy, strong, rugged, brawny, powerful, strapping, able-bodied, healthy, lusty, vigorous, hale; *ant.* weak, fragile.

rock *n.* stone, boulder, cliff, crag, promontory.

rock *v.* sway, swing, pitch, reel, lurch, shake, tilt, toss; stun, astonish, astound, surprise, jar, dumbfound, shock, shake up.

rocket *n.* missile, projectile, spacecraft.

rocket *v.* climb, ascend, rise, soar, fly, sky-rocket.

rocky *adj.* **1.** jagged, craggy, bumpy, rough, rugged, stony; *ant.* even. **2.** difficult, formidable, rigorous, laborious, uphill; *ant.* effortless. **3.** weak, wobbly, shaky, staggering, faint, dizzy, sickly; *ant.* steady, strong.

rod *n.* staff, pole, stick, bar, cane, shaft, switch, mace, baton, scepter, wand.

rogue *n.* scoundrel, villain, rascal, scamp, knave, scapegrace.

roguish *adj.* **1.** criminal, corrupt, deceitful, shady, arch; *ant.* honest, scrupulous, principled. **2.** mischievous, playful, impish, tricky, confounded; *ant.* serious.

roguery *n.* tricks, bantering, badinage, fraud.

roisterous *adj.* boisterous, rowdy, uproarious, obstreperous, unruly, loud; *ant.* orderly, restrained, subdued.

role *n.* **1.** part, character, impersonation, portrayal, persona, representation. **2.** duty, function, job, post, position, task, capacity, office, station, responsibility, mandate, brief.

roll *n.* **1.** bread, pastry, bagel. **2.** noise, boom, resonance, drumbeat, grumble. **3.** list, roster, register, record, inventory, index, catalog, census.

roll *v.* **1.** turn, revolve, rotate, spin, spiral, reel, swirl, pivot, swivel, twirl, undulate, surge. **2.** advance, progress, move, proceed, propel. **3.** sound, echo, thunder, reverberate, cannonade.

romance *n.* **1.** adventure, mystery, fascination, excitement, appeal, allure, charm, interest. **2.** love affair, liaison, attachment, courtship, intrigue, amour.

romantic *n.* dreamer, idealist, visionary, sentimentalist, knight-errant; *ant.* realist.

romantic *adj.* **1.** adventurous, daring, chivalrous, legendary, enchanting, mythical, exotic, charming, idyllic, lyric, poetic. **2.** exagger-

ated, fabulous, fanciful, idealistic, optimistic, impractical, visionary, quixotic; *ant.* realistic. **3.** loving, affectionate, amorous, passionate, tender, devoted, sentimental.

romp *v.* frolic, cavort, sport, revel, rollick, caper, skip.

rook *v.* cheat, trick, deceive, swindle, defraud, slang; sting, rip off, con.

room *n.* **1.** chamber, compartment, enclosure, cubicle, office, salon, vault, cell, niche. **2.** space, accommodation, capacity, area, volume, measure, extent, allowance, scope, margin, play, latitude.

roomy *adj.* spacious, sizable, broad, large, wide, voluminous, extensive, capacious, generous, comfortable, ample, commodious; *ant.* cramped, crowded.

root *n.* origin, source, starting point, beginnings, stem, derivation, cause, basis, essence, nucleus, germ, seed, heart.

take root grow, start, commence.

root *v.* **1.** establish, set, fix, implant, anchor, embed, ground, entrench, sink, moor. **2.** dig, rummage, hunt, forage, pry, burrow, delve, poke, nose, grout, ferret.

root out 1. remove, erase, eliminate, eradicate, extirpate, expunge. **2.** unearth, discover, produce, uncover, reveal.

rooted *adj.* firm, fixed, deep, ingrained, confirmed, felt, rigid, radical; *ant.* superficial, temporary.

roots *n.* beginnings, origins, heritage, background, family, home, birthplace.

rope *n.* line, cord, cable, strand, string, thread.

at the end of one's rope desperate, hopeless, in despair, at the end of one's tether, at one's wit's end.

know the ropes comprehend, understand, know, be familiar with, know the ins and outs.

rope *v.* catch, bind, fasten, tie, tether, hitch, pinion.

rope in lure, involve, engage, persuade, enlist, embroil, entrap, inveigle.

rope off segregate, restrict, reserve, mark off.

roster *n.* register, list, roll, index, record, catalog, schedule.

rostrum *n.* stage, platform, podium, dais, pulpit, lectern, desk.

rosy *adj.* **1.** blushing, blooming, ruddy,

healthy. **2.** optimistic, bright, promising, hopeful, favorable, propitious, encouraging; *ant.* gloomy, dark.

rot *v.* **1.** decompose, decay, fester, putrefy, spoil, disintegrate, corrode, deteriorate, crumble. **2.** (lose health or strength) degenerate, deteriorate, decline, degrade, languish. **3.** (cause mental or moral decline) corrupt, deprave, pervert, blight, warp, ruin, impair, damage.

rotate *v.* **1.** revolve, spin, turn, pivot, reel, pirouette, gyrate, wheel. **2.** switch, alternate, interchange.

rotation *n.* sequence, succession, cycle, orbit, volution.

rote *n.* repetition, routine, custom, practice, habit, wont; memory.

rotten *adj.* **1.** putrid, rancid, rank, foul, contaminated, polluted, infected; *ant.* fresh. **2.** corrupt, fraudulent, crooked; inefficient, poor, inadequate, miserable, wretched; *ant.* honest, reliable.

rotund *adj.* **1.** round, rounded, circular, spherical, spheric, global, bulbous, orbicular; *ant.* flat. **2.** plump, corpulent, stocky, portly, stout, thickset, burly, chubby, pudgy, chunky, bloated; *ant.* slender, trim, thin, svelte, lean. **3.** resonant, vibrant, mellifluous, sonorous, rich, grandiloquent.

roué *n.* lecher, libertine, debauchee, rake, wanton, profligate.

rough *adj.* **1.** irregular, bumpy, jagged, corrugated, gnarled, broken; *ant.* uniform, smooth, level, plane. **2.** (said of weather or conditions) severe, intense, rigorous, harsh, agitated, violent, fierce, furious, stormy, tempestuous, turbulent, choppy; *ant.* gentle, serene, placid, calm, still. **3.** (said of speech, manners, etc.) rude, coarse, crude, ragged, gross, raw, crass; *ant.* delicate, elegant, refined, urbane. **4.** (being in an early state) unfinished, sketchy, rough-hewn, crude, unpolished, rudimentary, approximate, vague, amorphous; *ant.* crafted, perfected, exact. **5.** (hard to do) arduous, strenuous, laborious, trying, difficult, rugged, austere; *ant.* easy, light, lenient.

rough up manhandle, batter, beat up, mug, mistreat.

roughen *v.* scuff, graze, granulate, abrade, coarsen, harshen, rough; *ant.* smooth.

roughneck *n.* tough, rowdy, ruffian, bully, bruiser, thug, hooligan, lout, rough.

roughly *adv.* approximately, about, around, more or less, in round numbers.

round *n.* **1.** sphere, ball, globe, circle, disk, band, ring, loop, halo, crown, aureole. **2.** circuit, revolution, orbit, cycle, course, sequence, system, routine, schedule, process, procedure, arrangement. **3.** outburst, volley, barrage, spray, flare-up, burst, blast, rush, outbreak, eruption, salvo, fusillade.

round *v.* **1.** turn, wheel, spin, whirl. **2.** encircle, circle, compass, circumnavigate, skirt, flank. **3.** curve, arch, bend, bow, form, shape, mold.

round on attack, abuse, assail, retaliate, turn on, snap at, bite someone's head off (*slang*).

round up assemble, herd, muster, rally, marshal, gather, group, gather in, collect, drive; *ant.* disperse.

round *adj.* circular, rounded, spherical, spheroid, globular, orbed, orbicular, bulbous, rotund, orbiculate.

roundabout *adj.* **1.** indirect, circuitous, deviating, meandering, oblique, ambiguous, evasive, discursive, tortuous, devious; *ent.* direct, straightforward. **2.** surrounding, encompassing, circumambient, encircling, peripheral, outer, outside; *ant.* inner.

roundly *adv.* **1.** thoroughly, completely, entirely, totally, utterly, wholly, fully, altogether, absolutely, perfectly. **2.** vehemently, intensely, severely, bluntly, sharply, fiercely, violently, rigorously; *ant.* moderately, mildly, gently, lightly.

rouse *v.* **1.** awaken, arise, stir, wake, call, summon. **2.** stimulate, move, excite, provoke, incite, instigate, inflame, whip up, exhilarate; *ant.* calm.

rousing *adj.* lively, spirited, vivacious, animated, active, dynamic, vigorous, brisk; *ant.* dull, sluggish, slow.

rout *n.* flight, exodus, retreat, panic, riot, stampede, evacuation, reversal, defeat, ruin, debacle, fracas; *ant.* victory.

rout *v.* defeat, destroy, overthrow, beat, crush, conquer, subdue, subjugate, repel, repulse, dispel, scatter.

route *n.* **1.** course, itinerary, circuit, beat,

trajectory, run, passage, detour. **2.** road, street, avenue, boulevard, turnpike. **3.** means, agency, medium, system, method, procedure, process, steps, practice, protocol.

route *v.* send, direct, steer, head, maneuver, drive.

routine *n.* **1.** procedure, program, system, method, practice, schedule, protocol, sequence, arrangement, formula, recipe, prescription, rule, model. **2.** usage, wont, custom, tradition, convention.

routine *adj.* **1.** ordinary, everyday, regular, familiar, usual, normal, standard, conventional, accepted, accustomed; *ant.* extraordinary, original, exceptional, singular. **2.** (said of tasks, behavior, etc.) automatic, mechanical, perfunctory, compulsive, monotonous, numbing, dry, sterile, dull; *ant.* spontaneous, impulsive, creative.

rove *v.* roam, wander, ramble, stray, drift, meander, range, stroll, traipse, gallivant; *ant.* stay.

rover *n.* vagrant, transient, gypsy, nomad, traveler, itinerant, gadabout; *ant.* stay-at-home.

row *n.* sequence, series, succession, range, arrangement, file, rank, line, queue, run, course.

in a row consecutively, in succession, successively.

rowdy *n.* ruffian, troublemaker, brawler, hoodlum, hooligan, rough, tough, lout.

rowdy *adj.* boisterous, unruly, rambunctious, wild, disorderly, uproarious, obstreperous, rude, rough, boorish, mischievous, rebellious; *ant.* quiet, restrained.

royal *adj.* regal, imperial, majestic, stately, sovereign, monarchical, noble, grand, aristocratic.

rub *n.* **1.** stroke, touch, friction, wipe. **2.** difficulty, problem, dilemma, impediment, obstacle, hindrance, drawback, catch, hitch, snag, predicament, frustration.

rub *v.* **1.** stroke, massage, caress, knead, clean, scrub, polish, shine, spread, apply, smooth. **2.** abrade, chafe, irritate, inflame, grate, rasp.

rub out 1. erase, delete, efface, remove, eliminate, eradicate, expunge, cancel. **2.** (*slang*) kill, destroy, shoot, assassinate, bump off (*slang*).

rub the wrong way irritate, anger, annoy, peeve, irk, needle, bug, vex, *slang;* get to, get, get under one's skin; *ant.* placate, appease.

rubbish *n.* **1.** trash, garbage, litter, waste, junk, scrap, landfill, debris, refuse, offal, leavings. **2.** nonsense, bombast, gibberish, drivel, balderdash, claptrap, bunk, gobbledygook; *ant.* sense.

ruddy *adj.* healthy, florid, flushed, sanguine, robust; *ant.* sickly, pale, wan, pallid, ashen.

rude *adj.* **1.** (lacking social refinement) boorish, coarse, raw, crude, rustic, barbarous, awkward, clumsy, indecorous, graceless, common, vulgar, illiterate; *ant.* cultured, urbane, suave. **2.** impertinent, ill-mannered, insolent, fresh, blunt, brusque, churlish, surly, gruff, crass, arrogant, supercilious; *ant.* polite, courteous, gracious, civil. **3.** approximate, rough, gross, broad, imprecise, inexact; *ant.* accurate. **4.** (said of weather or conditions) violent, rough, harsh, severe.

rudimentary *adj.* **1.** primary, basic, fundamental, elementary, initial, original, introductory, early, germinal; *ant.* advanced. **2.** incomplete, half-done, imperfect, embryonic, inchoate, vestigial; *ant.* developed, finished.

rudiments *n.* essentials, principles, foundation, core.

rue *v.* regret, deplore, mourn, lament, bemoan, bewail, repent; *ant.* rejoice.

rueful *adj.* sorry, conscience-stricken, remorseful, grievous, regretful, contrite, penitent, self-reproachful, woeful, melancholy, lugubrious; *ant.* defiant.

ruffian *n.* thug, hoodlum, hooligan, bully, brute, villain, scoundrel, rogue, miscreant, hood (*slang*), criminal, crook.

ruffle *n.* frill, flounce, pleat, fold, crimp, tuck, gather, border.

ruffle *v.* **1.** disarrange, rumple, dishevel, tousle, muddle, stir, ripple, churn, roughen, flurry. **2.** irritate, provoke, aggravate, exasperate, upset, annoy, peeve, vex, gripe, gall, pique, psych (*slang*).

rugged *adj.* **1.** uneven, irregular, bumpy, rough, jagged, ridged, rippled, crinkled, corrugated. **2.** (as of a task) difficult, hard, laborious, rigorous, strenuous, severe, stringent, demanding, trying. **3.** (said of a physique) robust, sturdy, hardy, able-bodied, husky, brawny, stout, vigorous, stalwart.

ruin *n.* 1. collapse, destitution, decay, disintegration, ruination, failure, crash, demolition, dissolution, fall, breakup, extinction, subversion, havoc; *ant.* reconstruction. 2. undoing, downfall, affliction, curse.

ruin *v.* 1. demolish, destroy, devastate, defeat, wreck, ravage, damage, injure, exhaust, impoverish, deplete; *ant.* restore, develop. 2. shame, humiliate, embarrass, disgrace, dishonor, debase, humble, impoverish.

ruinous *adj.* disastrous, calamitous, catastrophic, cataclysmic, deleterious, destructive, wasteful, injurious, deadly, dire, noxious, pernicious.

ruins *n.* 1. remains, traces, foundations, remnants, relics, vestiges. 2. wreckage, shambles, debris, destruction, devastation, chaos.

rule *n.* 1. power, authority, jurisdiction, leadership, direction, sway, dominion, sovereignty, supremacy. 2. procedure, method, course, action, pattern, habit, custom, practice, protocol, regimen, regime. 3. regulation, law, statute, measure, directive, dictate, charge, ordinance, mandate, code, edict, maxim, tenet.

rule *v.* 1. govern, reign, command, control, dominate, manage, direct, guide, influence. 2. decide, determine, pronounce, find, decree.

rule out 1. (refuse to accept) eliminate, reject, ban, disallow, dismiss, exclude, debar, delete. 2. (render difficult or impossible) prohibit, prevent, preclude, discourage, exclude, hinder.

ruler *n.* leader, chief, head of state, president, monarch, dictator, king, queen, emperor, potentate, sovereign.

ruling *adj.* principal, main, dominant, chief, predominant, prevalent, preeminent, supreme, preponderant.

ruling *n.* judgment, decision, verdict, resolution, decree, pronouncement, adjudication, finding.

rumble *n.* noise, reverberation, roll, drumbeat.

rumble *v.* sound, resound, growl, thunder.

ruminate *v.* contemplate, muse, ponder, reflect, brood, think, mull over, cogitate, meditate, deliberate, consider, revolve.

rummage *v.* ransack, root, search, poke around, delve, examine, explore, rout, hunt, scour, turn inside out.

rumor *n.* hearsay, gossip, insinuation, tale, report, news, tidings, intelligence, the grapevine.

rump *n.* backside, rear, seat, haunch, hindquarters, buttocks, posterior, bottom.

rumple *v.* wrinkle, tousle, ruffle, crinkle, crumple, crease, scrunch, pucker, dishevel, muss, crush, disorder; *ant.* smooth.

rumpus *n.* disturbance, commotion, uproar, to-do, brouhaha, disruption, confusion, tumult; *ant.* calm.

run *n.* 1. (act or style of running) race, dash, jog, trot, pace, break. 2. series, sequence, cycle, continuity, succession, progression. 3. course, track, way, path, route, field.

in the long run finally, ultimately, eventually, at last.

run *v.* 1. race, jog, sprint, dash, speed, bound, charge, rush, hurry, scamper, flee, escape. 2. (applied to machinery) function, operate, work, perform. 3. flow, surge, rush, flood, course. 4. administer, head, manage, oversee, supervise, control, direct, lead. 5. (cover or apply to in area or extent) extend, reach, come, range, spread, cover, surround, encompass.

run after follow, chase, pursue, tail, stalk, hunt, shadow.

run down chase, pursue, hunt, capture, seize, apprehend.

run into 1. encounter, meet, see, contact; *ant.* miss. 2. contact, collide with, hit, ram, bash, strike.

run out 1. stop, expire, finish, end, cease, dry up, close, terminate. 2. leave, abandon, depart, run away, escape.

run out of exhaust, use up, spend, lose, squander, dissipate, waste.

run together unite, fuse, blend, combine, merge, join; *ant.* separate.

runaround *n.* delay, postponement, diversion, evasion, song and dance.

runaway *n.* fugitive, delinquent, truant, refugee, lawbreaker.

rundown *n.* summary, briefing, review, recap, synopsis, sketch, outline, overview.

run-down *adj.* 1. dilapidated, ramshackle, broken-down, shabby, makeshift, tumbledown, dingy, seedy, decrepit; *ant.* well-kept.

2. fatigued, weary, weak, debilitated, enervated, spent; *ant.* healthy.

run-in *n.* encounter, altercation, confrontation, fight, argument, dispute, skirmish, quarrel, brush, difference of opinion.

runner *n.* athlete, competitor, contestant, entrant, sprinter, racer, jogger, marathoner, hurdler, miler; messenger, courier, express, dispatch bearer.

run-of-the-mill *adj.* average, everyday, commonplace, routine, ordinary, modest, tolerable; *ant.* exceptional, impressive.

runt *n.* midget, shrimp, pygmy, dwarf, half pint (*slang*).

rupture *n.* 1. split, tear, fissure. 2. estrangement, rift, divorce, breach, falling-out, quarrel, altercation.

rupture *v.* burst, open, break, sever, cleave, divide, rend, crack.

rural *adj.* country, rustic, pastoral, bucolic, agrarian, backwoods, agricultural, sylvan; *ant.* urban.

ruse *n.* device, artifice, stratagem, maneuver, dodge, deception, hoax, trick, subterfuge.

rush *n.* urgency, swiftness, onslaught, surge.

rush *v.* hurry, hasten, speed, race, hustle, hightail, scurry, shoot, storm, tear, fly, press, stampede.

rush *adj.* 1. prompt, swift, rapid, expeditious,

urgent, emergency. 2. hurried, hasty, cursory, careless, superficial.

rust *v.* oxidize, deteriorate, corrode, decay, tarnish.

rust *adj.* russet, auburn, ginger, chestnut, copper, tawny.

rustic *adj.* 1. rural, country, pastoral, agrarian, sylvan, bucolic, agricultural; *ant.* urban. 2. coarse, rough, boorish, uncouth, lubberly, simple, awkward, dull; *ant.* cultured, refined.

rustic *n.* bumpkin, peasant, hillbilly, hick, yokel, rube (*slang*), swain; *ant.* sophisticate, manabout-town, dandy.

rustle *v.* swish, crackle, stir, murmur, susurrate.

rustle up assemble, round up, collect, get together.

rusty *adj.* inadequate, deficient, stiff, out of shape, out-of-practice, deteriorated; *ant.* polished, practiced, fluent.

rut *n.* 1. track, hollow, trench, furrow, groove, channel, ditch, indentation, wheelmark, gutter, pothole. 2. routine, habit, custom, pattern, practice, system.

rut *v.* mark, score, gouge, cut.

ruthless *adj.* pitiless, callous, inhuman, heartless, coldblooded, remorseless, implacable, cruel, relentless, severe, ferocious, vicious, cutthroat; *ant.* compassionate, merciful.

sabbatical *n.* leave, time off, vacation, holiday.
sable *adj.* black, ebony, jet, pitch-black, midnight, raven.
sabotage *n.* damage, vandalism, treachery, destruction, impairment.
sabotage *v.* undermine, subvert, disrupt, attack, impair, throw a monkey wrench into, cripple, disable, incapacitate, wreck, destroy, demolish.
sac *n.* pouch, bladder, sack, vesicle, pocket, capsule, cyst.
sack *n.* **1.** bag, pouch, container, pocket. **2.** plunder, ruin, destruction, rapine. **3.** (*slang*) dismissal, notice, discharge, *slang:* the boot, the ax, pink slip.
sack *v.* **1.** (*slang*) dismiss, fire, lay off, discharge, cashier, can (*slang*). **2.** pillage, loot, plunder, lay waste, raze, demolish, ravage, devastate, maraud, desecrate, despoil.
sacred *adj.* **1.** consecrated, ordained, divine, pure, reverend, saintly, holy, blessed, godly, hallowed; *ant.* mundane, profane. **2.** inviolate, protected, sacrosanct, solemn, defended.
sacrifice *n.* **1.** offering, tribute, hecatomb, immolation, oblation; atonement, penance. **2.** martyr, victim, scapegoat. **3.** renunciation, abnegation, surrender, yielding.
sacrifice *v.* **1.** consecrate, offer up, dedicate, devote. **2.** forfeit, yield, surrender, relinquish, renounce, forgo, abandon.
sacrificial *adj.* expiatory, conciliatory, atoning.
sacrilege *n.* blasphemy, desecration, disrespect, curse, heresy, mockery, profanity, violation; *ant.* piety, reverence, respect.
sacrilegious *adj.* irreverent, wicked, sinful, blasphemous, heretical, godless; *ant.* pious, respectful, holy.
sacrosanct *adj.* sacred, reverent, blessed, divine, hallowed, inviolate, sanctified, untouchable, precious.
sad *adj.* **1.** downcast, dismal, gloomy, desolate, melancholy, unhappy, dispirited, dejected, troubled, morose, depressed, despondent, wistful, crestfallen, pessimistic, down in the mouth, down in the dumps, blue (*slang*); *ant.* happy, cheerful. **2.** (evoking sadness) mournful, pitiful, sorrowful, moving, touching, heart-rending, pathetic; lugubrious, tear-jerking (*slang*); joyless, dreary, dark, funereal; *ant.* heartening, comforting, pleasant. **3.** (*slang*) inferior, cheap, common, poor, second-class, shabby.
sadden *v.* discourage, oppress, dishearten, deject, depress, aggrieve, upset, dispirit, disturb; *ant.* encourage, cheer, delight.
saddle *v.* burden, encumber, load, tax, task, impose.
sadism *n.* barbarity, cruelty, perversion, malice.
sadistic *adj.* cruel, brutal, vicious, perverted, malicious.
sadness *n.* sorrow, dejection, melancholy, grief, distress, despondence, regret, sorrow, oppression; *ant.* delight, happiness.
safe *n.* vault, strongbox, coffer, chest, repository, safe deposit box.
safe *adj.* **1.** secure, protected, guarded, housed, screened, invulnerable, impregnable, shielded; *ant.* endangered. **2.** harmless, tame, innocent, innocuous; *ant.* dangerous, risky. **3.** reliable, trustworthy, dependable, competent, sound, proven, loyal, faithful.
safeguard *n.* defense, guard, shield, surety, escort, precaution, preventive.
safeguard *v.* defend, guard, insure, assure, preserve, protect, screen, shield, secure, shelter; *ant.* endanger, jeopardize.
safekeeping *n.* care, charge, custody, keeping, guardianship, supervision, protection, security.
safety *n.* security, surety, reliability, immunity, assurance; deliverance, sanctuary, refuge, shelter; *ant.* danger, jeopardy.
sag *v.* sink, bend, warp, lean, decline, droop,

saga fail, weaken, flag, settle, wane, wilt; *ant.* bulge, rise.

saga *n.* epic, legend, adventure, chronicle, history, narrative, story, tale, yarn.

sagacious *adj.* perceptive, astute, intelligent, witty, discerning, insightful, shrewd, smart, judicious, wise, discerning, sage, perspicacious, farsighted; *ant.* foolish, obtuse, shortsighted.

sagacity *n.* acumen, judgment, discrimination, foresight, insight, sapience, sense, understanding, wisdom; *ant.* folly, foolishness.

sage *n.* philosopher, authority, elder, expert, guru, master, pundit, savant, teacher, wise man, maharishi; *ant.* ignoramus.

sage *adj.* prudent, judicious, learned, philosophic, discerning, knowing, politic, sensible, wise; *ant.* foolish.

sail *v.* 1. leave, embark, set sail, get under way, weigh anchor, put to sea. 2. cruise, voyage, travel, navigate, pilot, captain. 3. (as in the air) fly, soar, skim, scud, wing, sweep, glide, float, drift, waft.

sail into (*slang*) attack, assault, lambaste, lay or tear into.

sailor *n.* 1. seaman, mariner, seafarer, sea-dog, salt, tar. 2. (member of the military) navy man or woman, marine, midshipman, seabee, bluejacket, *slang*: leatherneck, gob.

saintly *adj.* 1. spiritual, pious, faithful, devout, blessed, holy, angelic, beatific, blest, godly, sainted, seraphic; *ant.* wicked, sinful. 2. virtuous, upright, pure, chaste, selfless, worthy.

sake *n.* 1. end, objective, result, consequence, aim, purpose, score, motive, principle, reason. 2. welfare, benefit, account, behalf, interest, advantage, welfare, well-being.

salacious *adj.* lewd, lascivious, wicked, wanton, lecherous, bawdy, obscene, raunchy, ribald; *ant.* clean, proper, decent.

salary *n.* pay, wages, earnings, stipend, recompense, remuneration.

sale *n.* 1. commerce, business, exchange, barter, marketing, vending, trade, transaction, negotiation, auction, buying, selling. 2. clearance, bargain, fire sale, bankruptcy sale, closeout, sellout.

for sale selling, on the market, on the auction block, advertised, listed.

saleable *adj.* marketable, vendible, desirable, sought-after.

salesperson *n.* clerk, sales assistant, peddler, shopkeeper, storekeeper, vendor, merchandiser.

salient *adj.* 1. remarkable, prominent, notable, striking, telling, conspicuous, famous, arresting, chief, significant; *ant.* retreat. 2. jutting, swelling, projecting, protruding.

sallow *adj.* pasty, sickly, wan, yellowish, waxy, ashen, pallid, colorless, jaundiced, bilious, anemic; *ant.* rosy, sanguine.

sally *n.* 1. foray, excursion, expedition, sortie, trip, jaunt, raid, assault; *ant.* retreat. 2. jest, joke, quip, wisecrack, witticism, bon mot, crack, retort.

sally *v.* venture, stroll, issue, erupt, surge, rush, charge, dash.

salt *v.* 1. season, flavor, spice, leaven, imbue, lace, ginger. 2. scatter, strew, pepper, spread.

salty *adj.* piquant, pungent, sharp, witty, acerbic; racy, ribald, coarse, vulgar, obscene; *ant.* bland, refined, delicate, prudish.

salubrious *adj.* advantageous, beneficial, healthy, helpful, profitable, timely, useful, valuable, tonic, curative.

salutation *n.* greeting, address, welcome, salute, respects, homage.

salute *n.* acknowledgment, bow, wave, tribute, honor, ovation, fanfare, commemoration, celebration, salutation, hello.

salute *v.* hail, address, recognize, greet, acknowledge, recognize, welcome.

salvage *v.* retrieve, recover, restore, reclaim, rescue, glean, conserve, preserve, save; *ant.* lose, waste.

salvation *n.* 1. deliverance, liberation, emancipation, rescue, reprieve, pardon, escape. 2. redemption, mercy, forgiveness, sanctification, work of grace, regeneration, rebirth.

salve *n.* balm, cream, dressing, liniment, ointment, medication, lubricant, emollient, lotion.

same *adj.* 1. identical, equal, alike, equivalent, duplicate, comparable, analogous, corresponding, matching, synonymous, uniform; *ant.* different. 2. changeless, immutable, constant, invariable, regular, consistent.

sameness *n.* repetition, monotony, tedium, predictability, uniformity, identity; *ant.* difference, variety.

sample *n.* example, representation, specimen, demonstration, illustration, instance, model.

sample *v.* test, examine, inspect, investigate, taste, sip, try.

sanctify *v.* **1.** consecrate, dedicate, hallow, anoint, bless, beatify; *ant.* desecrate, profane, defile. **2.** purify, absolve, cleanse, redeem, shrive; *ant.* condemn, damn, excommunicate.

sanctimonious *adj.* hypocritical, priggish, self-righteous, smug, superior, bigoted, deceiving, insincere, holier-than-thou, preachy; *ant.* humble.

sanction *n.* **1.** permission, consent, assent, accreditation, approval, authorization, endorsement, imprimatur, license, seal, indulgence; *ant.* disapproval, veto. **2.** decree, command, writ, sentence, injunction, ban, embargo.

sanction *v.* approve, countenance, endorse, confirm, ratify, authorize, accredit, warrant, permit, allow; *ant.* forbid, hinder, veto, censure.

sanctions *n.* restriction, embargo, boycott, prohibition, ban.

sanctity *n.* saintliness, purity, godliness, piety, spirituality, sacredness, holiness, grace, virtue, righteousness; *ant.* irreverence, sacrilege, worldliness.

sanctuary *n.* **1.** sanctum, shrine, temple, altar, tabernacle. **2.** refuge, asylum, haven, shelter, retreat.

sand *n.* dust, grit, powder, gravel, silt, loam, dirt.

sandy *adj.* **1.** loose, permeable, porous, light, granular, powdery, gritty. **2.** fair-haired, blond, tawny, sun-bleached, flaxen, towheaded.

sane *adj.* sound, sensible, wise, rational, lucid, reasonable, sober, normal, healthy, sapient, sage, judicious; *ant.* deranged, demented, disturbed, imprudent.

sang-froid *n.* composure, indifference, nerve, self-control, nonchalance, cool (*slang*), equanimity; *ant.* excitability, hysteria.

sanguinary *adj.* bloody, gory, cruel, ferocious, savage, bloodthirsty, merciless, pitiless, ruthless, murderous.

sanguine *adj.* **1.** enthusiastic, optimistic, hopeful, assured, spirited, unabashed, animated,

ardent, cheerful, buoyant; *ant.* cynical, pessimistic. **2.** flushed, pink, red, rosy, rubicund, ruddy, florid; *ant.* pale, sallow.

sanitary *adj.* hygienic, germ-free, clean, sterile, disinfected, antiseptic, sterilized, healthy, wholesome; *ant.* polluted, contaminated.

sanity *n.* rationality, common sense, lucidity, reason, marbles (*slang*), coherence, moderation; *ant.* folly, madness, dementia.

sap *n.* **1.** lifeblood, vital fluid, essence, blood, juice. **2.** (*slang*) fool, sucker, simpleton, dolt, gull, dupe.

sap *v.* weaken, debilitate, enervate, exhaust, devitalize, drain, deplete, diminish, reduce, undermine, subvert; *ant.* strengthen, restore, regenerate, fortify.

sapient *adj.* judicious, wise, sagacious, discriminating.

sarcasm *n.* satire, irony, scorn, cynicism, derision, ridicule, mockery, lampooning, scoffing; *ant.* flattery, approval, admiration.

sarcastic *adj.* taunting, caustic, bitter, biting, cutting, cynical, derisive, ridiculing, contemptuous, acerbic, acrimonious, disdainful.

sardonic *adj.* sarcastic, cynical, bitter, dry, ironical, jeering, contemptuous, malevolent, wry.

sass (*slang*) *n.* impudence, disrespect, impertinence, pertness, boldness, freshness, forwardness, brass.

Satan *n.* Lucifer, Mephistopheles, Beelzebub, the Devil, Prince of Darkness.

satanic *adj.* sinister, wicked, malicious, vicious, demonic, diabolical, evil, infernal, hellish, fiendish, malevolent, malignant; *ant.* benevolent, benign.

sate *v.* satiate, glut, gorge, gratify, saturate, slake, surfeit, cloy, overfill, sicken; *ant.* deprive, starve.

satellite *n.* **1.** moon, asteroid, planetoid; space station, sputnik, capsule. **2.** adherent, aide, dependent, disciple, follower, lackey, minion, subordinate, sycophant, vassal.

satiate *v.* satisfy, gratify, gorge, glut, sate, slake, stuff, cloy, nauseate; *ant.* deprive, underfeed.

satire *n.* ridicule, sarcasm, irony, exposure, mockery, sendup, takeoff, wit, burlesque, parody, caricature, spoof, humor.

409

satirical *adj.* sarcastic, caustic, derisive, taunting, cynical, sardonic, malicious, incisive, pungent.

satirize *v.* lampoon, ridicule, mock, parody, deride, mimic; *ant.* honor, acclaim, celebrate.

satisfaction *n.* **1.** (act of satisfying) fulfillment, achievement, expiation, restitution, compensation, reparation, amends, recompense, redemption, atonement. **2.** (good feeling) gratification, contentment, relief, serenity, comfort, pleasure, delight, heart's ease; *ant.* resentment, want.

satisfactory *adj.* adequate, acceptable, sufficient, suitable, passable, competent, fair.

satisfied *adj.* content, happy, pleased, comfortable.

satisfy *v.* **1.** comfort, cheer, delight, amuse, entertain, gratify; gorge, glut. **2.** (pay a debt) repay, settle, compensate, reimburse, remunerate, requite, square up. **3.** (fill a requirement or expectation) fulfill, discharge, meet, quiet, assuage, answer, appease, suffice, conform with, furnish, equip; *ant.* neglect. **4.** (make a point in argument) convince, persuade, inveigle, pacify, assure, reassure, mollify.

satisfying *adj.* pleasing, pleasant, enjoyable, fulfilling, gratifying, comforting; *ant.* frustrating.

saturate *v.* soak, suffuse, waterlog, immerse, douse, drench, overfill, infuse, permeate; *ant.* dry, drain, evaporate, dehydrate.

saturated *adj.* soaked, wet, soaking wet, drenched, sodden, sopping, waterlogged.

saturnine *adj.* morose, grave, austere, dour, heavy, melancholy, severe, somber, stern, taciturn; *ant.* cheerful, jovial.

satyr *n.* lecher, sensualist, debaucher, womanizer, wretch, rake, reprobate; *ant.* celibate, ascetic, puritan.

saucy *adj.* rude, sassy (*slang*), flippant, impudent, impertinent, brash, bold, pert.

saunter *v.* amble, stroll, wander, idle, meander, dawdle, mosey (*slang*), rove, dally.

savage *adj.* **1.** fierce, cruel, ferocious, merciless, brutal, cruel, inhuman, vicious, feral, wild, terrible, ruthless; *ant.* gentle, tender, mild, kind. **2.** primitive, crude, barbaric, ancient, rustic; *ant.* civilized, cultured, advanced.

savagery *n.* barbarity, bestiality, brutality, cruelty, inhumanity, viciousness, sadism; *ant.* decency.

savant *n.* philosopher, authority, intellectual, master, guru, pundit, sage, scholar, polymath; *ant.* amateur, dope, ignoramus.

save *v.* **1.** rescue, deliver, extricate, liberate, emancipate, release, free; *ant.* abandon, sacrifice, surrender, condemn. **2.** collect, cache, store, put aside, squirrel away, lay up, amass, accumulate, gather, hoard, husband, salt away; *ant.* spend, waste, squander, disperse.

savings *n.* reserves, resources, store, means, funds, investment, provision, accumulation, gleanings, hoard, cache, nest egg.

savior *n.* deliverer, rescuer, hero, preserver, protector, benefactor, champion, liberator; *ant.* nemesis, traitor, seducer.

savoir-faire *n.* tact, poise, manners, urbanity, finesse, grace, elegance, sophistication, discretion, courtesy, politesse.

savor *v.* **1.** enjoy, relish, fancy, appreciate, value, admire. **2.** taste, smell, smack, reek, betoken, indicate, suggest, resemble.

savory *adj.* palatable, pleasing, appetizing, delectable, delicious, luscious, piquant, salubrious, ambrosial; *ant.* tasteless, unappetizing.

saw *n.* proverb, saying, maxim, adage, axiom, aphorism, byword.

say *n.* voice, vote, authority, influence, power, clout.

say *v.* **1.** tell, speak, recite, state, utter, declare, remark, express, disclose, pronounce, articulate. **2.** allege, claim, hold, maintain, assert, imply.

saying *n.* **1.** utterance, statement, declaration, communication, collocation. **2.** maxim, proverb, aphorism, adage, motto.

say-so *n.* approval, authorization, backing, consent, permission, acquiescence, agreement, sanction, OK.

scald *v.* burn, char, sear, blister.

scale *n.* **1.** calibration, graduation, measure, system, degrees; sequence, order, continuum, gradation, ranking, progression, hierarchy. **2.** plate, crust, layer, flake, lamina.

scale *v.* **1.** ascend, climb, clamber, mount, escalate, surmount, shinny; *ant.* descend, dismount, fall. **2.** peel, exfoliate, strip off, skin, flake, scrape, clean. **3.** compare, balance, compute, estimate, deliberate, graduate, adjust, regulate, shift.

scam (*slang*) *n.* swindle, hoax, fraud, *slang:* con, con game, dodge.

scamp *n.* rascal, rogue, knave, scoundrel, prankster.

scamper *v.* hurry, run, hasten, speed, dash, rush, dart, scurry, scuttle, sprint; *ant.* lag, dawdle, loiter, crawl.

scan *v.* **1.** investigate, study, examine, peruse, scrutinize, search, survey, consider. **2.** browse, glance at, skim.

scandal *n.* shame, disgrace, embarrassment, outrage, offense, abomination, sham, crime.

scandalize *v.* outrage, affront, offend, shock, embarrass, appall.

scandalous *adj.* infamous, disreputable, ignominious, improper, scurrilous, exorbitant, immoderate, unseemly, slanderous.

scant *adj.* scarce, meager, bare, minimal, sparse, insufficient, slight, deficient, exiguous; *ant.* abundant, plentiful, ample, profuse, copious, adequate.

scanty *adj.* deficient, thin, skimpy, scant, parsimonious, paltry, ragged, few, restricted; *ant.* adequate, excessive.

scapegoat *n.* victim, dupe, *slang:* patsy, fall guy; whipping boy, sacrifice.

scar *n.* blemish, injury, lesion, wound, discoloration, disfigurement, defect, flaw, cicatrix.

scar *v.* mark, brand, disfigure, traumatize.

scarce *adj.* rare, unusual, uncommon, odd, unique, exceptional; limited, few, infrequent, scanty, sparse; *ant.* common, plentiful.

scarcity *n.* dearth, deficiency, lack, insufficiency, rarity, poverty, shortage, want; *ant.* abundance, glut, plenty, plethora.

scare *n.* fright, alarm, shock, start, terror, fear, consternation, panic, agitation; *ant.* reassurance.

scare *v.* frighten, alarm, shock, terrify, startle, dismay, unnerve, intimidate; *ant.* reassure, soothe, lull.

scared *adj.* afraid, frightened, fearful, startled, petrified, panic-stricken.

scary *adj.* frightening, alarming, disturbing, horrifying, upsetting, unnerving, creepy, spooky, spine-chilling.

scathing *adj.* withering, searing, caustic, cut-

ting, severe, excoriating, scornful, biting, acerbic, trenchant; *ant.* gentle, benign, bland.

scatter *v.* **1.** strew, disseminate, broadcast, sprinkle, spread, sow; *ant.* assemble, gather, cluster. **2.** (to break up, as a crowd) disperse, dissipate, dispel, rout, separate, diffuse; *ant.* rally, unite, converge, assemble, meet.

scatterbrained *adj.* silly, giddy, irrational, empty-headed, addled, addlepated, thoughtless, distracted, fey, frivolous, flighty, *slang:* dizzy, ditsy; featherbrained; *ant.* sensible, sober.

scavenge *n.* clean, forage, collect, salvage, rummage, sweep.

scenario *n.* summary, plot, outline, synopsis, sketch, plan, rundown.

scene *n.* **1.** landscape, view, prospect, picture, tableau, panorama; setting, set, scenery, backdrop, background, ambiance, environment. **2.** (public display of emotion) spectacle, exhibition, display, commotion, outburst, episode, incident, outburst, sight, tantrum, to-do.

scenery *n.* **1.** landscape, outlook, panorama, surroundings, terrain, view, vista. **2.** setting, mise en scène, backdrop.

scenic *adj.* picturesque, pretty, breathtaking, impressive, panoramic; *ant.* dreary, dull.

scent *n.* smell, odor, fragrance, perfume, redolence, aroma, bouquet, essence, whiff.

scented *adj.* aromatic, fragrant, odoriferous, redolent.

schedule *n.* agenda, timetable, outline, program, catalog, table, protocol, roll, inventory, list, plan.

schedule *v.* plan, organize, slate, appoint, book, engage, arrange, reserve, line up.

scheme *n.* plot, stratagem, intrigue, machinations, conspiracy, contrivance, subterfuge, ruse, plan.

scheme *v.* conspire, collude, contrive, angle, devise, maneuver, manipulate, machinate, mastermind.

schemer *n.* plotter, conniver, deceiver, Machiavellian.

scheming *adj.* artful, sly, tricky, cunning, crafty, calculating, devious, unscrupulous, wily; *ant.* honest, open.

schism *n.* division, split, breach, rupture, rift, faction, break, discord; *ant.* union, fusion, harmony, compromise.

scholar *n.* **1.** academic, professor, authority, intellectual, sage, savant, philosopher; *ant.* illiterate, ignoramus, philistine. **2.** student, pupil, apprentice, disciple.

scholarly *adj.* educated, learned, erudite, intellectual, cultured, studious, critical, analytical; *ant.* illiterate.

scholarship *n.* **1.** erudition, education, insight, knowledge, learning, lore, pedantry. **2.** endowment, grant, fellowship, award.

scholastic *adj.* academic, learned, literary, lettered, analytical, scholarly; pedagogic; pedantic; bookish.

school *n.* **1.** academy, institute, seminary, college, alma mater. **2.** group, sect, faction, denomination, persuasion, set.

school *v.* educate, coach, drill, instruct, prepare, prime, train, tutor, verse, inure, discipline, indoctrinate.

scientific *adj.* systematic, empirical, precise, accurate, methodical, analytical, objective, material, exact; *ant.* transcendental, spiritual, intuitive.

scintillate *v.* spark, flash, glimmer, shine, twinkle, gleam, wink.

scintillating *adj.* animated, vivacious, witty, bright, exciting, lively, sparkling, stimulating; *ant.* obtuse, dense, dull, stolid.

scoff *v.* belittle, mock, deride, jeer, ridicule, revile, scorn, taunt; *ant.* praise, commend, appreciate.

scold *v.* admonish, reprove, reprimand, chide, berate, chasten, castigate, rebuke, upbraid, dress down, disparage, chew out (*slang*); *ant.* praise, commend.

scoop *n.* **1.** ladle, trowel, spoon, dipper. **2.** (*slang*) exclusive, coup, exposé, inside story, revelation, latest, lowdown, gossip.

scoop *v.* bail, dig, empty, excavate, hollow, shovel, remove, scrape.

scoot *v.* dart, speed, rush, hurry, scamper, scurry, scuttle, sprint, bolt, career; *ant.* dawdle, lounge, amble.

scope *n.* reach, range, field, extent, area, breadth, compass, latitude, span, sphere.

scorch *v.* wither, sear, shrivel, parch, singe, char, scald, burn.

scorching *adj.* **1.** hot, searing, burning, fiery, blistering, scalding, sizzling. **2.** sarcastic,

scornful, derisive, caustic, curt, blistering, biting.

score *n.* **1.** tally, count, number, record, reckoning, average, sum, aggregate, account, amount, total. **2.** grievance, grudge, injustice.

score *v.* **1.** mark, cut, groove, nick, notch, scratch, tick. **2.** cross out, delete, eliminate, cancel, erase, expunge. **3.** (gain a point in sport) win, gain, achieve, register. **4.** (achieve as a ranking) grade, evaluate, rank, rate. **5.** (to prepare music) compose, orchestrate, arrange, adapt.

scorn *n.* contempt, derision, disdain, disgust, disparagement, sarcasm, mockery, slighting, sneering; *ant.* respect.

scorn *v.* **1.** (treat with scorn) hate, despise, deride, look down on, insult, vilify, disdain, ridicule, slight, sneer at; *ant.* admire, value. **2.** (refuse as a matter of principle) ignore, flout, defy, spurn, repudiate, reject, avoid, shun, renounce; *ant.* acknowledge, accept.

scornful *adj.* arrogant, defiant, derisive, haughty, disdainful, supercilious, contemptuous; *ant.* deferential, appreciative.

scot-free *adj.* undamaged, clear, unharmed, unscathed, without a scratch.

scoundrel *n.* rascal, miscreant, reprobate, rogue, villain, scamp.

scour *v.* **1.** scrub, clean, cleanse, wash, rub, abrade, buff, burnish, polish, furbish. **2.** search, probe, scrutinize, comb, forage, ransack.

scourge *n.* **1.** whip, strap, switch, cat-o'-nine-tails, cord, stick. **2.** punishment, correction, penalty, affliction, bane, curse, doom, torment, visitation; *ant.* benefit, blessing.

scourge *v.* **1.** flog, beat, thrash, cane, flail, lash, horsewhip, whip. **2.** castigate, punish, chastise, penalize, discipline.

scout *n.* patrol, emissary, escort, lookout, spy, vanguard, advance guard.

scout *v.* explore, investigate, case, search, reconnoiter, survey, track, watch, check out.

scowl *n.* frown, grimace, pout, glare, glower; *ant.* smile, grin.

scramble *v.* **1.** mix, combine, blend. **2.** clamber, push, struggle, climb, jostle, scrabble, strive, vie, contend.

scrap *n.* **1.** bit, fragment, particle, portion,

scrap (*slang*) *v.* **1.** abandon, reject, discard, cancel, forsake, drop, write off, ax, chuck (*slang*), dismiss. **2.** battle, argue, bicker, clash, spat, quarrel; *ant.* agree.

scrape *n.* **1.** abrasion, scratch, scuff, contusion, lesion, sear. **2.** (*slang*) difficulty, dilemma, distress, plight, mess, predicament, trouble, fix, *slang*: pickle, kettle of fish.

scrape *v.* **1.** abrade, scuff, rasp, rub, file, graze, grind. **2.** amass, gather, assemble, acquire.

scrappy *adj.* combative, pugnacious, aggressive, competitive, feisty, tough, mettlesome, resolute; *ant.* timid, pusillanimous.

scratch *n.* incision, cut, laceration, scrape, blemish, gash, contusion.

scratch *v.* **1.** abrade, lacerate, file, grate, damage, score. **2.** cancel, eliminate, annul, erase, retire, delete, withdraw.

scrawny *adj.* angular, gaunt, emaciated, bony, lean, skinny, spare, thin, undernourished, lanky; *ant.* plump, fleshy, muscular.

scream *n.* cry, howl, shriek, outcry, yell, ululation.

scream *v.* yell, whine, wail, bellow, screech.

screech *v.* scream, squawk, yelp.

screen *n.* **1.** sieve, mesh, lattice, netting. **2.** shield, barrier, partition, guard.

screen *v.* **1.** conceal, hide, veil, mask, cloak, conceal, cover, hide, shroud. **2.** select, choose, eliminate, weed out, cull, filter, process, scan, sort, audition.

screw *v.* **1.** twist, turn, twine, wind, contort. **2.** (*slang*) cheat, swindle, defraud, extort, coerce, oppress.

screw up (*slang*) botch, bungle, mismanage, mess *or* foul up, spoil, damage, break, derange; *ant.* repair, adjust, order, regulate.

screwed up (*slang*) *adj.* **1.** awry, messy, chaotic. **2.** deranged, demented, disturbed, neurotic, daft, crazy, *slang*: screwy, out to lunch.

screwy (*slang*) *adj.* crazy, nuts (*slang*), odd, eccentric, peculiar, daft, demented, confused; weird, queer; *ant.* sober, staid.

scribble *v.* scrawl, scratch, jot, pen, write, dash off.

scribe *n.* copyist, clerk, secretary, transcriber, notary, scrivener, author, correspondent, writer.

scrimmage *n.* fight, scrap, disturbance, fray, melee, scuffle, skirmish; *ant.* calmness.

scrimp *v.* economize, limit, reduce, save, stint, curtail, pinch, restrict; *ant.* spend, waste, squander.

Scrooge *n.* cheapskate, miser, niggard, pennypincher, tightwad; cynic, grouch, sourpuss (*slang*), misanthrope; *ant.* spendthrift, philanthropist.

scrounge *v.* beg, panhandle, freeload, sponge, wheedle, cadge, purloin, bum (*slang*).

scrub *v.* **1.** clean, rub, cleanse, scour, wash. **2.** abandon, cancel, scrap, discontinue, drop, abort, give up, forget, abolish.

scrub *adj.* inferior, mediocre, poor, secondrate; *ant.* important. **2.** little, stunted, puny, diminutive, deficient.

scruffy *adj.* shabby, seedy, ragged, slovenly, illgroomed, unkempt, squalid, tattered, mangy; *ant.* tidy, well-dressed.

scrumptious *adj.* delicious, appetizing, tasty, delectable, succulent, mouth-watering, luscious.

scrunch *v.* crumple, crush, crunch, squash, mash.

scruple *n.* doubt, compunction, qualm, misgiving, objection, reluctance, hesitation, uneasiness, pang.

scrupulous *adj.* **1.** cautious, principled, ethical, honest, conscientious, upright. **2.** exact, meticulous, precise, fastidious, strict, painstaking, punctilious; *ant.* careless, negligent.

scrutinize *v.* examine, study, stare, analyze, dissect, inspect, peruse, investigate, probe, scan.

scrutiny *n.* analysis, perusal, inquiry, research, study.

scuff *v.* abrade, scratch, graze, rub, skin, brush.

scuffle *n.* fracas, fight, brawl, fray, commotion, disturbance, rumpus, tussle, ruckus.

scuffle *v.* clash, contend, fight, grapple, jostle, struggle, scrap.

sculpt *v.* fashion, form, hew, model, mold, represent, shape, carve, engrave, chisel, cut.

scum *n.* **1.** residue, froth, film, flotsam, crust,

fraction, grain, iota, morsel, vestige. **2.** argument, fight, brawl, squabble, dispute, scuffle, wrangle, ruckus; *ant.* peace.

dregs, dross, spume. **2.** rabble, mob, riffraff, pariah; *ant.* elite, aristocracy.

scurrilous *adj.* lewd, indecent, vulgar, ribald, foul, salacious, obscene, slanderous; evil, offensive, coarse, malicious, vicious.

scurry *v.* hasten, run, race, scamper, rush, hurry, scuttle, sprint, whisk, dart, dash; *ant.* loiter, dawdle.

scuttle *v.* **1.** destroy, sink, submerge, abandon, dismantle. **2.** scurry, sprint, hurry, race, hasten, bustle, rush, scamper, scramble; *ant.* stroll.

seafaring *adj.* maritime, nautical, naval, oceanic, marine.

seal *n.* **1.** approval, authorization, permission, allowance, imprimatur. **2.** fastener, sticker, tie, tape, stamp, binding, ligature.

seal *v.* **1.** authenticate, confirm, assure, attest, ratify, validate, stamp. **2.** close, plug, cork, stop, shut, stopper, bind, secure, fasten, enclose, occlude; *ant.* loosen, open, leak.

seal off forbid, restrict, isolate, quarantine, segregate; *ant.* open up.

seam *n.* junction, ridge, groove, closure, joint, suture, ligature, scar.

seaman *n.* sailor, seafarer, navigator, tar, mariner.

seamy *adj.* sordid, squalid, degraded, disreputable, sleazy, vulgar, corrupt; *ant.* wholesome, pleasant, respectable.

sear *v.* **1.** wither, fade, dehydrate, blight, shrivel; *ant.* bloom, blossom, flourish. **2.** burn, scorch, cauterize, singe, char, blister.

search *n.* quest, hunt, pursuit, inquiry, inspection, scrutiny, research, investigation.

search *v.* explore, seek, comb, check, examine, inquire, investigate, probe, ransack, scour.

searching *adj.* penetrating, keen, sharp, poignant, curious, speculative, inquisitive.

season *n.* period, span, spell, term, time, era, interval.

season *v.* **1.** acclimatize, prepare, accustom, temper, habituate, discipline, train. **2.** spice, salt, lace, flavor, enliven.

seasonable *adj.* appropriate, opportune, timely, convenient, suitable, welcome, providential.

seasoned *adj.* **1.** spicy, tangy, sharp, aromatic. **2.** experienced, mature, established,

414

veteran, settled, ripe, hardened, weathered, well-versed, battle-scarred; *ant.* innocent, green.

seasoning *n.* spice, sauce, relish, flavoring, dressing.

seat *n.* **1.** chair, bench, pew, stool, settee, throne. **2.** buttocks, rear, breech, rump, ass (*slang*). **3.** (a central place) locus, location, site, headquarters, center, locale, place, citadel, mecca, home.

seating *n.* room, seats, chairs, reservations, accommodation, places, arrangement.

secede *v.* withdraw, retreat, defect, quit, retire, abandon, desert, leave, separate, retract; *ant.* join, unite with.

secession *n.* break, schism, split, rift, divorce, separation, disunion; *ant.* unification, affiliation.

secluded *adj.* withdrawn, sequestered, cloistered, monastic, reclusive, remote, private, solitary; *ant.* busy, public, accessible.

seclusion *n.* solitude, privacy, isolation, retirement, quarantine.

second *n.* **1.** instant, flash, moment, twinkling, wink, jiffy, trice. **2.** assistant, backer, supporter, helper.

second *v.* endorse, approve, assist, back, encourage, promote, support, help, further; *ant.* oppose, discourage, hinder.

secondary *adj.* **1.** consequent, subsequent, attendant, indirect, derived; contingent, dependent; *ant.* original. **2.** subordinate, lesser, subsidiary, auxiliary, alternate; minor, petty, trivial; *ant.* primary, important.

second-class *adj.* inferior, mediocre, second-rate, ordinary, deficient; *ant.* prime, distinguished.

second-hand *adj.* borrowed, derivative, handme-down, used, worn, plagiarized; *ant.* new.

second-rate *adj.* cheap, inferior, mediocre, poor, shoddy, substandard, tawdry; *ant.* first-rate, excellent.

secrecy *n.* **1.** intrigue, conspiracy, coverup, concealment, stealth; confidentiality. **2.** hiding, seclusion, privacy, solitude, mystery, isolation, stealth; *ant.* publicity.

secret *n.* **1.** mystery, enigma, conundrum. **2.** answer, key, cause, explanation, essence.

secret *adj.* **1.** hidden, mysterious, enigmatic, esoteric, arcane, dark, obscure, clouded, latent; *ant.* known, revealed, exposed. **2.** (said of activities) covert, clandestine, underhanded, stealthy, sly, surreptitious, undercover; *ant.* aboveboard, overt. **3.** (said of information) confidential, classified, restricted, private, privileged, hush-hush, under one's hat, under wraps.

secretary *n.* assistant, clerk, typist, stenographer.

secrete *v.* **1.** emit, emanate, discharge, perspire, swelter. **2.** conceal, hide, seclude, disguise, bury, cache, stow, cover, veil.

secretion *n.* excretion, discharge, issue, emission, flow.

secretive *adj.* reticent, taciturn, tight-lipped, reserved, enigmatic, quiet, withdrawn; *ant.* communicative, open.

sect *n.* denomination, faction, camp, ism, cult, school, splinter group, subdivision.

sectarian *adj.* partisan, parochial, fanatic, exclusive, skeptical, extreme.

section *n.* **1.** part, division, share, slice, segment, component, fragment, piece, portion, percent; *ant.* whole, entirety. **2.** area, region, sector, locality.

sectional *adj.* exclusive, factional, narrow, selfish, local, regional, partial, sectarian; *ant.* general, universal.

sector *n.* class, division, category, caste, segment, hierarchy, community.

secular *adj.* **1.** (devoted to things of this world) temporal, profane, earthly, material, worldly, mundane; *ant.* spiritual, pious. **2.** civil, civilian, lay, public, civic; *ant.* ecclesiastical.

secure *v.* **1.** fasten, settle, adjust, bind, tighten, attach, batten down, bolt, chain, fix, lash, lock, rivet. **2.** (make fast against intruders) protect, shelter, guard, defend, shield, ensure. **3.** (manage to acquire) obtain, achieve, acquire, grasp, get, land, procure, seize; *ant.* lose. **4.** (get, as a loan) guarantee, pledge, insure, underwrite.

secure *adj.* **1.** firm, tight, bound, fast, immovable, solid, fixed, stable; *ant.* loose, open. **2.** safe, immune, protected, invulnerable; *ant.* exposed. **3.** self-reliant, self-assured, determined, positive, confident, sure, certain; *ant.*

anxious, hesitant. **4.** (not subject to doubt) certain, definite, assured, conclusive, absolute; *ant.* tenuous.

security *n.* **1.** safety, protection, shelter, refuge, retreat, defense, safeguard, sanctuary, guard, salvation; *ant.* danger, exposure, risk, hazard. **2.** guarantee, collateral, forfeit, token, pawn, pledge, surety, bond, assurance, promise. **3.** stability, confidence, soundness, assurance, surety; *ant.* doubt.

sedate *adj.* calm, dignified, composed, sober, collected, earnest, serene, solemn, staid, tranquil, unflappable; *ant.* agitated, fidgety, hasty.

sedative *n.* tranquilizer, narcotic, opiate, sleeping pill, downer (*slang*).

sedentary *adj.* idle, stationary, settled, still, torpid, inactive, motionless; *ant.* active.

sediment *n.* residue, lees, dregs, silt, dross, sand, precipitate.

sedition *n.* revolt, mutiny, defiance, insurrection, subversion, treason, tumult, agitation.

seditious *adj.* dissident, insurgent, insubordinate, riotous, rebellious, mutinous, subversive, traitorous, revolutionary; *ant.* loyal.

seduce *v.* **1.** entice, allure, attract, tempt, bait, lure, captivate. **2.** defile, deprave, violate, debauch, rape, deflower, corrupt, ruin, beguile; *ant.* preserve, protect.

seducer *n.* cad, philanderer, womanizer, libertine, rake, roué, Don Juan.

seduction *n.* snare, charm, spell, enticement, lure, temptation.

seductive *adj.* attractive, flirtatious, irresistible, beguiling, appealing, entrancing, bewitching; *ant.* repellent.

see *v.* **1.** observe, behold, view, gaze, stare, espy, regard, notice, witness, scrutinize, survey, contemplate. **2.** comprehend, grasp, apprehend, perceive, understand, discern, ascertain, recognize. **3.** (come to realize) conclude, ascertain, verify, determine, decide. **4.** encounter, meet with, visit, interview, receive, escort, accompany, attend.

see to manage, arrange, attend, organize.

see through **1.** finish, conclude, execute, complete, consummate, achieve, wind up; *ant.* quit. **2.** (not be fooled by someone's façade) penetrate, be wise to, have one's number (*slang*). **3.** support, assist, second, protect, succor; *ant.* desert, abandon, forsake.

seed *n.* **1.** ovum, egg, gamete, embryo, spore. **2.** source, origin, root, basis, foundation.

seed *v.* plant, sow, scatter, strew, broadcast.

seedy *adj.* decaying, dilapidated, shabby, mangy, squalid, unkempt, worn, slovenly, sleazy, grubby, ticky tacky; *ant.* fresh, elegant, posh.

seek *v.* **1.** look for, search for, hunt, quest, pursue. **2.** (try to obtain information) inquire, solicit, request. **3.** try, aim, attempt, endeavor, strive for.

seem *v.* appear, pretend, resemble, look, manifest.

seeming *adj.* apparent, professed, illusory, ostensible, outward, superficial, surface, pseudo, quasi-; specious; *ant.* real.

seemly *adj.* **1.** appropriate, befitting, proper, suitable, conventional, polite, decent, decorous, civil, diplomatic; *ant.* rude, outrageous. **2.** attractive, becoming, pleasing, comely, pleasant, personable, graceful; *ant.* repulsive.

seep *v.* leak, drain, flow, trickle, exude, ooze, permeate, weep, percolate, well.

seer *n.* predictor, prophet, prognosticator, soothsayer, augur, sibyl.

seesaw *v.* alternate, fluctuate, oscillate, hedge, waver, swing, teeter, flip-flop.

seethe *v.* **1.** simmer, stew, boil, ferment. **2.** rage, smolder, bluster.

see-through *adj.* sheer, translucent, filmy, flimsy, transparent, gossamer, diaphanous; *ant.* opaque.

segment *n.* section, fragment, part, component, fraction, portion, slice; *ant.* whole.

segregate *v.* divide, separate, sever, isolate, quarantine, set apart, sequester, dissociate, discriminate, differentiate; *ant.* unite, integrate.

segregation *n.* separation, estrangement, exclusion, ostracism, apartheid; *ant.* unification.

seize *v.* **1.** grasp, take, lay hold of, grip, catch, clinch, clasp, embrace, grab, snatch; *ant.* leave, let alone. **2.** understand, comprehend, realize, perceive, register, apprehend. **3.** (take over by force) occupy, conquer, subdue, overwhelm, overrun, annex, appropriate, confiscate; capture, apprehend, abduct, nab.

seizure *n.* convulsion, fit, spasm, spell, paroxysm

seldom *adv.* rarely, occasionally, at times, sporadically, infrequently, scarcely, now and then, off and on; *ant.* often, frequently, regularly.

select *v.* choose, elect, determine, distinguish, cull, single out.

select *adj.* elite, distinguished, exclusive, choice, superior, preferable, top-notch, top-drawer.

selection *n.* **1.** choice, decision, specification, preference, prerogative, option. **2.** collection, anthology, miscellany, excerpt.

selective *adj.* discriminating, particular, judicious, careful, discerning, scrupulous.

self *n.* identity, personality, character, essence, ego, soul, person.

self-assurance *n.* confidence, self-confidence, equanimity, self-possession, poise, presence, savoir-faire; *ant.* doubt, anxiety, timidity.

self-assured *adj.* confident, self-possessed, assured, cocksure, certain; *ant.* anxious, frightened.

self-centered *adj.* egotistic, selfish, self-absorbed, self-interested, self-serving, narcissistic; *ant.* altruistic.

self-confidence *n.* aplomb, assurance, poise, nerve, courage; *ant.* humility.

self-confident *adj.* secure, self-reliant, composed, sure, self-possession, calm, poised; *ant.* humble.

self-conscious *adj.* shy, humble, ill at ease, shamefaced, embarrassed, diffident, nervous, anxious, uptight (*slang*); affected.

self-control *n.* restraint, reserve, composure, discipline, poise, discretion, dignity, stability, sobriety.

self-esteem *n.* pride, dignity, self-assurance, self-confidence, amour-propre; vanity, haughtiness, egotism.

self-evident *adj.* obvious, plain, visible, apparent, clear, given, manifest, incontrovertible, inescapable; *ant.* doubtful, hypothetical, ambiguous.

self-government *n.* **1.** self-control, discipline, restraint, conduct, character, stability. **2.** autonomy, freedom, independence, home rule, democracy, self-sovereignty; *ant.* subjection.

self-important *adj.* proud, conceited, self-righteous, egotistical, arrogant, conceited, overbearing, pompous, swaggering, vain; *ant.* humble.

self-indulgence *n.* greed, excess, extravagance, incontinence, hedonism, high-living; *ant.* self-denial.

self-indulgent *adj.* dissipated, dissolute, extravagant, profligate, intemperate; *ant.* abstemious.

selfish *adj.* **1.** egocentric, egotistical, self-indulgent, self-seeking, self-centered, self-serving. **2.** miserly, niggardly, stingy, parsimonious, greedy, acquisitive, mean, mercenary; *ant.* generous.

selfless *adj.* generous, magnanimous, altruistic, considerate, self-sacrificing, self-denying, compassionate, charitable, open-hearted.

self-possessed *adj.* calm, aloof, placid, collected, confident.

self-possession *n.* composure, poise, presence of mind, serenity, tranquillity.

self-reliant *adj.* able, independent, autonomous, self-sufficient, self-contained; *ant.* dependent.

self-respect *n.* worth, pride, confidence, dignity, self-esteem, self-regard; *ant.* self-doubt.

self-restraint *adj.* patience, endurance, control, forbearance, abstemiousness, moderation, self-control, self-denial.

self-righteous *n.* sanctimonious, hypocritical, affected, smug, complacent, superior, pious, holier-than-thou; *ant.* understanding, tolerant.

self-seeking *adj.* greedy, rapacious, avaricious, acquisitive, mercenary, opportunistic, self-serving; *ant.* altruistic.

self-styled *adj.* professed, self-appointed, so-called, would-be.

sell *v.* vend, market, auction, hawk, barter, exchange, trade, peddle, retail; *ant.* buy, purchase, obtain.

sell out betray, deceive, cheat, trick, fail, violate, double-cross (*slang*).

seller *n.* merchant, vendor, dealer, peddler, salesperson, retailer, shopkeeper, agent; *ant.* buyer.

semblance *n.* likeness, look, resemblance, affinity, similarity, similitude, appearance, aspect, exterior, image, mien, guise.

seminal *adj.* important, influential, major, primary, basic, root, fundamental, formative, innovative, creative, productive, germinal, generative, original; *ant.* derivative.

send *v.* **1.** transmit, dispatch, ship, mail, convey, forward, expedite, hasten, accelerate, confer, entrust, bestow. **2.** throw, propel, fling, project, hurl, discharge, emanate, emit, radiate. **3.** relay, wire, cable, broadcast, televise, conduct, communicate.

send for request, summon, command, order.

sendoff *n.* departure, farewell, leave-taking, valediction, launching, start; *ant.* arrival.

senile *adj.* doddering, failing, imbecile, aged, superannuated, ancient, infirm, feeble.

senior *n.* **1.** (one who is first in rank or experience) superior, veteran, head, master, founder, dean, chief. **2.** oldster, senior citizen, elder, matriarch, patriarch.

seniority *n.* precedence, priority, rank, standing, advantage, preference.

sensation *n.* **1.** (sensory impression) impression, sense, feeling, response, reaction. **2.** (the capacity to perceive) awareness, consciousness, perception, sentience, sensibility; *ant.* obliviousness. **3.** commotion, agitation, excitement; hit, scandal, stir, surprise, thrill.

sensational *adj.* **1.** exciting, fascinating, marvelous, incredible, astonishing, superb, breath-taking, dramatic, spectacular; *ant.* routine, bland, run-of-the-mill. **2.** melodramatic, exaggerated, excessive, lurid, startling.

sense *n.* **1.** (ability to perceive) appreciation, capability, talent, discernment, understanding, sensitivity, capacity, faculty. **2.** (vague feeling, as of impending danger) perception, awareness, impression, aura, scent, apprehension, prescience, intuition. **3.** reason, logic, judgment, common sense, discretion, tact, intelligence, diplomacy, sanity, coherence. **4.** meaning, import, definition, denotation, signification, connotation, implication, content, intention. **5.** consensus, opinion, drift, tendency, direction, sentiment.

sense *v.* detect, perceive, observe, divine, realize, comprehend, understand, grasp, appreciate, guess.

senseless *adj.* **1.** unconscious, comatose, anesthetized, paralyzed, anoxic, numb, out cold (*slang*); *ant.* responsive, conscious, sentient. **2.** illogical, nonsensical, stupid, ridiculous, silly, foolish, inane, moronic, simple; *ant.* wise, sensible, rational.

sensibility *n.* awareness, judgment, sensitivity, taste, tact, intuition, appreciation, insight, feeling, understanding.

sensible *adj.* **1.** (showing good sense) reasonable, judicious, rational, discerning, thoughtful, levelheaded, practical, reasonable, sober. **2.** (able to recognize or detect things) perceptive, aware, discriminating, sagacious, shrewd, wise, informed, attentive.

sensitive *adj.* **1.** (hurting when touched) tender, delicate, sore, painful. **2.** high-strung, nervous, irritable, touchy, temperamental, thin-skinned. **3.** (responding to stimuli) impressionable, sensible, perceptive, reactive, responsive, sentient, tuned in (*slang*).

sensual *adj.* **1.** tactile, sensory, carnal, corporeal, worldly; *ant.* cerebral, spiritual, ascetic. **2.** sexual, voluptuous, erotic; licentious, lewd, salacious.

sensuality *n.* sexiness, eroticism, animal magnetism, ardor.

sensuous *adj.* sensual, physical, sensory; receptive, responsive.

sentence *n.* decree, judgment, pronouncement, verdict, opinion, ruling, decision, edict, dictum.

sentence *v.* punish, convict, ordain.

sentient *adj.* alive, responsive, conscious, observant, perceptive, aware, alert, sensitive.

sentiment *n.* **1.** sensibility, attitude, opinion, view. **2.** sentimentality, mawkishness, bathos, nostalgia, emotion, feeling.

sentimental *adj.* idealistic, emotional, romantic, melodramatic, nostalgic, maudlin, tender, weepy, *slang*: schmaltzy, drippy, sappy; corny, dreamy; *ant.* practical, sensible, realistic.

sentiments *n.* message, verse, salute, respects, congratulations.

sentry *n.* sentinel, guard, lookout, patrol, warden, watch.

separate *v.* part, divide, split, section, sever, sunder, rive; distinguish, isolate, sequester, seclude, segregate; *ant.* unite, connect, homogenize.

separate *adj.* individual, apart, autonomous,

solitary, estranged, divorced, riven, discrete; *ant.* attached.

separation *n.* **1.** break, detachment, division, rift, partition, severance, dissociation, divorce, estrangement; *ant.* integration. **2.** departure, leave-taking, farewell, parting.

septic *adj.* infectious, contaminated, toxic, noxious, putrid, rotten, rancid; *ant.* sanitary.

sepulchral *adj.* dismal, funereal, somber, grave, melancholy, morbid, gloomy, dreary, lugubrious; *ant.* cheerful.

sequel *n.* consequence, continuation, progression, development, supplement, outcome, result, upshot.

sequence *n.* **1.** (the way things follow one another) arrangement, order, placement, progression, graduation. **2.** (group of activities, events, etc.) series, cycle, course, schedule, round, chain.

sequester *v.* **1.** separate, isolate, segregate, quarantine, exile; *ant.* include, invite. **2.** (isolate oneself) retire, seclude, hibernate, cloister, retreat; *ant.* participate.

seraphic *adj.* angelic, celestial, divine, holy, heavenly, saintly, pure, beatific, sublime; *ant.* demonic.

serene *adj.* placid, tranquil, calm, peaceful, undisturbed, quiet, halcyon; *ant.* agitated, tumultuous.

serenity *n.* tranquillity, calm, composure, peace, peacefulness, quiet, placidity; *ant.* confusion, anxiety, disruption.

series *n.* succession, order, cycle, sequence, circuit.

serious *adj.* **1.** dangerous, acute, alarming, grim; momentous, urgent, critical, weighty, complex; *ant.* slight, trivial. **2.** earnest, sincere, sober, solemn, grave, deliberate, thoughtful; *ant.* facetious, smiling.

sermon *n.* speech, lecture, harangue, homily, address, exhortation, discourse.

serpentine *adj.* snakelike, spiral, coiling, crooked, meandering, tortuous, devious, circuitous, winding, sinuous; *ant.* straight.

servant *n.* attendant, domestic, help, handmaid, hireling, lackey, maid, manservant, steward, valet; *ant.* master, mistress.

serve *v.* **1.** obey, honor, follow, revere. **2.** assist, help, attend, satisfy, wait on.

service *n.* **1.** aid, assistance, help, coopera-tion. **2.** rite, ceremony, sermon, worship, observance.

service *v.* maintain, care for, sustain, repair, overhaul, recondition.

serviceable *adj.* helpful, useful, beneficial, ad-vantageous, convenient, dependable, durable, functional, utilitarian.

servile *adj.* humble, obsequious, menial, cring-ing, abject, base, fawning, groveling, submis-sive, slavish, bootlicking; *ant.* aggressive, bold, defiant.

servility *n.* self-abasement, sycophancy, sub-mission, obsequiousness, fawning, abjectness, groveling.

servitude *n.* enslavement, bondage, subjection, confinement, subjugation, obedience, thrall-dom; *ant.* freedom.

session *n.* assembly, conference, meeting, hear-ing, seminar, get-together.

set *n.* **1.** class, clique, faction, coterie, com-pany, crowd, cohort. **2.** collection, kit, assem-blage, assortment, mélange, congeries.

set *v.* **1.** insert, deposit, establish, anchor, fasten, fix, install, embed, sink; *ant.* loosen, dislocate. **2.** harden, stiffen, thicken, congeal, solidify, jell, crystallize, condense, gelatinize; *ant.* liquefy. **3.** rate, price, value, estimate, adjust, determine, specify.

set about begin, start, initiate, undertake, get started, prepare.

set apart isolate, segregate, separate, distin-guish.

set aside **1.** save, reserve, put away, lay up *or* away. **2.** discard, reject, repeal, cancel, abro-gate, annul, nullify, overrule, repudiate.

set back hinder, retard, reverse, slow down, delay, hamper, impede, check, frustrate; *ant.* encourage, promote.

set down write, record, transcribe, register.

set off **1.** depart, embark, leave, begin. **2.** detonate, explode, ignite. **3.** initiate, begin, inaugurate, trigger, let loose.

set out start, commence, begin, set off.

set straight inform, explain, reeducate, dis-abuse; correct, revise, amend.

set up assemble, build, arrange, compose, construct, install.

set *adj.* **1.** settled, solid, entrenched, firm,

stable, established, steadfast, determined, reso-lute; *ant.* free, moveable, spontaneous. **2.** obstinate, stubborn, harrow, obdurate, unyield-ing, relentless; *ant.* flexible.

setback *n.* problem, delay, misfortune, disap-pointment, hitch, snag, reverse; *ant.* advan-tage, advance, progress.

setting *n.* **1.** position, angle, placement, tilt. **2.** mounting, frame, border. **3.** surroundings, environment, background, mise en scène, mi-lieu, ambiance.

settle *v.* **1.** decide, choose, determine, re-solve, conclude, judge, establish, verify, prove. **2.** (bring to a satisfactory resolution, as a dispute or debt) finish, end, complete, resolve, discharge, quit, square up, make good. **3.** sink, descend, decline, fall, drop, lower, sub-merge, plunge, immerse. **4.** quiet, calm, com-pose, pacify, soothe, tranquilize, sedate, relax, quell, lull, hush. **5.** (find a home) lodge, locate, reside, dwell, colonize, inhabit, live in, populate.

settlement *n.* **1.** compensation, payment, re-imbursement, restitution, remuneration, de-frayal. **2.** colony, principality, plantation, community, encampment, hamlet, outpost, kibbutz, Bantustan.

settler *n.* frontiersman, immigrant, home-steader, pioneer, planter, squatter, sharecrop-per; *ant.* native.

setup *n.* arrangement, organization, structure, system, order, conditions, circumstances, hier-archy, taxonomy.

sever *v.* cut, divide, split, rend, cleave, sunder, bisect; *ant.* join, unite, connect.

several *adj.* **1.** some, a few, divers, a number of, a handful. **2.** various, manifold, multi-form, assorted, sundry, disparate, diverse.

severally *adv.* discretely, individually, ex-clusively, alone, singly; *ant.* simultaneously, together.

severe *adj.* **1.** (as in the exercise of authority) harsh, strict, rigid, brutal; *ant.* gentle, merci-ful, lenient. **2.** (said of conditions, tasks, etc.) difficult, extreme, acute, arduous, demanding, grievous, intense, profound; *ant.* mild, pleas-ant. **3.** (severe in manner) serious, austere, grave, staid, formal, earnest, repressed; *ant.* frivolous, affable. **4.** (as in style) plain, func-

419

tional, classic, ascetic, minimal, spare; *ant.* ornate, fancy.

severity *n.* acerbity, rigor, asceticism, stringency; *ant.* compassion.

sew *v.* stitch, seam, tailor, embroider, darn, mend, piece.

sex *n.* sexual intercourse, coitus, sexual congress, lovemaking, copulation, fornication, reproduction, carnal knowledge, mating, union.

sex appeal *n.* allure, magnetism, sensuality, glamour, nubility, charm.

sexual *adj.* **1.** reproductive, generative, procreative, coital, genitive. **2.** erotic, passionate, loving, carnal, wanton, intimate.

sexuality *n.* lust, desire, carnality, eroticism, sensuality, passion, libido.

sexy *adj.* sensuous, arousing, flirtatious, nubile, curvaceous, foxy (*slang*), inviting, provocative, seductive, titillating, alluring, attractive.

shabby *adj.* **1.** ragged, run-down, dilapidated, shoddy, frayed, tattered, worn, neglected, dingy, dirty, threadbare; *ant.* neat, new. **2.** contemptible, low, mean, paltry, sordid, disreputable, shameful; *ant.* kindly, noble.

shack *n.* hut, shed, hovel, cabin, shanty, lean-to, dump.

shackle *v.* bind, chain, fetter, handcuff, manacle, tether; constrain, encumber, restrain, restrict.

shade *n.* **1.** shadow, murk, obscurity, twilight, umbra. **2.** hue, color, tint, brilliance, tinge. **3.** hint, trace, nuance, suggestion, suspicion, degree, variation. **4.** cover, shelter, shield, canopy, screen, curtain, blind. **5.** ghost, spirit, wraith, manes, specter, phantasm, apparition.

shade *v.* **1.** screen, protect, block, conceal, cover, hide, mute, veil, overshadow, eclipse. **2.** shadow, darken, blacken, cloud, dim, adumbrate.

shadow *n.* darkness, dusk, gloom, adumbration.

shadow *v.* **1.** screen, shade, shelter, dim, veil, darken, obscure. **2.** watch, trail, tail, follow, stalk, pursue, dog.

shadowy *adj.* **1.** dark, shady, gloomy, somber; *ant.* bright, sunny. **2.** (hard to see or discover) dim, cloudy, indistinct, obscure, murky, nebulous, vague; *ant.* distinct, sharp, definite. **3.**

420

(not definable or readily present to the senses) eerie, spectral, mysterious, otherworldly, evanescent, wraithlike, dreamlike; *ant.* real, tangible, substantial, corporeal.

shady *adj.* **1.** dusky, shaded, darkened, shadowy. **2.** (*slang*) suspicious, questionable, suspect, disreputable, sleazy, sneaky, crooked; *ant.* honest, reliable.

shaft *n.* **1.** rod, pole, arrow, spear, lance, handle, shank, haft, bar, stem. **2.** beam, ray, streak, arc. **3.** passageway, tunnel, vent, flue, chimney.

shaggy *adj.* hairy, tousled, unkempt, furry, hirsute; *ant.* bald, shorn.

shake *n.* tremor, twitch, vibration, shock, quaking, shudder, oscillation, jerk.

shake *v.* **1.** tremble, quiver, quake, shiver, shudder, palpitate, oscillate, flutter. **2.** (to cause to shake) agitate, concuss, rock, sway, jounce, bounce, disturb, jar; settle, compose.

shake off elude, lose, leave behind, outdistance, outpace, give the slip.

shake up upset, disturb, unsettle, overturn.

shake-up *n.* rearrangement, reorganization, disturbance, upheaval.

shaky *adj.* **1.** jumpy, jittery, nervous, quivery, faltering, insecure; *ant.* confident. **2.** doubtful, questionable, dubious; *ant.* certain, reliable, dependable.

shallow *adj.* slight, superficial, surface, simple, silly, trifling, frivolous, puerile, ignorant, lightweight; *ant.* deep, profound, considerable.

sham *n.* fraud, forgery, pretense, counterfeit, fake; charlatan.

sham *adj.* **1.** false, artificial, ersatz, imitation, mock, pseudo, simulated, synthetic; *ant.* genuine. **2.** misleading, lying, false, bogus; *ant.* true.

shambles *n.* disarray, confusion, mess, hodgepodge, muddle, wreck, bedlam, confusion; *ant.* order.

shame *n.* **1.** disgrace, stigma, dishonor, blot, degradation, humiliation; *ant.* distinction, honor, credit. **2.** (a feeling of shame) mortification, embarrassment, regret, chagrin, remorse, self-reproach, self-reproof, guilt; *ant.* pride.

shame *v.* humiliate, ridicule, disgrace, mortify, dishonor, humble, abash, debase, smear,

shamefaced *adj.* ashamed, crestfallen, discomfited, embarrassed, chagrined; *ant.* proud, comfortable.

shameful *adj.* corrupt, immoral, abominable, atrocious, contemptible, disgraceful, ignominious, indecent, lewd, carnal, gross, wicked, vile; *ant.* worthy, admirable.

shameless *adj.* brazen, bold, forward, audacious, defiant, impudent, insolent, incorrigible, unabashed, unblushing; *ant.* meek, contrite.

shanty *n.* cabin, hovel, hut, cottage, shack, shed, lean-to; *ant.* mansion.

shape *n.* 1. form, contour, cut, appearance, aspect, configuration, pattern, template, stamp, frame, figure. 2. health, fitness, state, condition.

shape *v.* 1. mold, cast, fashion, form, construct, forge, make, model, produce, create; define, characterize. 2. take shape, become, grow, develop, adapt, modify.

shapeless *adj.* 1. amorphous, indefinite, inchoate, nebulous; *ant.* formed, distinct. 2. misshapen, irregular, mutilated, disfigured, deformed, abnormal; *ant.* symmetrical, shapely.

shapely *adj.* comely, curvaceous, elegant, pretty, voluptuous, well-proportioned, trim; *ant.* shapeless.

share *n.* portion, percentage, part, allowance, cut, ration, allotment, quota, serving, helping, due.

share *v.* 1 allot, divide, split, distribute, apportion, deal, dispense, assign. 2. participate, partake, have in common.

sharp *adj.* 1. honed, edged, fine, cutting, pointed, barbed, thorny, spiky; *ant.* dull, blunt. 2. clever, astute, alert, discerning, nimble-witted, observant, keen, bright, intelligent; *ant.* slow, stupid. 3. caustic, biting, acrimonious, sarcastic, crafty, sly, acerbic, acrid, bitter, tart, trenchant.

sharpen *v.* 1. grind, file, hone, whet, taper; *ant.* blunt, dull. 2. focus, intensify, clarify, make more distinct; *ant.* confuse, obscure.

sharp-sighted *adj.* aware, perceptive, attentive, perspicuous.

shatter *v.* 1. break, splinter, smash, crack, burst, split, damage, ruin. 2. (cause distress to) stun, devastate, overwhelm, paralyze, destroy, crush.

shave *v.* barber, crop, trim, shear, skin, peel, pare.

sheaf *n.* bundle, collection, stack, bunch, cluster, fagot.

shear *v.* shave, cut, sever, cleave.

shed *n.* barn, hut, shack, outhouse, woodshed, lean-to.

shed *v.* 1. cast off, discard, molt, slough, drop, scatter, divest, sprinkle. 2. exude, emit, radiate.

shed light on clarify, elucidate, clear up, explain, illuminate.

sheen *n.* luster, polish, brilliance, gloss, brightness, burnish, gleam, shimmer; *ant.* dullness, tarnish.

sheepish *adj.* timid, shy, tame, docile, self-conscious, embarrassed, ashamed, crestfallen, shamefaced, abashed; *ant.* bold, comfortable.

sheer *adj.* 1. steep, precipitous, abrupt, perpendicular, vertical. 2. thin, transparent, diaphanous, delicate, gossamer, gauzy, flimsy; *ant.* heavy, thick. 3. absolute, utter, complete, downright, total, unmitigated, unadulterated; *ant.* qualified.

sheet *n.* 1. cloth, cover, blanket, covering. 2. lamina, leaf, foil, veneer, coat, film, membrane, shroud, skin.

shelf *n.* 1. ledge, shoal, reef, ridge, sandbank, sandbar, terrace. 2. counter, cupboard, mantlepiece, rack, bracket.

shell *n.* 1. carapace, husk, pod, case, casing. 2. hull, skeleton, structure, framework, chassis.

shell *v.* 1. strip, peel, husk, shuck, exfoliate. 2. bomb, attack, bombard, barrage, strike.

shelter *n.* refuge, haven, sanctuary, retreat, asylum, safety, security, custody, aegis.

shelter *v.* protect, defend, safeguard, guard, shield, harbor, lodge, conceal, screen, cover, hide; *ant.* expose.

shelve *v.* postpone, defer, delay, put off, suspend, halt, put on ice, table.

shepherd *v.* guide, lead, conduct, usher, escort, supervise, marshal, herd.

shield *n.* buffer, safeguard, shelter, aegis, defense, screen.

shield *v.* protect, conceal, fend off, defend, guard, shelter, armor; *ant.* expose.

shift *n.* variation, rearrangement, metamorphosis, reversal, switch, alteration, change, reposition, realignment, permutation.

shift v. **1.** move, stir, change, alter, fluctuate, relocate, reposition, swerve, veer. **2.** (cause to be moved) displace, remove, substitute, exchange, dislodge, rid, transfer, transpose.

shiftless adj. idle, inactive, indolent, aimless, feckless, lazy, slothful; ant. industrious, eager, ambitious.

shifty adj. sly, tricky, cunning, sneaky, contriving, devious, evasive, furtive, scheming, wily, disingenuous; ant. honest, open.

shimmer v. glisten, glow, twinkle, sparkle, glimmer, shine, gleam, scintillate, phosphoresce.

shimmering adj. incandescent, iridescent, luminous, lustrous; ant. dull.

shine v. **1.** radiate, glimmer, sparkle, glow, flash, blaze, illuminate. **2.** polish, burnish, scour, wax, buff.

shine n. brightness, polish, gloss, glow, luster, radiance, sheen, luminosity, burnish, effulgence.

shining adj. **1.** bright, radiant, glowing, luminous, refulgent. **2.** illustrious, eminent, remarkable, celebrated, distinguished, outstanding.

shiny adj. bright, polished, aglow, glossy, satiny; ant. dull.

ship n. boat, bark, steamer, tanker, trawler, yacht.

shipshape adj. neat, orderly, spruce, tidy, trim, organized.

shirk v. avoid, evade, dodge, shun, malinger, duck.

shiver v. shake, quiver, quake, shudder, tremble, palpitate.

shock n. **1.** impact, jolt, blow, concussion, trauma. **2.** confusion, hysteria, excitement, breakdown, collapse, consternation, dismay, distress, fright, perturbation.

shock v. **1.** startle, disturb, agitate, confound; ant. settle, gratify. **2.** insult, outrage, horrify, revolt, offend, appall, astound, anger, disgust, scandalize; ant. comfort, humor, please.

shocking adj. repulsive, frightful, offensive, deplorable, distressing, execrable, horrible, loathsome, odious, repugnant; ant. delightful, pleasant.

shoddy adj. cheap, poor, flimsy, inferior, slipshod, junky, tacky, tawdry, meretricious, trashy; ant. high-quality, well-made.

shoot n. branch, bud, twig, sprig, sprout.

shoot v. **1.** fire, discharge, ignite, blast, set off, explode. **2.** dart, hasten, hurry, rush, dash, charge, race, sprint, streak. **3.** murder, execute, kill, knock off (slang,) wound.

shop n. boutique, emporium, store, market.

shore n. beach, seashore, seaside, waterfront, waterside, coast, littoral, strand, bank.

shore v. brace, buttress, prop, reinforce, strengthen, support, underpin.

short adj. **1.** undersized, small, little, dwarfish, stubby, squat, stunted, diminutive, pint-sized; ant. large, ample. **2.** (said of time) brief, fleeting, curtailed, condensed, terse, succinct, pithy, abridged, compressed, short-lived; ant. sustained, lasting. **3.** (said of funds) inadequate, deficient, lacking, wanting; ant. sufficient. **4.** curt, rude, cantankerous, quarrelsome, impatient, irascible, petulant.

shortage n. lack, dearth, deficiency, inadequacy, paucity, poverty, scarcity, want; ant. abundance, excess.

shortcoming n. fault, defect, deficiency, drawback, failing, lapse, weakness, imperfection.

shorten v. lessen, reduce, curtail, condense, abbreviate, abridge, summarize, abstract, trim, truncate; ant. extend, protract.

short-lived adj. brief, momentary, fleeting, short, transient, fugitive, ephemeral, evanescent; ant. enduring, permanent.

shortly adv. **1.** soon, presently, quickly, anon, directly.

short-sighted adj. hasty, careless, foolish, rash, stupid, precipitate, thoughtless, headlong; ant. wary, prudent.

short-tempered adj. touchy, irritable, irascible, testy, choleric, cranky, impatient; ant. calm, placid.

shot n. **1.** discharge, gunfire, blast, explosion, detonation. **2.** bullet, ball, projectile, slug, pellet, buckshot. **3.** (slang) chance, attempt, opportunity, turn, crack, go, stab.

shoulder v. **1.** shove, jostle, elbow, push, thrust. **2.** accept, assume, bear, carry, sustain, take on.

shout v. yell, holler, scream, roar, bellow, shriek, screech, bawl, bay.

shout down quiet, silence, heckle, shut up, overcome, defeat.

shove v. shoulder, crowd, force, push, elbow.

shove off leave, depart, clear out, push off, *slang:* beat it, skedaddle, vamoose.

shovel v. dig, dredge, ladle, load, move, scoop, trowel, toss.

show n. **1.** exhibition, exhibit, exposition, sight, spectacle, pageant, carnival, production, concert. **2.** pretense, sham, semblance, affectation, façade, illusion, pose.

show v. **1.** (cause to be seen) exhibit, display, manifest, evidence. **2.** (cause to benefit by) bestow, grant, confer, endow. **3.** tell, divulge, explain, illustrate, instruct, reveal, explicate, clarify, elucidate, demonstrate, convince, persuade.

showdown n. crisis, confrontation, clash, climax, culmination, turning point.

shower v. deluge, pour, douse, inundate, heap, lavish, load, overwhelm.

showing n. **1.** exhibit, show, display, exhibition, production. **2.** impression, appearance, performance, effect.

showoff n. braggart, boaster, exhibitionist, egoist.

showy adj. flashy, gaudy, glaring, flamboyant, garish, glitzy, pretentious, tawdry; *ant.* quiet, restrained.

shred n. fragment, bit, grain, iota, tatter, scrap, piece, sliver, wisp.

shrewd adj. astute, sharp, keen, canny, clever, crafty, cunning, sly, sagacious, wily; *ant.* naive, obtuse.

shrewdness n. acumen, judgment, wisdom, sagacity, canniness, perspicacity, smarts (*slang*).

shriek v. cry, yell, scream, screech, howl, squeal, wail.

shrill adj. piercing, penetrating, treble, strident, harsh, hysterical; *ant.* gentle, mild, temperate.

shrine n. chapel, sanctuary, temple, tabernacle, church, altar.

shrink v. **1.** contract, dwindle, shrivel, condense; *ant.* expand, stretch. **2.** recoil, flinch, cower, cringe, quail, shy away, withdraw.

shrivel v. wither, parch, shrink, wilt, wrinkle.

shriveled adj. shrunken, emaciated, sere, desiccated; *ant.* swollen.

shroud v. blanket, cloak, swathe, veil, envelop; *ant.* expose.

shudder n. tremor, spasm, convulsion.

shudder v. quiver, quake, shiver, convulse, heave, tremble.

shuffle v. **1.** mix up, rearrange, change, confuse, jumble, shift, intermix. **2.** (drag one's feet) scuffle, scuff, hobble, limp, scrape.

shun v. evade, avoid, elude, spurn, ostracize, ignore, neglect, give the cold shoulder; *ant.* embrace, accept.

shut v. close, lock, bar, bolt, fasten, latch, secure, slam; *ant.* open.

shut down close, discontinue, halt, abandon, stop, suspend, terminate.

shut out banish, bar, exclude, ostracize.

shut up silence, quiet, hush, gag, muzzle.

shut-in n. invalid, convalescent, cripple, sufferer, valetudinarian.

shuttle v. commute, travel, go to and fro, alternate.

shy v. recoil, shrink, rear, balk, quail, flinch, wince.

shy adj. bashful, humble, reserved, timid, diffident, timorous, cautious, hesitant, reticent; *ant.* confident, assertive.

sick adj. **1.** ill, ailing, indisposed, infirm, invalid, feeble, weak, laid up, bedridden, under the weather; *ant.* healthy, well. **2.** satiated, bored, disgusted, fed up, sick and tired.

sicken v. **1.** be stricken, fall ill, take sick, ail, languish, break out. **2.** disgust, offend, revolt, nauseate, repel; *ant.* attract, delight.

sickening adj. disgusting, putrid, foul, loathsome, repellent, vile; *ant.* pleasing.

sickly adj. **1.** ailing, weak, faint, feeble, frail, invalid, valetudinarian, languid; *ant.* robust, sturdy. **2.** pallid, wan, anemic, ashen, drawn.

sickness n. illness, ailment, disorder, malady, infirmity, affliction, disease, indisposition; *ant.* health.

side n. **1.** edge, rim, boundary, border, margin, perimeter, limit, verge. **2.** opinion, viewpoint, position, angle, stance, version. **3.** surface, plane, face, facet, flank, slant. **4.** (a competing group) party, faction, team, camp, contestants.

side *adj.* indirect, secondary, subordinate, incidental, marginal, subsidiary, contingent; *ant.* significant.

sidelong *adj.* sideways, indirect, covert, oblique; *ant.* overt.

sidestep *v.* evade, avoid, shun, bypass, circumvent; *ant.* confront.

sidetrack *v.* distract, divert, head off, deflect.

sideways *adv.* sidewards, askance, laterally.

side with *v.* agree with, support, favor, second, incline to.

sidle *v.* creep, inch, slink, sneak, steal, wriggle, insinuate.

sieve *n.* colander, strainer, screen, mesh.

sieve *v.* separate, sift, strain, remove.

sift *v.* 1. evaluate, investigate, scrutinize, probe, examine, review. 2. sort, filter, sieve, pan, separate, winnow.

sigh *n.* moan, cry, suspiration.

sigh *v.* gasp, breathe, groan, suspire, lament, grieve.

sight *n.* 1. vision, seeing, perception, apprehension. 2. (something seen) spectacle, scene, show, image, display. 3. (the art of looking) glimpse, view, glance, impression.

at first sight superficially, on the surface, to the outsider, on first acquaintance, prima facie.

sight *v.* behold, discern, distinguish, glimpse, observe, perceive, espy.

sightsee *n.* tour, travel, visit, wander, voyage, observe.

sign *n.* 1. signal, indication, portent, clue, augury, omen, premonition, foreshadowing, harbinger. 2. emblem, symbol, insigne, insignia, badge, crest.

sign *v.* authorize, approve, confirm, endorse, acknowledge.

sign over *v.* deliver, entrust, transfer, surrender, consign, convey.

sign up *v.* 1. employ, hire, contract, appoint, engage, recruit. 2. join, enlist, enroll, volunteer.

signal *n.* sign, beacon, flag, flare, watchword, alarm, omen.

signal *v.* beckon, motion, gesture, nod, wave, alert.

signature *n.* autograph, endorsement, John Hancock, inscription, mark, sign, trademark.

significance *n.* consequence, importance, rele-

424

vance, import, weight, force, implication, solemnity.

significant *adj.* meaningful, crucial, critical, profound, signal, momentous, noteworthy, vital; *ant.* trivial.

signify *v.* mean, imply, import, purport, connote, betoken, represent, symbolize, indicate, express.

silence *n.* stillness, quiet, calm, hush, peace, lull, quiescence; *ant.* noise, furore.

silence *v.* suppress, quiet, still, subdue, stifle, quell, extinguish, gag, muzzle; *ant.* agitate.

silent *adj.* quiet, mute, still, hushed, speechless, aphonic; *ant.* loud, noisy, talkative.

silhouette *n.* outline, profile, contour, shape, delineation.

silly *adj.* ridiculous, nonsensical, foolish, absurd, frivolous, stupid, preposterous, harebrained, fatuous, puerile; *ant.* sensible, wise, mature.

silt *n.* residue, sediment, deposit, sand, sludge, alluvium, mud.

similar *adj.* alike, analogous, comparable, congruous, related, homologous, parallel, close; *ant.* different.

similarity *n.* affinity, correspondence, likeness, resemblance, similitude, kinship, concurrence, equivalence; *ant.* variance.

similarly *adv.* likewise, by the same token, in like fashion, furthermore.

simmer *v.* 1. stew, boil, smolder, bubble. 2. rage, fume, seethe.

simpering *adj.* affected, arch, silly, coy.

simple *adj.* 1. (without embellishment or artifice) plain, natural, homely, modest, simplistic, pure, unadored, homespun; *ant.* fancy, gaudy. 2. (easy to understand) easy, clear, elementary, manageable, unvarnished, straightforward; *ant.* obscure, complicated, convoluted. 3. innocent, trusting, ingenuous, naive, childlike, artless, green, guileless; *ant.* sophisticated, pretentious. 4. stupid, inane, dull, ignorant, shallow, feebleminded; *ant.* clever.

simple-minded *adj.* moronic, imbecilic, dull, naive, addle-brained; *ant.* bright, clever.

simpleton *n.* fool, idiot, clod, dolt, bungler, dimwit.

simplify *v.* clarify, explain, decipher, elucidate; *ant.* complicate, elaborate.

simplistic *adj.* childish, naive, shallow, oversimplified, superficial; *ant.* analytical, complex.

simply *adv.* merely, absolutely, utterly, solely, just.

simulate *v.* imitate, affect, feign, assume, counterfeit, dissimulate, fabricate.

simulated *adj.* artificial, synthetic, imitation, ersatz, pseudo, mock, bogus, phony, manmade; *ant.* authentic, genuine, real.

simultaneous *adj.* coincident, concurrent, contemporaneous, synchronic, coeval; *ant.* sequential.

sin *n.* error, wrongdoing, evil, crime, offense, venality.

sin *v.* err, offend, trespass, transgress, misbehave, fall.

sincere *adj.* ingenuous, candid, honest, truthful, faithful, trustworthy, earnest, frank, natural; genuine, real, bona fide; *ant.* hypocritical, counterfeit.

sincerity *n.* candor, honesty, honor, veracity, probity; *ant.* cunning, guile, deceit.

sinewy *adj.* 1. strong, powerful, athletic, muscular, robust, sturdy. 2. stringy, wiry, tendinous, elastic.

sinful *adj.* immoral, corrupt, wicked, depraved, abandoned, vicious, iniquitous; *ant.* righteous, pious.

sing *v.* chant, hum, croon, carol, warble, chirp, caterwaul.

singe *v.* burn, sear, scorch.

singer *n.* vocalist, minstrel, troubadour, balladeer, crooner.

single *adj.* 1. individual, singular, distinct, particular; whole, unitary; *ant.* mixed, composite. 2. solitary, alone, isolated, separate, discrete, sole; *ant.* accompanied. 3. eligible, unattached, free; *ant.* married.

single-minded *adj.* determined, stubborn, dedicated, dogged, monomaniacal, resolute, steadfast, hell-bent (*slang*); *ant.* indecisive.

single out select, prefer, pick out, choose, distinguish, separate, winnow, target, elect.

singsong *adj.* dull, tiresome, repetitious, monotonous.

singular *adj.* 1. single, separate, individual, discrete, unique, particular; *ant.* compound, composite, plural, universal. 2. curious, bizarre, unusual, peculiar, remarkable, extraordi-

nary, exceptional, outstanding; *ant.* ordinary, usual.

sinister *adj.* evil, corrupt, perverse, malevolent, ominous, threatening, baneful, pernicious, deleterious; *ant.* innocent.

sink *n.* basin, washbasin, tub, pan, bowl.

sink *v.* 1. descend, submerge, slip, immerse, drown, penetrate; *ant.* float, rise. 2. decrease, lessen, diminish, wane, decline, deteriorate, degenerate, lapse; *ant.* increase, improve.

sink in penetrate, impress, influence, take hold, have an effect.

sinless *adj.* innocent, pure, perfect, upright, immaculate, virtuous; *ant.* corrupt.

sinner *n.* wrongdoer, delinquent, miscreant, evildoer, malefactor, reprobate.

sinuous *adj.* 1. twisted, circuitous, curved, meandering, serpentine, tortuous, undulating, winding; *ant.* straight, direct. 2. devious, vagrant, erring; *ant.* straightforward.

sip *n.* mouthful, drop, spoonful, swallow, taste, drink, sample.

sire *n.* parent, begetter, progenitor, creator, father.

siren *n.* 1. alarm, signal, whistle, horn. 2. temptress, seductress, charmer, femme fatale, vamp.

sissy *n.* coward, weakling, *slang:* wimp, chicken, pansy.

sit *v.* 1. perch, squat, be seated; *ant.* rise, stand. 2. (stay in place) rest, relax, remain, settle. 3. convene, assemble, meet.

site *n.* locality, ground, lot, plot, spot, section.

site *v.* locate, place, position, situate, install.

sit-in *n.* protest, demonstration, strike, march, display.

sitting *n.* assembly, meeting, session, gathering, consultation.

situation *n.* 1. condition, circumstance, status, state of affairs, predicament, plight, difficulty, problem. 2. location, site, position, spot, place, berth, locale, locality, setting.

sixth sense *n.* foresight, intuition, clairvoyance, ESP, telepathy, second sight, prescience.

sizable *adj.* large, considerable, substantial, great, grand, significant.

size *n.* dimension, measurement, area, extent, amplitude, scope, breadth, mass, bulk.

size up examine, judge, scrutinize, evaluate,

survey, appraise, look over, give the once over to (*slang*).

sizzle *v.* hiss, sputter, crackle, fry, spit, scorch, sear.

skate *v.* slide, glide, skim, skid, slip, race; rollerskate, rollerblade, blade.

skeletal *adj.* gaunt, haggard, drawn, wasted, emaciated, cadaverous.

skeptic *n.* cynic, dissenter, rationalist, agnostic, doubter; *ant.* believer.

skeptical *adj.* cynical, doubtful, suspicious, dubious; *ant.* certain.

sketch *n.* **1.** portrayal, picture, drawing, scenario, illustration, cartoon. **2.** summary, survey, description, plan, draft, outline.

sketch *v.* paint, depict, draw, pencil, portray, represent, delineate.

sketchy *adj.* preliminary, introductory, crude, rough, cursory, superficial, perfunctory; *ant.* detailed, finished.

skid *v.* slide, slip, glide, skate, skim.

skill *n.* **1.** ability, dexterity, facility, talent, aptitude, competence, savvy, knack. **2.** trade, craft, work, job, profession, occupation.

skilled *adj.* able, accomplished, experienced, proficient, talented, capable, schooled, trained, professional, adroit, adept.

skim *v.* **1.** soar, float, sail, dart, fly, coast, glide. **2.** scoop, dip, ladle, brush, separate, remove.

skimp *v.* conserve, economize, stint, scrimp, save, cut corners.

skimpy *adj.* **1.** scanty, sparse, meager, tiny, short, thin; *ant.* sufficient, adequate. **2.** stingy, miserly, tight, niggardly, tight-fisted, penny-pinching; *ant.* generous.

skin *n.* epidermis, derma, cuticle, bark, peel, husk, rind, coat, covering, casing, pelt, hide.

by the skin of one's teeth barely, narrowly, scarcely, just.

get under one's skin anger, upset, irritate, annoy, bother, irk, disturb, bug (*slang*).

skin *v.* peel, pare, scalp, flay, strip, husk, shuck, fleece, excoriate.

skin-deep *adj.* shallow, superficial, artificial, empty, desultory.

skinflint *n.* tightwad, miser, penny-pincher, Scrooge.

skinny *adj.* lean, gaunt, slender, thin, underweight; *ant.* fat, portly.

426

---

skip *v.* **1.** prance, bob, bounce, cavort, caper, gambol. **2.** miss, omit, eschew, overleap, cut.

skirmish *n.* engagement, encounter, conflict, clash, scrimmage, fracas, spat, tussle, brush.

skirt *v.* evade, avoid, bypass, circumvent, steer clear of, circle, circumambulate; *ant.* meet.

skit *n.* sketch, burlesque, parody, satire, caricature, spoof.

skittish *adj.* **1.** frivolous, capricious, lively, whimsical, playful, fickle. **2.** nervous, highstrung, afraid, restive, coltish, shy, timid.

skulduggery *n.* trickery, underhandedness, chicanery, duplicity, double-dealing, swindling, fraudulence.

skulk *v.* lurk, prowl, slink, creep, sneak, loiter.

sky *n.* air, atmosphere, azure, heavens, firmament, empyrean.

slab *n.* portion, slice, wedge, piece, part, hunk, chunk, lump.

slack *n.* excess, give, leeway, room, play, relaxation.

slack *adj.* **1.** relaxed, limp, flaccid, loose, lax; *ant.* rigid, stiff. **2.** remiss, negligent, inattentive, idle, lazy, sluggish, tardy; *ant.* diligent, active, busy, quick.

slacken *v.* slow down, relax, tire, abate, decrease, reduce, diminish, lessen, flag, fall; *ant.* tighten, quicken, increase.

slacker *n.* idler, loafer, shirker, dawdler, donothing.

slake *v.* allay, satisfy, assuage, quench, mitigate, reduce, moderate.

slam *v.* **1.** bang, crash, throw, push, close. **2.** criticize, attack, castigate, pan, lambaste, excoriate, vilify, excoriate.

slander *n.* calumny, scandal, aspersion, backbiting, libel, misrepresentation, smear, traducement.

slander *v.* defame, malign, defile, disparage, revile, sully, traduce, besmirch, denigrate, vilify, blacken; *ant.* praise, honor.

slang *n.* jargon, cant, shoptalk, argot, colloquialism, vernacular.

slant *n.* **1.** angle, diagonal, incline, slope, gradient, pitch. **2.** bias, attitude, opinion, viewpoint, judgment.

slant *v.* lean, tilt, list, veer, bend, distort, warp, skew.

slap *n.* smack, whack, blow, wallop, cuff, clap.

slap in the face insult, affront, rebuke, indignity, offense.

slap v. hit, strike, spank, whack, pat, clout, clobber, paw.

slapstick adj. farcical, absurd, comical, droll.

slash n. gash, cut, laceration, incision, rip.

slash v. cut, slit, sever, incise.

slatternly adj. messy, sloppy, unkempt, slovenly, dirty, frumpy, bedraggled; ant. tidy.

slaughter n. carnage, bloodshed, massacre, murder, mayhem.

slaughter v. butcher, kill, massacre, murder, slay.

slave n. captive, bondservant, serf, chattel, vassal.

slave v. labor, toil, struggle, sweat, drudge.

slavery n. bondage, captivity, subjugation, servitude, thralldom, impressment; ant. freedom, liberty.

slavish adj. 1. servile, submissive, obsequious, fawning, cringing, docile, sycophantic; ant. independent. 2. uninspired, imitative, dull, conventional, laborious, literal, menial; ant. original, imaginative.

slay v. kill, slaughter, butcher, murder, execute, assassinate.

sleazy adj. shoddy, poor, cheap, run-down, shabby, squalid, seedy, sordid.

sleek adj. smooth, silky, satin, glossy, lustrous, shiny.

sleep n. rest, repose, shut-eye (slang), forty winks (slang), nap, siesta.

sleep v. slumber, doze, drowse, rest, nap, snore, turn in, hit the sack or the hay (slang), nod off.

sleeping adj. asleep, dormant, inert, inactive, idle; ant. alert, awake.

sleepless adj. insomniac, wide-awake, restless, alert, vigilant, watchful, wakeful.

sleepy adj. tired, drowsy, dull, sluggish, lethargic, slow, soporific, torpid; ant. alert, restless.

slender adj. 1. thin, slim, svelte, small, slight, spare, willowy; ant. fat, thick. 2. (having little likelihood) remote, tenuous, poor, narrow, faint, meager, flimsy, scanty; ant. considerable.

slice n. piece, section, sliver, wedge, portion, share, segment.

slice v. carve, cut, sever, divide, chop, whittle.

slick adj. 1. oily, smooth, sleek, glossy; ant. coarse. 2. adroit, sharp, polished, deft, skillful, dexterous; ant. clumsy, amateurish. 3. glib, tricky, cunning, smooth-talking, slippery, sly.

slide v. 1. glide, skate, skim, coast, skid, toboggan. 2. push, thrust, impel, propel, drive, launch, start.

slight v. scorn, insult, affront, snub, disdain, neglect, overlook; ant. compliment, flatter.

slight adj. 1. minor, inconsiderable, trivial, petty, trifling, paltry, small, piddling; ant. major, significant. 2. delicate, frail, dainty, slender, flimsy; ant. large, bulky.

slighting adj. derogatory, abusive, derisive, maligning, disparaging, dismissive, opprobrious.

slim adj. slender, trim, thin, lean, lank, narrow.

slime n. mire, ooze, muck, slang: gunk, goo.

slimy adj. clammy, glutinous, oily, viscous.

sling n. cast, strap, support, dressing.

sling v. 1. throw, hurl, heave, catapult, fling, toss, pitch, put, shoot. 2. hoist, raise, hang, suspend, dangle, weight.

slink v. creep, lurk, sneak, prowl, cower, skulk.

slinky (slang) adj. lean, sinuous, sleek, serpentine, skin-tight, clinging, feline.

slip n. 1. error, mistake, blunder, indiscretion, oversight, gaffe, lapse. 2. scrap, piece, strip, sliver, cutting, sprig, sprout.

slip v. 1. slide, glide, shift, move, creep, skate, sneak, slither, slink. 2. fall, tumble, trip, lurch, sprawl, do a turn.

slippery adj. 1. smooth, glazed, slick, sleek, oily, greasy, glassy, icy, wet; ant. rough, sticky. 2. devious, wily, capricious, elusive, double-talking, glib, slick, cunning, canny; ant. reliable.

slipshod adj. careless, negligent, sloppy, slovenly, rough, makeshift; ant. fastidious, tidy.

slit n. cleft, tear, gash, fissure, crevice, incision, split, vent.

slit v. cut, slice, slash, split, incise, lance, rip, knife.

slither v. glide, slide, slink, slip, snake, undulate.

sliver n. splinter, fragment, shaving, shred.

slobber v. drool, drivel, salivate, dribble.

slogan n. motto, proverb, catchword, jingle, rallying cry, watchword.

slop v. refuse, trash, overflow, swill, spill.

slope *n.* incline, rise, hill, grade, ramp, declivity.

slope *v.* slant, lean, tilt, rise, pitch.

sloping *adj.* askew, oblique, angled, beveled; *ant.* level.

sloppy *adj.* 1. clumsy, awkward, slipshod, careless, mediocre, banal, poor, amateurish; *ant.* careful, exact, precise. 2. messy, slushy, muddy, sludgy.

slot *n.* slit, space, aperture, opening, groove.

slot *v.* assign, place, position, fit, insert, adjust, pigeonhole.

sloth *n.* indolence, inertia, languor, laziness, inactivity; *ant.* industry, activity.

slothful *adj.* lazy, lethargic, sluggish, listless, idle, torpid; *ant.* industrious.

slouch *v.* hunch, slump, droop, stoop, hobble.

slovenly *adj.* sloppy, careless, slipshod, slatternly, messy, unkempt.

slow *v.* 1. slacken, lag, relax, brake, decelerate, wind down; *ant.* rise, accelerate. 2. delay, postpone, retard, hinder, impede, hold back, curtail, check, curb, detain.

slow *adj.* 1. (slow in motion) laggard, sluggish, slack, listless, hesitant, gradual, moderate, deliberate, idle, torpid, apathetic, lackadaisical; *ant.* fast, rapid, active. 2. (slow in starting) tardy, late, belated; *ant.* immediate, instant. 3. (said of a person) dull, stupid, simple, obtuse, retarded; *ant.* clever. 4. (hard to maintain interest in) tedious, boring, endless, dull; *ant.* interesting.

slowly *adv.* leisurely, languidly, haltingly, ponderously.

sludge *n.* mud, muck, ooze, silt, sediment, residue, slop, refuse, filth, swill.

sluggish *adj.* torpid, indolent, lazy, slow, listless, lethargic; *ant.* brisk, vigorous.

sluggishness *n.* sloth, fatigue, languor, torpor, apathy, somnolence, lassitude, stagnation; *ant.* eagerness.

sluice *v.* cleanse, drain, flush, irrigate, swill, wash, drench.

slumber *v.* sleep, doze, nap, snooze, rest, drowse.

slump *n.* decline, descent, depression, downturn, recession, depreciation, crash, trough; *ant.* boom.

slump *v.* 1. plummet, plunge, sag, fall, collapse, cave in. 2. slouch, hunch, bend, stoop.

slur *n.* insult, affront, slight, aspersion, smear, slander, stain, stigma, blot, insinuation, reproach.

sly *adj.* 1. cunning, shrewd, wily, crafty, tricky, scheming, deceitful, cagey, canny, double-crossing; *ant.* honest, fair. 2. secretive, furtive, evasive, stealthy; *ant.* candid.

smack *n.* blow, stroke, clap, box, whack, slam, slap, punch, hit.

smack *v.* hit, slap, spank, whack, cuff, crack.

small *adj.* 1. little, diminutive, tiny, miniature, petite, short, minute, minuscule, bantam. 2. petty, trivial, insignificant, minor, secondary. 3. (intending to hurt or disparage) mean, base, small-minded, vulgar, shallow. 4. (said of profits, assets, etc.) humble, modest, meager, inadequate, scanty, poor, pitiful.

small fry children, infants, toddlers.

small-minded *adj.* intolerant, parochial, narrow-minded, rigid, petty, bigoted, insular; *ant.* liberal, tolerant.

small talk chitchat, banter, pleasantries, gossip, chatter.

small-time *adj.* petty, piddling, inconsequential, insignificant, minor; *ant.* important, major.

smart *v.* sting, burn, throb, hurt, twinge.

smart *adj.* 1. clever, intelligent, bright, quick, acute, astute, keen, shrewd, witty; *ant.* dumb, stupid. 2. impudent, bold, brazen, forward, impertinent, saucy, smart-alecky. 3. (as a pace) vigorous, brisk, lively, energetic, active, jaunty, pert, spirited, vivacious; *ant.* slow. 4. fashionable, stylish, chic, dandy, elegant, modish, spruce, trim, well-appointed; *ant.* dowdy.

smarts (*slang*) *n.* cleverness, savvy, shrewdness, street smarts, intelligence.

smash *n.* collision, crash, breakup, disaster, failure, ruin.

smash *v.* crash, shatter, crush, burst, fracture, splinter, wreck, demolish, destroy.

smattering *n.* bit, trace, dash, rudiment.

smear *n.* distortion, lie, deception, slander, libel, fabrication.

smear *v.* 1. spread, apply, smudge, paint, cover, coat. 2. slander, malign, insult, libel, defame, stain, tarnish, blacken, soil, vilify.

smell *n.* fragrance, scent, aroma, perfume, bouquet, odor, mustiness.

smell *v.* 1. stink, reek, stench, emanate. 2.

scent, sniff, inhale, get a whiff of, perceive, detect.

smelly *adj.* stinking, foul, putrid, rank, rancid, odorous, malodorous, rotten, fetid, miasmic.

smirk *n.* grin, leer, sneer, snigger, simper.

smitten *adj.* struck, infatuated, charmed, captivated, beguiled, bewitched, swept off one's feet (*slang*); afflicted, beset.

smog *n.* haze, air pollution, mist.

smoke *n.* exhaust, fume, smog, mist, vapor, fog.

smoke *v.* burn, fume, vaporize, smolder, vent, fumigate.

smoke out force out, drive out, ferret, detect, uncover.

smoky *adj.* sooty, grimy, dingy, gray, dirty, hazy, murky, thick, black, begrimed.

smolder *v.* burn, smoke, steam, fume, seethe, simmer.

smooth *v.* **1.** flatten, iron, plane, grade, polish, glaze, varnish, gloss; *ant.* wrinkle, roughen. **2.** alleviate, ease, calm, soften, mitigate, allay, appease, assuage, mollify.

smooth *adj.* **1.** even, level, flat, sleek, glassy; *ant.* steep, rough, wrinkled. **2.** (as a journey or climatic conditions) easy, effortless, placid, serene, calm, tranquil, uneventful; *ant.* difficult. **3.** suave, glib, fluent, oily; urbane, polite; *ant.* awkward, naive. **4.** (as wine) mild, mellow, bland.

smooth-talking *adj.* suave, slick, glib, facile, oily, persuasive.

smother *v.* **1.** suffocate, stifle, strangle, choke, asphyxiate. **2.** suppress, muffle, repress, extinguish, consume.

smudge *n.* blemish, mark, spot, blot.

smudge *v.* dirty, blacken, smear, soil, blur, daub.

smug *adj.* complacent; conceited, egotistical, self-satisfied, vainglorious, priggish, superior, cocksure; *ant.* modest, retiring.

smutty *adj.* pornographic, obscene, vulgar, lewd, crude, coarse, salacious, risqué, racy, bawdy, ribald; *ant.* decent.

snag *n.* complication, hitch, difficulty, glitch, obstacle, hindrance, impediment, barrier, stumbling block, bug (*slang*).

snap *v.* fasten, clasp, catch, close, lock.

snare *n.* trap, net, noose, lure, decoy, trick.

snare *v.* catch, seize, trap, capture, entrap, nab, collar.

snarl *n.* confusion, tangle, complication, entanglement.

snarl *v.* growl, grumble, mutter, bark, snap, yap.

snatch *v.* seize, jerk, grasp, steal, pluck, wrench, wrest.

snazzy (*slang*) *adj.* flamboyant, flashy, jazzy, ritzy, sophisticated, stylish, fashionable, dashing, snappy; *ant.* drab.

sneak *n.* rascal, scoundrel, snake in the grass, informer, cheater.

sneak *v.* prowl, lurk, slink, cower, hide, skulk, steal.

sneaking *adj.* unscrupulous, sinister, crafty, sly, furtive, surreptitious, private.

sneaky *adj.* tricky, deceitful, devious, dishonest, underhanded, two-faced, sly, guileful, shifty; *ant.* reliable, ethical, honest, open.

sneer *n.* grimace, smirk, grin, face.

sneer *v.* deride, disdain, affront, mock, slight, disparage, taunt, scoff.

snide *adj.* base, malicious, mean, scornful, cynical, derogatory, disparaging, spiteful, nasty, superior, disdainful, dismissive.

sniff *v.* smell, inhale, breathe, scent.

snip *n.* bit, fragment, scrap, clipping, shred, piece.

snip *v.* clip, slice, cut, notch, prune, shave, trim.

snippet *n.* particle, fragment, scrap, shred, section, segment.

sniveling *adj.* blubbering, mewling, moaning, sniffling, weeping, whimpering, whining, crying, puling.

snob *n.* braggart, pretender, upstart, parvenu, elitist.

snobbery *n.* pretension, pomposity, arrogance, condescension, loftiness, disdain, elitism.

snobbish *adj.* arrogant, pretentious, pompous, condescending, elitist, overbearing, high and mighty, uppity, *slang:* snooty, hoity-toity.

snoop *v.* interfere, pry, sneak, spy.

snooze *n.* siesta, catnap, shut-eye, forty-winks (*slang*).

snooze *v.* sleep, doze, nap, slumber, rest, drowse, sack out (*slang*).

snort *v.* grunt, snore, puff, blow.

snout n. nose, muzzle, proboscis, nozzle.

snub n. affront, insult, rebuke, rebuff, humiliation, brushoff, cold shoulder, slap in the face (slang).

snub v. ignore, neglect, disregard, slight, shun, disdain, scorn, ostracize, cut.

snug adj. 1. (said of a space) cozy, comfortable, warm, intimate, sheltered. 2. (as a garment) close, compact, tight, close-fitting, trim.

snuggle v. cuddle, hug, nestle, nuzzle, curl up.

soak v. 1. drench, immerse, moisten, drown, flood, saturate, marinate, permeate, dip. 2. soak up, sponge, absorb, dry, mop.

soaked adj. sodden, wet, soggy, waterlogged, steeped, sopping, dripping.

soar v. sail, fly, glide, mount, tower, wing, ascend, escalate, rocket.

sob v. weep, wail, bawl, blubber, cry, moan, mewl, snivel, whimper.

sober adj. 1. solemn, earnest, grave, serious, sensible, somber, placid, calm, staid, dispassionate, rational, sedate, realistic; ant. excitable, frivolous. 2. temperate, abstemious, abstinent, moderate, clearheaded, nonindulgent; ant. drunk.

sobriety n. 1. continence, teetotalism, self-denial; ant. drunkenness, alcoholism. 2. serenity, restraint, composure, rationality, seriousness; ant. frivolity.

so-called adj. alleged, professed, supposed, pretended, nominal, ostensible, self-styled, soi-disant.

sociable adj. friendly, affable, genial, cordial, warm, hospitable, convivial, gregarious; ant. distant, cold.

social adj. 1. secular, worldly, human, philanthropic, political, racial, humane, collective, common, communal. 2. genial, companionable, polite, amusing, friendly, civil, mannerly, sociable, convivial, pleasant, communicative.

social climber parvenu, upstart, status seeker, nouveau riche.

socialism n. communism, collectivism, Leninism, Marxism, Stalinism, Trotskyism.

socialize v. entertain, fraternize, mix, party, get together, go out.

society n. 1. civilization, culture, nation, community, people, population, humanity, group. 2. (high society) aristocracy, elite, gentry, haut monde, upper classes, slang; upper crust, jet set, beautiful people, smart set, top drawer. 3. (group formed for a special purpose) organization, association, federation, confraternity, union, guild, club, fraternity, sorority. 4. friendship, fellowship, camaraderie, brotherhood, companionship, fraternity, sisterhood.

sodden adj. saturated, drenched, soaked, steeped, soggy, sopping, waterlogged; ant. dry.

sofa n. couch, divan, davenport, love seat.

soft adj. 1. (easily bent or shaped) malleable, pliant, elastic, flexible, bendable, lax, limp, plastic, yielding; ant. rigid, hard. 2. smooth, satiny, velvety, silken, delicate, feathery, downy, supple, tender, cushy; ant. rough. 3. (said of color, light, or sound) muted, shaded, pale, pastel, dusky, dull; low, melodious, mellifluous, faint, quiet; ant. bright, harsh, loud. 4. pampered, spoiled, cossetted, indulged, flabby, weak, overindulged; indulgent, liberal, lenient, permissive, yielding, compliant; ant. tough, tough-minded, strong.

soft spot fondness, liking, partiality, penchant, weakness.

soften v. 1. dissolve, disintegrate, thaw, melt. 2. moderate, relax, relent, lessen, diminish. 3. mollify, appease, temper, alleviate, assuage, calm, ease, quell, soothe, subdue.

soften up persuade, conciliate, win over, disarm, weaken.

soggy adj. soaked, wet, mushy, saturated, dripping, sodden, waterlogged.

soil n. earth, dirt, loam, clay.

soil v. 1. stain, dirty, sully, spoil, muddy, tarnish, smear. 2. shame, debase, degrade, disgrace, slander, defile, besmirch.

soiled adj. tainted, ruined, dirty, grimy; ant. clean, immaculate.

sojourn n. vacation, visit, stopover, layover, stop, stay, peregrination.

sojourn v. dwell, reside, rest, abide, stop, tarry, lodge, hole up (slang).

solace v. soothe, console, comfort, allay, alleviate, mitigate, succor, support.

sole adj. exclusive, only, one, lone, singular, solitary, unique, individual; ant. multiple, shared.

solely adv. only, simply, just, entirely, totally, wholly, alone, exclusively.

solemn *adj.* **1.** grave, serious, sober, earnest, somber, staid, pensive, brooding, grim; *ant.* lighthearted, jolly. **2.** (as a ceremony) imposing, impressive, grand, ceremonious, august, majestic, reverential, venerable, portentous, stately. **3.** (as a rite or obligation) sacred, religious, holy, hallowed, divine, devotional, sanctified.

solemnity *n.* **1.** sobriety, gravity, seriousness, portentousness; *ant.* frivolity. **2.** impressiveness, dignity, grandeur, majesty, pomp, stateliness.

solemnize *v.* consecrate, sanctify, bless, honor, commemorate, dignify.

solicit *v.* **1.** beseech, entreat, implore, importune, request, query, inquire, ask, beg, supplicate. **2.** seduce, proposition, accost, entice, hustle (*slang*).

solicitous *adj.* kind, thoughtful, devoted, tender, loving, attentive, concerned, considerate, caring, compassionate; *ant.* indifferent.

solicitude *n.* anxiety, care, heed, worry, concern, compassion.

solid *adj.* **1.** stable, fixed, rooted, firm, sturdy, compact, substantial, stocky. **2.** reliable, dependable, trustworthy, steadfast, sound, upstanding. **3.** continuous, consecutive, unbroken, constant; *ant.* interrupted, broken, liquid, varying.

solidarity *n.* accord, cohesion, concordance, consensus, harmony, esprit de corps, unity, camaraderie, fraternity, brotherhood; *ant.* discord, division.

solidify *v.* harden, set, fix, crystallize, thicken, congeal, jell, clot, coagulate; *ant.* dissolve, soften.

solitary *adj.* **1.** (being the only one) sole, lone, single, individual, separate; *ant.* accompanied. **2.** reclusive, alone, isolated, lonely, private, hermitic, sequestered; *ant.* gregarious.

solitude *n.* isolation, privacy, reclusiveness, retirement, seclusion; *ant.* companionship.

solution *n.* **1.** explication, elucidation, interpretation, resolution, explanation. **2.** mixture, compound, concoction, solvent, emulsion.

solve *v.* explain, answer, clarify, resolve, decipher, unfold, unravel, fathom, sort out, get to the bottom of (*slang*).

somber *adj.* **1.** (said of weather) dark, drab, dim, dull, dusky, cloudy; *ant.* bright. **2.** solemn, serious, grave; gloomy, melancholy, dismal, dreary, funereal, joyless, lugubrious, mournful, dire; *ant.* happy, cheerful.

someday *adv.* sometime, eventually, one day, ultimately, finally; *ant.* never.

somehow *adv.* in some way, one way or another, somehow or other, by hook or by crook, by fair means or foul, come hell or high water (*slang*).

sometimes *adv.* now and then, at times, occasionally, off and on, once in a while, on occasion.

somnolent *adj.* drowsy, fatigued, sleepy, tired, soporific, languid, torpid.

son *n.* boy, descendant, offspring, dependent, scion, heir, chip off the old block.

song *n.* melody, lyric, verse, tune, ballad, air, anthem, hymn, ditty, madrigal.

for a song (*slang*) cheap, at a bargain, for almost nothing.

song and dance pretense, drivel, lie, performance, nonsense, runaround, evasion.

sonorous *adj.* resonant, resounding, vibrant, full-throated, ringing, rich; *ant.* cacophonic.

soon *adv.* presently, promptly, early, shortly, in a minute, before long, forthwith, in short order.

soothe *v.* **1.** quiet, calm, pacify, console, appease, mollify, placate, lull, salve; *ant.* annoy, irritate, vex. **2.** (reduce pain) alleviate, lessen, allay, assuage, relieve; *ant.* aggravate, intensify, exacerbate.

soothsayer *n.* seer, prophet, oracle, fortuneteller, sibyl, augur.

sophisticated *adj.* **1.** cultured, refined, well-bred, experienced, couth, urbane, cultivated, blasé, worldly, world-weary; *ant.* artless, naive. **2.** (advanced in structure or technology) involved, complicated, complex, intricate; modern, state-of-the-art; *ant.* simple.

sophistication *n.* savoir-faire, poise, refinement, finesse, composure, elegance; *ant.* naiveté, simplicity.

sophistry *n.* disingenuousness, casuistry, fallacy, pedantry, delusion; *ant.* rationality, consistency.

sophomoric *adj.* puerile, childish, adolescent, immature, callow, brash, foolish, naive, young, reckless; *ant.* mature.

soporific *adj.* **1.** soothing, balmy, hypnotic, tranquil, dull; *ant.* invigorating, stimulating. 2. drowsy, somnolent, torpid, sleepy, languid, dozing, slumberous; *ant.* alert, awake.

sopping *adj.* drenched, soaked, saturated, damp; *ant.* parched.

sorcerer *n.* witch, wizard, alchemist, enchanter, magician.

sorcery *n.* magic, witchcraft, enchantment, divination, necromancy, voodoo, black magic.

sordid *adj.* 1. degraded, vile, wretched, low, unscrupulous, contemptible, base, mean, corrupt; *ant.* upright. 2. slovenly, rundown, foul, dirty, sleazy, squalid, filthy. 3. mercenary, venal, avaricious, covetous.

sore *n.* inflammation, swelling, ulcer, wound, lesion, ulcer, abscess, boil, canker, carbuncle.

sore *adj.* 1. sensitive, irritated, painful, tender, raw, aching, inflamed, smarting. 2. irked, angry, resentful, offended, indignant, peeved, vexed, hurt, upset.

sorely *adv.* extremely, crucially, critically, urgently, severely, gravely, acutely.

sorrow *n.* 1. sadness, anguish, pain, grief, mourning, heartache; *ant.* happiness, joy. 2. catastrophe, misfortune, affliction, trial, hardship, blow, difficulty, trouble.

sorrow *v.* bemoan, bewail, regret, agonize, lament, mourn, pine, grieve; *ant.* rejoice.

sorrowful *adj.* sad, mournful, melancholy, despondent, crestfallen, grieving, disconsolate, piteous, woebegone; *ant.* happy, joyful.

sorry *adj.* 1. penitent, contrite, repentant, conscience-stricken, remorseful, regretful, apologetic. 2. inadequate, poor, paltry, trifling, cheap, mean, shabby, trivial, beggarly, worthless; *ant.* adequate, important. 3. sad, grieved, mournful, unhappy, melancholy, miserable, disconsolate; regretful; *ant.* happy, glad.

sort *n.* brand, category, class, breed, family, genre, genus, kind, species, type, variety. **out of sorts** 1. irritated, upset, angry, troubled, in a bad mood, sullen, grouchy, grumpy, cross. 2. ill, ailing, under the weather.

sort *v.* order, arrange, catalog, file, systematize, assort, distribute, select.

sortie *n.* attack, foray, encounter, charge, incursion, probe.

so-so *adj.* ordinary, average, adequate, common, tolerable, mediocre.

soul *n.* 1. ghost, phantom, shade, spirit, appa-

rition, specter, wraith, spook. 2. essence, heart, personality, ego, psyche, genius.

soulful *adj.* sensitive, eloquent, profound, expressive, heartfelt, meaningful; *ant.* mechanical, callous, cruel.

sound *n.* 1. noise, din, racket, resonance, reverberation, intonation, tenor. 2. bay, strait, channel, estuary, fjord, inlet, canal.

sound *v.* 1. vibrate, echo, resound, reverberate, murmur, blare, thunder, hum, quaver. 2. measure, examine, inspect, investigate, plumb, probe, gauge, auscultate.

sound *adj.* 1. healthy, hearty, well, robust, fit, vigorous, hale; firm, solid, stable, sturdy. 2. sensible, reasonable, rational, prudent, judicious, wise, level-headed, logical. 3. (backed by social convention) sanctioned, established, allowed, proper, well-founded, fair, valid, legal, correct, orthodox. 4. dependable, loyal, true, faithful, reliable, trustworthy, responsible, reputable.

sour *adj.* 1. tart, acidic, acrid, bitter, sharp, lemony, harsh, pungent, vinegary, spoiled, curdled; *ant.* sweet. 2. ill-natured, grouchy, irritable, acrimonious, crabby, cynical, churlish, embittered, jaundiced, peevish, down, ill-tempered.

sour *v.* disenchant, embitter, envenom, ferment, spoil, acerbate.

source *n.* 1. beginning, cause, root, origin, derivation, core, basis, fountainhead, spring. 2. informant, expert, specialist, authority, reference.

sourpuss (*slang*) *n.* grouch, killjoy, curmudgeon, shrew, whiner, grump.

souse *v.* 1. soak, drown, wet, dunk, immerse, douse, drench, steep. 2. preserve, pickle, marinate, brine.

souvenir *n.* gift, keepsake, memento, relic, remembrance, token, reminder.

sovereign *n.* king, queen, monarch, autocrat, potentate, ruler, prince, princess, kaiser, czar, head of state.

sovereign *adj.* 1. absolute, unlimited, chief, dominant, imperial, monarchical, predominant, supreme. 2. autonomous, independent, self-governing, free.

sovereignty *n.* supremacy, sway, domination, primacy, suzerainty.

sow *v.* **1.** seed, plant, inseminate, propagate, scatter, strew. **2.** disperse, broadcast, circulate, disseminate.

space *n.* **1.** outer space, infinity, the heavens, void, beyond. **2.** room, expanse, scope, range, dimension, extent, capacity. **3.** (place to live or for sleeping) place, area, site, location, reservation, berth, accommodation. **4.** (extent in time) period, duration, cycle, span, term, tenure, interval.

spacious *adj.* capacious, roomy, vast, large, ample, expansive, extensive, commodious; *ant.* confined, narrow.

span *n.* length, duration, extent, distance, spread, scope, reach, compass, measure.

span *v.* cross, traverse, ford, bridge, overarch, link.

spank *v.* beat, whip, belt, cuff, slap, smack, tan, punish.

spar *v.* wrestle, fight, bicker, contend, squabble, wrangle.

spare *v.* **1.** forgive, reprieve, pardon, allow, acquit. **2.** afford, donate, contribute, give, yield.

to spare excess, left over, remaining, in abundance.

spare *adj.* **1.** extra, superfluous, additional, remaining, leftover; *ant.* needed. **2.** lean, lank, slender, slight, sparse, meager, modest, scanty, frugal; *ant.* ample, full.

sparing *adj.* **1.** frugal, niggardly, stingy, tight, avaricious, chary, thrifty, economical, prudent. **2.** merciful, humane, compassionate, mild, tolerant.

spark *n.* flash, flicker, sparkle, glitter, flare, glow.

spark *v.* **1.** flash, flare, sparkle, flicker, glitter. **2.** excite, provoke, stimulate, start, stir, kindle, inspire, animate, precipitate.

sparkle *v.* glitter, glisten, twinkle, shine, shimmer, effervesce, fizz, scintillate.

sparse *adj.* scanty, meager, inadequate, scattered, slight, exiguous; *ant.* dense, lush, thick.

spartan *adj.* austere, abstemious, strict, stern, rigorous, spare, disciplined, self-denying, stringent; *ant.* indulgent, hedonistic.

spasm *n.* fit, convulsion, seizure, contraction, paroxysm.

spasmodic *adj.* **1.** jerky, convulsive, spastic,

fitful. **2.** irregular, sporadic, periodic, occasional, intermittent, erratic; *ant.* certain, continuous.

spat *n.* disagreement, quarrel, dispute, difference, tiff, scrap.

spate *n.* deluge, flood, torrent, rush, cascade.

spatter *v.* splash, splatter, sprinkle, spray, dirty, soil.

spawn *v.* produce, reproduce, generate, bring forth, issue.

speak *v.* **1.** express, utter, voice, vocalize, pronounce, say, enunciate, articulate, talk, converse, chat. **2.** lecture, preach, address, expound, harangue, sermonize, exhort, orate.

so to speak that is to say, as the saying goes, in a manner of speaking.

speak out assert, declare, make oneself heard, insist.

speak for itself be self-evident, be obvious, vindicate, justify, explain.

speaker *n.* orator, rhetorician, lecturer; spokesperson, spokesman, spokeswoman, mouthpiece, master of ceremonies, MC.

spearhead *v.* begin, originate, create, launch, head, lead, pioneer.

special *adj.* **1.** (being one of a kind) peculiar, unique, unusual, individual, exceptional, extraordinary, sui generis; *ant.* standard, typical. **2.** (limited in application) specific, particular, restricted, definite; *ant.* general. **3.** significant, memorable, important, notable, conspicuous, critical.

specialist *n.* expert, master, veteran, ace, savant, authority, professional; *ant.* novice, beginner.

specialty *n.* forte, metier, strength, pursuit, practice.

species *n.* class, genus, variety, kind, breed, sort, category.

specific *adj.* particular, distinct, characteristic, peculiar, distinguishing, precise, exact, definite, explicit, clear-cut; *ant.* general, vague.

specification *n.* term, condition, requirement, stipulation.

specify *v.* name, cite, designate, stipulate, enumerate, itemize, define, delineate.

specimen *n.* example, exhibit, model, paradigm, representative, sample, type.

specious *adj.* deceptive, misleading, fallacious,

false, counterfeit, sophistic, unsound; *ant.* valid, true.

speck *n.* particle, bit, spot, iota, mite.

speckled *adj.* mottled, dappled, specked, variegated, motley, mosaic.

spectacle *n.* display, pageant, parade, performance, scene, exhibition, display.

spectacular *adj.* sensational, awesome, striking, magnificent, dramatic, breathtaking, dazzling, splendid, marvelous, fabulous, grand; *ant.* ordinary.

spectator *n.* viewer, onlooker, observer, bystander, witness; *ant.* contestant, player.

specter *n.* ghost, apparition, phantom, spirit.

spectral *adj.* phantasmal, supernatural, ghostly, disembodied; *ant.* corporeal.

speculate *v.* 1. contemplate, meditate, muse, reflect, ponder, conjecture, theorize, think, cogitate, surmise. 2. hazard, risk, venture, scheme, gamble.

speculative *adj.* 1. suppositional, hypothetical, abstract. 2. risky, dangerous, tentative, iffy; *ant.* safe, secure, certain, predictable.

speech *n.* 1. conversation, talk, utterance, discourse, oratory, parlance, intercourse, locution, diction. 2. lecture, oration, harangue, sermon, dissertation, recitation, tirade, diatribe, peroration, spiel.

speechless *adj.* 1. mute, silent, wordless, inarticulate, dumb. 2. amazed, astounded, shocked, dumbfounded, aghast, dazed, thunderstruck, nonplussed.

speed *n.* haste, hurry, acceleration, rapidity, alacrity, tempo, promptness, velocity; *ant.* slowness, tardiness.

speed *v.* expedite, facilitate, hasten, quicken, hurry, rush, hurtle, race, sprint; *ant.* delay, hamper, restrain.

speedy *adj.* quick, swift, rapid, fast, hasty, nimble, fleet, winged, precipitate, summary; *ant.* slow, tardy.

spell *n.* 1. charm, enchantment, hex, bewitchment, trance, magic, sorcery, witchery. 2. interval, term, period, season, stint, time, stretch.

spell *v.* signal, indicate, suggest, imply, mean, presage, portend, herald, augur, prefigure.

spellbound *adj.* entranced, amazed, fascinated,

captivated, charmed, mesmerized, rapt, transfixed.

spend *v.* 1. (pay out) expend, disburse, allocate, shell out, cough up (*slang*). 2. (use up) consume, deplete, liquidate, exhaust; *ant.* hoard, save. 3. (use up time) pass, kill, while away, idle, fritter away, drift, waste, squander; *ant.* slow.

spendthrift *adj.* extravagant, lavish, profligate, improvident, prodigal, wasteful, free-spending.

spendthrift *n.* big spender, squanderer, wastrel; *ant.* miser.

spent *adj.* 1. used, finished, gone. 2. drained, tired out, exhausted, weakened, wearied, worn out, debilitated, *slang:* dog-tired, bushed, out of gas, zonked; *ant.* fresh, energetic.

spew *v.* spread, scatter, spit, blow out, disgorge, belch, vomit.

spherical *adj.* 1. circular, globular, round, rotund, orotund. 2. stellar, celestial, astrological, planetary, heavenly.

spice *n.* seasoning, savor, relish, tang, flavoring, color, gusto, kick, life, pep, zest, zip, piquancy.

spick and span *adj.* clean, immaculate, neat, polished, scrubbed, spotless, tidy, well-kept; *ant.* dirty.

spicy *adj.* 1. pungent, piquant, seasoned, tangy, savory, flavorful, aromatic, fresh; *ant.* bland. 2. erotic, risqué, racy, ribald, suggestive, titillating, scandalous, indecorous, provocative.

spiel *n.* speech, harangue, recital, pitch, sermon, line.

spike *n.* barb, prong, stud, nail, spire, tine, peg, pin.

spill *v.* overflow, overturn, upset, scatter, shed, slop, discharge, disgorge.

spin *v.* 1. turn, whirl, revolution, rotation, twist, pirouette, circuit. 2. (*slang*) point of view, slant, viewpoint, angle, approach.

spin *v.* 1. revolve, whirl, twirl, rotate, turn, gyrate, gyre. 2. concoct, invent, produce, shape, mold, form, unfold.

spindle *n.* axis, rod, shaft, pivot, stem.

spindly *adj.* gangly, lanky, thin, skinny, leggy, attenuated; *ant.* stocky, thickset.

spine *n.* 1. backbone, vertebrae, spinal column. 2. thorn, spike, barb, needle, quill, thistle.

spine-chilling *adj.* frightening, horrifying, scary, terrifying, nightmarish, bloodcurdling, eerie, spooky.

spineless *adj.* weak, timid, fearful, cowardly, irresolute, feeble, weak-willed, vacillating, weak-kneed, squeamish, lily-livered, gutless, wimpish (*slang*); *ant.* brave, strong.

spiny *adj.* pointed, barbed, spiked, thistly, thorny, briery.

spiral *adj.* winding, circular, coiled, whorled, corkscrew, helical, scrolled, wound.

spire *n.* tower, steeple, pinnacle, cone, spike, summit, top.

spirit *n.* 1. vitality, vivacity, animation, breath, life, verve, zest, vigor. 2. (inner being or driving force) essence, soul, substance, character, gist, core, heart, force. 3. apparition, vision, specter, ghost, ghoul, phantom, pneuma, shade. 4. courage, enthusiasm, ardor, resolution, resolve, spunk, grit.

spirit *v.* abduct, kidnap, purloin, steal, seize, carry, convey, remove, whisk.

spirited *adj.* active, lively, vivacious, animated, effervescent, plucky, sprightly; *ant.* dull, despondent, languid.

spiritless *adj.* indifferent, despondent, pathetic, lackluster, languid, torpid.

spirits *n.* alcohol, *slang:* moonshine, the hard stuff, hooch, firewater.

spiritual *adj.* 1. incorporeal, spectral, astral, disembodied, psychic, mental; *ant.* physical, material. 2. sacred, holy, religious, devotional, ecclesiastical; *ant.* secular, worldly.

spit *v.* eject, expectorate, spew, splutter, drivel, drool.

spite *n.* malice, resentment, ill will, hatred, contempt, enmity, animosity, rancor, pique, umbrage; *ant.* affection, good will.

spite *v.* offend, provoke, peeve, irk, gall, discomfit, pique, vex, nettle.

spiteful *adj.* vindictive, malicious, cruel, rancorous, malefic, splenetic, barbed, villainous; *ant.* charitable.

splash *v.* bespatter, spray, sprinkle, moisten, wet.

spleen *n.* anger, wrath, resentment, venom, acrimony, bile, animosity, bitterness, gall.

splendid *adj.* grand, marvelous, illustrious, celebrated, exalted, distinguished, excellent, admirable, exceptional, glorious, wonderful, sublime; *ant.* ordinary.

splendor *n.* luster, brilliance, radiance, brightness, dazzle, effulgence, éclat.

splenetic *adj.* irritable, peevish, cross, testy, sullen, fretful, bilious, choleric, crabbed, irascible, sour.

splice *v.* join, graft, mesh, entwine, interlace, knit, marry, plait, tie.

splinter *n.* fragment, shaving, sliver, piece, flake, chip, paring.

splinter *v.* break, smash, shatter, rive, fracture, fragment, shiver, split.

split *n.* 1. separation, severance, breaking up, disruption, rift, dissension, estrangement, divergence. 2. crack, fissure, rent, breach, cleft, gap, rift, slash, slit, tear.

split *v.* cut, divide, rend, cleave, splinter, break, burst.

spoil *v.* 1. decay, rot, decompose, putrefy, deteriorate, curdle, mildew, go bad. 2. ruin, destroy, damage, wreck, debase, defile, upset, mar, deface, blemish, disfigure, plunder.

spoils *n.* winnings, prizes, acquisitions, gain, haul, loot, booty, pickings, profits, pillage, plunder.

sponge *v.* 1. clean, wash, mop, wipe, wet. 2. leach, cadge, *slang:* scrounge, mooch, bum, freeload.

sponger *n.* dependent, freeloader, parasite, bloodsucker, cadger, sycophant, schnorrer (*slang*).

spongy *adj.* porous, absorbent, wet, cushioned, springy.

sponsor *n.* patron, guarantor, backer, supporter, booster, advocate, adherent, champion.

sponsor *v.* finance, fund, support, back, promote, subsidize, underwrite, guarantee, boost, stand behind.

spontaneous *adj.* impromptu, involuntary, offhand, natural, ad hoc, instinctive; *ant.* premeditated, deliberate, forced.

spoof *n.* satire, caricature, parody, burlesque, joke, lampoon, sendup.

spook *n.* ghost, spirit, visitant.

spook *v.* frighten, alarm, startle, start, shake up, terrorize.

spooky *adj.* mysterious, uncanny, weird, eerie, ominous, chilling, hair-raising, scary, blood-curdling; *ant.* normal.

spoon-feed *v.* indulge, pamper, spoil, baby, cosset, coddle.

sporadic *adj.* erratic, random, occasional, intermittent, interrupted, discontinuous, scattered, spasmodic; *ant.* frequent, regular.

sport *n.* **1.** game, amusement, entertainment, recreation, diversion, festivity, revelry, pleasure, enjoyment. **2.** mockery, teasing, raillery, joshing, jest, pleasantry, mirth, drollery, badinage, trifling.

sport *v.* wear, don, display, exhibit, show off.

sportive *adj.* gay, playful, sprightly, frisky, frolicsome, carefree, lively, merry.

spot *n.* **1.** speck, mark, discoloration, stain, smudge, blemish, flaw, blot, daub. **2.** place, locality, site, area, region, scene, point, position. **3.** pinch, iota, bit, morsel, splash.

spot *v.* sight, detect, find, locate, discern, espy, observe, see, make out, recognize, identify.

spotless *adj.* clean, pure, immaculate, flawless, virgin; *ant.* stained, sullied, blemished.

spotted *adj.* **1.** dotted, marked, dappled, blotchy, speckled, flecked, mottled. **2.** dirty, blemished, soiled, smudged, smeared.

spotlight *n.* attention, publicity, fame, limelight, notoriety, stardom.

spotlight *v.* accentuate, emphasize, highlight, illuminate, feature, focus on, throw into relief.

spotty *adj.* blotchy, irregular, dotted; *ant.* even, uniform.

spouse *n.* mate, husband, wife, partner, companion, consort, better half.

spout *n.* fountain, geyser, spray, chute, nozzle.

spout *v.* **1.** emit, squirt, erupt, spurt, discharge, surge, pour, stream. **2.** pontificate, sermonize, preach, orate, rant, spiel, declaim, ramble on.

sprain *v.* twist, wrench, strain.

sprawl *v.* slouch, flop, lounge, spread, slump, loll, relax.

spray *n.* mist, drizzle, fog, droplets, froth; aerosol.

spray *v.* splash, scatter, spatter, sprinkle, shower, diffuse, douse, drench.

spread *n.* **1.** extent, scope, range, expanse,

436

reach, span, sweep, measure, compass. **2.** meal, feast, banquet, array, repast.

spread *v.* **1.** scatter, diffuse, sow, radiate, disseminate, disperse, distribute, circulate, advertise, publish, broadcast, proclaim, promulgate; *ant.* contain. **2.** unfurl, open, expand, flatten, even out, widen, enlarge; *ant.* close, fold. **3.** cover, coat, daub, overlay, gloss, enamel, paint, spray, veneer, wax, varnish, plaster. **4.** (cause to move apart) separate, divide, part, sever.

spree *n.* **1.** celebration, revel, frolic, orgy, bacchanalia. **2.** celebration, splurge, binge, indulgence.

sprightly *adj.* animated, active, perky, vivacious, lively, agile, nimble, brisk, jaunty, spry, saucy, blithe; *ant.* dull, morose.

spring *n.* bounce, elasticity, rebound, recoil, buoyancy, resilience, vitality, zip.

spring *v.* **1.** bounce, bound, hop, jump, leap, vault, dance. **2.** originate, stem, come, start, emerge, issue, arise, proceed, appear, derive, emanate.

springy *adj.* pliable, flexible, resilient, rubbery, stretchy, elastic, buoyant; *ant.* rigid, stiff.

sprinkle *v.* **1.** moisten, dampen, spray, bedew, shower. **2.** dust, pepper, powder, scatter, seed, strew, dot.

sprinkling *n.* handful, few, smattering, dusting, trace, touch, dash.

sprint *v.* rush, dash, dart, gallop, scamper, race, tear, whiz, hotfoot.

sprite *n.* fairy, nymph, elf, goblin, imp, sylph.

sprout *v.* germinate, grow, spring, take root, bud, burgeon.

spruce *adj.* neat, trim, tidy, well-groomed, dapper, elegant, natty, slick; *ant.* disheveled.

spruce up *v.* preen, primp, groom, neaten.

spry *adj.* active, vigorous, fleet, nimble, sprightly, alert, energetic, brisk; *ant.* doddering, feeble.

spume *v.* froth, spray, foam, scum.

spunk *n.* courage, spirit, nerve, mettle, pluck, chutzpah (*slang*), resolution, backbone, guts, heart, grit, toughness.

spur *v.* stimulate, induce, incite, motivate, impel, push, goad, drive, catalyze; *ant.* block, stymie.

spurious *adj.* deceptive, false, specious, coun-

spurn *v.* terfeit, bogus, simulated, contrived, feigned, forged, mock, pseudo, sham, apocryphal; *ant.* authentic, genuine, real.

spurn *v.* despise, disdain, scorn, shun, rebuff, reject, slight, put off, snub; *ant.* embrace.

spurt *n.* discharge, squirt, jet, stream, explosion, outbreak, burst, surge, fit, rush, acceleration, effusion.

spurt *v.* spew, burst, gush, spout, jet, flow.

sputter *v.* stammer, stutter, stumble, falter.

spy *n.* operative, detective, undercover agent, double agent, emissary, scout, wiretapper, plant.

spy *v.* **1.** view, behold, descry, glimpse, notice, observe, spot, see, discover. **2.** watch, pry, peer, examine, scrutinize, search, trail, hunt, hound.

squabble *n.* dispute, spat, quarrel, feud, tiff.

squabble *v.* argue, quarrel, bicker, wrangle, fight, brawl.

squad *n.* group, team, force, troop, company, crew, band, outfit, gang.

squalid *adj.* dirty, slovenly, broken-down, dingy, foul, fetid, musty, nasty, odorous, seedy, sleazy, sordid; *ant.* clean, pleasant.

squall *n.* gale, blast, gust, storm, hurricane, tempest.

squalor *n.* filth, wretchedness, decay, neglect, poverty; *ant.* order.

squander *v.* waste, blow (*slang*), fritter away, spend, dissipate, consume.

square *v.* align, adjust, match, adapt, harmonize, reconcile, settle, agree, accord, satisfy, conform, suit.

square *adj.* **1.** honest, straightforward, aboveboard, on the level, fair, ethical, disinterested, reliable, upright, unequivocal. **2.** (*slang*) straitlaced, conservative, stuffy, dated, old-fashioned, conventional, bourgeois, orthodox, out of touch.

squash *v.* **1.** crowd, press, compress, flatten, crush; *ant.* elongate, stretch. **2.** annihilate, suppress, quell, silence, quash, humiliate.

squat *v.* stoop, bend, hunch, crouch, hunker, bow, cower.

squat *adj.* stocky, heavy, chunky, thickset, stubby, stumpy.

squawk *v.* cry, crow, cackle, shriek, squeal, yelp, yap.

squeak *v.* creak, peep, shrill, whine, pipe, squeal.

squeal *v.* **1.** cry, wail, screech, yell, shout. **2.** (*slang*) betray, inform on, *slang:* blab, rat on, snitch.

squeamish *adj.* queasy, delicate, prudish, prissy, fussy, finicky, scrupulous, mincing, fastidious.

squeeze *n.* pressure, influence, restraint.

put the squeeze on compel, coerce, urge, force.

squeeze *v.* clasp, pinch, clutch, grip, hug, nip, wring.

squeeze through survive, accomplish, get by, succeed, endure.

squelch *v.* censure, suppress, crush, oppress, thwart, put down.

squire *v.* attend, assist, conduct, escort, accompany.

squirm *v.* fidget, wriggle, wiggle, twist, writhe.

squirt *v.* shoot, ejaculate, spit, emit, discharge, spurt, jet, expel, eject.

stab *n.* puncture, incision, jab, rent, thrust, wound, prick, cut.

stab *v.* knife, pierce, stick, gore, puncture, spear.

stability *n.* steadiness, durability, perseverance, solidity, constancy, permanence, strength, sturdiness; *ant.* shakiness, instability.

stable *adj.* **1.** steady, stationary, firm, steadfast, constant, sound, solid, resolute, reliable; *ant.* weak. **2.** enduring, permanent, durable, abiding, deep-rooted, immutable, lasting, longlasting, sturdy, unalterable, unchangeable, unwavering; *ant.* transitory, volatile.

stack *n.* heap, pile, mass, accumulation, mountain.

stack *v.* accumulate, amass, assemble, gather, load, save, stockpile, store.

stack the deck (*slang*) prearrange, stagemanage, set up, load the dice (*slang*), trick, deceive.

staff *n.* **1.** personnel, workers, employees, assistants, crew, team, cadre, cast, organization. **2.** stick, club, pole, wand, cane, rod, stave.

stage *n.* **1.** step, grade, plane, juncture, period, phase, level, position. **2.** frame, scaffold, staging, platform, tier, shelf.

stage *v.* arrange, engineer, orchestrate, organize, present, manage, produce, put on, give.

stagger *v.* **1.** totter, waver, vacillate, reel, hesitate, lurch, falter, teeter. 2. amaze, astonish, astound, dumbfound, flabbergast, nonplus, overwhelm, shock, stun, stupefy.

staggering *adj.* monstrous, huge, tremendous, large, unbelievable, enormous, immense, immeasurable; crushing, unbearable.

stagnant *adj.* 1. still, becalmed, lethargic, motionless, sluggish, stale, standing, torpid, listless, inert. 2. dirty, filthy, putrid, foul.

stagnate *v.* decay, deteriorate, rot, putrefy, fester, languish, vegetate.

staid *adj.* sober, grave, steady, calm, composed, sedate, self-restrained, solemn, decorous, demure, dignified; *ant.* frivolous, jaunty.

stain *n.* 1. blot, spot, mottle, splotch, smudge, spatter, drip, speck. 2. stigma, brand, disgrace, dishonor, infamy, reproach, shame, slur, blot, mark.

stain *v.* 1. soil, spot, discolor, taint, besmirch, blemish, defile, sully, tarnish, tinge. 2. color, dye, tint, lacquer, paint, varnish.

stake *n.* 1. rod, post, stick, pale, picket, spike, stave. 2. ante, bet, wager, venture, pledge, investment, risk, peril.

at stake endangered, risked, in jeopardy, at issue, involved.

stale *adj.* 1. musty, spoiled, dried, smelly, old, decayed, fetid, stagnant; *ant.* fresh. 2. hackneyed, mawkish, dull, banal, clichéd, commonplace, platitudinous, stereotyped, threadbare, trite, vapid; *ant.* novel.

stalemate *n.* deadlock, standoff, standstill, impasse, halt, stop, tie; *ant.* progress.

stalk *n.* stem, branch, shoot, trunk, pedicle, spire.

stalk *v.* hunt, pursue, track, chase, follow, shadow, tail, track, haunt.

stall *v.* delay, postpone, hamper, hinder, obstruct; hedge, prevaricate, stonewall (*slang*), equivocate, temporize, put off; *ant.* advance.

stalwart *adj.* brave, valiant, bold, daring, intrepid, resolute, indomitable, redoubtable, determined; *ant.* timid.

stamina *n.* endurance, strength, indefatigability, energy, drive, perseverance, vitality, vigor, resilience, grit, toughness, tenacity, purpose; *ant.* weakness.

stammer *v.* stutter, falter, stumble, hesitate, pause, halt, hem and haw.

stamp *n.* emblem, brand, impression, imprint, mark, cast, earmark, hallmark, signature.

stamp *v.* impress, imprint, brand, inscribe, label, mint, print, categorize, characterize, identify.

stampede *n.* run, rush, charge, rout.

stampede *v.* bolt, panic, rush, flee, gallop, scurry.

stance *n.* 1. deportment, carriage, bearing, posture. 2. opinion, position, attitude, standpoint, stand, viewpoint, point of view, slant, bias.

stand *n.* 1. belief, position, notion, view, attitude, opinion, determination, stance. 2. stage, platform, frame, grandstand.

stand *v.* 1. put up with, endure, hold, abide, bear, suffer, sustain, tolerate, weather, withstand, brook. 2. exist, remain, persist, stay, last, survive, obtain; *ant.* fall, perish.

stand by champion, support, defend, uphold, back.

stand for 1. bear, brook, countenance, endure, suffer, tolerate. 2. exemplify, epitomize, represent, betoken, denote, embody, mean, personify, signify, symbolize.

stand out loom, catch the eye, stick out.

stand up to oppose, challenge, confront, withstand.

standard *n.* measure, criterion, rule, test, example, average, gauge, guideline, model, specification, yardstick.

standard *adj.* regulation, basic, customary, normal, official, prevailing, recognized, orthodox, stock, typical; *ant.* abnormal, irregular.

standard-bearer *n.* leader, commander, boss, flagship, demagogue.

standardize *v.* systematize, regulate, institute, regiment, unify, regularize, stereotype, homogenize, normalize; mass-produce; *ant.* differentiate, diversify.

standards *n.* ethics, ideals, morals, principles, mores.

standing *n.* position, status, rank, reputation, estimation, footing, level, grade.

standoff *n.* delay, pause, impasse, stalemate, deadlock, dead end.

standoffish *adj.* cool, aloof, distant, indifferent, haughty, remote, reserved, uncommunicative, unsociable; *ant.* friendly.

standpoint *n.* opinion, attitude, point of view, judgment, position, stance, slant, viewpoint, angle.

standstill *n.* delay, pause, stop, halt, cessation, impasse, lapse, moratorium, reprieve, respite, logjam; *ant.* progress.

star *n.* **1.** sun, asteroid, comet, meteor, nova, planet, quasar, starlet, supernova, shooting star. **2.** celebrity, headliner, idol, leading man, leading lady, starlet, luminary.

stare *v.* look, watch, gaze, gawk, gape, glare.

stark *adj.* plain, severe, stern; austere, bald, bare, barren, bleak, cold, desolate; *ant.* mild, slight.

stark *adv.* totally, utterly, absolutely, altogether, completely, entirely, wholly; *ant.* mildly, slightly.

start *n.* inception, commencement, origin, inauguration, source, derivation, beginning, birth, dawn, outset; *ant.* finish, end.

start *v.* **1.** begin, set out, commence, open, pioneer, embark on; rise, issue, spring, originate. **2.** (create, as an organization) inaugurate, begin, cause, activate, establish, engender, father, instigate, launch, found, create, institute; *ant.* finish, stop.

startle *v.* frighten, surprise, alarm, shock, astonish, astound, start, amaze, agitate; *ant.* soothe, reassure.

startling *adj.* unexpected, sudden, unforeseen, dramatic, alarming, jolting, staggering, electrifying; *ant.* boring, ordinary.

starvation *n.* hunger, deprivation, need, want, famishment, malnutrition, undernourishment; *ant.* plenty.

starve *v.* **1.** fast, go hungry, diet; perish, die, weaken. **2.** underfeed, undernourish, famish, emaciate; *ant.* feed.

starve for crave, desire, yearn for, hunger for, long for, thirst for.

starving *adj.* famished, ravenous, hungry, underfed; *ant.* full.

stash *v.* conceal, cache, closet, hide, hoard, stockpile, stow away; *ant.* uncover.

state *n.* **1.** republic, country, nation, kingdom, land, federation, commonwealth, body politic. **2.** status, circumstance, situation, case, footing, standing, condition, element. **3.** (a precarious or difficult position) predicament, plight, difficulty, quandary.

state *v.* pronounce, affirm, declare, assert, enumerate, explain, propound, voice, aver, asseverate.

stately *adj.* **1.** lordly, proud, dignified, noble, solemn, august, regal; *ant.* unassuming, modest. **2.** large, grand, spacious, lofty, imposing, majestic, palatial, opulent, luxurious, monumental; *ant.* poor, cheap, lowly.

statement *n.* **1.** utterance, comment, declaration, allegation, remark, assertion, avowal, asseveration, pronouncement, proclamation. **2.** bill, charge, reckoning, account, record, report, budget, affidavit.

statesman *n.* diplomat, politician, legislator, administrator, official.

statesmanship *n.* tact, diplomacy, statecraft.

static *adj.* constant, fixed, immobile, inert, motionless, unmoving, stagnant, stationary, still, dormant, latent; *ant.* active, dynamic.

station *n.* **1.** site, situation, location, position, place, post. **2.** occupation, duty, calling, service, employment. **3.** (the level of a job) standing, order, rank, state, sphere, status. **4.** depot, terminal, stop, stopping-place.

stationary *adj.* fixed, stable, permanent, inert, moored, anchored, settled, unmoving, sedentary; *ant.* moving.

statue *n.* cast, figure, bust, statuette, likeness, image, sculpture, effigy, icon.

statuesque *adj.* stately, beautiful, grand, graceful, dignified, regal, shapely; *ant.* small.

stature *n.* **1.** height, size, growth, tallness. **2.** importance, eminence, prestige, prominence, rank, standing, consequence.

status *n.* **1.** rank, situation, standing, station, degree. **2.** distinction, eminence, stature, position, influence, clout (*slang*); *ant.* unimportance.

status seeker opportunist, manipulator, social climber, nouveau riche.

statute *n.* ordinance, law, enactment, decree, edict, regulation, rule.

statutory *adj.* legal, sanctioned, lawful, rightful.

staunch *adj.* steadfast, strong, constant, faithful, firm, dependable, loyal, resolute, sound, stout, sure; *ant.* unreliable, wavering, weak.

stave off avert, delay, fend off, hold off, keep at bay, parry, ward off; *ant.* cause, encourage.

stay *n.* 1. truss, prop, hold, support, brace, buttress, stanchion, shoring, reinforcement. 2. visit, stop, sojourn, halt, visit, holiday. 3. deferment, delay, continuance, pause, postponement, reprieve, remission, suspension.

stay *v.* 1. visit, wait, tarry, linger, sojourn, linger, dwell, loiter. 2. delay, adjourn, defer, postpone; hold back, hinder, arrest, check, curb, suspend, obstruct; *ant.* advance, release. 3. buttress, prop, support, sustain.

steadfast *adj.* faithful, loyal, stalwart, unwavering, stable, constant, staunch, fast, firm, fixed, persevering, steady, unfaltering, unswerving; *ant.* wavering, weak.

steady *v.* brace, fix, secure, stabilize, support, firm, balance.

steady *adj.* 1. uniform, unvarying, patterned, constant, regular, ceaseless, incessant, unremitting, persistent; *ant.* wavering. 2. cool, calm, self-possessed, poised, reserved, equable, sensible, serene, staid, steadfast, unflappable.

steal *v.* filch, thieve, loot, rob, purloin, embezzle, defraud, rifle, cozen, poach, swindle, fleece, pillage, pilfer; *ant.* return.

stealth *n.* secrecy, slyness, furtiveness, underhandedness, clandestinity, covertness, surreptitiousness; *ant.* openness.

stealthy *adj.* secret, enigmatic, clandestine, furtive, surreptitious, covert.

steam *n.* mist, vapor, condensation, dampness, fumes, haze.

steel *v.* brace, fortify, harden, nerve, toughen; *ant.* weaken.

steep *v.* imbue, immerse, infuse, permeate, pervade, saturate, soak, submerge, suffuse.

steep *adj.* abrupt, sheer, perpendicular, precipitous, extreme, high; *ant.* gentle, moderate.

steer *v.* point, direct, control, govern, guide, pilot.

stem *n.* branch, shoot, stalk, trunk, peduncle, petiole.

stem *v.* check, contain, curb, restrain, stay, head off, stop, tamp; *ant.* encourage, increase.

stench *n.* odor, stink, redolence, reek, miasma, effluvium.

step *n.* 1. pace, stride, gait, footfall, tread, walk. 2. measure, action, move, process, phase, stage, notch, position.

in step alike, similar, in agreement, coinciding.

step by step carefully, slowly, tentatively, cautiously, gradually.

take steps act, start, do something.

watch one's step be careful, take precautions, look out, watch out.

step down leave, quit, resign, abdicate, retire, withdraw.

step up intensify, accelerate, augment, escalate, speed up; *ant.* decrease.

step *v.* pace, stride, advance, recede, tread, march, move, stalk, mince.

stereotype *v.* define, pigeonhole, catalog, typecast; conventionalize, standardize, normalize; *ant.* differentiate.

stereotype *n.* convention, formula, mold, pattern, fashion, model, paradigm, average, custom.

sterile *adj.* 1. infertile, impotent, childless, fruitless, barren, fallow; *ant.* fertile, productive, potent. 2. antiseptic, sterilized, disinfected, decontaminated, sanitary, hygienic; *ant.* dirty, infected, contaminated. 3. (void of novelty or freshness) uninspired, stale, dull, shallow, vapid, old hat, unproductive; *ant.* fecund, rich.

sterilize *v.* clean, disinfect, fumigate, purify; *ant.* contaminate, infect.

sterling *adj.* genuine, authentic, real, true, pure; *ant.* false, poor.

stern *adj.* severe, rigid, austere, strict, authoritarian, flinty, grim, unrelenting, unsparing, unyielding; *ant.* mild, lenient.

stew *v.* 1. boil, simmer, steam, fricassee. 2. fume, fret, fuss, chafe, worry, agonize, perspire, swelter, worry.

stick *n.* branch, twig, stem, stalk.

stick *v.* 1. adhere, cling, fasten, attach, cleave, cohere, hold; *ant.* loosen, let go. 2. prick, pierce, impale, penetrate, stab.

stickler *n.* 1. zealot, devotee, fanatic, follower, maniac, martinet, nut (*slang*). 2. enigma, riddle, paradox, puzzle.

sticky *adj.* viscous, gluey, adhesive, clinging, glutinous, gummy, syrupy; *ant.* dry.

stiff *adj.* 1. solid, rigid, congealed, petrified,

firm, ossified, unyielding, inflexible, hard, stony, cemented, steely; *ant.* flexible, soft. **2.** formal, awkward, ungainly, ungraceful, artificial, forced, labored, mannered, wooden; *ant.* graceful, informal. **3.** (said of a drink or potion) strong, potent, hard, powerful, having a wallop.

stiffen *v.* solidify, freeze, crystallize, petrify, harden, anneal; *ant.* soften, melt, relax.

stifle *v.* **1.** choke, smother, asphyxiate, suffocate, extinguish, strangle. **2.** dampen, check, curb, hush, muffle, repress, restrain, suppress, silence; *ant.* encourage.

stigma *n.* blemish, blot, disgrace, reproach, blame, slur, smirch, spot, stain, imputation; *ant.* credit.

stigmatize *v.* disgrace, blame, defame, discredit, pillory, vilify, condemn; *ant.* praise.

still *v.* alleviate, appease, calm, allay, lull, pacify, settle, silence, soothe, subdue; *ant.* agitate, stir up.

still *adj.* silent, calm, tranquil, noiseless, quiet, hushed, serene, untroubled, motionless, unstirring; *ant.* agitated, busy.

still *adv.* nevertheless, anyway, however, even, yet.

stillness *n.* peacefulness, peace, quiet, still, silence, serenity, tranquillity; *ant.* agitation.

stilted *adj.* affected, pompous, artificial, bombastic, forced, staged, high-flown, inflated, labored, pretentious, graceless, wooden; *ant.* flowing, fluent.

stimulant *n.* tonic, bracer, energizer, *slang:* upper, pick-me-up; reviver; *ant.* depressant.

stimulate *v.* support, foster, incite, excite, urge, animate, arouse, goad, instigate, provoke, spur, accelerate, agitate; *ant.* discourage.

stimulating *adj.* inspiring, provocative, rousing, intriguing, enlivening, electrifying, energizing, refreshing, galvanic; *ant.* dull, weary, enervating.

stimulus *n.* inducement, provocation, motive, incentive, spur, impetus, catalyst; *ant.* discouragement.

sting *v.* prick, prickle, tingle, hurt.

stingy *adj.* parsimonious, covetous, mean, miserly, scrimping, tightfisted, penurious, avaricious, grasping, penny-pinching, churlish, rapacious; *ant.* generous, bountiful.

stink *n.* stench, smell, fetor, foulness, miasma, effluvium.

stint *n.* assignment, job, consignment, term, time, work, tour of duty.

stipulate *v.* designate, specify, condition, arrange, bargain, postulate, pledge, require, promise, insist upon, contract.

stipulation *n.* arrangement, requirement, clause, condition, prerequisite, proviso, qualification, sine qua non.

stir *n.* agitation, bustle, excitement, activity, commotion, to-do, uproar, hustle, tumult; *ant.* calm.

stir *v.* **1.** provoke, excite, inflame, awaken, agitate, electrify, hasten, inspire; *ant.* bore, calm. **2.** beat, mix, move, bestir, agitate, blend, flutter, quiver, rustle.

stirring *adj.* stimulating, lively, exhilarating, heady, spirited, thrilling; moving; *ant.* calming, uninspiring.

stock *n.* **1.** merchandise, produce, commodity, accumulation, goods, inventory, property, selection, supply, wares. **2.** funds, property, capital, stocks and bonds, investment.

stock *adj.* trite, hackneyed, common, banal, dull, clichéd, worn-out, overused, bromidic; *ant.* original.

stocky *adj.* short, solid, stubby, chunky, sturdy, broad, thickset; *ant.* skinny, tall.

stodgy *adj.* boring, uninteresting, tedious, dull, labored, leaden, turgid, unimaginative; *ant.* exciting, informal.

stoical *adj.* impassive, enduring, calm, dispassionate, imperturbable, resigned, stolid, phlegmatic, patient; *ant.* anxious, depressed, irascible.

stoicism *n.* impassivity, patience, acceptance, fatalism, forbearance, long-suffering, resignation; *ant.* anxiety, fury.

stolid *adj.* impassive, wooden, unemotional, sober, apathetic, indifferent, plodding, unimaginative, unexcitable; obtuse, slow; *ant.* interested, lively.

stomach *n.* abdomen, paunch, belly, gut, potbelly, *slang:* spare tire, tummy.

stomach *v.* abide, bear, endure, suffer, submit to, swallow, tolerate, put up with.

stone *n.* boulder, rock, pebble.

stony *adj.* **1.** adamant, inflexible, unrelenting,

firm, unyielding, hard, inexorable, obdurate, steely. **2.** heartless, hostile, callous, merciless, pitiless, unfeeling, icy, cold, unforgiving, frigid; *ant.* forgiving, friendly, softhearted, warm.

stoop *v.* bend, bow, lean, incline, crouch, slant, descend, hunch, kneel, squat.

stop *n.* **1.** halt, standstill, pause, stay, discontinuation, rest, stoppage, cessation, termination, break. **2.** depot, station, terminus, way station, whistle stop.

stop *v.* **1.** halt, pause, stay, tarry, rest, pull up, check, discontinue, cease, suspend; *ant.* continue, proceed, advance. **2.** prevent, terminate, arrest, bar, block, forestall, frustrate, impede, obstruct, prevent, repress, staunch; *ant.* start.

stopgap *n.* substitute, makeshift, expedient, improvisation, resource.

stopgap *adj.* impromptu, emergency, provisional, temporary, expediential, improvised, makeshift; *ant.* finished, permanent.

stoppage *n.* abeyance, check, closure, desistance, halt, interruption, shutdown, standstill.

store *n.* **1.** shop, market, outlet, emporium, grocery, department store. **2.** reserves, wares, stock, accumulation, cache, hoard, stockpile, provision, supply; *ant.* scarcity.

store *v.* deposit, cache, stock, stow away, garner, hoard, stockpile, husband, squirrel away, amass; *ant.* use, spend.

storehouse *n.* warehouse, depository, granary, magazine, silo, barn, depot, armory, arsenal, repository, vault.

storm *n.* tempest, cloudburst, downpour, blizzard, snowstorm, squall, hurricane, cyclone, gust, gale, monsoon, northeaster.

storm *v.* **1.** rain, squall, drizzle, howl, blow a gale. **2.** assail, assault, charge, beset, rush, stalk, stomp.

stormy *adj.* **1.** rainy, wet, damp, cold, bitter, frigid, windy, blustery, tempestuous, pouring, threatening; *ant.* mild, clement. **2.** savage, agitated, turbulent, violent, riotous, chaotic, unruly.

story *n.* tale, myth, anecdote, narrative, legend, parable, fiction, novel, epic, saga, yarn.

storyteller *n.* author, narrator, relator, teller, bard, poet, biographer, chronicler, novelist.

stout *adj.* **1.** fat, corpulent, fleshy, portly,

plump, obese, rotund, tubby; *ant.* slim, lithe, lean. **2.** strong, sturdy, hardy, husky, brawny, athletic, muscular, strapping; *ant.* weak. **3.** staunch, enduring, dependable, reliable, trusted, loyal.

straggle *v.* lag, loiter, amble, drift, scatter, spread, stray, wander, ramble.

straggly *adj.* loose, untidy, messy, tangled, dispersed.

straight *adj.* **1.** level, plumb, vertical, perpendicular, upright, erect, even, unbent, unswerving; *ant.* bent, curved. **2.** direct, uninterrupted, continuous, through, nonstop, unrelieved, successive; *ant.* indirect, roundabout, circuitous. **3.** (of good character) honest, good, reliable, honorable, decent, honest, moral, upright, respectable, fair, equitable, just, straightforward; *ant.* dishonest, evasive. **4.** (said if a substance, as a drink) undiluted, pure, unmixed, unadulterated, concentrated, plain; *ant.* diluted.

straight *adv.* candidly, directly, frankly, honestly, outspokenly, point-blank.

straightaway *adv.* immediately, directly, at once, instantly, presently, now, right away, there and then, this minute; *ant.* eventually.

straighten *v.* arrange, neaten, order, untwist, rectify, unsnarl, unravel, put straight; *ant.* bend, curl.

straightforward *adj.* sincere, candid, frank, honest, direct, plain, forthright, guileless, truthful, uncomplicated; *ant.* devious, evasive.

strain *n.* **1.** exertion, effort, struggle, endeavor, force, struggle, wrench. **2.** (the result of effort or stress) anxiety, tension, pressure, stress. **3.** ancestry, blood, descent, lineage, extraction, stock, family, pedigree. **4.** melody, song, theme, tune, air, measure.

strain *v.* **1.** twist, hurt, wrench, sprain, distort, tear, pull, injure, distend. **2.** filter, refine, purify, screen, sift, sieve, squeeze, separate, percolate.

strained *adj.* artificial, awkward, false, forced, labored, self-conscious, stiff, tense, uneasy, unnatural, unrelaxed, difficult; *ant.* natural, easy.

strait *n.* **1.** channel, inlet, canal, sound, narrows. **2.** predicament, difficulty, distress, crisis, plight.

strait-laced *adj.* proper, strict, severe, stiff, prudish, moralistic, narrow-minded, prim, puritanical, stuffy, upright, Victorian; *ant.* liberal, broad-minded, easygoing.

strand *n.* lock, string, tress, thread, filament, fiber.

stranded *adj.* abandoned, aground, ashore, marooned, shipwrecked, helpless, beached.

strange *adj.* **1.** foreign, alien, unfamiliar, exotic, remote, unknown, detached, apart; *ant.* familiar. **2.** unusual, exceptional, rare, uncommon, weird, singular, queer, remarkable, curious, bizarre, astonishing, wonderful; *ant.* common, familiar, ordinary.

stranger *n.* foreigner, outsider, newcomer, intruder, visitor, alien, guest, immigrant; *ant.* inhabitant, citizen, native.

strangle *v.* **1.** choke, asphyxiate, suffocate, kill. **2.** suppress, subdue, stifle, repress, restrain, hold in.

strap *n.* belt, leash, thong, strop, band.

strap *v.* bind, buckle, fasten, secure, tie, truss.

strapping *adj.* brawny, burly, hefty, big, tall, powerful, hulking, husky, robust, stalwart, robust, muscular, athletic; *ant.* puny.

stratagem *n.* scheme, plot, artifice, device, intrigue, maneuver, ploy, ruse, subterfuge, trick.

strategic *adj.* **1.** cunning, clever, tricky, calculated, deliberate, planned, diplomatic. **2.** vital, crucial, decisive, imperative, important, necessary, cardinal, key.

strategist *n.* schemer, tactician, contriver.

strategy *n.* tactics, maneuvering, approach, procedure, design, campaign, plan, program, game plan, policy, scheme, artifice.

stratum *n.* layer, tier, level.

stray *v.* rove, roam, deviate, digress, drift, err, meander, straggle, wander.

stray *adj.* abandoned, lost, vagrant, scattered, roaming, wandering.

streak *n.* band, strip, stripe, vein, ridge, line, slash, smear.

streak *v.* **1.** flash, hurtle, slash, speed, sprint, tear, whistle, dart, fly, gallop. **2.** (form streaks) band, striate, stripe, ridge.

streaked *adj.* lined, smudgy, veined, flecked, banded.

stream *n.* river, rivulet, brook, creek, run, tributary, rillet.

stream *v.* cascade, emit, flood, flow, gush, run, issue, pour, spill, surge, well out.

streamer *n.* flag, banner, standard, pennant, ensign, plume, ribbon.

streamlined *adj.* modernized, sleek, smooth, efficient, graceful, elegant; *ant.* clumsy, inefficient.

street *n.* road, avenue, boulevard, thoroughfare, route, artery, highway, parkway.

strength *n.* **1.** power, vigor, brawn, might, energy, vitality, stamina, sturdiness; *ant.* weakness, feebleness. **2.** backbone, fortitude, stalwartness, tenacity, determination, persistence, fervor, spirit; *ant.* timidity. **3.** intensity, concentration, potency, force, effectiveness; depth, vehemence.

strengthen *v.* intensify, add, fortify, buttress, empower, augment, invigorate, reinforce, stiffen, steel, toughen, rejuvenate; *ant.* weaken, cripple.

strenuous *adj.* arduous, demanding, exhausting, laborious, hard, taxing, tough, uphill; *ant.* easy, effortless.

stress *n.* **1.** strain, tension, pressure, anxiety, apprehension; *ant.* peace, calm. **2.** emphasis, significance, importance, weight, import, urgency.

stress *v.* accentuate, emphasize, underscore, repeat, reiterate, belabor; *ant.* relax.

stretch *n.* extent, range, reach, compass, distance, time, term, period.

stretch *v.* **1.** grow, expand, spread, unfold, swell, open, burst forth, strain; *ant.* relax. **2.** (cause to become stretched) elongate, inflate, extend, lengthen, widen, draw tight, tauten, distend, pull.

stricken *adj.* hurt, wounded, injured, harmed, smitten, struck, afflicted, hit; *ant.* unaffected.

strict *adj.* stringent, stern, austere, firm, harsh, rigorous, diligent, unbending, rigid; *ant.* mild, easygoing, lenient.

stricture *n.* **1.** censure, criticism, rebuke, blame, reproach, admonition, reproof; *ant.* praise. **2.** constriction, tightness, choking, squeezing, binding, compression, shrinking, contraction.

strident *adj.* shrill, grating, loud, clamorous, jarring, discordant, vociferous, raucous, screeching, cacophonous; *ant.* quiet, sweet.

443

strife *n.* conflict, quarrel, disagreement, fight, bickering, dissension, animosity, friction, squabbling; *ant.* peace.

strike *n.* **1.** walkout, slowdown, deadlock, mutiny, refusal, stoppage. **2.** hit, stroke, blow, punch, wallop; attack, sortie, assault, bombardment, raid.

strike *v.* **1.** punch, thump, beat, hit, box, assault, assail, clout, cuff, knock, pound, smite, slap. **2.** walk out, picket, boycott, stop, quit, revolt, sit down, sit in, slow down. **3.** kindle, inflame, ignite, burn, light.

striking *adj.* attractive, noticeable, impressive, singular, memorable, salient, extraordinary, arresting; *ant.* common.

string *n.* **1.** strand, fiber, rope, cord, twine. **2.** sequence, succession, procession, chain, line, order, series, train.

stringent *adj.* **1.** strict, severe, rigid, harsh, demanding, exacting, inflexible, rigorous. **2.** (said of an argument) compelling, forceful, powerful, poignant, convincing, valid.

strip *n.* piece, band, belt, ribbon, shred, slat, strap.

strip *v.* **1.** disrobe, undress, divest, bare, denude, doff, expose, unclothe, uncover; *ant.* dress, cover. **2.** displace, remove, tear, peel, defoliate, despoil, dismantle, empty, gut, husk, pillage, sack, skin, excoriate; *ant.* provide.

stripe *n.* line, strip, band, border, demarcation, ribbon, layer, striation, belt.

stripling *n.* youth, fledgling, youngster, minor, adolescent.

strive *v.* try, endeavor, attempt, contend, strain, struggle, labor, toil, work.

stroke *n.* **1.** apoplexy, attack, seizure, collapse. **2.** blow, box, cuff, rap, hit, knock, pummel.

stroke *v.* rub, caress, pat, pet, fondle.

stroll *n.* walk, excursion, saunter, constitutional, turn, dawdle, ramble.

stroll *v.* roam, ramble, saunter, walk, dawdle, toddle, wander, gallivant, amble.

strong *adj.* **1.** robust, muscular, stout, hardy, sinewy, husky, athletic, powerful, brawny, strapping; *ant.* weak, emaciated. **2.** (said of a material or product) solid, sturdy, firm, wellbuilt, secure, tough, durable, sound, reinforced, rugged, well-made; *ant.* flimsy, slipshod. **3.** (strong in purpose) determined,

444

resolute, steadfast, staunch, tenacious, unyielding. **4.** (said of a drink) undiluted, powerful, potent, stiff, inebriating, intoxicating, straight, rich, unmixed, concentrated.

stronghold *n.* bastion, bulwark, citadel, fortress, redoubt, refuge.

structure *n.* **1.** arrangement, composition, formation, hierarchy, fabrication, construction, configuration, design, makeup. **2.** house, edifice, building.

structure *v.* arrange, assemble, build, construct, design, form, organize, shape.

struggle *n.* fight, contest, conflict, strife, battle, war.

struggle *v.* strive, grapple, cope, compete, contend, labor, strain, toil, work; *ant.* give in, rest.

strut *v.* swagger, prance, parade, stalk, peacock.

stubborn *adj.* obstinate, resolute, dogged, headstrong, inflexible, intransigent, obdurate, recalcitrant, willful, bullheaded, pigheaded, mulish; *ant.* compliant.

stubby *adj.* stout, stocky, fat, short, chubby, squat, stumpy, thickset; *ant.* long, tall, thin.

stuck *adj.* **1.** fast, fastened, cemented, tight, fixed, glued; *ant.* loose. **2.** perplexed, puzzled, baffled, stumped, stymied, nonplussed.

stuck-up *(slang) adj.* conceited, condescending, haughty, arrogant, overweening, snobbish, uppity; *ant.* humble.

student *n.* pupil, scholar, undergraduate, disciple, apprentice.

studied *adj.* deliberate, premeditated, planned, calculated, rehearsed, intentional, conscious; *ant.* unplanned, spontaneous.

studio *n.* workshop, workroom, atelier.

studious *adj.* thoughtful, contemplative, industrious, well-read, scholarly, academic, learned, bookish, assiduous, attentive, reflective; *ant.* lazy.

study *n.* **1.** research, investigation, learning, reading, inquiry, consideration, questioning, analyzing, comparison, thought, reasoning. **2.** subject, interest, field, branch of learning, discipline, area, thesis.

study *v.* examine, learn, compare, analyze, cogitate, peruse, ponder, scan, scrutinize, survey.

stuff *v.* fill, pack, compress, cram, jam, load, shove, wedge.

stuffy *adj.* **1.** confined, close, stagnant, muggy, airless, fusty, oppressive, stale; *ant.* airy. **2.** conservative, conventional, stodgy, humorless, priggish, prim, staid, old-fashioned; *ant.* informal, modern.

stultify *v.* prevent, frustrate, check, stop, repress, thwart, stifle, smother, negate, nullify, blunt; *ant.* encourage, boost.

stultifying *adj.* numbing, stupefying, dulling; *ant.* electrifying.

stumble *v.* blunder, flounder, lurch, fall, tilt, topple, trip, reel, stagger.

stumbling block obstacle, barrier, difficulty, hindrance, hurdle, impediment, snag.

stump *v.* baffle, bewilder, confound, mystify, nonplus, perplex, puzzle, stymie; *ant.* assist, help.

stumped (*slang*) *adj.* bewildered, uncertain, bamboozled, at a loss, flummoxed, nonplussed, up a tree (*slang*); *ant.* enlightened.

stun *v.* **1.** hit, knock out, daze, dazzle, deaden, paralyze, benumb, drug. **2.** astonish, astound, amaze, surprise, dumbfound, flabbergast, shock, stagger, stupefy.

stunned *adj.* shocked, dazed, astonished, amazed, nonplussed, dumbfounded, flabbergasted.

stunning *adj.* striking, remarkable, impressive, beautiful, charming, dazzling, gorgeous, lovely, ravishing; *ant.* poor, ugly.

stunt *n.* feat, exploit, deed, enterprise, performance, trick.

stunt *v.* hamper, hinder, impede, restrict, slow, stop, arrest, check, dwarf; *ant.* promote.

stunted *adj.* dwarfed, small, tiny, undersized, runtish, diminutive; *ant.* full-grown.

stupefaction *n.* astonishment, amazement, surprise, wonder, stupor, awe, bafflement.

stupefy *v.* **1.** stun, dull, numb, deaden. **2.** amaze, astound, astonish, startle, confound, stagger, nonplus.

stupendous *adj.* grand, breathtaking, marvelous, enormous, gigantic, colossal, prodigious, tremendous, vast, phenomenal; *ant.* unimpressive.

stupid *adj.* idiotic, simple, witless, inane, daft, doltish, addled, moronic, asinine, imbecilic, vacuous, vapid.

stupidity *n.* denseness, dimness, brainlessness, inanity, foolishness, puerility, thickheadedness; *ant.* alertness, cleverness.

stupor *n.* insensibility, lethargy, apathy, torpor, somnolence, coma, daze, inertia; *ant.* alertness.

sturdy *adj.* **1.** (said of a material or product) solid, well-made, durable, sound, strong, secure, unbreakable; *ant.* rickety, flimsy. **2.** (said of character) resolute, stalwart, firm, staunch, reliable, solid, unyielding, determined. **3.** athletic, brawny, hearty, husky, muscular, powerful, robust; *ant.* puny, decrepit.

stutter *v.* stammer, falter, sputter, hesitate, splutter.

style *n.* **1.** way, form, technique, method, habit, custom, practice, approach, modus operandi; bearing, manner, persona, life style. **2.** fashion, vogue, chic, dash, elegance, flair, sophistication, stylishness, taste, pizzazz, dress-sense, élan.

stylish *adj.* fashionable, chic, smart, dapper, natty, snazzy, trendy, urbane, in vogue; *ant.* frumpy, out-of-date, dowdy.

stymie *v.* hinder, block, impede, obstruct, confound, stump, frustrate, thwart, puzzle, nonplus; *ant.* assist.

suave *adj.* sophisticated, cultured, pleasant, urbane, affable, charming, gracious, polite, unctuous, bland; *ant.* crude.

subconscious *adj.* intuitive, latent, repressed, subliminal, hidden; *ant.* conscious, expressed.

subdue *v.* control, discipline, tame, humble, reduce, suppress, conquer, vanquish, break; *ant.* arouse.

subject *n.* matter, topic, theme, point, issue, gist, argument, substance, question.

subject *v.* control, tame, master, govern, dominate, suppress, subdue, vanquish, enthrall; *ant.* liberate, release.

subject *adj.* **1.** ruled, directed, submissive, servile, slavish. **2.** dependent, subordinate, contingent; answerable, accountable, beholden.

subjection *n.* bondage, captivity, oppression, slavery, thralldom.

subjective *adv.* **1.** biased, prejudiced, personal, emotional, prejudiced, instinctive, preconceived, intuitive; *ant.* objective, impartial. **2.** illusory, fanciful, idiosyncratic, personal, private, mental, impressionistic; *ant.* public, real.

subjugate *v.* suppress, enslave, master, subdue,

tame, conquer, crush, overcome, defeat, vanquish; *ant.* free.

sublimate *v.* **1.** purify, cleanse, refine, heighten, transmute. **2.** repress, hide, conceal, obscure, suppress.

sublime *adj.* transcendent, grand, noble, exalted, lofty, stately, eminent, majestic, empyrean; *ant.* lowly.

submerge *v.* **1.** (put below a liquid's surface) submerse, immerse, deluge, dunk, engulf, flood, inundate, overwhelm, swamp; *ant.* raise. **2.** (go down below a liquid's surface) sink, descend, subside, plunge, drown; *ant.* surface.

submerged *adj.* concealed, hidden, obscured; underwater, subaquatic.

submission *n.* obedience, deference, capitulation, compliance, assent, prostration, servility, cringing, tractability, subordination; *ant.* defiance.

submissive *adj.* passive, docile, acquiescent, humble, ingratiating, meek, pliant, supine, yielding; *ant.* defiant, refractory.

submit *v.* **1.** offer, advance, volunteer, tender, proffer, present, suggest, propose, propound. **2.** capitulate, surrender, relinquish, resign, yield, accede, bend, comply, defer, knuckle under, succumb; *ant.* struggle.

subordinate *n.* assistant, aide, junior, underling, adjunct, inferior, second banana (*slang*), subaltern; *ant.* superior.

subordinate *adj.* minor, subsidiary, supplementary, auxiliary, accessory, ancillary; *ant.* main, chief.

subpoena *v.* summon, cite, arraign, call.

subscribe *v.* **1.** advocate, support, second, approve, endorse, countenance. **2.** contribute, donate, give, offer, pledge, promise.

subscription *n.* consent, approval, agreement, acceptance, contribution, donation, dues, payment.

subsequent *adj.* succeeding, following, ensuing, resulting, consequent; *ant.* previous.

subservient *adj.* submissive, obsequious, servile, slavish, cringing, sycophantic.

subside *v.* ebb, recede, wane, sink, dwindle, abate, decline, diminish, settle, slake; *ant.* increase.

subsidiary *n.* affiliate, branch, division, section, offshoot.

subsidiary *adj.* auxiliary, subordinate, supplemental, backup, ancillary; *ant.* chief.

subsidy *n.* assistance, support, aid, backing, help, honorarium, gratuity, endowment, indemnity, subvention.

subsidize *v.* finance, fund, sponsor, underwrite, promote, support.

subsist *v.* survive, endure, eke out an existence, continue, last.

subsistence *n.* **1.** life, existence, being, presence, continuance. **2.** sustenance, means, circumstances, resources, property, wealth, capital, salary, income.

substance *n.* **1.** essence, matter, core, gist, import, meaning, heart, meat, significance, pith. **2.** material, matter, stuff, body, element, fabric, being.

substandard *adj.* inferior, cheap, poor, second-rate, shoddy, tacky, tawdry; *ant.* first-rate, adequate.

substantial *adj.* **1.** (large or strong in appearance) solid, firm, stout, durable, sound, well-built, strong, hefty, full-bodied. **2.** important, valuable, extraordinary, material, considerable, significant, weighty, worthwhile. **3.** (apparent to the senses) real, actual, material, tangible, corporeal, visible; *ant.* imaginary, fictitious. **4.** (great in number) considerable, ample, abundant, plentiful, sizable, multitudinous, numerous; *ant.* scanty.

substantially *adv.* **1.** essentially, mainly, in essence, for all intents and purposes; *ant.* slightly. **2.** extensively, heavily, largely.

substantiate *v.* **1.** confirm, ratify, attest, verify, affirm, prove, corroborate, authenticate. **2.** realize, complete, incarnate, embody.

substitute *n.* alternate, replacement, stand-in, reserve, understudy, surrogate, proxy, equivalent, pinch-hitter, fill-in, backup.

substitute *v.* change, replace, supplant, swap, superseded, step in, go to bat for, fill someone's shoes.

substitution *n.* replacement, change, switch, swap, exchange.

subterfuge *n.* deception, trick, artifice, ploy, machination, device, ruse, stratagem; *ant.* honesty.

subtle *adj.* **1.** suggestive, implied, insinuated, inferred, faint, elusive, understated, abstruse;

ant. direct, obvious, plain. **2.** (showing a refined understanding) sophisticated, perceptive, discriminating, skillful, shrewd, precise, astute; complex, deep, wily, devious.

subtlety *n.* nuance, delicacy, refinement, finesse, discrimination.

subtract *v.* deduct, decrease, debit, diminish, take away, remove, withdraw; *ant.* add.

subversive *n.* dissident, insurrectionary, seditionist, terrorist, freedom fighter, fifth columnist.

subversive *adj.* rebellious, riotous, insurgent, disruptive, seditious, incendiary; *ant.* loyal.

subvert *v.* overthrow, supplant, supersede, destroy, upset, undermine, topple, capsize, disrupt, demoralize, debase, pervert; *ant.* uphold, boost.

succeed *v.* **1.** make good, win, triumph, prevail, arrive, prosper, thrive; make it (*slang*); *ant.* fail. **2.** supplant, displace, supersede, replace, postdate, become heir to, be subsequent to, result.

succeed to *v.* accede, inherit, replace, take over, come into; *ant.* precede.

succeeding *adj.* ensuing, following, subsequent, successive, to come; *ant.* previous.

success *n.* **1.** consummation, resolution, accomplishment, progress; *ant.* failure. **2.** celebrity, star, hit, VIP, somebody, winner; *ant.* loser.

successful *adj.* prosperous, thriving, flourishing, auspicious, fortunate, wealthy, *slang:* ahead of the game, over the hump; *ant.* beaten.

successfully *adv.* well, happily, favorably, fortuitously, swimmingly.

succession *n.* continuation, sequence, series, progression, chain, line, inheritance, lineage, accession.

successive *adj.* consecutive, serial, succeeding, following.

succinct *adj.* terse, concise, brief, curt, compact, condensed, pithy, laconic; *ant.* wordy.

succor *n.* help, aid, sustenance, assistance, relief, support, comfort, ministrations.

succor *v.* help, assist, relieve, befriend, foster, nurse.

succulent *adj.* delicious, juicy, lush, moist, mouthwatering, rich, luscious, fleshy; *ant.* dry.

succumb *v.* yield, submit, surrender, give up, accede, capitulate, knuckle under, cease, drop; *ant.* overcome.

suck *v.* extract, drain, absorb, swallow up, imbibe.

suck up to *v.* (*slang*) fawn, flatter, ingratiate, bootlick.

sucker (*slang*) *n.* dupe, fool, pushover, victim, cat's-paw, stooge, *slang:* sap, patsy.

suckle *v.* nurse, breast-feed, nourish, sustain, nurture.

sudden *adj.* hasty, swift, abrupt, hurried, immediate, instantaneous, precipitate, impromptu, startling; *ant.* slow, expected.

suds *n.* froth, foam, bubbles, lather.

sue *v.* prosecute, claim, demand, solicit, litigate, petition, accuse, charge, indict, appeal, claim, entreat, plead, haul into court.

suffer *v.* **1.** experience, endure, undergo, bear, sustain, ache, agonize, grieve, hurt, languish, droop, flag. **2.** permit, allow, tolerate, acquiesce, admit, indulge, license, sanction, yield, bow, submit, brook, sustain; *ant.* prohibit, draw the line at.

suffering *n.* distress, misery, affliction, difficulty, hardship, pain, anguish, torment, ordeal, agony.

suffice *v.* serve, satisfy, answer, avail, do, measure up.

sufficiency *n.* competence, adequacy, enough, plenty.

sufficient *adj.* enough, adequate, ample, satisfactory.

suffocate *v.* choke, stifle, smother, strangle, asphyxiate.

suffuse *v.* permeate, pervade, infuse, imbue, steep, flood, bathe, cover.

sugary *adj.* sweet, sticky, candied, syrupy.

suggest *v.* recommend, propose, hint, intimate, imply, submit, advise, insinuate, connote.

suggestion *n.* **1.** hint, allusion, intimation, innuendo, insinuation. **2.** plan, proposal, scheme, idea, outline, motion, submission, advice, opinion. **3.** bit, trace, touch, taste, breath, whisper.

suggestive *adj.* **1.** symptomatic, indicative, reminiscent, redolent, symbolic, evocative. **2.** risqué, indecent, racy, titillating, ribald, prurient, provocative.

suit *n.* **1.** series, set, group, suite. **2.** case, trial, lawsuit, proceeding, appeal, litigation, prosecution, petition. **3.** clothes, ensemble, outfit, costume, uniform, dress.

follow suit imitate, accord with, conform, copy, fall into line, take a cue from.

suit *v.* **1.** befit, agree, correspond, fit, harmonize, match. **2.** adapt, change, accommodate, revise, adjust, modify; tailor.

suit up dress, prepare, get ready.

suitable *adj.* fitting, appropriate, right, proper, correct, fit, satisfactory, apt, becoming, suited, consonant, correspondent, congruent; *ant.* uncalled-for.

suite *n.* **1.** attendants, retinue, staff, servants, followers, entourage. **2.** sequence, series, order, set, train, line.

suited *adj.* fit, adapted, right, matched, satisfactory.

suitor *n.* beau, admirer, lover, wooer, swain, supplicant.

sulk *v.* brood, mope, pout, scowl, glower, despond.

sulky *adj.* grumpy, surly, cross, morose, irritable, sullen, despondent, petulant, peevish, churlish; *ant.* cheerful.

sullen *adj.* silent, moody, glum, sour, cross, surly, resentful, melancholy, despondent, depressed, low, saturnine; *ant.* cheerful, sociable.

sully *v.* soil, blot, stain, dirty, befoul, besmirch, blemish, defile, mar, taint, tarnish; *ant.* cleanse, honor.

sultry *adj.* **1.** stifling, oppressive, close, hot, humid, muggy, sweltering, sticky; *ant.* cool. **2.** seductive, passionate, provocative, sensual, sexy, torrid, voluptuous, erotic; *ant.* frumpy.

sum *n.* amount, tally, result, score, reckoning, quantity, whole, aggregate, totality.

sum up close, conclude, recapitulate, review, summarize, perorate, précis.

summarily *adv.* promptly, readily, speedily, immediately, abruptly, expeditiously, forthwith, hastily, peremptorily.

summarize *v.* abbreviate, abridge, condense, encapsulate, outline, review, abstract, put in a nutshell.

summary *n.* outline, synopsis, abstract, précis, digest, syllabus, essence, summation, recap,

condensation, compendium; *ant.* extension, elaboration.

summary *adj.* brief, cursory, hasty, perfunctory, short, pithy, succinct; *ant.* lengthy.

summit *n.* peak, top, apex, pinnacle, crown, head, zenith, apogee, culmination; *ant.* bottom, nadir.

summon *v.* call, beckon, send for, bid, invite, ask, convene, gather, muster, rally, direct, command, order, enjoin; *ant.* dismiss.

summons *n.* **1.** indictment, writ, subpoena, warrant. **2.** call, invocation, bell, cry.

sumptuous *adj.* lavish, magnificent, elegant, splendid, luxurious, plush, extravagant, costly, posh, opulent; *ant.* mean.

sunbathe *v.* tan, bake, bask, brown.

sunburned *adj.* tanned, burned, bronzed, ruddy, blistered, sunbaked.

sunder *v.* divide, separate, split, part, cleave, dissever, cut, chop; *ant.* join.

sundry *adj.* various, several, manifold, assorted, miscellaneous, varied, divers.

sunken *adj.* **1.** immersed, submerged, buried, lower, recessed. **2.** emaciated, gaunt, haggard, hollow, concave, drawn.

sunless *adj.* dark, overcast, cloudy, gray, hazy, bleak, dismal, cheerless, dreary, gloomy, somber, depressing; *ant.* sunny.

sunny *adj.* **1.** shining, brilliant, bright, clear, radiant, summery, sunlit; *ant.* cloudy. **2.** buoyant, cheerful, genial, merry, gay, optimistic, pleasant; *ant.* gloomy.

sunrise *n.* daybreak, dawn, morning, sunup, aurora, crack of dawn.

sunset *n.* evening, dusk, nightfall, twilight, sundown, gloaming.

super (*slang*) *adj.* excellent, glorious, wonderful, marvelous, superb, terrific, peerless; *ant.* poor.

superannuated *adj.* obsolete, outdated, old-fashioned; decrepit, antiquated, retired, put out to pasture; *ant.* new, young.

superb *adj.* grand, magnificent, splendid, elegant, exquisite, august; *ant.* poor, mediocre.

supercilious *adj.* disdainful, haughty, contemptuous, superior, condescending, arrogant, insolent, overbearing, patronizing; *ant.* humble.

superficial *adj.* trivial, desultory, summary, cursory, passing, slight, surface, shallow, flimsy, cosmetic; *ant.* detailed, learned, profound.

superficially *adv.* outwardly, at first glance, apparently, seemingly, ostensibly, extraneously.

superfluity *n.* excess, surplus, abundance, glut, surfeit, plethora, plenty; *ant.* lack.

superfluous *adj.* overflowing, redundant, inordinate, needless, supererogatory, exorbitant, profuse, lavish, overcharged; *ant.* necessary.

superhuman *adj.* great, herculean, divine, preternatural, phenomenal; *ant.* average, ordinary.

superintend *v.* oversee, manage, watch, administer, control, direct, steer, supervise, conduct, guide, care for.

superintendent *n.* administrator, chief, conductor, operator.

superior *adj.* **1.** higher, better, preferred, exceeding, finer, distinguished, prevailing, surpassing; *ant.* inferior. **2.** disdainful, condescending, haughty, pretentious, snobbish, supercilious; *ant.* humble.

superiority *n.* preponderance, advantage, ascendancy, edge, lead, supremacy; *ant.* inferiority.

superlative *adj.* **1.** supreme, highest, prime, greatest, best, excellent, consummate, matchless, transcendent, unrivaled, nonpareil; *ant.* poor. **2.** extreme, excessive, exaggerated, effusive.

supernatural *adj.* preternatural, spectral, ghostly, paranormal, otherworldly, metaphysical, transcendental, miraculous, unfathomable; *ant.* earthly, natural.

supernumerary *adj.* excessive, exaggerated, extra, superfluous, redundant, supererogatory, spare, surplus; *ant.* necessary.

supersede *v.* replace, succeed, displace, oust, supplant, usurp, outmode.

superstition *n.* fallacy, illusion, myth, delusion, notion, fear; *ant.* fact.

superstitious *adj.* credulous, gullible, uncritical, irrational, unscientific.

supervise *v.* manage, oversee, conduct, control, head, administer, tend, run.

supervision *n.* guidance, direction, administration, care, stewardship, auspices, instruction.

supervisor *n.* administrator, director, superintendent, chief, foreman, manager, boss.

supine *adj.* **1.** recumbent, prostrate, flat, reclining, horizontal; *ant.* prone, upright. **2.** indolent, listless, lazy, passive, languid, indifferent, apathetic, bored, slothful, sluggish, torpid; *ant.* alert.

supplant *v.* supersede, replace, take over for, usurp, displace, unseat, topple, overthrow.

supple *adj.* flexible, pliant, yielding, limber, rubber, elastic, lithe, willowy; *ant.* rigid, arthritic.

supplement *n.* sequel, continuation, addition, addendum, postscript, codicil.

supplement *v.* augment, compliment, fortify, strengthen, buttress, increase, enhance, enrich, fill up; *ant.* deplete.

supplementary *adj.* additional, extra, supplemental, auxiliary, secondary, ancillary, completing; *ant.* primary, main.

suppliant *adj.* importunate, entreating, imploring, begging, craving.

supplicate *v.* beg, petition, appeal, beseech.

supplication *n.* entreaty, solicitation, prayer, request, suit, appeal.

supplier *n.* retailer, vendor, wholesaler, dealer, peddler.

supplies *n.* materials, matériel, equipment, necessities, rations, provisions, stores, provender.

supply *n.* stock, hoard, accumulation, cache, fund, reserve.

supply *v.* furnish, stock, store, replenish, outfit, provide, contribute, endow, fulfill, purvey; *ant.* take.

support *n.* **1.** help, aid, assistance, relief, protection, comfort, succor. **2.** (something used to stabilize or secure in place) reinforcement, buttress, underpinning, prop, strut, pillar, post, stanchion, stay, abutment, fulcrum. **3.** (financial aid) subsidy, upkeep, maintenance, living, provision, sustenance, keep, alimony. **4.** backer, patron, supporter, booster.

support *v.* **1.** bolster, buttress, brace, sustain, gird, prop, bear up, shore; *ant.* drop, let fall. **2.** defend, guard, sustain, comfort, hearten, boost, encourage, promote, abet, advance, champion, approve; *ant.* discourage, deter. **3.** (provide a home for) provide for, finance, subsidize, sponsor, underwrite, bring home the bacon (*slang*); *ant.* neglect.

supporter *n.* advocate, adherent, benefactor, confederate, champion, patron, ally, booster, fan; *ant.* opponent.

supportive *adj.* attentive, caring, reassuring, sympathetic, helpful, understanding.

suppose *v.* surmise, assume, guess, hypothesize, imagine, infer, presume, postulate.

supposed *adj.* likely, rumored, reputed, professed, putative, alleged, presupposed; *ant.* known.

supposed to expected to, required to, obliged to, intended, meant to.

supposedly *adv.* apparently, seemingly, purportedly, avowedly.

supposition *n.* surmise, notion, guess, hypothesis, ideal, theory, opinion, conjecture; *ant.* knowledge.

suppress *v.* crush, overcome, put down, extinguish, smother, quash, repress, stifle, quell, subdue, restrain, destroy, terminate, censor; *ant.* incite, encourage.

suppression *n.* defeat, crackdown, prohibition, abolition.

suppurate *v.* decay, fester, putrefy, gather, maturate, ooze.

supremacy *n.* domination, mastery, command, ascendancy, predominance, preeminence, sway, sovereignty.

supreme *adj.* highest, greatest, paramount, chief, cardinal, crowning, ultimate, utmost, matchless, peerless, nonpareil; *ant.* lesser.

sure *adj.* **1.** confident, positive, assured, convinced, certain, definite, secure, ant; doubtful, wavering. **2.** inevitable, bound, decided, fixed, guaranteed, ineluctable, irrevocable; *ant.* disputable, avoidable.

make sure determine, fix, guarantee, establish.

sure-fire *adj.* reliable, dependable, good, infallible, fail-safe.

surely *adv.* indubitably, inevitably, undoubtedly, certainly, assuredly, doubtlessly.

surety *n.* pledge, guarantee, bail, forfeit, security, deposit.

surface *n.* exterior, covering, face, façade, skin, veneer, superficies, top; *ant.* interior.

surface *v.* rise, appear, emerge, materialize, transpire, come to light; *ant.* sink.

surface *adj.* superficial, apparent, external, outer, outward.

surfeit *n.* excess, glut, satiety, superabundance, superfluity, profusion, luxuriance; *ant.* lack.

surfeit *v.* satiate, gorge, overindulge, stuff, overfeed.

surge *n.* rush, swell, roll, flood, billow, breaker, surf, wave.

surge *v.* **1.** rise, mount, tower, arise, climb. **2.** billow, swell, heave, eddy, roll, seethe, swirl, undulate.

surly *adj.* morose, testy, crabby, irritable, sullen, brusque, rude, insolent, churlish, gruff; *ant.* pleasant, civil, gracious.

surmise *v.* infer, opine, presume, speculate, suppose, suspect, guess; *ant.* know.

surmount *v.* conquer, overcome, subdue, master, vanquish, defeat.

surmise *n.* conjecture, supposition, theory, hypothesis, inference, notion, guess, suspicion; *ant.* certainty.

surpass *v.* excel, outdo, transcend, better, exceed, eclipse, outstrip, best, top, match, rival.

surplus *n.* residue, excess, remainder, overage, surfeit; *ant.* lack.

surprise *n.* **1.** shock, revelation, bolt from the blue, bombshell (*slang*). **2.** astonishment, awe, wonder, amazement, incredulity.

surprise *v.* amaze, astonish, astound, shock, stun, dumbfound, stupefy, nonplus, daze, floor, make one's head swim.

surprised *adj.* bewildered, confounded, staggered, disconcerted, incredulous, speechless, thunderstruck, flabbergasted.

surprising *adj.* unexpected, unusual, extraordinary, remarkable; *ant.* ordinary.

surrender *n.* yielding, capitulation, submission, cessation.

surrender *v.* capitulate, yield, submit, abandon, concede, give up, forgo, cease, quit, relinquish, renounce, wave, give in, let go; *ant.* persevere, hold out.

surreptitious *adj.* clandestine, private, confidential, covert, hidden, secret, furtive, stealthy, sly, veiled; *ant.* open, authorized.

surrogate *n.* replacement, representative, substitute, stand-in, deputy, proxy, delegate.

surround *v.* circle, ring, encompass, encircle, enclose, gird; fence in, hem in, blockade, besiege.

surrounding *adj.* nearby, neighboring, bordering, adjacent, ambiant.

surroundings *n.* environment, setting, environs, vicinity, locale, milieu, background, ambiance.

surveillance *n.* supervision, direction, inspection, monitoring, scrutiny, vigilance, watch.

survey *n.* study, critique, outline, review, examination, appraisal, assessment, scrutiny.

survey *v.* **1.** view, see, peruse, look upon. **2.** study, scan, inspect, examine, scrutinize, reconnoiter, appraise, estimate, prospect, measure.

surveying *n.* measurement, triangulation, geodetics.

survive *v.* endure, withstand, sustain, outlive, pull through, persist, persevere, last, remain, weather the storm; *ant.* succumb.

susceptibility *n.* weakness, liability, predisposition, penchant, vulnerability, proclivity; *ant.* resistance.

susceptible *adj.* responsive, receptive, disposed, given, inclined, prone, subject; tender, vulnerable, defenseless, open; *ant.* impregnable, resistant.

suspect *v.* **1.** distrust, mistrust, doubt, question, call in question; *ant.* believe. **2.** presume, suppose, surmise, speculate, conjecture, guess, infer, conclude.

suspect *adj.* dubious, debatable, questionable, suspicious, unlikely; *ant.* acceptable, straightforward, reliable.

suspend *v.* **1.** reject, exclude, omit, bar, refuse, disbar, dismiss, expel, defrock. **2.** defer, postpone, delay, halt, interrupt, adjourn, retard, protract, pigeonhole, shelve, waive; *ant.* continue, carry on. **3.** hang, dangle, swing, wave.

suspended *adj.* **1.** hanging, pendulous, pendent, pensile. **2.** undecided, postponed, on ice, on hold, hanging fire, up in the air.

suspense *n.* anticipation, apprehension, hesitancy, anxiety, excitement, tension, confusion, perplexity; *ant.* certainty, knowledge.

suspension *n.* **1.** delay, pause, interruption, intermission, respite, remission, stay, abeyance, dormancy; *ant.* resumption.

suspicion *n.* **1.** misgiving, mistrust, doubt, qualm, jealousy, resentment; *ant.* trust. **2.** conjecture, guess, hint, impression, intuition, notion, surmise.

above suspicion honest, trustworthy, noble, cleared.

suspicious *adj.* **1.** suspecting, jealous, doubting, uneasy, wary, leery, skeptical; *ant.* trusting. **2.** shady, questionable, queer, suspect, irregular, peculiar, equivocal, debatable, specious, fishy; *ant.* innocent.

sustain *v.* **1.** carry, bear, uphold, keep afloat, convey, transport, transfer, pack, tote, lug; *ant.* abandon, drop. **2.** nourish, maintain, provide for, nurture, support, foster, parent; *ant.* neglect. **3.** defend, befriend, favor, stand by, sanction, endorse, side with, back up, stand up for; *ant.* oppose, forsake.

sustained *adj.* backed, maintained, continued, constant, continual, continuous, prolonged, regular, unremitting; *ant.* broken, sporadic.

sustenance *n.* food, nourishment, nutrition, subsistence, fare, edibles, provender, provisions, victuals.

svelte *adj.* slender, lithe, shapely, lean, streamlined, lissome, willowy; *ant.* bulky, ungainly.

swab *v.* scrub, clean, wash, mop, sweep.

swaddle *v.* clothe, wrap, swathe, sheathe, enwrap.

swagger *n.* arrogance, bluster, braggadocio, vainglory, boasting, show, ostentation; *ant.* modesty, diffidence.

swagger *v.* **1.** sway, saunter, strut, prance, parade. **2.** boast, gloat, brag, show off, crow, bluster.

swallow *v.* gulp, swig, swill, choke down, imbibe, consume, devour, engulf, quaff.

swallow up engulf, envelop, absorb, overwhelm, overrun, take in.

swamp *n.* bog, fen, marsh, moor, bottoms, mire, morass, quagmire, swale; *ant.* desert, high ground.

swamp *v.* deluge, flood, inundate, overwhelm, engulf, drench, waterlog, capsize, sink, submerge, beset, besiege.

swampy *adj.* muddy, wet, soggy; *ant.* dry, arid.

swank *n.* ostentation, display, boastfulness, conceit, show, swagger, vainglory, spectacle, array; *ant.* modesty, restraint.

swanky *adj.* showy, ostentatious, rich, flashy, glamorous, plush, posh, pretentious, sumptuous, ritzy; *ant.* discreet, unobtrusive.

swap *v.* trade, barter, exchange, traffic.

swarm *n.* throng, crowd, multitude, horde, pack, troop, drove, flock, host, multitude, myriad.

swarm v. congregate, crowd, mass, stream, throng, cluster, teem.

swarthy adj. dark, black, brown, dark-skinned, dusky, tawny; ant. fair, pale.

swashbuckling adj. adventurous, bold, dashing, flamboyant, gallant, exciting, spirited, roistering, swaggering; ant. tame.

swat v. slap, hit, knock, beat.

swath n. stripe, track, strip, row, ribbon.

swathe v. wrap, swaddle, bind, drape, clothe, enshroud, fold, bandage, furl, wind.

sway n. 1. undulation, pulsation, vibration, oscillation, reverberation. 2. authority, power, jurisdiction, rule, sovereignty, dominion, command, predominance, rule.
hold sway govern, reign, rule, control, dominate.

sway v. 1. fluctuate, oscillate, waver, swagger, swing, lurch, swerve, veer, bend, lean. 2. influence, persuade, guide, incline, induce, affect, direct, impress.

swear v. 1. curse, blaspheme, imprecate, cuss. 2. avow, affirm, testify, vow, attest, vouch, assert, depose, promise, give witness.

swear by trust, believe, be committed to, have faith in.

swear off quit, abstain from, abjure, stop, halt.

swearing n. profanity, expletives, maledictions.

sweat v. 1. perspire, swelter, wilt, exude, secrete. 2. work, toil, exert, slave.

sweat it out endure, suffer, agonize, worry.

sweaty adj. clammy, damp, moist, perspiring, sticky, sweating; ant. cool, dry.

sweep n. 1. course, movement, progress, stroke, swing. 2. compass, range, scope, breadth, extent, length.

sweep v. brush, clear, clean, dust, skim, tidy, ready.

sweep under the rug hide, conceal, neglect, ignore, put out of sight, whitewash, stonewall (slang).

sweeping adj. extensive, complete, comprehensive, broad, all-embracing, wholesale, wide-ranging, global, blanket, universal, catholic, ubiquitous; ant. limited, measured.

sweepings n. trash, dirt, litter, refuse.

sweet adj. 1. sugary, candied, honeyed, syrupy, succulent, fresh, rich, delicious, toothsome; ant. bitter, sour, acidic. 2. agreeable, pleasant, engaging, delightful, companionable, charming, gracious, lovable, gentle, generous, considerate, amiable; ant. nasty. 3. harmonious, melodious, lyrical, musical, mellifluous, tuneful, smooth; ant. discordant.

sweeten v. 1. sugar, flavor, mull, honey, mellow. 2. purify, freshen, fumigate, disinfect, cleanse, rinse, revive, renew.

sweetheart n. beloved, admirer, boyfriend, girlfriend, lover, beau, dear, darling, suitor.

sweets n. candy, confection, bonbons, sweetmeats, comfit.

swell n. bulge, billow, distension, rise, surge, swelling.

swell v. increase, bloat, protrude, expand, distend, puff, enlarge, grow, inflate, balloon, fatten, blister, tumefy, dilate; ant. contract, dwindle.

swelling n. blister, distention, welt, carbuncle, inflammation, lump, bunion, tumor, abrasion, tumescence, wheal.

sweltering adj. scorching, sultry, humid, oppressive, stifling, torrid, tropical, broiling; ant. airy, breezy, chilly.

swerve v. move, veer, stray, wander, bend, deviate, incline, sheer, skew, swing, warp.

swift adj. agile, fast, fleet, nimble, quick, rapid, winged, hurried, speedy, expeditious, sudden, prompt, precipitate; ant. slow, sluggish, tardy.

swiftly adv. speedily, posthaste, hurriedly, expeditiously, double-quick; ant. slowly.

swiftness n. alacrity, celerity, dispatch, expedition; ant. delay.

swill n. trash, garbage, waste, offal, refuse, hogwash.

swill v. drink, imbibe, drain, quaff, gulp, guzzle.

swimmingly adv. easily, quickly, successfully, smoothly, effectively.

swindle n. fraud, racket, con game, chicanery, knavery, slang: scam, rip-off; skin game.

swindle v. cheat, trick, gyp, cozen, victimize, defraud, deceive, rook, hoodwink, bamboozle, dupe, slang: con, clip; fleece.

swindler n. cheat, impostor, charlatan, counterfeiter, forger, rogue, sharper, scammer, grifter (slang).

swine n. 1. pigs, porkers, hogs, boars, beasts,

peccaries. **2.** scoundrel, cad, brute, miscreant, reprobate, pig (*slang*).

swing *v.* **1.** sway, undulate, sweep, rotate, pivot, revolve, fluctuate, waver, palpitate, oscillate, veer. **2.** wield, flourish, brandish, twirl, wave, hurl.

swinging *adj.* (*slang*) vivacious, sophisticated, stylish, trendy, *slang:* groovy, hip, with it; fashionable, modern.

swinish *adj.* gross, coarse, beastly, bestial, rude, repulsive, vile.

swipe (*slang*) *v.* steal, pilfer, purloin, filch, appropriate, *slang:* lift, pinch.

swirl *v.* eddy, whirl, surge, churn, agitate, coil.

switch *n.* **1.** alteration, substitution, swap, exchange, reciprocation. **2.** rod, whip, birch, cane.

switch *v.* **1.** change, shift, divert, rearrange, deflect. **2.** exchange, trade, swap, reciprocate. **3.** flog, lash, beat, whip, strike.

swivel *v.* pivot, gyrate, pirouette, revolve, rotate, spin, turn, twirl, wheel.

swollen *adj.* distended, puffed, inflated, bloated, tumescent; *ant.* contracted, emaciated.

swoon *v.* faint, pass out, languish, black out, lose consciousness.

swoop *v.* descend, drop, fall, dive, plunge, plummet, pounce.

sword *n.* saber, foil, rapier, cutlass, bayonet, machete, broadsword.

sworn *adj.* dedicated, avowed, eternal, implacable, inveterate, relentless.

syllabus *n.* plan, digest, outline, curriculum, synopsis.

syllogism *n.* argument, dialectic, logic, deduction, proposition.

sylph *n.* fairy, hobgoblin, nymph, dryad.

sylvan *adj.* rural, wooded, shady, forestlike.

symbol *n.* type, badge, emblem, image, logo, token, sign.

symbolic *adj.* allusive, metaphorical, indicative, emblematic, referential, allegorical, characteristic, typical, representative, exemplary.

symbolize *v.* represent, signify, connote, denote, exemplify, personify, mean, betoken, stand for.

symmetrical *adj.* parallel, isometric, regular, even.

symmetry *n.* correspondence, proportion, balance, equilibrium, harmony, regularity, conformity, arrangement, order; *ant.* imbalance, asymmetry.

sympathetic *adj.* compassionate, considerate, thoughtful, caring, sensitive, responsive, humane, supportive, warmhearted; *ant.* callous, indifferent.

sympathize *v.* condole, comfort, commiserate, empathize, feel for, identify with, understand; *ant.* disregard, ignore, oppose.

sympathizer *n.* advocate, benefactor, backer, partisan, patron, supporter, adherent; *ant.* enemy, opponent.

sympathy *n.* **1.** compassion, comfort, pity, solace, tenderness, solicitude, warmth, consolation, cheer, encouragement, reassurance, support; *ant.* indifference. **2.** harmony, unity, concord, alliance, accord, agreement.

symptom *n.* mark, token, indication, evidence, manifestation, expression, warning; sign, complaint, finding.

symptomatic *adj.* characteristic, significant, typical, suggestive, representative, suggesting.

syndicate *n.* association, alliance, cartel, company, partnership, consortium, union.

synonymous *adj.* like, similar, equivalent, identical, corresponding, alike, interchangeable, apposite, compatible; *ant.* conflicting, divergent.

synopsis *n.* summary, outline, digest, brief, abstract, précis, condensation, review, compendium.

synthesis *n.* blend, composite, pastiche, union.

synthesize *v.* merge, fuse, combine, integrate, incorporate, coalesce, amalgamate; *ant.* separate, dissect.

synthetic *adj.* artificial, counterfeit, ersatz, fake, plastic, simulated, imitation; *ant.* genuine, real.

system *n.* **1.** (a set of principles) order, regularity, rules, structure, worldview, Weltanschauung. **2.** (a way of operating) method, mode, scheme, way, custom, practice, modus operandi, plan, procedure, routine, technique. **3.** (a way of organizing) organization, structure, method, protocol, framework, hierarchy, construct, edifice, taxonomy.

systematic *adj.* precise, efficient, organized, rule-based, standardized; *ant.* erratic.

systematize *v.* arrange, classify, regiment, regulate, standardize, design; *ant.* confuse, jumble.

tab *n.* tag, sticker, flag, label, marker.

tabby *adj.* striped, variegated, banded, mottled, streaked.

table *n.* **1.** board, counter, sideboard. **2.** chart, graph, schedule, synopsis, report, record, register, index, appendix, table of contents.
put one's cards on the table be candid, level with, confess, reveal, display, show, tell all, let it all hang out (*slang*).

table *v.* postpone, delay; put off, put on the back burner.

tableau *n.* diorama, scene, representation, vignette, portrayal, spectacle.

tablet *n.* **1.** paper, pad, sheets, memo book, ream, folder. **2.** pill, capsule, dose, medicine.

taboo *adj.* forbidden, proscribed, prohibited, banned, out of bounds, illegal, restricted; immoral, indecent, pornographic, vile.

tabulate *v.* categorize, classify, catalog, order, arrange, systematize, list, index, codify, sort.

tacit *adj.* implicit, implied, inferred, silent, unspoken, unstated, unuttered, unexpressed, voiceless, wordless; *ant.* explicit, stated, spoken.

taciturn *adj.* silent, reticent, uncommunicative, reserved, quiet, laconic, withdrawn, aloof, antisocial, distant, cold, quiet, tight-lipped; *ant.* talkative, forthcoming, sociable, communicative.

tack *n.* **1.** pin, thumbtack, nail, pushpin. **2.** deviation, tangent, digression, variation, alteration, swerve, zigzag, turnabout.

tack *v.* pin, baste, mount, fasten, tie, piece together.

tackle *n.* apparatus, rigging, gear, paraphernalia.

tackle *v.* undertake, attempt, try, take on, confront, deal with, grapple with, engage in, face up to; *ant.* avoid, sidestep.

tacky *adj.* **1.** gluey, gummy, adhesive, sticky.

2. tasteless, kitschy (*slang*), sleazy, cheap, shabby, seedy, tawdry, vulgar, meretricious.

tact *n.* diplomacy, sensitivity, discretion, consideration, delicacy, finesse, grace, thoughtfulness, adroitness, judgment; *ant.* indiscretion, clumsiness.

tactful *adj.* diplomatic, sensitive, polite, discreet, considerate, delicate, graceful, thoughtful, perceptive, discerning, judicious; *ant.* rude.

tactic *n.* method, approach, way, means, stratagem, maneuver, device, ploy, course, move, scheme, subterfuge.

tactician *n.* strategist, mastermind, coordinator, orchestrator, planner, campaigner, director, brains (*slang*).

tactics *n.* strategy, approach, procedure, plans, game plan, campaign, policy.

tactile *adj.* palpable, tangible, physical, real.

tactless *adj.* inconsiderate, impolite, coarse, crude, inappropriate, insensitive, indiscreet, careless, gauche, blundering, inept, discourteous, rude, thoughtless; *ant.* considerate.

tag *n.* badge, identification, voucher, label, sticker, stamp, trademark, stub.

tag *v.* **1.** earmark, designate, check, hold, mark. **2.** (*slang*) pursue, track, chase, trail, shadow, dog.

tail (*slang*) *v.* follow, track, trail, spy on, shadow, stalk, dog (*slang*).

tailor *n.* clothier, seamstress, outfitter, costumer, dressmaker.

tailored *adj.* fitted, tailor-made, made-to-measure.

tailor-made *adj.* **1.** custom-made, made-to-measure, fitted, suited. **2.** perfect, right, exacting, on the mark.

taint *n.* stain, stigma, contamination, defect, blot, smear, flaw, fault, blemish, imperfection.

taint *v.* tarnish, stain, spoil, besmirch, defile, stigmatize, smear, adulterate, infect, pollute, ruin, sully, damage.

T

take v. **1.** acquire, attain, secure, obtain, possess, get, earn, win; seize, appropriate, absond with, confiscate. **2.** (understand to be) consider, interpret, regard, look upon, hold. **3.** (select among several things) pick out, choose, select, opt for; purchase, buy. **4.** (*slang*) cheat, defraud, hoodwink, trick, swindle, deceive.

take after resemble, look like, be like, seem like.

take apart dismember, dissect, reduce, analyze.

take in 1. understand, comprehend, apprehend, perceive, see, absorb. **2.** (*slang*) cheat, deceive, swindle, lie to, defraud.

take off 1. doff, remove, divest. **2.** subtract, deduct, take away, decrease by, lessen by. **3.** (*slang*) mock, satirize, mimic, ridicule, parody, burlesque, send up. **4.** leave, blast off, ascend, soar, fly, rise.

take on 1. hire, employ, engage, give work to. **2.** (acquire as a characteristic) become, seem, emerge, develop, turn. **3.** undertake, attempt, handle, endeavor, try.

take out extract, remove, excise, delete, pull out.

take over take control, usurp, take command, take charge, commandeer, lead.

take to like, be fond of, admire, enjoy, appreciate.

take up 1. begin, start, initiate, commence. **2.** raise, lift, elevate, hoist. **3.** (take out material from a garment) shorten, decrease, reduce, lessen, tighten. **4.** occupy, use, consume, engage, fill. **5.** (come to appreciate, as an activity) adopt, become involved in *or* with, embrace, assume, appropriate.

taken *adj.* **1.** captured, arrested, seized, appropriated, collared. **2.** (no longer available) reserved, occupied, engaged, held, contracted for, spoken for, employed, hired, rented; *ant.* vacant, free.

takeoff (*slang*) n. **1.** parody, burlesque, caricature, comedy, sendup, ridicule. **2.** ascent, departure, fly-off, climb, rise.

takeover n. coup, incorporation, merger, amalgamation, putsch, coalition, combination.

takings n. proceeds, revenue, yield, profits, gain, income, earnings, *slang*: take, haul.

tale n. story, yarn, narrative, fable, legend,

fiction, anecdote, fabrication, myth, rumor, old wives' tale.

talent n. aptitude, ability, forte, knack, gift, capability, skill, endowment, flair, expertise.

talented *adj.* gifted, accomplished, adept, adroit, capable, artistic, skilled, brilliant; *ant.* maladroit, inept.

talisman n. amulet, charm, mascot, juju.

talk n. **1.** speech, communication, articulation, locution; parlance, dialect, lingo. **2.** conference, symposium, parley, consultation, discussion. **3.** gossip, rumor, whispers, hearsay. **4.** (empty rhetoric) babble, hot air (*slang*), bombast, noise, cant, jargon, nonsense, rubbish. **5.** lecture, address, speech, sermon, oration.

talk v. converse, discuss, communicate, confer, chat, dialogue, interview, speak, chatter, gossip, yammer (*slang*), remark, have an exchange.

talk someone into persuade, influence, convince, sway, win over, affect.

talkative *adj.* communicative, forthcoming, verbose, effusive, prolix, expansive, vocal, conversational, garrulous, loquacious, prating, chatty, gabby (*slang*), long-winded, gossipy.

talker n. speaker, lecturer, orator, conversationalist, communicator, chatterbox.

talking-to n. reprimand, scolding, reproach, reproof, reprimand, dressing-down, lecture, rebuke, *slang*: telling-off, earful; *ant.* commendation, praise.

tall *adj.* **1.** big, giant, high, great, elevated, steep, towering, lofty; leggy, lanky; *ant.* short, small, low. **2.** (*slang*) far-fetched, embellished, exaggerated, implausible, unbelievable, grandiloquent, absurd, unlikely, overblown, preposterous, dubious, incredible; *ant.* reasonable, believable.

tally n. account, summation, reckoning, score, poll.

tally v. compute, total, reckon, figure.

tame v. break in, domesticate, bridle, curb, subdue, quell, master, discipline, temper, train, house-train.

tame *adj.* **1.** domesticated, obedient, disciplined, compliant, cultivated, manageable, subdued, submissive, docile, gentle, amenable, tractable, unresisting; *ant.* wild, unmanageable. **2.** dull, bland, insipid, vapid, bloodless, lifeless, prosaic, uninspired, humdrum, boring, wearisome, spiritless; *ant.* exciting, fresh.

tamper *v.* interfere, alter, meddle, corrupt, fiddle, rig, tinker, manipulate, mess.

tandem *adv.* back to back, single file, behind, in back of, in sequence, sequentially, in order.

tang *n.* piquancy, bite, spiciness, kick (*slang*), pungency, tinge, overtone, flavor.

tangible *adj.* palpable, concrete, substantial, actual, definite, discernible, perceptible, tactile, solid, physical, real, definable, manifest, evident, substantive, quantifiable; *ant.* intangible.

tangle *n.* entanglement, muddle, jumble, snarl, web, labyrinth, maze, confusion, mix-up; embroilment, *slang:* fix, jam.

tangy *adj.* piquant, tart, sharp, biting, bitter, pungent, spicy, strong; *ant.* bland.

tank *n.* container, cistern, basin, reservoir, vat, aquarium.

tantalize *v.* titillate, entice, bait, lead on, provoke, charm fascinate, lure; play upon, tease, torment, frustrate.

tantamount *adj.* equal, same, synonymous, equivalent, commensurate, comperable.

tantrum *n.* hysterics, outburst, temper, rage, fit, scene, fury, flare-up, paroxysm.

tap *n.* **1.** rap, knock, beat, pat, touch. **2.** faucet, spigot, valve, spout.

tap *v.* **1.** rap, pat, dab, touch, probe. **2.** (use as a resource) draw upon, make use of, use, consume, realize, take advantage of.

tape *n.* binding, ribbon, band, tape measure, magnetic tape.

tape *v.* **1.** fasten, bind, seal, secure, stick, wrap. **2.** record, tape-record, videotape.

taper *v.* decrease, lessen, wane, subside, fade, dwindle, peter out, die out, weaken, thin; *ant.* increase, swell, widen.

tar *n.* pitch, asphalt, resin, mineral pitch, coal tar, wood tar.

tardy *adj.* late, dilatory, overdue, belated, delayed, dawdling, eleventh-hour, last-minute, slack, slow, sluggish; *ant.* prompt, punctual.

tardiness *n.* lateness, dilatoriness, slowness, sluggishness, procrastination.

target *n.* goal, bull's-eye, aim, end, ambition, purpose, objective, purpose, intention, destination; mark, quarry, victim, prey.

tariff *n.* tax, levy, toll, customs, charges, duty.

tarnish *v.* taint, sully, stain, mar, dull, spoil, blemish, discolor, darken, rust; *ant.* enhance, brighten, polish.

tarry *v.* linger, lag, dawdle, pause, dally, delay, remain, rest, stay, stop, wait, loiter.

tart *adj.* sour, acid, tangy, piquant, vinegary, bitter, sharp, pungent, astringent.

task *n.* assignment, duty, work, job, chore, undertaking, toil, labor, employment, enterprise, burden, mission.

taste *n.* **1.** flavor, relish, savor. **2.** appetite, penchant, inclination, bent, partiality, choice, predilection, preference, desire, fondness, liking, palate. **3.** gustation, mouthful, morsel, nibble, sample, sip, nip, spoonful, swallow, tidbit. **4.** (an informed sense of civility) style, tact, grace, sensitivity, decorum, correctness, cultivation, discretion, polish, propriety, refinement, judgment, discrimination.

taste *v.* savor, relish; perceive, discern, experience; nibble, sample, try, sip.

tasteful *adj.* refined, graceful, cultured, stylish, sensitive, discriminating, polished, aesthetic, correct, harmonious, discreet, judicious; *ant.* vulgar.

tasteless *adj.* **1.** flavorless, watered-down, uninteresting, vapid, dull, bland, diluted, flat, weak, stale, mild; *ant.* tasty, delicious. **2.** coarse, crude, vulgar, garish, gaudy, cheap, tacky, unseemly, improper, rude, tawdry, flashy, crass; *ant.* refined.

tasty *adj.* flavorful, delicious, savory, scrumptious, appetizing, delectable, succulent, luscious, sapid, mouthwatering, yummy (*slang*).

tatters *n.* rags, shreds, duds, ribbons.

tattle *v.* **1.** gossip, blab, *slang:* tell on, snitch. **2.** chatter, babble, prattle, jabber, blather, *slang:* gab, yap, yak.

tattler *n.* gossip, rumor-monger, tell-tale, tale-teller, busybody, scandalmonger, snitch (*slang*).

tattered *adj.* frayed, ragged, ripped, threadbare, torn, in shreds, lacerated; *ant.* neat, trim.

taunt *n.* derision, barb, insult, provocation, jeer, sneer, teasing, ridicule, cut, gibe, dig (*slang*).

taunt *v.* tease, provoke, mock, ridicule, deride,

jeer, insult, gibe, sneer, bait, torment, rib (*slang*).

taut *adj.* tight, stretched, rigid, contracted, strained, stressed, tense, unrelaxed; *ant.* slack, loose, relaxed.

tautological *adj.* redundant, repetitive, superfluous, self-evident, pleonastic; *ant.* concise.

tautology *n.* repetition, duplication, redundancy, repetitiveness, superfluity, pleonasm; *ant.* succinctness, economy.

tavern *n.* bar, alehouse, pub, inn, *slang:* dive, joint; hostelry, taphouse.

tawdry *adj.* tacky, garish, tasteless, gaudy, vulgar, tatty, showy, flashy, cheap, meretricious; *ant.* fine, superior.

tawny *adj.* golden, tan, sandy, fawn, yellow.

tax *n.* levy, duty, tariff, toll, charge, customs, assessment, excise, rate, contribution.

tax *v.* **1.** assess, charge, levy, overtax. **2.** burden, exhaust, impose, try, strain, weaken, load, push, sap, weary, drain, enervate; *ant.* lighten, alleviate.

taxing *adj.* stressful, trying, burdensome, exhausting, tiring, strenuous, wearisome, draining, demanding, enervating, tough, heavy; *ant.* easy.

teach *v.* educate, instruct, train, tutor, enlighten, inform, advise, coach, demonstrate, school, verse, edify, instill.

teacher *n.* educator, instructor, tutor, professor, guide, coach, mentor, schoolteacher, trainer, lecturer, master, mistress, guru.

team *n.* group, squad, band, set, crew, gang, company, troupe, lineup.

team *v.* combine, band, match, join, link, couple, yoke.

team up with band together, join, combine, cooperate, unite.

teamwork *n.* joint effort, collaboration, cooperation, fellowship, team spirit, esprit de corps; *ant.* disharmony, disunity.

tear *n.* rip, hole, laceration, rupture, snag, run, split, scratch.

tear *v.* **1.** lacerate, rip, shred, rend, gash, mangle, scratch, sever, claw, sunder, mutilate. **2.** rush, bolt, dart, dash, hurry, run, speed, race, fly, sprint, zoom.

tearful *adj.* weepy, crying, emotional, sorrow-

ful, maudlin, mournful, sad, lamenting, lachrymose, woeful, sobbing, whimpering, blubbering; *ant.* cheerful, happy.

tease *v.* **1.** taunt, mock, goad, provoke, ridicule, rib (*slang*), irritate, annoy, vex, plague, torment. **2.** tantalize, excite, arouse, provoke.

technical *adj.* scientific, specialized, special, professional, scholarly, mechanical, methodological, technological, industrial; *ant.* artistic, nontechnical, simplified.

technician *n.* professional, engineer, practitioner, craftsman, specialist.

technique *n.* method, procedure, system, routine, protocol.

tedious *adj.* monotonous, soporific, banal, humdrum, wearisome, dull, laborious, long-drawn-out, fatiguing, boring, tiring, uninteresting, vapid; *ant.* exciting, interesting.

tedium *n.* monotony, routine, sameness, banality, boredom, ennui, tediousness, dullness, lifelessness.

teeming *adj.* brimming, abundant, replete, bursting, chock-full, bristling, overflowing, packed, swarming, pregnant, proliferating, fruitful, alive; *ant.* sparse, lacking, devoid.

teenage *adj.* adolescent, juvenile, immature, pubescent, young, youthful.

teenager *n.* adolescent, juvenile, minor, youth.

teeny *adj.* tiny, minute, miniature, diminutive, wee, microscopic, minuscule, *slang:* teensy-weensy, teeny-weeny.

teeter *v.* totter, wobble, waver, pivot, rock, sway, lurch, stagger, pitch, seesaw.

telegram *n.* cable, wire, telegraph, telex, telemessage.

telegraph *n.* cable, telegram, wire, teleprinter, telex, radiotelegram.

telegraph *v.* cable, wire, transmit, send, signal, telex.

telepathy *n.* mind-reading, ESP, sixth sense, clairvoyance, thought transference.

telephone *v.* call, contact, phone, ring, get in touch, dial.

television *n.* TV, receiver, TV set, *slang:* boob tube, small screen, idiot box; telly (*Brit.*).

tell *v.* **1.** inform, relate, report, depict, confess, describe, disclose, divulge, notify, reveal, state, command, instruct. **2.** discern, deduce, apprise, differentiate, understand, reckon, discover, foresee, predict, identify.

tell apart distinguish, differentiate, characterize, discriminate, disambiguate.

tell off (*slang*) upbraid, berate, dress down, reprimand, reproach, lecture, scold, take to task, bawl out (*slang*).

teller *n.* cashier, clerk, bank clerk, bank employee, bank assistant.

telling *adj.* revealing, significant, crucial, important, effective, persuasive, compelling, conspicuous, devastating.

telltale *adj.* revealing, disclosing, indicative, exposing, significant.

temerity *n.* rashness, recklessness, heedlessness, impulsiveness, daring, nerve, pluck; impudence, gall, audacity, effrontery, chutzpah (*slang*).

temper *n.* **1.** disposition, state of mind, humor, mood, attitude, feeling, composure, constitution, disposition, nature, passion, temperament. **2.** irascibility, irritability, ill humor, churlishness, impatience, excitability, grouchiness, peevishness, huffiness, crossness, touchiness, cantankerousness, acerbity; *ant.* patience, calmness, equanimity.

temper *v.* **1.** qualify, moderate, soften, mitigate, pacify, appease, compromise, abate, mollify, ease, curb, restrain. **2.** harden, toughen, strengthen, steel, bake, chill, stiffen, cement, vulcanize, solidify, congeal, starch, petrify, mold, set, dry; *ant.* melt, dissolve, soften.

temperament *n.* disposition, personality, nature, character, mettle, makeup, humor, moods, tendencies, excitability, bent, outlook, spirit.

temperamental *adj.* emotional, excitable, hypersensitive, mercurial, volatile, moody, passionate, capricious, erratic, highstrung, unpredictable, explosive, inconsistent; *ant.* calm, serene.

temperance *n.* self-restraint, moderation, discretion, self-discipline, forbearance, self-abnegation, abstinence, prohibition, self-denial; *ant.* excess, hedonism, intemperance.

temperate *n.* moderate, regulated, reasonable, fair, modest, controlled.

temperature *n.* thermal reading, heat, warmth, cold, body heat.

tempest *n.* **1.** storm, squall, gale, hurricane, typhoon, tornado, cyclone. **2.** upheaval, uproar, commotion, disturbance, furor, tumult.

tempestuous *adj.* turbulent, tumultuous, uncontrolled, emotional, impassioned, raging, wild, troubled, violent, furious, intense.

temple *n.* sanctuary, shrine, church, mosque, tabernacle.

tempo *n.* beat, rhythm, pace, cadence, pulse, measure, time, meter, rate, speed.

temporal *adj.* **1.** impermanent, fleeting, momentary, fugitive, passing, temporary, transient, short-lived. **2.** worldly, secular, carnal, earthly, fleshy, material, profane, terrestrial, unspiritual, civil, mundane; *ant.* spiritual.

temporarily *adv.* for the time being, briefly, in the interim, momentarily, fleetingly, transitorily; *ant.* permanently.

temporary *adj.* momentary, brief, ephemeral, interim, provisional, stopgap, makeshift, passing, transient, transitory.

temporize *v.* pause, delay, stall, hem and haw, procrastinate, play for time, hang back.

tempt *v.* entice, lure, bait, tantalize, seduce, coax, enamor, woo, incite, try, draw, allure; *ant.* discourage, dissuade.

temptation *n.* enticement, lure, forbidden fruit, attraction, appeal, persuasion, pull, bait, snare, draw, inducement.

tempting *adj.* enticing, inviting, alluring, tantalizing, attractive, appetizing, mouthwatering; *ant.* unattractive, uninviting.

tenable *adj.* defendable, justifiable, supportable, credible, viable, maintainable, sound, arguable, believable; *ant.* indefensible, unjustifiable.

tenacious *adj.* resolute, steadfast, inflexible, persistent, unswerving, unyielding, dogged, pertinacious, sure, unshakable, fast, adamant, stubborn; *ant.* weak-willed, irresolute.

tenant *n.* occupant, resident, inhabitant, leaseholder, renter, lessee, landholder.

tend *v.* **1.** manage, handle, maintain, keep, guard, protect, minister to, nurse, serve, comfort, cultivate, control; *ant.* neglect. **2.** be predisposed, incline, lean, graviate, head, aim, bend.

tendency *n.* predilection, inclination, leaning, predisposition, bent, penchant, purport, readiness, propensity, susceptibility, bias, readiness, tenor.

tender *v.* offer, give, extend, submit, volunteer, present, proffer, advance.

tender *adj.* **1.** soft, delicate, fragile, frail, gentle, supple. **2.** young, green, impressionable, immature, inexperienced, new, childish, childlike. **3.** tenderhearted, softhearted, kind, gentle, compassionate, sympathetic, caring; *ant.* insensitive.

tenderness *n.* kindness, benevolence, compassion, sympathy, humanity, caring, mercy, love, sensitivity, care, loving-kindness, warmth, affection; *ant.* cruelty, harshness.

tenet *n.* belief, article of faith, conviction, principle, view, creed, doctrine, dogma, canon, rule, teaching, maxim.

tenor *n.* inclination, tendency, course, purpose, direction, essence, meaning, intent, gist, drift, purport, sense.

tense *adj.* overwrought, stressful, nervous, uptight (*slang*), edgy, uneasy, anxious, jittery, apprehensive, taut, rigid.

tension *n.* stress, unease, anxiety, nervousness, pressure, edginess, worry, apprehension, suspense.

tentative *adj.* speculative, conjectural, experimental, unsettled, indefinite, unconfirmed; cautious, hesitant, uncertain, faltering, timid; *ant.* definite, conclusive, decisive.

tenuous *adj.* insubstantial, nebulous, fine, delicate, gossamer; slight, thin, dubious, questionable, shaky, flimsy, sketchy, weak; *ant.* substantial, strong, significant.

tenure *n.* term, time, duration, possession, occupancy, incumbency, holding, proprietorship, tenancy.

tepid *adj.* lukewarm, indifferent, half-hearted, unenthusiastic, apathetic, cool; *ant.* passionate, hot, animated.

term *n.* **1.** name, title, designation, denomination, expression, locution, appellation, phrase, epithet, word. **2.** interval, period, span, duration, session, semester, season; culmination, end, limit, finish.

terminal *n.* **1.** computer, monitor, data terminal, CRT, cathode ray tube. **2.** depot, station, end of the line.

terminal *adj.* **1.** fatal, mortal, lethal, incur-

able, deadly. **2.** final, concluding, ultimate, extreme, utmost; *ant.* initial.

terminate *v.* **1.** abolish, eliminate, annul, cancel, stop, end. **2.** finish, complete, end, conclude, wind up; perfect, achieve.

termination *n.* end, finish, close, terminus, resolution, conclusion.

terminology *n.* lingo, jargon, phraseology, language, nomenclature, cant, vocabulary, words, terms.

terminus *n.* boundary, limit, end, extremity, goal, target, close.

terms *n.* **1.** conditions, details, items, points, particulars, circumstances. **2.** agreement, understanding, treaty, conclusion.

come to terms compromise, arbitrate, agree.

terrace *n.* patio, garden, landscape, platform, green, lawn, yard.

terrain *n.* landscape, topography, territory, land, country, countryside, ground.

terrestrial *adj.* earthly, worldly, global, mundane, sublunary; *ant.* cosmic, heavenly.

terrible *adj.* horrible, dreadful, abhorrent, awful, severe, horrendous, horrific, loathsome, distressing, revolting, frightful, extreme; *ant.* pleasant, wonderful, great.

terribly *adv.* awfully, frightfully, shockingly, desperately, exceedingly, extremely, greatly, gravely, seriously, thoroughly.

terrific *adj.* tremendous, great, immense, shocking, thunderous, world-shaking; *ant.* common, ordinary, conventional.

terrified *adj.* frightened, terrorized, shocked, horrified, petrified, panic-stricken, alarmed, scared.

terrify *v.* scare, frighten, terrorize, shock, horrify, panic, alarm.

territorial *adj.* localized, regional, sectional, zonal, area, district, geographical, topographic.

territory *n.* region, district, domain, area, province, sector, zone, jurisdiction, community, neighborhood, section.

terror *n.* fear, horror, panic, shock, alarm, dread, panic.

terrorist *n.* subversive, revolutionary, incendiary, rebel.

terrorize *v.* menace, scare, frighten, petrify, threaten, intimidate, oppress, strong-arm (*slang*).

terse *adj.* curt, clipped, short, snappy, abrupt, brusque, elliptical, concise, succinct, brief, economical, laconic; *ant.* voluble.

test *n.* examination, evaluation, assessment, analysis, trial, tryout, check, moment of truth, hurdle.

test *v.* assess, check, examine, analyze, experiment, investigate, verify, prove, screen.

testament *n.* testimony, evidence, attestation, exemplification, proof, witness, will.

testify *v.* swear, bear witness, affirm, corroborate, declare, state, show, vouch, attest, assert.

testimonial *n.* 1. commendation, recommendation, endorsement, plug (*slang*). 2. tribute, memorial, commemoration.

testimony *n.* deposition, statement, witness, evidence, affidavit, verification, corroboration, attestation, declaration, support, affirmation, avowal.

testy *adj.* irritable, peevish, snappy, quick-tempered, cross, cantankerous, petulant, touchy, quarrelsome, grumpy, irascible; *ant.* equable, even-tempered.

tether *v.* restrain, fetter, secure, bind, lash, fasten, tie, manacle, shackle.

text *n.* contents, matter, body, passage, theme, topic, motif, verse, wording, words, sentence, paragraph, textbook.

texture *n.* consistency, composition, feel, surface, weave, grain, quality.

thankless *adj.* unappreciated, ungrateful, unrecognized, unrequited, unrewarding, fruitless, useless; *ant.* rewarding.

thankful *adj.* appreciative, grateful, pleased, relieved, indebted, beholden, obliged; *ant.* unappreciative, ungrateful.

thanks *n.* gratitude, appreciation, gratefulness, acknowledgment, credit, recognition, grace, thanksgiving.

thanks to because of, due to, through, on account of, as a result of, owing to.

thaw *v.* defrost, soften, warm, melt, dissolve, liquefy, unthaw; *ant.* freeze.

theater *n.* playhouse, amphitheater, auditorium, hall, opera house, cinema.

theatrical *adj.* dramatic, extravagant, melodramatic, thespian, showy, stagy, unreal, stilted, ostentatious, affected, artificial, exaggerated, histrionic.

theft *n.* stealing, thievery, larceny, robbery, heist, embezzlement, pilfering, purloining, plunderage, fraud, rip-off (*slang*).

theme *n.* motif, subject, thesis, topic, idea, keynote, text, matter, subject, essay, paper.

thematic *adj.* conceptual, taxonomic, classificatory, notional.

theological *adj.* religious, doctrinal, ecclesiastical, divine.

theology *n.* dogma, religion, creed, theism, belief, faith.

theorem *n.* proposition, rule, postulate, hypothesis, dictum, thesis, formula, principle, deduction.

theoretical *adj.* hypothetical, academic, conjectural, speculative, abstract, doctrinal; *ant.* concrete, practical, applied.

theorist *n.* speculator, ideologist, philosopher, scientist.

theorize *v.* hypothesize, conjecture, speculate, postulate, project, propound, suppose, guess, estimate, guesstimate.

theory *n.* 1. assumption, hypothesis, conjecture, speculation. 2. foundations, principles, postulates, data, conditions, basis, plan, ideas, method, approach, rationale.

therapeutic *adj.* restorative, healing, curative, beneficial, medicinal, tonic, corrective, recuperative.

therapy *n.* treatment, physical therapy, psychotherapy, rehabilitation, healing, cure.

thermal *adj.* warm, tepid, hot.

thesaurus *n.* synonymy, wordbook, repository, storehouse, treasury, vocabulary, lexicon, dictionary.

thesis *n.* 1. dissertation, paper, study, research, exposition. 2. argument, hypothesis, opinion, belief, principle, position.

thespian *n.* actor, player, performer, tragedian.

thick *adj.* 1. dense, condensed, compact, compressed, crowded, packed, impervious, close. 2. (as a fluid substance) syrupy, coagulated, viscous, dense, turbid, clotted, gummy; obscure, muddy, cloudy. 3. (said of speech or accent) inarticulate, muffled, garbled, indistinct; pronounced, conspicuous. 4. stupid, obtuse, ignorant, dull, doltish. 5. (*slang*) intimate, friendly, familiar, fraternal, cordial.

thicken *v.* condense, coagulate, congeal, cake, clot, set, deepen.

thicket *n.* grove, wood, bosk, copse.

thickheaded *adj.* dense, slow, obtuse, imbecilic, dimwitted, slow-witted, stupid, idiotic, doltish, brainless, dopey (*slang*).

thickness *n.* density, bulk, viscosity; breadth, diameter, width; *ant.* thinness.

thickset *adj.* squat, stocky, burly, dense, brawny, sturdy, heavy, muscular, strong, solid, stubby, beefy; *ant.* lanky, lean.

thick-skinned *adj.* callous, hard, tough, hardened, impervious, stolid, hard-boiled, hard-nosed (*slang*), inured; unfeeling, insensitive; *ant.* thin-skinned, sensitive.

thief *n.* robber, burglar, stealer, crook, mugger, pilferer, plunderer, embezzler, bandit, cheat, larcenist, swindler.

thieve *v.* rob, steal, heist, rip off (*slang*), pilfer, plunder, misappropriate, *slang:* lift, swipe, pinch; purloin, plunder, filch, poach.

thievery *n.* theft, larceny, robbery, crime, burglary, embezzlement, pilfering.

thin *adj.* 1. slim, slender, lanky, skinny, gaunt, lean, bony, wizened, starved; *ant.* fat, obese, heavy. 2. insufficient, scarce, inadequate, sparse, slight, meager, mere.

thing *n.* 1. object, article, item, entity, something, anything, commodity, device, gadget, thingamajig, whatchamacallit, doohickey, thingamabob, gizmo (*slang*). 2. condition, circumstance, matter, situation. 3. action, act, feat, deed, accomplishment. 4. idea, thought, notion, opinion, impression.

things *n.* stuff, paraphernalia, realia, odds and ends, bits and pieces, effects, impedimenta, junk, possessions, gear, goods, equipment.

think *v.* 1. cogitate, muse, deliberate, ruminate, meditate, ponder, consider, reflect. 2. believe, be convinced, hold, deem.

think about study, ponder, consider, contemplate, examine, evaluate.

think much of admire, esteem, respect, prize, value, venerate.

think up create, invent, conceive, visualize, imagine, concoct, design, devise, dream up.

thinkable *adj.* imaginable, feasible, conceivable, possible, reasonable, likely.

thinking *n.* reasoning, thoughts, idea, assess-

ment, judgment, philosophy, outlook, position, theory, view, conclusion, conjecture.

thin-skinned *adj.* sensitive, hypersensitive, touchy, vulnerable, tender, soft, susceptible; paranoid, irascible, testy, difficult; *ant.* thick-skinned, tough.

third-rate *adj.* inferior, shoddy, cheap, low-grade, mediocre, poor, bad.

thirst *n.* thirstiness, drought, dryness; appetite, craving, yearning, desire, longing, hankering, eagerness, keenness, yen.

thirsty *adj.* dehydrated, arid, parched, dry, burning; craving, yearning, longing, desirous, eager.

thorn *n.* 1. barb, prickle, spike. 2. irritation, annoyance, bane, torment, curse, scourge, torture, affliction, plague.

thorny *adj.* 1. barbed, bristly, spiky, spiny. 2. difficult, vexatious, awkward, problematic, ticklish, troublesome, complex.

thorough *adj.* comprehensive, exhaustive, inclusive, absolute, intensive, entire, painstaking, meticulous, sweeping, total, utter, all-embracing; *ant.* partial, haphazard, careless.

thoroughbred *adj.* purebred, pedigreed, of good breed, full-blooded.

thoroughfare *n.* concourse, highway, turnpike, roadway, street, avenue, boulevard.

thought *n.* 1. thinking, reflection, meditation, cogitation, introspection, deliberation, assessment. 2. concept, belief, view, idea, dream.

thoughtful *adj.* 1. pensive, contemplative, musing, introspective, meditative, ruminative, reflective, deliberate, careful, heedful, prudent; *ant.* heedless, impulsive. 2. kind, caring, helpful, unselfish, considerate, tactful, solicitous; *ant.* thoughtless, selfish, tactless.

thoughtless *adj.* 1. inconsiderate, rude, selfish, undiplomatic, uncaring, impolite, remiss, tactless, unkind, insensitive. 2. absent-minded, unthinking, inadvertent, ill-considered, rash, negligent, foolish, reckless, careless; *ant.* responsible.

thralldom *n.* servitude, slavery, serfdom, bondage, enslavement, subjugation; *ant.* freedom.

thrash *v.* trounce, whip, chasten, beat, flail, wallop, thresh, defeat, overwhelm, rout, punish, spank, tan.

461

thrash out debate, negotiate, resolve, discuss, settle, get to the bottom of.

thrashing *n.* trouncing, whipping, beating, hiding (*slang*), whaling, tanning, flogging, punishment, dressing-down.

thread *n.* **1.** strand, string, yarn, filament, fiber. **2.** story line, motif, theme, plot, line, tenor, drift, direction, course.

thread *v.* string, weave, wind, meander, pass, inch, ease.

threadbare *adj.* **1.** shabby, seedy, ragged, tattered, scruffy, frayed, down-at-the-heels, worn-out, moth-eaten. **2.** trite, clichéd, stale, old, overused, hackneyed, commonplace, stereotyped, stock.

threat *n.* menace, warning, omen, foreshadowing, foreboding, danger, peril, risk.

threaten *v.* menace, intimidate, terrorize, bully, imperil, endanger, jeopardize; warn, foreshadow, forbode, presage, portend.

threatening *adj.* menacing, sinister, terrorizing, grim, baleful, bullying, warning, cautionary, ominous.

thresh *v.* **1.** loosen, separate, sift, winnow. **2.** whip, hit, beat, chastise, punish, trounce.

threshold *n.* brink, start, verge, outset, onset, beginning, inception, opening, entrance, doorway, dawn, starting point, inauguration.

thrift *n.* frugality, thriftiness, economy, conservation, prudence, saving, carefulness; *ant.* waste, extravagance.

thrill *n.* excitement, pleasure, stimulation, titilation, charge, tingle, buzz (*slang*), tremor, tremble, throb, vibration.

thrill *v.* excite, arouse, stimulate, titillate, move, send, stir, wow (*slang*); tingle, tremble, throb, vibrate.

thrilling *adj.* exciting, exhilarating, rousing, stimulating, gripping, hair-raising, rip-roaring (*slang*), stirring.

thrive *v.* flourish, prosper, grow, succeed, profit, increase, develop, burgeon, bloom, blossom, luxuriate; *ant.* stagnate.

thriving *adj.* flourishing, growing, prosperous, successful, burgeoning, developing, healthy, wealthy, affluent, well, booming, blossoming, blooming, expanding.

throat *n.* gullet, gorge, throttle, larynx, esophagus, windpipe.

throaty *adj.* husky, raspy, hoarse, guttural, low, deep, gruff, thick, raucous.

throb *n.* pounding, pulsation, thumping, beat, pulse, thump.

throb *v.* pound, pulsate, palpitate, thump, beat, pulse, vibrate.

throes *n.* suffering, travail, agony, anguish, distress, torture, pain, death-agony.

throne *n.* authority, dominion, royal power, sovereignty, sway.

throng *n.* crowd, multitude, mob, herd, pack, mass, horde, crush, swarm, congregation, assemblage, flock.

throng *v.* mill, assemble, gather, flock, crowd, press, jostle, cram.

throttle *v.* **1.** strangle, strangulate, gag, stifle, smother, asphyxiate, choke. **2.** silence, gag, stifle, suppress, censor, inhibit, control.

through *adj.* finished, done, completed, over.

through *prep.* during, throughout, for the period of.

through and through completely, thoroughly, entirely, fully, totally, utterly, wholly, unreservedly, to the core, from top to bottom, from beginning to end.

throughout *adv.* everywhere, extensively, widely, ubiquitously.

throw *v.* **1.** hurl, fling, pitch, toss, heave, lob, put, launch; propel, thrust, project, discharge, start, drive, impel.

throw away discard, dispose, of, dispense with, cast off, reject, jettison, fritter away, squander, dump, *slang:* blow, ditch.

throw off 1. cast off, discard, drop, abandon, shake off, throw. **2.** (set on the wrong track) confuse, unsettle, upset, disconcert, frustrate.

throw out dismiss, expel, turn down, reject, evict, scrap, dump, ditch (*slang*).

throw up 1. vomit, regurgitate, spew out, disgorge, retch, *slang:* puke, barf. **2.** quit, give up, cease, terminate, abandon, stop.

throwaway *adj.* disposable, cheap; casual, offhand, passing, careless.

thrust *n.* core, meat, gist, sense, point, objective, goal, end.

thrust *v.* **1.** plunge, ram, shove, jam, poke, prod, stab. **2.** urge, propel, force, impel, press.

thud *n.* thump, crash, knock, clonk, wham, smack, thwack, wallop.

thug *n.* hoodlum, hooligan, ruffian, gangster, robber, bandit, mugger, murderer, assassin, goon, *slang:* bruiser, tough, heavy.

thumb *n.* first digit, preaxial digit.

all thumbs clumsy, inept, awkward, maladroit, fumbling, butterfingered, ham-handed.

thumbs down rejection, disapproval, rebuff, negation, no, turn-down.

thumbs up acceptance, approval, encouragement, go-ahead, affirmation, OK, yes, sanction.

under one's thumb under one's control, controlled, governed, managed, dominated, supervised.

thumbnail *adj.* short, small, concise, succinct, brief, pithy, quick.

thump *n.* thud, bang, crash, clunk, bang, knock, cuff, whack, wallop, blow.

thump *v.* pound, throb, beat, thrash, knock, hit, batter, rap, crash, lambaste, strike, smack.

thunder *n.* clap, cracking, rumbling, boom, crash, detonation, explosion, pealing, roll.

thunder *v.* roar, shout, threaten, bellow, blast, rail, curse, denounce, explode, yell, bark.

thundering *adj.* enormous, monumental, great, tremendous, unmitigated, remarkable, excessive.

thunderous *adj.* roaring, reverberating, deafening, resounding, ear-splitting, booming, tumultuous.

thunderstruck *adj.* amazed, flabbergasted, astonished, aghast, dumbfounded, staggered, astounded, open-mouthed, floored, shocked, stunned, paralyzed.

thus *adv.* consequently, therefore, hence, so, in this way, accordingly, ergo, then.

thwack *v.* whack, smack, slap, cuff, bash, buffet, beat, flog, thump, wallop.

thwart *v.* prevent, impede, hinder, obstruct, stymie, frustrate, check, defeat, foil, oppose.

tic *n.* spasm, twitch, jerk, tic douloureux.

tick *n.* **1.** beat, clicking, tick-tock. **2.** insect, pest, parasite, bloodsucker, arachnid, louse, mite.

tick *v.* **1.** click, tap, clack, beat. **2.** choose, mark, tally, count, score.

tick off (*slang*) anger, provoke, vex, aggravate, irritate, madden, outrage, enrage, infuriate, incense, get under one's collar (*slang*).

ticket *n.* **1.** certificate, token, voucher, stub, pass, document, label, tag, license, permit. **2.** candidates, party list, party slate, choice, schedule, ballot, roster.

tickle *v.* amuse, cheer, please, delight, entertain, thrill, titillate, divert, enchant, excite.

ticklish *adj.* sensitive, touchy, tricky, delicate, awkward, precarious, difficult, risky, thorny, controversial.

tidbit *n.* bit, bite, morsel, mouthful.

tide *n.* flow, current, ebb, course, direction, stream, tenor.

tidings *n.* news, message, information, intelligence, report, word.

tidy *adj.* **1.** neat, orderly, clean, uncluttered, shipshape, spruce, trim, spic-and-span, well-kept, well-groomed, methodical, systematic; *ant.* disorganized. **2.** large, ample, substantial, generous, goodly, respectable, sizable.

tie *n.* **1.** fastening, band, strap, bond, brace, yoke, zipper. **2.** necktie, cravat, bowtie, neckerchief, bow, scarf. **3.** deadlock, stalemate, draw, even game, dead heat, neck-and-neck contest.

tie *v.* **1.** join, fasten, bind, attach. **2.** knot, make a bow, do up (*slang*), make a hitch. **3.** equal, be on a par with, match, keep up with, parallel, break even, draw, come to a deadlock. **4.** (*slang*) marry, unite, join in holy matrimony.

tie in relate to, go with, be appropriate.

tie one on (*slang*) drink, get drunk, imbibe, go on a drinking spree *or* binge, *slang:* get hammered, get smashed, fall off the wagon, get rocked, drink oneself blind.

tie up **1.** bind, lash, secure, tether, truss, restrain, attach, rope. **2.** settle, conclude, end, finish off, terminate, wind up. **3.** engross, engage, occupy, absorb.

tie-in *n.* association, connection, relationship, affiliation, link.

tier *n.* level, stratification, stratum, layer, echelon, rank, stage, story, floor.

tiff *n.* quarrel, squabble, disagreement, battle, run-in, dispute, falling-out, words, spat (*slang*).

tight *adj.* **1.** firm, taut, secure, fast, bound up, close, clasped, fixed, steady, unyielding; *ant.* loose, shaky. **2.** closed, sealed, airtight, impenetrable, impermeable, impervious, water-tight; *ant.* open, penetrable, unprotected. **3.** (said of clothes) snug, close-fitting, pinching, uncomfortable, skintight, cramping, cutting; *ant.* loose, ample, wide. **4.** stingy, cheap, penny-pinching, miserly, parsimonious.

tighten *v.* constrict, narrow, squeeze, close, fasten, secure, tense; *ant.* loosen, relax.

tight-fisted *adj.* cheap, miserly, stingy; penny-pinching, parsimonious, tight, close-fisted; *ant.* generous.

tight-lipped *adj.* reticent, quiet, reserved, secretive, close-mouthed, mum, taciturn, uncommunicative; *ant.* talkative, garrulous.

timbre *n.* resonance, tone, tonality, voice quality.

till *n.* safe, vault, cash box, money-box.

till *v.* dig, plow, cultivate, dress.

tilt *v.* incline, slant, tip, turn, set at an angle, lean, slope, shift, dip.

timber *n.* wood, logs, planks, beams, trees, forest.

time *n.* **1.** duration, continuance, lastingness, extent, while. **2.** (a particular time) occasion, moment, instance. **3.** leisure, spare time, freedom, opportunity, free moment, ease, liberty, chance. **4.** (an extended period or a character-ization of such a period) age, era, period, epoch; conditions, circumstances.
ahead of time fast, ahead of schedule, earlier than expected, fast, early.
time and again over and over again, time after time, frequently, repeatedly, recurrently, often.
behind the times old-fashioned, out of date, archaic.
do time (slang) serve time, serve a sentence, be incarcerated *or* in jail.
for the time being temporarily, for the present, provisionally.
from time to time occasionally, sometimes, at times, once in a while.
time *v.* measure time, clock, pace.
time-honored *adj.* traditional, long-established, customary, established, accustomed, ordained, age-old, historic, venerable.
timeless *adj.* perpetual, eternal, permanent, immortal, ceaseless, ageless, endless, enduring, immutable, everlasting, undying; *ant.* ephemeral.

timely *adj.* punctual, prompt, well-timed; convenient, fortuitous, appropriate, opportune; *ant.* ill-timed, inappropriate.

timetable *n.* schedule, agenda, calendar, curriculum, diary, roster.

timeworn *adj.* dated, aged, passé, stale, out of date, tired, hackneyed, well-worn; *ant.* fresh, new.

timid *adj.* **1.** irresolute, indecisive, vacillating, compromising, wavering, capricious, fluctuating, flighty, uncertain. **2.** cowardly, faint-hearted, fearful, submissive, timorous, apprehensive, frightened, intimidated, bullied, cowed; *ant.* bold, assertive.

timorous *adj.* **1.** fearful, timid, cowardly, afraid, apprehensive, faint-hearted, shrinking, spineless. **2.** shy, bashful, coy.

tincture *n.* tint, tinge, shade, stain, trace, hue, suggestion, hint, touch, dash.

tinge *n.* smattering, dash, drop, trace, pinch, sprinkling, bit, touch, wash.

tinge *v.* color, dye, stain, rinse, taint, tincture, tinge, streak, influence, affect.

tingle *v.* prickle, sting, itch, tickle, thrill, vibrate.

tinker *v.* fiddle, dabble, putter, toy, play, monkey (*slang*), trifle, fuss.

tinkle *v.* jingle, clink, ring, chime.

tint *n.* shade, cast, hint, tone, trace, hue, rinse, wash, touch, stain, dye, tincture.

tiny *adj.* little, small, miniature, minute, trifling, slight, infinitesimal, petite, mini, wee, *slang:* teensy, teeny.

tip *n.* **1.** point, apex, peak, apogee, top, summit, cap, stub, nib. **2.** gratuity, compensation, reward. **3.** information, hint, pointer, suggestion, knowledge, advice, inside information, *slang:* dope, lowdown.

tipple *v.* drink, quaff, imbibe, swig, indulge.

tippler *n.* drinker, drunkard, inebriate, *slang:* lush, wino, boozer.

tipsy *adj.* drunk, inebriated, addled, muddle-headed, fuddled, *slang:* woozy, buzzed, feeling no pain.

tiptop *adj.* **1.** highest, topmost, uppermost. **2.** (*slang*) best, excellent, superior, prime, choice.

tirade *n.* diatribe, harangue, denunciation, outburst, lecture, rant, abuse, excoriation.

tire *v.* exhaust, fatigue, weary, drain, exasper-

tired ate, irritate, annoy, jade, bore; *ant.* enliven, exhilarate, energize.

tired *adj.* exhausted, fatigued, sleepy, weary, beat (*slang*), drowsy, spent, bushed (*slang*), worn out, flagging, drained, dog-tired (*slang*); *ant.* energetic, rested, fresh, lively.

tireless *adj.* industrious, diligent, energetic, determined, unflagging, indefatigable, untiring, resolute, vigorous.

tiresome *adj.* monotonous, tedious, wearisome, boring, exasperating, irksome, laborious, trying, uninteresting, flat, dull.

tissue *n.* **1.** web, network, mesh, interweaving, reticulum. **2.** (fabric) gauze, gossamer, chiffon, webbing.

titan *n.* colossus, leviathan, superman, giant, Atlas, Hercules.

titanic *adj.* enormous, huge, gigantic, mammoth, monstrous, colossal, stupendous, giant, towering, prodigious, herculean, vast.

tit for tat retaliation, revenge, counterblow, measure for measure, quid pro quo, an eye for an eye, requital.

tithe *n.* tax, levy, tariff, toll, impost, assessment.

titillate *v.* arouse, tantalize, stimulate, excite, captivate, tease, intrigue, thrill, turn on (*slang*).

title *n.* **1.** name, designation, appellation, heading, caption, inscription. **2.** deed, ownership, holding, rights, claim, license.

titter *v.* giggle, snigger, chuckle, chortle, mock, laugh.

titular *adj.* honorary, nominal, formal, token, so-called.

to *prep.* **1.** (in the direction of) toward, via, through, directed toward, traveling to, facing. **2.** (in respect of space) in front of, over, upon, on. **3.** (in respect of time) until, till, up to, extending to, stopping at. **4.** so that, in order to, that one may, for the purpose of.

toady *n.* sycophant, yes-man, fawner, flatterer, brown-noser (*slang*), parasite, minion, flunkey, bootlicker (*slang*).

toast *n.* **1.** salutation, tribute, compliment, drink. **2.** hero, heroine, darling, favorite.

toast *v.* grill, brown, broil, heat, warm, roast.

to-do *n.* uproar, fuss, commotion, furor, turmoil, rumpus, bustle, tumult, flurry, brouhaha, hubbub.

together *adv.* **1.** jointly, mutually, collectively, unitedly. **2.** simultaneously, at the same time, concurrently, coincidentally, at once, in connection with, in unison.

togetherness *n.* closeness, fellow *or* family feeling, affection, friendship, congeniality, love, society, brotherhood, sisterhood, gemütlichkeit.

togs *n.* clothes, apparel, suit, outfit, attire, duds.

toil *n.* labor, work, drudgery, travail, exertion, effort, elbow grease (*slang*).

toil *v.* labor, work, drudge, slave, slog, struggle, grind, persevere, plug away (*slang*), keep one's nose to the grindstone.

toiler *n.* laborer, worker, drudge, menial, workhorse, workaholic.

toilet *n.* latrine, privy, urinal, bathroom, lavatory, washroom, restroom, john (*slang*), outhouse, powder room, can (*slang*).

token *n.* gift, favor, memento; sample, sign, mark.

by the same token similarly, likewise, furthermore, besides.

tolerable *adj.* endurable, bearable, acceptable, adequate, passable, sufferable, middling, mediocre, OK, not bad, so-so.

tolerance *n.* open-mindedness, liberality, compassion, understanding, sensitivity, benevolence, humanity, good will.

tolerant *adj.* understanding, liberal, receptive, accepting, patient, open-minded, broadminded; *ant.* narrow-minded, bigoted.

tolerate *v.* allow, permit, consent to, accept, authorize, put up with.

toll *n.* **1.** charges, fee, duty, customs, price. **2.** loss of life, damage, casualties, deaths.

tomb *n.* crypt, vault, mausoleum, grave, burial place.

tombstone *n.* gravestone, headstone, monument, memorial, marker.

tome *n.* book, volume, opus, work.

tomfoolery *n.* foolishness, silliness, inanity, clowning, horseplay, buffoonery, childishness, shenanigans, hijinks.

tone *n.* **1.** sound, pitch, timbre, resonance. **2.** quality, character, nature, trend, temper.

tone down soften, modulate, reduce, moderate, subdue, assuage, play down, soft-pedal.

tone *n.* shape up, limber up, invigorate, touch up.

tongue *n.* speech, language, discourse.

hold one's tongue keep silent, hold back, shut up, clam up, button one's lip (*slang*).

tongue-tied *adj.* stunned, dumbstruck, speechless, mute, silent, dumb, voiceless; inarticulate.

tonic *n.* refresher, restorative, boost, stimulant, bracer, *slang:* pick-me-up, shot in the arm.

too *adv.* 1. also, as well, likewise, in addition, additionally, furthermore, besides. 2. excessively, exceedingly, extremely, beyond measure.

tool *n.* gadget, instrument, apparatus, machine, appliance, device, utensil.

tooth *n.* denticle, fang, incisor, molar, tusk.

tooth and nail energetically, fiercely, fervently, vigorously, hammer and tongs.

toothless *adj.* 1. edentulous, fangless, gummy. 2. powerless, ineffectual, unenforceable.

toothsome *adj.* delicious, appetizing, mouthwatering, scrumptious, tempting, ambrosial, delectable, luscious, savory, tasty; *ant.* disagreeable, unpleasant.

top *n.* 1. peak, summit, crown, head, crest, tip, apex, apogee, crowning point; *ant.* bottom. 2. toy, spinner, dreidel.

top *v.* exceed, better, beat, excel, surpass.

top *adj.* highest, uppermost, topmost; *ant.* bottom.

top-heavy *adj.* unstable, bulky, disproportionate, unbalanced, overloaded, cumbersome; *ant.* balanced, equalized, ballasted.

topic *n.* issue, subject, point, thesis, theme, motif.

topical *adj.* current, relevant, newsworthy, up-to-date, up-to-the-minute; *ant.* passé.

topple *v.* upset, capsize, overturn, tumble, overbalance, totter.

topsy-turvy *adj.* jumbled, mixed-up, chaotic, disorganized, messy, inside-out, upside-down.

torment *n.* suffering, affliction, torture, bane, scourge, anguish, misery, agony, trouble, worry.

torment *v.* plague, bother, annoy, harass, irritate, pester, provoke, torture, vex, distress, persecute, bedevil.

tormentor *n.* oppressor, persecutor, enemy.

torn *adj.* 1. ripped, split, cut, lacerated, ragged, rent, slit. 2. undecided, wavering, unsure, irresolute, vacillating, uncertain, up in the air, of two minds.

torpid *adj.* sluggish, slow, dull, apathetic, lackadaisical, indolent, listless, lethargic, slothful, languorous, supine, dormant.

torpor *n.* 1. stupor, coma, dormancy, inactivity. 2. apathy, indifference, dullness, sluggishness, listlessness, lethargy.

torrent *n.* barrage, gush, deluge, effusion, cascade, flow, downpour, outburst, volley, tide, stream.

torrid *adj.* passionate, erotic, fervent, ardent, intense, hot, sizzling, sultry, sexy, scorching, fiery.

tortuous *adj.* 1. winding, snaky, sinuous, twisting, crooked, roundabout, circuitous. 2. immoral, wicked, deceitful, devious, perverse.

torture *n.* torment, suffering, pain, anguish, misery, agony, distress.

toss *v.* hurl, throw, fling, cast.

tot *n.* toddler, child, baby.

total *n.* entirety, whole, all, aggregate, lot, mass, sum, amount.

total *v.* add up, sum, count, amount to, reckon.

total *adj.* complete, absolute, entire, whole, consummate, integral, sweeping, thorough, comprehensive, undivided, unmitigated; *ant.* partial, limited.

totalitarian *adj.* dictatorial, authoritarian, despotic, oppressive, tyrannical; *ant.* democratic.

totality *n.* completeness, entirety, whole, total, everything.

totally *adv.* absolutely, completely, entirely, utterly, wholly, comprehensively, thoroughly, unmitigatedly, consummately; *ant.* partially.

tote *v.* carry, take, haul, transport.

totter *v.* teeter, sway, waver, falter, stumble, shake, tremble, stagger.

touch *n.* 1. (sense of touch) feeling, touching, feel, tactility, perception. 2. (act of touching) contact, rub, stroke, pat, petting, fondling, rubbing, stroking, handling, caress. 3. skill, technique, ability, method, talent, knack. 4. trace, bit, suggestion, hint, inkling. **out of touch** 1. isolated, cut off, incommunicado. 2. naive, inexperienced, ignorant, oblivious.

touch *v.* 1. contact, feel, stroke, graze, rub,

pat, pet, caress, fondle. **2.** discuss, touch on *or* upon, treat, go over.

touch off initiate, start, arouse, provoke, begin, cause, ignite, set off, kindle.

touch on mention, refer to, broach, remark on, speak of, allude to.

touch up improve, fix up, polish up, retouch, patch up, perfect, enhance.

touch-and-go *adj.* risky, uncertain, tricky, iffy, up in the air; hazardous, dangerous, antsy (*slang*).

touched *adj.* **1.** affected, moved, stirred, impressed. **2.** insane, odd, eccentric, peculiar, neurotic, unhinged, bizarre; *ant.* sane, normal.

touching *adj.* moving, poignant, emotional, emotive, affecting, pathetic, stirring, pitiful, tender, heartbreaking.

touchstone *n.* gauge, norm, standard, measure, criterion, yardstick, benchmark.

touchy *adj.* irritable, irascible, captious, peevish, testy, petulant, thin-skinned, querulous, grouchy, grumpy, splenetic, quick-tempered; *ant.* calm, serene, unflappable.

tough *adj.* **1.** (said of a person's body) strong, wiry, robust, taut, mighty. **2.** (hard to resolve) difficult, hard, troublesome, laborious, resisting, thorny, vexatious, onerous, puzzling; *ant:* easy, simple. **3.** (marked by determination) stubborn, perseverant, determined, unyielding, obstinate, relentless, set. **4.** unsentimental, *slang:* hard-boiled, hard-nosed; thick-skinned.

tour *n.* expedition, excursion, trip, drive, jaunt, journey, circuit, course, progress.

tour *v.* travel, explore, visit, sightsee, ride, drive.

tourist *n.* traveler, voyager, globe-trotter, excursionist, sightseer, sojourner, jet-setter (*slang*).

tournament *n.* competition, championship, contest, match, tourney, event.

tousled *adj.* rumpled, disheveled, tangled, messed up, disarranged, ruffled.

tout (*slang*) *v.* praise, laud, promote, endorse, *slang:* plug, hype.

tow *v.* transport, haul, pull, lug, drag, tote.

toward *prep.* **1.** with respect to, concerning, regarding. **2.** coming up to, en route to, approaching, nearing; facing; away from.

towel *n.* wiper, drier, toweling, cloth, rag.

tower *n.* steeple, belfry, turret, citadel, observation tower, lighthouse, obelisk.

tower *v.* rise, soar, loom.

tower over surpass, transcend, exceed, dominate, eclipse.

towering *adj.* high, colossal, imposing, magnificent, transcendent, monumental, paramount, gigantic, soaring, tall, lofty, elevated.

town *n.* city, burg (*slang*), municipality, township, borough, settlement.

toxic *adj.* harmful, noxious, poisonous, lethal, deadly, miasmic, unhealthy; *ant.* harmless.

toy *n.* plaything, doll, game, trifle, trinket, gewgaw.

toy *v.* play, dally, fiddle, flirt, trifle, tinker, sport, tease.

trace *n.* **1.** fragment, bit, sprinkling, tinge, pinch, shade, hint, nuance, suggestion, touch, smidgen (*slang*). **2.** track, proof, mark, evidence, footprint.

trace *v.* **1.** discover, investigate, determine, ascertain. **2.** draw, outline, sketch, draw.

track *n.* **1.** course, path, road, route, passage, lane, walk, railroad. **2.** trail, footprint, impression, trace, mark, remnant, clue.

make tracks (*slang*) leave, depart, set out, dash off, hurry, make off, hit the road, *slang:* scram, split.

off track mistaken, wrong, ill-advised, off base (*slang*).

track *v.* follow, hunt, trail, pursue, stalk, dog (*slang*).

track down find, trace, hunt down, expose, discover, apprehend, capture, catch, unearth.

tract *n.* **1.** area, expanse, plot, region, stretch, lot, field. **2.** booklet, pamphlet, discourse, dissertation, leaflet, treatise.

tractable *adj.* docile, compliant, malleable, controllable, obedient, persuadable, biddable, pliable, submissive, yielding, governable; *ant.* feral, wild.

traction *n.* pull, drawing, drag, resistance, grip, propulsion.

trade *n.* **1.** craft, vocation, job, work, profession, occupation, line of work, avocation. **2.** commerce, exchange, market, barter, dealing, transactions, commodities.

trade *v.* exchange, swap, deal, barter, bargain, transact, do business, peddle.

trademark *n.* logo, brand, insignia, name, label, emblem, identification.

trader *n.* merchant, dealer, seller, buyer, barterer, broker.

tradition *n.* custom, institution, convention, ritual, way, habit.

traditional *adj.* customary, time-honored, long-established, accustomed, fixed, usual, ancestral, orthodox.

traduce *v.* defame, slander, vilify, disparage, decry, denigrate, malign, misrepresent, asperse, blacken, smear.

traffic *n.* **1.** travel, passage, transportation, flux, movement, transit. **2.** dealings, business, commerce, transactions, exchange, intercourse. *v.* deal, barter, bargain, do business, trade, exchange, peddle.

trafficker *n.* broker, dealer, merchant, trader, peddler, monger.

tragedy *n.* misfortune, doom, disaster, catastrophe, calamity, bad end; *ant.* happiness, fortune, success.

tragic *adj.* catastrophic, disastrous, calamitous, grievous, wretched, lamentable, sorrowful, dire, fatal, deadly, ill-fated, heartrending; *ant.* comic, triumphant.

trail *n.* path, route, way, road, track, footpath. *v.* **1.** trace, track, pursue, hunt, follow. **2.** tarry, lag behind, fall back, loiter, linger, dawdle.

train *n.* **1.** sequence, series, string, chain, succession. **2.** locomotive, subway, el, elevated, local, express.

train *v.* teach, educate, instruct, tutor; raise, nurture, rear, lead, discipline, mold, guide, shape.

trainer *n.* coach, instructor, teacher, tutor, drillmaster.

training *n.* instruction, schooling, education, coaching, guidance, preparation, practice, discipline, teaching, tutelage.

traipse *v.* walk, tramp, gad, ramble, stroll; trudge, plod.

trait *n.* characteristic, idiosyncrasy, mannerism, quality, feature, quirk, peculiarity, peccadillo, sign, feature, mark.

traitor *n.* turncoat, betrayer, double-crosser, quisling, defector, apostate, miscreant, deserter, informer, Benedict Arnold.

traitorous *adj.* disloyal, double-crossing, double-dealing, dishonorable, renegade, unfaithful, false, apostate; *ant.* loyal.

trajectory *n.* path, course, route, flight, line, trail, track.

tramp *n.* vagrant, vagabond, wanderer, bum, hobo, outcast, panhandler, loafer.

tramp *v.* march, plod, trudge, traipse, trek, hike, slog, roam, ramble.

trample *v.* squash, flatten, crush, infringe, stamp, tread, violate.

trance *n.* stupor, daze, spell, reverie, rapture, ecstasy, dream.

tranquil *adj.* serene, calm, peaceful, sedate, silent, quiet, still, undisturbed, untroubled, restful, composed; *ant.* agitated, tumultuous.

tranquilize *v.* calm, pacify, sedate, compose, quell, quiet, lull, soothe, relax; *ant.* agitate, upset, disturb.

tranquilizer *n.* sedative, barbiturate, narcotic, opiate, bromide, downer (*slang*).

tranquillity *n.* peacefulness, peace, quiet, calmness, stillness, serenity, sedateness, silence, composure, hush, repose, rest; *ant.* agitation, disturbance, noise.

transact *v.* execute, carry on, perform, conduct, manage, negotiate, handle, do, enact.

transaction *n.* affair, concern, goings-on, proceeding.

transcend *v.* surmount, surpass, exceed, excel, outdo, outshine, outstrip, eclipse.

transcendence *n.* supremacy, superiority, excellence, greatness, incomparability, predominance, preeminence.

transcendent *adj.* superior, unsurpassed, sublime, extraordinary, overarching, consummate, unparalleled, unequaled, unique.

transcribe *v.* write down, take down, note, record, copy, translate, interpret, render.

transcript *n.* notes, record, manuscript, transcription, translation, copy, reproduction.

transfer *n.* **1.** ticket, token, fare, check. **2.** shift, move, reassignment, translocation, relocation.

transfer *v.* **1.** carry, transport, convey, shift. **2.** (change owners) assign, give, sell, hand over.

trammel *v.* shackle, restrain, fetter, curb, hamper, restrict, impede, pinion, snag, catch, check.

transfigure *v.* **1.** transform, convert, transmute, modify, change, transmogrify, metamorphose. **2.** exalt, glorify, dignify, idealize.

transfix *v.* fascinate, captivate, bewitch, hypnotize, absorb, enrapture, engross.

transform *v.* change, change over, alter, metamorphose, transmogrify, redo, reconstruct, renew, remodel; *ant.* preserve.

transformation *n.* change, alteration, transmutation, metamorphosis, sea change, conversion.

transfuse *v.* transfer, instill, permeate, suffuse, pervade, imbue.

transgression *n.* offense, sin, wrong, violation, wrongdoing, crime, infraction, misdeed, lapse, encroachment, infringement.

transgressor *n.* wrongdoer, culprit, criminal, felon, villain, miscreant, lawbreaker, perpetrator, delinquent, malefactor.

transient *adj.* brief, temporary, ephemeral, impermanent, fugitive, momentary, passing, short-lived, transitory, fleeting.

transit *n.* passage, transition, transference, conveyance, transportation, infiltration, penetration, osmosis.

transition *n.* change, conversion, metamorphosis, progression, shift, transformation, evolution, flux, development, passage; *ant.* beginning, end.

transitional *adj.* developmental, temporary, passing, intermediate, changing, provisional, unsettled; *ant.* final, initial.

transitory *adj.* brief, temporary, fleeting, impermanent, momentary, short-term, passing, ephemeral; *ant.* lasting.

translate *v.* **1.** interpret, decode, transliterate, decipher, paraphrase, render, transpose, gloss. **2.** transform, transmute, alter, transpose, change.

translation *n.* interpretation, transcription, rendition, rewording, rephrasing, paraphrase, version, decoding, elucidation.

translator *n.* interpreter, linguist, paraphraser, glosser.

translucent *adj.* transparent, clear, diaphanous, sheer, see-through; *ant.* opaque.

transmigration *n.* rebirth, reincarnation, transformation, metempsychosis.

transmission *n.* **1.** transportation, transference, conveyance, carrying, hauling, sending, transmittal, communication, deliverance. **2.** broadcast, conduction, telecast, simulcast, radiocast, hookup.

transmit *v.* send, radio, broadcast, dispatch, communicate, convey, relay; *ant.* receive.

transmute *v.* alter, change, metamorphose, transfigure, remake, convert, transform, transmogrify; *ant.* retain.

transparency *n.* photograph, slide, picture, plate.

transparent *adj.* **1.** translucent, lucid, crystalline, gauzy, thin, clear; *ant.* dark, smoky. **2.** obvious, plain, clear, unmistakable, manifest, apparent; *ant.* obscure, hidden, difficult.

transpire *v.* **1.** happen, occur, take place, arise, befall. **2.** (become known) come to light, leak out, spread *or* get around.

transplant *v.* relocate, resettle, transfer, uproot, displace, shift, repot.

transport *v.* move, haul, carry, bring, take, transfer, fetch, ship, convey.

transpose *v.* interchange, switch, exchange, swap, shift, rearrange, transfer, reorder, relocate, substitute.

transverse *adj.* crosswise, diagonal, transversal, oblique.

trap *v.* snare, entrap, catch, ambush, beguile, deceive, corner, tangle.

trapped *adj.* caught, snared, stuck, cornered, duped, beguiled, inveigled, surrounded; *ant.* free.

trapper *n.* hunter, backwoodsman, frontiersman.

trappings *n.* **1.** trimmings, adornments, decoration, trim, accoutrements, embellishments. **2.** equipment, rigging, outfit, gear, matériel.

trash *n.* waste, rubbish, garbage, refuse, dregs, litter, dross, offal, leavings, excess.

trashy *adj.* shabby, tawdry, cheap, third-rate, worthless, shoddy, flimsy, inferior; *ant.* first-rate.

trauma *n.* shock, outburst, ordeal, confusion.

traumatic *adj.* upsetting, disturbing, agonizing, distressing, shocking, wounding, hurtful.

travail *n.* hardship, exertion, toil, tribulation, effort, labor, trial, slavery, grind, pain.

travel *v.* journey, roam, tour, voyage, trek, wander, traverse, commute, go.

traveler *n.* voyager, excursionist, explorer,

globetrotter, journeyer, wayfarer, tourist, migrant, nomad, jet-setter (*slang*).

traveling *adj.*: itinerant, wandering, roving, vagrant, migrant, nomadic, touring, cruising, commuting, moving.

traverse *v.*: cross over, pass through, move over.

travesty *n.*: distortion, perversion, sham, lampoon, parody, burlesque, mockery, caricature, *slang*: send-up, takeoff.

treacherous *adj.*: **1.** dangerous, risky, tricky, precarious, difficult, unreliable, deceptive, unstrustworthy, unstable; *ant.* reliable, dependable, steady. **2.** traitorous, falsehearted, deceitful, unfaithful, two-faced, Janus-faced, duplicitous, deceiving, false.

treachery *n.* dishonesty, treason, faithlessness, duplicity, betrayal, deceitfulness.

tread *v.* walk, pace, stride, tramp, hike, march, plod, trudge.

treason *n.* duplicity, disloyalty, treachery, mutiny, traitorousness; *ant.* loyalty.

treasure *n.* valuables, fortune, wealth, jewels, money.

treasure *v.* cherish, adore, prize, revere, value, esteem, worship, venerate; *ant.* disparage.

treasurer *n.* cashier, bursar, purser.

treasury *n.* bank, repository, resources, revenues, assets, capital, funds, finances, hoard.

treat *n.* pleasure, delight, enjoyment, thrill, gratification, enjoyment, celebration, surprise, fun.

treat *v.* **1.** entertain, play host to, escort, indulge, amuse. **2.** care for, heal, attend, administer, prescribe, dose, nurse, minister to. **3.** (have to do with) deal with, negotiate, manage, handle, address; *ant.* neglect, ignore.

treatment *n.* **1.** usage, handling, processing, dealing, approach, execution, procedure, method, manner, way, mode. **2.** care, therapy, remedy, regimen, protocol, modality.

treaty *n.* agreement, covenant, contract, pact, alliance, bond.

trek *n.* expedition, hike, walk, journey, odyssey, march.

trek *v.* hike, traipse, march, tramp, walk, journey, range, roam.

tremble *v.* shake, quiver, shiver, shudder, heave, oscillate, quake, vibrate.

tremendous *adj.* **1.** huge, enormous, colos-

470

sal, immense, formidable, gargantuan, monstrous, towering, vast, gigantic, mammoth. **2.** extraordinary, fabulous, amazing, fantastic, incredible, sensational, terrific, super (*slang*), awe-inspiring.

tremor *n.* quake, quiver, tremble, shock, shake, shiver, oscillation, agitation, vibration; *ant.* steadiness.

tremulous *adj.* **1.** shaking, trembling, quivering, palpitating. **2.** timid, cowardly, fearful, shy, timorous.

trench *n.* ditch, channel, gullet, drain, furrow, trough, pit, gully, gulch.

trenchant *adj.* cutting, sharp, caustic, biting, sarcastic, acerbic, astringent, sardonic.

trend *n.* fashion, fad, rage, style, vogue, mode, craze; inclination, direction, tendency, movement.

trendsetter *n.* pacesetter, initiator, leader, vanguard, groundbreaker, pioneer.

trendy (*slang*) *adj.* fashionable, in (*slang*), stylish, up to the minute, voguish, latest, with-it (*slang*).

trepidation *n.* **1.** quaking, tremor, quivering, shaking, agitation. **2.** anxiety, nervousness, dread, fear, alarm, apprehension, panic, terror.

trespass *n.* misdeed, offense, transgression, breach, infraction, infringement, iniquity, error, crime, sin, peccadillo, fault.

trespass *v.* transgress, violate, infringe, intrude, invade, encroach, poach.

trespasser *n.* intruder, interloper, invader, infringer, poacher, transgressor, malefactor, wrongdoer, sinner.

trial *n.* **1.** lawsuit, hearing, action, case, indictment, legal proceedings, claim, litigation. **2.** ordeal, difficulty, suffering, agony, tribulation, affliction, misfortune.

tribal *adj.* ethnic, kindred, familial.

tribe *n.* ethnic group, clan, stock, people, race, nation, association.

tribulation *n.* travail, trouble, woe, burden, affliction, trial, adversity, distress, ordeal, misfortune, misery; *ant.* happiness, rest.

tribunal *n.* court, bench, hearing, trial, examination, inquisition, bar.

tribute *n.* **1.** recognition, praise, applause, testimonial, endorsement; memorial service, offer-

trick ing, eulogy. **2.** fee, payment, ransom, levy, bribe.

trick *n.* deceit, wile, fraud, deception, ruse, feint, hoax, artifice, trap, stratagem, double-dealing, subterfuge.

trick *v.* dupe, fool, deceive, mislead, delude, cheat, outwit, gull, bamboozle, hoodwink, *slang:* pull a fast one, pull someone's leg.

trickery *n.* pretense, deception, cheating, swindling, hanky-panky (*slang*), dupery, shenanigans, flim-flam, hocus-pocus, sleight-of-hand.

trickle *n.* drip, dribble, seepage, dribs and drabs; *ant.* flood, stream.

trickle *v.* drip, run, dribble, leak, ooze, seep, drop, filter; *ant.* gush, stream.

trickster *n.* deceiver, joker, wag, pretender, cheat, con artist (*slang*), swindler, fraud, impostor, practical joker.

tricky *adj.* **1.** difficult, complicated, delicate, touchy, touch-and-go, involved, ticklish, thorny. **2.** shrewd, clever, sharp, keen-witted, devious, wily; *ant.* straightforward, guileless.

trifle *n.* little, dash, pinch, bit, drop, spot, touch, jot, trace.

trifle *v.* toy, play, sport, fool, flirt, tease, dally, fritter, meddle, dabble, idle.

trifler *n.* dallier, loafer, idler, dilettante, layabout, good-for-nothing, ne'er-do-well.

trifling *adj.* frivolous, shallow, trivial, insignificant, piddling, silly, slight, tiny, worthless, negligible.

trigger *n.* lever, release, catch, switch; spur, stimulus, impetus, catalyst.

trigger *v.* initiate, set off, start, actuate, generate, cause, activate, release.

trill *v.* warble, tweet, chirp, sing, whistle, twitter.

trim *n.* decoration, embellishment, ornament, garnish, fittings, trappings, adornment.

trim *v.* **1.** prune, crop, clip, shear, pare down, lop, shave, cut, snip. **2.** adorn, decorate, embellish, beautify.

trim *adj.* slender, slim, svelte, streamlined, compact, neat, well-dressed, orderly, shipshape, smart, spruce, trig.

trimmings *n.* accompaniments, extras, frills, garnish, ornaments, trappings, accessories, additions, extras.

trinity *n.* trilogy, triune, triad, trio, threesome.

trinket *n.* bauble, trifle, doodad, gewgaw, knick-knack, ornament.

trio *n.* threesome, trinity, triad, triplet, triptych.

trip *n.* excursion, tour, voyage, travel, jaunt, expedition, foray, junket.

trip *v.* stumble, tumble, slip, lurch, founder, fall, pitch, topple.

tripe *n.* nonsense, inanity, drivel, garbage, balderdash, rubbish, poppycock, hogwash, *slang:* guff, bunk, bull; *ant.* sense.

triple *n.* triad, trilogy, trio, triune, threesome, triumvirate.

triple *adj.* triplicate, threefold, three-ply, three-way, three-branched, treble.

triplet *n.* trio, threesome, triplicate, triad, triune, trinity, trilogy.

trite *adj.* banal, common, clichéd, run-of-the-mill, stale, tired, dull, stock, uninspired, ordinary, pedestrian, overused.

triumph *n.* victory, conquest, success, accomplishment, conquest, win, feat, tour de force, ascendancy, coup; *ant.* defeat.

triumph *v.* prevail, vanquish, defeat, overcome, succeed, best, dominate, revel, celebrate, rejoice; *ant.* succumb.

triumphant *adj.* victorious, successful, exultant, glorious, jubilant, rejoicing, celebratory, joyful, swaggering, boastful.

trivia *n.* trivialities, details, irrelevancies, minutiae, trifles.

trivial *adj.* insignificant, trifling, trite, inconsequential, negligible, meaningless, piddling, minor, paltry, unimportant, slight.

trivialize *v.* play down, underestimate, minimize, scoff at, belittle, depreciate, underplay, undervalue; *ant.* exalt.

troop *n.* crew, squadron, group, company, band, division, unit, pack, contingent, team, assemblage.

troop *v.* march, go, traipse, parade, throng, flock, crowd.

troops *n.* military, soldiers, army, armed service.

trophy *n.* award, prize, laurels, cup, booty, spoils.

tropical *adj.* equatorial, lush, hot, sultry, luxuriant, steamy, sweltering, torrid.

trot *v.* canter, lope, jog, run, pace, scamper, scuttle, bustle, scurry.

471

troubadour *n.* poet, singer, bard, minstrel, balladeer.

trouble *n.* **1.** difficulty, strain, stress, cares, worries, distress; predicament, plight, fix, *slang:* pickle, jam, hot water. **2.** conflict, fighting, feuding, agitation, unrest, rioting, bickering, dispute, argument, quarreling.

trouble *v.* **1.** annoy, disturb, irritate, bother, vex, worry, harass, disconcert. **2.** care, be concerned with, make an effort, take pains.

troubled *adj.* disturbed, worried, agitated, apprehensive, anxious, perplexed, afflicted, confused, overwrought, bothered, vexed, harassed, harried, preoccupied, concerned; *ant.* carefree.

troublemaker *n.* agitator, mischief-maker, instigator, meddler, rabble-rouser, provocateur, ringleader, gadfly, dissenter.

troubleshooter *n.* specialist, efficiency expert, mediator, arbitrator.

troublesome *adj.* **1.** (causing trouble) bothersome, trying, irksome, plaguing, vexations, vexing, pestilential, worrisome. **2.** (being the cause of trouble to others) rebellious, difficult, demanding, inconvenient, fractious; *ant.* helpful, accommodating.

trough *n.* channel, gully, ditch, trench, conduit, furrow, gutter, hollow, manger.

trounce *v.* **1.** beat, flog, pummel, thrash. **2.** defeat, conquer, beat, win, overcome.

troupe *n.* cast, company, repertory company *or* group, band, group, troop.

trouper *n.* old hand, veteran, actor, entertainer, player, thespian, performer.

trousers *n.* pants, slacks, breeches, dungarees, jeans, flannels.

truancy *n.* absence, malingering, shirking, dodging; *ant.* attendance.

truant *adj.* absent, malingering, missing, runaway.

truce *n.* armistice, cease-fire, peace, respite, treaty, suspension, intermission, lull, moratorium.

truck *v.* **1.** transport, haul, drive, carry, freight, ship. **2.** deal, traffic in, peddle, exchange, sell, push (*slang*).

truculent *adj.* fierce, cruel, savage, hostile, violent, belligerent, combative, bellicose, warlike, aggressive, antagonistic, quarrelsome, defiant; *ant.* cooperative, good-natured, mild-mannered.

trudge *v.* tramp, traipse, hike, march, plod, trek, lumber, walk.

true *adj.* **1.** accurate, valid, precise, exact, right, correct; *ant.* inaccurate. **2.** loyal, stalwart, faithful, trustworthy, reliable, sure, constant, steady, devoted, dependable, sincere; *ant.* faithless. **3.** real, bona fide, genuine, authentic; *ant.* fake, false.

truism *n.* axiom, platitude, bromide, cliché.

trumped-up *adj.* fabricated, made-up, invented, phony, bogus, concocted, contrived, falsified, fake, untrue.

trumpet *v.* bellow, proclaim, announce, call, shout, tout, roar, advertise, broadcast, extol.

truncate *v.* cut, shorten, clip, crop, pare, prune, trim, lop, maim, curtail, abbreviate, abridge.

trunk *n.* **1.** case, chest, footlocker, traveling case, baggage, luggage. **2.** torso, body, thorax. **3.** proboscis, nose, beak, snout, snoot, prow.

truss *n.* bundle, brace, shore, support, binding, buttress, prop.

trust *n.* **1.** reliance, faith, confidence, dependence, credence, honor. **2.** organization, corporation, monopoly, cartel, holding company, institution, business, syndicate.

trust *v.* **1.** believe, swear by, confide in, esteem, depend upon, lean on, put faith in; *ant.* doubt, mistrust, disbelieve. **2.** consign, lend, put in safekeeping, entrust, commit, give over, store with.

trustee *n.* executor, custodian, agent, guardian, keeper, administrator, fiduciary.

trustworthy *adj.* dependable, steadfast, true, responsible, loyal, honest, mature, reliable, sensible, upright, trusty, level-headed, principled; *ant.* unreliable.

trusty *adj.* dependable, responsible, reliable, faithful, loyal, true, upright, staunch, supportive, steady, solid.

truth *n.* truthfulness, veracity, correctness, sincerity, candor, honesty, fidelity, frankness, genuineness, accuracy, verisimilitude.

truthful *adj.* honest, sincere, forthright, true, candid, frank, straight, accurate, correct, veracious, reliable, exact, precise; *ant.* false, mendacious.

try *n.* attempt, endeavor, effort, test, trial, shot, stab, *slang:* crack, go, whack.

try *v.* **1.** endeavor, attempt, undertake, exert oneself, contend, strive, make an effort, have a try, aspire, make every effort. **2.** test, assay, analyze, examine, investigate, put to the proof.

trying *adj.* exasperating, taxing, vexing, vexatious, wearisome, bothersome, irksome, aggravating, annoying, arduous, hard, tough; *ant.* calming, easy.

tubby *adj.* chubby, pudgy, paunchy, plump, stout, overweight, portly, roly-poly, fat, corpulent; *ant.* slim.

tube *n.* hose, pipe, shaft, duct, spout, conduit.

tuck *v.* insert, cram, push, stuff, crease, fold, gather.

tuft *n.* cluster, bunch, clump, truss, tassel, topknot.

tug *v.* pull, drag, tow, lug, heave, haul, jerk, wrench, yank.

tumble *v.* stumble, topple, roll, pitch, fall.

tumble-down *adj.* broken-down, dilapidated, ramshackle, rickety, crumbling, disintegrating, decrepit, ruinous; *ant.* well-kept.

tumbler *n.* **1.** acrobat, gymnast, athlete, trampolinist. **2.** glass, cup, goblet, mug.

tumid *adj.* **1.** swollen, bulging, tumescent, distended, bloated, enlarged, inflated. **2.** pompous, bombastic, egotistic, inflated, bloated.

tumor *n.* lump, growth, neoplasm, cancer, malignancy, melanoma, sarcoma, carcinoma.

tumult *n.* upheaval, fracas, commotion, clamor, turmoil, strife, disturbance, bedlam, altercation, riot, din, fray.

tumultuous *adj.* turbulent, raging, agitated, stormy, tempestuous, violent, passionate, clamorous, hectic, rowdy, wild; *ant.* calm.

tune *n.* song, melody, air, aria, strain, theme, jingle, ditty, number, harmony.

tune *v.* regulate, synchronize, attune, harmonize, adapt, adjust, set.

tuneful *adj.* harmonious, melodious, mellow, musical, catchy, pleasant, sonorous.

tunnel *n.* burrow, passage, shaft, channel, underpass.

turbid *adj.* muddy, cloudy, thick, dense, murky, agitated, opaque, unclear, unsettled, hazy, impure.

turbulence *n.* upheaval, confusion, commotion, agitation, pandemonium, turmoil, unrest, disruption, tumult, chaos; *ant.* peace, order.

turbulent *adj.* tempestuous, riotous, anarchic, tumultuous, raging, disordered, chaotic, stormy, violent, wild, confused, agitated; *ant.* calm.

turf *n.* grass, sod, green, clod, divot.

turgid *adj.* bombastic, pompous, grandiloquent, inflated, pretentious, affected, overblown, grandiose, flowery, fustian.

turmoil *n.* uproar, turbulence, tumult, chaos, bedlam, confusion, disquiet, disorder, brouhaha, trouble, commotion; *ant.* calm.

turn *n.* **1.** (change in direction) bend, curve, winding, twist, wind, hook, shift, angle, corner, fork, branch. **2.** (change in circumstances) turning point, juncture, climax, crisis, crossing, change, shift, twist. **3.** deed, accomplishment, service, aid.

turn *v.* pivot, revolve, rotate, roll, spin, wheel, whirl, gyre, swivel.

turn against revolt, oppose, rebel, disobey, defy.

turn back go back, retreat, retrace one's steps, revert, return; *ant.* go on, stay.

turn down reject, rebuff, spurn, decline, repudiate; *ant.* accept.

turn into become, grow into, change into.

turn on **1.** start, begin, set going, set in motion, switch on. **2.** (*slang*) arouse, excite, titillate, stimulate, stir up.

turn over **1.** invert, upset, overturn, reverse, subvert. **2.** transfer, give, hand over, deliver.

turncoat *n.* traitor, defector, deserter, fink, renegade, apostate, quisling.

turning point *n.* crossroads, crisis, crux, cusp, watershed, moment of truth, critical point.

turnout *n.* crowd, audience, number, assembly, showing, throng, attendance, company, congregation.

turnover *n.* productivity, revenue, production, yield, volume, business, output, flow, movement, profits.

turpitude *n.* baseness, vileness, degeneracy, foulness, corruptness, evil, rascality, vice, viciousness, iniquity, immorality; *ant.* honorableness.

tussle *n.* fight, fracas, battle, brawl, struggle, scuffle, conflict, bout, fray, scrap.

tutelage *n.* guardianship, parenting, care, protection, custody, charge, wardship, patronage, instruction, preparation, education.

tutor *n.* teacher, instructor, educator, mentor, guide, coach.

TV *n.* television, *slang:* small screen, boob tube, idiot box; telly (*Brit.*).

twaddle *n.* nonsense, inanity, blather, balderdash, rubbish, rigmarole, drivel.

tweak *v.* pinch, squeeze, twist, nip, snatch, tug, jerk.

tweezers *n.* pincers, tongs, forceps.

twig *n.* branch, offshoot, stick, spray, switch, whip.

twilight *n.* dusk, sunset, sundown, gloaming, half-light, evening, ebb.

twilight *adj.* dim, evening, declining, ebbing, dying, darkening, crepuscular, shadowy, final, last.

twin *n.* lookalike, duplicate, match, mate, double, clone, counterpart, doppelgänger, corollary.

twin *adj.* identical, symmetrical, matching, paired, parallel, corresponding, dual, duplicate.

twine *n.* cord, string, yarn, rope.

twine *v.* braid, interlace, interweave, plait, splice, coil, spiral, snake, wind, zigzag.

twinge *n.* pang, spasm, pinch, stab, twitch, prick, throb, pain, ache.

twinkle *v.* sparkle, glisten, glitter, gleam, flicker, blink, shine, wink, vibrate, flash, glint.

twirl *v.* spin, whirl, gyrate, twist, rotate, pirouette, turn.

twist *v.* **1.** spin, turn, twirl, pivot, swivel, entwine, revolve. **2.** misquote, misrepresent, pervert, warp, contort, alter, change.

twisted *adj.* **1.** crooked, contorted, wrenched, bent, knotted, braided, twined, wound; *ant.* straight, even. **2.** (said of meaning or reasoning) confused, erroneous, perplexing, wrongheaded, puzzling, perverted.

twit *n.* idiot, dope, fool, nitwit, simpleton, chump (*slang*), nincompoop, ass, blockhead, airhead (*slang*).

twitch *v.* jerk, shiver, shudder, convulse, palpitate, tremble.

twitter *v.* titter, chatter, prattle, giggle, chirp, cheep, tweet, trill, warble.

two *adj.* twin, dual, binary, both, double. **in two** halved, divided, split, separated.

two-faced *adj.* deceitful, duplicitous, double-dealing, Janus-faced, lying, insincere, untrustworthy, hypocritical, underhanded, false; *ant.* sincere.

tycoon *n.* capitalist, captain of industry, mogul, magnate, industrialist, potentate, entrepreneur, financier.

type *n.* **1.** (the collective characteristics that define something) kind, variety, sort, nature, character, genus, class, genre, species. **2.** model, representative, specimen, example, prototype.

type *v.* **1.** transcribe, typewrite, copy, teletype, touch-type, hunt-and-peck. **2.** classify, systematize, categorize, typecast, stereotype; group, catalog.

typhoon *n.* storm, tempest, hurricane, tornado, cyclone, twister, whirlwind.

typical *adj.* usual, standard, stock, conventional, average, normal, representative, archetypal, classic, orthodox, ordinary, regular, mainstream; *ant.* extraordinary, exceptional.

typify *v.* epitomize, illustrate, exemplify, embody, represent, characterize, personify, symbolize.

tyrannical *adj.* authoritarian, despotic, domineering, iron-handed, oppressive, overbearing, dictatorial, absolute, inexorable.

tyrannize *v.* oppress, subjugate, domineer, dictate, intimidate, coerce, browbeat, bully.

tyranny *n.* authoritarianism, despotism, dictatorship, autocracy, oppression, coercion, imperiousness, injustice; *ant.* democracy, liberality.

tyrant *n.* oppressor, despot, bully, authoritarian, dictator, monarch, sovereign.

tyro *n.* beginner, learner, apprentice, novice, amateur, greenhorn; *ant.* veteran.

U

ubiquitous *adj.* everywhere, ever-present, omnipresent, pervasive, universal, global, common; *ant.* rare, usual.

ugly *adj.* **1.** (aesthetically displeasing) homely, unsightly, vile, repulsive, hideous, horrid, monstrous, repugnant, revolting; *ant.* beautiful, attractive. **2.** ominous, sinister, forbidding, threatening, menacing, malevolent, dangerous, terrible; *ant.* comforting. **3.** (said of behavior, situations, etc.) nasty, unpleasant, disagreeable, distasteful, bitter; vicious, brutal, savage, inhuman.

ulcer *n.* sore, canker, boil, abscess.

ulterior *adj.* secret, undisclosed, covert, concealed, hidden, unsaid; *ant.* declared, clear.

ultimate *adj.* **1.** supreme, topmost, greatest, maximum, utmost, extreme, perfect, consummate, superlative. **2.** conclusive, final, eventual.

ultimately *adv.* finally, eventually, at last, at long last, in the end.

ultimatum *n.* demand, requirement, condition, terms.

ultra *adj.* radical, extreme, excessive, immoderate, revolutionary, way-out.

umbrage *n.* offense, indignation, anger, displeasure, resentment, grudge, disgruntlement.

umbrella *n.* **1.** parasol, sunshade, bumbershoot. **2.** (anything that shields) protection, cover, shield, disguise, barrier.

umpire *n.* **1.** arbiter, arbitrator, moderator, mediator, adjudicator. **2.** field judge, line judge, referee, linesman, *slang:* ref, ump.

umpire *v.* judge, moderate, arbitrate, adjudicate, call, referee.

umpteen (*slang*) *adj.* countless, innumerable, many.

unabashed *adj.* unembarrassed, unashamed, brazen, bold, undaunted, confident; *ant.* sheepish.

unable *adj.* incapable, ineffectual, impotent, incompetent, inept, unqualified, unfit, powerless, helpless.

unabridged *adj.* uncut, uncondensed, whole, complete, full-length, unexpurgated, entire.

unacceptable *adj.* intolerable, impermissible, inadmissible, unsatisfactory, objectionable, offensive, unwelcome.

unaccountable *adj.* unusual, odd, strange, peculiar, mysterious, incomprehensible, baffling, inexplicable, puzzling, unfathomable.

unaccustomed *adj.* inexperienced, unacquainted, green, unpracticed, unfamiliar, new, unwonted; *ant.* customary.

unacquainted *adj.* unaccustomed, unfamiliar, ignorant.

unadorned *adj.* simple, plain, austere, stark, unornamented, straightforward; *ant.* decorated, embellished.

unadulterated *adj.* pure, untouched, uncorrupted, unalloyed.

unaffected *adj.* **1.** genuine, real, natural, unpretentious, artless, honest; unsophisticated, naive; *ant.* affected. **2.** uninfluenced, untouched, unchanged, unresponsive, unconcerned; *ant.* impressed, moved.

unafraid *adj.* fearless, daring, intrepid, confident, bold, imperturbable, unshakable.

unalterable *adj.* permanent, unchangeable, immutable, fixed, written in stone, invariable; steadfast, unyielding, firm; *ant.* flexible.

unanimous *adj.* unified, agreed, concerted, undisputed, consensual, universal, concordant; *ant.* split.

unanswerable *adj.* undeniable, indisputable, incontestable, indubitable, absolute, unarguable, final; *ant.* refutable.

unanswered *adj.* ignored, tabled, unnoticed.

unappetizing *adj.* unpalatable, distasteful, unappealing, uninviting, disagreeable, insipid, tasteless, off-putting.

unapproachable adj. inaccessible, aloof, distant, standoffish, withdrawn, unsociable.

unarmed adj. defenseless, helpless, vulnerable, weak, assailable, exposed, unprotected, pregnable.

unashamed adj. unabashed, shameless, brazen, unrepentant, open.

unasked adj. voluntary, unsolicited, unbidden, gratuitous.

unassailable adj. 1. invincible, inviolable, invulnerable, impregnable, sacrosanct, secure. 2. (said of reasoning or evidence) undeniable, incontrovertible, indisputable, sound, irrefutable; ant. flimsy.

unassuming adj. humble, modest, unpresuming, unobtrusive; ant. presumptuous, pretentious.

unattached adj. single, available, unmarried, free, independent, unaffiliated, footloose; ant. committed, engaged.

unattractive adj. unappealing, undesirable, repellent, unsightly, offensive, disgusting, ugly.

unauthorized adj. unsanctioned, unofficial, illegal, unlawful, illicit, unwarranted, unapproved.

unavoidable adj. inescapable, inevitable, fated, certain, inexorable, necessary; ant. optional, contingent.

unaware adj. oblivious, inattentive, ignorant, heedless; unknowing, forgetful, uninformed, unsuspecting, incognizant.

unawares adv. by surprise, off guard, unexpectedly, accidentally, inadvertently, unintentionally, unwittingly, unconsciously.

unbalanced adj. 1. deranged, crazy, demented, mad, disturbed, psychotic, erratic, eccentric, touched; ant. sane. 2. shaky, unstable, wobbly; ant. sound, steady.

unbelievable adj. astonishing, preposterous, implausible, incredible, unlikely, improbable, questionable, unimaginable, unthinkable; ant. credible.

unbeliever n. skeptic, doubter, cynic, agnostic, atheist, doubting Thomas.

unbelieving adj. unconvinced, doubting, suspicious, skeptical, dubious, distrustful; ant. credulous, trusting.

unbending adj. unyielding, uncompromising, stubborn, unyielding, obstinate, inflexible, rigid, firm, stiff.

unbiased adj. impartial, objective, neutral, unprejudiced, even-handed, equitable, just, fair, disinterested.

unbidden adj. voluntary, willing, spontaneous; unasked, uninvited, unwelcome; ant. invited, solicited.

unblemished adj. clear, immaculate, unmarked, unsullied, unstained, untarnished, pure, perfect, unspotted, unimpeachable, irreproachable; ant. flawed.

unblinking adj. unflinching, unwavering, unafraid, impassive, imperturbable; ant. fearful.

unborn adj. fetal, embryonic, in utero.

unbounded adj. 1. infinite, limitless, vast, immeasurable. 2. unrestrained, unbridled, uncontrolled, unconstrained.

unbowed adj. stubborn, defiant, resisting, undefeated, proud.

unbreakable adj. indestructible, shatterproof, durable, strong, resistant, rugged, permanent; ant. fragile.

unbridled adj. rampant, unchecked, unrestrained, uncontrolled, excessive, intemperate, licentious, unconstrained, wanton, profligate.

unbroken adj. 1. whole, entire, complete, total, intact; uninterrupted, continuous, ceaseless; ant. divided, intermittent. 2. untamed, unconquered, proud, defiant; ant. cowed.

unburden v. 1. unload, dump, dispose of, empty. 2. reveal, confess, disclose, lay bare, confide, tell all, get something off one's chest; ant. conceal, hide, suppress.

uncalled-for adj. unprovoked, unwarranted, undeserved, unjust, unwelcome, gratuitous, inappropriate, incorrect, objectionable, rude, uncivil, impolite, improper.

uncanny adj. unusual, astounding, incredible, fantastic, prodigious, singular; bizarre, weird, supernatural, strange, eerie; ant. ordinary, usual.

uncaring adj. callous, unsympathetic, indifferent, unconcerned, inconsiderate, negligent; ant. concerned, solicitous.

unceasing adj. nonstop, relentless, continuous, unbroken, uninterrupted, persistent, unremitting, incessant; unending, perpetual; ant. intermittent, spasmodic.

unceremoniously *adv.* informally, casually, familiarly; carelessly, rudely, briefly, abruptly, curtly, matter-of-factly, hurriedly.

uncertain *adj.* ambivalent, ambiguous, vague, indefinite, irresolute, undecided; unpredictable, changeable, precarious, vacillating, unsettled, variable, unsure.

uncertainty *n.* **1.** doubt, indecision, misgiving, skepticism, dubiety, inconclusiveness, diffidence, hesitation, confusion. **2.** ambiguity, indeterminacy, vagueness, fuzziness; unpredictability, iffiness, chanciness.

unchangeable *adj.* irreversible, permanent, eternal, final, intransmutable, immutable, fixed, unalterable.

unchanged *adj.* consistent, invariable, constant, perpetual, unaltered, same, maintained; *ant.* altered, modified.

unchanging *adj.* fixed, immutable, enduring, imperishable, unvarying, abiding, continuing, steadfast, steady.

uncharitable *adj.* stingy, callous, unchristian, unsympathetic, cruel, captious, hardhearted, censorious; *ant.* giving.

uncharted *adj.* unknown, unexplored, undiscovered, strange, new, novel, virgin, foreign; *ant.* familiar, well-known.

uncivilized *adj.* barbaric, savage, primitive, wild, untamed, brutish, boorish, barbarous, vulgar, uneducated, uncultured, philistine.

unclassifiable *adj.* indefinable, undefinable, unidentifiable, indescribable, elusive, indistinct, vague, ill-defined, indeterminate, doubtful; *ant.* conformable.

unclean *adj.* dirty, soiled, filthy, contaminated, defiled, corrupt, stained, spotted, polluted, impure, unhygienic, unwholesome, nonkosher.

unclear *adj.* ambiguous, equivocal, dubious, indefinite, indiscernible, indistinguishable, obscure, muddy, vague.

uncomfortable *adj.* painful, ill-fitting; awkward, self-conscious, ill at ease.

uncommitted *adj.* neutral, uninvolved, nonaligned; *ant.* biased, partisan.

uncommon *adj.* rare, scarce, infrequent, unusual, extraordinary, abnormal, exceptional, atypical, singular, unparalleled, distinctive, strange, odd, peculiar, unique, superior, inimitable, sui generis.

uncommonly *adv.* exceptionally, remarkably, extremely, outstandingly, unusually, abnormally.

uncommunicative *adj.* reticent, taciturn, unresponsive, tight-lipped, guarded, secretive, curt, laconic; *ant.* forthcoming, talkative.

uncompromising *adj.* obstinate, obdurate, inexorable, intransigent, unaccommodating, diehard, hard-core, steadfast; *ant.* flexible, open-minded.

unconcealed *adj.* overt, open, admitted, blatant, frank, visible, evident, apparent, conspicuous, noticeable, obvious; *ant.* hidden, secret.

unconcerned *adj.* unsympathetic, uncaring, cool, blithe, aloof, callous; untroubled, oblivious, indifferent, apathetic, uninvolved, unmoved, complacent.

unconnected *adj.* **1.** unattached, detached, discrete, disjointed, separate, divided, independent. **2.** irrelevant, unrelated, incoherent, irrational; *ant.* logical.

unconscionable *adj.* **1.** unethical, amoral, unprincipled, unscrupulous, unpardonable, criminal. **2.** unreasonable, immoderate, excessive, extreme, exorbitant.

unconscious *n.* psyche, mind, subconscious, preconscious, subliminal self, ego.

unconscious *adj.* **1.** ignorant, heedless, senseless, oblivious, deaf to, unaware, unknowing, unwitting; *ant.* cognizant. **2.** comatose, insensible, inanimate, insensate, inert, numb, entranced, in a stupor, in a trance, in a coma, motionless.

unconstitutional *adj.* undemocratic, lawless, illegal.

uncontrollable *adj.* wild, violent, ungovernable, frantic, unruly, recalcitrant, irrepressible, refractory, froward, intractable; *ant.* tractable, manageable, tame.

unconventional *adj.* different, eccentric, unique, unusual, unorthodox, original, offbeat, alternative, individualistic, nonconforming, idiosyncratic, atypical; *ant.* commonplace, pedestrian.

unconvincing *adj.* doubtful, improbable, questionable, unpersuasive, dubious, unlikely, specious, fishy, tall (*slang*); *ant.* plausible, credible.

uncoordinated *adj.* awkward, ungainly, inept, table, sui generis.

clumsy, bumbling, lumbering, maladroit, desultory; disjointed, diffuse; *ant.* graceful.

uncounted *adj.* many, numerous, countless, limitless, innumerable, unrecorded; *ant.* few, numbered.

uncouth *adj.* crude, barbaric, barbarian, unrefined, vulgar, uncivilized, ill-mannered, gauche, unseemly, boorish, rustic, coarse, rough; *ant.* mannerly, proper.

uncover *v.* reveal, disclose, divulge, expose, bare, unwrap, unveil, unmask, leak, unearth, exhume; *ant.* conceal, suppress.

unctuous *adj.* 1. oily, slippery, greasy, waxy, smooth, slick; *ant.* dry, rough. 2. ingratiating, fawning, sanctimonious, smarmy, sycophantic, obsequious, glib, gushing.

uncultivated *adj.* uncultured, rough, natural, wild, fallow.

uncultured *adj.* unrefined, coarse, uncultivated, awkward, provincial, boorish, rustic, crude, vulgar, hick, uncivilized; *ant.* sophisticated.

undaunted *adj.* undeterred, undiscouraged, steadfast, resolute, courageous, indomitable, fearless, brave, bold, intrepid, unbowed; *ant.* cowed, timorous.

undecided *adj.* unsure, ambivalent, hesitant, uncommitted, unsettled, tentative, wavering, debatable, irresolute; *ant.* certain, definite.

undecipherable *adj.* illegible, unintelligible, unreadable.

undefeated *adj.* triumphant, unbeaten, victorious, winning.

undefended *adj.* unprotected, unguarded, endangered, open, naked, vulnerable, defenseless, exposed; *ant.* armed, fortified.

undefiled *adj.* chaste, virginal, unsullied, inviolate, intact, pure, clean, immaculate, unsoiled, spotless; *ant.* violated, blemished.

undefined *adj.* unspecified, unexplained, unclear, vague, nebulous, tenuous, shadowy, inexact, imprecise.

undemocratic *adj.* repressive, authoritarian, totalitarian, autocratic, dictatorial.

undemonstrative *adj.* unresponsive, impassive, restrained, aloof, cold, reticent, stolid, reserved, distant, withdrawn, phlegmatic, unemotional, uncommunicative.

undeniable *adj.* incontestable, irrefutable, evident, indubitable, unmistakable, clear, certain, manifest, obvious, sound, sure, unquestionable, patent, proven.

undependable *adj.* irresponsible, untrustworthy, unreliable, unpredictable, fickle, capricious, mercurial, fair-weather, erratic, volatile, uncertain, changeable, variable, unstable; *ant.* reliable.

under *prep.* 1. beneath, below, lower than, less than, inferior to. 2. subject to, subordinate to, governed by, subservient to, secondary to.

under way going, in motion, in operation, moving, begun, started, launched, afoot.

underage *adj.* minor, juvenile, adolescent, teenaged, young; *ant.* of-age, old.

underbrush *n.* thicket, growth, copse, scrub, bush, cover, coppice, furze.

underclothes *n.* underwear, underthings, undergarments, lingerie, undies, unmentionables.

undercover *adj.* secret, concealed, clandestine, surreptitious, hidden, covert, confidential, furtive, underground, stealthy, hush-hush.

undercurrent *n.* undertone, feeling, *slang*: vibrations, vibes; overtone, atmosphere, trend; tinge, hint, suggestion, drift.

undercut *v.* 1. undermine, weaken, impair. 2. excavate, gouge out, hollow out. 3. underbid, undercharge, sacrifice, undersell.

underdeveloped *adj.* retarded, unformed, weak, puny, backward, little.

underdog *n.* failure, loser, underling, victim, low man on the totem pole; *ant.* winner, VIP.

underdone *adj.* raw, uncooked, rare; *ant.* overdone, burnt.

underestimate *v.* undervalue, underrate, minimize, deprecate, belittle, dismiss, sell short; *ant.* exaggerate, overestimate.

underfed *adj.* starving, hungry, skinny, malnourished.

underfoot *adj.* down, below; annoying, in the way, impeding.

undergo *v.* sustain, endure, go through, meet with, brook, bear, suffer, weather, stand, withstand, experience.

underground *adj.* 1. alternative, avant-garde, experimental, revolutionary, radical. 2. subversive, surreptitious, undercover, concealed, covert, subterranean, clandestine.

undergrowth *n.* underbrush, brush, scrub, ground cover, bracken.

underhand *adj.* unethical, unscrupulous, improper, immoral, crooked, deceitful, furtive, fraudulent, deceptive, shady, sneaky, shifty, sly, crafty; *ant.* aboveboard.

underline *v.* stress, emphasize, underscore, accentuate, italicize, highlight; *ant.* de-emphasize.

underling *n.* subordinate, hireling, servant, slave, inferior, flunky, menial, minion; *ant.* boss, leader, master.

underlying *adj.* **1.** basic, primary, root, fundamental, intrinsic, elementary, substructural, substratal. **2.** concealed, hidden, subliminal, latent.

undermine *v.* **1.** enfeeble, impair, sap, debilitate, weaken, sabotage, undercut, subvert, disable; *ant.* strengthen. **2.** excavate, mine, tunnel, undercut, wear away, erode.

underneath *adj.* beneath, below, down, lower.

underneath *prep.* lower than, covered by, under, beneath.

undernourished *adj.* hungry, underfed, malnourished.

underpass *n.* tunnel, bridge, culvert, cave.

underpinning *n.* foundation, base, basis, support, infrastructure.

underprivileged *adj.* disadvantaged, impoverished, poverty-stricken, needy, deprived, poor, indigent, destitute; *ant.* affluent, fortunate.

underrate *v.* disparage, underestimate, undervalue, belittle, dismiss, depreciate; *ant.* exaggerate, overrate.

underscore *v.* emphasize, stress, underline, italicize, reiterate; *ant.* de-emphasize.

undersell *v.* discount, mark down, slash, undercharge, undercut, depreciate.

undersized *adj.* little, small, miniature, puny, underweight, underdeveloped, stunted, dwarfed, runty, atrophied; *ant.* big, oversized, overweight.

understand *v.* comprehend, grasp, learn, conceive, follow, get it, get the message, realize, perceive, see, recognize, take in.

understandable *adj.* comprehensible, logical, reasonable, congruous, justifiable, acceptable, coherent, expected, imaginable; *ant.* irrational, obscure.

understanding *n.* **1.** comprehension, grasp, knowledge, intelligence, awareness, wisdom, insight, viewpoint, perception. **2.** agreement, pact, accord, harmony, meeting of the minds.

understanding *adj.* sympathetic, compassionate, considerate, tolerant, forgiving, forbearing, patient, tender, kind; empathetic; *ant.* insensitive.

understate *v.* minimize, play down, make little of, underplay, make light of, soft-pedal, downplay; *ant.* exaggerate.

understatement *n.* oversimplification, underestimation, litotes, meiosis; *ant.* overstatement, amplification.

understudy *n.* substitute, alternate, double, replacement, surrogate, reserve, stand-in.

undertake *v.* try, endeavor, begin, commence, tackle, embark on, set out, accept, shoulder, covenant, pledge.

undertaken *adj.* begun, initiated, launched, set in motion, essayed, started, ventured, hazarded.

undertaker *n.* mortician, funeral director, cremator, embalmer.

undertaking *n.* project, enterprise, endeavor, job, task, program, adventure, venture.

undertone *n.* undercurrent, atmosphere, current, hint, suggestion, tinge, touch, trace, murmur, whisper.

undervalue *v.* underestimate, underrate, minimize, depreciate, misjudge, dismiss, discount, disparage; *ant.* overrate.

underwater *adj.* sunken, marine, submarine, submerged, undersea, subaquatic, subaqueous; *ant.* above-water, on-land, high-and-dry.

underwear *n.* underclothes, undergarments, lingerie, undies, unmentionables, skivvies (*slang*).

underweight *adj.* skinny, thin, emaciated, undersized, puny, undernourished; *ant.* fat, well-fed.

underworld *n.* **1.** organized crime, gangland, the Mafia, the mob, the Syndicate, Cosa Nostra, criminals, riffraff, rackets. **2.** Hell, Hades, the nether world, the Inferno, Avernus.

underworld *adj.* illegal, wicked, criminal, mobruled, shady.

underwrite *v.* **1.** endorse, guarantee, initial, sign, seal, authorize, validate, sanction, okay.

2. finance, fund, insure, sponsor, subsidize, back.

undesirable *adj.* unwanted, unattractive, disagreeable, disliked, unsavory, unwelcome; *ant.* attractive.

undeveloped *adj.* immature, unformed, stunted, embryonic, latent, primordial, dwarfed, inchoate; *ant.* full-grown.

undifferentiated *adj.* similar, uniform, homogeneous, alike; *ant.* varying.

undignified *adj.* unrefined, indecorous, unseemly, inappropriate, foolish, unladylike, ungentlemanly, unbecoming, petty.

undisciplined *adj.* disobedient, unruly, wayward, willful, refractory, froward, uncontrolled, unrestrained, untrained, unschooled.

undisguised *adj.* unconcealed, explicit, obvious, open, overt, outright, apparent, unashamed, evident, manifest, naked, blatant; *ant.* concealed, hidden, secret.

undisputed *adj.* unchallenged, unquestioned, incontestable, acknowledged, accepted, certain, undeniable, unmistakable, sure, irrefutable, conclusive; *ant.* dubious.

undistinguished *adj.* ordinary, commonplace, plain, pedestrian, run-of-the-mill, unimpressive, everyday, banal, unexceptional, prosaic, unremarkable, mediocre; *ant.* extraordinary.

undisturbed *adj.* calm, tranquil, placid, unperturbed, unruffled, unflappable, untroubled, composed, serene, unaffected; *ant.* troubled.

undivided *adj.* 1. undistracted, engrossed, concentrated, intent, absorbed, steady, fixed, exclusive. 2. unified, entire, whole, total, altogether, solid, integral, complete; unanimous, united, collective; *ant.* separate, split.

undoing *n.* ruin, collapse, destruction, defeat, downfall, disgrace, weakness, humiliation, misfortune; *ant.* triumph, victory.

undomesticated *adj.* wild, untamed, savage, uncivilized, feral, natural; *ant.* tame, broken-in.

undoubtedly *adv.* of course, surely, certainly, undeniably, assuredly, definitely, indubitably, unmistakably, unquestionably.

undress *v.* disrobe, shed, unclothe, strip.

undue *adj.* undeserved, disproportionate, overmuch, uncalled-for, extravagant, immoderate, needless, excessive, unwarranted, inordinate, intemperate; *ant.* reasonable.

undulate *v.* roll, heave, ripple, billow, rise and fall, swell, surge, wave.

undulating *adj.* rolling, sinuous, billowing, wavy, rippling; *ant.* unmoving, flat.

unduly *adv.* unnecessarily, immoderately, inordinately, extravagantly, overly, disproportionately, unjustifiably, overmuch; *ant.* reasonably.

undutiful *adj.* negligent, careless, delinquent, remiss, neglectful, unfaithful, unfilial, disloyal; *ant.* attentive.

undying *adj.* everlasting, perpetual, eternal, perennial, unending, indestructible, immortal, infinite; *ant.* impermanent.

unearned *adj.* unmerited, undeserved, free, gratis.

unearth *v.* exhume, dig up, dredge up, excavate; ferret out, discover, uncover, reveal, find, expose, detect; *ant.* bury, cover, hide.

unearthly *adj.* supernatural, surreal, otherworldly, ethereal, heavenly; ghostly, nightmarish, eerie, ghoulish, haunted, spooky, heavenly; ungodly.

uneasy *adj.* nervous, anxious, troubled, disturbed, unsettled, apprehensive, tense, on edge, worried; *ant.* calm, composed.

uneducated *adj.* illiterate, ignorant, unschooled, uncultivated, uncultured, unread, untaught, unlettered, lowbrow, philistine; *ant.* learned.

unembellished *adj.* plain, unadorned, stark, simple, austere, bare, undecorated, modest, severe, unvarnished; *ant.* ornate, decorated.

unemotional *adj.* dispassionate, unfeeling, unresponsive, cold, cool, reticent, apathetic, impassive, indifferent, reserved, stolid, undemonstrative, laid-back (*slang*); *ant.* excitable.

unemployed *adj.* out of work, laid off, fired, terminated, excessed, jobless, on the dole, idle, loafing; *ant.* working.

unemployment *n.* layoff, furlough, work stoppage, lockout.

unending *adj.* interminable, ceaseless, incessant, unceasing, constant, unrelenting, perpetual, unremitting, never-ending, undying, eternal, everlasting, infinite; *ant.* intermittent, transient, momentary.

unendurable *adj.* unbearable, intolerable, insufferable, overwhelming.

unenthusiastic *adj.* indifferent, half-hearted,

blasé, nonchalant, lukewarm, unmoved, unimpressed, neutral, uninterested; *ant.* excited.

unequal *adj.* uneven, unbalanced, unmatched, asymmetrical, differing, disparate, disproportionate, inequitable, irregular; *ant.* similar, alike, comparable.

unequaled *adj.* unrivaled, incomparable, unmatched, peerless, unparalleled, exceptional, supreme, inimitable, unique, nonpareil; *ant.* common, ordinary.

unequivocal *adj.* definite, clear, express, explicit, unambiguous, distinct, certain, absolute, clear-cut, straightforward, crystal-clear, direct, evident; *ant.* vague, ambiguous.

unerring *adj.* faultless, impeccable, infallible, accurate, certain, sure, reliable, perfect.

unerringly *adv.* accurately, infallibly, unfailingly.

unethical *adj.* unscrupulous, dishonest, immoral, dishonorable, unfair, underhand, illegal, unprincipled, illicit, disreputable, shady; *ant.* reputable.

uneven *adj.* 1. irregular, one-sided, lopsided, rough, bumpy, jagged, patchy, broken; *ant.* smooth. 2. variable, disparate, intermittent, fluctuating, erratic, desultory; *ant.* consistent.

uneventful *adj.* ordinary, routine, commonplace, unremarkable, mundane, boring, uninteresting, dull, unexciting, tame, humdrum; *ant.* exciting, memorable.

unexceptional *adj.* average, normal, unremarkable, ordinary, typical, run-of-the-mill, conventional, mediocre, pedestrian, commonplace; *ant.* impressive.

unexcitable *adj.* calm, cool, composed, impassive, serene, easygoing, dispassionate, imperturbable, unflappable, phlegmatic, self-possessed; *ant.* high-strung, temperamental.

unexpected *adj.* surprising, startling, unanticipated, unforeseen, accidental, sudden, chance, abrupt, fortuitous; *ant.* predictable.

unexpectedly *adv.* surprisingly, suddenly, unpredictably, without warning, by chance, out of the blue, abruptly, fortuitously.

unexpressive *adj.* inscrutable, vacant, blank, deadpan, poker-faced, impassive, apathetic, expressionless, phlegmatic, indifferent; *ant.* lively, demonstrative, energetic.

unfailing *adj.* dependable, loyal, reliable, true, steadfast, staunch, unfading; endless, ceaseless; *ant.* fickle, transient.

unfair *adj.* inequitable, unjust, biased, one-sided, prejudiced, partisan, discriminatory, bigoted, unethical, unmerited; *ant.* evenhanded, impartial.

unfaithful *adj.* dishonest, false, untrue, deceitful, adulterous, disloyal, two-timing, traitorous, perfidious, inconstant, two-faced, deceitful, recreant; *ant.* dependable, chaste.

unfaltering *adj.* resolute, firm, steadfast, unflagging, stalwart, reliable, unflinching, constant, steady, unfailing; *ant.* unreliable, wavering.

unfamiliar *adj.* 1. new, novel, unusual, strange, foreign, alien, uncharted, unexplored; *ant.* customary, familiar, known. 2. (lacking knowledge or experience) unacquainted, unversed, unpracticed, unaccustomed.

unfashionable *adj.* outmoded, outdated, passé, old-fashioned, dated, antiquated, obsolete, out (*slang*); *ant.* in style, in.

unfathomable *adj.* 1. incomprehensible, inexplicable, impenetrable, mysterious, baffling, inscrutable. 2. immeasurable, bottomless, unknowable, unplumbed.

unfavorable *adj.* inopportune, untimely, untoward, adverse, disadvantageous, threatening, ominous, discouraging; *ant.* promising, auspicious.

unfeeling *adj.* uncaring, unsympathetic, insensitive, inhuman, apathetic, cold, callous, cruel, heartless, pitiless, hard-hearted; *ant.* good-hearted.

unfeigned *adj.* genuine, real, sincere, heartfelt, unforced, unaffected, wholehearted; *ant.* pretended.

unfettered *adj.* free, uninhibited, unrestrained, unhampered, unhindered, unchecked, unshackled, unbridled; *ant.* constrained, confined.

unfinished *adj.* bare, crude, natural, raw, rough.

unfit *adj.* 1. incompetent, incapable, feeble, ineligible, unequal to, inept, untrained, useless, unprepared, unqualified, ill-equipped; *ant.* able. 2. unhealthy, out of shape, feeble, decrepit, infirm, sickly; *ant.* robust, able-bodied. 3. inappropriate, unsuitable, inadequate, wrong, incorrect.

unflagging *adj.* constant, steady, persevering, tireless, indefatigable, staunch, unceasing, never-failing; *ant.* faltering.

unflappable *adj.* imperturbable, self-possessed, calm, collected, cool, level-headed, phlegmatic, impassive; *ant.* excitable, nervous.

unflinching *adj.* steadfast, courageous, firm, resolute, stalwart, staunch, unblinking, unshrinking, unfaltering, unwavering, constant; *ant.* cowed, scared.

unfold *v.* **1.** unfurl, open, undo, unbend, stretch out. **2.** reveal, transpire, expose, disclose, show, explain, present, elucidate; *ant.* obscure, conceal. **3.** (come about in stages) develop, evolve, mature.

unforeseen *adj.* surprising, startling, unanticipated, unpredicted, unheralded, fortuitous, accidental, abrupt; *ant.* expected, predictable.

unforgettable *adj.* memorable, momentous, extraordinary, impressive, exceptional, notable, noteworthy, historic.

unforgiven *adj.* unredeemed, unabsolved, unregenerate, unshriven.

unforgiving *adj.* avenging, revengeful, relentless, cruel, ruthless; *ant.* compassionate, forbearing.

unforgivable *adj.* inexcusable, unconscionable, indefensible, reprehensible, unjustifiable, unpardonable, deplorable, inexpiable; *ant.* venial.

unfortunate *adj.* **1.** unlucky, doomed, ill-fated, star-crossed. **2.** regrettable, adverse, unfavorable, untimely, disastrous, calamitous, lamentable; *ant.* felicitous, promising.

unfortunately *adv.* sadly, sad to say, regrettably, grievously, accidentally, perversely, calamitously.

unfounded *adj.* groundless, baseless, spurious, unmerited, unsubstantiated, unproven, gratuitous, trumped-up, fabricated, false; *ant.* supported, justified.

unfrequented *adj.* isolated, remote, secluded, desolate, deserted, sequestered; *ant.* crowded, populous.

unfriendly *adj.* unsociable, standoffish, antagonistic, cool, unapproachable, aloof, inhospitable, inimical; *ant.* agreeable, amiable.

ungainly *adj.* clumsy, awkward, uncoordinated, gawky, unwieldy, gangling, lumbering; *ant.* graceful.

482

ungentlemanly *adj.* rude, crude, uncivil, rough, coarse, boorish, sexist; *ant.* polite, polished, gallant, refined.

ungodly *adj.* **1.** sinful, blasphemous, vile, immoral, impious, irreligious, profane, depraved, malevolent; *ant.* righteous, virtuous. **2.** outrageous, unreasonable, intolerable; dreadful, wicked, horrendous; unearthly; unseasonable.

ungovernable *adj.* unmanageable, uncontrollable, disorderly, refractory, rebellious, unruly, wild.

ungrateful *adj.* ingrate, thankless, unappreciative, selfish, ill-mannered, ungracious, self-centered; *ant.* thankful, obliged.

unguarded *adj.* **1.** careless, rash, foolish, thoughtless, unthinking, imprudent, foolhardy, impulsive, indiscreet, impolitic; *ant.* cautious, careful. **2.** defenseless, exposed, vulnerable, unprotected, pregnable, unparrolled; *ant.* shielded, safeguarded.

unhappiness *n.* sadness, sorrow, woe, melancholy, misery; *slang:* blues, dumps.

unhappy *adj.* sad, dejected, despondent, miserable, wretched, crestfallen, downcast, depressed; *ant.* cheerful.

unharmed *adj.* unhurt, uninjured, intact, sound, unscathed, unimpaired, undamaged.

unhealthful *adj.* toxic, noxious, poisonous, virulent, harmful, dangerous, detrimental; *ant.* wholesome, salubrious.

unhealthy *adj.* **1.** sickly, ailing, unwell, infirm, invalid, weak, frail, feeble; *ant.* robust. **2.** unhealthful, polluted, insalutary; *ant.* hygienic.

unheard-of *adj.* unprecedented, unique, new, novel; unimaginable, unthinkable, outrageous, disgraceful, shocking, preposterous, unbelievable; *ant.* normal, usual, acceptable.

unheralded *adj.* unforeseen, surprising, unexpected, unannounced, unadvertised, unsung, unpublicized; *ant.* trumpeted.

unhesitating *adj.* prompt, immediate, instantaneous, automatic, unquestioning, unreserved, certain, resolute, steadfast, unfaltering, unwavering, unswerving; *ant.* tentative.

unhinge *v.* **1.** detach, remove, disjoint; *ant.* unite, fasten. **2.** upset, drive mad, confuse, craze, madden, unnerve, unsettle, shake, distract; *ant.* pacify, placate.

unholy *adj.* evil, immoral, depraved, wicked,

vile, heinous, profane, base, appalling, unconscionable, irreligious, sinful, ungodly; *ant.* holy, pious.

unhoped-for *adj.* undreamed-of, unforeseen, unanticipated, unlooked-for, surprising; *ant.* expected.

unhurried *adj.* leisurely, relaxed, deliberate, calm, slow, laid-back (*slang*), sedate, nonchalant, easy; *ant.* hasty, hectic.

unhygienic *adj.* dirty, unsanitary, unhealthful, polluted, unclean, unwashed; *ant.* clean, germfree, disinfected.

unidentifiable *adj.* unrecognizable, obscure, incognito, disguised, imperceptible; *ant.* known.

unidentified *adj.* nameless, anonymous, unfamiliar, unclassified, unrecognized, incognito, mysterious, pseudonymous; *ant.* known, named.

unification *n.* alliance, union, affinity, coalition, merger, incorporation, federation, confederation; fusion, coalescence, blending, integration, combination, amalgamation; *ant.* separation, dissolution.

unified *adj.* joined, synthesized, wedded, made one, combined, coalesced, consolidated, centralized, allied, incorporated, integrated, federated; *ant.* separated, distinct, disjoined.

uniform *n.* costume, outfit, dress, suit, attire, outfit, garb, gear, regalia, habit, livery, insignia, regimentals.

uniform *adj.* same, similar, like, alike, consistent, homogeneous, undeviating, unvarying, equal, even, equable, identical; monotonous; *ant.* changing, varied.

unify *v.* join, merge, marry, weld, bind, unite, consolidate, confederate, fuse, amalgamate; *ant.* separate, split.

unilateral *adj.* one-sided, unipartite, single.

unimaginable *adj.* inconceivable, incredible, incomprehensible, impossible, fantastic, mindboggling, unheard of, unthinkable, unknowable, undreamed-of, unhoped-for; *ant.* believable, plausible.

unimaginative *adj.* uncreative, unoriginal, uninspired, common, pedestrian, myopic, banal, prosaic, vapid, tame, ordinary; *ant.* creative.

unimpaired *adj.* uninjured, sound, whole, perfect; *ant.* damaged, hurt, handicapped.

unimportant *adj.* insignificant, irrelevant, im-

material, marginal, inconsequential, trifling, negligible, trivial, petty, minor, paltry; *ant.* meaningful, primary, foremost, salient.

unimpressive *adj.* unexceptional, unremarkable, mediocre, so-so, average, commonplace, dull; *ant.* memorable, notable.

ninformed *adj.* ignorant, naive, unaware, unenlightened, unacquainted, in the dark, benighted.

uninhabitable *adj.* unlivable, unoccupiable, untenantable, unimproved.

uninhabited *adj.* abandoned, deserted, desolate, unsettled, isolated; *ant.* populous, populated.

uninhibited *adj.* liberated, abandoned, open, relaxed, unself-conscious, free, emancipated, informal, candid, frank, spontaneous, unrestrained; *ant.* subdued, guarded, withdrawn.

uninitiated *adj.* uninformed, ignorant, naive, callow, inexperienced, green; *ant.* experienced, aware, enlightened.

uninspired *adj.* unimaginative, boring, dull, commonplace, ordinary, stock, trite, humdrum, unoriginal, prosaic, pedestrian, undistinguished.

unintelligible *adj.* illegible, indecipherable, incomprehensible, jumbled, garbled, incoherent, inarticulate; *ant.* plain, understandable, lucid.

unintentional *adj.* unthinking, accidental, involuntary, unwitting, inadvertent, fortuitous, unconscious; *ant.* deliberate, meant, planned.

uninterested *adj.* indifferent, apathetic, impassive, blasé, unenthusiastic, unconcerned, unresponsive, bored.

uninteresting *adj.* boring, flat, dull, dry, humdrum, tame, monotonous, tiresome, tedious, wearisome; *ant.* exciting, stimulating, engaging.

uninterrupted *adj.* unbroken, unending, continuous, nonstop, continual, constant, quiet, peaceful, undisturbed; *ant.* intermittent, fitful.

uninvited *adj.* unwanted, unasked, unwelcome, unsought, unsolicited, unbidden.

uninviting *adj.* unpleasant, disagreeable, unwelcoming, off-putting, repellent, offensive, repulsive, unsavory, unappetizing, unattractive.

uninvolved *adj.* disengaged, free, unattached, uncommitted, footloose, independent, unhampered, unhindered.

union *n.* **1.** junction, unification, uniting, joining, coupling, annexation, congregation, merging, fusion, synthesis, incorporation; *ant.* alienation, separation, severance. **2.** group, organization, federation, association, society, confederacy, league. **3.** marriage, wedlock, matrimony, cohabitation, match; *ant.* divorce, estrangement, legal separation.

unique *adj.* single, sole, matchless, nonpareil, peerless, incomparable, unequaled, unprecedented, inimitable, anomalous, unusual, bizarre, only; *ant.* commonplace.

unison *n.* unity, concert, conjunction, accord, harmony, cooperation, agreement, unanimity, concord; *ant.* discord.

unit *n.* **1.** whole, one, unity, entirety, total, totality, assembly, assemblage, system, complement. **2.** section, segment, part, fraction, component, constituent, piece, module, portion, element, factor, digit, layer.

unite *v.* come together, join, merge, pool, coalesce, combine, ally, wed, unify, conjoin, confederate, couple, link; *ant.* separate, sever, divide, part.

unity *n.* concord, agreement, harmony, oneness, peace, solidarity, wholeness, union, unification, accord, consensus, concurrence.

universal *adj.* **1.** global, worldwide, omnipresent, widespread, extensive, common, general, catholic, sweeping, ubiquitous, prevalent, all-embracing, across-the-board; *ant.* specialized, limited, peculiar. **2.** cosmic, astronomical, stellar, celestial, empyrean.

universality *n.* predominance, commonness, generality, prevalence, totality, ubiquity, entirety, comprehensiveness, all-inclusiveness, wholeness.

universally *adv.* totally, entirely, prevailingly, completely, extensively, invariably, uniformly, everywhere, always, ubiquitously; *ant.* occasionally, sometimes, partially.

universe *n.* world, creation, firmament, nature, the natural world, heavens, cosmos, macrocosm, everything.

university *n.* college, academy, educational institution, school, institute, institution of higher learning, varsity, academia, Athenaeum.

unjust *adj.* unfair, inequitable, biased, one-sided, partisan, prejudiced, unethical, wrong, undeserved, unjustified, unmerited; *ant.* impartial, righteous.

unjustifiable *adj.* inexcusable, indefensible, unpardonable, unforgivable, unacceptable, steep, outrageous, unreasonable; *ant.* culpable.

unkempt *adj.* disheveled, ungroomed, sloppy, tousled, uncombed, rumpled, bedraggled, slatternly, messy, disordered, disarranged; *ant.* neat, tidy.

unkind *adj.* mean, malicious, hardhearted, inhuman, cruel, callous, nasty; inconsiderate, insensitive, unchristian, unsympathetic, uncharitable; *ant.* amiable, thoughtful.

unknowable *adj.* unpredictable, unforeseeable, unimaginable, unfathomable; incalculable, infinite, untold; *ant.* comprehensible.

unknown *adj.* unfamiliar, alien, foreign, unidentified, nameless, incognito, unnamed, strange, obscure, mysterious, unheard-of, undisclosed; *ant.* recognized.

unladylike *adj.* indelicate, unfeminine, ungracious, unseemly, unrefined, unmannerly, impolite, ill-bred, rough, rude, coarse, uncivil.

unlawful *adj.* illegal, outlawed, banned, criminal, prohibited, forbidden, illegitimate, illicit, unauthorized, unsanctioned, unconstitutional, unlicensed; *ant.* allowable, permissible.

unleash *v.* release, loose, unloose, free, untie; *ant.* bind, confine.

unlettered *adj.* illiterate, unlearned, uneducated, ignorant, benighted, unschooled, untaught, untutored; *ant.* enlightened.

unlike *adj.* different, diverse, divergent, unequal, opposite, opposed, unrelated, incompatible, disparate, ill-matched; *ant.* similar.

unlikely *adj.* improbable, doubtful, dubious, questionable, improbable, tall (*slang*); *ant.* plausible.

unlimited *adj.* infinite, immeasurable, vast, endless, countless, unfathomable, unbounded, uncircumscribed, incalculable, boundless; *ant.* controlled.

unload *v.* dump, empty, unpack, unburden, relieve, discharge, void, disgorge; *ant.* fill.

unlock *v.* open, unfasten, unlatch, free, release, disengage.

unloved *adj.* rejected, spurned, forsaken, unwanted, uncherished, neglected, uncared-for, disliked.

unmade *adj.* disorderly, disheveled, messy, tousled.

unmanageable *adj.* **1.** (hard to manage or educate) uncontrollable, ungovernable, recalcitrant, refractory, intractable, uncooperative, fractious, unruly; *ant.* docile. **2.** (hard to handle, as a crate or carton) inconvenient, cumbersome, bulky, unwieldy, difficult, awkward.

unmannerly *adj.* rude, uncouth, uncivil, discourteous, boorish, graceless, ill-mannered, ill-bred; *ant.* polite, considerate, urbane, well-behaved.

unmarried *adj.* single, unattached, unwed, available, bachelor, footloose, fancy-free, eligible.

unmask *v.* reveal, bare, expose, discover, disclose, uncover, show, unveil, uncloak, out (*slang*); *ant.* camouflage, obscure, screen, hide.

unmatched *adj.* incomparable, unequaled, unsurpassed, consummate, supreme, paramount, unrivaled, unparalleled, nonpareil; *ant.* poor, run-of-the-mill.

unmentionable *adj.* unspeakable, unutterable, unnameable, taboo, disreputable, shameful, scandalous, disgraceful, indecent.

unmerciful *adj.* cruel, callous, hard, brutal, pitiless, sadistic, unsparing, ruthless, relentless, unfeeling, monstrous; *ant.* beneficent, pitying, compassionate, humane.

unmistakable *adj.* explicit, clear, crystal clear, indisputable, manifest, obvious, conspicuous, plain, undeniable, unequivocal, pronounced.

unmitigated *adj.* **1.** thorough, absolute, unabridged, out-and-out, clear-cut, pure, complete, utter, downright, outright, unabated. **2.** austere, grim, harsh, oppressive, unmodified.

unmotivated *adj.* lazy, indifferent, purposeless, indolent, unenterprising; *ant.* stimulated, aroused, prompted.

unmoved *adj.* impassive, unfeeling, dispassionate, dry-eyed, indifferent, unaffected, cold, obdurate, unresponsive.

unnatural *adj.* **1.** abnormal, strange, bizarre, aberrant, anomalous, queer, freakish, odd, outlandish, monstrous, perverted, supernatural, uncanny; wicked, cold-blooded. **2.** synthetic, artificial, false, phony, imitation, manufactured, ersatz, fake, fabricated, concocted, feigned.

unnecessary *adj.* superfluous, nonessential, inessential, dispensable, unneeded, useless, expendable, redundant, uncalled-for; *ant.* required, exigent.

unnerve *v.* scare, frighten, shake, upset, worry, fluster, rattle, unhinge, disconcert; discourage, dismay, dispirit; *ant.* brace, nerve, steel.

unnoticed *adj.* unseen, overlooked, disregarded, ignored, neglected, passed over, unobserved, inconspicuous, unrecognized; *ant.* noted.

unobtrusive *adj.* unassuming, modest, quiet, restrained, subdued, self-effacing, meek, lowkey, humble, inconspicuous, retiring; *ant.* ostentatious, blatant, interfering.

unobtrusively *adv.* surreptitiously, inconspicuously, quietly, humbly; *ant.* openly, ostentatiously.

unoccupied *adj.* **1.** vacant, empty, deserted, blank, void, uninhabited, tenantless. **2.** idle, dormant, inactive, unengaged, at leisure, loitering, free, jobless; *ant.* busy, employed.

unofficial *adj.* unauthorized, unconfirmed, informal, ulterior, wildcat, illegal; *ant.* sanctioned, proper.

unopposed *adj.* unchallenged, unhampered, unrestricted, free; *ant.* resisted, obstructed.

unorganized *adj.* disordered, chaotic, confused, random; *ant.* systematic.

unoriginal *adj.* copied, derived, derivative, plagiarized; stale, trite, second-hand, cliché-ridden, uninspired; *ant.* imaginative, innovative.

unorthodox *adj.* different, unconventional, alternative, unusual, novel, nonconformist, radical, innovative, eccentric, abnormal, fringe, irregular; *ant.* standard, traditional.

unpack *v.* empty, remove, unwrap; *ant.* stow.

unpaid *adj.* **1.** overdue, outstanding, payable, owing, due, unsettled. **2.** unsalaried, voluntary, amateur, freewill, donated, contributed, pro bono.

unparalleled *adj.* consummate, supreme, matchless, peerless, unequaled, unrivaled, unsurpassed, exceptional, unique, nonpareil, superlative, incomparable, singular; *ant.* outdone, exceeded, improved upon.

unpardonable *adj.* inexcusable, unforgivable,

indefensible, unconscionable, deplorable; *ant.* understandable.

unperturbed *adj.* composed, tranquil, passive, impassive, calm, collected, placid, undisturbed, unruffled, untroubled, unworried; *ant.* anxious, agitated, disconcerted, unsettled.

unpleasant *adj.* repulsive, objectionable, unpalatable, distasteful, disagreeable, unattractive; *ant.* enjoyable, pleasurable.

unpolished *adj.* unrefined, uncultured, uncivilized, coarse, uncultivated, unsophisticated, vulgar, crude, rough, uncouth, rude.

unpopular *adj.* shunned, disliked, hated, rejected, avoided, detested, hated, unwelcome, unfashionable, undesirable, unaccepted; *ant.* favored.

unprecedented *adj.* revolutionary, unheard-of, unparalleled, extraordinary, singular, novel, new, original, unusual; *ant.* commonplace, pedestrian, undistinguished.

unpredictable *adj.* changeable, erratic, fickle, iffy, random, unreliable, inconstant, unforeseeable, variable, chance; *ant.* likely, foregone.

unprejudiced *adj.* open-minded, unbiased, objective, impartial, disinterested, nonpartisan, just, fair, uncolored, dispassionate; *ant.* narrow-minded, influenced, chauvinist.

unpretentious *adj.* plain, simple, unaffected, humble, modest, unadorned, honest, straightforward; *ant.* ostentatious, grandiose.

unprincipled *adj.* immoral, dishonest, corrupt, amoral, unethical, venal, underhand, devious, deceitful, unscrupulous, crooked, unprofessional, dishonorable, discreditable; *ant.* ethical, upright, virtuous.

unproductive *adj.* useless, worthless, barren, fruitless, infertile, ineffective, unprofitable, arid, futile; *ant.* prolific, fruitful.

unprofessional *adj.* amateurish, inexperienced, incompetent, inexpert, unskilled, negligent, lax, unprincipled, unseemly, unacceptable, unethical; *ant.* proficient, virtuosic.

unprotected *adj.* unguarded, unarmed, defenseless, helpless, unfortified, vulnerable, exposed, open, pregnable; *ant.* immune, safe.

unqualified *adj.* 1. absolute, downright, utter, outright, certain, wholehearted, unreserved, unmitigated, thorough, out-and-out, consummate, total; *ant.* conditional, tentative. 2. in-

competent, untrained, ill-equipped, ineligible, unfit, incapable, unprepared; *ant.* practiced, qualified.

unquestionable *adj.* absolute, certain, sure, clear, obvious, conclusive, definite, undeniable, unequivocal, indisputable, indubitable, manifest, irrefutable; *ant.* indeterminate, arguable.

unquestioning *adj.* wholehearted, unhesitating, unconditional, full, complete, thorough, unqualified.

unravel *v.* 1. separate, untangle, undo, unknot, disentangle, extricate, free. 2. solve, resolve, explain, sort out, figure out; *ant.* complicate.

unreal *adj.* imaginary, illusory, fictitious, visionary, dreamlike, artificial, fake, made-up, phantasmagorical, fanciful, mythical, pretended; *ant.* genuine, factual.

unrealistic *adj.* impractical, unworkable, improbable, unplausible, idealistic, romantic, quixotic, starry-eyed, half-baked; *ant.* pragmatic, rational.

unreasonable *adj.* 1. illogical, nonsensical; arbitrary, biased, unjust; foolish, silly; *ant.* rational, fair. 2. extreme, immoderate, preposterous, excessive, exorbitant, extravagant, inordinate.

unrefined *adj.* vulgar, crude, boorish, uncultured, coarse; unpolished, uncultivated, unsophisticated.

unrelated *adj.* irrelevant, extraneous; unassociated, unconnected, inapplicable; unlike, different, distinct, dissimilar, disparate.

unrelenting *adj.* 1. ceaseless, perpetual, unabated, incessant, continuous; *ant.* intermittent, spasmodic. 2. insistent, uncompromising, inexorable; pitiless, ruthless.

unreliable *adj.* 1. (said of persons) undependable, untrustworthy, fallible, unsound, unstable, irresponsible. 2. (said of information) erroneous, inaccurate, mistaken, specious.

unremitting *adj.* unrelenting, continual, incessant, perpetual, relentless, unceasing, constant; diligent, assiduous, conscientious, indefatigable, sedulous; *ant.* spasmodic, irregular, occasional.

unrequited *adj.* unanswered, unrecompensed, unthanked, unpaid.

unreservedly *adv.* utterly, completely, entirely, wholeheartedly, outright, unhesitatingly.

unresolved *adj.* unsettled, up in the air, undecided, unanswered, undetermined, problematical, doubtful, pending, hanging fire.

unresponsive *adj.* indifferent, apathetic, uninterested, unmoved, aloof, cool, unaffected; *ant.* receptive, sensitive.

unrest *n.* discontent, turmoil, rebellion, discord, protest, disquiet.

unrestrained *adj.* boisterous, free, rampant, natural, abandoned, uninhibited, unconstrained, unchecked, irrepressible, unreserved, unhindered; *ant.* subdued, guarded.

unruly *adj.* rowdy, uncontrollable, wayward, wild, willful, insubordinate, disobedient, rebellious, turbulent, mutinous, obstreperous, lawless, refractory, intractable; *ant.* manageable, submissive, governable.

unsaid *adj.* unspoken, undeclared, unmentioned, implicit.

unsatisfactory *adj.* insufficient, inadequate, disappointing, inferior, mediocre, poor, deficient, weak, unacceptable, unsuitable; *ant.* excellent.

unscathed *adj.* intact, uninjured, unharmed, unhurt, safe, sound.

unschooled *adj.* amateur, untrained, untutored, ill-educated, ignorant, naive.

unscientific *adj.* illogical, irrational, invalid, superstitious.

unscrupulous *adj.* ruthless, corrupt, dishonest, dishonorable, shameless, unethical, improper, crooked, discreditable, immoral, unprincipled; *ant.* upright.

unseat *v.* dethrone, depose, overthrow, displace, oust.

unseemly *adj.* undignified, inappropriate, improper, unbefitting, indecorous, unbecoming, ungentlemanly, unladylike.

unsettle *v.* disconcert, agitate, bother, perturb, upset, throw, shake, confuse, trouble, ruffle, rattle, fluster, disrupt.

unsettled *adj.* 1. undetermined, uncertain, undecided, debatable, unresolved, iffy, pending, up in the air. 2. (said of persons) confused, unbalanced, unsteady, precarious, shaky, disturbed, troubled, tense, disoriented; *ant.* composed, stable.

unshakable *adj.* adamant, staunch, immovable, resolute, stalwart, determined, unwavering, un-

assailable, absolute, sure, steadfast, firm, unswerving.

unsightly *adj.* ugly, revolting, repugnant, repellent, repulsive, unattractive, hideous, horrid, off-putting.

unsolicited *adj.* unwanted, unsought, officious, unwelcome, uninvited, spontaneous, voluntary, gratuitous, unforced, offered.

unsound *adj.* 1. unsafe, shaky, weak, wobbly, defective, faulty; erroneous, fallible. 2. ailing, unhealthy, ill, frail.

unsparing *adj.* 1. generous, lavish, profuse, bountiful, abundant, liberal, openhanded, munificent, unstinting; *ant.* tightfisted, parsimonious. 2. severe, stern, scathing, ruthless, harsh, hard, implacable, merciless, unforgiving, relentless, stringent; *ant.* flexible, yielding, genial.

unspeakable *adj.* dreadful, horrible, heinous, horrid, shocking, appalling, abhorrent; unbelievable, indescribable, inexpressible, ineffable.

unspoiled *adj.* preserved, pristine, natural, intact, unaltered, unharmed.

unspoken *adj.* understood, assumed, implicit, implied, tacit, inferred.

unstable *adj.* vacillating, variable, fluctuating, inconsistent, unreliable, erratic; shaky, rickety, tottering; *ant.* firm, steady.

unsteady *adj.* 1. wobbly, shaky, treacherous, precarious, shifting, teetering, wavering, unsafe; *ant.* firm, sound. 2. inconsistent, changeable, fluctuating, variable, erratic, vacillating, capricious, inconstant; *ant.* fixed.

unstinting *adj.* generous, lavish, bountiful, abundant, ungrudging, profuse, plentiful, prodigal, ample, unsparing, abounding, liberal, munificent; *ant.* stingy.

unstructured *adj.* confused, disorderly, disorganized, chaotic.

unstudied *adj.* 1. natural, spontaneous, instinctive, unaffected, unforced. 2. unversed, untrained, untaught, ignorant.

unsubstantial *adj.* superficial, illusory, imaginary, impalpable, tenuous, vaporous, airy, immaterial, inadequate, slight.

unsubstantiated *adj.* unproven, unconfirmed, uncorroborated, questionable, unsupported, unestablished, unverified, debatable, dubious, unattested.

unsung *adj.* unacknowledged, overlooked, disregarded, forgotten, neglected, slighted, unknown, unnamed, anonymous, unrecognized; *ant.* famous, well-known, esteemed, celebrated.

unsure *adj.* skeptical, suspicious, unconvinced, mistrustful; hesitant, undecided, uncertain, tentative; *ant.* assured, resolute.

unsurpassed *adj.* exceptional, incomparable, matchless, unparalleled, unrivaled, unequaled, supreme, consummate, sublime, transcendent, peerless, paramount, nonpareil.

unsuspecting *adj.* unwitting, unsuspicious, innocent, trusting, naive, gullible; *ant.* knowing.

unswerving *adj.* constant, dedicated, immovable, single-minded, staunch, steady, steadfast, true, sure, firm, unflagging, devoted; *ant.* irresolute.

unsympathetic *adj.* antipathetic, uncompassionate, inhuman, soulless, unfeeling, unmoved, heartless, apathetic, insensitive.

untamed *adj.* wild, savage, unbroken, feral, fierce; *ant.* domesticated.

untangle *v.* **1.** undo, unsnarl, disentangle, unravel, extricate. **2.** resolve, explain, solve, clear up; *ant.* complicate.

untarnished *adj.* impeccable, immaculate, pure, pristine, unsullied, stainless, clean, bright, shining, spotless.

untaught *adj.* **1.** ignorant, uneducated, inexperienced, unread, untutored, unlearned. **2.** natural, spontaneous, artless, simple, instinctive.

unthinkable *adj.* preposterous, unheard-of, impossible, absurd, unimaginable, inconceivable, unbelievable, unreasonable.

unthinking *adj.* **1.** inadvertent, automatic, impulsive, instinctive; *ant.* conscious, deliberate. **2.** inconsiderate, insensitive, thoughtless, tactless, undiplomatic, indiscreet.

untimely *adj.* inconvenient, inopportune, premature, unseasonable, inappropriate, ill-timed, inauspicious, malapropos, mistimed.

untiring *adj.* devoted, dedicated, dogged, indefatigable, persistent, persevering, unremitting, tenacious, steady; *ant.* inconstant, capricious.

untold *adj.* countless, inexhaustible, innumerable, boundless, unnumbered, incalculable, infinite, myriad; unimaginable, unthinkable, inexpressible.

untouched *adj.* **1.** safe, intact, undamaged, unharmed, unhurt, unaffected, unaltered; virgin, immaculate. **2.** unconcerned, unmoved, unimpressed, indifferent.

untoward *adj.* **1.** annoying, irritating, disturbing, inimical, vexatious, troublesome, worrying. **2.** unyielding, obstinate, perverse, unpliable, refractory.

untried *adj.* new, novel, experimental, exploratory, innovative; *ant.* proven, tested.

untroubled *adj.* peaceful, placid, serene, tranquil, undisturbed, impassive, unconcerned, composed, cool; *ant.* anxious.

untrue *adj.* wrong, false, incorrect, mistaken, dishonest, lying, disloyal, traitorous, deceitful, unfaithful, two-faced, perfidious, mendacious.

untrustworthy *adj.* unreliable, undependable, dishonest, deceitful, dubious, devious, duplicitous, shady, disloyal, false, fly-by-night, fair-weather.

untruth *n.* lie, falsehood, fabrication, perjury, falsification, deceit, fib, fiction, prevarication, mendacity.

untruthful *adj.* deceitful, false, deceptive, lying, dishonest, crooked, dissembling, fraudulent, untrustworthy, mendacious; *ant.* veracious, sincere.

untutored *adj.* untaught, unschooled, inexperienced, ignorant, illiterate, inexpert, artless; *ant.* educated, trained.

unused *adj.* **1.** remaining, leftover, extra, available. **2.** idle, unemployed, unutilized, fallow. **3.** intact, new, fresh, brand-new.

unusual *adj.* phenomenal, extraordinary, remarkable, singular, strange, different, eccentric, peculiar, rare, uncommon, bizarre, abnormal, odd, atypical, unconventional; *ant.* ordinary.

unusually *adv.* strangely, oddly, peculiarly, curiously, especially.

unutterable *adj.* unspeakable, incredible, remarkable, impossible, unbelievable, indescribable, unimaginable, overwhelming, extreme, ineffable.

unvarnished *adj.* plain, simple, unadorned, bare, candid, frank, honest, straightforward, naked; *ant.* disguised, embellished.

unwarranted *adj.* unjustified, groundless, unprovoked, uncalled-for, unreasonable, inexcusable, indefensible.

unwavering *adj.* unshakable, tenacious, unflagging, dedicated, determined, undeviating, unswerving, resolute, single-minded, unfaltering, staunch, steadfast; *ant.* fickle, wavering.

unwelcome *adj.* unwanted, excluded, rejected, uninvited, unacceptable, undesirable, unpopular, upsetting; *ant.* appreciated.

unwell *adj.* ill, ailing, sick, under the weather, unhealthy, indisposed, diseased.

unwieldy *adj.* awkward, cumbersome, clumsy, bulky, inconvenient, ungainly, weighty, hefty, unhandy, burdensome, ponderous, gangling; *ant.* manageable.

unwilling *adj.* opposed, resistant, disinclined, averse, reluctant, loath, grudging, indisposed, refractory; *ant.* consenting, agreeable, disposed.

unwind *v.* **1.** undo, separate, uncoil, unravel, free, loosen, loose, disentangle, slacken. **2.** relax, calm down, quiet down, rest, let down one's hair.

unwitting *adj.* unknowing, inadvertent, involuntary, unintentional, accidental, innocent, unplanned, unsuspecting, unthinking, unaware, ignorant; *ant.* conscious, deliberate.

unwonted *adj.* unexpected, unfamiliar, atypical, extraordinary, uncommon, strange, exceptional, unheard-of, uncustomary, rare, singular, unaccustomed; *ant.* usual, habitual, normal.

unworldly *adj.* extraterrestrial, otherworldly, metaphysical, surreal, surrealistic, spiritual, unearthly, visionary, celestial, ethereal, transcendental; *ant.* temporal, fleshly.

unworthy *adj.* undeserving, ignoble, dishonorable, unsuitable, ineligible; *ant.* commendable, meritorious.

up *adj.* expired, lapsed, elapsed, done.

up against it (*slang*) in trouble, badly off, suffering.

up and around improving, getting better, recuperating.

up in the air undecided, uncertain, indecisive, irresolute, hanging fire.

up to one's eyes overwhelmed, inundated, busy, up to one's ears.

up *adv.* upward, skyward, uphill, perpendicularly.

up-and-coming *adj.* promising, ambitious, enterprising, eager, assertive.

upbeat *adj.* optimistic, hopeful, positive, cheerful, encouraging, promising, heartening, cheery, rosy; *ant.* downbeat, gloomy.

upbraid *v.* admonish, lecture, castigate, reproach, call on the carpet, reprove, scold, criticize, berate, vituperate, reprimand, chide, rebuke; *ant.* commend, praise.

upbringing *n.* rearing, raising, parenting, bringing-up, childhood, training, instruction, education, nurture, care, breeding, background.

upcoming *adj.* forthcoming, expected, imminent, future.

update *v.* modernize, refresh, renovate, revise, revamp, amend, renew.

upgrade *n.* incline, rise, ascent, slope, grade.

upgrade *v.* improve, enhance, make better, advance.

upgrading *n.* improvement, betterment, advancement, promotion, elevation, enhancement, amelioration.

upheaval *n.* outbreak, outburst, eruption, revolution, chaos, cataclysm, disruption, earthquake, turmoil, disorder, overthrow, shake-up.

upheld *adj.* backed, maintained, supported, confirmed, advanced.

uphill *adj.* tough, grueling, arduous, punishing, strenuous, taxing, exhausting, laborious; *ant.* downhill, easy.

uphold *v.* defend, sustain, champion, advocate, back, aid, stand by, support, endorse.

upholster *v.* pad, stuff, cushion, pillow, bolster, cover, drape, dress, accoutre, overlay.

upholstery *n.* covering, stuffing, filling, padding, cushioning, pillows.

upkeep *n.* maintenance, care, conservation, preservation, support, subsistence; overhead, outlay, expenses, operating costs.

upland *n.* hill, mountain, peak, summit, crest, elevation, ridge, altitude, hilltop, plateau, high ground, highland, barrow.

uplift *n.* improvement, enhancement, enrichment, advancement, betterment, boost, enlightenment, edification, cultivation.

upper *adj.* higher, greater, loftier; top, uppermost, topmost, elevated; superior, senior; *ant.* inferior, junior, lower.

upper class *n.* aristocracy, elite, ruling class.

upper-class *adj.* genteel, well-bred, high-class, patrician, aristocratic, blue-blooded, elite, noble, top-drawer, swanky.

upper hand *n.* edge, advantage, control, sway.

uppermost *adj.* greatest, highest, predominant, supreme, chief, dominant, leading, preeminent, topmost, first, foremost; *ant.* lowest.

uppish *adj.* self-important, affected, conceited, cocky, supercilious, bigheaded, arrogant, stuck-up, impertinent, snobbish, assuming.

upright *adj.* 1. vertical, erect, perpendicular, upended, straight, elevated, exalted, steep, upward; *ant.* flat, horizontal, prone, supine. 2. honorable, ethical, trustworthy, moral, virtuous, honest, principled, incorruptible, aboveboard, circumspect, upstanding.

uprising *n.* 1. revolt, revolution, rebellion, riot, upheaval, mutiny, insurrection, rising, insurgence. 2. slope, ascent, upgrade, incline, hill.

uproar *n.* pandemonium, commotion, tumult, riot, racket, clamor, din, furor, outcry, ruckus, rumpus, hubbub.

uproarious *adj.* riotous, hysterical, rollicking, riproaring, boisterous, clamorous, deafening, tumultuous, wild, rowdy; *ant.* sedate, quiet, sober.

uproot *v.* rip out, remove, extract, exterminate, eliminate; eradicate, destroy, extirpate.

uprooted *adj.* displaced, exiled, disoriented, adrift.

ups and downs *n.* vicissitudes, uncertainties, fortunes.

upset *n.* 1. defeat, subversion, upheaval, overthrow, reversal. 2. worry, distress, agitation, disturbance, shock.

upset *v.* 1. overturn, topple, tip over, upend, invert, capsize; *ant.* stand, erect, elevate. 2. disturb, trouble, agitate, fluster, perturb, bother, distress, grieve, disconcert, unnerve, dismay, shake, ruffle.

upset *adj.* pained, distressed, troubled, grieved, worried, disconcerted, bothered, dismayed.

upshot *n.* outcome, result, conclusion, payoff, culmination, consequence.

upside down 1. overturned, upset, topsy-turvy, upturned, inverted. 2. chaotic, jumbled, disordered, at sixes and sevens.

upstage *v.* eclipse, draw attention from, detract from, overshadow.

upstanding *adj.* upright, moral, principled, honest, ethical, incorruptible, honorable, trustworthy, stalwart.

upstart *n.* opportunist, social climber, status seeker, nouveau riche, Johnny-come-lately, parvenu, pretender, new rich.

upswing *n.* growth, boom, increase, acceleration, improvement; *ant.* downturn.

uptight (*slang*) *adj.* 1. anxious, edgy, tense, uneasy, nervous, irritated, hung up (*slang*); *ant.* relaxed, laid back (*slang*). 2. conventional, conservative, old-fashioned.

up-to-date *adj.* in vogue, fashionable, current, in (*slang*), modern, trendy, up-to-the-minute, contemporary, latest, now (*slang*), popular, stylish; *ant.* old-fashioned, outdated, out.

upturn *n.* upswing, upsurge, recovery, revival, advancement, increase, rise, boost, amelioration, improvement; *ant.* downturn, drop, setback.

upward *adj.* higher, skyward, uphill.

urban *adj.* metropolitan, city, town, municipal, civic, inner-city; *ant.* country, rural, rustic.

urbane *adj.* sophisticated, suave, debonair, mannerly, polished, cosmopolitan, civilized, refined, well-mannered, well-bred, elegant; *ant.* gauche, uncouth.

urchin *n.* waif, brat, ragamuffin, guttersnipe, youngster, gamin, child, kid.

urge *v.* impel, encourage, implore, beg, beseech, entreat, push, instigate, press, spur, prod, compel, stimulate.

urgency *n.* importance, gravity, exigency, need, seriousness, necessity, importunity.

urgent *adj.* critical, crucial, important, pressing, top-priority, imperative, exigent, cogent.

urinate *v.* go to the bathroom, excrete, make water, relieve oneself, micturate, *slang:* pee, piss, piddle, take a leak, tinkle, peepee, weewee, go to the little boy's *or* girl's room.

urine *n.* water, *slang:* pee, piddle, piss.

urn *n.* jar, pot, container, vessel.

usable *adj.* functional, operational, serviceable, practical, working, valid, available, operating, utilizable.

usage *n.* **1.** application, employment, management, regime, handling, operation, control, procedure, treatment, practice, custom, method, mode, protocol. **2.** (said of languages) locution, idiom, dialect, expression, form.

use *n.* **1.** employment, exploitation, utilization, application, practice, performance, exercise, handling, management, treatment, technique, manipulation. **2.** utility, usefulness, helpfulness, serviceability, practicality, convenience, effectiveness, expedience, merit, value, advantage.

use *v.* utilize, employ, exercise, exploit, handle, manipulate, wield; spend, expend, exhaust, waste.

use up exhaust, squander, consume, waste, spend.; *ant.* conserve.

used *adj.* **1.** employed, utilized, applied, adopted, adapted, accepted, put in service; secondhand, worn; *ant.* discarded, rejected. **2.** accustomed, habitual, customary, practiced, suited.

useful *adj.* handy, helpful, serviceable, advantageous, practical, valuable, productive, beneficial, effective, worthwhile, convenient, fruitful; *ant.* inefficient.

useless *adj.* worthless, ineffectual, of no use, unserviceable, nonfunctional, expendable; *ant.* efficient, operative.

usher *n.* escort, guide, attendant.

usher *v.* show in, show out, lead, escort, receive.

usher in introduce, launch, precede, initiate, herald, ring in.

usual *adj.* ordinary, conventional, everyday, stock, typical, standard, familiar, common, normal, regular, frequent, expected; *ant.* unheard-of.

usually *adv.* generally, ordinarily, normally, as a rule, by and large, on the whole, mostly, habitually, mainly, commonly, routinely, typically, chiefly; *ant.* rarely.

usurer *n.* extortionist, loan shark, moneylender, Shylock.

usurp *v.* annex, appropriate, commandeer, seize, steal, take over, assume, wrest, arrogate, confiscate.

utensil *n.* instrument, implement, device, apparatus, tool, gadget, gizmo, contrivance, appliance, equipment.

utilitarian *adj.* functional, serviceable, practical, useful, efficient, convenient; down-to-earth, pragmatic, unpretentious; *ant.* decorative.

utilities *n.* services, public utilities, facilities, conveniences.

utility *n.* practicality, advantageousness, use, usefulness, value, benefit, expedience, serviceableness, convenience.

utilize *v.* use, employ, appropriate.

utmost *adj.* highest, maximum, extreme, farthest, outermost, ultimate, supreme, paramount, greatest, last, final.

utopia *n.* heaven, bliss, Eden, paradise, land of milk and honey, seventh heaven, heaven on earth, Shangri-La, Garden of Eden, Elysium.

utopian *adj.* visionary, ideal, idealistic, romantic, chimerical, wishful, imaginary, fantastic, fanciful, Elysian.

utter *v.* say, state, speak, declare, express, proclaim, articulate, tell, voice, verbalize, vocalize.

utter *adj.* absolute, total, entire, out-and-out, downright, consummate, unmitigated, thorough, unqualified, arrant, perfect, sheer.

utterance *n.* remark, statement, announcement, opinion, articulation, declaration, expression, delivery, pronouncement, verbalization, vocalization.

uttered *adj.* spoken, said, pronounced, asserted, announced, affirmed, enunciated; *ant.* withheld, suppressed.

utterly *adv.* absolutely, completely, entirely, totally, wholly, extremely, fully, perfectly, thoroughly, diametrically.

uttermost *adj.* furthest, utmost, farthest.

U-turn *n.* about-face, reversal, about-turn, backtrack, turnaround.

491

vacancy *n.* opening, position, post; room, space, accommodation; emptiness, gap.

vacant *adj.* **1.** empty, void, devoid, blank, free, available; *ant.* inhabited, occupied. **2.** empty-headed, stupid, thoughtless, vacuous, inattentive, absent-minded; *ant.* intelligent, witty.

vacate *v.* abandon, quit, leave, depart, go away, evacuate, withdraw.

vacation *n.* holiday, time off, recess, sabbatical, respite, rest.

vaccinate *v.* immunize, inoculate, prevent, mitigate.

vaccination *n.* inoculation, immunization, shot, injection, hypodermic.

vacillate *v.* fluctuate, waver, hesitate, pause, dawdle, falter, tergiversate.

vacillating *adj.* inconstant, fickle, changing, irresolute, hesitating, uncertain, unresolved, wavering, capricious, volatile; *ant.* constant, steady.

vacuity *n.* **1.** emptiness, nothingness, void, nullity, vacuum. **2.** vacuousness, inanity, stupidity.

vacuous *adj.* **1.** empty, vacant, void, blank; *ant.* filled. **2.** unintelligent, stupid, shallow, mindless, uncomprehending, inane.

vacuum *n.* emptiness, nothingness, void, space, chasm.

vagabond *n.* vagrant, beggar, gypsy, bum, outcast, wanderer, wayfarer, itinerant, nomad, tramp.

vagabond *adj.* aimless, wandering, migratory, nomadic, roving, drifting, errant, transient, hobo.

vagary *n.* notion, whim, impulse, whimsy, caprice, fancy.

vagrant *n.* itinerant, tramp, wanderer, nomad, beggar.

vagrant *adj.* homeless, itinerant, traveling, wandering, nomadic, footloose, wayward, erratic.

vague *adj.* unclear, indefinite, amorphous, obscure, fuzzy, hazy, doubtful, enigmatic; *ant.* definite.

vaguely *adv.* imprecisely, faintly, slightly, obscurely.

vain *adj.* egotistical, egocentric, narcissistic, arrogant, conceited, self-important, full of oneself, haughty, proud; *ant.* modest, self-effacing.

vale *n.* glen, dale, dell, valley.

valediction *n.* sendoff, farewell, goodbye; *ant.* greeting, welcome.

valedictory *adj.* last, final, terminal, parting.

valet *n.* attendant, servant, manservant.

valiant *adj.* courageous, brave, heroic, gallant, chivalrous, dauntless, valorous, fearless, indomitable; *ant.* cowardly.

valid *adj.* sound, logical, accurate, cogent, right, convincing, compelling, genuine, authentic, legitimate, official, lawful; *ant.* fallacious.

validate *v.* sanction, confirm, legalize, authorize, authenticate, certify, corroborate, endorse.

validity *n.* strength, weight, substance, efficacy, soundness, accuracy, correctness, truth, authority, legitimacy.

valley *n.* glen, dale, dell, hollow, gulch, canyon, lowland, channel, river valley; *ant.* mountain, hilltop.

valor *n.* courage, bravery, prowess, heroism, fearlessness, gallantry, chivalry, determination, spirit; *ant.* cowardice, fear.

valorous *adj.* brave, intrepid, fearless, courageous, dauntless, heroic, stalwart, valiant, lion-hearted; *ant.* cowardly.

valuable *adj.* expensive, costly, high-priced, prized, precious, dear, cherished, invaluable, profitable; *ant.* useless.

value *n.* **1.** expense, cost, price, rate, charge, assessment, appraisal. **2.** worth, desirability, utility, usefulness, benefit, esteem, estimation, quality, advantage, importance, significance.

valued *adj.* prized, esteemed, treasured; appraised, evaluated, priced, marked.

values *n.* ethics, morals, principles, standards, mores.

valve *n.* lid, flap, plug.

vamoose (*slang*) *v.* quit, vanish, leave, *slang:* make oneself scarce, split, scram, get lost.

van *n.* truck, trailer, delivery truck, small truck, recreational vehicle, **RV**, camper.

vandal *n.* thief, despoiler, graffiti artist, hoodlum, pirate.

vandalism *n.* destruction, demolition, piracy, spoliation.

vanguard *n.* forerunners, precursors, leaders, spearhead, avant-garde, cutting edge, forefront.

vanish *v.* dissolve, disappear, fade out, go away; *ant.* materialize.

vanity *n.* conceit, narcissism, self-love, egotism, pride, egocentricity, ostentation, show, pretension, smugness, foppishness; *ant.* modesty.

vanquish *v.* defeat, conquer, beat, master, overcome, overpower, overwhelm, subdue, subjugate, quell, humble.

vapid *adj.* flat, bland, insipid, boring, dull, colorless, limp, stale, trite, tasteless, dead, uninteresting.

vapor *n.* steam, mist, condensation, breath, fog, exhalation, gas, haze, smoke, smog.

vaporous *adj.* foggy, hazy, misty, wispy, fleeting, unsubstantial, fanciful.

vapors *n.* despair, blues, melancholy, depression.

variable *adj.* fickle, mutable, inconstant, unsteady, fitful, shifting, fluctuating, vacillating, volatile, labile.

variance *n.* inconsistency, divergence, deviation, change, difference, modification, incongruity, oscillation; *ant.* agreement, sameness, unity.

variant *n.* alternative, exception, variation, development, deviant, modification.

variant *adj.* exceptional, varying, differing, irregular, divergent; *ant.* normal, standard, usual.

variation *n.* change, modification, deviation, aberration, alteration, elaboration, digression, volatility, lability; *ant.* uniformity, stability, monotony.

varied *adj.* diverse, different, variegated, miscellaneous, mixed, various, separate; *ant.* similar, uniform.

variegated *adj.* various, diverse, diversified, kaleidoscopic, mottled, multicolored; *ant.* plain, monochrome.

variety *n.* type, kind, sort, class, genre, assortment, array, range, diversity, miscellany.

various *adj.* miscellaneous, diverse, assorted, different, heterogeneous, differing; *ant.* alike, identical.

varnish *n.* coating, lacquer, shellac, glaze, polish, gloss.

varnish *v.* paint, shellac, lacquer, finish, wax, surface, coat, enamel, glaze, gloss over.

vary *v.* change, alter, modify, differ, disagree, fluctuate.

vase *n.* container, jar, urn, vessel, pitcher, jug, receptacle.

vassal *n.* servant, serf, liege, subject.

vassalage *n.* subjugation, subjection, servitude, slavery, bondage, dependence.

vast *adj.* large, enormous, huge, expansive, extensive, ample, widespread, comprehensive; infinite, boundless, eternal; *ant.* limited, narrow, confined.

vastness *n.* expanse, extent, enormity, hugeness, greatness, reach.

vat *n.* tank, container, vessel, cistern, tub.

vault *n.* crypt, tomb, catacomb, mausoleum, grave, repository, strongroom, safe, safe deposit box.

vault *v.* jump, spring, leap, hurdle, bound, clear.

vaulted *adj.* arched, domed, hemispheric, peaked.

veer *v.* swerve, curve, turn, bend, shift, tack, deviate, deflect, avert.

vegetable *n.* plant, herb, edible root, greens.

vegetable *adj.* floral, growing, flourishing, blooming, plantlike, herblike.

vegetate *v.* **1.** sprout, germinate, go to seed, bud, blossom, bloom, grow. **2.** degenerate, deteriorate, decay, stagnate, languish, idle, hibernate.

vegetation *n.* plants, trees, shrubs, grasses, flowers, herbs, weeds, crops, pasturage, vegetables.

vegetative *adj.* inert, stationary, inactive, unthinking, lowly, passive, monotonous, dull; comatose, unconscious.

vehemence *n.* intensity, frenzy, passion, fervor, eagerness, enthusiasm, impetuosity, force, fire, urgency; *ant.* indifference.

vehement *adj.* emphatic, impassioned, passionate, heated, intense, powerful, forceful, urgent, zealous, strong, violent; *ant.* apathetic, indifferent.

vehicle *n.* means, mechanism, channel, medium, apparatus, conveyance.

veil *n.* curtain, gauze, shade, screen, film, mist, cover, mask, blur, obscurity.

veil *v.* cover, conceal, cloak, hide, mask, disguise, obscure, camouflage, shade, shield.

vein *n.* **1.** lode, streak, course, current, thread, strain, hint; trait, style. **2.** channel, cleft, cavity.

veined *adj.* streaked, marbled, variegated, mottled.

velocity *n.* speed, quickness, rapidity, pace, rate, swiftness, momentum.

velvet *adj.* silken, shiny, plushy, fine-textured, soft.

venal *adj.* mercenary, corrupt, greedy, bribable, dishonorable, dishonest, crooked, on the table (*slang*); *ant.* incorruptible.

vend *v.* sell, trade, auction, peddle.

vendetta *n.* feud, quarrel, squabble, dispute, fight, grudge, bad blood, bitterness, rivalry.

vendor *n.* peddler, salesperson, salesman, saleswoman, huckster, merchant, businessperson, supplier.

veneer *n.* appearance, façade, front, mask, pretense, coating, surface, layer, covering, exterior.

venerable *adj.* revered, respected, esteemed, dignified, wise, sage, honored, august; ancient, aged.

venerate *v.* honor, respect, esteem, revere, worship, adore; *ant.* disregard.

vengeance *n.* revenge, retaliation, retribution, return, an eye for an eye, tit for tat.

vengeful *adj.* vindictive, spiteful, rancorous, punitive, revengeful, relentless; *ant.* forgiving.

venial *adj.* minor, insignificant, negligible, slight, trivial, mild, forgivable, pardonable, allowable, justifiable; *ant.* mortal, deadly, serious.

venom *n.* poison, toxin; acrimony, bitterness, spite, hatred, spleen, anger, malice, malevolence, ill will, vindictiveness.

venomous *adj.* envenomed, poisonous, toxic, noxious; hostile, malicious, vicious, savage, spiteful, vindictive, hurtful.

vent *n.* chimney, duct, passage, outlet, hole, aperture, opening, flue, drain.

vent *v.* release, emit, discharge, express, voice.

ventilate *v.* **1.** air out, freshen, cool, free, oxygenate. **2.** (open for discussion) air, open up, put on the table, discuss, debate, express, examine; *ant.* suppress.

venture *n.* enterprise, operation, project, adventure, chance, hazard, risk.

venture *v.* risk, wager, dare, undertake, attempt, try, experiment, invest, speculate, chance, gamble, hazard.

veracious *adj.* honest, truthful, truth-telling, trustworthy, reliable, accurate, credible, dependable, frank, genuine; *ant.* mendacious.

veracity *n.* truth, trustworthiness, honesty, integrity, credibility, verity, accuracy, frankness, exactitude; *ant.* dishonesty, error.

veranda *n.* porch, piazza, portico, gallery, terrace.

verbal *adj.* oral, spoken, told, word-of-mouth, verbatim, rhetorical, lexical.

verbatim *adv.* word for word, exactly, precisely, to the letter, literally.

verbiage *n.* verbosity, repetition, loquacity, periphrasis, circumlocution; *ant.* succinctness, economy.

verbose *adj.* wordy, redundant, tedious, diffuse, bombastic, prolix, long-winded, garrulous, talkative, windy, full of hot air (*slang*); *ant.* terse, precise, succinct.

verdant *adj.* green, grassy, leafy, flourishing, fresh, lush.

verdict *n.* decision, finding, judgment, sentence, opinion, adjudication, assessment, conclusion.

verdure *n.* vegetation, foliage, greenery, grass, flora, herbage.

verge *n.* brink, boundary, edge, extreme, limit, threshold.

verge *v.* approach, touch, border on, near, come close to.

verifiable *adj.* provable, testable, valid, correct.

verification *n.* proof, confirmation, affirmation, corroboration, authentication, validation, attestation, substantiation.

verify *v.* establish, prove, substantiate, attest, corroborate, support, confirm.

verily *adj.* certainly, undoubtedly, unquestionably, surely, in fact.

verisimilitude *n.* believability, likelihood, plausibility, appearance, resemblance, authenticity.

veritable *adj.* true, real, authentic, genuine.

vermilion *adj.* red, chrome-red, cinnabar.

vernacular *n.* speech, dialect, idiom, tongue, parlance.

vernacular *adj.* informal, colloquial, common, popular, local.

versatile *adj.* flexible, adaptable, dexterous, adjustable, multifaceted, many-sided, handy, resourceful, talented.

verse *n.* poetry, stanza, rhyme, lyric, ode, jingle, iambs, canto, doggerel, poesy.

versed *adj.* knowledgeable, learned, acquainted, familiar, proficient, tutored, educated, practiced, qualified, skilled, accomplished; *ant.* ignorant.

version *n.* rendition, translation, interpretation, reading, adaptation, account, report, tale.

vertebrae *n.* spinal column, spine, backbone.

vertex *n.* top, crown, zenith, peak, apex, pinnacle, summit, culmination, apogee; *ant.* nadir, bottom.

vertical *adj.* perpendicular, upright, erect, plumb, on end; *ant.* horizontal.

vertigo *n.* dizziness, lightheadedness, faintness, giddiness.

verve *n.* energy, vigor, strength, liveliness, enthusiasm, zeal, zest, zip, drive, gusto.

very *adj.* simple, sheer, mere, unqualified, utter, precise, plain, exact, same, appropriate.

very *adv.* extremely, excessively, exceedingly, greatly, terribly, truly, really, absolutely, particularly, unusually.

vessel *n.* 1. container, urn, pitcher, canister, receptacle, jar. 2. ship, craft, boat. 3. vein, artery, capillary; canal, duct.

vestibule *n.* lobby, foyer, entryway, anteroom, antechamber, entrance, hall.

vestige *n.* trace, sign, hint, remains, residue, evidence, track, clue, remainder, telltale.

vestigial *adj.* undeveloped, rudimentary, incomplete, imperfect.

veteran *n.* expert, master, professional, pro, old hand, trooper.

veteran *adj.* experienced, seasoned, versed, skilled, weathered, accomplished.

veto *n.* denial, refusal, interdiction, prohibition, ban, rejection, demurral, declination; *ant.* acceptance.

veto *v.* reject, ban, forbid, prohibit, refuse, deny, decline, demur, stop, kill.

vex *v.* trouble, bother, aggravate, agitate, annoy, disturb, beset, irritate, distress, provoke, plague, worry; *ant.* soothe.

vexation *n.* irritation, annoyance, bother, displeasure, anger, exasperation, frustration, problem, trouble, worry, distress.

vexatious *adj.* bothersome, irritating, annoying, infuriating, upsetting, worrisome, distressing, disturbing, provoking.

viable *adj.* possible, feasible, workable, achievable, operable, practicable, doable, achievable; *ant.* impossible, unworkable.

vibes (*slang*) *n.* feelings, atmosphere, aura, emanation.

bad vibes (*slang*) discord, foreboding, rejection, disharmony, antipathy, misunderstanding.

good vibes (*slang*) acceptance, accord, comfort, concordance, seeing eye to eye, appreciation, sympathy, understanding, harmony, the same wave length.

vibrant *adj.* bright, spirited, vivacious; colorful, vivid, electrifying.

vibrate *v.* pulsate, resonate, reverberate, throb, undulate, oscillate.

vibration *n.* pulsation, shaking, tremor, oscillation, tremulousness.

vicarious *adj.* surrogate, substituted, standby, empathetic, acting, manqué.

vice *n.* sin, evil, defect, depravity, failing, fault, weakness, wickedness; *ant.* virtue.

vicinity *n.* area, district, environs, precinct, neighborhood, proximity, community.

vicious *adj.* 1. wild, untamed, unruly, feral, bestial. 2. corrupt, brutal, fiendish, malicious, heinous, bad, debased, cruel, bloodthirsty.

viciousness *n.* cruelty, brutality, corruption, depravity, malice, rancor, venom, wickedness, violence, savagery; *ant.* gentleness, goodness, virtue.

vicissitudes *n.* alteration, change, deviations, diversion, fluctuations, shift, turn of events, twists, fortunes, ups and downs.

victim *n.* casualty, fatality, sufferer, dupe, *slang:* patsy, sitting duck, sucker.

victimize *v.* exploit, oppress, persecute, cheat, deceive, discriminate against, dupe, prey on, swindle, pick on.

victor *n.* champion, conqueror, subjugator, winner, vanquisher, champ, top dog (*slang*); *ant.* loser, vanquished.

victorious *adj.* triumphant, champion, conquering, first, successful, winning; *ant.* losing, unsuccessful.

victory *n.* triumph, success, conquest, laurels, mastery, prize, subjugation, vanquishment, win; *ant.* defeat, loss.

victuals *n.* food, edibles, provisions, rations, sustenance, *slang:* nosh, eats, grub.

vie *v.* compete, rival, fight, contend, contest, struggle, strive.

view *n.* **1.** see, sight, espy, glimpse, peek, glance, look. **2.** show, picture, tableau, spectacle; landscape, diorama, panorama, scene; prospect, distance, stretch. **on view** displayed, on display, on exhibit, exposed, shown.

view *v.* behold, see, look, observe, survey, inspect, take in.

viewer *n.* observer, spectator, watcher, onlooker.

viewpoint *n.* opinion, perspective, position, point of view, angle, standpoint, slant, bias.

vigil *n.* lookout, sentry duty, wakefulness, watchfulness, watch, sleeplessness.

vigilant *adj.* careful, cautious, attentive, wakeful, watchful, diligent, on the alert; *ant.* forgetful, lax, negligent.

vignette *n.* scenario, scene, sketch, novelette.

vigor *n.* **1.** (forcefulness of action) force, intensity, lustiness, vim, strength, determination, drive, vehemence; *ant.* weakness, impotence, slothfulness. **2.** (healthy energy) health, energy, hardiness, stamina, endurance, vitality, gusto, robustness; *ant.* feebleness, decrepitude.

vigorous *adj.* energetic, brisk, lively, robust,

active, flourishing, hardy, healthy, hearty, lusty, spirited, virile, strong; *ant.* feeble, lethargic, weak.

vile *adj.* repulsive, contemptible, despicable, loathsome, horrid, offensive, revolting, sickening, vulgar, wretched, depraved, foul.

vilification *n.* defamation, aspersion, denigration, disparagement, criticism, mudslinging, slander.

vilify *v.* defame, asperse, malign, slander, berate, criticize, denigrate, denounce, disparage, stigmatize, smear, bad-mouth (*slang*); *ant.* compliment, glorify, eulogize, adore.

village *n.* hamlet, township, settlement, community.

villain *n.* evildoer, miscreant, criminal, rascal, heavy, scoundrel, reprobate, rogue, wretch.

villainous *adj.* diabolical, vicious, fiendish, cruel, depraved, heinous, vile, mean, wicked; *ant.* heroic, angelic, good.

vindicate *v.* **1.** clear, acquit, free, absolve, exculpate. **2.** defend, plead for, second, excuse.

vindication *n.* exoneration, apology, plea, assertion, defense, alibi, justification; *ant.* accusation, conviction.

vindictive *adj.* malicious, spiteful, vengeful, malevolent, resentful, retributive, unforgiving; *ant.* charitable, forgiving, merciful.

vintage *n.* collection, harvest, crop, origin, year, era, epoch, generation, period.

vintage *adj.* prime, classic, choice, venerable, select, quintessential, mature, fine, rare, superior.

violate *v.* **1.** assault, defile, infringe, rape, desecrate, ravish, transgress, dishonor, invade, pollute. **2.** (go against a law, convention, etc.) break, disobey, defy, flout, disregard, thumb one's nose at; *ant.* uphold, observe.

violation *n.* **1.** transgression, infringement, infraction, negligence, trespass, breach. **2.** rape, ravishment, defilement, assault, degradation, invasion.

violence *n.* brutality, conflict, destructiveness, bloodshed, ferocity, fighting, frenzy, hostilities, savagery, terrorism, turbulence, wildness; *ant.* passivity, peacefulness.

violent *adj.* brutal, cruel, destructive, vicious, abusive, tempestuous, maniacal, rag-

violet *adj.* lavender, mauve, purple, purplish.

VIP *n.* very important person, luminary, *slang*: big shot, big cheese, honcho, high muck-a-muck, celebrity, dignitary; *ant.* nonentity, nobody.

virgin *n.* celibate, vestal, maiden, bachelor.

virgin *adj.* chaste, pure, undefiled, fresh, intact, untouched.

virginity *n.* chastity, virtue, maidenhead, purity.

virile *adj.* masculine, manly, potent, strong, rugged, lusty, forceful, macho; *ant.* effeminate, impotent.

virility *n.* masculinity, potency, vigor, machismo; *ant.* effeminacy, impotence, weakness.

virtual *adj.* essential, implicit, practical, effective, usable, workable.

virtually *adv.* in effect, in essence, practically, nearly, to all intents and purposes, as good as.

virtue *n.* honor, integrity, attribute, excellence, goodness, morality, purity, worthiness.

by virtue of because of, on the grounds of.

virtuosity *n.* expertise, mastery, panache, skill, finesse.

virtuoso *n.* maestro, artist, genius, master.

virtuous *adj.* righteous, saintly, just, upright, honorable, responsible, ethical, moral, scrupulous.

virulent *adj.* **1.** (said of a disease) acute, robust, strong, severe, quick-acting, overwhelming, violent; deadly, lethal. **2.** (said of criticism) venomous, acrimonious, bitter, hostile, malicious, poisonous, vicious, vindictive.

virus *n.* **1.** germ, microorganism, bug. **2.** sickness, illness, infection.

viscera *n.* bowels, intestines, entrails, innards, guts, vitals.

viscous *adj.* sticky, glutinous, adhesive, gluey, gummy, mucous, tacky; *ant.* runny, thin, watery.

visible *adj.* observable, noticeable, discernible, perceptible, detectable, conspicuous, distinguishable, evident, clear, apparent, obvious.

vision *n.* **1.** sight, perception, eyesight, range of view. **2.** foresight, understanding, wisdom, prescience, farsightedness, astuteness, insight,
discernment, imagination. **3.** revelation, fantasy, apparition, mirage, hallucination, illusion.

visionary *n.* prophet, seer, mystic, theorist, dreamer, idealist, enthusiast; *ant.* pragmatist.

visionary *adj.* fanciful, fantastic, romantic, dreamy, idealized, idealistic, utopian, prophetic, quixotic.

visit *n.* stay, stop, sojourn, excursion, stopover, layover.

visit *v.* stay, stop by, be the guest of, call on *or* upon, drop in on.

visitation *n.* affliction, calamity, misfortune, adversity, trouble.

visitor *n.* guest, company, caller, tourist.

vista *n.* panorama, view, perspective, prospect.

visual *adj.* visible, optical, observable, discernible.

visualize *v.* picture, envisage, conceive, imagine, call up, see.

vital *adj.* **1.** necessary, needed, essential, requisite, indispensable, exigent. **2.** alive, live, animate.

vitality *n.* energy, exuberance, vivacity, liveliness, vim, drive, lustiness, pep, robustness, vigor, oomph (*slang*).

vitalize *v.* energize, strengthen, invigorate, reanimate; *ant.* debilitate, enervate.

vitals *n.* organs, intestines, entrails.

vitiate *v.* contaminate, spoil, invalidate, blemish, corrupt, pollute, impair, mar, taint.

vitriolic *adj.* caustic, acerbic, scathing, biting, sardonic, envenomed, malicious, venomous, virulent, withering, acid.

vituperate *v.* abuse, reproach, upbraid, denounce, berate, excoriate, vilify, malign; *ant.* praise, eulogize, extol, applaud.

vivacious *adj.* lively, spirited, animated, effervescent, bubbly, scintillating, frisky, gay, high-spirited; *ant.* languid, listless.

vivid *adj.* bright, clear, colorful, vibrant, animated; distinct, dramatic, expressive, flamboyant, memorable, sharp, striking; *ant.* dull, lifeless.

vividly *adv.* **1.** clearly, distinctly, strongly, sharply. **2.** brightly, glowingly, strikingly, brilliantly.

vixen *n.* shrew, spitfire, harpy, hellcat, bitch, fury.

vocabulary *n.* language, words, lexicon, nomenclature, terminology; idiom; dictionary, glossary, thesaurus.

vocal *adj.* oral, spoken, voiced; articulate, eloquent, expressive, frank, outspoken, freespoken; *ant.* inarticulate, quiet.

vocation *n.* career, employment, profession, job, work, calling, position, business, niche, office, post, role.

vociferous *adj.* clamorous, noisy, uproarious, ranting, loud, boisterous, loud-mouthed, shouting, shrill, thundering, vehement, vocal; *ant.* quiet, silent.

vogue *n.* fashion, style, trend, fad.

voice *n.* **1.** speech, articulation, vocalization, tone, intonation, expression, inflection. **2.** representative, spokesperson, spokesman, spokeswoman, agent, press agent, mouthpiece (*slang*). **3.** vote, say, say-so, choice, consideration, franchise; approval, sanction.

with one voice unanimously, consensually, all together.

voice *v.* assert, declare, say, disclose, divulge, express, exclaim, state, announce, intone.

void *n.* vacuum, chasm, cavity, emptiness, opening, gap.

void *adj.* **1.** emptied, vacant, bare, drained, dead, blank; *ant.* full. **2.** rescinded, canceled, invalid, ineffective; *ant.* valid.

void *v.* **1.** cancel, nullify, invalidate, annul, rescind. **2.** empty, evacuate, defecate, eject, discharge.

volatile *adj.* erratic, unstable, explosive, mercurial, changeable, temperamental, volcanic, hotheaded, hot-tempered; *ant.* constant, steady, even-tempered.

volition *n.* choice, will, resolution, determination, purpose.

volley *n.* barrage, bombardment, fusillade, explosion, blast.

voluble *adj.* glib, articulate, fluent, talkative, garrulous, long-winded, loquacious, gabby (*slang*).

volume *n.* **1.** quantity, amount, bulk, capacity, mass, body. **2.** book, publication, tome, edition. **3.** (of sound) loudness, amplitude, intensity.

voluminous *adj.* ample, copious, prolific,

abounding, billowing, commodious, full, large, massive, vast; *ant.* slight, scanty.

voluntarily *adv.* of one's own accord, of one's own free will, by choice, intentionally, freely, willingly, consciously, on one's own initiative; *ant.* unwillingly.

voluntary *adj.* conscious, deliberate, willing, free, unforced, optional, volitional, unpaid, pro bono; *ant.* compulsory, unwilling.

volunteer *v.* come forward, sign up, enlist, offer oneself.

voluptuary *n.* hedonist, sensualist, bon vivant, debauchee, epicurean, pleasure-seeker; *ant.* ascetic.

voluptuous *adj.* sensual, hedonistic, pleasure-loving, erotic, seductive, luxurious; ample, buxom, curvaceous; *ant.* ascetic.

voracious *adj.* ravenous, insatiable, greedy, devouring, gluttonous, unquenchable.

voracity *n.* greed, ravenousness, hunger, acquisitiveness, predatoriness.

vortex *n.* whirl, whirlpool, whirlwind, maelstrom, eddy.

votary *n.* devotee, aficionado, follower, disciple, fan.

vote *n.* **1.** decision, election, balloting, will, wish, referendum, plebiscite, choice. **2.** (the right to vote) suffrage, franchise, enfranchisement.

vote *v.* enact, establish, grant, confer; ratify.

vote down decide against, kill, defeat.

vote in elect, put in office, choose.

vote out reject, turn out *or* remove from office, defeat.

votive *adj.* pledged, committed, dedicated.

vouch *v.* verify, affirm, attest, confirm, assert, testify, endorse.

voucher *n.* confirmation, declaration, certification, affirmation.

vouchsafe *v.* bestow, grant, confer, deign, impart.

vow *n.* oath, pledge, promise, troth.

vow *v.* swear, affirm, pledge, promise, devote, maintain.

voyage *n.* journey, expedition, trip, travels, cruise, passage.

vulgar *adj.* **1.** (said of manners or behavior) crude, unrefined, gross, impolite, uncivil, base, mean, uncouth, low, coarse, rude; *ant.* polished, refined. **2.** pornographic, salacious, licentious, suggestive, provocative, indecent, immoral, earthy. **3.** (applied to things) tacky, gaudy, flashy, cheap, tawdry. **4.** common, ordinary, vernacular, popular.

vulnerable *adj.* defenseless, exposed, accessible, susceptible, unprotected, weak, sensitive; *ant.* strong.

wacky (*slang*) *adj.* crazy, daft, *slang;* loony, goofy, nutty; wild, zany, screwy, silly; *ant.* sensible.

wad *n.* hunk, chunk, bundle, mass.

waddle *v.* wobble, shuffle, totter, rock, sway, strut.

waffle *v.* hedge, evade, equivocate, hem and haw, sidestep, tergiversate, sit on the fence.

waft *v.* drift, float, sail, fly, glide, breeze, carry.

wag *v.* shake, nod, bob, waggle, rock, wave.

wage *n.* earnings, salary, allowance, fee, payment, compensation, recompense, stipend.

wage *v.* engage in, carry on, conduct, undertake, practice, pursue.

wager *n.* bet, venture, gamble, speculate, stake, hazard.

waggish *adj.* jesting, jocular, comical, frolicsome, funny, mischievous, humorous, playful, bantering, impish, puckish.

wagon *n.* cart, buggy, carriage, truck, van.

waif *n.* orphan, foundling, stray, street urchin.

wail *v.* cry, howl, yowl, caterwaul, lament, moan.

wail *v.* howl, yowl, cry, weep, grieve, lament, moan.

wait *n.* interval, delay, halt, hiatus, pause, rest, stay, holdup, hesitation.

wait *v.* **1.** expect, anticipate, watch for. **2.** pause, delay, stay, linger, tarry, bide one's time, cool one's heels; *ant.* leave, hurry.

wait on attend, serve, help.

waiter *n.* server, waitress, headwaiter, counterman, garçon, host.

waitress *n.* server, waiter, headwaitress, counter girl, hostess.

waive *v.* defer, relinquish, forgo, give up, do without, resign, renounce, surrender.

wake *n.* **1.** track, waves, aftermath, trail, wash, backwash. **2.** funeral, vigil, death watch.

wake *v.* **1.** arise, get up, rouse, stir; *ant.* sleep. **2.** stimulate, provoke, enliven, galvanize.

wake up arise, awaken, rise and shine, get up.

wakeful *adj.* attentive, watchful, unblinking, vigilant, wary, alert; sleepless, restless; *ant.* inattentive; sleepy.

walk *n.* **1.** stride, gait, tread, pace, step, saunter. **2.** path, trail, sidewalk, pavement, pathway, footpath, track, promenade, street. **3.** stroll, ramble, hike, trek.

walk *v.* go on foot, stride, amble, stroll, trek, traipse, saunter, tread, hike, perambulate, promenade, tramp, trudge, hoof it (*slang*).

walk out on abandon, desert, leave, walk away from, forsake.

walk off with steal, take, appropriate, purloin, filch, abscond with.

walkover (*slang*) *n.* (easy win) conquest, triumph, victory, pushover (*slang*).

walker *n.* pedestrian, hiker, wayfarer, backpacker, rambler, footslogger (*slang*).

walking *adj.* strolling, sauntering, hiking, ambling, treking, trudging, sauntering, tramping, touring, promenading, roaming, wandering, wayfaring.

walking papers (*slang*) dismissal, discharge, pink slip.

walkway *n.* path, lane, sidewalk, footpath, promenade, esplanade.

wall *n.* divider, enclosure, partition, barricade, barrier, obstacle, obstruction.

wall up enclose, close up, wall in *or* out, surround.

wallet *n.* billfold, purse, pocketbook, pouch.

wallop *v.* hit, punch, pound, strike, beat, slug, pummel, lambaste, trounce, swipe, smack.

wallow *v.* bask, revel, relish, luxuriate, indulge, glory.

wan *adj.* sickly, pale, drawn, colorless, ashen, waxen, pasty, anemic, cadaverous, faint, weak.

wand *n.* staff, stick, baton, scepter, rod.

wander *v.* **1.** stroll, ramble, roam, hike, walk, saunter. **2.** digress, ramble, stray, shift.

wanderer *n.* drifter, nomad, vagabond, rambler, gypsy, itinerant, wayfarer, traveler.

wandering *adj.* aberrant, drifting, rambling, meandering, rootless, roving, homeless, wayfaring, itinerant, nomadic, traveling.

wane *v.* fade, ebb, abate, dim, dwindle, subside, diminish, taper off, weaken.

wangle *v.* manipulate, contrive, scheme, maneuver, finagle, engineer, pull off.

want *v.* **1.** desire, crave, long for, lust for, have an urge for, aspire, covet, thirst *or* hunger after, incline toward, fancy, hanker, have a yen *or* an itch for. **2.** lack, need, require, be deficient in, be deprived of.

wanted *adj.* needed, necessary, desired, sought after, in demand, requested, asked for; *ant.* satisfied, fulfilled.

wanting *adj.* inadequate, insufficient, lacking, deficient, incomplete, substandard, inferior, unsatisfactory; *ant.* adequate, sufficient.

wanton *adj.* unrestrained, abandoned, reckless, unreserved, capricious, extravagant, free, unfettered, frivolous, licentious, libertine.

war *n.* battle, combat, hostilities, fighting, action.

war *v.* fight, battle, wage *or* make war, combat, attack, bombard.

warble *v.* sing, trill, yodel.

ward *n.* **1.** division, district, territory, precinct, diocese, neighborhood, parish. **2.** dependent, juvenile charge, foster child, orphan, godchild, adopted child.

ward off repel, deflect, fend off, evade, stave off, avert, block, thwart, turn aside, turn away *or* back.

warden *n.* guardian, keeper, caretaker, curator, administrator, custodian, superintendent.

wardrobe *n.* **1.** apparel, clothes, outfit. **2.** closet, clothespress, armoire, cabinet.

warehouse *n.* storehouse, depository, depot, entrepôt, stockroom.

wares *n.* merchandise, products, stock, commodities, goods, vendibles.

warfare *n.* military operations, combat, battle, hostilities, fighting, struggle, discord, arms.

warily *adv.* guardedly, carefully, cautiously, apprehensively, hesitantly, watchfully, distrustfully, gingerly; *ant.* recklessly, heedlessly, thoughtlessly.

warlike *adj.* combative, bellicose, pugnacious, martial, military, antagonistic, bloodthirsty, inimical, jingoistic, aggressive, belligerent, saber-rattling.

warlock *n.* sorcerer, witch, wizard, conjurer, enchanter, magician.

warm *v.* **1.** heat, heat up, reheat; *ant.* cool. **2.** arouse, stimulate, agitate, excite, inflame.

warm *adj.* **1.** heated, lukewarm, mild, tepid, temperate, clement. **2.** (marked by growing excitement *or* anger) glowing, perspiring, flushed, ardent, hot, passionate, excited; angry, inflamed, hot under the collar; *ant.* cool, chilly. **2.** friendly, gracious, cordial, empathetic, sympathetic, outgoing.

warmblooded *adj.* passionate, emotional, fervent, ardent, hotblooded, spirited, enthusiastic.

warmhearted *adj.* kind, generous, compassionate, loving, sympathetic, tender, affectionate, genial; *ant.* cold, unsympathetic.

warmth *n.* affection, kindliness, affability, tenderness, hospitality; fervor, intensity, spirit, effusiveness, passion, enthusiasm; *ant.* coldness, unfriendliness.

warn *v.* caution, alert, put on one's guard, counsel, advise, apprise, notify, inform, tip off (*slang*).

warning *n.* notice, caution, monition, admonishment, alert, tip, tip-off, word to the wise, notification, omen, handwriting on the wall, sign, threat, premonition.

warp *n.* irregularity, kink, bend, deviation, distortion, twist, perversion.

warp *v.* deviate, distort, deform, contort, bend, kink, pervert.

warrant *n.* **1.** permit, authorization, license, sanction. **2.** voucher, guarantee, warranty, assurance.

warrant *v.* **1.** justify, explain, give grounds for, call for, deserve, merit, bear out. **2.** authorize, approve, sanction, license, empower.

warranted *adj.* **1.** allowable, permissible, justified, authorized; *ant.* unjustified. **2.** attested, guaranteed, certified.

warranty *n.* guarantee, contract, pledge, assurance, certificate, covenant.

warring *adj.* contending, antagonistic, hostile,

belligerent, opposing, fighting, conflicting, at war, embattled.

warrior *n.* soldier, combatant, war horse, war-dog, champion, fighter.

warship *n.* fighting ship, armored vessel, gun-boat.

wary *adj.* leery, guarded, heedful, suspicious, cagey, cautious, circumspect, distrustful, on the lookout, prudent, watchful; *ant.* heedless, impulsive.

wash *n.* **1.** laundry, soiled clothing, wash-ing. **2.** current, eddy, surge, flow, lapping, wave, gush, spurt. **3.** liquid, rinse, swab, coating.

wash *v.* **1.** clean, cleanse, bathe, soak, scrub, scour, wipe, take a bath *or* shower, freshen up, clean up. **2.** (apply a liquid coating to) moisten, swab, paint, whitewash, color, coat, dye, tint, stain, touch up, daub. **3.** (*slang*) be plausible, be reasonable, be convincing, stand up to examination, hold water.

wash one's hands abdicate responsibility, have nothing to do with, give up, leave to one's own devices, lose patience.

washable *adj.* launderable, colorfast, pre-shrunk, Sanforized (Tm).

washed *adj.* cleaned, scrubbed, soaped, laun-dered, put through the wash; *ant.* dirty, soiled, foul.

washed up (*slang*) finished, defeated, ruined, done for (*slang*).

washed-out **1.** tired, pale, wan. **2.** dismissed, discharged, let go, dropped, cashiered, drummed out.

washout (*slang*) *n.* failure, disaster, fiasco, disap-pointment, mess, bust (*slang*).

waspish *adj.* peevish, ill-tempered, testy, can-tankerous, cross, crotchety, irritable, petulant, bitchy (*slang*), grouchy, crabby.

waste *n.* **1.** refuse, debris, leavings, dregs, dross, offal, scrap, spoilage, garbage, rubbish, trash, litter. **2.** destruction, devastation, loss, ruin. **3.** misapplication, misuse, squandering.

waste *v.* **1.** deplete, squander, exhaust, fritter away, drain, throw away, consume, dwin-dle. **2.** ravage, destroy, devastate, eat away, lay waste, ruin.

waste time malinger, loaf (*slang*), dawdle, drift.

waste *adj.* desolate, barren, discarded, worth-less, valueless, useless, empty, dreary, uninhab-ited, futile, pointless, purposeless; *ant.* usable, preserved, valuable.

wasted *adj.* **1.** depleted, dissipated, ex-hausted, spent; cadaverous, gaunt, withered, washed-out; *ant.* healthy, robust. **2.** (*slang*) drunk, inebriated, intoxicated, stoned (*slang*).

wasteful *adj.* prodigal, extravagant, lavish, prof-ligate, spendthrift, thriftless; *ant.* frugal, eco-nomical, thrifty.

wasteland *n.* barrenness, void, desert, wilder-ness, waste.

watch *n.* **1.** clock, timepiece. **2.** lookout, sur-veillance, guard, patrol, vigil, observation; vigi-lance, alertness, watchfulness; *ant.* neglect, sleepiness, apathy.

watch *v.* **1.** observe, see, take notice, view, pay attention, concentrate, attend. **2.** guard, keep an eye on, patrol, police.

watchdog *n.* guard dog, protector, guardian, custodian, vigilante, inspector, monitor.

watchful *adj.* alert, observant, on the lookout, on the qui vive; cautious, careful, circumspect, suspicious, wary, guarded; *ant.* inattentive.

watchman *n.* guard, security guard, caretaker, custodian.

watchword *n.* buzzword, catch phrase, catch-word, maxim, motto, byword, battle-cry, slo-gan; password, shibboleth.

water *v.* moisten, dampen, soak, douse, drench, hose, irrigate.

water down dilute, weaken, thin, mitigate, qualify, tone down, soften; *ant.* strengthen, purify.

waterproof *adj.* water-repellent, water-resistant, impermeable, impervious; *ant.* leaky.

watertight *adj.* hermetic, waterproof, airtight, impregnable, sound, unassailable, foolproof; *ant.* leaky, unsound.

watery *adj.* diluted, watered-down, thin, weak, soggy, tasteless; rheumy, tearful, weepy, in-sipid; *ant.* solid, strong.

wave *n.* **1.** swell, crest, whitecap, breaker, comber, curl, billow. **2.** undulation, rippling, sway, winding, coil, curl, roll, twirl, loop, swirl, corkscrew.

wave *v.* flutter, ripple, sway, weave, oscillate, undulate, wag; flourish, gesture, signal, wield.

waver *v.* vacillate, fluctuate, hesitate, falter, waffle, hem and haw, sway, blow hot and cold, shilly-shally, seesaw, go back and forth.

wavering *adj.* doubting, hesitant, dithering, of two minds, uncertain, shilly-shallying, agonizing; *ant.* determined.

wavy *adj.* undulated, sinuous, curvy, ripply, curly; *ant.* flat, smooth.

wax *v.* expand, increase, magnify, develop, swell, enlarge; *ant.* wane.

waxen *adj.* pale, livid, wan, ashen, anemic, colorless, bloodless, white; *ant.* ruddy.

waxy *adj.* impressionable, soft; pasty, pallid.

way *n.* **1.** road, trail, walk, highway, byway. **2.** means, method, mode, plan, technique, design, system, procedure, process, contrivance, step, idea, policy.

wayfarer *n.* wanderer, itinerant, nomad, gypsy, globetrotter, traveler, trekker, voyager; *ant.* resident, homebody.

waylay *v.* lie in wait for, intercept, hold up, accost, ambush, seize, set upon, mug.

way-out *adj.* unorthodox, outlandish, freaky, bizarre, weird, eccentric, offbeat, avant-garde, experimental, progressive; *ant.* ordinary.

ways and means *n.* funds, capital, cash, resources, wherewithal; methods, procedure.

wayward *adj.* incorrigible, disobedient, ungovernable, fractious, capricious, unruly, willful, rebellious, headstrong, contrary; *ant.* compliant.

weak *adj.* **1.** debilitated, sickly, frail, delicate, enervated; *ant.* strong, healthy, robust. **2.** (said of a mixture or a light) thin, low, soft, indistinct, feeble, faint, dim, pale.

weaken *v.* abate, diminish, lessen, fade, thin, mitigate, undermine, emasculate, reduce, water down; *ant.* strengthen.

weakling *n.* coward, wimp (*slang*), mouse, milksop, sissy; *ant.* hero, stalwart.

weakness *n.* **1.** flaw, frailty, fault, deficiency, failing, vulnerability, Achilles' heel; *ant.* strength. **2.** predilection, penchant, proclivity, soft spot, inclination, fondness, craving.

weak-willed *adj.* spineless, submissive, pliable, complaisant, compliant, irresolute, weak-minded; *ant.* strong-willed.

weal *n.* welt, wound, contusion, scar, cicatrix, mark.

wealth *n.* fortune, richness, capital, property, possessions, means, abundance, affluence, bounty, prosperity, riches, opulence; *ant.* poverty.

wealthy *adj.* affluent, prosperous, rich, opulent, moneyed, well-heeled, well-off, well-to-do.

wean *v.* break of, disaccustom, detach.

weapon *n.* armament, protection, weaponry, military hardware, ordnance.

wear *n.* depreciation, erosion, damage, corrosion, dilapidation; *ant.* growth, accretion.

wear and tear damage, depletion, depreciation, loss.

wear *v.* **1.** dress, put on, don, be clothed in, have on, cover, wrap, get into. **2.** erode, decline, decay, deteriorate, waste, fade, go to seed.

wear down chip away at, erode, corrode, diminish, reduce; overcome, undermine.

wear off subside, diminish, dwindle, fade, lessen, peter out, wane, ebb.

wear out exhaust, deteriorate, fray, use up, consume, tire, tucker out.

wear the pants dominate, run things, boss, control, keep under one's thumb.

weariness *n.* lethargy, tiredness, exhaustion, fatigue, drowsiness, sleepiness, tiredness, listlessness, languor.

wearisome *adj.* exhausting, bothersome, vexatious, annoying, trying, irksome, protracted, tedious, boring, dull, monotonous; *ant.* refreshing.

weary *adj.* **1.** tired, fatigued, drained, spent, *slang*: beat, dead on one's feet, dog-tired, whacked; *ant.* fresh, lively. **2.** jaded, bored, sick and tired, fed up. **3.** taxing, irksome, wearisome.

weather *n.* climate, temperature, conditions, rainfall.

under the weather sick, ailing, ill, indisposed.

weather *v.* **1.** expose, harden, petrify, patinate, dry, bleach, blanch, whiten, tan, burn. **2.** overcome, endure, become toughened, grow hardened, stand up against, bear the brunt of, acclimate oneself, grow strong through; *ant.* fail, be overcome, fall victim to.

weather-beaten *adj.* weathered, old, worn, decayed, battered.

weave *v.* **1.** criss-cross, interlace, intertwine,

wreathe, mesh, spin, knot, braid, plait, twist. 2. (put together mentally) contrive, fabricate, form, construct, compose, piece together, manufacture, create.

web *n.* net, mesh, lattice, interlacing, screen, snare, tangle, trap, weave.

wed *v.* 1. marry, unite, espouse, tie the knot, get hitched, jump the broomstick; *ant.* divorce. 2. fuse, unify, merge, yoke, commingle.

wedding *n.* nuptials, matrimony, marriage, bridal, espousals; *ant.* divorce.

wedding *adj.* matrimonial, nuptial, marriage, bridal, epithalamial, hymeneal.

wedge *n.* chunk, lump, block, piece.

wedge *v.* force, jam, squeeze, lodge, thrust, cram, crowd, ram, stuff, push, pack; *ant.* dislodge, take out, space out.

wedlock *n.* marriage, matrimony, holy matrimony, union.

weed *n.* 1. cigar, cigarette, tobacco, *slang:* coffin nail, fag, joint. 2. marijuana, ganja, *slang:* pot, Mary Jane, locoweed.

weed *v.* hoe, garden.

weed out thin out, get rid of, eliminate, purge, remove, root out, eradicate.

week *n.* seven days, hebdomad, sennight.

weekly *adv.* once a week, every week, by the week, hebdomadally.

weep *v.* cry, sob, lament, moan, mourn, whimper, bewail, snivel, blubber, boo-hoo; *ant.* rejoice.

weepy *adj.* tearful, crying, sobbing, morose, teary, blubbering; *ant.* dry-eyed.

weigh *v.* think over, mull over, give thought to, consider, cogitate, contemplate, ponder, reflect on, study, deliberate, evaluate.

weigh down burden, depress, worry, oppress, afflict, bear down, trouble, weigh upon; *ant.* lighten, hearten, refresh.

weight *n.* 1. heaviness, load, heft, burden, mass, density, ponderousness, tonnage, substance. 2. ballast, counterbalance, counterweight, sinker, anchor, sandbag. 3. importance, influence, authority, power, sway, clout (*slang*).

weight *v.* encumber, impede, overburden, handicap, hold down, charge, keep down, unbalance, weigh down.

weightless *adj.* insubstantial, light, airy, imponderous, unsubstantial.

weighty *adj.* 1. burdensome, oppressive, onerous, taxing. 2. important, serious, significant, ponderous, solemn, grave, revered, critical; *ant.* trivial, unimportant.

weird *adj.* bizarre, strange, freakish, queer, outlandish, odd, eerie, unnatural, mysterious.

weirdo (*slang*) *n.* oddball, freak, crackpot, eccentric; *slang:* nutcase, fruitcake, queer fish, loony, nut.

weld *v.* fuse, connect, bind, unite, link, solder, make fast, join.

welcome *n.* greeting, reception, hospitality, acceptance, salutation, red carpet.

welcome *v.* greet, receive, accept, meet, approve of, embrace, roll out the red carpet for; *ant.* reject, snub.

welcome *adj.* accepted, allowed, appreciated, entitled; pleasant, agreeable; *ant.* unwelcome.

welfare *n.* health, happiness, well-being, benefit, profit, prosperity, good fortune.

well *n.* waterhole, shaft, fountain, spring, pool, source, repository.

well *v.* spring, flow, gush, swell, rise, brim over, stream, flood, seep, trickle.

well *adj.* 1. healthy, fit, fine, flourishing, robust, strong, in good health, thriving, sound; *ant.* ill. 2. pleasant, favorable, satisfactory, agreeable, fortunate.

well *adv.* splendidly, admirably, favorably, comfortably, heartily, glowingly, nicely, fittingly, pleasantly; *ant.* badly, poorly.

as well as 1. similarly, like, equally, as much as, as good as. 2. including, together or along with, plus, in addition to.

as well also, in addition, additionally, to boot.

well-being *n.* comfort, happiness, welfare, contentment; *ant.* discomfort, harm.

well-bred *adj.* mannerly, refined, cultivated, polite, well-brought-up, aristocratic, noble, upper-crust, blue-blooded, titled, civil, courteous; *ant.* ill-bred.

well-defined *adj.* definite, distinct, specific, clear, sharp, outlined.

well-deserved *adj.* rightful, just, justified, appropriate, due, condign, merited; *ant.* undeserved.

well-disposed *adj.* agreeable, friendly, sympathetic, amicable, favorable; *ant.* ill-disposed.

well-favored *adj.* good-looking, attractive, handsome, comely.

well-fixed *adj.* rich, wealthy, comfortable, well-to-do, well-heeled (*slang*).

well-informed *adj.* educated, learned, advised, well-read.

well-intentioned *adj.* honorable, high-principled, good-hearted, well-meaning, noble.

well-known *adj.* famous, notable, illustrious, celebrated, reputable, popular, renowned, notorious, familiar; *ant.* unknown.

well-off *adj.* affluent, wealthy, rich, prosperous, successful, moneyed, well-to-do, fortunate, *slang*: well-heeled, loaded, in the money; *ant.* poor.

well-rounded *adj.* well-informed, educated, literate, cultivated.

well-timed *adj.* timely, appropriate, opportune, seasonable.

well-thought-of *adj.* respected, venerated, honored, admired, esteemed, revered, highly regarded; *ant.* despised.

well-to-do *adj.* affluent, wealthy, rich, prosperous, comfortable, moneyed, *slang*: well-heeled, loaded; *ant.* poor.

welt *n.* cicatrix, weal, contusion, mark, scar, ridge, streak, burn.

welter *n.* turmoil, confusion, muddle, tangle, web, mess, jumble, mish-mash, hodge-podge.

welter *v.* wallow, roll, flounder, tumble, pitch, writhe, heave, wade, stumble.

wend *v.* walk, ramble, saunter, stroll.

wend one's way make one's way, progress, move, wander, travel, plod, hike; *ant.* stay.

wet *v.* moisten, water, soak, drench, douse, saturate, dampen, souse, irrigate; *ant.* dry.

wet *adj.* waterlogged, sodden, soppy, clammy, moist, watery, dripping, soggy, saturated, drenched, soaking; *ant.* dry.

wet behind the ears inexperienced, naive, untrained, new, callow, immature, innocent, green; *ant.* experienced.

wetness *n.* dampness, moisture, liquid, water, condensation, soddenness, sogginess; *ant.* dryness.

whack *n.* hit, smack, blow, buffet, slug, belt, bash, sock, slap, crack, wallop, rap.

out of whack out of order, not working, inoperative; mixed up, on the blink (*slang*); out of sync (*slang*).

take a whack at attempt, try, endeavor, give it a shot *or* try.

whack *v.* clobber, hit, smack, lambaste, buffet, cuff, strike, wale, wallop, slap, slug, rap.

wharf *n.* dock, pier, marina, quay, landing-stage, jetty.

wheedle *v.* cajole, persuade, entice, importune, coax, charm, inveigle.

wheel *n.* **1.** circle, disk, ring, hoop, roller, caster. **2.** vehicle, bicycle, tandem, bike.

at the wheel in control, running things, driving.

wheels (*slang*) *n.* car, automobile, vehicle.

wheeze *v.* gasp, cough, rasp.

whereabouts *n.* location, place, vicinity, site, position.

wherewithal *n.* resources, capital, means, funds, cash, money.

whet *v.* **1.** sharpen, hone, file, grind, strop; *ant.* blunt. **2.** incite, arouse, awaken, stimulate, titillate, kindle, pique, stir, increase; *ant.* dampen.

whiff *v.* smell, inhale, sniff.

whim *n.* impulse, caprice, quirk, fad, notion, urge, whimsy, fancy.

whimper *v.* cry, mewl, snivel, whine, sob, weep, blubber.

whimsical *adj.* fanciful, quaint, playful, fantastical, droll, mischievous, curious.

whine *v.* complain, gripe, carp, grouse, grumble, moan, sob, whimper, cry, *slang*: beef, bellyache, kvetch.

whip *n.* lash, switch, cat-o'-nine-tails, riding-crop, horsewhip, jambok, cane, thong, rawhide.

whip *v.* **1.** flog, thrash, flagellate, lash, paddle, prod, punish, spank, strap, switch, tan. **2.** (defeat soundly) conquer, defeat, smash, lick, trounce, outdo, overpower, bury. **3.** (blend a food mixture) agitate, beat, stir, whisk.

whip into shape polish, fix, finish, complete, get together, get one's act together.

whirl *n.* **1.** twirl, gyration, twist, reel, rotation, spin, stir. **2.** (mental confusion) flurry, dither, tizzy, confusion, hubbub, tumult.

whirl *v.* twirl, gyrate, twist, reel, rotate, spin, swirl, swivel.

whisk v. sweep, swipe, brush, whip, beat, flick; dart, scoot, hasten, rush.

whisker n. hair, bristle, seta, vibrissa.

whiskers n. (facial hair) beard, mustache, sideburns, muttonchops, goatee.

whiskey n. bourbon, rye, John Barleycorn, Scotch, malt, slang: mountain dew, moonshine.

whisper v. divulge, gossip, insinuate, intimate, murmur, hint, hiss, breathe, buzz; ant. shout.

whisper n. secret, rumor, insinuation, suspicion, suggestion, gossip, buzz, hint, hiss, breath.

whistle v. warble, sing, call, cheep, chirp.

whistle n. warble, call, cheep, chirp, song, siren.

whit n. iota, speck, mite, atom, fragment, particle, pinch, trace, dash, crumb, bit, drop, slang: hoot, damn; ant. lot.

white adj. **1.** ivory, bleached, pale, silvery, snow-white, frosted, milky, chalky, pearly, blanched, ashen, wan; ant. dark, black. **2.** colorless, clear, transparent, blank, spotless, unalloyed, achromatic; ant. colored, chromatic. **3.** Caucasian, Caucasoid, fair-skinned, light-complexioned.

white-collar adj. service, clerical; professional, executive, managerial; ant. blue-collar, manual.

whiten v. blanch, bleach, whitewash, fade, pale; ant. blacken, darken, color.

whitewash n. coverup, stonewall, red herring, camouflage, concealment, deception; excuse, rationalization, extenuation; ant. exposure.

whitewash v. cover up, stonewall, camouflage, conceal, gloss over, make light of, euphemize; ant. expose.

whittle v. carve, pare, shape, trim; wear away, diminish, erode, undermine.

whiz (slang) n. prodigy, genius, star, marvel, wonder, wunderkind.

whole n. entirety, entity, total, everything, all, aggregate, lot, unit, Gestalt.

whole adj. complete, full, intact, total, unabridged, uncut, flawless, sound, integral, inviolate, perfect.

wholehearted adj. unreserved, sincere, earnest, true, devoted, unfeigned, committed, genuine; zealous, passionate, warm, enthusiastic; ant. halfhearted, feigned.

wholesale adj. comprehensive, indiscriminate,

506

extensive, far-reaching, sweeping, broad, massive; ant. partial.

wholesome adj. **1.** healthy, beneficial, invigorating, edifying, nourishing, nutritious, hygienic. **2.** respectable, decent, honorable, exemplary, innocent, moral, pure, virtuous; ant. depraved, wicked.

wholly adv. thoroughly, completely, in toto, entirely, comprehensively, completely, totally, utterly, through and through.

whoop v. shout, holler, roar, scream, hoot, hurrah, cheer, yell, shriek.

whoop it up (slang) celebrate, get drunk, get noisy, party, slang: kick up one's heels, paint the town red.

whopper n. lie, tall tale or story, falsehood, fabrication, untruth, fib.

whopping adj. enormous, monstrous, gigantic, massive, staggering, tremendous, monumental, mammoth, huge, extraordinary.

whore n. prostitute, hooker, call girl, streetwalker, tramp, tart, hustler, harlot, strumpet, working girl (slang).

whorehouse n. brothel, bordello, bawdy-house, cathouse (slang), house of ill repute, bagnio.

whorl n. spiral, vortex, helix, coil, corkscrew, turn, twist, convolution.

wicked adj. immoral, sinful, evil, depraved, corrupt, abominable, fiendish, vile, impious, nefarious, devilish; ant. good.

wide adj. **1.** broad, extended, extensive, spacious, deep. **2.** inaccurate, far, dissimilar, off course, aside, out; ant. on target.

wide adv. astray, off target, off the mark, off target.

wide-awake adj. alert, roused, sharp, astute, aware, watchful, vigilant, wary, on one's toes, on the ball, on the qui vive; ant. asleep.

widen v. broaden, extend, expand, open out, distend, enlarge, splay, spread, dilate; ant. narrow.

wide-open adj. exposed, vulnerable, defenseless, unprotected, unfortified, splayed, expansive.

widespread adj. pervasive, extensive, broad, sweeping, common, universal, prevalent, far-reaching, far-flung, popular, rife.

width n. wideness, thickness, breadth, diameter, girth, span, scope, amplitude, extent, reach.

ful, cunning, deep, foxy, shifty, cagey, crafty, Machiavellian, deceptive, tricky; *ant.* guileless.

wimp (*slang*) *n.* sap, milksop, marshmallow, drip, nebbish (*slang*).

win *n.* victory, triumph, conquest, success.

win *v.* 1. succeed, be victorious, prevail, get the best of, triumph, conquer, overwhelm, overcome. 2. obtain, acquire, gain, secure, get. 3. (succeed in persuading) convince, persuade, sway, win over, bring around, talk into, influence.

win over persuade, convince, influence, sway, talk into.

wince *v.* flinch, recoil, shrink, quail, draw back, cower, cringe.

wind *n.* air current, breeze, gust, gale, blast, flurry, draft.

get wind of hear of, learn, sense, understand, be clued in.

wind *v.* coil, furl, twine, bend, reel, twist, encircle, serpentine, zigzag, meander, ramble.

wind down unwind, relax, slacken off, quiet down, slow down, subside; *ant.* increase, tense.

wind up conclude, end, finalize, close down, wrap up, finish, terminate; *ant.* begin.

windbag *n.* gossip, braggart, bigmouth, blowhard (*slang*), bore.

winded *adj.* breathless, out of breath, panting, *slang*; pooped, out of gas; *ant.* fresh.

windfall *n.* bonanza, jackpot, godsend, manna, pennies from heaven, stroke of luck, treasuretrove.

winding *adj.* curving, bending, spiral, serpentine, turning, twisting, circuitous, meandering, indirect.

window *n.* pane, glass, dormer, opening, skylight.

windy *adj.* 1. blustery, breezy, gusty, squally, stormy, windswept. 2. long-winded, loquacious, verbose, prolix, wordy; boastful, bombastic.

wing *n.* annex, addition, ell, hall, division, section, part.

take wing leave, go, depart, run off, flee, exit, make tracks (*slang*).

take under one's wing help, nurture, adopt, foster, favor, protect, sponsor, look after.

wing *v.* wound, hurt, injure, bring down.

wield *v.* brandish, hold, maintain, possess, manipulate, exercise, control, exert, handle, use, utilize.

wife *n.* spouse, woman, bride, helpmate, mate, consort, partner, better half.

wiggle *v.* wriggle, squirm, shimmy, writhe, twist, twitch.

wild *adj.* 1. uncontrolled, unrestrained, unmanageable, unruly, fractious, disorderly; uncivilized, primitive, savage, barbarous, feral, undomesticated. 2. inaccurate, erratic, mistaken, wrong, unsound, off; bizarre, strange, daft, crazy, lunatic, way out (*slang*).

wilderness *n.* wild, jungle, desert, forest, wasteland, maze, tangle, jumble, confusion.

wildlife *n.* animals, fauna, game.

wilds *n.* wilderness, wasteland, back-veld, outback, desert, boondocks, the sticks, the back of beyond, the middle of nowhere.

wile *n.* trickery, artifice, craftiness, guile, cunning, slyness; ruse, lure, device, ploy, subterfuge, contrivance, stratagem; *ant.* guilelessness.

will *n.* 1. desire, inclination, volition, want, wish, pleasure, yearning, craving, longing, hankering; *ant.* indifference. 2. instructions, command, directions, order, insistence, injunction.

will *v.* 1. command, insist, decree, order, demand, enjoin, request. 2. wish, want, incline to, prefer.

willful *adj.* 1. deliberate, intentional, premeditated, meant, contemplated; *ant.* accidental. 2. obstinate, stubborn, intractable, ornery, determined.

willing *adj.* amenable, open, compliant, consenting, voluntary, disposed, inclined, ready, enthusiastic, eager; *ant.* reluctant.

willingly *adv.* freely, eagerly, unhesitatingly, voluntarily, readily, by choice, cheerfully, gladly, happily.

willowy *adj.* lithe, graceful, limber, lissome, sylphlike, supple, slim, slender, svelte; *ant.* buxom.

willpower *n.* self-control, discipline, self-discipline, determination, resolution, grit, drive, resolve, single-mindedness, heart, mettle.

wilt *v.* languish, wane, atrophy, droop, sag, wither, diminish; *ant.* perk up.

wily *adj.* sly, shrewd, scheming, guileful, deceit-

wink *n.* moment, instant, jiffy, split second, flash.

wink *v.* **1.** blink, squint, nictate; flirt, make eyes at, bat eyes at. **2.** sparkle, twinkle, gleam, flash.

wink at (pretend not to see) gloss over, condone, excuse, overlook, look the other way, permit, forgive; *ant.* censure, frown upon, revile.

winner *n.* champion, victor, master, conqueror, vanquisher, first; *ant.* loser.

winning *adj.* alluring, captivating, charming, disarming, engaging, fetching, fascinating, taking, winsome, bewitching, endearing; *ant.* unappealing.

winnings *n.* prizes, spoils, takings, profits, gains, proceeds; *ant.* losses.

winnow *v.* sift, separate, diffuse, divide, comb, cull, select, fan, part.

winsome *adj.* engaging, endearing, attractive, winning, alluring, comely, prepossessing, taking; *ant.* unattractive.

wintry *adj.* cold, frozen, Siberian, snowy, icy, freezing, frosty, bleak, desolate; *ant.* summery.

wipe *v.* clean, sponge, wash, remove, clear, swab.

wipe out eradicate, abolish, annihilate, obliterate, extirpate, exterminate, expunge, erase, blot out.

wire *n.* **1.** coil, cable, line, aerial, conductor, filament. **2.** telegram, cablegram, message. **down to the wire** to the very end, at last, finally, eventually.

get in under the wire just make it, succeed, arrive, squeak through.

wire *v.* telegraph, cable, fax, notify, inform.

wiry *adj.* sinewy, lean, strong, tough, bristly; *ant.* puny, soft.

wisdom *n.* intelligence, knowledge, enlightenment, astuteness, comprehension, sagacity, learning, erudition, judgment, reason, common sense, understanding; *ant.* folly.

wise *adj.* **1.** prudent, sensible, careful, tactful, discreet, politic, wary. **2.** sage, sagacious, erudite, learned, educated, scholarly, smart, reasonable, rational, sensible. **3.** (*slang*) impudent, rude, bold, fresh, forward, offensive, impertinent.

wiseacre *n.* smart aleck, *slang:* wise guy, wiseass; wisenheimer, smarty-pants.

wisecrack *n.* barb, jibe, joke, one-liner, witticism, gag, jest, quip.

wise up (*slang*) learn, get informed, get the message or the picture, figure things out.

wish *n.* aspiration, hope, whim, inclination, desideratum; hankering, yen, desire, yearning, want, hunger, urge; *ant.* dislike, fear.

wish *v.* **1.** aspire, yearn, hope, crave, yen, hunger, long for, want, need, desire; *ant.* dislike, fear. **2.** require, order, ask, bid, request, command.

wishy-washy *adj.* vapid, ineffectual, weak, insipid, bland, thin, tasteless, watered-down, namby-pamby; *ant.* strong.

wisp *n.* strand, lock, thread, snippet, piece, twist.

wispy *adj.* diaphanous, ethereal, flyaway, gossamer, delicate, insubstantial, fragile, light, thin, faint, fine; *ant.* substantial.

wistful *adj.* pensive, dreamy, contemplative, longing, wishful, yearning, reflective, nostalgic, musing, meditative, disconsolate, soulful.

wit *n.* **1.** cleverness, intelligence, intellect, reason, discernment, common sense, brains. **2.** *slang:* wisecracker, wise guy. **3.** humor, whimsicality, drollery, banter, repartee; witticism, sally, bon mot, joke, jest, quip, pun, wisecrack (*slang*), gag.

at one's wit's end desperate, helpless, hopeless, at the end of one's rope, troubled, downhearted.

witch *n.* sorceress, enchantress, magician, hag, occultist, necromancer.

witchcraft *n.* magic; sorcery, necromancy, enchantment, spell, incantation, voodoo, occult, conjuration, divination, witchery, wizardry.

witch doctor *n.* medicine man, shaman, magician.

witch hunt *n.* inquisition, McCarthyism, hounding, hue and cry, fishing expedition.

withdraw *v.* retract, take back, revoke, rescind, recant; disengage, secede, pull back, retreat, back out, back off, draw back, go away; *ant.* advance.

withdrawal *n.* disengagement, extraction, exodus, retreat; retraction, disclaimer; *ant.* advance.

withdrawn *adj.* taciturn, introverted, reserved,

shy, solitary, reclusive, uncommunicative, distant, aloof, detached, private; *ant.* outgoing.

wither *v.* **1.** shrivel, wilt, languish, disintegrate, droop, fade, decline, shrink; *ant.* thrive. **2.** snub, humiliate, abash, shame, mortify, put down; *ant.* boost.

withering *adj.* snubbing, scathing, scornful, devastating, mortifying, humiliating, deadly, murderous, wounding; *ant.* supportive.

withheld *adj.* held back, concealed, hidden, kept under wraps, checked, restrained, delayed; *ant.* free, opened.

withhold *v.* hold back, retain, reserve, keep, suppress, repress, check, conceal, hide, secrete; *ant.* give, release.

with-it (*slang*) up to date, au courant, modern, contemporary, in fashion.

withstand *v.* endure, bear, tolerate, cope with, face, brave, stand one's ground, hold out, stay the course, survive, weather; *ant.* collapse, yield.

witless *adj.* idiotic, imbecilic, senseless, empty-headed, obtuse, moronic, cretinous, daft, foolish, half-witted, stupid; *ant.* intelligent.

witness *n.* observer, spectator, corroborator, testifier, voucher, attestant, bystander.
bear witness attest, testify, vouch for, confirm, evidence.

wits *n.* reason, judgment, faculties, sense, intelligence, intellect, comprehension, cleverness, brains, smarts; *ant.* stupidity.

witticism *n.* quip, pun, repartee, bon mot, one-liner, sally, jibe.

witty *adj.* amusing, funny, jocular, clever, droll, humorous, waggish, comic; *ant.* dull, unamusing.

wizard *n.* **1.** sorcerer, warlock, magician, necromancer, enchanter, conjurer, occultist. **2.** expert, master, ace, genius, virtuoso, star, maestro, *slang:* whiz, hotshot; *ant.* duffer.

wizardry *n.* sorcery, witchcraft, magic, enchantment, occultism, necromancy, the black art, incantation, divination, voodoo.

wizened *adj.* wrinkled, gnarled, shriveled, lined, dried up, weazened, worn; *ant.* smooth, plump.

wobble *v.* sway, teeter, totter, seesaw, oscillate, fluctuate; shilly-shally, waver, hesitate.

wobbly *adj.* teetering, tottering, doddering, unbalanced, unsteady, uneven, unsafe, rickety, ramshackle, shaky; *ant.* stable.

woe *n.* suffering, misery, heartbreak, pain, grief, depression, melancholy, tribulation, wretchedness, sorrow, anguish, agony; *ant.* joy, happiness.

woebegone *adj.* crestfallen, downcast, gloomy, forlorn, blue, grief-stricken, disconsolate, dispirited, mournful, miserable, down in the mouth, hangdog; *ant.* joyful.

woeful *adj.* deplorable, distressing, pitiable, tragic, catastrophic, heart-rending, calamitous, dreadful, lamentable, disastrous, sorrowful, agonizing; *ant.* joyful.

woman *n.* female, lady, girl, mother, daughter, sister, wife.

womanly *adj.* feminine, ladylike, matronly, motherly; *ant.* manly.

women *n.* womankind, womanhood, womenfolk, sisterhood.

wonder *n.* **1.** (appreciation of something extraordinary) fascination, amazement, astonishment, awe, curiosity. **2.** (something extraordinary) rarity, spectacle, miracle, curiosity, marvel, sight, sight to see.
wonder *v.* **1.** speculate, conjecture, ponder, query, question, inquire, cogitate, ruminate. **2.** marvel, gape, gawk, stare.

wonderful *adj.* marvelous, incredible, extraordinary, astounding, amazing, astonishing, miraculous, terrific, tremendous, awe-inspiring, fantastic, fabulous, stupendous.

wondrous *adj.* remarkable, extraordinary, unusual, miraculous, fascinating, marvelous, amazing, astounding.

wont *adj.* accustomed, given, used, habituated.

wonted *adj.* accustomed, customary, habitual, conventional, regular, routine, normal, usual, familiar.

wood *n.* **1.** lumber, timber, log, planks. **2.** forest, grove, thicket, woods, woodland, copse, trees.
out of the woods safe, out of danger, free and clear, secure, in the clear.

wooded *adj.* forested, tree-covered, timbered, sylvan; *ant.* open.

wooden *adj.* **1.** lifeless, unemotional, expressionless, vacant, flat, empty, spiritless, stiff, deadpan, enigmatic, blank, unresponsive; *ant.* lively, expressive. 2. obtuse, dull, thick, dense, stupid, dull-witted; *ant.* bright.

woody *adj.* sylvan, forested, tree-covered, bosky.

woodland *n.* forest, woods, boscage.

wool *n.* fleece, yarn.

pull the wool over someone's eyes (*slang*) deceive, con (*slang*), dupe, fool, delude, trick, lead up the garden path, put one over on, *slang*; snow, pull a fast one on.

woolen *adj.* worsted, sheepskin, fleecy.

woolly *adj.* fleecy, fuzzy, nappy, frizzy, shaggy.

word *n.* 1. expression, form, name, term, designation, concept, lexical form, definiendum. 2. promise, pledge, declaration, commitment, word of honor. 3. report, news, information, tidings, message, announcement, account, advice, intelligence.

a good word endorsement, testimonial, recommendation, support, boost, plug (*slang*).

have words with argue, differ with, bicker, fight, quarrel, disagree.

in a word briefly, succinctly, in short, in a nutshell, thus, viz.

the word information, knowledge, truth, the facts, the lowdown (*slang*).

word *v.* express, say, put in words, write, phrase, explain, couch.

word-for-word *adv.* verbatim, exactly, literally, accurately, precisely.

wordiness *n.* verbiage, wordage, long-windedness, verbosity, prolixity, perissology, logorrhea.

wording *n.* phrasing, diction, terminology, choice of words, verbiage, syntax.

word-perfect *adj.* exact, accurate, letter-perfect, verbatim, true, faithful; *ant.* inaccurate.

words *n.* 1. dispute, argument, contention, wrangle, quarrel, tiff. 2. conversation, discussion, chat, communication.

wordy *adj.* verbose, loquacious, rambling, discursive, garrulous, long-winded, prolix; *ant.* concise, laconic.

work *n.* 1. job, task, chore, assignment, project, commitment, duty, obligation. 2. (product of someone's labor) performance, handiwork, output, endeavor, production, job, vocation, line, occupation, profession, job, vocation, line. 3. calling, employment, craft, trade, business, skill, avocation, pursuit.

in the works planned, prepared for, ready, budgeted, in the cards, coming, primed.

make short work of finish off, deal with, dispose of, prevent, stop, put paid to.

work *v.* 1. (do a job or task) labor, toil, do; slave, sweat, punch a time clock, work one's fingers to the bone, buckle down, work like a horse *or* a dog, put one's nose to the grindstone. 2. (operate effectively, as a machine) function, go, run, serve, operate. 3. (bring about a result) accomplish, achieve, effect, manage, control.

work in include, squeeze in, find a place for, introduce.

work out turn out, pan out, be resolved.

work over 1. fix, repair, redo. 2. beat, punish, thrash, abuse, beat up *or* upon, assault, mug.

work up develop, produce, elaborate, refine, get *or* pull together, assemble, collect, gather.

workable *adj.* possible, practical, feasible, realistic, viable, doable, practicable, conceivable; *ant.* impossible, visionary.

workaday *adj.* routine, everyday, commonplace, run-of-the-mill, humdrum, familiar, mundane, ordinary, dull; *ant.* exciting, extraordinary.

worker *n.* laborer, employee, tradesperson, workman, workwoman, staffer, craftsperson, artisan; *ant.* idler.

work force personnel, labor force, employees, staff, hands.

working *n.* operation, routine, method, functioning, action, running, system.

working *adj.* functioning, operational, active, busy, humming; employed, laboring; *ant.* inoperative, idle; retired, unemployed.

workings *n.* excavations, shaft, mine, pit, diggings, quarry.

workmanlike *adj.* skilled, professional, expert, proficient, efficient, adept, thorough, painstaking; *ant.* amateurish.

workmanship *n.* skill, craft, technique, expertise, craftsmanship, execution, artistry, artisanship.

workout *n.* tryout, drill, rehearsal, practice, exercise, conditioning, training.

works *n.* **1.** parts, cogs, wheels, gears, pistons, springs, coils, chains, rods, pulleys, wires. **2.** everything, all, totality, entirety, the whole, the whole shebang.

workshop *n.* **1.** seminar, conference, class, symposium. **2.** studio, atelier, workroom.

world *n.* **1.** earth, globe, planet, terrestrial sphere. **2.** universe, cosmos, creation, nature. **3.** (an individual's reality) environment, atmosphere, milieu, society, human intercourse; experience, inner life, memory.

for all the world 1. seemingly, to all appearances, apparently. **2.** for everything and anything, no matter what, regardless.

on top of the world exuberant, delighted, triumphant, happy, ecstatic, jubilant.

out of this world extraordinary, excellent, remarkable, superb, fabulous, great, incredible, fantastic.

worldly *adj.* **1.** worldly-wise, sophisticated, urbane, cosmopolitan, knowing. **2.** carnal, earthy, temporal, material, secular, fleshly, materialistic, greedy, avaricious; *ant.* spiritual.

worldwide *adj.* international, global, universal, ubiquitous, international, catholic; *ant.* local.

worm *v.* insinuate oneself, sidle, sneak, inch, crawl.

worm out of avoid, evade, get out of, escape.

worn *adj.* **1.** (said of a garment) ragged, frayed, tattered, threadbare, shabby; *ant.* new. **2.** spent, haggard, fatigued, weary, careworn, played-out; *ant.* fresh, renewed, refreshed.

worn-out *adj.* **1.** (said of a garment) shabby, spent, tattered, threadbare, useless, frayed, moth-eaten, decrepit, on its last legs; *ant.* new. **2.** exhausted, fatigued, prostrate, played out, tuckered out, tired, weary, dog-tired, dead on one's feet; *ant.* fresh.

worried *adj.* nervous, anxious, ill at ease, uneasy, on edge, apprehensive, distraught, troubled, strained, tense, agonized, uptight (*slang*); *ant.* calm, unconcerned.

worrisome *adj.* disquieting, bothersome, troublesome, irksome, disconcerting, upsetting, agonizing; jittery, nail-biting, uneasy; *ant.* calm, reassuring.

worry *v.* upset, distress, agonize, vex, faze, disturb, badger, harass, pester, torment, hassle, annoy; *ant.* comfort, reassure.

worrywart *n.* nervous Nellie, fretter, *slang:* neurotic, paranoid.

worse *adj.* poorer, inferior, deteriorated.

worsen *v.* decline, deteriorate, degenerate, retrogress, sink, go downhill, take a turn for the worse, go from bad to worse; exacerbate, aggravate; *ant.* improve.

worship *n.* praise, adoration, exaltation, honor, love, reverence, homage, glorification, deification, laudation, prayer; *ant.* vilification.

worship *v.* praise, adore, adulate, exalt, idolize, venerate, love, glorify, put on a pedestal, laud, honor, revere; *ant.* despise.

worshiper *n.* devotionist, churchgoer, communicant, congregant, supplicant, celebrant, pilgrim; *ant.* atheist, agnostic, skeptic.

worst *v.* vanquish, subdue, overpower, defeat, conquer, best, subjugate, beat.

worst *adj.* poorest, lowest, least.

worth *n.* value, quality, goodness, excellence, merit.

worth *adj.* deserving of, meriting, equivalent to, rated.

for all one is worth vigorously, powerfully, mightily, hard, greatly.

worthless *adj.* ineffectual, insignificant, unimportant, meaningless, pointless, wretched, useless, feckless, good-for-nothing, no-account; *ant.* valuable.

worthwhile *adj.* beneficial, useful, productive, helpful, positive, efficacious, valuable; *ant.* useless.

worthy *adj.* deserving, honorable, respectable, virtuous, admirable, reliable; fit, suitable, appropriate; *ant.* disreputable, unworthy.

would-be *adj.* hopeful, anticipated, manqué, supposed, wannabe (*slang*).

wound *n.* injury, lesion, laceration, scar, gash, cut, insult; hurt, damage, distress, torment, pang, harm, pain.

wound *v.* **1.** injure, lacerate, gash, slash, cut, damage, traumatize. **2.** (insult by one's actions or words) pain, hurt, mortify, offend, insult, cut.

woven *adj.* spun, intertwined, interlaced, worked into, wreathed.

wow (*slang*) *v.* impress, win over, bowl over, flabbergast, astound.

wraith n. apparition, spirit, ghost, phantom, specter, spook.

wrangle v. quarrel, disagree, squabble, bicker, argue, brawl, fight, row, fall out, scrap; ant. agree.

wrap n. shawl, cloak, cape, stole, mantle, robe.

wrap v. enclose, bundle up, package, encase, surround, swathe, muffle, shroud, cloak, cocoon, sheathe, cover.

wrap up conclude, end, finish, terminate, bring to a close, wind up.

wrapper n. packaging, sleeve, sheath, paper, cover, jacket.

wrapping n. packaging, paper, tinfoil, bubble wrap, carton.

wrath n. rage, anger, temper, fury, indignation, resentment, passion, exasperation, ire, displeasure, spleen; ant. calm, pleasure.

wrathful adj. enraged, incensed, infuriated, irate, furious, pissed off (slang), angry, bitter, beside oneself; ant. calm, pleased.

wreak v. cause, create, execute, inflict, unleash, perpetrate, bring about, carry out, consummate.

wreath n. garland, crown, festoon, lei, band, loop, ring.

wreathe v. entwine, adorn, festoon, swathe, wind, wrap, crown, encircle.

wreck v. devastate, ravage, demolish, destroy, ruin, spoil, quash, subdue, break, shatter, smash, play havoc with; ant. repair, save.

wreckage n. debris, rubble, remains, ruin, fragments, pieces, flotsam.

wrench n. pang, sorrow, pain, ache, upheaval, sadness, blow, shock.

wrench v. force, jerk, wrest, tear, wring, rip, pull, yank, tug.

wrest v. wrench, extract, take, force, pull, seize.

wrestle v. struggle, tussle, grapple, scuffle, vie, fight, battle, combat, contend.

wretch n. ruffian, scoundrel, rogue, miscreant, cad, villain, blackguard, rapscallion, rascal, good-for-nothing, ne'er-do-well.

wretched adj. 1. (said of conditions or situations) pitiful, pathetic, dismal, miserable, intolerable, abject. 2. (said of character or behavior) contemptible, abject, base, despicable, shameful, vile, vicious, deplorable. 3. (feeling extremely unhappy) dejected, depressed, miserable, downcast, gloomy, forlorn, disconsolate, crestfallen, melancholy, broken-hearted; ant. content, happy.

wriggle v. squirm, wiggle, writhe, twist, worm, snake, extricate, dodge, edge, sidle, talk one's way out.

wring v. twist, squeeze, coerce, extract, extort, force, rend, wrench, mangle, strangle.

wrinkle n. crease, line, furrow, crow's foot, rumple, crinkle, pucker, gather.

wrinkle v. crinkle, crease, furrow, line, rumple, fold, corrugate; ant. smooth.

writ n. decree, summons, court order, subpoena.

write v. 1. compose, draft, formulate, create, communicate, correspond. 2. inscribe, copy, jot down, pen, record, scribble, take down, transcribe.

write off disregard, cancel, cross out, destroy.

write up develop, expand, work up, describe, compose.

writer n. author, littérateur, librettist, scribe, wordsmith, columnist, novelist, poet, playwright.

writhe v. thresh, squirm, wriggle, contort, thrash, wreathe, struggle, coil, contort, twist, jerk, wiggle.

writing n. 1. literature, publication, letters, belles lettres, opus, work, composition. 2. calligraphy, penmanship, holography; scribble, script, scrawl, holograph.

written adj. recorded, set down, documented, transcribed; ant. oral.

wrong n. transgression, sin, inequity, error, injustice, offense, abuse, crime, misdeed, infraction, trespass.

wrong v. abuse, harm, hurt, injure, malign, mistreat, oppress, ill-use.

wrong adj. 1. improper, inappropriate, bad, unethical, dishonest, dishonorable, reprehensible, unseemly, immoral, illicit, criminal, illegal, felonious; ant. ethical, right. 2. inaccurate, erroneous, false, incorrect, amiss, askew, awry, malapropos, mistaken, off-base, wide of the mark; ant. accurate, correct.

wrongdoer n. offender, transgressor, culprit, miscreant, perpetrator, delinquent, criminal, evildoer, sinner.

wrongdoing *n.* transgression, offense, mischief, error, delinquency, iniquity, crime, sin.

wrongful *adj.* immoral, dishonest, illicit, improper, reprehensible, dishonorable, unethical, unlawful, illegal, felonious, criminal; *ant.* rightful.

wrongheaded *adj.* biased, prejudiced, narrowminded, stubborn, obstinate, opinionated, unyielding.

wrongly *adv.* incorrectly, inaccurately, erroneously, mistakenly; *ant.* rightly.

wrought *adj.* ornamental, decorative, ornate, shaped, beaten, hammered.

wrought-up *adj.* anxious, nervous, excited, disturbed, tense, agitated.

wry *adj.* droll, sardonic, sarcastic, ironic, mocking, dry, subtle.

xenophobia *n.* insularity, isolationism, ethnocentricism, racism.

xenophobic *adj.* ethnocentric, racist, parochial, narrow-minded.

Xerox (Tm) *v.* copy, photocopy, reproduce, duplicate, ditto.

X-rated *adj.* risqué, off-color, blue, adult, pornographic.

x-ray *n.* radiograph, x-ray film, roentgenogram, skiagram.

xylophone *n.* vibraphone, vibes, glockenspiel, marimba.

yacht *n.* boat, ship, pleasure boat, sloop.

yak (*slang*) *n.* prattle, blather, gossip, hot air.

yak (*slang*) *v.* prattle, blather, yap, run on, chatter, jabber, gossip.

yahoo *n.* brute, savage, beast, boor, barbarian.

yammer *v.* **1.** complain, whine, grumble, whimper, *slang:* bitch, kvetch. **2.** prattle, babble, yak (*slang*), blather.

yank *v.* tug, wrench, pull, jerk, draw, snatch.

Yank (*slang*) *n.* American, Yankee, soldier, GI Joe, Joe, GI, doughboy.

Yankee *n.* Northerner, New Englander, Easterner, American, North American, Yank (*slang*).

Yankee *adj.* American, North American, westernized, individualistic.

yap *v.* jabber, blather, yammer, babble, rant, jaw, chatter.

yard *n.* grounds, lawn, garden, backyard, court, quadrangle; corral, pen, stockyard; terminal.

yardstick *n.* measure, gauge, standard, norm, criterion, model, pattern, rule, benchmark, touchstone, paradigm.

yarn *n.* **1.** fiber, spun thread, spun wool, cotton fiber. **2.** tale, story, narrative, tall story, fabrication, *slang:* cock-and-bull story, fish story.

yaw *v.* pitch, swerve, deviate, veer, bank, turn.

yawl *n.* sailboat, boat, ship, vessel.

yawn *v.* gape, open, gap, split, part, diverge; *ant.* shut, close, come together.

yawning *adj.* gaping, wide, vast, cavernous; *ant.* narrow.

yearling *n.* suckling, nursling, weanling, baby.

yearly *adv.* annually, every year, once a year, per year, per annum.

yearn for *v.* long for, desire, lust, passion, want, lust for, pine for, crave, hunger for, have a yen for, hanker for, wish for; aspire to.

yearning *n.* desire, longing, craving, lust, passion, want, wish.

years *n.* age, oldness, maturity, senility, seniority.

yeast *n.* leaven, ferment, zyme, barm.

yeasty *adj.* frothy, foamy, lathery, sudsy, bubbly.

yell *v.* shout, holler, bellow, scream, raise one's voice, whoop, yowl, howl, hoot, shriek, cheer.

yellow *adj.* **1.** yellowish, xanthous, flaxen, golden, lemon, saffron; jaundiced. **2.** cowardly, craven, cringing; sneaky, tricky, deceitful, treacherous, low, *slang:* chicken, wimpy. **3.** (said of journalism) sensational, tabloid, unethical, unprincipled, chauvinistic, lowbrow.

yelp *v.* bark, cry, yap, yip, yowl, howl, bay, hoot.

yen *n.* desire, longing, yearning, craving, hankering, passion, need, want, lust.

yes *interj.* affirmative, agreed, okay, OK, right, surely, of course, certainly, yeah, uh-huh, yep (*slang*).

yes-man *n.* lackey, sycophant, bootlicker, minion, toady.

yesterday *n.* the day before, the other day, the past, times gone by, the old days.

yesterday *adv.* before, earlier, previously, recently, not long ago.

yet *adv.* still, all the same, even so, nevertheless.

as yet not yet, still, till now, so far.

yield *n.* **1.** harvest, crop, produce. **2.** profit, earnings, income, return, revenue, output, proceeds.

yield *v.* **1.** surrender, succumb, capitulate, give up, knuckle under, cry uncle, submit, concede; quit, throw in the towel, resign, abdicate; *ant.* resist. **2.** (result in) produce, bear, bring forth, give; profit, return, bring in, sell for, pay. **3.** (lose an argument) give in, grant, concede, defer, concur, allow, admit, accept, acquiesce, assent, comply.

yielding *adj.* **1.** productive, fruitful, fecund, fertile, green. **2.** (giving under pressure, as a substance) flexible, malleable, pliable, softening, loosening; *ant.* firm, impervious. **3.** submissive, compliant, compliant, obedient, wavering, budging, passive; *ant.* defiant, obdurate.

yodel *v.* warble, trill, sing.

yoke *n.* **1.** bond, chain, link, coupling. **2.** oppression, subjugation, servility, serfdom, bondage, enslavement, slavery; burden.

yoke *v.* link, connect, bind, attach, join, couple, wed, conjoin, fix, secure, fasten; enslave; *ant.* separate, sever, divorce.

yokel *n.* bumpkin, rustic, hick, hayseed, hillbilly, clodhopper, yahoo.

yonder *adv.* farther, remote, over there, thither.

young *n.* offspring, children, babies, brood, litter, progeny; *ant.* parents.

young *adj.* youthful, juvenile, childlike, pubescent, immature, green, callow, wet behind the ears (*slang*); growing, fresh, raw, new, modern.

youngster *n.* child, little boy, little girl, youth, kid.

youth *n.* **1.** adolescent, teenager, minor, child, junior, boy, girl, student, pup, kid. **2.** (time or state of being young) adolescence, childhood, boyhood, girlhood, juvenility, teens, salad days. **3.** (young people collectively) children, the younger generation, kids, youngsters.

youthful *adj.* young, adolescent, juvenile, immature, naive, inexperienced; zestful, vigorous, active, full of life, fresh, limber, spry.

youthfulness *n.* vivacity, vigor, liveliness, energy, enthusiasm.

yowl *v.* caterwaul, wail, howl, yelp, cry, screech.

yucky (*slang*) *adj.* disgusting, gross (*slang*), filthy, dirty, repulsive, grotty (*slang*); *ant.* nice, pleasant.

yule *n.* Christmas, Nativity, holiday season, yuletide, Noel.

zany *adj.* wacky, madcap, humorous, comical, funny, crazy, loony, odd, goofy; *ant.* serious.

zeal *n.* enthusiasm, eagerness, fervor, gusto, verve, spirit, passion, intensity, zest, dedication, enterprise; *ant.* apathy.

zealot *n.* fanatic, extremist, enthusiast, partisan, devotee, follower, disciple, fan.

zealous *adj.* ardent, fervent, fanatical, passionate, devoted, eager, enthusiastic, militant; *ant.* apathetic.

zealously *adv.* assiduously, vigorously, industriously, fiercely.

zenith *n.* top, summit, pinnacle, peak, apex, apogee, climax, acme, vertex; *ant.* base, bottom, nadir.

zephyr *n.* wind, west wind, draft, breeze.

zeppelin *n.* blimp, airship, dirigible, balloon.

zero *n.* nothing, null, naught, cipher, *slang:* zip, zilch, nix, goose egg.

zero in on concentrate on, focus on, home in on, aim for, pinpoint.

zero hour target day, D-day, appointed hour, now.

zest *n.* **1.** gusto, relish, appetite, joie de vivre, enjoyment, zip, brio, delight, zeal, élan; *ant.* apathy, objection, disgust, distaste. **2.** piquancy, pungency, taste, spice, bite, tang, zing, punch, kick.

zigzag *v.* meander, wind, snake.

zigzag *adj.* serpentine, sinuous, meandering, circuitous, twisted, serrated, jagged, erratic, crooked, devious, irregular.

zing *n.* energy, animation, verve, sparkle, spirit, vitality.

zip *n.* vigor, energy, vim, drive, enthusiasm, pizzazz (*slang*).

zip *v.* rush, dash, run, fly, scoot, hurry, race.

zone *n.* area, district, region, territory, section, community, neighborhood, sector, tract, meridian, latitude, belt.

zoned *adj.* planned for, plotted, restricted.

zoo *n.* zoological garden, menagerie, animal park, safari park.

zoom *v.* dash, rush, race, speed, streak, zip.